THE
BIBLICAL WORLD

THE

BIBLICAL WORLD

A DICTIONARY OF
BIBLICAL ARCHAEOLOGY

Edited by
CHARLES F. PFEIFFER

Consulting Editors
E. Leslie Carlson, Claude F. A. Schaeffer,
and J. A. Thompson

BAKER BOOK HOUSE
Grand Rapids, Michigan

THE BIBLICAL WORLD

Library of Congress Catalog Card Number: 66-19312
Copyright 1966 by Baker Book House Company

PRINTED IN THE UNITED STATES OF AMERICA

Introduction

THE BIBLICAL WORLD, A Dictionary of Biblical Archaeology, deals with the lands of the eastern Mediterranean and the Fertile Crescent — the areas in which the events of Biblical history took place. In its widest sense the world of the Old and New Testaments extends from Iran to Italy. It includes Egypt, the land of Israel's bondage, and the Tigris-Euphrates Valley where Assyria and Babylonia had their days of world power. Asia Minor, Greece, and Rome are the focus of our attention as we move into the New Testament with its description of the journeys of Paul and the growth of the earliest church. Canaan, or Palestine — the promised land — remains, of course, the center of THE BIBLICAL WORLD.

Our studies will take us to Palestine mounds where archaeologists study the pottery and trace the city walls of centuries ago. They also take us to the scholar's study where texts are deciphered and their significance for history and religious faith is appraised. Geography, history, literature, art — all come within the scope of Biblical archaeology. Ancient law codes, books of wisdom, stories, and records of military campaigns help us to reconstruct the history of a people. Hymns and religious epics along with the altars and temples which the archaeologist discovers, help us to understand a people's faith.

While it has been necessary to be selective in presenting the results of modern archaeological discovery, through the use of numerous cross references the editor has attempted to provide some material on the nature and significance of major discoveries. Biblical persons and places are mentioned only if archaeology has added to our knowledge of them. Major archaeological terms are defined to help the reader with no professional training in the subject to get the most out of the many valuable archaeological books that are now available.

For the most part contributors have been permitted to speak for themselves on subjects they know best. The editor wishes to express appreciation to the contributors of articles, to the museums and other agencies which have provided the photographs which illustrate the articles, and to his consulting editors, and to Mr. Cornelius Zylstra and the editorial staff of Baker Book House in making this volume possible. Acknowledgment of the sources of photographs and major articles is appended. The editor is responsible for articles not credited.

Charles F. Pfeiffer

Central Michigan University
Mount Pleasant, Michigan

Contributors

Butrus Abd al-Malik, American University, Cairo: Egypt, Arabia (with John Alexander Thompson)

Dimitri C. Baramki, American University of Beirut: Baalbek, Palmyra

Roy Beaman, New Orleans Baptist Theological Seminary: Behistun Inscription

Andrew C. Bowling, Haigazian College, Beirut: Wen-amon

Joseph A. Callaway, Southern Baptist Theological Seminary, Louisville: Jericho (Old Testament), Jerusalem

E. Leslie Carlson (Consulting Editor), Southwestern Baptist Theological Seminary, Fort Worth: Archaeologists, Hammurabi

A. Dudley Dennison, Physician, Indianapolis: Medicine

Harvey E. Finley, Nazarene Theological Seminary, Kansas City: Nineveh

Clyde T. Francisco, Southern Baptist Theological Seminary, Louisville: Enuma Elish

George Giacumakis, Jr., Orange State College, Fullerton, California: Alalakh

Victor R. Gold, Pacific Lutheran Theological Seminary, Berkeley: Gibeon, Ezion-geber, Serabit el-Khadem

Carl Graesser, Jr., Concordia Seminary, St. Louis: Taanach

William Hallo, Yale University, New Haven: Aleppo, Carchemish, Gozan, Habor, Haran, Nimrud Dagh, Til Barsib, Ura, Zinjerli, Qatna

George W. Harrison, New Orleans Baptist Theological Seminary: Ramesses, Suppilu-liumas

Roy Hayden, Huntington College, Huntington, Indiana: Hurrians

Andrew Helmbold, Frederick College, Portsmouth, Virginia: Nag Hammadi

Harry Hoffner, Brandeis University, Waltham, Massachusetts: Hittites, Hittite Law

Siegfried H. Horn, Andrews University, Berrien Springs, Michigan: Capernaum, Gibeah, Scarab, Seal

Horace Hummel, Lutheran School of Theology, Chicago: Shechem, Qatna

James L. Kelso, Pittsburgh Theological Seminary: Ceramics, Jericho (New Testament), Metallurgy, Pottery

Gerald A. Larue, University of Southern California, Los Angeles: Babylon, Petra

William S. LaSor, Fuller Theological Seminary, Pasadena: Dead Sea Scrolls

Menahem Mansoor, University of Wisconsin: Jewish Sects

Henry R. Moeller, Central Baptist Theological Seminary, Kansas City: Sargon, Sargon of Akkad

William H. Morton, Midwestern Baptist Theological Seminary, Kansas City: Dibon, Moab

Anton T. Pearson, Bethel Theological Seminary, St. Paul: Lachish, Funerary Customs Customs

Anson F. Rainey, University of Tel Aviv, Israel: Arad, Beth-haccherem, Gath, Tell Sheikh el-Areini, Ramat Rahel

Francis R. Steele, North Africa Mission: Law (Mesopotamian)

Gerald G. Swain, Huntingdon College, Huntingdon, Indiana: Phoenician Inscriptions

Marvin E. Tate, Southern Baptist Theological Seminary, Louisville: Ipuwer, Hordedef, Merikare

John Alexander Thompson, American University, Cairo: Egypt, Arabia (with Butrus Abd al-Malik)

J. A. Thompson (Consulting Editor), Baptist Theological College, Eastwood, New South Wales: Archaeology, Bethshan, Covenant, Debir, Edom, Nabateans, Samaritan ostraca, Tirzah, Sela

Merrill F. Unger, Dallas Theological Seminary: Damascus

Bastiaan VanElderen, Calvin Theological Seminary, Grand Rapids: Oxyrhynchus Papyri, Sardis, Derbe, Lystra

Jerry Vardaman, Southern Baptist Theological Seminary, Louisville: Herodium, Bethesda, Pilate

Howard Vos, Trinity College, Chicago: Rome, Athens, Ephesus

Donald Wiseman, University of London: Babylonian Chronicles

George Ernest Wright, Harvard University: Shechem, Beth-shemesh

Edwin Yamauchi, Rutgers University, New Brunswick, New Jersey: Descent of Ishtar

Kyle M. Yates, Jr., Golden Gate Baptist Theological Seminary, Mill Valley, California: Ur

Dwight W. Young, Brandeis University, Waltham, Massachusetts: Shipwrecked Sailor, Sinuhe

Fred E. Young, Central Baptist Theological Seminary, Kansas City: Gezer, Gezer Calendar

Ronald Youngblood, Bethel Theological Seminary, St. Paul: Moabite Stone, Siloam Inscription

James H. Zink, Harding School of Bible and Religion, Memphis: 'Araq el-Emir, Tell Hesy, Tell en-Nasbeh

Acknowledgments of Illustrations

Illustrations

Tomb at Abu Ghosh 17
The Great Temple at Abu Simbel . . . 17
The Acropolis at Athens 19
Calcinated Grains Found Near Beer-sheba 23
Ancient Egyptian Model of Plowman . . 23
Sitting Statue of Akhenaton 27
Adze with Ugaritic Alphabetic Inscription 34
·Canaanite Shrine, Megiddo 35
The Ruins of Amarna Today 37
Pharaoh Akhenaton 37
The Head of a Princess 37
The Amarna Letters 38
Inside View of Colosseum in Rome . . . 42
Amphora Depicting Heracles and the
  Cretan Bull 42
Roman Aqueduct 46
Map of Arabia 49
Archaeologists and Students 63
Israeli Archaeologists 63
Yigael Yadin Examining a
  Bar Kochba Letter 66
One of Egypt's Great Pyramids . . . 85
Tripylon Stairway to Darius' Palace
  at Persepolis 87
The Parthenon at Athens 88
Solomon's Temple and Its Environs . . . 90
Model of a Palestinian House 90
Bronze Implements and Weapons
  from Persia 92
Horses' Heads in Relief from Sargon's Palace 95
Bust of Queen Nefertiti 95
Libation Bowl of Gudea of Lagash . . . 95
Winged Bull from the Palace of Sargon II 95
A Griffin Carved on an Ivory Plaque . . 96
The Asclepium at Pergamum 97
Statue of Asclepius, the God of Medicine . 97
Gold Pendant Depicting Asherah . . . 98
Ramesses II Storming Ashkelon 99
Winged Bull from Gateway of Ashurbanipal 103
Shamshi-adad V under Symbols of His Gods 105
Two Eunuchs from Sargon's Palace . . . 107
Bas Relief of Bacchus 111
Stoa of Attalos 113
Odeon of Herodes Atticus 115
Porch of the Maidens, the Erechtheum . 115
Hadrian's Gate 117
Theater of Dionysus, Athens 117
Avdat as It Appears from the Air . . . 119
Baal, the Storm God 121
The Temple of Venus at Baalbek . . 122
Reconstruction of the Temple at Baalbek . 122
Model of the Ziggurat at Babylon . . . 125
Babylon in the Sixth Century B.C. . . . 128
Babylon Today 128
Dragon from the Istar Gate 130

Bronze Figure of a Four-faced God . . . 131
Tablet of the Babylonian Chronicle . . . 133
Bas Relief Panel from Black
  Obelisk of Shalmaneser 137
Beni Hasan Tomb Painting 138
Excavations at Bethel 140
The Church of St. Anne, Jerusalem . . . 141
The Mound of Beth-shan 144
Cult Objects from a Temple at Beth-shan . 145
Site of Ancient Beth-shemesh 147
The Black Obelisk of Shalmanezer . . . 150
Egyptian Book of the Dead 151
Roman Amphitheater at Byblos 153
The Harbor of Caesarea 155
Ivory Panel from Calah 156
A Woman from Calah 157
·Land of Canaan 160
Lid of Canopic Jar 162
Ruins of Synagogue at Capernaum . . . 163
Excavations at Carchemish 165
Hittite Soldier on Sculptured Slab,
  from Carchemish 166
Monument of Merodach-Baladin 169
One Mina Weight from the Time
  of Nebuchadnezzar 170
Throne Room in the Palace of Minos . . 172
The Lechaeum Road at Corinth 173
The Temple of Apollo at Corinth . . . 173
Alabaster Vases from Corinth 174
Cyrus Cylinder 178
Panoramic View of Damascus Today . . 179
Wall of Damascus 183
The Street Called Strait 184
A Jar from Cave 1 at Qumran 186
Isaiah Scroll from Cave 1, Qumran . . . 187
Parchment Fragment of the
  Thanksgiving Hymns 187
The Copper Scrolls from Cave 3, Qumran . 187
Writing Table and Bench from
  the Qumran Scriptorium 192
Excavators Examine an Ancient Dye Vat . 193
Air View of Dura Europus 203
Map of Ancient Egypt 208
Valley of the Kings 210
King Mycerinus 211
·Canaanite Foes of Seti I 212
Deir El Bahari Temple of Queen Hatshepsut 214
Horemhab with Papyrus Scroll 216
Sealed Contract from Elephantine 220
Cuneiform Tablet containing a part of
  the Babylonian Creation story 223
The Great Theater of Ephesus 230
The Marble Street of Ancient Ephesus . . 231
Sarcophagus of Eshmunezer, King of Zidon 240

Ossuaries in the Museum of the Israel
  Department of Antiquities 242
A Tomb from Palmyra 243
The Family Tomb of the Herods . . . 245
Game Board from Ancient Ur 249
Panorama of Gerasa 252
Stone Serpent Discovered at Gezer . . . 255
Gezer Agricultural Calendar 257
Air View of Excavations at Tell el-Fûl . . 258
Citadel of Saul at Gibeah 260
The Great Pool at Gibeon 265
A Portion of the Gilgamesh Epic . . . 268
Relief Showing Camel Rider from Gozan . 271
Portrait of Hammurabi on Limestone Tablet 277
Stele of the Code of Hammurabi 278
Haran and the Ancient
  Mesopotamian Trade Routes 281
A View of Hebron 286
Excavations at Hazor 284
Canaanite Shrine at Hazor 285
Rolling Stone Sealing
  "Herod's Family Tomb" 288
Hittite Relief Showing a Deer Hunt . . 291
Stele of the Hittite God Teshub 293
Step Pyramid at Saqqara 298
Aqueduct of Sennacherib 301
Excavations at Old Testament Jericho . . 304
Aerial View of Jerusalem 310
Outline Map of Ancient Jerusalem . . . 312
Conjectured Floor Plan of Solomon's Temple 316
The Antonia, Herod's Fortress 319
Greek Inscription in the Temple 320
The Lithostroton beneath the Church of
  the Sisters of Zinn in Jerusalem . . . 322
Detail of Stone in the Lithostroton . . . 323
Caves in the Judean Wilderness 328
Inside a Qumran Cave 331
Judean Landscape 332
Painted Plaster Decoration 337
The Prime Minister and an Attendant
  on a relief from Sargon's Palace . . . 338
Guardian Deity from Sargon's Palace . . 340
The Mound of Lachish 344
Artist's Reconstruction of Lachish . . . 344
Relief Showing Sennacherib on His Throne 346
Lachish Letter 4 347
Stele of the Vultures 349
Gudea of Lagash 350
An Assortment of Ancient Lamps . . . 351
A Worshiper Kneeling. From Larsa . . . 353
Code of Lipit-Ishtar 358
Sardis, Capital of Lydia 361
A Fertility Goddess, Mari 363
Statue of Intup Ilum, Mari 364
Air View of the Hill of Masada 366
Herod's Palace at Masada 367
Corinthian Capital from Herod's
  Palace, Masada 368
Air View of Megiddo 374
Horned Animal Incised on a Limestone Slab 375
Model Restoration of the Stables at Megiddo 376
An Ivory Game Board from Megiddo . . 377

Ruins of Canaanite Megiddo 378
The Merneptah Stele 381
Copper Mining in the Negeb 383
Gold Medallion Showing Winged Lion
  with Horns 384
Golden Mask Found at Mycenae 387
Walls of Tell en-Nasbeh. A Reconstruction 390
Foundations of City Gate at
  Tell en-Nasbeh (Mizpah) 391
The Moabite Stone 396
Musicians Playing a Lute 397
The Lion's Gate at Mycenae 398
The Golden Cup from Mycenae 399
Nabatean Inscription from a Tomb at Petra 401
A Part of the Gospel according to Thomas 405
Mary's Well at Nazareth 411
Traditional Tomb of Joseph at Nazareth . 412
The Harbor at Neapolis 413
Ivory Plaque Discovered at Nimrud . . . 415
Lions Springing at Ashurbanipal during
  a Lion Hunt. From Nineveh 416
Ashurbanipal and His Queen Feasting . 418
Ashurbanipal's Soldiers Lead Away
  Prisoners of War 420
Bronze Coat of Mail from Nuzi 423
Brickmaking in 18th Dynasty Egypt . 426
An Olive Press from Capernaum 427
Assyrian Fishing with a Line 427
First Century Ossuary from Azor . . . 428
Hebrew Letter on Ostraca 429
Panorama of Palmyra 434
The Agora at Palmyra 436
The Theater of the Asclepium at Pergamum 438
Reconstruction of Altar of Zeus
  at Pergamum 439
The Apadana at Persepolis 440
Silver Drachmae 441
The Gate of Xerxes in Persepolis . . . 442
El Khazneh 445
The Ancient Philistine City of Ashkelon . 448
Two Prisoners from among the Philistines 449
Phoenician Tombs at Ancient Byblos . . 450
Crusader Castle at Sidon 453
Theater Inscription from Caesarea . . . 456
Silver Dishes and Utensils from Pompeii . 459
An Ancient Egyptian Potter 461
Water Jar at Capernaum Synagogue . . 462
An Oil Storage Jar from Jaffa Museum . 462
Pottery Incense Stand from Megiddo . . 464
Great Pyramid of Khufu and Sphinx . . 466
The Caves at Qumran 470
Domestic Quarter at Qumran 471
Ramat Rahel 474
Stele of Ramesses II 477
Osiris Columns in the Great Temple
  of Ramesses II 480
Ramesses II Represented as Victor . . . 480
The God Horus Guards the Entrance
  to the Horus Temple 481
Diagram of a Temple to the God Mekal . 482
Bronze Model from Susa 483
The Old Appian Way 485

Augustus Caesar 486
Head of Nero 487
Arch of Titus in Rome 489
Julius Caesar 490
The Rosetta Stone 492
Remains of the City Gate of Samaria . 494
Phoenician Sarcophagus from Byblos . 497
Cylinder Seal from the Akkadian Period . 500
Palace of Sargon II at Khorsabad . . . 503
Facade of the Inner Temple of Nabu . 505
Procession of Horses and Captives
    en route to Sargon's Capital . . . 506
A Commemorative Scarab from Thebes . 509
Impression of a Cylinder Seal . . . 510
Seal Impression on a Jar Handle . . 514
Record of Shishak's Campaign in Palestine 526
The Pool of Siloam 529
Inside the Siloam Tunnel 532
Map of the Route of the Exodus
    and the Conquest of Canaan . . . 534
Jebel Musa (in the Sinai Peninsula) . 537
Jebel Usdum 542
Stele of Esarhaddon 543
Stele of Seti I 544
Standing Male Figure in the Act of
    Worship. From Tell Asmar 546
A Sumerian Priest from Tell Asmar . . 547
The Standard of Ur (showing scenes
    of war) 548
The Standard of Ur (showing scenes
    of peace) 549
Bronze Statuette of King Ur-Nammu . 550
The Sumerian King List 551
The Mound of Susa from the Air . . 554
Seven Branched Candlestick 556
Tell Taanek after Plan by Schumacher . 557
Debris from Storeroom of a
    "Cultic Structure" 559

Astarte Figurine Mold with Modern Cast . 560
Incense Altar from Taanach 562
Step Trench at Tell Jedeidah, Syria . . 564
A Palestinian Tell (Tell el-Mutesellim) . 567
Revetment Built to Strengthen the
    Wall at Tell en-Nasbeh (Mizpah) . . 568
Stele from Tell Halaf, Showing a
    Wheeled Chariot 571
Excavations at Tell Nagila 572
Archaeologists at Tepe Gawra 574
The Acropolis at Tepe Gawra 577
Roman Amphitheater at Caesarea . . . 580
The Temple of Amun at Karnak 581
Bas Relief from the Amun Temple . . . 583
Tiberias on the Sea of Galilee 585
Covered Wagon Excavated at Tepe Gawra 588
Boats Transporting Logs 589
Map of Ugarit (Ras Shamra) 592
Ugarit Text with the Legend of Aqhat . 593
A God from Ugarit 594
Stele from Ugarit Depicting
    Two Officials with Offerings 595
The Ruins of Ur 597
The Ziggurat of Ur-Nammu at Ur. A
    restoration 598
Game Board from Ur 599
Gold Dagger and Sheath from Ur . . . 600
Gold Helmet of Mes-Kalam-dug 601
Goat Eating Leaves. A Figure from Ur . 602
The Ur-Nammu Stele 604
Stele Showing a Lion-hunting
    Scene from Uruk 605
Assyrian Archers and Siege Engines . . . 606
Writing Equipment of an Egyptian Scribe 609
The Pallette of Narmer 610
The Ziggurat at Ur 611

Abbreviations

AASOR	*Annual of the American Schools of Oriental Research*
AJA	*American Journal of Archaeology*
ANEP	*Ancient Near East in Pictures,* J. B. Pritchard, ed.
ANET	*Ancient Near Eastern Texts,* J. B. Pritchard, ed.
APEF	*Annual of the Palestine Exploration Fund*
BA	*Biblical Archaeologist*
BASOR	*Bulletin of the American Schools of Oriental Research*
IEJ	*Israel Exploration Journal*
JAOS	*Journal of the American Oriental Society*
JBL	*Journal of Biblical Literature*
JEA	*Journal of Archaeology*
JNES	*Journal of Near Eastern Studies*
JPOS	*Journal of the Palestine Oriental Society*
PEFQ	*Palestine Exploration Fund, Quarterly Statement*
PEQ	*Palestine Exploration Quarterly*
QDAP	*Quarterly of the Department of Antiquities in Palestine*
RB	*Revue Biblique*
RSV	Revised Standard Version
VT	*Vetus Testamentum*
ZAW	*Zeitschrift für die alttestamentliche Wissenschaft*
ZDPV	*Zeitschrift des deutschen Palästina-Vereins*

A

ABGAR. An old tradition states that Abgar V of Edessa (48 B.C.-A.D. 50) wrote a letter to Jesus, asking that Jesus visit him in Edessa and heal him. Jesus, in his reply, declined to make the trip but promised Abgar to send a disciple to effect the cure and preach the gospel following his resurrection. One version of the tradition claims that Christ sent with his letter a portrait of himself, miraculously imprinted on canvas.

The historian Eusebius (*ca.* A.D. 263-339) records the tradition that the apostle Thomas delegated Thaddaeus, one of the Twelve, to go to Edessa. Under his ministry the king was cured and many of the inhabitants of Edessa became Christians.

By the third century A.D. Edessa had become a center of Syrian Christianity, and in subsequent years it became one of the major religious centers of the Byzantine Empire. It was in this environment that the legend of an exchange of letters between an early king of Edessa and Jesus developed. Contemporary scholars find no historical basis for the legend.

ABRAHAM. Although the names of the Biblical patriarchs do not appear outside the Bible, archaeology has been able to throw light upon the period in which they lived. Excavations have revealed the nature of the material culture of the Patriarchal Age, and written documents provide additional details.

The name Abraham is paralleled by such West Semitic names as Abiram, Abamram, and Abarama found in cuneiform literature. An Old Babylonian business document states that a man named Abarama, son of Awel-Ishtar hired an ox for a month. Another cuneiform tablet of twenty-one lines tells the terms under which Abamrama leased a farm. A third, dated two years after the ox was hired, is a receipt for payment of one shekel by Abamrama as rent for his field. Names with the same components are also found at °Mari.

Abraham and his descendants ethnically represent a number of strains. Laban, a grandson of Nahor, Abraham's brother, is specifically termed an Aramean (Gen. 25:20; 31:20, 24). The Israelites were later to confess, "A wandering Aramean was my father . . ." (Deut. 26:5). The homeland to which Abraham sent his servant to secure a bride for Isaac was Mesopotamia, or Aram Naharaim (Gen. 24:10). Jacob, in fleeing to his uncle Laban journeyed to Paddan-aram, "The fields of Aram" (Gen. 28:5, 6).

About the year 2000 B.C. great changes took place throughout the Near East due to incursions of a Northwest Semitic people known as °Amorites ("Westerners") by the people of Mesopotamia. With the fall of Ur (*ca.* 1950 B.C.), Amorites pushed into southern Mesopotamia and they soon controlled its principal city-states. Between the Early and Middle Bronze Age there is archaeological evidence of a break in the occupation of many Palestinian cities. Albright's excavations at °Tell Beit Mirsim, Kathleen Kenyon's work at °Jericho, and Nelson Glueck's explorations in Transjordan show a rapidly declining density of settlement, followed before the end of the twentieth century B.C. by virtually complete abandonment of the country to nomadic peoples (cf. W. F. Albright, *The Archaeology of Palestine*, p. 82). Similarly the Egyptian °Execration Texts show that nomadic and semi-nomadic peoples were in Palestine during the twentieth century B.C.

Among the Amorites and related peoples, who pressed into Canaan during the twentieth century B.C., we should probably place the patriarch Abraham. The term Amorite probably included a number of subgroups, including the °Arameans with whom the patriarchal family was clearly related. In speaking of the origin of Jerusalem, Ezekiel in his allegory of the unfaithful wife said, "Your origin and your birth are of the land of the Canaanites; your father was an Amorite and your mother a Hittite" (Ezek. 16:3).

Although the prophet was not making a pronouncement on national origins, he did recollect something of the mixed background of the chosen people.

On but one occasion (Gen. 14:13) is Abraham spoken of as "the Hebrew," a word which seems to be related to the °Habiru or Hapiru which appeared in various parts of the Fertile Crescent during the second millennium B.C. Etymologically the word may mean "those who cross over," in the sense of trespassers or immigrants. Probably the term Hebrew did not refer to a particular racial group, but to a social class. A Hapiru-Hebrew was a foreigner, and such a term often had an evil connotation to settled inhabitants of a country. In the °Amarna Letters the Hapiru are described as marauding raiders who threaten the peace of the city-states of Syria and Palestine.

Although the area around Haran, designated as Paddan-aram or Aram Naharaim was the place which the patriarchs considered their ancestral home (Gen. 24:4, 10), we are told that Abraham's immediate ancestors came from "Ur of the Chaldeans" (Gen. 11:31). The Septuagint version speaks of "the land of the Chaldeans" without reference to Ur.

A great Sumerian city named °Ur was located in southern Mesopotamia at the mound al-Muqaiyar. Following World War I a joint expedition by the British Museum and the University of Pennsylvania conducted a series of expeditions there under the direction of Leonard Woolley. Since this Ur is in the land that was known in Neo-Babylonian times as Chaldea, Biblical scholars were largely convinced that al-Muqayyar was the site of Abraham's childhood.

An Akkadian tablet from Ugarit contains a letter from the Hittite king, Hattusilis III (ca. 1275-1250 B.C.), to King Niqmepa' of Ugarit. These traders are called, "merchant men, citizens of the city of Ura." That Chaldeans were known in the northwest as well as in southern Mesopotamia is attested by Xenophon who mentions them as neighbors to the Armenians (Anabasis IV. iii. 4; cf. V.v.17; Cyropaedia III. i. 34). Cyrus H. Gordon presents the case for a northern Ur and identifies Abraham as a merchant prince in his "Abraham and the Merchants of Ura" (JNES, XVII, 1958, pp. 28-31). An older interpretation identified Ur with Urfa (Edessa), twenty miles northwest of Haran, but this is unlikely on philological grounds. Several places in Asia Minor bore the name Ura, but Abraham in journeying to Haran from one of them would have gone out of his way if Canaan was his ultimate destination as is indicated in Scripture (Gen. 12:31).

Although positive proof is lacking, most scholars still identify Biblical Ur with al-Muqaiyar. Both Ur and Haran were dedicated to Nannar, the moon god, and shared the same religious emphases. A migration toward Canaan from al-Muqaiyar would take Abraham through the Fertile Crescent to the vicinity of Haran. It is possible that a group of Northwest Semitic clans had migrated southward to Ur and subsequently (perhaps after the fall of the Ur III dynasty), migrated northward again to the Haran area where they would have felt most at home. This fact may explain the reluctance of Terah to move on to Canaan, and suggest the reason for the place Haran had in the affection of the patriarchs. It is significant that Ur itself is never considered the patriarchal home, whatever its location.

The Biblical patriarchs are often described as being nomads or semi-nomads. This is, indeed, one aspect of their lives as they are depicted in Genesis. They have herds of cattle and flocks of sheep and goats and they move about in the hill country of Palestine between Dothan and Beer-sheba seeking pasturage and springs. On the other hand, the Bible describes the patriarchs as rich in gold and silver. When his nephew Lot was in trouble, Abraham was able to raise a personal army, challenge the combined forces of a confederacy of eastern kings, and gain a military victory (Gen. 14). At Sarah's death, Abraham paid for a burial plot with "four hundred shekels of silver, according to the weights current among the merchants" (Gen. 23:16). Although he possessed no real estate, Abraham was a man of wealth and influence.

During the period of the Biblical patriarchs the Central Range of Palestine was thinly populated. There were vast areas in which semi-nomads such as Abraham could pasture their flocks and herds. The towns mentioned in the Biblical narratives — Dothan, Bethel, Shechem, and Jerusalem — are known to have existed in the Middle Bronze Age. The patriarchs often sojourned near the towns. We read of Lot that he "dwelt among the cities of the valley and moved his tent as far as Sodom" (Gen. 13:12). Similarly Abraham "moved his tent and came and dwelt by the oaks of Mamre, which are at Hebron" (Gen. 13:18).

According to the Biblical account, the age of Abraham was one of great mobility. Abraham himself traveled from Ur to °Haran, to Canaan, to Egypt, and back to Canaan. By the nineteenth century B.C. Assyrian merchants had penetrated Cappadocia in Asia Minor for purposes of trade. Their records have been preserved on the °Cappadocian Tablets. Contacts between Palestine and Egypt, whose famed Twelfth Dynasty began *ca.* 1991 B.C., were frequent. Palestinian tombs of the period from 2000-1800 B.C. contain numerous Egyptian artifacts. The Execration Texts show in a negative way the relationship between Egypt and Palestine during the twentieth and nineteenth centuries B.C. In the earliest series, imprecations against various foes were inscribed on jars or bowls which were then smashed to make the curse effective. In the second series the imprecations were inscribed on clay figurines representing bound captives. The first group (known as the Berlin Texts) name Jerusalem and Ashkelon as enemies of Egypt; the second (or Brussels Texts) list Jerusalem, Shechem, Accho (Acre), Ashshaph (near Acre), Tyre, Hazor, Ashtaroth (in Bashan), and Pella (across the Jordan from Bethshan).

From the twentieth century B.C we also have the famed °Sinuhe Story telling how a noble of high rank fled from Egypt and journeyed toward Kedem ("the East"). He was favorably received by a local prince in Upper Retenu (the Egyptian name for Syria and Palestine). There he was happily settled and prospered until he was invited back to Egypt. From the same period (*ca.* 1900 B.C.) are the tomb paintings from °Beni Hasan in Egypt which depict thirty-seven Semites bringing gifts and desiring trade. The dress and equipment of these Asiatics was probably similar to that of Abraham who visited Egypt about the same time.

Before entering Egypt, Abraham instructed Sarah to declare herself to be his sister, fearing that the Egyptians might kill him if they knew that he was her husband (Gen. 12:11-13). Subsequently Pharaoh did take her to his harem until a series of plagues came upon his household (Gen. 12:17-20). The motif of a Pharaoh exerting great effort to secure a beautiful woman as his wife, even though she already had a husband, appears in the Tale of the °Two Brothers. Pharaoh sent messengers to the Valley of the Cedar (i.e. Lebanon) to bring the woman to him. Bata, the woman's husband, killed all of the messengers but one who was spared to bring the message to the Pharaoh. Pharaoh, however, sent a second expedition including this time a woman who brought such ornaments as might entice a young lady to come to the Egyptian court. The messenger was successful, for "the woman came back to Egypt with her, and there was rejoicing over her in all the land, and His Majesty loved her very much and he gave her the rank of Great Favorite." Although the papyrus containing the Egyptian tale dates only from the twelfth century B.C., the strange tale it records is doubtless much older. A man such as Abraham might well fear that Pharaoh would use any means to add a beautiful woman to his harem.

After returning from Egypt, Abraham and Lot separated, Lot taking the Jordan Valley and Abraham settling in Canaan. Genesis 13:10 records that Lot saw "that the Jordan valley was well watered everywhere like the garden of the Lord, like the land of Egypt . . ." This area is now hot and barren, the least desirable part of Palestine. Archaeology has shown that this was not always so, however. Between 1932 and 1939, Nelson Glueck, while Director of the American Schools of Oriental Research in Jerusalem, made a thorough study of Southern Transjordan east and south of the Dead Sea. He discovered that nomadic peoples settled down in villages there in the centuries before 2000 B.C. Suddenly, about the twentieth or nineteenth century B.C. the villages were abandoned and for some reason the people in the area became nomads.

It is known that there was a large city at Khirbet Kerak at the southern end of the Sea of Galilee between 2500 and 2000 B.C. °Beth-shan has a history which dates back to 3000 B.C. The once great cities of Sodom, Gomorrah, and Zoar are probably beneath the shallow waters at the southern tip of the Dead Sea. W. F. Albright excavated two sites nearby and found that they were abandoned about the twentieth century B.C. as were other cities in southern Transjordan. These discoveries show why Lot would have chosen to settle in the Jordan Valley and help us to date Abraham in the twentieth or nineteenth century B.C.

Abraham's fear that his slave Eliezer might be his heir (Gen. 15:1-4) may be explained by adoption procedures described in the °Nuzi Tablets. A childless couple might adopt a son, often a favored slave. If a natural son were subsequently born, the adopted son would yield his rights to the natural son, although certain of the interests of the adopted son were guarded. It would appear that Eliezer was Abraham's adopted son but the patriarch wanted a natural son as heir.

In Nuzi marriage contracts we often read that a childless wife would be required to provide her husband with a concubine who night become a mother to his children. A similar situation prevailed in the Code of °Hammurabi: "If a man takes a priestess and she does not present him with children and he sets his face to take a concubine, that man may take a concubine and bring her into his house. That concubine shall not rank with the wife" (Paragraph 145). These laws and customs provide the cultural background against which we may understand Sarah's suggestion to Abraham, ". . . go in to my maid; it may be that I shall obtain children by her" (Gen. 19:2).

The Code of Hammurabi realistically faced the situation in which such a maid would bear children to the husband of her mistress and aspire to a higher position in the household: "If a man takes a priestess and she gives to her husband a maidservant and she bears children, and afterward that maid servant would take rank with her mistress; because she has borne children her mistress may not sell her for money, but she may reduce her to bondage and count her among the female slaves" (Paragraph 146). After Hagar had conceived, Sarah "dealt harshly with her, and she fled from her" (Gen. 16:6). Later Abraham was grieved when Sarah urged, "Cast out this slave woman with her son" (Gen. 21:10-11), a request contrary to prevailing law and custom.

Abraham's purchase of a burial plot from Ephron the Hittite may be understood in the light of the Hittite Law Code found at °Boghazkoy in Turkey. The code stipulates that a buyer must render certain feudal services if he purchases all of the seller's property. If a portion of the property was sold, the seller continued to bear the obligation. Although Abraham only required the cave at the edge of Ephron's field as a burial place (Gen. 23:9), Ephron insisted that he take the entire field (Gen. 23:11). Ephron evidently saw an opportunity to rid himself of his obligations, causing Abraham to become feudatory for the entire field.

BIBLIOGRAPHY. Leonard Woolley, *Abraham: Recent Discoveries and Hebrew Origins*, Faber and Faber, London, 1935. Dorothy B. Hill, *Abraham: His Heritage and Ours*, Beacon Press, Boston, 1957.

ABU GHOSH. Eight and one-half miles north of Jerusalem, on the main highway from the Mediterranean coastal plain, is an Arab village known as Abu Ghosh. It is named for an early nineteenth century sheikh who terrorized the area and exacted a toll from all pilgrims bound for Jerusalem. Abu Ghosh is thought to be the site of Biblical °Kirjath-jearim where the ark remained for twenty years between the time that the Philistines sent it back to Israel and the reign of David, who brought it up to Jerusalem (I Chron. 13:5-8).

BIBLIOGRAPHY. F. T. Cooke, "The Site of Kirjath-jearim," AASOR V, 1923-24, pp. 105-120. Roland De Vaux and A. M. Steve, *Fouilles a Qaryet El cEnab, Abu Ghosh, Palestine*, 1950.

ABU SIMBEL. Abu Simbel is located between the first and second cataracts of the Nile River, about thirty-six miles north of Wadi Halfa, in southern Egypt. In anc' times Egypt extended only to the first c.. aract of the Nile, and Abu Simbel was in the country known as Nubia. Here, *ca.* 1250 B.C., Ramesses II had two temples hewn from the sandstone of the mountains along the west bank of the Nile. The temple to the sun god had at its entrance four sitting statues of Ramesses, each sixty-five feet high. The ear of the Pharaoh is three feet high. A hypostyle hall is decorated with scenes depicting Egyptian religious ritual and battle scenes commemorating Ramesses' victories at °Kadesh on the Orontes.

Abu Simbel is in the region to be flooded by the artificial lake behind the Aswan High Dam which will alleviate the water shortage in Egypt and make possible the irrigation of lands now desert. Archaeologists have sought ways of preserving the monuments of

person buried in accord with the Osiris ritual symbolically took a pilgrimage to Abydos. The models of barques found in tombs all over Egypt were provided for this symbolic journey, as were pictures of journeys of the soul of the deceased painted on the walls of tombs.

The zenith of Abydos's influence was reached during the Ramesside Age when Sethi I rebuilt the Osiris temple and provided it with a heavy endowment. Sethi depicted seventy-six of his predecessors in reliefs in the Abydos temple, and he even built a palace there so that he could supervise the work. The limestone reliefs are the best preserved of any from pre-Ptolemaic times.

Sethi I died before his temple could be completed, but the work was continued by Ramesses II who left an inscription of 116 lines describing his labors. A short distance to the north of the Sethi temple, Ramesses built a second temple for himself. It was beautifully landscaped and richly endowed

according to an inscription which Ramesses left on the exterior of the south wall.

After Ramesses II, we read of little further work at Abydos. With the decline of Egyptian power, the magnificence of gifts to Osiris inevitably diminished. Other centers gradually replaced Abydos. Beautiful Philae became the center for Osiris worship in the days of the Ptolemies and the Romans. In the development of Egyptian religious thought, Osiris came to be regarded as the husband of Isis, and ultimately her popularity became such that he took second place.

ACROPOLIS. The acropolis ("high point of the city") in Greek antiquity was the name applied to any fortified stronghold or citadel overlooking a populated area. An acropolis was primarily a place of refuge and defense. For this reason it was fortified and built on a hill or eminence. The city would normally develop around the base of its acropolis.

When cities became large, walls were some-

THE ACROPOLIS still towers over the city of Athens. Courtesy, N. Stoupnapas

times built for defense and the acropolis lost its military significance. Under such circumstances temples and public buildings might be erected on the acropolis, as happened in ancient Athens.

Although there are Mycenaean remains (*ca.* 1500 B.C.) on the acropolis at °Athens, its period of greatness was the Periclean Age (fifth century B.C.) when it was adorned with important temples and civic buildings. A winding processional path led from the base of the acropolis upward to its western end where the impressive Propylaea stood. The road then passed a statue of Athena, the patron goddess of Athens, and the Athena temple before reaching the Parthenon. To the north was the Erechtheum and to the southwest the temple of the Wingless Victory. On the southern slope were the °Odeum of Herodes Atticus and the °theater of Dionysus. The plan of the Athenian acropolis was initiated by Pericles and carried out by Phidias.

ADANA. Adana, on the Seyhan River in southern Turkey, was the center of a kingdom in Asia Minor during the eighth century B.C. An inscription discovered at nearby °Karatepe tells of the activities of Asitawanda, a lieutenant of the king of Adana. The inscription is bilingual, one version being Phoenician, and the other hieroglyphic Luwian.

ADAPA LEGEND. The Adapa Legend has been preserved on four cuneiform fragments, three of which are from the library of °Ashurbanipal and the fourth from the state archives of Akhenaton at Tell el °Amarna. Although we do not possess the complete Adapa Legend, the presence of fragments of it in Egypt suggest its wide diffusion through the ancient East.

Adapa was a man of intelligence who did not possess immortality. Adapa was priest of the temple of the god Ea at Eridu in southern Mesopotamia. While fishing one day in the Persian Gulf his boat was overturned by the South Wind, and Adapa found himself in the water. Enraged, Adapa broke the wings of the South Wind. As a result, the wind was rendered powerless to blow its cool air over the parched land north of the Persian Gulf for seven days.

The great gods Anu and Ea were distressed and warned Adapa of the con-

sequences of his deed. Adapa was called to give an account of himself at the assembly of the gods, and Ea, in an apparent gesture of kindness, warned him not to eat or drink anything that might be offered to him lest he be offered the food and drink of death. As a matter of fact Adapa was offered the food and drink of life, but he remembered the counsel of Ea and refused it. Through this caprice of the gods, Adapa was robbed of immortality and had to return to earth and live as a mortal.

The loss of immortality is a theme common to both the Adapa Legend and the account of man's fall in Genesis 3. In the Biblical account man was banished from Eden and barred from eating of the Tree of Life because he had disobeyed the command of God and eaten of the Tree of the Knowledge of Good and Evil. Not only does the Adapa Legend have a polytheistic setting, in contrast to the monotheism of Genesis, but the Babylonian account has no moral basis. Adapa lost immortality by accident. He believed the words of a god who had lied to him. His loss of the blessing could be blamed on fate or the whim of the gods. There is a total absence of any thought of personal responsibility in the Adapa Legend. The Biblical account presents Adam as a transgressor against the divine law. Man lost immortality as a result of a moral choice.

BIBLIOGRAPHY. E. A. Speiser, "Adapa," in *ANET*, pp. 101-103. E. T. Harper, "Die babylonischen lengeden von Etana, Zu, Adapa, und Dibbarru," *Beitrage zur Assyriologie und vergleichenden semitischen Sprachwissenschaft*, II, 1894, pp. 390-521; H. Zimmern, "Zusatzbemerkungen zur legende von Adapa, *ibid.*, pp. 437-438.

ADOPTION. The discovery of the °Nuzi documents has illustrated adoption practices in the Near East, some of which are paralleled in Scripture. In Nuzi a property owner who had no son would adopt a son. The adopted son might be freeborn, or a slave. The father could expect service from his adopted son and, on the father's death, he would receive a proper burial. Then, if the father had no natural son, the adopted son would receive the property. If a natural son had been born to the father, however, the natural son would become heir and take the household gods — small clay figurines used in worship — which served as title deeds to the property.

Before Abraham had a child of his own

he named his servant Eliezer of Damascus as his heir (Gen. 15:2, 3). Subsequently, however, Isaac became the true heir. It appears that Laban adopted his son-in-law Jacob before Laban had sons of his own (cf. Gen. 31:1). After Laban had sons of his own, his relations with Rachel and Jacob were strained. Rachel determined to take the matter into her own hands and stole the household gods (teraphim) before she along with Jacob's household fled from Laban in the direction of Canaan. Rachel evidently felt that by stealing the teraphim she could secure the inheritance for her husband (cf. Gen. 31:30, 32, 34).

AEGEAN CIVILIZATION. See Minoans, Mycenae.

AERIAL PHOTOGRAPHY. Aerial photography is one of the means used by modern archaeologists in determining sites which should be excavated. By showing surface irregularities which cannot be observed at ground level, aerial photography reveals the lines of walls and buried buildings.

Crop marks, variations in the height or color of a growing crop, will also appear in aerial photographs. These variations are discernable from the air at certain stages of a crop's growth. The nature of a crop of grain depends on the depth of top soil. A buried wall will tend to produce a line of poor soil, whereas an ancient ditch will result in deeper top soil and better crop growth.

Through the data assembled as a result of aerial photography the plans of a buried building can often be drawn in surprisingly accurate detail before the excavator begins to dig.

AGRAPHA. The term agrapha means "not written" and is used of sayings attributed to Christ which do not appear in the New Testament writings. Paul, in Acts 20:35, reminded the Ephesian elders of a saying of Christ which is not recorded in our Gospels: "It is more blessed to give than to receive."

Late manuscripts of the Greek New Testament contain a few alleged sayings of Christ which do not appear in the older texts. The Codex Beza records such a saying after Luke 4 (cf. the footnote in Nestle's text). Church Fathers also record sayings of Jesus of unknown origin. Justin in his dialogue with Trypho quotes Jesus as saying, "In whatsoever things I shall take you, in these I shall judge you."

The *Oxyrhyncus Papyri discovered by Grenfell and Hunt in Egypt include about fourteen alleged sayings of Jesus, about half of which parallel the canonical Scriptures. Gnostic texts discovered at *Nag Hammadi include a text known as the Gospel of Thomas which is a collection of 114 sayings attributed to Jesus, some of which parallel the Biblical sayings of Jesus. The Nag Hammadi texts are thought to date from the second century B.C. (cf. Floyd L. Filson, BA, XXIV, 1961, pp. 8-18). They represent Gnostic ideas of Christ but do not supplement historical knowledge of the Person of Jesus or his teaching.

AGRICULTURE. Although we cannot trace the origins of agriculture, excavations at various sites in the Near East have shown the transition from a food-gathering to a food-producing culture which made possible urban living and the growth of civilization in the lands of the Fertile Crescent. A people known as Natufians (from the Wadi en-Natuf at Mt. Carmel where their artifacts were discovered) used a flint blade in a bone haft for gathering grain. There is evidence that these Natufians lived largely by hunting, for enormous quantities of gazelle bones have also been found in their caves. The sickles could have been used to gather wild grains, but some authorities are convinced that grain was actually cultivated by the Mesolithic Natufian culture (see Natufians). The skeleton of a dog in a Middle Natufian level is our earliest example of the domestication of animals.

Excavations by Kathleen Kenyon at *Jericho show that Natufians also settled there and that by ca. 7500 B.C. their descendants were engaged in agriculture. Excavations at Jarmo in Iraq and Sialk in Iran have also shown evidences of the transition from food-gathering to food-producing cultures.

The grains, notably wheat and barley, appear to have been the earliest agricultural crops, and they continued to be the staples of ancient Palestine. Wheat is the more valuable, but barley has a shorter growing season and will thrive on poorer soil. In later times a variety of crops was planted including lentils, peas, beans, onions, and garlic.

Life in ancient Palestine was largely determined by the agricultural year, as the *Gezer Calendar from about 925 B.C. indicates. During October and November the farmer awaited the "early" rains which softened the parched ground and enabled him to sow his winter crops (wheat and barley). December and January are the months of the heavy rains when the soil is saturated and the wells, cisterns and pools are filled. January and February are the months for planting the summer grain (millet, sesame) along with melons and cucumbers. The "latter" rains come in March and April, assuring the winter grain and fertilizing the summer crop. The summer months, May to October are usually rainless and the plants are kept alive by the heavy dew brought by the west wind.

Irrigation was more common in Egypt and Mesopotamia than in Palestine during the Biblical period. Predynastic Egyptians and the Sumerians of the lower Euphrates valley were building dams and digging canals as early as the Neolithic age. The earliest Sumerian and Babylonian law codes show a concern for water rights. The Code of *Hammurabi states: "If a man has opened his sluice for watering and has left it open and the water destroys the field of his neighbor, he shall measure out grain to him on the basis of that produced by neighboring fields" (Paragraph 55).

The earliest plows were simply forked, crooked limbs of trees which were driven through shallow soil. Copper and bronze plowpoints appear before the tenth century B.C. With the introduction of iron, plowpoints could be made larger, and they were less easily dented. The typical plow was drawn by two oxen (cf. I Kings 19:19). It could not plow a furrow, but merely scratched the surface of the ground for three or four inches.

In Mesopotamia a primitive type of seeder was attached to the plow, permitting seeds to be dropped down a tube which was attached behind the plowpoint, but we do not know of such a device in Israel. Probably most seed was scattered by hand over the plowed ground, and a second plowing covered it. Harrowing and leveling the ground (cf. Isa. 28:24-25; Hos. 10:11; Job 39:10) was performed by dragging branches after the plow to smooth the ground over the seed.

Sickles were used in reaping throughout the Near East. Prehistoric Mesopotamian sickles were made of flint teeth set in wood. Natufian flint sickles in bone handles are among the oldest known. This type of sickle was used until the tenth century B.C. when small curved iron blades replaced the earlier flint. A wooden handle was affixed by rivets.

The reaper would grasp the stalks of grain with one hand (cf. Ps. 129:7; Isa. 17:5), and with the other cut them off close to the ear. Later a number of the small bundles of grain would be gathered together and bound with pieces of straw. They were then carried to the nearest threshing-floor, located in the open air outside the village. The grain was spread on this floor, and the kernels separated from the straw by oxen trampling upon it and pulling a threshing-sledge. Two types of sledges are known, one made of flat boards, and the other running on small wheels or rollers (cf. Isa. 28:27-28). In sections inaccessible to a threshing-floor, women beat the grain from the ears with heavy wooden mallets or long sticks called flails.

From May through September a strong breeze from the Mediterranean penetrates as far as two hundred miles inland. Farmers used it to separate grain from chaff. They stood on the threshing floor and tossed bunches of threshed wheat into the air, letting the wind blow away the chaff, while the heavier grain fell to the ground.

After winnowing, and at times sifting through a sieve, grain was placed in storage jars. Large silos for storing grain have been discovered. One from Beth-shemesh (ca. 900 B.C.) was 25 feet in diameter at the top and nearly 19 feet deep. It had been dug through the debris of former cities to bedrock. Small, plastered silos dug through the floor of a home for private use were also common.

The Jewish religious calendar in large measure parallels the cycle of agricultural activities which began with the end of the dry summer. There were seasons of fasting at the beginning of the year, before the rains had started, and periods of rejoicing and thanksgiving as the crops were harvested.

The New Year comes in the present Jewish calendar during the autumn days of the siroccos when the rain is anxiously awaited. At an earlier period new year began in the spring, at the Passover season, but the

CALCINATED GRAINS of wheat, barley, lentils, and grapes were found in these underground silos dating back to 4000 B.C. The discovery was made near Beer-sheba. Courtesy, Consulate General of Israel

ANCIENT EGYPTIAN MODEL OF PLOWMAN. Courtesy British Museum

calendar was later made to conform to the agricultural year, beginning in the fall.

The Biblical Feast of Trumpets (Lev. 23:23-25) was adapted to mark the beginning of the agricultural year. Ten days later the Israelites observed the Day of Atonement, a time of solemn preparation for a year of life spent in obedience to God's laws. The Feast of Tabernacles which follows the Day of Atonement by a few days, contained a special prayer for rain. During the days of the Temple, water was drawn from the Pool of Siloam and ceremonially poured on the altar, symbolizing the need for rain.

Generally the rainy season would begin along the Mediterranean coast shortly after the Feast of Tabernacles. It would reach the hill country a little later. With the coming of rain, the crops would grow until the "latter rains" of April which would make possible their final growth and insure a good harvest. There was always the possibility of a poor year, however, so that the Israelite could not take it for granted that God would always bring an abundance of food to His people. Famines were frequent and Israel was constantly reminded that God was directly related to the supply of food.

The constant threat of famine was doubtless an important factor in the popularity of the Canaanite fertility cult during much of the pre-exilic period of Israel's history. *Baal was a fertility god, and the native Canaanites doubtless instructed their Israelite neighbors in the traditional means of securing adequate rain by the licentious Baal-worship. Prophets and psalmists of Israel insisted that it was Yahweh, God of Israel, and not Baal who "rode upon the clouds" and controlled the rains and winds.

At the close of the agricultural year, Israel had a cluster of special observances. Associated with the Passover, commemorating the Exodus from Egypt, was the Feast of First-fruits, when the first of the grain was offered to God in thanksgiving. In Pauline theology, Christ is both the "firstfruits" of the resurrection and the "Passover" lamb slain for His people. The "firstfruits" were consecrated to the Lord, and were ceremonially presented to Him each year.

Seven weeks later, in late May or early June, Israel observed the Feast of Weeks, or Pentecost. This marked the end of the season for harvesting grain. Shortly after the Feast of Weeks, the summer dry season set in, and the farmers' activities were curtailed.

There are two major seasons in Palestine — the dry summer, extending without interruption from mid-June to mid-September, and the rainy season which extends intermittently throughout the remainder of the year. The actual cold of winter is limited, however, to a period of three months beginning about mid-December.

Although rain never falls during the summer months, winds from the Mediterranean help to moderate the heat and bring dew along the coast and on the western slope of the mountains. The morning dew is an important factor in maintaining agriculture. Without it the growth of grapes during the summer drought would be impossible. Scripture mentions dew as an evidence of God's care for His people (Deut. 33:28). The fact that it is quickly dissipated before the heat of the day, makes it a fitting symbol of things transitory (Hos. 13:3).

The summer breezes are regular to a degree that surprises westerners who are accustomed to a constantly changing weather pattern. Cool air from the Mediterranean hits the Palestinian coastal cities early in the day. It is noon before it is able to pass over the mountains and enter the Jordan Valley. By about three in the afternoon it reaches the Transjordan plateau.

The winds not only bring refreshment to individuals sweltering in a tropical sun, they also are useful in the agricultural pursuits of the Palestinian farmer. The process of winnowing the grain makes use of the winds which drive away the chaff and permit the grain itself to fall back upon the threshing floor (cf. Ps. 1).

Soon after sundown the sea breeze stops and a period of calm lasts until nine or ten o'clock. Then a land breeze may begin, although it has to counter the general drift of air from the sea and may at times be indistinguishable. Summer nights are very warm along the coast, but blankets may be required for comfort in the hills.

Unlike the regularity of the three summer months, the Palestinian rainy season is unpredictable. It usually begins around the middle of October, but it has been known to begin as late as January. A delay such as this may be very harmful to crops which depend on the rainy season for their moisture.

Prolonged periods of drought after the first showers may also kill the young crops.

The first showers which usually begin in October are known in Scripture as the "former rain." They are usually accompanied by severe thunder storms which result from the rapid rise of damp air above the overheated ground.

Cold weather sets in by mid-December and light snow falls in some parts of the country. About once in fifteen years Jerusalem experiences enough snow to block the roads. Hail storms are quite frequent on the coastal plain, and they may cause considerable damage.

Rains taper off during March and April, and there is a corresponding rise in the temperature. The "latter rains" usually come during April. They constitute the final storm of the season and the temperature drops rapidly. The "latter rains" make possible the final growth of the crops, and form a complement at the end of the season to the "former rains" at its beginning.

Between seasons there are traditional periods which often are accompanied by violent storms. Navigation in the Mediterranean is relatively safe during the summer. The shipwreck described in Acts 27 was the result of a voyage prolonged into the dangerous transition season with its sudden changes of wind.

The winds which bring desert conditions to the whole of Palestine during the transition seasons are known as siroccos, from the Arabic word for "east wind." Sometimes the name "khamsin" is applied to them, but this word is properly used of a similar condition in Egypt.

The sirocco is a hot, dry wind from the desert which produces the highest temperatures of the year. A yellowish dust haze fills the air so that visibility is greatly reduced and the sun casts only the palest of shadows. The intense dryness of the atmosphere may cause much physical discomfort, even for those who can adapt to excessively high temperatures. Biblical references to the "east wind" are frequent. The judgment of God is likened to a "hot wind from the bare heights in the desert . . . not to winnow or cleanse" (Jer. 4:11). In speaking of the future of Judah, Ezekial asked, "Will it not utterly wither when the east wind strikes it — wither away on the bed where it grew?" (Ezek. 17:10).

Violent sandstorms may arise in the desert during the period of the siroccos. Herodotus records the fate of a Persian army which, setting out from Egypt against a rising south wind to subdue the oasis of Siwa, lost its way and was never heard from again.

BIBLIOGRAPHY: Denis Baly, *Geographical Companion to the Bible,* ch. 3, McGraw-Hill, 1963. *The Geography of the Bible,* Harper & Bros., New York, 1957. W. F. Albright, "The Gezer Calendar," *BASOR,* 92, pp. 16-26. G. E. Wright, *Biblical Archaeology,* pp. 180-184, *The Westminster Press, Philadelphia,* 1957.

AHASUERUS. *See* Persia.

AHIRAM. Ahiram is the Phoenician form of the Biblical name Hiram. A Phoenician sarcophagus of a ruler named Ahiram was discovered by a French expedition conducted by M. Montet at °Byblos (Gebal) during the 1923-24 season. The sarcophagus is thought to date from the eleventh or twelfth century B.C. and is thus considerably earlier than the Hiram of °Tyre with whom David and Solomon had treaties.

Around the edges of the lid is the following inscription:

If there be a king among kings, and a governor among governors and an army commander up in Byblos who shall uncover this sarcophagus, let his judicial staff be broken, let his royal throne be upset! May peace flee from Byblos, and he himself be wiped out.

The sides of the sacrophagus depict Ahiram sitting on a throne with his feet on a triple-staged footstool. The side of the throne is in the form of a winged sphinx. Winged creatures, or cherubim, were used on the veil, the walls, and other objects of the Temple in Jerusalem (cf. I Kings 6; II Chron. 3). Israel's God is depicted poetically as "enthroned upon the cherubim" (Ps. 99:1).

AI. A mile east of Beitin, ancient Bethel, rises the mound of Et-Tell, formerly identified with Ai, the site of Joshua's second encounter with the °Canaanites (Josh. 7 and 8). In 1928, John Garstang while director of the Department of Antiquities in Palestine, did some superficial digging on the Et-Tell mound. He and F. W. Albright of the American Schools concluded, on the basis of ceramic evidence, that the city fell to Joshua in the sixteenth or fifteenth century B.C.

From 1933 to 1935 the Rothschild Expedition excavated Et-Tell under the direction of Mme. J. Marquet-Krause and S. Yeivin. Excavations proved conclusively that Et-Tell was flourishing during the third millennium B.C. It had strong walls, well-constructed stone houses, and a porticoed palace on the top of the hill. Stone bowls and ivories discoverd there give evidence of contacts with Egypt at this early period. Some time before 2200 B.C., however, it was destroyed. Except for a small settlement which made use of the earlier ruins (*ca.* 1100 B.C.), there is no archaelogical evidence that the site was ever occupied again.

Some Biblical scholars suggest that the story of Joshua's conquest of Ai should actually be applied to nearby Bethel. Hugues Vincent has suggested that the Canaanites of Bethel used the site of the Bronze Age city at Et-Tell as a military outpost at the time of the Israelite conquest, and that the battle was actually fought there (*RB*, 1937, pp. 231-266).

On the other hand, the identification of Ai with Et-Tell has itself been challenged. J. Simons insists that the expression "beside Bethel" in Joshua 12:9 requires a location for Ai closer than the two miles which separate Et-Tell from Bethel (*The Geographical and Topographical Texts of the Old Testament*, Leiden, E. J. Brill, 1959, p. 270). Yehezkel Kaufmann denies the identity of Ai with Et-Tell and insists that the term Ai does not mean "ruin," but "a heap" in the sense of a pile of stones, rejecting the idea that Ai stood on the mound of an ancient city.

In 1964, Joseph A. Callaway directed excavations at Et-Tell. There was no evidence that the site was occupied in the Middle or Late Bronze periods. An Iron Age settlement was confined to the uppermost terraces of the tell, suggesting that security had to be provided by a nearby fortified city, possibly Bethel.

Early Bronze Age city walls were excavated at the eastern extremity of the lower city. Work was also done on the acropolis, the sanctuary, and the Iron Age city.

BIBLIOGRAPHY. Judith (Krause) Marquet, *Les Fouilles de 'Ay (et-Tell)* 1933-35, P. Geuthner, Paris, 1949; W. F. Albright, "Ai and Beth-aven," *AASOR* IV, 1924, pp. 141-49.

'AIN EL-QUEDEIRAT. *See* Kadesh-barnea.

'AIN ET-TABGHA. Along the Sea of Galilee between Tiberias and Capernaum is the site which tradition identifies as the place where Jesus multiplied the loaves and fishes to feed the multitude (Mark 6:30-44). Tabgha, the Arabic name for the site, is a translation of the Greek *Heptapeogon*, "seven springs." The miracle is commemorated by the Church of the Multiplication of Loaves and Fishes. Under the new altar are remnants of an ancient altar with an inscription of the sixth century dedicating the church to the memory of the Patriarch Martyrius. A mosaic floor, dating from the fifth century, is decorated with representations of birds and plants. Near the church is a Benedictine monastery.

'AIN FESHKHA. 'Ain Feshkha is the name of a spring in the neighborhood of the Wadi Qumran, northwest of the Dead Sea. It was in this area that the °Dead Sea Scrolls were discovered and the community center at Khirbet °Qumran was excavated.

'AIN KADEIS. *See* Kadesh-barnea.

'AIN KAREM. Tradition places the birthplace of John the Baptist at 'Ain Karem, a village four miles west of Jerusalem. The Franciscan Church of St. John is built over the grotto in which John is said to have been born. Beneath the present church are remains of earlier structures including one of which (dated to the fifth or sixth century A.D.) contains a Greek inscription which reads, "Hail, martyrs of God." The Franciscans also maintain the Church of the Visitation marking the presumed site of the summer house of Zacharias and Elizabeth which Mary visited (Luke 1:39-44).

The Bible simply states that Mary went "into the hill country, to a city of Judah" (Luke 1:39). Besides 'Ain Karem, both Hebron and Juttah have been suggested as the site of John's birth.

'AIN SHEMS. *See* Beth-shemesh.

'AIN SILWAN. *See* Siloam Inscription.

AKHENATON. Amenhotep IV (*ca.* 1370-1353 B.C.) began his career as coregent with his ailing father Amenhotep III. His interests, however, were not in government, but in philosophy and religion, with the result that the Egyptain Empire of his period lost effective control of its Asiatic provinces (*see* Amarna Letters). Amenhotep became a devotee of the god Aton, identified with the solar disk, and he determined to bring all Egypt to the worship of his deity (see Hymn to the Aton). He even changed his name Amenhotep ("Amun is satisfied") to Akhenaton ("He who is beneficial to Aton"). Thereupon Akhenaton sought to remove the names of Amun and all other gods except Aton from the monuments throughout Egypt.

In the sixth year of his reign, Akhenaton moved his capital from Thebes to Akhetaton, "the horizon of Aton." While his break with the priesthood at Thebes had political overtones, the sincerity of Akhenaton's religious convictions has never been questioned. Breasted called him, "the first *individual* in

SITTING STATUE OF PHARAOH AKHENATON.
Courtesy, the Louvre

history." He was a monotheist in religion, although his one god was identified with the sun disk, and Sigmund Freud's contention that Moses learned his monotheism from Akhenaton is not taken seriously today.

Akhenaton's revolt inspired a new realism in art and a hymnody which finds its highest expression in the Hymn to the Aton, ascribed in Akhenaton. His reforms were short-lived, however. Akhenaton's rigor in suppressing the Amun cult and alienating its priesthood brought about a reaction after his death. The capital was moved back to Thebes, the Aton cult was officially rejected, and things reached a full cycle when Tutankh-Aton, ("The living image of Aton") Akhenaton's son-in-law, became Tut-ankh-amon. Akhenaton's concern for religious reform had a negative effect politically. His neglect of the affairs of state resulted in the dismemberment of the Empire.

AKHETATON. *See* Amarna.

AKKAD, AKKADIANS. The exact location of Akkad, sometimes spelled Agade or Accad (cf. Gen. 10:10), is unknown, but it was probably near Sippar or Babylon in southern Mesopotamia. A Semitic ruler named Sargon (Sargon I or °Sargon of Akkad) founded an empire which eventually controlled Sumer, Elam, Syria, and southern Anatolia from its capital at Akkad (*ca.* 2350 B.C.). By the time of the Third Dynasty of Ur (*ca.* 2000 B.C.) all of lower Mesopotamia was known as Sumer and Akkad, Sumer being the region above the Persian Gulf, and Akkad the area farther north, reaching the area of Baghdad. The terms Sumer and Akkad were in use until the late Persian period, although the term Babylonia is the more familiar name for the entire region. The Akkadians were a Semitic people, and the language which was spoken by the dynasty founded by Sargon I is now known as Old Akkadian. Linguistically the term Akkadian applies to the language spoken by the ancient Assyrians and Babylonians. It was written in a cuneiform script derived from the *non*-Semitic °Sumerians. The Assyrian king °Ashurbanipal spoke of "the obscure Akkadian writing which is hard to master."

BIBLIOGRAPHY. W. F. Albright, "A Babylonian Geographical Treatise on Sargon of Akkad's

Empire," *JAOS*, XXXXV, 1925, pp. 193-245. A. Moortgal, in A. Scharff and A. Moortgat, *Agypten und Vorderasien im Altertum*, Verlag F. Bruckmann, Munchen, 1950, pp. 256-71. S. N. Kramer, *Schooldays: A Sumerian Composition Relating to the Education of a Scribe*, University Museum, Philadelphia, 1949.

ALALAKH. The excavation of Tell Atshana (Turkish: Açana) by an archaeological team under the supervison of Leonard Woolley unearthed the ancient city-kingdom of Alalakh. The site is on the Amq plain in northwestern Syria in the present day Turkish province of Hatay. The people of Alalakh established their city at the junction of the main highways which led from the Mediterranean to the Euphrates and southward, and from the Taurus down to the Orontes River. Woolley's original intention in choosing this area for excavation was to trace relationships between the Aegean world and the civilizations of the Near East. In fact, the chief value of his excavation is the extension of our knowledge of the North Syrian area in the middle of the second millennium B.C. In recovering a somewhat detailed history of Alalakh, many references appear to the empires of the Sumerians, the Hurrians, the Hittites, and the Egyptians.

The excavations were carried on in two stages which totaled seven seasons of digging. The first period, from 1937 to 1939, ended abruptly with the beginning of World War II. The second period began after the war and continued from 1946 to 1949. Woolley has published a detailed account of the expeditions outlining his extensive finds of pottery, architecture, and inscriptional materials.

Although some seventeen different levels were uncovered, two levels yielded most of the texts, including cuneiform tablets and a monumental inscription. The lowest level where tablets were found was Level VII whose inscriptions are from the eighteenth-seventeenth century B.C. The language of this group of tablets is similar to the Old Babylonian dialect of Akkadian. Level IV not only yielded cuneiform tablets from the fifteenth-fourteenth centuries B.C., but also an inscribed statue of King Idrimi. The inscribed statue is about three feet five inches high. It is composed of 104 lines, the longest of the Alalakh tests. L. Oppenheim says concerning the inscription:

All this seems to me to bespeak the existence of a specific literary tradition totally different in temper and scope from that of the ancient Near East; of this tradition we have known only the later, far more substantial but equally admirable, fruits in the narratives of certain sections of the Book of Genesis and especially in the story of King David (*JNES* 14, 1955, p. 200).

The statue records the events in the life of King Idrimi which led to his establishment as the king of Alalakh and his subsequent achievements. The statue-account begins by relating internal problems within the royal circles of Aleppo, where Idrimi's paternal relatives lived. This unrest caused Idrimi to flee southward in his endeavor to put distance between himself and his enemies. The first state of the flight brought him to the town of Emar where the ruling family was related to his mother.

Idrimi did not remain very long at Emar, for he soon continued his flight with his troops through a desert area to the land of Canaan. This is the earliest reference to the name "Canaan" (*ki-in-a-nim*) in either Biblical or non-Biblical literature. Idrimi finally reached his destination at the Canaanite city of Ammiya. Here he learned that some of the occupants were citizens of the kingdom from which he was an exile. The town apparently was in control of the °hābiru warriors. Idrimi dwelled with them for seven years interpreting the flights of birds and studying the insides of lambs for omens.

Idrimi went home by sea after receiving assurance that it was safe for him to return. His relatives welcomed him, but there was still hostility expressed by Barattarna, the king of the Hurrian warriors. The inscription clearly states that this hostility lasted about seven years and that Idrimi was not acknowledged as the king of Alalakh until he had negotiated a peace treaty with Barattarna. Many kings of both the north and the south honored Idrimi because of his achievement.

The next recorded event is an expedition against the Hittites. Idrimi's treaty with Barattarna may have included a clause agreeing to such a campaign. Seven cities are listed as having been plundered by Idrimi and his troops. The Hittites do not seem to have offered any resistance.

Idrimi boasts of his accomplishments at home:

I built a palace. I made my throne like the throne of (other) kings; my servants like the servants of (other) kings. I made my sons to correspond like their sons and my comrades like their comrades. I caused the families who lived in the midst of my land to dwell happily, and I found a dwelling for those who had no homes . . . The borders which the gods of Alalakh had established and the sacrifices which our fathers had devotedly carried out, I continue to uphold.

After a reign of thirty years Idrimi established a co-regency with Adadnirari, his son, to whom he began to pass on the responsibilities of the kingdom. The text does not indicate what caused this turn of events.

The last section of the inscription contains a curse which is to be visited by the gods of heaven and earth upon any who would steal the statue. However, the gods were to bring only blessing and protection into the life of Sharruwa the scribe for writing the inscription.

Donald J. Wiseman has published the basic work on the remaining Alalakh tablets. In his original publication he included copies, transliterations, and translations of some of the tablets and summaries of the rest. Later, Wiseman edited tablets not included in his original publication.

Approximately 466 inscribed tablets were discovered at two levels. Even though the language of the cuneiform texts is the Babylonian dialect of Akkadian, there are many evidences which lead to the conclusion that the scribes' native language must have been one of the West Semitic dialects. This is understandable in light of the fact that this was a period of international communication during which the language of diplomacy was Akkadian.

A small number of tablets are agreements dealing with land and city exchanges. Certain historical events can be gleaned from these. Evidently Alalakh was in control of Abba'il of Yamhad in the Level VII period. In a treaty with Yarimlim, he agreed to give the city of Alalakh to Yarimlim in exchange for the city of Irridi which was east of the Euphrates. Another text describes the treaty provisions and the events of the uprising in the city of Irridi.

Contracts are found among the inscriptions where one ruler agrees to return any fugitives to the ruler from whose land they have fled. Besides these contracts of exchange and return, there are texts that involve loans, sales, and surety for loans.

Marriage accounts are found only among the Level IV or later period tablets. A written contract was the basis of civil marriage and was executed before witnesses. Two texts reveal that a bride price was sometimes required before a marriage could be consummated. One problematic inscription relates that the father, upon receiving the bride price, would then pass it to the possession of the daughter about to be married. In another text a betrothal gift is presented to the future father-in-law. This custom was practiced in the Old Testament when Eliezer offered gifts to Laban for the hand of Rebekah (Gen. 24). Likewise Shechem (Gen. 34) was willing to give gifts for the consent of Jacob and his sons to marry Dinah.

Most of the remaining texts are lists of landowners, classes of people, animals, clothing, metal and wooden objects, etc. A few Hittite documents appear along with the Akkadian tablets. It should be noted that many hundreds of Hurrian words occur throughout the inscriptions.

The king was at the top of the social structure of Alalakh. He owned villages and whole towns outside of his own immediate area of rule. These villages and towns could be sold at the discretion of the king either for personal or political purposes. This was similar to the Solomon-Hiram transaction involving the exchange of twenty cities as reported in I Kings 9:11.

The upper class of society was composed of the *maryannu*, the "chariot-owning nobility." In the census lists the *maryannu* are frequently designated as those "possessing chariots." Another indication of their high rank in society is found in a tablet which lists the *maryannu* as owning servants. The social levels appear to be somewhat flexible, because in a text consisting of a marriage settlement case before King Niqmepa, certain women and their offspring are appointed for *maryannu* status.

The most interesting of the *maryannu* tablets is the text in which King Niqmepa appoints a certain Qabia to the *maryannu* status. The context states that this status shall apply to his grandsons and that no one can rescind it at any time. An added feature is the statement that Qabia and his offspring are also to be priests of the goddess Enlil.

The second class of society is expressed under two names. The census lists provide the proof that this class was permitted to go under either name. In the columns of the lists certain individuals are identified as *shūzubūtu*, while in the totals the same individuals are referred to as *eḫelena*. *Shūzubūtu* is the Semitic title for the group, whereas *eḫelena* is the Hurrian designation, another proof of the strong Hurrian infiltration into all areas of society. Since the Semitic root means "to release or free," the second class of society can be defined as "the freedmen." This is largely a professional class and includes shepherds, grooms, singers, stonecutters, and leatherworkers. Since this class is not known outside the Alalakh texts, and then only in lists, it is difficult fully to realize the extent of their power and privileges.

The third class of society and by far the most numerous is the *ṣābē namē*. Namu which is the same as the word *nawu* denotes "pasture ground" or "habitation." The Hebrew cognate of this word, *nāweh*, can refer to a meadow or to the abode of a shepherd. This term is the technical designation for people who lived on the land, i.e., the rural population. However, the occupations of this class were not completely limited to the soil, in that some professions are listed for this class.

The *ṣābē namē* is a general term for several different groups of people in the Alalakhian society. The two main sub classes of this startification are the *ḫupshu*, and *ḫanū* or *ḫanyahu*.

The *ḫupshu* are found mentioned in the °Amarna letters, in the Assyrian law code, and in late Assyrian texts. They appear at °Ugarit, at °Nuzi, and in the Old Testament. This term appears to carry with it the idea of being free and yet, subservient to a degree. It is a low class in the Old Testament (*hopshi*), even though the individual is free.

In Alalakh the *ḫupshu* along with the *ḫanyahu* possessed cattle, agricultural implements, houses, and vineyards. Not much is known about the derivation of *ḫanyahu* which seems to be a Hurrian word. The *Assyrian Dictionary* considers this class to have been comprised of people who were once citizens of Hana which was a small kingdom located on the Euphrates. "Semi-free" would be the best definition to give to this lower class of society.

The fourth class and the lowest rung of the social ladder is the slave class. The two main sources of slaves as indicated in the tablets, are prisoners of war and natives who could not pay their debts.

The average slave price at Alalakh appeared to be about twenty-five shekels. An exception to this is found in text 66 which states that one slave costs fifty shekels. A slave was usually worth thirty shekels at Nuzi and in the Old Testament (Ex. 21:32), whereas in Ugarit the average price was forty shekels. Tablet 70 presents a problem. It states the cost of the slave mentioned in that text as one thousand shekels. Either this slave had rare professional ability or a scribal error has been committed.

Besides the social classes discussed above, another group of people occur in the sociological pattern of Alalakh. This group, the famous °ḫābiru, must be dealt with as a distinct social class, and yet this class can be placed under two categories already mentioned. In tablets 29 and 30 the *ḫapiru*, which are connected with the military, are composed of *eḫelena* and *ḫanyahu*.

The social stratification at Alalakh was not as rigid as it might appear. There are examples of status seekers, especially those desiring to progress to the *maryannu* class.

BIBLIOGRAPHY. *The Assyrian Dictionary*, III-VII, XVI, XXI. The Oriental Institute of the University of Chicago, 1956-   . Sidney Smith, *The Statue of Idri-mi*, Occasional Publications of the British Institute of Archaeology at Ankara, No. 1, London, 1949. E. A. Speiser, Review of *The Alalakh Tablets, Journal of the American Oriental Society,* LXXIV, 1954, pp. 18-25. Matitiahu Tsevat, "Alalakhiana," *Hebrew Union College Annual*, XXIX, 1958, pp. 109-134. Donald J. Wiseman, *The Alalakh Tablets*, Occasional Publications of the British Institute of Archaeology at Ankara, No. 2, London, 1953; "Supplementary Copies of Alalakh Tablets," *Journal of Cuneiform Studies*, VIII, 1954, pp. 1-30; "Abban and Alalakh," *Journal of Cuneiform Studies*, XII, 1958, pp. 124-129; "Ration Lists From Alalakh VII," *Journal of Cuneiform Studies*, XIII, pp. 19-33; "Ration Lists From Alalakh IV," *Journal of Cuneiform Studies*, XIII, pp. 50-62. Leonard Woolley, *Alalakh: An Account of the Excavations at Tell Atchana in the Hatay, 1937-1949*, The Society of Antiquaries, London, 1955; *A Forgotten Kingdom*, Penguin Books, Baltimore, 1953.

ALEPPO. Aleppo in northern Syria stood on the main road from the Euphrates and the east to the port of °Ugarit, the Mediterranean, and the west. It came under Hittite influence when Hattusilis I (1650-1620 B.C.) clashed with the kingdom of Yamhad which ruled the rich plane between the Upper Euphrates and the Mediterranean. Aleppo, known in ancient times as Halab or Halap, was the capital of Yamhad. The Hittites were interested in Yamhad because it was situated immediately to the south of their vassal state of Kizzuwatna. Its fertile plains and its lucrative trading routes made it particularly attractive.

Hattusilis made use of his chariotry, battering rams, and mobile towers as he attacked the strongly fortified cities of Yamhad. Aleppo itself finally fell, but the king succeeded in escaping to the east where he appeared as a refugee in Babylon. The capture of Yamhad brought the Hittites a step closer to control of western Asia, and hastened the day when the Egyptians and the Hittites would fight for the right to rule Syria and Palestine.

Six years after his campaign against Yamhad, Hattusilis died and was succeeded by Mursilis. The exiled king of Yamhad left Babylon with an army sympathetic to his cause. He attacked Aleppo and, with the aid of loyal followers within the city drove the Hittites out. Mursilis, however, struck back promptly. He sacked the cities of Yamhad, razed their walls, and mercilessly slaughtered their garrisons. Again Aleppo fell and its king sought refuge in Babylon. Mursilis and his chariots dashed five hundred miles down the Euphrates valley to Babylon. The Babylonians were taken by surprize, and after a short but fierce battle the Hittites had control of the city. The Hittite lines were overly extended, however, and Mursilis retraced his steps to Aleppo and then back to Hattusas (°Boghaskoy). Within a matter of weeks he was murdered.

Aleppo was never thoroughly incorporated into Hittite domains, but the Hittites continued to lay claim to the city. Tudhaliyas II (1460-1440 B.C.), the founder of the dynasty which later created the Hittite Empire, attacked Aleppo, ostensibly as punishment for its defection to Hanigalbat, a °Hurrian state which was organized around 1500 B.C.

Under °Suppiluliumas (1380-1340 B.C.), the Hittites entered a new era of strength. During his expedition dated ca. 1370 B.C.,

Aleppo and °Alalakh were restored to the Hittite domains, although °Carchemish held out until ca. 1340 B.C. After that date Syria from the Euphrates to the Mediterranean was a Hittite dependency. The Hittite Empire of Asia Minor came to an end as a result of invasions by the "Peoples of the Sea" during the twelfth century B.C., but Hittite culture lasted five more centuries in northern Syria. Assyrian records referred to Syria and the Taurus Mountain area as the "Land of Hatti," and kings of principalities in Syria appear in the Old Testament as "Kings of the Hittites" (II Kings 7:6; II Chron. 1:7).

BIBLIOGRAPHY. Roger T. O'Callaghan, *Aram Naharaim*, Pontifical Biblical Institute, Rome, 1948.

ALEXANDRIA. Alexander the Great founded the city of Alexandria on the site of Rakotis, a small Egyptian village on the northwest coast of the Egyptian Delta near the Canopic mouth of the Nile. It became the most successful of the many Alexandrias which Alexander established throughout the Near East. Egyptian Alexandria was about four miles long, built with streets intersecting at right angles. Colonnades adorned its principal streets. In order to preserve the best in Hellenistic culture, Alexander encouraged Greeks to settle there. The population of the city continued to have an Egyptian substratum, however, and a few years later a large and influential Jewish element moved into its northeastern sector. This intermingling of Greek, Jew, and Egyptian made Alexandria the most cosmopolitan city of the ancient world.

Located on a narrow isthmus between the Mediterranean Sea and Mareotis Lake, Alexandria early became a major Mediterranean port. Within thirty years after it was founded (332 B.C.) it became capital of Ptolemaic Egypt (304-30 B.C.). At the same time Alexandria served as the literary and scientific center of the Greek world.

Ptolemy I (Soter) not only made Alexandria his capital, but he also established a library and a museum in the city. Under his successor, Ptolemy II (Philadelphus), the library was enlarged and Alexandria became a seat of learning unrivaled in the East. Legend states that it was Ptolemy Philadelphus who made provision for the translation of the Old Testament into Greek. Although

31

the initiative was probably taken by the Jewish community in Alexandria, it is certain that the Jewish Scriptures did find their way into the great Alexandrian library.

Many of the great names of antiquity were associated with the Alexandrian library. Its first librarian was Zenodatus of Ephesus who made a specialty of the classification of poetry. Callimachus, a poet, classified, arranged, and labelled a library which numbered a hundred thousand manuscripts. Eratosthenes, Strabo, Hipparchus, Archimedes and Euclid were among the scholars who used its facilities. The library, which is said to have numbered 750,000 volumes, was destroyed at the time of Caesar's siege of Alexandria.

Ptolemy II (Philadelphus) employed a noted architect, Sostratus of Onidus, to construct a lighthouse on an island off the coast of Alexandria. The Pharos, as it was called, made use of a variety of architectural designs, and is regarded as one of the wonders of the ancient world. The lowest level was in the form of a rectangle, the second level an octagon, and the upper level a circle with a fire beacon amplified by a mirror, which flashed out into the sea. Its 445 foot height makes it comparable in size with a thirty-six story skyscraper of modern times.

Another engineering feat was the hepastadium, a causeway which joined the island to the Alexandrian mainland. The causeway, built either by Ptolemy Soter or Ptolemy Philadelphus, made two harbors: one facing east, largely used for small Egyptian boats; and a larger western harbor, bearing the name Eunostos, which was protected by a breakwater. Here vessels from the entire Mediterranean world brought their wares to Alexandria.

One of the most beautiful buildings of the ancient world was the Serapeum, built in Alexandria by Ptolemy Soter. The Serapeum was built to house the statue of a god from Sinope whom the Egyptians called Osiris-Apis, or Serapis. Eventually the shrine was filled with statuary and other works of art and it had a library of three hundred thousand manuscripts in its own right. The Serapeum was destroyed by Theophilus, Patriarch of Alexandria during the reign of Theodosius II. Theophilus was intolerant of the pagan nature of the Serapeum and

thought of himself as a partisan for true Christianity. The library was burned by another religious reformer, 'Amr ibn el-'Asi, the Arab commander under Chalif Omar (A.D. 641). Legend says that a request was made to Omar asking that the library be spared, whereupon he replied, "If these writings of the Greeks agree with the book of God, they are useless and need not be preserved; if they disagree they are pernicious and ought to be destroyed." The volumes of paper and parchment were then distributed to the four thousand baths of the city, and they are said to have provided fuel to heat the public baths for six months.

After the Ptolemaic period, Alexandria had a checkered history. In 48 B.C. Caesar landed his troops, four thousand in all, on the famed island:

I immediately embarked some troops, and landed them on Pharos. The island of Pharos gives its name to a lighthouse, a miracle of size and engineering. Lying opposite Alexandria, it forms one side of the harbor, and earlier monarchs had connected it with the city by means of a narrow causeway. The channel (of the harbor) is so narrow that anyone controlling the Pharos may close the harbor to shipping from whatever quarter. This alarming prospect decided me . . . to land troops on the island; a move that ensured the safe arrival of our food and reinforcements, which had been ordered by the neighboring provinces (*Commentaries,* Warrington translation).

Although Caesar destroyed the great Alexandrian library, Marc Antony rebuilt it and gave to Cleopatra two hundred thousand volumes which he brought from Pergamum. The library there had been built by Eumenes II in 197 B.C.

Following the defeat of Cleopatra at the Battle of Actium (31 B.C.), Alexandria fell to Octavian, later to serve as the Roman Emperor Augustus. Egypt was placed under Roman control, and made subject to a Roman prefect.

With the disintegration of Roman power in the East, Alexandria fell to Chosroes of Persia, A.D. 619. Persian power was short-lived however. Islam was on the march, and 'Amr ibn el-'Asi took the city in the name of Omar in A.D. 641. The Moslem conquerors moved their capital to Cairo, at the head of the Delta, and Alexandria declined in importance. At the time of the conquest,

Alexandria had a population of three hundred thousand and that progressively descreased until the early nineteenth century saw but twelve thousand people there. During the fourteenth century the canal to the Nile River was silted up, and this hastened Alexandria's decline. The canal was re-opened under Mohammed Ali in the nineteenth century, and today the city has grown to a population of one million and serves once more as Egypt's major seaport.

BIBLIOGRAPHY. A. Weigall, "The Alexandria of Antony," *Wonders of the Past,* II, 1924, pp. 477-90; E. M. Forster, *Pharos and Pharillon,* New York: Alfred A. Knopf, 1962.

ALPHABET. Although all problems concerning the origin and early history of the alphabet have not been solved, there is no question that it originated in the ancient Near East. Our word "alphabet" is derived from the first two letters of the Greek alphabet, alpha and beta. These, in turn, are derived from a Semitic alphabet. The first two letters of the Hebrew alphabet are Aleph and Beth.

The alphabet was preceded by other methods of written communication. Prehistoric caves contain pictures etched on their walls and ceilings, which conveyed meaning. By 3000 B.C., two systems of writing, both based on pictorial art, made possible written communication at the two extremities of the Fertile Crescent. The Egyptian system of hieroglyphic writing was a combination of picture writing, alphabetical and syllabic elements. The Egyptians, however, never dropped the non-alphabetical elements from their writing, so that hieroglyphic writing remained in part pictographic and in part syllabic throughout its over three thousand years of history.

In the Tigris-Euphrates valley, the Sumerians of the third millennium before Christ used a system of wedge-shaped characters which they impressed with a stylus on clay or cut into stone. This, too, was originally a system of picture writing, but the soft clay on which the pictures were inscribed was adaptable to the hasty drawing of pictures by groups of wedges which in time, lost their pictorial quality. Cuneiform syllabaries resulted, and they were adopted by the successors to the Sumerians — Assyrians, Babylonians, Hittites and others. The Assyro-Babylonian language known as *Akkadian

became the *lingua franca* of the Amarna Age (fifteenth and fourteenth centuries B.C.)

Inscriptions at *Serabit el-Khadem, in the Sinai Peninsula where turquoise mines were worked by the Egyptians during the early second millennium B.C., were once thought to be the oldest examples of alphabetic writing. W. F. Albright dates the Sinai inscriptions in the early fifteenth century B.C., by which time several systems of alphabetic writing had already developed.

Excavations at Tell ed-Duweir (Biblical *Lachish) have produced alphabetic writing, including an inscription on a dagger which dates to the sixteenth century B.C. Comparable material has been found at Gezer, Shechem, Megiddo, and Beth-shemesh.

In 1929 a new alphabet was discovered at Ras Shamra, ancient *Ugarit in northern Syria. Texts dating from *ca.* 1400 B.C. contained a type of writing which differed both from the alphabet of the Serabit el-Khadem texts and the cuneiform syllabaries of Mesopotamia. It seems to have been self-consciously invented by someone who knew the alphabetical principle and the cuneiform method of writing. He combined both ideas, inventing an alphabet of cuneiform symbols which would be suitable for alphabetic writing on clay tablets. Other texts in the same alphabet were subsequently discovered at Beth-shemesh and in the vicinity of Mount Tabor. In 1949, C. F. A. Schaeffer found at Ras Shamra a tablet containing the thirty letters of the Ugaritic alphabet in their proper order. The arrangement of the Ugaritic letters is similar to that used for the Phoenician alphabet with which the Sinai script is related.

The Old, or Palaeo-Hebrew script is the form of writing which is similar to that used by the *Phoenicians. A royal inscription of King Shaphat-baal of Gebal (Byblos) in this alphabet dates from about 1600 B.C. The sarcophagus of *Ahiram of Byblos contains an inscription in the Phoenician alphabet.

The oldest extant Hebrew writing is the *Gezer Calendar, dated about 1000 B.C. It is written in the Old Hebrew script, as is the *Moabite Stone (*ca.* 840 B.C.) which gives the Moabite version of the revolt against Israel mentioned in II Kings 1:1.

A variant of this Phoenician-Old Hebrew method of writing was used by the *Aramaeans whose alphabet used square letters in contrast to the more angular shape of the North Semitic alphabet. About 200 B.C. the Hebrews, under influence from the Aramaic language which was commonly spoken by post-exilic Jews, adopted the square letters. This form of the Hebrew alphabet is used, with few exceptions, in the *Dead Sea Scrolls dated from the second century B.C. to the first century A.D. It is used today both in the Old Testament and in modern Hebrew literature.

According to Greek tradition, the alphabet was brought to Boeotia by a Phoenician named Cadmus. In view of the fact that *kedem* is the Semitic word for "east," this tradition seems to reflect the memory that Greece received her alphabet from the East. The Semitic origin of the alphabet is also demonstrated by the names of the letters. Alpha, beta, and gamma are meaningless in Greek, but their Semitic equivalents aleph, beth, and gimmel mean, respectively, ox, house, and camel.

The Greeks probably first learned of the alphabet through trade with Phoenician mariners. From utilitarian usage, the alphabet slowly was adapted to literary purposes so that by 700 B.C. even painters of pottery jars had learned the use of the alphabet. The hundreds of signs used in cuneiform and hieroglyphic writing made the art of reading and writing the secret of the privileged few. The simplicity of the alphabet made it possible for every normal human to communicate with his contemporaries, and write for posterity. It appears that the Biblical writers all used alphabetic writing, and by the time of the Judges the ability to write had become so commonplace that a chance young man whom Gideon met could write the names of the chief men of his city (Judg. 8:14). See also Writing.

BIBLIOGRAPHY. David Diringer, *The Alphabet*, Philosophical Library, New York, 1948; *The Story of the Aleph Beth*, Thomas Yoseloff, New York, 1960; *Writing*, Frederick A. Prager, New York, 1962. I. J. Gelb, *A Study of Writing*, University of Chicago Press, Chicago, 1952. W. F. Albright, "The Early Alphabetic Inscriptions from Sinai and their Decipherment," *BASOR*, 110, 1948, pp. 6-22.

ALTAR. The altar of the ancient Near East was a place of sacrifice. Although the Mosaic Law limited Israelite sacrifice to the Tabernacle and, subsequently, the Temple, the

ADZE with Ugaritic alphabetic inscription. Courtesy, the Louvre

patriarchs customarily built altars wherever they settled. We read that Noah built an altar as soon as he left the ark (Gen. 8:20).

Archaeologists have discovered altars in ancient Egypt, Mesopotamia (notably Eridu, Ur, Ashur), Ras Shamra, and Palestine. In the excavations at Et-Tell Mm. J. Marquet-Krause discovered a small Early Bronze Age temple with an altar of plastered stones on which animal and food offerings were made. The great altar at Megiddo, dating from about 1900 B.C. was 6½ feet high and 29 feet in diameter at the base, with six steps leading to the top. At the foot were animal bones which were the remains of sacrifices which had been made there in ancient times. Late Bronze Age altars have been excavated at Lachish, Bethshan, and Hazor.

Small limestone altars with four horns at the upper edges are thought to have been used for incense. One of these, two feet three inches high, from the time of David has been discovered at Megiddo.

The infamous High Places denounced by the Israelite prophets were hills on which altars were built. The worshiper would bring the product of his field, his flocks, or his herds, to make an offering at the High Place. Prayers and vows were made and a sacrificial feast was enjoyed. The choicest portions of the animal, especially the fat (cf. Lev. 17:6), were burned. Other portions were reserved for the priests and the re-

CANAANITE SHRINE with a large altar, Megiddo. Courtesy, Oriental Institute

mainder eaten by the worshiper and his friends. Not only were the Canaanite gods worshiped at the High Places, but in times of apostasy Israel worshiped Yahweh there as well.

In addition to altars for sacrifice, archaeology has discovered many clay stands thought to have been incense burners. Relatively small stone altars, many of which have horns at their upper corners, discovered at Megiddo, Tell Beit Mirsim, and Shechem, are also regarded as altars of incense.

The Greeks as well as the peoples of the Fertile Crescent made use of altars, and Paul observed one with the inscription, "To an unknown god" (Acts 17:23) while on the way to Athens. Pausanias, who wrote his *Description of Greece* about a century after Paul's visit, wrote that there were in Athens "altars of gods called unknown" (i. 1.4). The Neo-Pythagorean philosopher Apollonius of Tyana, who died A.D. 98, observed the same altars. His biography, written by Flavius Philostratus (A.D. *ca.* 170-245), speaks of the necessity of speaking well of all the gods "especially at Athens, where altars are set up in honor even of unknown gods" (Phil-

ostratus, *The Life of Apollonius of Tyana* VI.3.).

Although the Athenian altar which Paul noted at *Athens has not been discovered, a comparable one was found in 1909 in the sacred precincts of the temple of Demeter at Pergamum. Although a corner of the stone is broken off, the inscription probably read, "To unknown gods, Capite, torchbearer."

AMARNA. The mound of Tell el-Amarna, ancient Akhetaton ("The Horizon of Aton") is located on the east bank of the Nile, about 190 miles south of Cairo. Here the reforming Pharaoh Amenhotep IV (Akhenaton) built his new capital after renouncing the Amun priesthood at Thebes and devoting himself exclusively to the Aton cult.

The ruins of Akhetaton are not imposing today. The city extended about five miles along the Nile, but its width was only about 1,100 yards. The lines of the city streets and the ground plan of the houses may still be traced. The great Temple to the Aton has left few remains, but the lines of the royal palace are clear. W. M. Flinders Petrie discovered four pavements of painted stucco during his expedition at Amarna in 1891. They were maliciously destroyed by a disgruntled guard in 1912, and the portions that were salvaged are now in the Cairo Museum.

To the west of the palace was the so-called House of Rolls which contained the records of the Egyptian foreign office from the time of Akhenaton and his father Amenhotep III (ca. 1400-1353 B.C.). It was while digging in this area that a woman accidentally discovered the first of the *Amarna Letters in 1887.

Excavations at Tell el-Amarna suggest that the city was built in haste. The workmanship is shoddy, although this fact is often disguised by the beauty of the naturalistic pictures of birds and vegetation painted on plaster walls and floors. Akhenaton's revolt brought about a change in the conventions of Egyptian art which is reflected in the Amarna discoveries. The older stylized figures give way to realistic representation. The bust of Queen Nefertiti, now in the Berlin Museum, is regarded as one of the finest specimens of ancient art.

Cut into the side of the hills to the east of Akhetaton were twenty-five tombs in which Akhenaton's officials were buried. They lack the variety of the tombs at Thebes, for the royal family and the worship of the Aton appear with monotonous regularity. The plaster relief figures which line the walls do give us some conception of life in the court of Akhenaton and his beautiful wife Nefertiti.

BIBLIOGRAPHY. Edward F. Campbell, Jr., "The Amarna Letters and the Amarna Period," BA, 1923, 1960, pp. 2-22. Charles F. Pfeiffer, Tell Amarna and the Bible, Baker Book House, Grand Rapids, 1963. J. A. Knudtzon, Die El-Amarna Tafeln, Leipzig, 1907-15. S. A. B. Mercer, The Tell el-Amarna Tablets, Macmillan Co., Toronto, 1939. Edward F. Campbell, Jr. The Chronology of the Amarna Letters, John Hopkins Press, Baltimore, 1964.

AMARNA LETTERS. At Tell- el-*Amarna, about midway between Cairo and Luxor in Egypt, a peasant woman accidentally discovered a deposit of cuneiform tablets in 1887. The tablets are rectangular in shape, measuring from 2 x 2¼ inches to 3½ x 9 inches. They are made of clay, inscribed on both sides and sometimes along the edges. The quality of the clay and the style of writing varies, depending on the place of origin. The language is uniform, the Assyro-Babylonian tongue which is now known as *Akkadian. In letters from Canaanite city-states, Canaanite words frequently appear as glosses to explain Akkadian words. These form our earliest examples of the language of Palestine.

The tablets passed from hand to hand until most of them were in the possession of Cairo merchants. E. A. Wallis Budge, representing the British Museum, realized the value of the tablets and procured 82 of them for the Museum. Another group of 160 found their way to the Berlin Museum, and 60 remained in the Cairo Museum.

The tablets comprise the diplomatic correspondence between the Egyptian Pharaohs Amenhotep III and Amenhotep IV (Akhenaton) and the kings of city-states in western Asia, including Syria and Palestine. Modern Amarna was the site of Akhetaton, the capital city established by Akhenaton after his rupture with the Theban priesthood.

Akhenaton neglected the interests of his empire, and the Amarna Letters indicate that Canaan was in a state of chaos. Egyptian authority was breaking up, and each petty kinglet was looking after his own interests. To add to the confusion, a people known as *Habiru were overrunning the country. The king of Jerusalem Abdi-Heba, wrote a number of letters to Akhenaton. In one of them he pleads:

. . . Let the king turn his attention to the archers so that archers of the king, my lord, will go forth. No lands of the king remain. The Habiru plunder all lands of the king. If archers are here this year, then the lands of the king, the lord, will remain; but if archers are not here, then the lands of the king, my lord, are lost. . . . All the lands of the king, my lord, are going to ruin.

Letter after letter was addressed to Akhenaton, but there is no evidence that Abdi-Heba's pleas were ever heeded. The Amarna letters give us our first non-Biblical reference to *Jerusalem. Aside from the political chaos which they exhibit, they show that Canaan enjoyed a high state of culture. They mention copper, tin, gold, and silver. Mulberries, olives, and grain appear as food products, and the agate seems to have been highly prized. Ships and chariots are mentioned, along with capital cities, provincial cities, fortresses, towns, and villages.

THE RUINS OF AMARNA TODAY. *Courtesy, Zion Research Library*

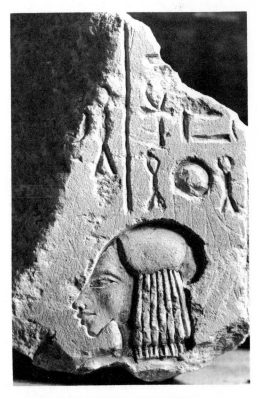

PHARAOH AKHENATON who established Akhetaton as his capital. Courtesy, the Louvre

THE HEAD OF A PRINCESS in limestone relief from Akhetaton, modern Amarna. Courtesy, Museum of Fine Arts, Boston

In addition to Canaan, the Amarna correspondence includes letters from the kings of Babylon, Mitanni, and the land of the Hittites. Much of it appears trivial, dealing with such matters as the exchange of gifts and the arrangement of royal marriages.

The Amarna Letters give us a first-hand picture of conditions in Canaan during the fourteenth century B.C. We learn that the land was nominally subject to Egypt, but that Egyptian control had completely broken down. The word Habiru, used of the bands of outlaws who were threatening the cities of Canaan, may be related to the Biblical word Hebrew, but the two peoples cannot be equated. Within the Bible the Hebrews, or sons of Eber (Gen. 11:15-16), are an earlier, and more inclusive group than the Israelites, or sons of Jacob (Gen. 32:28; 35:10, 11).

Communication between such lands as Egypt and Babylon, documented in the Amarna correspondence, is in accord with the mobility which is evident in the Biblical records of the Patriarchal Age. Abraham travelled freely throughout the *Fertile Crescent. Hittite penetration as far south as Hebron is seen in the fact that Abraham purchased a burial plot for Sarah from "Ephron the Hittite" (Gen. 23). The Amarna age king, Abdi-Heba of Jerusalem, has a name which suggests homage to a Hittite goddess. Hepa was known as "queen in heaven and queen of the Hatti (i.e. Hittite) lands."

AMENEMOPET, THE INSTRUCTION OF. The Egyptian book of Wisdom Literature commonly called Amenemopet (or Amenemope) was brought to the British Museum by E. A. Wallis Budge in 1888. It is written in Hieratic Egyptian on a papyrus 12 feet 1½ inches long and 10 inches wide, and is said to have been discovered at Thebes. The text occupies twenty-seven columns, bearing the Egyptian title, "Teaching

THE AMARNA LETTERS from governors of the city-states of Palestine appeal for help from Egypt against rebels and semi-nomadic Hapiru. Courtesy, British Museum

how to live." It is classified as British Museum Papyrus 10474. A portion also appears on a writing tablet in Turin.

Scholars disagree concerning the date of Amenemopet, but the weight of current opinion suggests some time between the tenth and the sixth centuries B.C. The original may be much earlier than our copies.

Biblical students have shown considerable interest in Amenemopet because of its numerous parallels with the Book of Proverbs, particularly Proverbs 22:17 — 23:14. Amenemopet says:

Do not carry off the landmark at the boundaries
   of the arable land,
Nor disturb the position of the measuring-cord;
Be not greedy after a cubit of land,
Nor encroach upon the boundaries of a widow.

The parallel passage in Proverbs (22:28; 23:10) reads:

Remove not the ancient landmarks which your
   fathers have set. . . .
Do not remove an ancient landmark or enter
   the fields of the fatherless.

A proverbial saying from Amenemopet reads:

Better is poverty in the hand of the god
Than riches in a storehouse;
Better is bread when the heart is happy,
Than riches with sorrow.

This may be compared with Proverbs 15:16-17:

Better is a little with the fear of the Lord,
Than great treasure, and trouble with it.
Better is a dinner of herbs where love is,
Than a fatted ox, and hatred with it.

Scripture bears witness to the fact that the Egyptians were noted for their wise men. Solomon's wisdom, we read, "surpassed the wisdom . . . of Egypt" (I Kings 4:30). Israel had contacts with Egypt during the Solomonic era, as it did both before and after, and it should not be surprising that similar thoughts appear in the literature of the two peoples. It is harder to determine whether the Biblical text or Amenemopet had priority. W. O. E. Oesterley in The Wisdom of Egypt and the Old Testament, p. 104, suggests that an Egyptian wise man incorporated the Biblical ideas into his Egyptian book of Wisdom. These ideas may very well have been in oral form prior to both our Book of Proverbs and the Egyptian Amenemopet. Oesterley sees a common stock of wisdom material which was abundant in the Near East providing the materials for the literature of many peoples. The specific ideas of Amen-

emopet seem on a higher level than those of other Egyptian books of wisdom and could, conceivably, have had their origin in Israel.

BIBLIOGRAPHY. E. A. Wallis Budge, The Teaching of Amenemopet, Son of Kanakht, M. Hopkins and Co., London, 1924. Francis Llewellyn Griffith, "The Teaching of Amenophis, the son of Kanakht (Papyrus BM 1074)" JEA XII, 1926, pp. 191-231. Ludwig Keimer, "The Wisdom of Amen-em-ope and the Proverbs of Solomon," AJSL, XXXXIII, 1926-27, pp. 8-21. Robert Oliver Kevin, The Wisdom of Amen-em-opet and its Possible Dependence upon the Hebrew Book of Proverbs, University of Pennsylvania, Philadelphia, 1931. James Martin McGlinchey, The Teaching of Amen-em-ope and the Book of Proverbs, Catholic University of America, Washington, 1939. W. O. E. Oesterley, The Wisdom of Egypt and the Old Testament in the Light of the Newly Discovered Teaching of Amen-em-ope, Society for promoting Christian Knowledge, London, 1927. David C. Simpson, "The Hebrew Book of Proverbs and the teaching of Amenophis," JEA, XII, 1926, pp. 232-239.

AMMAN (RABBAH, RABBATH AMMON, PHILADELPHIA).

Amman, ancient Rabbah-ammon, is located near the headwaters of the Jabbok, about twenty-three miles east of the Jordan River. Flint implements found on hills surrounding the city indicate that man has occupied the site since Palaeolithic times. A few *dolmens from the Neolithic or Chalcolithic Age are still standing.

The oldest occupation was in the area of the Citadel Hill, southwest of which are tombs which date from Hyksos times (ca. 1600 B.C.). When the airport was built for modern Amman, the workmen came upon ruins of a late Bronze Age temple.

The first Biblical reference to "Rabbah of the Ammonites" is in Deuteronomy 3:11 where we read that the great iron bed (sarcophagus?) of Og, the king of Bashan was in Rabbah. It is likely that the famed bedstead was carried off as a trophy of war and kept in the Ammonite capital.

At the division of the land of Canaan, half of the land of Ammon was allotted to the Gadites but there is no mention of them ever occupying Rabbah. Gad presumably occupied only the portion of its inheritance closest to the Jordan River, never moving as far east as Rabbah.

About 1050 B.C. the Ammonite king Nahash attacked Jabesh-gilead, northwest of

Rabbah, and threatened to put out the right eye of all its inhabitants (I Sam. 11:1-4). Saul aroused his fellow Israelites, rescued the people of Jabesh-gilead, and thereby proved his fitness to be king.

Nahash subsequently befriended David (II Sam. 10:1-2), but his son Hanun rejected a kindly visit of David's ambassadors and insulted them. Joab defeated a contingent of Ammonites and Aramean mercenaries and, the next year, besieged the city of Rabbah (II Sam. 11). It was during the siege of Rabbah that David acted shamefully in the Uriah incident.

The prophet Amos denounced the Ammonites for their brutality, threatening fire on the wall of Rabbah (Amos 1:13-14). Jeremiah also uttered prophecies of judgment, mentioning that Milcom (the god of Ammon) had dispossessed Gad (Jer. 49:1-2). Evidently the Ammonites had regained territory which had been lost to the tribe of Gad at the time of the Conquest.

Under Ptolemy Philadelphus (285-246 B.C.) Amman was rebuilt and renamed Philadelphia. It became an important trading center and was a member of the league of Hellenistic cities known as the *Decapolis.

Amman is now the capital of Jordan, and its population has multiplied in recent years. Its chief archaeological monument is the Roman theatre which was built into the side of 'a cliff which was partly cut out to accommodate it. The theatre seats six thousand people. The columns nearby were part of a colonnade which originally surrounded a plaza. On the east side of the plaza was an Odeum, a smaller theatre used for concerts and recitals. There are also remains of the Nymphaeum on the banks of a nearby stream. These buildings bear no inscriptions but they are thought to date from the second or third century A.D.

Older remains have survived at the Citadel Hill which was enclosed by a wall, some stretches of which may still be seen. At the northeast corner, part of the Iron Age wall remains; the rest is Roman or later. Outside the wall to the north is the cistern which provided water for the garrisons during times of siege. At the northwestern corner is a Roman temple to Hercules. Bare rock exposed within the temple indicates that the Roman structure may have been built on the site of earlier temples in which the rock served as an altar or a high place. Fragments of a statue found beside the Roman temple indicate that a thirty foot statue of Hercules once stood there.

When the Romans rebuilt the city they removed most of the remains of earlier cultures. Sherds from the Early and Middle Bronze Ages, the Iron Age and the Hellenistic period were found mixed with Roman sherds when deep cuttings were made on the slopes of the Citadel Hill. Evidently the Romans threw the remains of earlier ages over the edge of the hill.

AMMON, AMMONITES. The origin of the Ammonite people is traced in Scripture to Lot's incestuous relation with his younger daughter (Gen. 19:36-38). Ammonites dwelt in the area north and east of Moab in the area between the Arnon and the Jabbok. Their capital city was known as Rabbah, or Rabbath Ammon, modern *Amman.

Ammon was frequently hostile to Israel (cf. Deut. 23:3, 4; Judg. 8:13; II Sam. 10: 1-19; Neh. 4:3). The Assyrian king Sennacherib conquered Ammon during his campaign in western Asia (705 B.C.), and Pudiel of Ammon paid tribute to Esarhaddon (690 B.C.). An Ammonite, Tobiah, obstructed the rebuilding of Jerusalem by the Jews who had returned from exile (Neh. 2:10, 19; 4:3, 7). The Ammonites were incorporated into the Roman Empire and survive today as one of many strains which form the ancestry of Palestinian Arabs.

AMORITES. Amorites are first mentioned in Sumerian and Akkadian inscriptions dating from the last half of the third millennium B.C. At that time they were a Semitic nomad people from the regions of Syria north of Palmyra. The cultivated peoples of lower Mesopotamia looked upon them as uncivilized barbarians.

About 2000 B.C. groups of Amorites migrated southward into the Tigris-Euphrates valley, and soon we find Amorite names among the rulers of important city-states. The Sumerian rulers of the Third Dynasty of Ur lost their power ca. 1960 B.C. Larsa became an Amorite state and after 1800 B.C. an Amorite ruled in Ashur, the earliest capital of Assyria.

The *Beni-hasan tomb paintings from

Egypt (*ca.* 1900 B.C.) depict bearded Amorites with shaven lips bringing their wares into Egypt. They are dressed in elaborately woven, striped garments. The men wear simple loincloths and the women full garments reaching below the knee. The ass serves as the beast of burden, and the Amorites bring with them their musical instruments (the lyre, or "harp" of the English Bible), spears, bows, and skin water bottles.

During the latter half of the eighteenth century B.C. the most important Amorite state was °Mari on the middle Euphrates. Among the twenty thousand cuneiform tablets discovered there since 1936 is a sizable collection of diplomatic correspondence between the kind of Mari and his vassals in Mesopotamia and Syria. One of the earliest known references to chariotry appears in this correspondence.

The First Dynasty of °Babylon was also Amorite in origin. Its illustrious sixth king, °Hammurabi, conquered his fellow Amorite, Zimri-lim, the last king of Mari. Shamshi-adad I (1748-1716 B.C.), of Assyria, another contemporary of Hammurabi, was also an Amorite.

The period of Amorite control of southern Mesopotamia was paralleled by Amorite incursions into Palestine. Archaeological evidence indicates a break in the occupation of numerous Palestinian cities in the period between 2100 and 1800 B.C. The nomadic folk who entered the land at this time left few artifacts. Their pottery was similar to that used in Syria and seems to have Amorite affinities. The journeys of Abraham can be understood as part of the Amorite migrations of the period.

Amorites were in Canaan during the age of the Biblical Patriarchs (cf. Exod. 33:2). They were among the allies of Abraham at the time of the routing of the four kings from the East who had plundered Sodom and taken Lot captive (Gen. 14:1-16). Amorites were so plentiful in Palestine that the °Amarna Letters use the term *Amurru* of the entire Syria-Palestine territory. Later, however, Egyptian usage tended to restrict the term *Amurru* to the far north of Palestine, the area which had as its capital Kadesh-on-the-Orontes.

At the time of the Israelite invasion of Canaan, Amorite rulers (Sihon of Heshbon and Og of Bashan) controlled Transjordan (Josh. 12:1-6; Judg. 1:36). Significant victory over these Amorites formed a prelude to the conquest of Palestine proper. West of the Jordan, however, there were other Amorites with whom Israel fought. The men of Ai are called Amorites (Josh. 7:7) and the confederation of southern city-states (Jerusalem, Hebron, Jarmuth, Lachish, and Eglon) which challenged Joshua at Gibeon was lead by "the five kings of the Amorites" (Josh. 10:5). Amorites also took part in the northern alliance under Jabin of Hazor which fought Joshua at the Waters of Merom (Josh. 11:3-5).

The term Amorite seems to have become a general name for the inhabitants of *Amurru,* and need not always have a specific ethnic connotation. At times it seems to have been used as a synonym for °Canaanite but frequently the two peoples are clearly distinguished (cf. Josh. 11:3; Judg. 3:5). By the time of the United Kingdom (*ca.* 1000 B.C.) the Amorites lost all significance to Israel (cf. I Kings 9:20-21). At the same time they were displaced in other areas by °Kassites, °Hurrians, and °Arameans.

BIBLIOGRAPHY. George A. Barton, "The Place of the Amorites in the Civilization of Western Asia," *JAOS,* XXXXV, 1925, pp. 1-38. E. Dhorme, "Les Amorrhéens," *RB,* XXXVII, 1928, pp. 161-180; XXXIX, 1930, pp. 161-178; XXXXX, 1931, pp. 161-184. W. F. Albright, "Western Asia in the 20th Century B.C.: the Archives of Mari," *BASOR,* LXVII, 1937, pp. 26-30. Martin Noth, *Die Ursprunge des alten Israel in Lichte neuer Quellen,* Westdeutecher Verlag, Köln, 1961.

AMPHITHEATER. Amphitheaters were open structures which served for the exhibition of gladiatorial contest, struggles of wild beasts, sham sea battles and other spectacles designed for the entertainment of the populace of Rome and other cities of the Empire. The typical amphitheater was elliptical in shape with seats supported on vaults of masonry rising in many tiers around an arena in the center. Under the arena was storage space and quarters for gladiators and wild animals. The earliest amphitheaters were built of wood, but that built at Pompeii (*ca.* 70 B.C.), and the Flavian Amphitheater at Rome, better known as the Colosseum (A.D. 80), are stone amphitheaters which have left significant remains that can be studied today. *See also* Theater.

INSIDE VIEW of Colosseum (the Flavian Amphitheater) in Rome. Courtesy, Italian State Tourist Office

AMPHORA. An amphora is a tall, two-handled earthenware jar used by the ancient Greeks for wine and oil. The body is egg-shaped, with a narrow neck at the top. The bottom of the jar either forms a base or ends in a point which can be inserted into the ground.

Amphorae painted with figures of Athena and athletic subjects were awarded as prizes at the Panathenaic Games. Many of these decorative amphorae are now in museum collections.

AMRAPHEL. Amraphel, "king of Shinar," was an ally of Chedorlaomer of Elam, Arioch of Ellasar, and Tidal "king of nations" in attacking Sodom, Gomorrah and the other cities in the area south of the Dead Sea. (Cf. Gen. 14.) Although some scholars attempted to identify Amraphel with *Hammurabi of Babylon, any relationship between the two is now seriously questioned.

AMPHORA depicting Heracles and the Cretan Bull, ca. 520 B.C. Courtesy, Museum of Fine Arts, Boston

AMULET. The term amulet is used of anything worn by a person in order to drive away evil spirits and to insure health, prosperity, and fertility. Jewelry and amulets may not be readily distinguished, and superstitious people would doubtless consider some magic inherent in any jewel they wore. Common amulets were in the form of gems, stones, beads, seals, and plaques with an inscribed prayer or incantation. Excavations in Palestine have produced thousands of amulets made of pierced shells, pearls, and animal teeth. Figurines of deities (particularly Egyptian), animals shaped in gold, and lunar disks or crescents are plentiful. The inverted crescent was associated with the fertility goddess and was worn by women and hung on the necks of animals to guarantee offspring (cf. Judg. 8:21). The prophetic teachers in Israel frowned on the use of amulets. When Jacob urged the women of his household to put away the foreign gods in preparation for the return to Bethel they buried their earrings as well (Gen. 35:4). Isaiah pronounced judgment on the haughty women of Jerusalem, bedecked in finery and wearing amulets (A.V. "earrings").

ANAT. Anat was the Canaanite goddess of war and fertility, the sister and consort of Baal. *See* Baal, Ugarit.

BIBLIOGRAPHY: W. F. Albright, "The Evolution of the West Semitic Divinity 'An-'Anat-'Atta," *AJSL*, LXI, 1925, pp. 73-101.

ANATHOTH. Near the village of 'Anata, three miles northeast of Jerusalem is the mound known as Ras el-Harrubeh. At the suggestion of William F. Albright two students of the American Schools of Oriental Research in Jerusalem, A. Bergman and A. C. Blair, made preliminary soundings in the mound early in 1936. Although the results were inconclusive, the identification of Ras el-Harrubeh with Anathoth, the home of Jeremiah, is presupposed by modern students of Biblical geography such as E. G. Kraeling and L. H. Grollenberg. Ras el-Harrubeh was a walled town of some strength located on a broad ridge of hills overlooking the Jordan valley and the northern part of the Dead Sea. Settlements there date from ancient Israelite times to the seventh century A.D. The report of the soundings by Bergman and Blair appears in *BASOR*, numbers 62 and 63.

ANCYRA (ANKARA). Modern Ankara, the capital of Turkey, is built on the site of ancient Ancyra, situated in the heart of the Hittite country. There is no evidence, however, that Ancyra was occupied in Hittite times. A necropolis discovered in 1925 by Macridi Bey suggests that an important Phrygian town was located at the site of Ancyra at the end of the second millennium B.C.

The name Ancyra first appears during the Achaemenid Persian period (540-332 B.C.). The city was occupied by Alexander the Great (334 B.C.) after his victory at the Grannicus. Following Alexader's death Ancyra was ruled by Seleucids until the invasion by the Gauls during the third century B.C. Ancyra became the principal city of the Tektosages, one of the tribes of the Galatian confederacy. Foundations of their fortress were discovered beneath the present fortifications above the town.

Mithridates of Pontus (88-63 B.C.) occupied Ancyra and at his death the city came under Roman control. Augustus changed the name of the city to Sebastus. An important building of the Roman period was known as the Temple of Augustus and Rome. In pre-Roman times it was consecrated to the Phrygian god, Men. By the beginning of the Christian era it was an Augustus temple and bore Greek and Latin inscriptions commemorating the achievements of Augustus. In later centuries it served as a Christian church and a Moslem mosque.

Architects making soundings for a public building accidentally came upon the remains of Roman baths in 1926. The area was subsequently excavated by archaeologists from the University of Ankara (1937-41) who also discovered fragments of Phrygian ceramics from the seventh century B.C.

ANI, INSTRUCTION OF. The Instruction of Ani is a selection from the Egyptian Wisdom Literature which is now in the Cairo Museum ("Boulaq #4"). Fragments are preserved in Paris and Berlin. The Cairo manuscript, in Hieratic Egyptian, dates somewhere between the eleventh and the eighth centuries B.C.

The author of the Instruction of Ani writes as a father giving counsel to his son. Most of the advice pertains to the practical details of life: "Take to thyself a wife while thou art still a youth. . . . Be on thy guard against a woman far abroad [cf. the Biblical 'strange woman' Prov. 5:3 A.V.] . . . Do not talk a lot. Be silent and thou wilt be happy. . . . Thou shouldst not sit when another who is elder than thou is standing. . . . Thou shouldst not eat bread when another is waiting. . . ." The lad is taught to have a high regard for his mother and his wife, and to make the prescribed offerings to the gods. Of his mother, the youth is reminded, "She put thee into school when thou wert taught to write."

The Instruction of Ani does not have the close parallels to Proverbs that we meet in the Wisdom of °Amenemopet. The form of writing, in which a father gives counsel to his son, is found in Proverbs: "Hear, O sons, a father's instruction, and be attentive, that you may gain insight . . ." (Prov. 4:1).

ANI, PAPYRUS OF. The Papyrus of Ani is our fullest version of the Egyptian funerary texts known collectively as the °Book of the Dead. It dates from the Eighteenth Dynasty (1570-1310 B.C.) and was discovered at °Thebes. The papyrus is 78 feet long, 15 inches wide, and is profusely illustrated.

ANTIOCH (SYRIAN). Antioch-on-the-Orontes was the most famous of sixteen Antiochs founded by Seleucus (I) Nicator (312-280 B.C.) in honor of his father. It was established in 301 B.C. after the victory of Seleucus over Antigonus at Issus (310 B.C.). The navigable Orontes connected Syrian Antioch with its nearby port city Seleucia Pieria.

Jews were encouraged to settle at Antioch, which was a cosmopolitan city with a culture that evoked the admiration of Cicero himself. Pompey captured the city in 64 B.C. Subsequently it became capital of the Roman province of Syria and, with a population of 500,000, was the third largest city of the Roman Empire. It boasted magnificent buildings and temples and lamp-lighted streets, earning the epithets "Antioch the beautiful" and "Queen of the East."

Religiously Antioch was a mixture of the best and the worst. The groves of Daphne and the Apollo sanctuary were scenes of orgiastic rites. Juvenal made of the Orontes a symbol of the corruption which was entering Rome from the East:

Obscene Orontes, diving under ground
Conveys his wealth to Tiber's hungry shores,
And fattens Italy with foreign whores.

Here, however, Christians were able freely to preach to Jew and gentile, and from the Antioch church the first foreign missionaries went forth as heralds of the cross.

Ancient Syrian Antioch is now a Turkish city of 42,000 known as Antakya. Archaeologists have here discovered about twenty churches dating from the fourth century A.D.

ANTIPATRIS, APHEK. Antipatris, about twenty-six miles south of Caesarea, on the road to Lydda, was the site of a Canaanite stronghold as early as 2000 B.C. Known in the Old Testament as Aphek, it was here that the Israelites suffered the tragic loss of the ark to the Philistines (I Samuel 4). Herod the Great rebuilt the city about 35 B.C. and named it Antipatris for his father Antipater. It was here that the apostle Paul stopped on his way from Jerusalem to Caesarea (Acts 23:31). Water from ancient Antipatris, now known as Ras el-'Ain, is piped thirty miles upland to Israeli Jerusalem.

The site was excavated in 1946 by the Palestine Department of Antiquities.

APHEK. *See* Antipatris.

AQUEDUCT. Proximity to a satisfactory water supply was a prerequisite to every human settlement, however small. Biblical patriarchs settled near springs or sank wells to provide water for their encampments. The building of a channel to convey water was an important step in freeing man from the necessity of living beside a well or a stream of water. Such channels, or troughs (termed aqueducts, "conveyers of water" by the Romans) were a necessity whenever large populations assembled in a place of limited water supply.

Although earlier rulers concerned themselves with canals and reservoirs, it was Sennacherib of Assyria who built the first aqueduct in Mesopotamia. His Jerwan Aqueduct was a great causeway, one thousand feet wide which conveyed water for thirty miles to the gardens of Nineveh. Its stone arches are considered to be the world's oldest bridge. The Jerwan Aqueduct was

the inscription of the name "Tobiah" (t-w-b-y-h) on the face of the cliff where the caves are located. Albright considers the inscription to be Aramaic characters of the third century B.C. and identifies this Tobiah with the Tubias of the Zenon Papyri (*Archaeology of Palestine*, p. 149). B. Mazar, however, dates the inscription at the end of the sixth or beginning of the fifth century B.C. He regards the *teth* as transitional form between the ancient Hebrew form and the Aramaic of the Persian period and calls attention to the archaic form of the *yod* ("The Tobiads," *IEJ*, VII, 1957, pp. 141-142). The *teth* is essentially the later form of the le , and the form of the *yod* can probably b explained by the nature of the writing; that is, it is a formal inscription which would be likely to utilize an archaic form.

The fact that the literary references to 'Araq el-Emir date from the mid-third century, thus indicating that this was the time of its prominence, and the lack of archaeological evidence of an extensive building activity before the beginning of the second century should be considered in this case. It seems unnecessary to date the inscription earlier than the third century B.C., although it might go back as early as the time of Tobiah the contemporary of Nehemiah. (See: R. A. Bowman, "The Book of Nehemiah [Exposition]," *IB*, III, Abingdon Press, New York, 1954, p. 676.)

V. *Relevance to Biblical Study.* The association between 'Araq el-Emir and the Bible is quite clear. The name Tobiah is first mentioned in Zech. 6:9-14 as one of the rich, well-connected Judeans and a supporter of the Zadokite high-priest. The origins of the family probably go much farther back (ben Tabeel in Isa. 7:6 has been suggested as a member of the family), but the most prominent period for them begins about 520 B.C. (For a detailed discussion of the origins of the family see: Mazar, "The Tobiads.")

A. Nehemiah. In the Book of Nehemiah the Tobiads appear to be well established in the Transjordan. Tobias is called "the Ammonite servant" in Neh. 2:19, as a derisive term. The expression "servant," however, as it appears on seals of the period, designated a royal officer. In this case, Tobiah could be the Persian-appointed governor of Ammonite territory. This same Tobiah was related, by marriage, to the high-priest,

Eliashib, and was highly regarded by him (Neh. 13:4-7). Also, he was prominent in the affairs of Jerusalem (Neh. 6:17-19). It has long been debated whether Tobiah was a Jew, an Ammonite or of mixed blood, but no firm conclusions can be made on the subject.

There was great rivalry between Nehemiah and Tobiah. Tobiah first appears as one of the opponents to the rebuilding of the walls of Jerusalem (Neh. 2:17-20; 4:7-9; 6:1ff); but, when they were completed he moved into the city. A decisive action was finally taken by Nehemiah who, learning that Eliashib had given Tobiah chambers in the Temple during his absence from the city, drove Tobiah out, threw out his furniture, and cleansed the rooms where he had been (Neh. 13:6-9).

B. The Maccabees and Josephus. Even after the episode in Nehemiah 13 the influence of the Tobiads in Jerusalem had not ended. According to Josephus, it was simply because it was unsafe for him to go to Jerusalem that Hyrcanus went to the Transjordan where he built his fortress. When Antiochus IV Epiphanes came to the throne of Syria, Hyrcanus committed suicide for fear of reprisals, for he had been of the Egyptian faction. His lands were confiscated by Antiochus (Josephus, *Antiquities* XII.236). From this period there are only two references to the area, both of which relate to the time of Antiochus' invasion: I Macc. 5:9-13 which refers to the "land of Tob," and II Macc. 12:17 which refers to Jews called "Toubiani."

BIBLIOGRAPHY. Paul W. Lapp, "Soundings at 'Araq el-Emir (Jordan)," *BASOR*, No. 165, 1962, pp. 16-34. C. C. McCown, "The 'Araq el-Emir and the Tobiads," *BA*, XX, 1957, pp. 63-76. B. Mazar, "The Tobiads," *IEJ*, VII, 1957, pp. 137-145, 229-238. L.-H. Vincent, "La Palestine dans les papyrus ptolemaïques de Gerza," *RB*, XXIX, 1920, pp. 161-202.

ARARAT. *See* Urartu.

ARCHAEOLOGY. Archaeology is the scientific study of the material remains which have been left behind by men during past ages. Most modern countries have undertaken a study of their ancient past by excavating ancient towns, graves, etc. so that today there is a vast storehouse of knowledge about ancient man all over the world. There are many branches of the science of archaeology. "Biblical Archaeology" is concerned with the understanding of the history, life, customs, and literature of the Israelites and of those peoples in the neighborhood of ancient Israel who influenced them. Valuable material is available, therefore, from ancient °Egypt, °Moab, °Edom, °Ammon, Syria, °Canaan, °Assyria, °Babylonia, °Persia, Greece and the Roman world. Any discoveries from these lands which throw light on Biblical history, religion, customs or literature come within the purview of Biblical archaeology.

I. *Sources of Information.* The archaeologist obtains his information from the material remains left behind by men in past ages. These are of two broad classes: the written documents which were inscribed on stone, clay, metal, papyrus, parchment, wood, etc.; and the unwritten documents which comprise all other kinds of remains — buildings of various kinds, fortifications, sculptures, household vessels, tools, personal ornaments, coins, weapons, clothing, art pieces, food, animal and human bones, etc. These are found in association with buildings which have become completely or partially covered or in graves and tombs.

Numerous buildings are still more or less exposed, among which may be noted such monuments as the °Pyramids and temples of Egypt, the Parthenon and other buildings on the °Acropolis in Athens, the great °ziggurat at °Ur of the Chaldees and various Roman temples, °aqueducts, roads and walls, which are to be seen in many lands. In these cases, any inscriptions, art work, or general architectural features are available for study with little or no excavation.

In some cases building remains are partly covered with the accumulated debris of the centuries which gathers about their lower portions. This has to be cleared away before the complete structure is visible. Some of the buildings already mentioned were of this type.

Other remains are completely covered and need to be exposed to view by the skill of the excavator. For example, in the course of the centuries it sometimes happened that a deserted town which lay at the foot of a hill or a mountain was gradually covered by silt brought down by the rains. The buildings of the ancient market place at Athens and of the forum in Rome were covered in this way. In some cases, deserted towns were covered by wind blown dust or sand, as in the case of ancient settlements in Arabia and Egypt. Occasionally a town was covered by volcanic ash, as were Pompeii and Herculaneum which were destroyed by the eruption of Mt. Vesuvius in 79 A.D.

Perhaps the most significant of all the covered ruins is the so-called °"tell" which is comprised of the remains of several towns lying one on top of the other. In the ancient world, when a walled town was burned, beaten down by battering rams, or destroyed by earthquake or any other means, the new-comers who rebuilt did not remove all the debris and the foundations of the old city. Some of the best materials were re-used, but the remains of the old city were levelled out and a new town was built on the ruins of the old one. In this way several feet of debris from the previous town were sealed off leaving behind the general pattern of buildings and streets as well as a great variety of the common items of daily use.

Most of the important towns of ancient Palestine are in this category — Bethel, Jericho, Ai, Samaria, Jerusalem, Megiddo, Bethshan, Beth-shemesh, Debir, Gezer, Hazor, and so on. In some cases there may be ten, twelve or even twenty strata of destroyed towns, each of which tells us its own story. It is the task of the archaeologist to dig through successive layers of occupation in order to unravel the story of centuries of history. In area, these mounds vary from three or four acres up to fifteen or twenty.

Tombs of various kinds provide a valuable source of information whether these are the spectacular tombs of kings, such as the Royal Tombs at Ur of the Chaldees, or the tomb of the Pharaoh Tutankhamon on the one hand, or the small tombs of lesser citizens. In the vicinity of ancient towns lies the burial ground. One of the tasks of the archaeologist is to search the hillsides and surrounding country for the ancient cemetery. In the case of a tell with several layers of occupation there may be several cemeteries, or, in some cases, several areas in the same cemetery. Whereas pottery is often broken in the tell, complete pieces are found in the graves along with many other items which, because of their value, would normally have been plundered from the city after its destruction.

II. *Method of Excavation.* A site is generally chosen for a particular purpose. Sometimes more information may be required about the sequence of events in a particular region. Or perhaps more detail is required about a particular nation such as the Assyrians. If the site is clearly identifiable, it may be excavated in order to discover the archaeological history of this particular site.

Where identification is possible from references in written records the archaeologist is anxious to compare his archaeological discoveries with the written record. Sometimes the name of a site becomes clear as written records bearing its name come to light during excavation (*e.g.* °Gibeon).

Normally permits to excavate must be secured from the appropriate government authority and the particular site must be purchased or rented from its owners. Once all formalities are complete the excavation may begin.

Excavation in mounds begins by a preliminary survey of the mound and its division into smaller areas about five metres square. Each area is then excavated stratigraphically, that is, each layer of debris must be dealt with as a unit. Normally a trial trench is cut across the area to a depth of a few feet. By observing the layers in the sides of this trench the nature of the area is determined. This trial trench then acts as a key to the rest of the area which is excavated layer by layer. All the items of each layer belong together and are kept in separate baskets. When walls appear the excavator begins to look for floors since objects on top of the floor belong to its final period of occupation, while those beneath the floor belong to an earlier period.

Once a reasonable area of a given period has been laid bare down to the floor, and all the small items have been collected, surveyors' plans are drawn and the whole is photographed. Only then are the floor and walls dismantled in order to proceed to the next level. At each stage detailed records are kept since all archaeology is basically destruction. Once the area has been dug it cannot be restored.

Normally, only limited areas of a large mound are excavated, although frequently several of these are opened up at different points in the mound and dug in depth in order to provide a comparison between the various strata revealed in the several areas. It is generally necessary to return to a given mound for several seasons before a reasonably clear picture emerges.

A search for the tombs which correspond to each layer is normally carried on at the same time as the excavation of the mound is being undertaken. Cemeteries are seldom marked and are difficult to find, but once they are discovered their excavation is not as complex as is excavation of the mound. The chief difficulty lies in the fact that the space is generally very confined. But the objects in the tombs are generally intact, although frail objects such as those of wood or bone have to be chemically treated before removal.

As the excavation proceeds, a considerable amount of data accumulates, including photographs, sketches, surveyor's plans, and a great number of objects in pottery, wood, stone, bone, etc., all of which are marked to define their exact origin. It is from this data that the archaeologist compiles his final report for official publication.

III. *Archaeological Periods.* In the course of thousands of years great changes have taken place in the structure of buildings, in the shape and decoration of pottery and art pieces, in the shape and nature of weapons, in the style of writing, etc. Archaeologists distinguish various periods of time during which there was reasonable uniformity of culture in a particular area. Change in culture may have been due to invasions by other peoples or to an era of invention or to some other cause.

In Palestine the commonly recognized periods are as follows:

Mesolithic (Natufian)	*ca.* 8000-6000 B.C.
Pre-Pottery Neolithic	*ca.* 6000-5000 B.C.
Pottery Neolithic	*ca.* 5000-4000 B.C.
Chalcolithic	*ca.* 4000-3200 B.C.
Early Bronze (EB)	
EB I	*ca.* 3200-2800 B.C.
EB II	*ca.* 2800-2600 B.C.
EB III	*ca.* 2600-2300 B.C.
EB IV (or III B)	*ca.* 2300-2100 B.C.
Middle Bronze (MB)	
MB I (or EB-MB	
Intermediate)	*ca.* 2100-1900 B.C.
MB IIa	*ca.* 1900-1700 B.C.
MB IIb	*ca.* 1700-1600 B.C.
MB IIc	*ca.* 1600-1550 B.C.

Late Bronze (LB)	
LB I	*ca.* 1550-1400 B.C.
LB IIa	*ca.* 1400-1300 B.C.
LB IIb	*ca.* 1300-1200 B.C.
Iron I	*ca.* 1200- 900 B.C.
Iron II	*ca.* 900- 600 B.C.
Iron III	*ca.* 600- 300 B.C.
Hellenistic	*ca.* 300- 63 B.C.
Roman	*ca.* 63 B.C.-A.D. 323
Byzantine	*ca.* A.D.323-636
Islamic	*ca.* A.D. 636-present

The methods used for dating these periods are various. The existence of broad periods of cultural stability is easily recognizable in the separate strata of mounds. Comparison between many different mounds in the one area establishes these broad culturally stable eras so that items may be placed early or late in a relative sequence. For more exact dating the excavator is dependent on many lines of evidence. Very often literary references in the Bible or in non-Biblical texts enable an event to be dated. Thus the fall of Samaria in 721 B.C. is fixed by external history so that one of the destructions of Samaria may be dated to 721 B.C.

Sometimes inscriptions occur in excavations which refer to kings or events which may be dated. Coins, also, provide dating evidence, particularly for periods after about 500 B.C. Once clear dating evidence is available for a particular level, items of pottery, jewelry, architecture etc. which occur in that level are associated with the same general age. Thereafter, similar items found elsewhere provide a clue to the date of the environment in which they occur. In more recent years the physicists have provided the archaeologist with the method of radio-carbon dating, a method which is of greater value for early periods, since the later periods may be dated by other means. Finally, a comparison with the information obtained from lands which were geographically in close proximity to the country being studied enables the archaeologist to reach a reasonable degree of certainty in regard to the dating of the various cultural periods of his own area. At the same time he is able to attach an approximate date to a wide variety of items of daily use — pottery, tools, ornaments, etc. as well as to architectural features. With such knowledge as this he is able to conduct preliminary surface surveys in order to determine the approximate period of occupation for sites which have not been excavated. This procedure has proved particularly useful in Transjordan and the *Negeb where Nelson Glueck has visited thousands of ancient sites in the course of several years. From the pieces of broken pottery (potsherds) which lie scattered on the mounds in these areas he has been able to suggest a general cultural history of the area without actual excavation.

IV. *Exploration and Excavation in Bible Lands.* During the nineteenth century interest in Biblical sites all over the Near East grew apace. In Palestine proper as well as in Transjordan, Syria, Turkey, Iraq, Persia and Egypt travellers set out to survey many ancient towns known from the Bible. For convenience, brief reference will now be made to three areas of exploration and excavation.

A. Exploration and Excavation in Palestine. In 1838 Edward Robinson and Eli Smith undertook the first serious surface exploration of Palestine and were able to identify several Bible towns. In 1850-51 and 1863 F. de Saulcy explored and excavated in several places. In 1865 the Palestine Exploration Fund was established and significant work was carried out by Charles Warren, Charles Wilson, Charles Clermont-Ganneau, C. R. Conder and others.

In 1890 Flinders Petrie hit upon the idea that pottery could be used for dating. He was able to show from his excavation at *Tell el Hesi that the separate strata in the mound had their own characteristic pottery. F. J. Bliss confirmed Petrie's view in the years following. In the period between 1890 and 1914 a good deal of pioneering work was done. Notable excavations were carried on by R. A. S. Macalister at *Gezer and at four sites in the old Philistine area; by E. Sellin at *Taanach and *Shechem; by G. Schumacher at *Megiddo; by Sellin and C. Watzinger at *Jericho; and by G. A. Reisner at *Samaria. This latter worker developed new techniques such as careful surveying, accurate recording, attention to details of architecture, etc. in each stratum.

Great advances were made between the two world wars from 1920 to 1939. Techniques improved, pottery chronology was accurately established notably by W. F. Albright from his work at *Tell el-Ful in 1922 and *Tell Beit Mirsim (1926-32). Some of

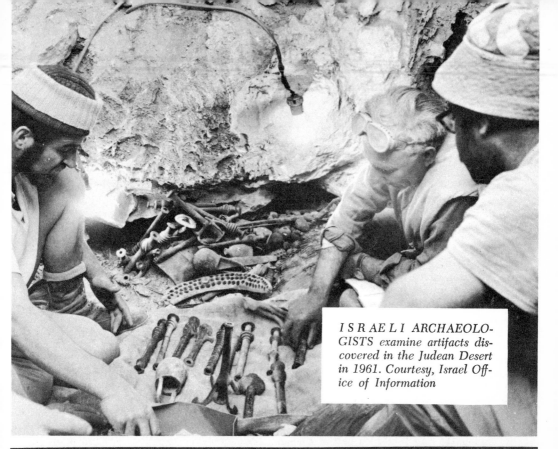

ISRAELI ARCHAEOLO-
GISTS *examine artifacts discovered in the Judean Desert
in 1961. Courtesy, Israel Office of Information*

ARCHAEOLOGISTS AND STU-
DENTS *from the Hebrew University
searching for remains of the past in
the Judean Desert, 1961. Courtesy,
Israel Office of Information*

the other important excavations of this period were those of W. F. Badè at °Tell en-Nasbeh (1926-35), E. Grant at °Beth-shemesh (1928-33), J. Garstang at °Jericho (1929-36), J. W. Crowfoot, Miss K. Kenyon and E. L. Sukenik at °Samaria (1931-35), J. L. Starkey at °Lachish (1932-38), C. S. Fisher, Alan Rowe and G. M. Fitzgerald at °Beth-shan (1921-33), C. S. Fisher, P. L. O. Guy and Gordon Loud at °Megiddo (1925-39), and Nelson Glueck at *Tell el Kheleifeh* (°Ezion Geber) (1937-40). Numerous smaller excavations were conducted during the same period among which those at Tell Jemmeh (possibly Gerar), *Tell el-Far'ah* (possibly Sharuhen), °Petra, Bethzur, *Tell Abu Hawam* (possibly Salmonah), Et-Tell (°Ai), °Bethel, *Khirbet et Tannur* may be mentioned.

Since the close of World War II many significant excavations have been carried on. One of the most striking of all archaeological discoveries is that associated with the caves and the ancient buildings in and around Qumran where, since 1948, the now famous °Dead Sea Scrolls have been coming to light. Since 1950 ancient °Caesarea has been under excavation. During 1950-51 a part of Roman °Jericho at *Tulul Abu el- Alayiq* was unearthed. In 1951 a series of campaigns was commenced at °Dibon in Transjordan. In 1952 Kathleen Kenyon commenced to dig again at Jericho and has continued there for several seasons with startling results. Since 1953 J. P. Free has been working at °Dothan, and since 1956 G. E. Wright and others have worked at °Shechem. Other excavations of note during these years are those of J. B. Pritchard at °Gibeon, Pere de Vaux at *Tell el-Far'ah* (probably Tirzah), Kathleen Kenyon at °Jerusalem, B. Mazar at *Tell Qasile*, Avi-Yonah, N. Avigad and others at Masada (Herold's palace), and Y. Yadin and his colleagues at Hazor in Galilee. Some of these excavations are still in progress. There is a rapidly accumulating amount of archaeological data from Palestine and our knowledge of Biblical life and times is being enriched every year.

B. Exploration and Excavation elsewhere in the Near East. Excavation has been carried out in many ancient sites all over the Near East. Some of these like °Ur, °Babylon, °Susa, °Nineveh, Nimrud, °Haran, °Damascus, and Jebeil are known from the Bible.

But many others, not mentioned in the Old Testament, have produced valuable information for our understanding of Bible times. In particular, important documents and inscriptions have been found at Ur, Babylon, Nineveh, Nimrud, °Alalakh (in North Syria), Amarna (in Egypt), °Mari (on the Euphrates River), °Nuzi (near Kirkuk in Iraq), Ras Shamra, the ancient °Ugarit (on the North Syrian Mediterranean coast), and Hattusas (in Turkey). See Boghazkoy. All of these sites have produced significant documentary evidence about the history and culture of the peoples who lived in these lands during the years from 2000 B.C. onwards. The non-inscriptional records such as pottery, architectural features, tools, weapons, art motifs, etc. are useful for comparative purposes and enable the archaeologist to gain a much clearer picture of the position and role of Palestine in the ancient Near East. A great deal of excavation is continuing in these lands which provides further enrichment of our knowledge of Biblical life and times.

C. Exploration and Excavation in classical lands. Of particular significance for our understanding of the New Testament are the excavations which have been carried out in classical lands. Many of the towns known from the New Testament have been excavated in recent years. Among the more important of these are °Ephesus, °Sardis, °Pergamum, °Philippi, °Corinth, °Athens and °Rome. Fascinating insights into the significance of statements in the Book of Acts come from such excavations. But inscriptional and documentary evidence in the form of coins, papyri, monumental inscriptions, etc. from anywhere in classical lands are likely to throw light on the language, law and religion of the classical age and thus fill out the background to the New Testament age. Indeed New Testament scholarship has probably gained as much from archaeological discovery as has Old Testament study.

IV. *Archaeology and the Bible*. The contribution of archaeology to the understanding of the Bible is considerable. It is not too much to say that our knowledge of the Bible has been revolutionised by modern archaeological discovery. Today it is possible to study Biblical history and culture against the contemporary background in a way that was not possible prior to the modern era of archaeological discovery. The following discussion is intended to indicate some of the main areas in which archaeology has contributed to our understanding of both the Old Testament and the New Testament.

In the first place archaeological discovery has filled out, in considerable detail, the total background not only to life in Palestine in Bible times but also to life in Egypt, Syria, Assyria, Babylonia, Persia, Greece and Rome. Numerous allusions to local customs are now clearly understandable. Thus the patriarchal stories and the Joseph narratives are now known to contain a considerable variety of references to practices that were current in Mesopotamia and Egypt during the second millennium B.C. Such items as law, social custom, religious practices and theological ideas have been preserved on documents which have come to light in dozens of ancient sites all over the Near East. By way of illustration reference may be made to the customs which were current at Nuzi in Northern Mesopotamia during the second millennium B.C. in reference to inheritance. A man who had no son might adopt one of his slaves as his heir. He might, however, adopt a relation or take a subsidiary wife in the hope that a son might be born from such a union. Should a true son be born in due course, this son became the true heir although the other individuals were to be given some share in the inheritance. The patriarchal stories of Abraham and Eliezer (Gen. 15:2-4), Laban and Jacob (Gen. 29-31), Abraham and Hagar (Gen. 16:1-5), and Abraham and Isaac (Gen. 21: 1-12) take on new meaning against such a background, which was, of course, the background which Abraham knew so well.

In the purely historical realm, important international events which are referred to in the Bible are described in non-Biblical documents which have been discovered in the course of archaeological work. Thus the invasion of Shishak (I Kings 14:25-26) in *ca.* 918 B.C., the assault on Samaria in 722/1 B.C. (II Kings 17:5-6) and the capture of Jerusalem in 587 B.C. (II Kings 24) are well attested in non-Biblical records and described from another viewpoint.

At times, non-Biblical documents refer to important events which are not mentioned in the Bible. Thus King Ahab was involved in a great battle against the Assyrians along with eleven other kings at Qarqar in 853 B.C.; Jehu, king of Israel became a vassal of Shalmaneser III of Assyria in 842 B.C; Omri, king of Israel conquered Moab at some time during the years 876-869 B.C. (*see* Moabite Stone).

Sometimes the exact significance of a Biblical event only becomes clear after other historical documents become available.

It is now clear that Pharaoh Necho was on his way to help the Assyrians rather than to oppose them (II Kings 23:29) so that the Hebrew preposition *'al* in this verse should be translated "alongside" rather than "against."

One of the most important contributions of archaeology to our understanding of the Bible lies in the discovery of texts in various ancient Near Eastern languages such as Hittite, Canaanite, South Arabic, Akkadian, Ugaritic, Hurrian, Sumerian, Egyptian, etc., all of which provide comparative material for the study of the Old Testament text. It is now possible to provide more accurate translations of a variety of Hebrew words and phrases. Thus the word *'ed* translated "mist" in Genesis 2:6 means "river" in Sumerian or "river (god)" in Akkadian. The meaning "river" suits the Old Testament passage admirably.

Again, the difficult passage in I Kings 10:28 makes much easier reading once it is realised that there was an ancient state of Kue (QWH) in Asia Minor. The passage can now be translated "And Solomon's import of horses was from Egypt and from Kue, and the king's traders received them from Kue at a price" (RSV). Or again, Proverbs 26:23 may now be translated ". . . like glaze covering an earthenware vessel" since the word *spsg* has been discovered in Ugaritic meaning "glaze." This kind of discovery finds many dozens of applications in recent translations of both Old and New Testaments.

It is evident that the contribution of archaeology to Biblical studies is considerable. The volume of evidence that has become available has led to a new approach to the historical value of the Biblical records. Naturally, archaeological support is not available for every Biblical event. Yet it is true to say that it has corroborated the substantial historicity of the Biblical record from the patriarchal age to the apostolic age. Despite this, however, exaggerated claims should not be made for the achievements of archaeology. If it has compelled scholars to exercise more caution in their judgments about the historicity of the Biblical records, it has at times made the interpretation of the Biblical record more difficult rather than less difficult. At times, earlier interpretations have had to be modified, as for example in the case of Garstang's interpretation of the Joshua story in the light of his Jericho excavations.

But the contribution of archaeology to our understanding of the Bible is only beginning. As more pieces of the jigsaw puzzle come to light it becomes evident that adjustments have to be made in our earlier arrangements of the pattern. The achievements of the past half century have been so spectacular that the Bible student awaits with keen anticipation the discoveries of the next half century.

BIBLIOGRAPHY. K. M. Kenyon, *Beginning in Archaeology*, London, 1952; *Digging up Jericho*, London, 1957; *Archaeology in the Holy Land*, London, 1960. G. E. Wright, *Biblical Archaeology*, London, 1957. W. F. Albright, *The Archaeology of Palestine* 2nd Ed., London, 1960; *Archaeology and the Religion of Israel*, Baltimore, 1956; *From the Stone Age to Christianity*, 2nd Ed., New York, 1957. N. Glueck, *The Other Side of Jordan*, New Haven, 1940; *Rivers in the Desert*, London, 1959. M. Burrows, *What Mean These Stones*, 1941. A. G. Barrois, *Manuel d'Archéologie Biblique*, I-II, Paris, 1939, 1953. G. L. Harding, *The Antiquities of Jordan*, London, 1959. M. Wheeler, *Archaeology from the Earth*, London, 1956. L. H. Grollenberg, *Atlas of the Bible*, 1956. G. E. Wright and F. V. Filson, *Westminster Historical Atlas to the Bible*, 2nd Ed., London, 1956.

YIGAEL YADIN, Israeli archaeologist, examining a Bar Kochba letter from the Judean Wilderness. Courtesy, Israel Office of Information

ARCHAEOLOGISTS AND THEIR WORK

PALESTINE AND SYRIA

Archaeologist	Sites Excavated	Principal Activities and Discoveries
William F. Albright	Gibeah (Tell el Ful), 1922-23 Kirjath-sepher (Debir), 1926-43 Petra, 1934 Lower end of Dead Sea, site of Sodom and Gomorrah (with Melvin Grove Kyle), 1924 Bethel, 1934	Director, Jerusalem School, ASOR, 1920-29; 1933-36. Writer in the field of Palestinian archaeology, Semitic linguistics, and the Dead Sea Scrolls.
William F. Badé	Tell en-Nasbeh, 1926-35	Jar handles stamped with the word "Mizpeh" helped identify Tell en-Nasbeh with Mizpah of Benjamin. Cf. Judges 20:1.
Frederick Bliss	Tell es-Safi, 1898-1900 Marissa, 1898-1900 Azekah, 1898-1900 Tell el Hesi 1890-92	Cuneiform tablet discovered that was from the period of the Amarna tablets.
	Jerusalem, 1894-97	Bliss excavated the south wall which had been rebuilt under Nehemiah.
J. L. Burckhardt	Petra, 1812	Burchardt rediscovered Petra.
Millar Burrows		Director, Jerusalem School, ASOR, 1947-48. Edited Hebrew text of Dead Sea Scrolls.
J. Calloway	Ai, 1964	
C. E. Clermont-Ganneau	Dibon	Secured remains of Moabite Stone. Explored and verified Biblical sites from Joppa to Jerusalem in 1873-74.
C. R. Conder		Led survey of Palestine with Lord Kitchner; 1872-74 in preparation of Palestine Exploration Fund map.
Frank M. Cross, Jr.		Member of team of international scholars working on Scroll materials in Palestine Archaeological Museum in Palestine Museum in Jerusalem.

Archaeologist	Sites Excavated	Principal Activities and Discoveries
J. W. Crowfoot	Jerusalem, 1927 Jerash, 1928-30 Samaria, 1931-33, 1935	Director of British School of Archaeology, 1927-35. Discovered the famous ivories at Samaria.
Maurice Dunand	Amrit, Syria, 1954, 1955 Byblos, 1933-38; 1960-62	Directed Amrit excavation.
René Dussaud	Dura, 1928-37	
George W. Elderkin	Antioch (on the Orontes), 1932-36	
C. S. Fisher	Samaria, 1908-10 Bethshan, 1921-23 Megiddo, 1925-27 Garasa, 1930 Antioch on the Orontes, 1932	Associate Director of Antioch expedition.
Joseph Free		Director, Excavation of Dothan, 1953-
A. Frova	Caesarea, 1958, 1959, 1960-62	
A. Gabriel	Palmyra (Tadmor), 1927	
Dorothy Garrod	Mt. Carmel, 1929-34	Exploration and discovery of stone age human remains in the Wadi el Mugharah caves.
John Garstang	Jericho, 1907-9, 1930-36 Hazor, 1922-28 Ashkelon, 1921, 1922 Gerar, 1922	
Nelson Glueck	Ezion Geber, 1938-40 Shiloh, 1932 Khirbet et Tannur, 1937, 1938 Negeb, 1954—	
Elihu Grant	Beth-shemesh, 1928, 1929, 1931-39	
P. L. O. Guy	Megiddo, 1935-39	
Philip Hammond	Petra, 1954-63	Director of excavations at Petra in cooperation with Jordan Dept. of Antiquites, 1959-63. In 1961, the main theater was excavated.

Archaeologist	Sites Excavated	Principal Activities and Discoveries
G. Lankester Harding	Lachish, 1938-40	Director of Dept. of Antiquities. Assisted in exploring Caves I and II near Qumran, 1949, 1951. Directed excavation of Essene monastery at Qumran, 1951-56.
George Horsfield	Petra, 1929	First to excavate Petra.
Edward Hull		Surveyed and explored the valley of the Dead Sea and Arabah.
John H. Iliffe		First director of Palestine Archaeological Museum in Jerusalem. He initiated the first display of Palestinian archaeological treasures.
Charles H. Inge	Lachish, 1938	
J. W. Jack	Samaria, 1935	
J. L. Kelso	Bethel, 1934, 1954-60 N. T. Jericho, 1950, 1952-55	
Kathleen Kenyon	Jericho, 1952-58 Ophel, 1961-	
Hans Kjaer	Shiloh, 1926, 1929, 1931 (with A. Schmidt)	
Melvin G. Kyle		Co-director with Albright in exploring lower end of Dead Sea, 1924. Assisted Albright at Debir, 1926-30.
Paul Lapp	Araq el Emir, 1961, 1962, 1963 Taanach, 1964	Director, Jerusalem School, ASOR, 1961-64. Excavated cave north of Jericho and found important papyri from Samaria (722 B.C.) in 1963.
T. E. Lawrence	Carchemish (Syria), 1912-14 1919	During winters of 1913-14, he, with C. L. Woolley, explored the wilderness of Sin for Kadesh-Barnea; tentatively identified Qoseimeh at Kadesh-barnea.
Gordon Loud	Megiddo, 1937	Discovered the famous Megiddo ivories.

Archaeologist	Sites Excavated	Principal Activities and Discoveries
W. F. Lynch		In 1848 explored Jordan River and Dead Sea and ascertained the depth and location below sea level (1292 ft.) of the Dead Sea.
D. G. Lyon	Samaria, 1908-10	
R. A. S. Macalister	Gezer, 1902-08 Beth-shemesh, 1911, 1912 Ophel, 1923-24	
D. Mackenzie	Gezer, 1902-05, 1907-09 Beth Shemesh, 1911, 1912	
Mme. Marquet-Krause	Et-Tell, 1933-35	
Theodore McCown	Mt. Carmel, 1932 Gerasa, 1930 (with C. S. Fisher)	Discovered prehistorical burials at Mt. Carmel.
J. T. Milik		Member of international group of scholars working on Dead Sea Scroll materials in Palestine Museum in Jerusalem, Jordan.
Pierre Montet	Byblos, 1921-24	Found tomb of Ahiram.
William Morton	Dibon, 1950-56	Director, Jerusalem School, ASOR, 1954-55.
E. H. Palmer		Surveyed Sinai and route of the Exodus, 1868-69.
Peter J. Parr		Director, Excavations at Petra, 1957, 1960-63. British School of Archaeology.
André Parrot	Mari, Syria (Tell Hariri)	Began excavations in 1933 and continued to 1955. Over 20,000 tablets found.
Flinders Petrie	Ancient Gaza, 1927, 1930-34 Tell el Ḥesi (Ekron), 1890, 1891 Tell el Farah, 1927	
James B. Pritchard	N. T. Jericho, 1951 Gibeon, 1956-63	
O. Puchstein	Baalbek, 1898-1905	
B. Ravani	Ancient Tiberius, 1957	Excavated baths

Archaeologist	Sites Excavated	Principal Activities and Discoveries
William L. Reed	Dibon, 1950-56	
George A. Reisner	Megiddo Samaria, 1908-1910	
Ernest Renan		In four campaigns in Lebanon, he explored and started excavations at Aradus, Byblos, Tyre and Sidon
Edward Robinson		Geographical and archaeological exploration of Palestine and Syria as recorded in his *Biblical Researches*. He identified "Robinson's Arch," an arch of a bridge across the Tyrophean Valley in Jerusalem. He identified the remains of a large city in Petra. First to report windings of Siloam Tunnel at Jerusalem. Found remains of synagogue in Capernaum. Located 3rd wall of Jerusalem. Located and identified Megiddo, Jezreel, Anathoth, Bethel, Shiloh, Beth-shemesh, and foundations of Samaritan temple on Mt. Gerizim (1838, 1852).
George L. Robinson	Petra, 1900, 1907, 1913, 1914, 1928	Discovered and excavated the great High Place.
Alan Rowe	Gezer, 1934 Bethshan, 1924-29	Found rock cover used as dwellings in 3000-2800 B.C. at Gezer.
M. de Saulcy		Excavated so-called Tombs of Kings, north of Jerusalem.
C. F. A. Schaeffer	Ras-Shamra (Ugarit), 1929-	Discovered and deciphered the cuneiform alphabet
Aage Schmidt	Shiloh, 1922, 1926, 1929, 1931, (with Hans Kjaer)	
K. Schoonover	Et-Tell, 1964	
G. Schumacher	Megiddo, 1903-5	
O. R. Sellers	Bethzur, 1931, 1962	
Ernest Sellin	Taanach, 1902, 1903 Jericho, 1907-09 Shechem, 1913-34	

ARCHAEOLOGISTS AND THEIR WORK

Archaeologist	Sites Excavated	Principal Activities and Discoveries
James L. Starkey	Lachish, 1933-38	Lachish letters
E. L. Sukenik	Third wall of Jerusalem, 1925-27	Did significant work on important scrolls he purchased for the Hebrew University in 1948
Charles C. Torrey	Necropolis of Sidon, 1901	
John C. Trever		Secured permission to photograph the scrolls of Isaiah A, Habakkuk and Manual of Discipline (1QS), 1947. These were published by ASOR in 1950.
Père Roland de Vaux	Tirzah (Tell el Farah), 1946-	Directed group of scholars in identifying 60 mss. from Qumran caves, 1954-57
Père L. H. Vincent	Jerusalem Fortress of Antonia and pavement of court, 1936, 1937 Pool in Bethesda, 1909-10	
Charles Warren	Site of Solomon's Temple, 1865 Temple area in Jerusalem, 1865, 1866 Ophel	In Temple area in Jerusalem, he ascertained Solomonic and Herodian walls. At Ophel he found the staircase to Virgin's fountain (Ancient Gihon).
Charles Wilson		One of important leaders in formation of Palestine Exploration Fund and 1st secretary.
C. Leonard Woolley	Carchemish, 1912-14, 1919 Tell Atchana, 1937-49	
G. Ernest Wright	Balata (Shechem) 1956-	
Yigael Yadin	Hazor, 1955-59 Megiddo, 1941-43	
S. Yeivan	Caesarea, 1955 Tell Gat, 1956-59, 1960	
N. Zori	Bethshan, 1958	Excavated a Roman-Byzantine villa with mosaics and attached bath.

EGYPT

Archaeologist	Sites Excavated	Principal Activities and Discoveries
Alessandro Barsanti		The Egyptian temple of Kalabsha excavated, 1907-09. It is the site of ancient Talmis, Nubia. This temple is the finest in Nubia. He restored the great temple of Abu Simbel in 1910.
G. B. Belzoni		Found opening to the 2nd pyramid built by Pharaoh Khafle (4th dynasty) at Gezeh in 1818. Found and plundered alabaster royal tombs in the western valley of the Kings at Thebes in 1927. Among the tombs found was that of Seti I. First to enter the great temple of Ramesses I at Abu Simbel in 1817.
M. Boussard	Rosetta mouth of Nile, 1799	At St. Julian, he discovered the Rosetta stone, the key to the Egyptian language.
James H. Breasted		Founder of Oriental Institute of University of Chicago. Found and translated the Edwin Smith Surgical Papyrus (17th cent. B.C.) in 1920. This is a copy of the original that dates about 3000-2500 B.C.
Howard Carter		Found and excavated the tomb of King Tutankhaten, 1922, 1923.
Jean F. Champollion		Discovered key to the two unknown scripts used in the Rosetta Stone.
C. S. Clermont-Ganneau	Island of Elephantine, 1907-08	Excavated eastern half of island, where papyri were found.

Archaeologist	Sites Excavated	Principal Activities and Discoveries
Walter B. Emery	Sakkara, 1937 Armant, 1927 Abydos, 1954	At Saqqara, he excavated the intact tomb of Hemaka, vizier of king of 1st dynasty, in 1936, then the tomb of Sabu, nobleman of 1st dynasty in 1937, and most important, the large tomb of Aha. In Armant, excavated the temples and tomb of the sacred bull. Discovered and cleared first dynasty tomb of Pharaoh Ka-a at Abydos. Found funerary boat at great tomb thought to be that of Pharaoh Udimu of 5th dynasty in 1955. Returned and continued work at Saqqara and found mastaba tomb of Queen Her-Neit of 1st dynasty in 1956. Began extensive excavation of the 12th century Egyptian dynasty strongly fortified town of Buhen in the Sudan in 1958, 1959, 1960.
Clarence Fisher	Memphis, 1919-24	
Henri Frankfort	Tell el Amarna, 1926-29 Abydos, 1925-26	Finished excavating the great building (called the "Osireion") of Seti I at Abydos.
Alan H. Gardiner	Thebes	Excavated tomb of royal scribe Amenemhet. It is one of the most important and beautifully decorated with mural designs. He also excavated other tombs here.
J. Garstang	Beni Hasan, 1902-04 Beit Khallaf, 1901	At Beit Khallaf, he excavated two large mastaba tombs, one of Neterket (same as Djoser) and the other of his brother and successor, Sanakht.
Zakarie Goneiun	Saqqara, 1954	Discovered an untouched but empty alabaster sarcophagus in an unfinished step pyramid. Jewelry of gold and precious stones as well as stone vessels were found with it.

Archaeologist	Sites Excavated	Principal Activities and Discoveries
B. P. Grenfell	Oxyrhynchus, 1897-1900 (with A. S. Hunt)	Excavated rubbish heaps for papyri.
Salimbey Hassan	Saqqara, 1938 Gizeh, 1936 Gizeh, 1935	At Saqqara, discovered and excavated a large necropolis of 20,000 mummies. The 22,000 tombs date from period of Pharaoh Unas, last king of 5th dynasty. In 1944, the pyramid complex of this king was excavated. At Gizeh, found tomb of daughter of Chephren. The body was nearly perfectly preserved and a cache of jewelry and 2 piles of gold (at her feet) were found. The tomb of Ra-Wer of 5th dynasty, largest subterranean tomb ever found in Egypt, was found.
U. Holscher	Gizeh, 1909	Co-director (with Steindorff) of excavation that found pyramid temple of Chephren.
Kamal el Mallakh	Gizeh, 1954	Discovered burial boat of Cheops alongside of west side of pyramid of Cheops.
George M. Legrain	Karnak, 1896, 1897, 1903	Cleared the temple of Ramesses III at Karnak of rubbish. He and Maspero found over 7000 stone monuments: statues, busts, stone vases, etc. in a large water-filled pit.
Richard Lepsius	Sinai Thebes, 1844 Napata, 1844	Made exhaustive general topographical study of Egypt. Visited and found the copper mines in Sinai. Made copies of the inscriptions by the Egyptian expeditions that worked there. Made survey of the Valley of the Kings near Thebes and partially cleared tombs of Ramesses II and Merneptah. Partially cleared the great temple of Abu Simbel in 1842-45. Explored Napata, capital of Ethiopia kings who like Taharqa ruled Egypt and invaded Palestine.

Archaeologist	Sites Excavated	Principal Activities and Discoveries
M. Loret	Thebes, 1898	Discovered tomb of Amenhotep II in the Valley of the Kings.
Auguste F. F. Mariette (Bey)	Saqqara, 1850	Discovered the Sarapeum (Tomb of the sacred bulls of Apis) at Saqqara. Established the Bulaq Archaeological Museum which later became the National Museum at Cairo. He was the great preserver of the antiquities which he gathered from Saqqara, Tanis, Karnak, Abydos, Medinet Habu, Deir el-Bahri. He was the director of the Antiquities Dept., 1858-81. In 30 years he excavated and found 15,000 monuments from Memphis to Karnak in 37 sites. Excavated temple of Edfu in 1860 and temple of Hatshepsut at Deir el Bahri in 1858. Partially cleared the Temple of Abu Simbel in 1869.
Gaston Maspero		Director of Dept. of Antiquities, 1881-86, and 1889-1910. Began the work on the Meydum pyramid and opened it in 1881. In the same year, he opened the pyramid of Unas (5th dynasty) at Saqqara.
Pierre Montet	Tanis, 1940, 1945	Tomb of Pharaoh Psusennes excavated Triple anthropoid coffins — 1st of black granite and 2nd and 3rd of silver.
Edward Naville	Deir el-Bahi, and Temple of Queen Hatshepsut, 1893-1908 Pithom (Tell el Maskhutat), 1882-83 Tell el Yahudiya, 1887 Abydos, 1911-14	At Abydos, partially excavated great building, called "The Osireion" of Seti I.
P. E. Newberry	Bene Hasan, 1907 Hatnub, 1891	Restored the tombs of Beni Hasan. Found alabaster quarries at Hatnub, 10 mi. east of Tell el Amarna.
T. Eric Peet	Tell el Amarna, 1921-22	Conducted excavations in south part of city, with C. L. Woolley.

Archaeologist	Sites Excavated	Principal Activities and Discoveries
J. D. S. Pendlebury	Tell el Amarna, 1930-37	Completed excavations in central and northern parts of city. Director of Egyptian Exploration Society excavations, 1928-34.
F. E. Perring	Gizeh, 1837	Carefully measured the great pyramids of Gizeh, with H. Vyze.
Flinders Petrie	Gizeh, 1881-82 Tanis, 1884 Nabasha, 1886 Hawara, 1888 Tell el Amarna, 1891, 1892 Temple of Amun, Karnak, 1896 Abydos, 1899-1901 Tell el Yehudiya and nearby Hyksos camp, 1905-06 Memphis and palace of Hophra, 1907-09 Tombs in necropolis at Meydum, 1931-32	Excavated pyramids of Gizeh and studied triangulation and engineering of them. At Hawara, studied pyramids and portraits of mummies. Discovered Semitic (Canaanite-Hebrew) writings used by miners on Sinai peninsula, 1904. Led in most of excavations at Memphis. Noted as an archaeologist and writer, 1880-1937.
George A. Reisner	Nag el Deir, 1899-1903 Kerma (Sudan), 1913-15 Napata (Sudan), 1916-23	Excavated pre-dynastic cemetery, at Nag el Deir. At Kerma two large mounds, fortified trading stations, and factories, were found. Very important as to business, artistry and manufacture of products of Middle Kingdom period. Explored pyramids of Meroe and capital city, Napata, capital of Ethiopian kings.
Alan Rowe	Pyramid of Seneferu at Meydum, 1929, 30.	
George Steindorff	Gizeh, 1909	With Holscher, he directed excavations of the pyramid temple of Chephren.
Howard Vyse	Gizeh, 1937	Assisted F. E. Perring in measuring the great pyramids.
A. E. P. Weigall	Thebes, 1895	Excavated mortuary temple of Thutmose III at Thebes. Discovered tomb of Prince Yuya and his wife, Thuyu, parents of Queen Tiy, favorite wife of Amenhotep III, in the Valley of the Kings.

Archaeologist	Sites Excavated	Principal Activities and Discoveries
J. A. Wilson	Abu Simbel, 1960-	Leader in rescue of archaeological remains in Upper Egypt and Sudan (near lake made by new Aswan Dam.
C. Leonard Woolley	Tell el Amarna, 1921-22	Co-directed excavation in south part of city with T. E. Peet.

IRAQ AND IRAN

W. Andrae	Ashur, 1902-14 (Qal'at-Sharqhat)	
George A. Barton	Nuzi and Tepe Gawra	Director of Baghdad School, ASOR, 1923-34.
Paul Emile Botta	Khorsabad, (Palace of Sargon II), 1843-44	
Robert Braidwood	Qal'at Jarmo (Kurdestan Mts.), 1948, 1954, 1955, 1958 Karim Shahir (near Jarmo), 1950-51	
George G. Cameron		Made accurate copy of Behistan inscription in 1943, using modern method of spraying quick-drying liquid rubber.
Edward Chiera	Khorsabad, 1928, 1929 Nuzi, 1927, (Hurrians identified) 1930-32	
Gaston Cros	Telloh (Lagash), 1901-27	Lagash was found to be a short distance north of Telloh, in 1953.
M. A. Dieulafoy	Susa, 1884-96	Excavated palace of Xerxes
Robert Dyson	Hasanlu (Iran), 1957-60	Began excavation there, finding pottery and other evidences of Sassanian and Parthian periods. In 1957-59, 1960, the site yielded materials of the Bronze Age.
Henri Frankfort	Khorsabad, 1929-36 Tell Asmar, 1930-36 Khafaje, 1932, 33	At Tell Asmar (Eshnunna), found legal code.

Archaeologist	Sites Excavated	Principal Activities and Discoveries
C. J. Gadd		When Director of Assyrian-Babylonian Dept. of British Museum, found a tablet that gave real date of fall of Babylon in 612 B. C.
Hade de Genouillac	Kish, 1914 Telloh, 1928-34 (Lagash)	Discovered the great ziggurat at Kish.
Roman Ghirshman	Tepe Siyalk, 1933-37 Susa, 1946- Choga-Zambil, 1952-60	Cleared much of the elaborate ziggurat at the Elamite city of Chaga-Zambil, Iran, in 1952.
André Godard	Persepolis (Iran), 1954	Finished clearing the royal palace there.
Richard Haines	Nippur, 1954-63	Discovered the famous Inanna Temple at Nippur.
H. R. Hall	Tell al-'Ubaid, 1919	
John H. Haynes	Nippur, 1899-1900	Excavated there and found large number of tablets.
Ernest Herzfeld	Persepolis (Iran), 1931-34	
Julius Jordan	Warka (Erech), 1912-14, 1919-31	
Robert Koldewey	Babylon, 1899-1914	
Stephen Langdon	Kish, 1923 Nippur, 1899, 1900	
Austin Henry Layard	Calah (Nimrod), 1845-47 Nineveh (Palace of Sennacherib), 1849-51	
Heinrich Lenzen	Warka (Erech), 1954-	The German Archaeological Society renewed work there and sent him to direct it in 1954.
W. K. Loftus	Warka (Erech), 1850, 1854	Explored Nuffar, Mugheir (Ur) and other sites never before visited by Europeans.
Ernest Mackay	Jemdet Nasr, 1923	Over 200 tablets of ancient cuneiform script found.

Archaeologist	Sites Excavated	Principal Activities and Discoveries
M. E. L. Mallowan	Nineveh, 1931, 1932 Calah, 1949, 1950 Tell Arpachiyah, 1933-34 Tell Chagar Bazar, 1934-35 Tell Brak, 1936 Nimroud, 1955-60	
John Marshall	Mohenjo-Daro, 1922-31 Harrapa, 1922-31	
D. E. McCown	Nippur, 1959-62 Tell Agrab, 1930-36	
J. de Morgan	Shushan (Iran), 1897-1912	Continued excavations there and in 1901, found stele with code of Hammurabi.
Max von Oppenheim	Tell Halaf, 1899, 1911-13, 1927-29, 1960	
H. H. von der Osten	Takhi-Suliman (Iran), 1959	Worked on the Sassanian fire temple.
André Parrot	Mari, 1934-39 Tello (Lagash), 1948	
John P. Peters	Nippur, 1888-96	
Victor Place	Khorsabad, 1851-1855	Succeeded Botta. Completely excavated palace of Sargon II.
Hormuzd Rassam	Nineveh, 1853-1877 Telloh, 1879-82	Found palace of Sennacherib in 1877. Found library of Ashurbanipal at Telloh.
Henry C. Rawlinson	Zagros Mts. (Iran), 1835 Erech, 1851-55	Discovered Bethistun inscription in Zagros Mts.
C. J. Rich	Babylon, 1811	Made survey in Babylon. Visited Nineveh and Nimroud in 1820, and Persepolis in 1821, where he copied inscriptions.
Sayid Fuad Safar	Eridu (Tell Abu Shahrain)	Found ziggurat of Ur-Nemmu, 1st king of 3rd dynasty (c. 2000 B.C.) of Ur and in the excavation found 16 temples built one above the other.
Ernest de Sarzec	Telloh (Lagash), 1877-1901	Discovered statues of early governors at Lagash, Victory Stele of Eannatum, business documents.

Archaeologist	Sites Excavated	Principal Activities and Discoveries
Erich Schmidt	Persepolis, 1935-39	
George Smith	Nineveh, 1873, 1874	Found important inscriptions at Nineveh. At British Museum in 1872 he found the "flood" tablets, the Chaldean account of the flood.
E. A. Speiser	Tepe Gawra, 1927, 1931-39 Tell Billah, 1927, 1931-39 Khafaje, 1930-36	
Richard Starr	Nuzi (Yorgan Tepe), 1925	
Maurel Stein	Khotan, 1907 Serinidia, 1921 Innermost Asia, 1928 Baluchistan, 1928 South Persia, 1936	The explorations and excavations he made are helpful in tracing the route of the Sumerians to Iraq.
R. Campbell Thompson	Eridu, 1918	
Leroy Waterman	Tell Umar, 1927, 1936, 1937	
Leonard Woolley	Ur (Muquiyar), 1922-34	Excavated Ur with its great ziggurat, temples and tombs of Shubad and the lady Meskalam-dug.

ASIA MINOR, GREECE AND ITALY

Otto Benndorf	Ephesus, 1897-1914	
Kurt Bittel	Boghazkoy, 1954-1963	
Carl Blegen		In 1954, 1955, at Pylos he cleared a large Holos Tomb and a building which was probably King Nestor's. In 1957 he recovered many tablets in Linear B script, and in 1960 there were further excavations.
Oscar Broneer	Athens, 1931-39 Corinth, 1957	In Athens, the Agora was excavated by the American School of Classical Studies, directed by Broneer. At Isthmia, near Corinth, he completed clearance of the Temple of Poseidon in 1955, 1959. In old Corinth he found a 7th century B.C. fort in the Temple of Poseidon.

Archaeologist	Sites Excavated	Principal Activities and Discoveries
Howard C. Butler	Sardis, 1909-1914	Found temple of Artemis.
L. P. Cesnola	Paphos (on Isle of Cyprus) 1878	Uncovered large ancient temples and large Mycean tombs in Paphos.
John Cook	Smyrna (Izmir), 1947-1960	Directed excavations with assistance of Ekrem Akurgal.
A. H. Detweiler	Sardis, 1958-63	Associate director of excavation.
P. Dikaias	Erimi (Cyprus), 1933, 1934	Director of Cyprus Museum. Directed excavations at Erimi, where 13 layers of the town were found.
W. Dörpfeld	Corinth, 1886-91 Troy, 1902	
George W. Ederkin	Antioch (on the Orontes), 1932	He directed the excavations.
Arthur Evans	Cnossus and other sites, 1894-96; 1898-1905; 1906-10; 1926-1938	Spent his fortune restoring the great palace at Cnossus.
John Evans	1959	Reopened Neolithic level at Cnossus.
G. Fiorelli	Pompeii, 1860	First archaeologist to excavate there using technological methods.
John Garstang	Mersin (Turkey), 1934-39	
Einer Gjerstad	Enkomi (Cyprus) Lapethos (Cyprus), 1927-31 Vouni (Cyprus)	Directed the excavations and excavated large palace (Minoan influence seen) at Vouni
Hetty Goldman	Tarsus, 1934-37	Directed excavations where six layers of cities were found.
G. M. A. Hanfmann	Sardis, 1958-63	Director of excavations.
D. G. Hogarth	Ephesus, 1904, 1905	
Sinclair Hood	Cnossus (Crete), 1958	Found a large cache of ivories.
Ludwig Kaas	Rome, 1950-1957	Director of excavation of cemetery under basilica of St. Peter in Vatican City.
Emil Kunze	Olympia (Greece), 1955	Excavated portions of the clay mould used by Phidias for casting the giant statue of Zeus.

Archaeologist	Sites Excavated	Principal Activities and Discoveries
Seton Lloyd	Beycesultan (Turkey), 1954, 1955, 1958	Directed excavations of a mound of a second millennium B.C. people contemporary with the Hittites. Palaces indicating Mycenean and Minoan influence were cleared.
A. Maiuri	Pompeii, 1931-57 Herculaneum, 1932-59	
James Mellaart	Konya (Iconium), 1961-63	
Franz Miltner	Ephesus, 1958	Directed the excavations.
Charles Morey	Antioch, 1933-1939 (On the Orontes)	Excavated Roman villa with mosaic panels in floor and also two churches. In 1939 he excavated a Roman bath and found over 250 mosaics in the city.
J. D. S. Pendlebury	Cnossus (with Arthur Evans), 1928-40	Curator of Cnossus Museum, 1928-34.
A. Puglish	Rome, 1954	Excavated an "Early Iron Ape" hut on Palatine Hill.
W. M. Ramsay	Antioch of Pisidia (Turkey), 1912-14	
David Robinson	Antioch of Pisidia, 1924-26	
Claude F. Schaeffer	Enkomi (Alasiya), 1933, 1934; 1946-49	Excavated this Anatolian city noted for its copper and bronze industry as early as 2nd millennium B.C. Walls of the city, houses, alabaster mortars, etc. found.
Heinrich Schliemann	Troy, 1870-82 Mycenae, 1874, 1876 Tiryns, 1884	
T. Leslie Shear	Athens, 1930-37	Director of American School of Classical Studies in Athens, 1926-. Directed excavations of the Athenian Agora, 1930-37. American School of Classical Studies excavated in Athens 1931-.
H. F. Squarciapino	Ostia, 1962	Excavated a 4th century A.D. synagogue, the oldest found in Western Europe.

83

Archaeologist	Sites Excavated	Principal Activities and Discoveries
Richard Stillwell	Corinth Antioch (on the Orontes), 1933-39	Directed excavations at Corinth.
A. J. B. Wace	Mycenae, 1920-22	In 1953, he discovered a seventh shaft grave and houses. In 1954, he cleared two houses and recovered a wealth of small ivory carvings, and in 1955, three large houses. Excavations continued in 1959 and 1962.
Saul S. Weinberg	Old Corinth, 1959, 1961, 1962	
T. Wiegand	Pergamum and its Asklepion, 1928-31	
Hugo Winckler	Boghazkoy (Hittite capital), 1906	
J. T. Wood	Ephesus (Turkey), 1863-74	
Rodney Young	Gordium (Turkey), 1957-62	Excavated burial ground dating 700 B.C. A royal tomb was opened and believed to be that of King Gordius, c. 700 B.C.

ARCHITECTURE. Excavations in the Near East have revealed considerable information concerning the palaces, temples, private houses, walls, city gates, and fortifications of the Bible lands. As in other areas of material culture, Egypt and Mesopotamia provide our earliest architectural achievements, and it is not until the time of the Monarchy that Israel developed a distinctive architecture.

I. *Egyptian Architecture.* Concern for the welfare of the dead motivated the earliest Egyption stone structures. The Egyptian pyramids were tombs in which the bodies of deceased Pharaohs were placed, and mortuary temples nearby served as shrines for the offering of appropriate sacrifices. Such a structure is the step pyramid of Djoser at Saqqara, near Cairo, built about 2800 B.C., the oldest free standing stone structure known to man.

Pyramid building in Egypt reached its zenith during the Fourth Dynasty (2720-2560 B.C.). The Great Pyramid of Khufu (Cheops) took twenty years to complete. It covers thirteen acres and originally towered 481 feet above the western desert. The pyramid contained nearly two and one-half million blocks of stone, each averaging two and one-half tons in weight. The four corners are almost perfect right angles.

Sir Alan Gardiner, the noted Egyptologist, calls the mortuary temple of Hatshepsut at Deir el-Bahri, west of Thebes, the noblest architectural achievement in the whole of Egypt. The architect Senmut built the sanctuary for his queen above three separate terraces. The first fronted by a pylon which has disappeared, was planted with rare trees brought from Punt (Somaliland). The terraces are connected by ramps. Under the square-pillared portico that forms the back of the first terrace are engravings of scenes from Hatshepsut's maritime expeditions. The upper terrace is lined in front with a double row of columns, and comprises a large central court, behind which is an opening leading to the shrine.

ONE OF EGYPT'S GREAT PYRAMIDS with the sphinx in the foreground. Courtesy, Trans World Airlines

The best known structures of Thebes, the capital of Egypt after the Eleventh Dynasty, are the temples of Karnak and Luxor. The great temple of Amun at Karnak was in process of construction for many years. Pharaohs Seti I and Ramesses II are the names associated with the temple proper with its massive columns. Thutmose I and Hatshepsut erected obelisks and Amenhotep III set up an avenue of ram-headed sphinxes leading from the main gate to the Nile.

Luxor, which means "the castles," has given its name to the Egyptian town which occupies the site of ancient Thebes. The Luxor temple was built by Amenhotep III on a three hundred yard site at the southwest of Thebes. Ramesses II added an extensive court in which he erected obelisks and carved scenes commemorating his victories over Hittites and Syrians.

In Nubia, 166 miles south of the First Cataract of the Nile, Ramesses II built a temple which was hewn from a sandstone cliff which overlooked the Nile. The surface of the rock, which originally sloped down to the river, was cut away to form the front of the temple. In this area, about ninety feet square, Ramesses caused four colossal statues of himself to be carved from living rock. The sixty-six foot high statues depict him seated on thrones, with the royal wife and children represented by small statues at his feet. Between the middle two statues is a door which leads into the temple. The Ramesseum, as it is called, is in the area which will be flooded at the completion of the High Dam at Aswan, at the First Cataract of the Nile River.

II. *Mesopotamian Architecture.* The oldest known architecture of Mesopotamia comes from the Sumerian city of Uruk (Biblical Erech, Gen. 10:10), modern Warka, about a hundred miles southeast of Babylon. A pavement of limestone blocks and a *ziggurat at Urak are thought to date back to the early fourth millennium B.C. The ziggurat at Uruk was simply a mass of clay stamped down and strengthened with layers of asphalt and unburned bricks. Rows of pottery jars were embedded in the upper edges to support them and prevent them from crumbling away. The ziggurat measured 140 by 150 feet and stood about 30 feet high. On its summit was a shrine 65 feet long, 50 feet wide, built around a narrow court 14 feet across. It was dedicated to the Sumerian goddess Eanna, known to the Semites as Ishtar.

The best preserved Ziggurat of Mesopotamia was that begun by Ur-Nammu at Ur about 2350 B.C. This gigantic structure was made of solid brick, 200 by 150 feet in length and breadth and about 70 feet high. The Sumerians of Ur built their houses of burned brick and surrounded their city with walls for defense.

At Ashur, the first capital of Assyria, a temple to Ishtar has been excavated which dates to about 3000 B.C. The temple is known to have been rebuilt by Tukulti-Ninurta I (ca. 1234-1197 B.C.) who added a subsidiary shrine. The statue of the goddess stood in an alcove at the top of a flight of stairs. A second temple at Assur was dedicated to the worship of the god Asshur, the patron deity of the city and of the later Assyrian Empire.

Nineveh, the later capital of Assyria, attained the height of its magnificence under Sennacherib (705-681 B.C.). This dynamic ruler built extensive fortifications and brought water into the city by means of an °aqueduct. The palace of °Sennacherib, discovered by Austin Henry Layard in 1847, had seventy-one rooms and ten thousand feet of walls lined with sculptured reliefs.

Twenty miles southeast of Nineveh was ancient Calneh (Calah, modern Nimrud) where Ashur-nasir-pal II (883-859 B.C.) built his palace. Layard began his Assyrian excavations here in 1845 and discovered one of the colossal winged man-headed lions which guarded the palace at the very beginning of his campaign.

Two years before Layard's work at Calneh, the French consul at Mosul, Paul Elime Botta, excavated the palace of Sargon II (721-705 B.C.) at Khorsabad (Dur-Sharrukin), twelve miles northeast of Mosul. His successor, Victor Place, excavated three gates flanked by large winged bulls and other sculptures. Their arches were decorated with friezes of blue and white enameled tiles representing winged genii and animals or plants and rosettes.

Mari, on the middle Euphrates, was one of the most flourishing cities of Mesopotamia during the third millennium B.C. In addition to its famous Ishtar temple and ziggurat, Mari boasted a royal palace which covered fifteen acres. The palace complex contained administrative offices and a school for scribes in addition to its royal apartments. It was adorned with murals which include a painting of the king of Mari receiving a staff and ring, emblems of authority, from the goddess Ishtar.

The ancient city of Babylon attained its first period of importance under °Hammurabi. The period of Babylon's greatest achievement and, that represented best by her archaeological remains, is the Babylon of °Nebuchadnezzar, the period of the Jewish Exile. The beautiful Ishtar Gate, opening into the principal street of the city, the Processional Way, was built of bricks so moulded that they produce bas reliefs of bulls and dragons. The surface of the bricks was overlaid with thick colored enamel.

The ziggurat of the city, sometimes spoken of as the Tower of °Babel, stood in a spacious courtyard on the north side of the street leading to the Euphrates Bridge. At the top of the ziggurat was a temple to Marduk, the god of Babylon, and on the opposite side of the street was a second sanctuary, the E-soq-ila with a seated figure of Marduk which, according to Herodotus, weighed eight hundred talents.

Eight miles east of Babylon was the ancient Sumerian city of Kish. The excavation of palaces, temples, canals, and the ziggurat at Kish shed light on the earliest Mesopotamian culture. The city was the birthplace of Sargon of Akkad (ca. 2360 B.C.) and was later adorned by Hammurabi.

The most impressive evidence of Persia's ancient achievements in architecture come from Persepolis where Darius I established his capital. The chief buildings of Persepolis were erected on a rectangular terrace. The palace of Darius (the Tachara) had an entrance hall extending across the entire width of the building, and a main hall that was fifty feet square, adorned with relief sculptures.

The Reception Hall (Tripylon) has stairway reliefs showing rows of ascending dignitaries. The eastern gate jamb shows Darius I on the throne with Xerxes, the crown prince, standing behind him. The Apadana, or hall of Xerxes, had a wooden roof supported by seventy-two stone columns of which thirteen are still standing. The hall itself was 195 feet square and surrounded by vestibules on three sides. It was mounted on a platform which was ascended by two sculptured stairways, representing envoys of subject nations bringing their gifts to the Persian ruler. The Hall of One Hundred Columns was a room 229 feet square with a roof once supported by the one hundred columns. Huge stone bulls flanked the northern portico, and the hall was originally approached through any of eight ornamented stone gateways.

An inscription tells that Darius I brought wood from Lebanon, silver from Egypt, gold from Bactria, ivory from India, and stone columns from Aphrodisias of Ogia (?) to build his royal palace at Susa, Old Testament Shushan (Neh. 1:1; Est. 1:20; Dan. 8:2). A French expedition under Jacques DeMorgan excavated Susa in 1901 and was able to outline the general plan of the palace which had three courts surrounded by rooms decorated with glaced brick showing spearmen and winged bulls and griffins. It was during the excavation of this palace that the Code of *Hammurabi was discovered.

III. *Greek architecture,* like so much of Greek culture, finds its highest expression in Periclean *Athens. The rigidity and squatlike appearance of earlier Greek temples gave way to the marvelous proportions of the Parthenon with its impressive Doric columns, eight across the ends and seventeen along the sides. The entire structure, except for its wooden roof and doors, was made of Pentelic marble, a stone containing veins of iron. It measures approximately 100 by 230 feet and is divided into two chambers or cellas.

Pericles dedicated the Parthenon in 438 B.C. and began immediately to construct the gateway to the Acropolis which is known as the Propylaea. This was followed with the temple of Athena Nike at the western bastion of the Acropolis. During a break in the Peloponnesian War (421 B.C.) work on the Erechtheum was begun. The Erechtheum was built of Pentelic marble and blue limestone. On the south side it has a Caryatid porch with stately maidens supporting the roof.

IV. *Roman architecture* was a synthesis of many elements, including the arch which they learned from the Etruscans and the

TRIPYLON STAIRWAY to Darius' palace at Persepolis. Courtesy, Oriental Institute

decorative column which had been developed in Greece. Roman theaters and amphitheaters can be seen wherever Roman influence spread. They are among the principal surviving ruins at Amman in Jordan and Byblos in Lebanon. Vespasian's amphitheater, better known as the Colosseum, was opened by Titus in A.D. 80. It seated 45,000 people and was in the form of a four-storied oval 620 by 500 feet, enclosing an arena 290 by 180 feet. Gladiatorial contests were frequently held there. Shafts in the floor of the arena served for the introduction of wild beasts which were brought up from vaults below by means of lifts. Although tradition suggests that Christians were thrown to the lions in the Colosseum, contemporary historians are skeptical of any such use.

One of the most beautiful buildings of imperial Rome was the Basilica of Trajan, with its central hall 280 feet long and 80 feet in breadth. It was divided into double aisles colonnaded with granite columns. An apse was located at each of the shorter ends of the basilica. The building was lighted by clerestory windows under the wooden roof.

The Basilica of Trajan was but one of the complex of buildings which comprised the Roman Forum. Trajan's Forum included a variety of shops, libraries, law courts, and places of worship. Wide thoroughfares and colonnaded promenades made it a place of both beauty and comfort. The architects of these buildings were often Greeks, but Roman organization made possible the integrated whole.

The eruption of Mt. Vesuvius in A.D. 79 overwhelmed and partly preserved commercial Pompeii and residential Herculaneum, making it possible to reconstruct the houses and other buildings of the period. These were insignificant, in comparison with the Rome of that era, but they exhibit the splendor of first century Italy nevertheless.

V. *Architecture of the Israelites.* Culturally, the Israelites were largely dependent upon their neighbors. During the period of the Biblical patriarchs, as in the subsequent wilderness wandering, Israel lived in tents. After the settlement in Canaan they built more permanent houses of brick and stone, probably similar in material and design to the houses of the earlier Canaanite residents of the land.

Canaanite cities were defended by double or triple walls. Those of Tell Beit Mirsim were eleven feet thick, laid in rough courses and strengthened by towers. The highest point of a town was usually occupied by a citadel where the palace, temple, and other public buildings were located. This area was fortified and formed an inner line of defense when the city was attacked. It was this citadel ("fastness" or "stronghold") of Zion which David captured in order to incorporate Jerusalem into his kingdom (I Chron. 11:5-7).

Both David and Solomon maintained close links with Hiram of Tyre and made use of Phoenician artisans in their building projects (cf. II Sam. 5:11). David built "a house of cedar" (II Sam. 7:2) in the southeast corner of Jerusalem and began to fortify and build the city itself.

Although David did not build a Temple as he had purposed to do before being dissuaded by Nathan (II Sam. 7), Solomon included a magnificent sanctuary among the complex of royal buildings which he erected. Solomon's Temple was designed by a Tyrian architect (I Kings 7:13-15) and is comparable with sanctuaries of the period between 1200 and 900 B.C. excavated in northern Syria.

The Temple itself, measuring 100 by 30 feet, was erected on a nine foot platform which was about 7½ feet wider than the building. The Temple was approached by ten steps, at the top of which were two free standing pillars such as were used in Phoenicia and Syria. Between the pillars were high doors which led into a vestibule or entrance porch. A set of double doors, 33 by 15 feet, opened into the sanctuary itself which measured 60 by 30 feet and was 45 feet high and illuminated by high clerestory windows below the ceiling. The walls, floors, and doors of this sanctuary, known as the Holy Place, were lined with wood and overlaid with gold. Beyond further steps a door led to the Holy of Holies, a room without windows in the shape of a thirty foot cube. This was the throne room of Israel's God. It was dominated by gilded cherubim, fifteen feet high, over the Mercy Seat which formed the cover to the sacred Ark of the Covenant.

Solomon's reign marked the peak of Israel's material prosperity. Although serving the same function as the earlier wilderness Tabernacle, the Temple was built of the most expensive materials and Solomon was able to bring in expert artisans to supervise its construction. Solomon was also responsible for impressive building operations in other parts of his empire. Ezion-geber became a prosperous port on the Gulf of Aqaba and chariot cities were established at strategic places to provide for defense (I Kings 9:26-28; II Chron. 9:25).

Following the division of the kingdom a period of cultural decay set in, and we read little of architectural advances. Samaria, the capital of the Northern Kingdom has been excavated and the ruins of the palace erected by Omri, with additions by Ahab and Jeroboam II, have been identified. It had a wide court with a reservoir or pool 33½ by 17 feet.

The Jews who returned from Exile were dependent upon the good graces of the Persian Empire and had few resources of their own, with the result that the Second Temple was regarded as far inferior to that built by Solomon. Herod, however, showing a patronizing attitude toward the Jews,

planned to rebuild the Temple on a grand scale. The project lasted from 20 B.C. until A.D. 64 — just six years before the whole was completely destroyed by the armies of Titus (A.D. 70). The Bible gives no details concerning the Herodian Temple, but information has been preserved in the Talmud and in the writings of Josephus.

The Temple and its courts were erected in an area about 500 yards from north to south and 325 yards from east to west. On the lower level was the Outer Court, or Court of the Gentiles which could be entered by gates from the west. The whole court was surrounded by porticoes of marble pillars and roofed with cedar. Gentiles and unclean persons were permitted only as far as the Outer Court. An east gate led to the Court of the Women and, through the western gate of the Outer Court, Israelite men could enter the Court of Israel by walking up fifteen steps to a higher level. Crowning the whole was the Temple itself which was twelve steps higher yet. As in the earlier Temple, it was divided into a Holy Place and a Holy of Holies.

In addition to his buildings in Jerusalem, Herod rebuilt Samaria and Caesarea. Roman architecture became common throughout the Near East, and Palestinian buildings of New Testament times are generally influenced by Roman and Greek designs.

In Patriarchal times the Israelites lived in tents, although the city dwellers lived in more substantial houses. Archaeological data indicates that houses of the period were rectangular with an entrance on the longer side. The house had but one room, and it was primarily used for eating and sleeping. The foundation was of unhewn stones, above which three to five rows of flat stones were laid. The wall was then built of unbaked brick. Holes were left in the walls for a door and windows. The roof was flat. Larger houses were built around a courtyard with an oven for baking and a well.

The older style houses were preserved in later periods of Biblical history with important modifications. By the time of David and Solomon the standard of living among the Israelites was raised and we find larger and more elegant homes, some with three rectangular rooms laid side to side, with a perpendicular fourth room stretched along

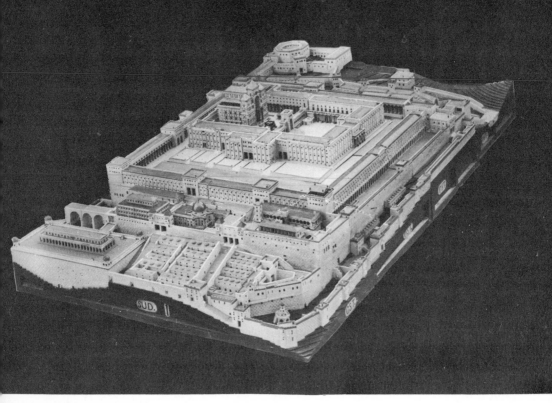

SOLOMON'S TEMPLE and its environs according to
Shick's model. Courtesy, Matson Photo Service

MODEL OF A PALESTINIAN HOUSE, reconstructed
on the basis of excavations at Tell en-Nasbeh. Courtesy,
Palestine Institute, Pacific School of Religion

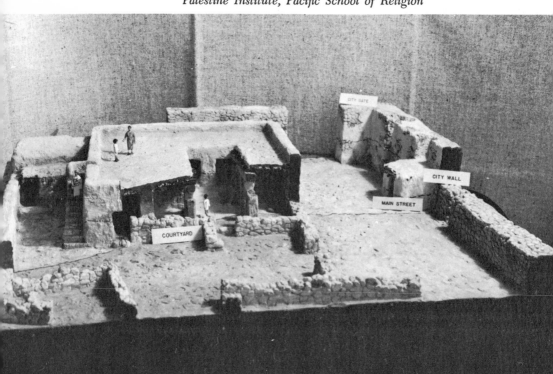

their combined width. In Hellenistic and Roman times the old styles were continued, with pillars, plastered walls, and mosaic tiles added. The modern Arab house in Palestine is basically a continuation of the old style with the addition of a vaulted roof.

AREOPAGUS. The name Areopagus was applied to a rocky hill, 370 feet high, northwest of the Athenian Acropolis, and to the council of elders which convened there. Legend states that Athena, goddess of wisdom presided over the Areopagus when Orestes was acquitted of blood guilt in the murder of his mother Clytemnestra.

During the fifth and sixth centuries B.C. the Areopagus was the stronghold of the Athenian aristocracy. In subsequent years its power was gradually lessened, although the prestige of the Areopagus was maintained until well into the Roman period.

The Areopagus court met in the open air with accuser and accused standing on platforms hewn from rock. It was here that Paul preached his famous sermon to the Athenians (Acts 17:21-34).
See also Athens.

ARMAGEDDON. See Megiddo.

ARMS AND WEAPONS. Archaeology has thrown considerable light on the nature of weapons used in the ancient Near East. In addition to actual weapons discovered in tombs or the debris of excavated cities, bas reliefs frequently depict the battles of Assyrian kings showing the combat weapons. Literary texts, including the Bible, give details concerning the nature and use of arms and weapons.

The bow and arrow ranks as the most common weapon of the Near East during Biblical times. They were used at both ends of the Fertile Crescent — Sumer and Egypt. Bas reliefs depict archers of Shalmaneser's army besieging a Syrian city. Archers are also prominent in a relief showing Sennacherib's attack upon Lachish in Judah. Egyptians used seasoned wood five feet long for their bows, and made their string of animal hides or catgut. To string the bow, the archer held the lower end down with his feet, and bent the upper end down so that he might fasten the string in a niche. The Egyptian hieroglyph representing the word "soldier"

depicts a crouching man with a bow and quiver.

Arrows which have been excavated throughout the Near East appear in a wide variety of shapes and materials. The earliest arrowheads were made of flaked flint or slivers of bone. Later metal, first bronze and then iron, became the usual material for arrowheads which were fitted on a shaft made of reed or light wood. To keep the arrow on its course two halves of a feather were placed at the back of the shaft. The arrows were kept in a quiver at the warrior's left side or on his back.

The bow and arrow were used in hunting game. Isaac in his old age sent Esau into the field with the command: "Now then, take your weapons, your quiver and your bow, and go out to the field and hunt game for me" (Gen. 27:3). Philistine archers at Mt. Gilboa wounded Saul and killed his son Jonathan (I Sam. 31:1-3) On the battlefield of Ramoth-gilead a Syrian archer "drew his bow at a venture" and mortally wounded Ahab of Israel (I Kings 22:34). Later, on the battlefield of Megiddo, archers in the army of Pharaoh Neco mortally wounded King Josiah (II Chron. 35:23). The bow was an important weapon in the Near East until the battle of Marathon (490 B.C.) when Greek spears proved more effective than Persian bows.

Bowmen were honored among the Israelites. Jonathan, the son of King Saul, was known as an expert bowman (II Sam. 1:22). Arrows could wound and kill of themselves, but at times they were dipped in poison to make them even more deadly. Still another way of spreading destruction was achieved by piercing the arrowhead in several places and filling the holes with tow soaked in oil. At the time of battle the oily tow was ignited and the arrow shot bearing its fire to the predetermined target. The Psalmist speaks of the judgments of God who "has prepared his deadly weapons, making his arrows fiery shafts" (Ps. 7:13). Paul urged the Ephesian Christians to take "the shield of faith" in order that they might "quench all the flaming darts of the evil one" (Eph. 6:16).

The sling was used by shepherds to protect their flocks from the attacks of wild beasts. David as a shepherd boy had learned the use of the sling, and he drew upon that knowledge when confronting the Philistine champion Goliath (I Sam. 17:1-54). Ancient slings were made of two strings of sinew, leather, or rope, with a leather receptacle in the middle in which a stone or a lead plummet was placed. To operate the sling, the shepherd or warrior would whirl it once or twice around his head, then discharge the stone by releasing one of the strings. An expert marksman such as David would see the stone head straight for its target. Great care was taken in the choice of stones. Flint sling stones discovered during the excavations of Tell Beit Mirsim had been carefully worked and polished by the ancient warriors. The Benjaminites were noted for their ability with a sling. During the war between Benjamin and the other tribes, there were "seven hundred picked men who were left-handed; every one could sling a stone at a hair and not miss" (Judg. 20:16; cf. I Chron. 12:2).

During the conquest of Canaan utter destruction frequently was meted out to Israel's neighbors "with the edge of the sword" (cf. Josh. 7:21; 10:28-38; 11:12). The sword, or dagger, was the deadly weapon used in hand to hand combat. Richly ornamented swords have been excavated both in Mesopotamia and in Egypt. Egyptian swords were two and one-half to three feet long, double-edged, and tapering to a point. The king, however, wore a somewhat smaller sword in his girdle. Frequently, it was ornamented with one or two heads of a falcon, representing the god Horus.

The swords used in Israel seem to have been quite short. Ehud used one that was but a cubit long (18 to 22 in.) when he killed Eglon, the Moabite oppressor of Israel (Judg. 3:16-23). The sword was normally worn in a sheath held by a girdle (I Sam. 17:39; II Sam. 20:8). Blades were normally of iron, a fact which gave the Philistines an advantage over the Israelites until their monopoly of iron was broken during David's reign (I Sam. 13:19). The "two-edged" sword is noted as a particularly formidable weapon (Judg. 3:18; Ps. 149:6).

Daggers have been discovered at *Lachish

BRONZE IMPLEMENTS AND WEAPONS from Persia. Courtesy, Sculpture Masterworks Company, New York

and *Megiddo from the period before the Biblical patriarchs entered Canaan. Specimens of a curved sword, sharpened on two sides, found at *Shechem date from *ca.* 1800 B.C. A Hyksos-type dagger, common in Palestine from *ca.* 2000 to 1500 B.C., has its blade in the shape of a leaf. Hittite daggers discovered at *Bethshan date to the fifteenth century B.C. A Lachish dagger from the sixteenth century B.C. bears an inscription which is one of our earliest examples of alphabetic writing (*see* Alphabet).

During his excavations at Gerar, Flinders Petrie discovered a sword factory and an iron-smelting center. Near one furnace he discovered spearheads, daggers, and arrowheads dating from 1300 to 800 B.C.

Egyptian spears were five to six feet long with heads of bronze or iron. Javelins were lighter and shorter, hardly four feet long. The spearhead had a socket into which the wooden shaft was fitted. Many spearheads of varying shapes have been found in Palestinian excavations.

Goliath of Gath was armed with an enormous spear (I Sam. 17:7), but David felled him with his sling. Saul, in his insane jealousy over David's popularity, cast a spear at the lad hoping to pin him to the wall (I Sam. 18:10-11; 19:9-10). Later, in a fit of anger, Saul cast his spear at his own son Jonathan (I Sam. 20:33).

The battle-ax was a developed version of the primitive club. In Egypt the battle-ax of historical times comprised a handle from two to two and one half feet in length with a bronze or iron blade secured to the handle by bronze pins. The handle was bound to prevent splitting. Battle axes are also known among the Hittites, Assyrians, Babylonians, and Elamites. In Jeremiah 51:20 (AV), Babylon is termed a "battle-ax" in the hand of the Lord, by means of which God humbles the nations that are ripe for judgment. The RSV translates "You are my hammer. . . ." Probably the prophet had a club in mind, rather than the more sophisticated battle-ax.

Battering rams were used to make a breech in the wall of a besieged city. Such battering rams (cf. Ezek. 4:2; 21:22) were made by attaching a metal head to an enormous beam. As many as two hundred men would lift the beam and attempt to use it in breeching the wall. Machines were contrived to throw large stones and shoot arrows. Movable towers could bring men and missiles to the wall of the besieged city.

The most used piece of defensive armor was the shield, and the smaller version of the same which is designated the "buckler" in the English Bible. The large shield was designed to cover the whole body. It was either oval or rectangular in shape and, in the instance of Goliath at least, a shield-bearer actually went ahead of the warrior to protect him in battle (I Sam. 17:7). The armies of Judah in Asa's time (I Sam. 17:7) included shield-carrying bowmen.

Shields were normally made of wood or wicker work overlaid with leather. Ezekiel pictures a day when "shields and bucklers" along with other weapons will be burned (Ezek. 39:9). Shields of bronze were in use as early as the time of Rehoboam (I Kings 14:27) but they were probably too costly to be used on a large scale.

From earliest times the Sumerians, Elamites, and their successors in southern Mesopotamia wore helmets when going to battle. The head of a wild ox or bull was sometimes used, perhaps with the magical purpose of obtaining the strength of the animal whose likeness the soldiers bore. Later a leather headdress was adopted, but horns were continued. Sometimes Babylonian soldiers are depicted with several pairs of horns.

Elamites introduced metal helmets which were adapted in varying ways by Babylonians and Assyrians. Hittite helmets depicted on the walls of the Karnak temple in Egypt are in the shape of a skull cap. The Egyptians themselves did not use helmets until late in their history.

The Philistine champion Goliath wore a bronze helmet as he challenged the Israelite armies (I Sam. 17:5). David was unarmed save for his sling, but after he had killed Goliath Saul placed "a helmet of bronze" on his head (I Sam. 17:38). During the prosperous days of Uzziah the army of Judah was equipped with helmets (II Chron. 26:14).

Coats of mail used for protecting the body of the soldier while in combat have been discovered at Ras Shamra, Boghazkoy, and Alalakh dating from about the fifteenth century B.C. The Nuzi tablets, from the same period, mention armor for chariots and horses. In the Maccabean period war elephants were protected by armor (I Mac. 6:43).

Goliath wore a bronze coat of mail (I Sam. 17:5), although common soldiers of the time probably wore leather coats. Coats of mail are mentioned as part of the equipment of Uzziah's army (II Chron. 26:14) and of Nehemiah's armed workmen who were prepared to ward off attacks from the Samaritans (Neh. 4:16).

BIBLIOGRAPHY. Yigael Yadin, *The Art of Warfare in Biblical Lands,* 2 vol., McGraw-Hill, New York, 1963. A. G. Barrois, "L'Outillage et la Metallurgie," *Manuel d' Archeologie Biblique,* I, Editions Auguste Picard, Paris, 1939.

ART. Thousands of years before the invention of a system of writing, art in its varied forms was used by man. The first hieroglyphs of Egypt were pictures of the objects they represented, and the cuneiform method of writing in Mesopotamia developed from a similar pictorial script.

From the earliest historical period, the Egyptians produced primitive figures of men and animals in ivory. By the First and Second Dynasties, sculptors were producing massive stone statues of human beings. Limestone and wood were used during the Old Kingdom to make statues on which the human face was reproduced with fidelity. Reliefs were also common, and a stylized posture was assigned to the characters. The head is seen in profile, with a front view of the shoulders. The other parts of the body exhibit a mixture of profile and full face.

During Egypt's famed Middle Kingdom (Twelfth and Thirteenth Dynasties) her art reached its zenith. Colossal statues of forty or fifty feet in height were made of Pharaoh Amenemhet III, and a great premium was placed on massiveness. At the same time individuality was lost, and artists tended toward a stereotyped woodenness in their representations of both gods and men. Such realism as they used was reserved for the animals they portrayed. There were, of course, artists who showed true skill in bringing out the distinctive features of their subjects. Middle Kingdom jewelry shows both technical skill and refined taste.

The reforms of °Akhenaton had important results in the field of art. The Pharaoh himself was realistically portrayed by his court artists. Realism was insisted upon, with the result that a bust of Akhetaton's

beautiful wife Nofretete remains an all time specimen of artistic beauty.

In general, Egyptian art was massive in its dimensions and largely concerned with the afterlife. It was this latter factor that has caused so many specimens of art to be preserved, for the walls of the tombs were richly ornamented, and art objects were placed in the tombs with a view to making more blessed the state of the deceased.

Mesopotamian art dates back to the protoliterate period of °Uruk. The marble head of a person, and a basalt relief depicting a bearded man with spear and bow and arrow hunting a lion, date to about the thirty-second century B.C. A statue of a human being from °Jemdet-Nasr in northern Babylon dates from about 3000 B.C.

Sumerian art flowered during the second millennium B.C. The royal tombs of °Ur, excavated by Leonard Woolley, have yielded beautiful golden vessels, jewelry, and an ornamented dagger of exquisite workmanship. The "Standard of Ur" is a rectangle, 19 x 8 inches with three rows of pictures made in mosaic on each side. It illustrates the armament and organization of the earliest field army of which we have knowledge.

Naram-sin, the grandson of °Sargon of Akkad, produced a victory stele which is considered our finest piece of early west Asiatic art. It depicts a victorious campaign against the mountain-dwelling Lullubians. The soldiers advance up the slope with lances and standards, while the king himself, colossal in size, wearing a horned helmet and carrying a battle axe and bow and arrow, climbs victoriously upward.

The Sumerian ruler Gudea of Lagash (*ca.* 2000 B.C.) was something of a patron of the arts, and eighteen statues bearing his likeness are currently in existence. He was clean shaven, evidently short of stature and kindly in facial expression. In the centuries that follow we have numerous examples of monumental art from °Mari and the famed stele containing the Code of °Hammurabi which depicts King Hammurabi standing before Shamash, the sun god.

The early excavations of Layard at °Nineveh brought from the ground immense human headed winged bulls which flanked doorways to temples and palaces. The walls of Assyrian palaces were decorated with bas reliefs depicting mythological scenes, records

HORSES HEADS IN RELIEF
from Sargon's palace at Khorsabad.
Courtesy, Oriental Institute

BUST OF QUEEN NEFERTITI.
Courtesy, Oriental Institute

LIBATION BOWL of Gudea of
Lagash. Courtesy, the Louvre

WINGED BULL from the palace
of Sargon II at Khorsabad. Courtesy, Oriental Institute

of the military successes of the king, or his prowess in peacetime sports such as lion hunting. Only one perfect statue in the round has been discovered thus far, that of *Ashur-nasir-pal II (883-859 B.C.). Statues of the gods are common, but Assyrian art is best represented in its bas reliefs.

The art of Nebuchadnezzar's Babylon continued the traditions which Mesopotamia had inherited from the Sumerians. An original contribution was the adornment of the Ishtar temple with enameled bricks bearing the figures of lions and other beasts. A huge basalt lion was found in one of the palaces in Babylon.

Persian art was influenced by Sumer and later Mesopotamian forms which developed alongside native traditions. Its most impressive monument is the *Behistun Inscription which includes a gigantic relief cut into the mountainside showing the victory of Darius I over the rebels who challenged his right to take the throne.

Canaan does not abound in the monumental art found both in Egypt and Mesopotamia, but small representations of deities, particularly the goddess of fertility, are common. At Bethshan a basalt stele was discovered with a bas relief of a dog and a lion in fierce combat. The stele is three feet high and dates somewhere between 1500 and 1200 B.C. The art has close affinities to that of Mesopotamia.

Somewhat later we find coffins with lids containing a crude likeness of a human face (1200-900 B.C.). They exhibit Egyptian influence. In 1937 nearly four hundred beautifully carved ivories dating from the twelfth century B.C. were discovered at Megiddo. Bronze lamps and stands are also among the art objects from Megiddo. Mounted on a tripod is the representation of a nude woman playing a pipe.

From Taanach comes a clay incense burner, three feet high, adorned with protruding animal heads. At the front stands a palm tree with an ibex on either side and the figures of a man and a serpent. Among Hyksos fortifications at Tell el-Farah an elaborately carved ivory panel, originally part of a box, was discovered. The style was distinctly Egyptian.

Our knowledge of the art of ancient Israel is quite limited. The prohibition against making graven images as objects of idolatry (Exod. 20:4) discouraged such monumental art as developed in Egypt and Mesopotamia. The command was not always obeyed, however, and the fashioning of a molten calf at Sinai (Exod. 32:2-4) is evidence that the Israelites were not lacking in artistic ability.

The earliest specifically Israelite art of which we have knowledge was that associated with the Tabernacle. A man named Bezalel had the ability "to devise artistic designs, to work in gold, silver, and bronze, in cutting stones for setting and in carving wood, for work in every craft" (Exod. 31:4).

A GRIFFIN CARVED ON AN IVORY PLAQUE. This composite animal with a lion's body and an eagle's head and wings is of Greek Mycenaean style. From Megiddo (1400-1250 B.C.). Courtesy, Oriental Institute

Under his leadership the furnishings of the Tabernacle and the garments for the priests were prepared.

When Solomon prepared to build the Temple in Jerusalem he sought skilled artisans from Phoenicia to supervise the work. He wrote to Hiram of Tyre: ". . . send me a man skilled to work in gold, silver, bronze, and iron, and in purple, crimson, and blue fabrics, trained also in engraving, to be with the skilled workers who are with me in Judah and Jerusalem, whom David my father provided" (II Chron. 2:7). Hiram was able to answer Solomon's request "Now I have a skilled man . . . trained to work in gold, silver, bronze, iron, stone, and wood . . . and to do all sorts of engraving and execute any design that may be assigned him . . ." (II Chron. 2:13-14). Israelites worked with the Phoenician artisan whom Hiram sent to supervise the building of the Temple.

Excavations at Samaria reveal animal and floral decorations in ivory and metal which are similar to contemporary Phoenician work. Culturally, Israel recognized the superiority of Phoenician artisans and sought to imitate their work.

Art and *architecture were highly developed in the Herodian age, largely under the impact of Graeco-Roman style. The frescoes from the *Dura Europus synagogue depicted scenes from Old Testament history. The synagogue is dated in the third century A.D.

BIBLIOGRAPHY. Henri Frankfort, *The Art and Architecture of the Ancient Orient*, Penguin Books, Baltimore, 1954. W. Stevenson Smith, *The Art and Architecture of Ancient Egypt*, Penguin Books, Baltimore, 1958. A. Reifenberg, *Ancient Hebrew Arts*, Schocken Books, New York, 1950. Setin Lloyd, *The Art of the Ancient Near East*, Frederick A. Praeger, New York, 1961. C. Leonard Woolley, *The Art of the Middle East including Persia, Mesopotamia, and Palestine*, Crown Publishers, New York, 1961.

ARTIFACT. Etymologically, any thing made by human art or skill is an artifact. The term is applied to any object made by man, who has shaped or fashioned it for his own use. The tools, utensils, agricultural implements and furniture of a people are among the artifacts which an archaeologist studies in order to reconstruct their history and means of livelihood.

ASCLEPIUS. Asclepius was a legendary Greek hero, the son of Apollo and Coronis, who learned from Hermes the art of healing. He became a skilled surgeon and was particularly successful in prescribing drugs. When he became so skillful in healing that he could revive the dead, Zeus killed him. Apollo, however, persuaded Zeus to make Asclepius the god of medicine.

STATUE OF ASCLEPIUS, the god of medicine. Courtesy, National Museum, Naples

E ASCLEPIUM AT PERGA-'M, dedicated to the god of licine it served as a combination pital and cult center. Courtesy, Gökberg

The worship of Asclepius, which is thought to have originated in Thessaly, spread throughout the Graeco-Roman world. The serpent, because of its ability to annually renew itself by shedding its skin, is sacred to Asclepius. Temples and shrines to Asclepius served as hospitals and health resorts. At Epidaurus, Cos, Pergamum and other places the sick would come for treatment which included massage and baths. The Roman form of the name is Aesculapius.

GOLD PENDANT depicting Asherah, the Canaanite Fertility Goddess. Courtesy, the Louvre

ASHERAH. In Canaanite mythology Asherah, Ugaritic *Athirat,* was the chief consort of El, the father god. Asherah served as a mother goddess and was associated in Biblical times with °Baal, the god of fertility. Her symbol was the sacred tree or pole (translated "groves" in AV), which corresponded to the *maṣṣebah* or stone pillar used in the Baal cult (cf. Judg. 6:28). Among the idolatrous prophets whom Jezebel, the idolatrous wife of Ahab, supported were "four hundred prophets of Asherah" (I Kings 18:19). Asherah was the chief goddess of Tyre, the town from which Jezebel had come.

The names Ashtoreth, Anath, Astarte, and Asherah, all related to sex and motherhood, were often interchanged to the point where the goddesses were no longer differentiated. Hundreds of plaques of the nude fertility goddess have been found during the excavation of Canaanite towns.

The *asherim* (pl. of Asherah), wooden cult objects, have not survived and no description of their form is given in Scripture. A bronze relief found in Susa represents an ancient Semitic high place and, among other ritual furnishings, three tree trunks without branches may be identified. This relief, dating from the twelfth century B.C., is the closest representation of an asherah which we have.

ASHKELON. Ashkelon, on the coastal plain about twelve miles north of Gaza, has had a history stretching back to Neolithic times. Kings of Ashkalon are mentioned in Egyptian °Execration Texts and in the °Amarna Tablets. In 1280 B.C., Ronesses II sacked Ashkelon. During the time of the judges it was temporarily occupied by Judah (Judg. 1:18) but by the time of Samson it had reverted to Philistine rule (Judg. 14:19).

Under Tiglath-pileser III, Ashkelon became a vassal to Assyria (734 B.C.). It rebelled and enjoyed a brief period of freedom until Sennacherib sacked the city. With the disintegration of the Assyrian Empire following the fall of Nineveh (612 B.C.), Ashkelon enjoyed a period of independence. The rising Chaldean power (*see* Chaldeans) posed a new threat, however, and in 604 B.C. the army of Nebuchadnezzar destroyed Ashkelon, slew its king, and took prisoners to Babylon (cf. Jer. 47:5-7).

During Persian times Ashkelon was subordinate to Tyre, but it became a free Hel-

RAMESSES II STORMING ASHKELON. *Ladders have been placed against the city wall and a soldier is hacking at a door with an axe. The limestone relief is from the exterior of the south wall of the Great Hall in the Karnak temple.*

99

lenistic city in 104 B.C. Ashkelon was the birthplace of Herod the Great and the residence of his sister Salome. Herod embellished the city with ornate buildings and colonnaded courts. It is Herodian Ashkelon that has yielded the most impressive ruins.

Archaeological work began at Ashkelon at the beginning of the nineteenth century when Lady Hester Stanhope, an English noblewoman, began excavating the site in the hope of finding silver and gold which tradition said were buried there. Although this romantic adventure proved fruitless, it was followed in 1920 by serious excavations under the direction of John Garstang representing the Palestine Exploration Society. On the summit of the mound, Garstang discovered remains of Roman Ashkelon. A sampling of other levels was gained by cutting sections in the face of the mound, thus revealing a succession of settlements. A complete break marked the disruption brought about by invading °Philistines between the end of the Late Bronze Age and the beginning of the Early Iron Age (see Archaeology). With the Philistine settlement at Ashkelon, the city became a part of Biblical history.

ASHUR, ASSYRIA. The city of Ashur was located on the western bank of the Tigris above its junction with the Little Zab River, about sixty miles south of Nineveh. Ashur seems to have been colonized by Sumerians as early as the third millennium B.C. The remains of temples to the gods Ishtar and Ashur date from about 3000 B.C. Ashur is first mentioned by name on a cuneiform tablet from °Nuzi written during the Old Akkadian period (ca. 2350 B.C.).

The site of Ashur was identified in 1853 when Hormuzd Rassam dug under the base of the ziggurat at Qalat Sharqat and found two cylinders of Tiglath-pileser I (1115-1077 B.C.) which mentioned the city by name. Systematic excavations were conducted by Robert Koldewey and Walter Andrae for the German Orient Society from 1903 until the outbreak of World War I in 1914. During those years the excavators were able to plot the successive layers of the city and study the plans of its palaces and temples.

One of the finest examples of Assyrian architecture is the Anu-Adad temple built on a double °ziggurat at Ashur during the twelfth century B.C. Among the literary discoveries is an Assyrian version of the Akkadian Creation Epic (see Enuma Elish) written about 1000 B.C. While the Babylonian version exalts Marduk, the god of Babylon, as the supreme deity, the god Ashur is the hero of the Assyrian account.

Andrae's excavations at Ashur have revealed to us the nature of Assyrian law. Two large tablets and a number of fragments dating from the time of Tiglath-pileser I (twelfth century B.C.) give us a corpus of law which is about one-quarter the length of the better known code of °Hammurabi. The laws themselves may go back to the fifteenth century B.C. Our texts are badly broken, however, and thus far we have not discovered other texts to help us fill the lacunae. The penalties of the Assyrian code are more severe than those of their Babylonian counterparts.

The kings of the city state of Ashur ruled over a limited area until the end of the Ur III period (see Sumer), when they began a policy of conquest. Assyrian merchants established settlements at Kanish, Kultepe and other centers in Cappadocia which brought both wealth and prestige to Ashur (see Cappadocian Texts). Although we do not know the reason, this period was short lived. Within three generations the Assyrian merchants were cut off from communication with their capital, and Ashur entered a period of decline.

Assyrian power was on the rise again when Shamshi-Adad I (ca. 1812-1780 B.C.) subdued °Mari and placed his son Yasmakh-Adad on its throne. Caravan routes stretched from Ashur to the Mediterranean during Shamshi-Adad's reign. He built a great Enlil temple in Ashur. After his death, however, the empire disintegrated. °Hammurabi of Babylon became master of Mesopotamia.

During the °Amarna Age Ashur-uballit I (1365-1330 B.C.) of Ashur corresponded with °Akhenaton of Egypt, and Assyria emerged from its period of quiescence. From the fourteenth to the seventh centuries B.C., the armies of Assyria spread panic throughout much of western Asia. Assyrian kings imposed heavy tribute on subject peoples and sent punitive expeditions to collect tribute when it was withheld. The Assyrian monarchs boasted of their cruelty in the annals which recorded their campaigns.

Tiglath-pileser I (1115-1077 B.C.) campaigned vigorously throughout western Asia, but he met fierce resistance from the Aramaean states which temporarily checked Assyrian imperialism. It was during this period that Israel was able to emerge as an independent monarchy and, under David and Solomon, to control much of Syria. With the rise of Tukulti-Ninurta II (890-885 B.C.), Assyria began to take more vigorous action against her foes. Names such as Ashur-nasir-pal II (885-860 B.C.), Shalmaneser III (859-824 B.C.), Shalmaneser IV (781-772 B.C.), Tiglath-pileser III (745-727 B.C.), Shalmaneser V (727-722 B.C.) and Sargon II (723-705 B.C.) bespeak the period during which Assyria demanded tribute of the states of western Asia and succeeded in conquering the Arameans of Damascus (732 B.C.) and the Israelite capital at Samaria (722 B.C.).

While the city of Ashur was the titular capital of the Empire, *Nineveh was established as early as the twelfth century B.C. as an alternate royal residence. During the period of Assyria's greatest power, it was to Nineveh that the tribute of the nations came. The years following the fall of Samaria saw Assyrian power at its zenith. Sennacherib (705-681 B.C.) conquered most of Judah but he was unable to take Jerusalem (II Kings 18:17 − 19:9). The Assyrians had to lift the siege and Sennacherib returned home where he was murdered by his sons (II Kings 19:38).

Esarhaddon (680-669 B.C.) continued his father's policies but he met increasing opposition. His son Ashurbanipal (669-627 B.C.) fought hard to maintain the rapidly slipping prestige of Assyria. *Ashurbanipal's library was his significant bequest to posterity, but his kingdom was fast approaching its end. Cyaxeres the Mede and Nabopolassar of Babylon took the city of Ashur in 614 B.C., and Nineveh itself fell in 612 B.C. By 609 B.C. the Assyrians had suffered defeat again at Haran and their empire was at an end.

ASHURBANIPAL. Ashurbanipal (672-631? B.C.) succeeded to the throne of Assyria at the death of his father Esarhaddon. Early in his career (663 B.C.) he conducted a campaign in Egypt, briefly occupying both *Memphis and *Thebes (mentioned in Nah. 3:8 as No-Amon). His annals describe raids against Syrians, Phoenicians and Arabs who periodically rebelled against Assyrian rule. It was probably Ashurbanipal who freed the Judean king Manasseh from exile in Nineveh (II Chron. 33:13), thus insuring a loyal vassal in Jerusalem. In 641 B.C. Ashurbanipal sacked Susa, the Elamite capital.

Ezra 4 quotes an Aramaic document which refers to the "great and noble Asnapper" who settled various peoples in Samaria including men of Susa and Elam (Ezra 4:9-10). It is probable that Ashurbanipal is the Asnapper of Ezra 4, and that Elamites were transported to Samaria following his sack of Susa.

Ashurbanipal is best known for the excellent library which he assembled (see Ashurbanipal, library of). The end of his reign is obscure. After 652 B.C. he was at war with his twin brother Shamash-shum-ukin of Babylon, and Assyrian power in western Asia was weakened.

BIBLIOGRAPHY. A. C. Piepkorn, *Historical Prism Inscriptions of Ashurbanipal*, University of Chicago Press, Chicago, 1933. R. Campbell Thompson, *The Prisms of Eserhaddon and Ashurbanipal found at Nineveh, 1927-28*, British Museum, London, 1931.

ASHURBANIPAL, LIBRARY of. The Assyrian king *Ashurbanipal was both scholar and soldier. In his youth he received a good education, which gave him occasion to boast, "I read the beautiful clay tablets from Sumer and the obscure Akkadian writing which is hard to master. I had my joy in the reading of inscriptions on stone from the time before the flood." Ashurbanipal created a large library by gathering and copying texts from royal archives and religious centers.

In 1852-53, Hormuzd Rassam one of the successors of Sir Henry Layard excavator of *Nineveh, came upon the remains of Ashurbanipal's library in the ruins of the royal palace and Nabu temple there. The fragments of cuneiform tablets numbered about 26,000, representing some 10,000 different texts. They included historic, scientific and religious literature, official dispatches and archives, business documents and letters. Ashurbanipal's scribes had been faithful in copying and translating literature dealing with every conceivable subject.

Many of our most valuable cuneiform texts were first known to modern man as a result of the discovery of Ashurbanipal's library.

The tablets were taken to the British Museum where scholars began the task of decipherment. George Smith, then a young assistant at the Museum, found that one text contained a Babylonian version of the Biblical flood story. His discovery, published in 1872 (*see* Gilgamesh Epic), proved a stimulus to further excavation and study of the cuneiform literature.

Other Epic literature from Ashurbanipal's library includes the Babylonian Creation Epic (*see* Enuma Elish), the *Descent of Ishtar into the Netherworld and the legend of *Etana who flew to heaven on an eagle. A legend tells that *Sargon of Akkad was saved at birth, like Moses, by being placed in a reed basket on the river Euphrates until rescued by the goddess Ishtar.

Also represented is a large corpus of Wisdom Literature including a poem of the righteous sufferer, often described as the Babylonian Job. Hymns, parables, proverbs, and popular tales are well represented.

Tablets reveal how the peoples of the Near East interpreted omens which were derived from the study of the liver or entrails of sacrificial animals, or the movements of men, animals, birds, or heavenly bodies. Of more scientific value are the texts which deal with medicine, botany, geology, chemistry and mathematics. King lists and astronomical data are of help to scholars in establishing an accurate chronology of the ancient world.

The discovery of Ashurbanipal's library, and the subsequent publication of its texts made possible the development of *Assyriology as a serious study with language, script, and a significant body of literature.

ASHUR-NASIR-PAL II.

Ashur-nasir-pal II (883-859 B.C.) was an Assyrian king who campaigned ruthlessly throughout Western Asia. His palace at *Calah (cf. Gen. 10:11), now known as Nimrud, was excavated by A. H. Layard in 1845.

In a small Nimrud temple the excavators found a statue of Ashur-nasir-pal, about half life-size, bearing an eight line cuneiform inscription on its breast. The inscription contains the boast that Ashur-nasir-pal had conquered the region from the Tigris River to Lebanon and the "Great Sea," i.e. the Mediterranean.

At the entrance to the Ninurta temple in Nimrud were pavement slabs inscribed with the annals of Ashur-nasir-pal. In describing a campaign in the West, he says, "At that time I seized the entire extent of the Lebanon mountains and reached the Great Sea of the Amurru country. I cleaned my weapons in the deep sea and performed sheep-offerings to the gods." Ashur-nasir-pal claims to have received tribute from numerous states, including Tyre, Sidon, Byblos, Amurru, and Arvad.

ASIA.

In New Testament usage, the term Asia refers to the Roman senatorial province comprising the territory between Bithynia, Lycia and Galatia to the east, and the Aegean to the west. It included the territory of Mysia, Lydia, Caria, Phrygia and the coastal areas of Aeolia, Ionia, and the Troad. Many Aegean islands, including Rhodes and Patmos, were a part of the province of Asia. Pergamum was its capital until the time of Augustus when the capital was moved to Ephesus. Asia was ruled by a governor with the title Proconsul. It had a high culture, dating back to the Greek settlements of Ionia, and was the richest of the Roman provinces. The Book of the Revelation (2-3) mentions seven churches of Asia, including those of the three chief cities of the province: Ephesus, Smyrna, and Pergamum.

ASITAWANDAS.

Asitawandas is described in the *Karatepe Inscriptions as vassal or lieutenant of the king of Adana (Hittite version) or *Dnnym* (Phoenician version). The latter may be vocalized "Danunians," and identified as one of the "Peoples of the Sea" mentioned in Egyptian inscriptions of the twelfth century B.C.

ASSYRIA.

Assyria proper was the country in the upper Mesopotamian plain bounded on the north and east by Armenia (ancient Urartu), on the west by the Syrian Desert and on the south by Babylonia. Its great cities *Ashur and *Nineveh were located along the central Tigris River (the Hiddekel of Gen. 2:14). At the height of its power, during the eighth and seventh centuries B.C., the Assyrian Empire comprised southern Anatolia, Cilicia, Syria, Palestine, Elam, Media, Babylonia and parts of Arabia.

The racial origins of the earliest inhabitants of Assyria are not known, although Sumerians

WINGED BULL FROM GATEWAY OF ASHURBANIPAL *at Nineveh. Courtesy,*
British Museum

are known to have been in Ashur as early as 2900 B.C. Prehistoric pottery (*ca.* 5000-3000 B.C.) has been found at such Assyrian cities as Ashur, Nineveh, and Calah.

Immigrants from Babylon founded the cities of *Ashur, *Nineveh and *Calah according to Genesis 10:11-12. Later Assyrian culture was in large measure in debt to both Sumerian and Semitic Akkadian influences from the south. Other elements of Assyrian culture came from the deserts to the west and the northern hill country.

The Semitic empire builder *Sargon of Akkad is known to have occupied Nineveh (*ca.* 2350 B.C.) and Assyrian princes were engaged in trade with Cappadocia in Asia Minor during the eighteenth and nineteenth centuries B.C. (*see* Cappadocian Tablets).

Assyrian power grew under the Amorite ruler Shamshi-Adad I (1813-1781 B.C.), whose sons Yasmah-Adad and Zimri-Lim ruled the Amorite state of *Mari. We learn from the Mari letters that Shamshi-Adad was a contemporary and rival of the Babylonian lawgiver Hammurabi. With the influx of *Hurrians into Mesopotamia, Assyria suffered a period of decline. During the fifteenth century B.C. Assyria was a vassal to *Mitanni and it was only after Mitanni was overthrown by the Hittites that Assyria was again free to develop into a strong independent state.

Under Ashur-uballit I (1365-1330 B.C.), whose correspondence with Akhenaton has been preserved in the *Amarna Letters, Assyria regained her power. Northern trade routes were again open to Assyria. Territories as far west as Carchemish, lost since the days of Shamshi-Adad were recovered during the reigns of Arik-den-ilu (1319-1308 B.C.) and Adad-Nirari I (1307-1275 B.C.).

Shalmaneser I (1274-1245 B.C.) was a vigorous fighter who fought the Iranian tribes in the hill country east of Assyria and the Hurrians at Hanigalbat to the northwest. His son, Tukulti-Ninurta I (1244-1208 B.C.) determined to rule Babylon as well as Assyria, and in the process devastated Babylon. After Tukulti-Ninurta, Assyrian expansion was arrested for about a century.

The next strong Assyrian ruler was Tiglath-pileser I (1115-1077 B.C.) who campaigned northward as far as the Black Sea and Lake Van, southward to Babylon, and westward to the Mediterranean where he received trib-

ute from Byblos, Sidon, and Arvad on the Phoenician coast. After Tiglath-pileser, pressure exerted by the Aramaeans kept Assyria in check for a century and a half when Ashur-nasir-pal II restored its power.

A new Assyrian dynasty began with Tukulti-Ninurta II (890-885 B.C.) whose son *Ashur-nasir-pal II (885-860 B.C.) began a policy of sustained pressure on the West. The city states of Syria and Palestine were kept under tribute, and the Assyrians sought to control the roads to Egypt and the sea. At the same time Assyria had to secure control of the northern mountain passes to forestall invasion, and placate Babylon lest revolt flare up there.

Under Shalmaneser III (859-824 B.C.), Ashur-nasir-pal's policies were continued and Assyria ruled territory from Armenia to the Persian Gulf, from Media to the Syrian coast, including Cilicia in southern Asia Minor. In 857 B.C. Shalmaneser took the city of Carchemish whereupon he was faced with a coalition of city states that determined to resist Assyrian encroachments. In 853 B.C. a battle was fought at *Qarqar in which Ahab of Israel supplied two thousand chariots and fourteen thousand men (according to the Assyrian annals). Although Shalmaneser claimed victory, the battle was indecisive. By 841 B.C., however, the coalition had broken up and Shalmaneser was able to overrun the territory of Hazael, although the city of Damascus was bypassed. Shalmaneser continued westward to the Dog River in Lebanon where he received tribute from the states of Tyre and Sidon and from Jehu of Israel. This event, not recorded in Scripture, is recorded and depicted on the *Black Obelisk of Shalmaneser.

Shamshi-Adad V (823-810 B.C.) was largely occupied with putting down revolts in the eastern provinces. After a short reign he died and his widow Sammuramat (the legendary Semiramis) acted as regent until 805 B.C. when their son Adad-nirari III became king.

During a brief lull in Assyrian strength in western Asia, the Aramean ruler, Hazael of Damascus, sought to build an empire by subduing Israel and other states. When Adad-nirari attacked Hazael (804 B.C.) it seemed a blessing to the smaller states of western Asia, for it relieved them of pressure from the Arameans. Adad-nirari's annals claim

SHAMSHI-ADAD V stands under symbols of his gods. From Nimrud. Courtesy, British Museum

that he received tribute from Hatti (northern Syria), Amurru (eastern Syria), Tyre, Sidon, the land of Omri (Israel), Edom, and Philistia as far as the Mediterranean. Joash of Israel was able to recover territory which had been lost earlier to Hazael (II Kings 13:25).

Assyrian pressure on Damascus continued under Shalmaneser III (781-772 B.C.). Jer-

oboam II profited from this Assyrian policy and was able to extend Israel's borders northward to include the Beq'a Valley (II Kings 14:25-28).

Early in the reign of Tiglath-pileser III (745-727 B.C.) he took the throne of Babylon under the name Pulu, or Pul (II Kings 15:19; I Chron. 5:26). Among the revolts which he had to put down was one organized by "Azariau of Yaudi" in league with Hamath. It is tempting to see in this name the Biblical Azariah (a variant of the name Uzziah) of Judah. There was a small city state in northern Syria named Yaudi, and it is probable that the king of that state is meant, although the Judean king cannot be positively ruled out. Tiglath-pileser's annals contain his claim that he received tribute from Menahem of Israel (cf. II Kings 15) and Hiram of Tyre — a descendant of the Hiram of Davidic and Solomonic Tyre.

By 732 B.C., Tiglath-pileser had captured Damascus and put an end to the once powerful Aramean state which was centered there. His annals also tell us that he replaced Pekah, the murderer of Pekahiah, son of Menahem by 'Auzi (Hoshea, II Kings 15:3). The Assyrians advanced down the Phoenician coast, through "the border of Israel" to Gaza, whose king fled across the Wadi el-Arish into Egypt. Ahaz of Judah joined the kings of Ammon, Moab, Edom, and Ashkelon in paying tribute to the Assyrian rather than run the risk of combat.

While Damascus was a potential threat to Assyria, its king Resin joined Pekeh of Israel in an effort to remove Ahaz of Judah and put an anti-Assyrian king on the throne of Judah (Isa. 7). Ahaz doubltess sought help from Tiglath-pileser when his throne was threatened. Such help would have been quickly forthcoming. We know that Israel was attacked, Hazor destroyed (II Kings 15:29) and many taken into exile. Even Ahaz was obligated to Tiglath-pileser, and we read of religious innovations which took place as a result of Assyrian influence or pressure (cf. II Kings 16:10).

Shalmaneser V (727-722 B.C.), son of Tiglath-pileser III, continued to campaign in western Asia. Hoshea of Israel accepted the counsel of his pro-Egyptian courtiers and refused to pay tribute to Shalmaneser, expecting Egypt to back him up in the event of trouble. Trouble came, for Shalmaneser besieged Samaria, and the Israelite capital fell to the Assyrians three years later. During the siege Shalmaneser evidently died, for Sargon II (722-705 B.C.) claims to have taken the city and to have deported 27,270 people, settling them in the eastern provinces of his empire.

Sargon was a vigorous ruler. After the fall of Samaria (722 B.C.) he defeated Carchemish (717 B.C.), sacked Ashdod and Gath (715 B.C.) and conducted raids on his tribes in the Lake Van area (714 B.C.). Early in his reign he invaded Elam (720 B.C.) and sacked Susa. A decade later he drove Marduk-apal-iddina II (Biblical Merodach-baladan) who attempted to organize an independent Babylon into the marshlands at the head of the Persian Gulf. Sargon built a large palace at °Khorsabad near Nineveh, but died before it was completed.

Sennacherib (705-681 B.C.) spent the first years of his reign in suppressing revolts which followed the death of his father Sargon. Marduk-apal-iddina seized the throne of Babylon (703-701 B.C.) and Sennacherib had to rally all his forces to dislodge him. In the process the city of Babylon was sacked and Marduk-apal-iddina fled to Elam and died there.

With problems in the eastern part of his empire resolved, Sennacherib marched westward in 701 B.C., besieged Sidon and marched down the Mediterranean coast as far as °Ashkelon. It was probably at this time that he besieged °Lachish. The siege of Lachish (cf. II Kings 18:13-14) is depicted on bas reliefs discovered in Sennacherib's palace at Nineveh.

Scripture makes it clear that Hezekiah of Judah paid tribute to Sennacherib — three hundred talents of silver and thirty talents of gold (II Kings 18:14-16). Sennacherib's annals boast of the tribute received from Hezekiah. It was probably later in the same campaign that Sennacherib boasted in his annals, "As for Hezekiah, the Judean, I shut him up as a bird in a cage" (cf. II Kings 18:17–19:9). Both the Bible and the Assyrian annals state that the siege was lifted and Sennacherib withdrew without punishing Hezekiah for his rebellion (II Kings 19:35). The Bible credits the deliverance of Hezekiah to the miraculous intervention of God, and a statement in Herodotus has been interpreted to mean that the secondary cause may have been an attack of bubonic plague in the Assyrian camp (cf. Herodotus ii. 141). According to the Babylonian account Sennacherib was subsequently murdered by his son. The Bible (II Kings 19:37) mentions two sons who killed their father while he was worshiping in the temple of Nisrock — possibly the temple of Nusku or Ninurta at Nineveh.

Sennacherib was a builder as well as a soldier. In addition to extensive palaces, temples, and gateways, he was responsible for the Jerwan Aqueduct (see Aqueduct) which brought water to irrigate large parks around Nineveh. Prisoners of war were used in these building projects.

Esarhaddon (680-669 B.C.), Crown Prince and Viceroy of Babylon under Sennacherib, had to put down the usual revolts following the death of his father before he could effectively rule the Empire. Babylon and Elam gave trouble, as did the northern tribes. Tirhakah of Egypt dreamed of bringing back lost glories to his land and encouraged the city states of western Asia to revolt. When Baal of Tyre refused to pay tribute, Esarhaddon attacked. Abdi-Milki of Sidon also heeded the counsel of Tirhakah and suffered a three year siege (676-673 B.C.). According to his annals, Esarhaddon claimed tribute from "Baal of Tyre, Chemosh-gabri of Edom, Musuri of Moab, Sili-Bel of Gaza, Metinti of Ashkelon, Milki-ashapa of Gabal . . . Ahi-Milki of Ashdod. . . ."

Realizing that much of his trouble in western Asia could be traced to Tirhakah, Esarhaddon invaded Egypt in 672 B.C. and installed Assyrian governors at Memphis and Thebes. With political wisdom, Esarhaddon summoned his vassal states and proclaimed his son Ashurbanipal as Crown Prince of Assyria, and Shamash-shum-ukin as Crown Prince of Babylon. In this way he sought to forestall the usual revolts which took place whenever a new government came into power.

Esarhaddon's plans met obstacles, however. Tirhakah stirred up trouble in Egypt, and Esarhaddon set out to bring the Egyptians to their knees. While on his way, Esarhaddon died at Haran. It was up to his son Ashurbanipal (669-627 B.C.) — famous in legend as Sardanopolis — to march against Tirhakah. After three hard campaigns, and the sack of Thebes (the "No" or "No-Ammon" of Nahum

3:8) in 663 B.C., control of Egypt was again in Assyrian hands.

Rebellion continued, however, in other places. Esarhaddon fought at Tyre, Arvad, and in Cilicia. Gyges of Lydia sent emmissaries to Nineveh seeking an alliance with Assyria, but this was only one bright spot in a generally dark picture. Medes were threatening in the East and in 652 B.C., Shamashshum-ukin led the Babylonians in another revolt. Ashurbanipal turned his attention toward Babylon, which he sacked in 648 B.C. °Susa the capital of Elam which had been an ally of Babylon was sacked in 639 B.C.

Assyrian's troubles in the East gave western Asia a period of respite. Josiah was free to institute his reforms and pursue an independent policy in Judah. Egypt, again independent, sought to weld the city-states of Syria and Palestine into an anti-Assyrian coalition.

Records for the next two decades are scanty and we are uncertain concerning the date of Ashurbanipal's death. Scythians moved down into the Middle Euphrates area, and Median power grew in the East. In 625 B.C. the Assyrians were driven out of Babylon. Thereupon the Babylonians and the Medes joined forces to capture Ashur (614 B.C.) and Nineveh (612 B.C.). Sinshar-ishkan, a son of Ashurbanipal, perished in the flames of Nineveh and the Assyrian capital was hurriedly moved to Harran where Ashur-uballit held out for two years. The Egyptians under Pharaoh Necho, desiring now to support a weakened Assyria against a new giant, Babylon, arrived too late to prevent Babylon and her Scythian allies from taking Haran and thereby bringing Assyrian history to an end.

The Assyrian kings were absolute rulers. They were not deified as were the Egyptian Pharaohs, but the king of Assyria was considered to be the agent on earth of the national god Ashur. The king was also chief priest of Ashur and commander of the armies of Assyria. In times of peace it was his

TWO EUNUCHS FROM SARGON'S PALACE, Khorsabad. Courtesy, Oriental Institute

responsibility to plan for the welfare of the people. Provincial and district governors collected and forwarded taxes and tribute to the capital at Nineveh.

Assyrian law was largely dependent on the earlier Sumerian and Babylonian codes, but they show greater severity and a lower cultural level than the °Code of Hammurabi. Business made use of written agreements and disputes were adjudicated by the courts.

The Middle Assyrian Law Code was discovered by German archaeologists at the site of ancient °Ashur from 1903 to 1914. They are not preserved on a stele, as was Hammurabi's Code, but on clay tablets, some of which are badly broken. The tablets date from Tiglath-pileser I (1115-1077 B.C.) but the laws themselves may go back to the fifteenth century B.C.

As representative of the god Ashur, the king waged holy wars against those who failed to acknowledge his sovereignty. The Assyrian war machine was the cruelest that the world had ever seen. The army included a highly trained force of chariotry, bowmen, spearmen, and slingers. Ramps and battering rams were used to capture walled cities, and the spoil of captured peoples, including people taken as slaves, would go to Nineveh to enhance the Assyrian capital. Hostile rulers were sometimes impaled or skinned alive as a warning to potential rebels.

The religion of Assyria was similar to that of Babylon and other ancient Semitic nations. Although Ashur was the deity to whom Assyria was devoted — Assyrians are, by definition, "the people of Ashur" — other deities had interests that were not be be neglected. Anu and Adad had temples at Ashur; Ishtar — goddess of war and love — was accorded special worship at Nineveh. Nabu, the god of wisdom and patron of the sciences had shrines at Nineveh and Calah. The moon god, Sin, honored of old by the Sumerians at Ur, was still the patron deity of Assyrian Harran. Ninurta, god of war and hunting, was worshiped at Calah.

BIBLIOGRAPHY. Georges Contenau, La Civilisation d'Assur et de Babylone, Payot, Paris, 1937. Georges Contenau, Everyday Life in Babylon and Assyria, Edward Arnold, London, 1954. Jorgen Laessoe, People of Ancient Assyria, Barnes and Noble, New York, 1963. Sabatino Moscati, Ancient Semitic Civilizations, Elek Books, London, 1957. André Parrot, The Arts of Assyria, Golden Press, New York, 1961. A. T. Olmstead, History of Assyria, Charles Scribner's Sons, New York, 1923. A. Leo Oppenheim, Ancient Mesopotamia: Portrait of a Dead Civilization, University of Chicago Press, Chicago, 1964. Robert W. Rogers, A History of Babylonia and Assyria, 2 vol., Eaton and Mains, New York, 1901. Georges Roux, Ancient Iraq, George Allen and Unwin, London, 1964.

ASSYRIOLOGY. The study of the history, culture, and language of the Semitic inhabitants of ancient Mesopotamia is known as Assyriology. During the mid-nineteenth century Paul Emile Botta discovered an Assyrian palace at Khorsabad and Austen Henry Layard discovered two more at Nimrud. Both of these sites were within a few miles of ancient °Nineveh (modern Kuyunjuk) across the Tigris from Mosul. Among these ancient Assyrian ruins the science of Assyriology was born.

Subsequent discoveries were made at °Babylon and its environs — ancient Babylonia — but the relationship between the language and culture of Assyria and Babylonia was such that the word Assyriology was broadened to include both areas. The Assyro-Babylonian language is now termed °Akkadian and the specialized study of the non-Semitic Sumerian culture of southern Mesopotamia is known as Sumerology.

ASTROLOGY, ASTRONOMY. Historically, astrology and astronomy are related although their methods and results differ markedly. Astrology is concerned with interpreting the bearing of the heavenly bodies upon the world and its events. It is a form of divination and survives only as a pseudoscience. When the observation of the heavenly bodies was used for measuring time intervals and when it became mathematically precise it gave rise to the science of astronomy.

The origins of astrology elude us, but we know that around 700 B.C. systematic reports of the movements of the heavenly bodies were given to the Assyrian kings. The reports were not, however, limited to the movements of the stars. Cloud formations were deemed as significant as eclipses. No mathematical computations were made, and the horoscope had not been invented. There were many means of divination in the ancient world. The examination of the liver of an animal that had been sacrificed was common, and some diviners were expert in interpreting the signs made during the flight of birds. That astronomical and meteorological phenomena should be put to such use is understandable.

In Roman times the term Chaldean came to mean astrologer and the Babylonians were considered to be the great experts on the heavenly bodies. Studies in the astronomical and mathematical texts of ancient Mesopotamia by O. Neugebauer, J. A. Sachs and others conclude that early Mesopotamian astronomy was very crude and it was not until the last three centuries B.C. that texts reveal a consistent mathematical theory of lunar and planetary motion.

It was during Classical and Hellenistic times that astronomy developed into a true science and astrology adopted the vagaries which have characterized it in succeeding generations. Thales enunciated the theory of the earth's roundness and predicted the year of a solar eclipse. The sixth century (B.C.) Greek mathematician Anaximander taught that the earth moves about on its own axis and that the light of the moon reflects that of the sun. Pythagoras and his school (530-400 B.C.) held that the sun is the center of the planetary system, and that the earth rotates on its axis.

The names of the heavenly bodies go back to Babylonian astrologers, but the concept of the zodiac itself appears to have developed during Hellenistic times. Hellenistic horoscopes concern specific individuals and depend upon the computed position of the seven celestial bodies (sun, moon, Mars, Mercury, Jupiter, Venus, Saturn) and their zodiacal signs in their relation to the given horizon for the moment of birth. Most of the texts give simply the results of such computations, and do not give us insight into astronomical method or theory.

Egyptian astronomy, like that of Babylon, was crude before the Hellenistic era. With the Ptolemaic period the zodiac appears on the monuments. Beginning with the second century B.C. astronomical and astrological papyri appear. Planetary texts from the time of Augustus to Hadrian record the dates when specific planets enter given zodiacal signs. Astronomy and astrology were among the cultural elements shared throughout the East in Hellenistic and Roman times.

Astrology was banned in Israel, and Isaiah predicted that the Babylonian stargazers would become "as stubble" (Isa. 47:13-15). Observers did watch for the "new moon" so that they might announce the sacred seasons of the Hebrew calendar, but it was not until after the time of Christ that astronomical knowledge was such that a fixed calendar could be adopted. The Biblical records made it clear that the heavenly bodies were created by the Lord, and Israel was warned against worshiping them. Israelite monotheism may well have discouraged a serious concern about the heavenly bodies in pre-Christian times. The heavens showed forth the glory of God, but they were not considered to have messages for man in their own right.

ASWAN. Ancient Aswan marked the frontier between Egypt and Nubia. It was located at the First Cataract of the Nile, where red granite, syenite, and other hard stone formed a natural boundary between the two peoples. It early became a center for trade, commerce, and warfare. Princes of Elephantine bore the titles "Caravan Conductor," and "Keeper of the Gate of the South," and conducted expeditions from Egypt into the unknown southern regions to enhance the glory and comfort of Egypt. Aswan, located on the east bank of the Nile, was largely a commerial city. Elephantine Island was the religious and military center of its district, and is presumed to have been the older settlement.

The origin of the name Elephantine is itself problematical. Some scholars relate it to the fact that Egyptians first saw the elephant there. Others follow the suggestion of Arthur Weigall that the name comes from the totem of the tribe which settled at Elephantine. There are numerous drawings of elephants on the rocks near Elephantine, many dating to prehistoric times. The Egyptian word for Elephant is *Yeb* or *Yebu*, and it was that name which the town bore in ancient times.

As the island was probably crowded, Nubian traders brought their wares to the mainland market town which came to be called *Swn*, or "Market." The Egyptians pronounced the word "Swani," and the Greeks gave as their approximation *Svene*. In Coptic it was called *Swan*.

The area around Aswan is rich in hard stone: red and grey granite, and diorite being plentiful. The Egyptians were the great builders of antiquity, and they were not slow in learning to quarry stone from Aswan and float it northward on Nile barges. As early as the First Dynasty, the tomb of Den Semti at Abydos was provided with a red granite floor. This red granite became the most familiar of hard stones to the craftsmen of the Egyptian Middle Kingdom and Empire period.

The pyramid builders made use of limestone and sandstone, which were quarried locally. Nevertheless, they appreciated the value of the harder granite and used it for linings and other furnishings. Mycerinus attempted to case his entire pyramid in granite, although this project was never completed.

During the Pyramid Age, Aswan was evidently an important quarrying community. Local workmen would be augmented as the need arose by special gangs sent in by the reigning Pharaoh who had a special project to be accomplished.

During the latter days of the Old Kingdom, Aswan and Elephantine became important centers of military expeditions. From Aswan, Egyptian soldiers were led by the frontier lords deep into Nubia, and there is some evidence that expeditions reached as far as central Africa.

Pharaoh Pepi I used Nubian mercenaries as the spearhead of the forces which he put into the field from time to time. Uni, an officer of Pepi, traveled south to Elephantine to organize a force to repel "the Asiatic sand-dwellers." Ultimately his army included "the Irthet negroes, the Mazoi negroes, the Yam negroes, the Wawat negroes, the Kau negroes" and the Temeh of Libya. Aside from the Libyans, all these warriors were recruited from the Negro tribes south of Aswan.

Throughout subsequent history, the Nubian mercenaries played an important role in Egyptian military campaigns.

BIBLIOGRAPHY. James H. Breasted, *Ancient Records of Egypt, I,* p. 142, University of Chicago Press, Chicago, 1906.

ATHENS. While Athens controlled hundreds of eastern Mediterranean States at its height in the fifth century B.C. under the leadership of Pericles, the city's political and economic greatness were gone by the time the Apostle Paul arrived in the middle of the first century A.D. The fortunes of the city were destined to decline still further under Byzantine and Turkish rule. When Athens became the capital of the newly independent Greek state in 1833, it had sunk to an insignificant village of less than 5,000. Since then it has climbed back to major city status and today has a population of some 630,000.

Athens is located about five miles from the Aegean on the roughly triangular peninsula of Attica. It is in the driest region of Greece and enjoys an annual rainfall of only sixteen inches. But the city's resources anciently included excellent clay beds for pottery manufacture, the famous marble of mount Pentelicus, the lead and silver mines of Laurium in the south of Attica and excellent harbor facilities. The great port of classical times was located at the Piraeus.

When the Apostle Paul arrived in Athens (probably in A.D. 50 or 51), the city still enjoyed great fame as a center of arts and pagan learning. Although the ravages of Sulla in 86 B.C. had been great and several other eastern Mediterranean cities had cut into her trade, the great classical structures of Athens were still intact. The university enjoyed a good reputation, and emperors and private citizens alike bestowed large benefactions upon the city. Moreover, Nero's raids on Athenian sculpture did not occur until after the great fire of Rome in A.D. 64, when the Emperor sought art pieces for his capital that was being rebuilt.

Apparently Paul had no intention of founding a church in Athens but merely went there to ride out the storm of opposition raised against him in Thessalonica and Berea. While in Athens the Apostle became exercised about the idolatry everywhere in evidence and sought to make converts. He ministered in the synagogue and the Agora (market place) and spoke before the Areopagus. Moreover, he apparently went sightseeing; Acts 17:23a may be translated, "For as I went about and examined objects of your religious devotion. . . ."

Thus, Paul was certainly familiar with the °Areopagus, the old Greek and the newer Roman marketplaces, the structures of the °Acropolis and those along the south side of the Acropolis, the great temple of Zeus, and possibly the stadium. Since these structures or areas have a direct or implied connection

BAS RELIEF OF BACCHUS, God of wine. Courtesy, N. Stoupnapas

with the Biblical narrative, all of them are considered here.

I. *Archaeological Activities.* Soon after Greek independence, interest was kindled in antiquities of the country. The Greek Archaeological Society was founded in 1837. Of foreign archaeological schools the French was founded in 1846, the German in 1874, the American in 1882, the British in 1886, the Austrian in 1898, the Italian in 1909 and the Swedish since World War II.

As might be expected, these schools were established because scholarly interest in things Greek had already been aroused in the western world. Systematic study of the topography of ancient Athens began in the seventeenth century. Later a particularly important contribution was made by James Stuart and Nicholas Revett who published four large volumes on *The Antiquities of Athens* on the basis of three years of work there (1751-1754). In the nineteenth century W. M. Leake's *Topography of Athens* (2nd ed., 1841) introduced the period of modern research.

For decades now, with the exception of war years, archaeological work has been continually in progress in Athens. A few of the more important excavations may be noted. Greek (1870 ff.) and later German (1907-16, 1926-39) archaeologists excavated the Dipylon cemetery northwest of the city. Athens' finest burial ground, the district was also called the "outer Kerameikos" from the fact that potters' quarters were located there in early times. Graves examined in this cemetery dated from the eleventh century B.C to Roman times. A number of Jewish grave stones were found. But where the synagogue was located in which Paul may have preached is another question. A stone slab bearing Psalm 118:20 was found in the eastern section of the city; some have thought it may have been incorporated in a synagogue.

During the years 1884-91 the whole Acropolis area was examined down to bed rock by Greek archaeologists. The Greek Archaeological Society also excavated the remains of Pericles' *Odeum at the southeast corner of the Acropolis in the 1920's. Several German scholars studied the adjacent theater of Dionysus. The north slope of the Acropolis was excavated by the American School of Classical Studies 1931-39 under the direction Oscar Broneer.

The most prodigious excavation in Athens was centered on the Agora. The area was examined earlier by German and Greek archaeologists, but expense of purchasing the land and demolishing homes prevented thorough excavation until 1930. Then the Greek government offered to allow the American School to undertake the task. The project was largely financed by John D. Rockefeller, Jr., and Ward Canaday and was directed between 1931 and 1940 by T. Leslie Shear and since 1946 by Homer A. Thompson. Some 4,000-5,000 people were moved from the area, sixteen acres cleared and about 250,000 tons of earth removed. About 68,000 objects were discovered and cataloged in addition to 94,000 coins. The Stoa of Attalus (discussed below) was reconstructed as the Agora museum and work was also done on the Hephaesteion.

Considerable repair work has also been done on structures standing above ground. For instance, between 1922 and 1933 the Greek government devoted considerable attention to rehabilitation of the Parthenon so that by the latter date it was as complete and in as good condition as it can ever be short of actual reconstruction.

II. *The Agora.* As Paul docked at the Piraeus and traveled the five miles into Athens, he would have entered by the Dipylon Gate and probably would have continued southeast on the main road leading to the Agora. As well oriented as he was to the Greek city, it would have been most natural for him to go first to the political, commerical and social center to get the feel of the metropolis and to arrange for lodging. The sights there would have become very familiar to the Apostle as he reasoned "daily" with the crowds in the Agora (Acts 17:17). Fortunately, the very meticulous work of the American School of Classical Studies makes it possible for us to visualize the Agora as Paul would have known it.

The avenue he traveled led diagonally across the Agora from northwest to southeast and is called the Panathenaean way, for along this route the annual procession in honor of Athena made its way toward the Parthenon. As the Apostle entered the Agora, he would have noticed the "Painted Stoa" extending across the north of the area. Built in the fifth century B.C., it was so-called because of the paintings of Polygnotus

and Micon on its walls. These depicted battle scenes from the Trojan War, the struggle with the Persians at Marathon, and contests between Athenians and Amazons, among others. This stoa was a haunt of philosophers in the fourth and third centuries B.C. Zeno, founder of the Stoic school, held forth here. Unfortunately a road and a railroad running here have prevented excavation of the north side of the Agora.

All along the east side of the Agora to the Apostle's left stretched the magnificent Stoa of Attalus, now reconstructed and serving as the Agora museum. Attalus II, king of Pergamum (195-138), a Philhellene, built this structure for the Athenians about 150 B.C. Some 38 feet long and 64 feet wide, it was faced with a two story colonnade of 45 columns, Doric at the base and Ioniac at the top. The second story was reached by stairs at either end. Behind the colonnade were twenty-one shops. In front of the stoa, about half way along the east side of the Agora, stood the Bema or public rostrum where officials could address crowds gathered in the square.

Directly west of the Bema, in the middle of the Agora, stood the Odeum or music hall or theater of Agrippa, built about 15 B.C. The auditorium had seats for 1000 placed in eighteen rows. The seats were comfortable, with scooped tops. The structure apparently had a second story.

South of the Odeum sprawled the commercial agora. Constructed in the second century B.C., it included south, east and middle stoas facing an open market area. The east stoa connected the south and middle stoas and screened the commercial agora from the Panathenaean way. Entrance to the commercial agora was gained by means of a broad stairway that led through this stoa to the lower level of the open market area. The south stoa consisted of a single wide aisle with Doric columns along its north side; its back wall acted as a retaining wall against the slopes of the Acropolis to the south. At the west end of the south stoa was located the Heliaia, largest of the law courts of Athens. Next to that was the southwest fountain house. A southeast fountain house stood next to the mint at the southeast corner of the south stoa. The middle stoa faced both northward on the commercial agora and on the larger agora area to the north. The largest structure in the Agora, it was about 450 feet long and like the south and east stoas was faced with unfluted Doric columns.

The road along the west side of the Agora passed the important political structures of Ancient Athens. Moving from south to north, first comes the circular Tholos, the office and dining room of the prytany, a committee of the city council. At the expense of the state, prytany members spent the night there so responsible administrators were always on duty. Built around 470 B.C., this building was the real headquarters of the Athenian government. Also, the official set of standard weights and measures was kept here.

A few feet away against a steep hillside, called Kolonos Agoraios, stood the Bouleuterion or Senate house, where the full council of 500 met. This building was constructed in the form of a theater with raised banks of seats in semicircular form. Between the Bouleuterion and the Agora stood the Metroon which housed the state archives and sanctuary of the mother of the gods. It was built in the second century B.C. Across the road from the Metroon in the open area of the Agora was a fenced enclosure surrounding a long base, on which statues of the tribal heroes of Attica are thought to have been located. The base of these statues served as a public bulletin board.

Between the Metroon and the Temple of Apollo to the north is a wide passageway that provided access to the Temple of Hephaestus (god of the forge) on the Kolonos Agoraios. One of the best preserved of all Greek temples, it is 104 feet long, 45 feet wide and 34 feet high. The Doric colonnade consists of six columns at the ends and thirteen on the sides. On the east pediment above the entrance were sculptures representing the labors of Hercules. Plants were set out in flower pots sunk into the rock and carefully spaced around the temple to provide a formal garden.

As one continues north along the west side of the Agora once more, he passes the fourth century Temple of Apollo Patroos, reputed father of the Athenians. Across from this in the open square of the Agora was the Temple of Ares, god of war, whom the Romans called Mars. North of the Temple of Apollo was the Stoa of Zeus, a large u-shaped structure housing administrative offices. Before it stood a colossal statue of Zeus. And opposite it in the open Agora

STOA OF ATTALOS, originally built in the 2nd century B.C. by Attalos II of Pergamum. Reconstructed with funds given by John D. Rockefeller, Jr. augmented by other gifts and a grant from the Marshall Plan. Courtesy, N. Stoupnapas

stood the Altar of the Twelve Gods, considered to be the very center of Athens, from which distances to outside points were measured.

III. *The Roman Market.* A few hundred feet to the east of the Greek Agora lay the Roman Market or Agora. Planned by Julius Caesar in 44 B.C., it was completed by Augustus Caesar. As an inscription on the main gate (western) indicates, it was erected between 10 and 2 B.C. Excavation of this agora was undertaken by the Greek Archaeological Society in 1890 and work was carried on there intermittently until 1931, but it is still unfinished because of lack of funds.

The Market consists of a rectangular open area with a series of shops and arcades along the sides. Exterior dimensions are 367 feet by 315 feet. The interior courtyard, paved with marble, is 269 by 187 feet. This courtyard is surrounded by an Ionic colonnade, through which entrance was gained to the shops. Monumental entrances were constructed both at the east and west ends of the Market. There the Doric columns were almost twenty-six feet high and carried a pediment. Between the columns three passages led into the Market, the one in the center for chariots and those on the sides for pedestrians.

At the east end of the Market stands the Tower of the Winds or the Andronicus Clock. It was a hydraulic clock arranged with sundials. The octagonal tower in white marble measured twenty-six feet in diameter and about forty feet in height. Each of its faces is turned toward one of the points of the compass and each face bears a sculptured figure representing a personification of that respective wind.

IV. *The Areopagus.* According to Acts 17:22-31, Paul appeared before the *Areopagus. That Areopagus referred to a court is sure; that it also referred to a hill is equally certain. In early times the court met on the hill but by New Testament times it also occasionally met in the Royal Stoa in the Agora. There is some question as to how that stoa is to be identified. Normally, however, in Paul's day the Areopagus met on the hill, and Paul probably appeared before the court there.

Areopagus ("hill of Ares") is a 377 foot eminence west of the Acropolis and north of the Agora. Ares (Roman Mars), the god of war, supposedly stood trial here for the slaying of the son of the sea-god Poseidon. Later the hill served as the meeting place of the most ancient court and council of Athens. On two stones on top of the hill the accuser and defendant sat facing each other. The hill was ascended by sixteen steps cut in the rock. To the right of these at ground level a bronze plate bearing the Greek text of Paul's speech to the Areopagus is affixed to the rock. In Paul's day the Areopagus apparently had responsibility for religious and educational affairs and presumably had the right to audition prospective lecturers (Paul?) coming to the city.

V. *The Acropolis.* As Paul preached on the Areopagus, he referred to "temples made with hands" (Acts 17:4). Perhaps he gestured toward the beautiful structures on the Acropolis as he did so. No effort had been spared to make the Acropolis the crown and glory of Athens and her empire. And those temples were still intact in New Testament times. But the southern slopes of the Acropolis supported structures almost as important as some of those on the sacred hill.

A. The South Slope. At the southeast corner of the Acropolis stood the Odeum of Pericles. Originally constructed about 440 B.C., the Odeum was destroyed during the First Mithradatic War in 86 B.C. and rebuilt shortly thereafter on the same plan by Ariobarzanes of Cappadocia. It was a rectangular building (possibly square) some 270 feet long on its north side, which is the only side completely excavated. In the interior were many seats, apparently banked against the walls, and the roof was supported by a forest of columns which must have interfered greatly with the spectators' view. Located just to the east of the Theater of Dionysus, the Odeum was probably used for rehearsals of presentations in the theater. But it was no doubt also used for musical contests which Pericles himself introduced.

West of the Odeum of Pericles was the great Theater of Dionysus, which was the "mother" of other Greek theaters and the place where Greek drama was developed. The evolution of the theater need not detain us here. Suffice it to say that Lycurgus is credited with a reconstruction of the theater about 330 B.C. When he finished with it, the auditorium was a little more than a half

ODEON OF HERODES ATTICUS, *built A.D. 161 to serve as a theater and concert hall. Courtesy, N. Stoupnapas*

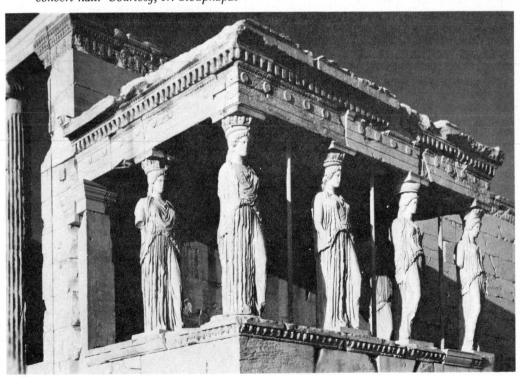

PORCH OF THE MAIDENS, *the Erechtheum, Athens. Courtesy, N. Stoupnapas*

circle fitted with stone seats and supported by retaining walls on the south, east and west sides. The seats were arranged in semicircular fashion and divided into thirteen wedges by twelve stairways. Presumably the seating was arranged in three vast horizontal bands. The seventy-eight rows of seats are estimated to have held 17,000 persons. Occupying the front row were sixty-seven Pentelic marble arm chairs for officials. The orchestra, some sixty feet in diameter, was paved by Roman times and was backed by a raised stage and scene building (*skene*).

Extending westward from the theater Eumenes II, king of Pergamum (197-159 B.C.) had built a great stoa or portico some 535 feet long and 85 feet wide. It was designed to serve as a shelter for the theater audience. Behind this, on the slope of the Acropolis, several small temples were located.

B. The summit. The entrance to the Acropolis was on the west and looked much different in Paul's day than it does now. The modern visitor has to think away the great pylons jutting out seventeen feet which were added about 200 A.D. But the Agrippa monument was there — a figure mounted on a chariot drawn by four horses atop a thirty-nine foot rectangular pedestal of marble. Overhanging the entrance path on the right was the beautiful little Ionic temple of Athena Nike (victory) sculptured with figures of victories in a variety of poses.

Passing through the impressive ornamental gateway called the Propylaea, a visitor to the Acropolis would see the colossal bronze figure of Athena made by Phidias from the spoils taken from the Persians at Marathon. As one walked the sacred way to the entrance to the Parthenon on the east, the Parthenon was on his right. On his left was the Erechtheum, temple of Athena Polias (of the city) and Poseidon-Erechtheus with its beautiful porch of the maidens. The main part of this structure is a rectangle seventy-eight feet long by forty-two feet wide, with an Ionic colonnade at either end standing twenty-five feet in height. The porch with its six maidens whose heads support the roof, extends from the southwest of the temple.

Next on the left was the great altar of Athena. As the sacred way turned toward the eastern entrance of the Parthenon it passed a circular structure surrounded by nine Ionic columns, which housed the altar

of Roma and Augustus. This was built between 27 and 14 B.C.

Now one turns into the Parthenon. Begun in 447, it was dedicated to the goddess Athena in 438. The great marble structure measured at its base 238 feet in length and 111 feet in width. Its encircling row of 46 fluted Doric columns (17 on each side and 8 on each end) stood to a height of 34 feet, each having a diameter at the base of six feet. The top of the pediments rose to a height of 65 feet. Both pediments were filled with sculpture, the eastern depicting the birth of Athena and the western portraying the contest of Athens and Poseidon for Attica. Encircling the entire structure above the colonnade was the Doric frieze. Divided into ninety-two panels, it consisted of groups of sculptures depicting legendary and mythological scenes dear to the hearts of Greeks. Inside the colonnade the Ionic frieze encircled the temple below the roof. This continuous frieze 524 feet in length consisted of 600 figures and portrayed the annual Panathenaic procession up to the Parthenon. Two tremendous bronze doors gave entrance to the east room or holy of holies, where stood the great ivory and gold image of Athena. This room measured 98 feet long, 63 feet wide and 43 feet high. The west room or treasury was 44 feet long and 63 feet wide.

The beautiful structures of the Acropolis remained fairly intact until the seventeenth century. During a Venetian-Turkish war the Turks used the Parthenon as a powder magazine. A Venetian mortar blew up the magazine on September 26, 1687, causing extensive and irreparable damage to the whole structure. At the beginning of the nineteenth century Lord Elgin carried off to London a large part of the remaining sculpture; it is now housed in the British Museum. The Erechtheum suffered its greatest destruction much later than the Parthenon. A Turkish house for several hundred years, it was used as a Greek headquarters in 1826-27 during the Greek war of independence. As a result it suffered ruinous Turkish bombardment.

VI. *Temple of Zeus.* Southeast of the Acropolis stood the Temple of Zeus, one of the greatest of ancient temples. Significant archaeological work was done here by the Greek Archaeological Society 1886-1901 and the German School 1922-23. This massive structure was begun by the Peisistratids in

HADRIAN'S GATE at the foot of the acropolis, Athens. Courtesy, Elly Athanasso-poulou

THEATER OF DIONYSUS. Courtesy, N. Stoupnapas

the latter part of the sixth century B.C. and was continued by Antiochus IV of Syria (175-164 B.C.). Still open to the sky in Paul's day it was completed by Hadrian during the second century A.D.

The temple itself measured 286 by 62 feet and stood on a platform 353 by 13 feet. A total of 104 Corinthian columns 56 feet high and 5 feet 7 inches in lower diameter supported the roof. They stood in two rows of twenty columns on the sides and in three rows of eight columns at the ends. Today fifteen of these columns are standing and one is overturned; the rest have been used in other building projects.

VII. *The Stadium.* Southeast of Athens in a ravine near the Ilissus River, stood the horseshoe shaped stadium of ancient Athens. Here the annual athletic festival in honor of Athena was held — including such events as foot races, wrestling, boxing and javelin throwing. A rounded arc at the southern end, the stadium opened to the north and had a race track about 200 yards (a stade) long and 36 yards wide. Lycurgus, about 330 B.C., marked out the track with stone. But it was not until about 140 A.D. that Herodes Atticus built the spectators' seats on the adjacent hillsides in marble. His stadium could hold about 50,000. Used as a quarry for many centuries, the stadium was rebuilt for the first Olympic games in 1896 by the wealthy Alexandrian Greek G. Vroutos.

VIII. *To The Unknown God.* Paul mentioned seeing an altar in Athens dedicated to the Unknown God (Acts 17:23), and it is frequently asked whether that altar has been found. Unfortunately one has not yet been recovered. One such was discovered at Pergamum (closely tied with Athenian development); and Pausanias, who visited Athens about A.D. 150, mentions seeing one on the road between Athens and its harbor at Phaleron and also at Olympia.

BIBLIOGRAPHY. Oscar Broneer, "Athens, City of Idol Worship," *BA*, XXI, 1958, 2-28. William B. Dinsmoor, *The Architecture of Ancient Greece,* B. T. B. Batsford, Ltd., London. 3rd ed. rev., 1950. Robert S. Kinsey, *With Paul in Greece,* Parthenon Press, Nashville, 1957. Mabel Lang and C. W. J. Eliot, *The Athenian Agora,* American School of Classical Studies, Athens, 1954. A. W. Lawrence, *Greek Architecture,* Penguin Books Inc., Harmondsworth, England, 1957. William A. McDonald, "Archaeology and St. Paul's Journeys in Greek Lands, Part II. Athens," IV, 1941, pp. 1-10. Paul MacKendrick, *The Greek Stones Speak,* St. Martin's Press, New York, 1962. William M. Ramsay, *St. Paul the Traveller and the Roman Citizen,* Hodder and Stoughton, London, 8th ed., 1905. D. S. Robertson, *A Handbook of Greek and Roman Architecture,* The University Press, Cambridge, 1929. Charles H. Weller, *Athens and Its Monuments,* The Macmillan Company, New York, 1913. R. E. Wycherley, *How the Greeks Built Cities,* Macmillan & Co., Ltd., London, 2d ed., 1962.

ATON, HYMN TO THE. Composed either by *Akhenaton or by courtiers who had assimilated his religious reforms, the Hymn to the Aton is our fullest expression of Atonism. The hymn was inscribed on the walls of the tomb prepared for the courtier Eye east of Akhetaton, modern *Amarna. James H. Breasted suggested that the hymn was an excerpt from the ritual of the Aton temple.

Although the Hymn to the Aton clearly grants a favored position to Egypt, Aton is pictured as holding sway over all peoples, for the sun brings light and heat to men of every nation. The Hymn begins:

> Thou dawnest beautifully on the horizon
> of heaven,
> Oh living Aton, the beginner of life.
> When thou risest on the eastern horizon
> Thou fillest every land with thy beauty.

Parallels between the Hymn and Psalm 104 suggest that the poetic expressions which Akhenaton used became a part of the literary heritage of the Near East. Although Atonism as a religion died a short time after the death of Akhenaton, poetic utterances used in praise of Aton could readily be incorporated into Egyptian devotional literature and eventually find an echo in the literature of other lands. The numerous contacts between Israel and Egypt suggest that devotional literature as well as proverbs (cf. I Kings 4:30) were common knowledge to the two peoples.

Akhenaton's god, Aton, is identified with the disk of the sun. While Akhenaton seems to have spiritualized sun worship, he never divorced himself from it. In Biblical monotheism the "lights in the firmament of heaven" (Gen. 1:15) were created by God, who is never identified with natural phenomena.

BIBLIOGRAPHY. Charles F. Pfeiffer, *Tell el-Amarna and the Bible,* Baker Book House, Grand Rapids, 1963. John A. Wilson, "The Hymn to the Aton," in *ANET,* pp. 369-371.

AUGUSTUS. Augustus was the title given to Gaius Julius Caesar Octavianus (63 B.C.

— A.D. 14), the first Roman Emperor and ruler of the Mediterranean world at the time of the birth of Jesus (Luke 2:1). *See* Rome.

AVARIS. *See* Raamses.

AVDAT. Avdat was a Nabatean city south of Beer-sheba in the section of the Negeb known in Biblical times as the Wilderness of Zin. It was occupied from the second century B.C. to the sixth century A.D. Nabatean rule ended in A.D. 106 when Trajan annexed the region to the Roman Empire. Under Diocletian (284-305) Avdat was fortified and was chosen as the site for a Roman camp with a watchtower and a colonnaded terrace. By the sixth century, Avdat was at the peak of its prosperity, with two Christian churches and a monastery. With the Moslem conquest of the Negeb (A.D. 634) Avdat entered a period of decline from which it never recovered.

The Israeli archaeologist Michael Avi Yonah of the Hebrew University has excavated and restored Avdat. Among the remains of the city are Nabatean caves and Byzantine fortifications, churches, and a bath house.

'AZARIYEH, EL. *See* Bethany.

AZEKAH (TELL EZ-ZAKARIYEH). Tell ez-Zakariyeh, the site of ancient Azekah, is a triangular mound about one thousand feet long by five hundred feet in maximum breadth, standing in the Wadi es-Sunt (Old Testament "Valley of Elah"). The mound was excavated in 1899 by Frederick J. Bliss for the Palestine Exploration Fund. The largest building on the site was a citadel or fortress with masonry on the top level that was comparable to Herodian buildings in Jerusalem. Pottery at the bottom of the structure caused Bliss to date the foundations to early Israelite times. He discovered a jar containing a number of scarabs bearing the names of the Egyptian Pharaohs Thutmose III and Amenhotep III.

Azekah was a Canaanite stronghold during the time of Israel's conquest of the land. Joshua, after the victory at Beth-horon, pursued the enemy as far as Azekah (Josh. 10:10-11). When David met the challenge of the Philistine champion Goliath, the foes of Israel were encamped "between Socoh and Azekah" (I Sam. 17:1). The inner citadel which Bliss discovered may go back to

AVDAT as it appears from the air after excavation and restoration. Courtesy, Israel Office of Information

Rehoboam who is said to have strengthened the Azekah fortress (II Chron. 11:9). There is evidence, however, that it was subsequently repaired or enlarged. When Nebuchadnezzar invaded Judah, Azekah was one of the last Judaean strongholds to fall to the Babylonians (Jer. 34:7). A letter discovered at *Lachish speaks of the correspondent's failure to see the signals from Azekah. The absence of smoke signals seems to indicate that the city had fallen. Soon Lachish also fell, and finally Jerusalem, after which the remnants of the Jews who survived the war were taken into exile in Babylonia. Excavations were conducted at Azekah by F. J. Bliss and R. A. S. Macalister in 1898 and 1899. They found evidence that the site was occupied before the Israelites arrived in Canaan. It was fortified twice during Israel times and was occupied for a short time by the Romans.

AZOR. Excavations were conducted during 1961 and 1962 by the Israeli Department of Antiquities at an ancient cemetery in Azor, near Tel Aviv. Burials there date from the fourth millennium B.C down to the Middle Ages. A tomb excavated in 1962 contained Philistine pottery at the head of a young man who wore an Egyptian *scarab at his throat. The scarab represents the Nile god Hapi, surrounded by three crocodiles. It dates from the Twentieth Egyptian Dynasty and is contemporary with the major wave of Philistine migration to Canaan. Family burial plots were common during the Solomonic era. One such was discovered with a large number of Cypro-Phoenician vessels, indicating the foreign commerce of Israel during the Monarchy. A later tomb, dated about the time of the Exile (587 B.C.), yielded a jar with a clear inscription which was written on wet clay before the jar was fired. It read: LSHLMY, "to Shelmay," evidently the name of the owner of the jar. Shelmay is a shortened form of Shelemiah, the name of several Old Testament personages of the period of the Exile and subsequent years (Jer. 37:13; Neh. 3:30; Ezra 10:39, 41).

B

BAAL. Baal, a Semitic word meaning "lord" or "master," was the chief god worshiped by the Canaanites at the time of Israel's entrance into the land of promise. The nominal head of the Canaanite pantheon was El who was regarded as the father of the seventy *elim* or gods.

The popularity of Baal was doubtless due to his association with fertility in its varied aspects — human, animal, and vegetation. As the "rider of the clouds" Baal was identified with Hadad, the Semitic storm god.

The worship of Baal tended to be localized so that each community worshiped its local Baal. This gave rise to the concept of Baalim, a plural form used to denote the multiplicity of Baal shrines and idols. These include Baal-peor (Num. 25:3, 5); Baal-zephon (Num. 33:7) and Baal-hazor (II Sam. 13:23).

The Baal cult was conducted by priests who conducted licentious rites in fields or on high places. Wine, oil, first fruits, and firstlings of flocks were brought to the priests at the shrines. Dances and ritualistic meals formed a part of the ceremony which had an attraction to the Hebrews from the time of their entrance into Canaan until the destruction of Jerusalem (587 B.C.).

Near the Baal altar a sacred pole or tree was erected to the goddess Astarte. These are the "groves" of the King James Bible, more properly the cultic poles of the Asherah, the female counterpart to Baal. Cultic stone pillars (*masseboth*) of Baal also formed a part of the cultic pattern.

At Baal-peor (Num. 25:1-5), Israel took part in the religious prostitution rites which characterized Baalism. This pattern was continued after the entrance into Canaan, where idolatry was the cause of humiliations of Israel before her enemies during the time of the Judges (Judg. 2:11-14).

A crisis in Israelite history took place during the reign of Ahab, when the wife of the king, Jezebel, attempted to suppress the worship of Israel's God, and place Baal as the god of the nation. Jezebel was a daughter of Itto-baal, the priest-king of Tyre, who was a devotee of Melchart, the Tyrian Baal. Elijah's faithfulness to God and his successful challenge to the Baal priests at Mount Carmel (I Kings 18) brought defeat to the purposes of Ahab and Jezebel.

A similar crisis occurred in the kingdom of Judah when Athaliah, daughter of Jezebel and wife of King Jehoram, sought to secure the throne for herself by killing "all the royal seed" (II Kings 11:2). The young prince Joash was spared, and the godly Jehoiada kept him in the Temple until he was old enough to present to the loyal guard who

proclaimed him king. Athaliah was slain, and Baalism suffered defeat.

The prophets Hosea (2:8) and Amos (5:26) denounced Baalism as an act of disloyalty to Israel's God. Josiah effected a reform which included the destruction of Baal images by casting them into the Kidron valley and burning them (II Kings 23).

Although Baalism was a threat to Israel and Judah to the time of the captivity, the Babylonian exile was regarded as a divine punishment for apostasy. The mission of Israel as a witness to the one God was increasingly emphasized in the years that followed the exile. Baal is mentioned only once in the New Testament, and then in a context in which the Old Testament is quoted (Rom. 11:4).

Baalism is known through the study of the epic literature from °Ugarit dating to the fifteenth century B.C. Excavations of Palestinian cities have brought to light many images of Baal and the corresponding female deities.

BAALBEK. The ancient city of Baalbek lies in the Valley of the Beqa'a, which separates the Lebanon from the Anti-Lebanon mountain ranges. This valley was called Coele-Syria by the Greeks and Romans and was notable for its great fertility. Baalbek itself stands on a commanding view of the valley; it rose around a shrine dedicated to Baal of the Beqa'a, or to the "Lord of the Plain." There is no doubt that there was a temple dedicated to the lord of the valley from the earliest times and the present Roman temples actually stand over the ruins of earlier structures. Soundings in the court of the Temple of Jupiter have revealed remains of temples of the Persian and the Hellenistic Periods.

The existing monuments at Baalbek include three temples: one dedicated to Jupiter Heliopolitanus, one to Bacchus and the third to Venus. In addition to these temples, other remains of the Roman Period, such as founda-

BAAL, the storm god, is represented holding a club in his right hand and a lance in his left hand. The lance extends upward in the form of a tree, or stylized lightning. Found at Ras Shamra in 1932. Courtesy, the Louvre

121

THE TEMPLE OF VENUS at Baalbek and general view of the city. Courtesy, Azad, Beirut

(inset) RECONSTRUCTION OF THE TEMPLES AT BAALBEK. Drawing courtesy Photo Sport, Beirut

tions of villas, Roman statuary, and coins, keep turning up from time to time. Also on an outcrop of rock to the north of the temples, the stairs, cut in the rock, and a section of the foundations of yet another temple have come to light; it is suspected that these may belong to the lost temple of Mercury which was known to have existed in the city.

When the Seleucid Kings reigned over Syria they gave Greek names to all the cities in the area, and identified the local gods with Greek gods. Thus the name of Baal, the Sun-god, was changed into Helios, and the city came to be called Heliopolis, or the city of the sun-god. The Romans kept the name of the city but changed the name of the god into Jupiter Heliopolitanus. The worship of this god was widespread but naturally his most important shrine lay in the city of Baalbek.

Evidence shows that a temple dedicated to Jupiter was built during the reign of Nero, and remains of that temple have come to light in recent years in the course of excavations. There was an oracle in the temple, which was consulted by Trajan in A.D. 116 on the eve of his campaign against the Parthians. But the present gigantic edifice was built during the reign of Antoninus Pius. To this structure some additions were made by the Caracalla, the Syrian Emperor, in memory of his mother Julia Domna.

The temple built by Antoninus Pius consisted of a large rectangular court, flanked on the north, east and south sides by a colonnaded porch, at the back of which there were rooms of all types. The entrance of the court stood in the middle of the east side, and at the other extremity or west side of the court rose the cella proper. Immediately in front of the cella, there was an altar of burnt offerings, and behind it a structure for the offering of libations. On either side of the altars, there was a shallow basin built of stone for purifying the sacrificial animals. The walls of the basins were carved on the outside with representations of mythological figures especially marine deities and other motifs such as dolphins.

The *cella itself was built on an artificially raised platform (podium), at the top of a flight of broad stairs on an east-west axis. Unfortunately apart from six columns together with the entablature above them, only a few bases remain to indicate the position of most of the other columns. But like most temples of the second century A.D. the cella had a row of columns in front (*prostyle in antis*) and another row of columns running around the structure on all sides (*peristyle*). Inside, it must have had an altar set on a raised platform at the west end of the cella and approached by a flight of stairs. The cella was probably roofed with a gable roof consisting of slabs of marble supported on a timber framework. At each corner of the roof, and at the top of the gable there were ornaments resembling acanthus leaves (*acroteria*) decorating the roof. This reconstruction is based on representations of the temple which appear on the coins of Baalbek, struck during the reign of the Emperors Septimius Severus and Philip the Arab. Some of the stones used in the construction of the podium are as much as fifty-seven feet in length, nine feet high and eight feet deep and weigh over sixty tons. The Emperor Caracalla added the hexagonal court and the monumental porch (*propylaea*), which now stand at the east end of the hexagonal court.

The Temple of Bacchus was built a short distance south of the Temple of Jupiter, and like the latter, it also stood on a raised platform or podium, and was constructed on an almost identical plan, but on a smaller scale, and is far better preserved than the Temple of Jupiter. A flight of stairs at the east end led up to the porch of the cella consisting of two rows of columns, the first set between the projecting sides of the side walls, and the other in front of it completing the circuit of columns which surrounded the entire building.

The walls of the temple are preserved as far up as the springing of the roof. The temple was provided with three doors, one main monumental entrance which was about fourteen meters high, and eight meters wide, and had two small lateral entrances. Stairs built in a narrow stairwell and starting from these two lateral doors led up to the roof. The door-jambs were profusely carved with vine and ivy patterns set in a border of ovules, while the soffit or lower part of the lintel over the door was carved with an eagle carrying a caduceus in its beak and claws.

The walls of the temple on the inside were decorated with columns between which there were niches for statues. The west section of the temple is occupied by a raised altar approached by a flight of stairs set in the middle section and contained within two panels, one on either side carved with Bacchanalian scenes of drunken women in states of utter abandon. Below the altar and approached by a door on the right, there is a cellar for storing wine used in the Bacchanalian orgies.

The roof of the porch surrounding the temple is preserved on the north side, either in its original position, or fallen between the columns and the walls of the temple. The soffit is richly carved with hexagonal panels, in each of which appears one of the deities worshipped by the ancient inhabitants of Lebanon. One can recognize the city-goddess Tyche, the Goddess of Medicine Hygiea, the Goddess Atargatis, the God Mars, the God Mercury and so on.

Some distance south of the Temple of Bacchus stands the dainty Temple of Venus, which is built on a circular plan, and contrasts sharply with its gigantic neighbors. Like the other two it is built on a raised podium, and was surrounded by a row of columns. It is approached from the court by a flight of stairs and was roofed by a masonry dome, part of which is still preserved in the original position.

BIBLIOGRAPHY. Hoyningen-Huene and David M. Robinson, *Baalbek, Palmyra,* J. J. Augustin Publishers, New York, 1946. R. Dussaud, "Temples et cultes de la triade heliopolitaine a Baalbek," *Syria,* XXIII, 1942-43.

BABEL, Tower of. The account of the building of the Tower of Babel (Gen. 11:1-8) reflects building techniques of lower Mesopotamia where both stone and wood are scarce, and bricks made of the local clay form the principal building material. Asphalt ("slime," A.V.; "bitumen," R.S.V.) serves as mortar.

The tower itself is reminiscent of the staged towers or ziggurats which were built in the principal cities of Mesopotamia. Such a °ziggurat in the Babylon of Hammurabi's day (*ca.* 1700 B.C.) is described on a cuneiform tablet now in the Department of Oriental Antiquities at the Louvre (Tablet AO 6555). The ziggurat was known as E-temen-an-ki, "the house of the terrace platform of heaven and earth." Its base was 295 feet square, and it rose in seven stages to a height of 295 feet. The tablet describing the

structure dates from the Seleucid Period (*ca.* 229 B.C.).

Koldewey discovered the ground plan of the ziggurat during his excavations at °Babylon. The Biblical Tower of Babel was left in ruins, but later generations seem to have rebuilt the tower, on the top of which was a temple. In this way they hoped to approach their god and seek his favor.

BAB ED-DRA. During February and March of 1924 W. F. Albright representing the American School of Oriental Research and M. G. Kyle representing Xenia Theological Seminary (now Pittsburgh) conducted an expedition to explore the region south of the Dead Sea in search for Sodom, Gomorrah and the other "Cities of the Plain." They found the site of Byzantine and Arab Zoar, but concluded that the Dead Sea covered ancient Zoar as well as Sodom and Gomorrah. They did, however, find remains of a sanctuary at Bab ed-Dra which they dated between 2800 and 1800 B.C. Here, east of the Dead Sea, they found six prostrate °menhirs, with broken pieces of a seventh. Open air hearths and enclosures were discovered, along with large quantities of sherds, vases, flint artifacts, bones and skulls. The archaeologists interpret these as remains from a sanctuary in which religious services were conducted during the Early and Middle Bronze Ages.

BIBLIOGRAPHY. W. F. Albright and M. G. Kyle, "Results of the Archaeological Survey of the Ghor in search for the Cities of the Plain," *Bibliotheca Sacra,* LXXXI, 1925, pp. 276-291.

BABYLON. The capital city of the empire to which it gave its name was situated on the banks of the ancient course of the Euphrates fifty-four miles south of modern Baghdad, west of the present river bed. The flat river-deposit terrain without minerals or stone is reduced by the hot dry climate to relative unproductivity, unless fed by irrigation canals. By its very location Babylon was destined to become important commercially. Access routes to the north and west followed the Tigris and Euphrates. On the south the Persian Gulf made naval communication with maritime nations possible. Eastward, through the Zagros gates, was the road to Iran.

I. *History of the City.* The earliest history of the city is unknown. The Akkadian creation epic, *Enuma elish,* provides a mythical account of the founding, describing Babylon as the first city to come into existence, its shrines designed as dwelling places for the gods (VI:50 ff.). Flint and stone artifacts testify to the antiquity of the site but archaeologists have been unable to penetrate below the strata of the third millennium due to the high water table. An early Mesopotamian text indicates that during the third millennium the city was known by the Sumerian name *Ka-dingira,* the equivalent of the Akkadian *Bab-ilum,* "gate of god."

By the second millennium under the Semitic *Amorites, "People of the West," Babylon was the capital of a small *Akkadian kingdom dedicated to the god Marduk, ruled by a dynasty founded by Sumu-abum. The sixth king of this dynasty, Hammurabi, a military, administrative, and economic genius, strengthened and beautified Babylon. During the sixteenth century Hittites attacked and destroyed the city, terminating the First Dynasty. Then Cassites, who had been settling in Babylon in great numbers, assisted by an invasion of countrymen from the Zagros mountains, established a new dynasty that was to rule for five hundred years continuing, so it would seem, Hammurabi's governmental patterns. *Assyria brought the Cassite under control and Cassite rule was replaced by the Second Dynasty of Isin. The greatest monarch of this 125-year period, Nebuchadnezzar I, came to the throne at the end of the twelfth century.

For the next centuries Babylon's history is obscure. Rulers appear to be those acceptable to Assyria. In the eighth century reign of Tiglath-pileser III of Assyria, Ukin-zer, the Chaldeans, whose tribes controlled the territory south of Babylon, seized the city, but within three years Tiglath-pileser had retaken it. Six years after Tiglath-pileser's death (*ca.* 721 B.C.), when King Sargon was defending northern frontiers, Merodoch-baladan (*cf.* II Kings 20:12 ff.), a Chaldean, claimed the throne. For ten years the usurper went unchallenged, then Sargon moved southward, and was proclaimed vice-regent of Babylon. Merodoch-baladan, promising loyalty, returned to his tribe only to make another bid for the throne during the reign of Sennacherib, Sargon's successor. The attempt failed and Bel-ibni became king. Insurrection involving Hezekiah of Judah (II Kings 8:13 ff. and Isa. 30:1 ff.) necessitated the movement of Assyrian troops to Palestine, and immediately Merodoch-baladan incited rebellion. Bel-ibni failed to cope with the situation, but Assyrian armies quickly regained control. A series of insurrections tried Assyrian patience beyond endurance and Babylon

MODEL OF THE ZIGGURAT AT BABYLON, often called the Tower of Babel. Courtesy, Oriental Institute

was destroyed (*ca.* 689 B.C.). Sennacherib's record of the event boasts of the utter devastation. His son Esarhaddon was given charge of the area. When Sennacherib was murdered in 681, Esarhaddon was crowned, the restoration of Babylon was begun, and Shamash-shum-ukin, Esarhaddon's son was proclaimed Crown Prince. At Esarhaddon's death his son Ashurbanipal became king of Assyria, and Shamash-shum-ukin king of Babylon. After nearly twenty years of the diarchy Ashurbanipal besieged Babylon, holding supreme kingship until defeated by the Chaldeans, Nabopolassar, in 627-626. In 612 Assyria crumbled and the Neo-Babylonian empire was established.

Nebuchadnezzar II, Nabopolassar's son, crowned in 605 B.C., made Babylon one of the most beautiful cities in the world. Nebuchadnezzar died in 562, and by 556 a new dynasty was begun by King Nabu-naid, whose son Bel-shar-uṣur was for a time regent in Babylon (*cf.* Dan. 5, 7, 8). Cyrus of Persia conquered Babylon in 539 and until 331 Babylon was under Achemenid rule. Alexander the Great, having defeated Persia, planned to rebuild Babylon and restore it to its former greatness but after his death in 323 B.C. Babylon was neglected and finally abandoned.

Frequent reference to Babylon is found in ancient texts and in the writings of Herodotus, Cestius, Strabo, and Pliny. Herodotus' detailed description of the city, while exaggerating the dimensions, appears to be accurate in the discussion of walls, towers, bridges, and buildings, and has been invaluable in determining the identity of buildings.

II. *Excavations.* Scientific interest in Babylon began in 1616 when Pietro della Valle, an Italian nobleman, collected inscribed bricks and produced a fairly accurate description of the ruins. Archaeological exploration commenced with Abbe de Beauchamp, vicar-general for the Pope at Baghdad from 1780-90, who hired workmen to dig in the ruins uncovering the so-called "Lion of Babylon," some clay cylinders, and a portion of the Ishtar gate. The publication of de Beauchamp's memoirs in 1790 made a great impact on the scholarly world, and on the British East India Company. Cladius James Rich, Resident for the Company at Baghdad, authorized to conduct exploratory studies,

visited Babylon in 1811, the date on which modern scientific study of the site can be said to have begun.

Rich measured mounds, collected inscribed tablets and cylinders for the British museum, and determined that the city measured two miles, one thousand yards from north to south, and two miles, six hundred yards from east to west. Within this nearly square area he recognized four mounds. Babil, an oblong tell or irregular height about 950 yards from the river bank, was at the north end of the city. One mile southward, in the center, was the Kasr (the Palace), a seven hundred yards square conglomeration of mounds. Separated from the Kasr by a valley five hundred fifty yards long and rising only fifty feet above the plain was Tell Amran ibn Ali, named for a commemorative dome in the center. The southernmost mound was called Jumjuma, for the nearby Arab village.

Robert Ker Porter, successor to Rich (1817-20), drew a plan of the entire area. In 1828 Robert Mignan opened a twelve-foot square area to a depth of twenty feet, recovering a clay cylinder, coins, and some gems. Austin Henry Layard did limited exploratory work in 1850.

In 1852 a French expedition under Fulgence Fresnel, Jules Oppert, and Felix Thomas investigated three mounds. From Kasr came enameled tiles, inscribed bricks, and a clay cylinder. At Amran, Parthian tombs were opened, Neo-Babylonian bricks gathered, and terra-cotta, clay, glass, copper, and a few gold items recovered. Babil yielded bricks and artifacts in stone and glass. Unfortunately, in 1855, the boat returning the material gathered by the expedition to France sank, and the artifacts were lost. On the whole the French expedition was disappointing. Oppert, misled by Herodotus' expanded dimensions, included within the city limits such mounds as Birs Nimrud (Borsippa), and El Ohemir (Kish).

Shortly afterward, Arabs digging for bricks in the Amran-Jumjuma area discovered clay jars containing nearly three thousand clay tablets from the time of Nabopolassar and his successors. These were acquired by George Smith for the British Museum. In 1879 Hormuzd Rassam, former assistant to Layard, began excavations. From Jumjuma he extracted thousands of inscribed tablets in-

cluding records from the days of Nabopolassar and Nebuchadnezzar of the great banking house of Egibi, thus furnishing valuable
information about Babylonian businesss life.
From this location came the °Cyrus cylinder
(see below). Unfortunately many unbaked
clay tablets crumbled upon exposure to air.
At Kasr, Rassam conducted a limited investigation, but at Babil discovered aqueducts
and wells of imported red granite, beautifully
cut and fitted. Remains of a wall in one
area were erroneously identified as a remnant
of Nebuchadnezzar's gardens.

The most extensive investigation of Babylon was conducted by Robert Koldewey. In
1898, sponsored by Kaiser Wilhelm II and
the German Oriental Society, Koldewey began an eighteen-year study which was terminated in 1917 by World War I. His colleagues included W. Andrae, F. Baumgarten,
G. Buddensieg, J. Grossmann, J. Jordan, F.
Langenegger, B. Meissner, K. Müller, A.
Nöldeke, O. Reuther, F. Weissbach, and F.
Wetzel. Almost all of the results of the
German expedition relate to the period subsequent to Sennacherib's destruction. Only
in one quarter was earlier material discovered.

Koldewey identified five mounds: Babil,
Kasr, and Amran, previously identified by
Rich, and Homera and Merkes, slightly to
the east. The plain between Amran and
Merkes known as the Sachn (the pan) was
also excavated.

Nebuchadnezzar's Babylon, straddling the
Euphrates, was protected by a huge wall
more than eleven miles long and eighty-five
feet thick. The outer twenty-five feet was
composed of baked brick set in asphalt, the
inner surface of crude brick was twenty-
three feet thick, and the intervening space
was filled with rubble. Reinforcing towers
were spaced every sixty-five feet, and a cir-
cumjacent moat lined on the city side with
baked bricks to a thickness of ten feet
tapped the Euphrates and strengthened defenses. Secondary inner walls of sun-dried
brick flanked the Euphrates where the river
divided the city.

Literary sources mention that eight gates,
each named for a deity, pierced the walls.
Koldewey excavated four, the Gate of Ishtar
on the north, on the east the Gates of Marduk
and Ninurta, and on the south the Gate of
Urash. The four remaining gates were identified with reasonable certainty: the Gate of
Sin, on the north, the Gate of Adad, on the
west, the Gates of Enlil and Shamash, on the
south. The Ishtar Gate appeared to be the
entrance most frequently used, and the road
leading through the Gate was known as "The
Processional Way."

The excavation of Babil, identified through
inscriptions as the site of Nebuchadnezzar's
summer palace, was not rewarding. Work
on the Kasr uncovered Nebuchadnezzar's central palace and the little temple of Ninmakh.
Homera, the red mound, yielded little other
than a Greek theater. Massive debris to the
north of the theater was interpreted as waste
material dumped by Alexander's men in the
restoration of the ziggurat. The Merkes provided the key to the archaeological history
of the city. A few feet below the surface
Parthian artifacts were found, and then in
succession, Hellenistic, Persian, Neo-Babylonian, Assyrian, and Kassite. Forty feet below
the top remains of buildings and tablets from
the First Dynasty appeared but due to the
water level it was impossible to go lower.
Small, windowless, cube-like houses from this
period, although crowded together in island
blocks separated by relatively straight streets,
appeared to have been well built and provided with adequate water and good drainage. Artifacts of the First Dynasty included
numerous business documents demonstrating
that this area had been a business center,
omen literature, bowls, storage flasks, bronze
weapons, and jewelry. Destruction had come
through fire, but it was impossible to determine whether the disaster was due to Assyrian or Hittite enemies. On the Neo-Babylonian level an Ishtar temple was found.

In the Amran a temple dedicated to Marduk was discovered, and on the plain Sachn,
the ruins of the great ziggurat were found.

III. *Temples.* Of forty-three temples mentioned in documents, fifteen named in Nebuchadnezzar's inscriptions, only five were
excavated. Each stood within walled precincts entered through gates opening on inner
courts flanked by buildings. The shrine room
or cella, often with the raised dais for statuary still in place, was approached through
an antecella. A long corridor, entered through
the courtyard or the antecella, bordered either
two or three sides of the holy place. Few
artifacts were recovered from temple sites.

Emah, the temple of Ninmah, goddess of
the underworld, located in the Kasr just

BABYLON IN THE SIXTH CENTURY B.C. *The Ishtar Gate is in the foreground and the ziggurat appears on the horizon. Photo of painting by Maurice Bardin, courtesy Oriental Institute.*

BABYLON TODAY. *The excavators have been able to trace the streets of the city and the walls of its buildings, but Babylon is a waste today. Courtesy, The Oriental Institute.*

east of the Ishtar Gate, was a small structure (175 by 115 feet) in such excellent preservation that it became the model for interpreting ground plans of shrines. Military architectural influence was discernible in the towers and battlements, but the walls were niched with long upright indentations absent in military structures. Before the flanking towers of the entrance stood a small street altar of mud brick, originally covered with white plaster. The entrance led through a small room to a court with a brick-lined well, and immediately opposite the doorway was the shrine, approached through a vestibule and antecella. Circular depressions in the asphalt paving of the courtyard may have been made by cult objects. Brick offering containers stood on either side of the entrance to the cella and within was the pediment for the statue of Ninmah. Both cella and antecella had side chambers, and around one side and to the back of the cella was a long room entered through the court or antecella. Cuneiform tablets listing building materials and workmen, numerous figurines and a pottery figure of a male with a gold staff, were recovered. A clay cylinder stating that Ashurbanipal built the temple identified the site.

E-patutila, "The house of the scepter of life" dedicated to Ninurta was an oblique-angled complex, 190 by 133 feet, lying beneath the southeastern part of Amran. A foundation cylinder reported Nabopolassar's completion of the building, and an inscription recorded Nebuchadnezzar's restorations. Before the eastern gate which opened on the street leading to the Ninurta gate was a small street altar. The precincts contained a central court, the usual building complex and three shrines linked by connecting doors, presumably cellae sacred to Ninurta, his consort Gula and their son. Terra-cottas of bearded males, nude females, and apes are believed to symbolize the three deities.

Temple Z, standing west of the Ninurta temple, could not be identified for the single inscription found failed to designate the god for whom the building was intended. The complex was enclosed within heavy walls with two entrances opening into a courtyard. On the southern side of the court a vestibule led to an antecella and cella. Two small courts with adjacent rooms were uncovered on the western side. Few artifacts apart

from a clay dove and a figurine were discovered.

The Temple of Ishtar of Akkad stood among houses in the Merkes, east of the Processional Way. South and east entrances led through vestibules to an open court with a well. Opposite the eastern gate were the antecella with a brick chest containing a statuette, and the cella surrounded by a long passageway.

Esagila, "The House with the Uplifted Head," the most important temple in Babylon sacred to Bel-Marduk, the patron god, was uncovered in 1900 at a depth of sixty-five feet in the Amran mound. An area 260 by 280 feet was cleared but tunnelling made wider investigation possible. Two adjoining rectangular structures with numerous chapels formed the building complex. The eastern annex, approached through a gate in the wall fronting on the Processional Way, consisted of a rectangular central court surrounded by rooms as yet unexcavated. A smaller court flanked by unexcavated buildings lay to the south. A doorway on the west side led to the main temple area — a square courtyard bordered on the north and south by double rows of rooms. Across the court and opposite the doorway a huge gate led through the antecella to the cella, called Ekua, a rectangular room 130 by 65 feet. In this sanctuary Marduk's statue must have stood, probably on the raised postament in the niche of the cella opposite the main entrance. In the brick offering containers a clay figure of a bearded man with bull's feet, holding a palm was recovered. Which gods occupied other rooms is conjectural except, perhaps, for a single chapel in which Ea symbols were discovered. Four entrances, one on each side, provided entrance to the temple area, while the eastern annex had five doorways.

IV. *The Processional Way and the Ishtar Gate.* The great seventy-five-foot wide Processional Way which served as the main artery of city life was almost entirely the work of Nebuchadnezzar, although it had existed earlier. Foundation layers of brick covered with asphalt were surfaced with slabs of imported limestone three and one-half feet square. Side walks of veined red breccia blocks each two feet square bordered the road. The bevelled edges of each stone bore inscriptions stating that Nebuchadnezzar had

DRAGON FROM THE ISHTAR GATE, *Babylon. Courtesy, Staatliche Museen zu Berlin.*

built this roadway for Marduk. The road led through the Ishtar gate, past the palace of Nebuchadnezzar to the temple of Marduk.

The double gates with walls still standing to a height of about forty feet formed a solid block with doors separated by a narrow court or passageway. Towers flanked each gate. Walls of blue enameled brick were adorned with yellow and white bulls and dragons (*sirrush*) in alternating rows. A replica of the gate found on a gold plaque from a grave in Nabopolassar's palace depicts the arched doorway with two towers overtopping the wall. An inscribed limestone block between the gates announced that the Gate had been built for Marduk by Nebuchadnezzar. Beyond the gate the Processional Way continued between high defensive walls of blue enameled bricks adorned with white lions with yellow manes and yellow lions with red manes, each over six feet in length.

V. *Nebuchadnezzar's Palace* stood between the Processional Way and the Euphrates, a huge complex of buildings protected by a massive double wall. A smaller palace beneath the ruins, probably Nabopolassar's pal-

ace, had been razed by Nebuchadnezzar according to an inscription. Five major courts lay within the walls. The first was entered from the Processional Way by a doorway in a shallow recess between protective towers through a diminutive access-court with flanking rooms. To the north and south were dwellings accessible only through narrow alleys. Numerous alabastra and cylindrical cores found near the northern dwellings led Koldewey to conclude that a manufacturing center must have been located there. A second court, entered from the first through a large gateway, was adjoined by large buildings. A wide passage led to the northeast corner of the citadel where Koldewey excavated fourteen cells similar in size and shape, one containing a well, all surrounded by a strong wall. Here, Koldewey believed, was the site of the hanging gardens with the water system for irrigation. As his conjecture has not been accepted, the location of this legendary marvel is still unknown.

Beyond the second court the central court, encircled by strong walls and entered through a large gate, was distinguished by a water basin cut into it, although this may have come from the Persian period. To the north were two major dwellings, one with two courts, one with four. To the south was the white-plastered throne room (55 by 170 feet) with a great central entrance and two flanking doors. The doubly-recessed niche opposite the main door, believed to be the site of the throne, would be visible from the court. The external enameled tile facade depicted yellow columns and bright blue capitals, connected by a series of palmettos, topped with a frieze of white double palmettos against a background of dark blue. The whole was bordered by a band of alternating squares of yellow, black and white tile. West of the central court were two more courts, both of impressive size, surrounded by buildings.

Tile fragments pieced together produced motives of scorpions, lions, birds, serpents, and panthers. Remnants were found of cedar doors overlaid with bronze threshholds, and an inscription stated that Nebuchadnezzar imported the cedar from Lebanon.

Artifacts included a coarse-grained dolorite Hittite stele depicting the weather god, a basalt figure of a lion trampling a man, and a stele representing a local governor recording before Ishtar and Adad the restoration of the canal Sukhi, the laying out of a town, and the planting of date palms in the neighborhood of Khabur on the Euphrates.

VI. *The Ziggurat of Babylon,* E-temen-an-ki, "House of the Foundation of Heaven and Earth," excavated in the Sachn between 1908 and 1911, was a vast complex over 1340 feet square surrounded by a heavy casemate wall. Ornamental towers adorned the inner walls and ten elaborate gateways, two on the north, two on the east, two on the west, and four on the south, each with inner courts, led to the interior. Within the peribolos were three divisions, a court with numerous small houses on the north, a long western court, and the principal court of the ziggurat and other large buildings.

The ziggurat itself may date to the third millennium. After Sennacherib's siege it was restored by Nabopolassar and Nebuchadnezar, only to be destroyed by Xerxes. Kolde-

wey found the structure to be a huge mass of mud brick set in layers of bitumin and matting, with an outer shell of baked brick. The base measured approximately three hundred feet square, but it was impossible to determine the nature of the superstructure. A stairway at right angles to the southern face indicated an approach, and Koldewey's reconstruction, based on the plan known from Ur, added two stairways flanking the central steps. There can be little doubt that this was the tower of Babel mentioned in Genesis 11:1-9. *See* Babel, Tower of.

VII. *The Bridge.* Seven piers of the famous bridge which spanned the Euphrates and united the two parts of the city were excavated. Built of small bricks set in asphalt each pier measured sixty-nine feet in length, and twenty-eight feet in width and were spaced at twenty-eight foot intervals. The

BRONZE FIGURE OF A FOUR-FACED GOD from the Old Babylonian period (ca. 1800 B.C.) Courtesy, Oriental Institute

gateway to the bridge was in the huge protecting wall between the land and the first river pier.

VIII. *Babylon and the Bible.* Numerous Biblical references to Babylon relate to the period of the subjugation of Judah by Nebuchadnezzar (e.g. II Kings 17-25, II Chron. 36, Jer. 20-51, Ezek., etc.). Other passages are more general. The tower of Babel (Gen. 11) is surely to be associated with the ziggurat of Babylon. In the Revelation of John, Babylon is an eschatological symbol.

Limited contributions have come from the excavation itself and little first dynasty material has direct significance for Bible study. The attempts to associate Amraphel (Gen. 14:1) with Hammurabi have been abandoned. First dynasty tablets dealing with the rental of an ox, and the leasing of a field by a certain Abarama, son of Awel-Ishtar, obviously do not refer to the Abraham of the Bible. Abarama and Abraham are, essentially, the same names, demonstrating that the Biblical name need not be treated as a coined term ("father of the people") but represents nomenclature not unique in the ancient near east.

Two first dynasty texts are important for the study of the Sa.Gaz-Hab/piru problem. One refers to the provision of clothing for °Habiru mercenaries, and the other, a letter written by Hammurabi, mentions the overseer of the Sa.Gaz. There is at present no way to relate these references to the Hebrews of the Bible.

Of more direct significance are materials from the Neo-Babylonian period such as the Jehoiachin Tablet. In the ruins of the vaulted buildings of the royal citadel, identified as the hanging gardens of Nebuchadnezzar, some three hundred clay tablets dating from 595 to 570 were found. Many listed rations for captive peoples from Egypt, Ashkelon, Phoenicia, Syria, Cilicia, Lydia, Elam, Media, Persia, and Judah, including such staples as oil and barley. Often the status or craft of the recipient was designated. One tablet, measuring approximately three by six inches, broken into three pieces, referred to King Jehoiachin of Judah as "Yaukin, king of Yahud," and mentioned his five sons and other Judaean captives. This tablet, dated in 592 B.C. makes it clear that in exile Jehoiachin was still regarded as the Judaean monarch.

The Cyrus Cylinder, a baked clay barrel about nine inches long, records the conquest of Babylon by Cyrus of Persia. Despite the loss through breakage of several lines, the main account is clear. Having set forth problems encountered by Babylonian priests in King Nabonidus the text tells of Marduk, seeking a righteous man, pronouncing the name of Cyrus thus destining him to be ruler of the world. Babylon was taken without battle and Cyrus welcomed by the populace. By royal edict captives were released and permitted to return to their homelands, sanctuaries restored, statuary and cultic implements returned to shrines.

Much of what is related in the cylinder can be correlated with Biblical accounts. Isaiah 44:24-28, 45:1-6 proclaim Cyrus' actions as a fulfillment of Yahweh's will, whether or not Cyrus realized this (45:4). Under the law of return some Jews journeyed to Jerusalem, and by virtue of Cyrus' interest and encouragement in shrine restoration, Yahweh's temple was rebuilt (II Chron. 36:22 f., Ezra 1).

A tablet known as the °Babylonian Chronicle covering the history of the period between 605 and 594 B.C. is of significance for dating the fall of Jerusalem. Noting the defeat of Nineveh by Babylonians and Medes in 612 the account delineates Egyptian-Babylonian relationships until the Battle of Carchemish in 605 (*cf.* Jer. 46:2) when Pharaoh Necho was defeated by Nebuchadnezzar, crown prince of Babylon. The account records the conquest of Syria and Palestine (II Kings 24:7). Nabopolassar died on August 15, and by September 7 Nebuchadnezzar had been enthroned. The payment of tribute by kings of Hatti land, which would include Judah, is recorded, and possibly Jehoiakim was among the contributors (II Kings 24:1). Egypt's defeat of the Babylonians in 601, duly noted on the tablet, may have encouraged Jehoiakim to rebel. After attacking the Arabs of Kedar (Jer. 49:28-33) Nebuchadnezzar moved on Jerusalem, commencing the siege December 18, 598 B.C. On March 16, 597, the city capitulated, and having installed a king "after his own heart" Nebuchadnezzar withdrew, taking captives and heavy tribute (II Kings 24:10-17). There can be little doubt that the reference is to the capture of Jehoiakin and the installation of Zedekiah as the new monarch. The chronicle reports

TABLET OF THE BABYLONIAN CHRONICLE confirms the conquest of north Arabia by Nebuchadnezzar. Courtesy, British Museum

other raids upon Hatti-land but terminates before the time of Zedekiah's revolt.

BIBLIOGRAPHY. Walter Andrae, *Babylon, die versunkene Weldstadt und ihr Ausgräber Robert Koldewey*, De Gruyter, Berlin, 1952. Albert Champdor, *Babylon*, translated by Elsa Coult, G. P. Putnam's Sons, New York, 1958. Friedrich Delitzsch, "Discoveries in Mesopotamia," *Annual Report of the Board of Regents of the Smithsonian Institute*, 1900, pp. 535-550. Claude H. W. Johns, *Ancient Babylonia*, G. P. Putnam, New York, 1913. L. W. King, *The Letters and Inscriptions of Hammurabi*, 3 vols., London, 1898-1900. Robert Koldewey, *The Excavations at Babylon*, translated by Agnes St. Johns, Macmillan & Co., London, 1914; *Das Ischtar-Tor in Babylon*, J. C. Hinrichs, Leipzig, 1918; *Die pflastersteine von Aiburschabu in Babylon*, J. C. Hinrichs, Leipzig, 1901; *Die tempel von Babylon und Borsippa*, J. C. Hinrichs, Leipzig, 1911; *Das wieder erstehende Babylon*, 4th ed., J. C. Hinrichs, Leipzig, 1925. Joachim Menant, *Ninive at Babylone*, Hachette, Paris, 1888. Jules Oppert, *Expedition scientifique en Mesopotamie*, Paris, 1856. Oscar Reuther, *Die Innenstadt von Babylon (merkes)*, 2 vols., J. C. Hinrichs, Leipzig, 1926. James Claudius Rich, *Narrative of a Journey to the Site of Babylon*, London, 1839. H. W. F. Saggs, *The Greatness That Was Babylon*, Hawthorne, New York, 1962. E. Unger, *Assyrische und babylonishce Kunst*, De Gruyter, Berlin, 1927; *Babylon Die Heilige Stadt*, De Gruyter, Berlin, 1931.

BABYLONIAN CHRONICLES. The political history of Babylonia is largely recon-

structed from references in the Annals of Assyria which dominated its southern neighbor for many centuries. The one outstanding exception is a series of inscribed clay tablets generally known as "Babylonian Chronicles" after the title given to the first of this class of texts published in 1887. These present concise accounts of major internal events in Babylonia. The precise dates of the accession and death of a king, his length of reign and usually a synopsis of a major event in each year are given. Foreign affairs are introduced where they are considered to indicate a change in the control of Babylon or in her relations with her neighbors, principally Assyria and Elam.

These Chronicles are objective and accurate, if sometimes showing a nationalistic bias. They follow a long-established practice of historiography, the data, selected or abstracted from a full history, kept on tablets or writing-boards, being used for a particular purpose (e.g. the Religious Chronicle covers only cultic relations between Assyria and Babylonia). While the purpose of all the tablets cannot yet be ascertained, it is likely that the majority, compiled in the sixth century B.C. were notes to aid an inquiry on behalf of the Chaldaean of Achaemenid kings for which a knowledge of the history was required. That is, the circumstances were similar to those described in the reign of Darius II (Ezra 5:18) and Xerxes (Esth. 6:1, 23). Only one of these texts bears a date of composition (500/499 B.C. if Darius I) and one the name of the secular scribe who copied it. They are, however, all easily identified by their form, subject matter and the type of tablet used, while the date is roughly ascertainable from the script. All extant copies are now preserved in the British Museum.

I. *Classification.* The Chronicles are generally divided into three groups. *Summary Chronicles* include the so-called "Babylonian Chronicle" of the years 747-668 B.C. (BM 92502 = II A below); The Nabonidus Chronicle (557-520 B.C.) BM35382 = II E). These are large two-columned tablets. *Detailed Chronicles* are written on small single-columned tablets. These comprise the Chronicles of Chaldean Kings; Nabopolassar (626-605 B.C.), originally on four tablets, of which three survive (BM 25127, BM 21901 – "The Fall of Nineveh Chronicles" = II B,

BM 22047); Nebuchadrezzar II for the first 11 years of his reign only (605–595 B.C.), see II C and D; Neriglissar, Year 3 only (556/5 B.C.). *Extract Chronicles* were written on small tablets giving date of miscellaneous kinds, not always for consecutive years. These include the "Chronicle of Early Babylonian kings" recounting Sargon of Akkad's campaigns in the West. *ca.* 2350 B.C., the First Dynasty of Babylon, including Hammurabi, and events to 1650 B.C. (BM 26472, 96152). The "Chronicle for some years *ca.* 1080–681 B.C." (BM 27859); The Esarhaddon Chronicle (BM 25091); The Chronicle of the Years 680-626 B.C. (BM 86379) and the extract Chronicle for the years 996, 758-6, 693, 654-650 B.C. (A. R. Millard, *Iraq* XXVI 1964), BM 96273.

II. *Relevance to the Old Testament.* These Chronicles give a number of fixed points for the Chronology of Babylonian and Biblical history. While they show the existence of detailed historical records from the third to first millennia B.C. with which the Old Testament records may be compared, the main points of direct comparison lie in the seventh-sixth centuries B.C. when Babylon had direct relations with Judah and the west. It is these aspects of the Chronicles which are emphasised below.

A. Chronicle of the Years 747-668 B.C. After describing in some detail the relations of Sennacherib of Assyria with Babylon, the death of Sennacherib is given: "On the 20th of the month Tebet during a rebellion, his son killed Sennacherib, the king of Assyria. Sennacherib had ruled Assyria for twenty-three years. The rebellion lasted from the 20th of Tebet to the 2nd of Adar and on the 18th of the month of Adar, his son Esarhaddon sat on the throne of Assyria."

While the last statement accords with II Kings 19:36, and Isaiah 37:37, the apparent discrepancy in the number of the murderers can be explained in a number of possible ways. Either Esarhaddon, as head of a pro-Babylonian party, contrived the murder through the agency of others or one of two brothers mentioned in the Old Testament may have been counted as the actual killer or as the elder, and temporary occupant of the throne. It is known from other Assyrian sources that Esarhaddon ascended the throne only after the flight of elder brothers.

This Chronicle also records the sack of Sidon in Esarhaddon's fourth year (665 B.C.). In his seventh year Assyria was defeated by Egypt and three years later Esarhaddon avenged this in three fierce battles, capturing Memphis and looting Egypt. This forms the background to the varying claims of Egypt and Assyria on the allegiance of Manasseh of Judah. Finally, the Chronicle tells how Esarhaddon died at Haran while on the way to Egypt on the 10th day of the 8th month of his twelfth year (669 B.C.). There followed the partitioning of the Assyrian state between Ashurbanipal (Assyria) and Shamash-shum-ukin (Babylonia) as agreed in the Vassal-treaties found at °Nimrud. This led to the weakening of Assyrian control over her colonies and thus enabled Josiah to take the first steps to asserting the renewed independence of Judah.

B. The Fall of Nineveh (612 B.C.). The Nabopolassar Chronicle records that "(in the fourteenth year = 612 B.C.) the king of Babylonia called out his army . . . met the king of the Umman-manda (Medes and/or Scythians) . . . marched upstream along the Tigris river bank and pitched camp at Nineveh. From the month of Sivan to the month of Ab (= June-August) they progressed only 3. . . . In the month of Ab they made a strong attack on the citadel . . . and the city was taken, a great defeat being inflicted on the people and their leaders. On the same day Sin-shar-ishkun, the king of Assyria (perished in the flames). Much spoil was taken from the city and temple-area and then the city was reduced to a mound of ruins and heap of rubble . . . Ashur-uballit, the (new) king of Assyria had moved out before the final attack . . . and established his seat of government in Harran."

Thus the ancient capital, subject of many prophecies, fell as recorded by Nahum and Zephaniah. The present ruins remain a silent witness to this event (*see* Nineveh).

The Chronicle continues: "In the month Iyyar of his sixteenth year (Nabopolassar) king of Babylon called out his army and marched to Assyria. In Marcheswan he joined forces with the Umman-manda and marched after Ashur-uballit to Harran. Fear of them fell on him and on the army of Egypt which had come to his help. They abondoned the city which . . . was captured." This extract shows that the Biblical account of the same event (II Kings 23:29; Jer. 46:2) is to be translated "the king of Egypt went up on behalf of the King of Assyria to the river Euphrates." Josiah, forseeing the weakness of the Assyrian position and rising Babylonian strength sought to intervene and regain part of the lost Israelite territory. He thus met his death at the hands of the Egyptians in Megiddo (II Chron. 35:20-25).

C. The Battle of Carchemish (605 B.C.).

In 607/6 B.C. the elderly Nabopolassar handed over command of the Babylonian army to the crown-prince Nebuchadrezzar, except for one expedition up the Euphrates to establish a garrison at Kimuhu. Soon after Nabopolassar's withdrawal, the Egyptian garrison from nearby Carchemish attacked and captured this strong-point. The Chronicle for the next year reads: "In the 21st year of the king of Babylon he remained at home while the crown-prince Nebuchadrezzar his eldest son, took personal command of his troops and marched to Carchemish which lay on the banks of the Euphrates. He crossed the river to march against the Egyptian army which lay in Carchemish. . . . they fought with each other and the Egyptian army withdrew before him. He defeated them and annihilated them. As for the remnant of the Egyptian army which had escaped from the defeat so hastily that no weapon could reach them, the Babylonian army overtook and defeated them in the district of Hamath, so that not a single man escaped to his own country. At that time Nebuchadrezzar conquered the whole of the Hatti-land. For 21 years Nabopolassar had ruled Babylonia. On the eighth of Ab he died; in the month of Elul Nebuchadrezzar returned to Babylon and on the first day of Elul (= 6 September 605 B.C.) he sat on the royal throne in Babylon.

"In his accession year Nebuchadrezzar returned to Hatti-land and moved victoriously through it until Sebat when he took the heavy spoils back to Babylon.

"In his first year Nebuchadrezzar . . . marched about as victor in Hatti-land until Kislev. All the kings of the Hatti-land (= Palestine) came before him and he received tribute from them. He advanced on Ashkelon, capturing it in the month of Kislev."

The date of this epic battle is therefore to be certainly dated in May-June of 605 B.C. The swiftness of the occupation of the west accords both with the words of Jeremiah and with II Kings 24:7 that "the king of Babylon took all the area claimed by the King of Egypt from the River of Egypt (= Wadi el Arish) to the River Euphrates."

Since the Chronicle makes no mention of any attack on Jerusalem itself in this (Jehoiakim's third) year, the accuracy of Daniel 1:1 has been questioned. It is possible that the Babylonian force which pursued to the Egyptian frontier may have made a swift siege of the Judean capital with the successful results described in Daniel 1:2. Others assume a different method of dating, but this does explain the words "and besieged it!" The Hebrew text might be simply translated "and showed hostility to it" (Akkadian ṣrr). If the last suggestion is correct then Jehoiakim would have been with the kings of Damascus, Tyre and Sidon who, says the Babylonian text, brought tribute in Nebuchadrezzar's accession year. It is certain that by this year Jehoiakim was a vassal, for three years later (II Kings 24:1) he had broken away. Despite the warnings of Jeremiah, Jehoiakim seems to have succumbed to the approaches from Egypt perhaps, encouraged by the defeat of the Babylonians by the army of Necho II in a battle known only from the Chronicle for the year 601. "In open battle they smote each other and inflicted a severe defeat on each other." The Babylonians rested at home re-equipping his army throughout the next year.

The sack of Ashkelon in 604 B.C. may be reflected in an Aramaic papyrus from Saqqarah in which a Phoenician city pleads for help at this critical time. The fall of the city may have occasioned the public fast proclaimed in Judah at this time (Jer. 36:9).

D. The Capture of Jerusalem (597 B.C.).

In 599/8 this text describes the Babylonian attack on the Arab tribes east of Jordan. These raids were the subject of Jeremiah's oracles (49:28-33). They were, perhaps, but a step taken in preparation for the punitive expedition against rebellious Judah, and this in its turn was an action designed to safeguard the line of march when the Babylonians were later to invade Egypt.

It was not until the month of Kislev (= December), late in his seventh regnal year (598 B.C.) that Nebuchadrezzar called out his army for yet another march to the west ("Hatti-land"). According to the Chronicle "he besieged the city of Judah, capturing the city on the second day of the month Adar. He seized the king and appointed there a ruler of his own choice. He took away heavy tribute and sent it off to Babylon."

The date of this conquest of Babylon is thus known precisely (March 16, 597 B.C.). The siege must have been brief since it would have taken the Babylonians some weeks to gather forces and reach Jerusalem. It is possible that the death of Jehoiakim (three months and ten days before the fall of the city, II Chron. 36:9), which we now know must have occurred on December 7, 598, may have occasioned the Babylonian expedition. The Babylonian account agrees with, and supplements, the Hebrew historian. The captured king was Jehoiachin, the Babylonian appointed substitute being Mattaniah-Zedekiah (II Kings 24:17, Jer. 37:1). The heavy tribute included the temple vessels and among the human deportees were Jehoiachin, his mother, wives and family, leading officials and craftsmen whose presence in exile at Babylon is attested by other cuneiform inscriptions found there.

A few days appear to have elapsed before this large group of prisoners was assembled and marched off, for the exile is said to have begun "at the turn of the year" (II Chron. 36:10), that is, in the month following that in which the city fell which also marked the beginning of Nebuchadrezzar's eighth regnal year (so II Kings 24:12). Some apparent discrepancies between the Babylonian and Biblical account and that recorded by Josephus (*Antiq. Jud.* X. 6-7) may be due to the brevity of each writer and there are insufficient details to reconcile all accounts in our present state of knowledge.

The remainder of the Nebuchadrezzar Chronicle describes further marches on Syria in January 596 and again in the following year. In 595/4 Nebuchadrezzar faced a revolt at home which was suppressed. There is an unfortunate gap in the Chronicle series from 599 to 556 B.C. (when the conquest of E. Cilicia in Neriglissar's third year is outlined in one tablet). It is to be hoped that one day tablets giving the events in these intervening years will come to light and so clear up many questions relating to the last thirty-three years of Nebuchadrezzar's reign.

E. The Fall of Babylon (539 B.C.) is recounted in the text chronicling the reign of Nabonidus (555-539 B.C.). This tells of the rise of Cyrus to power in the East, of campaigns in Cilicia, E. Syria and Edom and then of ten years in which Nabonidus stayed in Tema (in Arabia) while the crown-prince, Belshazzar, as co-regent, ruled in Babylon. An inscription from Haran implies that this exile was not voluntary and ended in 546 only when the priests and people of Babylonia, with the consent of the kings of Egypt and "the king of the Medes" (= Cyrus), agreed to the return. The government was opposed by tribes in the southern marshes.

The Chronicle for Nabonidus' seventeenth year runs: ". . . the gods of Babylonia entered Babylon from every direction. Those from Borsippa, Cutha . . . and Sippar did not come in. In Teshrit, when Cyrus attacked the Babylonian army at Opis on the Tigris river, the people of Babylonia revolted, but he (Nabonidus) slew (some of) the people. On the 15th day, when Sippar had been captured without a battle, Nabonidus fled. On the 16th day, Ugbaru, the district-governor of Gutium, and the troops of Cyrus entered Babylon without battle. Later Nabonidus was captured when he returned to Babylon. Till the end of the month, the shield-bearing Gutians were in Esagila, but none carried arms within Esagila or its temple precincts and no prescribed religious ceremonies were missed. On the third of Marcheswan Cyrus entered Babylon and they spread green branches before him. A peace-settlement was imposed on the city and Cyrus proclaimed peace to Babylon. Gubaru, his governor, appointed sub-prefects in Babylon. . . the Babylonian gods returned to their cities. In the month of Marcheswan, in the night of the eleventh, Ugbaru died. . . ."

The advent of Cyrus and the downfall of Babylon were the constant theme of the later Hebrew prophets (Isa. 13, 21; Jer. 50-51). The fall of the city is mentioned in Daniel 5:30.

The date of Cyrus' entry into the capital is here given as 29 October 539 B.C., sixteen days after the city capitulated to Gubaru. The latter is regarded by some as the Darius of the book of Daniel (J. C. Whitcomb, *Darius the Mede*), though another theory equates Cyrus with "Darius the Mede" as a bi-name.

BIBLIOGRAPHY. A. L. Oppenheim, "Babylonian and Assyrian Historical Texts" in *ANET*. Sidney Smith, *Babylonian Historical Texts relating to the capture and downfall of Babylon,* Methuen, London, 1924. D. J. Wiseman, Chronicles of Chaldaean Kings (626-556 B.C.), The British Museum, London, 1956; "Records of Assyria and Babylonia," *Documents from Old Testament Times,* ed. D. W. Thomas, Nelson, New York and London, 1958.

BACTRIA, BACTRIANS. Bactria was a country in the region of the upper Oxus river of central Asia, now the Balkh district of Afghanistan. It was incorporated into the Persian Empire and prospered as an area for the transmitting of Siberian and Indian metals and goods to Persia. Darius III, following his defeat by Alexander, fled to Bactria where he was murdered by Bessus, the Bactrian satrap. Alexander, took Bactria and married Roxanna, a Bactrian princess. Following the death of Alexander and the murder of Roxanna and her infant son, Bactria became a part of the Seleucid empire. In 256 B.C., under the satrap Diodotus I, Bactria became an independent Greco-Bactrian kingdom. By 130 B.C., however, the nomadic Sakas occupied Bactria, and the Bactrian kingdom was ended. During its period of greatness Bactria served as an intermediary between the Greek world and India and China. Its ancient capital Bactra is modern Balkh in northern Afghanistan.

BASILICA. The basilica was one of the buildings which commonly surrounded the forum in towns within the Roman Empire. It was a rectangular structure divided by columns into a nave and two side aisles. At one end was a rounded apse. The Roman basilica was used as a court of justice and administrative center. The design influenced early Christian architecture, and some basilicas were actually used for church services.

BAS RELIEF. The term bas relief is used to describe that form of sculpture in which the figures project only slightly from the background. On the °Black Obelisk of Shalmaneser the figure of Jehu is carved in bas relief.

BEER-SHEBA. Beer-sheba is the principal city in the Judean Negeb, located at the junction of the road running southward from Hebron to Egypt and the route that ran northeastward from the Arabah to the coast. It served as the southern limit of Israelite population, so that the entire land could be designated as the territory "from Dan to Beer-sheba" (Judg. 20:1).

Excavations at the southern sector of the city have uncovered remains from the chalcolithic period (4000-3000 B.C.). In 1954 the Israel Department of Antiquities found evidence of the use of stone and copper at this early period, when the inhabitants of the region dwelt in subterranean dugouts. Later huts were built with storage pits. Above the level of the huts were remains of timber-roofed cottages with walls of beaten earth built on rough masonry footings. They made good pottery with the aid of an elementary turn-table, and worked bone and stone into utensils and ornaments. Smiths in the region made copper articles from ores imported from Arabia. Wheat, barley, and lentils were grown, and sheep, goats, and oxen were domesticated. The fertility goddess was worshiped at chalcolithic Beer-sheba.

BEHISTUN. Twenty miles east of Kermanshah, on the main highway to Tehran, is the village of Bisitun or Behistun, famed for the nearby bas-relief of Darius I (521-485 B.C.). The boastful king had a record of his exploits engraved 345 feet above a spring, and 100 feet above the highest point to which a man can climb. To insure that his

BAS RELIEF PANEL from Black Obelisk of Shalmaneser, showing tribute of Jehu. Courtesy, British Museum

BENI HASAN TOMB PAINTING showing Semites entering Egypt during the 19th century B.C. Courtesy, Oriental Institute

inscription would not be defaced by later generations, Darius evidently had the ascent to the inscription sheered off after the work was completed.

In 1835, Henry Rawlinson, a British officer stationed near Bisitun, began the hazardous task of copying the inscription. Risking his life in the process, he continued until 1847, when the work was completed. To copy the top lines, Rawlinson had to stand on the top-most step of a ladder, steadying his body with his left arm and holding his notebook in his left hand while writing with right hand.

In 1904, the British Museum sent L. W. King and R. Campbell Thompson to Bisitun to check Rawlinson's readings by making fresh copies of the inscription. A further study was made in the fall of 1948 when George C. Cameron made fresh copies of the inscription under the auspices of the American Schools of Oriental Research and the University of Michigan. (Cf. W. C. Benedict and Elizabeth von Voightlander, "Darius' Bisitun Inscription, Babylonian Version, Lines 1-29," *J.C. 5.* X (1956), pp. 1-10.)

The top register of the inscription contains a winged disk and twelve figures. Darius is depicted treading on his rival Gaumata, a pretender to the throne. In front of Darius are nine captive rebels. To the right of the relief are four columns in Elamite.

The main inscription is given in Persian in five columns directly under and to the right of the relief. To the left of the Persian, on the face of the rock projecting one inch further out, is the Elamite translation. Above this, projecting out still further, is the Akkadian (Babylonian) version.

This tri-lingual inscription unlocked the Assyrio-Babylonian system of cuneiform writing in the same way the Rosetta Stone made possible the decipherment of the Egyptian hieroglyphs. After the Old Persian inscription was deciphered, scholars worked on the hypothesis that the other two texts were but different versions of the same text. Through the labors of Edward Hincks, rector of a parish church at Killyleagh, County Down, Ireland, and Henry Rawlinson himself, a list of values for cuneiform characters was issued and the key to the decipherment of other inscriptions was made available to the world of scholarship.

In part, the Behistun inscription reads:
I am Darius (descendant of Achmenes, for which reason we are called Achemenians. By the grace of Ahura-Mazda I am ruler of 23 lands including Babylonia, Sparda (Sardis?), Arabia, Egypt. I put down the rebellions of Gaumata and (8) others in (19) battles . . .

A copy of the Behistun inscription was also found at Babylon on black diorite, and an Aramaic papyrus version was discovered among the Jews of Elephantine. Darius evidently spared no effort to tell of his might in the most remote corners of his empire.

BEIRUT. Beirut and Gebal (*Byblos) were the two principal centers of the ancient Giblites. The *Amarna Tablets refer to Beirut, but the principal remains date from Roman times. Herod the Great and his successors built temples, baths, and theaters there. From the middle of the third century on, Beirut was the seat of a law school. Christianity early gained a foothold there, and the town became the seat of a bishopric.

BEISAN. *See* Beth-shan.

BELSHAZZAR. Belshazzar, Babylonian Bel-shar-uṣur ("May Bel protect the king"), was the son of Nabonidus and may have been, through his mother, a grandson of Nebuchadnezzar. According to the °Nabonidus Chronicle, Nabonidus entrusted the army and the kingship to Belshazzar (*ca.* 556 B.C.), while Nabonidus campaigned in central Arabia where he remained for ten years. Legal documents from the twelfth and thirteenth years of Nabonidus record oaths sworn by the life of Nabonidus "and by the life of Bel-shar-uṣur the crown prince."

According to Daniel 5, it was following Belshazzar's impious feast that the Persians entered Babylon, killed the king, and assumed control of Babylon (Oct. 539 B.C.).

BIBLIOGRAPHY. R. P. Dougherty, *Nabonidus and Belshazzar,* Yale Oriental Series, New Haven: Yale University Press, 1929.

BENI HASAN. The rock tombs of Beni Hasan, 169 miles south of Cairo, extend several miles along the face of cliffs on the eastern bank of the Nile. The northernmost tombs date from the Second and Third Dynasties, and the most southerly are from the Fifth Dynasty. Other tombs in the area date as late as the Thirtieth Dynasty. Of particular interest, however, is a series of Twelfth Dynasty tombs comprising the necropolis of courtiers and officials of the Oryx nome excavated from 1902 to 1904.

In all there are thirty-nine Middle Kingdom tombs at Beni Hasan, twelve of which mention the names of those for whom they were made. Eight of these were chieftains or monarchs, two were princes, one the son of a prince, and one a royal scribe. The tombs are cut from limestone and decorated with some of the finest examples of Egyptian art. Wrestlers, dancers, and girls playing ball are depicted with a naturalism only paralleled by that of the Greeks in their finest period of vase painting.

Beni Hasari tomb three, belonging to Khnumhotep, contains the famous painting of a group of thirty-seven Semites coming to Egypt with merchandise for trade. The men have black hair and pointed beards. They are wearing long cloaks and are carrying bows and throw sticks. Their leader is identified as Ibsha, "the ruler of a foreign land." The inscription reads, "The arriving, bringing eye-paint, which thirty-seven Asiatics brought to him."

W. F. Albright has suggested that the traveling Semites were metalworkers, reminiscent of the occupation of Tubal-Cain (Gen. 4:22).

The painting dates from the sixth year of Senusert II, about 1892 B.C. It gives us an authentic appearance of the dress and appearance of Semites during the Patriarchal Age.

BIBLIOGRAPHY. Newberry, P. E., *Beni Hasan I,* London, 1893; *ANEP* No. 3.

BEROSSOS. Berossos was a priest of Marduk at Babylon under Antiochus I (281-161 B.C.). He was a contemporary of the Egyptian priest °Manetho and the two priests were rivals in proclaiming the greatness and antiquity of their respective lands. Berossos preserved earlier Mesopotamian myths regarding the Creation of the world (*see* Enuma Elish) and the early history of his people. The original writings of Berossos have not been preserved, but fragments are quoted by Josephus and Eusebius of Caesarea, the church historian.

BETHANY. Modern *El 'Azariyeh,* on the east slope of the Mount of Olives, on the road from Jerusalem to Jericho, is the site of Biblical Bethany. The traditional tomb of Lazarus was mentioned in A.D. 333 by the Bordeaux pilgrim. To reach the tomb the visitor descends twenty-four steps which were cut into the rock in 1613. The Franciscans have excavated part of the site of the ancient village of Bethany.

BIBLIOGRAPHY. S. J. Saller, *Excavations at Bethany* (1957).

BETHEL. The ruins of ancient Bethel have been identified on the north side of the Arab village of Beitin where W. F. Albright made soundings during 1927 while director of the American Schools of Oriental Research in Jerusalem. Full scale excavations were conducted from July to September, 1934 by Albright and J. L. Kelso of Pittsburgh-Xenia Theological Seminary (now Pittsburgh Theological Seminary).

The earliest level contained a Late Bronze Age wall and houses with some of the best-laid masonry of that period yet discovered in Palestine. This was the Bethel of the age

139

of the Biblical patriarchs. Its occupation is thought to have begun about 2200 B.C. During the thirteenth century the Canaanite city was destroyed in a tremendous conflagration which left debris five feet thick in places. Albright attributes this to the Israelites at the time of their conquest of Palestine. The Israelite levels that follow are inferior to the Canaanite city. Twice Bethel seems to have been burned by the Philistines, or other early enemies of Israel. The city of the ninth century — the time of Jeroboam I — was built with evidences of finer workmanship than that in the comparatively primitive earliest Israelite levels. Early in the sixth century the city was again burned, this time by the armies of Nebuchadnezzar. For a time the site was unoccupied, but a humble village was built there during the Persian period. Vespasian captured it in A.D. 69, but it was re-occupied as a Roman town

and continued to flourish until the Arab conquest.

BETHESDA, Pool of. Bethesda is mentioned once in the New Testament (John 5:2). But Josephus in his first century description of Jerusalem (cf. *War* V, iv. 1-4) says nothing concerning it. Moreover, while some ancient Greek texts read "Bethesda" others read "Bethsaida" ["house of fish"], "Bethzatha" ["house of olives"] or Belzetha. Eusebius reads "Bezatha" in his *Onamasticon*. Josephus knows a hill by the name of Bethzatha located north of the temple.

I. *The Meaning of the Name Bethesda.* The Copper Scroll from Qumran Cave 3 (discovered in 1952) enables modern Biblical students to choose among these confusing variants, and this new evidence provides the clue for determining the meaning of the name as well. The Copper scroll lists 64 dif-

EXCAVATIONS AT BETHEL reveal house walls from the time of the Judges. Courtesy, Matson Photo Service

THE CHURCH OF ST. ANNE, Jerusalem. Excavations adjacent to the church have revealed the pool now believed to be the Biblical pool of Bethesda.

ferent places where hidden treasure is supposedly located. Hiding places 57-60 are located in and around double pools known as Beth-Eshdatain. The text reads:

(57) Nearby, at Beth-Eshdatain, in the reservoir where you enter into the small basin: a case of aloes wood (and a vase of) resin from the white pine. (58) Just nearby, at the western entrance to the lodging of the triclinium (where is found) the platform for the portable stove, close by [. . .]: nine hundred [talents of silver], five talents of gold. (59) Sixty talents: on circling around from the west side beneath the black rock. (60) Nearby, under the threshhold of the stepped cistern: 42 talents.

See J. T. Milik, "The Copper Document from Cave III of Qumran," *Annual of the Department of Antiquities of Jordan,* IV and V (1960) 142; cf. also *Petites Grottes* ("Minor Caves"), *Discoveries in the Judean Desert,* III, 297ff.; cf. also, Joachim Jeremias, "The Copper Scroll from Qumran," *Expository Times,* LXXI (May, 1960), 227-228.

Thus, as Jeremias notes "*Beth Eschdathajin* is a dual form of Bethesda, which (in agreement with the finding of archaeology) gives the information that the site of Bethesda

comprised two pools." The correct reading "Bethesda" is established by this new evidence. At the same time, the old theory that "Bethesda" meant "house of mercy" must be abandoned. A once unpopular theory that the name derived from the Hebrew *Beth 'Ashda,* "place of 'pools'," "overflowing water" (suggested as early as Reland and supported by Conder, see E. W. G. Masterman, "The Pool of Bethesda," *Palestine Exploration Fund Quarterly Statement* (1921), p. 92) is strengthened. The theory of Robinson, Conder, and Masterman that Bethesda was located below the Virgin's Fountain (Gihon) which afforded it water must be rejected, however.

II. *The Identification, Arrangement and Time of Construction of the Pool of Bethesda.* The accompanying chart with its dimensions will serve in a general way to give the layout and arrangement of the Pool of Bethesda.

Contemporary scholarship generally accepts the identification of the excavated pools of the Church of St. Anne in Jerusalem (on the right [north] as one enters St. Stephen's Gate) as the correct site. Other places suggested as Bethesda include: (1) the Birket

Israel [north of the temple area on the south as one enters St. Stephen's Gate] 360 feet by 126 feet in size; (2) the pools under the Convent of the Sisters of Zion; (3) an adjunct pool which was related to Gihon, whether Siloam or a pool closer to Gihon itself. As early as Eusebius, Bethesda is referred to as having double pools: "Bezatha, a pool in Jerusalem, which is (called?) the sheep, formerly having five porches." It is now identified with the twin reservoirs, of which one is supplied by the seasonal rains, while the water of the other is of a muddy color — a trace, they say, of carcasses of the sacrifices which were formerly cleansed in it before offering, whence also it is called *probatike* ("sheep place"). This mention of double pools at Bethesda in Eusebius and other ancient writers fits perfectly with modern archaeological work there.

The Pilgrim of Bordeaux (writing *ca.* A.D. 333) also refers to these twin pools (*piscinae gemellares*). The excavation work done over the decades (starting in the 1880's) by the "White Fathers" of Saint Anne's Church in recovering the ancient location and arrangement of Bethesda is truly a service to Biblical scholarship. A poorly-made Hebrew inscription found at the site serves to indicate that the construction of the pools preceded the Hadrianic period since Hadrian excluded Jews from Jerusalem after A.D. 135. The style of the architecture would suggest that the pools were built during the period of Herod the Great, or at least remodeled then. A church was built over the pools in the Byzantine period (Fifth Century).

III. *Bethesda As a Place of Healing*: The passage that deals with the angel stirring the water is an interpolation (John 5:3b, 4) and does not appear in the best texts. Even so, Bethesda was clearly a resort for the infirm who hoped to find the cure for their sicknesses there. It was regarded in the same way that temples of the pagan god, Asclepius, were in other locales. A miniature votive foot, dedicated by a certain Pompeia Lucilia, likely on the occasion of the restoration of an infirm foot, was found at Bethesda and is now in the Jewish museum at the Louvre. Such replicas were commonly placed in the temples of Asclepius, the Greek god of healing.

BIBLIOGRAPHY. J. Jeremias, *Die Weiderentdeckung von Bethesda,* Göttingen, Vandenhoeck & Ruprecht, 1949. See his useful bibliography on p. 27 for older sources. C. R. Conder, *PEFQS,* 1888, 115-134; A. M. Schneider, *Beitrage zur biblischen Landes und Altertumskunde,* 68, 1951, 282; M. Avi-Yonah, *Views of the Biblical World, The New Testament,* Jerusalem, International Publishing Company, 1961, p. 142.

BETH-HACCHEREM. The earliest reference to Beth-haccherem, which means "House of the Vineyard," is Joshua 15:59b (according to LXX; the passage is missing in the MT), where *Karem* appears along with Bethlehem, Etam, Beth-zur, and Tekoa in the tenth district of Judah. This would locate it somewhere to the south or southwest of Jerusalem. Likewise, Jeremiah seems to indicate that Beth-haccherem was situated on a vantage point from which fire signals could be seen from Jerusalem, and perhaps also from Tekoa (Jer. 6:1). In Nehemiah's day a district governor resided there (Neh. 3:14). A Mishnaic tradition records that the stones for the altar were quarried from virgin soil in the valley of Beth-haccherem since no iron was allowed to touch them (Middoth iii. 4; cf. Exod. 20:25, Deut. 27:5). The list of hidden treasure on the Dead Sea Copper Scroll (*see* Dead Sea Scrolls) mentions Beth-haccherem just before the Tomb of Absalom, which was in the Valley of the King (II Sam. 18:18; J. T. Milik, "Le rouleau de cuivre de Qumran (3Q 15)," *RB* 66 (1959), p. 327). In another of the Scrolls, the *Genesis Apochryphon*, the Valley of the King is identified with the Valley of Beth-haccherem (N. Avigad and Y. Yadin, *A Genesis Apochryphon,* The Magnes Press, Jerusalem, 1957, pl. xxii, lines 13-14). St. Jerome, in commenting on Jeremiah 6:1, stated that the place called Bethacharma in Hebrew was located on a mountain between Jerusalem and Tekoa.

None of these references favors the identification of Beth-haccherem with the village of 'Ain Karim which is west of Jerusalem. The latter place is on a low-lying knoll surrounded by higher hills. Furthermore, no tell has been found there. On the other hand, the ancient sources all support the suggestion that the Biblical Beth-haccherem was in the vicinity of the modern day °*Ramat Rahel* between Jerusalem and Bethlehem, both of which can be seen from its summit. Today, as in the past, its slopes and the adjacent hills provide an excellent site for viticulture.

BETHLEHEM. The birthplace of Jesus and the home of King David is a village about six miles south of Jerusalem near the road which leads to Hebron and the Negeb. Bethlehem is mentioned in the °Amarna Letters as *Bit-Lahmi* which had gone over to the *'Apiru* people.

The tradition that Jesus was born in a cave in Bethlehem dates back to the second century. In 325 the emperor Constantine built a basilica over a group of caves in Bethlehem. When Constantine's basilica was destroyed, a new and larger church was built by Justinian (527-565). The present Church of the Nativity is basically the structure built by Justinian.

BIBLIOGRAPHY. R. W. Hamilton, "Excavations at the Atrium of the Church of the Nativity, Bethlehem," *QDAP*, III (1933), pp. 1-8; E. T. Richmond, "Basilica of the Nativity: Discovery of the Remains of an Earlier Church," *QDAP*, V (1936), pp. 75-81; J. W. Crowfoot, *Early Churches in Palestine* (1941), pp. 22-30; 77-85.

BETH-SHAN. The town Beth-shan was situated at the junction of the Valley of Jezreel and the Jordan Valley and was counted with the towns of Taanach, Dor, Ibleam, and Megiddo in the list of the cities of Manasseh (Judg. 1:27). The modern village of *Beisan* preserves the name, while the ancient site is represented by a tell known as *Tell el-Hosn*. The site may be identified both from its geographical situation in the Old Testament and from two Egyptian texts found during excavations, where the name is mentioned. Otherwise, the name occurs with several linguistic variations in Egyptian, Akkadian and Hebrew documents from the fifteenth century B.C. onwards.

I. *Archaeological Investigation.* The site was excavated by the University of Pennsylvania under the direction of C. S. Fisher (1921-23), Alan Rowe (1925-28) and G. M. Fitzgerald (1930-33). At one point a deep sounding revealed settlement reaching back to the fourth millennium B.C.

There was an important Canaanite town here in the Early and Middle Bronze Age. During the period from about 3300 B.C. to about 1500 B.C. the available evidence suggests that the city was unwalled.

The main excavations were concerned with Levels IX to I, extending from the fourteenth century B.C. to Islamic times.

II. *Levels of Occupation.* Level IX, dating probably from the fourteenth century B.C. was occupied by an Egyptian garrison, and from about the time of Amenhotep III (1390-1353), was protected by a city wall. The gateway was partly of stone construction. An extensive temple dedicated to "Mekal, the Lord (Baal) of Beth-shan" was found here with a variety of temple implements and the remains of a bull that has been sacrificed.

Egyptian influence began, however, in the fifteenth century B.C. for Thutmose III refers to it among the towns in Upper Retenu which he occupied after the Battle of Megiddo *ca.* 1468 B.C. His scarabs have been found in the city. One of the °Amarna letters from the fourteenth century B.C. refers to the reinforcement of the garrison there (EA 289 in *Ancient Near Eastern Texts*, ed. by J. B. Pritchard, Princeton, 1955, p. 489).

Level VIII dates from the end of the fourteenth century in the days when Seti I of Egypt was seeking to restore Egyptian control in Western Asia. He took Beth-shan in his first year. Two of his royal °stelae were found in this level, one of which refers to an attack on Beth-shan by some neighboring petty kings while the other refers to a clash with the *Apiru* people (*See* Habiru).

Level VII (thirteenth century B.C.) contained a temple of Ramesses II (*ca.* 1290-1224 B.C.) in which the excavators found a stele depicting a goddess with a two-horned head-dress. This temple persisted through into Level VI which probably dates to the twelfth century B.C., the time of Ramesses III (*ca.* 1198-1167 B.C.). A seated statue of this Pharaoh may have been set up there, originally, to commemorate his defeat of the "Sea Peoples" in Galilee *ca.* 1182 B.C. To the same period belong a number of anthropoid clay coffins which were found in the city cemetery. Similar coffins were found in Philistine areas further south. Some writers have therefore suggested that the Egyptians used Philistine mercenary troops at Beth-shan. In any case, Beth-shan was too strong for the Israelites to take (Josh. 17:11, 16; Judg. 1:27). When Saul was killed by the Philistines in the battle of Mt. Gilboa, his armor was placed in the house of Ashtaroth, and his body, along with the bodies of his sons, was fastened to the wall of Beth-shan (I Sam. 31:10, 12). In Level V (*ca.* eleventh century) two

THE MOUND OF BETH-SHAN, over-looking the Jordan Valley. Courtesy, Religious News Service

temples were discovered, the southern one dedicated to the god Resheph, and the other to the goddess Antit. These are possibly the temples referred to in I Samuel 31:10.

It is not quite certain when Beth-shan fell into Israelite hands although it was probably in the time of David. By Solomon's time the city was counted along with *Megiddo and *Taanach in the taxation district of Baana, son of Ahilud (I Kings 4:12). The town of those days is represented by Level IV. It was attacked by Sheshonk I (Shishak) in the days of Rehoboam I (I Kings 14:25) *ca.* 925 B.C. Sheshonk recorded the fact on his temple at Karnak in Egypt.

Thereafter Beth-shan was unoccupied till Hellenistic times when it was called Scythopolis (Level III). Level II of the tell and the rock cut tombs on the north side of the valley contained evidence of later Hellenistic and Roman occupations, while Level I contained the remains of the restored city walls, the remnants of a circular Christian church, and extensive mosaic floors with many inscriptions which formerly belonged to a monastery founded in the sixth century A.D. The city finally fell into the hands of the Arabs in 636 A.D.

BIBLIOGRAPHY. *Publications of the Palestine Section of the Museum of the University of Pennsylvania* (1930-40); I. A. Rowe, *The Topography and History of Beth-shan* (1930); II. A. Rowe, *Beth-shan, Four Canaanite Temples* (1940); III. G. M. Fitzgerald, *Beth-shan Excavations 1921-23, Arab and Byzantine Levels,* 1931; IV. G. M. Fitzgerald, *Beth-shan, Sixth Century Monastery,* 1939. W. F. Albright, "The smaller Beth-shan Stele of Sethos I, (1309-1290 B.C.)," *BASOR,* 125, 1952, pp. 24-32.

BETH-SHEAN. See Beth-shan.

BETH-SHEMESH. According to Joshua 15:10 Beth-shemesh is a town located on the northern border of the tribal area of Judah between Chesalon in the hills and Timnah near Ekron in the coastal plain. Its name is not Israelite, however, but is much older. As "the House of the Sun" it evidently designated a city where once there was a temple to the sun-god. In Josh. 19:41 it is called "Ir-shemesh," "City of the Sun."

I. *Identification and History.* Eusebius in his *Onomasticon* (*Bethsamis*) identified it in the fourth century A.D. with a site ten miles from Eleutheropolis (*Beit Jibrin*) in the direction of Nicopolis to the "east." The city

CULT OBJECT DEPICTING SNAKES AND BIRDS from the Southern Temple at Beth-shan, level 5. Courtesy, University Museum, Philadelphia

of Gezer subsequently, in the same source, is said to be north of Nicopolis. Hence it is difficult to understand Eusebius' reference to "east" unless it is simply an error. In any event, the site would surely lie in the Shephelah between Eleutheropolis and Gezer, with the towns of Zorah, Zanoah and Jarmuth nearby, inasmuch as they are assigned approximately the same distance from Eleutheropolis.

In modern times it was Edward Robinson who identified the ancient site with the low mound immediately west of an Arab village called *Ain Shems,* the latter preserving the ancient name: "Here are the vestiges of a former extensive city, consisting of many foundations and the remains of ancient walls of hewn stone." This mound, once known to Arabs locally as *Tell er-Rumeilah,* lies in the midst of the broad valley which was designated the "Valley of Sorek." The low ridge,

250 meters above sea level, on which it stands is between two wadis in the valley which meet a short distance west of the site. The one to the north was known to Arabs as *Wâdi es-Sarâr*, and that to the south as *Wadi 'Ill'n*. On the northern ridge which borders the valley, ca. 125 meters higher than the tell, is the site of Zorah, the home of Samson (modern *Sar'ah*). The ancient city was not large, ca. seven acres on the summit. Its mound rises only some thirty meters above the wadis. The valley was so large and the nature of the site and its water supply being what they were, the development of a city here adequate for defense of the area was impossible. Between ca. 1700 and 900 B.C. a fortified town was erected, but in the Bronze Age it could never have been the center of a city-state. It was probably always a dependency of a larger city to the north, west, or south. During the tenth century it was a defensive outpost and provincial center of the Kingdom of Judah.

II. *The Archaeology of the City.* Beth-shemesh was first excavated by Duncan Mackenzie for the Palestine Exploration Fund in 1911-12. A Bronze Age city wall was followed throughout its course around the city, and a city-gate belonging to it, with three entries, was excavated on the south side of the tell. Four strata were distinguished. The earliest was Bronze Age, ending with the cessation of Mycenean and Cypriote importations. The Second City was characterized by Philistine ware, which Mackenzie for the first time was able to interpret and adequately describe. This city was destroyed by a conflagration which was the most conspicuous feature of every section through the tell. The Third City was believed to contain two phases, the first interpreted as ending with the invasion of Sennacherib in 701 B.C., and the second as reoccupation in the "late Israelite Period." The first level of occupation consisted of a Byzantine monastery at the southeastern edge of the tell.

Five seasons of excavation by the Haverford College Expedition, under the direction of Elihu Grant, were conducted in 1928-31 and 1933. Clarence S. Fisher served as architect and archaeologist in 1929; Alan Rowe was archaeologist in 1933. Preliminary reports of the first four seasons of work were published by Grant as: *Beth-shemesh,*

a Report of the Excavations Made in 1928 (Haverford, 1929); *Ain Shems Excavations,* Part I (Haverford 1931), and Part II (Haverford, 1932), the last mentioned being a condensed registry of objects. Part III, appearing under the title Rumeileh (Haverford, 1934), was a report of the excavations in 1933. Parts II and III contain the only plans of the excavation which were published.

In 1937, after consultation with W. F. Albright, Grant engaged G. Ernest Wright for a six-month period to prepare a comprehensive report of the work. This was published as *Ain Shems Excavations,* Parts IV and V (Haverford, 1938-39). The first is the plate volume of the latter, and the comparatively small size of the whole represented what could be done in the time available with the surviving records. The summary report was only possible because of the stratigraphical work of Alan Rowe in 1933 together with his extensive selection of carefully recorded pottery. In 1961 this valuable collection was shifted from Haverford College to its permanent home in the University Museum in Philadelphia. In the sectors dug in 1931 and 1933 in the central portion of the mound the phases of Stratum II were better preserved than along the western portion dug in 1929-30. The result was a confusion in the numbering of the strata within the preliminary reports which was corrected in AS V, p.15.

Except for occasional Neolithic and Chalcolithic flint implements which turned up in later contexts, the earliest occupation of the site was during the nomadic irruptions of Middle Bronze I. This material together with sherds of MB II A was found on the rock surface or virgin soil and was accorded the designation "Stratum VI."

Stratum V was the Hyksos period of Middle Bronze II B and C (late 18th through the mid-16th century.). At this time a well-built city wall was erected around the summit of the city on bedrock, ca. 2.20 to 2.4 meters wide, the lowest course consisting of large boulders, some almost a meter in thickness. The upper part of the wall was brick on the stone foundations, masses of it having been encountered in excavation. The city-gate of three entries is a comparatively small example of the typical Bronze Age type (*APEF* I, p. 90, Fig. 28; II, Pl. 3). Three towers were recovered, one at the northeast, one at the west and one at the southwest. They protected critical points in the fortification plan, though at least one of them, that at the southwest, is a later addition, while the western one was rebuilt at least once after destruction. Three tombs, Nos. 9, 17 and 13, dating from the late eighteenth through the mid-seventeenth century, appear to antedate the city wall. Another tomb, No. 12, from the seventeenth-sixteenth centuries is perhaps contemporary with it. If so, then the wall was erected not before the middle or second half of the seventeenth century. This type of fortification in the period suggests that below it along the slope of the tell there was a *glacis* and a lower battered wall against the mound, but insufficient work along the slopes was done to recover it. One fine house, erected against an offset in the western wall, was excavated.

In 1933 Rowe included in V loci a few groups which contained bichrome ware of the early fifteenth century. This would mean that the destruction of the Middle Bronze city could not have been much before *ca..* 1500 B.C. at the very earliest. These few loci, however, may well contain mixed material from Strata V and IVa. Indeed, it would now appear more likely that the end of City V occurred at the Egyptian recon-

quest of Palestine during the mid-sixteenth century, such a date being more in accord with the other pottery found in the stratum.

A most prosperous period in the city's history was that of *Stratum IV* in the Late Bronze Age. The debris from it reached nearly two meters in depth. Two phases were present: one from the fifteenth and early fourteenth century, and one from the fourteenth-thirteenth centuries. A large building was recovered in the second phase, one room of which contained two brick smelting furnaces with holes in the sides where air could be forced into the fire by a blowpipe. Nearby was a furnace of a different type, long, narrow, and probably open; it was filled with ashes and drops of crystallized slag adhered to the side walls. Numerous cisterns for the first time were dug into the rock, with narrow necks built up through the debris to the occupation level. Each had a small depression in the center as a sump hole. The number of the cisterns is such that one must presume the invention of a cement efficient enough to keep the water from seeping away through the rock. The most interesting objects found were a tablet written in the Ugaritic cuneiform script, the signs being impressed on it backwards (AS III, Pl. XX and p. 29, Fig. 2A), and an ostracon bearing letters in early Canaanite alphabetic

SITE OF ANCIENT BETH-SHEMESH. Courtesy, Gerald Larue

147

script (AS I, Pl. X). Tombs 10 and 11 preserve a fine series of thirteenth century pottery which belongs to the end of City IV's era.

The city of Stratum IV was destroyed at the end of the thirteenth or beginning of the twelfth century, but the data is not sufficiently precise to identify those who conquered it. Two silos, Nos. 515 and 530, contain transitional pottery of the period *ca.* 1200 B.C. and are later than IVb but earlier than City III which was built over them. They suggest the same pre-Philistine phase of Iron I as does Albright's Tell Beit Mirsim B, whence it follows that City IV was destroyed in the late thirteenth century, presumably by the Israelites whose life is represented by these silos.

In any event *Stratum III,* with debris *ca.* 1.00 meters in depth, contains a fine collection of Philistine ware. It was a flourishing age for the town. The city wall on the west side had been breached, but was repaired at this time. Houses were simply built, but one large residence with courtyard was recovered. Copper smelting like that in City IV was in evidence, furnaces being laid out in a north-south direction to catch the west wind, and portions of several ceramic blowpipes were recovered. It was a time of cisterns under private houses, as had been the preceding age. This evidence of prosperity, together with the city's geographical location and its quantity of Philistine pottery, suggest that it was under the political and economic domination of the Philistines, in spite of its Israelite population. Since we now know that during the second half of the eleventh century fine Philistine pottery ceased to be made, we must infer that the terrible destruction which laid the city waste occurred not later than the early part of the third quarter of the eleventh century. If so, then Beth-shemesh may be assumed to have been destroyed with great violence by the Philistines shortly after their destruction of Shiloh and the subsequent removal of the Ark from Beth-shemesh to Kirjath-jearim (I Sam. 6:1–7:2). The quantities of Philistine pottery were thus found because the city was destroyed at a time when the broken fragments of the ware were preserved in quantity within the thick layers of the debris of destruction.

The city of *Stratum IIa* dates from the early tenth century B.C., when the site had been retaken by the Davidic government for Israel. A casemate repair of the old city wall was found, the dimensions of walls and casemates being so close to those at Tell Beit Mirsim (Debir) that one must presume the erection of both under common direction. A large residence for the district governor was erected, and reused in subsequent periods, though it was never completely or carefully excavated. Southeast of the residence for the governor was an even larger government granary, consisting of three long parallel rooms surrounded by well-built walls, 1.50-1.75 meters thick. The residence is raised and may have been built on a filling (*millô?*), as was the residence of similar age and type at Lachish and also a major piece of construction in Jerusalem. Beth-shemesh without doubt was a center for the provincial administration of Israel's United Monarchy, and the structures above mentioned are evidence of that fact. Additional confirmation of the unusual nature of these installations is a large stone-lined silo for grain storage found east of the residence but within its precincts. Its diameter was *ca.* 7.50 meters on the N-S axis and 6.50 meters on the E-W. It was lined to a depth of *ca.* 4 meters, and bedrock appeared at 5.70 meters. Where the floor of the structure was, whether between these two points or on bedrock, is not recorded. Whether this great silo was erected in IIa or IIb is also unknown. Its size is such, however, as to suggest governmental, rather than private, use.

City IIa appears to have been burned, at least in the sections where it was found. The pottery of the stratum, however, is close in type to much of the common pottery found in the destruction layers of Stratum III. It seems to be earlier than that part of the tenth century when chordal and spiral burnishing of red-slipped bowls had become the common decoration. Consequently, the writer affirmed in 1937-38 that the brief interruption in the city's life at the end of IIa must have happened either late in the reign of David or early in that of Solomon — that is, before the end of Tell Beit Mirsim B3 and the invasion of Shishak (*ca.* 918 B.C.). Only further excavation with new methods of digging can determine whether this conclusion is the correct one.

Stratum IIb and c are the writer's artificial separation of pottery horizons without clear architectural correlation. After the tenth century it is quite evident that the site was occupied by an unfortified village. The building remains of the seventh century are so incoherent and eroded that little can be made of them. Quantities of pottery, however, from the end of Iron II suggest that the site was destroyed in the Babylonian capture of Judah, presumably in 587 B.C. Houses of the period between the tenth and eighth centuries were published as though of one level, and an occasional structure was well preserved (AS V, pp. 71 ff.). On the western side, the town's outline, established in the time of Stratum IIa and continued subsequently, shows houses built around the edge of the mound and facing inward upon a street which turned in a large semi-circle within the occupied area. Evidences of reconstruction were plentiful in the houses, but they cannot now be dated. From the 1933 expedition large numbers of sherds from the late tenth or early ninth century were recovered, indicating an interruption in the life of the town at that time, perhaps occasioned by the Shishak invasion. Indeed it can be maintained that there is little published from the town whch requires a ninth century date. In any event, it is clear that Rehoboam did not consider the site sufficiently defensible as to aid in the protection of Judah, for he fortified Zorah in its stead (II Chron. 11:10). From the data which survive from the excavation it is certainly wisest to assert that the precise history of the city between *ca.* 950 and 587 B.C. cannot now be reconstructed. Copper working continued, and vats for the olive oil and dying industries were recovered. The most important economic activity, however, was surely that of wine, large numbers of grape presses having been discovered. A fine series of tombs from the period of Stratum II were dug by Mackenzie. Tomb I is the earliest, from the tenth century B.C. The others belong to the eighth-seventh centuries. The latter are excellent examples of late Judean tombs: a room in a rock slope, entered by a square-cut door, with steps leading down into it, and with benches for the burials on three sides. At the rear a "silo" or "repository" was dug, perhaps as a place to store older bones when new

burials were made. The entrance was sealed by a stone plug, its edges carefully rabetted to fit snugly. The unusual feature of the main group of the Mackenzie tombs is that they form a coherent family group opening around a central area. The usual number of eighth-seventh century seals and royal stamped jar handles was found in the town. Of special interest was the stamped handle with the inscription: *l'lyqm (n)'r ywkn,* "Belonging to Eliakim, steward of Jehoiachin (Xawkin)." It was stamped with the same seal as two stamped handles found by Albright at Tell Beit Mirsim.

BIBLIOGRAPHY. Elihu Grant, *Beth Shemesh (Palestine),* Biblical and Kindred Studies, Haverford, Pa., 1929. Frank M. Cross, Jr. and G. Ernest Wright, "The Boundary and Province Lists of the Kingdom of Judah," JBL LXXV, 1956, pp. 202-226. E. Grant and G. E. Wright, *Ain Shems Excavations,* I - V, Haverford, 1931-39.

BETH-ZUR. Beth-zur, or Bethsura, has been identified with Khirbet et-Tubeiqah, four and one-half miles north of Hebron on a hill 3,325 feet above sea level. During Hellenistic times Beth-zur was a strategic frontier fortress between Judea and Idumea.

O. R. Sellers and W. F. Albright partially excavated Beth-zur in a series of campaigns beginning in 1930. The city seems to have been founded during the seventeenth century B.C. It had massive fortifications similar to those of the Hyksos period at Bethel and Shechem. Beth-zur was destroyed in the fifteenth century, perhaps during the campaigns of Pharaoh Thutmose III. It remained unoccupied until the Israelite conquest during the early twelfth century. The Israelites reused the walls and buildings of the earlier city, but by the mid-eleventh century the city was again destroyed, perhaps by the Philistines. There is an occupation gap during the tenth and ninth centuries, but much material has been discovered that dates from the eighth and seventh centuries. Again the city was destroyed — perhaps during Nebuchadnezzar's invasion of Palestine. Little evidence of the Persian period has been discovered, but coinage enables use to trace its history during the Ptolemies and Seleucids. The first six Ptolemies and most of the Seleucids are represented in coins from Beth-zur. The city was a stronghold of the Maccabees, but it seems to have been abandoned around 100 B.C. After John

Hyrcanus annexed Idumea, Beth-zur lost its significance as a military garrison.

BIBLIOGRAPHY. O. R. Sellers, and W. F. Albright, "The First Campaign of Excavation at Beth-zur," *BASOR*, 43, 1931, pp. 2-13; O. R. Sellers, "The 1957 Campaign at Beth-zur," *BA*, XXI, 1958, pp. 71-76.

BISITUN. *See* Behistun.

BLACK OBELISK OF SHALMANESER III. In his campaign at Calah (Nimrud) in 1846, A. H. Layard discovered a four-sided black limestone pillar, 6½ feet high, with five rows of roughly executed bas reliefs extending around the pillar. Cuneiform inscriptions explaining the reliefs were inscribed between and below the reliefs.

The pillar, or obelisk as it is called, was erected in a public place near Shalmaneser's palace to commemorate the achievements of the first thirty-one years of his reign. The reliefs show representatives of five regions subject to Shalmaneser bringing him their tribute. In the second row of reliefs on the front of the obelisk we see Jehu of Israel kneeling before Shalmaneser. Jehu is pictured with a short rounded beard, clothed with a sleeveless jacket and a long, fringed skirt with a girdle. A soft cap is on his head. Following Jehu we see a group of Israelites in long robes carrying precious metals and other tribute. The inscription reads,

> Tribute of Jehu, son of Omri. I received from him silver, gold, a golden bowl, a golden vase with pointed bottom, golden tumblers, golden buckets, tin, a staff for a king. . . .

Shalmaneser doubtless used the expression "son of Omri" in the sense of successor, for in fact the Jehu dynasty was bitterly opposed to the earlier Omri dynasty which had sought to introduce Baalism as the religion of Israel in the days of Ahab and Jezebel.

BOGHAZKOY. The capital of the ancient Hittite Empire was located ninety miles east of modern Ankara, on the great bend of the Halys River. The ruins of ancient Hattusas, modern Boghazkoy, were discovered by a Frenchman, Charles Felix Marie Texier, early in the nineteenth century and published in his *Description of Asia Minor* (Paris, 1839). At that time the existence of a Hittite Empire in Asia Minor was not suspected. During the following decades, however, William Wright, a missionary to Damascus, and A. H.

THE BLACK OBELISK OF SHAL-MANESER III, discovered at Nimrud (Calah). The original is in the British Museum. Courtesy, Oriental Institute

Sayce of Oxford suggested that a number of monuments which had come to light in Syria and Asia Minor were of Hittite origin, and that the Hittites had once ruled a mighty empire.

The ruins of Boghazkoy suggested that it was an immense city with strong fortifications. Its walls had a series of towers pierced by gateways ornamented with extraordinary sculptured reliefs. The visitor could make out the form of crude sphinxes, sculptured lions, or a Hittite warrior — all in the squat, heavy style that has come to characterize Hittite art.

In 1906 Hugo Winckler of Berlin began the excavation of Boghazkoy. Hittite studies were significantly advanced by his discovery of a collection of cuneiform tablets with inscriptions in many languages, including one that proved to be the tongue of the ancient Hittites. The decipherment of Hittite was the combined work of many scholars, with a major contribution provided by Friederich Hrozny, a Czech scholar.

The documents discovered at Boghazkoy include Hittite legends and myths, historical annals, and a law code. The latter actually formed a body of legal precedents which served as guidelines for local judges. Scholars were particularly interested in the discovery of a copy of the peace treaty between the Hittite king Hattusilis III (*ca.* 1275-1250 B.C.) and the Egyptian Pharaoh Ramesses II, the oldest such treaty known to students of ancient history. An Egyptian text of the same treaty is also extant.

With brief interruptions during war years, the German Orient Society has continued excavations at Boghazkoy to the present.

See also Hittites.

BIBLIOGRAPHY. Hugo Winckler and P. Puchstein, "Excavations at Boghaz-keui in the Summer of 1907," *Smithsonian Institute Annual Report, 1908*, Washington, 1909. Hans G. Guterbock, "Participation in the excavation of Boghazkoy, Turkey, ancient Hattusa, capital of the Hittite Empire," *Yearbook, 1933*, pp. 271-276, American Philosophical Society, Philadelphia, 1933. Kurt Bittel, *Bogazkoy, die Kleinfunde der Grabungen*, 1906-12, J. C. Heinrichs, Leipzig, 1937. Kurt Bittel and Hans G. Gutterbock, *Bogazkoy: Neue untersuchungen in der hethischen hauptstadt*, Verlag der Akademie der wissenschaften, Berlin, 1935.

BOOK OF THE DEAD. The Book of the Dead is the name given to hundreds of funerary texts discovered in New Kingdom tombs. They developed from the Old Kingdom Pyramid Texts, written on the walls of pyramids, which were followed by inscriptions on Middle Kingdom coffins known as Coffin Texts. The Pyramid Texts, Coffin Texts, and the Book of the Dead give us

EGYPTIAN BOOK OF THE DEAD depicting balances. Courtesy, British Museum

our most extensive body of Egyptian religious literature.

In its later history the Book of the Dead could be written on leather or papyrus in any form of writing — hieroglyphic, hieratic, or demotic. It reflects Egyptian ideas concerning the afterlife, but it is in no sense an Egyptian Bible. Actually a rather haphazard collection of magical texts, the Book of the Dead is designed to insure for the deceased body with which it is placed a "coming forth by day," i.e. the emerging into the light from the darkness of the tomb.

The Theban recension of the Book of the Dead contains one hundred ninety spells. Among them are hymns to the gods Re and Osiris; speeches addressed to various gods, and to the deceased; and magical spells such as were inscribed on *scarabs.

The best known part of the Book of the Dead is the Negative Confession (chapter 125) in which the deceased denies the commission of a series of evil actions before the gods. The deceased affirms that he has not committed theft, murder or adultery, that he has not moved boundary stones or interfered with irrigation controls. While the denial itself may have had magical qualities, the moral standards reflected in the confession suggest that the gods are concerned with more than ceremonial religion.

The deceased is pictured as he is led by the hand before his forty-two judges, each of whom he addresses by name, affirming his innocence of a particular crime. In front of the god Osiris is a balance attended by Anubis. Thoth, the scribe of the gods, is depicted calculating on his palette the result of the weighing of the dead man's heart against Truth. If the scales balance, the deceased is declared to be "true of voice" like Osiris, and entitled to a future life of happiness. If the test is unsatisfactory, the deceased is destroyed by the "devourer of the dead," a monster waiting beside the balances.

The Book of the Dead is itself evidence of a democratic tendency in Egyptian religious life. In the Pyramid Texts only the Pharaoh could hope to be identified with Osiris in the after life. By the end of the Sixth Dynasty, queens and other members of the royal family could be so identified. In the last period of Egyptian history any private individual could hope for the identification which would assure him a blessed future.

BIBLIOGRAPHY. Thomas George Allen, ed., *The Egyptian Book of the Dead: Documents in the Oriental Institute Museum at the University of Chicago*, University of Chicago Press, 1959. E. A. Wallis Budge, ed., *The Book of the Dead. The Hieroglyphic Transcript of the Papyrus of Ani, The Translation into English, and An Introduction*, University Books (reprint) New Hyde Park, N. Y., 1960.

BORSIPPA (BIRS NIMRUD). Borsippa, located about seven miles southwest of Babylon boasts an impressive ruin that still rises 154 feet above the level of the plain. Early travelers such as Rich and Rawlinson thought of the "tower" at Birs Nimrud as a possible remnant of the Biblical Tower of *Babel. Later study, while assuming that the Biblical tower would be found in Babylon itself, has noted the remains of the Borsippa *ziggurat, a temple known as the E-zida, "the enduring house," and a palace of Nebuchadnezzar. A. H. Layard, Hormuzd Rassam and others excavated Borsippa for the British Museum in campaigns during 1850, 1854, and 1880.

BIBLIOGRAPHY. H. Rassam, *Ashur and the Land of Nimrod*, 1897.

BRAK. See Habor River.

BRONZE AGE. See Archaeology III.

BUBASTIS. Bubastis is the Pi-beseth mentioned by Ezekiel as an idolatrous city ripe for divine judgment (Ezek. 30:17). It was dedicated to the worship of Bast, a cat-headed lioness whose sacred emblem was the cat. So popular was the worship of Bast that as many as 700,000 pilgrims would come for the annual festival which Herodotus graphically describes:

Now when they are being conveyed to the city of Bubastis, they act as follows: for men and women embark together, and great numbers of both sexes in every barge: some of the women have castenets on which they play, and the men play on the flute during the whole voyage; the rest of the women and men sing and clap their hands together at the same time. When, in the course of their journey, they come to any town, they lay their barge near to land, and do as follows: some of the women do as I have described; others shout and scoff at the women of the place; some dance, and others behave in an unseemly manner; this they do at every town

RUINS OF SYNAGOGUE AT CAPERNAUM. Courtesy, Israel Office of Information

Jordan, while others identified it with *Khirbet Minyeh*, two and one-half miles farther to the southwest. Modern excavations have settled the question in favor of *Tell Hum*. *Khirbet Minyeh* was excavated in 1932 by D. A. Mader and A. M. Schneider. First the excavators thought that the ruins were the remains of a Roman castle, but the pottery proved that the site had not been occupied before the early Moslem period (C. C. McCown, *The Ladder of Progress in Palestine*, New York, 1943, pp. 257-263). On the other hand, the excavations at *Tell Hum* — property of the Franciscans since 1894 — conducted by H. Kohl and C. Watzinger in 1905, and in later years by Father Gaudence Orfali, proved that a flourishing city had been at that site in the days of Christ, for which reason Capernaum must be identified with *Tell Hum*.

Although Orfali was mainly concerned with the excavations of the Jewish synagogue, he also cleared a basalt-paved street, west of the synagogue, as well as houses in which he found many mills and olive presses. Unfortunately, these ancient remains have neither adequately been published nor have they been preserved, with the exception of the movable objects, which are now set up in rows near the synagogue as in a museum.

The main attraction of all ancient remains of *Tell Hum* has always been the impressive remains of an early Jewish synagogue. The first excavations of this structure were made in 1866 by Charles Wilson, who believed that this building was the synagogue of Jesus' day mentioned in Luke 7:5. However, H. H. Kitchener, who from 1874-77 worked in the survey of western Palestine, recognized the synagogue correctly as a structure of the second or third century A.D. Later G. Orfali tried to prove its first-century date, but all scholars agree now that it comes from a later period, probably the third century, although it is possible that it rests on remains of the synagogue in which Jesus taught. The

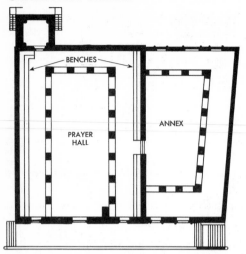

PLAN OF SYNAGOGUE at Capernaum

first correct plan of the building was made during the excavations of Kohl and Watzinger in 1905. In 1925 the Franciscan owners of the property received permission from the Department of Antiquities of Palestine to restore parts of the building. This work was carried out by Father Orfali.

The whole structure, built of white limestone, consisted of two parts: a main roofed building, 24.00 x 18.65 m in size, and an adjoining court surrounded on three sides by columned halls. The actual synagogue building, two stories high, was a basilica-type structure of three aisles with a gallery for the women on the second floor running around all walls except the southern one. This gallery rested on sixteen columns which stood at a distance of about 3.50 m from the walls. The gallery was reached by a stairway attached to an outside extension at the northwestern corner of the building. The room formed by this extension was probably used as storeroom. A double row of stone benches runs along the eastern and western walls in the main building. Access to it was obtained through three doorways in the southern wall. In front of the building was an outside platform that was reached on either end by means of several steps. The western wall had no door, although a street ran outside it. The northern wall was also without any entrance, except that a small door led from the inside of the synagogue to the storeroom already mentioned. The eastern wall had a door which led

into the adjoining court. This court was open to the sky, and surrounded on three sides, north, east and south, by columned halls, open toward the court. This court with its halls had the same length as the main building, but its northern side being 11.00 m long, was longer than the southern side, which had a length of only *ca.* 9.00 m. Doorways to the columned halls were found in all three exterior walls.

In the main hall of the synagogue and near the south wall, several sculptured stones were found which seem to have belonged to the Ark of the Torah Scrolls. This Ark had stood with its back to the great central doorway so that the worshipers facing it looked toward Jerusalem.

The synagogue of Capernaum was richly ornamented. A great variety of sculptured stones were found, such as capitals of columns, lintels and posts of doorways, window frames, friezes and cornices. They show representations of animals, plants, and of mythological and geometric figures. One sculptured block coming from a frieze is of extraordinary interest, since it depicts a columned object on wheels which looks like a temple, but has been interpreted to be either a movable ark, shrine, or chariot. No interpretation so far advanced with regard to this object is entirely satisfactory.

Two columns bear inscriptions of people who made donations for the building. One is in Greek and reads, "Herod, son of Mo[. .]mus and Justus his son, together with the children erected this column." The other inscription is in Aramaic and is of special interest because of the New Testament names mentioned, "Alphaeus, son of Zebedee, son of John, made this column; on him be blessing."

BIBLIOGRAPHY. H. Kohl and C. Watzinger, *Antike Synagogen in Galilaea*, Leipzig, 1916. G. Orfali, *Caphernaum et see ruins*, Paris, 1922. E. L. Sukenik, *Ancient Synagogues in Palestine and Greece*, London, 1934, pp. 7-21, 71-72.

CAPPADOCIAN TABLETS. The Cappadocian Tablets comprise a collection of several thousand business documents and letters written in Akkadian cuneiform during the nineteenth century B.C. by Assyrian merchants who had settled at Kanish, modern Kultepe, one hundred fifty miles south of Ankara. In 1907, Hugo Winckler reported the discovery of the texts in the *Communi-*

cations of the German Orient Society, adding, "Difficult to interpret and yielding little information, these tablets nevertheless proved the influence of the cuneiform script countries in Asia Minor, and so they added welcome evidence to the few letters from Asia Minor to the Egyptian Pharaoh which had been found at Tell el Amarna."

Julius Lewy and others have carefully studied the Cappadocian tablets with the result that we can now follow the commercial and legal transactions of the Assyrian merchants and their relation with the population of eastern Asia Minor in considerable detail. The Assyrians were permitted to operate a *karum* or market place in an area assigned to them outside the Cappadocian city of Kanish. The *Karum* was self governing, comprising a small walled suburb occupied exclusively by Assyrian merchants. The texts indicate that the merchants exported metalic ores from Cappadocia and imported metal products and textiles from °Ashur. With the rise of Hittite power *ca.* 1770 B.C. Assyrian commercial activity in Asia Minor came to an end.

The Cappadocian Tablets illustrate the extreme mobility of peoples during the Biblical Patriarchal Age. Trade routes extended up the valleys of the Tigris and Euphrates Rivers. The Assyrians were able to journey up the Tigris, through °Hurrian territory into Asia Minor.

Excavations have continued intermittently at Kultepe. Bedrich Hrozny of Prague directed an excavation in 1925, and since 1948 a Turkish archaeologist named Ozguc has worked there.

BIBLIOGRAPHY. Julius Lewy, "Aspects of Commerical Life in Assyria and Asia Minor," *JAOS*, LXXVIII, 1958, pp. 89-101. Ferris J. Stephens, "Notes on Cappadocian Tablets," *JAOS*, XLVI, 1926, pp. 179-181. Albert T. Clay, *Letters and Transactions from Cappadocia*, Yale University Press, New Haven, 1927. Kemal Balkan, ed., *Letter of King Anum-hirbi of Mama to King Warshama of Kanish*, Türk Tarik Kuruma yayinlarindan, Ankara, 1957.

CARBON 14. *See* Radio Carbon Dating.

CARCHEMISH. Carchemish, today an imposing mound just north of the Syrian village of Jerablus (Jerabis), was for more than a thousand years the dominant city of the upper Euphrates. Already the seat of a kingdom in the early second millennium B.C., it was a vassal of its more powerful Mitanni and Hittite neighbors from *ca.* 1500-1200 B.C., and a leading Hittite successor state in the early second millennium. In all this time, it controlled much of the territory bordering on the westernmost part of the Euphrates and called Ursum in the cuneiform sources. Incorporated into the Assyrian empire in 717 B.C. (cf. Isa. 10:9), it was the site of a decisive battle in 605 B.C. (II Chron. 35:20) which left a lasting impression on Israel (Jer. 46).

EXCAVATIONS at Carchemish. Courtesy, British Museum

I. *Location and Name.* The mound of Carchemish is situated on the right (western) bank of the Euphrates at the point where the Berlin-Baghdad railway and hence, since 1920, the Turko-Syrian frontier, cross the river, most of it lying on the Turkish side of the border. It commands the plains, once heavily wooded and still fertile today, which stretch southward along the river, as well as the river-crossing of the shortest route from Assyria toward Cilicia. The nearest modern village, known variously as Jerabis or Jerablus, may preserve the ancient name, which was written Karkamis(h) in Old Babylonian, Kargamis(h) in Middle Assyrian, Gargamis(h) in neo-Assyrian, Krkmsh or Qrqmsh in Egyptian, Kargamis(a) in Hieroglyphic Hittite, and *Karkemish* in Hebrew. Since the etymology of the name is uncertain — a proposal to connect it with the name of °Gilgamesh notwithstanding — it is uncertain which of these spellings is to be preferred. The popular English transliteration Carchemish is an amalgam of various Septuagint readings.

II. *History of Discovery.* The prominent ruins of Carchemish were visited as early as 1699 by Henry Maundrell of the East India Company and at intervals thereafter in the seventeenth and early eighteenth centuries by other English travellers. Their identification with ancient Carchemish was first proposed in 1876, when George Smith surveyed the site, sketching many of its free-standing monuments before death overtook him on his way back to Aleppo. His discoveries inspired the excavations of 1878-1881 which yielded a number of monuments for the British Museum. A more serious undertaking was envisaged by D. G. Hogarth's survey in 1908, and he returned in 1911 to begin formal excavations with R. C. Thompson and T. E. Lawrence. These were continued, until the outbreak of the war, by Sir Leonard Woolley, and resumed by him in 1920, when they were interrupted for good by the Turkish War of Independence. The results, as far as they survived these interruptions, have been fully published in three volumes by the excavators (see Bibliography). The identification of Carchemish was confirmed by a cuneiform inscription from the site published in the last of these volumes.

HITTITE SOLDIER ON SCULPTURED SLAB, from Carchemish. Courtesy, British Museum

III. *History of the Site.*

A. Old Babylonian Period. Although there are traces of prehistoric occupation in and around Carchemish in the form of pottery and kilns thought to be of the Halaf type or even earlier, the recorded history of the site begins with the Old Babylonian period. The earliest reference to Carchemish dates from the time of Yahdun-Lim of °Mari (*ca.* 1800 B.C.). Subsequently, as the Mari letters show, a certain Aplahanda, whose name sounds "Anatolian," ruled Carchemish. He is the subject of a letter of Shamshi-Adad I (*ca.* 1815-1782 B.C.) to his son Yashmah-Adad at Mari; in another letter he appears as contemporary of Yarim-Lim of Yamhad (see *Aleppo*), and no less than nine letters of his own addressed to Yashmah-Adad, are known. They suggest that Aplahanda was an ally, perhaps even a vassal, of the Assyrian viceroy at Mari, and in return counted on the latter to police the Euphrates below Carchemish. A cylinder seal inscribed by his daughter already acknowledges Kubaba as her deity; this goddess later headed the pantheon at Carchemish. Aplahanda was succeeded by his son Yatar-Ami, a contemporary of Zimri-Lim, who received his allegiance when he reconquered Mari from the Assyrians. Other kings of Carchemish about this time are [Bi]n-Ami and his son [X-d]a-Lim, but nothing is known of them beyond their names. Perhaps they were contemporary with °Hammurabi of Babylon, (*ca.* 1792-1750 B.C. who does not list Carchemish among his conquests and thus presumably did not penetrate so far north; thereafter and for at least a century, nothing is known about the city.

B. The Hurrian-Hittite Period. When it first re-emerges from obscurity late in the seventeenth century, Carchemish appears allied with the Hurrians and Aleppo against the rising power of the Hittites of Anatolia. Hittite sources that probably date to Hattusilis I (*ca.* 1650-1620 B.C.) show the antagonists in action at Urshu, north of Carchemish. If correctly dated, this siege may have been a prelude to the famous campaign of the next Hittite king, Mursilis I (*ca.* 1620-1590 B.C.) who destroyed Aleppo, marched all the way to Babylon which he sacked (*ca.* 1595 B.C.) and fought off the Hurrians on the way back to his capital; the implication is that Carchemish was, at the least, neutralized during or prior to this campaign.

In the sixteenth and fifteenth centuries B.C., Carchemish probably formed part of the great Hurrian empire of Mitanni, (Naharina to the Egyptians) which stretched from the Mediterranean to the Tigris, and we do not hear of the city in the geographical lists and military biographies of the time of Thutmose III and Amenhotep III of Egypt who repeatedly invaded Syria. In the next two centuries, however, Carchemish passed decisively into the sphere of influence of the new Hittite empire.

The Hittite sources from the fourteenth and thirteenth centuries B.C. are now supplemented by important evidence from Ugarit, another Hittite vassal at this time, which maintained a continuing contact with Carchemish. Suppiluliumas, the founder of the new Hittite empire (*ca.* 1375-1335 B.C.), conquered Carchemish about 1355 B.C. and installed as its subject king his own younger son Piyashilli, also known as Sharru-Kushuh, whom he bound to himself by a treaty and who in turn proposed to ally himself with Niqmadu of Ugarit. His Hittite overlords assigned most of the country west of the Euphrates to Sharru-Kushuh. He was succeeded by his two sons Shahurunuwa and x-Sharruma (sometimes thought to be the same king under two names); one of them may have been the king of Carchemish who figures as the sixth ally of Muwatallis of Hatti at the great battle of °Kadesh in 1285 B.C. Shahurunuwa's son and grandson succeeded as Ini-Teshub (whose name is preserved in hieratic Egyptian on a contemporary ostracon from Egypt) and Talmi-Teshub; these Hurrian royal names, like those of some of the Hittite kings themselves, may have had Hittite doublets. At the end of the thirteenth century, Carchemish, together with much of the Ancient Near East, was overrun by the invasion of the Sea Peoples and once more plunged into obscurity.

C. Carchemish as a Late Hittite Successor State. The Hittite Empire collapsed under the onslaught of the Sea Peoples, but its language and art found a curious survival in Northern Syria where, mixed with Assyrian and Aramean elements, it formed a new culture employing the so-called hieroglyphic Hittite script. It was this area which henceforth was known as the land of Hatti in the Assyrian records, and it is probably its inhabitants which the Bible calls *Hittīm*. Carchemish turned out to be the most important center of this Late Hittite culture, and has produced more hieroglyphic Hittite inscriptions than any of the other far-flung sites where these have been found. Its kings were called "great king" in their own inscriptions, and "King of great Hatti (= Hittite Land)" by the Assyrians, and their territories must have been considerable for Tiglath-pileser I of Assyria (1114-1076 B.C.) battled Carchemish east of the Euphrates, again ruled by an Ini-Teshub, together with the Mushki (Biblical Meshek; Gen. 10:2, etc.) who had penetrated the area. By about 1000 B.C., we can see the emergence of the first of several local dynasties which maintained Carchemish's independence in the face of the Assyrian expansion for nearly three hundred years. It is headed by Luhas or Suhas I, who called himself simply prince, and continued by his direct descendants, Asatuwatimais, Luhas II and Katuwas, under the more imposing title of lord of the land. Katuwas, who ascended the throne about 900 B.C., claimed to have dispersed the Mushki and rebuilt Carchemish. He was followed by a very long-lived ruler attested, so far, only in the Assyrian sources, for these claim that King Sangara of Carchemish paid tribute to Ashur-nasir-pal as early as 874 B.C. and to Shalmaneser III as late as 827 B.C. The latter king, thwarted by Carchemish and its allies at the Battle of Lutibu in 858 B.C., even attempted the first' Assyrian siege of the city (852, 849-8) but massive fortifications resisted his efforts and he had to content himself with accepting a face-saving mass of tribute, also illustrated at Balawat. Where the two great conquerors failed, their weak successors certainly could not succeed and thus the native sources for the period of *ca.* 820-750 B.C. reveal two more local dynasties who ruled as lords of the land of Hatti and kings of the land of Carchemish respectively. The former consisted of Asadarus (Astarus) and his son(s?), the latter of the priest Araras (or Atatas) and his son Kamanas and a grandson (Astarus II?). Araras was a contemporary of Ashur-dan III of Assyria (772-755 B.C.), whose name seems to occur in one of his inscriptions; in view of the weakness of Assyria at the time, he seems to have sided with the rising power

of Urartu (Armenia). Kamanas was, in fact, a vassal of Sarduris III of Urartu (*ca.* 760-733) on the evidence of an inscription found near Aleppo which, nevertheless, shows Carchemish in control of this fairly distant area.

D. The Fall of Carchemish. Pisiris, the last independent king of Carchemish, is again known from Assyrian sources. It was his fate to be matched against a resurgent Assyria, first under Tiglath-pileser III, who defeated him in 743 B.C., and later under Sargon II who finally captured him, once more allied with the Mushki, and his capital in 717 B.C. (cf. Isa. 10:9). Brick-inscriptions of Sargon from Carchemish show that he helped rebuild the city, which now became the headquarters of an Assyrian province. By 691 B.C. and again in 649 B.C. its governors served as eponyms. Nor did Carchemish lose its strategic importance with the collapse of Assyria in 615-609 B.C., for it was here that the great battle for the succession to Assyria's hegemony was fought out between Pharaoh Necho of Egypt and the crown-prince Nebuchadnezzar of Babylon in 605 B.C. By his decisive victory, Nebuchadnezzar established Babylonia as the dominant power in the Near East for the next seventy years, a turn of events fraught with significance for Israel, where the Battle of Carchemish did not pass unnoticed (Jer. 46; II Chron. 35:20). Thereafter the city must have declined rapidly for, by Seleucid times, it was possible to found a new city on the site which Seleucus I Nicator called Europos, like several of his other Asiatic foundations, after his birthplace in Macedonia.

BIBLIOGRAPHY. D. G. Hogarth and Leonard Woolley, *Carchemish,* The British Museum, London, 1914-1952, 3vv. Leonard Woolley, "The prehistoric pottery of Carchemish," *Iraq,* I, 1934, pp. 146-62 and pls. xviii-xxi; "The Iron-Age Graves of Carchemish," *Annals of Art and Archaeology,* XXVI, 1939-40, pp. 11-37 and pls. iii-xxv. Georges Dossin, "Aplahanda, Roi de Carkémiš," *Revue d'Assyriologie,* XXXV, 1938, pp. 115-121. Édouard Dhorme, "Lettre du Roi de Kargamish au Roi d'Ugarit," *Melanges Syriens . . . Dussaud,* I, 1939, pp. 203-7. R. D. Barnett and J. Černy, "King Ini-tešub of Carchemish in an Egyptian Document," *JEA,* XXXIII, 1947, p. 94. H. Th. Bossert, "Zur Geschichte von Karkamis," *Studi Classici e Orientali,* I, 1951, pp. 35-67. Pietro Meriggi, "I nuovi framenti e la storia di Kargamis," *Athenaeum,* XXX, 1952, pp. 174-181; "La Ricostruzione di Kargamis," *Rivista degli Studi Orientali,* XXIX, 1954, pp. 1-16, pls. i-iv. Mario Liverani, "Karkemiš nei testi di Ugarit,"

MONUMENT OF MERODACH-BALA-DIN. *Courtesy, Staatliche Museen zu Berlin*

ibid, XXV, 1960, pp. 135-147. H. G. Güterbock, "Carchemish," *JNES*, XIII, 1954, pp. 102-114. E. Laroche, "Rois de Kargamiš et d'Amurru," *Ugaritica*, ed. Claude F. A. Schaeffer, III, 1956, pp. 121-133.

CARMEL, MOUNT. *See* Mugharah.

CARRHAE. *See* Haran.

CATACOMBS. Catacombs are underground burial places consisting of passages and small rooms with recesses in their walls into which coffins were placed. The catacombs were used by Christians in Rome from the second century until 412 when Alaric ravaged the countryside around the city and the catacombs — located a mile or so outside the walls of Rome — were no longer accessible. Some of our earliest examples of Christian art come from the catacombs. There we see the Good Shepherd; Christ under the guise of Orpheus, the radiant sun; the Feeding of the Five Thousand; and Old Testament figures such as the Three Hebrew Children of the fiery furnace (Dan. 3).

CELLA. Cella is an architectural term used of the inner part of ancient temples, as distinguished from open porticoes and other outside parts. The statue of the deity would be placed in the cella of his temple.

CHABUR. *See* Habor River.

CHALDEA, CHALDEANS. The Chaldeans were a Semitic people who first appeared in southern Mesopotamia about 1000 B.C. Beginning about the ninth century B.C. we read of Chaldeans struggling with Assyrians for control of Babylonia. References to Chaldeans occur in Assyrian records from the time of Ashur-nasir-pal II (883-859 B.C.). In 731 B.C., a Chaldean prince named Ukinzer successfully attacked Babylon and seized the throne. Tiglath-pileser III of Assyria (745-727 B.C.), supported by the priests, launched a counter-attack and deposed Ukinzer (728 B.C.).

During the reign of Shalmaneser V (727-722 B.C.) the Chaldeans were restive, and under his successor Sargon II (722-705 B.C.) a Chaldean named Marduk-apal-iddina (Biblical Merodach-baladan) who had ruled a small principality named Bit Jakin, dominated Babylon (721-710 B.C.). During the reign of the Judean king Hezekiah (715-687 B.C.), Merodach-baladan sent an envoy to Judah to congratulate the king on his recovery from sickness and, at the same time, to urge him to ally himself with the Chaldeans against Assyria. Hezekiah injudiciously showed his treasures to the visiting Chaldeans, and the prophet Isaiah warned him of the consequences of his folly. The very Chaldeans whom Hezekiah had befriended would one day conquer Judah (II Kings 20:12-19; Isa. 39:1-8).

Sennacherib of Assyria (705-681 B.C.) was able to conquer Marduk-apal-iddina in 703 B.C. While Assyrians sought to rule with an iron hand, the Chaldeans remained the dominant ethnic group in Babylonia and they awaited the opportunity to declare their independence again.

About 626 B.C., Chaldean power was reestablished in Babylonia when Nabopolassar (626-605 B.C.) rebelled against his Assyrian overlord and established what was to become the Neo-Babylonian, or Chaldean Empire. He joined forces with Cyaxeres the Mede (625-585 B.C.) and attacked °Nineveh, the Assyrian capital. When Nineveh fell (612 B.C.), Assyrian power was forever broken. Nabopolassar rebuilt the ancient city of Babylon and made it the capital of his empire.

The Neo-Babylonian empire attempted to take control of the vast territories which had been tributary to Assyria. After the fall of Nineveh, Assyria could offer no effective resistance to Nabopolassar. Egypt feared the rising Chaldean power and sent armies into the field. At the crucial battle of °Carchemish on the Euphrates (609 B.C.) Nebuchadnezzar, the son of Nabopolassar inflicted a crushing defeat on the Egyptian forces. Josiah of Judah (640-609 B.C.) sought to prevent the Egyptians from passing the fortress of °Megiddo. It is not known whether Josiah had a formal treaty with the Chaldeans or if he merely acted in what he considered the best interests of Judah. Josiah was killed in the battle, but the delay may have prevented the Egyptians from joining forces with the remaining Assyrians at a time when they might have challenged the rising Chaldean power (cf. II Chron. 35:20-24).

In 605 B.C., Nebuchadnezzar received word of the death of his father, and hastened home to assume power in his own name. He returned to the battlefield after securing his succession to the throne and, by the end of 604 B.C., his armies were on the Philistine plain. Ashkelon was taken (cf. Jer. 47: 5-7) and Jehoiakim of Judah (609-598 B.C.) became a vassal (II Kings 24:1). Trusting Egyptian promises of aid, Jehoiakim rebelled (II Kings 24:1) but Egypt was in no position to defend Judah from an attack by Nebuchadnezzar. During the time of the Chalddean march against Judah, Jehoiakim died. Some have suggested that he was assassinated by some of his own subjects in the hope that they might gain more lenient treatment from the Chaldeans (cf. Jer. 22:18-19; 36:30). Eighteen year old Jehoiachin succeeded his father as Judah's king (II Kings 24:8) but within three months Judah surrendered to the Chaldeans. The king, the queen mother, high officials, leading citizens and large amounts of booty were taken to Babylon. The king's uncle Mattaniah (or Zedekiah) was named king of Judah (597-587 B.C.).

When rebellion flared up in Babylon (595 B.C.). both those Judaeans in exile and those still in Judah hoped for an end of Nebuchadnezzar's rule. False prophets encouraged such hopes, but Jeremiah made it clear that the exiles would remain in Babylon for a long time (Jer. 29).

The pro-Egyptian party in Zedekiah's court encouraged the king to rebel against Nebuchadnezzar, but Egypt was unable to help Judah when she defied the Chaldeans. In 589 B.C. Zedekiah rebelled and the armies of Nebuchadnezzer reacted swiftly. The outlying cities of Judah were taken one by one and Jerusalem, the capital, was besieged. By summer, 587 B.C. the walls of Jerusalem were breached, the city was destroyed, and its king and people taken into exile.

While best known from the Bible as a conqueror, Nebuchadnezzar is depicted in the Neo-Babylonian documents as a great builder. During his reign, Babylon became the most beautiful city of the ancient world (cf. Dan. 4:30). His son and successor, Awil-Marduk (Evil-Merodach of II Kings 25:27-30) released Jehoiachin from prison and dealt kindly with the Jews. After a reign of but two years he was murdered by his brother-in-law Neriglissar who seized the throne (560-558 B.C.). His successor, Labashi-Marduk, reigned but three months and was succeeded by another usurper, Naboni-

ONE MINA WEIGHT from the time of Nebuchadnezzar. Courtesy, British Museum

dus, whose son Belshazzar (Dan. 5) was coregent until the fall of the Chaldean Empire to Cyrus (538 B.C.). The rulers after Nebuchadnezzar were not strong, and in the latter days of the Empire the priests of Marduk, the god of Babylon, were bitterly opposed to the Chaldean rulers. Cyrus was actually welcomed as a liberator when his armies marched on Babylon.

The term Chaldean is used in the book of Daniel to describe the learned astrologers of Babylon. They are equated with magicians, soothsayers, and enchanters (Dan. 2:2, 4, 5, 10; 4:4; 5:7-11). Herodotus (464-424 B.C.) distinguished between the ordinary Babylonians of his day and the Chaldeans, identified by him with the priests of Bel-Marduk (*Histories* i. 181, 183). Chaldean astrology was not differentiated from astronomy. Along with prognostications which must be dismissed as frivolous, they arrived at some amazingly exact computations. Chaldean astronomers estimated a year of 365 days, 6 hours, 15 minutes and 41 seconds — within 30 minutes of the computation of modern instruments.

The Chaldeans of the Neo-Babylonian empire used the °Akkadian language which had been used by the earlier Babylonians and the Assyrians. Daniel and his companions learned this language and its literature while at the Babylonian court (Dan. 1:4).

BIBLIOGRAPHY. A. Leo Oppenheim, *Ancient Mesopotamia: Portrait of a Dead Civilization,* University of Chicago Press, Chicago, 1964. Georges Roux, *Ancient Iraq,* George Allen and Unwin, London, 1964. H. W. F. Saggs, *The Greatness that Was Babylon,* Hawthorn Books, New York, 1962. D. J. Wiseman, *Chronicles of Chaldaean Kings (626-556 B.C.),* British Museum, London, 1956.

CHENOBOSKION. *See* Nag Hammadi.

CHORAZIN. About two and one-half miles north of °Capernaum (Tell Hum) is Kerazeh, identified with ancient Chorazin, one of the cities in which Jesus preached (Matt. 11:21). Rabbis of the second century boasted of the excellent wheat of Chorazin. Ruins of a black basalt synagogue, dating to the third and fourth century A.D. are still visible.

CLEOPATRA. *See* Egypt.

CLOTHING. Man early used a variety of readily available materials to clothe himself.

The Bible mentions leaves (Gen. 3:7) and skins (Gen. 3:21). In addition, hair, grass, and bark-cloth were probably used. Since it was made of perishable materials, man's earliest clothing has disappeared and left no remains for archaeological study.

By the Biblical Patriarchal Age, known to archaeologists as the Middle Bronze period, we read of Joseph's "long robe with sleeves" (Gen. 37:3, AV, "coat of many colors"). The invention of spinning and weaving long antedated the patriarchs, and probably should be dated in Neolithic times.

Nomadic peoples could make clothing from hides and leather, but sedentary people had easier access to vegetable fibers, notably flax and cotton. Flax grew in Egypt, where the Pharaohs gave garments of fine linen as presents, along with gold and jewels (Gen. 41:42). Cotton was introduced into °Assyria around 700 B.C. by Sennacherib. It was indigenous to Upper Egypt and the Sudan. Wool was readily available throughout the Near East, and it was commonly employed for outer garments (Lev. 13:47; Deut. 22:11).

Linen and cotton were usually used undyed, but wool was used either in its natural state (of which there was a variety of coloration, cf. Gen. 30:32-34), or dyed. The Bible speaks of "blue and purple and scarlet stuff" (Exod. 26:1), all of which was produced by dyeing wool.

Egyptian men wore a loincloth or kilt, and their women wore cloaks or dresses. The loincloth was common dress throughout most of the ancient world. The °Beni Hasan tomb painting depicts Semites entering Egypt during the Patriarchal Age.

In general, garments used in the Near East were loose and flowing. The °Minoans constitute an exception, for Minoan women wore clothes that were skillfully shaped to fit the figure. They had wide flounced skirts and low cut blouses or jackets.

CNOSSUS. Cnossus, the chief city of ancient Crete was on the north shore of the island, near modern Candia. Arthur Evans began the excavation of Cnossus in 1900 and work has continued to the present time.

The site was occupied long before 3000 B.C., and it served as the center of an extensive Bronze Age culture. From 2000 to 1600 B.C. Cnossus enjoyed a high culture

THRONE ROOM IN THE PALACE OF MINOS at Cnossus, showing an elaborate griffin fresco. Courtesy, Foto Marburg

and marked prosperity. Some time before 1500 B.C. the city was destroyed, possibly by an earthquake. It was magnificently rebuilt, but it was destroyed a second time *ca.* 1400 B.C., possibly by invaders from the Greek mainland. This marked the end of Minoan culture (*see* Minoans).

Cnossus later became a flourishing Greek city, and its history continued until the fourth century A.D. In Greek mythology, Cnossus was the capital of Minos and the site of the labyrinth. The excavation of the palace of Minos, by Arthur Evans, has revealed an elaborate building and evidences of the high °Minoan culture.

BIBLIOGRAPHY. A. J. Evans, *Palace of Minos,* 4 vol., 1921-35.

COFFIN TEXTS. See Book of the Dead.

CORACLES. See Transportation.

CORINTH. Ancient Corinth was located on the Gulf of Corinth about five miles southwest

of the modern canal that cuts the Isthmus. The excavation of the city began in 1896 under the supervision of the American School of Classical Studies in Athens.

Corinth was one of the great seaports of ancient Greece because of its favorable position on two harbors. Its eastern Harbor, Cenchreae, was on the Saronic Gulf, an arm of the Aegean Sea; its western harbor, Lechaeum, was on the Gulf of Corinth, an arm of the Ionian Sea. Thus Corinth served as a crossroads between east and west. It had a reputation for moral corruption to the point where the expression "Corinthian girl" came to mean "prostitute" and the verb "to live like a Corinthian" signified the living of a dissolute life. Ritual prostitution in the temple of Aphrodite on the Acropolis of Corinth (termed the Acrocorinth) was in part responsible for this reputation. According to Strabo (VII. 378-82) who visited the city soon after its restoration by the Romans in 44 B.C., there were about a thousand female temple slaves in Corinth. In the ruins of the theater a stone seat was unearthed bearing the inscription "of the girls" showing that the temple slaves had their own reserved seats in the theater.

The excavation of stone implements and pottery vessels indicate that the site of Corinth was occupied as early as the Neolithic period. The presence of metal tools shows the transition to the Early Bronze Age around 3000 B.C. About 2000 B.C. the site was devastated, and there are no significant remains until the beginning of the first millennium when remains of the Dorian Greeks begin to appear. Corinth was a flourishing city during the age of the tyrants (8th to 6th century B.C.) and again in the Hellenistic period until the Romans destroyed the city in 146 B.C. On the ruins of old Corinth, Julius Caesar founded a Roman colony in 44 B.C. which became the capital of the province of Achaia in 27 B.C. Gallio (Acts 18:12-17) became proconsul of Corinth in A.D. 52.

When the Romans under L. Mullius destroyed Corinth (146 B.C.) they destroyed most of the Greek monuments, with the result that it is largely the remains of Roman Corinth that have been brought to light in the excavations. In A.D. 174 the Roman traveler Pausanius wrote his *Description of Greece*, book two of which has served as a guide to archaeologists working at Corinth.

THE LECHAEUM ROAD *leading to the harbor 1½ miles west of Corinth. Courtesy, Gerald Larue*

The Lechaeum Road led directly to the center of Corinth where it was colonnaded and lined with shops on each side. Above the shops on the west side of the road was the °basilica, beyond which on a separate eminence stood the great Temple of Apollo built in the sixth century B.C. Seven of its original thirty-eight columns still stand. At the head of the Lechaeum Road stood the agora surrounded by shops, basilicas, and other monuments. Between the upper and lower areas of the agora was a row of central shops in the midst of which was the bema, a high platform raised on two steps with a superstructure and benches. The bema, built of white and blue marble, served as a platform for public speaking. This is without doubt the place where Paul

THE TEMPLE OF APOLLO *at Corinth, ca. 590 B.C. Courtesy, N. Stoupnapas*

ALABASTER VASES from Corinith, ca. 600 B.C. Courtesy, N. Stoupnapas

was brought "before the tribunal" in Corinth (Acts 18:12-17).

Colonnades of a southern stoa gave access to additional shops and buildings. Many of these shops seem to have been taverns, for the pottery discovered here consisted largely of drinking vessels inscribed with such words as Dionysus, Zeus, Health, Security, and Love.

Near the theater at Corinth was a sixty-foot plaza paved with limestone. On one of the blocks is an inscription, thought to date from the middle of the first century A.D.: ERASTVS-PRO-AED/S-P-STRAVIT. This Latin inscription would be read, *Erastus pro aedilitate sua pecunia stravit.* "Erastus, in return for the aedileship, laid the pavement at his own expense." The Roman official known as the "Aedile" was in charge of various public works. Paul, in Romans 16:23 mentions an Erastus "the city treasurer," probably of Corinth from which the apostle was writing. Since the term rendered "treasurer" can have the wider connotation of "steward, manager," it is at least possible that the two men named Erastus are the same person who became a friend of Paul.

Inscriptions discovered in the vicinity of the agora identify shops as *macellum* and *piscario,* "meat market," and "fish market." Paul used the Greek term *makellon,* "meat market" in I Corinthians 10:25. Another inscription, now partially destroyed, bears the words "Synagogue of the Hebrews." The style of writing indicates that it was made after the time of Paul, who first arrived in Corinth in A.D. 50, yet the inscription may have been carved on the lintel of the synagogue which was the successor to the one in which Paul preached (Acts 18:4).

BIBLIOGRAPHY. T. H. Shear, "Excavations in the Theatre District and Tombs of Corinth in 1929," *AJA, XXXIII* (1929), pp. 525-526; O. Broneer, "Corinth, Center of Paul's Missionary Works in Greece," *BA,* XIV, 1951, pp. 77-96; W. A. McDonald, "Archaeology and St. Paul's Journey in Greek Lands. Part III: Corinth," *BA,* 5, 1942, pp. 36-48; H. J. Cadbury, "Erastus of Corinth," *JBL,* L, 1931, pp. 42-58; "The Mecellum of Corinth," *JBL* LIII, 1934, pp. 34-41.; American School of Classical Studies at Athens, *Ancient Corinth, A Guide to the Excavations* (6th ed., 1954).

COVENANT, COVENANTS. The Hebrew word *berith*, which occurs over 280 times in the Old Testament, is used to describe a wide variety of agreements between participating parties. The same term is used to describe the relationship that existed between God and Israel.

Documents from many different ancient Near Eastern sites extending from Babylon to Asia Minor and Palestine in area, and from the late third millennium B.C. to the middle of the eighth century B.C. in time, provide a valuable background against which to study the various Old Testament covenants. Of particular value are those documents which define inter-tribal, inter-state and international treaties. There are many resemblances, at least in their formal and legal aspects, between the Near Eastern Suzerain-vassal treaties and the covenant between God and man.

I. *Near Eastern Treaties Available for Study.* Two treaties which go back to the period when the Sumerian states flourished in Lower Mesopotamia *ca.* 2500 B.C. show that at this early date there were parity treaties between states of more or less equal strength, as well as treaties imposed by a victorious ruler on a defeated enemy. Both types were well known in the second millennium. Fragments of a treaty imposed by Rim-Sin of Akkad on an Elamite prince towards the end of the eighteenth century B.C. have been preserved. Documents from °Mari on the Middle Euphrates, dating to *ca.* 1750-1700 B.C., show that treaties of friendship were common between small states or tribal groups, although no complete treaties are extant. From °Alalakh, a little to the east of modern Antioch, come three texts which deal with interstate treaties, one from the eighteenth century B.C., and two from the fifteenth century B.C. There are references to treaties between early Assyrian kings and the rulers of Mari in the eighteenth century B.C. and between Assyria and Babylonia in the fifteenth century B.C. The famous °Amarna correspondence makes it clear that in the fourteenth century B.C. the rulers of Egypt were requiring their vassals in West Asia to undertake vassal treaties, although no formal treaty documents have so far been discovered.

By far the most significant of all second millennium treaties were those between the

Hittites and their vassals. Two important archives have been discovered in recent years, that at the ancient Hittite capital of Hattusas in Turkey, and that at the ancient Canaanite town of °Ugarit, the modern Ras Shamra, on the Syrian coast. The Hittite rulers Suppiluliumas (*ca.* 1380-1350 B.C.), Mursilis (*ca.* 1339-1306 B.C.), Muwatallis (*ca.* 1306-1282 B.C.), Hattusilis III (*ca.* 1275-1250 B.C.) and Tudhalia IV (*ca.* 1250-1220 B.C.) entered into treaties with many neighboring petty kings. Numerous treaty documents have been preserved intact.

From the first millennium B.C. come several Assyrian vassal treaties, the most important being those of Ashur-nirari V (754-725 B.C.) and Esarhaddon (681-669 B.C.) with their vassals.

Finally a valuable Aramaic treaty between Mati'ilu of Arpad and his vassal Bar-ga'ayah has been preserved in three separate documents.

II. *Characteristics of the Near Eastern Treaties.* The Hittite suzerainty treaty may be taken as giving a general picture of the literary structure of the Near Eastern treaty. The following elements were regularly present in the Hittite treaty texts, and presumably in other treaty texts; (a) the preamble, which identifies the author of the treaty and gives his titles and attributes; (b) the historical prologue, in which the benevolent deeds of the great king on behalf of his vassal are recounted and made the ground of the suzerain's appeal to the vassal to render future obedience in gratitude for past benefits; (c) the treaty stipulations — (i) general clauses which were in the nature of principles on which future relations between the parties were to be based, (ii) specific stipulations; (d) the divine witnesses and guarantors of the treaty; (e) the maledictions (curses) and benedictions (blessings). In addition to these standard elements there was normally some provision for depositing the treaty document in the sanctuary, for a periodic reading of the treaty document, for an oath of acceptance of the treaty by the vassal, and for a religious ceremony of ratification, often involving blood sacrifices.

The historical prologue was of special significance. Whereas it was normally brief in the parity treaties, perhaps for the reason that the previous relations between the parties were not very happy, in the suzerainty treaties it was often of considerable length. It seems clear that it was regarded as a vital element in the whole treaty document for it provided the *raison d'être* for the establishment of the treaty. It was on the basis of favors extended to the vassal and his subjects by the great king and his predecessors that the suzerain founded his claim to the acceptance of the treaty by the vassal and also to his loyal service in future days.

One further point of interest for Old Testament studies is that in the Hittite treaties the literary pattern was not a rigid one. There was a considerable variation possible both in the order in which the elements occurred and in the wording of each section. In some cases elements were omitted, whether deliberately or by accident it is difficult to say. This allowance for variation permitted the adaptation of the literary pattern to each particular situation.

III. *The Treaties in the Old Testament.* The patriarchal records refer to several inter-tribal covenants (Gen. 14:13; 21:22-24; 26:26-32; 31:44-55) which probably followed the pattern of the Mari inter-tribal covenants. The Mari practice of receiving neighboring tribal groups into a relationship of peace may provide an explanation of the acceptance of Joshua by the men of Gibeon (Josh. 9) or of David by Achish, king of Gath (I Sam. 27:1-3). Parity treaties may be seen in those between Solomon and Hiram (I Kings 5:12), between Baasha and Ben-hadad of Damascus (I Kings 15:19) and between Ahab and Ben-hadad (I Kings 20:34).

Examples of vassal treaties may be seen in the case of David's arrangements with defeated Aramean states (II Sam. 8:6, 14) and with the states of Moab, Ammon and Edom. Solomon likewise ruled over these states (I Kings 4:21). When Omri conquered Moab he must have imposed a vassal treaty to judge from the fact that Mesha paid tribute to Israel (II Kings 3:4f.). See Moabite Stone.

During the ninth century B.C. the people of Israel began to feel the effects of Assyrian expansion. Jehu of Israel submitted as a vassal to Assyria in 841 B.C. The last kings of Israel were vassals of the Assyrian rulers Tiglath-pileser III (745-727 B.C.) (II Kings 15:19 f., 29 f.), Shalmaneser V

(727-722 B.C.) and Sargon (722-705 B.C.).

Judah too was a vassal of Assyria, first to Tiglath-pileser III (II Kings 16:7-10), and then to Sennacherib (II Kings 18:19), Esarhaddon (II Chron. 33:11f.) and Ashurbanipal. After Judah broke free from Assyria she soon became a vassal of Egypt (II Kings 23:29-35) and then of Babylon (II Kings 24:1, 10-17). It was when Judah's last ruler Zedekiah broke his covenant and despised the curses of the covenant that Judah was finally destroyed by Nebuchadnezzar (Ezek. 17:13-21).

The nature of all these vassal treaties may be understood by comparison with the extant treaties between the Assyrians and their vassals.

IV. *The adaptation of the Near Eastern Treaty Pattern to Define the Covenant between God and Israel.* The Near Eastern Treaty pattern may be discerned in many areas of the Old Testament where the covenant between Yahweh, the God of Israel, and his people is under discussion (*e.g.* Exod. 19-24; Josh. 24). Yahweh takes the place of the Great King who sets before his vassals the stipulations and commandments which will ensure fellowship and peace. The first clear application in the Old Testament of the Near Eastern Treaty pattern to the covenant between Yahweh and Israel is in reference to the Sinai Covenant which constituted the whole nation as Yahweh's covenant people. There were preceding mighty delivering acts which formed the basis of Yahweh's appeal to Israel. There were stipulations, namely, the Decalogue (Exod. 20), there was a religious ceremony (Exod. 24), and an oath of allegiance. This covenant was renewed again and again (Josh. 24; I Sam. 12; II Kings 23; Neh. 9, 10, etc.). At each covenant renewal, the acts of Yahweh were recited, the covenant stipulations declared, and the oath of allegiance taken. There were "blessings" for those who obeyed and "curses" for those who disobeyed (Deut. 27; Lev. 26; Josh. 8). Indeed, it was a fundamental part of Israel's view of history that in obedience to Yahweh and his covenant Israel would find prosperity and peace, while the rejection of that covenant could only lead to disaster. Prophets, priests, and poets reiterated the point again and again. In particular, the continuing burden of the prophets of Israel was that sin was a rejection of the covenant and would lead to judgment.

It seems clear that a picture which was widely known and understood in the secular environment in the realm of international law, was taken over and adapted to give concrete expression to the deeper concept of the divine election of Israel.

V. *The Significance of the Near Eastern Treaties for Old Testament Studies.* The Near Eastern treaties in their literary structure, their vocabulary, their historical setting, and to some extent in their general spirit, have significance for Old Testament studies in several areas. First of all they provide a clue to the probable content of many of the "secular" treaties of the Old Testament for which, in general, details are not given in the Old Testament itself. Secondly, they provide a literary pattern which may be used in the interpretation of certain Old Testament passages. In particular, in certain areas of the Old Testament where literary critics have, at times, desired to remove sections of a passage which are said to be editorial, there is a growing hesitancy to exclude passages which fit into a total Near Eastern treaty pattern. Thirdly, important comparative materials are available for vocabulary studies. It is evident that there was a widespread standard covenant vocabulary all over the ancient Near East, although Israel had her own peculiar covenant terms. Finally the fact that the covenant or treaty pattern was already widely known in the Near East before the Exodus makes its presence in the Exodus narratives more easily understandable and lends support to the view that the covenant idea in Israel was at least as old, if not considerably older, than the time of the Exodus.

BIBLIOGRAPHY. G. E. Mendenhall, *Law and Covenant in Israel and the Ancient Near East,* Pittsburg, 1955. V. Korosec, *Hethitische Staatsvertrage,* 1931. K. Baltzer, *Das Bundesformular,* 1960.

CREATION EPIC. See Enuma Elish.

CRETE. See Minoans.

CUNEIFORM. See Writing.

CYCLOPEAN MASONRY. Walls made of huge uncut blocks of limestone with a filling of smaller stones and rubble are called Cyclopean because of the belief of the Greeks

of Homer's day that they were erected by the mythological one-eyed giants known as Cyclops. Cyclopean masonry was much used by the people of °Mycenae.

CYLINDER SEALS. See Seals.

CYPRUS. Cyprus is an island at the northeastern end of the Mediterranean, about forty-five miles from the coast of Asia Minor and sixty miles from Syria. On clear days the mountains of the mainland can be seen from Cyprus. The island is 148 miles long, and its width varies from five to fifty miles. Its area comprises 3,600 square miles of largely mountainous terrain.

Since ancient times, Cyprus has been a source of timber and valuable mineral deposits. Its forests provided lumber for ship building, and Cypriots boasted that they could build their vessels without aid from foreign countries. In addition to its valuable deposits of copper, the mountains of Cyprus produced iron, lead, zinc, and silver. Pliny (*Natural History,* xxxiv. 2) states that brass was invented on Cyprus. Diamonds, emeralds, and other precious stones were also found there.

From prehistoric times Cyprus was exploited by its neighbors from the mainlands of Asia Minor and Syria. Shortly after 3000 B.C. the Island's copper attracted settlers from Anatolia (Asia Minor). Later it was subject to a succession of peoples including the Hyksos, the Egyptians and the Hittites. Thutmose III of Egypt claims to have conquered Cyprus. Mycenaean traders and settlers came to the Island, as did later Achaeans from Greece. The Greek settlements remained independent and emerged in historic times as separate kingdoms possessing Cypriot, Greek, and oriental elements.

After 1000 B.C., Cyprus suffered a period of eclipse probably brought on by the use of iron which replaced copper as the common metal. The Cypriots used their timber to construct ships and became a sea power until eclipsed by the Phoenicians. In the eighth century B.C. the Phoenicians established trading stations on Cyprus.

Subsequently Cyprus was tributary to Assyria (under Sargon); Egypt (under Ahmose II); and Persia (under Cyrus). The Cypriots supported Alexander the Great in his siege of Tyre and, after Alexander's death fell to Ptolemy and became part of the Egyptian kingdom. In 58 B.C. the Romans annexed Cyprus and made it a senatorial province under a proconsul. Salamis was its principal town, and Paphos its administrative capital.

The Kittim (Gen. 10:4) listed among the sons of Javan (i.e. the Ionians) are primarily the people of Cyprus, designated as Chittim in Isaiah 23:1. Barnabas was a Cypriot (Acts 4:36), and the Island was among the first places outside Palestine to hear the gospel (Acts 11:19-20). It was visited by Paul and Barnabas during the First Missionary Journey (Acts 13:4-13). Later Barnabas and John Mark returned to Cyprus (Acts 15:39). Three bishops from Cyprus were present at the Council of Nicaea (A.D. 325).

BIBLIOGRAPHY. Stanley Casson, *Ancient Cyprus: Its Art and Archaeology*, London, Methuen and Co., 1937. Claude D. Cobham, *An Attempt at a Bibliography of Cyprus*, Nicosia, Government Printing Office, 1900. G. F. Hill, *A History of Cyprus*, Cambridge, England, Cambridge University Press, 1940. L. and H. A. Mangolian, *The Island of Cyprus*, Nicosia, Mangolian Brothers, 1947.

CYRUS. *See* Persia.

CYRUS CYLINDER. During his excavations at Babylon (1879-82), Hormuzd Rassam discovered a clay barrel inscription in which Cyrus describes and justifies his policies. Concerning his conquest of Babylon, Cyrus says:

Marduk . . . looked through all the countries, searching for a righteous ruler. . . . He pronounced the name of Cyrus king of Anshan, declared him to be the ruler of all the world. . . . He made him set out on the road to Babylon, going at his side like a real friend. His widespread troops — their number, like that of the water of a river, could not be established — strolled along, their weapons packed away. Without any battle, he [i.e. Marduk] made him [Cyrus] enter his [Marduk's] town, Babylon, sparing Babylon any calamity. He delivered into his hands Nabunaid, the king who did not worship him.

Having taken Babylon, Cyrus made it his policy to allow captive peoples to return to their homelands and rebuilt their temples. It was in the spirit of this policy that the Jews were encouraged to return to Jerusalem (II Chron. 36:23; Ezra 1:2-4). The Cyrus Cylinder says:

As to the region from . . . as far as Ashur and Susa, Akkad, Eshnunna, the towns Zamban, Me-Turnu, Der, as well as the region of the Gutians, I returned to these sacred cities on the other side of the Tigris, the sanctuaries of which have been in ruins for a long time, the images which used to live in them, and I established for them permanent sanctuaries. I also gathered all their former inhabitants and returned to them their habitations. Furthermore, I resettled upon the command of Marduk, the great lord, all the gods of Sumer and Akkad whom Nabunaid has brought into Babylon to the anger of the lord of the gods [i.e. Marduk], unharmed, in their former chapels, the places which make them happy.

CYRUS CYLINDER. Courtesy, British Museum

D

DAMASCUS. Damascus is a very ancient city of Syria (Aram) located in the fertile oasis region east of the Antilebanon range with snowy Mt. Hermon rising majestically on the southwest. Its Hebrew (*Dammeseq*) and Aramaic name (*Darmeseq*) occur in the Bible (II Kings 16:10). In the °Amarna Letters it occurs as *Dimashqa, Dumashqa,* Egyptian *Timashgi.* Its Arabic name is *Dimashq* or *Dimaskq ash-Sham.* The present-day city is the capital of Syria, representing one of the oldest continuously occupied cities in the world.

I. *Damascus in the Patriarchal Age (ca.* 1850-1600 B.C.). The first mention of the district (*Apum*) in which the ancient city was located occurs in the °Execration Texts dating about 1850-1825 B.C. and belonging to the first half of the reign of the Pharaoh Amenemhet III (*ca.* 1837-1789 B.C.). The district of *Apum* is well-known as *Api* (*Upe*) of the Amarna Letters as the designation of a land (*mâtu*) in which Damascus was located. The name *Apum* also is attested some three generations after the Execration Texts in the °Mari Tablets from Tell el-Hariri on the Middle Euphrates, discovered in 1936. This early name of the Damascene region is apparently from the Akkadian word *âpum,* later *âpu* (often written *abi* or *api*), denoting a "forest or thicket of reeds (canebrake)." This is a singularly fitting description of the eastern Damascene, a region the Arabs call *El Merj* ("the meadow land"), which is dotted with reed-filled lakes and marshes.

The name of Damascus at the time of Abraham *ca.* 2,000 B.C. was probably *Mesheq,* as the difficult reference in Genesis 15:2, 3, apparently suggests. W. F. Albright's reconstruction of the text of this passage runs: "And the 'son of my house' [heir presumptive] is the 'son of Mesheq,' (inhabitant of Mesheq), which is Damascus . . . and behold the 'son of the house' shall be my heir." (See Merrill F. Unger, *Israel and the Aramaeans of Damascus,* London, 1957, p. 4).

II. *Damascus under Egyptian Control (ca.* 1475 B.C.). The city is first mentioned extra-biblically among the Asiatic conquests of the great empire-builder Thutmose III (1490-1436) in his Annals preserved in the great Karnak temple of Amun at Thebes. The city appears as *Timasku,* thirteenth in order in the enumeration of conquered Palestinian-Syrian city states taken on Thutmose' "first victorious campaign," when Megiddo, the key fortress in Esdraelon, fell to Egyptian control.

III. *Damascus in the Amarna Age (ca.* 1375 B.C.). The °Amarna Letters, discovered in Egypt in 1886, introduce us to an uprising against Egyptian control of Syria in the general region of Upe and furnish

PANORAMIC VIEW OF DAMASCUS TODAY. Courtesy, Photo Sport, Beirut

an intimate glimpse of the political status of Damascus and the contiguous city-states at the time, especially Qatna, just south of Hamath on the Orontes. King Akizzi of Qatna, whose realm bordered on the north of Damascus, pays high tribute to the loyalty of Damascus to the Pharaoh Amenhotep IV (ca. 1375-1370 B.C.), for he uses its fidelity as a standard of comparison for that of his own realm. "O Sire, as Damascus [al Timashgi] in the land of Upe [ina mat Upe] is faithful to the pharaoh, so Qatna is likewise loyal" (EA 53:63-65).

Biriawaza, the representative of Egyptian government in Upe and Damascus, employed °Habiru (mercenary soldiers) to maintain his country's authority in this region (EA 195:27 ff.). If there was a king in Upe, as seems clear from the °Boghazkoy texts (E. F. Weidner, Politische Dokumente aus Kleinasien Boghazkoi-Studien, Helt 8, p. 14, lines 40 ff.), he is not mentioned in the Amarna Letters. Biriawaza, on the other hand, was apparently a prince or noble of Mittani (a Mesopotamian kingdom) linked in some way by marriage to the Egyptian royal family, as was common in this period.

IV. Damascus in the Period of Hittite Ascendancy (ca. 1350 B.C.). Egyptian control of Damascus was to suffer a temporary disruption with the upsurge of Hittite power, under Shuppiluliumas (ca. 1380-1346 B.C.), who sacked several cities of Mittani and invaded Syria. Ariwana, mentioned as king of the land of Apina at this time, resisted the Hittite invasion. Although the Hittites claimed victory and the despoilment of Apina, which is clearly to be identified with Upe (Ape), the land of Damascus mentioned in the Amarna Letters (cf. Weidner, Boghazkoi-Studien VII, p. 14), they withdrew from the region. In Shuppiluliumas' reorganization of his Syrian conquests, he established a series of small vassal kingdoms, but his dominion did not extend to Damascus and the land of Upe, which must have again reverted to Egyptian control, as in Amarna days.

The aggressive Pharaohs Seti I (1319-1301 B.C.) and Ramesses II (1301-1234 B.C.) attempted to regain Egypt's Asiatic domains north of Upe. The latter clashed with the Hittites in the famous battle of Kadesh. So far from a brilliant victory as painted by the fulsome Egyptian eulogist,

the Hittite army under Mutwatallis is said to have driven the disordered enemy as far as "the land Apa," the region of Damascus (Albrecht Gotze, OL XXXII, 1929, p. 837). Eventually Ramesses II and the Hittites concluded a treaty of peace in 1280 B.C., a cuneiform copy of which was found by Hugo Winckler at Boghazköy, the Hittite capital in Asia Minor. In the delimited spheres of influence Egypt apparently controlled the region of Damascus and the country south of Hamath, although the treaty mentions no specific boundary. Lack of Hittite remains south of Hamath shows that the Hittites exercised no permanent control over the Damascene.

V. Damascus under Hebrew Control (ca. 1000-930 B.C.). Aramean settlement in Syria and northeastern Palestine took place in the several centuries following the Exodus and Israel's conquest of Canaan. Damascus in this era became settled by Arameans. A reminiscence of an early clash between Aram and Israel is preserved in Judges 3:7-11. By Saul's time, 1020 B.C., powerful Aramean kingdoms such as Zobah, Abel, Beth-maacah, Tob and Geshur had grown up on Israel's northeastern frontiers. Saul clashed with these principalities (I Sam. 14:47) (LXX). David conquered them, (II Sam. 8:1-18), so that under the Davidic-Solomonic Empire Damascus became a part of the Hebrew kingdom.

However, during the latter years of Solomon's reign Rezon, a former official of Hadadezer of Zobah, established a strong Aramean center of power in Damascus and flouted Solomon (I Kings 11:24). This aggressive city-state, emboldened to defy even the mighty Solomon, after his death was destined to enjoy rapid growth and to prove a serious threat to Israel, especially since the latter was weakened by the division of the twelve-tribe kingdom.

VI. Damascus as a Rival of Israel (ca. 930-879 B.C.). Rezon, who established Damascus as a dominant Aramean power (I Kings 11:24), was evidently not its first king, unless he is to be identified with Hezion, the father of Tabrimmon, the father of the famous Benhadad I, mentioned in the Dynastic list preserved in I Kings 15:18. This order of early Aramean kings is corroborated extra-Biblically by the important Benhadad Stele discovered in 1940 north of Aleppo in North Syria (see *BASOR* 87, October 1942, pp. 23-29; 90, April 1943, pp. 30-32; Maurice Dunand, "Stele araméenne didiée à Melquart," *Bulletin de Musée de Beyrouth* Vol. iii, 1941, pp. 65-76). Hezion and Tabrimmon quickly took advantage of the division of the Israelite kingdom to seize political ascendancy in Syria and to bequeath Benhadad I (*ca.* 883-843 B.C.) with a kingdom strong enough to challenge all foes. Asa of Judah (917-876 B.C.) actually sent the latter a bribe to attack Baasha king of Israel (*ca.* 900-877 B.C.). Hard-pressed Judah obtained immediate relief. Baasha had to abandon his fortification of Ramah, as a threat to Jerusalem, and retire to his capital Tirzah (I Kings 15:16-22), as Benhadad I seized the golden opportunity for extending the power of Damascus, and invaded northeastern Israel (*ca.* 879 B.C.).

VII. *Damascus in Conflict with Israel* (*ca.* 879-843 B.C.). Although Benhadad I's power substantially increased as a result of his victory over Baasha and the period of dynastic weakness that followed, the founding of a new aggressive dynasty by Omri (*ca.* 876-869 B.C.) resulted in the strengthening of Israel as a formidable foe to Aramean expansion. Foremost among Omri's achievements were the founding of the fortress capital city of Samaria and his control of Transjordanian trade routes, attested by the Mesha Stone (lines 4-8), which shows he conquered northern Moab, exacting heavy annual tribute (cf. II Kings 3:4). Evidently Benhadad I hesitated to invade Israel during Omri's reign, but did so some five years before the end of the reign of Ahab (*ca.* 869-850 B.C.), suffering a defeat that nearly cost Benhadad his life (I Kings 20:1).

The return of the Syrians the next year (*ca.* 854 B.C.) to retrieve their humiliating defeat resulted in a worse defeat near Aphek, modern Fiq east of the Sea of Galilee (I Kings 20:23-34). Ahab magnanimously spared the life of the defeated Benhadad. The next year 853 B.C. found Ahab allied with Benhadad to stop the formidable invasion of Assyria under Shalmaneser III (858-824 B.C.) at *Qarqar on the Orontes, guarding the approaches to the city of Hamath and all lower Syria. The famous battle of Qarqar is recorded on the Monolith Inscription of Shalmaneser, now in the British Museum. "Hadadezer of Aram" (Benhadad I, as now is known from the evidence of the *Melcarth Stele, see above) heads the anti-Syrian coalition followed by Irhuleni of Hamath and *Ahabbu Sir'elai* (Ahab of Israel). Resistance to the Assyrian was evidently discouraging to Shalmaneser, despite his claims of victory, for he not only failed to follow up his boasted successes, but did not resume attack on Hamath or Damascus till some half-dozen years later.

The three-year period of peace between Syria and Israel (I Kings 20:1) terminated in Ahab's attempt to recover Ramoth in Gilead (*ca.* 851 B.C.). Benhadad's inexcusable perfidy in failing to restore the Israelite towns which had been taken by Damascus, in accordance with the terms of the treaty of Aphek (I Kings 22:1-53), provoked Ahab into an attack that resulted in his death (*ca.* 850 B.C.).

In the anti-Assyrian coalitions of 849, 848 and 845 B.C. "Adadidri" (Benhadad I) is mentioned prominently, but Israel is not mentioned as such, although it may have sent contingents under Ahaziah (*ca.* 850-849 B.C.) or Joram (*ca.* 849-842 B.C.).

VIII. *Damascus as Master of Israel* (843-801 B.C.). Benhadad I's long reign came to an end in 843 B.C. by the hand of a usurper Hazael, whom the Assyrians aptly called "son of nobody." By 841 B.C. Hazael had gained control. In the confusion Ahab's son, Joram, was able to regain Ramoth in Gilead. But the Omride dynasty was soon wiped out by Jehu (*ca.* 842-815 B.C.), the extirpator of the Baal Melcarth cult from Israel. Jehu earned the implacable hatred of Hazael when he refused to ally with Syria in the Assyrian advance under Shalmaneser III in 841 and 837 B.C. Damascus had to face the Assyrian advance alone, while Jehu is pictured on the *Black Obelisk as humbly prostrating himself and paying tribute to the Assyrian emperor.

When Shalmaneser had to abandon his Syrian campaigns to attend to other pressing problems after 837 B.C., Hazael at last found himself free to use his power of conquest against Israel and Judah. During Jehu's reign he relentlessly harassed Israel, especially the country east of the Jordan (II Kings 10:32, 33). Later he reduced Jehu's son Jehoahaz (815-801 B.C.) to an extreme state of humiliation (II Kings 13:1-9, 22, 25) in which Israel was nothing more than a menial vassal.

IX. *Damascus and a Revitalized Israelite State* (801-746 B.C.). Benhadad II succeeded his father Hazael as king of Damascus after the latter's decease (*ca.* 801 B.C.). Adadnirari III's conquests in Northern Syria (805-802 B.C.), including his successful campaign against Damascus, so weakened Aramean power that Joash, the son of Jehoahaz (*ca.* 801-786 B.C.) was able to recoup Israel's fortunes (II Kings 13:25). However, Damascus was able to recover from the Assyrian blow as shown by the Zakir Stele discovered in 1903, which names "Birhadad [Benhadad II] son of Hazael, king of Aram" as heading a coalition of more than a dozen kings of North Syria against "Zakir king of Hamath and Lu'ash" (*ca.* 870 B.C.).

Meanwhile Joash's successes against Benhadad II were continued by his son Jeroboam II (*ca.* 876-746 B.C.). The latter not only recovered all Israelite territory which had been lost to Aram, but was able to lift Israel to the acme of political and economic power not enjoyed since Solomonic days. Uzziah (Azariah) of Judah (*ca.* 783-742 B.C.) enjoyed a similar prosperity.

According to II Kings 14:28 Jeroboam II "recovered Damascus and Hamath . . . for Israel." This can only mean Israel became master of Aram in the days of Jeroboam II as Damascus had become master of Israel in the days of Hazael and Jehoahaz. Only by so doing could Jeroboam be said to have "restored the frontier of Israel from the pass of Hamath" (between Kadesh and Riblah) "as far as the sea of Arabah" (II Kings 14:25).

X. *Damascus and Its Fall to Assyria* (746-732 B.C.). After the events preserved in the Zakir Stele, practically nothing is known of Benhadad II and his successors on the throne of Damascus. The next monarch encountered in extant sources is Rezen (*ca.* 750?-732 B.C.). His name occurs as *Raṣunnu* in the Assyrian sources, making his debut in the Annals of Tiglath-pileser III (745-727 B.C.). The weakness of Israel occasioned by the extermination of the Jehu dynasty and the ensuing civil war from *ca.* 746-743 B.C. gave Damascus a chance to throw off Israelite control and to regain some of its former vitality before a final crushing

blow from an awakened Assyria would bring both it and the kingdom of Israel to an end.

Meantime the balance of power had shifted to the south. Azariah of Judah (*Azriyua of Yaudi*) in 843 B.C. headed a coalition of Syrian-Palestinian states against Assyria, as is learned from Tiglath-pileser's Annals (E. Schrader, *The Cuneiform Inscriptions and the O. T. I.,* 208 ff., H. M. Haydn, "Azariah of Judah and Tiglath-pileser III," *JBL,* 28, 1909, pp. 182-199, E. Forrer, *Die Provinzeinteilung des assyrisches Reiches,* p. 57). Meanwhile Menahem of Israel (*ca.* 745-738 B.C.) paid tribute to Tiglath-pileser III, whose name was also Pul (Pulu), shown from a Babylonian king list and the Babylonian Chronicle (II Kings 15:19, 20; I Chron. 5:26).

Tiglath-pileser's preoccupation in Urartu (737-735 B.C.) gave a breathing spell to Syria Palestine and the opportunity to form a new anti-Assyrian coalition headed by Pekah of Israel and Rezin of Damascus. Ahaz of Judah (*ca.* 735-715 B.C.) adamantly refused to join, so Pekah and Rezin advanced against him, precipitating the Syro-Ephraemite war *ca.* 735 B.C. (II Kings 16:5; Isa. 7:1-3). Ahaz dispatched an embassy with heavy tribute to Tiglath-pileser III to bribe him to attack Aram and Israel. The Assyrians invaded Northern Israel, deporting the inhabitants to Assyria (II Kings 15:29).

With Israel duly castigated Tiglath-pileser now turned to Damascus to punish the other prominent rebel, Rezin. Events center there in the next two years 733, 732 B.C., as the Assyrian eponym list indicates. Despite the mutilated condition of Tiglath-pileser's records dealing with the siege and fall of Damascus, the essential facts are evident. The Assyrians overthrew the Aramean state and its capital city, Damascus. In the long siege, concerning which little is known, for not even Tiglath-pileser's description of it has survived, Panammu of Samal, one of the loyal Syrian tributaries of the Assyrian king, perished, as is known from an Aramaic inscription of the Syrian vassal. This bit of evidence supplies a hint how intense the struggle was before Damascus finally capitulated in 732 B.C.

Assyrian records reveal a terrific destruction. Some 591 towns of the "sixteen districts of Aram," the Assyrian declares, "I destroyed like the mounds left by a flood"

(*ARAB* I, 177). Hadaru, southeast of Damascus, said to be the birthplace of Rezin, was wiped out and eight hundred of its citizens deported.

The Bible connects the fall of Damascus with Ahaz's appeal and payment of tribute to Assyria. "And the king of Assyria hearkened unto him . . . and went up against Damascus and took it, and carried the people of it captive to Kir, and slew Rezin" (II Kings 16:9). The tablet recording Rezin's death, found and read by Henry Rawlinson, a pioneer Assyriologist, was unfortunately lost (E. Schrader, *The Cuneiform Inscriptions and the O. T.*, I, pp. 252, 257).

With Rezin's death terminated the long and powerful line of kings that sat on the throne of Damascus and which interacted influentially both in war and peace with the kingdoms of Israel and Judah for almost two centuries. With Rezin's death the Aramean kingdom of Damascus passed away forever.

XI. *Damascus As an Assyrian Province* (732-612 B.C.). With the capture of Damascus in 732 B.C. its entire territory was incorporated into the Assyrian Empire. Out of its area four new Assyrian provinces were formed — Subutu, Dimashqu (Damascus), Qarninu and Haurena. Subutu lay north of Damascus and Qarninu and Haurena to the south. The province of Magidu (Galilee) was ruled from Megiddo and the province of Du'ru (Sharon) from Dor. Besieged under Shalmaneser (726-722 B.C.), Samaria fell to Sargon II by 721 B.C., and Israel also was added to the Assyrian Empire.

Even under Assyrian domination Damascus displayed its inveterate love of freedom. The Assyrian Eponym canon in 727 B.C. lists an expedition against the city, apparently to crush some civil commotion. Moreover, there was a last intrepid attempt at revolt in 720 B.C., known from the records of Sargon II (721-704 B.C.). It was, of course, put down as the city's spirit was finally quelled under Assyrian political and military might.

XII. *Damascus in Later Pre-Christian Times.* With its fall to Assyria Damascus entered upon a period of comparative political unimportance. However, under Assyrian rule till 612 B.C. and then under Babylonian control (612-539 B.C.) and Persian rule (539-323 B.C.) it continued as a wealthy trading center. Not until the establishment of the Seleucid Kingdom with its capital at Antioch, did Damascus lose its position as the chief city of Syria. Through Roman policy Damascus became the capital of an independent Nabatean kingdom in 85 B.C. In 65 B.C. as a result of Rome's conquest of Syria, Damascus was placed under a Nabatean governor.

XIII. *Damascus in New Testament Times.* When Paul came to Damascus (Acts 9:2-8), the city was a free town and member of the Decapolis, a chain of ten autonomous cities of the general region. Like its free sister towns Damascus coined its own money, extant examples surviving from the reigns of Augustus, Tiberius and Nero, but none from the reign of Caligula A.D. 37-41. Some

WALL OF DAMASCUS. Although the Syrian city of Damascus was superseded in importance by Antioch, it remained a favored city of the Decapolis. Courtesy, E. Leslie Carlson

THE STREET CALLED
STRAIT. *Courtesy, Merrill
Unger*

scholars think the paranoiac emperor handed over the free city to Aretas IV (9 B.C. — A.D. 40) for I Corinthians 11:32 mentions that "the governor of King Aretas was guarding the city of the Damascenes" when Paul escaped. Others deny that Aretas was in possession of the city, and assume that the governor of Aretas was merely waiting outside the city, perhaps a neighboring sheikh, to catch Paul as he emerged (cf. C. S. C. Williams, *The Acts of the Apostles* in *Harper's New Testament Commentaries,* 1957, p. 126; H. J. Cadbury, *The Book of Acts in History,* 1955, pp. 19-21).

XIV. *Damascus in Later Times.* During the following centuries the city became a center of Christianity. One of the famous edifices was the Church of Saint John Baptist, begun by Emperor Theodosius and completed by Arcadius. It was erected on the site of an ancient temple of Hadad, the West Semitic storm-god.

With the rise of Islam in the seventh century A.D. Damascus came under Moslem influence. Today the city is the capital of modern Syria, a tourist mecca since it is one of the most thoroughly Oriental cities in the Near East. It is situated on a fertile plain rich in beautiful gardens and orchards, forming a well-watered grove more than fifteen miles in circuit.

BIBLIOGRAPHY. R. Hartmann, *Enzyklopaedie des Islam* I, 1908-1913, pp. 941-49; Sina Schiffer, *Die Aramäer,* Leipzig, 1911; Emil Kraeling, *Aram and Israel,* New York, 1918; H. von Kiesling, *Damaskus. Alter und Neues aus Syrien,* 1919; C. Watzinger and K. Wulzinger, *Damaskus die antike Stadt und die islamische Stadt,* 2 vols., 1921-24; E. Honigmann, *Historische Topographie von Nordsyrien im Altertum,* ZDPV, 1923, pp. 149-93; 47, 1924, pp. 1-64; J. Sauvaget, *Les monuments historique de Damas,* 1932; Alfred Jepsen, "Israel Und Damaskus," *Archiv für Orientforschung* XIV, 1942, pp. 141-161; Merrill F. Unger, *Israel and the Aramaeans of Damascus,* London, 1957.

DARIUS. *See* Persia.

DATING. For discussions of the dating of archaeological materials see Archaeology, Fluorine Dating, Pottery, Radio Carbon Dating.

DEAD SEA SCROLLS. This name is used to designate: (a) the original scrolls discovered in a cave at Qumran, near the northwestern end of the Dead Sea, probably early in 1947; (b) fragments of scrolls, and later, additional scrolls, found in nearby caves as a result of careful exploration of the region; (c) fragments of scrolls found at Wadi Murabbaʿât, about twelve miles SSW of °Qumran; and (d) fragments of scrolls found at Wadi Mird, about six miles WSW of Qumran. Since these latter two sets of discoveries come from quite different periods and locations than the Qumran materials, they should not be included in the same term. However, they were discovered in the exploration that resulted from the Qumran discoveries, and were studied at the same time (and, in fact, are being published in the same series), hence, they have been included in the term "Dead Sea Scrolls." For several reasons, the term is not descriptive, (nor are the terms, "Scrolls from the Judean Desert," and " 'Ain Feshkha Scrolls"), and it might better be replaced with the more accurate term "Qumran manuscripts and fragments." (For the location of Qumran and the archeological excavations that resulted from the Scrolls discovery, *see* article Qumran.)

The Wadi Murabbaʿât discoveries — to dispose of the non-Qumran materials first — included Biblical manuscripts, letters, contracts, etc., from the second century A.D. The type of handwriting was important for

THE GENERAL AREA IN
WHICH THE DEAD SEA
SCROLLS WERE DISCOV-
ERED

comparative chronology, and assisted in dating the paleography of the Qumran materials. Two letters signed by Bar-Kokba, the leader of the Second Jewish Revolt (A.D. 132-135), and other letters that mention his name, establish the date. More important for Biblical studies is the text of the Biblical materials from this location. Scholars have long been convinced that the Hebrew consonantal text of the Old Testament was standardized about the end of the first century A.D. The Murabba'ât materials are entirely of the "Masoretic" or standard text, whereas the Qumran materials, a century or two earlier than those from Murabba'ât, represent at least three text types, as we shall see below.

The Wadi Mird discoveries contain Biblical materials written in Greek and Aramaic, dating from the fifth to the eighth centuries A.D. Their value for Qumran studies at present seems to be marginal. The New Testament materials found at Mird — the only New Testament documents found in the Dead Sea Scrolls, it should be emphasized — add little or nothing to our already vast supply of materials for the study of the New Testament text.

The Original "Dead Sea Scrolls" were discovered accidentally by Bedouin of the Ta'âmireh tribe. Their treasure, which at first they thought might be used for making sandals, was ultimately placed in the care of Mar Athanasius Y. Samuel, Metropolitan of the Syrian Orthodox Church. Part was sold to Prof. Eleazar L. Sukenik, of the Hebrew University, Jerusalem, and part, after having been taken to the American School of Oriental Research at Jerusalem for examination, was carried to America for safe-keeping. Ultimately these scrolls, too, were bought by Hebrew University. The scrolls bought and subsequently published by Sukenik were: (a) an incomplete scroll of Isaiah (identified commonly by the *siglum* 1QIs^b, meaning the "b" or second manuscript of Isaiah from Cave 1 of Qumran); (b) portions of a scroll of *Thanksgiving Hymns,* called by the Hebrew name *Hodayot,* 1QH; and (c) a scroll called *The War of the Sons of Light against the Sons of Darkness,* or the *War Scroll* 1QM (for *Milḥamah,* "war"). The scrolls published by Millar Burrows for the American Schools of Oriental Research were the following: (a) a complete Isaiah scroll, 1QIs^a (b) a description of the rules of membership, called commonly the *Manual of Discipline,* 1QS (for *Sérek,* 'order, rule'); (c) a commentary on the prophecy of Habakkuk, 1QpHab (p for *pésher,* "commentary"). A fourth scroll in the lot taken to the American School could not be opened at the time, but from a fragment broken from it which contained the name Lamech, it was called the "Lamech Scroll." Later, when it was opened and published, it was identified as a *Genesis Apocryphon,* or an expanded work using Biblical and apocryphal materials for Genesis, 1QApGen.

These manuscripts were written on leather or parchment, in good handwriting, and are, except for the *Genesis Apocryphon,* in a good

185

state of preservation. Some idea of the sizes of the manuscripts can be gained from the following facts: The widest of the scrolls is the *Hodayot,* which contains thirty-five to forty-one lines in a column or about thirteen inches in height. (Scrolls are held with the rolls vertical, so that the "width" of the scroll actually becomes the height of the column, and the "length" of the scroll is the horizontal measurement.) The narrowest is the *Habakkuk Commentary* which has only eighteen lines in a column or about six inches in height (but about two or three lines have been eaten away along the bottom edge). The complete Isaiah manuscript contains about twenty-nine lines to a column, and the column is about ten inches high (i.e., the scroll is ten inches wide). This same Isaiah manuscript is the longest, consisting of fifty-four columns written on seventeen sheets of leather sewn together to form a continuous scroll twenty-four feet long. The original length of the *Hodayot,* or *Thanksgiving Hymns,* is not known, for it was found in several pieces, and was written in two different hands. In some manuscripts, the columns and the lines were ruled, using a pointed instrument that left an impressed line (like that of a ball-point pen that has refused to write), and the letters were hung from the lines. The excellent condition of the scrolls is at least in part due to the fact that they had been placed in jars which obviously had been made for the purpose, and the covers had been sealed. The *Genesis Apocryphon,* on the other hand, had not been placed in a jar.

Dating handwriting is the task of a specialist (called, in the case of ancient writing, a paleographer), and the results are comparative, unless other evidence is found. In other words, the expert can say that a certain specimen of writing is "earlier than *a* and later than *b,*" and if he has approximate dates for *a* and *b,* he can use them to bracket the subject of his study. Experts dated the Qumran manuscripts in the middle of the second century B.C., with some manuscripts possibly a bit later (and some of the

subsequent discoveries dated a century or more earlier). This estimate is now established beyond reasonable doubt by at least five independent lines of evidence: (a) the cloth wrappings on the scrolls have been dated to 20 B.C. $\pm$ 200 years, by radiocarbon (Carbon-14) analysis; (b) several hundred coins found in the excavations at Qumran can be dated between 135 B.C. and A.D. 68; (c) pottery chronology for the jars that contained the scrolls and for the pottery found in great quantity in the excavations yields a date in the early Roman period, i.e., the second and first centuries B.C.; (d) comparative paleography, which now includes dated materials from Wadi Murabbaʿât is more firmly established for the relevant period than it was when the first estimates were made; (e) linguistic analysis of the Aramaic documents found at Qumran indicates a relative date of about the beginning of the Christian era for the stage of development of the language. The archeological excavation of the Qumran "monastery" added two other facts that corroborate this evidence, namely, the destruction by an earthquake, which can be dated 31 B.C.

A JAR FROM CAVE ONE. This jar was used to store scrolls from the Qumran library. Courtesy, Oriental Institute

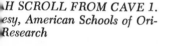

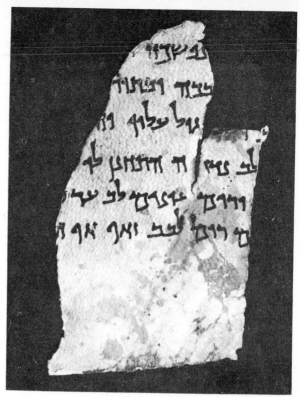

H SCROLL FROM CAVE 1.
esy, American Schools of Ori-
Research

PARCHMENT FRAGMENT OF THE
THANKSGIVING HYMNS. Courtesy, Oriental Institute

THE COPPER SCROLLS from Cave 3Q. Courtesy The Palestine Archaeological
Museum

and the destruction by fire, which can be dated to the time of the march of the Roman Tenth Legion from Jericho to Jerusalem, or about A.D. 67.

Because many fragments of similar manuscripts continued to appear in the bazaars, an all-out exploration of the entire region around Qumran was undertaken in 1952, and several caves (out of nearly 250 that were found) yielded manuscript fragments. Père Roland de Vaux, who led the archaeological work, says "This exploration could not have been exhaustive," (*L'achéologie et les manuscrits de la Mer Morte,* p. 42) for two other caves containing fragments, and even entire manuscripts, were discovered subsequently. To date, eleven caves have yielded literary materials, and the contents of two caves (Cave 4 and Cave 11) are probably far more important than the contents of Cave 1.

It is not yet possible, and probably would be of doubtful value, to give a complete catalog of the materials found in the eleven Qumran caves. More useful would be a classification of the types of materials found, together with some description and an evaluation of the significance of the types. The following classification is preliminary, and may need further clarification as the discoveries are studied in detail.

(a) *Biblical texts.* In addition to the Isaiah manuscripts found in Cave 1, schools of Leviticus and some Psalms have been found in Cave 11. Tens of thousands of fragments of other manuscripts have been found in the Qumran caves, most of them from Cave 4. Approximately five or six hundred different manuscripts are represented among these fragments, about one-quarter of them being Biblical books. Every Old Testament book except Esther is represented, including at least seventeen different copies of Deuteronomy, and nearly as many of Isaiah and of Psalms.

At least three text-types are found in the Biblical manuscripts. One type is clearly related to the Masoretic Text, which is the text of our present Hebrew Bible. (It is not accurate to call this the "Masoretic Text" at a period that was at least six hundred years before the Masoretes; what we mean is that this text was the text used by the Masoretes when they added the traditional pronunciation. But "Masoretic" — and oc-casionally "proto-Masoretic" — is simple, and clear, and firmly established by usage.) A second type is closely related to the Hebrew text that was used for the Greek version (the Septuagint) of the Old Testament. The third type has been compared by some scholars with the Samaritan text (i.e., the Samaritan recension of the Pentateuch, written in Hebrew; not the Samaritan version, which is an Aramaic dialect). Once again it is necessary to use terms cautiously. The Samaritan schism had occurred some centuries before the establishment of the Qumran Community. Since the Samaritan recension contains only the Pentateuch, some scholars have suggested that the rest of the Old Testament was not yet canonized. At any rate, the textual evidence of the Samaritan indicates the existence of a second non-Masoretic Text type. It is conceivable that this type extended into the Prophets and the Writings.

To avoid the use of names which are not accurate, we might indicate these three text types by *sigla,* as follows: —M= the ancestor of the Masoretic Text; L = the text used in making the Septuagint (or LXX); S = the text which bears resemblance to the Samaritan recension. We can therefore say that during the time the Qumran Community was in existence, the Old Testament text was found in at least three recensions, M, L, and S. The New Testament corroborates this evidence, as an analysis of the Old Testament quotations will prove. Some quotations in the New Testament agree with the Masoretic Text (i.e., they were made from M); some agree with the Septuagint (they were made from L): and some do not agree with either the Masoretic Text or the Septuagint (they were made from S or some other text type). According to tradition, the Council of Jamnia, in A.D. 90, standardized the Hebrew text, giving us the consonantal text which was later used by the Masoretes. The fact that only the proto-Masoretic text (or M) was found in the second century A.D. materials at Wadi Murabba'ât lends strength to this tradition.

(b) *Commentaries on Biblical books.* In addition to the Commentary on Habakkuk, fragments of similar commentaries on Isaiah, Hosea, Micah, Nahum and Psalm 37, have been identified, and Zephaniah and several other books are possibly to be identified.

The commentaries are without doubt original compositions of the Qumran Sect, for the Scriptures are distorted to show the persecution of the Community by the wicked, the favor of God enjoyed by the Community, and the punishment that will come upon the wicked. This gives us an important insight into the use of Scripture, at least by the Qumranians, in the period just prior to the New Testament. The fact that no commentary has been found that is based on a noncanonical book may be valid to support the view that the Qumran canon was the same as the canon of Palestinian Judaism.

(c) *Apocrypha and Pseudepigrapha.* These terms are variously used, and signify different things to Protestant and to Catholic. As used here, they refer to religous works produced by the Jews which are not included in the Hebrew canon, without distinguishing "Apocrypha" from "Pseudepigrapha" for present purposes. Among the fragments found at Qumran the following works are represented: Ecclesiasticus (or the Wisdom of Jesus ben Sira) in Hebrew, Tobit in Hebrew and Aramaic, Jubilees in Hebrew, Enoch (excepting Part II or the Similitudes) in Hebrew, and what appears to be the Testament of Levi, a part of a larger work known as the Testaments of the Twelve Patriarchs. The "Zadokite Fragments," sometimes included with the Pseudepigrapha, will be considered separately with the documents that specifically belong to the Qumran Community.

It is not yet clear what significance we must place on the finding of these materials — in some cases several copies of the work — at Qumran. Since the time of Julius Wellhausen, some scholars have been inclined to attribute some of these works to the Essenes. Today, most scholars identify the Qumran sect with the Essenes, and as a result the theory of an Essene origin for at least some of these Apocrypha and Pseudepigrapha has gained considerable strength. At the same time, the theory of gradual development or growth of some of the compositions is likewise strengthened. It is possible that the Testaments of the Twelve Patriarchs developed out of the Testament of Levi. On the other hand, it is almost certain that Book II (the Similitudes) was a later addition to Enoch. This is of particular significance, for the Son-of-Man doctrine appears in Enoch only in Book II. It is clear that the Qumranians have left no evidence of the heavenly or apocalyptic Son-of-Man concept in their Messianic doctrine. We may also infer that the Son-of-Man doctrine in the New Testament, rather than being the result of the doctrine in Enoch, was the inspiration for the addition of the doctrine to Enoch. The view that Jesus originated the Son-of-Man concept, or rather, that He was the first to combine the ideas of the Messianic Son of David, the Suffering Servant, and the heavenly Son of Man into one Messianic Person, has therefore gained considerable strength.

(4) *Writings on the religious life of the Community.* Among the original discoveries were the *Manual of Discipline*, the *Thanksgiving Hymns*, and the *War Scroll*, which can be specifically related to the members of the Qumran Community. The *Manual of Discipline* contains rules governing admission to the Community and life in the Community. The *Thanksgiving Hymns* appear to be expressions of devotional life, possibly hymns sung by the members in public or private worship. The *War Scroll* describes the preparations for and conduct of a war (whether actual or symbolic is a matter of interpretation) at the impending end of the age, hence called the eschatological war. To these writings must be added another that had been known for decades, formerly called the *Zadokite Fragments* and now generally known as the *Damascus Document* (CD). This work was discovered in a genizah in a Cairo synagogue in 1897 and published in 1910. As soon as the Manual of Discipline from Qumran was published, scholars recognized a close connection between the two documents, but it was not until fragments of the *Damascus Document* were discovered in the caves at Qumran that the work could positively be identified as Qumranian. At least nine manuscripts of the *Damascus Document* have been found in Caves 4, 5, and 6. The work contains a history of the origin of the Sect, provisions for admission, and rules of conduct for members. The *Damascus Document* and the *Manual of Discipline* provide the material for reconstruction of the faith and life of the Community. Other fragments of manuscripts belong in this category of literature, notably the larger fragments called the

Rule of the Congregation (IQSª) and the *Benedictions* (IQSᵇ). Much of the detail of the Messianic doctrine of the Community has been reconstructed from these fragments, but the condition of the text and the problems of interpretation leave some scholars with the conviction that the last word has not yet been said on the subject.

(e) *Miscellaneous writings.* In this category we place the *florilegia*, or collections of Biblical texts, and the *testimonia*, or proof-texts for certain ideas (for example, a Messianic *testimonium* contains Deut. 5:28-29; Deut. 18:18-19; Num. 24:15-17; and Deut. 33:8-11); as well as phylacteries (the *Shema*, or "creed" of Judaism, recited at every time of prayer). Other fragments, many of them representing works that were not known prior to the Qumran discoveries, and which are still too fragmentary for satisfactory identification, may temporarily be included in this category. For want of a better description we may also include the *Genesis Apocryphon*, identified as a Midrash by some scholars, but differing considerably from the Midrashim we know in Jewish Haggadic literature. Fragments of Septuagint texts, and the Aramaic Targum (i.e., translation) of Job, not yet published at this writing, may also be provisionally included in this category.

(f) *The Copper Scrolls.* Early in 1952 two badly oxidized copper scrolls were found in a cave identified as 3Q, and it was easy to assume that they were part of the Qumran products. They were accordingly assigned the *siglum* 3QX or 3Q15 (i.e., "unknown" or the 15th item from the cave). After several years of experimentation, the scrolls were finally cut, layer by layer, and laid open. The Hebrew inscription embossed in the copper, which had been visible from the outside of the roll (the back of the sheets), was an inventory of great treasure, about twenty-six tons of gold and sixty-five tons of silver buried in sixty-four locations in various parts of Palestine. (This "inventory" was therefore assigned a new *siglum*, namely 3QInv.) From the beginning there were problems concerning the Copper Scrolls: the amount of treasure was not consonant with the stated views of the Community concerning wealth; the use of sheets of copper could not be explained; the type of epigraphy was not like that of other Qumran materials; the language was Mishnaic Hebrew and as

such was unique among the Qumran documents; why had such an inventory been placed so casually in the front part of a cave?, etc., etc. Explanations were suggested The writing on copper was merely an exercise in writing (but why use such valuable material for such a purpose, and why the fantasy about such treasure?). This was an inventory of the Temple treasure (but why would it have been entrusted to the Qumranians who despised the Temple priesthood?), etc. A recent theory seems more acceptable than any of the others the copper scrolls were not part of the Qumran materials; rather, they were a later composition — probably about the end of the first century A.D. — in Mishnaic Hebrew, by persons unknown, possibly describing the location of Temple treasure that had been hidden before the Roman legions destroyed the Temple. That the scrolls were discovered at the same time as the Qumran materials was a sheer accident, just as were the discoveries at Wadi Murabba'ât and Wadi Mird. This is not an unreasonable theory, and it is not merely an attempt to avoid or cover up a serious problem. Rather it is the conclusion provisionally indicated by all the facts at present known.

Having described at some length the Scrolls, we can now proceed to describe the Community that served as custodian of, and in some cases at least, provided the authors of, the Dead Sea Scrolls. Our knowledge is derived from the contents of the scrolls, particularly the *Manual of Discipline*, the *Damascus Document*, the *Habakkuk Commentary*, and other documents that appear to be compositions of the Community. To this we can add the indications of archeological discoveries and possibly the descriptions of the Essenes found in Philo, Josephus, and other ancient writers.

The Community was a Jewish sect that had separated from the main stream of Judaism in the early second (or possibly late third) century B.C. Their pious practices suggest that they were in some way related to the Hasidim, precursors of the Pharisees. At the same time their stress on the priesthood and their use of the name, "sons of Zadok," suggest to some scholars that there may have been an early relationship with the Sadducees. An attractive compromise is the suggestion that the original chism began with the Sadducees, possibly first joining the Hasidim (which would explain the presence of priests among the Pharisees), and then a second schism occurred in which some ex-Sadducees (the "the sons of Zadok") and some Hasidim formed the new sect. Because of close relationships between the Qumranians and the Essenes as described in Philo and Josephus it would seem that the new movement was either the Essenes or the parent group from which the Essenes later developed. If we assume that the descriptions in Philo and Josephus are accurate, it seems best to consider the Qumranians and the Essenes as two closely related sects, rather than attempting to force them into single identity.

The Damascus Document, in a vague statement (CD 1:6), places the foundation of the Sect 390 years after the Exile. If we assume that this refers to the destruction of Jerusalem, and if the figure is to be taken literally (it may be only a symbolic number drawn from Ezekiel 4:5), then we could put the date of origin *ca.* 197 B.C. While this date is compatible with other evidence, most scholars are not inclined to take the figures in the *Damascus Document* seriously. About twenty years after the foundation, according to the same *Damascus Document,* God raised up a "Teacher of Righteousness" to lead the Sectarians (CD 1:10-11).

Membership in the sect was carefully regulated by the rules set forth in the Manual of Discipline. It included a probationary period in two stages of a year each (1QS 6:13-23). When a probationer was finally accepted, his wealth was permanently assigned to the Community. An annual examination determined the promotion or demotion of members, and each had an assigned rank according to his achievement. At meetings of the Community, members were not permitted to speak out of the order of their rank. A system of fines, spelled out in the *Manual of Discipline* (1QS 6:24–8:1), was imposed on members for minor infractions, and for serious offenses members could be banished from the membership. Meals were taken in common, and much of the life was devoted to reading of the Scriptures. According to provisions in the *Rule of the Congregation,* women and children could be admitted to membership (IQS^a 1:4). Nothing in any other document contradicts this; neverthe-

less, most scholars, because of a commitment to the Essene identification which involves applying all of the statements concerning the Essenes to the Qumran sect, insist that this was a "monastic" sect.

The Community either lived in tents on the plateau where the compound of buildings was located, or in the numerous caves in the cliff that extends along the western side of the Dead Sea. Their flocks were probably watered at 'Ain Feshkha, a copious source of fresh water on the very edge of the Dead Sea, about two miles south of the Qumran buildings. Grain was probably grown in the Buquê'an above the cliffs, and after harvest was ground in the mills and baked in the ovens found in the ruins at Qumran. Leather may have been tanned at 'Ain Feshkha. To judge from the number of dishes and bowls found alongside the refectory, corroborated by the number of graves in the cemetery, we may estimate the number of members at any given time to have been between two hundred and four hundred.

The place of the Teacher of Righteousness in the Community has been enlarged out of all proportion to documentary evidence. Nearly all of the statements concerning this person (or office?) are found in the *Habakkuk Commentary* and the *Damascus Document.* The entire body of material can be typed on one page, double-spaced. From this plus devotional statements in the *Thanksgiving Hymns* that are supposed to be from his lips, he has been built into a fantastic person, of whom, according to one writer at least, Jesus is only "a pale carbon copy." The Teacher was doubtless a deeply devoted member of the Community, who took a prominent place in its life at one period. He was persecuted, and died. He was not the founder of the Community, and theories concerning his virgin birth, crucifixion, resurrection, and second coming, have been woven whole-cloth by sensationalists who have taken their ideas from the New Testament and read them into the Dead Sea Scrolls.

The Community believed it was living in the end-time. It expected a "teacher of righteousness" as one of the eschatological persons involved in the end of the age. It looked for the Messiah, who was the Davidic prince of Jewish eschatology, but not the Son of Man of Jewish apocalyptic. Many scholars, on the evidence of one passage and

WRITING TABLE AND BENCH FROM THE QUMRAN SCRIPTORIUM. *Courtesy, Palestine Archaeological Museum*

textual emendation of several other passages, are convinced that the Sect also looked for another Messiah, the Messiah of Aaron or priestly Messiah, who was greater in priority than the Davidic Messiah, or Messiah of Israel. However, the term "Messiah of Aaron" is not found in the Dead Sea texts, and the reading "Messiahs of Aaron and Israel" does not occur in the fragments of another copy of the Manual of Discipline. The whole theory is feebly supported. (For detailed discussion, see W. S. LaSor, "The Messianic Idea in Qumran," in *Studies and Essays in Honor of Abraham A. Neuman*, pp. 343-364.)

The Dead Sea Scrolls are of importance in two principal areas of study: in textual criticism of the Old Testament, and in understanding the developments in Judaism in the intertestamental period. The former has been sketched in connection with the description of the texts, above. The significance for our understanding of Judaism, which of course includes the backgrounds of the New Testament, is a highly complex problem that

is demanding the efforts of many scholars. While it is yet too early to attempt to set forth the results, it has nevertheless become clear that the New Testament — significantly the problematic areas of the Fourth Gospel and the Pauline Epistles — belongs to the same milieu as the Dead Sea Scrolls. Matters which were once identified as "Hellenistic" and placed in the latter part of the second century A.D. (such as Gnosticism) can now be recognized as elements of first-century Judaism. Numerous parallels of language or idea have been pointed out, and some scholars have concluded that John the Baptist (and probably some of his disciples) and Jesus were members of the Qumran Community. John's attitude toward the world, as a society to be redeemed, is markedly different from that of Qumran, but it would be possible to suppose that the specific part of the Wilderness of Judea in which he grew up was the Qumran Community. On the other hand, that Jesus grew up at Nazareth and was well known to the inhabitants of that village is an essential part of the Gospel account, and the reaction of the Nazarenes at the beginning of Jesus' ministry can only be explained on this basis.

BIBLIOGRAPHY. G. Vermès, *The Dead Sea Scrolls in English*, Pelican Books, Baltimore, 1962. M. Burrows, *The Dead Sea Scrolls*, and *More Light on the Dead Sea Scrolls* (full discussion of the discoveries and problems arising therefrom), Viking Press, New York, 1955, 1958 W. S. LaSor, *Bibliography of the Dead Sea Scrolls, 1948-1957*, Fuller Library, Pasadena, 1958. C. F. Pfeiffer, *The Dead Sea Scrolls*, Baker Book House, Grand Rapids, 1962.

DEBIR (KIRJATH-SEPHER). The ancient town of Debir, or Kirjath-Sepher (Josh. 15: 15) was a Canaanite city in the hill country of Southern Judea (Josh. 10:38; 12:13). It was occupied by the Anakim at the time Joshua took it (Josh. 11:21). In some narratives the conquest of the city is attributed to the Calebites (Josh. 15:15-17; Judg. 1:11-15). Possibly they were the actual conquerors under Joshua, although the accounts of their conquest may refer to a re-capture of the town following its loss after an early victory over the occupants.

When Israel organized the land for administrative purposes the town Debir was a center for administration (Josh. 15:49). It is also featured as one of the Levitical cities (Josh. 21:15; I Chron. 6:58).

I. *Identification.* The exact identification of the city has proved difficult. Topographically, a site in the Hebron area must be sought (Judg. 1:10f). Historically, the site was occupied in pre-Israelite times and was later occupied by the Israelites although the Old Testament does not indicate how late it was occupied. Now in the general area of Hebron there are a number of sites which are topographically suitable — *Zahariyeh* (twelve miles south of Hebron), *Khirbet Rabud, Khirbet Zanuta,* and *Khirbet Tarrameh.* Soundings at *Zahariyeh* showed no trace of a Canaanite city (*BASOR,* 47, 1932, p. 16). The most acceptable identification is, however, that proposed in 1924 by W. F. Albright, namely, *Tell Beit Mirsim,* eleven miles southwest of Hebron. Excavations during the years 1926 to 1932 revealed a long period of occupation extending from the later part of the Early Bronze through

the Middle Bronze and Late Bronze ages and on into the end of the Iron II Age.

II. *The Archaeological Story.* The archaeological story may be correlated with the Biblical story comparatively easily.

Tell Beit Mirsim was occupied in the Middle Bronze I Age (*ca.* 2100-1910 B.C.) and is representative of towns that existed in Palestine in Abraham's day. The land was dominated by Egypt during this and the subsequent Middle Bronze II Age. It seems clear that the city was destroyed at the time of the Hyksos invasion, the probable period of Jacob's migration to Egypt. These people built on the same site and protected the town by a beaten earth wall. Well constructed houses, and artistic work in metal, ivory, bone and stone attest a considerable prosperity. When the Hyksos rulers in Egypt were finally cast out *ca.* 1550 B.C., *Tell Beit Mirsim* was again

EXCAVATORS EXAMINE AN ANCIENT DYE VAT at Tell Beit Mirsim, believed to be Biblical Debir (Kirjath-Sepher). Courtesy, Matson Photo Service

destroyed although it was later rebuilt. The late Bronze Canaanite city was a poor one compared with the rich Hyksos city. This city was destroyed in the late thirteenth century by a fire so great that it left three feet of ashes in some areas. The destruction was probably due to the Israelites (Josh. 10:38).

The next town was built by the Israelites. It evidently came within the sphere of Philistine influence judging from Philistine pottery found in the city. It was finally burned *ca.* 1050 B.C., probably at the time of the Philistine invasion when °Shiloh was destroyed (I Sam. 4). David rebuilt the city and fortified it with double walls, braced at intervals (casemate walls). The city was destroyed again, probably by Pharaoh Shishak, in 918 B.C. (I Kings 14:25-28; I Chron. 12:9 ff.). It was rebuilt in due course, possibly by Asa (*ca.* 913-873 B.C.; *cf.* I Kings 15:23; II Chron. 14:6-7). In subsequent years the city once again became prosperous. Excavations suggest that a flourishing textile industry was carried on here which reached its height in the eighth century B.C. There is evidence of later attacks, possibly by Sennacherib the Assyrian in 701 B.C., and by two other invaders during the next century. Towards the end of the seventh century the city declined rapidly. It was destroyed by Nebuchadnezzar in 587 B.C. and never rebuilt.

BIBLIOGRAPHY. W. F. Albright, *The Excavation of Tell Beit Mirsim, Annual of the American Schools of Oriental Research*, XII, 1930-31; XIII, 1931-32; XVII, 1936-37, XXI-XXII, 1941-43; *The Archaelogy of Palestine*, 1960.

DECAPOLIS. The term Decapolis ("ten cities") is used of a confederation of cities, all except Beth-shan (Scythopolis), located east of the Jordan. While they may have been settled by Greek colonists as early as 200 B.C., during the Maccabean struggle they came under Jewish rule. Pompey liberated three of the cities — Hippos, Scythopolis, and Pella, and annexed them to the province of Syria with guarantees of municipal freedom. At the beginning of the Christian era the cities of the Decapolis formed a league for mutual defense. Pliny states that the original members included Scythopolis, Pella, Dion, °Gerasa, Philadelphia, Gadara, Raphana, Kanatha, Hippos, and Damascus. Philadelphia was the old

Rabbath-Ammon (modern °Amman) chief city of the Ammonites. Pella was probably founded by Greeks and named for Pella in Macedonia, the birthplace of Alexander the Great. Jewish Christians fled to Pella before the destruction of Jerusalem (A.D. 70).

DEIR 'ALLA. The mound known as Tell Deir 'Alla is situated on the east bank of the Jordan north of the Zerqa (Biblical Jabbok). During his surface exploration of Transjordan in the 1930's, Nelson Glueck identified the ten acre Tell Deir 'Alla with Biblical Succoth.

In 1960 a Dutch expedition financed by the Netherlands Organization for Pure Science Research and directed by H. J. Franken of Leiden University began a series of excavations which ended in May 1964. The original purpose of the expedition was to apply scientific methodology in determining the stratigraphic sequence of pottery types. The discovery of a Late Bronze Age sanctuary caused the excavators to broaden their purpose to include a cultural history of the site. Soundings were made to virgin soil, and they revealed that the Late Bronze Age sanctuary was the last of a series of sanctuaries, the first of which was probably built during the sixteenth century B.C. They were built on an artificial platform raised above the natural surface of the soil. Highly decorated objects from the early levels were superior in artistic qualities to those of the later period.

The latest sanctuary was destroyed by an earthquake and fire. It had been built of mud brick with the roof made of reeds, plaster, and some wood. The earthquake had caused a landslide and it produced cracks in walls and floors. Upper levels of the walls were knocked down, sometimes landing upright beside the remaining lower levels, giving the appearance of double walls. The fire had fused the bricks into formless masses of green, white, and red color. Melted pots were found in the ruins.

The sanctuary complex covered a large area, and there is no room on the tell to accommodate ordinary dwellings. This has caused Franken to suggest that he has discovered a central sanctuary for tribes of the area. The absence of defensive walls also suggests that the tell was exclusively devoted to a sanctuary.

On the floor of the cella of the sanctuary a vase was discovered with the cartouche of Tewosret, the widow of Pharaoh Seti II who reigned *ca.* 1190 B.C. In the cella were bronze scales of armor, perhaps a trophy of victory brought to the sanctuary by a grateful hero. The Philistines are said to have taken Saul's armor to the temple of their god Ashtoreth following victory at Mount Gilboa (I Sam. 31:10).

The store rooms contained plain vessels that would prove serviceable for the ordinary needs of the functionaries at the sanctuary. The "treasury" however had finer pottery, including Mycenaean ware. A flask, decorated in dull red paint, depicts a man leading a goat, with a dog in the background. Other objects include cylinder seals, scarabs, juglets, and bone cones. The most important find was three inscribed clay tablets. The texts are in a hitherto unknown script. Another tablet was found with evidence that it had been crushed in the scribe's hand before it had a chance to harden. Eight smaller tablets were discovered with rows of five or seven impressed dots. The dots may have had some magical significance.

The dwellings adjoining the "treasury" also contained cylinder seals and a variety of pottery, including Mycenaean juglets. Bone spindle whorls and spindles were also in evidence. Only one recognizable metal object was discovered: a bronze ring handle which may have come from a leather or wooden bucket. Under fallen roof fragments was a badly charred skeleton.

Identification of Deir 'Alla is still uncertain, but Franken states, that in the light of his excavations, "there is no less reason to identify Deir 'Alla, with the Gilgal to which Saul went with the men of Jabesh-Gilead after their victory over Nahash the Ammonite (cf. I Sam. 13:15) than with "Succoth." Franken suggests that a semi-nomadic tribe of smiths made use of the iron age furnaces discovered at Deir 'Alla. This might further suggest that Deir 'Alla is within the area mentioned in I Kings 7:46 as the source of metal vessels for the Temple: "In the plain of the Jordan the king cast them, in the clay ground between Succoth and Zarethan."

BIBLIOGRAPHY. H. J. Franken, "A Bronze Age Shrine and Unknown Script," *Illustrated London News*, 246, No. 6559, April 17, 1965, pp. 34-35. A. van den Branden, "Essai de dechiffrement des inscriptions de *Deir 'Alla*," *Vetus Testamentum*, XV, 1965, pp. 129-152. H. J. Franken, "Iron Age Jordan Village," *Illustrated London News*, 246, No. 6561, May 1, 1965, p. 27.

DEMOTIC. *See* Writing.

DERBE. The ancient city of Derbe, located in south-central Asia Minor, is mentioned in the Bible only in connection with Paul's missionary activities. Following his persecution and stoning in Lystra on his first missionary journey, Paul and Barnabas went to Derbe (Acts 14:21). From Derbe they retraced their steps and visited again the churches organized on the first missionary journey. Paul revisited Derbe on his second missionary journey (Acts 16:1) and possibly on his third missionary journey (Acts 18:23). In Acts 20:4 a disciple and companion of Paul from Derbe is mentioned. Lystra and Derbe are identified as cities of Lycaonia in Acts 14:6. Derbe is mentioned in some secular sources (Cicero *Ad Fam.* 13. 73; Strabo 535, 569). It is identified by Strabo as the city of Antipater, the "robber-king."

That a church flourished at Derbe for some time is indicated by the identification of four bishops from Derbe who attended the early councils of the church: Daphnus (Constantinople, A.D. 381), Thomas (Ephesus), Paulus (Chalcedon), and Cyricus (le Quien, *Oriens Christianus* I, Paris, 1740, p. 1081).

I. *Traditional Location of Derbe.* It was near the end of the nineteenth century that a site was suggested for ancient Derbe. J. R. Sitlington Sterrett first suggested locating Derbe in the neighborhood of the large mound of Gudelisin. Shortly after that, William M. Ramsay advanced the theory that the mound of Gudelisin is the site of Derbe (*The Cities of St. Paul*, pp. 393-97). There was no epigraphical or extensive archaeological evidence for this identification, but the proximity to Lystra seemed to fit the data of Acts 14:20. Nevertheless, there has always been a measure of uncertainty about this identification, although it is the one given in practically all the maps describing Paul's missionary journeys. Gudelisin is located in the Taurus foothills about forty-seven miles south of Konya (ancient Iconium), and about thirty miles southeast of the mound of ancient Lystra.

II. *Evidence for the New Site of Derbe.* In 1957 M. Ballance published an inscription which he had found in 1956 at Kerti Hüyük (*Anatolian Studies,* 7, 1957, pp. 147-51). The inscription, cut on a sizeable limestone block, contained sixteen lines of text. On the basis of names mentioned, Ballance was able to date the inscription in the year A.D. 157. In lines 9 and 10 the *boule* and *demos* of the people of Derbe (*derbeton*) are mentioned. This stone has been moved to Konya and is housed in the Archaeological Museum there.

Kerti Hüyük is a large mound located about fifteen miles north-northeast of Karaman (ancient Larande), which is about sixty-five miles south of Konya. This new site is about thirty miles east of the area suggested by Ramsay as the territory of Derbe. The mound has not been excavated, but surface exploration clearly points to extensive occupation during the Roman and Hellenistic periods.

In 1962 another inscription was found which mentions the name of Derbe. This inscription was found inside a small house in the village of Suduraya. The natives maintained that the stone had been taken from the mound of Kerti Hüyük, which is only a short distance away. On the basis of the date-line and paleography, this inscription can be dated in the latter part of the fourth century after Christ. The text mentions the name of a "most God-loving" bishop of Derbe. The name appears to be Michael.

With these two inscriptions mentioning Derbe, the location of Derbe at Kerti Hüyük is rather definitely established. Acts 14:20b must be interpreted as implying a journey of more than one day. The second inscription further substantiates the significance of Derbe in the early church. Undoubtedly future excavation of Kerti Hüyük could throw some more light on the ancient city of Derbe.

DESCENT OF ISHTAR. The famous myth — the Akkadian "Descent of Ishtar to the Nether World," and its Sumerian prototype, the "Descent of Inanna to the Nether World" — is one of the most important documents for our understanding of the Mesopotamian concepts of the afterlife. It has been held as the prototype of the fertility-god cycles. Scholars have attempted to discover allusions to this myth both in the Old and in the New Testament.

I. *Comparison of the Sumerian and Ak-*

kadian Versions. As history's first literate civilization the *Sumerians bequeathed a number of important myths to the Semitic Babylonians who became the dominant ethnic group in Babylonia during the second millennium. Although the basic features of the story are the same, the Semitic version has omitted some elements and has added others. The most important difference of the extant reconstructions come at the end of the myth. The Akkadian version remains obscure here, but we now have a good reconstruction of the end of the Sumerian, thanks to newly published tablets. As a whole, the temper of the Sumerian version is "calm, subdued, passive and unemotional; the incidents are recited impassively and repeated to the point of monotony. The Semitic version, on the other hand, glosses over many of the particulars, but expands with language that is characteristically passionate and intense those details which are rich in emotional possibilities (Samuel N. Kramer, 'Ishtar in the Nether World According to a New Sumerian Text,' *BASOR* 79, 1940, p. 20)."

II. *History of the Texts.* The Sumerian text of nearly four hundred lines comes from about 2000 B.C. The tablets which have been used to reconstruct the myth were discovered by the University of Pennsylvania at Nippur at the turn of the century. Unfortunately the tablets were arbitrarily divided between the Museum at Istanbul in Turkey and the University Museum at Philadelphia. Arno Poebel first published three fragments in 1914, that same year Stephen Langdon published the upper half of a four-column tablet which he found at Istanbul. A few years later Edward Chiera discovered the bottom half of the same tablet in Philadelphia. It is largely through the efforts of Samuel Noah Kramer that we have a complete text today. He first published a translation of the text in 1937. His second edition published in *ANET* (1950, 1955) is not the most complete edition now available. His third edition with the inclusion of an important tablet from Yale was published in *JCS* V, 1951, pp. 1-17. A translation of the Yale tablet may also be found in his *History Begins at Sumer,* pp. 165-167. In 1960 Kramer succeeded in assembling 30 fragments of the myth "The Death of Dumuzi" dating from about 1750 B.C. This is not an integral part of the Descent of Inanna but is nonetheless intimately connected with it. Translations of this important myth may be found in *Mythologies of the Ancient World,* edited by Kramer, pp. 110-115, and in his latest book, *The Sumerians,* pp. 156-160.

The Akkadian version, containing a little more than 100 lines, comes to us from about 1000 B.C. There are two major recensions: one comes from the library of Ashurbanipal at Nineveh in the middle of the seventh century B.C., and the other from about 1000 B.C. from Ashur. In 1949 eleven lines of an older and possibly independent recension from Ashur was published. The text was published as early as 1896. The most recent English translations are those by Alexander Heidel, *The Gilgamesh Epic and OT Parallels,* pp. 121-128, and by E. A. Speiser in *ANET,* pp. 107-109.

III. *The Characters.*

A. Inanna-Ishtar. The Sumerian goddess Inanna — and her Akkadian representation Ishtar — was the most important goddess in the Mesopotamian pantheon. She was the goddess of love and the goddess of war. In her first capacity she had male and female prostitutes attached to her temples. As the patroness of war she is often pictured with a lion. She was also the "Lady of Heaven" and was identified with the planet Venus. The Sumerian-Akkadian bilingual "The Ascension of Ishtar" refers to the rise of Venus to its zenith (F. Thureau-Dangin, "L'Exaltation d'Ištar." *Revue d'Assyriologie,* XI, 1914, pp. 141-158). Although the name Ishtar itself does not occur in the Old Testament the related plural form transliterated Ashtaroth occurs in Judges 2:13, 10:6; I Sam. 7:3, 4, 12:10, 31:10, and Ashtoreth in I Kings 11:5, 33 and II Kings 23:13. It is well known that the Phoenicians worshipped Astarte at Tyre, Sidon, and Byblos. The phrase "the queen of heaven" in Jer. 7:18, 44:17, 18, 19, 25 is probably a title of Ishtar. (See also, J. Reider, "New Ištar epithet in the Bible," *JNES,* VIII, 1949, pp. 104-7.) It is furthermore believed that the Greek goddess Aphrodite owes much of her character to Ishtar. Her center at Corinth with one thousand sacred prostitutes was quite unhellenic (Lewis R. Farnell, *The Cults of the Greek States,* Vol. II, Clarendon Press, Oxford, 1896, pp. 626 f.).

B. Dumuzi-Tammuz. The Sumerian Dumuzi was originally a king of Uruk (Erech, Gen. 10:10) early in the third millennium B.C. who was deified as the consort of the city's protectress, Inanna. Although he was a shepherd figure, he was thought by scholars to be the prototype of the dying and rising vegetation god, largely on the belief that the purpose of Inanna's descent was to resurrect him from the dead. We have Sumerian love songs which were used in the *hieros gamos* or "sacred marriage," in which the king was addressed as Dumuzi and a hierodule as Inanna (*see* Samuel N. Kramer, "The Biblical 'Song of Songs' and the Sumerian Love Songs," *Expedition,* V, 1962, pp. 25-31). Lamentations for Tammuz (the Akkadian name for Dumuzi) are well known. In Ezekiel 8:14 the prophet finds some women of Jerusalem weeping for Tammuz. Since Tammuz was associated with Adonis in Syria he was identified by Sir James Frazer in 1906 along with Adonis, Attis, and Osiris as a type of the dying god. In 1952 P. Lambrechts showed that even the belief in the resurrection of Adonis and of Attis was a late development, probably borrowed from the Egyptian Osiris during the period of widespread syncretism under the Seleucids (323-64 B.C.).

C. Ereshkigal. The older sister of Inanna, known among the Semites also as Allatu, was the queen of the Underworld and the goddess of death. A myth entitled "Nergal and Ereshkigal" (*ANET,* pp. 103-4) relates how Nergal was summoned to the Underworld because he failed to pay proper respects to Ereshkigal's messenger Namtar. Nergal, however, posted his own forces at the various gates and overpowered Ereshkigal. He spares her and accepts her proposal to rule the Underworld with her. The Underworld deities were greatly feared because of their baneful powers, and were often entreated in prayers and magical incantations.

IV. *The Plot*

A. The Motive of the Goddess. It is not clear from the Akkadian version why the goddess made her descent. The Sumerian text reads: "My daughter *has demanded* the '[great] above,' *has demanded* the 'great below,'. . . ." It appears that Inanna wished to have dominion not only over Heaven but also over the Underworld as well.

B. The Preparation. The Sumerian text

devotes about a hundred lines to Inanna's preparations for the descent. She abandons her temples in seven cities and gathers the decrees and various adornments. The *me* or decree was "a set of rules and regulations assigned to each cosmic entity and cultural phenomenon for the purpose of keeping it operating forever. . . ." (S. N. Kramer, *The Sumerians*, p. 115). Inanna tells her vizier Ninshubur what to do in case she does not return. The Akkadian text does not spend time to describe Ishtar's preparations.

C. The Arrival. Her arrival at the "palace, the lapis lazuli mountain" is more graphically described in Akkadian than in Sumerian. The dread place is vividly described as a place:

> Where dust is their fare and clay their food,
> (Where) they see no light, residing in darkness,
> (Where) they are clothed like birds, with wings for garments.

Ishtar then threatens the gatekeeper, warning him:

> If thou openest not the gate so that I cannot enter,
> I will smash the door, I will shatter the bolt,
> I will raise up the dead, eating the living,
> So that the dead will outnumber the living.

The last lines are extremely interesting. The Ashur version reads, "So that the living will outnumber the dead." In either case Ishtar threatens to raise and to liberate the dead. It is interesting that the promise of a resurrection is viewed here not as a hope but as a calamity. This was especially feared by Ereshkigal, who was concerned lest her food supply which was offered by the living for the dead should be cut off. She groans, "Should I eat clay for bread, drink muddied water for beer?"

D. The Removal of the Garments. In both versions the goddess is led through seven gates at each of which one of her seven objects of clothing or adornment is removed until she is rendered naked. Evidently the rules of the Underworld permitted no one to approach Ereshkigal's presence except in that condition. The lists of objects worn by the goddess differ in the two versions. They are as follows:

Sumerian	Akkadian
1. crown	1. crown
2. measuring rod and cord of lapis lazuli	2. earrings
3. necklace of lapis lazuli beads	3. necklace of egg-shaped beads
4. pendant with double egged-shaped beads	4. breast ornaments
5. golden bracelet	5. girdle with the Stone-of- (easy) Birthgiving
6. breastplate	6. clasps around hand and feet
7. *pala*-garment of ladyship	7. loincloth

In the Sumerian version the description of her preparations includes two other items: either a "wig" or "locks of hair," and ointment which she daubed on her eyes. The descriptions of the ointment and of the breastplate are strikingly modern. The former is called "Man, come, come!" and the latter "He (the man) shall come, he shall come," that is, "man-alluring" and "man-enticing" much as a woman's perfume would be called "Temptation" in our day. A much larger catalogue of objects associated with the statue of the goddess is discussed by W. F. Leemans in his monograph, *Ishtar of Lagaba and her Dress*, E. J. Brill, Leiden, 1952. Among the objects of precious stones and metals and the garments, gold and silver *vulvae*, point to the worship of Ishtar as a fertility deity.

E. The Slaying. According to the Sumerian text the slaying takes place before the Anunnaki, the seven judges, as Ereshkigal fastened her eye upon her sister. The corpse was then hung on a nail. The Akkadian text speaks of Namtar attacking Ishtar with his sixty maladies. Upon the death of the goddess all reproduction ceases among man and beast.

F. The Appeal. In the Akkadian text Ishtar's vizier Papsukkal goes to Ea for help. In the Sumerian account, Inanna's minister Ninshubur follows his instructions "after three days (and) three nights had passed," and raises a commotion:

Played for her the drum in the assembly shrine,
Wandered about for her in the houses of the gods,
Tore at his eyes for her, *tore at* his mouth for her.

He seeks for help first from Enlil at Nippur, and then from Nanna at Ur but without success. He receives help, however, from Enki at Eridu. He appeals to Enki by pointing out the possible loss of the heavenly ornaments:

Let not your good metal be covered with the dust of the nether world.
Let not your good lapis lazuli be broken up into the stone of the stone-worker.
Let not your *boxwood* be cut up into the wood of the wood-worker.

These may be poetical descriptions of the body of the goddess herself rather than references to her ornaments.

G. The Rescue. In the Sumerian account, Enki creates two sexless creatures, the *kurgarrû* and the *kalaturru*, to whom he entrusts "the food of life" and "the water of life." After refusing to be bribed by gifts they succeed in reviving the goddess by sprinkling her with the elements of life. In the Akkadian account, Ea creates a eunuch, *Asushunamir* — "His appearance is brilliant" — who evidently dazzles Ereshkigal. A. Leo Oppenheim suggests that the rescuers were made sexless creatures to circumvent any curse Ereshkigal may have made, a curse which "presumably enumerated all the deities of the pantheon by name, including expressly their yet unborn offspring, male as well as female in short, everything born from a womb" (Mesopotamian Mythology III, *Orientalia*, XIX, 1950, p. 132)."

H. The Ascent. Once brought back to life again, the goddess' troubles were not yet over. She needed to get a substitute to take her place in the Underworld. This is clearly stated in the Akkadian version: "If she does not give thee her ranson price, bring her back."

I. The Search for Dumuzi. The Yale tablet of ninety-one lines, thirty-one of which are new, which Kramer published in *JCS* (IV, 1950, pp. 199-214), relates how Inanna is accompanied in her search for a suitable substitute by a company of ghoulish demons, small and large, who are very eager to do their duty. In fact, they almost drag off Ninshubur, Inanna's faithful minister, before she intercedes for him. Likewise they want to take her barber Shara but she intervenes. They come to Kullab where she finds that her husband Dumuzi, instead of mourning her absence, had "dressed himself in a noble garment, seated himself nobly on (his) seat." In a fury, Inanna "fastened the eye upon him, the eye of death," and says, "As for *him*, carry him off." In desperation Dumuzi asks Inanna's brother Utu to change him into a snake that he might escape.

J. The Death of Dumuzi. At this exciting juncture the available tablets had broken off, until 1960 when the new poem, "The Death of Dumuzi," clearly revealed to us the tragic end. This myth shows that Dumuzi had premonitions of his death through dreams, which his sister Geshtinanna interpreted for him. He attempts to hide among the plants, and then begs Utu to turn him into a gazelle that he might escape the *galla* demons who are pursuing him. He eludes them once and then escapes a second time to the goddess Belili. The third time five demons catch up with him as he comes to the sheepfold of Geshtinanna. The demons enter one after the other. One "strikes Dumuzi on the cheek with a *"piercing nail*," and another "strikes Dumuzi on the cheek with the shepherd's crook."

The holy churn lies (shattered), no milk is poured,
The cup lies (shattered), Dumuzi lives no more
The sheepfold is given to the wind.

K. The Akkadian Conclusion. The last twelve lines of the Akkadian text have usually been taken as an indication of the resurrection of Tammuz. The first four lines speak of the funeral of Tammuz. The next four lines are about the goddess Belili, who has been considered to be Ishtar. The Sumerian myth "The Death of Dumuzi" now indicates that Belili was probably another goddess. The last four lines conclude:

My only brother, bring no harm to me!
On the day when Tammuz comes up to me,
When with him the lapis flute (and) the carnelian ring came up to me,
When with him the wailing men and The wailing women come up to me,
May the dead rise and smell the incense.

This may not be a case of a real resurrection but rather the ascent of spirits to smell the burning incense and to partake of the offerings made for the dead. Similarly neglected and famished spirits would rise and feed on the garbage thrown into the streets, and other spirits such as that of Enkidu in the Gilgamesh Epic would be recalled for information. (See Alexander Heidel, *The Gilgamesh Epic and O.T. Parallels*, p. 207.)

V. Relevance to Biblical Studies

There was a time when some scholars sought to reduce the Old Testament to a collection of Babylonian myths. Alfred Jeremias, for example, saw the Tammuz myth in the Joseph story (*The O.T. in the Light of the Ancient East*, G. P. Putnam's Sons, New York, 1911, Vol. II, chap. 17). He wrote, "The sojourn with the slave-dealers is held to be a tarrying in the Underworld. . . . The prison is likewise the Underworld" (p. 65).

Many writers have also seen in Tammuz a prototype of Christ. For example Paul Carus says, "The ancient Tammuz is one of the most important prototypes of Christ. He is a god-man, an incarnation of the deity who is born as a human being, dies in the course of time and wakes to life again (cited by Wilfred Schoff, 'Tammuz, Pan, and Christ,' *The Open Court*, XXVI, 1912, p. 545)."

These parallels can no longer be maintained for: (1) Tammuz did not rise from the dead, and (2) Ishtar did not descend to deliver the dead. Ishtar died and needed a substitute so that she herself could get back to Heaven.

BIBLIOGRAPHY. O. R. Gurney, "Tammuz Reconsidered: Some Recent Developments," *Journal of Semitic Studies*, VII, 1962, pp. 147-159. Alexander Heidel, *The Gilgamesh Epic and O.T. Parallels*, University of Chicago, Chicago, 1949. S. N. Kramer, " 'Inanna's Descent to the Nether World' Continued and Revised," *JCS*, V, 1951, pp. 1-17; *History Begins at Sumer*, Doubleday & Co., Inc., Garden City, New York, 1959; *The Sumerians*, University of Chicago, Chicago, 1963. E. A. Speiser, "Descent of Ishtar to the Nether World," *Ancient Near Eastern Texts*, ed. J. B. Pritchard, Princeton University Press, Princeton, 1955.

DIBON. The Moabite city of Dibon is represented by the modern ruin of Dhībân in the Kingdom of the Jordan and is situated approximately forty miles south of Amman, three miles north of the *Wadi Mojib* (River Arnon), and thirteen miles east of the Dead Sea. It is near the southern end of the gently rolling tableland which constituted the major granary of ancient Moab and just west of the north-south highway traversing the region in both Biblical and modern times.

I. *Literary History.* Sometime prior to the Israelite Conquest in the thirteenth century B.C. Dibon and all Moab north of the Arnon River was overrun by Sihon, the Amorite ruler of Heshbon, and incorporated into his kingdom (Num. 21:26-30). The Israelites, in turn, dispossessed Sihon of the region and allotted it to the tribes of Reuben and Gad (Num. 32:2-5; 32:34-38; Josh. 13:9). Although it was to Reuben that Dibon was specifically given (Josh. 13:17), it was the sons of Gad who are reported to have rebuilt it (Num. 32:34). The role of the Gadites in its reconstruction is further attested by the appearance of the form Dibon-gad in a later reference to one of the campsites of Israel in her northward trek toward Nebo (Num. 33:45f).

Moabite dominion over the district of Dibon and other former territories north of the Arnon was regained during the period of the Hebrew "judges," probably during the Moabite resurgence to power under Eglon (Judg. 3:12-14). The area was apparently recaptured by David when he subjugated Moab (I Sam. 8:2), but reverted to independent Moabite control with the division of the Hebrew monarchy.

For the events of the following ninth century B.C., the Old Testament record is supplemented by the Mesha Stele (*ca.* 830 B.C.), which informs us that Omri reconquered the Moabite territory north of the Arnon and for forty years thereafter Israelites again occupied the region of Medeba and Dibon (*See* Moabite Stone.) Moreover, Israel imposed a heavy annual tribute in sheep and wool upon the conquered land (II Kings 3:4). The death of Ahab, however, signaled the resurgence of Moab under Mesha, her Dibonite King (II Kings 3:4). Having freed Moab from the humiliation of Israelite oppression, Mesha rebuilt many captured cities (some with Israelite prisoners) which he had added to his domain and ruled over them from his capital city of Qarhoh, which seemingly is to be identified with the citadel of Dibon.

Mesha's account of his building of Qarhoh-Dibon affords an intriguing list of archaeological expectations from the site. He claims credit for the construction, among other things, of its city walls, gates, and towers, the king's palace, and two reservoirs for water. Earlier in his inscription he also stated that he made there a high place to his god Chemosh.

During the following centuries Isaiah (ch. 15) and Jeremiah (ch. 48) pronounced judgment upon Dibon in their prophetic oracles against Moab. However, neither in these references nor in subsequent literary evidences is the history of the site distinguishable from the general fortunes of the land of which it was a part.

II. *Excavation History*. Dibon was untouched by scientific excavation until the autumn of 1950. Beginning with that date the American School of Oriental Research at Jerusalem conducted yearly campaigns at the site through 1956, with the single exception of 1953/54. Its occupational history, as indicated by the cultural strata, dates from the beginning of the Early Bronze Age — E.B. I, II, and III all being represented. Thereafter, a long cultural gap is indicated by the absence of both Middle and Late Bronze materials. Heavy occupation is indicated for Iron Age I and II (The Moabite Period) — again followed by a period of abandonment. The °Nabataeans succeeded in resettling the site near the beginning of the Christian Era and it was rather heavily occupied during the succeeding cultural periods until its final abandonment in late Arabic times. This occupational pattern is in agreement with the cultural history of Transjordan as a whole as discerned by Glueck from his surface survey of the region — in spite of the appearance of isolated examples of Middle and Late Bronze materials near °Amman.

During the first three campaigns the enormous and exceedingly complex defenses on the eastern and southeastern perimeter of the mound were probed. Though it has not yet been possible to assign dates to all of a series of such defenses the outermost wall on the east is, nevertheless, worthy of special note. It is an enormous, sloping wall of squared, roughly dressed stones, which still stands to a height of several meters and which is one of the most impressive examples of the defensive strength of ancient cities.

Ground-plans of structures of particular interest unearthed in the southeastern sector of the mound include a gateway, a Nabataean-Roman temple, and a Byzantine church.

Incorporated into the church pavement was a re-used stone containing a Greek inscription dating the construction of a yet undiscovered Roman defensive tower to the year 557, which, assuming the Seleucid Era, would represent A.D. 245-46.

Samples of carbonized grain (presumably wheat) from a cache found in the Iron Age levels were dated by the radio-carbon process. The result, 858 B.C., ± 165 years, is quite in harmony with the date determined for these levels by a study of the pottery finds.

During the 1955 and 1956 seasons the scene of operations was shifted to the central and northern sectors of the site. In the northern area an entranceway to the city was laid bare revealing three successive roadways leading through huge corner guardroom towers up into the city. This entranceway saw service during various periods of the city's history, the period of greatest usage being from the tenth to the eighth centuries B.C. Adjacent to the Iron Age entranceway were found huge bins and nearby destruction levels produced large quantities of charred grain. Moabite city walls of brick and stone were encountered, one of the latter remaining standing to a height of over four meters.

Chief interest on the summit and center of the site focused upon the foundation of a Moabite official building of imposing but yet undetermined extent. The walls averaged approximately one and one-half meters in thickness and the floors were of flat stones covered with a type of packed *huwar*. In a small central room was a very fine incense stand and two adjacent rooms each produced fertility figurines. The quality of the best Moabite pottery recovered from this building challenges the finest and thinnest ever produced in the ancient world. Of interest, also, was the first Moabite ostracon to be recovered from the site. The interior plan of the structure plus the nature of the finds recovered make it most probable that this building was a Moabite temple or palace-temple combination. Since it is the only such Moabite structure ever recovered, it should be of very considerable importance to students of Moabite and Old Testament culture.

BIBLIOGRAPHY. William H. Morton, "Dhiban, 1956," *RB*, Tome, LXIV, 1957, pp. 221-223.

R. E. Murphy, "A Fragment of an Early Moabite Inscription from Dibon," *BASOR*, no. 125, 1952, pp. 20-23. William L. Reed, "A Recent Analysis of Grain from Ancient Dibon in Moab," *BASOR*, no. 146, 1957, pp. 6-10. William L. Reed and Fred V. Winnett, "A Fragment of an Early Moabite Inscription from Kerak," *BASOR*, no. 172, 1963, pp. 1-9. A. D. Tushingham, "Excavations at Dibon in Moab, 1952-53," *BASOR*, no. 133, 1954, pp. 6-25; "An Inscription of the Roman Imperial Period from Dhiban," *BASOR*, no. 138, 1955, pp. 29-33. F. V. Winnett, "Excavation at Dibon in Moab, 1950-1951," *BASOR*, no. 125, 1952, pp. 7-20. G. R. H. Wright, "The Nabataean-Roman Temple at Dhiban: A Suggested Reinterpretation," *BASOR*, no. 163, 1961, pp. 26-30. A. H. Van Zyl, *The Moabites*, E. J. Brill, Leiden, 1960.

DILMUN. Dilmun is the Sumerian paradise, the home of the gods. Mythology describes it as good, clean, and bright. It is a land of the living which knows neither sickness nor death. It is located at "the place where the sun rises." Dilmun is not solely a figment of the imagination, however, for the Sumerians engaged in extensive trade with Dilmun. Sumerian documents record the cargo of ships from Dilmun — gold, copper, copper utensils, lapis lazuli, tables inlaid with ivory, "fish eyes" (probably pearls), ivory, and ivory objects.

The location of Dilmun has puzzled scholars. It has been frequently identified with the island of Bahrein in the Persian Gulf, but S. N. Kramer argues for a site in the Indus Valley (Pakistan and India) where a remarkable, literate, urban culture flourished toward the end of the third millennium B.C. From the vantage point of °Sumer, this would fit the description of Dilmun as "the place where the sun rises." As a remote land, it would lend itself to the mythological embellishments which depicted Dilmun as a paradise.

BIBLIOGRAPHY. Samuel Noah Kramer, *The Sumerians: Their History, Culture, and Character*, University of Chicago Press, Chicago, 1963, pp. 147-49; 277-286.

DIVORCE. See Marriage.

DOLMEN. A dolmen is a prehistoric table-like structure consisting of two or more large upright stones set with a space between and capped by a horizontal stone. Dolmens are usually regarded as tombs.

DOR. The Egyptian tale of °Wenamon tells how an official of the Amun temple at Karnak journeyed to Phoenicia to procure lumber for the ceremonial barge of his god. He stopped at Dor, "a town of the Tjeker" and was given a fitting reception by its prince, who evidently felt it necessary to show honor to a visiting Egyptian dignitary. While at Dor, one of Wenamon's men stole the gold and silver which was to have been used in paying for the lumber, and ran away. The prince of Dor was courteous, but he disclaimed any responsibility in the matter. The Tjeker who inhabited Dor were Sea Peoples who, like the Philistines, settled in various places in Asia Minor, Syria, and Palestine between the fifteenth and twelfth centuries B.C.

A king of Sidon wrote in praise of his gods in the fifth century B.C., saying, "And further, the Lord of kings gave to us Dor and Jaffa, the glorious cornlands which are in the field of Sharon, in accordance with the great things which I did; and we added them to the borders of the land that they might belong to the Sidonians." Dor had access to the Plain of Esdraelon through the Fureidis Gap in the Carmel Range, but it could not compete with the port of Accho which was superior to Dor and provided a more natural outlet from Esdraelon.

DOTHAN. Dothan is situated about thirteen miles north of Shechem in a fertile plain which separates the hills of Samaria from the Carmel range. The main caravan route between Damascus and Egypt passes through the Dothan Plain.

It was at Dothan that Joseph found his brothers pasturing their flocks. In their jealousy, however, they cast him into a pit and subsequently sold him to passing Midianites (Gen. 37:17-28). The Egyptian empire builder Thutmose III (*ca.* 1490-1435 B.C.) lists Dothan among the places he captured during the course of his campaigns in Palestine. The prophet Elisha was besieged by a band of Syrians (Arameans) at Dothan. The army was smitten with blindness and the prophet directed them to Samaria where their sight was restored and they were sent home without further punishment (II Kings 6:8-23).

Excavations have been conducted at Dothan since 1953 by Joseph P. Free of Wheaton College. The mound itself is about one thousand feet above sea level, 175 feet

AIR VIEW OF DURA EUROPUS. Courtesy, Yale University

above the surrounding plain. The top of the mound covers ten acres, with about fifteen more acres on the slopes.

Dothan has been occupied since the end of the Chalcolithic Period (*ca.* 3000 B.C.). Fifty feet from the top of the mound the excavators came upon a wall dating to the Bronze Age (3000-2000 B.C.), sixteen feet high. A Middle Bronze Age wall and an abundance of pottery date from the time of Joseph and the Biblical patriarchs. The site was occupied until the Iron Age, and again in the Hellenistic and Roman periods.

DURA EUROPUS. Dura Europus was founded by a general of Seleucus I, one of Alexander's successors, in the Syrian desert east of Tadmor about 300 B.C. It was situated on the Euphrates and gained importance as a caravan stopping point. Although a Greek city, Dura Europus was successively occupied by Parthians (2nd cent. B.C.) and Romans (2nd cent. A.D.). When the Romans defeated the Parthians, Dura was incorporated into the province of Syria, and in A.D. 167 a Roman garrison was settled there.

Dura was again besieged when the Sasanian Persians challenged Roman power in the East. The Persian Ardashir (224-241) nearly took the city in A.D. 238. In 256 the Persians invaded again. The Roman garrison built a mud brick embankment on either side of the walls to strengthen them. The walls were built higher and strengthened further, but Dura fell to the Persians and the Roman Emperor, Vakerian, was made a prisoner of the Persian ruler Shapur I (A.D. 241-272). The Persians occupied Dura for a short time, but the city was soon deserted. It is said that the Roman Emperor Julian (361-363) hunted lions among its ruins.

The ruins of ancient Dura were discovered by accident in 1921 when the British army dug trenches at the site while fighting the Arabs nearby. The trench diggers uncovered a section of a temple, and seven years later archaeologists began the serious excavation of the site.

Yale University and the French Academy of Inscriptions and Letters sponsored a series of expeditions at Dura under the direction of M. I. Rostovtzeff, beginning in 1928. Aerial photography indicated that the city was surrounded by a wall, and that the main gate faced westward, toward the desert. In a series of campaigns the excavators discovered eleven temples, two small shrines, a Christian church with murals, two synagogues, the second of which had walls covered with frescoes, a market, baths, houses, and the remains of the Roman garrison.

In 1932 the excavators came upon a church which had first served as a private house.

One room had first served as a chapel, and later other rooms were used for religious purposes. The chapel was decorated with wall paintings. The 1932-33 campaign brought to light a synagogue which was originally a private house. It was enlarged and dedicated as a synagogue in A.D. 245 (the year 556 of the Seleucid era as an inscription relates).

A second synagogue replaced the earlier one, and it is this second synagogue, completed in 255, that is the best known structure from Dura. Franz Cumont of the French Academy of Inscriptions and Letters excavated the synagogue from 1932 to 1935. In 1936 the structure was removed to Damascus where it was reconstructed as part of the national museum in Syria's capital.

The synagogue was entered through a courtyard to the east and the worshiper found himself in a room of approximately twenty-five by forty feet in size. In the middle of the west wall was a niche where the Ark of the Law was placed during services. Along the other wall were benches. The walls were decorated with frescoes depicting Old Testament themes. Around the niche are representations of a shrine in which the Law was kept, a seven-branched lampstand, and Abraham's offering of Isaac. Abraham has a knife in his hand as he is about to slay his son who is bound to the altar. God intervenes, however, as a hand interrupts Abraham and a ram waits in a bush nearby. Other scenes depict Moses and the burning bush, Moses leading the Israelites from Egypt, the Egyptians drowning in the waters, Joshua and the angel who met him before the battle of Jericho, the miracle of the sun standing still, David playing his harp, the sacrifice of Elijah on Mount Carmel, the vision of Ezekiel, and many more Old Testament scenes. The painting of the Return of the Ark (I Sam. 5) shows the Philistine leaders sending away the ark on a cart drawn by two oxen. On the ground, amid the rubble, are broken images of the gods of °Palmyra which were worshiped by the people of Dura. In the picture of the story of Job, one of his friends is depicted as a king. The

Jews of Dura were evidently familiar with a midrash which states that Job's friends were kings.

On the same street with the synagogue was a church which had once been the private house of a man of means in Dura. A graffito in the plaster indicates that the house was built in the year A.D. 232-233. When the original chapel was enlarged by the addition of two other rooms, the meeting place could accommodate about one hundred people. Three inscriptions cut into the wall read, "One God in heaven," "Remind Christ of the humble Siseos," and "Remind Christ of Proclus among yourselves." The last two are requests that the congregation remember Siseos and Proclus in prayer.

At the west end of the chapel was a niche with a sunken receptacle which may have been a baptismal font. If this interpretation of the find is correct, the church at Dura practiced affusion, since the font is too small for immersion. Some have denied that this was a baptismal font, suggesting that it marked the tomb of a martyr.

The chapel was decorated with frescos similar to those of the synagogue, except that both Old Testament and New Testament scenes are depicted. At the back of the niche are two scenes: Adam and Eve, and the Good Shepherd. Evidently the two are chosen to show that death entered the world through Adam, but salvation came through Christ. Other pictures include David and Goliath, the Samaritan Woman, and the Healing of the Paralytic. The last mentioned includes one of our earliest representations of Christ. Jesus is shown as young and beardless, with short hair and wearing the usual costume of the day. This painting may be dated definitely in the first part of the third century.

BIBLIOGRAPHY. René Dussaud, "La campagne 1933-34 a Doura-Europos," *SYRIA*, XV, 1934, pp. 393-394. Mikhail Ivanovitch, *Dura-Europos and its Art*, Clarendon Press, Oxford, 1938. M. I. Rostovtzeff, A. R. Bellinger, F. E. Brown, C. B. Welles, *The Excavations at Dura Europos Conducted by Yale University and the French Academy of Inscriptions and Letters*, Yale University Press, New Haven, 1943.

EEDFU

E

ECBATANA. Hamadan, on the site of ancient Ecbatana, is a modern city with a population of 130,000, high in the Zagros Mountains of western Iran. Although cold in winter, it has a delightful summer climate and Cyrus made it his summer capital. The name Ecbatana is ultimately derived from Akkadian *Agamatanu*, from *hangmatana*, "gathering place." It is mentioned in Ezra (6:2) as Achmetha, the place where Darius I found the Decree of Cyrus which authorized the Jews to return to Jerusalem and rebuild their temple.

The apocryphal book of Judith states that King Arphaxad who ruled the Medes during the time of Nebuchadnezzar had his capital at Ecbatana (Judith 1:1-14). A tradition preserved in II Maccabees (9:3) states that Antiochus Epiphanes stopped at Ecbatana after retreating from °Persepolis where he had suffered defeat. The Judith story is fictious, and there is no outside evidence to corroborate the statement in II Maccabees, for the more reliable account in I Maccabees (6:4) does not mention Ecbatana.

Ecbatana plays an important part in the apocryphal legends contained in the Book of Tobit where we read that the younger Tobit, or Tobias, was guided by the angel Raphael on a journey from Nineveh to collect the equivalent of $30,000, which the elder Tobit, his father, had deposited with Gabel at Rages (i.e. Rayy, near Tehran). Stopping at Ecbatana, Tobias was entertained at the home of Raguel, his father's brother. Sarah, Raguel's daughter was of marriageable age but her seven husbands had died on their wedding night. Armed with a formula for driving away the evil demons, Tobias married his charming cousin, and the story ends on a happy note.

Cuneiform documents from Tiglath-pileser I (1100 B.C.) mention Ecbatana as *karkassi*, "Kassite town." The Greek writer Ctesias (cf. *Diodorus* 2.3) ascribes the founding of Ecbatana along with Babylon and other important cities to Semiramis, a legendary figure who is probably to be identified with Sammuramat, described as "lady of the palace" in the days of the Assyrian king Adad-nirari III (*ca.* 800 B.C.). She was either the king's mother, and regent

during the early years of Adad-nirari's reign, or his wife.

At the northeastern sector of Hamadan is the area known as *Sar Qal'a,* "cliff castle," where the citadel of Cyrus once stood. Excavations at Sar Qal'a have revealed remains of the walls and foundations of the towers of the palaces of Median and Achaemenian kings. A gold plate discovered in the same area contains our earliest Achaemenian document, an inscription of Ariarmenes (640-590 B.C.) written a century before the time of Cyrus. Southeast of the town is an imposing "stone of the lion," Persian *Sang i-Shir,* which dates to Achaemenian or Parthian times.

Hamadan also boasts a traditional tomb of Esther and a tomb of Mordecai. The latter may be that of a Jewish physician and prime minister named Mordecai who was martyred in Tabriz in A.D. 1291. In later years his tomb was evidently ascribed to the Mordecai of the Book of Esther. The presence of a traditional "tomb of Esther" is probably due to the erroneous idea that ancient Susa was located at the sight of modern Hamadan. The archaeologist Ernst Herzfeld maintained that a godly woman named Shushan migrated to Hamadan, and that her Esther-like qualities caused her to be called "Shushan-Esther." Her tomb, Herzfeld suggests, is the one now identified as the tomb of the Biblical Esther.

EDESSA. The city of Edessa in northern Mesopotamia (mod. Urfa, Turkey) emerged into history in the fourth century B.C. Beginning *ca.* 137 B.C., Edessa was the capital of an independent kingdom (Osroene). It subsequently became a Roman city until A.D. 260 when Shapur I of Persia defeated the Roman Emperor Valerian and took him prisoner. By the third century A.D. Edessa was a center of Syrian Christianity, but in A.D. 639 it fell to the Arabs. Except for a brief period during the Crusades, Edessa has remained a Moslem center.

EDFU. Edfu, on the west bank of the Nile halfway between Luxor and Aswan, was capital of the second nome of Upper Egypt. The Greeks called it Appolonopolis

205

Magna equating the god Horus of Edfu with Apollo. Auguste Mariette discovered Edfu in 1860 and cleared the Temple of Horus which is the most perfectly preserved monument of the ancient world. It was begun by Ptolemy III, Euergetes in 237 B.C. and not completed until 57 B.C. Its towers rise to a height of 112 feet, and the walls enclose a space 450 by 120 feet. The front of the Propylon is 252 feet high. Early temples had been built at Edfu by Pharaohs Seti I, Ramesses III and Ramesses IV, but they have left no remains.

Horus, the god of Edfu, is represented on the monuments of Egypt by a winged solar disk. Legend says that he was assisted in a war with the god Seth and his followers by men who understood the art of metal working. The legend seems to reflect an account of a tribe of primitive users of stone weapons and implements being defeated by people who had learned to use metal.

BIBLIOGRAPHY. Henri Henne, Octave Guerade, Maurice Alliot, *Rapport sur les fouilles de Tell Edfou (1921-22)*. Impr. de l'Institute francaise d'archeologie orientale, Le Caire (Cairo), 1924.

EDOM, EDOMITES. The ancient kingdom of Edom lay to the south of the Wadi Zered below the Dead Sea. Both the land and its people are frequently mentioned in the Old Testament. Up to the present no written records from ancient Edom have been recovered so that our knowledge of this ancient kingdom comes from the records of the Israelites, Egyptians, Assyrians and Babylonians, and from archaeological discoveries in the area.

I. *The Land of Edom* was a mountainous and extremely rugged land mass about one hundred miles long extending from the River Arnon, which was the southern boundary of Moab, as far south as the Gulf of Aqabah. In width it included the mountains and fertile plateaux both to the east and the west of the Arabah, the great depression connecting the Dead Sea with the Gulf of Aqabah. The most important area was the plateau to the east of the Arabah. The highest point was Mount Seir which rises to about 3500 feet above the Arabah. In the days of the Hebrew monarchy the capital was Sela, which lay at the southern end of the secluded valley which eventually became *Petra. Other important towns were Bozrah and Teman. The economic strength of the kingdom lay in its agriculture, its mineral resources and in the tolls it levied on caravans traversing its roads, especially the King's Highway.

II. *Edom in the Old Testament.* According to Genesis 36:1-17 the Edomites were descendants of Esau. The land was occupied, however, before the arrival of Esau's descendants (Gen. 14:6). Tribal chiefs emerged here quite early (Gen. 36:15-19, 40-43; I Chron. 1:51-54), and the Edomites had kings "before there reigned any king over Israel" (Gen. 36:31-39; I Chron. 1:43-51).

In the days of the Exodus, Israel sought to pass through Edom, travelling on the King's Highway but was refused permission (Num. 20:14-21; 21:4; Judg. 11:17-18). Some kinship with Edom was recognized however (Deut. 23:7, 8). The prophet Balaam promised that Israel would one day possess Edom (Num. 24:18).

Joshua allotted Judah the lands to the west of the Dead Sea as far as the borders of Edom (Josh. 15:1, 21). Two hundred years later Saul fought Edom (I Sam. 14:47) although there were Edomites in his service (I Sam. 21:7; 22:9, 18). David conquered Edom and placed garrisons in the land (II Sam. 8:13, 14. Emend *'ăram* in verse 13 to *'edom* because of the scribal confusion of resh "*r*" and daleth "*d*." Cf. I Chron. 18:13.) David's methods were ruthless (II Sam. 8:13). He left Joab in Edom for six months "until he had cut off every male in Edom" (I Kings 11:15, 16). Some fled to Egypt, including a royal prince Hadad who later troubled Solomon (I Kings 11:14-22). In his day Solomon had a port on the Red Sea at *Ezion-geber and exploited the copper mines in the region (I Kings 9:26-28).

In the time of Jehoshaphat, Edomites raided Judah in company with others but were overcome (II Chron. 20). Jehoshaphat sought to re-open the port of Ezion-geber without success (I Kings 22:48). The "deputy" of Edom (I Kings 22:47) acknowledged the rule of Jehosaphat and joined him in an attack on Mesha, king of Moab (II Kings 3:4-27).

Under Joram (Jehoram) Edom gained her independence (II Kings 8:20-22; II Chron. 21:8-10) but Amaziah later captured Sela their capital and killed many (II Kings 14:7;

II Chron. 25:11, 12). His son Uzziah restored the port at Elath (II Kings 14:22) although this was lost in the days of Ahaz and never recovered (II Kings 16:6). After 736 B.C. Edom became a vassal state of Assyria.

When Judah fell in 586, Edom rejoiced (Ps. 137:7). For her bitter hatred of Judah the prophets foretold her destruction (Jer. 49:7-22; Lam. 4:21, 22; Ezek. 25:12-14; 35: 15; Joel 3:19; Amos 9:12; Obad. 10 ff.). Some Edomites entered Southern Judah and settled to the south of Hebron under pressure from Arab invasions during the fifth century B.C. In the third century B.C. the °Nabateans occupied old Edom and drove out more of the people into Judah. Judas Maccabeus later subdued them (I Macc. 5:65), and John Hyrcanus compelled them to be circumcised and incorporated into the Jewish people. The family of Herod was of general Edomite stock.

III. *Archaeological Discoveries and Edom.* Surface surveys have shown that between the twenty-third and the twentieth century B.C. there was a flourishing civilization in Edom. But this was destroyed, possibly by desert invaders. Little evidence of urban settlement is found before the thirteenth century B.C. The destruction of the older civilization may be related to the invasion of Genesis 14. The presence of ancient sites along the main central road — the King's Highway — points to the existence of this road during this early period. The discovery of pottery of the Late Bronze and Early Iron Ages on many sites in Edom points to a date in the thirteenth century for the establishment of the later kingdom of Edom. These people built a series of walled fortresses around their highland home, especially on the eastern position which was exposed to raids from the desert. They were strategically placed so as to enable communication by fire signals in case of attack. They point to a well organized military system under a strong government. Egyptian records from as early as the days of Thutmose II (*ca.* 1495-1490 B.C.) speak of contact with the *Shasu* nomads. Later records from the days of Merenptah (1224-1215 B.C.) and Ramesses III (*ca.* 1198-1167) show that at least some of the *Shasu* people were to be found in the region of Edom, for Mount Seir is specifically mentioned.

Archaeological discovery has produced a good deal of evidence from the days of Solomon, *i.e.* from Iron I Age. The port at °Ezion-geber (Phase I) and numerous mining and smelting sites in the Wadi Arabah, dating to the early Iron Age, point to considerable activity in southern Edom. The complex smelting plant at Ezion-geber which used the north winds for draught, argues for a high degree of technical knowledge. Items found in the excavations indicate that trade was carried on between the port and such places as Egypt and South Arabia. The destruction of Ezion-geber I during the tenth century can be attributed to the invasion of Shishak (I Kings 14:25).

During the period between the seventh and the fourth centuries (Phases IV and V), Elath remained Edomite. Several seventh century Edomite seals bearing the title "Qos 'anal, servant of the King" have been found. Under later Persian rule, trade still flourished at this port to judge from Aramaic ostraca of the fifth and fourth centuries B.C., some of which were receipts for wine. Attic Greek pottery sherds suggest trade with the Greeks. Eventually the port fell into Nabatean hands.

While the picture of Edomite cultural achievements is slowly emerging, a good deal more excavation will need to be undertaken before the picture is clear.

BIBLIOGRAPHY. N. Glueck, *The Other Side of Jordan,* New Haven, 1940; *Annual of the American Schools of Oriental Research,* XV, XVIII, XIX; articles in *BASOR,* 71, 72, 75, 76, 79, 80, 82, 84, 85. F. M. Abel, *Géographie de la Palestine,* II, Paris, 1933, pp. 281-285. M. Du Buit, *Géographie de la Terre Sainte,* Paris, 1958, pp. 143f.

EGNATIAN WAY. The Egnatian Way was the military highway which linked Rome with the East. Vessels crossing the Aegean from Asia Minor would dock at Neapolis, the port of Philippi in northern Greece. There they would connect with the Egnatian Way which ran westward through Philippi, across Macedonia to Dyrrachium (Durazzo) opposite Brundisium in Italy. A sea journey across the Adriatic would bring the traveler to Brundisium where he could take the Appian Way to °Rome.

EGYPT. I. *Name.* The name Egypt is probably derived from a name of Memphis, *Hi-ku-Ptah,* "the house of the spirit of Ptah," through the Greek form *Aigyptos.* The an-

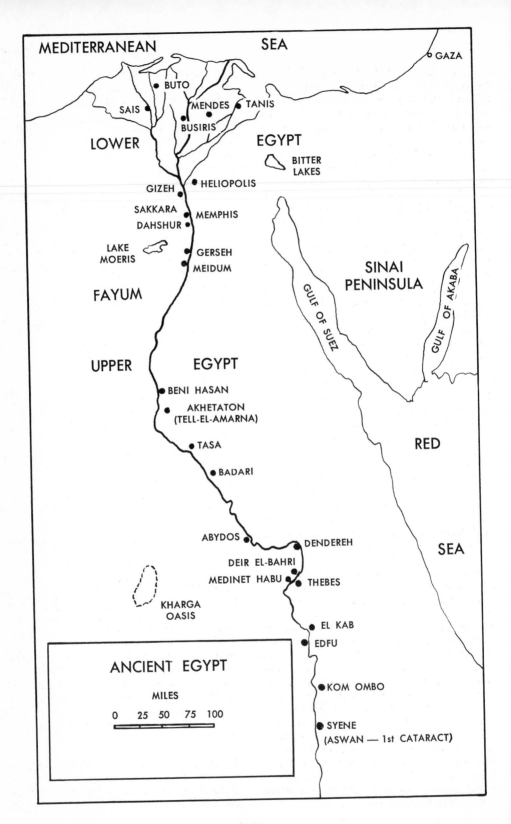

MEDITERRANEAN SEA

GAZA

BUTO

SAIS

MENDES TANIS

BUSIRIS

LOWER EGYPT

BITTER
LAKES

GIZEH HELIOPOLIS

SAKKARA MEMPHIS
DAHSHUR

LAKE
MOERIS

GERSEH
MEIDUM

FAYUM

SINAI
PENINSULA

GULF OF SUEZ

GULF OF AKABA

UPPER EGYPT

BENI HASAN

AKHETATON
(TELL-EL-AMARNA)

TASA

BADARI

RED

ABYDOS DENDEREH

DEIR EL-BAHRI
MEDINET HABU THEBES

SEA

KHARGA
OASIS

EL KAB

EDFU

ANCIENT EGYPT

MILES

0   25 50 75 100

KOM OMBO

SYENE
(ASWAN — 1st CATARACT)

208

cient Egyptians had several names for their country, such as *Kemi* "the black land," and "the two lands" (of Upper and Lower Egypt). The modern Arabic name for Egypt, *Misr*, is related to Hebrew *Miṣrāyim*, a dual form probably referring to Upper and Lower Egypt. Since February, 1958, the official name of the country has been *al-Jumhuriyah al-'Arabiyah al-Muttahidah*, "the United Arab Republic."

II. *Geography.* Modern Egypt is roughly a rectangle in the northeast corner of Africa. It is bounded on the south by the Sudan, on the east by the Red Sea and Palestine, on the north by the Mediterranean Sea, and on the west by Libya.

"Egypt," wrote Herodotus in the fifth century B.C., "is the gift of the Nile." Ninety-nine percent of the population live on the four percent of the area which can be irrigated by the Nile water, and the rest is desert, with the exception of a few oases. The average rainfall in Cairo is about one inch and in Aswan practically nil. The dryness of Egypt has helped to preserve many ancient monuments, especially papyri, wood, and mummies, which would have perished in a damper climate. The annual overflow of the Nile during the summer has deposited fertile soil and also freed thousands of laborers for such gigantic projects as the pyramids, the temples, and the royal tombs. The Nile also furnished a water highway for easy transportation of goods and people.

The difference between the narrow valley of the Nile and its broad Delta has divided the habitable area into two distinct geographical and political regions. In Upper Egypt from Aswan to Cairo the valley averages about twelve miles in width between desert hills. About twelve miles north of Cairo the Nile divides into two main branches, from which many canals water the flat Delta, which reaches a width of about 150 miles.

Some of the products of Egypt are mentioned in the Bible. The sandstone and limestone hills on either side of the Nile furnished stone for the pyramids and temples. Granite from Aswan was used for obelisks, statues, and sarcophagi. Alabaster from near Bani Suwayf was made into perfume jars (Matt. 26:7). Copper from Sinai furnished tools and weapons during the period of Egypt's Empire, the late Bronze Age. Gold (Gen. 41:42) from the eastern desert

and turquoise and lapis lazuli from Sinai were used for jewelry. Wheat was usually abundant, and some was bought by foreigners from the time of Abram (Gen. 12:10) to that of Paul (Acts 27:6, 38). Other vegetable food included cucumbers, melons, leeks, and onions (Num. 11:5). Fish was also an important item of diet as illustrated by the Bible (Num. 11:5; Isa. 19:8) and the monuments. Cattle (Gen. 41:2) are mentioned or depicted in the earliest records. Horses (Exod. 14:9) were not introduced till the Hyksos period. The chief beast of burden was the ass (Gen. 45:23). Along the Nile and the canals grew papyrus reeds, which were split and pressed to make the earliest paper (II John 12). The most common source of cloth was flax (Gen. 41:42; Isa. 19:9), and fine pieces of linen have been found in tombs.

Cities and districts in Egypt mentioned in the Bible include: Baalzephon (Exod. 14:2), perhaps near Tell Defenneh, Biblical *Tahpanhes; Goshen (Gen. 47:6, 27) a district in the eastern part of the Delta; Hanes (Isa. 30:4), perhaps the classical Herakleopolis Magna, modern Ihnasiyah al-Madinah; Migdol (Exod. 14:2), near the Red, or Reed Sea; No (Jer. 46:25), or No-Amon (Nah. 3:8), Greek *Thebes, capital of Upper Egypt and center of worship of Amun, modern Luxor; Noph (Isa. 19:13), or Moph (Hos. 9:6), Greek *Memphis, capital of the Old Kingdom, modern Mit Raḥinah: On (Gen. 41:45), or Aven (Ezek. 30:17), or Beth-shemesh, "house of the sun" (Jer. 43: 13), Greek *Heliopolis, center of worship of Re', the sun-god, modern al-Maṭariyah; Pathros (Isa. 11:11), from Egyptian *p'-t'rsy*, the southland, Upper Egypt; Pi-beseth (Ezek. 30:17), modern Tell Basṭa in the eastern part of the Delta; Pi-hahiroth (Exod. 14:2), near the Red, or Reed, Sea; Pithom (Exod. 1:11), identification with either Tell al-Maskhuṭah or Tall al-Raṭabah in Wadi Tumilat has been proposed; Raamses (Exod. 1:11), perhaps modern Qantir, or Ṣan al-Ḥajar, both in the northeastern part of the Delta; Sin (Ezek. 30:15, 16), classical Pelusium, modern Tell al-Faramā, about eighteen miles east of the Suez Canal; Succoth (Exod. 12: 37), perhaps modern Tell al-Mashkuṭah in Wadi-Tumilat; Syene (Ezek. 29:10), modern Aswan; *Tahpanhes (Jer. 43:7), or Tehaphnehes (Ezek. 30:18), modern Tell Defen-

VIEW OF THE VALLEY OF KINGS. *Graves of the New Kingdom era. Courtesy, E. Anrich*

neh in the northeastern part of the Delta; Zoan (Num. 13:22), Greek Avaris or Tanis, modern Ṣan-al-Ḥajar in the northeastern part of the Delta.

III. *History.*

A. Prehistoric Egypt. Several prehistoric cultures developed in Egypt from *ca.* 5000 B.C. to the beginning of the First Dynasty, *ca.* 3200 B.C. Centers of these predynastic cultures have been found at al-Fayyum, Marimdah Bani Salamah, Dair Tasa, al-'Umari near Ḥilwan, al-Badari, al-'Amrah (Amratian Culture), Jarzah (Gerzean Culture), and al-Ma'adi. These settlements show advances in the making of implements and pottery.

Egyptian writing developed during the predynastic period. Hieroglyphic writing consisted of pictures used first to represent objects or actions, then to represent syllables, and finally to represent single sounds as an alphabet. These three stages of hierglyphic writing continued together throughout three millennia. In 1905 W. M. Flinders Petrie discovered at *Sarabit el-Khadem some Semitic inscriptions using signs borrowed from Egyptian hieroglyphs. This Sinaitic alphabet is a link between Egyptian hieroglyphics and our modern alphabets.

During this period the Egyptians devised a solar calendar. This calendar was later standarized during the reign of Djoser of the Third Dynasty, perhaps by his famous chancellor, Imhotep.

B. Early Dynastic Period, *ca.* 3200-2780 B.C. An Egyptian priest *Manetho, in *ca.* 280 B.C. compiled a formal history of Egypt, extracts of which have been preserved by Josephus, Julius Africanus, Eusebius, and others. Manetho grouped the kings of ancient Egypt into thirty families, or dynasties,

down to the conquest by Alexander in 332 B.C.

The early dynastic period comprises Dynasties I and II. Materials from this period have been found in tombs at Saqqara, Naqadah, Memphis, Ḥilwan, and al-Fayyum, and in the ancient temple enclosure at Abydos.

The first king of the First Dynasty, Menes or Narmer, united Upper and Lower Egypt under a fully-organized central government. Written records were carefully kept, a meticulous inventory of government supplies was made, and a census of the population and an assessment of the national property were taken every two years for levying taxes. Religious festivals were celebrated at appointed intervals.

C. The Old Kingdom (*ca.* 2780-2280 B.C.). This period comprises Dynasties III, IV, V, and VI, of Manetho's list, and the capital was at Memphis. Djoser (*ca.* 2780-2761 B.C.), founder of the Third Dynasty, is best known for his step-pyramid and mortuary temple at Saqqara. These were designed by his physician, architect, and chancellor, Imhotep.

The Fourth Dynasty (*ca.* 2680-2560 B.C.) is one of the great high points of Egyptian history. The annals of its first king, Snefru, are preserved in part on the Palermo Stone. He constructed two pyramids at Dahshur.

Three kings of the Fourth Dynasty, Khufu, Khafre, and Menkaure, known in Greek as Cheops, Chephren, and Mycerinus, built three great mortuary pyramids at Gizeh, eight miles southwest of Cairo. The *pyramid of Khufu, or the Great Pyramid, is the largest single building ever constructed by man. It covers an area of thirteen acres, its original height was 481 ft., and it is composed of about 2,300,000 great blocks of limestone, each weighing about two and one-half tons. The four faces of this pyramid are very accurately directed to the four cardinal directions. To the southwest of Khufu's pyramid, his son, Khafre, built a pyramid more pointed and slightly smaller than his father's. To the west of his pyramid, and beside his mortuary temple Khafre had the Great Sphinx carved out of solid limestone, with the likeness of his own head and the body of a recumbent lion. Some think that Job 3:14 refers to Egyptian pyramids.

During the Sixth Dynasty Egyptian power expanded in Nubia, and Egypt's trade increased with the African countries to the south and with eastern Mediterranean lands to the north.

D. First Intermediate Period (*ca.* 2280-2052 B.C.). During the Seventh and Tenth Dynasties minor kings ruled in Memphis, Thebes, or Herakleopolis.

E. Middle Kingdom (*ca.* 2134-1178 B.C.). Mentu-hotep I (*ca.* 2079-2061 B.C.) reunited the two lands and paved the way for the Middle Kingdom, including Dynasties Eleven and Twelve.

During the Twelfth Dynasty (*ca.* 1991-1778 B.C.) new and larger copper mines were worked at Sarabit el-Khadem in Sinai. Senusert III made a foray into Palestine as far as Shechem. The tomb of Khnumhotep, a noble of the Twelfth Dynasty, at *Beni Hasan has a painting of Asiatics entering Egypt to get food. It was probably during this period that Abram visited Egypt for the same purpose (Gen. 12:15-20).

F. Second Intermediate Period (*ca.* 1778-1567 B.C.). This second period of deterioration comprises Dynasties Thirteen to Seventeen. The Hyksos, meaning "shepherd kings," or "rulers of foreign countries," conquered Egypt (*ca.* 1675-1567). These seem to have been chiefly Semites who invaded Egypt from Asia, bringing the horse, the chariot, and new weapons. Perhaps Joseph rose to power (Gen. 41:14-45) during this period of foreign domination. Goshen, where Jacob and his family settled (Gen. 47:27), was near Avaris, the Hyksos capital in the Delta.

G. New Kingdom (*ca.* 1567-1085 B.C.). This period comprised Dynasties Eighteen,

Nineteen, and Twenty. Ahmose I (*ca.* 1570-1546 B.C.) a Theban prince, first king of the Eighteenth Dynasty, drove the Hyksos out of Egypt. It has been suggested that he might be the "new King over Egypt, that knew not Joseph" (Exod. 1:8). In pursuing the Hyksos he besieged Sharuhen in southwestern Palestine. Thutmose I (*ca.* 1526-1508 B.C.) campaigned in Syria as far as the upper reaches of the Euphrates. Thutmose II died leaving a young son, Thutmose III (*ca.* 1490-1436 B.C.). Because of the latter's youth, Hatshepsut, the royal widow, assumed power. About 1469 B.C. her rule and her life ended, and Thutmose III attained sole rule. He campaigned successfully in Palestine, Syria, the Hittite lands, and the Mitanni land. These conquests initiated the golden age of ancient Egypt. According to the fifteenth-century dating of the Exodus, Thutmose III would be the Pharaoh from whom Moses fled (Exod. 2:15). He was succeeded by Amenhotep

KING MYCERINUS between the goddess Hathor and the personification of the 7th district of Upper Egypt. Courtesy, Foto Marburg

CANAANITE FOES OF SETI I. A fortre
situated on a hill, bears the name, "the to
of the Canaan." The bearded foes of t
Egyptian Pharaoh are the Shasu-bedou
The relief is from the exterior of the nor
wall of the temple at Karnak.

II (*ca.* 1436-1411) who resumed his father's campaigns in Palestine and Syria. According to Manetho the Pharaoh of the Exodus was Amenophis, the Greek form of Amenhotep. Taking I Kings 6:1 (Exodus 480 years before Solomon's temple) and Judges 11:26 (Conquest 300 years before Jephthah) at their face-value would put the Exodus in the middle of the fifteenth century about the time of Amenhotep II. His stela discovered in Memphis in 1943 refers to the capture of 3,600 Apiru during a campaign in Palestine. Some think that this indicates that the Exodus had already taken place, but the name Apiru, though related to "Hebrews," has a wider reference.

After Thutmose IV and Amenhotep III the latter's son, Amenhotep IV (*ca.* 1370-1353 B.C.) ascended the throne. He deserted Thebes and built a new capital, which he called Akhet-Aten, modern Tell el-Amarna in Middle Egypt. He and his beautiful wife, Nefertiti, launched a religious revolution. He adopted the worship of Aton, a god of Heliopolis, discarded that of Amun of Thebes, and changed his name to Akhenaton. Contention naturally arose between Akhenaton and the priests of Amun in Thebes. While he was engaged in religious reforms, the possessions of the Empire in Palestine and Syria were falling away. The death of Akhenaton dealt a fatal blow to the religious reformation.

The international correspondence of Amenhotep III and of his son, Amenhotep IV, or Akhenaton was discovered in 1887 in Tell el-Amarna. These archives were in the form of baked clay tablets, written mostly in Akkadian cuneiform. These tablets mention the Habiru who were making trouble in Palestine and Syria and who are probably related in name to the Hebrews. Some associate the rebellious activity of the Habiru with the Hebrew Conquest of Palestine and so support the fifteenth century date for the Exodus. However the Habiru were active in a much wider area than the Hebrews.

The second successor of Akhenaton, his son-in-law, Tut-'ankh-Aton, was obliged to relinquish Atenism. He changed his name to Tut-'ankh-Amun, "Beautiful in Life is Amun." He was also forced to abandon the royal residence in Akhet-Aton and to restore the court to Thebes. His tomb, crammed with magnificent mortuary furniture, was discovered by Howard Carter in 1922.

Egypt's military power was restored by two generals who became Pharaohs, Haremhab, the last king of the Eighteenth Dynasty, and Ramesses I, the first of the Nineteenth Dynasty. Seti I carried on campaigns in Palestine and Syria. He erected a temple and a triumphal stela at Beth-shan, in which he refers to the Apiru. He vanquished the rebellious princes of Galilee. In a campaign against the Hittites he forced their king, Mursilis II, to make peace.

Ramesses II (*ca.* 1290-1223 B.C.) fought a battle near Kadesh against the Hittites and their confederates and drove them to the Orontes. Finally in the twenty-first year of his reign war between the Hittites and the Egyptians was ended by a peace treaty between Ramesses II and Hattusilis, king of the Hittites. According to this treaty, Palestine and southern Syria were to remain under the control of Egypt. Some think that this great builder is the Pharaoh for whom the Hebrews constructed the city called by his name Raamses (Exod. 1:11), and he records using Apiru slaves in his building projects. On the basis of the dating of the destruction of cities in Palestine some also wish to place the Exodus in his reign during the early part of the thirteenth century.

Some think that the Pharaoh of the Exodus was Ramesses II's son, Merneptah (*ca.* 1223-1211 B.C.). This identification, like that with Amenhotep II mentioned above, is consonant with Exodus 2:23 which indicates that the Pharaoh who had wished to kill Moses and who preceded the Pharaoh of the Exodus died after Moses had been in the wilderness almost forty years. Merneptah's victories in Palestine are commemorated in a stele preserved in the Egyptian Museum in Cairo. This stele has the only direct mention of the children of Israel in any Egyptian inscription: "Israel is laid waste; his seed is not." The Exodus must have taken place *before* the date of this stele, *ca.* 1220 B.C.

Ramesses III (*ca.* 1192-1160 B.C.) of the Twentieth Dynasty recorded on the walls of his temple at Medinat Habu his repulse of the migrating sea peoples from the north, among whom were the Pelesti, the Biblical Philistines. The Philistines were able to establish themselves only in some cities of the coastal plain of Palestine, such as Gaza, Ashkelon, Ashdod, Ekron, and Gath.

H. Late Dynastic Period (*ca.* 1085-332 B.C.). This period includes Dynasties Twenty-one through Thirty and end with the conquest of Egypt by Alexander the Great. It was initiated by Herihor, high priest of Amun, who established an ecclesiastical control which lasted over four hundred years (1085-670 B.C.), a time of general decline. During the Twenty-first Dynasty (1085-945 B.C.) the capital was at Tanis. The Pharaoh who received Hadad of Edom (I Kings 11:18) was either Amenemope or Siamun of this Dynasty. The Pharaoh who gave his daughter in marriage to Solomon (I Kings 3:1) was either Siamun or Psusennes II of the same Dynasty. The latter's tomb and silver coffin have been discovered at Tanis.

The Pharaohs of the Twenty-second Dynasty were of Libyan origin, and their capital was Bubastis. Shishak, who harbored the rebellious Jeroboam in the time of Solomon (I Kings 11:40) was Sheshonq (*ca.* 945-924 B.C.), first king of this Dynasty. Later he invaded Palestine and took treasure from Jerusalem in the time of Rehoboam (I Kings 14:25, 26; II Chron. 12:2-9). A relief on the exterior of the southern wall of the temple of Amun at Karnak depicts this campaign and lists Palestinian cities captured. Zerah, the Ethiopian, who invaded Judah and was defeated by Asa (II Chron. 14:9-15; 16:8), was probably a general of Osorkon I (924-895 B.C.). During the Twenty-second, Twenty-third, and Twenty-fourth Dynasties the Ethiopians set up an independent kingdom with its capital at Napata and began to push into Egypt. So of Egypt to whom Hoshea of Israel sent ambassadors (II Kings 17:4) may have been Osorkon IV (727-716 B.C.) of the Twenty-third Dynasty, or the vizier of Egypt, or Sais a capital in the

DEIR EL BAHARI TEMPLE of Queen Hatshepsut. Courtesy, E. Anrich

Delta (*BASOR*, 171, Oct. 1963, pp. 64-66).

The Ethiopians finally gained control of all of Egypt and established the Twenty-fifth Dynasty (712-663 B.C.). During this time Assyria was the expanding power in the Near East. The Assyrian besiegers of Jerusalem warned Hezekiah against relying on Tirhakah (II Kings 19:8-13), Egyptian Taharqa, who was probably then a general and who later became a Pharaoh of the Twenty-fifth or Ethiopian Dynasty. The Assyrians defeated Taharqa several times and finally sacked Thebes in 663 B.C. (Nah. 3:8-10).

Under the Twenty-sixth Dynasty (663-525 B.C.), whose capital was Sais, there was a revival of Egyptian power and of archaizing art and literature. Necho II (610-595 B.C.) marched through Palestine to try to help Assyria against rising Babylonia. Josiah of Judah opposed him at Megiddo and was defeated and killed (II Kings 23:29-30 RSV). Pharaoh Necho removed Jehoahaz, Josiah's successor, and put Jehoiakim on the throne of Judah, exacting tribute from him (II Kings 23:33-35). An Aramaic letter from a Palestinian city-king, found in Saqqara in 1942, reports to Necho about Babylonian advances in southern Palestine, which are also described in I Kings 24:1-17 and II Chron. 36:6-10. Pharaoh Hophra, called in Greek Apries, (589-570 B.C.) came to the aid of Zedekiah besieged in Jerusalem by the Babylonians (Ezek. 17:11-21; Jer. 37:5). Nebuchadnezzar temporarily stopped the siege to repulse Hophra (Jer. 37:7, 11). Hophra was finally killed by his co-regent Ahmose, according to the prophecy in Jeremiah 44:30. In the reign of Ahmose II (570-526 B.C.) Nebuchadnezzar marched against Egypt as predicted by Jeremiah (43:10-13; 46:13-26).

In 525 B.C.. A Persian army led by Cambyses conquered Egypt, and the following Persian monarchs constituted the Twenty-seventh Dynasty down to Alexander's conquest. Egyptian rulers who revolted against the Persians in the later part of this period made up Dynasties Twenty-eight through Thirty. The fifth-century B.C. papyrus records of the Jewish colony on Elephantine Island near Aswan mention some Biblical characters: Johanan the priest (Neh. 12:22, 23), sons of Sanballat (Neh. 2:10), and Anani (perhaps I Chron. 3:24). These records indicate that the Jews in this frontier city were a military garrison under the Persian governor and that they had their own temple and observed the passover according to directions from the high-priest in Jerusalem. A silver bowl from Tell el-Maskuṭah refers to Qainu, son of Geshem (Neh. 2:19) and shows that the latter was king of the Arab tribe of Kedar, who evidently maintained a garrison on the eastern frontier of Egypt for the Persians.

I. Alexander and the Ptolemies (332-30 B.C.). When Alexander and his army reached Egypt in 332 B.C., he was acclaimed as a liberator. Soon after his arrival he went to Memphis, sacrificed to the Apis bull, and was accepted as Pharaoh. Returning to the coast, he laid out the city of Alexandria.

When Alexander died in Babylon in 323 B.C., his empire was divided, and his general Ptolemy took Egypt and became the founder of the Ptolemaic Dynasty, which ruled Egypt till the Roman conquest. This first Ptolemy established the famous library of Alexandria, which became a center of Greek culture. Daniel 11 refers to many of the Ptolemies down to Ptolemy VI (180-145 B.C.) under the title kings of the South and describes especially their conflicts with the Seleucids. The Apocryphal books mention several Ptolemies: IV (III Mac. 1:1), VI (I Mac. 1:18), VII (I Mac. 15:16), and VIII (Est. 11:1). A stele of Ptolemy V (203-181 B.C.), inscribed in hieroglyphic, demotic, and Greek and found near Rosetta, furnished Champollion with the key to Egyptian hieroglyphics, which he published in 1822.

The last of the Ptolemies was Queen Cleopatra. Julius Caesar came to Egypt in 48 B.C., then Mark Antony in 41 B.C. Cleopatra tried devious ways with both these Roman generals to preserve Egypt's sovereignty. Octavian defeated Antony and Cleopatra in the naval battle of Actium in 30 B.C. He refused to be influenced by Cleopatra's charms, she took her own life, and Egypt became a Roman province.

J. Egypt as a Roman Province and the New Testament. According to Matthew 2:13-15, the Holy Family fled to Egypt to save the infant Jesus from Herod. They are said to have rested under a tree in Heliopolis. Their traditional stay in Old Cairo, commemorated in the crypt of the Church of St. Sergius is plausible because of the Jewish community there. Local traditions claim that

HOREMHAB *with papyrus scroll across his lap. The future king is reading a psalm to Thoth. On the base are prayers to Thoth and other gods. Courtesy, Metropolitan Museum of Art*

they also visited Upper Egypt as far south as Drunkah, near Asyut. Various representatives of the large Jewish community in Alexandria are mentioned in the New Testament: visitors to Jerusalem at Pentecost (Acts 2:10), opponents of Stephen (6:9), the learned and eloquent Apollos (18:24-28), a revolutionary in Jerusalem (21:38). According to tradition, John Mark preached in Alexandria and was martyred there. Coptic Orthodox patriarchs are counted in succession from him and are called patriarchs of the Marcan preaching. Some believe that I Peter 5:13 refers to Old Cairo, called Babylon in Greek, one of the oldest Christian centers in Egypt, but many think that the reference is to Rome.

IV. *Art.* Much of the preserved art of Egypt has been found in tombs, because of the belief that a representation of food or servants and of the article of daily life could be utilized by the deceased. Architecture is characterized by massiveness, as in the pyramids of the Old Kingdom and the great temples of the New Kingdom. Sculpture, bas-relief, painting, and jewelry, reached a high degree of refinement. The Egyptian artist represented the object without perspective, in its most characteristic aspect or from several aspects at once. Certain poses of the body became conventional and were retained through the three millennia of ancient Egyptian art. The art of *Amarna broke with tradition in being more realistic. In Ptolemaic times Greek influences appeared, for example in a more plastic treatment of the human body.

Egyptian art may have influenced the Hebrews at certain points. (1) The golden calf made by Aaron and the children of Israel at Sinai (Exod. 32) may have been modeled after the Egyptian Apis or Mnevis. (2) The design of some Egyptian temples and portable shrines resembles that of the Tabernacle (Exod. 25-27). (3) Egyptian winged sphinxes may have looked like the cherubim which were represented over the ark (Exod. 25:18-22) and on the curtains of the Tabernacle (Exod. 26:1). (4) Tutankhamun's throne is decorated with lions, like that of Solomon (I Kings 10:19, 20). (5) Bound prisoners from different countries are represented on Tutankhamun's footstool, a symbolism which is also found in Psalm 110:1. (6) The diorite statue of Khafre is protected by the wings

of a hawk, and the same figure is used for God's protection in Psalm 17:8.

V. *Literature.* Among the types of Egyptian literature which have been preserved are: funerary texts from tombs, the Book of the Dead (directions for vindication in the judgment), hymns to the gods, laudations of royal victories, proverbs, stories, poems of love, letters, business documents, mathematical, medical, and magical texts.

Some of the relationships between literature produced in Egypt and the Bible are as follows. (1) Some words in the Hebrew Old Testament are derived from ancient Egyptian, like the word for Nile, *ye'or* (from *'irw*), Moses (perhaps from *msw*, "born of" which appears in Kings names like Ramesses, "born of Re'"), and Phinehas (from *p'nshy*, "the Nubian"). (2) The similarities between the Egyptian tale of *The Two Brothers and the story of Joseph and Potiphar and between the negative confessions of the Book of the Dead and the Ten Commandments are outweighed by dissimilarities. (3) The parallels between Akhenaton's Hymn to the Aton and Psalm 104 may be the result of a similar subject, creation and providence by one god, and direct literary affinity cannot be proved. (4) Many of the proverbs of *Amenemopet (written *ca.* 1100-950 B.C.) are similar to the "words of the wise" in Prov. 22:17-24:22. (5) In the Inter-Testament period the Jewish community in Alexandria produced important writings and translations into Greek: among the Apocrypha, Wisdom and II Maccabees, and the Greek translation of Ecclesiacus or Sirach; among the Pseudepigrapha, Letter of Aristeas, Sybilline Oracles, II and IV Maccabees, II Enoch, and III Baruch; and the Septuagint Greek translation, begun according to tradition under Ptolemy II Philadelphus (285-246 B.C.), which opened the Old Testament to Greek-speaking Jews and Gentiles and later to Christians. (6) Philo, the Alexandrian Jewish philosopher of the first century A.D., who tried to harmonize Plato and the Bible, uses some expressions and methods of interpreting the Old Testament which are also found in John and Hebrews. For example Philo speaks of the Logos, or Word, as the agent in Creation, like John 1:3, but the great difference is that in John the Word is personal, historical, and incarnate in Jesus Christ. Philo,

217

like Hebrews 9:11, 23, 24, refers to the earthly sanctuary as a shadow of the heavenly, and he uses Melchizedek as an allegory of right reason, while the writer to the Hebrews (5:10; 6:20; 7:1-28) uses him as a type of Christ the supreme mediator. (7) Some of the sayings of Jesus in the Coptic Gnostic Gospels of the fourth and fifth centuries A.D. recently discovered near Nag' Hammadi in Upper Egypt are practically the same as passages in the canonical Gospels, but other sections show ascetic and dualistic tendencies foreign to the New Testament.

VI. *Religion.* The many Egyptian gods have been classified under three types: (1) gods of place, such as Ptah of Memphis, the crocodile god Sobek of al-Fayyum, and Amun the ram-headed god of Thebes; (2) cosmic gods such as the sky goddess Nut, the earth god Geb, and the sun god Re; (3) gods responsible for some function in life, such as Ma'at the goddess of truth and justice, Sekhmet the lioness-headed goddess of war and disease, Hathor the cow goddess of love, and Thoth the ibis-headed god of wisdom.

In the Old Kingdom Ptah and Re were the paramount gods, but in the New Kingdom Amun predominated and was identified with Re. The monotheistic worship of Aton by Akhenaton was temporary. The most popular myth was that of Osiris. He was killed by his brother Set. Isis found the body of Osiris and embalmed it, and then he revived and became king of the underworld. Isis bore Horus to Osiris after the latter's death. The worship of Serapis (a combination of Osiris, Apis, and Greek elements) was introduced in Ptolemaic times.

There are similarities between Egyptian and Biblical religion, but also great contrasts. (1) Circumcision, which was an ancient practice in Egypt, was first adopted by Abraham according to divine command for Ishmael his son by the Egyptian Hagar (Gen. 16:3; 17:23). (2) The accounts of embalming for forty days and mourning for seventy days (Gen. 50:3) and of putting in a coffin (Gen. 50:26) agree exactly with Egyptian practices. (3) One of the purposes of the plagues was to show the superiority of the one Yahweh to the many so-called gods of Egypt (Exod. 9:14). (4) It is difficult to establish direct relationship between the monotheism of Aton and that of Yahweh. The latter religion is distinguished by more moral demands, by more direct relationship between the worshipper and God, and by the imageless worship, not of the sun disk but of the Creator of the sun. (5) Some of the early Christian Fathers saw in the cult of Osiris a preparation for the gospel. However, the Egyptian story of the dying and reviving Osiris is mythical, and the account of Jesus Christ in the New Testament is historical. The mythical and polytheistic triad of Osiris, Isis, and Horus is of a very different nature from the monotheistic Holy Trinity.

VII. *Biblical Texts from Egypt.* Before the discovery of the Qumran manuscripts the oldest known Hebrew texts of the Old Testament were from Egypt, like the Nash Papyrus, the Genizah fragments from the Ben Ezra Synagogue in Old Cairo, the Codex Cairenses of the Karaite community in Cairo, and the Codex Leningradensis used as the basis for Kittel's *Biblia Hebraica.* Among the ancient Greek Biblical manuscripts originating in Egypt are: the Scheide papyri of Ezekiel, probably the great Codices Vaticanus and Sinaiticus, the John Rylands papyrus fragment of John dated about 125 A.D., the °Oxyrhynchus papyri, the Chester Beatty papyri, and the recently published Bodmer papyri of John, Luke, and the Catholic Epistles. The Coptic translations are also among the earliest witnesses to the Biblical text.

BIBLIOGRAPHY. A. Erman, *A Handbook of Egyptian Religion,* translated by A. S. Griffith, Archibald Constable, London, 1907; *The Literature of the Ancient Egyptians,* translated by A. M. Blackman, Methuen, London, 1927. H. Frankfort, *Ancient Egyptian Religion,* Harper and Brothers, New York, 1961. Alan Gardiner, *Egypt of the Pharaohs,* Oxford University Press, Oxford, 1961. W. C. Hayes, *The Scepter of Egypt,* Parts I and II, Harvard University Press, Cambridge, 1953, 1959. O. F. A. Meinardus, *In the Steps of the Holy Family,* Dar al-Maaref, Cairo, 1963. C. F. Pfeiffer, *Tell el-Amarna and the Bible,* Baker Book House, 1963. G. Steindorff, and K. C. Seele, *When Egypt Ruled the East,* 2nd ed., University of Chicago Press, Chicago, 1957. J. A. Wilson, translator of Egyptian texts in *Ancient Near Eastern Texts,* edited by James P. Pritchard, 2nd ed., Princeton University Press, Princeton, 1955; *The Burden of Egypt,* University of Chicago Press, Chicago, 1951.

EKRON. Ekron, the northernmost city of the Philistine pentapolis, was temporarily occupied by the men of Judah during the period of the Judges (Judges 1:18), but it reverted to the Philistines. From Gath, the ark of the Covenant was taken to Ekron, after which it was sent to *Beth-shemesh in Israel (I Sam. 5:10 — 6:12).

The fortunes of Ekron varied through its long history. Padi, its king in the days of Sennacherib, remained loyal to the Assyrians, but a group of rebels seized the throne and turned Padi over to Hezekiah, who was evidently a leader in the opposition to Sennacherib. The Annals of *Sennacherib tell how the Assyrians took Ekron and restored Padi to his throne. Esarhaddon also mentions Ekron as a Philistine city loyal to its Assyrian overlord.

The god of Ekron was Baal-zebub. Ahaziah of Israel was on his way to the shrine of Baal-zebub, when Elijah intercepted him, demanding to know if Israel was without a god that the god of Ekron was being consulted (II Kings 1:1-6; 16). Baal-zebub, "lord of flies," may be an intentional Hebrew alteration of the Canaanite name Baal-zebul, "Exalted Baal," or, "Lord of the high Place." Baal-zebub (or Zebul), in the New Testament appears as a synonym for Satan, "the prince of demons" (Matt. 12:24-29).

In 147 B.C., Alexander Balas, king of Syria, transferred Ekron to the Maccabean ruler Jonathan (I Macc. 10:89). According to the historian Eusebius it had a large Jewish population during the third century A.D. In subsequent centuries the site was abandoned and its identification has been lost. Edward Robinson, in the nineteenth century, suggested that it be identified with 'Akir, ten miles northeast of Ashdod. Others identify Ekron with Khirbet el-Muqenna', six miles southeast of 'Akir, although el-Muqenna' is usually thought to contain the remains of Eltekeh.

ELAM. During the third and second millennia before Christ a people known as Elamites developed a high culture in the territory east of Babylon, comprising a rich plain and adjacent hill country. Elamites were neither *Sumerian nor *Semitic, although they derived many of their cultural elements from the inhabitants of Mesopotamia. Elamites were known as a warlike people, and they periodically threatened the Babylonians and the Assyrians. The stele of Naram Sin and the code of *Hammurabi are among the treasures the Elamites took to their capital, *Susa, as trophies or victory.

Early in the second millennium B.C. the Elamites invaded Mesopotamia and established a dynasty at Larsa. Shortly afterward they became masters of *Erech, *Babylon, and Isin, although Hammurabi of Babylon was able to check further expansion. By the fourteenth century B.C. the Elamites had reached the peak of their culture. With the rise of *Assyria, the Elamites faced their most serious threat. Sargon, Sennacherib, and Esarhaddon all waged campaigns against the Elamites. Ashurbanipal sacked Susa and almost exterminated the Elamites. Although Elamite history ends at this time, the territory of Elam was to become a favored part of the later Persian Empire, and Susa one of its capitals.

In the third millennium B.C. a Proto-Elamite cuneiform literature existed alongside the Sumerian cuneiform. This died out during the *Akkadian period (ca. 2360-2180 B.C.) after which the Elamites used the Akkadian (Assyro-Babylonian) signs for their syllabary. Elamite was one of the languages used by Darius the Great in his *Behistun Inscription.

Among Elamite texts we find a treaty between Naram-Sin, the grandson of *Sargon of Akkad, and kings of the Elamite Avan dynasty. Some Proto-Elamite and Akkadian bilingual texts date from the reign of Puzur-Shushinak (ca. 2280 B.C.), a king of the Avan dynasty.

The Biblical Table of Nations (Gen. 10) associates Elam with the line of Shem, perhaps reflecting a cultural fusion between Elamites and Semites. A "king of Elam" named Chedorlaomer is mentioned among those who invaded the cities south of the Dead Sea, including Sodom (Gen. 14). An Elamite ruler, Kudur-mabug, has a name comparable with that of the Biblical text, although positive identification cannot be made.

Jeremiah's prophecy against Elam (Jer. 49:34-39) probably refers to the Persians who ruled the land that had earlier been called Elam. From this time on Elam serves as a part of the Persian Empire, and Elamites are subject politically to Persia.

ELATH. *See* Ezion-geber.

ELEPHANTINE. *See* Aswan.

219

ELEPHANTINE PAPYRI. Elephantine, known to the Egyptians as Yeb, is an island at the first cataract of the Nile opposite °Aswan. During January and February 1893, Charles Edwin Wilbour, an American student of Egyptian antiquities acquired some papyri from an Arab woman on Elephantine Island. He examined the papyri and sent them to an unnamed Semitic scholar for his appraisal of their nature. In 1896, however, Wilbour died and the papyri were forgotten. They were sent to New York with his possessions, and they remained in storage there until the death of his daughter, who bequeathed them to the Egyptian Department of the Brooklyn Museum. Other papyri from Elephantine found their way to the Cairo Museum and the Bodlein Museum at Oxford. Both German and French archaeological expeditions worked at Elephantine, but the principal discovery was the correspondence of the Jewish colony of mercenary soldiers stationed at Elephantine. The documents purchased by Wilbour, along with others discovered by the archaeologists who followed him, have given us fresh insights into the Jewish community in Egypt during the fifth century B.C.

The Jewish colony at Elephantine seems to have been composed largely of mercenary soldiers, although the papyri indicate that

SEALED CONTRACT FROM ELEPHANTINE. Courtesy, Brooklyn Museum

some members engaged in trade. They evidently settled in Egypt during the reign of Pharaoh Hophra (588 B.C.-569 B.C.) or Amasis (569 B.C.-525 B.C.). The Elephantine colony had built a temple to Yahweh, whom they called Yahu, which was standing when Cambyses took Egypt in 525 B.C. When Judah fell to Nebuchadnezzar (587 B.C.) and the Jerusalem temple was destroyed, Egypt seemed a suitable haven for those Jews who had been pro-Egyptian and

anti-Babylonian. Although Jeremiah had counseled the Jews not to go to Egypt (Jer. 42:18-22), many rejected his counsel, and even the prophet himself was taken to Egypt (Jer. 43). The Egyptians evidently welcomed the Jews during the years immediately following their defeat at the hands of Nebuchadnezzar.

After Cambyses took Egypt and incorporated it into the Persian Empire (525 B.C.) the fortunes of the Jews changed. The Persians favored the Jews and used them as mercenary soldiers, a fact which the native Egyptians resented. The papyri tell us that the priests of Khnum, an Egyptian god, had the Yahu temple at Elephantine destroyed around 410 B.C. In 408 B.C. the Egyptian Jews addressed letters to Palestine asking the officials there for help in rebuilding their temple. We know that the temple was rebuilt for Papyri #12, dated in December of 402 B.C. records the fact that "Yahu" dwells in "Yeb, the fortress" in his sanctuary.

It is noteworthy that the Elephantine community addressed letters both to Jerusalem and Samaria, suggesting that they were not limiting their associations to their compatriots in Jerusalem. An undated memorandum, signed by five Jews, promised the Persian governor that no animal sacrifices would be offered if permission were granted to rebuild the temple. This seems to have been a concession to the Jerusalem Jews who would oppose the offering of sacrifices anywhere except in the Jerusalem temple. There was evidently a Jewish commissioner in the court of the Persian governor. Earlier (419 B.C.) such a commissioner addressed the Jews at Elephantine stating that the governor had ordered that the passover be observed in accord with practices of the Jerusalem temple (cf. Exod. 12:1-20).

Among the papyri listing contributions to the Egyptian temple we read of one portion set aside for the worship of Yahu, a second for Ishumbethel, and a third for Anathbethel. Another text mentions Herembethel. These names, compounds of Bethel, "House of God," may be interpreted as an attempt to personalize or give a separate existence to certain qualities or aspects of Yahweh. Herembethel, meaning "Sacredness of the House of God," and Ishumbethel, meaning "Name of the House of God" might thus be identical with Yahweh, or Yahu. Yet this very tendency was a step away from the rigid monotheism of the Old Testament, and the very existence of a Jewish temple in Egypt suggests that the Elephantine Jews were moving away from the orthodoxy which came to characterize the Jews of Jerusalem in the days of Ezra and Nehemiah.

Among the papyri a copy of a Jewish marriage contract has come to light, as well as a copy of the °Behistun Inscription of Darius. Aramaic was the language of the texts, as it was the language of the Palestinian Jews after their return from Babylonian exile. Aramaic was the official language of the Persian Empire, and the Book of Ezra quotes in Aramaic official documents of the Persian government (cf. Ezra 4:8 — 6:18; 7:12-26).

The Elephantine colony came to an end during the reign of Pharaoh Nepherites I (399 B.C.-393 B.C.). Judaism in °Egypt, however, continued to exercise a cultural influence, and after Alexander's conquest, °Alexandria became a major Jewish center.

BIBLIOGRAPHY. A. E. Cowley, *Aramaic Papyri of the Fifth Century B.C.,* Clarendon Press, Oxford, 1923. E. G. Kraeling, *The Brooklyn Museum Aramaic Papyri,* Yale University Press, New Haven, 1953. G. R. Driver, *Aramaic Documents of the Fifth Century B.C.,* Clarendon Press, Oxford, 1957. E. G. Kraeling, "New Light on the Elephantine Colony," *BA,* XV, 1952, pp. 50-67.

ELOQUENT PEASANT. The tale of the Eloquent Peasant has survived in Egyptian texts dating from before 1800 B.C. The story relates how a peasant was robbed of his donkey and merchandise while on a trip to Heracleopolis. Thereupon he sought out the local magistrate to plead for justice, but the magistrate turned out to be the thief's liege lord. The magistrate was so impressed with the peasant's eloquence, however, that he detained him so that his supplications, reproaches, and invective might be written down for the king. After passing from official to official the peasant's case was ultimately brought to the king, and the peasant himself was accorded justice.

The tale of the Eloquent Peasant is of interest not only for its human interest, but also as a demonstration of Egyptian concepts of justice at the time of the Biblical patriarchs. The peasant pleads for consideration of the plight of the orphan and the widow, as did the Biblical prophets. It is significant that a humble peasant could appeal to the king himself with the assurance that he would be given a fair hearing.

ELTEKEH. Eltekeh was a city in Dan (Josh. 19:44), mentioned by Sennacherib as one of his conquests during his campaign of 701/700 B.C. Some identify it with modern Khirbet el-Muqannaᶜ twenty-five miles west of Jerusalem.

BIBLIOGRAPHY. W. F. Albright, *BASOR,* 15, 1924, p. 8.

EMMAUS. A village in Judea mentioned only in Luke 24:13. One of the appearances of Jesus on Resurrection Sunday was to two men walking from Jerusalem to Emmaus. The Lucan passage locates this village 60 stades from Jerusalem, or approximately 6¾ miles away. A variant reading, 160 stades, is found in a few uncial manuscripts, Sinaiticus (fourth century), N (sixth century), K, Pi, and Theta (ninth century), and a number of minuscules. The reading "60 stades" is found in P75 (late second or early third century), B (fourth century), A (fifth century), C (fifth century), and others. The evidence of P75 (recently-published Bodmer papyrus) and B (Codex Vaticanus) together establishes rather definitely the reading "60 stades."

Three identifications of Emmaus have been proposed: (1) the modern village of 'Amwas (definitive publication: H. Vincent and F. M. Abel, *Emmaus: sa basilique et son histoire,* Librairie Ernest Leroux, Paris, 1932). However, this location would require the reading "160 stades," which is very doubtful in the light of the newer manuscript evidence. (2) A military colony of Vespasian, possibly present-day Kaloniye, called Ammaous by Josephus. The distance from Jerusalem is about 34 stades — rather difficult to correlate with the Biblical record. (3) Present-day el Kubebe (definitive publication: P. B. Bagatti, *I Monumenti di Emmaus El-Qubeibeh e dei dintorni,* Franciscan Press, Jerusalem, Jordan, 1947). The remains here are definitely from the New Testament period, and the distance from Jerusalem agrees fairly well with the Lucan record, making this identification the preferred one.

EN GEDI. En Gedi, the largest oasis on the western shore of the Dead Sea, is watered by a spring which causes narrow green belts of vegetation to spring up in the barren wasteland. The fame of the En Gedi oasis caused the author of the Song of Solomon to exclaim, "My beloved is unto me as a cluster of henna in the vineyards of En Gedi" (S. of Sol. 1:14). Yet the region around En Gedi was anything but fruitful. To its barren wastes David fled when Saul was seeking his life, and in one of its numerous caves the former shepherd boy found a place of refuge (I Sam. 24:1-6).

Although David's flight to En Gedi was a temporary expedient, and he left the Wilderness as soon as it was safe to do so, others in Israel looked upon the Judean Wilderness as an ideal abode, apart from the corrupting influences of society. Such were the Rechabites who determined to live a life of asceticism in an environment removed from the temptations of civilized life. The Rechabites dwelt in tents and abstained from the fruits of the vineyard and crops that were sown by man (cf. II Kings 10:15-18; Jer. 35:5-10).

The Rechabites were forerunners of the Essenes who established a communal settlement at Qumran, north of En Gedi, within sight of the Dead Sea. To the people of Qumran, the wilderness was the ideal place to live a life of pious preparation for the advent of the Messiah. In their Manual of Discipline they quote Isaiah 40:3: "Clear ye in the wilderness the way of the Lord, make plain in the desert a highway for our God."

En Gedi became an important base during the Second Jewish Revolt (A.D. 132-135) of which Shimeon ben Cosba (Bar Kochba) was the leader. Many in Israel, including the renowned Rabbi Akiba, looked upon ben Cosba as the promised messiah and deliverer of his people. Recently discovered letters contain orders to the commander and people at En Gedi to provide supplies for the Jewish army. Ben Cosba exercised control for about two and a half years, but again the might of Rome prevailed, and En Gedi suffered defeat along with Jerusalem and the rest of Jewish Palestine.

Later Roman writers continued to speak of the date palms of En Gedi, and as late as the fifth century, Jerome spoke of En Gedi as a "large Jewish village," famous for its henna, dates, and vineyards. During Roman times En Gedi served as the agricultural, commercial, and territorial administrative center for the west coast of the Dead Sea.

Beginning in 1949 systematic excavations have been carried on at En Gedi. A campaign in 1962 organized by the Hebrew University and the Israel Exploration Society under the direction of Binyamin Mazar, Emanuel Dunajevsky and Trude Dothan traced levels of occupation at Tell Goren, the principal site of occupation in the oasis, from the time of Josiah of Judah to the destruction of Jerusalem by Nebuchadnezzar (587 B.C.). Among the discoveries were rows of large jars, numerous pottery vessels, and iron and bronze utensils which were evidently used in the manufacture of perfume from balsam which grows in the En Gedi region. Josephus speaks of the balsam of En Gedi, and Pliny mentions its palm trees.

In a house identified by an inscription as belonging to a man named Tovshalom, a cooking pot was discovered containing a hoard of silver ingots. An oil lamp was used as a lid to cover the pot. Other finds included stone weights, jewelry, and pottery vessels of excellent craftsmanship.

On the basis of his campaigns at En Gedi, Mazar suggests that the Jewish settlement at En Gedi was destroyed in the time of Nebuchadnezzar, but rebuilt after the return from Babylon. During the fifth century B.C. it was the site of a prosperous settlement. Among the remains of a large house from the period are ostraca with Aramaic inscriptions, fragments of imported Attic pottery, and jar handles containing the inscription *Yehud*, denoting the Persian province of Yehudah, or Judah.

Citadels from the Hellenistic Period (3rd to 2nd centuries B.C.) and the Hasmonean Period (*ca.* 100-70 B.C.) have been excavated. The Hasmonean citadel, dated to the period of Alexander Jannaeus, was surrounded by a stone wall about six feet thick. The earliest remains at En Gedi are a Chalcolithic Period enclosure — about 30 by twenty yards in size, dating to the last third of the fourth millennium B.C. It is possible that this was a central place of worship for the inhabitants of the Judean Desert and the Dead Sea area at the time. The most recent remains date from the Roman-Byzantine period — the fourth to sixth centuries A.D.

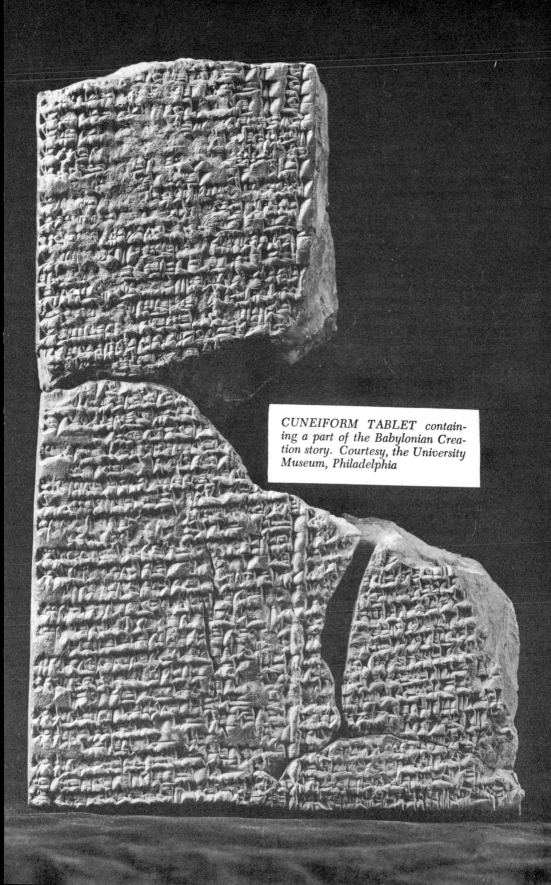

CUNEIFORM TABLET containing a part of the Babylonian Creation story. Courtesy, the University Museum, Philadelphia

ENUMA ELISH. The Babylonian Creation account begins with these two words, which in English are translated "when above" or "when on high." This great epic was unknown to the modern world until the years 1848-76, when Austen H. Layard, Hormuzd Rassam and George Smith discovered fragments of the seven clay tablets upon which the story was written in the library of Ashurbanipal, king of Assyria in the seventh century B.C. Further discoveries of copies in other places have continued until the present time so that almost the entire document can be read today. The only tablet that is still seriously lacking is Tablet V, which treats the establishment of the heavenly bodies.

I. *Date of Writing.* When the poem in its classic Semitic form was completed, we cannot be sure. Although the copies from Ashurbanipal's library are from the seventh century B.C., copies that date back to 1000 B.C. have been found in Ashur. Our present samples are clearly copies of earlier material. Since the principal burden of the poem is to prove that Marduk, the god of Babylon has won the right to be the supreme deity, and since Babylon rose to political supremacy during the first Babylonian Dynasty (1894-1595 B.C.), especially during the reign of Hammurabi (1792-1750 B.C.), most authorities conclude that the original was probably composed about 1800 B.C. In all probability the Babylonian epic is in turn based upon Sumerian stories of creation that are even earlier, although the extent of the borrowing is not known due to the scarcity of Sumerian materials.

II. *Summary of the Story.* The story begins when only Apsu, fresh water; and Tiamat, his wife, salt water, were in existence, and nothing else. From their mixing came the other gods. When the grandchildren became so noisy that Apsu could stand it no longer, he determined to destroy them that there might once more be peace in heaven. Before his plan could be put into effect, Ea, a wise and strong descendant of Apsu, drugged his forefather and slew him, taking over his divine prerogatives. To him was born the mighty Marduk, god of Babylon, his rightful heir.

Then Tiamat the widow organized war against Ea and Marduk. For this purpose she created many terrible monsters. As commander of her hosts she appointed a god named Kingu, who became her consort. At first Ea resolved to engage the approaching armies, but when he saw their terrible array, he turned away in terror. Finally Marduk was summoned, but he would agree to do battle only if he was made ruler of the gods. Accordingly the gods assembled in holy conclave and drunken stupor and declared Marduk to be the king of the gods. At once Marduk began to prepare for combat, his principal weapons being a huge net and the winds of the storms. When Kingu saw him approaching he fell away, but Tiamat did not hestitate to challenge Marduk. However, when she opened her mouth to swallow him, he caught her in his net and drove the storm wind down her throat followed immediately by a dart that pierced her heart.

Then Marduk split the carcass of Tiamat asunder. One half he used to form the firmament of heaven, the other to form the earth. Above the firmament and below the earth there was water that the severed body kept under control.

Then the chief god assigned the various gods to their stations in the heavens to determine days and seasons. Soon the gods complained that they were forced to work, but had no servants of their own. In answer to their complaint Marduk decided to create man, who would serve the needs of the gods. It was agreed that one of them would supply the blood, so Kingu was selected, his head cut off, his veins slit; and from his blood and bone man was formed.

In gratitude to Marduk the gods built the city of Babylon and still return yearly on New Year's Day to pay homage anew to him. On this day he decides the destinies of the whole world.

III. *Similarities to Old Testament Account.* The most striking phenomenon confronting the reader is the conspicuous correspondence of outline. Both accounts have the following order.

(1) Primeval chaos
(2) Coming of light
(3) Creation of the firmament
(4) Appearance of dry land
(5) Creation of luminaries
(6) Creation of man
(7) Deity rests

There has been much discussion about the relation of *Tiamat* to the Hebrew word *tehom* ("deep") in Genesis 1:2. However, there is disagreement concerning any close relationship etymologically. It seems best to conclude that *tehom*, rather than being a derivative of Tiamat is related to an older word from which both *tehom* and *Tiamat* are derived.

In Tablet IV:20-27 a test is made of Marduk's ability. The gods tell him to exercise his power upon a garment. He must speak a word and it is to be destroyed, another word and it is to be restored. This feat he performs readily. Does he make the garment completely disappear? Some translations say so; others contend that he only tears it to shreds. Whatever opinion one forms about this, there still remains a striking correspondence between the effective word of God in Genesis 1, and that of Marduk in the passage under study.

There is every evidence that the picture of the three-storied universe in the Enuma Elish is reflected in the Hebrew account. In both sources a fixed firmament divides the waters above it from those below it. Under the earth there are the waters of the deep. Thus there are three levels of water, kept in bounds by the firmament and the dry land. The Hebrew word firmament carries the idea of "something hammered out" as a metal is worked. The English word literally means something firm or solid.

In Tablet V, when the moon is caused to shine, the seven day week is emphasized. In fact there is a progression from six to seven (V:16-17). The Babylonian word for full moon in V:18 is *sapattu*, which is clearly a kindred word to the Hebrew word for Sabbath, although here the *sapattu* comes only once a month, not every seventh day as in the Old Testament. Yet it is obvious that there is some sort of relationship between the concepts of the two accounts. Although that relationship is apparently quite remote, yet it is clearly a matter to be seriously considered for the light it may throw upon the history of the Biblical material.

In the Enuma Elish mankind was created only that the rebel gods might be at ease after they had performed their various functions. Men were to bring their sacrifices and gifts to them that the gods might not have to provide for their own needs. After the creation of men, the divine beings were thus provided with servants to do their menial tasks. In the Old Testament account man is also portrayed as a servant of God. He is to represent God upon the earth and extend his dominion over all the created world. He is to care for the garden that God has made, and is responsible to God for its cultivation. The Old Testament in its opening passages pictures man as God's steward, responsible to him for his faithfulness. The purpose of man's efforts, however, is not to provide an opportunity for God to be at ease, but to give man a healthy incentive for living, and a part in the dominion of the universe that God has established. It remains true, however, that man is to serve under God. He is a creature, and is to remain ever conscious of this.

In the Babylonian story, before man was created, there was a great assembly of the gods. It was this conclave that established the guilt of Kingu and passed the death sentence upon him. In their presence mankind was formed from the blood of Kingu under the direction of Marduk and Ea. Some scholars see a similarity in Genesis 1:26 where God says, "Let us make man in our image." Who is the "us" to whom God addresses himself? Could it be the heavenly court, comprised of angelic divine beings even as in the Enuma Elish? In some original sense this may be true, but by the time Genesis 1 was written such ideas were certainly not present among responsible Israelites. The passage now stands in the Old Testament to guard against gross anthropomorphism. If man were told only that he was made in the image of God himself, it would increase his tendency to deify himself. Being made in the image of divinity as well as after the likeness of the one God accomplishes a two-fold result in man's estimate of himself. It reveals man as above all creation but still leaves him responsible to serve under his creator. He shares in the nature of God, but he is not God.

IV. *Differences in the Accounts.* Although the similarities in the stories are striking, the differences are even more significant. At every turn it is obvious that the Hebrew concepts are advanced over that of the Babylonian, and stem from a concept of God that is utterly different.

There is a marked difference in the purpose behind the writing of the two accounts. The Hebrew story is told in order to tell how all things came into being within the purpose of their God. The Babylonian material was not written primarily to tell how things began. Strictly it is not a creation *story*, for it is more concerned with praise of Marduk and the primacy of Babylon than with how the world began. Not even a total of two out of the seven tablets actually deals with the works of creation. Most of the space is consumed in describing Marduk and his various exploits, particularly his fifty names in Tablets VI and VII. There appears to be a political purpose behind the Enuma Elish as well as religious. Marduk is the god of Babylon, and his primacy over the gods corresponded to Babylon's primacy over the nations. The Enuma Elish lacks the simple directness and unadorned piety of the Hebrew portrayal of first things.

Although both accounts agree that creation began with watery chaos, here the similarity ceases. Order, in the Babylonian account, is achieved only after a titanic battle with Tiamat, and there is always the threat of a return to chaos that must be averted by the proper ritual. In fact, the primary purpose for the annual reciting of the Enuma Elish at the Babylonian New Year's Festival was to furnish magical aid for the renewal of the Marduk conquest of chaos.

At the end of the fourth day of the Festival, which was held in the Spring, the first to the eleventh of the month Nisan, the Enuma Elish was recited in its entirety by the high priest before the statue of Marduk. Later it was recited again. Parts of the story would even be dramatized with the king playing the significant role as Marduk. The purpose for the first recital is not mentioned in our sources. It was intended either to be used as a magical formula to guard against the annual inundation of the Tigris and Euphrates, or as an appeal to Marduk to turn his favor upon his people. The more they sang the song of his glorious conquests, the more they could expect his help.

The second recitation is more carefully documented, for the express reason for its use is stated in E. Ebeling's *Keilschrifttexte aus Assu religiösen Inhalts* (1915 ff.). Nos. 143:34 and 219:8: "*Enuma Elish* which is recited before Bel (Marduk) which they chant in the month Nisan, because he is held prisoner." Here the purpose of the use of the epic is clear. It is to give magical aid to Marduk's deliverance from imprisonment. If he is not freed, chaos will return again to his established world. This allusion makes clear the fact that the gods in the Babylonian account are themselves a part of the creation. The original gods, Apsu and Tiamat, are personifications of fresh water and salt water. Marduk is really a personification of imperialistic Babylon, but is also so closely associated with the natural world that he can be said to be in prison when winter has conquered autumn and can only be freed when spring returns.

Sublimely different is the Old Testament story. Although the watery chaos is there, it offers no resistance to the divine will. There is no struggle against order, but there is an immediate yielding to the purpose of God. Natural order is established once and for all, and there is no threat of a return to chaos. The God of Israel is clearly not a part of nature, but is above it, and has complete control of all its processes. To a Hebrew it would have been utterly inconceivable that God could ever be imprisoned as was Marduk. For God to be God his power must be incontestable and his purpose immutable.

From whence did the deep (*tehom*) come? There is no question but that for the Babylonians matter was eternal. Apsu and Tiamat being fresh and salt water, have always been. There is no suggestion of a time when there was only deity, a nonmaterial being. What does the Hebrew account have to say on this subject? Did God create the *tehom*, or was it there when he began the process? Volumes have been written upon this problem, seeking to prove that *bara* (create) means create from nothing, but the word itself does not carry such a meaning. Others would suggest that the declaration, "In the beginning God created the heavens and the earth," implies that he formed the cosmos as a rudimentary state first, before he began to form the earth as it now is. Mesopotamian creation stories open with a subordinate clause beginning with "on the day," "when." If the Hebrew account were following such an analogy the expression *beyom* (on that day) would have been appropriate, and it occurs in Genesis 2:4 and 5:1-2. The word *bereshith* (in beginning) is not paralleled in any Mesopotamian account, and convincingly argues for everything being new when the cosmos was brought into being. Certainly in other places the idea of "creation from nothing" is proclaimed in the Bible (Prov. 8:22 ff.; John 1:1-3; Heb. 11:3). Such a concept is certainly rooted in Genesis 1.

Crude polytheism permeates the Enuma Elish. The earliest stages of creation are ascribed to sexual union. In every way the gods behave like the worst of human beings. A grandfather decides to kill his grandchildren because they desturb his rest. Jealousy and uncontrolled ambition throw the gods into constant turmoil. They even get drunk when they are supposed to participate in a serious assembly with their minds clear and alert.

They are characterized by fear when confronted by superior forces, and are not above any method of dealing with a foe. Cosmic events result from the whim of this god or that. When the various rebel deities are assigned their tasks in the universe, they complain about the difficulty of the task, and are silenced only when a new race of slaves is provided, called mankind.

The contrast in the Old Testament is so apparent that it is hardly necessary to mention it. The God of Israel is never pictured with a female consort. Only masculine pronouns are associated with deity. Even angels are always masculine, contrary to popular opinion. Although God is sometimes pictured in anthropomorphic terms, he is never characterized by the vices or sensual pursuits of man. There is a oneness in his nature that leaves no room for a divided heaven. In his person he transcends all nature, is never a part of it.

Although in both accounts light in the universe preceded the creation of the heavenly bodies, there is a different picture of the origin of the light. In the Mesopotamian story a dazzling glory surrounded Apsu (I:68) and Marduk was originally a solar deity (I:102). Thus the light that permeated the world came from the god himself. In the Old Testament account light appeared as the result of the creative activity of God himself. It is not an emanation from his person, but the result of the divine fiat.

It is important to notice that although Genesis mentions the creation of the sun, moon, and stars in that order, that the arrangement is reversed in the Enuma Elish, stars, moon, sun. This was probably due to the fact that more emphasis was put upon the stars among the astrologically inclined Babylonians. Also the Babylonian descriptions are charcterized by astronomical terminology and mythological allusions. The Hebrew story is written in laymen's language with all mythological allusions missing.

Until the present time no portion of the Enuma Elish has been found which pictures the creation of normal vegetation, animals, birds, reptiles and fishes. Such an account might have been written as the missing part of Tablet V, but there is no way of determining this. There is one passage that describes Marduk as "the creator of grain and legumes" (VII:2), but there is no attempt to establish an order of creation for the rest of life on the earth. Other materials mention the creation of animals, but not Enuma Elish itself. Thus it appears that only the Old Testament account attempts to give a complete picture of creation. Absolutely nothing is left out of the creative work of Israel's God. As he moved from lower forms to higher, he finally arrived at man. This view impressively parallels the theories of modern science. There are many minor differences between Genesis 1-2 and modern scientific hypothesis, but the principle of proceeding from lower to higher forms in creation has no place in the ancient Near East except in the Old Testament.

In both sources the creation of man is a significant moment. Yet in the Babylonian account the forming of man was not in the original plan of the gods. It was an afterthought. The result was an amazing achievement, but all events were not pointing to this event. In fact, in the Enuma Elish the universe is primarily for the use of the gods; man is never more than a servant. For the Hebrews man was the climax of all creation. The world was fashioned for his use and dominion. He is a servant of God, but also lord of all the created world. To him is accorded a dignity that the average Babylonian could never know. The Genesis story centers in the creation of man, the Babylonian in the ways of the gods. Man is responsible to God in the Hebrew account, but it is for his own good and that of his world, not because God needs his services to survive. Man is to tend the garden, but God asks for none of its fruit. He is to be a good steward for his own sake, and for the benefit of the good world into which he has been placed.

Above all man has been put in a world that has been planned by God to its every detail. To live successfully he must fulfill his own place in those plans. The Babylonian lived in a world that had struggled into existence and might revert any moment. The Hebrew lived in an established world order that he could defy and taint but could never shake. Rebellion would only destroy him, not God's creation.

There is no parallel in the Enuma Elish to the account of man's fall in Genesis 3. In fact, the epic vividly deals with the fall of the gods. The gods being the way they were, one could not expect any difference in the men who were created by them as a sort of punitive act from the blood of a criminal. From what could man fall? Only the Old Testament, with its concept of a pure and holy God, could conceive of a man who was "very good" and whose present condition of sin must be self-derived. Here indeed is a Biblical distinctive.

V. *Relation of Genesis and Enuma Elish.* There is no doubt that there is a genetic relationship between the two accounts. The problem centers in the nature of that relationship. There are obviously several opinions. First, there are those who seek to prove that the Babylonians borrowed from the Hebrews, but this is hardly likely, since the Babylonian epic is much older than the final form of the Hebrew. However, we know little of the history of the Biblical account, and the core of it could be much older than the final recension. All of this remains in the realm of conjecture where nothing can be proved. Certainly the Babylonian material could not be based upon the final form of the Hebrew.

A second theory supposes that the Hebrew borrowed from the Babylonian. This view has been very popular since the discovery of the Enuma Elish. However, the correspondences are not so striking as to make such a conclusion inevitable. Many of the characteristics held in common could be due to the tendency of people everywhere to take similar approaches to the problems of origin. However, such an ex-planation does not explain all the facts, particularly the similarity of basic outline in the accounts. Besides it is well known that close literary affinity exists between the Babylonian flood accounts and that of the Old Testament. Such knowledge naturally affects one's opinion of the question immediately under consideration. Indeed, it is most likely that people living in Palestine from the fifteenth century B.C. onward were quite familiar with Babylonian culture. During the first part of this period Babylonian was the diplomatic language of Egypt and Canaan, as evidenced in the Tell el-Amarna correspondence.

However, it is erroneous to suggest that the Hebrew borrowed from the Babylonians. It is quite possible that such literature as the Enuma Elish had been appropriated by Hebrew culture itself. With the adoption of the Canaanite language as their own, the Hebrews assimilated a great deal of the culture of the area at the same time. Such material had to be sifted through the basic Mosaic theology, but it must have been always at hand.

However, there is still another position: It is quite possible that both the Hebrew and the Babylonian have sprung from a source older than either one of them. It is well known that the Babylonian account is based upon an older Sumerian story. It is quite possible that the two accounts are based upon old creation motifs that go much further back into history. If this did occur, centuries of independent development should have left fewer correspondences than now exist. A most plausible conclusion would be that the patriarchs brought with them a creation story from a similar background to that of the Enuma Elish. Later literary contact with Babylonian further modified the Hebrew account and influenced its approach as the counterpart of the prevailing story of creation.

Whatever dependence the Hebrew story has upon the Babylonians, it is only literary. A study of literary correspondences only makes more conspicuous the vast difference in the presuppositions and outlook of the accounts. In its analysis of man and his task, its concept of the God who made and ruled the world, and its perception of stability and purpose in the founding of the world, the Biblical account startlingly surpasses the Mesopotamian. A study of similarities eventually results in an astounding mass of significant differences, all of which point to the superiority of the Hebrew concepts. It is clearly a wondrous miracle that out of such an environment as the Enuma Elish reveals, the Hebrews could arrive at such an exalted idea of God and man. If they borrowed from the Babylonians, the finished product far exceeded the raw materials. The Hebrew faith never suffers by comparison with contemporary thought. Inferior in culture they were, yet in religion they drank from a fountain of knowledge unknown to cultures otherwise far more advanced.

BIBLIOGRAPHY. Peter Jensen, *Assyrisch — babylonische Mythen and Epen*, Berlin, 1900. L. W. King, *The Seven Tablets of Creation*, London, 1902. A. Ungnad, *Die Religion der Babylonien und Assyrer*, Jena, 1921. S. Langdon, *The Babylonian Epic of Creation*, Oxford, 1923. E. A. Wallis Budge, *The Babylonian Legends of Creation*, London, 1931. René Labat, *Le Poeme Babylonien de la creation*, Paris, 1935. Alexander Heidel, *The Babylonian Genesis*, Chicago, 1942, 1963. ed. H. Frankfort, *The Intellectual Adventure of Ancient Man*, Chicago, 1946 ed. J. B. Pritchard, *Ancient Near Eastern Texts*, Princeton, 1950. S. H. Hooke, *Babylonian and Assyrian Religion*, London, 1953. Norman K. Gottwald, *A Light to the Nations*, New York, 1959.

EPHESUS. Ephesus is especially significant to the Bible student as the city where the Apostle Paul carried on his most extensive ministry (two years and three months, Acts 19:8, 10) and from which he evangelized much of Asia. It was also the headquarters of the Apostle John during the latter years of his life.

Ephesus was one of the greatest cities of the Mediterranean world during New Testament times. Reliable historians and archaeologists have estimated its peak population during the second century all the way from 200,000 to 500,000. The reasons why the city drew so many to its bosom were at least threefold: political, economic and religious. The Roman governor resided there and for all practical purposes Ephesus became the capital of Asia, though it is a question whether the capital was officially transferred there in New Testament times. Its economic prowess lay in the fact that Ephesus stood on the great north-south road of western Asia Minor and controlled trade flowing into the interior of Asia Minor along the Maeander and Lycus valleys. Religiously, it was a great cult center for the worship of Diana or Artemis.

Ephesus was located four miles from the Aegean and possessed an inland harbor connected with the Cayster River. The harbor was kept large enough and deep enough only by constant dredging. The city felt the general economic decline of the Empire during the third century, and after the raid by Goths in 263 was unable to put the necessary effort into maintaining the harbor. By the fourth century the port was silting up fast and by the tenth century the prosperous city of Roman times was completely deserted and invaded by marshes. Of course the inevitable happened: Ephesus served as a first-class stone quarry for nearby communities.

Archaeologists did not begin to lift the veil from the ruins of Ephesus until 1863. In that year John T. Wood, an English architect, started his long search for the Temple of Diana, one of the wonders of the ancient world. He finally came upon the ruins on December 31, 1869 and then spent five more years working at the temple site. D. G. Hogarth excavated there in 1904-5. The excavators found that the temple had passed through five phases of construction (the earliest beginning about 600 B.C.) and that the edifice Paul and John would have known was begun about 350 B.C. and destroyed by the Goths during the third century invasion. The temple itself was 180 feet wide and 377 feet long. The roof was supported by 117 sixty-foot columns. These columns were six feet in diameter and thirty-six of them were sculptured at the base with life size figures. The temple stood on a platform 239 feet wide by 418 feet long. The holy of holies was apparently open to the sky and contained an altar twenty feet square, behind which the statue of Artemis no doubt stood. Artemis or Diana was equated with the Asia Minor Cybele, the mother goddess. As worshiped in Ephesus the goddess was a considerably orientalized fertility deity. Her statue was a many-breasted figure (or as some think fronted with ostrich eggs, symbolizing fertility). During the Artemision (March-April), a month dedicated to the worship of the goddess, devotees came from many other provinces to participate in religious festivals.

While Wood was looking for the Temple of Diana, he cleared the theater of Ephesus, specifically connected with Paul's ministry (Acts 19:31). The structure, located on the western slope of Mount Pion, measured about 495 feet in diameter and held some 25,000 spectators. The seating arrangement was divided into three bands with twenty-two rows of seats in each.

Between the two stages of British excavation at the Temple of Diana, the Austrian Archaeological Institute began work on the city proper. Starting in 1897, they excavated there continuously for sixteen years. They worked at Ephesus again in 1926-35 under the direction of Joseph Keil. Keil resumed the excavation in 1954 and continued until his death in 1959. Since then F. Miltner has been in charge.

In apostolic times a street 1735 feet long led from the theater to the harbor. This was greatly enhanced during the second century. To the right (north) of this street the Roman agora was built between the days of Paul and John. And during John's day Domitian built baths and gymnasia in the same area. At the southwest corner of the theater lay the older Hellenistic agora, main center of the city in apostolic times. A total of 360 feet square, it was lined with porticoes behind which were small shops. To date most of the shops, as well as the central part of the agora, are not excavated. But Miltner did find there shops of silversmiths.

Other structures excavated at Ephesus and dating to New Testament times include the town hall, a stadium and the Magnesian Gate at the southeast of the city. Most of the impressive ruins cleared by the Austrians date to the second century A.D., when the city was at its height.

EPISTLE OF JAMES. *See* Nag Hammadi.

EPONYM LISTS. Eponym lists comprise the names of the years of Assyrian history, each of which was named for the reigning king or some other high official. The eponyms were used for dating much as the Greeks used the names of their archons, and the Romans of their consuls to establish a chronology. In the Assyrian Eponyms short remarks referring to military campaigns or

THE GREAT THEATER of Ephesus. Courtesy, H. Gökberg

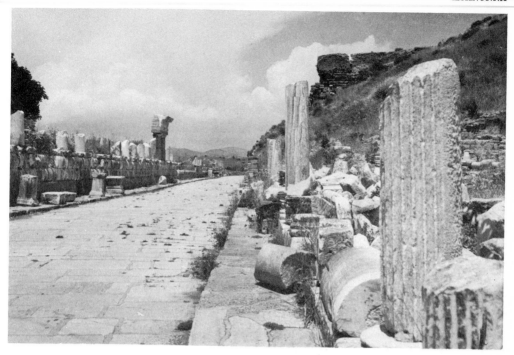

THE MARBLE STREET of ancient Ephesus as it appears today. Courtesy, H. Gökberg

natural calamities were frequently appended. One of these mentions an eclipse at Nineveh, which astronomers have been able to date in May/June 763 B.C. From this fixed date it is possible to calculate other dates from about 900 B.C. to 600 B.C. on the basis of the Eponym Lists.

ERECH. *See* Uruk.

ERIDU. A few miles south of Ur is the mound of Tell Abu Shahrain, ancient Eridu, mentioned in the *Sumerian King List as the location of the first dynasty before the flood. Fuad Safar excavated Eridu in 1946 and 1949 for the Iraq Department of Antiquities. The lowest levels of the mound date to *ca.* 4500 B.C. and contain specimens of pottery older than ᶜUbaid ware. These include shallow dishes, deep bowls and tall goblets (chocolate colored or red) decorated with ornamental designs. Checks, cross-hatching, and zig-zag lines appear frequently.

At the lowest level Safar found traces of reed huts, probably the first type of construction in lower Mesopotamia. In the *Gilgamesh Epic we read of the god Ea warning Utnapishtim of a coming flood while he sat in his reed hut. Safar also discovered the ruins of a ten foot square shrine built of sun-dried bricks, the first of a series of fourteen shrines which successively served the needs of the people of Eridu.

BIBLIOGRAPHY. R. C. Thompson, British Museum Excavations at Abu Shahrain, 1920; *Sumer III,* 1947. *Sumer VI,* 1950.

ESHNUNNA. Ancient Eshnunna was a city located on the sight of modern Tell Asmar, in the Diyala River region fifty miles northeast of Baghdad. Henri Frankfort and his associates excavated Tell Asmar for the Oriental Institute of the University of Chicago in a series of campaigns beginning in 1930. Polychrome pottery characteristic of the *Jemdet Nasr period was found at the lowest level of Tell Asmar. Above this, in a layer marking the transition from Jemdet Nasr to later times, was an archaic temple, which was subsequently rebuilt into a square temple. Hidden under the floor of the square temple was a hoard of cult statues. One of these, representing the god Abu wearing a full black beard, is thirty inches high.

A second statue represents Abu's wife, a mother goddess, with a one piece cloak passing under her right arm and fastened on her shoulder. Another represents a worshiper holding a cup.

The figures are made of gypsum. The eyes have disks of black limestone set with bitumen into eyeballs cut from shell. Black wavy hair and a full beard are fashioned from black pitch, giving us a representation of the Sumerian people as they visualized themselves.

Eshnunna had contacts with India as early as 2500 B.C. A seal from Eshnunna gives representations of Indian animals: the elephant, the rhinoceros, and the crocodile.

A law code attributed to Bilalama of Eshnunna was excavated at Tell Abu Harmal, near Baghdad by the Iraq Department of Antiquities. The code, written during the twentieth century B.C. in the Akkadian language, contains sixty paragraphs of law dealing with such subjects as the price of commodities, the hire of wagons and boats, the wages of laborers, marriage, divorce and adultery, assault and battery, and the placing of responsibility for the ox that gores a man and the mad dog that bites a man. The problem of the goring ox is settled as follows: "If an ox is known to gore habitually and the ward authorities have had the fact made known to its owner but he does not have his ox dehorned, it gores a man and causes his death, then the owner of the ox shall pay two-thirds of a mina of silver." The problem of the goring ox was also faced in the Mosaic legislation (Exod. 21:28-32).

BIBLIOGRAPHY. Henri Frankfort, Seton Lloyd and Thorkild Jacobsen, *The Gimilsin Temple and the Palace of the Rulers at Tell Asmar,* University of Chicago Press, Chicago, 1940. Henri Frankfort, Thorkild Jacobsen, and Conrad Preusser, *Tell Asmar and Khafaje: the First to the Fifth Seasons' Work at Eshnunna, 1930/31 to 1934/35,* 5 vol., University of Chicago Press, Chicago, 1932-36. Henri Frankfort, "Tell Asmar, Iraq," *Antiquity,* VIII, 1938, pp. 226-227. Henri Frankfort, "The Work of the Oriental Institute in Iraq," *AJA,* XXXVII, 1933, pp. 529-539. Thorkild Jacobsen, *Philological Notes on Eshnunna and its Inscriptions,* University of Chicago Press, Chicago, 1934. Albrecht Goetze, "The Laws of Eshnunna," *ANET,* pp. 161-163.

ESSENES. *See* Jewish Sects.

ETANA. Etana appears in the *Sumerian King List as a ruler of the First Dynasty of Kish. He is also the subject of legend in which he is described as "a shepherd, the one who to heaven ascended." Etana did not reach heaven, for the story tells how he soared upward on the back of an eagle on a quest for the "plant of birth," only to fail in his quest. When he reached the point where he could not distinguish the sea he became frightened and fell back to earth.

BIBLIOGRAPHY. Oliver Robert Gurney, "A Bilingual Text concerning Etana," *Journal of the Royal Asiatic Society,* 1935, pp. 459-466.

ET TELL. *See* Ai.

EVIL-MERODACH. Awil-Marduk, Biblical Evil-Merodach, succeeded his father Nebuchadnezzar in October 562 B.C. He released Jehoiachin of Judah from prison and dealt kindly with him (II Kings 25:27-30). The only references to him in Babylonian literature are in administrative tablets. He was killed in 560 B.C. in a plot led by his brother-in-law Neriglissar. Josephus quotes the tradition of *Berosses that he ruled "lawlessly and wantonly." *See* Chaldeans.

EXECRATION TEXTS. Execration texts are pottery bowls or clay figurines on which were inscribed curses against the enemies of Egypt in the Egyptian Hieratic script. These objects were used in a magical rite in which the Egyptian Pharaoh would smash the bowl or figurine on which the enemy's name was written. In this way it was thought that the power of the enemy would be broken, and the enemy himself would come to grief. Among the places named is one Aushamem, thought to be an Egyptian writing of Jerusalem.

The texts inscribed on bowls date from the twentieth century B.C. They were published by Kurt Sethe in 1926 and are now in Berlin. The figurines of bound captives are thought to date from the nineteenth century B.C. They were published, in part, by G. Posener in 1940 and are now in Brussels.

EXODUS. The term Exodus refers to the departure of the people of *Israel from Egypt. *Joseph, an Israelite, entered Egypt as a slave but attained the position of vizier, probably under a *Hyksos Pharaoh. Following his death, however, members of his family who had migrated to Israel became slaves under oppressive Pharoahs. Moses was the Israelite leader who led his people from Egypt through the Sinai Peninsula and Transjordan to the mountains of Moab where he died within sight of the Promised Land. *See* Egypt, Pithom, Raamses, Succoth, Sinai, Ramesses II.

EZION-GEBER. Ezion-geber (AV: Gaber) is first mentioned in the Bible as one of Israel's campsites en route from Kadesh-bar-nea to Moab (Num. 33:34-35) after having been refused transit through Edom (Deut. 2:8, where it is mentioned with Elath). It apparently was near the Gulf of Aqabah, the eastern arm of the Red Sea (*cf.* Num. 21:4). At this time, Ezion-geber did not lie in the territory of Edom, though it may have been considered within the Edomite "sphere of influence."

Nothing further is heard of Ezion-geber until the reign of Solomon (I Kings 9:26-28). Now Ezion-geber is designated as located in the land of Edom; it became Israelite territory as a result of David's victory in the Valley of Salt (perhaps es-Sebkha, south of the Dead Sea; II Sam. 8:13-14, *cf.* I Chron. 18:12-13). In the course of his reign, with Phoenician aid, Solomon built a fleet of ships as a part of his foreign trade program. These ships went to Ophir (perhaps a part of Somaliland), carrying goods brought from Egypt, Arabia, Mesopotamia, Israel, Canaan, and elsewhere for exchange at various ports of call en route to Ophir and return, finally bringing as much as 420 talents of gold (about 31,500 lbs. @ 75 lbs. / talent, or $17,640,000 @ $35.00 / oz.) to Solomon's treasury as proceeds of voyages of perhaps two to three years' duration.

The Biblical record does not report the fate of Solomon's fleet. During the troubled years after his death, Edom led by Hadad, presumably attempted to declare her inde-pendence after some years of guerilla war-fare (I Kings 11:14-22, 25; *cf.* II Kings 8:20-22, II Chron. 21:8-10). The fleet may have been destroyed during this uprising, or by Pharaoh Shishak in 918 B.C. in the course of his sweep through Judah and Israel (I Kings 15:25-28), or by a storm. In any event, Jehoshaphat (873-849 B.C.) attempt-ed to rebuild the fleet after putting down an attempted revolt by Edom (II Chron. 20). Before it could set out for its maiden

voyage, a storm drove it on near-by rocks and destroyed it. Within a few years of Jehoshaphat's disastrous effort, Edom suc-cessfully revolted against his son, Jehoram (849-842; II Kings 8:20-22; II Chron. 21: 8-10).

Almost a half-century later, Amaziah (800-783) recaptured Edom (I Kings 14:7; II Chron. 25:11-16, 20). His son Azariah (Uzziah; 783-742) rebuilt the city, now called Elath, an indication of his effective control of the territories east and west of the Arabah (II Chron. 25:1-15; *cf.* II Kings 14:21-22). That Elath is the later name of Ezion-geber is suggested both by the parallel references in Deuteronomy 2:8 and I Kings 9:26 and by archaeological evidence (see below).

Except that it was near the Gulf of Aqabah, the location of Ezion-geber was unknown in modern times. Several writers and scholars accepted as factual a tale told the intrepid German explorer Alois Musil by some Be-douin. For our purposes, it resulted in the assumption that the Gulf of Aqabah reached much farther north than it does today so that Ezion-geber was thought to be located at Khirbet el-Mene'iyyeh, about 18½ miles from the present shoreline, or even at Ghadyan, several miles farther north. In 1934 Fritz Frank published his suggestion that the site was to be identified with the low mound of Tell el-Kheleifeh, about two miles west of the village of Aqabah and 550 yards north of the present seashore. This suggestion has been corroborated by the ex-cavation of the site by Nelson Glueck, then Director of the American School of Oriental Research in Jerusalem, during three seasons, 1938-40. Though no inscription was found absolutely to confirm the identification of Tell el-Kheleifeh with Ezion-geber, no other site along this coast is known whose arch-aeological history agrees with the Biblical narrative. The site of Aila, the successor to Ezion-geber, about 1½ miles to the east, has no surface pottery earlier than the Nabatean period (fourth century B.C., *ff.*) — though the possibility of earlier occupation is not thereby absolutely precluded.

In the excavation of Tell el-Kheleifeh five major occupation periods with some sub-periods were discovered extending from the tenth century B.C to the fourth century B.C. Excavation to virgin soil turned up no trace of an earlier — Edomite (?) — settlement

233

to be associated with the Exodus. The earlier settlement may have been located at some presently unidentified site, or it may have been located at Tell el-Kheleifeh but was unfortified, its mud-brick buildings dissolving into the earth from which they had been taken, leaving no trace of man's presence. Period I is to be equated with the time of Solomon (962-922) and some years following. During the years immediately after his death, the city was damaged by rebellious Edomites, Shishak, or Judahite troops recovering control of the area (see above).

Most tantalizing was the discovery in the northwest corner of the tell of a building, about 40 feet x 40 feet, divided into three small rooms to the north and three large rectangular rooms to the south. All of the walls of this building had two rows of tile set into the mud-brick walls, one row five bricks (about 20 inches) above the other. The lower row of tile (about 3 feet to 4 feet above floor level) went through the walls while the upper row led into a channel within the wall. Glueck concluded that the building was a (copper) refinery, the rows of tile being flues. The lower row conducted heated air into adjacent rooms to pre-heat semi-refined ("roasted") copper ore as part of the smelting process. The upper row led into an air-draft channel whose northern opening admitted the wind, almost constantly blowing down the Arabah, the location of the city — at the western edge of available sweet water — being calculated to take advantage of the wind at its strongest force.

The refinery was surrounded by an enclosure 12½ feet to 19 feet from the building, one room deep which rooms were perhaps used for industrial purposes. The outer wall of this enclosure was re-inforced to serve as a fortification wall for the complex. The entrance gate was presumably in the southwest corner of the enclosure. Pottery of this period consisted of crude, hand-made, rather straight-sided jars, fashioned on a mat, the impression of which can be seen on the bottom. This type of primitive, very break-

THE WILDERNESS NEAR EZION-GEBER. Israel's journey to Ezion-geber took her through this barren, mountainous terrain. Courtesy, Consulate General of Israel.

able pottery with horn (button) or ledge handles has become well-known from other sites in the Negeb. In addition, examples of more conventional Iron I (1200-900 B.C.) pottery were found. According to the excavator, all indications pointed to the conclusion that this was the city built by Solomon to complete the refining of copper mined in Sinai and in the hills of the Arabah. This copper, together with goods brought to this junction point of trade routes, became part of the materials traded by Solomon's men for gold.

Sometime during the period of Ezion-geber I, minor modifications were made in the main building; e.g. a wall divided the long west room into two smaller rooms, but the basic plan and flue system remained as before. Some repairs were also made. It is possible that this occurred in consequence of Shishak's attack or some other circumstance suggested above. Still later in this period, the flue system was discarded, the openings being plastered over and the outer walls of the building strengthened with a glacis of mud-brick laid in a crisscross fashion and reaching nearly to the top of the 12 foot walls. Glueck suggested that soot, dust, and settlement of walls made the flues inoperative and that the stress of heat or some other factor necessitated the reinforcement of the walls. It would also require a return to the more primitive method of heating by using hand bellows rather than the more sophisticated air-draft system. Ezion-geber I was destroyed by fire, perhaps to be associated with the abortive Edomite revolt in Jehoshaphat's day (see above) or by hostile action even earlier.

Ezion-geber II retained use of the large main building but in the new scheme, it was located in the northwest corner of the compound. The interior disposition of the main building was further modified by the building of partition walls to make the long southeast room into two rooms and the three northern rooms into five. Southeast of the building was an angle of the earlier industrial square which continued in use. The remainder of the now enlarged enclosure seems to have been open, serving as a place for caravans to tether camels and asses and to pile goods awaiting trans-shipment, perhaps on the ill-fated fleet Jehoshaphat had hoped would re-establish Judahite sea commerce.

The fortification system was radically changed. It became a double-walled system with regularly spaced insets and offsets, often parallel to the earlier outer wall of the enclosure, strengthened by a glacis built of brick laid in a crisscross fashion for additional strength, rather than header-stretcher as used elsewhere in the walls and buildings. The north wall of the main building was incorporated into the inner circumvallation. This inner wall, whose foundations were laid 2 feet to 3 feet deep in virgin soil, was about 25 feet high and 15 feet thick at the base (including the glacis, the wall itself being 7½ feet to 9 feet thick). The outer wall was about 10 feet high and about 3 feet thick, plus a glacis similarly constructed as the inner one. The northern section of the west outer wall incorporated the outer west wall of the earlier industrial square. Thus on the north and west the new walls cut through, and in part incorporated, earlier walls of the main building and industrial square. At the southwest corner was the main gateway, opening to the sea and leading to the large open area noted above. The gateway consisted of three massive piers with guardrooms between the piers on either side. At one time three gates barred entrance to this heavily fortified complex whose total area was only about 1½ acres.

On the northern side, not far from the main building, in the 10 feet wide dry moat between the two walls, a larger mastaba-like grave was discovered. Its mud-brick roof was covered by granite boulders. Though robbed of valuables in antiquity, it contained the bones of a man, his camel, and bowls with bones of a fish, a bird, and a small animal — remnants of a funerary meal for the deceased or an offering to his divine judge. A millstone, mortar and cosmetic palette were also found, but no clue to the identity of a man sufficiently important to be the only one, apparently, to be buried in this impressive way between the city walls.

Ezion-geber II was also destroyed by fire. This catastrophe was perhaps a part of Edom's successful revolt against Jehoshaphat's son, Jehoram.

Ezion-geber III is presumably to be connected with the time of Amaziah (Uzziah) and his son Jotham. As Amaziah changed the name of the Edomite capital, Sela', to Joktheel (II Kings 14:7; II Chron. 26:1-2) after regaining control of it, so also he changed the name of Ezion-geber to Elath. When the writers of our present books of Deuteronomy, I Kings and II Chronicles arranged the materials at hand, they identified the earlier Ezion-geber by relating it to its successor, Elath.

Ezion-geber III (Elath I) used the same fortification walls as its predecessor and the disposition of the main building remained the same. The ninth century gateway was modified by walling up the entrances to the two sets of facing guardrooms, producing a sort of casemate effect. The third (inner) gate was narrowed by placing a mud-brick pillar against both piers. The once-open courtyard was now filled with dwellings, some of them in the southeast section built over a brickyard in which some of the bricks prepared for use in the massive fortification walls still remained intact. Had the restorers of the city dug a foot below the debris level, they could have used bricks moulded seventy or more years earlier. This circumstance made it possible for the excavator to distinguish between Ezion-geber II and Ezion-geber III, the two being so similar in most other respects.

Unique is a ring with a copper-enclosed seal bearing the inscription LYTM — "Belonging to Jotham" — with a ram depicted on it. The ram (Heb. 'ayil) is perhaps a symbol of the city name, Elath (Heb. 'eylat). Another figure in front of the ram was first thought to represent a man, but N. Avigad has suggested bellows, comparing it to the famed Beni Hasan relief. The ring perhaps belonged to the governor of Elath during the administration of Jotham.

In the ruins of the eighth century city were found two large jars on which were South Arabic, probably Minaean, letters, the first found in Palestine. These attest to the trade connections with South Arabia whose history dates back at least to the days of Solomon. In this level were items from Sinai and Egypt such as carnelian, agate, amethyst, and crystal beads, a tiny faience amulet of the god Bes (Bast), another amulet — an Uzat eye of Horus, and fragments of alabaster cups, plates and buttons. Iron and copper nails, about 1½ inch long, various sizes of rope made of twisted palm fibers,

metal fish hooks, lance and spear heads, knives and fibulae bear mute testimony to the life and activity of the people living here.

It was during the reign of Jotham's successor Ahaz that we are specifically told of Elath's recapture by Edom. The Edomite city (Ezion-geber IV — Elath II) re-used the fortification walls of the previous two periods. It had at least three phases. The first of these extended down into the seventh century B.C., coming to an end perhaps during Ashurbanipal's expedition against Egypt in 663 (cf. Nah. 3:8) or his punitive raids in the west following the revolt of Shamash-shum-ukin (652-648). In this level were found many jar handles stamped with the inscription LQWS'NL 'BDMLK — "Belonging to Qaus'anal, servant of the king [of Edom]." Qaus (Qos) was the name of one of the gods of Edom, and later of the Nabataeans (cf. Barkos, Ezra 2:53; Neh. 7:55). On a fragment of another jar was a graffito in Edomite characters, the precise reading of which remains uncertain.

In a storeroom of a later phase of this city were four large storage jars, three of them intact. One of them contained sweet-smelling resin which melted in the sun from which it had been hidden for 2½ millennia. The intended use of the resin remains unknown. The small finds of the earlier city (see above) find their analogues in this later one. A pottery plaque bearing a crude representation of the pregnant mother-goddess was found in another house, as well as foundation offerings beneath the walls of some of the houses consisting of pots with fruit, fish, and fowl. Finally, one of the Aramaic ostraca (see below) has been provisionally assigned to the early sixth century, just before the destruction of the city, perhaps by Nebuchadrezzar's forces as part of his campaign against Egypt in 568 B.C., or some other raid, perhaps by Arabs during Nabonidus' reign (556-539).

Ezion-geber V (Elath III) was built on its predecessor's ruins later in the same century, perhaps during the reign of Cyrus (d. 530) or a successor. It was built along different lines with a new fortification system. It seems to have had two phases with the last ending in the fourth century B.C. During this period it may have been under Arab domination, perhaps controlled by Nehemiah's enemy Geshem in the fifth century (Neh. 2:19; 6:1 ff.). Some red-figured and degenerate black figured Attic ware sherds were found in this level calling attention to the greatly expanded trade activity of the Persian period. Their route may have taken them from Athens to Gaza by ship, to Elath and Arabia by camel train. Wines and other products were exchanged for incense and spices. Several Aramaic ostraca, one of them a wine receipt, were found in this last level of occupation.

With the fall of the second occupation of the fifth city, the history of the site comes to an end. Later mud-brick houses may have been built atop the ruins but there is no trace of them. The city was moved to a place 1½ miles east by the Nabateans who continued the name Elath, known to later history as Aila, which in Roman times became the important terminus for Trajan's famous highway.

Recently, Beno Rothenberg has adduced certain observations which seem to call for a reconsideration of the original description of the function of Ezion-geber as a great smelter complex. First of all, only minimal amounts of slag were found at the site, and none on any pottery fragment. In the ancient smelting process there would have been slag in considerable quantity regardless of the relative purity of "roasted" ore — and there would surely have been some identifiable vestiges of the proper kind of smelting crucibles, metal working implements, casting molds, etc. There is some question as to the efficiency of a system of flues in all of the walls of the building for developing the necessary draft to raise the heat of the ore to the minimal requisite 1083° C. for refining, and even more about the possibility of a bellows operator's surviving in a small room at such elevated temperatures and in the presence of released gases with the flue or ventilating system now plastered over. The discoloration of the bricks of the "refinery" would be the result of the burning of roof,

roof supports, and stored goods when the city was destroyed, rather than by gases released by the smelting process. The industrial enclosure with its fortified outer wall may well be a Solomonic casemate wall, typical for the period of Ezion-geber I, with some of the casemate "rooms" being used for storage or other purposes.

Meteorological data indicate that the difference in wind velocity between the sides of the Arabah and the location of Tell el-Kheleifeh is not sufficiently great to justify the location of the installation there, if it be a refinery. The southerly path of the sandstorms which expands from the east (Aqabah) across toward modern Eilat suggests that Ezion-geber was placed as far west in the Arabah as water was available and almost (within about a mile) of the usual limit of sandstorm intensity. Another reason for its location may have been easy access to a sandy shore up-on-to which (Tarshish) boats could be drawn.

It may thus be that the interpretation first rejected by the excavator is correct after all. The site was perhaps a fortified storage depôt for goods being shipped along the trade routes which intersected at Ezion-geber, and a garrison for securing the safety of the routes and the caravans which travelled them. Only the definitive publication of the excavation reports can really provide the data for the solution to the problem of the function of the city of Ezion-geber — Elath.

BIBLIOGRAPHY. Nahman Avigad, "The Jotham Seal from Elath," BASOR 163, 1961, 18-22. Fritz Frank, "Aus der 'Arabah, I," ZDPV 57, 1934, 191-285, esp. 243-44. Nelson Glueck, "The First Campaign at Tell el-Kheleifeh (Ezion-Geber)," BASOR 71, 1938, 3-17. "The Second Campaign at Tell el-Kheleifeh, (Ezion-Geber)" BASOR 75, 1939, 8-22; "The Third Season at Tell el-Kheleifeh," BASOR 79, 1940, 2-18; The Other Side of the Jordan, New Haven:American Schools of Oriental Research, 1940, pp. 89-113; "Ostraca from Elath," BASOR 80, 1940, 3-10; 82, 1941, 3-11. B. Mazar (Maisler), "The Campaign of Pharaoh Shishak to Palestine," VTS IV, 1957, 57-66. Beno Rothenberg, "Ancient Copper Industries in the Western Arabah," PEQ 94, 1962, 5-61.

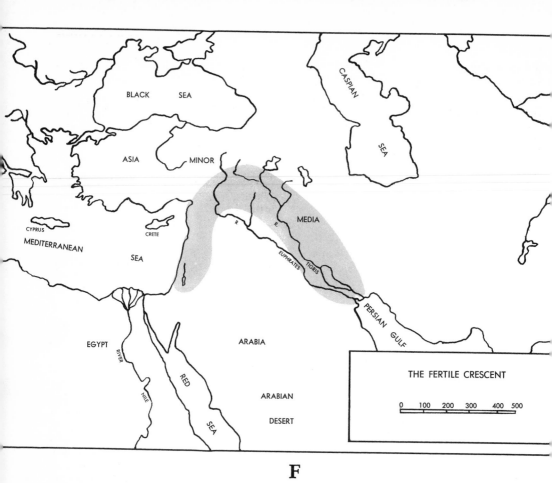

The map shows: BLACK SEA, ASIA MINOR, CASPIAN SEA, CYPRUS, CRETE, MEDITERRANEAN SEA, MEDIA, EUPHRATES, TIGRIS, PERSIAN GULF, EGYPT, RIVER, NILE, RED SEA, ARABIA, ARABIAN DESERT, THE FERTILE CRESCENT, 0 100 200 300 400 500

F

FERTILE CRESCENT. No part of the Biblical World is far removed from desert. Stretching northwestward from the Persian Gulf is the narrow strip of land, skirting the Arabian and Syrian deserts, which James H. Breasted named the Fertile Crescent. Its northern boundary is the three thousand foot high tableland of Anatolia and Iran, separated from each other by the mountains of Armenia, the *Urartu* of ancient cuneiform inscriptions and the Ararat of the Bible (Gen. 8:4). Cross movement is almost impossible due to the mountain ranges which hem in the tablelands — the Tauras, Pontio, Elburz, and Kurdistan Ranges.

South and east of the Fertile Crescent are the desert areas which forbid access to the merchant and the soldier alike. The historic trek of Abraham from Ur of the Chaldees through Haran to Canaan approximates the way by which people have journeyed from southern Mesopotamia to Palestine since the beginning of history. As man moved from either the mountains or the desert into

the river valleys of the Fertile Crescent he became a part of the culture which produced Sumerian city states or Assyrian and Babylonian empires.

As the Euphrates River swings northwestward it reaches a point in northern Syria not far from the Mediterranean coast. Here rainfall is more plentiful and the summer drought shorter than in the regions farther south. Here, too, there is but one mountain barrier, and the rain is carried farther inland, so that a broad area of fertile steppeland connects the Mediterranean with the Euphrates.

As the Fertile Crescent swings southeastward along the coasts of Syria and Palestine, rainfall diminishes and cultivated land gradually passes into desert. The desert begins at Gaza (*cf.* Acts 8:26) and this, technically speaking, also marks the end of the Fertile Crescent. Actually, however, the fertile Delta and valley of the Nile is but a short distance southwest. The Fertile Crescent has historically been the connecting road between the

the figurine of a thrown deer, an erotic statuette, and a phallic pestle.

3. Neolithic. Jericho (Tell-es-Sultan), located at an oasis eight hundred feet below sea-level to the northwest of the Dead Sea, abounds in Neolithic (6000-4000 B.C.) remains. From the pre-pottery period have come the amazing plastered skulls, discovered by Kathleen Kenyon in 1951. The detached skulls were filled with clay and painted. One which had the lower jaw intact was of outstanding delicacy and showed careful anatomical observation. These are forerunners of funerary masks. Forty individuals, from many of which the skull had been removed, were found beneath another house. Were these the heads of slain enemies, or more likely of venerated ancestors? The separation of the skulls and skeletons suggests that the physical body had no place in the concept of the after-life, while the modelled skull recalled the appearance of the dead person and made his presence and influence on the living very strong.

Megallithic graves are another characteristic of the Neolithic Age. There are four thousand dolmens (Breton, "table stones") in the Golan and Bashan regions of Jordan and in "Moab," but only a few in western Palestine. These cube-like tombs have single slabs on three sides and a single slab as a roof. They belonged to pastoral peoples of different races who herded cattle, sheep, and goats. Many dolmens have cup marks on the roofs, but owing to the absence of sculpture, pottery, and offerings in the tombs, nothing is known about the religion of their builders except that they laid emphasis on an after-life.

B. Chalcolithic Burials. Sukenik, digging through a five foot layer of *kurkar*, solidified sand, at Hadera in the Plain of Sharon in 1934, found box-like pottery vessels protruding. This proved to be the first man-made cave used for burials, dating from the Chalcolithic Age (4000-3000 B.C.). The pottery urns were identified as ossuaries or bone-boxes. The best preserved was a house shaped ossuary two feet long, one foot wide, and two feet high, decorated with bands and triangles. Many of them were also unearthed at Bene Baraq, Givatayim, and Azor, in the vicinity of Tell Aviv. Some were animal and ovoid shaped, but the great majority were house shaped. When there was no more room for burial under houses, the ossuary burial

developed. After the decay of the flesh, the bones were put into a house of the dead. The urn was lowered into a collective grave, and eventually there was a village of houses under the earth. These are the first elaborate secondary burials. They suggest the preservation of the individual's remains after death and a community of the dead who needed houses and bowls of food and drink.

Stone Age burial practices persisted at Ghassul, east of Jericho, and numerous burials of children in jars beneath the floors occurred. At Adeimeh, one and one-half miles east of Ghassul, Stekelis in 1933 excavated 168 "cist" type burial chambers. The chamber from two to five feet in length, to fit the individual, was lined with upright flat stones to form a *cist* (Lat., "chest"). Individuals were buried in a crouching position, resting on the back. Table-like flat stones were laid across the top of the cist. Hearths associated with the cist-chambers were apparently for ceremonial funerary meals, since there are no traces of

C. Bronze Age Burials. The Early (3000-1900 B.C.), and Late Bronze Ages (1550-1200 B.C.) are designated Early (3300-1850 B.C.), Middle (1850-1550 B.C.), and Late Urban (1550-1200 B.C.) Periods by Anati.

1. Much racial and cultural amalgamation took place in Palestine in the *Early Urban Period*. It was a time of the building of walled cities, of the proliferation of city states, of the erection of shrines and temples, and of trade with Egypt, Syria, and Mesopotamia.

Elaborate communal tombs were in widespread use from 3300-3000 B.C., reflecting the wide variety of the backgrounds of the people. Some form of partial cremation was definitely known from the Troglodyte Crematorium of Gezer, explored by Macalister in 1902, and from Jericho tomb A 94. The skulls were preserved, and cremation was the method of disposing of accumulated skeletons to make room for more burials. The community burial, common throughout Palestine by 3000 B.C., implies development in a concept of the realm of the dead, which succeeding cultures until the Post-Exilic period also held.

Despite the multiplication of affluent cities in the period 3000-2400 B.C., tombs became less elaborate. Even the pottery was miniature. The disturbance of the bones after the burial represents varied customs prac-

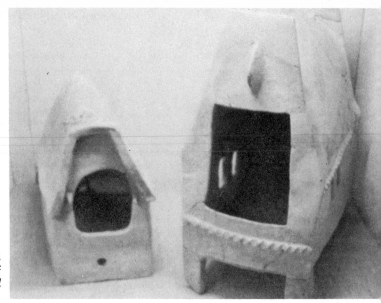

OSSUARIES in the museum of the Israel Department of Antiquities. Courtesy, Gerald Larue

ticed, as well as a shift of interest away from life after death to the prosperous urban present.

In the period 2300-1900 B.C., nomadic invaders ended the prosperous urban culture of the Early Bronze Age. Apparently they were the Amorites, the most prolific tomb builders of ancient Palestine. Over 400 of the 505 tombs excavated at Jericho between 1952-58 belong to this period. Single burials predominate in the rather elaborate rock cut tombs. Rows of *maṣṣebahs* or *menhirs (roughly hewn upright columns), cairns, and shaft graves are common. The "Dagger" tombs of Jericho contain a single copper dagger but no pottery. The chambers were relatively small, neatly cut, and holding the body in a reclining attitude on the side. "Pottery" tombs contained pottery but no daggers, with burials unarticulated and secondary. Apparently after a season's nomadic wanderings, the group reburied the bones of its dead.

The unusual multi-chambered shaft tombs in Megiddo may have served a family unit. Altars at Jericho and Bethel, and a temple structure at Megiddo, in connection with these tombs may point to a cult of the dead.

2. The *Middle Urban Period* (1850-1550 B.C.) witnessed the conquest of Palestine and Egypt by the powerful Hyksos invaders,

an amalgam of Semitic and Indo-European tribes, who ruled about 1720-1550 B.C. They buried horses and donkeys with their dead (an Indo-European practice), as evidenced at Tell el-Ajjul (Gaza) and Jericho. Communal and single Hyksos tombs have been found outside Jerusalem, at Tell el-Farah (Sharuhen), Jericho and Lachish, with grave goods and sacrificed animals.

2. At the end of the *Late Bronze Age* (*ca.* 1200 B.C.), some Canaanites had begun to adopt the Egyptian practice of burying the dead in anthropoid clay coffins, on the upper part of which were molded human features, the face and hands. One of these with an hieroglyphic inscription was found at Lachish. In the twelfth and eleventh centuries, these tombs appear with Philistine pottery, in Tell el-Farah, Beth-shan, Tell el-Yahudiyeh, and Tell Nebesheh, having been adopted by the Philistines.

In the Late Bronze Age, Canaan was exposed to the raids of the *Habiru (*ca.* 1400-1350 B.C.) referred to in the Amarna Letters, and then about a century later to the Hebrew conquest.

II. *Post-Old Testament Burials.* The Israelite period described in the Old Testament

A TOMB from Palmyra Courtesy, Azad, Beyrou

embraces the period from the Conquest of Canaan to the work of the Chronicler, from about 1200 to 400 B.C. We shall now survey the burials of Persian and Hellenistic Palestine, and then come back to the Biblical funerary practices.

The contents of tombs from the Persian period (539-332 B.C.) are often rich. Petrie discovered at Tell el-Farah a tomb containing a bronze bed, a beautiful fluted silver bowl, and a dipper, the handle of which was a slender nude maiden.

During the Hellenistic period (332 B.C.-A.D. 70), large chambers were hollowed out of the rock with niches (Hebr. *kôkîm*) or *loculi* cut out of the walls to receive the ossuaries and with ledges or *arcosolia* on which to place the bodies. The *loculi* often have Hebrew, Aramaic, or Greek inscriptions, including the deceased's name, and a warning, "Do not open." The ossuaries are often elaborately decorated with rosettes and other figures.

The tombs of Marissa (Mareshah), about 250-200 B.C., discovered in 1902, of the *kôkîm* type, have walls richly decorated with figures of animals, vases, musical instruments, and humans. *Graffiti* (writings scratched on walls) in Greek indicate the names of the buried.

At *'Araq el-Emir, west of Amman in Jordan, is located the mausoleum of the Tobiad family, founded by Tobiah the Ammonite (Neh. 2:19, etc.). The name Tobiah in third century Aramaic character is cut into it. Josephus connects the building with Hyrcanus, the last Tobiah, *ca.* 175 B.C. (*Antiquities* XII. iv. 11).

The *Qumran community, famed for the Dead Sea Scrolls, occupied an area at the northwest shore of the Dead Sea seven miles south of Jericho within the period 110 B.C.-A.D. 68. The main cemetery is to the east of the settlement, with smaller groups of graves to the north and south. There are 1200 individual graves in rows. They consist of a shaft two meters long, a half meter wide, and two meters deep, in the bottom side of which is a shallow loculus for the body. Stones were placed over the grave, with a standing stone at the head and the foot. Nothing was ever buried with the body.

The "Tombs of the Judges" are situated in the Sanhedria garden in the northeast section of Jerusalem, Israel. There are about twenty-five rock-hewn caves, some of three stories, dating from the Maccabean and Herodian era. Niches or *kôkîm* are hollowed into the cave walls to accommodate the stone sarcophagi and ossuaries. In one of the largest caves, tradition says the members of the Jewish Sanhedrin were buried. It has a Greek style facade with a frieze of acanthus leaves, pomegranates, and citrons. There are no inscriptions to identify the graves.

The so-called tombs of St. James, Zechariah, Absalom, and Jehoshaphat, in the Valley of Kidron, belong to the time of Herod the Great.

Since the fourth century the tomb of Jesus has been located beneath the dome of the Church of the Holy Sepulchre. Some Protestant scholars prefer the "more natural looking" Garden Tomb adjoining "Gordon's Calvary," to the north of the Damascus Gate. There are no known Christian burials of New Testament times in Palestine. The *Catacombs in Rome are the oldest known Christian burials.

The so-called "Tomb of the Kings of Judah," investigated by De Saulcy in 1850 and 1863, is in the northern part of Jerusalem, Jordan, to the east of the Nablus Road, close to the Anglican Cathedral of St. George. It is actually the *hypogeum* ("underground" cave or structure) of Helen, Queen of Adiabene in Upper Mesopotamia. She was converted to Judaism, came to Jerusalem in A.D. 44, and built this tomb for her family. It has a rolling stone *in situ*. (Cf. Josephus *Wars* V. iv. 2; *Antiquities* XX. ii. 1-4, iv. 3.)

The colored sandstone cliffs of *Petra are lined with mausoleums cut out of the solid rock, many of monumental type, showing Roman influence. They were made by the Nabatean Arabs, whose greatest king, Aretas IV Philodemus (9 B.C.-A.D. 40), ruled Edom, the Transjordan, and Syria in the days of the Apostle Paul (II Cor. 11:32). The Nabatean capital was built on the site of the Edomite city Sela (II Kings 14:7; II Chron. 25:11f), sixty miles north of Aqaba. The mausoleums indicate a cult of the dead.

Herod's Cave, to the west of the Valley of Hinnom and south of the King David Hotel in Jerusalem, Israel, was the tomb for members of King Herod's family. Beautiful stone coffins were within. A large rolling stone (yet *in situ*) closed the entrance to the

THE FAMILY TOMB of the Herods in Jerusalem. Note the stone that rolls to form a door. Courtesy, Gerald Larue

tomb. Herod himself was interred in the spectacular *Herodium* on Frank Mountain four miles southeast of Bethlehem. (cf. Josephus *Antiquities* XVII. viii. 4; *Wars* I. xxiii. 9.

Beth-Shearim, the Jewish necropolis between Nazareth and Haifa, was excavated in 1936-40, 1956 by Mazar, and in 1953-55 by Avigad. The twenty-six rock-hewn catacombs date from the second to the fourth centuries A.D. One of the catacombs contains four hundred burial places. It shows the influence of Hellenistic culture on the Jews in the first centuries of the Christian era. Most of the burial inscriptions are in Greek rather than Hebrew or Aramaic. The tomb decorations and architecture is Hellenistic. Pagan deities and scenes, including "Leda and the Swan," are depicted. They were apparently for decorative purposes only, and were tolerated by the prominent rabbis and their families who were subsequently buried there.

The Mishna's instructions regarding burials and tombs and their making are in *Baba Bathra* VI. 8; *Oholoth* XV. 1; *Ma'aser Sheni* V. 1; *Shekalim* I. 1; *Mo'ed Katan* I. 2.

III. *Israelite Funerary Customs of the Bible.* Death was probably a more familiar part of daily life in Israel than it is to us, because families were larger and lived under one roof. Final illnesses were not prolonged by the use of drugs. War, malnutrition, and poverty accounted for many early deaths. Infant mortality was high. Probably few people reached three score years and ten.

A. Burial of the Corpse. There were elaborate burial and mourning customs in Israel. Upon death the eyes of the dead were closed in a semblance of sleep (Gen. 46:4), relatives embraced the body (Gen. 50:1), and began preparations for the burial, the washing, anointing, and wrapping of the corpse (Acts 9:37; Mark 16:1; Matt. 27:59; John 11:44; 19:39f.).

Embalming, the art of preserving dead bodies from decay, was not practiced in Israel, probably because of theological beliefs, antipathy to Egyptian religion, and the great cost of embalming. Of the Hebrews, Jacob and Joseph alone received Egyptian funerals (Gen. 50:2f., 26; cf. also Josephus *Antiquities* XIV. viii. 4).

Cremation was abhorrent to the Hebrews, meted out only to grievous sinners (Gen. 38:24; Lev. 20:14; 21:19; Josh. 7:25). The men of Jabesh Gilead are said to have burned the bodies of Saul and Jonathan to spare them further Philistine indignities, and then to have buried them (II Sam. 31:12. But contra. I Chron. 10:12). The burning of a pagan corpse by an enemy was considered inhuman (Amos 2:1). There are references to the burning of incense and spices, but not bodies, at funerals (II Chron. 16:14; 21:19; Jer. 34:5). The Mishna *Aboda Zarah* I, 3 forbids cremation.

Burial was the regular method for the disposal of the body. Lack of burial was considered a great tragedy (I Kings 14:11; Jer. 16:4; 22:19; Ezek. 29:5), while to provide burials was a virtue (Tob. 1:17-19; 2:8f.). Burials usually took place on the day of death (Deut. 21:22f.; Num. 19:11-14; Acts 5:6, 10). The corpse was carried on a bier to the grave (II Sam. 3:31; II Chron. 16:14; Luke 7:14), and deposited there coffinless (II Kings 13:21). Pins and ornaments found in tombs show that the dead were buried fully clothed (I Sam. 28:14; Ezek. 32:27). Herod buried Aristobulus in full armor (Josephus *Antiquities* XV. iii. 4), and was himself buried in purple, with diadem, crown, and scepter (Josephus *Wars* I. xxxiii. 9). Lazarus was wrapped in some type of winding sheet (John 11:44), as were Ananias and Sapphira (Acts 5:6-10).

The tomb was a natural or artificial cave shaped as a burying place for the dead. Abraham purchased the Cave of Machpelah in Hebron from Ephron the Hittite (Gen. 23), and it became a family tomb (Gen. 49:29-32). The tomb was family property (Josh. 24:30, 32; I Sam. 25:1; I Kings 2:34), and a man was buried in the tomb of his father (Gen. 25:9f.; 49:29-32; Judg. 8:32; 16:31; II Sam. 2:32; 17:23; 19:38; 21:12-14). To be excluded from the family tomb was punishment (I Kings 13:21f.). Various Israelite worthies buried in certain tombs or cities include Joshua (Josh. 24:30; Judg. 2:9), Gideon (Judg. 8:32), Jephthah (Judg. 12:7), Samson (Judg. 16:31), Saul and Jonathan (I Sam. 31:13; II Sam. 21:14), Asahel (I Sam. 2:32).

Except for the royal necropolis inside the old city of David (I Kings 2:10; 11:43; 14:31; 15:8, 24; II Kings 8:24; 12:21; 14:20), tombs were not located in cities. They were scattered over slopes (II Chron. 32:33), where the soil was favorable (II Kings 13:21; II Chron. 34:4), on elevated places (II Kings 23:16; Isa. 22:16), and in gardens (II Kings 21:18, 26; John 19:41).

Graves for the common people of Jerusalem were located in the Kidron Valley (II Kings 23:6; Jer. 26:23), while the rich frequently planned great burial places for them-

selves during their life-time (Isa. 22:15f.; Job 3:14).

There are references to the grave monuments or stelae of Rachel (Gen. 35:20), Absalom (II Sam. 18:18) and the wicked oppressors (Job 27:15), and kings in their °High Places (Ezek. 43:7).

B. Mourning Rites. The Bible relates many different practices which were customary on occasions of great sorrow, whether death or public calamities. There was the tearing of the garments (Gen. 37:34; II Sam. 1:11; 3:31; 13:31; Job 1:20); sackcloth was put on (Gen. 37:34; II Sam. 3:31); sandals and headdresses were removed (II Sam. 15:30; Ezek. 24:17, 23; Micah 1:8). A man covered his beard (Ezek. 24:17, 23), or veiled his face (II Sam. 19:5). Putting the hands on the head was an expression of sorrow or shame (II Sam. 13:19; Jer. 2:37). Putting earth on the head (Josh. 7:6; I Sam. 4:12; Neh. 9:1), or sitting or lying in the dust and ashes (Esth. 4:3; Job 16:15; Isa. 58:5; Jer. 6:26; Ezek. 27:30; Micah 1:10) was common. Mourners refrained from washing and using perfumes (II Sam. 12:20; 14:2). Shaving of the hair and beard and making cuts in the body were condemned as savoring of heathenism (Luke 19:27f.; 21:5; Deut. 14:1; Isa. 22:12; Jer. 16:6; 41:5; Amos 8:10).

Fasting was a part of mourning (II Sam. 1:12; 3:35; I Sam. 31:13), and neighbors brought food and drink to the relatives of the deceased (Jer. 16:7; Ezek. 24:17, 22; Hosea 9:4), for food could not be prepared in a house rendered unclean through death. The Hebrew law forbade the offering of food to the dead (Deut. 26:14).

The chief funeral ceremony was lamentation for the dead (Jer. 4:8; Micah 1:8, Amos 5:16), for a brother, sister, or king (I Kings 13:30; Jer. 22:18; 34:5), for an only son (II Sam. 19:1, 5; Jer. 6:26; Amos 8:10; Zech. 12:10). Weeping (Mal. 2:13; Matt. 11:17; Luke 7:32) and lamentation began at death (Matt. 9:23; Mark 6:58), and continued on the way to the grave. The usual period of mourning was seven days (the *ší b' a*, Gen. 50:10; I Sam. 31:13; I Chron. 10:12; Ecclus. 22:12). For Moses and Aaron the mourning lasted 30 days (Num. 20:29; Deut. 34:8), and for Jacob, the Egyptian custom of 70 days (Gen. 50:3).

Professional mourners were a part of a funeral, especially women, as being more emotional and sensitive (II Chron. 35:25; Eccl. 12:5; Jer. 9:17-20; Ezek. 27:32; Amos 5:16). The mourners composed poetic laments, *qînôt*, for the dead (II Sam. 1:18-27; 3:33f; I Macc. 9:21). The most elaborate of these elegies is the Book of Lamentations, a dirge over the fall of Jerusalem, mainly in the *qinah* meter, the lines being divided into hemistichs of three and two beats respectively. Satirical laments were uttered over Babylon, Tyre, and Egypt (Isa. 14:4-41; Ezek. 27:2-36; 32:2-16). Dialogue formed a part of the lament (II Sam. 1:19, 25, 27; Ezek. 32:19ff; Rev. 18:10ff; Matt. 11:17), and musical instruments were used, especially the flute (Jer. 48:36; Matt. 9:23; Josephus *Wars* III. ix. 9; Mishna *Kethuvoth* IV. 4).

IV. *The Meaning of Funerary Practices.* There is no foundation for the idea of a cult of the dead in the Old Testament. The dead were honored in a religious spirit, but no worship was paid to them.

The Old Testament indicates that a man cannot worship two masters, Yahweh and the spirits of the dead, and so all the practices connected with death were deemed unclean and as far as possible suppressed (Lev. 21:14; 22:4; Num. 19:11-14; Hag. 2:13; Isa. 38:17-19; Ezek. 43:7).

Israel, like her ancient and contemporary neighbors believed in a life beyond the grave, a hope which grew steadily throughout the Old Testament, until it found complete fulfillment in Christ who abolished death, and brought life and immortality to light through the gospel" (II Tim. 1:10).

BIBLIOGRAPHY. Emmanuel Anati, *Palestine before the Hebrews*, N.Y., Knopf, 1963. Joseph A. Callaway, "Burials in Ancient Palestine: From the Stone Age to Abraham," *BA* 26, Sept. 1963, pp. 74-91. Roland de Vaux, *Ancient Israel: Its Life and Institutions:* N. Y., McGraw-Hill, 1961. William F. Albright, *The Archaeology of Palestine*, Baltimore, Penguin Books, 1951; *From the Stone Age to Christianity,* Garden City, N. Y., Doubleday, 1957. Jean Perrot, "Le mésolithique de Palestine et les récentes découvertes à Eynan ('Ain Mallaha)," *Antiquity and Surviva*l (II: 203; 1957), pp. 91-110. T. Dothan, "Archaeological Reflections on the Philistine Problem," *do.,* pp. 151-164. N. Avigad, "The Beth She'arim Necropolis," *do.,* pp. 244-261. E. W. Heaton, *Everyday Life in Old Testament Times,* N. Y., Scribner, 1956. G. Lankester Harding, *The Antiquities of Jordan,* London, Lutterworth, 1960. *The Interpreter's Dictionary of the Bible,* N. Y., Abingdon, 1962, under the headings, "Burial," "Dolmens," "Mourning," "Mughara, Wadi el-," "Ossuaries," "Tomb."

G

GABBATHA. Gabbatha is the transliteration of an Aramaic term which, in John 19:13, is described as the equivalent of the Greek *lithostrōton,* meaning a paved area. Gabbatha was the place where Jesus stood trial before Pontius *Pilate, somewhere outside the governor's residence or *praetorium* which has not been identified with certainty.

In the basement of the Convent of Our Lady of Zion an extensive paved court has been excavated. Each stone is more than a yard square and a foot thick. Some are marked for use in playing games, and others are cut for drainage. The central area measures 2,500 square yards. The court extends eastward beneath the Convent of the Flagellation.

If Pilate was residing at the Castle of Antonia at the time Jesus was brought to trial before him, then the Antonia was the "Praetorium" and the courtyard pavement may have been the Gabbatha mentioned in John's Gospel. The so-called Ecce Homo arch, built later, is outside the Convent of Our Lady of Zion. Although the name of the arch is an anachronism, if the paving stones under the convent mark the true Gabbatha, the traditional Via Dolorosa, or "Way of Sorrows" running from the Ecce Homo arch to the Church of the Holy Sepulchre may preserve the true general direction of the journey of Jesus from the Judgment Hall to Golgotha.

GALILEE. North of the Plain of Esdraelon and the Valley of Jezreel was the fertile hill country known as the *galil,* literally "the circle" or "the district." It is a land of rivers and wells, and the olives of Galilee were so numerous that the ancient rabbis maintained that it was easier to support an entire legion there than to raise one child in the more barren country to the south.

In pre-exilic times, the area north of Esdraelon was occupied by the tribes of Asher, Zebulun, Issachar, and Naphtali. These were the tribes most exposed to the nearby Phoenicians and Syrians, as well as the more distant Assyrians who periodically invaded western Asia. Following the exile, comparatively few Jews settled in Galilee, and even they were resettled in Judaea in 164 B.C. by Simon the Maccabee (I Macc. 5:23). Under John Hyrcanus and his successors, Galilee was incorporated into the Hasmonean State, and many Jews settled there. The inhabitants of Judea, however, continued to look upon the Jews of Galilee as slightly unorthodox. Jesus and his disciples were despised as Galileans, who were identified by a peculiar accent (cf. Mark 14:70). Nothing good could be expected from Nazareth (John 1:46), and they could not take seriously the claims of a Messiah who was from Nazareth in Galilee (cf. Matt. 21:11).

The people of Galilee, however, were as intensely loyal to the Jewish faith, and as intensely anti-Roman, as any in Judea. Judas of Galilee (Josephus, Jewish War II. viii. 1; cf. Acts 5:37) was the founder of the Zealots, an intensely anti-Roman sect whose fanaticism and violence under Florus, the last of the procurators, brought on the war with Rome. Although Josephus was writing with a view to winning the favor of the Romans, he makes it clear that these Galilean insurrectionists were motivated by the same spirit as their Maccabean predecessors. It was loyalty to the Jewish Law, the Torah, that proved the rallying point for the Zealots (Josephus, Life 12 (65); 13 (74); 27 (134)).

Galilee awakes within the Christian the reminiscence of Jesus' boyhood in Nazareth, his ministry at Capernaum, and his miracles and teaching along the shores of the Sea of Galilee. To the Jew, also, Galilee ultimately became a place of sanctified associations, for the rabbinic sages migrated northward following the destruction of Jerusalem. Tiberias, on the western shore of the Sea of Galilee, became a center of talmudic scholarship and the capital of Jewish Palestine. The families of Ben Asher and Ben Naphtali at Tiberias made important contributions to the preser-

vation of the traditional (or Masoretic) text of the Old Testament. During the fifteenth century, Safed in Upper Galilee was the home of Jewish mystics whose religious ideas found expression in the Kaballah.

During the time of Christ, the province of Galilee was a rectangle, forty miles from north to south and twenty-five miles from east to west. It was bounded on the east by the Jordan River and the Sea of Galilee, and on the west by the Coastal Plain which had been assigned to the tribe of Asher. South of Galilee was the fertile Plain of Esdraelon with the main road from the coast to the Jordan Valley. Galilee itself is divided into two parallel strips, comprising Upper Galilee and Lower Galilee. Between them is the fault of Esh-shaghur, now known as the plain of er-Rameh, cutting across the country from Accho to the region south of Safed. North of this plain the plateau of Upper Galilee reaches three thousand feet, with its highest point, Jebel Jarmuk, thirty-nine hundred feet high. The hills of Lower Galilee, however, have no elevations in excess of two thousand feet. The border between modern Israel and Lebanon passes through Upper Galilee. In New Testament times, however, Upper Galilee extended northward to the gorge of the Leontes River which enters the Mediterranean north of Tyre.

GAMES. While athletics as such were not a part of ancient Israelite life, prowess on the field of battle and physical strength were highly regarded. Formalized games were of importance in the Greek and Roman world and the New Testament makes occasional allusions to them.

The Olympic Games were the chief national festival of the Greeks. They were given at Olympia in honor of Zeus every four years. While chiefly gymnastic, equestrian and music contests were also held. In the second and fourth year of each Olympiad the Isthmian games were held at Corinth in a grove dedicated to Poseidon. At the end of each first and third year of the Olympiad, the Nemean games were given in honor of Zeus in the valley of Nemea. Next in importance to the Olympian games were the Pythian games, played in the third year of each Olympiad below Delphi.

In Roman times the number of games increased until, by the middle of the second

Christian century, a total of 135 days out of the year was given over to games. The priests usually superintended the games and they were paid for from the public treasury. While the Greeks favored athletic games, the Romans favored contests that involved danger and bloodshed. The Greeks in particular enjoyed races, wrestling matches, and throwing the discus and javelin. Boxing was also a favorite. Chariot races in the arena were popular with the Romans. The Circus Maximus in Rome accommodated 400,000 spectators. Large sums of money exchanged hands as the people bet on the outcome of the races. A successful charioteer might amass a fortune.

Gladiatorial shows made use of prisoners of war and slaves for massive fights in the arena. Circular arenas, or amphitheaters were designed for the combats of gladiators with wild beasts. The Colosseum in Rome was used for mock battles in which entire armies were engaged in mock battle, fights with wild animals were staged, and occasionally the arena was flooded so that small ships could conduct naval battles before the eyes of the crowd, which might number 87,000.

The Greeks and Romans both had ball games, and people played various games of chance using dice. A game similar to chess was used, in which people moved stones on a board divided into spaces.

GATE. The gates of ancient walled cities were important gathering places where business was transacted. At Tell-en-Nasbeh (see Mizpah) stone benches lining the walls forming the gate provided seats for those with business to transact (cf. Ruth 4:1). City gates were usually of wood (Neh. 2:8; cf. 1:3, 2:13) strengthened with copper bands, or sheathed in copper plates.

The Solomonic-type gateways at Megiddo, Hazor, and Gezer were elaborate defensive structures. They were actually a series of gates hung on piers jutting out from a side wall. The outer gate was protected by a tower. When closed the doors to gates were secured by a bar, sometimes made of copper. The doors themselves were formed to pivot at jambs in stone sockets.

Houses excavated at °Tell Beit Mirsim in the period from 2200 to 1600 B.C. give evidence of heavy doors, but many of them from the period from 900 to 600 B.C. did not have door sockets. We may surmise that in the earlier unsettled times heavy doors were needed, but that with the establishment of the Davidic monarchy (cf. I Sam. 25:7-9) order was enforced and a simple hanging at the doorway was all the gate that was needed to a dwelling. Lot had a strong door on his house in Sodom, suggesting the need for special precaution there (Gen. 19:9-11).

GATH (1). Gath, meaning "wine press," is a place name widely used in the Levant. Administrative documents from Ugarit list twenty-nine different towns with a name of which the first element is gt (Gath) followed by a second element, e.g., "The wine

GAME BOARD from ancient Ur, ca. 2500 B.C. Courtesy, University Museum, Philadelphia

press of Ashtaroth," "The wine press of Gilead." Therefore, it is not surprising to find several places with the name Gath in Palestine, since viticulture was a major industry in antiquity just as it is today. There are numerous references to these towns in both Biblical and secular sources. Sometimes an additional element is added to the name to distinguish it from other Gaths, but in numerous instances the name Gath stands alone, and it is difficult for the interpreter to decide just which Gath is meant. The Bible gives numerous compound names with the word Gath, viz, Gath-hepher, Gath of the Philistines, and Gath-rimmon. The locative ending -ayim may be added to produce the form: Gittaim. The name Moresheth-gath contains this term as a second element, though it, too, may possibly be called simply Gath (II Chr. 11:8).

At least four, or perhaps five, other Gaths are known from sources outside the Bible. One of these is called Gittipadalla in the Amarna Tablets (EA 250:12) and is written ddptr in Shishak's list (No. 34). From its position in the latter text, between Borim (No. 33; Khirbet Burin) and Yehem (No. 35; Khirbet Yamma) it is evident that this "Gath-padilla" should be identified with the village of Jatt. The same place is listed as knt in the list of Thutmose III (no. 70) in close association with other places known to be located in the northern Sharon, e.g. Soccho (No. 67; swk, Khirbet Shuweikat ar-Ras, and Yehem (No. 68). The Gintikirmil, Gath-carmel, of the Amarna Tablets (EA 288:26, 289:18) may possibly refer to the same town as Gath-padalla. Another Galilean Gath is indicated by No. 44 of Thutmose III's list, written knt'isn, listed after Ibleam (No. 43, Khirbet Bal'ama, 177-205), which appears in an Amarna Tablet (EA 319:5) as Ginti-ashna. The fourth "Gath" in Thutmose's inscription is knt'it (No. 93), probably represents the plural form Gattoth. Due to its position in the list alongside other towns in northern Galilee, Aharoni has associated it with "Gath Asher," written qt'isr in two topographical lists of Ramesses II. He suggests that this Gath be identified with Jatt, a village in the ancient tribal territory of Asher; Yohanan Aharoni, The Settlement of the Israelite Tribes in Upper Galilee, Jerusalem: Magnes Press, 1957, p. 65 (Hebrew).

GATH (2). The Philistine city of Gath ("wine press") was the home of Goliath, the giant who was felled by a stone from David's sling (I Sam. 17). Later, in fleeing from Saul, David came to Gath and feigned madness before Achish, the king of the city (I Sam. 21:10-15). David, with a company of six hundred men, spent more than a year in Gath where Saul could not reach him. After the death of Saul, David was able to add Gath to his territory (I Chron. 18:1). David seems to have enjoyed friendly relations with the people of Gath, or Gittites as they are called in Scripture. At the time of the rebellion of Absalom, six hundred Gittites served among David's mercenaries (II Sam. 15:18).

Rehoboam fortified Gath (II Chron. 11:8), but it fell to Hazael of Damascus during the ninth century (II Kings 12:17). It was evidently in Philistine hands again when Uzziah broke down its walls (II Chron. 26:6). Sargon II besieged and conquered Gath during the eighth century B.C. The city then dropped out of history (cf. Amos 6:2) and its very location is a matter of dispute.

The Israeli Department of Antiquities conducted excavations at °Tell Sheikh el-'Areini, twenty miles northeast of Gaza, under the direction of S. Yeivin beginning in 1956. Diggings at the top and the foot of the mound yielded building foundations, potsherds, Hebrew seals on jar handles from the kingdom of Judah, and similar remains. There were no artifacts which could be traced to the Philistines, however, with the result that most scholars doubt the identification of Tell el-'Areini with Gath. °Tell Najila, also suggested as the possible sight of Gath, has not yielded Philistine remains either. As a result scholars are looking with favor on the older identification of Gath with Tell es-Safi, ten miles southeast of Ekron and ten miles east of Ashdod. 'Araq el-Menshiyeh, six miles west of Beit Jibrin, is also suggested as the site of Gath.

GAZA. Gaza was the southernmost of the cities of the Philistine pentapolis, and marked the southern limit of Canaan on the Mediterranean coast (Gen. 10:19). It was the center of busy caravan routes which led southwest into Egypt, south to Arabia by way of Beersheba, southeast into Edom, and north, along the Mediterranean and thence overland to Damascus and beyond. In the days of the Egyptian Empire (1550-1225 B.C.), Gaza served as an administrative center for protecting Egyptian interests in Canaan. When the Philistines were repulsed in their attempt to enter Egypt during the reign of Ramesses III, they moved northward and occupied Gaza and its environs.

During the period of the Judges, Gaza was a Philistine stronghold. There blinded Samson worked at the prison mill (Judg. 16:21) and, when his strength was revived, brought about the death of the assembled multitude (Judg. 16:28-30).

Although Gaza was nominally a part of the kingdoms of David and Solomon (cf. I Kings 4:24), Israelite control of the city was tenuous. The Assyrian annals record a series of battles for Gaza. Tiglath-pileser III captured it in 734 B.C., but Hanno, the ruler of Gaza, succeeded in fleeing to Egypt. When Assyrian pressure was relieved, Hanno returned to support a rebellion against Assyria. Sargon marched against the city in 722 B.C. and took Hanno as a prisoner to Assyria. At the time of Sennacherib's campaign against Judah (701 B.C.), Gaza was evidently loyal to Assyria for Sennacherib gave to Sillibel, king of Gaza, territory which was taken from Judah. By the time of Jeremiah, Gaza had fallen into Egyptian control (Jer. 47:1). It later was subject to *Babylon, and then became a part of the Persian Empire until it fell to Alexander the Great after a five-month siege (332 B.C.). Alexander colonized Gaza as a Hellenistic city but sovereignty was disputed by the Egyptian Ptolemies and the Syrian Seleucids after his death. In 198 B.C. it was annexed by Antiochus III of Syria. Under the Maccabean ruler Alexander Jannaeus, Gaza was destroyed along with other coastal cities (93 B.C.). Pompey, however, declared Gaza a free city in 61 B.C.

Gaza became an important trading city in the days of the *Nabatean Arabs. In 57 B.C. Pompey's general, Gabinius, rebuilt the city at a new site, to the south of the old and nearer the ocean. It was on the road to old, or "desert" Gaza that Philip met an Ethiopian (i.e. Nubian) eunuch and led him to Christ (Acts 8:26-40). Gaza is now the principal city of the Gaza Strip, administered by Egypt and populated largely by Arab refugees.

The mound Tell el-'Ajjul, long assumed to be the site of ancient Gaza, was excavated by Flinders Petrie from 1930 to 1934. Pottery indicated settlements from the Middle Bronze and Late Bronze Ages, and there was evidence that the site had once been a Hyksos stronghold, but nothing was found to identify the mound with Gaza. The numerous artifacts which Petrie found there included gold jewelry and bronze daggers, toggle pins, and horse bits. Tell el-'Ajjul is now tentatively identified with Beth-eglaim.

GEBAL. See Byblos.

GENESIS APOCRYPHON. See Dead Sea Scrolls.

GERAR. During the Patriarchal Age the Philistine center in Palestine was at Gerar, in the foothills of the Judean mountains south of Gaza. Both Abraham and Isaac enjoyed cordial relations with Abimelech of Gerar, although Isaac's relations were strained because he had lied concerning the identity of his wife (Gen. 21:32, 34; 26:1, 8). Although there are no extra-Biblical references to Philistines in Canaan before the twelfth century B.C., it is known that trade was common between western Asia and Crete early in the second millennium B.C. One of the Mari Tablets (eighteenth century B.C.) records the sending of gifts by the king of Hazor to Kaptara (Caphtor). Philistines did not have a dominant position in southern Palestine during the Patriarchal Age, but early trading centers appear to have been established at that time.

The site of Gerar has been identified with Tell Jemmeh, about eight miles south of Gaza. This mound was excavated in 1922 by W. J. Phythian-Adams and in 1927 by W. M. Flinders Petrie. Petrie's excavation produced remains from the time of Egypt's Eighteenth Dynasty (sixteenth to fourteenth centuries B.C.). More recently, however, Y. Aharoni has argued that Gerar should be located at Tell Abu Hureira, a mound about eleven miles southest of Gaza (Y. Aharoni, "The Land of Gerar," *IEJ* VI, 1956, pp. 26-32.) An Israeli archaeologist, D. Alon, made a survey of Tell Abu Hureira and found evidence from potsherds that the city had enjoyed a period of prosperity during the Middle Bronze Age, the period of the Biblical patriarchs.

GERASA, JERASH. Gerasa was a city of the *Decapolis, located two hundred feet high in the plateau of Transjordan, twenty miles east of the Jordan River, twenty-six miles north of *Amman. Although not on any of the ancient trade routes, Gerasa was near iron mines which may have encouraged its growth. It was abandoned in the thirteenth century, and lay untouched until a German traveler named Seetzen came upon its ruins in 1806. Gerasa proved to be the best preserved example of a small colonial town in the Near East. A modern Arab village was established on the eastern sector of the old town of Gerasa in 1878.

The earliest settlement of Gerasa goes back to the Early Iron Age when it was the site of an Ammonite village. In the third century B.C. it was controlled by the Ptolemies of Egypt. Subsequently it was refounded by Antiochus IV of Syria and named Antioch on the Chrysorrhoas, because of its location on a tributary of the Jabbok River which bore the name Chrysorrhoas.

About 82 B.C. the Maccabean ruler Alexander Janneus captured Gerasa and added it to his Jewish state. The Roman general Pompey intervened in the affairs of Palestine, however, and in 63 B.C. Gerasa was taken and made a part of the Decapolis. Gerasa flourished under the Romans. The city was rebuilt in A.D. 65, and during the second and third centuries it was adorned with impressive temples, theaters, and public structures which have left their ruins until modern times. Gerasa enjoyed trade with *Petra, *Palmyra, and lands farther east. In A.D. 129 the Roman Emperor Trajan visited Gerasa. The Triumphal Arch erected to commemorate his visit is still standing at the entrance to the city.

During the second century Gerasa was largely a pagan city. A magnificent temple to Artemis was erected toward the end of the century. By the fourth century, however, Gerasa had become a strong Christian center. The remains of thirteen churches have been identified at Gerasa, the earliest of which is the Cathedral, dating between A.D. 350 and 375. By A.D. 635 the Moslem conquest had reached Gerasa, and its days were numbered. After the earthquake of *ca.* A.D. 746 the city was abandoned and almost forgotten until the nineteenth century. The ruins so impressed the Arab population of Palestine that even today when they wish to describe something that is in total ruin they say, "It is like the ruins of Jerash."

PANORAMA OF GERASA, one of the cities of the Decapolis.
Courtesy, Holy Views

The systematic excavation and study of the remains of Gerasa began in the 1920's and was a co-operative enterprise. Beginning in 1925 John Garstang, then director of the Department of Antiquities of the Palestine Government, and director of the British School of Archaeology in Jerusalem, in association with George Horsfield of the Department of Antiquities, J. W. Crowfoot of the British School of Archaeology, C. S. Fisher of Yale University and Chester C. McCown of the American School of Oriental Research conducted excavations at Gerasa. The work continued under the sponsorship of Yale University and the British School of Archaeology in Jerusalem from 1928 to 1930. Yale Univeristy and the American Schools of Oriental Research directed the work in the 1930-1931 and 1933-1934 seasons. Directors and fellows of the American School supervised the excavations which were summarized in a volume edited by C. H. Kraeling, *Gerasa, City of the Decapolis,* published in 1938.

The city of Gerasa is enclosed by the ruins of the town wall which is for the most part preserved, following the slopes and contours of the valley on both sides. It consists of solid bastions, set at regular intervals, joined together by walls of well cut stones, filled in with rubble and earth. The wall was built to protect the city against raids or sudden attack. It had no ditch and would not have afforded protection against siege engines.

The Triumphal Arch built in honor of Hadrian's visit is still standing at about half its original height. It is actually a triple arch, the center of which is 39 feet high, 21 feet wide, and 22 feet deep. The whole width is 85 feet. To the left of the Triumphal Arch are ruins of a hippodrome, with a semicircular end toward the north. The hippodrome was built in Roman times, but it appears to have been adapted as a polo field after the Persian conquest of A.D. 614.

North of the hippodrome, which is outside the walls of the city, are the remains of the South Gate, a triple arch similar in design to the Triumphal Arch only much smaller. The South Gate has been excavated and the door of the room of the ancient gate keeper may be seen today. Beyond the gate was the *Forum, erected early in the first century and surrounded by Ionic columns.

In the southern part of the city are the South Theater and the Temple of Zeus. The theater was built in the first century and has a long inscription in Greek describing a statue of Victory erected during the reign of Domitian (A.D. 81-96) by a non-commissioned officer who had served in the army of Titus during the Jewish War (A.D. 70) which resulted in the destruction of Jerusalem. The theater had thirty-two tiers of seats and accommodated between four and five thousand spectators. The lower tiers are numbered, presumably so that the seats could be reserved.

The Temple of Zeus was built between A.D. 161 and 166, probably on ground that had been deemed sacred since earlier times. The structure was originally surrounded by columns, but all but one of them have fallen in times of earthquake. The temple was approached by a great flight of steps.

The whole length of the town from the Forum to the North Gate can be traversed on the Street of Columns, with more than one hundred columns. The Street of Columns, a north-south street, is intersected by two east-west streets. At each intersection is a tetrapylon. The South Tetrapylon consists of four square piers, each supporting four columns, on top of which was a step *pyramid, probably surmounted by a statue. The North Tetrapylon consisted of four piers joined by arches and surmounted by a dome. This was dedicated to Julia Domna, the Syrian wife of the Emperor Septimus Severus (A.D. 193-211). On the north and south faces were freestanding columns. From the lions' heads on the bases, water spouted to the basin below.

Along the street at regular intervals were fountains, the most elaborate of which was at the Nymphaeum, which served as a temple to the Nymphs and the chief ornamental fountain of the city. It was built of two stories, the lower of which was covered with marble. The upper story was plastered and painted. In the niches of the lower story stood statues, probably holding vessels from which water flowed to the great tank below. Surplus water from the tank flowed out through lions' heads into drains on the sidewalk.

The finest and most prominent building in Gerasa was the Temple of Artemis, the patron goddess of the city. Its columns, which stand majestically above everything else in the ruins, are fifty-four feet high. Both exterior and interior are plain. The statue of the goddess stood on a raised platform under the arches at the west end.

The North Theater, still unexcavated, is smaller than the South Theater. The North Gate connects the Street of Columns, the main street of Gerasa with the road to Pella, another of the Decapolis cities. The gate is much wider on the west than on the east due to the fact that the architect wished to present a facade at right angles to each road. The Pella Road meets the Street of Columns at an obtuse angle.

The earliest of the thirteen churches is the Cathedral, built in the usual *basilica style. The church was built on the site of an earlier temple of Dionysius. The columns and stones of the Cathedral were taken from earlier structures including, no doubt, the temple of Dionysius. A fourth century Christian writer (Epiphanius by name) claimed that there was a fountain at Gerasa at which was enacted yearly the miracle of the changing of water into wine. This is evidently a reference to the fountain in the courtyard west of the Cathedral. Evidently some rite of Dionysius, god of wine, was transferred to Christian tradition and associated with the miracle recorded in John 4.

BIBLIOGRAPHY. C. H. Kraeling, *Gerasa, City of the Decapolis,* American Schools of Oriental Research, New Haven, 1938. C. C. McCown, *The Ladder of Progress in Palestine,* Harper and Bros., New York, 1943, pp. 309-325. G. Lankester Harding, *Official Guide to Jerash,* Department of Antiquities, Amman, 1955.

GEZER. One day Charles Clermont-Ganneau, a French orientalist, was studying the Chronicle of Mujir ed-Din, a medieval Arab historian, and came upon a passage describing the action taken by a governor of Jerusalem against some Bedouin who had raided the coastal plain. The historian stated that the governor, following his lieutenant, came after a few hours from Ramleh to the mound of Jezar and there heard the shouting of the combatants at nearby Khuldeh. Clermont-Ganneau recognized in Jezar the soft Arabic "j" taking the place of the Hebrew "g" and surmised that he could find Gezer. Since Khuldeh and Ramleh were identified, he further reasoned that Gezer must be within earshot of these places. In 1871 he visited

Ramleh and Khuldeh and was shown a nearby mound called by the local Arabs *Tell el Jazar.* His subsequent announcement to a French society of biblical scholars was met with the suggestion from the chairman of the society that if some inscription with the name of the place were to be found on the site, Clermont-Ganneau's identification would command more respect.

In 1874 Professor Clermont-Ganneau was led to a spot on the mound three quarters of a mile east of the foot of the hill to see an inscription written in two languages; in Greek, "Alkios"; in Hebrew, "the boundary of Gezer"!

Gezer was a frontier town in the Shephelah, in the extreme east of the territory of the Philistines. It commanded the plain to the north and the west, overlooking both the coastal road to Lydda and Aphek, and the road which came down from Jerusalem. A watch tower several miles to the southeast also enabled the Gezerites to observe the road that went toward Egypt.

Archaeological excavations have given evidence that the site was destroyed and rebuilt four times before the reign of Solomon. It was occupied both in his time and centuries later in the period of the Maccabean revolt. It was also the site of Mount Gisart, scene of a brilliant victory of the Crusaders over Saladin. He, however, soon afterwards dealt a death blow to the Latin Kingdom in Palestine with a resounding victory over the Christians at Hattin, near Tiberias.

Thutmose III, Pharaoh in the Eighteenth Dynasty, recorded on the walls of the temple of Amun at Karnak his capture of Gezer. Scarabs and other Egyptian data found at Gezer verify his report. Nine of the Tell el *Amarna tablets refer to Gezer. Five of these letters are from Milki-ili, the King of Gezer, and three are from his heir Yapahu. They are addressed to Amenhotep III and Amenhotep IV, pleading for aid against the Sagaz and the Sutu. There was also a letter from Abdi-Hiba of Jerusalem to the Pharaoh complaining about Gezer being anti-Pharaoh. He complained that the men of Lachish and Gezer had invaded his territory and invoked Egyptian aid. Concerning the participation of Gezer in the Canaanite rebellion against Egyptian control and its reconquest by Mer-ne-ptah (*ca.* 1230 B.C.),

STONE SERPENT *discovered at Gezer. The snake was an object of worship among the Canaanites. Courtesy, Alva Studios*

information is preserved in the °Merneptah Stele. " . . . Canaan is despoiled, Ashkelon is taken, Gezer is seized . . . Israel is laid waste, his seed is not . . . ."

In Shishak's own list of conquered cities on the southern wall of the temple of Amun-Re in Karnak, Gezer is mentioned. This action took place in the days of Rehoboam, King of Judah (cf. I Kings 14:25ff.; II Chron. 12:2ff.).

Gezer is mentioned frequently in the Biblical sources dealing with the conquest. Although Horam, King of Gezer, came to the aid of nearby Lachish, he and his people were defeated by Joshua in his southern campaign (Josh. 10:33). This defeat is listed in the war annals of Joshua (12:12). Apparently the defeat of Horam was not final for the Canaanites continued to dwell in Gezer, although in enslavement (Josh. 16:10; Judg. 1:29) to the tribe of Joseph (Josh. 16:3). Joshua eventually designated it as a levitical city (Josh. 21:21). During the expansion of the Philistine empire, Gezer was an important boundary city of the Philistines. David routed the Philistine army from Geba to Gezer (II Sam. 5:25; I Chron. 14:16) and in a later encounter between the Israelites with the Philistines at Gezer, an Israelite hero, Sibbecai, slew Sippai, a Philistine

descendant of the giants. During the reign of Solomon, Pharaoh, King of Egypt, captured the city, slew its Canaanite population and presented it as a dowry to his daughter, the wife of Solomon (I Kings 9:16). Solomon, recognizing its strategic location on his highway system, rebuilt the destroyed areas (I Kings 9:15, 17), fortified it and assigned it to the First District, namely, the mountains of Ephraim (cf. I Kings 4:8).

Gezer is mentioned several times in Maccabees. It was considered an important border station between Ashdod and Judah (I Macc. 14:34). Several times it is mentioned in the wars of the Hasmoneans. Bacchides fortified Gezer (I Macc. 9:52) and Simon settled Jews there and built for himself a house on the site (I Macc. 13:33-38). Gezer apparently remained under Jewish control until Roman times, then was more or less deserted and slowly became a tell.

Gezer was excavated by R. A. S. Macalister on behalf of the Palestine Exploration Fund in 1902-1905; 1907-1909; and for the space of a little over a month in 1934 by Alan Rowe, under the sponsorship of Charles Marston and Herbert Bentwick. When Macalister arrived at the site he found a small local cemetery, the shrine of a local Moslem saint, the farm home of a Mr. Bergheim and a mulberry plantation. With the help of local personnel, Macalister began the excavation. In 1903 he wrote to the Athenaeum in London stating that an epidemic of cholera had stopped the work temporarily. He also learned by experience that the excavation would progress more rapidly when he executed it in the off season, for local help preferred the higher wages paid to harvest the crops to the lower pay for dragging the soil. Funds were often slow in coming and in 1909 he completed his final season on the mound.

Several boundary inscriptions were found at Gezer. After the original one was found by Clermont-Ganneau in 1874, someone chipped away part of it, thus making it quite illegible.

The earliest occupants on the site lived in caves, natural and artificial. Tombs found in the caves give evidence of the cremation of the dead. Egyptian and Philistine tombs built of masonry were also found. The bodies surrounded with deposits of artistic value were oriented east-west with bodies laid out at full length rather than in a contracted position. High quality Philistine art may be observed in the tombs. Contrary to Semitic burials, these were found within the city wall. In one tomb was found the skeleton of a girl cut in half. Scholars have speculated murder, sacrifice or cannibalism, but the mystery remains. In at least two other excavations half skeletons have been found. The other half was not found at Gezer or at these sites. In foundation jars the remains of both infants and adults have been found. With the bones were lamps, bowls and white sand from a particular spot. One giant skeleton was uncovered, suggesting the account of the Philistine giants reputed to have lived in the vicinity. Several Hebrew tombs were uncovered. One was inscribed, "Sar, son of Eliezer;" another, "Hanun, son of Jechoni." A tear bottle was lying in one of the Hebrew tombs (cf. Psa. 56:8). Christian tombs with lamps on which were engraved crosses and Bible verses in Greek characters were also found. On one was written John 1:9; another contained Psalm 27:1 with these additions, "the light of Christ shines for all. The Lord is my light." Greek words were sometimes con-

tracted and sometimes were actually misspelled.

The ancient Gezerites developed their water supply by constructing a stepped tunnel twenty feet down to a landing from which another flight of stairs descended at a right angle to a depth of seventy-five feet. These steps led into a long cave containing a spring. Apparently earlier the waters of the spring rose to the surface, indicating the abundant water supply beneath the surface. The abundance of the spring led ancient natives to call Gezer "The city of our Lord Noah," from the legend based on the bursting through to the surface of the waters of the spring. The underground tunnel shows the ingenuity of Gezer's architectural engineers before the Jebusite tunnel at Jerusalem.

Macalister found a row of eight standing stones. The tallest of these was over ten feet high, the smallest was over five feet. Their size and arrangement, coupled with the discovery of ten infant burials in Middle Bronze Age jars led Macalister to conclude that this was a religious center. A high pedestal, caves nearby with connecting chambers, and burials of humans and animals together confirmed in his mind that he had found a Canaanite high place. W. F. Albright, viewing the same materials, called it a common cemetery. Similar monoliths have been found in Assyria and at °Ugarit with names inscribed upon them indicating funeral stelae. It is interesting that human and animal bones rest in the same tombs at Gezer (cf. Jer. 22:19 "the burial of the ass," that is, buried where animals are interred!). A snake pit with several brazen serpents (cobras?) was found (cf. II Kings 18:4 and the brazen serpent of Moses in the wilderness).

The excavators discovered an Assyrian tablet with an Egyptian governor's name from 649 B.C. The Egyptian name indicates that the handing over of Gezer as a dowry (cf. Laban's dowry to his daughters) to Solomon's wife did not necessarily imply handing the city over completely to Solomon. It was the wife's dowry; she must have retained the revenue.

An ancient time piece which told time by the angle of the sunlight rather than the more ancient methods of the gnomon which told time by measuring the length of the shadow was found. By some it was termed the Babylonian Zodiac Tablet.

Simon Maccabeus, the high priest, captured Gezer in 142 B.C., settled Jews there and built for himself a castle with its walls. The foundation of this building was discovered. Part of this structure which Macalister called the Maccabean Castle, Yadin had shown to be a casemate wall similar to those found at Megiddo and Hazor. In recent publications he has demonstrated that the city gates at Hazor and Megiddo are identical with the Gezer city gate. It seems likely that the same architect designed them all (cf. I Kings 9:15).

The excavations have revealed a long history for Gezer. From the period of the first cave men to the Crusaders, the mound was occupied. Semites, Egyptians, Canaanites, Philistines, and Hebrews lived there in considerable numbers over a lengthy period. The social and religious customs of these civilizations have been reconstructed.

BIBLIOGRAPHY. R. A. S. Macalister, *Biblical Sidelights from the Mound of Gezer,* Hodder and Stoughton, London, 1907. *The Excavation at Gezer, 1902-1905 and 1907-1909,* vols. I - III, Hodder and Stoughton, London, 1912.

GEZER CALENDAR.

In 1908, during excavation at *Gezer, R. A. S. Macalister discovered a small plaque of soft limestone, 4¼ inches long by about 3⅜ inches wide inscribed with Hebrew writing. It was evidently used by a schoolboy for his exercises about the time of Solomon (*ca.* 925 B.C.), and it shows signs of repeated scraping to clear the surface for a fresh inscription. The words which appeared on it at the time of its discovery are in Palaeo-Hebrew script. They enumerate the agricultural seasons, perhaps as an aid to memory. The entire text reads:

> The two months of (olive) harvest;
> The two months of planting (grain);
> The two months of late planting;
> The month of hoeing up flax;
> The month of harvest of barley;
> The month of harvest and festivity;
> The two months of vine-tending;
> The month of summer fruit.

The calendar begins with the fall olive harvest. This presumably would begin at the time of the Jewish New Year in the second or third week of September and extend to mid-November. Oil was an im-

GEZER AGRICULTURAL CALENDAR

portant part of Israel's economy. It served as a fat in cooking (cf. I Kings 17:14); it was burned in lamps to provide illumination; and it had important medicinal uses (cf. Isa. 1:6). Oil also was used as a cosmetic to keep the skin soft in a hot, dry climate.

The two months from mid-November to mid-January were used in planting grain. When the early rains began the farmer began to plow his field, after which he planted his wheat and barley. The following two months — January to March — were used for the planting of the summer crops: millet, sesame, chick-peas, lentils, melons, cucumbers and the like.

The next three months described in the calendar were those in which the main crops were harvested. March-April was "the month of hoeing up flax." The plant was cut with the hoe near the ground in order not to waste any of the stalk, which was dried and used to make cord and linen cloth (cf. Josh. 2:6). April or early May was the time of barley harvest, and this was followed by the wheat harvest which ended the harvest season and was celebrated by the "festivity" which later became known as Pentecost.

AIR VIEW of excavations at Tell el-Fûl, identified as Gibeah of Saul (1 Sam. 10:26). Courtesy, Matson Photo Service

The rainless months of summer were not wasted for they afforded opportunity for the farmer to prune and clean his vines. The remaining month was the time of "summer fruit" when figs, grapes, pomegranates and other fruit could be picked.

The Gezer calendar not only gives us an authentic description of the agricultural year as observed in ancient Israel, but also it gives us an example of the Hebrew script and language as used in Solomonic times.

BIBLIOGRAPHY. W. F. Albright, "The Gezer Calendar," *BASOR* 92, 1943, pp. 16-26. L. Finkelstein, "A Talmudic Note on the Word for Cutting Flax in the Gezer Calendar," *BASOR* 94, 1944, pp. 28-29. R. A. S. Macalister, *Bible Side Lights from the Mound of Gezer,* London, Hodder and Stoughton, 1906.

GHASSULIAN CULTURE.

Teleilat Ghassul, north of the Dead Sea in the vicinity of Jericho, is the type site for a Chalcolithic Age (4500-3000 B.C.) culture. The site was excavated from 1929 to 1938 by the Jesuit fathers, with Alexis Mallon, Robert Koeppel and their associates in charge. Before 3400 B.C. the people of Ghassul lived in well-constructed homes, some of them built of hand molded sun-dried bricks on a foundation of bricks, and others made entirely of bricks. The houses had wooden roofs which collapsed when the town was destroyed by fire. Many of the mud brick walls were covered with fresco paintings in elaborate geometric designs. One of these is an elaborate eight-pointed star around which was a field containing stylized dragons and geometric figures. Another well-preserved fresco depicts a bird with a naturalism unsurpassed in antiquity except in Egypt. Ghassulian pottery also was adorned with simple painted designs. No building which can be identified as a temple has yet been excavated at Ghassul.

BIBLIOGRAPHY. Alexis Mallon, Robert Koeppel and René Neuville, *Teleilat Ghassul, compte rendu des fouilles de l'Institut Biblique Pontifical,* I, *1929-1932,* Pontifical Biblical Institute, Rome, 1934. Robert Koeppel, *Teleilat Ghassul, compte rendu des fouilles de l'Institut Biblique Pontifical,* II, *1932-1936,* Pontifical Biblical Institute, Rome, 1940.

GIBEAH.

The name Gibeah means "hill." In a few Bible texts Gibeah is confused with the neighboring town of Geba, since the two names differ in Hebrew only by the absence or addition of one letter. Sometimes the city is called "Gibeah in Benjamin," or "Gibeah which belongs to Benjamin," but as King Saul's home town it also carries the designation "Gibeah of Saul."

Gibeah appears first in the period of the judges as the inhospitable town in which a traveling Levite's wife was ravished so badly that she died as the result. When the tribe of Benjamin refused to bring the culprits to judgment, the other Israelite tribes waged a punitive war against Benjamin which resulted in the destruction of Gibeah and in the near annihilation of the tribe (Judg. 19-20). That the crime committed in Gibeah and the ensuing war was still remembered in the eighth century B.C. can be seen from Hosea's prophecies (Hos. 9:9; 10:9). Later, the city is mentioned as the home town of Saul's family, and also as his residence during his reign (I Sam. 10:26; 11:4; 14:2, 16; 22:6; 26:1). From Gibeah came some mighty warriors who joined David (II Sam. 23:29; I Chron. 11:31; 12:2-3); also Micaiah, King Abijah's mother (II Chron. 13:2). That the place was inhabited in the eighth-seventh century B.C. is attested by Isaiah's mentioning its population as having fled when the Assyrians marched toward Jerusalem from the north (Isa. 10:29). The only other mention of Gibeah is found in Josephus' records of the Jewish War (*War* V.ii.1) in which he states that Titus in A.D. 70 spent the night at Gibeah before reaching Jerusalem.

A study of the various Old Testament passages in which Gibeah is mentioned shows that this city must have been located on the main road which leads from Jerusalem to the north. In 1843, Gross, a young German theologian, identified *Tell el-Fûl* a prominent mound (altitude 2,840 feet), 3½ miles north of Jerusalem, with Gibeah. Its location agrees with Josephus' statement that Gibeah lay at a distance of thirty furlongs from Jerusalem (*War* V .ii. 1). Although for a time not all scholars agreed with this identification, the excavations have proved it to be correct, and there is now general agreement about it.

In 1868 Charles Warren carried out some soundings on the mound of *Tell el-Fûl* on behalf of the Palestine Exploration Fund, but the results of that work were never published. During the years 1922 and 1923,

W. F. Albright intermittently carried out excavations for the American School of Oriental Research in Jerusalem, and dug up the Israelite fortress on the mound. Another season of excavations was conducted there by Albright in 1933. The archaeological and historical results of these two seasons are the following.

A few sherds and mace heads originating in the Middle Bronze Age were found. They showed that some people must have lived on the hill before the first Hebrew settlement took place in the twelfth century B.C., which was an unfortified village that found its end when it was destroyed by fire *ca.* 1100 B.C. or a little later. This catastrophe must be connected with the events recorded in Judges 19-20.

During the second half of the eleventh century B.C. the first fortress was built, probably by King Saul. This "Fortress I" was destroyed after Saul's death, evidently by the Philistines toward the end of that century. Albright excavated the southwest tower of the fortress, and found that it had served to protect a casemate wall, which seems to have surrounded an oblong open courtyard. The outer wall of the main structure had a thickness of 1.75 m while the inner wall was 1.20 m thick. The space between the two walls was 1.20 m. At the corner a strong tower jutted out from the casemate walls. Its walls were 2.00 m thick. Partition walls formed three rooms in the lower floor of this tower of which the largest one had a size of 8.00 x 2.50 m, while the other two had sizes of 4.10 x 3.10 and 4.10 x 2.50 m. The remains of a stairway indicated that the whole structure had been at least two stories high. An examina-

tion of the ash left from the interior wood construction of the fortress showed it to be carbonized cypress and pine.

Albright found no traces of the remainder of the fortress, which evidently had been completely removed in later building activities, but he reconstructed the overall plan of the citadel, and arrived at dimensions on the basis that "about 65 m east of the outer corner of the southwest tower the rock begins to fall away so rapidly that the citadel cannot have extended further in this direction." Furthermore, he reasoned that the total length of the southern side, including the towers, could not be reduced "to a point below which the distance between the towers becomes less than the length of the southwest tower itself." This reasoning led him to assume that the fortress had had a minimum length of 52 m at the south and north sides. By taking the ratio of length to breadth as about the same as the corresponding ratio between the dimensions of the southwest tower, he reached the length of 35 m for the shorter sides. The tenth century fortress at *'Ain el Qudeirât* (Kadesh-barnea) served Albright as a close example for the reconstructed fortress of Saul (Albright, *BASOR*, No. 52, Dec. 1933, 8).

The excavations revealed furthermore that the fortress of Saul, probably destroyed by the Philistines after Saul's death at the battle of Gilboa, was soon rebuilt on the same plan as the first. The masonry of this "Fortress II" was much less massive, but more regularly shaped and laid than that of the preceding structure. However, this fortress had only a very brief existence and must have been abandoned a few years after its construction. This leads to the conclusion that it was built by King David shortly after he became king of Judah, to protect his kingdom against the northern tribes who for a few years were ruled by Saul's son Ish-bosheth. As soon as these tribes joined Judah and enabled David to rule over a united kingdom which included all the inland areas of Palestine, the need for this border fortress ceased to exist, with the result that it was abandoned and gradually fell into ruins. The absence of a burned destruction level clearly showed that it had met no violent end.

After the first season of excavations Albright thought that the next rebuilding of

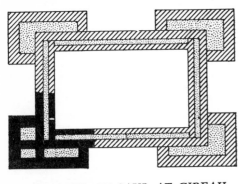

CITADEL OF SAUL AT GIBEAH

the site occurred under the reign of King Asa of Judah, who built Mizpah and Geba (which Albright at that time considered to be an error for "Gibeah") with building material amassed by Baasha of Israel for the fortification of Ramah, but which was left by him when an invasion of the Arameans diverted his attention from Judah (I Kings 15:16-22). During the period between the two seasons of excavations at Gibeah the dating of Palestinian pottery was refined, with the result that during the excavations of 1933 Albright recognized that *Tell el-Fûl* contained no transitional Iron I-II pottery (from the tenth-ninth century), and that therefore Gibeah was not rebuilt by King Asa, who lived in that period.

In the late ninth century or during the early eighth century a watchtower ("Fortress III") was built over the southwest tower of the former citadel. In this process the remains of the other towers of the preceding fortress may have been removed, so that nothing of them has been preserved. The new fortress was built around and upon the former southwest tower, with its outer walls being protected by a well-built sloping revetment. The outer dimensions of this watchtower were approximately 16 x 15 m, not including the revetment. It also must have possessed a second story, which was supported by wooden beams. The carbonized remains of this wood showed it to be almond, instead of the coniferous cypress and pine used in Saul's fortress. Evidently the coniferous woods had already disappeared from the area of Benjamin. This fortress was destroyed by fire in the eighth century, perhaps during the Syro-Ephraimite war against Judah (*ca.* 735 B.C.).

The watchtower was rebuilt in the seventh century on the same lines as the preceding one, and was again destroyed around 600 B.C., this time probably during one of the Chaldean invasions of Nebuchadnezzar, either in 597 or 586 B.C. From this period come thirteen royal stamped jar handles found during the excavations. They are of the "flying scroll" type which was in use during the late period of the kings of Judah down to the Babylonian Captivity.

The ruined site then remained uninhabited for several centuries, until the tower was reconstructed in the fourth century B.C. as "Fortress IV" according to a plan similar to that of Fortress III. At that time also a village was built on the eastern slope of the hill. The destruction of the fortress and its village came around 200 B.C., perhaps in the war between Ptolemy V and Antiochus III, as the result of which Palestine changed overlords. Gibeah thus again lay in ruins for more than a century, but in the Roman period a village was built on the site which seems to have existed until A.D. 70. At that time it was probably destroyed by Titus when he stopped there on his march to Jerusalem to capture that city (Josephus, *War* V.ii.1).

BIBLIOGRAPHY. W. F. Albright, "Excavations and Results of Tell el-Ful (Gibeah of Saul), *Annual of the American Schools of Oriental Research for 1922-23*, p. 1-89, Laurence A. Sinclair, "An Archaeological Study of Gibeah (Tell el-Ful), *Annual of the American Schools of Oriental Research for 1954-56*, pp. 5-52.

GIBEON, GIBEONITES. References to Gibeon or the Gibeonites occur forty-five times in the Bible. Among the more important narratives is that of the successful deception of Joshua by the Gibeonites, the execution of a covenant with them and the defeat of the south Canaanite coalition under Adonizedek of Jerusalem who was alarmed by the extension of Israelite control to the north. At this time Gibeon was the chief city of a confederacy which included Chephirah, Beeroth, and Kirjath-jearim. The consequence of the episode for Gibeon was that it was preserved from destruction by the Israelites or the Canaanite coalition, though the Gibeonites received only secondary status within the Israelite confederacy as the enigmatic "hewers of wood and drawers of water for the congregation and the altar of the Lord" seems to suggest (Josh. 9-10).

Nothing further is heard of Gibeon until the time of David, nearly two centuries later. Shortly after Saul's death, Esh-Baal (Ishbosheth), his son, was enthroned by Abner at Mahanaim, east of the Jordan, on the Jabbok (Nahr ez-Zerqa). David was in control of the territory south of Jerusalem centered at Hebron. For some reason, forces under Abner and under Joab, David's general, met at Gibeon, near "the pool." A contest between twelve men from each side was proposed in the course of which all twenty-four men were killed. Y. Yadin, on the analogy of the Goliath episode and a relief from Tell Halaf (Gozan) showing two men in the same type of combat, suggests that there was a contest between heroes, which resulted in a draw, with a resultant larger battle in which Abner's forces were defeated (II Sam. 2:12-17).

Later in David's reign, "the great stone which is in Gibeon" was the scene of Joab's execution of Amasa, the priest, whose delay in rallying the people of Judah for David for the defense of his throne against the revolt of Sheba, the Bichrite, aroused suspicions of loyalty and cost him his life (II Sam. 20:4-13).

Sometime during his reign, Saul had killed an unknown number of Gibeonites in apparent violation of the treaty made in Joshua's day (contrast I Chron. 9:35-39). This act was interpreted as the cause of a famine in Israel during David's reign. To rectify matters, the Gibeonites demanded the lives of seven of Saul's sons. David handed over five grandsons and two sons who were hanged "before the Lord at Gibeon on the mountain of the Lord." Though assigned to Benjamin (Josh. 18:25), from v. 4 it would appear that at this time Gibeonite territory was a semi-independent enclave within Israel (II Sam. 21:1-14).

The references above as well as the narrative of Solomon's sacrifice on the altar of the high place before his coronation indicate that Gibeon was a shrine of major importance in Israel. The tabernacle and altar of burnt offering are said to have been there after the Philistine destruction of Shiloh (I Chron. 16:39; 21:29; II Chron. 1:3, 13) while the ark was in Kirjath-jearim (I Sam. 7:1-2; cf. II Sam. 6:2; I Chron. 13:6), one of the cities of the earlier Gibeonite confederacy. The shrine to Yahweh may have replaced an earlier one to another deity, perhaps the sun-god Shemesh (cf. Josh. 10:12). Its cult significance is perhaps implied by its designation as one of the forty-eight Levitical cities (Josh. 21:17).

Gibeon was among those cities listed as conquered by the Egyptian pharaoh Shishak who pillaged both Israel and Judah in 918 B.C. Nothing more is heard of Gibeon for three centuries. It is given as the home of Hananiah, the prophet (Jer. 28:1) and the scene of the confrontation "at the great waters" between Ishmael, assassin of the Judean governor Gedaliah, and Johanan, his

avenger. Ishmael escaped but his captives were freed (Jer. 41:11-16). About a century and a half later, a group of Gibeonites assisted in the rebuilding of the walls of Jerusalem (Neh. 3:7). Josephus (BJ II. xix. 1, 7) concludes the ancient records concerning Gibeon by reporting that in the early skirmishes of the first revolt, the Roman governor of Syria, Cestius, in October A.D. 66, camped at Gabao (Gibeon) en route to Jerusalem, and again in November as he withdrew from Jerusalem. The route taken by Cestius from Gibeon to the coastal plain via the pass between Upper and Lower Beth Horon was the same as that used more than a thousand years earlier by the Canaanite forces under Adonizedek as they fled before Joshua, and probably by the Philistines in their flight from David (I Chron. 14:16; II Sam. 5:25; read Gibeon for Geba, cf. LXX).

The site of Gibeon is a hill rising more than two hundred feet above the surrounding plain (itself about 2500 feet above sea level), a bit more than five miles north of Jerusalem. On the northwestern part of the saddle-backed hill lies the small Arab town of el-Jib. The identification was first suggested by a Silesian nobleman, Franz Ferdinand von Troilo in 1666. In 1738, Richard Pococke, later Bishop of Meath, looked down on el-Jib from the nearby height of Nebi Samwil and suggested the identification with Gibeon. Edward Robinson visited el-Jib for about forty minutes on the afternoon of Saturday, May 5, 1838. He noted the fact that the first two letters of the Arabic name corresponded to the first two of the Hebrew (JB − GB.). In spite of the somewhat conflicting statements of distance and location by Josephus, Eusebius of Caesarea and Jerome, Robinson concluded that the place they had in mind and that which seemed to best correspond to the Biblical narrative was el-Jib. This suggestion was accepted by most scholars except in the period 1926-1956 when the great German scholar Albrecht Alt argued first that it should be identified with Tell en-Nasbeh, about four miles north of el-Jib. When Bade's excavations of Tell en-Nasbeh, demonstrated this untenable, he suggested el-Bireh, opposite modern Ramallah, for Gibeon and el-Jib continued to be suggested as the site of ancient Beeroth. The excavations led by James B.

Pritchard of Church Divinity School of the Pacific (then) and the University of Pennsylvania in five seasons (1956-57, 1959-60, 1962) have conclusively proven that el-Jib is the site of ancient Gibeon.

I. *Early Bronze Age* (3100-2100 B.C.) Gibeon was founded at the beginning of this period. Beneath the foundations of the Iron Age wall, a room was discovered in which were the sherds of fourteen storage jars, neatly crushed by the room as its beams burned and it collapsed. The typical EB jars have a distinctive "handle" on them, making it possible to associate this occupation with those at Ai, seven miles northeast, Tell en-Nasbeh (Mizpah?) three miles north, and Jericho, sixteen miles northeast. Below this room was bedrock. EB pottery and housewalls of sun-dried brick (3 inches high, 16 inches wide) were found at the top of the mound but the destruction of a Turkish artillery emplacement by British gunfire in 1917 destroyed the stratification. It is probable that Gibeon like other EB cities in Palestine was fortified with a strong city wall which has not yet been located. It appears that the EB city was destroyed by fire, the time of destruction as yet undetermined.

Gibeon's EB inhabitants were buried in rock-cut caves in the east side of the hill. Both the storage jars and the pottery in the tomb (jars and bowls) seem to have been formed first by hand and then turned on a slow wheel; it is similar to that found in tombs at Ai and Tell en-Nasbeh. Carbon on the rim indicates that at least three of the bowls had been used as lamps.

II. *Middle Bronze Age.* MB I is known from the shaft tombs cut into a soft limestone layer on the west side of the city. A cylindrical shaft, about 4 feet in diameter, was sunk into the rock an average depth of 6 feet (1'3" -- 8'6"). At the bottom a doorway (average size 2'7" by 2') leads into the tomb chamber whose floor averaged nearly six square yards and height 3 feet -- 4 inches (2'9" -- 4'5"). The tomb was closed with a flat stone and sealed by filling the shaft with limestone chips and *huwwar* (decayed limestone). A total of twenty-six tombs having MB I materials have been found. These materials include 4-spouted lamps, funerary jars in forms typical for the period, bronze javelin heads and daggers. The absence of elegance in design or workmanship

reflects the simplicity of the MB I inhabitants of Gibeon who may well have been semi-nomads who pitched their tents and buried their dead in this open, probably not fortified site. The pottery and metalwork, the disposition of the tombs, and the type of occupation find their counterparts at Tell el-Ajjul, Jericho, Lachish, and, in some ways, to a few examples at Megiddo and Beth-Shan. The cultural implications are thus consistent with what is known of this period elsewhere in Palestine and Transjordan.

The MB II, or Hyksos, period occupation is really the second city to have been built on the hill. At the northwest of the site, under thirteen feet of debris, a room was uncovered beneath a layer of ashes and burnt brick in which were sixteen large storage jars of typical MB II type. Analysis of the charcoal remnants of the central post which had held up the room showed the post to have been the trunk of an olive tree. The pottery of this period, which was abundant on the tell, was the finest ever made at Gibeon, both in design and workmanship. Some of it was so fine that it could pass for the shell of an ostrich egg.

Again tombs — twenty-nine of them — are the best source for the artifacts of this period which included pottery, fragments of bone inlay, bronze toggle pins, dagger blades and knives, faience beads and scarabs. MB II people used the same type shaft tomb as their MB I predecessors, indeed some of the same tombs. While single burials seems to have been typical in MB I, multiple burials in a tomb were the MB II practice. MB II Gibeon seems also to have been destroyed by fire, perhaps in the course of the empire-wide revolt which overthrew Egypt's Hyksos rulers in the mid-sixteenth century.

III. *Late Bronze Age* (1550-1200 B.C.). Seven tombs provide our only knowledge of this period, at the end of which Gibeon's leaders, in behalf of themselves and their allies, executed a treaty with Joshua and the invading Israelites. In contrast to Jericho and Ai, however, there is conclusive evidence of occupation in Joshua's day. Quantities of imported wares testify to Gibeon's participation in the commerce of the period whose routes extended from Cyprus to Egypt. Scarabs of Pharaoh Thutmose III (1490-1436 B.C.) and Amenhotep II

(1435-1414 B.C.) and a distinctive long-necked Cypriote jug, a *bilbil*, perhaps once filled with perfumed oil, are representative imports. Local potters attempted to imitate this and other forms of Mycenean and Cypriote pottery but the fabric is coarser, the design variant, and the painting distinctive. Other forms of local pottery, "pilgrim flasks" and pyxides appear as well as lamps, jugs, dippers and cooking pots. With the decline of LB Gibeon, painted pottery disappears; Iron Age pottery in Palestine is not painted. Comparison with materials from *Lachish, *Beth-Shemesh and *Tell Beit Mirsim indicates that the chief period of use was the fourteenth and early thirteenth centuries B.C. (LB IIA). Nothing is known of the fate of this city; the Biblical records suggest that it was not destroyed. Presumably it was "phased out" as the Iron I city was built.

IV. *Iron Age* (I. 1200-900; II. 900-550 B.C.). This period provides the most spectacular of the discoveries thus far made at Gibeon: the city wall, the tunnel to *'ein el-beled*, the "industrial areas" where wine was made, and the great "pool." The Iron I city wall, which may go back to Joshua's day, was only about five feet thick and at most fifteen feet high, though the two hundred feet scarp below it made it formidable beyond its own size. Of the total circumference of 1,105 yards, 165 yards have been excavated on the northeast and west sides of the hill. Two or three centuries later, perhaps in David's or Solomon's time, the fortification around the sixteen acre site (larger than Jerusalem) was strengthened by adding a much stronger inner wall. A foundation trench as much as 10 feet deep and 10 feet wide was dug and the new wall rose to at least 22 feet above ground level. The thickness of the new wall was 10 to 13 feet. At the northeastern corner, near the city entrance to the tunnel, the wall was strengthened by two towers increasing the total thickness to 23 feet. The main city gate may be on the north side; if so, it is inaccessible because it then lies below the modern cemetery. This wall protected the city until its destruction in the sixth century B.C. In one of the quarries from which the limestone for the city wall had been cut, three blocks, cut on all sides, were still in place, awaiting the insertion of wooden wedges which would be soaked, the

expansion of the wood breaking them free.

A large "patrician" house, just inside the line of the Iron I wall and contemporary with it, was among the houses of the period. In it, the stone pillars which had supported the roof beams were still in place along the center line of the building. In an adjacent room, the kitchen, were two large ovens. Among the houses of Iron II was a large house of the seventh century (fixed by a stamped jar handle), near the great "pool." A court separated side rooms (about 5 feet by 10 feet) to the left and right and led into a larger end room whose length was the combined width of the side rooms and court (about 18'). The room to the right was used as a kitchen and storage room; in it were hand mills of volcanic stone, flint sickle blades, a stone blade, and, of course, pottery. The left hand room was apparently used as a pantry. The long back room was used for weaving and other household tasks as shown by a loom weight, additional mill stones, etc. To the left there was a small compartment in which there was a plastered storage bin, 4 feet in diameter and 4'5" deep, in which grain had been stored. The unusually thick left outside wall suggests the possibility of a second story. In the court was a limestone roller used to roll the clay or *huwwar* which covered the matting laid over the roof beams.

Just inside the northeast corner of the Iron II wall is an opening leading to a tunnel 174 feet long (148 feet on the horizontal) leading beneath the city wall to *ein el-beled*, just northeast of the tell and the most important of 8 nearby springs. Its 93 steps (5 to 6 feet wide) were cut out of the living rock. Just below the outer side of the wall, one section of the tunnel was made by sinking a deep trench, covering it with stone slabs and concealing it by a covering of earth. From this section, workers tunneled downward to the spring and upward to the surface inside the city wall. The tunnel leads into a large cistern room about 39 feet long, 19 to 25 feet wide and 5 to 10 feet high. Into this room flowed water from the spring about 112 feet back in the rock of the hill; a "feeder" tunnel

THE GREAT POOL AT GIBEON, show the steps used for the descent to the wa level. Courtesy, James B. Pritchard

had been cut back in the hope of increasing the flow of water. A door led from the cistern room to the outside. Inside the door, in the sides and the floor were grooves into which flat stones could be fitted in case of attack. On the sides of the stepped tunnel and cistern room niches were cut at regular intervals for oil lamps. On the basis of the tunnel's opening just inside the Iron II wall and the blocking up of what seems to have been a "water gate" leading through the outside of the wall at about the same place as the tunnel opening, Pritchard feels that the tunnel system was dug during the Iron II period. The well-worn step treads and tunnel sides polished by the hands of water-carriers reaching for support suggest the possibility that it may be much older, perhaps a part of the original Iron I fortification and defense system, and thus contemporary with the tunnels at Megiddo and perhaps Gezer and Ibleam.

About eight feet south of the inner face of the northeastern section of the city wall and about the same distance from the entrance to the tunnel just to the northeast is the north rim of a huge "pool" 37 feet in diameter and 35 feet deep. Beginning on the north side with three steps of cut stones, a stairway of forty steps, 5 feet wide with an 18 inch balustrade, cut as the "pool" was dug, leads to the floor of this unique excavation; it continues another 11 steps and then leads into a tunnel, continuing in spiral fashion to a point 45 feet below the "pool" floor where it opens into a kidney shaped room, about 23 feet long, 11 feet wide and 7½ feet high, with lamp niches cut into the walls. Further lighting was provided by two light wells dug from the floor through the roof of the tunnel as it curved downward. The excavation thus leads to the water level some 80 feet below the streets of the city. Lying in the reservoir when it was discovered were two Iron II jars. G. E. Wright suggests that the little wear shown on the steps may well indicate that this system is later than the stepped tunnel (contra Pritchard). It was perhaps dug in the days of Hezekiah (715-687) or Manasseh (687-642) and filled with debris from the breached city wall, the streets and squares in the mid-sixth century, perhaps in consequence of Ishmael's assassination of Gedaliah, or later in the century (see below).

Gibeon's water supply for its 4,000 to 6,000 people was further augmented by a system of cisterns one of which was found at the end of a city street which led from the top of the hill. The water from the housetops and squares was led through a filtering basin and into the plastered cistern whose capacity was estimated at 150,000 gallons. This also explains the absence of storm drains through the city walls.

Of extraordinary importance was the recovery of fifty-six jar handles on twenty-four of which was inscribed the word GB'N — "Gibeon" — 19 times in combination with the word GDR - "Gedor" -, perhaps the name of a section of the city of Gibeon (cf. I Chron. 8:31; 9:37), or perhaps referring to that walled vineyard (cf. Ps. 80:13; Isa. 5:1-7) belonging to men whose names often appear with GB'N-GDR, such as Azariah, Amariah, and Hananiah, or the previously unknown Domla and Shebu'el. (F. M. Cross, Jr. and N. Avigad prefer the reading GDD - "Gaddud" - a personal name, to the reading GDR.) The handles come from jars of a type also found at Beth-shemesh and Shechem, appearing about the mid-sixth century B.C., thus indicating a date of later in the century for the filling of the "pool" - more properly, stairwell — with debris from the area south of the "pool." Forty clay stoppers were found along with a part of a funnel which fit perfectly into the 1½ inch-wide mouth of the jar which must have contained about six gallons of wine. The finding of the name of the city being excavated on artifacts found at the site is quite rare (cf. the stela at Beth-shan and the ostracon at Arad) and the number found at Gibeon is unparalleled.

In addition to these, there were also found eighty jar handles with the royal "lamelekh" — "belonging to the king" — seal stamped on them. Twelve of the seals are with the winged scarab or beetle; the rest have a winged sun-disk of flying scroll. In addition to the LMLK are the names of one of four cities — Hebron, Socoh, Ziph, and MMST (Mampsis-Kurnub, or Kh. el-Gharra, due east of Beer-sheba?). Y. Yadin has proposed that these are the key depot cities for the four major Judean military districts — the Negeb ("extreme south"), Shephelah ("lowland"), hill country and wilderness (cf. Josh. 15:21, 33, 48, 61). Gibeon thus exported produce to these cities. These royal stamped jar-handles come from the period about 650-587 B.C.

Other jar handles with the names of individuals, many pieces of female and of animal figurines and miscellaneous items were found in the debris of the "pool"-stairwell.

An area northwest of the "pool"-stairwell and another south of it were found to be honey-combed with vat-shaped pits dug into the rock to a depth of 3 feet to 10½ feet, ranging in diameter from 3 feet 3 inches to 11 feet 5 inches with openings of 1 foot 4 inches to 4 feet 9 inches across. The openings were closed with flat stones, some of them carefully shaped to fit tightly. Thus far sixty-five vats have been found in one of which three storage jars (approximate volume: nine gallons) were found still in place. Rock-cut basins, troughs, and settling tanks in these "industrial areas" together with the inferences to be drawn from the fact that a constant temperature of 65° F. is maintained in the pits, led to the conclusion that Gibeon was the center of a wine industry whose known storage capacity is already in excess of 30,000 gallons. Storage jars filled with wine were carefully stored in these pits for aging and awaiting shipment to other markets.

Thus far the location of the great high place at Gibeon remains unknown. Some suggest that it may be at near-by Nebi Samwil; if so, it is inaccessible to the archaeologist because of its present sacred use.

After more than a half-millenium of continuous and apparently prosperous existence, Iron II Gibeon was destroyed toward the middle of the sixth century B.C. Its walls were never rebuilt. Occupation during the *Persian period* (550-330 B.C.) is indicated by a jar-handle stamped in fifth century Aramaic script MṢH — "Moṣah" (identified by N. Avigad with Roman Colonia; mod. Qalunia-Moza, about four miles west of Jerusalem, or Kh. Beit Mizzah, a mile farther west), perhaps a Persian crown estate. Other Persian period finds include an 18 carat gold signet ring and a late sixth century silver ring with the owner's name LMRTSMN engraved on it as well as pottery of the period.

Except for a few coins (Ptolemy II, Antiochus III, John Hyrcanus I) there is little present sign of *Hellenistic occupation* (330-63 *B.C.*).

Early in the *Roman period* (63 B.C. — A.D. 325) Gibeon was extensively re-occupied but it was an open city, reflecting the security of the Pax Romana. A Roman road was built over part of the Iron II wall's foundation. Several baths with plastered walls and steps leading into them have been uncovered. Some of the wine storage pits were plastered and used for cisterns. Others had niches carved in the walls and became columbaria in which the bones of the deceased were placed. Another tomb, made of six of the storage pits, had an applied stucco moulding and a mural painted around it — unique in Palestine. Motifs and lamps found in these tombs suggest it was used about A.D. 300. While Iron Age Gibeonites reverted to the EB use of rock-cut caves in the scarp of the hill, those of the Roman period used more monumental types of tombs and coffins — as was customary for the period.

About 130 feet northeast of the outer entrance to the cistern room was a Roman reservoir (37 feet by 60 feet 8 inches deep). It had been plastered four times during its period of use. Two rows of jars (1st cent. B.C. — 1st cent. A.D. type) were embedded in the walls with the mouths of the jars opening into the pool; the purpose for these jars remains unknown. Robinson in 1838 thought that this might be the famous pool of Gibeon. Just to the northeast of the southeast corner of this reservoir is a smaller, oval-shaped reservoir (about 15 feet by 10 feet) whose date of construction cannot be fixed — except sometime in the Roman period.

Just when the curtain of history was drawn over Roman-Byzantine Gibeon is not known. The last reference is that of Paula, a friend of Jerome, who saw it as she ascended the ancient-pass by the Beth-Horons in the late fourth century. A small village of Gabaon (Gibeon) is located north of Jerusalem on the mid-sixth century mosaic map of Medeba. Almost fifteen hundred years later, the location and life of a city whose history spanned three thousand years is once more known.

BIBLIOGRAPHY: James B. Pritchard, *Gibeon, Where the Sun Stood Still,* Princeton: Princeton University Press, 1962, note bibliography, p. 174;

Hebrew Inscriptions and Stamps from Gibeon, Philadelphia: University of Pennsylvania Museum, 1959; "More Inscribed Jar Handles from El-Jîb" *BASOR* 160 (1960) 2-6; *The Water System of Gibeon,* Philadelphia: University of Pennsylvania Museum, 1961; *The Bronze Age Cemetery at Gibeon,* Philadelphia: University of Pennsylvania Museum, 1963; preliminary report on 1962 season, *idem, Illustrated London News,* Sept. 22, 1962. N. Avigad, review of *Hebrew Inscriptions . . .", IEJ* 9, 1959, 130-133. F. M. Cross, Jr., *ibid., BASOR* 168, 1962; J. Dus, "Gibeon — eine Kultstätte des šmš/und die Stadt des benjaminitischen Schicksals," *VT* 10, 1960, 353-374.

GIHON. Gihon is the name of a spring in the Kidron Valley which served as the principal source of water for ancient Jerusalem. The spring gushes forth intermittently from a natural cave once or twice a day at the end of the dry season, and four or five times a day after the rainy season.

A PORTION OF THE GILGAMESH EPIC, which contains a flood account with remarkable parallels to the account in Genesis. Courtesy, British Museum

In 1867 during early excavations of Jerusalem by Charles Warren for the Palestine Exploration Fund, the archaeologists discovered a forty foot shaft built by the pre-Israelite inhabitants of Jerusalem (*ca.* 2000 B.C.) to permit them to draw water without being exposed to a potential enemy. This ancient structure is now called Waren's Shaft. After David took the city the old shaft went out of use, and the waters were collected in a reservoir and conveyed by means of an aqueduct. At the time of the Assyrian threat, Hezekiah blocked the spring and the aqueduct, and built a tunnel to convey the water to new reservoirs within the fortified perimeter of the city. *See* Siloam, Pool of.

GILGAMESH EPIC. Tablets containing the epic adventures of Gilgamesh, the fifth king of the first dynasty which reigned in °Uruk after the flood, according to the °Sumerian King List, were discovered in 1853 by Hormuzd Rassam, collaborator and successor to Austen Henry Layard, among the cuneiform texts from the library of °Ashurbanipal in Nineveh. The epic was evidently very popular, for portions of it have been discovered at °Boghazkoy in Asia Minor, and a small but important fragment was accidentally discovered in 1955 in the debris of the Oriental Institute campaigns at °Megiddo in Palestine.

Although Gilgamesh may have been the name of an actual king of Uruk, the account of his epic adventure is a myth which probably dates from the beginning of the second

millennium B.C. As the story begins, Gilgamesh is the tyrant of Uruk, terrorizing its inhabitants. As the people cry to their gods for relief, the gods answer the people's prayers by sending Enkidu who serves as a companion and foil for Gilgamesh. Enkidu at first lives with the wild animals with whom he identifies himself. It is only after he is seduced by an harlot from the city that Enkidu comes to live like a human. After this event the animals reject him, and he learns to wear clothes, eat the food of humans, herd sheep, and make war with the lion and the wolf, once his friends.

We might expect Gilgamesh and Enkidu to have become rivals, but they became the closest of friends. They went out together to the Cedar Mountains (the Amanus Range) and destroyed the evil giant Humbaba. Gilgamesh was acclaimed as an hero, and the goddess Ishtar herself fell in love with him. Gilgamesh spurned her offers of love, reminding her of a succession of lovers that she had mercilessly cast away. In revenge Ishtar insisted that Anu create a monster named the Bull of Heaven. Enkidu and Gilgamesh met this new challenge. Gilgamesh slew the Bull, and Enkidu tore out the bull's right thigh and tossed it at the face of Ishtar.

Although the killing of the Bull of Heaven may be regarded as a victory for Enkidu and Gilgamesh, Ishtar was determined to have her revenge. Enkidu was taken sick and in a short time he had died. Gilgamesh mourned the loss of his friend, and he realized that he, too, one day would die. In this new crisis he thought of his ancestor Utnapishtim a mortal who had survived the flood and thus gained immortality. Gilgamesh determined to find Utnapishtim and seek from him the means to immortality. He undertook a hazardous pilgrimage across untraversed mountains and the waters of death to reach Utnapishtim. Along the way he was dissuaded by the barmaid Siduri, whose advice is reminiscent of Ecclesiastes 9:7-9. Siduri said,

Gilgamesh, whither dost thou rove? The life thou pursueth thou shalt not find. When the gods created mankind, they set aside death for mankind. Life they retained in their own hands. Let thy belly be full, Gilgamesh. Make merry by day and by night. Make a feast of rejoicing of each day; dance and play both day and night. Let thy garments be fresh, thy head washed, thy body bathed. Take heed to the little one that holds thee by the hand. Let thy wife delight in thy bosom, for this is the task of mankind.

Gilgamesh would not be dissuaded, however. He insisted on continuing his journey until he found himself in the presence of Utnapishtim. In the eleventh tablet of the Gilgamesh Epic, Utnapishtim tells Gilgamesh how he attained immortality. The story is the Akkadian version of the flood, based on Sumerian antecedents. The gods determined to destroy mankind with a flood, but the kindly Ea warned Utnapishtim of what was coming through his reed hut. Ea urged him to build a ship and take into it "the seed of all living things."

Utnapishtim proceeded to build the ark in the form of a giant cube, nearly two hundred feet on each side (120 cubits). It was divided into seven stories, each containing nine rooms. He then took silver, gold, living creatures, family and relatives into the ark. The storm began at the appointed time. It was so fierce that even the gods crouched like dogs along the wall of heaven. After six days and six nights the storm abated. Utnapishtim looked out and saw that "all mankind had returned to clay." Finally the ship came to rest at Mount Nisir. Utnapishtim sent forth successively a dove, a swallow, and a raven. The dove and swallow returned, but the raven saw that the flood waters were abating and did not

come back. Utnapishtim left the ark at Mount Nisir and offered sacrifices. The gods, who had been deprived of sacrifices during the flood, gathered like flies around Utnapishtim. Enlil was angry that anyone had escaped destruction in the flood, but Ea insisted that it was not right to destroy the righteous with the sinful. "On the sinner impose his sin," said Ea. Enlil then granted immortality to Utnapishtim and his wife: "Hitherto Utnapishtim has been human; henceforth Utnapishtim and his wife shall be like unto us gods. Utnapishtim shall reside far away at the mouth of the rivers."

Utnapishtim had gained immortality, but Gilgamesh still had not attained his goal. Utnapishtim challenged him to remain awake for six days, but he could not meet the test — Gilgamesh was indeed a mortal. Utnapishtim did offer Gilgamesh a ray of hope. He told him of a plant that would restore lost youth to a man. With great difficulty Gilgamesh found the plant and rejoiced at the thought of rejuvenation for himself and the elders of his city. While bathing, however, a serpent rose from the water and took the plant. Sloughing off its skin it was rejuvenated, but Gilgamesh had to return empty to his city. Like other mortals he would die one day.

The account of the flood in the Gilgamesh Epic has numerous parallels to that recorded in Genesis 6:9—9:19. In both accounts we read of a warning of a coming flood. An ark is built, the flood comes, the vessel settles on a mountain, and birds are sent out in each story. Both Noah and Utnapishtim offer sacrifices at the time they disembark. The similarities are so close that it would appear that one story drew on the other, or both went back to a common origin.

There are important differences between the two flood stories. The gods of the Gilgamesh Epic disagree with each other. They crouch like dogs and swarm like hungry flies. The monotheism of the Genesis account stands in sharp contrast to the polytheism of the Babylonian story. The names of the heroes differ. Mount Ararat and Mount Nisir are different, Ararat being the conventionalized rendering of the mountains of Urartu (Armenia). Each nation adapted the flood story to its own geography.

In the light of similarities and differences it appears that both the Biblical and the

Babylonian accounts refer to the same event. The Biblical account portrays a holy God bringing judgment on a sinful world but sparing Noah and his family. The Gilgamesh Epic presents a group of gods whose motivation is frequently selfish and who lack the quiet majesty of the God of Israel.

BIBLIOGRAPHY. Alexander Heidel, *The Gilgamesh Epic and Old Testament Parallels,* University of Chicago Press, Chicago, 1949. N. K. Sanders, *The Epic of Gilgamesh,* Penguin Books, Baltimore, 1964. R. Campbell Thompson, *The Epic of Gilgamesh,* Clarendon Press, Oxford, 1930. Sidney Langdon, "The Sumerian Epic of Gilgamesh," *Journal of the Royal Asiatic Society,* 1932, pp. 911-948. Thorkild Jacobsen, "How did Gilgamesh oppress Uruk?," *Acta Orientalia,* VIII, 1930, pp. 62-74.

GLACIS. A glacis is a sloping bank of earth built to make the approach to a fort more difficult.

GOSHEN. The territory in Egypt assigned to Jacob and his family is known as the land of Goshen. It was located in the eastern Delta area, including the Wadi Tumilat, a fertile region which connected the Nile to the Bitter Lakes. It is located in "the land of Rameses" (Gen. 47:11) and was near the royal palace where Joseph served as vizier.

GOSPEL OF PHILIP. *See* Nag Hammadi.

GOSPEL OF ST. THOMAS. *See* Nag Hammadi.

GOZAN, GUZANA (TELL HALAF). Located on the westernmost source of the river °Habor (or Khabor), Tell Halaf is a type-site for an important phase of Mesopotamian pre-history and, as Guzana (Biblical Gozan), a major center, first of the Arameans and later of the Assyrians and neo-Babylonians in the first half of the first millennium B.C. It is known in the Bible as one of the destinations of the Israelites exiled by Tiglath-pileser III from Transjordan in 734-2 B.C. and by Shalmaneser V and Sargon II after the fall of Samaria in 722 B.C. In Hellenistic times, it gave its name to the district of Gauzanitis.

I. *Location.* Tell Halaf and Tell Fakhariyah ("rich in sherds") are the two principal ruin mounds in the immediate vicinity of the modern village of Ras-el-Ayin, located at the sources of the °Habor River. It is situated just inside the Syrian side of the Berlin-Baghdad railway which, since 1920, marks the Turko-Syrian border in Mesopotamia.

II. *History of Discovery.* The discovery, exploration, excavation and restoration of Guzana is largely the life-work of one man, Baron Max von Oppenheim (1860-1946), whose numerous early travels acquainted him with all parts of the Near East and who gave up a diplomatic career to devote much of his life and resources to this site. The Tell Halaf Museum in Berlin which von Oppenheim built to house the reassembled finds was destroyed during World War II, but a foundation established by and named for him has carried on the publication of the surviving results of his expedition and the exploration of other sites in the same vicinity.

Tell Halaf was discovered by von Oppenheim in the course of one of his exploratory journeys in 1899, and his initial excavations convinced him of the importance of the site. He conducted the first organized excavations there from 1911-13, when the first World War and the subsequent battles at the site between Turkey and France interrupted his work. Among the finds of this campaign was the archive of the local Assyrian governor (see below); with its help, the site was identified with Guzana by 1918. In 1927, Oppenheim returned for a second campaign, removing no less than thirteen box-car loads of sculptures and smaller finds to the museums which he erected for the purpose in °Aleppo and Berlin. The final campaign of 1929 also included surveys of the surrounding mounds. Besides shorter or more popular works, von Oppenheim and his collaborators published four large volumes on the excavations between 1943 and 1962 (see Bibliography).

III. *History of the Site.*

A. Prehistoric period. Although the earliest finds at Halaf are neolithic in date, they are overshadowed in numbers and importance by those of the chalcolithic strata, when Halaf was a — perhaps the — center of the production of a magnificent glazed and polychrome pottery which has given its name to a whole phase of Mesopotamian pre-history. The Halaf period, in fact, designates an entire culture attested throughout northern Mesopotamia just prior to, and at its end contemporaneous with, the first evidences of settlement in southern Mesopotamia (so-called Ubaid period). It covered a long span of time, with at least three major sub-periods, of which only the last is well represented at Halaf itself.

B. Early Historic Periods. No doubt the site of Halaf was inhabited in the third and second millennia, but there is little arti-factual evidence to indicate this, and the historical records cannot help as long as the native name of the site at this period is unknown. What is clear is that the Upper Habor area in general was the focal point of Hurrian civilization about 1500 B.C. and that Washukanni, the capital of the Hurrian state of *Mitanni, cannot have been far from Halaf. It has even been proposed to identify Washukanni with Tell Fakhariyah. Neither the American soundings there in 1940, nor the German ones in 1955-56 have proved the proposal, but if correct it would explain the significance of Halaf at this period on the often confirmed observation that two important cities in immediate proximity to each other cannot both flourish at the same time. From dated tablets found at Fakhari-yah it is, at any rate, clear that this site was occupied in the thirteenth century, when it was subject to Shalmaneser I and Tukulti-Ninurta I (1265-1198 B.C.) of *Assyria. Thereafter Fahkariyah appears to have en-tered at least three centuries of decline until it re-emerged, perhaps as Sikani, in the neo-Assyrian period. It is in this interval, apparently, that the neighboring Tell Halaf first achieved independence and prominence.

C. The Kapara Dynasty. The principal monuments of Tell Halaf are the imposing sculptures which, on the testimony of the inscriptions repeatedly carved on them in a crude Assyrian cuneiform, belong to two great structures, the "palace" (i.e., temple) of the weather-god, Adad, and the "palace of Kapara, son of Hadianu," the Aramaic equivalent of Hebrew Ḥezyôn, the father of Ṭab-rimmōn and grandfather of Ben-Ha-dad of Damascus (I Kings 15:18), all of whose names have been restored by Al-bright with some degree of probability in a votive stele from Aleppo. If therefore the father of Kapara were demonstrably identi-cal with the grandfather of Bar-Hadad, he would be approximately contemporary with Rehoboam of Judah (ca. 920-900 B.C.), and Kapara and his palaces could be confidently dated to the early ninth century. In fact,

RELIEF SHOWING CAMEL RIDER from Gozan (ca. 1000 B.C.). Courtesy, Walters Art Gallery, Baltimore

however, the Assyrian records, which know of neither Hadianu nor Kapara, show that Gozan was ruled at this time by one Abisa-lamu, son of (i.e., of the house of) Bahianu who is, in turn, unknown in the inscriptions of Halaf itself. In the fifth campaign of Adad-nirari II, (i.e., in 894 B.C.), we are told Abisalamu occupied Guzana, which is here for the first time mentioned by that name. Moreover, it has long been a matter for discussion whether the buildings, the sculptures and the inscriptions are all of one date or not. Although the divergences in dating have been narrowed down, it thus remains an open question whether Kapara, his father, and his grandfather ruled before Abisalamu in the tenth century (so Al-bright) or after him in the ninth century.

Whatever the date of its principal in-dependent dynasty, Gozan in most of the ninth century continued to form a part of the territory of the Aramean tribe of Bahyan and it may have been the object of two campaigns by Ashur-nasir-pal II (883-859 B.C.) against an unnamed "son of Bahianu." An Aramaic inscription from the site about this time may supply the name, for Al-bright translates it "Zidant (?) lord of (the tribe of) Bahyan" and calls it the "oldest Aramaic inscription now [1942] known." But the cuneiform inscriptions of Kapara, according to his readings, prefer to designate the state by the more prestigious name of Hattê, the Hittite land.

D. Guzana as an Assyrian Province. In 808 B.C., the Assyrians recorded their first major attack on Guzana, under the energetic queen-mother Sammu-ramat (the Semiramis of Greek legend). This was the first of several decisive victories against the Arameans which marked her young son Adad-nirari III as a veritable deliverer in the eyes of Israel, traditionally the rival of the Arameans (II Kings 13:5). There is little reason to doubt that Guzana became the capital of a new Assyrian province at this time, for in the eighth century its governors took their regular turns among the eponyms. Four of them are known from the eponym lists, among them three who are famous in their own right. The first was Mannu-ki-Ashur, who gave his name to the year 793 B.C. His official archive, consisting of nearly one hundred tablets, was excavated at Gozan and shows that, through him, the royal Assyrian court at Kalah concerned itself with all the details of local administration. In 763 B.C., the governor of Gozan was Bur-Sagala and the solar eclipse recorded for his eponymate has provided a firm astronomical anchor for all neo-Assyrian dates. In 759 B.C. Gozan participated in the last of a succession of revolts against the weak king Assur-dan III but it seems to have been put down in the following year. And by 727 B.C., we again find the city's governor taking his accustomed place in the cycle of eponyms. His name, Bel-harran-bel-usur, is the same as that of the "palace herald," a high official ranking directly under the king and his *turtanu* (*see* Til-Barsib), under Shalmaneser IV and Tiglath-pileser III. Whether he is the same person may be doubted. About this time, too, Gozan and the whole Habor region figure in the Biblical record as the destination of some of the Israelite exiles, first from across the Jordan under Tiglath-pileser III in 734-2 (I Chron. 5:26) and then from Galilee and Samaria itself by Shalmaneser V and Sargon II (II Kings 17:6; 18:11). Presently Israelite names appear on both cuneiform and Aramaic documents from other Assyrian sites which suggest that the exiles found their way from Gozan to the capital cities of Assyria and did not dis-

appear quite as abruptly as we had assumed upon the basis of our reading of the history of the Lost Ten Tribes. The last dated Assyrian reference to the city is 706 B.C.; in the seventh century the city seems to have passed under the administration of the neighboring province of Naṣibina (Nisibis). Private documents from Gozan itself, and undated references in the royal correspondence from Nineveh attest to the continuity of its role otherwise. After the collapse of the Assyrian empire in 612 B.C., the city became a colony of the neo-Babylonian empire, and in Hellenistic time gave its name to the province of Gauzanitis, but thereafter it again lost its pre-eminence in the area to neighboring Fakhariyah (Resaina).

BIBLIOGRAPHY.

A. Works written or edited by or in honor of Max von Oppenheim: *Der Tell Halaf und die verschleierte Göttin* = *Der Alte Orient* X/1, 1908. "Tell Halaf, la plus ancienne capitale soubaréenne de Mésopotamia," *Syria*, XIII, 1932, pp. 242-254 and pls. xlvi-liii. *Tell Halaf, a new culture in ancient Mesopotamia*, G. P. Putnam's Sons, London and New York, 1933. *Archiv für Orientforschung*, Supplement I, 1933 (= Oppenheim Anniversary Volume, the articles by Hommel, Meissner, Opitz, Schmidt and Ungnad). *Führer durch das Tell Halaf-Museum*, Max Freiherr von Oppenheim-Stiftung, Berlin, 1934. "Die Embleme der Subaräischen Hauptgottheiten auf der Buntkeramik des Tell Halaf . . .," *Bibliothèque Archéologique et Historique*, XXX, 1939 (= René Dussaud Anniversary Volume), pp. 609-623 and 4 pls. *Tell Halaf*, 4 vols., Walter de Gruyter & Co., Berlin, 1943-62.

B. Works by others: E. Douglas van Buren, "A gaming-board from Tell Halaf," *Iraq*, IV, 1937, pp. 11-15 and pl. vi; J. Friedrich *et al, Die Inschriften vom Tel Halaf* (= *Archiv für Orientforschung*, Supplement VI, 1940). R. A. Bowman, "The Old Aramaic Alphabet at Tell Halaf," *AJSLL*, LVIII, 1941, pp. 359-67. W. F. Albright, "The Date of the Kapara Period at Gozan," *Anatolian Studies*, VI, 1956, pp. 75-85.

C. Works on Tell Fakhariya: Moortgat Anton, *Archäologische Forschungen der Max Freiherr von Oppenheim Stiftung . . . 1955, 1956* (2 vv.) Köln and Opladen, Westdeutscher Verlag, 1957-59, reprinted from *Les Annales Archéologiques de Syrie*, VI, 1956, pp. 39-50 and pls. i-viii; VII, 1957, pp. 17-30 and pls. i-vii. Calvin W. McEwan, *et al.*, *Soundings at Tell Fakhariyah* = *Oriental Institute Publications*, LXXIX, Barthel Hrouda, "Tell Fecherije: Die Keramik," *Zeitschrift für Assyriologie*, LIV, 1961, pp. 201-239.

GRAFFITO (pl. Graffiti). Graffiti are markings, scratched or cut into walls, pottery, tiles, or other surfaces. They frequently indicate ownership.

GUDEA. *See* Lagash.

H

HABAKKUK COMMENTARY. *See* Dead Sea Scrolls.

HABIRU, HAPIRU. A people known as Habiru or Hapiru are first mentioned in cuneiform documents from the third dynasty of Ur, *ca.* 2050 B.C., and in the centuries that follow they are found throughout the Near East. They appear at *Larsa, *Babylon, *Mari, *Alalakh, *Nuzi, *Boghazkoy, *Amarna, and *Ugarit. At Boghazkoy they appear among lists of social classes between free citizens and slaves. At Mari they operate as bands of semi-nomads. King Idrimi of Alalakh dwelt among Habiru soldiers for seven years. Kings of city states in Palestine who wrote the *Amarna letters complained of the Habiru as disturbers of the peace.

Originally the Habiru seem to have constituted a stratum of society rather than an ethnic group. While many of their names are Semitic, other names appear as well. According to George E. Mendenhall, the Habiru should be considered a people living outside the bounds of a given legal community, and not controlled by its laws and mores. The term would thus refer to unsettled, nomadic people who continually haunted the civilized communities around the Arabian Desert. In the Amarna letters the Habiru (or 'Apiru) are lawless gangs or ill paid mercenaries who were joined by people from the oppressed population in their attacks on the established cities.

The relationship between the Biblical Hebrews and the Habiru has been given careful study. Since the Habiru appear in contexts far removed from the Hebrews of the Bible, identification is impossible. It is possible, however, that the Hebrews were regarded in the same light as the Habiru in the period before the establishment of the Israelite monarchy. Abraham is called "the Hebrew" (Gen. 14:13) in a context in which he is involved in the political struggles of the day. Most of the Biblical uses of the term Hebrew appear in contexts in which Israelites identify themselves to other peoples, or in which other peoples discuss the Israelites (cf. Gen. 39:14, 17; 40:15; 41:12; 43:32). While all Habiru were not Hebrews, the Israelites were re-

garded as Habiru by the people among whom they lived.

BIBLIOGRAPHY. Moshe Greenberg, *The Hab/piru, American Oriental Society,* New Haven, Conn., 1955; Jean Bottero, *Le Probleme des Habiru.* Imprimerie Nationale, Paris, 1954.

HABOR RIVER. According to the Bible, the river Habor (II Kings 17:6) was one destination of the Israelites exiled by the Assyrians from the northern kingdom, traditionally the "Ten Lost Tribes." In Parthian times, the area briefly harbored a virtually autonomous Jewish state.

I. *Description and Location.* The river Habor may be divided into two very different parts. The upper half flows southeast from its source at Ras-el-Ayin near ancient *Gozan toward its junction with the river Jaghjagha, the two streams receiving, during the rainy season, numerous tributaries from the north along the way, so that they embrace what was once a very fertile area resembling a river delta in reverse; the lower half flows southward between the Abd-el-Aziz and Sinjar mountains and onward through a largely barren area until it joins the Euphrates above *Terqa. It is the valley of the Upper Habor, dotted with the remains of five hundred or more ancient settlements (tells), which in the Old Babylonian period sustained an estimated fifty thousand people, though it is now relatively depopulated, and which will be discussed here.

II. *Exploration of the Region.* Although numerous explorers and archaeologists had crossed the Habor region in earlier decades, it was a British expedition under M. E. L. Mallowan which first undertook a comprehensive survey of both the Habor "triangle" and the Lower Habor in 1934-35. The greater promise of the former area led to systematic excavations on two sites, Shagar Bazar and Brak, in the eastern half of the triangle. Further campaigns at these sites in 1936-38 brought the work to completion. French and Syrian efforts have succeeded in identifying some of the other sites in the area since World War II (see below). For the western part of the triangle *see* Gozan.

III. *The Habor Region in Pre-historic Times.* Surface finds throughout the "Habor

273

triangle" indicate that the area was occupied by the earliest agriculturalists, who probably left the rain belt of the Anatolian highlands to the north to penetrate as far south as they could without the aid of irrigation. At Shagar Bazar, as at Gozan the unpainted pottery goes back to the end of the neolithic period; by Chalcolithic times it is found as far south as Brak, and the Halaf ware takes its name from the region (see Gozan).

IV. *The Third Millennium.* The late proto-literate and entire Early Dynastic periods are well represented at Brak and Shagar Bazar, the most systematically dug sites in the region. Perhaps the most characteristic finds of the former period are the thousands of "eye-idols" from Brak which in some circles have been taken as evidence of a wide-spread cult of the sun and moon as twin "eyes" of heaven in the pre- and proto-historic Near East (see Bibliography). These idols and other objects including particularly beads were found in and under the foundations of a temple repeatedly rebuilt at the same site.

On this site too, the Brak excavations revealed an unexpected palace identified by its inscribed bricks as belonging to Naram-Sin of *Akkad (ca. 2252-2216 B.C.). There is both literary and inscriptional evidence for conquests by the Sargonic kings in northern Mesopotamia, but the extensive remains of the palace at Brak are by far the most impressive witness yet to the extent of Akkadian influence in the area. The neo-Sumerian rulers of the Third Dynasty of Ur (ca. 2111-2004 B.C.) seem to have perpetuated the southern rule here at the end of the millennium.

V. *The Mari Age.* In the early part of the second millennium, the whole Habor valley was dominated by *Mari, on the Euphrates, some fifty miles downstream from the confluence of the Habor. The Habor triangle was known as Idamaraz at this time. Numerous place names figuring in the Mari correspondence must be looked for in the area, though it is frequently difficult to establish definite correlations between ancient names and modern sites. During the period of Old Assyrian supremacy at Mari, one of the royal Assyrian residences was located at Shubat-Enlil in this area; some scholars would identify it with Tell Hamidi, or Tell Lelan, others with Shagar Bazar, while still

others think that Shagar Bazar is rather to be identified with Harsi or Kirdahat. Positive identifications so far are possible for only four sites in this area: Tell Barri (east of Shagar Bazar and north of Brak on the Jaghjagha River) with Kahat; Nisibis (where the Jaghjagha crosses the Turkish frontier) with Naṣibina; Amuda (west of Nisibis) with Urkish, and Tell Halaf with *Gozan.

Archaeologically, this period is well defined in the region, for it produced a characteristic painted pottery to which Mallowan has given the name of Habor (Khabur) ware. It is found also east and west of the Habor triangle but nowhere else in such great abundance; moreover it can all be dated fairly rigorously to the interval ca. 1900-1600 B.C. on the basis of cuneiform texts found associated with the ware at Brak and especially at Shagar Bazar.

VI. *The Hurrian Period.* The Habor triangle was the earliest seat of an independent Hurrian state in Mesopotamia, for the oldest Hurrian text now known is an inscription of a king called Dish-atal who ruled Urkish (see above) in the late Sargonic period. A few Hurrian names also appear in the Old Babylonian tablets from Shagar Bazar. It is thus not surprising to find the heart of the state of *Mitanni in this area in the middle of the second millennium (see sub Gozan), Mitanni was Hurrian in speech and to a large extent in population, though ruled by an Indo-Aryan aristocracy. Among its distinctive cultural traits was the prevalence of horse-raising and horse racing, and it is therefore interesting to note horses already mentioned in the Old Babylonian texts from Shagar Bazar. There are no texts, Hurrian or otherwise, from the region in this period, but those from Nuzi, Ugarit, Anatolia and Egypt attest to the vital role played by the Hurrians of Mitanni both culturally, as transmitters of Babylonian literature to the Hittites and even, it is thought, to the Israelites (see Bibliography), and politically. The ceramic record, on the other hand, is well documented here and again a distinctive style unites the Habor triangle with its eastern and western neighbors in the same latitudes; it is a luxury pottery variously known as Mitannian, Hurrian or Nuzi ware.

VII. *The Assyrian Period.* The collapse of Mitanni seems to have brought with it a marked decline in the fortunes of the Habor triangle, especially its eastern half, where the principal sites (Shagar Bazar and Brak) seem never to have been rebuilt after *ca.* 1400 B.C., perhaps because the top of their mounds had become too small. Lying, as it did, across the path of *Assyrian expansion to the west, the area in due time came under Assyrian rule, most of it being divided among the provinces of *Gozan, Izalla (Huzirina) and Naṣibina (Nisibis). Its importance for Biblical history lies chiefly in the fact that Israelites deported from Transjordan, Galilee and Samaria were successively settled on the Habor, "the river of Gozan," by Tiglath-pileser III (I Chron. 5: 26), Shalmaneser V and Sargon II (II Kings 17:6; 18:11). As in the case of the later Babylonian exile, these settlements must have been more durable than we had concluded from the history of the "Lost Ten Tribes," for not only do Israelite personal names occur in cuneiform and Aramaic documents of the neo-Assyrian period, but the area continued to constitute a thriving center of Jewish provincial life even after the fall of Assyria and Babylonia, no doubt strengthened by new accretions of emigrés from Palestine. Josephus, for instance, records the existence of a virtually autonomous Jewish enclave in the area in Parthian times, and it continued to flourish as a center of Jewish life and learning in the Sassanian period, as attested by the Babylonian Talmud.

BIBLIOGRAPHY. Allen H. Godbey, *The Lost Tribes a Myth,* Durham, North Carolina, Duke University Press, 1930. M. E. L. Mallowan, "The Excavations at Tall Chagar Bazar and an Archaeological Survey of the Habur Region, 1934-35," Iraq, III, 1936, pp. 1-86; IV, 1937, pp. 91-177 and pls. xii-xix; "Excavations at Brak and Chagar Bazar," *ibid.,* IX, 1947, pp. 1-266 and pls. i-lxxxvi. C. J. Gadd, "Tablets from Chagar Bazar (and Tall Brak)," *ibid.,* IV, 1937, pp. 178-185; VII, 1940, pp. 22-66. Margarete Riemschneider, *Augengott und Heilige Hochzeit,* Leipzig, Koehler und Ameland, 1953. E. A. Speiser, "The Hurrian Participation in the Civilization of Mesopotamia, Syria and Palestine," *Journal of World History,* I, 1953-54, pp. 311-327. W. J. Van Liere, "Nouvelle Propspection Archéologique dans la Haute Jézireh Syrienne," *Les Annales Archéologiques de Syrie,* IV-I, 1954-55, pp. 129-148 and pls. i-iv and map (with J. Lauffray); "Urkiš, Centre Religieux Hurrite," *ibid.,* VII, 1957, pp. 91-94; "Notice Géographique sur le Site de la Ville de Kahat - *Tell Barri," ibid.,* XI-XII, 1961-62, pp. 163f. and map. Georges Dossin, "Le Site de la Ville de Kahat," *ibid.,* pp. 197-206 and pls. i-ii.

HADATU (Arslan Tash).

Hadâtu was an Assyrian garrison post and royal residence in the second half of the eighth century B.C. commanding the plain of Sarug(i) whose name survives in the Biblical proper name Serug (Gen. 11:20-23; I Chron. 1:26) and in the modern village of Seruj.

I. *Name and Location.* The ruins of Hadâtu, called Arslan Tash ("black lion") by the semi-nomadic Kurdish population of the area after two colossal five-legged Assyrian lions dominating the site, are located some twenty miles due south of Sarug and some fifty miles due east of *Carchemish in Syria just south of the Turkish border. In its day, Hadâtu served as the last station before the Euphrates on the road from Assyria which reached the river at *Til-Barsib. Its identification is based on inscriptions of Tiglath-pileser III found *in situ.* Its name appropriately enough is an Assyrianized rendering of an Aramaic word for "new (town)."

II. *History of Discovery.* The first recorded visit to the site was by Lieutenants Lynch (US Navy) and Eden (Royal Navy) in 1836. From 1883 to 1925, numerous archaeologists returned to the site, and some of its monuments were recovered during this time. Formal excavations were conducted by Thureau-Dangin in 1928, after a short exploratory visit in the preceding year, and the results were published in 1931 (see Bibliography).

III. *History of the Site.* Apart from a small chapel of the Hellenistic period, the occupational evidence from Hadâtu is confined to the neo-Assyrian period. More specifically, the town flourished during the reign of Tiglath-pileser III (744-727 B.C.), who reconquered all of northern Syria for Assyria and founded provincial centers like Hadâtu to serve the multiple purposes of controlling the native population, securing the empire against foreign invasion, and checking the ambitions of local Assyrian governors. In addition, Hadâtu in particular also served as a station on the Assyrian road to Syria and as a royal residence during the brief stop-overs of the king on his western campaigns. As such it has left one of the finest examples of a royal Assyrian provincial residence and, in addition to the sculptures and reliefs which decorated this residence, the most important collection of "Assyrian" ivories outside of Calah. With the capture of nearby Carchemish in 717 B.C., Hadâtu lost most of its importance, though it is still mentioned in the Assyrian "census" of the Harran district which probably dates from the seventh century (see Haran), and Ashurbanipal (668-623 B.C.) seems to speak of it as the jumping-off place for his second campaign against Arabia. A memorial to this campaign may even be preserved among the finds from Hadâtu, for these include some ivory fragments inscribed in Aramaic with a dedication to a certain Hazael, "the master," i.e., king. This is hardly the Biblical Hazael, king of Damascus in the late ninth century B.C. (I Kings 19:15, 17, etc.) but more likely the Hazailu, ruler of Qidru (Biblical Qēdār) whose son (or brother) Uaite' was the target of Ashurbanipal's expedition. In the Hellenistic period, the site of Arslan Tash may have been occupied by the station called Banata or Balata in the Itineraries.

IV. *The Hadâtu Amulet.* In 1933, subsequent to the formal excavations of Hadâtu, Count du Mesnil du Buisson acquired there an amulet which probably dates from the seventh century B.C., and which well illustrates the cultural cross-currents of the whole region toward the end of the Assyrian period. In shape and type it approximates the Assyrian and Babylonian *lamashtu* tablets, intended as spells against diseases, etc.; the drawings of demons or deities on it are partly in the Syro-Hittite style, and the inscription itself is in a Canaanite dialect, quite possibly Hebrew. Yet the population for whom it was intended was almost certainly Aramaic.

BIBLIOGRAPHY. Eckhard Unger, *Die Reliefs Tiglatpilesers III. aus Arslan Tash* = *Publications des Musées d'Antiquités de Stamboul*, VII, 1925. Max Freiherr von Oppenheim, "Eine unbekante Statue aus dem Serudj," *Mitteilungen der Altorientalischen Gesellschaft*, IV, 1928-9, pp. 155-162 and pls. ii-vii. Francois Thureau-Dangin et al., *Arslan-Tash* = *Bibliothèque Archéologique et Historique*, XVI, 1931. William F. Albright, "An Aramaean Magical Text in Hebrew from the Seventh Century B.C.," *BASOR*, 76, 1939, pp. 5-11. Theodore H. Gaster, "A Canaanite Magical Text," *Orientalia*, XI, 1942, pp. 41-79.

HAMATH. Hamath, on the Orontes River in Syria, is located on the main trade route from Asia Minor to the south. It was the center of an independent kingdom, the southern border of which was the northern border of Israel (cf. Num. 13:21; Josh. 13:5; Judg. 3:3). King Toi of Hamath was friendly to David (II Sam. 8:9-10). Subsequently, however, Solomon controlled Hamath (II Chron. 8:4) and the territory was conquered by Jeroboam II (ca. 780 B.C., II Kings 14:28) and Sargon of Assyria (ca. 721 B.C., cf. II Kings 18:33-34). Some of the inhabitants of Hamath were settled by the Assyrians in Samaria (II Kings 17:24) in accord with their policy of transporting captured peoples.

A Danish archaeological expedition under H. Ingholt excavated Hamath in a series of campaigns between 1932 and 1938. Twelve occupation layers were uncovered, the earliest of which dated to Neolithic times. There is no evidence of Hyksos remains, suggesting that the city was destroyed during that period. Important Hittite hieroglyphic inscriptions have been discovered at Hamath (see Hittites).

HAMMURABI. See Babylon.

HAMMURABI, THE CODE OF. This famous code of laws was promulgated by Hammurabi, sixth king of the First Dynasty of Babylon. Of the eleven kings of this dynasty, his reign of forty-three years was the longest. Many inscriptions give a good account of his life and testify to his wise rule and his brilliant administration. He welded the small states of Babylonia into a unified and powerful kingdom. His conquests not only covered the Mesopotamian Valley, but even extended westward to the Mediterranian Sea. The date of his reign had been unsettled until *Mari, the city state on the west side of the Euphrates river about 260 miles north of Babylon, was excavated. The excavators found there many tablets which give an accurate history of the Patriarchal Age. An account of the conquest of Mari dates it during the thirty-second year of the reign of Hammurabi (1728-1686 B.C.).

Not only was Hammurabi a great military genius, but he is noted for his literary achievements. The extent of his kingdom and the needs of his people socially, economically, and legally demanded a code of laws to meet these situations, as the legal codes known to him were inadequate. A study of Hammurabi's code in comparison with earlier codes shows that he used them as a basis.

women, nuns, and artisans are especially named. Some of the crimes mentioned are (1) sorcery (cf. Ex. 22:18; Deut. 18:10; Num. 5:11-28); (2) false testimony (cf. Deut. 19:18, 19); (3) theft, as stealing property of the temple or state, receiving stolen goods, stealing at a fire, selling lost property, highway robbery (cf. Ex. 22:1-4, 9; Lev. 6:3-5; Deut. 21:1-9); (4) kidnapping (cf. Ex. 21:16; Deut. 23:15); (5) desertion or appropriating property of a soldier falsely; (6) overcharging and allowing outlaws to congregate in a wineshop conducted by women, or a nun visiting a wineshop (cf. Deut. 23:17); (7) faulty construction of a building that caused the death of the owner; (8) incest or adultery (cf. Lev. 19:20-22; 20:10; Num. 5:11-28); (9) striking a parent (cf. Ex. 21:5-6); (10) murder (cf. Ex. 21:15).

The method of execution is not always specified. The three types mentioned are burning, drowning and impalement on a stake.

Besides the death penalty, bodily mutilation was imposed for specified crimes not warranting death. This might take the form of branding upon different parts of the body; cutting off the ear, hand, tongue, or breast, or destroying an eye. The *lex talonis*, the law of retaliation was basic for both the Hammurabi and the Mosaic codes.

Some of the offences with their penalties are: (1) A son who strikes his father, loses his hand. (2) one who destroys the eye of a free-man has his own eye destroyed. (3) One who breaks a bone of a free-man has his own bone broken. (4) One who knocks out the tooth of a free-man has his own tooth knocked out. (5) A physician who causes the death or loss of an eye in a major operation, has his own hand cut off.

A third method of punishment was the assessing of fines, the amount depending upon the class of citizens to which the guilty person belonged. The guilty person was required to make restitution. If he was an aristocrat the penalty was thirty-fold; if a private citizen it was ten-fold. If a wealthy free-man cut down a tree of another without consent, the penalty was a monetary sum; if a wealthy free-man's ox gored a person, a cash fine was assessed.

The code contained laws regarding fees and wages. The physician received a payment for an operation. The amount paid by the free-man was ten shekels of silver; a freed-man five shekels; and a slave two shekels. Interest on money lent was the same for all classes (cf. Ex. 21:2-6; 22:17; Deut. 15:17-18; 25:11-13).

The wages of certain workers were fixed by law. The boatman, reaper, thresher, and herdsman were paid by the year; the wages of brickmaker, carpenter, stone cutter, artisan, milkman, and tailor were to be paid daily as was the hire of a domestic animal for plowing or threshing, an oxcart and driver, and a wagon, cart or boat (Ex. 22:10-13).

Most important are the laws relating to the family with reference to property rights, rights of the children and of divorce (cf. Ex. 21:17; Num. 27:8-11; 36:2-12; Deut. 21:15-21; 22:13-21).

Slavery was a recognized institution. There were two classes — temporary and permanent. The temporary slave was a person who sold himself or any member of his family to pay a debt to serve for three years and in the fourth year was restored to freedom (cf. Ex. 21:2-11; Deut. 15:12-18). Perpetual slaves were foreigners, usually captives of war. They were purchased at the slave market. They had a hard life and if one should rebel against his master, his ear was cut off (cf. Josh. 9:16-27).

The code closes with a long Epilogue in which Hammurabi tells of his noble deeds, his honest administration and his concern for the best interests of his people. He orders each officer and ruler under him to obey every law and commandment, pronouncing blessings upon the faithful administrator of the laws and terrible curses upon those who fail, neglect or seek to destroy them.

The Mosaic or Hebrew code has much in common with the Hammurabi code, yet it varies due to cultural and religious differences between Israel and Babylon. The Biblical code acknowledges Yahweh alone as Israel's God, and is particularly suited to a people who have just left a slave status. The Hammurabi Code presupposes the urban life of southern Mesopotamia with its merchants and highly civilized culture.

BIBLIOGRAPHY. *Encyclopedia Britannica*, 1954 edition, Vol. 2, pp. 862-64; Vol. 11, p. 134. Robert F. Harper, *The Code of Hammurabi, King of Babylonia*, 2nd edition, University of Chicago Press, 1904. Sabitino Moscati, *The Face of the Ancient Orient*, Quadrangle Books, Chicago, 1960, chapters

2 and 3. George Contenau, *Everyday Life in Babylon and Assyria,* St. Martin's Press, Inc., New York, 1954. *Encyclopedia Americana,* New York, 1941, Vol. 13, pp. 666-668. *Ancient Near Eastern Texts,* Revised edition, Princeton University Press, Princeton, New Jersey, 1955. Jack Finegan, *Light from the Ancient Past,* Princeton University Press, Trenton, New Jersey, 1959. Albert T. Clay, *Light on Old Testament from Babel,* 2nd edition, Sunday School Times, Co., Philadelphia, Pa., 1907. Ira M. Price, *The Monuments and the Old Testament,* Revised and enlarged by O. R. Sellers and E. L. Carlson, Judson Press, Philadelphia, Pa., 1958. G. R. Driver and John C. Miles, *The Babylonian Laws,* Clarendon Press, Oxford, England, 1952. Cyrus Gordon, *Hammurabi's Code, Quaint or Forward Looking?* Rinehart, New York, 1957.

HANA, HANAEANS, *See* Terqa.

HANGING GARDENS. *See* Babylon.

HARAN, HARRAN. The modern village of Haran in southern Turkey occupies the southeastern corner of the site of ancient and medieval Haran, an important station on the routes from Mesopotamia to the Mediterranean (cf. Ezek. 27:23). It was also the midpoint in the migration of Terah and his family from Babylonia to Canaan.

I. *Name and Location.* Haran is located some ten miles north of the Berlin-Baghdad railway and, hence, of the Syrian border, at the confluence of two wadi's which in winter join the Balikh River just below its source. It is strategically located about half-way between °Gozan and Carchemish on the east-west road which links the Tigris and the Mediterranean, at the very point where the north-south route along the Balih links the Euphrates to Anatolia. It is thus the traditional crossroads of the major routes from Mesopotamia to the west and the northwest, and its very name implies as much in Akkadian (and Sumerian). *Harrānu* (and Sumerian *harran* means route, journey, caravan, etc., and some of the earliest references to the place write the name with the plural, "routes," or with the sign depicting a crossroads. The Biblical name Paddan-Aram (Gen. 25:20, etc.) "The Aramean Highway" seems to identify the same site by a synonym reflecting its later role as a center of Aramean settlement.

II. *Occupation and Exploration of the Site.* From its recorded beginnings to the present day, Haran has been continuously occupied, retaining its original name through the millennia. One cannot therefore speak of the

discovery of the site. Even its exploration has been limited by the extensive and important medieval remains covering the more ancient strata. Although several archaeologists and explorers from R. C. Chesney in 1850 to T. E. Lawrence in 1911 made their way to the rather inaccessible site, actual excavations did not begin until 1950, when Seton Lloyd surveyed the site for the Joint Anglo-Turkish Expedition of 1951-52. Even then, the principal finds of interest for the Biblical periods at Haran consisted of three neo-Babylonian steles reused as paving slabs for three different entrances to the Great Mosque of Haran (see Bibliography). They were discovered in 1956 by D. S. Rice whose subsequent death put a temporary halt to the excavations.

III. *History of the Site.*

A. Haran in the "Patriarchal Age." In 1959, a single sounding near the center of the great mound of Haran yielded some pottery of Middle Bronze I type, but for the rest of its history the archaeological record is unavailable and we must rely on the evidence of the written sources. They first mention Haran in a letter addressed to Yashmah-Adad, the Assyrian viceroy at °Mari (ca. 1790 B.C.). Another letter between two officials of King Zimri-Lim of Mari (*ca.* 1780-1759 B.C.) shows that Haran, in a period generally equated with the Patriarchal Age of Israel, was an important center of the semi-nomadic "Benjaminites." Specifically, it alerts the king of Mari to the conclusion of a formal alliance between Asditakim, who according to other, as yet unpublished, letters was then king of Haran and the (other) kings of Zalmaqum on the one hand and the sheikhs and elders of the "Benjaminites" on the other hand. This alliance was concluded in the temple of the moon god Sin at Haran. It thus shows that the cult of the moon god, well-known for Haran in later ages, goes back at least to the Old Babylonian period and, in addition, that it was the center or border of the land of Zalmaqum on the Upper Balih River. This country was the object of an extended campaign by Shamshi-Adad I of °Assyria (*ca.* 1815-1782 B.C.) and probably became subject to him together with Haran. But with his death the Old Assyrian empire broke up, Mari became independent again and in its struggles with the other great powers as

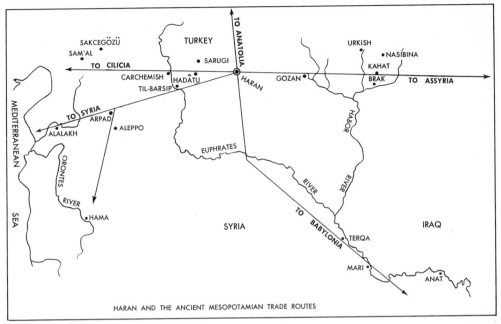

HARAN AND THE ANCIENT MESOPOTAMIAN TRADE ROUTES

well as with the nomads no doubt could not maintain its control over Haran. Nor did Hammurabi of Babylon (ca. 1792-1750 B.C.), who eventually emerged the victor from these struggles, claim the conquest of either Haran or Zalmaqum. It was thus, apparently, an independent principality at the very time when, we may suppose, the Biblical traditions reflect on the sojourn of Abraham and his family in the area (Gen. 11-25). These traditions also support the cuneiform evidence in at least two other ways: (1) the migration of Abraham's family parallels what appears to have been the movement of the Moon-cult from Ur to Haran, perhaps about the end of the neo-Sumerian period (ca. 2000 B.C.), and (2) the personal names of the patriarchs reflect the geographical names of the Haran area. Specifically Serug, the grandfather of Terah, may be compared with the town of Sarugi (modern Seruj) some thirty-five miles west of Haran and Nahor, his father (and second son) with the town of Nahur, probably located on the upper *Habor River, due east of Haran. Terah's own name has been identified with Til(-sha)-Turahi on the Balih south of Haran and his third son, Haran, recalls the name of Haran although the two names are spelled differently in Hebrew. At all events, the Mari letters document

a political, social, and economic state of affairs in the latitude of Haran which makes the settlement there of at least five generations of pastoral members of Abraham's family entirely plausible. Albright has further suggested that they took advantage of the strategic commercial position of Haran to engage in a far-flung trade based on donkey caravans (BASOR 163) in conjunction with Abraham and Lot, the son of his brother Nahor, who migrated onwards to Damascus, Canaan and Sinai.

B. Haran in the Late Second Millennium. Like the rest of Northern Mesopotamia, Haran enters a dark age during the late eighteenth century; in fact it is not mentioned in the cuneiform sources of the Mitannian period. But it probably belonged to that Hurrian state, since the moon god (Sin) of Haran (?) is invoked for *Mitanni in treaties with the *Hittites, and since Haran was captured along with other Mitannian centers when it is first heard of again in the fifteenth century. Nominally its conqueror is himself a Hurrian, Matiwaza, but in fact this son-in-law of *Suppiluliumas was no more than a pawn in the Hittite king's grand design; he conquered the legitimate Mitannian ruler, Shuttarna III, with the help of Suppiluliumas' son Piyashilli of *Carchemish and presently had to cede Haran and his other conquests west of the Habor River to the latter.

At Suppiluliumas' death many of the Hittite dependencies rose in revolt but his second son and successor, Murshilis II (*ca.* 1334-1306 B.C.), re-established the Hittite overlordship in most of them, including Haran. By this time, however, Assyria was again a force to be reckoned with in Northern Syria. The first mention of Haran in Middle Assyrian documents occurs under Adad-nirari I (*ca.* 1304-1273 B.C.), who briefly conquered the Hittite vassal-states as far as the Euphrates, and took the title of "king of the world" for himself. His son Shalmaneser I (*ca.* 1272-1243 B.C.) repeated these feats as did his grandson Tukulti-Ninurta I (*ca.* 1242-1206 B.C.) if we may believe the testimony of one of his descendants. But it is doubtful whether these were more than ephemeral conquests; they were directed as much at checking the newly entrenched waves of Aramean settlers who now began to make the region their own, as at completing the decay of Hurrian and Hittite authority in the area. For the latter, the real coup de grace came from another quarter, the invasions of the Sea Peoples (*ca.* 1200 B.C.), which shattered the Hittite empire in Anatolia and upset all the traditional balance of power in the Ancient Near East.

It was not till the end of the twelfth century that the Near East recovered from this blow. Like the rest of Northern Syria, Haran was now a center of Aramean settlement ruled by pretended or actual successors of the earlier Hittite royal houses. We do not, however, know of any of these rulers by name and in any case they must have often been virtual vassals of Assyria, at least in periods of Assyrian strength. Otherwise a ruler such as Tiglath-pileser I (*ca.* 1114-1076 B.C.) could hardly have hunted elephants in the area of Haran, as he reports. It is reasonable to suppose that he and his stronger successors laid the foundations of the concept of Haran as Assyrian crown land in the first millennium.

C. Haran and Assyrian Crown land. While it is uncertain precisely when Haran passed under direct Assyrian rule, it is clear that it was one of the first of the more distant provinces to do so, for it always enjoyed a special status within the empire; was loyal to the king when other provinces revolted;

never was the object of a recorded Assyrian campaign in the first millennium; and even harbored the last Assyrian defenders when the capital cities of the empire had already collapsed. The solicitude lavished on Haran by the Assyrian kings was probably due less to its religious importance (which admittedly goes back to Old Babylonian times at least, see above, III A) than to its strategic and commercial significance (see above, I).

"Westward the course of empire takes its way" might well have applied to Assyria in the tenth and ninth centuries B.C., when natural barriers and rival powers blocked all other directions. The Euphrates was the natural limit of these early conquests, as it had been in the second millennium, and Haran early became the administrative center of all the conquests on the Assyrian side of the river. Its governor was the *turtanu* (Hebrew *tartan*), the highest military commander in Assyria, who ranked second only to the king in the eponym lists. As early as 814 we know one of them, Belu-balaṭ, by name, and their influence grew with their province. This system was, however, fraught with danger, for in a period of Assyrian weakness such as the early eighth century, the turtanu's at Haran could rival the king at Calah himself, and at least one of them, Shamshi-ilu, ruled the area and much of the Assyrian empire besides in virtual independence (*see* Til-Barsib III D) between *ca.* 780 and 750 B.C. To prevent such situations, Tiglath-pileser III broke up the largest provinces into smaller enclaves shortly after his accession in 745 B.C., and Haran, though it remained the responsibility of the turtanu, was particularly reduced in size. (The Septuagint seems to preserve a memory of this event in Amos 1:15, where it reads Haran for Beth-Eden). Haran apparently did not take kindly to this demotion, which must have been adhered to also by Shalmaneser V, Tiglath-pileser's successor. These two kings formed a separate and perhaps not altogether legitimate dynasty in the native view, and the entrenched Assyrian nobility at Haran seems to have joined that of Ashur in the upheavals which installed Sargon II (literally, "the legitimate king") in 722 B.C. At any rate both cities were rewarded by the new monarch with special charter restoring their ancient privileges. After 686 B.C., the offices of *turtanu* and governor of Haran seem to have been separated, but this did not imply a further demotion, and the Assyrian kings' loyalty to the cult of Sin at Haran is both attested and rewarded by an oracular vision which encouraged Esarhaddon to proceed to the conquest of Egypt (*ca.* 673 B.C. cf. *ANET* p. 450). Ashurbanipal (668-623 B.C.) dutifully restored Sin's temple Ehulhul, and a kind of census of the province which has been compared to the Doomsday Book of Medieval England (see Bibliography) gives us a unique insight into the social and economic conditions of the whole area around Haran at this time. The cultural life of Haran also flourished during the seventh century; although we have no literary texts from the site, the impressive private library of an Assyrian priest discovered at Sultan Tepe, some fifteen miles to the north, shows signs of dependence on a larger school at Haran. Indeed, Haran even outlived the destruction of the great capital cities of Assyria in 614-612 B.C., for it was here that the last king of Assyria, Ashur-uballit II, made a last desperate attempt to save and restore the empire, and it was not until he fled Haran in 610 B.C. that the city was sacked and occupied by the Medes and the fate of Assyria finally sealed.

D. Haran after the Assyrians. Virtually alone among the great Assyrian strongholds, Haran recovered its glory under the neo-Babylonias and survived for many centuries thereafter as the center of successive forms of the worship of Sin the moon-god. Sin was particularly venerated by the pious Nabonidus, son and successor of Nebuchadnezzar II. To the chagrin of the old priests of Marduk at Babylon, he singled out the centers of moon-worship at Ur in Babylonia, Haran in northern Mesopotamia and the oasis Teima in Arabia for his particular attention. His own mother, Adad-guppi, served as high-priestess of Sin during most of her long life of 104 years, and in her own inscriptions as well as that of her son recorded the history of this momentous century. According to them, Haran lay desolate (i.e., in the possession of the Medes) for fifty-four years (610-556 B.C.) until, at the very beginning of the reign of Nabonidus (555-539 B.C.), a vision informed the new king, in words strangely reminiscent of Isaiah 44:28—45:1, that Marduk would raise up "his young ser-

vant" Cyrus to scatter the Medes. Some time thereafter, Nabonidus accordingly rebuilt Ehulhul and reconsecrated Haran to the worship of Sin. This role it retained after the fall of the neo-Babylonian empire as well. Celebrated as the Carrhae where Crassus met his death (54 B.C.) at the hands of the Parthians, Haran was successively ruled by Zoroastrians, (Nestorian) Christians, Moslems and Crusaders, but never ceased to perpetuate its old Assyrian cults, especially under the Sabeans (*ca.* ninth century A.D.), a peculiar sect of moon-worshippers, sometimes known simply as Harranians. Thus, after a fashion, Mesopotamian traditions survived at Haran longer than anywhere else.

BIBLIOGRAPHY. C. H. W. Johns, An Assyrian Doomsday Book (= *Assyriologische Bibliothek,* XVII), Leipzig, J. C. Hinrichs, 1901. William F. Albright, "The role of the postdiluvian patriarchs in Hebrew history," *JBL,* XLIII, 1924, pp. 385-393. Georges Dossin, "Benjaminites dans les textes de Mari," *Melanges Syriens . . . Dussaud = Bibliothèque Archéologique et Historique,* XXX, 1939, pp. 981-996. Julius Lewy, "The late Assyro-Babylonian Cult of the Moon . . .," *HUCA,* XIX, 1946, pp. 405-489. Roger T. O'Callaghan, *Aram Naharaim = Analecta Orientalia,* XXVI, 1948. Seton Lloyd and William Brice, "Harran," *Anatolian Studies,* I, 1951, pp. 77-111. D. S. Rice, "Medieval Harran," *ibid.,* II 1952, pp. 36-84. C. J. Gadd, "The Harran Inscriptions of Nabonidus," *ibid.,* VIII, 1958, pp. 35-92 and pls. i-xvi.

HASIDIM. *See* Jewish Sects.

HATTINA. *See* Tell Ta'yinat.

HATTUSAS. *See* Boghazkoy.

HAZOR. The most powerful Canaanite center in Upper Galilee at the time of Joshua was Hazor, a short distance southwest of Lake Huleh. The *Amarna letters indicate a rivalry during the fourteenth century B.C. between the king of Hazor and the king of Tyre. At the time of Joshua, Jabin of Hazor organized a coalition of Canaanite rulers to prevent Israel from expanding into northern Palestine (Josh. 11:1-5). Joshua surprised his foes at the waters of Merom (Josh. 11:7), once identified with Lake Huleh, north of the Sea of Galilee, but now more plausibly associated with the springs which flow southward by the village of Meiron west of Safed. The battle turned into a rout as the Canaanites fled northwestward toward the Phoenician coastal cities. Thereupon, "Joshua turned back . . .

and took Hazor and smote its king with the sword" (Josh. 11:10). The city was destroyed by Joshua, but it was evidently rebuilt soon afterward for another Jabin of Hazor oppressed Israel during the period of the Judges (Judg. 4:2). This time Hazor appears to have been permanently crushed (Judg. 4, 5), for it was incorporated into the tribe of Naphtali and was fortified by Solomon (I Kings 9:15).

Located in the far northern part of Israel, Hazor was exposed to dangers of invasion and, during the eighth century B.C., Tiglath-pileser III of Assyria conquered the city (II Kings 15:29). Its inhabitants were taken into exile and the city never regained its earlier importance.

The site of Hazor was identified by John Garstang with the mound known as Tell el-Qedah, five miles southwest of Lake Huleh, during a trial dig in 1926. Garstang returned to Tell el-Qedah in 1928, but the major archaeological undertaking there began in 1955 when Yigael Yadin conducted the first of a series of excavations for the James A. de Rothschild-Hebrew University Archaeological Expedition. The mound was one of the most impressive in Palestine covering twenty-five acres and reaching a height of one hundred thirty feet.

Yadin set out to locate the boundaries of ancient Hazor, to investigate the levels of occupancy, to fix the dates of the final destruction of the city, and to learn all that could be learned about the social, economic, political, and military history of Hazor. Before the excavation began, there was ample evidence that Hazor was one of the great cities of the past. It is mentioned in Egyptian *Execration Texts written about 1900 B.C. which list potential enemies of the Egyptian Empire among the provinces. Several letters from Mari (*Tell Hariri*) on the Middle Euphrates (*ca.* 1700 B.C.) mention Hazor. Somewhat later, we read of ambassadors who journeyed from Babylon to Hazor to see its king.

During the fifteenth and fourteenth centuries, Hazor was incorporated into the Egyptian Empire, and it is mentioned among the cities conquered by Pharaohs Thutmose III, Amenhotep II, and Seti I. Four of the Amarna letters mention Hazor, and it also is mentioned in the famous papyrus from thirteenth century Egypt known as Papyrus Anastasi I.

The excavators worked at two distinct places in the vicinity of Hazor. The first was the bottle-shaped tell itself, and the second was a rectangular plateau immediately to the north of the mound. Excavations began on the mound proper near a row

EXCAVATIONS AT HAZOR lead by Yigael Yadin, indicate that the city once had 40,000 inhabitants. Courtesy, Consulate General of Israel

of columns discovered by John Garstang in 1928. During 1955, Yadin uncovered four strata, the topmost of which proved to be the remains of a humble settlement of the late eighth and early seventh centuries B.C. The second level appears to have been that of the Israelite city destroyed by Tiglath-pileser III in 732 B.C. It contained beautiful basalt and pottery vessels, along with loom weights and other handicraft tools. Many were intact and in their original positions, suggesting that the population fled in haste and did not return. One interesting object from the third level (eighth and ninth centuries B.C.) was a handle of a mirror or a scepter made of bone depicting a winged deity grasping a "Tree of Life" of a type known from Phoenicia. The fourth level is from the period of Ahab (874-852 B.C.). Its most imposing structure was a public building, about forty-nine by sixty-six feet, containing two rows of stone columns, nine pillars to the row, each six and one-half feet high. Most were still intact.

The rectangular enclosure to the north yielded remains of a well-built city which was destroyed during the thirteenth century and never again occupied. Floors of the houses were littered with Mycenaean pottery from the Late Bronze Age. Two small Canaanite temples were also discovered on successive levels from the fourteenth and thirteenth centuries. One of them contained a sculptured male figure in basalt, seated on a throne in a central niche high above the floor. He holds a cup, and to the left is a basalt stele, the middle one depicting two hands outstretched in prayer, surmounted by a sun disk within a crescent. At the end of the row is a basalt orthostat bearing a sculpture of the head and forelegs of a lion on its narrow side, and a relief of a crouching lion with tail between its legs on its wide side. These are representative of the religion and art of Hazor before the conquest.

Excavations at the central and eastern parts of the enclosure revealed thirteenth century buildings constructed on the ruins of earlier cities, the oldest dating back to the Hyksos period (eighteenth century B.C.). A Middle Bronze Age cemetery had rock-hewn tombs with pottery and scarabs near the skeletons. Two furnaces were discovered, one of which served to smelt metals and the other, probably, was used as a kiln for pottery. Three late Bronze Age arrowheads were found in an excellent state of preservation. Most exciting of all was a small fragment of a thirteenth century jar bearing two letters of the so-called Proto-Sinaitic *alphabet, the predecessor of the

Old Hebrew script. This is the first instance of the use of this script in Galilee. The excavations indicate that Canaanite Hazor was one of the greatest cities in Canaan. Its population has been estimated at forty thousand.

HEBRON. Hebron, nineteen miles southwest of Jerusalem, is 3,040 feet above sea level, the highest town in Palestine. It was known to the Biblical patriarchs as Kirjath-Arba, "tetrapolis." Abraham spent much of his time in the vicinity of Hebron and purchased his family burial plot from a Hittite chieftain named Ephron, who lived nearby.

At the time of Joshua's invasion, Hebron was allied with Adonizedek of Jerusalem in an attempt to halt the Israelite advance (Josh. 10:1-27). After Joshua's death, Caleb succeeded in conquering the Hebron region from the Anakim (Num. 13:22, 28, 33).

David ruled as king of Judah from Hebron for seven and a half years before moving his capital to Jerusalem farther north. Absalom was born in Hebron, and when he revolted against his father David, he attempted to set up headquarters there (II Sam. 15:7-10).

Hebron did not occupy an important place in later Old Testament history, and it is not mentioned in the New Testament. Hebron seems to have been a royal pottery during the eighth century B.C., for numerous jar handles have been found throughout Palestine bearing the inscription "Belonging to the King: Hebron."

Following the Exile, Jews resettled in Hebron (Neh. 11:25) but in subsequent years the Idumeans pushed northward as far as Hebron when their homeland south of the Dead Sea was taken by the Nabataean Arabs. During the Maccabean wars, Hebron was conquered by the Jews (164 B.C.), and in subsequent years, buildings were erected at the traditional site of the Cave of Machpelah and at Mamre.

HELIOPOLIS. When Midianite traders brought the slave Joseph to Egypt, they sold him to an officer of the Pharaoh, who bore the name Potiphar (Gen. 37:36). Potiphar's name means, "The gift of Re," the Egyptian sun god whose worship centered in On, a city known to the Greeks as Heliopolis, "The City of the Sun." A variant of the name Potiphar is Potiphera, the name of the priest of On who gave his daughter Asenath in marriage to Joseph (Gen. 41:45).

A VIEW OF HEBRON. A mosque within the city, The Mosque Al-Haram Al-Ibrahimi, encloses the traditional site of Machpelah, where Abraham, Sarah, Isaac, Rebekah, Leah, and Jacob were buried. Courtesy, Jordan Tourist Department

On was sometimes given the fuller name On-mehit, "the northern On," to distinguish it from a southern On which the Greeks called Hermonthis. Jeremiah (43:13) uses the Semitic name Beth-Shemesh ("House of the Sun") in referring to Heliopolis.

Modern Heliopolis is located about seven miles northeast of the center of Cairo, not far from the airport. There are few ancient remains, and "the city of the sun" is now a fashionable suburb. Tradition says that the Holy Family sojourned at Heliopolis following the flight into Egypt (Matt. 2:13-14). The visitor may still see the so-called Virgin's tree and the well where Mary and the infant Jesus are said to have refreshed themselves during their sojourn. Actually the Sycamore tree which supposedly shaded Mary was planted during the seventeenth century, and the Virgin's Well was associated in pre-Christian times with the worship of the sun god, to whom Heliopolis was dedicated. Christian legend says that the child Jesus miraculously created the well after which his mother, Mary, washed his garments in it. A much older Egyptian legend states that the sun god bathed his face in the well when he rose upon earth for the first time.

About 730 B.C. a Sudanese (Cushite) warrior named Pi'ankhy marched northward from Napata, his capital, and gained control of Egypt. The Libyan dynasties which preceded him had left the nation in disunion and disorder so that Pi'ankhy met no united resistance. After bringing local rulers into subjection, he made a pilgrimage to Heliopolis where, in the words of his commemorative stele, "His purification was performed, and he was cleansed in the pool of Kebeh, and he bathed his face in the river of Nun, in which Re bathes his face." The legend of the river of Nun reflects the Egyptian concept of a primeval chaos from which the sun is said to have emerged. This legend was embellished in Christian times and applied to Christ. We are told that all the idols of Heliopolis fell upon their faces before the Virgin and her child.

Of the ancient splendor of Heliopolis nothing remains above ground except a granite obelisk erected to celebrate the jubilee of a Pharaoh of the twentieth century before Christ. Originally this obelisk marked the entrance to the great temple at Heliopolis which was second in size to that of Amun at *Thebes. It was in this Heliopolis temple that Potiphera, Joseph's father-in-law, functioned as a priest of Re.

During Egypt's New Kingdom, Pharaoh Thutmose III erected several obelisks at Heliopolis. Two were taken to Alexandria by the Roman prefect Barbarus in 23 B.C. One of these was knocked down during the earthquake of 1301. Mohammed Ali, Egyptian governor from 1805 to 1849, presented this fallen obelisk to the British who did nothing with it until 1877 when Erasmus Wilson paid John Wayman Dixon, an engineer, to move it to the Thames embankment in London. The second obelisk was taken to New York by Lieutenant Commander H. H. Corringe of the United States Navy, and it is now located in Central Park. Incongruously, these obelisks are popularly known as Cleopatra's needles. Actually they were carved a millennium before the time of Cleopatra. In 1912, while excavating at Heliopolis for the British School of Archaeology, Flinders Petrie and R. Engelbach discovered fragments of another obelisk. These were removed to the Cairo Museum.

Throughout Egyptian history, Heliopolis was noted both for its magnificent temple and for the wisdom of its priests. During the fifth century B.C., the Greek historian Herodotus visited Heliopolis and learned much from the priests there. He writes, "I went to Heliopolis . . . for the Heliopolitans are esteemed the most learned of all the Egyptians" (*Histories* ii.3). A tradition which has no basis in fact, but illustrates the reputation of Heliopolis, states that the philosopher Plato studied there for thirteen years.

HERODIAN TOMBS. Beyond the King David Hotel in Israeli Jerusalem are the remains of an ancient mausoleum built of large stones. Beside the mausoleum is a cave, in front of which is a large rolling stone which was used to block the burial place (cf. Luke 24:2). Josephus in his *Wars of the Jews* mentions a monument to Herod which may be identified with the cave. Members of the Herodian family were buried there, although Herod himself was buried at *Herodium, near Bethlehem.

HERODIUM. Herodium, located south of Jerusalem at a distance of 7½ miles (2½

ROLLING STONE SEALING "HEROD'S FAMILY TOMB" in Jerusalem. Courtesy, Gerald Larue

miles to the southeast of Bethlehem), is the burial place of Herod the Great (Matt. 2:20). Here on a mountain-top, Herod began construction of a palace-fortress-mausoleum around 24 B.C., the year of his 50th birthday. Most of the work on the palace complex must have been completed by 15 B.C. since Herod showed the place to his friend Agrippa in that year (*Ant.* XV. ix. 4). Early in his career (40 B.C.) Herod had defeated his Parthian enemies at this spot (cf. *Wars* I. xiii, 8), a fact which explains his desire to build here a monument to his name.

Around the base (2082 ft. high) of Mt. Herodium (2489 ft. high) on which one of Herod's palaces was located (he also had palaces at Caesarea, Machaerus, Masada, Jerusalem, Jericho, Samaria, etc.), there were various apartments, public buildings, granaries and fountains which served various administrative and aesthetic functions. Water had to be supplied to Herodium via an aqueduct which came down from Artas, remains of which are still visible. As Josephus notes:

> When this wedding was over (Herod's marriage, *ca.* 25/24 B.C., to Mariamme II), he built another citadel in that place where he had conquered the Jews when he was driven

out of his government, and Antigonus enjoyed it. This citadel (that is, Herodium) is distant from Jerusalem about three score furlongs (Gk. — "*stadia*"). It was strong by nature, and fit for such a building. It is a sort of moderate hill, raised to a further height by the hand of man, till it was of the shape of a woman's breast. It is encompassed with circular towers, and hath a straight ascent up to it which ascent is composed of steps of polished stone in number two hundred. Within it are royal and very rich apartments, of a structure that provided both for security and for beauty. About the bottom there are habitations of such a structure as are well worth seeing, both on other accounts, and also on account of the water which is brought thither from a great way off, and at vast expenses, for the place itself is destitute of water. The plain that is about this citadel is full of edifices, not inferior to any city in largeness, and having the hill above it in the nature of a castle (*Ant.* XV. ix. 4.).

Besides Herodium, Herod had a number of mountain-top fortresses spread over his territories (Alexandrium, Hyrcania, etc.). This enabled him to keep in touch with important events in his kingdom by means of signal fires, an ancient method of communication used in the Near East as early as the eighteenth century B.C., as we learn from the Mari Texts (cf. George Dossin, "Signaux lumineux au pays de Mari," *Revue d'Assyriologie* 35, 1938, 174-186).

I. *Archaeological Work at Herodium.* For approximately one hundred years archaeologists have expressed the hope that Herodium would be excavated. De Saulcy wanted to excavate it and expressed his intention to do so (see L. F. J. C. de Saulcy, *Histoire d'Herod*, Paris, Librairie de L. Hachette et Cie., 1867, p. 378). Watzinger also noted: "An archaeological exploration of the buildings of Herod [at Herodium] would not only clarify certain problems of ancient art history, but also would enable us for the first time to arrange a working, effective picture of the environment in which Jesus grew up and taught" (cf. Carl Watzinger, *Denkmaler Palastinas*, Leipzig, J. C. Hinrichs'sche Buchandlung, 1935, II, 56).

Watzinger, as is now known, was too optimistic in this opinion. For, starting in the summer of 1962, excavations have now been carried out at Herodium by an Italian expedition under Vergilio Corbo. (The 1962 and 1963 seasons represented the work done t the time of this writing.) Yet, the picture f the first century, which was once hoped or, was distorted somewhat by later occu-ants of the site. For, as the recent Dead ea Scroll material from Murabba'at informs s, Ben Koseba also used Herodium's installa-ions for collecting grain for his forces. The ollowing text is typical of a whole series of ew documents which tell us of Ben Kose-a's activities:

The twentieth of Shebat, year two, of the freedom of Israel by Simeon, son of Koseba, the prince of Israel. In the camp which is at *Herodium*, Eleazar, son of the Shilonite (i.e., one from Shiloh), declares to Hillel, son of Garis, 'I, of my own free will, have taken a farm-lease from your part, a parcel of land which becomes mine for the right of farming, and it is found at Ir Nahash. I have taken it in lease from the part of Simeon, the prince of Israel, for five years. (If the aforementioned land is not cultivated . . . it will be returned and lost) completely. I have taken it in lease from your part this day until the end of the eve of the year of Release. The rent I shall pay you here, each year, in grain of good quality and pure: four kor and eight seah, which are to be submitted for the "tenth" (religious tithe?) . . . after you have deducted the "tenth" (a rent levy?) which you shall send to the treasury at *Herodium* each year. This document is valid and binds me accord-ing to its terms.' Eleazar, son of the Shilonite, by himself; Simeon, son of Koseba, by his order. (Murabba'at 24B).

Milik's translation has been corrected here in the light of Y. Yadin's observations on this passage. Cf. J. T. Milik in P. Benoit, J. T. Milik and R. DeVaux, *Discoveries in the Judean Desert II, Les Grottes de Mur-abba'at,* Oxford: Clarendon Press, 1961, p. 125; Y. Yadin, "Were the Headquarters of Bar-Kokhba at Herodium?" (in Hebrew), *Ha'aretz,* Tel Aviv, March 10, 1961, p. 10, cf. also *I.E.J.* 11, 1961, 51, 52.

Corbo's excavations have also revealed that the site was inhabited again in the Byzantine period (fifth century) by a group of Chris-tians.

As far as the New Testament period it-self, the excavations not only revealed the damage done to the walls of Herodium by the powerful Roman siege machines (*ball-istae*) but several Greek and Hebrew ostraca (not yet published) arrowheads, and artisti-cally-moulded wall plaster decorations have been uncovered. This must be what Jose-phus had in mind when he spoke of the "more elaborate embellishment" of this "Ju-dean" Herodium. A well-planned Roman bath system with an apodyterium (dressing-room), a frigidarium (cold bath) and a tepidarium was also revealed. Evidence that Herodium was occupied by Ben Koseba's troops also came to light, as would be ex-pected by the document quoted above. (For Corbo's reports, see "Gebal Fureidis: Risul-tati della prima campagna di scavi all' Hero-dion", *La Terra Santa,* Agosto, Settembre, Ottobre, 1962, p. 231-235. See also *Liber Annuus,* 1962-63.

II. *Herod's Tomb at Herodium.* The tomb of Herod has not been discovered as yet at Herodium. Until recently, most schol-ars have been of the opinion that the tomb would have been located inside the palace proper on top of the mountain (cf. C. Schick, "Der Frankenberg," *Z-DPV,* 1880, pp. 88-99. De Saulcy conjectured that it was on the island in the midst of the pool or in nearby caves (*op. cit.,* pp. 374ff.). The question must still remain open. From Josephus, how-ever, we have some evidence as to the type of tomb in which Herod must have been buried. Rather than following the custom of the common people who gathered the bones of their dead and deposited them in small ossuaries after the flesh had decom-posed, Herod was more likely buried in a full-size coffin, which was more appropriate for royalty (like Helen of Adiabene, whose tomb chamber L. F. J. C. de Saulcy discov-ered). This probability becomes almost a certainty when it is remembered that Herod had a supply of such full-size coffins on hand in his palace at Jerusalem (cf. *Ant.* XV. iii.2 — which informs us that Alexandra and Aristobulus sought to escape from Her-od's palace by concealing themselves in sar-cophagi of this type).

HEZEKIAH'S TUNNEL. *See* Siloam In-scription.

HIERATIC. *See* Writing.

HIEROGLYPHS. *See* Alphabet, Writing.

HIGH PLACE. In ancient Canaan the High Place was the usual place of worship. Near each village, and sometimes within the cities (cf. Jer. 7:23; 19:6; Ezra 6:3) were such sanctuaries equipped with an altar, stone pillars or *maṣṣebot* which served as male cult objects, and *asherim* female cult objects in the form of wooden poles. A basin was provided for ceremonial washings. Some high places possessed special objects such as the golden calves set up by Jeroboam, an ephod, or an ark. These would require a temple for shelter. At Shiloh such a structure, termed the "house of God," was erected as a shrine for the ark of the covenant (I Sam. 1:9; 3:3).

The High Place was a place of sacrifice. In the earliest times each worshiper officiated at his own sacrifice, but later an order of priests was appointed. With the establishment of the temple in Jerusalem, the High Places were looked upon as illegitimate worship centers (cf. II Kings 23:4-20). The tendency to associate them with the worship of *Baal and the other Canaanite deities brought them into disfavor with the Israelite prophets. The central shrine at Jerusalem served as an object lesson in the unity of Yahweh, whereas the proliferation of High Places tended to encourage the concept of localized deities.

HIRAM. Hiram, king of *Tyre, came to the throne about 978 B.C. and became its most energetic ruler. He reclaimed land to the east of the principal island belonging to Tyre, improved the harbor and fortifications of the city, and rebuilt and beautified its Temples.

Hiram provided cedars from Lebanon and carpenters and masons from Tyre to build a palace for David (II Sam. 5:11, 12). In building his Temple, Solomon needed wood, gold, and a variety of artisans. Hiram provided these in exchange for agricultural products and land (I Kings 5:1-12; 7:13, 14). Twenty towns in Galilee were given in exchange for gold, but Hiram was not pleased with them (I Kings 9:10-14).

Solomon and Hiram co-operated in the building of a fleet of merchant ships to sail from *Ezion-geber. Tyrians had developed trade throughout the eastern Mediterranean, so they were in a position to help Solomon. By developing fresh routes to the south in co-operation with Solomon they gained access to products in southern Arabia and Africa (I Kings 9:25-28).

HITTITES. A people called "Hittites" has been known throughout the Christian era from the Old Testament, but most of the biblical references to them indicate nothing more than an insignificant ethnic group living in central Palestine (Gen. 15:19-21; Josh. 3:10; Num. 13:29). Only a very few passages suggested something more. Solomon's Hittite wives (I Kings 11:1) were foreigners of some consequence. Solomon sold horses to the kings of the Hittites and Arameans (II Chron. 1:17). A Syrian army was terrified, because they believed that Jehoram of Israel had hired against them the kings of the Hittites and Egyptians (II Kings 7:6-7). In the mid-nineteenth century the historical records of the Egyptians and Assyrians were carefully studied, and references to the mighty people of Hatti were found. In the 1870's basalt stones inscribed with strange hieroglyphs were found at Hamath and Aleppo in North Syria. A. H. Sayce attributed them to the Hittites. In the years which followed monuments inscribed with the same script and pictures cut in low relief were observed all over Asia Minor, but especially concentrated within the bend of the Halys River near the modern village of *Boghazköy. Excavations were begun at Boghazköy itself in 1906 by the German Orient Society under the direction of Hugo Winckler. Over ten thousand clay tablets unearthed at the site (many in the well-known Akkadian language of Babylonia) confirmed that this mound was indeed the site of ancient Hattusa, capital of the "Land of Hatti." The language of the Hittites, suspected as being Indo-European already by Knudtzon in 1902 on the basis of the letters from Arzawa in the *Amarna collection, was conclusively deciphered, identified as Indo-European, and presented in grammatical outline by a Czech named Hrozny in 1915. Hittite cuneiform texts began to be published in facsimile, and in the decades which followed a dedicated group of scholars (among them Hrozny, F. Sommer, H. Ehelolf, J. Friedrich, and A. Goetze) advanced the study of Hittite grammar and lexicography rapidly. Today the efforts of these scholars and others such as H. Güterbock, E. Laroche, and H. Otten have been incorporated in the standard Hittite grammars and lexicons (cf. Bibliography). Excavations have continued at Boghazköy under the auspices of the German Orient Society down to the present with brief interruptions during war years. In recent years excavations have been directed by Kurt Bittel and Heinrich Otten.

I. *History.*

A. Chronology. One's views on the absolute chronology of Anatolian (esp. Hittite) history will depend upon which of the three principal chronological schemes for the second millennium B.C. he holds. Generally speaking, Hittitologists prefer one of the two "higher" chronologies (that of Sidney Smith adopted by the New *Cambridge Ancient History,* or that of A. Goetze), because the lower chronology of W. F. Albright leaves little room for the reigns of many of the early Hittite kings. This sketch follows Smith's chronology.

B. Pre-Hittite Anatolia. If we date the arrival of the Luwians in western Asia Minor *ca.* 2300 B.C. (J. Mellaart in *CAH,* Vol. I, chap. XVIII) and that of the "Nesite" (Hittite-proper) group in eastern and central Asia Minor *ca.* 2000 B.C., we must conclude that the history of "pre-Hittite" Anatolia is to be reconstructed from non-literary remains. Principal sites from which archaeologists reconstruct the cultures of Neolithic and Chalcolithic Anatolia are Mersin, Tarsus, and Sakcegözü in the south; Beycesultan, Kumtepe, and Poliochni in the west;

and Alishar, Alaça Hüyük, and Büyük Güllücek in north-central Anatolia. The Early Bronze Age in Anatolia, which stretches from *ca.* 3500 (Mellaart) down to *ca.* 2000 B.C., is best represented in the following sites: Troy (Levels I-V), Yortan, Kusura, and Beycesultan in the west; Mersin and Tarsus in south-central; and Alishar and Alaça Hüyük in north-central Anatolia. It is to this period (*ca.* 2500 B.C.), roughly contemporary with the flowering of Sumerian culture in southern Mesopotamia, that the famous "royal tombs" of Alaça Hüyük belong.

C. Assyrian Colonies (*ca.* 1900-1750 B.C.). The first indications of the presence of Luwians in western Anatolia are the destruction levels found on many sites datable to *ca.* 2300 B.C. The first indications of the presence of Hittites (Nesites) in north-central Anatolia are Hittite personal names in the documents from the Old Assyrian trading colonies in the Cappadocian area. Although small colonies were spread all over eastern Anatolia and northern Syria, the principal Cappadocian colony was ancient Kanesh (modern Kültepe), also called Nesa by the Hittites. During the century and a half of Assyrian commercial activity in these colonies a number of kings ruled successively over Assyria, the most important of whom

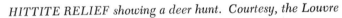

HITTITE RELIEF showing a deer hunt. Courtesy, the Louvre

were Erishum I and Sargon I. The decline and fall of the colonies in Asia Minor coincided with the emerging of the Hittite Old Kingdom and the eclipse of Assyria in its homeland by the first dynasty of Babylon.

D. The Hittite Old Kingdom (ca. 1680-1460 B.C.).

1. Old Kingdom Rulers.

Labarnas I - - -	1680-1650
Hattusilis I - - -	1650-1620
Mursilis I - - - -	1620-1590
Hantilis I - - - -	1590-1560
Zidantas I - - - -	1560-1550
Ammunas - - - -	1550-1530
Huzziyas I - - - -	1530-1525
Telipinus - - - -	1525-1500
Alluwamnas - - -	1500-1490
Hantilis II - - - -	1490-1480
Zidantas II - - - -	1480-1470
Huzziyas II - - -	1470-1460

2. Important Rulers and Their Accomplishments. Hattusilis I was the first Hittite king to lead his armies through the mountain passes of the Taurus into northern Syria. Early in his reign he subdued the North Syrian cities of *Alalakh and Urshu. But preoccupation with matters in western Anatolia (the kingdom of Arzawa) loosened his hold on the Syrian possessions. Hurrians from Hanigalbat invaded the Hittite homeland, while the king was in the west, and wrested every important city from him but Hattusa itself. The task of retaking the lost territory occupied Hattusilis throughout the rest of his reign. Eventually he managed to campaign again in the southeast, capturing Hashshu and Urshu, and defeating but not capturing Aleppo. It was at the beginning of Hattusilis' reign that the capital was moved from Kussara to Hattusas, whence the king derived his name Hattusilis.

Mursilis I was a vigorous leader and a worthy successor to his grandfather. He led the Hittite army down the Euphrates to conquer Aleppo, destroy *Mari, and plunder and sack Babylon itself (then ruled by Samsu-ditana, last of the Amorite rulers of the Hammurabi dynasty). According to the Smith chronology, the sack of Babylon by Mursilis took place ca. 1590. But certain rebellious elements in the homeland led by Hantilis, Mursilis' brother-in-law, were preparing a coup. When Mursilis returned victorious, he was assassinated. Mursilis' blood brought nothing but evil on the heads of his successors. During the reigns of the four kings between Mursilis and Telipinus the kingdom tottered and almost collapsed, for dissension and murder within the royal family were sapping away the kingdom's strength.

It was not until the accession of Telipinus (ca. 1525) that something was done to stabilize royal succession. Telipinus secured for the king the right to pass on his crown to an heir without interference from the council of nobles (the pankus). It is probable that during his reign important work was accomplished on the official collection of laws. He pushed back the barbarian Gasga tribes to a safe distance north and east of Hattusas, but realistically accepted the loss of Arzawa in the southwest and North Syria in the southeast. He is the first Hittite king whom we know to have made a treaty with a foreign power (with Isputahsu of Kizzuwatna).

E. The Hittite Empire (ca. 1460-1190 B.C.

1. New Kingdom (Empire) Rulers.

Tudhaliyas II - - -	1460-1440
Arnuwandas I - - -	1440-1420
Hattusilis II - - -	1420-1400
Tudhaliyas III - - -	1400-1380
Suppiluliumas - - -	1380-1340
Arnuwandas II - -	1340-1339
Mursilis II - - - -	1339-1306
Muwatallis - - - -	1306-1282
Urhi-Teshub (Mursilis III) -	1282-1275
Hattusilis III - - -	1275-1250
Tudhaliyas IV - - -	1250-1220
Arnuwandas II - -	1220-1190
Suppiluliumas II - -	1190-?

2. Important Rulers and Their Accomplishments. Revival of Hittite expansion began with Tudhaliyas II, who in cooperation with Thutmose III of Egypt, destroyed Aleppo ca. 1457. During the years that followed, however, the power of the Hurrian kingdom of Mitanni increased in Syria. In the west also the Luwian kingdom of Arzawa revived at the expense of the Hittites.

Perhaps the greatest, and certainly the most famous of the Hittite kings was *Suppiluliumas (ca. 1380-1340 B.C.). It was he who was responsible for the destruction of the great kingdom of *Mitanni and the annexation of most of the great cities of Syria as vassals. In his first attempt to invade North Syria over the Taurus passes, he was repulsed and defeated by the armies of Tushratta of Mitanni. Undaunted he planned a more circuitous approach. Reducing the North Anatolian tribes to submission, he crossed the upper Euphrates near Malatya and took Isuwa. Proceeding southward, he conquered Wassukkanni, Tushratta's capital and re-crossed the Euphrates into North Syria. Kadesh, Aleppo, Alalakh, Nuhasse, and Amurru soon came to terms. Only Carchemish and Ashtata in North Syria remained loyal to Tushratta. But now a rebellious faction in Mitanni assassinated Tushratta, and within eight days Suppiluliumas brought Carchemish to her knees, installing as governor over her his son Piyassilis (known also by his Hurrian name Sharrikushukh). Suppiluliumas bound all of these newly acquired vassal states to himself by treaty. Such treaties (called suzerainty treaties) were the foundation of Hittite foreign policy.

During the reign of Mursilis II there was little change in the territory of the realm. Kizzuwatna (Cilicia) apparently became a Hittite province during his reign, and Haremhab of Egypt continually agitated the vassals in Syria. But the great contest between Egypt and Hatti came during the reign of Muwatallis (*ca.* 1306-1282 B.C.). In 1268/5 Ramesses II of Egypt joined battle with the Hittite allied armies at Kadesh. Both sides claimed victory, but Muwatallis retained Syria and added Abina (Biblical Hobah) to his possessions.

Muwatallis was succeeded by an incompetent, Urhi-Teshub, who took the throne name Mursilis III. He ruled seven years and was driven from the throne by his uncle Hattusilis, who banished him first to Nuhasse in Syria and later to Alashiya (Cyprus). Growing pressure from the young Assyrian state forced Hattusilis into a treaty with Ramesses II, the latter receiving a Hittite princess in marriage (*ca.* 1286).

Tudhaliyas IV campaigned some in the west, annexing the land of Assuwa (the later Roman province of Asia). In his days the king of Ahhiyawa (possibly an Achean ruler) began to harrass the western possessions. The situation rapidly deteriorated for the Hittites. When Suppiluliumas II came to the throne (*ca.* 1190?), the days of the Hittite empire in Asia Minor were numbered. During his reign the Hittites waged two victorious sea battles with Alashiya, during which the Hittite

STELE OF THE HITTITE STORM GOD TESHUB. Courtesy, Aleppo Museum

sailors burned and sank the Alashiyan ships at sea. But the end came soon, and in Asia Minor Phrygian invaders soon replaced the Hittites as the dominant power. The North Syrian city-states became heirs to the culture of the Anatolian Hittites. Among these "neo-Hittite" states were Tabal (Biblical Tubal), Kammanu, Gugum, Arpad, Sam'al, *Carchemish, Aleppo, and Hamath.

BIBLIOGRAPHY.
1. *General.* A. Goetze, *Kleinasien*, 2nd ed., München, 1957. O. R. Gurney, *The Hittites*, 2nd ed. rev., Penguin Books, Baltimore, 1961.
2. *History.* A. Goetze, *Das Hethiter Reich (Der Alte Orient*, Band 27.), Leipzig, 1928. O. R. Gurney, "Anatolia: c. 1750-1600 B.C.," Vol. II, chap. VI in *The Cambridge Ancient History*, Cambridge, 1962. J. Mellaart, "Anatolia: c. 4000-2300 B.C.," Vol. I, chap. XVIII in *The Cambridge Ancient History*, Cambridge, 1962.
3. *Law.* J. Friedrich, *Die Hethitische Gesetze*, Leiden, 1959. A. Goetze, "The Hittite Laws," *Ancient Near Eastern Texts*, ed. J. B. Pritchard, Princeton University Press, Princeton, 1955. H. G. Güterbock, "Authority and Law in the Hittite Kingdom," *JAOS* Supplement 17 (1954). H. A.

Hoffner, *The Laws of the Hittites,* unpublished doctoral dissertation, Brandeis University, Waltham, Mass., 1963.

4. *Religion.* G. Furlani, *La religione degli Hittiti,* Bologna, 1936. H. G. Güterbock, "Hittite Religion," *Forgotten Religions,* ed. V. Ferm, New York, 1949.

5. *Art and Architecture.* E. Akurgal, *The Art of the Hittites,* Abrams, New York, 1962. R. Naumann, *Architektur Kleinasiens von ihren Anfängen bis zum Ende der hethitischen Zeit,* E. Wasmuth, Tübingen, 1955.

6. *Exploration and Excavation.* S. Lloyd, *Early Anatolia,* Penguin Books, Baltimore, 1956.

7. *Languages.* J. Friedrich, *Hethitisches Elementarbuch,* 2nd ed., Heidelberg, 1960. J. Friedrich, *Hethitisches Wörterbuch,* Heidelberg, 1952. E. H. Sturtevant and A. Hahn, *A Comparative Grammar of the Hittite Language,* 2nd ed., Philadelphia, 1951.

HIVITES. Hivites are described in the Bible as descendants of Canaan (Gen. 10:17). Their settlements existed in the vicinity of Tyre and Sidon (II Sam. 24:7), in the Lebanon and Hermon regions (Judges 3:8; Josh. 11:3), and in the regions around Shechem (Gen. 34:2) and Gibeon (Josh. 9:7; 11:19) in Palestine.

In Hebrew spelling the words Hivite °and Horite (°Hurrian) differ in only one letter — *w* (*v*) and *r* — both of which are shaped similarly in Hebrew, many scholars assume an early textual error and equate the Hivites with the Horites. This view is argued on the basis of such passages as Gen. 36:2 and 20 in the first of which Zibeon is termed a "Hivite," and in the second, a "Horite." Hurrian personal names are attested in the Palestinian regions where the Biblical Hivites were located.

HOR-DEDEF, INSTRUCTION OF. Hor-dedef was a son of the pharaoh Khufu (Cheops) who ruled Egypt as the second king of the Fourth Dynasty (*ca.* 2650-2500 B.C.). Hor-dedef is mentioned with several of the famous sages of ancient Egypt, and his proverbial wisdom was well known. He is linked most closely with Imhotep, the brilliant minister and architect of Djoser, a pharaoh of the Third Dynasty (*ca.* 2700 B.C.). Imhotep is credited with the architecture of the Stepped Pyramid, which seems to have been the first tomb of this kind constructed of hewn stone. Later generations regarded Imhotep not only as an architect, but also as a magician and the father of medicine. The Greeks identified him with

°Asclepius, the god of medicine. There is a reference to Hor-dedef in a text known as the "Satirical Letter" which seems to refer to a written collection of his sayings. However, the only known texts of his teaching extant are mere scraps of uncertain translation and content. The few sentences which can be read seem to offer advice common to other wisdom traditions: the dangers of boasting, the obligation of a man to provide for a family, the importance of religious duties.

The most extensive reference to Hor-dedef is found in the text known as the Westcar Papyrus. In this account, Khufu requests that his sons tell him about the wonders worked by great magicians of the past. Two sons tell him of patent acts of magic wrought by outstanding magicians. But Hor-dedef knows of a magician who is still living, a man named Djedi, who dwells in a town north of the Faiyum. Djedi is pictured as a prodigious and venerable man, 110 years old; but able to eat five hundred loaves of bread, a haunch of beef, and to drink one hundred jugs of beer as a day's (?) rations! Despite this diet, or perhaps, because of it, Djedi is a man of good health who sleeps well and is not bothered by coughs or other sickness. He is pictured also as a man of unusual skills, e.g., he knows how to put a severed head back on a body. Hor-dedef is dispatched to bring Djedi to the court. Hor-dedef is successful in his mission and presents Djedi to Khufu. The king requests some feats of magic and Djedi obliges. But he also predicts that the dynastic line of Khufu will be supplanted by a new line of kings (Fifth Dynasty) who will be begotten by the god Re. After his appearance, Djedi is assigned to live in the house of Hor-dedef and is given a huge food allowance. There is a strain of humor in this old account which is rather characteristic of the wisdom literature of the ancient Near East.

BIBLIOGRAPHY. Adolf Erman, *The Literature of the Ancient Egyptians,* translated by Aylward M. Blackman, Methuen and Company, Ltd., 1927, pp. 36-47. J. A. Wilson, "Egyptian Instructions," *Ancient Near Eastern Texts,* ed. J. B. Pritchard, Princeton University Press, Princeton, 1955, pp. 419-20.

HORITES. *See* Hurrians.

HURRIANS. The Hurrians first appear on

the scene of history about the middle of the third millennium B.C. Until the mid-twenties of our present century this people was virtually unknown outside of a few Biblical references, and no one dreamed that they were a part of a widespread ethnic group. But archaeological evidence from the past four decades reveals that the Hurrians played an important part in the history of the ancient Near East during the second millennium B.C. The history of this ethnic group can be traced fairly well through personal names which are found in documents scattered throughout the Near East. The earliest record of explicit Hurrian names comes from a dedicatory tablet of Samarra which dates from before Ur III. Geographical localities connected with these names point to an infiltration of Hurrians into the East-Tigris region during the Old Akkadian period. That this infiltration was gradual is indicated by the absence of Hurrian names during this period from important sites (e.g. *Nuzi, *Alalakh, and *Mari) which later became predominantly Hurrian. Many more names occur during the Ur III period (ca. 2060-1950). In the Old Babylonian period (beginning ca. 1830) some religious texts were written in the Hurrian language at Mari. A contract from Hana found at Mari is the earliest known reference to the Hurrians as a people. Hurrian names are found in considerable numbers during this period at sites as far west as Alalakh in northern Syria, as far north as Chagar Bazar in the *Habur valley between the Tigris and Euphrates rivers, and as far east as Dilbat near Babylon. The main Hurrian movement seems to have come during this period and may have coincided with the invasion of Akkad by the barbarian Guti from the Zagros mountains. However, since we have very little direct evidence, the period between the First Dynasty of Babylon (ca. 1800 B.C.) to approximately 1500 B.C. must be reconstructed on the basis of what is known from the period following 1500 B.C.

I. *Geographical Distribution.* The original home of the Hurrians was probably in the mountains of Armenia. As the texts mentioned above indicate, Hurrians were present in the population of Upper Mesopotamia in the early part of the second millennium B.C. The population itself, however, was predominantly Semitic. In the seventeenth and sixteenth centuries there was a great inflow of Hurrians into Upper Mesopotamia, the East-Tigris region, northern Syria, Palestine, and the Hittite land to the northwest. To be more specific, Nuzi (below the Little Zab River, east of the Tigris) was, by the fifteenth century, almost wholly Hurrian. Alalakh, in northern Syria, which had many Hurrians in its midst in the seventeenth century, now had an overwhelming majority of them in this later period. To the far west on the North Syrian coast of the Mediterranean at Ras Shamra (ancient Ugarit) numerous texts were found composed in Hurrian, and these date before 1400 B.C. Some of the Amarna letters mention Hurrian princelings at Qatna and Tunip in central Syria. Texts from Taanach and Shechem in Palestine gave evidence of Hurrians in that region also. The Egyptians called Palestine, and at times Syria, *Ḫuru.* The presence of Hurrians in Palestine can also be established from the Bible, where they are referred to as Horites (see below). So before the fifteenth century B.C. the Hurrians stretched across Upper Mesopotamia from Nuzi in the east to Ras Shamra in the west, and they had welded themselves into a large and powerful state — the kingdom of *Mitanni. "Mitanni" is primarily a political term, for the state included more than what is technically known as the land of Mitanni or (as in the Mesopotamian records) Hanigalbat. The center of the state was near Harran (*Haran) in the Middle Euphrates Valley, and the capital was called Washshukanni. This site is still uncertain, but Fekhkheriyeh is now generally accepted as the proper identification. Assyria at this time was a dependency and Mitanni dominated the kingdom of Arrapkha in the east, and the kingdom of Mukish in northern Syria. This state had a predominantly Hurrian population, but evidence from personal names indicates that most of the ruling class in general, and the kings in particular, were Indo-Aryans. This relationship between the more numerous Hurrians and the dominant Indo-Aryans can best be characterized as a complete symbiosis.

II. *Political History.* The kingdom of Mitanni probably reached its zenith under Saushsatar around the middle of the fifteenth century B.C. Hittite documents mention that Saushsatar took a precious door of gold and silver from Ashur to use in his palace at

Washshukanni. The kings of Assyria, Arrap-kha and Alalakh, were undoubtedly in sub-jection to him. Probably he controlled also the areas of Aleppo and Carchemish to the east of Alalakh, and such sites as Qatna and Tunip in Syria. Saushsatar came into conflict with Thutmose III of Egypt over the pos-session of Syria, and, it seems, was defeated by the Egyptians and lost much of his ter-ritory west of the Euphrates. However, peaceful relations existed between the two countries after this. Either under Thutmose III or his successor Thutmose IV a treaty of friendship was concluded between the two countries whereby Mitanni received Aleppo and North Syria. Artadama I, suc-cessor of Saushsatar, gave his daughter in marriage to Thutmose IV. This procedure was followed also by Sudarna II and his successor Tushratta who both gave daughters to Amenhotep III. On the death of that pharaoh, Tushratta gave his daughter to Amenhotep IV for a wife. Extensive cor-respondence was carried on between Tush-ratta and these two Egyptian rulers. The largest tablet found in the material from El Amarna was a letter composed almost entirely in Hurrian and addressed to Amen-hotep III. At this time Tushratta was still the overlord of Assyria, and Mitanni was still a powerful kingdom. Conflicts within Mitanni itself, however, and the rise to power of Shuppiluliumas, the great Hittite king, soon caused dark clouds to form on the horizon. Egypt failed to come to the aid of her ally. Tushratta suffered a military defeat at the hands of Suppiluliumas, and lost much land in the west, but he still retained his throne. His son, Mattiwaza, was reduced to a vassal of the Hittites by Sup-piluliumas around the middle of the four-teenth century. Mittiwaza was given the throne of Mitanni as his realm and the daughter of Suppiluliumas as his wife. At the same time in the east, Assyria under Ashur-uballit I seized her opportunity and reasserted her independence. Thus the king-dom of Mitanni as a political power passes from the pages of history.

III. *Cultural Contribution.* The cultural contribution of the Hurrians is as important as their political attainment, and it endured much longer. As was indicated above, some texts in Hurrian were found at the site of Mari on the Euphrates River in Central Mesopotamia, and these date from the period of Hammurabi. Six of these tablets have been published thus far, and they are re-ligious texts written in poetic style. These texts precede all other connected Hurrian texts by four to five hundred years. From the site of °Boghazköy have come pure Hur-rian texts, including a fragment of the Gil-gamesh Epic; short Hurrian passages scat-tered among Hittite texts; and longer Hurrian texts with Hittite passages in them. Most of this material is of a religious nature, and deals especially with rituals. Epic and historic-mythological passages are also pre-sent. Material from about this same period (*ca.* 1400 B.C.) was also found at Ras Shamra. The script is not syllabic, however, but consonantal in nature. The largest text contains sixty-two lines and is divided into seventeen paragraphs, each of which is an invocation to a deity or deities. Most of the other texts are short and fragmentary. A Sumero-Hurrian vocabulary tablet was also discovered, written in syllabic cuneiform with Sumerian in one column and the Hur-rian equivalent in another. Also, there is a Hurrian-Akkadian bilingual document. An-other tablet, as yet unpublished, was com-posed in four languages in parallel columns — Sumerian, Akkadian, Hurrian, and Ugari-tic. The Hurrian and Akkadian were written with the normal Akkadian syllabary. The most important Hurrian text is the letter of Tushratta found at El Amarna in Egypt. The first seven lines are written in Akkadian, and the rest of the nearly five hundred lines is in classical Hurrian. In-dividual Hurrian words are scattered through-out other of the Amarna letters, the Nuzi tablets, the long Qatna tablet, and the tab-lets from Alalakh.

The Hurrian language is unrelated to any of the other languages commonly associated with the Near East- Semitic, Sumerian, and Indo-European. Hurrian is exclusively a suffixing language. This means that all gram-matical elements are added to the end of the word and none are placed on the front as in other languages of the Near East. The verbal system is very complicated. Hurrian has a close connection in morphology, syn-tax, and vocabulary only with Urartian (the language of ancient Armenia).

The Hurrians served as the conduit through which much of the culture of Mesopotamia flowed to the west. They were the transporters of such typically Babylonian works as the Gilgamesh Epic and the Hymn to Nikkal. The large number of Hurrian loan words in Hittite is an example of the debt owed by the Hittites to their Hurrian teachers. The Hurrians borrowed extensively from their Babylonian neighbors, but they also made original contributions to their culture in the field of literature, social practice, and art. The latter area is well illustrated by Hurrian seal-cylinders. The Hurrian craftsmen borrowed style and subject matter from Syrian, Syro-Cappadocian, Kassite, and Babylonian art. The Mitannian style is a combination of many divergent elements, and is rich in themes and modes of expression. Unique to Mitanni are the stylized trees, small animals, and series of concentric circles. This Mitannian style influenced the glyptic art of the following centuries in both its stylistic features and its subject matter. The Hurrians produced a pottery (Mitannian ware) characterized in form by high and shouldered cups, vessels with thin walls and button base. The painted decoration was used most often on the cups of this thin, delicate ware. The pottery is of fine execution and usually is made of a very fine clay. The smooth surface was excellent for the application of color. The most common color was black, which was sometimes applied as plain bands around the vessel, but most often as a base on which the design was overlaid in white. Red was sometimes used as a base color, but not nearly as often as black. Brown is very infrequent. The design has a marked tendency toward geometrical patterns. The running scroll is a favorite motif. A simple zigzag line is common. Circles also are common motifs. Plant forms are sometimes used in conjunction with geometric designs. Animals are used in a number of designs. Because of the fine quality of this pottery, and because it is connected closely with royal buildings, it may have been a luxury ware.

The Hurrian religion has been hinted at above in the reference to the Hymn of Nikkal. This consort of the moon-god Sin, called Ningal at Harran, was a leading figure among the Hurrians, and this hymn to her was probably transmitted through them. From the treaty made between Suppiluliu-

mas and Mattiwaza we learn that the latter invokes the Vedic deities Mithra, Indra, Varuna and the Nasatyas. They adopted gods also from the Mesopotamians, among whom Ishtar was prominent. Besides these foreign gods, the Hurrians also worshipped their own gods. Teshup is the storm-god and Hepa, his consort, is the sun-goddess or mother-goddess. Also present were Shaushka and Shimiki, the sun-god. Kumarpi is the head of the Hurrian pantheon. The Hurrians were as successful in passing on their gods as they were other aspects of their culture, for the Hurrian gods are more prominent in Hittite texts than are the Hittite gods themselves. More important for the student of the Bible, however, is the Hurrian influence in the areas of legal practice and social custom. A very close similarity exists between the customs found in the book of Genesis and those found in the Hurrian city of Nuzi.

IV. *Biblical Material.* As indicated above, the cuneiform sources from Taanach, Amarna, and Shechem witness to a rather significant Hurrian population in central Palestine in the patriarchal age. The Bible also manifests this fact. In the Hebrew text of the Old Testament the name "Hivites" occurs several times. The Greek text of the Old Testament (LXX) substitutes the word *chorraios* for the Hebrew in Genesis 36:2 and Joshua 9:7. The Greek in these passages reflects the Hebrew "Horite," which is used to designate the ancient inhabitants of Edom or Mt. Seir who were defeated by Chedorlaomer (Gen. 14:6), and later driven out by the sons of Esau (Deut. 2:12, 22). Hamor, who is designated as a Hivite, is connected with Shechem. Gibeon (according to Josh. 9:7 and 11:19) had a Hivite population. But as we have seen, the Greek used the term "Horites" in Joshua 9:7, and extra-biblical material indicates the presence of Hurrians at Shechem. Therefore, it seems that the term "Hivites" really designates "Hurrians" in these passages. This may be further confirmed by the Hebrew text itself which interchanges "Hivites" (Gen. 36:2) with "Horites" (Gen. 36:20) when it speaks of the father of Zibeon. The term "Hivites" thus appears to be a local designation for Hurrians. But it may not be possible to lump all "Horites" and "Hivites" into one group of Hurrians. E. A. Speiser

STEP PYRAMID of Djoser at Saqqara, designed by Imhotep. Courtesy, E. Anrich

("Horites," *Interpreters Dictionary of the Bible*) indicates that there are valid reasons for distinguishing the early occupants of Mt. Seir or Edom from the west Horites of Palestine proper. The confusion may be due to accidental similarity in sound. The term as it refers to the pre-Edomite Horites may reflect the traditional Semitic etimology of "cave-dweller." As it refers to the people of Palestine, it goes back to a Hurrian stem (*ḫuru* or *ḫurw*).

Another name which occurs in the Old Testament is "Hittite." In Joshua 11:3 the Hebrew reads "Horites" and the Greek "Hittites." Is it possible that many, if not most, of the Old Testament passages referring to Hittites should be replaced by Horites? This would require a change of only one consonant — t to r. Since the extra-biblical material indicates the presence of a considerable number of Hurrians in Palestine, and this is confirmed by the Bible; and since we have no real evidence of Hittites so far south, perhaps "Horite" should be substituted for "Hittite" in many cases.

The ruler of Jerusalem bears a Hurrian name (Abdi-Hiba) in the Amarna Letters. The last part of his name stands for *Ḫiba* the Hurrian mother-goddess. Thus the Jebusites, as the inhabitants of ancient Jerusalem are called in the Old Testament (Josh. 15:63), have a Hurrian background. The Jebusite name in II Sam. 24:16 (Araunah) suggests the Hurrian *ewri* "lord," and would support the conclusion that the Jebusites were actually Hurrians.

BIBLIOGRAPHY. R. T. O'Callaghan, *Aram Naharaim*, Pontifical Biblical Institute, Rome, 1948. I. J. Gelb, *Hurrians and Subarians*, University of Chicago, Chicago, 1944. E. A. Speiser, "Introduction to Hurrian," *AASOR* XX, 1941 "Hurrians and Subarians," *JAOS* LXVIII, 1948, pp. 1-13; "Ethnic Movements in the Near East in the Second Millennium B.C.," *AASOR*, XIII, 1933, pp. 13-54; "Hurrians," *The Interpreter's Dictionary of the Bible*, Abingdon Press, Nashville, 1962. H. G. Güterbock, "The Hurrian Element in the Hittite Empire," *Journal of World History*, II, 1954, pp. 383-394.

HYKSOS. The fifteenth and sixteenth dynasties of °Egypt were comprised of Hyksos rulers, a term meaning "Rulers of Foreign Lands." They were largely Semitic of Canaanite and Amorite descent. Semites had infiltrated Egypt for centuries, and eventually they became powerful enough to establish their own government. The Hyksos capital was at Avaris-Tanis (*see* Raamses) from which they ruled a kingdom including Syria and Palestine. The horse drawn chariot and the composite bow were introduced into Egypt during Hyksos times, along with cultural and religious ideas. Hyksos type fortifications have been excavated at *Megiddo, *Shechem, and *Lachish. A native Egyptian dynasty under Ahmose I regained control of the government and forced the Hyksos out of the country. Tanis fell in 1550 B.C.

HYPOSTYLE. In Egyptian temples, such as the Amun Temple at Karnak, a number of columns supported a flat stone roof. The halls or chambers of such temples were named hypostyle, from the Greek words meaning "under a pillar."

I

IDAMARAZ. *See* Gozan, Habor.

IDRIMI. *See* Alalakh.

IDUMAEA. Idumaea is the term used by the Greeks and Romans to refer to the country occupied by the people known in the Old Testament as Edomites. When the Nabateans pushed the Edomites out of their traditional home, they moved northward to the Hebron region. Antipater, father of Herod the Great was an Idumaean.

IMHOTEP. Imhotep was vizier to Djoser, the first king of Egypt's Third Dynasty (*ca.* 2700 B.C.). His greatest material monument is the step *pyramid which he designed at Saqqara to serve as a royal mausoleum. In addition he was reputed to have been a priest, magician, and physician. Although none of his writings have survived he is also said to have been the author of wise proverbs. Bronze figurines of Imhotep depict him as a man seated and unrolling a papyrus on his knees.

In the Late Egyptian period Imhotep was worshiped as a god of healing and identified with Greek Asclepius. His chapel at Saqqara became a sanitarium to which cripples flocked from all Egypt. The Greeks, who called him *Imuthes*, as well as the Egyptians were devoted to the cult of Imhotep. Propaganda for his healing powers was circulated throughout Egypt. Ptolemy V built a chapel for Imhotep on the island of Philae.

INANNA, DESCENT OF. *See* Descent of Ishtar.

IPUWER, ADMONITIONS OF. The name of Ipuwer is known only from a defective manuscript which records a series of reports, rebukes, and admonitions for the Pharaoh of Egypt. The exact context in which Ipuwer delivered his address is unknown. The beginning and the ending of the text have not survived, and the extant text opens with a speech already in progress. The occupation of Ipuwer is also unknown, but it has been suggested that he was some sort of treasury official who appeared before the king in an attempt to make him aware of the true situation in his realm. One reference ("lies are told thee") may indicate that Ipuwer thought that the indifference of the king was due to a lack of accurate information.

The historical context of the speech is generally agreed upon by scholars. Ipuwer's harangue came out of the troubled period of Egyptian history following the dissolution of the Old Kingdom and frequently designated as the First Intermediate Period (*ca.* 2200-2050 B.C.). This was a chaotic time in which Egypt weltered in the backwash of the breakdown of the power and organization of the Old Kingdom. It was a time of change, challenge, and conflict. It was no time for a supine and uninformed king.

The prevailing conditions are set forth with considerable detail by Ipuwer. Internal security had broken down. Bandits roamed the country and there was a general disregard for law. Foreigners appeared everywhere and there seemed to be some threat of invasion. Economic impoverishment gripped the land. Foreign trade was greatly diminished and domestic productivity was at a very low level: the plowing was not done, the cattle were allowed to run free without care, the storehouse was empty and the storekeeper dead. These woes were accompanied by radical changes in the social structure. The poor had swapped places with the rich, the nobles were banished, and servants had little respect for their masters. Even the kingship itself was threatened by irresponsible men. The land was spinning like a potter's wheel, laughter had become wailing, suicides and internecine strife plagued the land.

Some of the literature from this period reflects the strong currents of despair which were running in the life of the people. Deep pessimism possessed the minds and will of some. But Ipuwer did not belong to these. He seems to have been nearer to those who sought constructive social change. For all were not caught in an immobilizing sense of doom. There were those who expressed a growing desire for the abundant life for more people and concern for the "little man." Even a serf was due his worth and his justice. It would be going too far to call Ipuwer a social reformer on the basis of the material preserved. His chief objective seems to have been a return of stability to a seething society. However, he was positive in his approach and dared to lay the responsibility for the deteriorated situation on the king while proposing that the problems be dealt with in a vigorous manner.

Attempting to stimulate the king into action, Ipuwer followed his lamentations with a series of adjurations (from which the "admonitions" of the title is derived) to remember various regulations concerning worship. He also described an ideal ruler who had no evil in his heart and cared for his people as a good herdsman. It is impossible to be certain whether he was thinking of an ideal ruler of the past (perhaps after the pattern of the sun-god Re) or expressing a hope for such a ruler in the future. The latter is the more probable, and some scholars have seen a form of Messianic prophecy in his words. Indeed, it has been rather common to find Ipuwer compared to the Old Testament prophets. His speech has been considered even as a sort of *schema* for Old Testament prophecy.

More recent study has tended to minimize the similarity between Ipuwer and the Old Testament. It is true that he reminds the reader of the Israelite prophets by the fearless way in which he confronted the king with a disturbing arraignment of social conditions. He may, also, long before the prophets, have had some hope for a future ruler who would correct current wrongs and restore the lost security of the land. But this universal and very human desire can be called "Messianic prophecy" only in the broadest sense. Unlike the prophets of Yahweh, Ipuwer did not speak in the name of a god, nor did he seek in any significant way to probe for spiritual causes beneath the contemporary turmoil. He deserves a place of honor among accurate appraisers of unhealthy and unpleasant social developments, but he hardly belongs with men like Amos, Isaiah, and Jeremiah.

BIBLIOGRAPHY. A. H. Gardiner, *The Admonitions of an Egyptian Sage,* J. C. Hinrichs, Leipzig, 1909. Adolf Erman, *The Literature of the Ancient Egyptians,* translated by Aylward M. Blackman, Methuen and Company, Ltd., London, 1927, pp. 92-108. J. A. Wilson, "Egyptian Oracles and Prophecies," *Ancient Near Eastern Texts,* ed. J. B. Pritchard, Princeton University Press, Princeton, 1955. J. H. Breasted, *Development of Religion and Thought in Ancient Egypt,* Harper and Brothers Publishers, New York, 1959, pp. 204-215; *The Dawn of Conscience,* Charles Scribner's Sons, New York, 1933, pp. 194-200.

IRAN. *See* Persia.

IRRIGATION. *Aqueducts, cisterns, dams, and canals were needed throughout the Near East to assure the greatest utilization of available water supplies. Both Babylon and Egypt depended upon the use of their rivers for water, which was conveyed through the land by canals. Generally the winter rains of Palestine and Syria were ample for the grains, but vegetable and fruit gardens would be parched by the long summer drought. Such gardens were planted near natural water supplies, and water was conveyed through the garden by little channels. When necessary the water was raised by an aqueduct or an endless chain of buckets drawn by a horse or donkey (cf. Num. 24:7). Such gardens usually had storage pools (cf. Eccl. 2:6). Most excavated sites in Palestine give evidence of the use of cisterns by their early inhabitants.

AQUEDUCT OF SENNACHERIB. Reconstruction of the Jerwan Aqueduct by Seton Lloyd. Courtesy, The Oriental Institute

ISHTAR, DESCENT OF. *See* Descent of Ishtar.

ISIN. Following the fall of the third dynasty of Ur, *Amorites gained control of the Mesopotamian region, including the territories of *Sumer and Akkad. A ruler named Ishbi-Irra from Mari took the throne of Isin, fifty miles northwest of *Uruk and established a dynasty which lasted 225 years. Ishbi-Irra began his reign about 1952 B.C., and his dynasty came to an end about 1728 B.C. when Rim-Sin of *Larsa conquered Isin. Rim-Sin was a contemporary of *Hammurabi of Babylon. *Lipit-Ishtar of Isin, who ruled from about 1864 to 1854 B.C. produced a law code in the Sumerian language. *See also* Hammurabi, Code of.

ISRAEL. The term Israel may be used as (1) an alternate name for the Biblical patriarch Jacob (Gen. 32:28), (2) the collective name for the twelve tribes which traced their ancestry back to Jacob (Gen. 32:32; 34:7; 49:16, 28) or (3) the Northern Kingdom which rebelled against Solomon's son Rehoboam and chose Jeroboam I as king (*ca.* 922 B.C.). In this sense the kingdom of Israel is distinguished from the southern kingdom, or Judah. The Northern Kingdom, Israel, fell in 722 B.C. when its capital, *Samaria, was taken by the Assyrians.

The earliest archaeological reference to the people of Israel appears in the *Merneptah Stele (*ca.* 1230 B.C.) Israelite kings Ahab and Omri are mentioned on inscriptions of Shalmaneser III of Assyria (*see* Black Obelisk of Shalmaneser). The inscription of Mesha of Moab contained on the *Moabite Stone describes relations between Moab and Israel.

ISRAEL STELE. *See* Merneptah.

ITALY. *See* Rome.

J

JARMO. In 1948, Robert J. Braidwood began a series of expeditions for the Oriental Institute of Chicago at Jarmo, in the highlands of eastern Iraq, thirty miles from modern Kirkuk. During successive years Braidwood discovered fifteen different levels of occupation at Jarmo. The top five contained pottery, but the lower levels date from a period before pottery had been invented. Even in the earliest levels, however, the people had tools made from flint and obsidian.

Although most of the earliest houses were crudely built of packed mud, archaeologists were able to trace the foundations of some which had stone foundations. The people of

Jarmo ground their cereals between grind-stones but they do not appear to have used hoes, a fact which suggests that grains were gathered wild. One of the flint sickles bears evidence that it had been fastened into a wooden handle with bitumen.

The presence of clay figurines of goats, sheep, dogs and pigs — and of pregnant women — suggests that the people of Jarmo practiced a fertility cult. They used stone in making decorative beads, rings, and arm-bands which probably served both a magical and an ornamental purpose. Bones of sheep, goats, pigs, and oxen discovered at Jarmo suggest that some progress had been made in the domestication of animals.

Tools made of obsidian provide evidence that the people of Jarmo were engaged in trade with other peoples, for the nearest source of obsidian was the region around Lake Van, 250 miles away. The Carbon 14 method of dating organic material has been useful in establishing dates for the Jarmo culture. The testing of snail shells discovered at Jarmo gives evidence that the settlement dates from the period between 5077 and 4537 B.C.

From their base at Jarmo, Braidwood and his staff also excavated Karim Shahir, a mile distant. Here, too, there were evidences of very early settlements, but life was even more primitive there than it had been at Jarmo. There were no sickles and no flint tools at Karim Shahir, which was probably settled around 6000 B.C.

About two thousand years passed between the pre-pottery neolithic settlements at Jarmo and the beginnings of history among the Sumerians of southern Mesopotamia. Archaeologists use the study of pottery as a convenient basis for studying the changes in culture during this time. The Jarmo culture appears to have been succeeded by one which was first identified at the mound of °Tell Hassuna on the Tigris River near ancient °Ashur.

BIBLIOGRAPHY. Robert J. Braidwood, "Jarmo; a Village of Early Farmers in Iraq," *Antiquity*, XXIV, 1950, pp. 189-195. Robert J. Braidwood, "From Cave to Village," *Scientific American*, CLXXXVII, 1932, pp. 62-66. Linda Braidwood, *Digging Beyond the Tigris*, H. Schulman, New York, 1953.

JAVAN. Javan, the name of one of Jephthah's descendants, appears as *Yamanu* in the Assyrian inscriptions of Sargon II, and is doubtless related to the *Ioanes* (Ionians) of Homer's *Iliad* (xiii, 685). A South Arabic inscription mentions *Ywnm* as a country from which female temple attendants were secured. Ezekiel also mentions Javan among nations involved in the slave trade (Ezek. 27:13).

JEBEL MUSA. *See* Sinai.

JEBUSITES. The Canaanites dwelling in the territory of °Jerusalem and its environs were termed Jebusites (Num. 13:29; Josh. 11:3). During the Amarna Age (15th, 14th centuries B.C.) the city of Jerusalem was ruled by Abdi-Hiba, whose name is non-Semitic, probably °Hurrian. Araunah, or Ornan, a later Jebusite ruler (II Sam. 24:24) also appears to have a Hurrian name. David's general Joab took Jerusalem from the Jebusites (II Sam. 5:6).

JEHOIACHIN. In the ruins of a vaulted building near the Ishtar Gate of °Babylon, three hundred tablets from the years 595-570 B.C. were unearthed. They list rations such as barley and oil paid to captives who lived in or near Babylon. Among the recipients are people from Egypt, Asia Minor, Elam, Media, Percia, Phoenicia, Philistia, and Judea. Among the Jews are such names as Gaddiel, Semachiah and Shelamiah. Along with five royal princes we read of Yahkin, king of Judah — the same name as the Biblical Jehoiachin. The tablets identify him as "Yaukin, king of the land of Yahud."

The tablets provide evidence that the Babylonians continued to regard Jehoiachin as the legitimate king of Judah, even after he was replaced by Zedekiah. Jehoiachin was the lawful, although exiled king. Biblical texts are dated in terms of the years of his exile (cf. II Kings 25:27; Jer. 52:31).

JEMDET NASR. The last period of Mesopotamian prehistory bears the type name of Jemdet Nasr, a mound near ancient Babylon. Jemdet Nasr pottery was painted with black and yellow designs, and a rapidly developing culture produced utensils of bronze as well as stone. The pictographic cuneiform script, first seen in °Uruk, appears in a more advanced form during the

Jemdet Nasr period, and sculpture in stone developed into a fine art. Trade and commerce were highly developed among the Jemdet Nasr people, and the art of writing spread to the point where we enter the full light of history. The Jemdet Nasr period extends from about 3500 to about 3000 B.C. The site was excavated by S. Langdon and L. C. Watelin during the 1925-26 season.

BIBLIOGRAPHY. Henry Field and Richard A. Martin, "Painted Pottery from Jemdet Nasr, Iraq," *AJA*, XXXIX, 1935, pp. 310-320. Henry Field, "Human Remains from Jemdet Nasr, Mesopotamia," *Journal of the Royal Asiatic Society*, 1932, pp. 967-970. Donald Benjamin Hardin, "A Typological Examination of Sumerian Pottery from Jamdet Nast and Kish," *Iraq*. I, 1934, pp. 30-44. E. MacKay, *Report on Excavations at Jemdat Nasr*, 1931.

JERABLUS, JERABIS. See Carchemish.

JERASH. See Gerasa.

JERICHO (NEW TESTAMENT). Ancient Palestine never saw a more prolific builder than Herod the Great. Indeed Solomon was only a poor second to Herod. New Testament Jericho was the most unique of all the cities that Herod built. It was actually an Italian city in Palestine. Its *opus reticulatum* architecture was the same that Augustus had introduced in Rome; and Jericho is actually the only city east of Italy where this type of architecture has been found. To appreciate New Testament Jericho one needs only to look at Pompeii and then expand that city into Herod's super luxurious winter capital of Palestine.

Jerusalem does not often have a temperature below freezing in winter but the city's air is so damp that its chill gets into the marrow of one's bones, and present day visitors seldom believe the winter recordings they see on the thermometer. Small charcoal braziers were the only heaters in ancient Palestinian houses and even then one had to sit near them to receive any warmth. This explains why Jerusalem's important government officials, the rich merchants and the high clergy spent their winters at Jericho where one can often go about in shirt sleeves in the middle of winter. Jerusalem is 2700 feet above sea level, Jericho 800 feet below sea level.

For this new winter capital Herod chose a site about a mile southward from Old Testament Jericho and at the extreme western edge of the Jordan plain where the Wadi Qelt burst forth from the lofty mountain ridge which towered high above the city and gave it a perfect setting. On both banks of the stream which ran a good flow of water in winter he erected his numerous public buildings. The private villas which must have been quite similar to those of Pompeii were concentrated on the north bank. Some of the public buildings had concrete walls forty-one inches thick, thus giving a clew to their size and magnificence. Parks and pools were there too and Herod had an influential brother-in-law drowned in a swimming party in one of the latter. The excavators found a large sunken garden about 350 feet long. Behind it was a great retaining wall which contained fifty statuary niches alternately rectangular and semi-circular in form. In the center of this retaining wall was a terraced garden whose benches were just the height of theater seats. Behind each row of seats were flowers; the flower pots, placed a foot or so apart, were still intact in their places. Here the royal court could watch Greek and Roman plays in the sunken garden. In front of the statuary niches and terraced garden ran a reflecting pool, the plaster of which was still waterproof when excavated. At each end of the sunken garden were massive buildings and from one of these a grand stairway thirteen feet wide climbed over 150 feet up the hill on barrel vaults and ended in a pleasant edifice erected on what had originally been a fort in Maccabaean times.

From an earlier period of building when Herod was using ashlar masonry instead of *opus reticulatum* the excavators discovered a great gymnasium with Roman baths in the quarters for the army officers. This building was approximately 170 x 145 feet. Literary references also speak of a theater, an amphitheater and a hippodrome. The ruins on the site, however, suggest that there were also other major buildings as well as the large villas of the rich. The city's water supply was always sufficient as it was supplied from different water sources high in the mountains behind the site. The city was set in balsam groves which were such a valuable source of income that at one time Mark Anthony had given them to Cleopatra as a flattering present.

EXCAVATIONS AT OLD
TESTAMENT JERICHO
with the Mount of Tempta-
tion in the background. Courtesy, Giovanni Trimboli

Herod died at Jericho and a revolt broke out there at once in which his palace and other buildings were burned. His son Archelaus, however, quickly repaired the damage and the city continued its prosperity. Jericho was the last city visited by Christ before he went up to Jerusalem to his crucifixion. Here was the setting of the Zacchaeus episode (Luke 19:1-10) and Christ was entertained by him in one of the city's finest villas. Sycamore trees still grow in Jericho and their earlier presence is proved by timber which was still preserved when a fort from the Maccabaean period was excavated. The synoptic Gospels all mention the story of Christ and the beggars here. The latter would naturally work any rich city such as Jericho. When Christ left the city he climbed up the steep south bank of the Wadi Qelt. Here he was soon in the midst of that wilderness where he had been tempted of Satan in the beginning of his ministry.

The ruins of New Testament Jericho are known today at Tulu Abu el-'Alayiq. Charles Warren who had expected to find New Testament Jericho here ran an east-west trench across the southern *tell* but was disappointed in what he found and thought he had the wrong site. Ernst Sellin worked here briefly before World War I while excavating Old Testament Jericho. He dug a north-south exploratory trench but failed to recognize the unique nature of the city. James L. Kelso excavated there in 1950 and the next year James B. Pritchard continued the work. Their findings are published in the *AASOR*, Vols. XXIX-XXX and XXXII-XXXIII.

The site was occupied in the Chalcolithic and Early Bronze Ages after which it seems to have been abandoned until inter-Testament times. The two *tells* on the site, one on each side of the wadi, were originally defensive towers in Maccabaean times (Macc.

9:50). The south *tell* was square on the exterior and circular within, an excellent form for military defense. This same *tell* was later reused by Herod as the site for the building which he erected at the head of the grand stairway which climbed the hill from the wadi bank below. Pompey captured both of these defensive towers in 63 B.C. On the mountain bastion above Jericho on the south bank of the wadi was Kypros, a citadel which Herod the Great gave to his mother. On the north side of the wadi only a small tower, however, guarded the corresponding peak.

Vespasian in his campaign against Jerusalem captured Jericho but did not destroy it. Instead he established large garrisons here and later Titus brought the 10th legion from Jericho to aid him in the capture of Jerusalem. Following the Roman conquest in A.D. 70 there were no wealthy Jews to keep Jericho flourishing and it quickly declined to the status of a county seat and military post. It again became of strategic military value for the Romans in the Jewish revolt against Hadrian in A.D. 132-135. Sometime late in the 4th century New Testament Jericho was replaced by Eriha or Byzantine Jericho less than a mile to the east. This is also modern Jericho. The Muslim conquerors erected a small military post on the south *tell* in the eighth century to guard the Jerusalem road. A marble slab found here during the excavations had been used as a copy book of some suras from the Quran. They are most valuable in the textual criticism of that book.

JERICHO (OLD TESTAMENT).

An elongated mound known as Tell es-Sultan covers the remains of Old Testament and prehistoric Jericho. It lies twelve miles north of the Dead Sea on the west side of the Jordan Valley. A copious spring bubbles perennially out of the east edge of the mound and waters the modern oasis of *Eriha* which stretches toward the Jordan River. The spring attracted settlers by 8,000 B.C. and by 7,000 B.C. a 7.8 acre walled city was built, the world's oldest known city.

Lying 825 feet below sea level, Jericho is semi-tropical in climate. Temperatures reach 120 F. in summer and the annual rainfall is four inches. However its strategic values have always outweighed its liabilities. The city dominated trade in salt, sulfur and bitumen, natural products of the Dead Sea region, and it sat astride the historic east entrance to the hill country of Palestine. Jericho was destroyed in the fourteenth century B.C., presumably by the army of Joshua, and it ceased to be a city of importance until New Testament times.

For nearly a hundred years the attention of archaeologists has been attracted to Jericho. Charles Warren put down an exploratory shaft in the south end of the mound in 1867 and, having dug plumb into the center of an Early Bronze Age mud brick wall, declared there was nothing to be found at the site. An Austro-German expedition led by E. Sellin and C. Watzinger carried out extensive excavations in 1907-1909 and penetrated Neolithic levels in the south trench. But because of limited technical knowledge available at the time the historical and chronological significance of finds eluded them.

John Garstang directed a British School of Archaeology expedition which excavated the site from 1930-36 and brought to light the pre-pottery Neolithic levels dating before 5000 B.C. Garstang discovered some twenty-five tombs spanning the period from Early Bronze to Iron Age II and excavations on the mound revealed the rich history of the city during the Early and Middle Bronze Ages. For Biblical scholars the most interesting discovery of Garstang was his City IV belonging in the Late Bronze Age which he said was destroyed about 1400-1385 B.C. by the army of Joshua.

A British School of Archaeology expedition led by Kathleen M. Kenyon excavated at Jericho from 1952-58. Advanced techniques in controlled stratigraphic excavation were perfected and utilized and much information hitherto lost to the dump was captured. The unique prehistoric city of Jericho was resurrected from the dust of decayed mud bricks and fallen stones. An accurate sequence of cultures from the first settlement by the spring about 8000 B.C. to the city which fell before the invading Israelites was recovered. From the phenomenal discovery of 505 additional tombs a wealth of grave goods such as pottery, personal ornaments, food deposits, clothing, weapons, furniture, skeletal remains and even rock drawings yielded information which gave life to the framework of successive cultures and peopled them again on the stage of history.

I. *Periods of Occupation.* It is apparent from the preliminary reports of the 1952-58 excavations that Garstang's level designations will be revised in Kenyon's forthcoming *Excavations at Jericho,* Vol. III. Therefore the periods of occupation indicated by the latest reports are described here.

A. Mesolithic. While *Natufian man inhabited caves at Mt. Carmel, a settlement was established by the spring at Jericho. Charred wood from a shrine-like structure at the base of the mound on bedrock yielded a Carbon-14 date of 7800 B.C. (plus or minus 210 years). Lunate flints and a bone harpoon head associated the settlement with Natufian culture at Mt. Carmel. Jericho thus appears to be the first Old Testament city that can be traced back archaeologically to the point in prehistory when man made the transition from life as a wandering hunter to that of a sedentary village dweller and probably agriculturist. Some thirteen feet of packed earth occupation layers remain in the nucleus of the mound from the circular, skin-wall dwellings of these people.

B. Neolithic. Four distinct Neolithic cultures have been identified at Jericho, covering roughly the period from 7000-4000 B.C. The two which precede the introduction of pottery about 5000 B.C. are designated Pre-pottery Neolithic A. and B, while the two cultures after 5000 B.C. are called Pottery Neolithic A. and B.

1. Pre-pottery Neolithic A. An incredibly energetic people captured the village of Jericho and built the world's first known walled city. A free-standing stone wall six and one-half feet thick and a half-mile in circumference was constructed without the aid of metal tools or transport machines. The wall survives in one spot twelve feet high, and it probably reached twenty-three feet in original height. Around the outside base of the wall was cut a moat in solid rock twenty-seven feet wide and nine feet deep. A circular stone tower, styled in keeping with the curvilinear stone houses, was built to a height of thirty feet inside the east wall. Charcoal timbers in a late phase of an associated house gave a Carbon-14 date of 6850 B.C. (plus or minus 210). The original tower and defences must date to 7000 B.C.

At first it was thought that an elaborate system of irrigation accounted for the sudden wealth evident in Jericho. It is more likely however that the city controlled trade in salt, sulfur and bitumen, natural products of the Dead Sea area, and from these products acquired the wealth necessary for its unique building enterprise.

2. Pre-pottery Neolithic B. By 6250 B.C. (plus or minus 200) the city was abandoned and, after a lapse of an appreciable period, was reoccupied by people with new cultural traditions. Characteristically they built rectangular houses of mud brick and floored them with plaster which was burnished to a glossy finish. Eventually the city walls were rebuilt on the ruins of the preceding culture. The long period of occupation by the so-called "plaster floor" people brought occupation debris in the mound to a height of forty-five feet above bedrock!

Like their predecessors the Pre-pottery Neolithic B. people buried their dead underneath the floors of their houses. It is probable that the dead were thought to have a future only in association with the living members of the family. A surprising discovery of ten plastered skulls emphasizes the close association between the living and the dead. Skulls were removed from certain individuals after initial burial and facial features were modeled on the skulls even to shells inserted into the orbits for eyes and paint daubed above the mouth for a moustache on one. The plastered skulls probably were held in veneration by the living members of the family, and the quasi-physical presence of the person represented by the skull must have been of considerable influence.

3. Pottery Neolithic A. and B. After a considerable occupation gap during which time wind-blown earth covered the ruins of the preceding culture, Jericho was settled about 4750 B.C. by pit-dwellers who knew the art of pottery-making. They represent a cultural retrogression because the half-subterranean houses and surface campsites were inferior to the architecture of the Pre-pottery cultures. Before 4000 B.C. the Pottery A people were joined by new cultural elements designated Pottery B, which introduced a crude type of free-standing mud brick architecture. The latter people provide a link with cultures at other sites. Similar pottery is found in the Yarmuk Valley, Shechem,

Byblos and other sites around the north fringe of the Fertile Crescent.

C. Early Bronze Age. Jericho was unoccupied during the Chalcolithic period (4000-3250 B.C.) of nearby Ghassul, but by 3250 B.C. nomads were camped on the mound. From the camping phase which Kenyon calls Proto-Urban several interesting rock-cut tombs remain. Tomb A 94 contained evidence of possible cremations. It is likely that accumulated skeletal remains were burned in the underground chamber to make room for additional burials. Thus the cremations were not of whole bodies. The discovery of over 300 skulls in Tomb K2, dating immediately after Tomb A 94, indicates that the cremation of accumulated bones was discontinued and most bones with the exception of skulls were simply thrown out of the tomb.

Jericho had a checkered history as a walled city between 2900 and 2300 B.C. Seventeen rebuilding phases are evident in west side walls. Earthquakes, occurring as often as four times a century, often flattened the mud-brick defences, and in one instance an enemy piled brushwood against the south wall and with an intense fire that left three feet of ashes burned the timber beams in the wall and the city. About 2300 B.C. nomadic invaders destroyed the city and introduced a new culture called Intermediate Early Bronze-Middle Bronze by Kenyon.

D. Middle Bronze Age. The intermediate phase from 2300-1900 B.C. is represented mainly by some 400 tombs which contained copper daggers, crude pottery and usually single burials. It was mainly a camping phase since only one meager level of architecture on the mound can be associated with it. The latter part of this period has been associated with Abraham by Glueck and Albright, but Albright's Middle Bronze II A, 1900-1750 B.C. with which Wright associates Abraham, is found at Jericho in the remains of only one tomb.

Five phases of the Hyksos period, 1750-1550 B.C., have been identified by Kenyon at Jericho. During most of the time the city was fortified with a huge sloping plastered scarp that reached down the mound. On top of the slope was the town wall, a part of which still survives on the north end of the mound as the highest remains. The long 35° slope was protection against the newly developed battering ram.

From the tombs of this period come the only preserved food deposits from ancient times. Platters of roasted sheep, trays of pomegranates and vessels lined with the sediment of an unidentified liquid were found. Strangely, ostrich eggs were deposited with the burials. There seems to be religious significance in the food deposits because pomegranates were symbols of fertility religion, with the tree sometimes representing the Tree of Life. The inclusion of meat from sheep only may indicate that Baalism with its bull symbols had not penetrated Jericho at this time. This is interesting in view of the fact that the patriarch Joseph must be placed somewhere in the Hyksos period.

E. Late Bronze Age. Following the Egyptian destruction of Hyksos Jericho about 1550 B.C., there was a lapse in occupation of the city until 1400 B.C. Pottery from Tombs 4, 5 and 13 indicates that the city was occupied at least nominally between 1400 and 1300 B.C. On the mound itself only the foundations of a wall and one square yard of a house floor have been found which can be dated in this period. No city walls or other structures survived the erosion of long centuries of abandonment after the fourteenth century B.C. Presumably this is the city whose walls fell before the army of Joshua.

F. Iron Age. There is no evidence of a walled Iron Age city of Jericho. A number of buildings datable to the eighth-seventh centuries B.C. were excavated by the Austro-German expedition and seventh century B.C. structures were found in the latest excavations. Pottery and structures were found on the lower slopes of the mound indicating that the settlement was extensive and unfortified. This occupation probably continued until the Babylonian captivity in 587 B.C.

II. *Joshua and the Fall of Jericho.* The dramatic account of the capture of Jericho is given in Joshua 6:1-27. Surrounded by Israelite forces the city was shut up in anticipation of an attack. Strangely, Joshua was ordered to march his army around the city instead of mounting an attack. For six days the priests led Joshua's warriors once each day around the city, and after marching around it seven times on the seventh day, the priests blew the trumpets, all the multitude shouted, and the walls of Jericho fell

307

down flat. The Israelites entered the city and took it. When the houses had been looted of valuables, the city was burned with fire and left in ruins under a curse.

Assuming the correct identification of the site of Old Testament Jericho with Tell es-Sultan, there are two facts related in the capture of the city by Joshua which should be illuminated by excavations. First it is indicated that the walls fell down flat, apparently in a major disruption which caused them to tip down the slope of the mound. And secondly, destruction of the entire city with fire should have left an appreciable deposit of ash upon the ruins of the Late Bronze Age city.

A. Garstang's Interpretation of the Fall of Jericho. The first archaeologist who tried to find evidence of the ruined city was John Garstang and his discoveries were apparently successful and accepted by scholarship in general, even in some of the latest Bible commentaries. Three major lines of archaeological evidence were used to reconstruct the sacking of Jericho by the Israelites under Joshua.

From Garstang's field report dated March 2, 1930 the following description is taken: "The main defences of Jericho in the Late Bronze Age followed the upper brink of the city mound, and comprised two parallel walls, the outer six feet and the inner twelve feet thick. Investigations along the west side show continuous signs of destruction and conflagration. The outer wall suffered most, its remains falling down the slope. The inner wall is preserved only where it abuts upon the citadel, or tower, to a height of eighteen feet; . . . Traces of intense fire are plain to see, including reddened masses of brick, cracked stones, charred timbers and ashes. Houses alongside the wall were found burnt to the ground, their roofs fallen upon the domestic pottery within." Good photographs and a scaled section of the casemate-type walls were published to support the above interpretation.

Inside the ruined walls was found evidence of the city burned with fire. On a brick ledge in the corner of a room was found a family provision of dates, barley, olives, a piece of bread, and a quantity of unbaked dough, all charred but unmistakable. It was sad evidence of a people cut off in full activity. Elsewhere the royal residence with its filled storerooms had been burned and a knee-deep layer of white ash and charred debris covered the ruins. The streaky ash layer was in fact so thick and the burning so thorough that Garstang conjectured that the fires had been set after deliberate preparation. A five-foot thick layer of ash between the city walls supported his theory. In devoting the city as a holocaust, "they burnt the city with fire and all that was therein" (Josh. 6:24).

Unfortunately pottery evidence for dating the fallen walls and the burned palace was indecisive. However, Tombs 4 and 5 provided scarabs of Amenhotep III who reigned alone in Egypt until about 1385 B.C., at which time the heretical Akhenaton, his son, became co-regent. Garstang concluded that no scarabs nor pottery from the City IV tombs or tell could be dated later than 1385 B.C., and that the sacking of Jericho occurred between 1411 and 1385 B.C. When this conclusion was placed alongside I Kings 6:1, which stated that the Exodus occurred 480 years before Solomon began building the temple, Biblical evidence for the fall of Jericho about 1400 B.C. was found to agree with the archaeological evidence. Thus the fall of City IV was that described in the Book of Joshua, and Garstang concluded that the narrative embodied the tradition of an eye-witness.

B. Revision of Garstang's work by Kenyon. Excavations at Jericho from 1952-58 require a radical re-examination of Garstang's interpretations. Careful stratigraphic analysis of the city walls in Trench I indicates that Garstang's parallel walls were in fact Early Bronze Age, belonging with the city one thousand years before the time of Joshua. Furthermore the walls were not contemporary because a layer of debris which overlay the inner wall curved downward and became a part of the foundation of the outer wall. A part of the Hyksos scarp covered both walls, but it was not recognized by the earlier excavators. The highest surviving wall remains on the site were Middle Bronze Age, datable at least 150 years before Joshua, and no Late Bronze Age city walls at all were found.

The palace of Garstang's City IV with its storerooms was found to belong in the Middle Bronze Age, and it apparently was destroyed by the Egyptians about 1550 B.C.

after the expulsion of the Hyksos from Egypt. The thick streaky layer of ashes covering the ruined palace derived from the Egyptian destruction. During the 150 year period of abandonment, 1550-1400 B.C., ashes and debris from the summit of the tell eroded down the slopes and covered the Middle Bronze Age ruins to depths up to five feet. This layer cannot be ascribed to the time of Joshua because it precedes the earliest possible arrival of the Israelites by 150 years.

C. Present Conclusions. What then remains of the city that fell to the Israelites? Unfortunately archaeology can offer little positive evidence. Garstang's "Middle Building" which was built upon the streaky layer of ashes that covered the Middle Bronze Age ruins probably was Late Bronze. It was erroneously ascribed to the Iron Age period of Eglon, king of Moab (see Judg. 3:12-26). Fragmentary remains of a house were found on the east slope during the 1954 excavations which may be dated to the mid-fourteenth century B.C. The foundations of a single wall with about a square yard of intact floor beside it were discovered. On the floor was a small clay oven with a dipper juglet lying beside it. Over the rest of the surrounding area, erosion had carried away all contemporary remains and the modern surface was lower than the level of the floor.

Elsewhere great gulleys were cut into the ruins of the Middle Bronze Age city, and in places the Early Bronze Age remains protruded. In fact there were places where Neolithic ruins lay scarcely over a yard under the present surface. No city walls at all datable to the time of Joshua were identified. The present conclusion is that the Late Bronze Age city which fell to the Israelites must have been quite small and that erosion over the five hundred year period of abandonment after its capture by the Israelites destroyed all but a trace of the city. The meager pottery and scarab evidence from both tombs and the mound suggest that the city was abandoned about 1325 B.C.

BIBLIOGRAPHY. John Garstang, *Liverpool Annals of Archaeology and Anthropology,* Vols. XIX-XXII, 1932-1935; "The Walls of Jericho," *PEQ,* 1931. John Garstang and J. B. E. Garstang, *The Story of Jericho,* London, Marshall, Morgan and Scott, Ltd., 1948. Kathleen M. Kenyon, *Archaeology in the Holy Land,* New York,, Frederick A. Praeger, 1960; *Digging Up Jericho,* London, Ernest Benn, Ltd., 1957; *Excavations at Jericho,* Vol. I, Jerusalem, British School of Archaeology, 1960; "Excavations at Jericho," *PEQ,* 1953-1960; "Some Notes on the History of Jericho in the 2nd Millennium B.C.," *PEQ,* 1951, Ernst Sellin and Carl Watzinger, *Jericho, Die Ergebnisse der Ausgrabungen,* Leipzig, 1913.

JERUSALEM. Sacred to Jews, Christians and Moslems, Jerusalem has been a great religious center since David established his capital there about 1000 B.C. It was probably a significant place of Canaanite worship for 800 years prior to David because Abraham worshiped there and paid tithes to Melchizedek (Gen. 14:18-20). Excavations in 1961 indicate that the Canaanite city of 1800 B.C. had walls far down the east slope of the southeast hill and was as extensive as the city of David. Thus for the last 1750 years Jerusalem has been a religious center, and in Biblical times it became the leading city of Israel.

I. *Names.* One of the Egyptian Execration Texts of the nineteenth century B.C. first mentions a name equivalent to *Urushalim.* Four hundred years later the name appears in the Tell el-Amarna tablets as *Urusalim.* Assyrian records of a later period use the name *Urusilimmu.* In the Bible the city is first mentioned as Salem or Shalem, the priestly kingdom of Melchizedek (Gen. 14:18). During the period of the Judges it was *Jebus* of the Jebusites (Judg. 19:10-11), and after its capture by David (II Sam. 5:6-9) the primary name was Jerusalem until it was rebuilt in A.D. 135 by the Roman emperor Aelius Hadrianus as Aelia Capitolina. The name Jerusalem was restored in the fourth century by Constantine whose mother, Helena, made a pilgrimage to the city in A.D. 326. Among Moslems today it is known as *El Kuds,* "the holy," but to Christians and Jews it is Jerusalem.

The Hebrew name *Yerushalaim* which is translated Jerusalem is derived from the Canaanite *Urushalim* meaning "the god Shalem founded (the city)." *Shalem* was a deity of the Amorites and his association with Jerusalem supports the saying of Ezekiel 16:3, ". . . Thus saith the Lord God unto Jerusalem; thy birth and thy nativity are of the land of Canaan; thy father was an Amorite and thy mother a Hittite." The names of David's sons Absalom and Solomon reflect the name of the Jerusalem deity.

II. *Location and Climate.* Nestled among

AERIAL VIEW OF JERUSALEM. You will find it interesting to compare this photograph of modern Jerusalem with the outline map of ancient Jerusalem on page 313. Courtesy, Matson Photo Service

the hills of the central plateau, Jerusalem lies astride the ancient route which led from Shechem to Hebron. It is 2500 feet above sea level and is located at about thirty one degrees north latitude, about fourteen miles west of the north end of the Dead Sea and thirty three miles east of the Mediterranean coast. High mountains surround the city and the traveler upon reaching the crest of Mount Scopus or the Mount of Olives is arrested momentarily by the sudden picture-like panorama of the crowded city and vast temple area that stretch before his eyes.

Geographically Jerusalem is not the natural center of the hill country. Major international routes led along the coastal region toward Egypt on the west, and on the east the King's Highway led through the Transjordan toward Arabia. Until the time of David, Shechem was a more important political, commercial and religious center than Jerusalem. The pre-eminence of Jerusalem as the First City of the Bible derives from the religious significance given it by David and Solomon in the establishment of the first temple.

Situated on the winding north-south course of the watershed which divides the hill country between the Dead Sea and the Mediterranean, Jerusalem suffers at times from capricious changes in climate. About twenty-four inches of rain falls between October and May. Occasionally in January and February the rain is driven by the wind in slashing sheets that seem to inundate the earth. Between May and October there normally is no rain and the summer heat becomes oppressive at times. Usually cool moisture-laden winds sigh through the narrow streets at night, as when Nicodemus came by night to see Jesus (John 3:1ff.). But occasionally the hot east wind blows in from the desert for periods of three to five days, and the excessive heat and dryness wilt the leaves of plants and cause both man and beast to become uncomfortable and easily irritated.

III. *Topography.* Jerusalem is a city built upon a closely knit series of hills. Deep valleys surround the city on all sides except the north and form natural moats which simplified the building of defences in ancient times. A central valley bisects the city from northwest to southeast, and lateral ravines cut through from the central valley to the deep valleys bounding the city on the east and west creating isolated but closely related hills in the original terrain. However occupation of the site for centuries has caused radical alterations in the topography of the inner city.

A. Valleys. On the east the Kidron Valley bounds Jerusalem along its entire length with slopes that reach an incline of forty degrees. Circling from the west side around the south limits of the city is the Valley of Hinnom with equally steep sides. It joins the Kidron at the southeast tip of the city near the *Bir Ayyub* or Job's Well, known in Biblical times as En-rogel (I Kings 1:9).

The central valley, known in Roman times as the Tyropoeon or Cheesemakers' Valley, runs from a point near the Damascus Gate southeastward to the Pool of Siloam where it joins the Kidron. A lateral branch of the Tyropoeon in ancient times cut across the north end of the temple area to the Kidron, and a second branch probably led to the Kidron at a point below Ophel, isolating somewhat the temple mount and the southeast hill. Another depression branched out westward from the central valley along the general line of David Street to a point near the Jaffa Gate.

The valleys inside the walls of the Old City have been filled with debris over the centuries until only traces of them remain. However, the course of the central valley can be discerned in the stepped streets of the Old City or by looking down upon the city from a high vantage point such as the tower of the Lutheran Church of the Redeemer.

B. Mountains. The relatively low southeast hill known in Biblical times as Mount Zion was the site of Canaanite Jerusalem. It is a narrow spur ridge bounded by the Kidron and the Tyropoeon and possibly cut off from Ophel by a small ravine in the time of David. Opposite Gihon Spring at the foot of the east slope, Mount Zion is hardly sixty yards across on top. Its steep sides were terraced in order to widen the city area to include a part of the slopes in the fortified area. Even with terracing, the fortified area of Mount Zion covered only six to eight acres.

Immediately north of Mount Zion is the temple mount dominated by the sacred rock over which the Moslem Dome of the Rock now stands. The temple mount is much higher than the southeast hill. In Biblical times it was more constricted than the present walled area indicates. Herod the Great widened the temple area artificially and supported the pavement at the southeast corner, just east of the *Al-Aksa* mosque, with arches which form the so-called Solomon's Stables underneath the courtyard. The rounded south ridge of the temple mount is probably Ophel of Biblical times. It is common today to call the southeast hill and south extension of the temple mount, both of which lie outside the present walled city, by the name Ophel.

The high southwest hill became known in post-Roman times as Mount Zion and it was believed until the end of the nineteenth century that the original Canaanite city was located there. It is still the commanding hill of the city with steep sides on the west and south that drop off into the Valley of Hinnom. The Tyropoeon separated the southwest hill from the lower hills to the east, and a ravine almost isolated it from hills on the north. Excavations now indicate that this site was occupied much later than the eastern hills, and that its southern extremity was first fortified in the reign of Herod Agrippa I, about A.D. 42, and connected with the southeast hill across the mouth of the Tyropoeon.

The Church of the Holy Sepulchre is built upon a hill north of the southwest hill. It is in the heart of the present walled city, but according to tradition it lay outside the city in the time of Christ and was the site of the crucifixion and burial. The city of Herod Agrippa I enclosed this area, and it has been a part of the walled city since about A.D. 42.

C. Springs. Jerusalem has always been limited by its meager water supply. Only Gihon Spring at the foot of the east slope of Mount Zion and En-rogel just off the south tip of the hill are perennial springs. Gihon is the major spring. It overflows intermittently three to five times a day in a gushing action caused by cavities in the recesses of the spring which fill up and initiate a siphonlike process. Tunnels and channels were dug to give access to Gihon in time of siege, and it is possible that Joab entered the Jebusite city through one of these tunnels

and captured the city for David (II Sam. 5:8; I Chron. 11:6). The Siloam Tunnel was cut through nearly 1800 feet of limestone to bring the waters of Gihon through Mount Zion to the Pool of Siloam in the reign of Hezekiah (II Kings 20:20; II Chron. 32:30).

IV. *Excavations.* Jerusalem has been excavated more than any Palestinian city and probably has yielded the poorest returns in both objects and information. The paucity of objects is due partly to the fact that Jerusalem has been besieged more than twenty times and partly to its poverty as a capital city. Little information has been garnered from the hundred years of excavations because scientific methods of digging came to Jerusalem last of all the cities in Palestine.

A. Pre-World War I. Captain Charles Warren, a mining engineer, first excavated around the temple mount area in 1867-70 with grudging support by the Palestine Exploration Fund. Warren probed the four sides of the *Haram esh-Sharif* with a system of shafts and tunnels, but he was not able to penetrate the forbidden temple area and learn what lay under the Moslem sanctuary area. A drawing of his famous eighty-foot-deep shaft at the southeast corner of the *Haram* adorns the title page of the *Palestine Exploration Quarterly.*

The tunnel method of excavating was used also by H. Guthe on the southeast hill in 1881, but almost no reliable information was gained. J. Bliss and A. C. Dickie explored the south limits of the western hill in 1894-97 with soundings and tunnels. A huge wall connecting the southeastern and southwestern hills was found across the mouth of the Tyropoeon Valley, but because pottery and stratification were ignored in the excavation method, it was not accurately dated. Excavations in the same area in 1961-62 indicated that Bliss and Dickie did accurately plan the walls and gates which they explored by means of tunnels, a remarkable feat indeed.

Montague Parker resumed work on the southeast hill in 1909-11 with the same shaft-boring method that Warren had used. His explorations above Gihon Spring of the tunnels leading from the spring yielded reliable information on the spring canal system, thanks to Père H. Vincent who interpreted and published the results of the excavation.

It was this expedition which discovered the tombs of the earliest inhabitants of the southeast hill, dating to the thirty-first century B.C.

Raymond Weill in 1913-14 began a systematic excavation of the southern part of the southeast hill and succeeded, by the time World War I broke out, in demonstrating that the southeast hill was the site of the original Mount Zion.

B. World War I to World War II. Weill led a second season of excavations on the southern point of the southeast hill in 1923-24, while J. Garrow Duncan and R. A. S. Macalister excavated in 1923-25 above Gihon Spring in Fields 5, 7, and 9 on top of the ridge. A large area was excavated to bedrock on the ridge, and the so-called "Solomonic tower" and "Jebusite ramp" were identified at the crest of the east slope. Excavations in 1961 indicated that these structures were from the second century B.C., but that Late Bronze Age structures lay deep in the earth beneath them.

J. W. Crowfoot and G. M. Fitzgerald, working with the British School of Archaeology in Jerusalem and the Palestine Exploration Fund as did Duncan and Macalister, began in 1927 a trench from the crest of the southeastern hill across the Tyropoeon. A city gate and wall were discovered on the west side of the hill, proving that the hill was encircled by walls. However, evidence dating the wall and gate to the time of David, as the excavators reported, is lacking.

North of the walled Old City, E. L. Sukenik and L. A. Mayer excavated three seasons (1925-27) and discovered sections of a wall attributed to Herod Agrippa I (A.D. 40-44),

OUTLINE MAP OF ANCIENT JERUSALEM

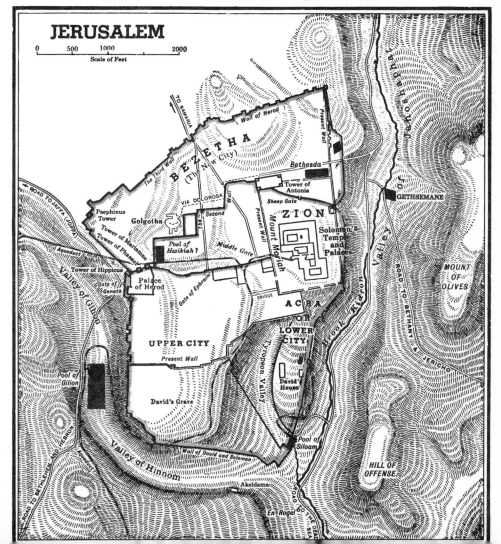

presumably built before the siege by Titus in A.D. 70. The line of this wall has been traced eastward past the American School of Oriental Research property, but its relationship to walls further south is still uncertain. One further excavation, possibly the best conducted before World War II, was led by C. N. Johns with the Department of Antiquities in 1934-40 at the Citadel on the west side of the Old City. A reliable history of the Citadel towers from the Hellenistic period was established, but no architecture traceable to the pre-exilic city was reliably identified.

C. Post World War II. Because of strife between Jews and Arabs following World War II, no large scale excavation in Jerusalem was undertaken until 1961. Under the leadership of Kathleen M. Kenyon of the British School of Archaeology in Jerusalem and Père R. de Vaux of École Biblique et Archeologique de St. Etienne, a seven-season project was begun in 1961. The centennial celebration of the first excavations in Jerusalem, sponsored by the Palestine Exploration Fund under Warren in 1867, coincides with the last phases of this significant excavation. Already the scientific techniques used by Kenyon at Jericho are yielding information on the walls and sequences of occupation in Jerusalem that is radically revising our knowledge of the history of the city. Principal areas being excavated are the southeastern hill above Gihon Spring, the area around the mouth of the Tyropoeon Valley, a site inside the walls of the Old City and immediately south of the *Haram* area, and the Armenian Gardens area just inside the west wall of the Old City and south of the Citadel on the southwestern hill. This last area is in the vicinity of the camp of the Roman Tenth Legion, and possibly in the gardens of Herod's palace.

V. *Early Bronze Age Jerusalem*. About 3000 B.C. nomadic tribes camped on the southeast hill and became the earliest known inhabitants of the site. Three of their tombs were discovered in 1909-11 in a cave near the east crest of the ridge above Gihon Spring. Culture similar to theirs is found at Tell en-Nasbeh, °Ai, Gezer, and at Jericho where Kenyon calls it Proto-Urban B.

Pottery from Early Bronze II and III has been found on bedrock on the east slope of the southeast hill, but no architecture

remains. A deep cave was found near the foot of the slope in 1962, and preliminary explorations indicate that Early Bronze people used the cave, possibly for burials.

VI. *Abraham and Middle Bronze Age Jerusalem*. The city that Abraham visited when he paid tithes to Melchizedek King of Salem (Gen. 14) was probably the *Urushalim* mentioned on one of the Egyptian °Execration Texts of the nineteenth century B.C. A section of the city wall of that time was excavated in 1961-62. Surprisingly it lay 161 feet below the crest of the ridge and outside the easternmost wall of Old Testament Jerusalem. No other remains datable to the time of Abraham have been found, except pottery, but the massive stone wall on the east slope of Mount Zion suggests that the city was as extensive in the Middle Bronze Age as it was during the time of the Jebusites, 800 years later.

The sacred area of Jerusalem in Abraham's time has not been found, but it is probably the temple mount area just north of Mount Zion. It is now fairly certain that the sacred areas at Shechem and Bethel were open air shrines which lay outside the walled cities. II Chronicles 3:1 identifies Mount Moriah where Abraham came to offer Isaac (Gen. 22:1-19) with the temple mount. There are other traditions which are less definite in the identification, but by the time II Chronicles 3:1 was written it was believed that the temple site was the place where Isaac was almost sacrificed. This area was outside the walled city until Solomon enclosed it when he built the First Temple.

On the occasion of Abraham paying tithes to Melchizedek, it is written that he met the king of Sodom and Melchizedek at the Valley of Shaveh or the King's Valley (Gen. 14:17-20). The Valley of Shaveh was apparently near the city of Jerusalem, as Melchizedek brought out bread and wine (Gen. 14:18) for the occasion. It may have been the open space at the juncture of the Kidron and Hinnom valleys possibly near the spring En-rogel. In any case it does not seem to have been the main place of worship associated with Jerusalem. Tradition gives the temple mount area priority for this claim even in the time of Abraham.

VII. *The Late Bronze Age*. Among the Tell el-Amarna letters from Egypt dating to the fourteenth century B.C. are five appeals from Abdi-Hiba king of Jerusalem for the Pharaoh to send military help. Warlike tribes known as the Habiru were taking the hill country by assault upon the cities and by entering into covenants with local rulers like Lab'ayu of Shechem. The Habiru are believed to have been associated with the Hebrews, although the two cannot be equated nor can the Habiru revolution of the fourteenth century B.C. be identified with the Israelite invasion led by Joshua.

During the fourteenth century B.C., under Abdi-Hiba or his Jebusite successors, radical changes were made in the topography of the southeast hill. There was a deep bay in the bedrock at the east crest of the ridge above Gihon Spring. An enterprising project was initiated to fill in the bay with a series of artificial terraces and bring the surface up to the level of the top of the ridge. Platform terraces which served as buttresses for the immense fill stepped down the slope toward Gihon Spring and houses were constructed on the terraces. Deep underneath the so-called Jebusite rampart, a late structure on the crest of the ridge erroneously dated to the Late Bronze Age by Duncan and Macalister, a series of rib walls interlaced the fill at right angles to the east face. On either side of the central spine, the series of walls leaned inward slightly to give strength to the structure.

The structure was obviously a major town-planning operation, such as would be required for royal buildings. It extended the width of the ridge area suitable for level building by sixty feet toward the east. The immense weight of the fill and steep slope down toward Gihon Spring made the structure vulnerable to earthquake and landslides caused by excessive rains. At the end of the 1962 excavations four phases of rebuilding were evident as a result of collapses. The final collapse was in the seventh century B.C., and houses destroyed by the Babylonian armies of Nebuchadnezzar in 587 B.C. were built upon the repair of the last collapse. These houses disappeared by erosion down the slope after 587 B.C., but the terraces remained until they were excavated in 1961-62.

VIII. *Iron Age I and the City of David.* Although Adoni-Zedek, king of Jerusalem, was defeated in the battle of Ajalon with Joshua (Josh. 10:1-26), the city was not taken by the Israelites. Judges 1:1-8 reports that Judah took Jerusalem and burned the city, but apparently the Jebusites recaptured the city because Joshua 15:63 indicates that the Jebusites remained in Jerusalem, presumably until the time of David.

A. The reign of David. The capture of Jerusalem by David is of interest to archaeologists because he used a stratagem that involved Gihon Spring on the east slope of Mount Zion. The accounts in II Samuel 5:6-9 and I Chronicles 11:4-8 are concise and obscure. Jerusalem is called the "stronghold of Zion," which implies a fortress. And the taunt of the Jebusites that the "blind and the lame" could defend the city implies that the fortress was secure against a frontal attack. How then did David capture the city?

A hint is in David's challenge to his men, "whosoever getteth up to the *tsinnor,* and smiteth the Jebusites, ..." (II Sam. 5:8). Joab went up first and was rewarded with command of David's army (I Chron. 11:6). The *tsinnor* has been identified with Warren's Shaft, a tunnel cut from Gihon Spring through the limestone of the east slope to the surface about eighty feet below the top of the ridge. On the basis of identification of the rampart on the crest of the ridge as Jebusite by Duncan and Macalister, some have interpreted David's objective as that of reaching the upper entrance to the tunnel eighty feet outside the wall and thus gaining control of the water supply. However it is now known that the rampart was post-Jebusite and that the Jebusite wall was probably eighty feet down the slope toward Gihon from the entrance to Warren's Shaft, providing access to the watershaft within the Jebusite city.

Discovery of the Jebusite wall well down the slope toward Gihon increases the possibility that Joab entered the city secretly, or with the aid of saboteurs, through Warren's Shaft. One of Parker's men in the 1909-11 explorations demonstrated that the shaft could be climbed. Thus many now hold to the view that Joab and his commando party seized the watershaft in a surprise maneuver, cut off the Jebusites from their water supply, and gained entrance into the fortress by clever stratagem instead of a frontal assault on the walls.

David occupied the city and "built round

about from the millo and inward" (II Sam. 5:9). The "Millo" which literally means "filling," has long been identified with a deposit of debris which widened the narrow ridge just south of the temple mount. However, no archaeological evidence of a planned artificial fill such as the Millo which underlies the temple area at Shechem supports the identification. It is more probable that the great terraced fill on the east side of the ridge above Gihon, first built by the Jebusites in the Late Bronze Age, is the Millo (see VII above).

B. The reign of Solomon. The city walls were repaired and the Millo was rebuilt or extended by Solomon (I Kings 9:15). In 1962 a massive buttressing terrace of huge stones weighing up to a ton each was found at the foot of the Late Bronze Age terrace system. This terrace was firmly based on bedrock and abutted on its upper side the older terraces stacked up the steep slope with bulging walls. Obviously it was a major effort to anchor the whole fill system and stabilize it on the upper slope. Pottery from the massive structure is Iron Age I, dated by Kenyon and De Vaux to the tenth century B.C. Quite possibly the structure may belong in the reign of Solomon and may represent a rebuilding and extension of the Millo.

Solomon's most important project in Jerusalem was the building of the temple and extension of the city to include the temple mount area. Nothing belonging with the temple of Solomon has ever been identified, and no walls around the temple area reliably dated to Solomon have been found. It is probably that the city of Solomon included only the temple mount and the southeast hill, and that the Tyropoeon valley bounded the city on the west. Walls around the temple area would have enclosed the north end of the city and connected it with Mt. Zion. Present evidence indicates that Millo should be located in the area of the so-called Water Gate above Gihon, and that the City of David should be wider than the plan indicates because 161 feet of the east slope was also enclosed in the city.

The temple of Solomon can be reconstructed conjecturally from Biblical descriptions and parallel evidence from sites like Tell Ta'yinat in Syria. A good reconstruction has been drawn by Charles F. Stevens based

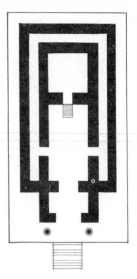

CONJECTURED FLOOR PLAN OF SOLOMON'S TEMPLE in Jerusalem

upon information furnished principally by G. E. Wright.

IX. *Iron Age II and Pre-Exilic Jerusalem.* Josephus thought the southwest hill was the original Mount Zion of David and Solomon and thus was a part of pre-exilic Jerusalem. Scholars and excavators followed Josephus until the southeast hill was proved to be the earliest site of Jerusalem by Weill at the beginning of World War I. It is certain that the southwest hill was an organic part of the city by the time of Herod the Great, but when was it added?

A. Extent of the Pre-Exilic City. Pottery of Iron Age II has been found mixed with later pottery on the southwest hill, but no city walls have been reliably dated earlier than the Hellenistic period. Bliss and Dickie believed that they found a pre-exilic city wall around the southwest hill and across the central valley, but their walls were found in 1962 to be A.D. first century and later. At the present time there is no reliable archaeological evidence that links the southwest hill with the Solominic city until the Hellenistic period. It is fairly certain that no city wall closed the mouth of the Tyropoeon Valley and encircled the lower slopes of the southwest hill in pre-exilic Jerusalem.

Deposits of Iron Age II pottery in the lower Tyropoeon suggest that a pre-exilic city wall may be found across the upper valley. possibly it is as far north as Crowfoot's Gate on the west side of the southeast hill. The walls could very well cross the Tyropoeon in the vicinity of Crowfoot's Gate and encircle the acropolis of the southwest hill. Excavations in 1963 may shed light on the problem.

B. Hezekiah's Tunnel. In preparation for the siege of Jerusalem in 701 B.C. when "Sennacherib king of Assyria came up against all the fenced cities of Judah" (II Kings 18:13), Hezekiah "made a pool and a conduit and brought water into the city" (II Kings 20:20). "He took counsel with his princes and his mighty men to stop the waters of the fountains which were without the city" (II Chron. 32:30). This undoubtedly is an 1800 foot tunnel cut through the solid rock of Mt. Zion which to this day brings the waters of Gihon to the pool of Siloam on the southwest side of the hill. Just inside the central valley opening was found in 1880 an inscription in the Hebrew of Isaiah's time recording the excavating of the tunnel by two teams which started at either end and met in the middle of the hill "one hundred cubits" under the surface overhead.

Other water canals were cut from Gihon around the slope of Mount Zion and through the south point of the hill before Hezekiah's Tunnel was excavated. It was probably by one of these canals "at the end of the conduit of the upper pool" (Isa. 7:3) that Isaiah the prophet met Ahaz in an historic confrontation. The reference in Isaiah 8:6 to "the waters of Shiloah that go softly" must also refer to one of the rock-cut channels which Weill calculated to have a fall of four millimeters per meter in a winding-course around the hill to the southwest side. Hezekiah's Tunnel brought water directly through the hill and eliminated the need for the vulnerable open channels outside the city walls (see Siloan inscription).

C. The Babylonian Destruction in 587 B.C. Hezekiah is reported to have "built up all the wall that was broken, and raised it up to the towers, and another wall without, and repaired the Millo in the city of David" (II Chron. 32:5). Also Manasseh "built a wall without the city of David, on the west side of Gihon, . . . and compassed about Ophel, and raised it up a very great height" (II Chron. 33:14). In 1962 a massive stone wall seventeen feet thick was discovered just inside the line of the Canaanite wall (see VI above). Three stages of use within the seventh-sixth centuries B.C. are evident. Thus the Canaanite wall which was in use from the eighteenth to seventh centuries B.C. was reinforced by a massive Israelite wall based on bedrock behind the older wall. In Site A of the 1962 excavations the older wall turns sharply up the slope on the north side and is incorporated into the Israelite wall in the north balk. It is possible that the Israelite wall may lie outside the Canaanite wall further north. Quite probably the building activities of Hezekiah and Manasseh were involved with these walls which in places were combined and in other places were separated.

The Babylonian army of Nebuchadnezzar breached the massive fortifications of Jerusalem and razed the houses on the slopes of Mount Zion. Pottery buried in ashes on the plaster floors of wrecked houses attests the violence of the destruction. There is no indication on the slopes of the southeast hill that the houses were rebuilt or the walls restored after 587 B.C.

X. *Nehemiah and the Post-Exilic City.* In the twentieth year of Artaxerxes I (*ca.* 444 B.C.) Nehemiah was commissioned to return to Jerusalem and rebuild the city walls (Neh. 2:1-8). The accounts of his work and that of Ezra comprise the most specific information in the Old Testament on the topography of Jerusalem (see Neh. 2:12-15; 3:1-32; 6:15; 8:1; 9:4; 12:31-43; Ezra 10:6-7). M. Avi-Yonah's plan of the city with its location of the various gates and walls is probably the most accurate in the light of present knowledge. It represents the city as much constricted on the southeast hill, which was true in the time of Nehemiah but not true of the pre-exilic city.

No structural remains dating after 587 B.C. are found below the crest of the hill. However a wall was located on the east crest of Mount Zion in 1962 which may be a wall of Nehemiah. It stands on a scarp of rock cut away at the base of the wall to prevent access to the wall on its outer side. There is no positive stratigraphic evidence linking the wall with multiple layers of debris from the Persian period at the base of the scarp, but it is quite clear that the city did not extend down the slope. The opinion of Kenyon and De Vaux is that here is a remnant of the wall built "in fifty and two days" (Neh. 6:15). Not only was the rebuilt temple of Ezra and Nehemiah only a shadow of its former glory, but the city of Jerusalem was restricted to the narrow crest of the southeast hill in an area of less than six acres.

XI. *The Maccabean City.* When the Maccabees gained power, Jerusalem was in ruins and a Syrian garrison occupied a citadel reported by Josephus to be in the "lower city" overlooking the temple courtyard. Jonathan dwelt in Jerusalem about 153 B.C. and began to rebuild the city. He encircled the southeast hill with a wall of "squared stones" (I Macc. 10:11).

The wall of ashlar masonry on top of the hill, which was called "Solomonic" by Duncan and Macalister, was found to be mid-second century B.C. in the 1961 excavations. It must be the work of Jonathan. Thus the Maccabean occupation of the southeast hill was limited to the small area on top of the ridge covered by the post-exilic city and did not extend down the slopes of the line of the pre-exilic city walls.

The citadel reported by Josephus in the "lower city" cannot be located. There is not a place south of the temple area where a citadel could conceivably be located high enough to overlook the temple courtyard. Some scholars believe it must have been on the northeast slope of the western ridge, site of the modern "Jewish Quarter" where the elevation of the ridge affords even today a view into the courtyard.

On top of the southwest hill was also a part of the Maccabean city. Underlying the towers at the Jaffa Gate on the west are foundations dating to the Hellenistic period. Thus the first positive evidence of incorporation of the western hill into the city comes from this time. The line of the First North Wall, along David Street, must mark the northern limits of the city.

XII. *The Reign of Herod.* In sheer physical magnitude the building enterprises of Herod the Great exceeded that of any ruler of Jerusalem, including Solomon. One of the first projects was to rebuild and enlarge a strategic fortress at the northwest corner of the temple area which guarded the north approach to the temple. The fortress was built foursquare with massive towers at each corner ranging from sixty to

one hundred feet high. A central courtyard was paved with large flat stones and probably became the arena for semi-public pronouncements by the local rulers. It is thought that Jesus appeared before Pilate (John 19:13) in this courtyard. Herod named the fortress Antonia in honor of Mark Anthony and made it his residence before he built a palace on the western hill.

The western hill was strongly fortified on its northern approach by the erection of massive towers which Herod named Hippicus, Phasael and Miriamne. Herodian masonry can be seen today in the three towers which still guard the western approach to the Old City at the Jaffa Gate. On the western hill south of the fortress towers Herod built a palace which became the residence of later Roman rulers of Jerusalem when they visited the city. The palace was supplied with water by an aqueduct from a source near Bethlehem, possibly "Solomon's Pools" south of the city.

Also inside the city Herod built a xystus or arena for athletic contests as well as an amphitheater and a theater. These may have been located in the Tyropoeon valley where the terrain would lend itself to the building of structures with elevated spectator seats, but no remains of the structures have been identified.

Herod's most notable building enterprise was the reconstruction of the temple, which he never finished. The sacred enclosure was enlarged to about twice its former size and new walls of characteristic Herodian masonry were built from bedrock. The stones were exceedingly large but closely fitted together without mortar. One massive block high in the wall at the southeast corner of the enclosure today is estimated to weigh near ninety tons.

By filling in the edge of the Kidron Valley at the southeast corner and constructing stone supporting pillars and arches, the courtyard area was extended both south and east. Underneath the paved area which lies on top of the pillars is a spacious ground level called "Solomon's Stables" today. At the southwest corner of the enclosure the Tyropoeon Valley was also partially filled in to allow extension of the paved courtyard on that side equal to that on the Kidron side. The so-called "Wailing Wall" along the west boundary of the sacred enclosure was built

THE ANTONIA, Herod's fortress in New Testament Jerusalem. Artist's reconstruction. Courtesy, Ecce Homo Orphanage, Jerusalem

by Herod and can be seen today. Apparently a bridge across the Tyropoeon to the western hill was connected with the southwest corner of the enclosure at the point of "Robinson's Arch," an anchor stone for an arch went in the massive wall.

The temple area was extended northward by filling in the ravine that once bounded the north side of the temple mount. At the northwest corner, the tower of Antonia guarded and overlooked the vast enclosure.

Only two stones known today can be related to the temple structure built by Herod. Both contain inscriptions forbidding the entry of Gentiles into the inner court of the temple upon pain of death and they must have been set in the walls of the inner court near entrances. No archaeological evidence of the temple building itself is known.

In addition to the impressive structures noted above, Herod rebuilt the remaining walls of Jerusalem. The western hill, where his palace was located, was occupied on the summit possibly as a royal quarter. A wall of debatable course ran from a point near the towers Hippicus, Phasaelus and Miriamne bounding the north side of the palace in a northeasterly direction to the tower of Antonia. Josephus notes that the wall began at the "Gennath Gate" on the west side of the city, a point not identified yet by archaeologists. This wall is significant because of its bearing upon the location of Golgotha and the garden tomb, discussed below.

XIII. *The Ministry of Jesus.* Surprisingly few of the places in Jerusalem associated with the ministry of Jesus have been reliably located by archaeologists. Jesus knew the city that Herod built, and that city was destroyed by the Romans in A.D. 70 and again in A.D. 132-135, after which it was radically replanned and rebuilt as Aelia Capitolina. Only in the fourth century did interest arise in locating the sacred places associated with the ministry of Jesus, and by that time the topography of the city had changed. Consequently we are largely dependent upon church traditions of uncertain value dating from the fourth century for most of the sites pointed out to pilgrims today. Archaeological investigation of some sites has been quite thorough, but in most cases, excavation has been either impossible or quite superficial and unsatisfactory. To illustrate the difficulties of identifying places, the Via Dolorosa with its fourteen stations of the cross is as much as twenty feet above the first century levels of the authentic Via Dolorosa.

Two pools of Jerusalem mentioned by John prior to the last week of Jesus' ministry may be located with some certainty. The pool called Bethesda, or Bethzatha (RSV), where Jesus healed the lame man (John 5:1-6) has possibly been located by excavations at the Church of St. Anne just north of the temple enclosure. (See Bethesda, Pool of.) Twin pools separated by a rock partition about twenty feet thick have been

319

GREEK INSCRIPTION IN THE TEMPLE forbidding Gentiles to enter the inner court under penalty of death. It dates from about A.D. 30 and was in the Temple at the time of Christ. Courtesy, the Louvre

found, supporting early church traditions of twin pools in the area called Bezeth by Josephus. The Biblical account suggests a water source of intermittent flow, but the source has not been located.

The man born blind (John 9:1-7) was instructed by Jesus to go and wash in the pool of Siloam. There is a pool of Siloam located today at the lower end of Hezekiah's tunnel from Gihon spring. The present pool structure is of more recent construction, but it is likely that the New Testament pool of Siloam was in the same vicinity.

Jesus appeared before Pilate at the Praetorium which has been located by tradition at Herod's palace on the southwest hill and also at Antonia adjoining the temple enclosure walls. Most authorities accept the location at Antonia, mainly on the basis of French excavations under the convent of the Sisters of Zion. A large stone pavement more than 150 feet square has been found in what was probably the courtyard of Antonia. Scratched in the stones of the pavement are the diagrams of what must have been Roman games played by the idle soldiers.

Here then is quite likely the place of which John 19:13 speaks: ". . . Pilate . . . brought Jesus forth, and sat down in the judgment seat in a place that is called the Pavement, but in the Hebrew, Gabbatha." The sentence of death may have been pronounced on Jesus here.

The present Via Dolorosa from the site of Antonia, where Jesus was sentenced, to the Church of the Holy Sepulchre where tradition holds that he was crucified, is of more emotional than historical value. The real Via Dolorosa is deep beneath the present one and probably follows a different course. However this is a technicality of little consequence to the thousands of fervent pilgrims who annually bear crosses in processionals from the site of the judgment seat of Pilate by way of the stations of the cross to the Church of the Holy Sepulchre and traditional Golgotha.

According to Eusebius the Roman Emperor Constantine in the fourth century directed Bishop Macarius to locate the places of the crucifixion and burial of Jesus. Reportedly he was led to the site through a vision of e Queen Mother Helena. Constantine rected two churches: Golgotha at the site f the crucifixion and Anastasis at the site of he tomb. The sprawling Church of the Holy epulchre covers today the sites of both he ancient structures. Traditions of the site annot be carried back earlier than the early urth century. Nevertheless there must have een a strong tradition associated with the te in the fourth century because it was cated then within the city walls, and Ha-ian's Temple of Aphrodite was demol-hed to make room for Constantine's Church f the Anastasis. It is likely that a strong adition, as well as visionary guidance, in-uenced the identification of the site. In the resent Church of the Holy Sepulchre, the levated rock pointed out as Golgotha and he tomb under the rotunda of the ancient tructure almost lose the interest of the west-n pilgrim because of garish adornments of old, crosses, relics, lights and the unrealistic tories told to tourists.

A second site has been promoted as the ite of Golgotha and the garden tomb. Char-s Gordon claimed that a rocky hill about 50 yards northeast of the Damascus Gate reviously pointed out by Otto Thenius of Dresden was the place of the skull. He was ided in the identification by an active ima-ination because cavities in the side of he hill did in fact suggest the appearance f a skull. A rock-cut tomb is located nearby. t is complete with a large stone shaped ike a solid wheel which can be rolled in its ewn track to close the tomb entrance. How-ver the tomb seems to be post-apostolic and erhaps is Byzantine in origin. No tradition arlier than the nineteenth century supports he authenticity of Gordon's Calvary or the omb. It is true nevertheless that the devout ilgrim may find more of a sense of rever-nce in the quiet simple outdoor surround-ngs of Gordon's Calvary and the associated epulchre than in the cluttered confines of he Church of the Holy Sepulchre, even hough the latter has more claim to authen-icity.

Location of Golgotha and the Garden Tomb is affected by the course of the "second vall" reported by Josephus. The first wall n the north seems to have run east from he towers of Herod at the present Jaffa Gate to the temple enclosure walls. Jose-phus said the second wall began at the Gen-

nath (or Garden) Gate, of the first wall presumably, and that it enclosed the north quarter of the city and ended at the for-tress Antonia. If the Gennath Gate was near the middle of the first wall, the second wall could have run northward on the east side of the Church of the Holy Sepulchre, then eastward to Antonia. A sounding ten meters square is being excavated in the courtyard of the Lutheran school which is a few yards north of a point near the middle of the first wall. Angled tip lines indicating fill have been found under Byzantine levels, but no certain evidence of a city wall has been identified.

If the Gennath Gate was near the west end of the first wall, the second wall could have turned to the east either north or south of the Church of the Holy Sepulchre. In either case there is the unusual situation of a fortification wall standing on lower ground than the surface outside it. The ab-sence of positive archaeological evidence of the course of the second wall leaves the site of the traditional Golgotha dependent mainly on tradition dating to the fourth cen-tury. This may be just as well for the devout pilgrim because of the tendency to make sacred places almost objects of idol worship. It is possibly more conducive to reverence to know only that somewhere in the vicinity Jesus was crucified, buried and rose again the third day.

XIV. *The Apostolic Period to A.D. 70.* Healing and preaching were done in the precincts of the temple by the apostles and clashes with temple officials occurred there. It was the same temple begun by Herod the Great and known to Jesus in his ministry.

One incident in Acts 6:9-15 involving Stephen has possible amplification from arch-aeological discovery. It is said that some of those who belonged to "the synagogue of the Freedmen" (v. 9) disputed with Stephen. A possible reference to this syna-gogue is contained in the Theodotus Inscrip-tion found near the tip of the southeast hill of Jerusalem in 1913-14. The text reads in part: "Theodotus son of Vettenus, priest and synagogue president, . . . has built the synagogue . . . and the hostelry and the chambers and the cisterns of water in order to provide lodgings for those from abroad who need them. . . ." Theodotus' family name is thought to be derived from the

Roman family of Vetteni, which suggests that he or an ancestor was a freedman from Italy. The inscription is believed to date prior to A.D. 70 and could refer to the synagogue of the Freedmen of Acts 6:9.

Stephen was stoned to death outside the city (Acts 7:58) and the Dominican church of St. Stephen just north of the Damascus Gate, built on the foundation of a fifth century basilica, is one traditional site of the martyrdom of Stephen. Another is the Greek chapel of St. Stephen in the Kidron Valley outside St. Stephen's Gate in the east wall of Jerusalem.

About A.D. 42 Herod Agrippa I began what Josephus called the "third wall," but he quickly abandoned it to avoid incurring the displeasure of Emperor Claudius. The wall was intended to enclose the suburb Bezeth north of the Herodian "second wall." Foundations of an ancient wall have been found in the garden of the American School of Oriental Research and at points to the east and west of the school, several hundred yards north of the Damascus Gate. These may be remains of Agrippa's "third wall," but dating evidence is not conclusive and the wall has not been traced to its junction with the known walls of the Herodian city.

The "third wall," found first by Sukenik and Mayer, may be a post-New Testament period fortification and the actual "third wall" of Herod Agrippa I may have followed near the course of the present north wall of the old city. Excavations in 1962 indicate that Herod Agrippa extended the city to the south and completely enclosed the southwest hill, the Tyropoeon Valley and the southeast hill with fortifications. Bliss and Dickie first located this line of walls and erroneously ascribed it to pre-exilic Jerusalem. Present evidence indicates that the first complete enclosure of the southwest hill and mouth of the Tyropoeon was in mid-first century A.D., probably by Agrippa I.

Jerusalem revolted against the Romans in A.D. 66, and the city became a hotbed of intrigue and revolution. Intra-mural strife among the people and leaders prepared the way for defeat by the Romans. The north wall of Agrippa I, now completed, was breached by the battering rams of the Romans with the aid of their siege towers and the fortress Antonia was captured and occupied. The temple area became the scene of a massacre followed by destruction of the temple itself. The entire city was plundered and burned in A.D. 70 and it must

THE LITHOSTROTON beneath the church of the Sisters of Zion in Jerusalem. Many modern scholars identify this with the pavement, or Gabbatha, of John 19:13. Courtesy, Ecce Homo Orphanage, Jerusalem

DETAIL OF STONE in the Lithostroton. Courtesy, Ecce Homo Orphange, Jerusalem

have seemed that not one stone remained upon another (see Luke 19:43-44). Christians in the city are reported to have escaped to Pella. Tens of thousands of Jews perished and were thrown outside the wall into the valley of Hinnom. Jerusalem ceased to play a significant role in either Jewish or Christian history because a curse seemed to have fallen upon it with the coming of the Roman Legions.

Not until after the conversion of Constantine in the early fourth century did Jerusalem begin to attract wide interest among Christians. And then it was significant more as a museum of early Christian history than as a dynamic center of Christian faith. The image of the museum has persisted until this day perhaps to remind us to look for a new Jerusalem that will come "down out of heaven from God" (Rev. 21:10).

BIBLIOGRAPHY. M. Avi-Yonah, *Jerusalem,* The Orion Press, New York, 1960. F. J. Bliss, and A. C. Dickie, *Excavations at Jerusalem, 1894-1897,* London, 1898. J. W. Crowfoot, and G. N. Fitzgerald, *Excavations in the Tyropoeon Valley, Jerusalem, 1927, Palestine Exploration Fund Annaul,* Vol V, London, 1929. Flavius Josephus, *Antquities of the Jews,* Whiston; *Wars of the Jews,* Whiston. R. W. Hamilton, "Excavations against the north wall of Jerusalem," *Quarterly of the Department of Antiquities of Palestine,* Vol. X, 1940, pp. 1-54. C. N. Johns, "Recent Excavations at the Citadel," *PEQ,* 1940, pp. 36-58. Kathleen M. Kenyon, "Excavations at Jerusalem, 1961," *PEQ,* 1962, pp. 72-90; "Excavations in Jerusalem, 1962," *PEQ,* 1963, pp. 7-21. R. A. S. Macalister, and J. G. Duncan, *Excavations on the Hill of Ophel, Jerusalem, 1923-1925, Palestine Exploration Fund Annual,* Vol. IV, London, 1926. George Adam Smith, *Jerusalem, The Topography, Economics, and History from the Earliest Times to A.D. 70,* 2 vols., London, 1907, 1908. E. L. Sukenik, and L. A. Mayer, *The Third Wall of Jerusalem, an Account of Excavations,* Jerusalem, 1930. J. Simons, *Jerusalem in the Old Testament,* E. J. Brill, Leiden, 1952. L. H. Vincent, and A. M. Steve, *Jerusalem à l' Ancien Testament,* 4 vols., J. Gabalda et Cei, Paris, 1954. L. H. Vincent, *Underground Jerusalem,* London, 1911. R. Weill, *La Cité de David . . . Campagne de 1913-1914,* Paris, 1920; *La Cité de David . . . Campagne de 1923-1924,* Paris, 1947. Charles Warren, *The Recovery of Jerusalem,* London, 1871.

JEWELRY. Both men and women in the ancient Near East adorned themselves with jewelry, some of which (e.g. *Amulets) had a magical significance. Shell, bone, and vertebrae of fish were fashioned into jewelry by the *Natufians as early as 8000 B.C. Significant discoveries of jewelry were made in the royal cemeteries at *Ur and in the tomb of King Tutankhamun. The Oriental Institute expeditions at *Megiddo discovered examples of Canaanite jewelry.

Among common articles of jewelry were gem *seals, bracelets, anklets, pendants, ear and nose rings, and gold nets for the hair.

323

When Abraham's servant was seeking a bride for Isaac he presented Rebecca with "a golden earring of half a shekel weight, and two bracelets for her hands of ten shekels weight of gold" (Gen. 24:22). While Moses was on Mount Sinai, Aaron asked the men of Israel to bring the golden earrings from the ears of their wives, sons, and daughters so that he might fashion them into a golden calf (Exod. 32:1-6). A legitimate use for such materials was found, however, in the building of the tabernacle when "they came, both men and women, as many as were willing, and brought bracelets, and earrings, and rings, and tablets, all jewels of gold; and every man that offered an offering of gold unto the Lord" (Exod. 35:27). In Judges 8:24 we read that the Ishmaelites wore earrings (or noserings).

Monarchs wore jewelry crowns and sat on richly ornamented, jeweled thrones. During his conquests David acquired the jeweled crown of the king of *Ammon (II Sam. 12:30). The queen of Sheba, in southern *Arabia brought gold and precious stones, along with the spices for which her land was famous, when she came to see Solomon (I Kings 10:2).

Among the Jews who returned from Babylon was "Malchiah the goldsmith's son" (Neh. 3:31). For centuries Semitic craftsmen have fashioned wires of gold and silver into beautiful, jewel-studded ornaments.

In speaking of the value of wisdom, the book of Job asserts that its value far exceeds the gold of Ophir, the precious onyx, the sapphire, topaz, pearls, and rubies (Job 28:15-20). All of these stones were valued for their beauty and scarcity, and were used in the manufacture of jewelry.

JEWISH SECTS. The *Assideans* or *Hassideans* (Greek form of Hebrew *Ḥasidim* — "The pious ones"), were a Jewish religious group organized during the fourth or third century B.C. to revive and promote the observance of Jewish rites, to study the Law, and to uproot paganism from the land. Their date of origin cannot be known with certainty, but they are first mentioned by this name when the members joined the Maccabean revolt against the Syrians in the second century, B.C. They formed the nucleus of the revolt and refused to compromise in any way with the Hellenizing policies of Syrians. The Assi-

deans were exposed to torture and death for their refusal to desecrate the Sabbath and other Jewish observances. Explicit reference to the Assideans in the Books of Maccabees describe them as mighty men in Israel, devoted to the Law, and welcoming peace with the Syrians when promised assurance of religious liberty. They ceased to cooperate with the Hasmoneans, the successors of Judas the Maccabee, in their fight for political independence. Certain passages in the Psalms speak of the "pious ones," but it is doubtful that these were the Assideans. Similar references in the Mishna and especially in the Talmud — their strict observance of the commandments, rigid adherence to the Sabbath, and their ardent devotion to prayers which they would not renounce even at the risk of their lives — may be to the Assideans or to merely pious individuals of a later period. Because of their meticulous observance the Assideans have been linked with the Essenes, but scholarly concensus places them as the spiritual forerunners of the Pharisees.

Pharisees. The Pharisees were a Jewish religious and political party during the Second Temple period which emerged as a distinct group shortly after the Maccabean revolt, about 165-160 B.C. Their origin may be traced to the Assideans (or *Ḥasidim*), an earlier Jewish sect which promoted the observance of Jewish ritual and the study of the Torah. The Pharisees considered themselves the traditional successors of Ezra, whom they cherished, after Moses, the founder of Judaism, maintaining the validity of the Oral Law as well as of the Pentateuch as the source of their religion. They tried to adapt old codes to new conditions, believed in a combination of free will and predestination, in the resurrection of the dead, and in recompense for this life in the next. Though at first relatively small in number, the Pharisees came to represent, by the time of the New Testament, the religious beliefs, practices, and social attitudes of the vast majority of the Jewish population. They attempted to imbue the masses with a spirit of holiness, based on a scrupulous observance of the Torah, by spreading traditional religious teaching. So greatly did religious values prevail over political in the Pharisaical framework that they were willing to submit to foreign domination — so long as it did not interfere with their inner way of life

– rather than to support an impious government of their own.

The Pharisees first made a bid for power in a period about two centuries after the Babylonian Exile, when men from the masses began to wage a long and bitter struggle to remove the Temple control and religious rule from the priests and the aristocratic Sadducees. Ceremonies originally part of the Temple cult were carried over to the home, and learned men of non-priestly descent began to play an important role in national religious affairs. While the priesthood exhausted itself in the round of Temple ritual, the Pharisees found their main function in teaching and preaching the Law of God. The inception of synagogue worship traced to this time may have been an attempt by the Pharisees to undermine the privileged authority exercised by the Sadducees. By the beginning of the second century B.C. a conflict was developing between the lay and priestly factions of the supreme council and tribunal, called the Sanhedrin, regarding the interpretation of the Torah for decisions to questions arising in daily life. The Pharisees exploited this opportunity to incorporate non-Biblical folk-customs into the Temple cult. In general, the Pharisees admitted the validity of an evolutionary and non-literal approach toward the legal decisions; they regarded the legal framework of the Oral Law, as equally as that of the Written Law. The antagonism between them and the Sadducees extended to many spheres outside of the religious, and eventually became a fundamental and distinctive one. Under John Hyrcanus the Pharisees were expelled from membership in the Sanhedrin and branded with the name *Perushim*, "the expelled ones," meant as a taunt, which they accepted, but in its alternate Hebrew significance, the "exponents" as Shammai and Hillel, and Ishmael and Akiba. When Pharisaism gave utterance to the hopes of the oppressed Jewish masses during the Maccabean revolt, it had become evident that its theological doctrines were affecting the entire life of the Pharisees. They held, in opposition to the Sadducees, doctrines which included belief in the resurrection of the dead on the Day of Judgment, reward and retribution in the life after death, the coming of the Messiah, and the existence of angels, and also Divine foreknowledge along with man's free choice of, and therefore responsi-

bility for, his deeds. These beliefs touched on the theological foundations of life.

Based on the sayings of the prophets, the Pharisees conceived of God as a spiritual Being, all-wise, all-knowing, all-just, all-merciful. He loves *all* His creatures and asks of man to walk in His ways, to act justly and to love kindness. Though all-knowing and omnipotent, He endowed man with the power to choose between good and evil. He created in him two impulses, a good and a bad one, advised him to do good and gave him the Torah as a guide. God is transcendant, therefore could not be comprehended, could not really be spoken of in anthropomorphic terms, nor could his totality of being be designated with a name. Two names taken over merely to describe some attribute of God, incomprehensible to man, were "The Divine Presence" and "The Spirit of Holiness."

For the Pharisees, the Torah God gave to Moses consisted of the Written and the Oral Law, and both were truth. The Divine Revelation in the first five books of Moses were to be supplemented and explained by the prophets and the unwritten tradition, and were intended to guide man in the right way of life. The Torah was the center of Pharisaic teachings, and since Divinely inspired, it comprised all law, and was sufficient for all men and all times. Their view of the Law was that its commandments must be interpreted in conformity with the standard of the teachers of each generation, and made to harmonize with advanced ideas. When a precept was outgrown, it was given a more acceptable meaning, so that it would harmonize with the truth resulting from God-given reason. When the letter of the Law seemed to oppose conscience, it was to be taken, according to the primary authority of the teachers, in its spirit. The Mosaic Law of "an eye for an eye" for instance, was interpreted to refer to monetary compensation and not retaliation. In insisting on the compulsory nature of the Oral Law (a set of traditions and practices which developed in preceding centuries without Scriptural backing), the Pharisees generated a ramified system of hermeneutics. They found no great difficulty in harmonizing Torah teachings with their advanced ideas, or in finding their ideas implied or hinted at in the words of the Torah. It was due to this progressive tendency, however, that the Pharisaic interpretation of Judaism continued to

325

develop and remain a vital force in Jewry.

The Pharisees believed that since God was everywhere, He should be worshiped both in and outside of the Temple, and was not to be propitiated by bloody sacrifices. They thus fostered the Synagogue as a place of worship and raised it to a central and important status in the life of the people which rivaled the Temple.

The Sadducees believed that God takes little cognizance of and little interest in human affairs, except to reward or to punish His people as a group. The Pharisees held that everything in the world is ordained by God, but that man has it in his power to choose between good and evil. Although "fate does cooperate in every action," and although God can determine man's choice of conduct, he leaves the choice open to man himself.

On the belief in man's responsibility for his actions is predicated the Pharisaic belief in Divine retribution. To the Pharisees, man would be rewarded or punished in the next life, according to his deserts, and this obviated the need to explain away the vexing problem of why the righteous suffer and the wicked prosper in this world. This belief in Divine retribution rests on the more basic one that man's existence is not limited to this life alone. Though evident in many Persian and Greek sources, the concept of the immortality of man is proper to the Scriptures, and can be found in many of their passages.

As there is one God, there is one humanity, and the only distinction between Jew and Gentile, in the Pharisaic system, is that of believing in the Torah. Israel was given the Torah while in the wilderness; her position among nations is now that of older brother; it was her duty therefore to help other people to recognize the Torah as God's Law. With this in mind, the Pharisees engaged in very active propaganda and proselytized widely.

While the Pharisees, as a whole, set a high ethical standard for themselves, not all lived up to it. New Testament references to them as "hypocrites" of "off-spring of vipers" should not be applied to the entire group. However, the leaders were well aware of the onerous presence of the insincere among their numbers, but had no means of getting at them. The Talmud contains denunciations on such Pharisees. St. Paul himself had been a Pharisee, was a son of a Pharisee, and was taught by one of the sect's most eminent scholars, Gamaliel of Jerusalem. Pharisaic doctrines have more in common with those of Christianity than is supposed, having prepared the ground for Christianity with such concepts as Messianism, the popularization of monotheism, and apocalypticism and with such beliefs as life after death, resurrection of the dead, immortality, and angels and spirits.

The active period of Pharisaism extended well into the second century A.D., and was the most influential in the development of orthodox Judaism. The Pharisees were the most deeply earnest in the religion of their forefathers, represented the most stable elements in their religion, and were the most instrumental in preserving and transmitting Judaism. Unlike the Zealots, they rejected the appeal to force and violence, believing that God was in control of history, and that every true Jew should live in accordance with the Torah. It is not surprising, therefore, that the Pharisees devoted much of their effort to education. After the destruction of the Temple and the fall of Jerusalem in A.D. 70, it was the synagogue and the schools of the Pharisees that continued to function and to promote Judaism. Pharisaism has persisted in its course as a liberal religious movement, both within and without Judaism, giving man a finer appreciation of religious ideas, a higher spiritual conception of God, and a greater recognition that God is his father and man his brother.

The *Sadducees* were a Jewish religious sect of the latter half of the Second Temple period, formed about 200 B.C. as the party of highpriests and aristocratic families, and was opposed by the Pharisees down to the time of the destruction of Jerusalem in A.D. 70. They represented the conservative position in religious matters, and so questioned the validity of oral tradition upheld by the Pharisees. Both in Josephus' writings and in the New Testament, Sadduceeism is associated with certain definite religious views, rejecting the doctrines of the resurrection of the body, the immortality of the soul, and the existence of angels and ministering spirits. The Sadducees laid great stress on the letter of the Mosaic Law, which they believed provided no basis for the Pharisees' supernatural beliefs. The early Christian Church then, having had more in common doctrinally with the Pharisees, had most to fear from the Sadduces (Acts 4 and 5).

The word "Sadducee" is probably derived from Zadok, the high priest in the time of David, to whose family the control of the Temple was later entrusted. His descendants, the Zadokites, and their sympathizers were known as Sadducees. Composed largely of the wealthier elements of the population — influential priests, wealthy merchants, and worldly aristocracy — the party was the most influential in the political and economic life of Palestine. The Sadducees dominated the Temple and its rites, and many were members of the supreme Jewish council and tribunal called the Sanhedrin. Thus not all priests were Sadducees and not all Sadducees were priests.

The rivalry between the Pharisees, who claimed the authority of piety and learning, and the Sadducees, who claimed that of blood and position, was in a sense a renewal of the conflict between prophets and priests of pre-exilic times. When the Temple and its sacrificial cult had been restored, the priests regained their position as religious leaders. This was later weakened by the rise of laymen and "scribes," i.e., learned men of non-priestly descent, and/or the influence of the Greeks. By the beginning of the second century B.C., the Sanhedrin was composed of both priests and lay leaders.

The basic difference between the Pharisees and the Sadducees concerned their *attitude* toward the Torah. Both acknowledged its supremacy. The Pharisees assigned to the Oral Law, however, a place of authority alongside the written, whereas the Sadducees refused to recognize any precept as binding unless found in the Torah. This difference led to a struggle between two concepts of God, seen as anthropomorphic to the Sadducees and as transcendant to the Pharisees. The Sadducees seemed to have believed that God is not concerned with human affairs, and, according to Josephus, that all actions are within the power of man. The Sadducees tended to adhere strictly to the letter of the Law. They acted severely in cases involving the death penalty. The Mosaic principle of *Lex Talionis* was interpreted literally and not construed as one of monetary compensation, as it was by the Pharisees.

Josephus and the Talmud say little about the Sadducean position on prayer, but the sect would naturally not favor a ritual of prayer and study alone, as this would diminish the importance of the sacrifice cult, and thus threaten its own priestly status. It is to be assumed that the Pharisaical institution of the Synagogue was viewed by the Sadducees as such a threat. Not only were the Sadducees opposed to innovations in and departures from the Written Law, but they denounced any reform in the functions of the Temple. They were, in effect, a conservative priestly group, cherishing highest regard for the sacrificial cult of the Temple.

In the New Testament, John the Baptist condemned jointly the Pharisees and the Sadducees, and Jesus denounced them together (Matt. 16:6-12). According to Acts 4:1; 5:17; and 23:6-8, Peter and John were imprisoned by them. There have been controversial references in Rabbinical literature to the Sadducees on the interpretation of the Law. The Sadducees have been represented as lax and worldly-minded aristocrats, primarily interested in maintaining their own privileged position, and favoring Greco-Roman culture. Unfortunately we have no statement from the Sadducean side of their belief and principles.

Historically the Sadducees came under the influence of Hellenism and later were in favor with the Roman rulers, though unpopular with the common people, from whom they kept aloof. Since the whole power and reason for existence of the Sadducees were bound up with the Temple cult, the group ceased to exist after the destruction of the Temple in A.D. 70. By the end of the first half of the second century, the Pharisees were the sole teachers and leaders of the Jewish people.

The *Essenes* were a religious communal Jewish sect or brotherhood in Palestine in the latter half of the Second Temple period (*ca.* 2nd century B.C. — end of 1st century A.D.). The members opposed the ownership of private property and adhered to celibacy; they clustered in monastic communities from which women were, with few exceptions, excluded, lived austerely, and held everything they owned in common. They kept no slaves and abhorred slavery. The proceeds of their own labor, exclusively manual and generally agricultural, replenished a common fund. The Essenes devoted their lives to a study of the Torah in its minutest details. Like the Pharisees, the Essenes, at first, withdrew from the defilements of everyday life and practiced a ritual purity, but even went so far as to gather in their own "purified" monastic centers, where emphasis was put on meticulous ceremonial purity, as in communal baptism and communal meals. In the course of time the communities developed into more closely-linked units until finally, in order to give undivided attention to the Torah, they divided into separate groups in several locales. By the end of the first century B.C. their main division was located on the northwestern shore of the Dead Sea region, organized as a genuine monastic order.

The Essenes were never numerous, numbering no more than four thousand in Philo's day. They replenished their numbers by adopting proselytes who had undergone a period of probation. Although the Essenes as a body preferred the country to the city, some took part in urban and political life, and some were known to have participated in the wars against the Romans, wherein they endured torture and death rather than forsake their religious precepts. The discovery of the *Dead Sea Scrolls has cast a new and interesting light on the nature of the Essenes or some sect closely related to them. The derivation of the name *Essenes* has not yet been ascertained, and the etymological problem it presents has elicited a wide variety of theories. Both Josephus and Philo connect the word *Essenes* with "holiness," but neither gives an etymological account for the connection between the two. In the nineteenth century scholars generally agreed that the word is associated with a Hebrew root meaning "pious," but none of the divergent views surrounding this seems sound enough for exclusive adoption. The popular designation of the Qumran sect, however, which has been identified as a branch of the Essenes, is related to the root 's' "to heal," which is supported by Philo in his metaphorical application of the Essenes' healing both the spiritual and physical sicknesses. Furthermore, the Aramaic stem *'syym* "healers" is used with reference to both the body and the soul; the etymology is traditional and corresponds to the general Jewish thought of the period as it appears in the Apocryphal, Pseu-

CAVES IN THE JUDEAN WILDERNESS once inhabited by members of the Qumran Community, who observed a communal life as did the Essenes. Courtesy, Palestine Archaeological Museum

depigraphic, and New Testament writings, and is expressly confirmed by Josephus. Moreover, the noun *mrp'* "healing" is found in the Qumran writings and appears to play an important role in Qumran theology.

In their emphasis given to the need for personal piety and separation from the impurities of daily life, the Essenes seem to have much more in common with the Pharisees than with the Sadducees, but the two differed in details of doctrine and practice. While the Essenes believed in immortality, they rejected the doctrine of bodily resurrection, one crucial to the Pharisees. The Pharisees took part in the active life of Israel among the masses; the Essenes, who deemed themselves as the only true Israel, considered the religious observances in city and Temple corrupt, and withdrew from them and commenced to seek God in the Wilderness of Judea. However the Essenes cannot be said to have at any time seceded from official Judaism.

It was doubtless the communal living of the Essenes, of men intent on a strict construction of the Torah, which led to their strong emphasis in ritual precision. They observed the Sabbath with particular rigor. On this day they listened to a reading of the Scripture with allegorical interpretations of the text. During the weekdays, the levitical laws of holiness were similarly rigidly kept. The Essenes arose at dawn, prayed, worked until about 11 A.M., then bathed in cold water. They took their midday meal in common, as their evening meal, with a grace recited before and afterward. Strict silence was maintained at the meals. The Essenes lived a simple life, devoting most of their time to study and prayer; yet every member was required to perform some manual labor, principally in handicrafts or farming.

The discipline of the Essenes is described in detail by Josephus. Seniority and learning were the basis of rank in the Essene community. The leaders directed the activities, and each member was assigned to live in constant submission to an overseer, who acted only with his consent and by his injunction. The only opportunity for personal initiative was in performing acts of mercy. Since the Essenes maintained that all oaths taken were absolutely binding, and since a member apparently entered the community by swearing to adhere to the laws of ritual purity, he

could, if refractive, be easily starved into obedience by the other members of the community. Disobedience, however, seems to have been rare and expulsion unknown.

Josephus, who underwent the probationary period prior to admission to the sect, but was not privy to the inner secrets of the order, can be considered authoritative in his accounts of the external life and the tenets of the Essenes. They declined to take part in the Temple rites involving animal sacrifice and brought to the altar offerings of only flour and oil. They zealously studied the books of their ancestors and had some knowledge of medicine. They despised luxury and pleasure, and would not even anoint their bodies with oil. Blasphemy was punishable by death. A candidate for admission waited a year before he was bestowed the emblems — a hatchet, belt, and white garment. If he proved worthy he was admitted, after two more years, to the society, but only upon the exaction of fearful oaths, among which were many ethical injunctions, a pledge of loyalty to the society, and a promise 'to keep the books of the sect and the names of the angels.'

The Essenes attributed all things to fate. They believed in the immortality of the soul only, that upon its resurrection after death it will be exposed to either reward or punishment. The doctrine of immortality seems to have been purely germane to Judaism, since it was likewise held by the Pharisees; this and the doctrine of the resurrection, in fact, may have been borrowed by them, from the Pythagoreans and the Stoics. Though the New Testament contains no references to the Essenes, it is probable that John the Baptist, who lived an ascetic life not far from an Essenic community on the Jordan was one of their exponents and that the Apostolic Church was influenced by them. To the student of the New Testament the very existence of a pre-Christian fraternal community is of importance, for, while asceticism was practiced widely in the ancient world, Essenism was the first form of organized monasticism.

The term Essene was used to characterize groups and individuals whose tenets and practices varied widely. Josephus speaks of an order whose members practiced restricted sexual intercourse; to Pliny the Essenes practiced celibacy exclusively. The Therapeutae were an Essenic order, as were the Hemeraobaptists, known for their daily ritual ablutions. Scholars have also noted that, like the descriptions of the Essenes in Josephus, Philo, and Pliny, the members of the Qumran sect had rules of discipline, appointed overseers over the lives of the members, practiced ritual washing, and imposed a period of probation on the newcomers. On the other hand the attitude at Qumran was that of complete separation from the Jerusalem priesthood, and the Essenes do not seem to have had priests in prominence in their community, nor any parallel to the "Teacher of Righteousness" of the Qumran sect. On the whole, little can be said of the Essenes which cannot equally be applied to the Pharisees. Pharisees were known to have individually lived the Essenic life while in society, such as John, a general in the Roman War. The Essenes and the Pharisees both probably sprang from the pre-Maccabean Assideans. The Essenes are depicted in Greek sources mainly as sects, in the Rabbinical writings as individuals or as informal groups; both were applicable to different varieties of Essenic living.

The *Therapeutae* were an ancient sect of Jewish ascetics who settled on the shores of Lake Mareotis near Alexandria, Egypt, during the first century, A.D. Though closely like the Essenes, they were more contemplative and allowed women into their community. The origin and fate of the Therapeutae are unknown; our only source for an account of them is Philo. The members engaged solely in prayer and spiritual exercise twice daily and in readings in the Holy Scriptures, whose allegorical significance they proposed to investigate beneath the level of the literal. Upon joining the sect, a man voluntarily assigned his property to his heirs, for he was no longer considered to be of this world. The sect was unusually severe in its mode of life. Its members were wholly occupied with prayer and meditation.

The Therapeutae lived in separate community dwellings. Women customarily maintained their virginity. Slaves or servants were never used, since the members believed any form of servitude to be contrary to nature. In each dwelling was a sanctuary consecrated to study or prayer, and into which nothing was permitted to be brought except the sacred books. The Therapeutae had the books of the Old Testament, but they composed

their own on the allegorical interpretation of Scripture and psalms in various meters and melodies.

Each member lived in solitude during the daylight hours, which he devoted to the pursuit of wisdom within his sanctuary. Food was taken only at dark. On the Sabbath only, all left their dwellings to attend a meeting in a common sanctuary, in which the men were separated from the women by a four-cubit high partition. All could, in this fashion, hear the voice of a single speaker, usually the eldest among them and the most skilled in their doctrines. After such services the members partook of coarse bread, flavored with salt or hyssop, and spring water — never wine or meat — which were the sole fare of the community, even at feasts.

As the most revered number of the Therapeutae was 50, the members on each fiftieth day assembled, white-robed and cheerful, for an all-night festival. First the men and women stood and prayed, then sat (separated by sex) to a banquet in the order of their admission. All listened devoutly as the president discussed a philosophical question proposed either in Scripture or by one of the members. Afterward he chanted a hymn, and each took it up in turn, the community singing the refrains. Then followed the meal, after which both men and women participated in antiphonal and joint singing of thanksgiving hymns, and in choral dancing, until dawn. At sunrise each stood facing the East with hands stretched to heaven and prayed for knowledge and the light of truth on his thinking.

Most scholars believe that the Therapeutae were a radical offshoot of pre-Christian Judaism, probably Essenism, though the discipline and regulations of the Therapeutae were notably more severe than those of the Essenes. The importance of both lies in the evidence they afford of Pre-Christian monastic existence, evidence which has been confirmed by the discovery of the Dead Sea Scrolls. Though Philo, who describes the Therapeutae in loving detail, gives no account of their origin, it is now generally assumed that they were an offshoot of the Essenes, for the first century Jewish philosopher seems to stress their distinctive quest for wisdom and their love of contemplative devotion. They shared with the Essenes two crucial characteristics: their dualistic view of the body and

INSIDE A QUMRAN CAVE. Discoveries connected with the Dead Sea Scrolls give evidence of pre-Christian monastic life. Courtesy, Palestine Archaeological Museum

the soul, and their affection for the secret doctrine which underlies the literal word of the Scriptures. Like the Essenes, the Therapeutae left no impression on Jewish life, but were influential, because of their semi-monasticism, on early Christian development. Their emphasis on individual salvation was a voluntary cleavage from Jewish national law and life which led to their absorption into the anti-national Christian body.

The *Zealots* were a Jewish sect whose members regarded themselves as the defenders of the Law and national life of the Jewish people, and thus relentlessly opposed the Roman attempt to bring Judea under her idolatrous role. The Zealots were most influential in Galilee and later in Jerusalem, especially from the time of Herod (37 B.C.-A.D. 4) until the fall of Jerusalem (A.D. 70). They were the members of what Josephus calls the "fourth philosophy," distinguished from the Pharisees, Sadduccees, and Essenes by their strong opposition to any foreign domination of Judea. Josephus informs us of incidents of Zealot activities in the time of Herod, according to one of which forty disciples sacrificed their lives rather than permit Herod's placing a large golden eagle over the gate of the Temple.

It was the introduction of Roman institutions entirely antagonistic to the spirit of Judaism — the gymnasium, the arena, and especially the trophies — which provoked the indignation of the people and which aroused among them an uncompromisingly aggressive policy toward Rome. The Zealots arose under the leadership of Hezekiah, later martyred by Herod, and were particularly active in A.D. 6 during the revolt of Judas of Gamala, in Galilee, who maintained that compliance with the Roman demand for a census would constitute an act of enslavement among Palestinians. Josephus refers to the Zealots also as being members of one of the parties that started a reign of terror in A.D. 66 against Rome. The Zealots are also mentioned, but not described, in the Gospels (Luke 4:15). The term *Zealots* is applied as a designation of Simon, a disciple of Jesus, in Luke 6:15 and Acts 1:13. The same disciple is called "The Canaanean" in Matthew 10:4.

The Zealots (who called themselves *Kanna'-eem*, from a Hebrew and Aramaic stem *kanna'* "to be zealous"), claimed the right to assassinate any Roman who dared to enter the consecrated parts of the Temple, a privilege which was officially recognized. They refused to pay taxes, in contrast to the Pharisees, and harassed the Roman administration with every means at their disposal. It was during the period immediately preceding the great rebellion against Rome in A.D. 66 that the Zealots won followers from all the social classes. The Jewish government, weakened by previous Roman successes, was not able to prevent them from establishing themselves in Jerusalem, and from strengthening the defenses of the city. The Zealots terrorized their political opponents who had accepted foreign rule, deposed the high priest and elected a successor by lot, and even went so far as to burn the storehouses containing provender for a siege, in order to stir the inhabitants to action against the Romans. The population at length arose against such terrorism and drove the Zealots under Eleazar Ben Simon into the inner court of the Temple. With the support of the Idumeans, the Zealots regained control of Jerusalem, under the leadership of John of Gischala, and resumed their acts of terror. It is from this sect that Sicarii, the ultra-extreme sect, was engendered. They were called *Sicarii* from their custom of going about with daggers (*sicae*), hidden beneath their cloaks with which they would stab any person found committing a sacrilegious act or anything provoking anti-Jewish feeling. One of the chief leaders of the revolt of A.D. 66, Menahem, son of Judah the Galilean, appeared to have claimed Messianic status. Surrounded by royal pomp, he went up to the Temple to be crowned, but was slain by rivals of his own party (*Wars* II, xvii, 8-9). When the final siege of Jerusalem by the Romans began, the Zealots advocated and used the most extreme measures, which brought about the collapse and destruction of the city in A.D. 70.

The Zealots were not as purely selfish and secularly motivated as Josephus pictured them, but like the early Maccabees, were deeply patriotic and motivated by a dynamic theology of zeal for the Torah. Traditional Jewish history has declared itself, however, in favor of the Pharisees, who regarded the house of study more important to the Jews than the State and Temple; historians give the Zealots recognition for their sublime type of steadfastness.

JOPPA. Joppa, in the Plain of Sharon, served as the seaport for Jerusalem, thirty-five miles distant. It was a walled town as early as the reign of Pharaoh Thutmose III (1490-1435 B.C.), who mentions Joppa in his town lists. The conquest of Joppa by a general of Pharaoh Thutmose III became the subject of a popular folk tale. The Egyptian general, Thoth, had two hundred of his soldiers placed in baskets (or sacks) and ordered five hundred men to carry them. Then he feigned a surrender, pretending that the baskets were filled with booty which the Egyptians were bringing to their conquerors. The gates of Joppa were opened to receive the men carrying the baskets, but once inside the city, the men were released from the baskets, and the Egyptians took the city of Joppa in the name of Thutmose.

At the division of the land, Joppa was assigned to Dan (Josh. 19:46), but it was not really a part of Israel until David gained effective control of the coast. Hiram of Tyre floated timber from Lebanon to the seaport of Joppa for Solomon's Temple (II Chron. 2:16) and, in the time of Cyrus, cedars were again transported by water to Joppa for the building of the Second Temple (Ezra 3:7). When Jonah embarked for Tarshish in order to avoid going to Nineveh, he took ship at Joppa (Jonah 1:3). Here Peter spent some time in the house of Simon the Tanner (Acts 9:43), and received the vision which told him he should not term unclean that which God had cleansed (Acts 10:5, 16). Joppa was twice destroyed by the Romans and changed hands several times during the Crusades. Jaffa, or Yafa, now forms the southern part of the combined Israeli metropolis Tel Aviv-Jaffa.

JOSEPH. Joseph was the favorite son of Jacob, the first child of Rachel. His jealous brothers sold him into Egypt where he was falsely accused of criminal asssault on the wife of his master, Potipher, and imprisoned. For an Egyptian parallel, *see* Tale of the Two Brothers. Subsequently Joseph became known for his ability to interpret dreams,

JUDEAN LANDSCAPE. This is a view of the Valley of Ajalon. Courtesy, Matson Photo Service

was released from prison and became vizier (Prime Minister) of all Egypt (Gen. 41:41).

While the Bible does not provide materials for an exact chronology, *Hyksos times are often suggested as the period when Joseph rose to power in Egypt. Since the Hyksos rulers were largely Semitic, it may be assumed that they would have been likely to have honored Joseph, a fellow Semite.

The career of Joseph as outlined in Genesis suggests that the Biblical writer was familiar with the Egyptian language and culture. Joseph, like other Semites, was bearded, but he shaved himself before appearing before Pharaoh (Gen. 40:14). Pharaoh honored Joseph by providing him with garments of fine linen (Gen. 41:42), characteristically Egyptian. The word which Pharaoh caused the couriers to call out before Joseph's chariot (Gen. 41:43), *Abrek*, is Egyptian, not Hebrew. It is usually translated, "Bow the knee" (because of its similarity to the Hebrew *berek*, knee), but in Egypt it probably meant, "Pay attention," or something similar. Joseph was given an Egyptian name, Zaphnath-paaneah, interpreted by some as meaning, "Says the God, he will live." His Egyptian wife Asenath has a name honoring an Egyptian goddess: "She is of Neith." Asenath was the daughter of a priest of *On (Heliopolis), a center for the worship of Re, the sun god (Gen. 41:50).

JUDAH. The term Judah may refer to (1) a son of Jacob by Leah (Gen. 29:35), (2) the tribe of Judah, one of the twelve Israelite tribes, and the one from which David and his dynasty of kings had come, or (3) the Southern Kingdom which remained true to the Davidic dynasty at the time that Jeroboam became king of the rival kingdom of *Israel in the north.

After the fall of *Damascus and *Samaria, Judah was threatened by Assyrian power. *Sennacherib, around 701 B.C., occupied most of the territory of Judah, but did not succeed in taking Jerusalem. With the fall of *Nineveh, the Assyrian Empire went into decline and the *Chaldean or Neo-Babylonian Empire took its place as the major power in western Asia. Judah fell to the armies of *Nebuchadnezzar, the Chaldean king, in 587 B.C. *See also* Judea.

JUDEA. In Persian times the term Judea was applied to the region south of Samaria, corresponding approximately to the territory of the pre-exilic kingdom of Judah, except for the coastal cities which were excluded. The name Judea was the Greek equivalent of the Aramaic *Yehud*.

K

KADESH-BARNEA. The name Kadesh, and its variant Kedesh, signifies a sanctuary or holy place. It was a common Semitic name and was carried as far west as Spain where it persists in the modern name Cadiz. Historically Kadesh-barnea is first mentioned in Gen. 14:7 where it is identified with En-mishpat near El-paran ("on the border of the wilderness," 14:6). Evidently Kadesh-barnea was a watering place used by the Patriarchs and other peoples of the Negeb (cf. Gen. 16:14).

During the wilderness wandering following Israel's Exodus from Egypt, Kadesh became a center for Israelite tribal life (Num. 13, 14; Deut. 1). At Kadesh the Israelites murmured because they lacked water. Here Moses struck a rock twice (Num. 20:11), but because of his lack of faith he was told that he could not enter the Promised Land. The waters were termed the waters of Meribah ("contention"), giving rise to the name Meribath-Kadesh, a name which Ezekiel used in describing the southern boundary of the ideal Israel (Ezek. 47:19; 48:28).

The Biblical data suggest that Kadesh-barnea was located near the Brook of Egypt (Wadi el-'Arish) south of the Israelite border (Num. 34:4-5). There are three springs in this area: 'Ain el-Quedeirat, 'Ain Qedeis, and 'Ain Qoseimeh. H. C. Trumbull surveyed the area during the nineteenth century and argued for 'Ain Qedeis as the site of Kadesh-barnea. The fact that the modern name retains the Arabic form of Kadesh argues for the identification, but the investigations

THE ZIGGURAT AT
KISH. Courtesy, Zion Research Library

along the King's Highway was evidently destroyed by Chedorlaomer, for the region was uninhabited for about six hundred years after the time of Abraham. The road was used by *Nabatean traders and rebuilt by Trajan (A.D. 106). In Arabic it is known as Tariq es-Sultani, a name approximating the Hebrew of the Old Testament. A modern road in Jordan closely follows the old King's Highway.

KIRDAHAT. See Habor.

KIRJATH-SEPHER. See Debir.

KIRJATH-JEARIM. See Abu Ghosh.

KISH. Kish, modern Tell el-Ukheimir, southeast of Babylon, was a rival to *Uruk in early Sumerian history. According to the *Sumerian King List, Kish was the city which produced the first dynasty after the flood. Historically Kish was in the ascendancy from ca. 3200 to ca. 3000 B.C. The legendary *Etana was a ruler of Kish. In the story of Gilgamesh and Agga we are told that Kish presented an ultimatum to Uruk. Gilgamesh presented the ultimatum to "the convened assembly of elders" which advised submission to Kish. Next he presented the ultimatum to the assembly of "the men of the city," evidently the men bearing arms. The assembly of men chose to fight. The episode shows the rivalry between Kish and Uruk and also suggests the concept of a parliament with two houses as the ruling body of a Sumerian city.

Early in 1914 a French expedition under H. de Genouillac excavated Ukheimir, dis-

covering a ziggurat and a temple. Work was stopped during World War I but resumed in 1923 when the Ashmolean Museum of Oxford and the Field Museum of Chicago began a series of campaigns which lasted until 1933. Stephen Langdon was scientific director of the excavation, with E. Mackay and L. C. Watelin serving as field directors. Among significant buildings excavated were a Sumerian palace which had been rebuilt by the Assyrians, and the temple of the Sumerian goddess Ninhursag. Cuneiform tablets discovered at the site contained fragments of the creation epic (see *Enuma Elish). Another tablet mentioned the ruler Marduk-apal-iddina, ("Marduk has given a son"), the Merodach-baladan of Isa. 39:1.

Langdon discovered a layer of flood silt one and one-half feet thick at Kish. This he interpreted as a deposit dating back to the Biblical flood, which he dated at 3300 B.C. This view has not proved defensible, however, in view of the fact that so-called "flood silt" from other sites, including Ur and Nineveh, do not correspond with those of Kish. They are, in fact, not dated in the same century. It is probable that the sediment found at various sites in Mesopotamia was deposited at the time of the overflowing of the Tigris or Euphrates rivers. These were local floods which may have been highly destructive but they should not be equated with the Biblical flood.

BIBLIOGRAPHY. L. C. Watelin and Stephen Langdon, *Excavations at Kish*, Oxford University Press, Oxford, 1925-30, 1934.

KITTIM. See Cyprus.

KNOSSUS. See Cnossus.

KUDURRA STONE from the time of Nebuchadnezzer I. Courtesy, British Museum

KUDURRU. The word *kudurru* is an Akkadian term used for boundary markers. They were oval or pillar shaped stones set up to publicize the fact that certain territory was given by the king in the form of a royal grant. Eighty such kudduru stones are extant from the period of the Assyrian king Kadashman-Enlil I (*ca.* 1380 B.C.) to Shamash-shum-ukin (668-648 B.C.).

The kudurru stones were set up in fields or placed in private agricultural buildings to publicize grants which the king made to private citizens. At times grants were made to temples, in which instance copies of the kudurru stones were made on clay tablets and deposited in the temple.

Symbols of the major deities of the Assyrian pantheon were inscribed on kudurru stones. These were meant to protect the monument and discourage its removal or defacement. Reliefs on the stones show the king alone or with the recipient of the grant. Sometimes they depict the recipient worshiping his deity. Inscribed on the kudurru were curses upon any who might remove or deface the stone, and blessings upon those who would honor and restore it. The presence of the kudurru guaranteed the validity of the royal grant, and it was necessary that they be preserved.

KULTEPE. Kultepe is the name of a mound near Kayseri, Turkey. The site was excavated by the Turkish archaeologist Tahsin Özgüç. Kultepe was known in ancient times as Kanesh, and was the site of an Assyrian trading colony whose business documents have been preserved in the °Cappadocian Tablets.

KUYUNJIK. *See* Nineveh.

L

LABYRINTH. A labyrinth is a building with irregularly built passages which comprize a maze. In Greek legend the labyrinth was a building erected at °Cnossus by Daedalus at the command of Minos, king of Crete. It was built as the palace of the Minotaur, a creature with a bull's head and a human body. Athenians were annually sacrificed to the Minotaur until Theseus, legendary king of Athens, slew the creature and escaped from the labyrinth with the aid of Ariadne, Minos' own daughter.

On the walls and furnishings of Minos' palace at °Cnossus the double axe appears repeatedly, suggesting that it was a symbol of his authority. The term labyrinth means, "place of the double ax," and the name itself may be historical. The many rooms of the palace and the difficulty of a stranger in finding his way out may have given rise to the legend which developed among the Greeks. See also Minoans.

LACHISH

I. Name and References. Lachish, one of the largest cities in ancient Judah, was a key site in the Judean defense system in the Shephelah in the tenth to the sixth centuries B.C. The meaning of the name is unknown, though explanations such as "height," "impregnable," and "captured" have been offered.

There is a reference to Ru-ki-ša in the hieratic papyrus no. 1116 A of the Hermitage collection, a document contemporary with Tuthmose III (1490-1436), and referring to a king of La-ti-ša (?). The Amarna correspondence of Pharaoh Akh-en-aton (1369-1353) five times refers to the city Lakisu or Lakišu (Winckler, T. A. Tablets, nos. 217, 218, 180, 181). It is possible that the Karnak lists refer to Lachish as Lu-ga-za. These are the only references in Egyptian materials. The Assyrian records refer to the city as Lakisi (cf. Sch. COT, on II Kings 18:14). The Greek Bible (LXX) calls the city Lacheis.

II. Identification and Location. The city was first sought at Umm Lâkis and then at Tell-el-Ḥesi, ca. thirty-three miles southwest of Jerusalem, by W. F. Petrie (1891) and F. J. Bliss (1894). It was later identified with the imposing mound Tell ed-Duweir (cf. W. F. Albright, Z A W 6 [1929], p. 3), thirty miles southwest of Jerusalem and fifteen miles west of Hebron, for the following reasons:

1. Tell ed-Duweir is the most prominent Bronze and Iron Age site in the region indicated by Eusebius for the contemporary village of Lachish, "in the seventh mile from Eleutheropolis," i.e., ca. five miles southwest of Beit Jibrin, the ancient Eleutheropolis.

2. Excavation has revealed striking resemblances between the Iron Age ruin at Tell ed-Duweir and pictorial representations of Lachish at Nineveh.

3. The literary sources disclose correspondences between the history of Tell ed-Duweir and Lachish.

The site lies toward the lower west slopes of the Judean hill country. It has been favored at all times by the presence of copious water near the surface. Excavation was begun by the Wellcome-Marston Archaeological Expedition in 1933, under J. L. Starkey, till his murder by brigands in 1938. It was continued by Charles H. Inge and Lankester Harding. The summit of the tell is about eighteen acres in size, as compared with Megiddo thirteen acres, the Ophel of Jerusalem eleven and a half acres, and Debir (Tell Beit Mirsim) seven acres.

III. History of the Site

A. *Earliest Traces.* The surrounding ridges give evidence of human habitation as early as the Upper Palaeolithic times (8000 B.C.), while cave dwellings were in use in the Chalcolithic (3000 B.C.), and Early Bronze Ages (3000-2000 B.C.).

Egyptian influence in the Middle Bronze Age (2000-1600 B.C.) is evident from the twelfth dynasty and on. By the Hyksos period (1720-1550 B.C.), Lachish was a military site protected by a fosse (an artificial ditch or moat) and a plaster-covered glacis (a defensive slope in front of a fortification) rising to a height of one hundred feet above the valley, and presumably crowned by a brick wall. According to the Amarna Letters (1375-1360), the city under its own rulers was favorable to the incoming Habiru and so caused the pro-Egyptian element to appeal for help from Egypt.

B. *The Late Bronze City.* With the renewal of Egyptian power in Asia, the Hyksos defenses fell into disuse. Early in the Late Bronze Age (1600-1200 B.C.), a small temple was built on the rubbish at the bottom of the fosse ("the fosse temple"), and twice enlarged, before finally being destroyed about 1200 B.C. by the Hebrews.

Originally built about 1550 B.C. of unhewn stones set in mud mortar, the temple was replaced by a larger structure in 1450 B.C. It had walls of stone plastered with lime, a floor of hard clay, and a roof supported by wooden columns. The cult room had a raised shrine on which the cult statue(s) stood. Long benches of mud, for the laying

THE MOUND OF LACHISH, *one of the last cities of Judah to fall to Nebuchad-nezzar. Courtesy, Trustees of the Wellcome Trust*

ARTIST'S RECONSTRUCTION *of Lachish before it fell to Nebuchadnezzer. Courtesy, Trustees of the Wellcome Trust*

of offerings, were placed along the north, east, and west walls. In 1350 B.C., a room was added to the south of the temple. Around the shrine and in the rubbish pits connected with the building were found large quantities of bones of birds, animals, and fish. There were bones of sheep, goats, oxen, gazelles, ibex, all young. Many were of the right foreleg or shoulder, corresponding to Leviticus 7:32.

Among the finds in Late Bronze Lachish were a broken bronze dagger blade of about 1550 B.C. with four signs, probably acrophonic; a paste seal bearing the name of Amenhotep II (1439-1406 B.C.); a lion-hunt scarab of Amenhotep III (1398-1361 B.C.), commemorating his feat of killing 102 lions with his own hand during the first ten years of his reign; and five pieces of pottery with alphabetic signs of the Sinaitic type, from 1350-1200 B.C., including the Duweir or Lachish ewer and the Lachish bowl. The ewer is decorated around the neck with wavy lines in red paint and carries an inscription of thirteen letters similar to those of Serabit el-Khadem (ca. 1500-1450 B.C.), the turquoise mines worked by Semitic people from near Tanis and akin to the earliest forms of Phoenician inscriptions of the tenth century.

The most important discovery for fixing the date of destruction of the Late Bronze Age Lachish was that of a broken bowl on which had been inscribed, apparently by an Egyptian tax collector, a record of certain wheat deliveries from the local harvests. There were three dates all "in the year four" of a certain Pharaoh. The hieratic characters of the thirteenth-twelfth century B.C. point to 1220 B.C., the fourth year of Pharaoh Merneptah (1224-1214 B.C.). All twenty-five fragments of the bowl were found together. Doubtless the bowl was broken when the city under King Japhia in league with four Amorite cities (cf. Josh. 10), fell to the Israelites in 1220 and was destroyed in conflagration. Cf. W. F. Albright, *BASOR 68* (Dec. 1937), pp. 22-26.

Olga Tufnell dates Level VIII 1567-1450 B.C.; Level VII 1450-1350 B.C.; and Level VI 1300-1225 B.C. The great majority of archaeologists equate Level VI of the tell with the Late Bronze Age city. Strata V, IV, and III are not clearly distinguished as yet. Miss Tufnell identifies Level V with Rehoboam's fortified Lachish; dates Levels IV-III 900-700 B.C., and Level II 700-586 B.C.; finds a period of abandonment; and dates Level I 450-150 B.C.

Starkey and G. E. Wright date Levels IV-II very differently. Because of these disagreements, we shall try merely to indicate the nature and the date of the various occupations of the tell, rather than assigning them to any Level.

C. *The Israelite City.* The mound was virtually deserted during the period of the Judges, the twelfth and eleventh centuries B.C. The presence of a scarab of Ramesses III (1168-1137 B.C.) in the city is not yet solved satisfactorily.

King David probably brought the city to life again in the early tenth century B.C. A palace for the provincial government official was erected on the ruins of the old Canaanite buildings. Practically nothing of the superstructure remains, but the platform on which it was built can still be seen, an earth-filled podium, about 105 feet square, and 23 feet in height. This is reminiscent of the citadel, the *millo* ("filling"?) which David built in Jerusalem (II Sam. 5:9). Adjacent to this palace was a thick-walled brick building with long parallel rooms and high floors to keep grain from spoiling, probably a government storehouse or royal granary. Similar remains of a palace and storehouse have been found at Beth-Shemesh, fifteen miles north of Lachish, also of the early tenth century. These "store-cities" are evidence for some sort of Judean provincial administration in the time of David before Solomon's organization of the northern part of the country (I Kings 4:7ff.).

After 922 B.C. Rehoboam fortified Lachish as one of fifteen defense centers to protect Judah from attack by the Philistines and Egyptians (II Chron. 11:5-12). The summit of the mound was surrounded by a wall of sun-dried mud brick about 19½ feet thick with alternating salients and recessed panels and a regular series of defense towers. Over fifty feet below it, half way down the slope of the mound, was an outer wall or revetment made of stone and brick, about thirteen feet wide, with alternate projecting and recessed panels and with towers located at strategic places. The battlements were built of wood.

Along the west side of the mound, was a roadway ascending to the city. The gate was protected by a large free-standing bastion, which by Nebuchadnezzar's time was incorporated into the line of the outer revetment.

The tenth century podium of Palace A from David's time was lengthened from 105-256 feet (= Palace B). Later a ten foot strip was added to the east side (= Palace C). These additions occurred between 900-750 B.C. Scratched on the limestone step in the stairs leading up to the citadel platform on the east side of Palace C were the first five letters of the Hebrew alphabet in traditional order. Diringer and Albright date these about 800 B.C.

Large numbers of stamped jar handles from the eighth and seventh centuries with script similar to that of the Siloam inscription of about 700 B.C. have been recovered in this level. They are stamped *lmlk*, "for the king," and followed by the name of Hebron Ziph, Socoh, etc. Cf. Diringer, *BA* 12 (Dec. 1949).

The Assyrian King Sennacherib (705-681 B.C.) attacked Judah in 70l B.C. He besieged Lachish (II Kings 18:13-17 = II Chron. 32: 1-9 = Isa. 36:1ff) to cut off Jerusalem from any support from Egypt. From Lachish he sent messengers to Hezekiah demanding surrender. The siege of Lachish was depicted on Sennacherib's palace walls at Nineveh. Discovered by A. H. Layard in the campaign of 1849-51, now in the British Museum, it shows Sennacherib the King of Assyria sitting on his throne while the spoil of Lachish passed before him. Cf. L. H. Grollenberg, *Atlas of the Bible*, New York, Nelson, 1956, plate 230; and plate 233 for H. H. McWilliam's reconstruction of Judean Lachish.

The debris outside the wall contains charcoal from the burned battlements. A bronze helmet crest was found in the mass of burned debris, such as worn by an Assyrian (or Chaldean?) soldier. Great ramps of soil, probably a part of the Assyrian siege ramps, were piled against the city-gate bastion.

On the northwest slope of the mound was a large pit (tomb #120) which held the remains of fifteen hundred bodies, the bones in a jumbled mass. They had been gathered up and flung into this repository, and over this solid mass of human bones was a layer of animal bones, mostly pig, probably part of the commissariat of the Assyrian army.

RELIEF SHOWING SENNACHERIB ON HIS THRONE before Lachish. Courtesy, British Museum

LACHISH LETTER 4. Correspondence in Hebrew on broken pieces of pottery between Lachish and its military outpost during the time of the Babylonian invasion of Judah (ca. 588 B.C.) Courtesy, Trustees of the Wellcome Trust

Starkey holds that the bones were from the clearance of the city after Sennacherib's siege. This is suggested by the conglomeration, the marks of burning, the almost total absence of remains of old persons (hence these were not from a previous cemetery), and the eighth and early seventh century pieces of pottery associated with the remains. Miss Tufnell holds that these were from Josiah's clearance of idolatrous burials, about 621 B.C. Cf. II Kings 23:4-14; II Chron. 34:3-7.

At least three of the skulls from this mass burial show an operation known as trepanning, in which a piece of bone was sawed off and removed from the skull to relieve pressure on the brain. On the third skull the bone had grown sufficiently to obliterate evidence of the saw marks.

Wiseman suggests that after Sennacherib's capture of Lachish, the city was administered by the Assyrian government and was the rallying point for levies from Philistia. Part of the citadel was cleared and a narrower gateway was constructed. There are indications of Scythian warriors in the city in the late seventh century.

By the time of Jehoiakim (608-597 B.C.), Lachish had been rebuilt. Evidences of two invasions by Nebuchadrezzar in 598/7 B.C. and 587/6 B.C. are to be seen at Debir (Tell Beit Mirsim, eight miles away) and at Lachish. In 598/7, the city-gate, fortification, and palace-citadel were violently destroyed, the brick superstructure of the palace collapsed and was spread about the courtyard. Cf. Albright, *BASOR* 132 (Dec. 1953), p. 146.

The inner wall was again rebuilt by quarrying material from the southeast corner of the mound, but the palace was left in ruins. In Nebuchadrezzar's capture of Judah, the fortified cities Jerusalem, Lachish, and Azekah resisted the longest (Jer. 34:7). The

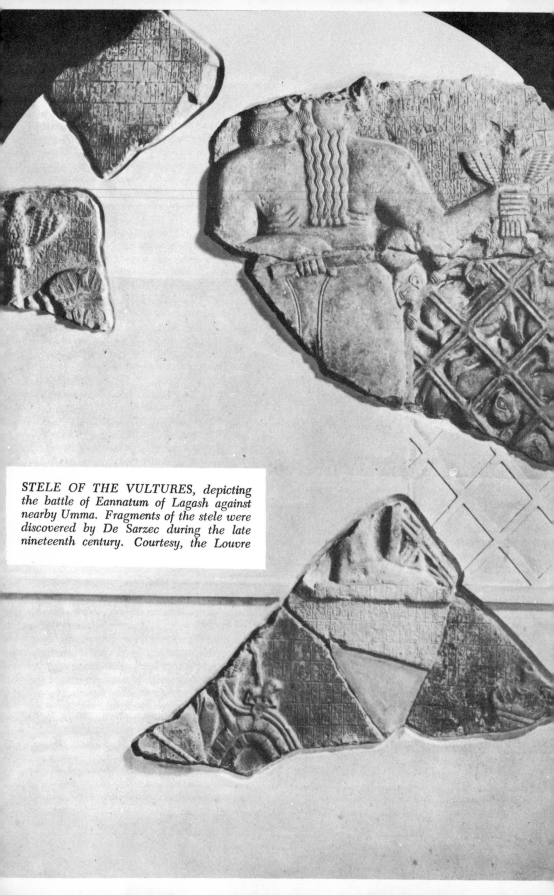

STELE OF THE VULTURES, depicting the battle of Eannatum of Lagash against nearby Umma. Fragments of the stele were discovered by De Sarzec during the late nineteenth century. Courtesy, the Louvre

destruction of Lachish in 589/8 B.C. was so thorough that the fire dissolved the masonry. Above the debris was found a seal impression reading, "to Gedaliah who is over the house" (cf. Isa. 22:15; 36:3). This was probably used by Gedaliah before the city fell to Nebuchadrezzar. He was one of the last prime ministers of Judah (II Kings 22:3, 8-12; 26:22-26; Jer. 39:14; 40-5f; 41:2).

IV. Lachish Letters. In a small room, probably a guard room, adjoining the outer gate and lying in the ashes of the burned city of Lachish, Starkey discovered in 1935 the eighteen *Lachish letters* (three more were discovered in 1938). These are pottery sherds, ostraca, on which messages were written in black ink in the cursive Phoenician script in the epistolary style of classical Hebrew prose, contemporary with the last years of Jeremiah. They are first hand documents of the political and military situation just prior to Nebuchadrezzar's destruction of Jerusalem. Only one third of them are intelligible. The most interesting are numbers 3, 4, and 6.

Letter 3 was written by Hoshaiah, a subordinate official in an outpost, to his superior Yaosh in the city. It refers to Koniah the son of Elnathan making a trip to Egypt for help and to a letter by Tobiah, a royal official, with a warning from a prophet (Urijah? Jeremiah?).

Letter 4 ends with the statement, "and let (my lord) know that we are watching for the signals of Lachish, according to all the indications which my lord hath given, for we cannot see Azekah" (= 12 m. NE of Lachish; Jer. 34:7).

Letter 6 says, "And behold the words of the pr[inces] are not good, (but) to weaken our hands [and to sla]cken the hands of the m[en] who are informed about them" (cf. Jer. 38:4).

There is a reference to the "9th year" of Zedekiah in letter no. 20. The letters thus have epigraphic, linguistic, and historical interest.

V. Post-Israelite Lachish. Between 586-450 B.C., Lachish was abandoned. Level I of the mound, dated 450-150 B.C., consists of two phases separated by a period of desertion. After the exile Judah became a part of the fifth Persian satrapy, "beyond the River." Lachish was not in this area but was in the province of Arabia or Idumaea.

The governor in Nehemiah's time was "Geshem (or Gashmu) the Arab" (Neh. 6:1). A fine villa, "the Residency," was built on the site of the old citadel as the home of the governor, 450-350 B.C. Here was found a stone altar with a three line votive text in the Aramaic script, beginning with the word *lbnt'*, "incense." The third line reads *lyh mr'*, "to Yah Lord [of heaven?]," similar to the Elephantine texts of the 5th Century B.C. (Albright, *BASOR* 132, Dec. 153 pp. 46f.).

Geshem's name was found on a Lihyanite inscription from Dedan in Arabia south of Edom, and on a vessel found at Tell el-Mashkutah (Biblical Succoth) near the Suez Canal in Egypt, which reads "Qainu, son of Geshem (Gusham), king of Qedar." This family ruled from Lachish the area of Edom and North Arabia to Succoth in the Nile Delta. South Arabic incense altars were found at Lachish, Gezer, and Tell Jemmeh, showing the extent of Arab trade.

After a period of withdrawal, the very latest phase of the late second century B.C. is attested by a "solar shrine" and a tomb of the Seleucid period. In about 150 B.C., Lachish was finally deserted, never to be reoccupied.

BIBLIOGRAPHY. H. Torczyner, O. Tufnell, C. H. Inge, Lankester Harding, *Lachish I—IV* (4 vol.), Oxford University Press, London, 1938-1958. W. F. Albright, "The Lachish Ostraca," *ANET*, p. 321-322. B. W. Buchanan, "Lachish (Tell ed-Duweir); the Iron Age," *JBL*, LXXV, 1956, pp. 335-339). H. G. May, "Lachish III (Tell ed-Duweir): the Iron Age," *JBL*, LXXV, 1956, pp. 704-706. G. E. Wright, "Judaean Lachish," *BA*, XVIII, 1955, pp. 9-17.

LAGASH (TELLOH). The earliest settlements at the mound of Telloh, Sumerian Lagash, date to the 'Ubaid period. Its period of greatness began when Ur-Nanshe founded a dynasty at Lagash, fifty miles north of Ur, *ca.* 2500 B.C. Ur-Nanshe's inscriptions describe his extensive building operations and the canals which he dug for irrigation purposes.

Under Ur-Nanshe's grandson, Eannatum, Lagash had the hegemony over most of Sumer. He claimed victories over Umma, Uruk, Ur, Kish, and Mari. The Stele of the Vultures, discovered at Lagash, depicts a battle of Eannatum against neighboring Umma. The soldiers are marching in a close-packed phalanx, with lances protruding from behind huge rectangular shields. Vultures

GUDEA OF LAGASH IN STANDING POSITION. *Courtesy, the Louvre*

bear the heads and limbs of the dead away from the field of battle.

Wars of conquest brought prosperity to Lagash. A richly ornamented silver vase and fine examples of terra cotta and stone work illustrate the wealth and artistic ability of the people of Lagash during the years following Eannatum's conquests.

With wealth, however, came political corruption, and Urukagina, the eighth ruler after Ur-Nanshe, is remembered for his reforms. Greedy local officials had seized boats, cattle, and fisheries from their owners. Exhorbitant fees were levied on the poor, and tax gatherers were universally detested. Urukagina removed these corrupt officials and tax gatherers and is remembered as history's first reformer. Shortly after the reign of Urukagina, however, Lagash suffered a period of eclipse as Lugalzaggisi of *Umma conquered its territories.

During the period of Sumerian revival, which began about 2070 B.C., an able and enlightened ruler named Gudea occupied the throne of Lagash. An inscription tells how Gudea was instructed in a dream to restore the Lagash temple known as Eninnu, "The House of Fifty (Gods)." Gudea undertook the extensive project and personally laid the first brick. He imported wood from the Amanus Mountains of Syria, a part of the range from which Solomon imported the famed Cedars of Lebanon for his Jerusalem Temple (I Kings 5:6).

In subsequent years Lagash was subject to a succession of rulers — Babylonians, Assyrians, and Persians. In the second century B.C. the city was finally deserted, and its ruins remained undisturbed until the nineteenth century A.D. when the people of Europe began to rediscover ancient Mesopotamia.

The excavation of the mound, then known as Telloh, was begun in secret during the year 1877 by Ernest de Sarzec, the French vice-counsul at Basra, whose principal interests were art and archaeology. Between 1877 and his death in 1901, de Sarzec directed eleven campaigns at Telloh. During the earliest campaigns he dug a series of trial trenches to determine the character of the ruins. His efforts were rewarded by the discovery of the Stele of the Vultures, several statues of Gudea, and numerous cuneiform inscriptions. The Stele of the Vultures was one of the first bas reliefs of the ancient orient to be discovered.

While visiting Paris in 1878, de Sarzec met Leon Heuzey, curator of the Department of Oriental Antiquities at the Louvre. Although the expeditions continued to be conducted in secret, Heuzey encouraged de Sarzec in his work which became semi-official in nature. By the time of de Sarzec's death the discoveries had been announced to the people of Europe, and France took national pride in the collection of antiquities from Telloh which had been placed in the Louvre. Others were kept in the East at the Imperial Ottoman Museum.

After de Sarzec's death, the excavation of Telloh was continued by Captain G. Gross, whose military duties forced him to relinquish the work in 1909. Nothing could be done during the years of World War I, and French archaeological activity was largely limited to Syria and Lebanon during the post-war years. The League of Nations had granted a mandate to France for the government of Syria and Lebanon, and that field seemed particularly important. By 1929, however, the French were ready to resume work at Telloh, and the Abbe de Genouillae reopened the work, which was continued after 1931 by André Parrot. In 1933, after a total of twenty campaigns, the excavation of the site was considered completed.

While Lagash is not directly related to Biblical history, its recovery has been particularly valuable in bringing into focus the life of the ancient Sumerians, the people whose culture was dominant in the area north of the Persian Gulf at the dawn of history. This Sumerian culture influenced the peoples of the Near East, including the Israelites, long after the Sumerian city states had been incorporated into the great empires of the second and first millennium B.C.

BIBLIOGRAPHY. Andrè Parrot, Tello; vingt campagnes de fouilles (1877-1933), A. Michel, Paris, 1948. M. Lambert and R. Tournay, "Gudea, Patesi of Lagash," Revue Biblique, LV, 1948, pp. 403-437. Francois Thureau-Dangin, Les cylindres de Goudea; transcription, traduction, commentaire, grammaire, lexique, E. Leroux, Paris, 1905.

LAMENTATION OVER THE DESTRUCTION OF UR.

The text of the Lamentation over the Destruction of *Ur has been reconstructed from twenty-two cuneiform tablets and fragments, all but one of which were excavated at *Nippur. The remaining tablet probably comes from Ur. The tablets date from the first half of the second millennium B.C. in the period following the fall of the Third Dynasty of Ur. There are 435 lines of text.

The lament states that the goddess Ningal tried to dissuade Anu and Enlil from their determination to destroy the city. Ningal was not successful and the gods dispatched Kingaluda, the lord of the storm winds, to carry out their decree. In another lament the singer implores Ningal and then Nanna to have the gods return to a new Ur with its temples restored. The king of Sumer, however, had fled to the mountains like a bird whose nest had been destroyed.

During the days of Ibi-Sin, last ruler of the Third Dynasty of Ur, Elamites stormed down out of the hills and sacked the city of Ur. The lament was probably written during the reign of Samsu-iluna, the son of *Hammurabi of Babylon.

BIBLIOGRAPHY. S. N. Kramer, "A Sumerian Lamentation," ANET, pp. 455-463. Lamentation over the Destruction of Ur, University of Chicago Press, Chicago, 1940.

LAMPS.

The earliest lamps were saucers filled with olive oil (cf. Ezek. 27:20) with a wick of twisted thread resting on the rim. About 2000 B.C. true lamps began to appear

AN ASSORTMENT OF ANCIENT LAMPS used in the Near East. The lamp burned oil. Illumination was provided by a lighted wick. Courtesy, Ancient Arts Division, Sculpture Masterworks Company

as the saucer had its rim pinched in four places to form lips for holding the wick. In subsequent centuries the lamp had but one lip which became increasingly pinched until it had the form of a covered appendage with a hole. During Israelite times the lamp acquired a base. The covered, spouted models of Hellenistic times were wheel-made with the spout formed from a lump of clay attached to the round body.

Lamps of the Old Testament period were made of pottery, but in later times bronze was also used. When used to illuminate buildings, lamps were placed in a niche in a wall or a shelf jutting out from the wall. Sometimes they were suspended by a cord from the ceiling (Eccl. 12:6). Palestinian excavations have produced a large variety of lampstands, usually made of pottery. Such stands were used for incense and offerings in the Near East. As lampstands they made the tending of lamps more efficient and provided better light (Matt. 5:15). Metallic stands discovered at Megiddo and Beth-shan consisted of an upright shaft arising from a tripod base. The lamp and the lampstand could be united in one piece. A seven-spouted lamp of this kind was found at °Taannah (cf. II Kings 4:10).

LAODICEA. Laodicea, a city in the extreme southwestern section of Phrygia in Asia Minor, is located in the valley of the Lycus, a tributary of the Maeander River. The city was built on an ancient highway leading from Ephesus eastward to Syria. Ten miles east of Laodicea is Colossae.

Laodicea was founded about 250 B.C. by the Seleucid ruler Antiochus III and named for his wife Laodice. After 190 B.C. it was ruled by Pergamum and suffered decline but, when the Romans took the city (133 B.C.) they made it the center of a judicial district and prosperity returned.

The area around Laodicea is fertile. Sheep with black wool grazed in its fields and woolen garments and carpets were woven in the city. Laodicea became a financial center. Beginning in the second century Laodicea struck her own coins. The population included Greek-speaking Syrians, Romans, Romanized natives, and Jews.

Laodicea along with its neighbors Colossae and Hierapolis (Col. 2:1; 4:13-16) was early evangelized, but our knowledge of Christianity there during apostolic times is limited to Biblical evidence. The Book of the Revelation describes the Laodicean church as rich in material things but lukewarm in things of the spirit (Rev. 3:14-22). By the fourth century Laodicea was the most prominent bishopric in Phrygia and the secular capital of western Phrygia. Under Seljuks and Turks the city suffered, and soon after the thirteenth century it was abandoned. The modern town of Denizili was built near the ruins of Laodicea, known in Turkish as Eski Hissar.

The lines of the ancient city walls can still be traced. An inscription states that the triple eastern gate was dedicated to Vespasian. A stadium, also dedicated to Vespasian (in A.D. 79), has two semicircular ends of about a thousand feet in length. Gladiatorial combats were staged in Laodicea as early as the first century B.C.

Near the stadium is a large building with arches, piers, and colonnades that have been badly weathered. It may have served as a gymnasium or baths and is thought to date from the time of Hadrian. Two theaters are better preserved. Water was brought to the city by an aqueduct from springs near Denizili. Arches of masonry conveyed the water part of the way, but stone barrel pipes were used to convey the water up and down the slopes.

While visitors have frequently described the ruins of Laodicea, the site has not been scientifically excavated and final identification of many of its buildings cannot be given.

LAQE. *See* Terqa.

LARSA. Larsa, a Sumerian town in southern Mesopotamia located between Ur and Uruk, was one of the leading powers in the °Mari age. An Amorite leader named Naplanum settled at Larsa (*ca.* 2025 B.C.). His fourth successor, Gungunum, conquered Ur, making Larsa, along with °Isin, a major power. The last ruler of Larsa, Rim-Sin, fell before °Hammurabi, and Larsa became an administrative capital of Hammurabi's Babylonian Empire.

W. K. Loftus, working for the Assyrian Exploration Fund, excavated Larsa, modern Senkereh, in 1854. He found a cemetery on the site and erroneously assumed that the clay tablets discovered in the area were related to the tombs. Actually the cuneiform documents range in date from the Ur III to the Neo-Babylonian periods, and the tombs are much later. Grave diggers accidentally struck hundreds of cuneiform tablets and seal cylinders, and moved them to upper strata of the mound where Loftus discovered them. One tablet proved to be a table of squares from one to sixty. Both "one" and "sixty" are represented by the same perpendicular wedge, evidence that the Sumerians and their successors used a sexagesimal system of calculation. Loftus also discovered the ziggurat of Larsa and a temple that had served the ancient city.

In 1932-33 Andrè Parrot conducted further excavations on behalf of the Louvre. Additional temples, palaces, and inscriptions excavated by the French prove the importance of ancient Larsa in Sumerian and Babylonian times.

LAW (HITTITE). I. *Nature of the Collection.* The laws of the Hittites which are known to us from clay tablets unearthed at Boghazköy during the past half-century represent a hetergeneous collection. Some of the ideas and practices contained in them undoubtedly originate in primitive Indo-European customary law. Other customs and procedures were acquired after the Hittites had arrived in their Anatolian homeland through contact with the other great cultures of the ancient Near East. The tablets themselves confront us with three distinct historical stages in the development of Hittite law. The main "version" of the law code represents those legal precedents which prevailed in the capital city and its environs during the early part of the Empire period (*ca.* 1450-1300). Within the text of this main version are references to an older version. A number of laws contain the following phraseology in the penalty clause: "Formerly (*karū*) . . ., but now (*kinuna*) . . . ." The sanctions contained in the *karū* clauses represent a stage of Hittite law earlier than the Empire period. Some scholars attribute this earliest known stage of Hittite law to the Old Kingdom period prior to the reign of Telipinus (*ca.* 1525-1500). Still other tablets unearthed at Boghazköy seem to represent a version composed later than the main version. This can be determined on the basis of the development of the script and further "modernizing" tendencies in the laws themselves.

A WORSHIPER KNEELING before his God. From Larsa. Courtesy, the Louvre

It should be understood that the collection of laws recovered from the ruins of ancient Hattusas does not represent a "code" in the strict legal sense of that term. Specialists in ancient Near Eastern law have long stressed that prescriptive (or constitutional) law was generally unknown in the Near East down to Hellenistic and Roman times. The most common type of law was case law (or casuistic law). Case law usually took the form of collections of legal precedents from a certain geographical area which had become normative and which served as guidelines for the local judges. Often such collections were made and propagated shortly after the creation of a new political entity which sought to unite in itself many smaller geographical and political units. A common, standardized body of laws served to cement the newly achieved political unity. Hammurabi's code is a good example of this practice. Nevertheless, the Hittite laws differ from Hammurabi's collection in that they were a private collection kept in the palace archives. They were not published on a *stele for the public to see and read, but rather were kept for the private consultation of the state judiciary officials in the palace. Still another reason why the Hittite laws cannot be viewed as a "code" is their incompleteness. A true code must legislate on every conceivable aspect of civil life. The Hittite laws lack legislation on such important aspects of civil life as adoption, inheritance, and laws of contract.

II. *Modernization of the Laws.* One of the conspicuous features of Hittite law is the manner in which laws were periodically adjusted in accord with changing concepts of the gravity of an offence and changes in the structure of society. Now it is true that in all societies governed by laws, these laws develop and change to accommodate themselves to new circumstances. What is unusual in the Hittite laws is that, unlike the other collections of ancient Near Eastern laws, the Hittite laws preserve the old rulings in the text, noting the changes, almost as though the scribes gloried in this progressive attitude. One can best observe the trend of these revisions by studying the changes in the laws from the earliest version (the *karū* clauses), to the main version, to the late version. On the basis of such a comparison it will be seen that the principal characteristics of the trend are: (1) general reduction of fines, (2) further specification as to the nature of the fines, and (3) elimination of corporeal punishment. In several cases (¶¶ 92, 101, 121, and 166) capital punishment was replaced by a monetary payment.

III. *Legal Categories.* It has often been pointed out that there are several important subjects which are not treated in the laws. Among these are adoption, inheritance, and laws of contract. This fact coupled with the limited treatment of other subjects, such as marriage, has led some scholars to suspect that there was yet another portion of the laws which we have not yet recovered. It would be strange, though, if this were the case, that among the many tablets that have come to light there should not be a single one which could be clearly and positively attributed to the missing laws. It is more likely that these matters were regulated by the customary law of the people and rarely gave rise to legal dispute. It is difficult to judge the manner in which judicial matters were handled and laws applied to specific cases, inasmuch as we lack the all-important private documents of suits and trials. Documents of this latter type are quite common in Mesopotamia and greatly facilitate the understanding of the manner in which "codified" law was actually applied. The extent of Hittite evidence outside of the Hittite "code" is a body of texts giving instructions to high military officials who travel through the realm and occasionally participate in local judicial proceedings (the so-called "Instructions Texts"), and a few isolated tablets recording a trial.

Those legal categories which are treated in the existing tablets are the following: homicide, assault, abduction, property damage, burglary, theft, sexual offences, sorcery, marriage and divorce, *iwaru*-inheritance (which is not true inheritance, but represents a legal fiction facilitating the sale of property), feudal obligations, wages, fees, and hire.

IV. *Some Interesting Features of Hittite Law.* Although the subject of homicide falls within the jurisdiction of written law, it is possible that murder fell rather within the jurisdiction of customary (or unwritten) law and was handled by blood revenge. Only two instances are recorded in the laws of what might constitute murder (at least they appear to be premeditated homicide). In one of these (¶ 43) the offender must become the slave of the slain man's heir or survivor. In the second case (¶ 44A) the offender must give his own son to the heir or survivor as a slave. Gurney (*Hittites,* p. 89) calls one of these "accidents at a river crossing" and the other "homicide," but it is clear from the laws themselves that these are not accidents, but rather intentional homicide. In determining the ruling on cases of homicide, Hittite judges took motivation into consideration: premeditated (¶¶ 43-44A), robbery (¶ 5), in a quarrel (¶ 5, later version), in a brawl (¶ 174), and accidentally or unintentionally (¶ 5, later version). In at least one case we know that a person might be held responsible for the death of another, simply because the latter was found dead on his property (¶ 6 and its later version; cf. Deut. 21:1-9).

The Hittites recognized the usual sexual offences (adultery, rape, incest) and prescribed punishments for them in accord with their gravity. But in certain respects the Hittites differed from other Near Eastern peoples as to the permissibility of certain types of sexual relationship. Whereas the ancient Hebrews forbad all forms of bestiality and homosexuality, the Hittites did not. Apparently in all three categories of sex (heterosexuality, homosexuality, bestiality) the criterion of degrees of kinship was employed to determine which relationships were permissible and which were not. The only homosexual relationship which is expressly forbidden in the laws is that between father and son (¶ 189), and this because of close blood ties, as its grouping with incestuous heterosexual relationships shows (¶ 189-195). As for bestiality, sexual relations between a man and an ox (¶ 187), sheep (¶88), pig (¶ 199), or dog (¶ 199) are punished. But if ox or pig leap on a man for sexual purposes, there is no punishment (¶ 199). And a man may freely engage in sexual acts with horse or mule with no fear of punishment (¶ 200A.). Just what distinction was felt to exist between the horse or mule and the others which made it permissible to engage in sexual relations with one and not with the others is not clear. The analogy with heterosexual and homosexual relationships makes the "degree of kinship felt to exist" theory plausible, but not incontrovertible.

The realm of magic was morally neutral. Magic was simply one of many means for accomplishing things. Accordingly, "white magic" was accepted and widely practiced. "Black magic," called "sorcery" (alwanzātar), was quite another matter. In the laws several forms of alwanzātar are described: molding clay into an image for sympathetic magic (¶ 111), leaving defiled remnants of a purification rite on another's property (¶ 44B.), and killing a snake while pronouncing an-

other's name (¶ 170). The term alwanzātar is not found in the last case, but the action is clearly "black magic." In most cases of sorcery the offender was brought before the king's court, a practice reserved for the gravest offences.

The established procedure for contracting and consummating marriage was very similar to that which is described in Mesopotamian law. Negotiations to obtain a wife are made by the groom or his father with the bride's parents. On the occasion of the initial agreement with the girl's parents, the groom makes a small payment of some kind, which is returned if the girl elopes with another man (¶ 28). The suitor receives a verbal promise from the girl's parents that she shall be his, and the girl is henceforth spoken of as tarants "spoken for" or "promised." The second step in the procedure is betrothal. The suitor or his father pays to the bride's parents the kusata, a kind of bride-price, roughly analogous to the Assyro-Babylonian terhatum. The girl is now called hamenkants (literally, "bound"), which means "betrothed." At this point the girl is legally obligated to the marriage. It is possible, after this, for the parents of the girl to withhold her and contest the marriage, but they must repay the young man's kusata double (¶ 29). At the time of marriage the parents of the girl give to her a dowry (iwaru), corresponding to the Assyro-Babylonian sheriktum. This appears to be the girl's share in her parents' estate, i.e., her inheritance portion. If her husband takes her to his home and lives independent of her parents, he will receive her iwaru, should she precede him in death. If he chooses to live under her parents' roof, or to let her do so, when she dies, her iwaru will belong to her children and not to her husband (¶ 27).

A kind of feudalism seems to have operated in ancient Hittite Asia Minor. The entire land belonged to the weather god, who had entrusted it to the administration of the king. The king leased portions of land out to various of his subjects in return for certain feudal duties. These services or payments are called sahhan and luzzi in Hittite. The former was a form of ground-rent; the latter was a more general type of service, sometimes involving corvée, levies, and military services. As an act of special favor the king could exempt certain individuals or professional classes (¶¶ 50-51) from *sahhan* and *luzzi* (cf. later versions of ¶ 47, and KBo X 2 iii 18-19, where Hattusili I exempts certain individuals from *sahhan* and *luzzi*).

In the rural areas court was held in the village gates, as it was among the Hebrews of Biblical times. The judges were the elders of the village. When the commander of a border garrison passed through the area, he would sit with the mayor and elders of the village as a judge, presumably representing the central government (cf. E. von Schuler, *Hethitische Dienstanweisungen*, p. 47 for more details). Even though the Hittite laws represent an official collection kept in the palace, there is mention in ¶ 71 of the elders of a village determining custody of stray cattle. Certain offences of a more serious nature demanded trial before the king. Such cases are designated by one of the following expressions: "court of the king" (¶¶ 44B, 102, 111, 176A.), "gate of the king" (¶¶ 187-8), or "gate of the palace" (¶¶ 198-9). On such occasions the king rendered the verdict, and it was irreversible (¶ 173).

LAW (MESOPOTAMIAN).

Of the two great river cultures, Egypt and Mesopotamia, which arose almost simultaneously yet grew along quite different lines, law plays a far more important part in the latter. This fact has been explained on the basis of geography which, it is said, had the effect of bringing about a centralized authoritarian religion and government in Egypt and made for ideological and artistic conservation in a relatively closed land, but led to a more flexible and adaptive society marked by the greater exercise of personal rights in the more open territory of Mesopotamia. To what degree geography is responsible is of course a matter of speculation. The fact remains that throughout its recorded history the characteristic element in Egyptian thought was that the ruler — the Pharaoh — was the incarnation of the sun-god who held the entire land and all its inhabitants in thrall. There were outstanding exceptions, to be sure, at various periods in history and generally in the actual practice of every day life. But they were really only practical exceptions to the commonly accepted view. So strong was the power of centralized control politically and economically there was no need in Egypt for elaborate machinery to regulate and control the exercise of individual personal and property rights which would lead to the development and systematization of law.

In Mesopotamia, on the other hand, god, king and people stood in an entirely different relationship to each other. We see this in the roots of religion, in the literature and in every day life. We can trace the successive stages in the economic and political growth from small settlements of largely self-sufficient food gatherers to large complex metropolitan units and empires. But we see it best in the many hundred thousands of clay tablets recording every conceivable type of business and legal transaction demonstrating beyond question the principle of individual personal private rights before the law. In fact, this need to identify personal property and record ownership and transfer of property is almost certainly the stimulus which led to the invention and development of writing.

The pattern of society in early Mesopotamia has been described as "primitive democracy." There was an assembly (Sumerian *ukkin*, Akkadian *puhrum*) of the elders and young men with whom the chieftain or leader (antecedant of the later king) must consult. All major decisions were put to a vote. In addition, the chieftain was obliged to give to his tutelary deity an annual account of his conduct of authority during the previous year. No doubt here also, as in the case of Egypt, there was drastic modification in practice especially in later years when, for example, such strong men as Sargon of Akkad, Hammurabi of Babylon or Sennacherib of Assyria ruled. But the principle remained in daily life as a unique characteristic of Mesopotamian civilization and spread into Syria and Anatolia as well.

Before turning to the documents themselves it might be well to consider briefly the basic concepts that underlay the structure of society and law. We begin with their expression in Sumerian for that is the earliest recorded material. In fact, the Sumerians were the ones who invented writing at about 3200 B.C. It is not known whether the ideas pre-date the arrival of the Sumerians and were adopted by them or whether the Sumerians introduced these ideas themselves. There is evidence of a remarkably cohesive civilization during the Ubaid period in Mesopotamia prior to their arrival and the idea of law persists throughout history long after Sumerian influence as such has ceased. So whether or not personal legal rights is a Sumerian import it is definitely a basic Mesopotamian characteristic.

Order in the universe which produced correct thinking and behavior was thought of in a remarkable manner. It is said that the gods established a norm (Sumerian *me*) for every conceivable function in civilization. There were norms for kingship, war, business and every kind of craft and human relationship. These norms, according to Sumerian legend, were handed down from heaven to the people of the city of Kish in the early post-diluvian age in order that they might organize themselves in a manner acceptable to the gods. Further, the guidelines of correct behavior in general were communicated to mankind in a two-fold form by the sun-god (Sumerian *Utu*, Akkadian *Shamash*) who is the god of law and the judge of the universe. The two-fold form in which these concepts were disclosed may best be translated as "truth" and "justice." The first word stands for the abstract concept of truth and is expressed by a term meaning basically "to be firm" that is "unchanging and unchangeable" (Sumerian *níg-gi-na*, Akkadian *kēttum*). The second word represents the exercise of the abstract idea which produces justice. It comes from a word meaning "to be straight" or "to be right." (Sumerian *níg-si-ša*, Akkadian *mâšarum*). These two terms describe the passive and active, the abstract and concrete aspects of human conformity to the heavenly norms. These concepts, conveyed to the ruler, gave him authority to exercise government over his people and also laid down the pattern for that government. Inscriptions from several rulers exist which state that the authority to "establish" (Sumerian *gar*, Akkadian *ša-kānu*) Truth and Justice in the land was given them by the sun-god. This statement is frequently followed by the boast that that is exactly what the ruler has done. And so we see the various levels of organization. Beginning at the bottom, there is the average citizen, owner of property and engaged in business with his fellows. Family and business transactions were controlled by law and recorded in contracts and receipts. Infractions were punished by law and noted

in the records. At the next level were the treaty arrangements between governments recorded and sworn to before the gods. Next there was the accounting the ruler must give of his exercise of government to his god reporting on the economic and political situation. In theory he would be removed if a plague or a drought overtook the land or if his army suffered severe military reverses. Everybody from the king down was held responsible for the proper discharge of his duties. At the top, the gods themselves were described as sharing responsibilities under the chief god An and his vice-gerent Enlil and meeting in council for major decisions.

The source materials from which our knowledge of law and legal procedure arises is varied. First, in point of discovery and numbers, are the various types of legal documents themselves ranging from very brief receipts of the earliest period to complicated contracts drawn up for the participating parties by scribes in the presence of witnesses and bearing their names and seals in order to insure accuracy and prevent attempts to alter any terms in the contract. Included in the general category of business and legal documents are receipts, lists, loans, sales, exchanges and contracts covering many different types of commercial and agricultural transactions. In addition, there are other hundreds of documents describing personal and family affairs such as marriages, adoptions, divorces, wills and such like. Very likely such tablets comprise from eighty to ninety percent of all cuneiform documents recovered from ancient towns and cities. Their number must run into several hundred thousand over the centuries and by their quantity and variety they permit a remarkably detailed reconstruction of daily life of long ago and also emphasize the high degree of legal organization in ancient Mesopotamia. In addition to the above mentioned documents which witness to the presence of law there are others which reveal the process of law. For want of a better name we shall include them all under the heading "Court Records." They consist of brief records of cases tried in court and "declarations" recording the agreement of the person who lost the suit not to raise claim again upon penalty of paying a double fine. There is frequent reference to "ordinances of the king" (*ṣimdāt šarri*) as establishing

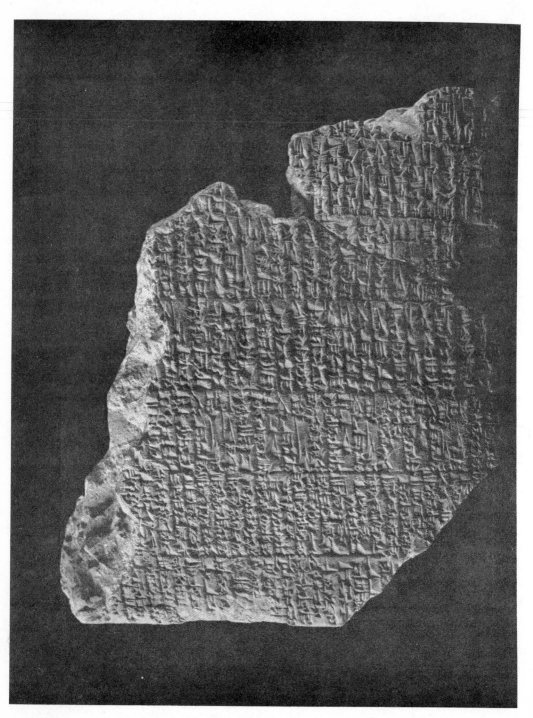

legal principles for specific situations but no documents containing such ordinances have themselves been found.

Insofar as the theory of law is concerned there are but few though well-known documents containing substantive law. The most famous of all, doubtless, is the large diorite monument upon which is inscribed the °Hammurabi Code. This stele is by far the most impressive and complete. It stands at 2.25 meters high and with a circumference ranging from 1.65 to 1.90 meters from top to bottom. At the top is a relief depicting King Hammurabi of Babylon (1728-1686 B.C.) standing before the sun god and giver of law Shamash. There follows an introductory paragraph of some five and a half columns, then the body of the legal text and finally a closing paragraph of about five columns. The text is written in columns which run in horizontal bands around the monument and the individual lines are set up in separate boxes by ruled lines as was the custom with official inscriptions on stone. This great stele was discovered during the 1901-02 season of excavations at the site of ancient Susa, capital of Elam. It appears certain that Shutruk-nahhunte, (1207-1171 B.C.) King of Elam, brought it back as a trophy of war from Sippar a prominent old Babylonian city. The bottom third of the Babylonian text was erased so that a dedicatory inscription in Elamite might be inscribed; but this was never carried out.

At first it was thought that this remarkable Code was unique in the history of Mesopotamia and therefore must be the prototype for Mosaic legislation. But many other collections of law in Babylonian, Assyrian and Hittite, some reaching down to the seventh century B.C., have been discovered since then. Two in particular are identified by name with royal codifiers of law earlier than Hammurabi. These are the Code of Lipit-Ishtar, King of Isin (1875-1865 B.C.) which was identified on seven tablets and fragments recovered at Nippur, and the Code of Ur-Nammu (2050-2032 B.C.) first king of the Third Dynasty of Ur also found in fragmentary form on a broken Nippur tablet. Both of these documents, though fragmentary, appear to follow the pattern of the Hammurabi Code. There is the prologue followed by the paragraphs of law and closing with an epilogue. However, these codes and collections are puzzling to the modern student of jurisprudence since they do not contain all the legislation current at the time and do not appear to follow any logical sequence in their arrangement. Evidence that they are not complete collections of existing law springs from the fact that there are many law contracts concerning matters not treated in the codes and few contracts dealing with matters contained in the codes. Further evidence that the so-called code did not contain the official statement of the law at that time is adduced from the fact that no known contract or case record makes any reference to an official canon of law. It appears now that the so-called code actually consists of selected paragraphs of law singled out for amendment or emphasis rather than constituting a collection of all of the law in force at any one time.

In any case, a definite relationship can be established between the laws thus collected by Lipit-Ishtar of Isin and Hammurabi of Babylon almost two centuries later which yield extraordinary information regarding social changes in Southern Mesopotamia. Of the thirty odd Lipit-Ishtar laws extant and reasonably intelligible nineteen are at least analogues to legislation in Hammurabi's collection and twelve of these are virtually identical. Furthermore, the two classes in society mentioned in the earlier laws (free man and slave; Sumerian *lú* and *arad*) have become three (free man, serf and slave; Akkadian *awīlum*, *muškēnum* and *wardum*). So we are able to trace the development of law in a changing society. Thus far legislation attributed to Ur-Nammu is insufficiently known to establish a firm relationship with later laws.

It is evident, then, that Biblical law as law is not unique to Near Eastern history. Rather, law is the basic framework for society throughout history in the Near East as distinguished from, say, Egypt. Nevertheless, the ethical character and motivation of Biblical law is unique.

BIBLIOGRAPHY. G. R. Driver and John C. Miles, editors, *The Babylonian Laws*, vol. I Legal Commentary, vol. II Text and Translation, Oxford, 1952-5. H. Frankfort, *Kingship and the Gods*, University of Chicago, 1948. F. R. Steele, *The Code of Lipit-Ishtar*, University of Pennsylvania (no date). H. W. F. Saggs, *The Greatness that was Babylon*, Hawthorn, 1962.

LEONTOPOLIS. In 162 B.C. Antiochus V (Eupator) of Syria appointed a man named Alkimus as High Priest in Jerusalem, although he was not of the priestly family. Alkimus was regarded as a usurper by many pious Jews, and Onias IV, the son of the High Priest Onias III who had earlier been deposed by Antiochus IV (Epiphanes) fled to Egypt with the hope of establishing a center of true worship there. According to Josephus, Onias addressed a letter to the Egyptian ruler, Ptolemy VI (Philometor) and his wife, Cleopatra, requesting permission to build in Egypt a temple similar to that in Jerusalem, with Levites and priests serving as ministrants (*Antiquities* xiii. 62-64). The reply was brief and favorable:

> King Ptolemy and Queen Cleopatra to Onias, greeting. We have read your petition asking that it be permitted you to cleanse the ruined temple at Leontopolis in the name of Heliopolis, called Bubastis-of-the-Fields. We wonder, therefore, whether it will be pleasing to God that a temple be built in a place so wild and full of sacred animals. But since you say that the prophet Isaiah foretold this long ago (cf. Isa. 19:19), we grant your request if this is to be in accordance with the law, so that we may not seem to have sinned against God in any way. (*Ibid.* xiii. 70-71.)

Josephus tells us that Onias built a temple at Leontopolis "similar to that at Jerusalem, but smaller and poorer" (*Ibid.* xiii. 72). Although the letters which Josephus records are not accepted as authentic, a Jewish temple is known to have been built in Egypt, and Tell el-Yahudiya is its traditional site.

The tell was excavated in 1887 by E. Naville and Llewellyn Griffin with no significant results, although the excavators were satisfied that they had identified the site of ancient Leontopolis. Flinders Petrie was more successful in his work there in 1906. He discovered the remains of a large building, and later observed, "The plan of the whole hill is strikingly modelled on that of Jerusalem; the temple had inner and outer courts, like that of Zion, but it was smaller and poorer in size. . . . The whole site was formed in imitation of the shape of the Temple hill of the Holy City. It was, in short, a New Jerusalem in Egypt" (Flinders Petrie, *Hyksos and Israelite Cities*).

Petrie also discovered remains of a large Hyksos fortified encampment, a mile in circumference, at Tell el-Yahudiya, with a Hyksos cemetery nearby. He considered this as evidence that he had discovered the Hyksos capital city, Avaris, but more recent scholars tend to identify Avaris with Tanis. We can be sure, however, that the Hyksos maintained a stronghold at Tell el-Yahudiya, whatever its name in ancient times.

LEVIRATE MARRIAGE. The term levirate marriage is derived from the Latin word *levir*, a husband's brother. We learn from the Nuzi tablets that when a father obtains a bride for his son, and the son dies, the girl is to be married to another son. The custom may have originated in the concept of a "bride price." Since the father had an investment in the girl, he would be free to give her to another of his sons.

The levirate marriage formula was incorporated into Biblical Law (Deut. 25:5-10). Its violation is illustrated in Genesis 38. Onan took his brother's wife, but refused to have a child by her, and died. Judah, having lost two sons, refused to give his third son in marriage to Tamar, with the result that she took matters into her own hands, dressed as an harlot, and had children by Judah, himself. The episode illustrates the fact that levirate marriage incurred obligations on the part of the father-in-law as well as of the bride. Judah acknowledged that he had done wrong in not permitting Tamar to marry his third son. The Book of Ruth provides another Biblical example of levirate marriage. There we learn that when there are no more brothers, a close relative of the deceased may marry the widow. The first child born in such circumstances is reckoned to the deceased husband, receiving his name and inheritance.

LIPIT-ISHTAR. The fifth king of *Isin was Lipit-Ishtar who reigned from *ca.* 1864 to 1854 B.C. Tablets containing a law code of Lipit-Ishtar were excavated at *Nippur by the University of Pennsylvania and they are now in the collection of the University Museum. Lipit-Ishtar was an *Amorite but he wrote his law code in Sumerian, and the laws themselves were probably derived from Sumerian antecedents.

The code begins with a prologue in which the king traces his rule to the will of the Sumerian gods Anu and Enlil. In accord with the command of Enlil, Lipit-Ishtar claims that he established justice throughout Sumer and Akkad.

There is a lacunae in the text, only half of which has been preserved. The legal text contains thirty-eight regulations, dealing with such subjects as the hiring of boats, treatment of slaves, the possession of real estate (including a date palm plantation), tax defaults, inheritance, and marriage. Regulations state: "If a man cut down a tree in the garden of another man, he shall pay one-half mina of silver" (Paragraph 10), and "If a man rented an ox and damaged its eye, he shall pay half of its price" (Paragraph 35).

An epilogue states that Lipit-Ishtar "erected this stele." It calls down a blessing on those who do not damage it, and invokes a curse on any who mutilate it. *See also* Law (Mesopotamian).

BIBLIOGRAPHY. Francis Rue Steele, "The Code of Lipit-Ishtar," *AJA* LII, 1948, pp. 425-450 (reprinted as a Museum Monograph, The University Museum, Philadelphia). S. N. Kramer in *ANET*, pp. 159-161.

LYDDA. Eleven miles southeast of Jaffa is the town of Lydda, Old Testament Lod mentioned by Thutmose III in the list of Palestinian towns conquered by his generals. Lydda was in territory assigned to Benjamin and was one of the most westerly of the Jewish towns of the post-exilic period. Peter cured a palsied man at Lydda and saw many of its people converted to Christ (Acts 9:32-35).

After the fall of Jerusalem (A.D. 70), Lydda served as a rabbinical center during the second and third centuries. In the early Christian centuries Lydda had a bishopric and it is the traditional site of the martyrdom of St. George (A.D. 303). St. George was honored by the Crusaders and, through Richard Coeur de Lion, he was adopted as the patron saint of England. The Church of St. George was built by the Crusaders at Lydda during the twelfth century.

Lydda was renamed Diospolis by the Romans. It is now an Israeli town and officially bears the ancient Old Testament name of Lod. It is two and one-half miles from Israel's principal airport, known as the Lod (or Lydda) Airport.

LYDIA. Lydia, the land of the Lydians, was located in southwestern Asia Minor. Greek colonies in Asia Minor bordered Lydia to the west, and the Phrygians disputed the eastern border. The capital and chief city of Lydia was *Sardis, in the Hermus Valley.

*Hittite influence extended into Lydia, but the Lydian Kingdom itself did not arise until the first millennium B.C. After describing a

SARDIS, CAPITAL OF LYDIA. Courtesy, Gerald Larue

legendary past, Herodotus (I, 6-86) mentions the historical figure of Gyges (*ca.* 685-652 B.C.) who maintained contacts with Delphi in Greece and with the Assyrian king Ashurbanipal whose annals speak of "Guggu of Luddu," i.e. Gyges of Lydia. Gyges died in battle, defending his country against raids from the Cimmerians, Indo-European nomads who invaded Asia Minor under pressure from the Scythians. The Medes under Cyaxeres also sought control of Asia Minor until the Halys River was accepted as the border between Lydia and the Median Empire. A daughter of the Lydian king Alyattes was married to Astyages, son of Cyaxeres the Mede.

The best known Lydian king was Croesus (560-546 B.C.) who sent spectacular gifts to Delphi and Hellenized his kingdom. The name of Croesus is preserved on the temple to Artemis which he subsidized at *Ephesus. Political independence came to an end for Lydia when Cyrus of Persia captured Sardis (546 B.C.). Lydia became a Persian satrapy until 334 B.C. when following the Battle of Granicus, Lydia fell to Alexander the Great. After a checkered history it became part of the Roman province of Asia. Three of the seven churches of Revelation (Thyatira, Sardis, and Philadelphia) were located in the territory of Lydia.

361

LYSTRA. Lystra is one of the cities in south-central Asia Minor where Paul established a church on his first missionary journey. Luke describes Paul's experiences in Lystra in Acts 14. Because of persecution in Iconium, Paul and Barnabas fled to Lystra. The healing of a lame man at Lystra caused the people to identify Paul and Barnabas as Hermes and Zeus and to worship them accordingly. After restraining them with difficulty. Paul preached to them the sermon partially recorded in Acts 14:15-17. Judaizers from Antioch and Romans instigated a riot in which Paul was stoned. From Lystra the missionaries went to Derbe and on their return trip visited Lystra again (Acts 14:21). Paul visited Lystra again on his second missionary journey, at which time Timothy, a native of Lystra, was circumcised and joined Paul. Paul vividly recalled his experiences at Lystra in II Timothy 3:11, written near the end of his life.

The location of ancient Lystra has been ascertained on the basis of an inscription found on a mound near the modern village of Hatunsaray, about twenty-five miles south of Iconium. This inscription was discovered and published by J. R. Sitlington Sterrett in 1885 (*The Wolfe Expedition to Asia Minor,* Amarell and Upham, Boston, 1888, p. 142). This Latin inscription contains the name LVSTRA, and is now housed in the new Archaeological Museum in Konya, Turkey. The text reads: "Divum Aug(ustum) Col(onia) Iul(ia) Felix Gemina Lustra consecravit. D(ecreto) D(ecuriorum)." Numerous other inscriptions can be found in and near the modern village of Hatunsaray.

The mound of Lystra has not been excavated. It is a typical mound of a fairly good-sized city. Surface exploration has indicated an extensive occupation during the Hellenistic and Roman periods. During the Roman period Lystra also struck her own coins. Lystra was also represented at the major councils of the early church — A.D. 325, 381, 451, 530, 692, 787, 879. This would indicate that a church flourished at this place for some centuries. Future excavation of the mound will undoubtedly throw significant light on the history of Lystra.

M

MACEDONIA. The kingdom of Macedonia was located north of Thessaly, northwest of the Aegean Sea. Its capital was Pella, twenty-four miles northwest of Thessalonica. Under Philip II (359-336 B.C.), Thrace and Greece were incorporated into the Macedonian Empire. Philip's son Alexander turned his attention eastward and conquered the Persian Empire which had once been a threat to Greece itself. The Macedonians adopted Greek culture, and Alexander was an apostle of Hellenism as well as a conqueror.

In 148 B.C. Macedonia became a Roman province. The apostle Paul ministered in numerous Macedonian cities including Neapolis, Philippi, Amphipolis, Apollonia, Thessalonica (the capital) and Berea.

MAMRE. Almost two miles north of Hebron is the place known in Arabic as Ramat el-Khalil ("height of the friend") reminiscent of the fact that Abraham was known as "the friend of God." This is the traditional site where Abraham erected an altar (Gen. 13:18).

Because of its association with Abraham, Mamre became a place sacred to the Jews. A pavement discovered there dates back to the ninth or eighth century B.C. Josephus (*War* IV. ix. 7; *Antiquities* I x. 4) mentions a terebinth said to have been at Mamre since creation which was pointed out as the tree beneath which Abraham entertained the angels (Gen. 18:4, 8). Constantine's mother-in-law, Eutropia was scandalized to find pagan altars at Mamre and, at her instigation, the Emperor ordered them demolished and replaced by a Christian basilica. Its remains were identified by Father A. E. Madar during excavations in the area. The walls of the enclosure were built in part by Herod, and in part during the reign of Hadrian. The church built under Constantine was a small basilica with a long narthex and the apse built within the rectangle of the church. Although later rebuilt, the present ruins are thought to represent the site and plan of Constantine's basilica.

MANETHO. Manetho, a priest at *Heliopolis under Ptolemy I and II, wrote (*ca.* 300 B.C.) a history of Egypt from the earliest times to 323 B.C. when the Ptolemies assumed control after the death of Alexander. Manetho's *Egyptian History* has not survived, but fragments are quoted by other ancient historians. Josephus quotes from them, and the list of dynasties together with notes on important kings and events was incorporated into the *Chronicle* (A.D. 221) of Sextus Julius Africanus. Further quotations appear in the *Chronicon* (A.D. 326) and in a history of the world from Adam to Diocletian by George Syncellus (*ca.* A.D. 800).

Although modern Egyptologists are aware of errors in Manetho's reckoning, they still find his schematic view of Egyptian history useful. Manetho's thirty dynasties form the basis for all contemporary discussions of the history of Pharaonic Egypt.

BIBLIOGRAPHY. W. G. Waddell, tr., *Manetho*, Loeb Classical Library, 1940.

MANUAL OF DISCIPLINE. *See* Dead Sea Scrolls.

MARI. According to the *Sumerian King List, Mari was the tenth city to exercise kingship after the flood. The ancient caravan route from the Tigris-Euphrates Valley westward to the Mediterranean intersected at the site of Mari, modern Tell Hariri, with the main route which extended southward from the Habor and the Upper Euphrates to Babylon and the Persian Gulf. Tell Hariri stands on the west bank of the Euphrates near Abu Kemal on the Syria-Iraq border.

Eannatum of *Lagash boasts of a victory over Mari on a cuneiform document dated to about 2500 B.C. By that time Mari had developed into an important city with a *ziggurat and numerous temples. Excavations have brought to light temples to Ishtar, Ninhurzag, Ishtarat, Shamash, and Ninnizaza.

When Lugalzaggisi of *Uruk, or *Sargon of Akkad conquered Mari they destroyed the city. Temples were desecrated and statuettes were shattered and strewn around. Recovery was rapid, however, and Mari became an important city during the Sargonid period. Naram-sin installed two of his daughters at Mari, probably as priestesses, a fact we learn from two inscribed vessels

A FERTILITY GODDESS excavated at Mari. Courtesy, Aleppo Museum

discovered in a house near the temple of Asherat.

About 2021 B.C., Ishbi-Irra of Mari conquered the city of *Isin and helped bring about the downfall of the Third Dynasty of Ur. Mari's period of independence was short lived, however, for she soon fell to Iahdun-Lim of Khana who, in turn, was conquered by Shamshi-Adad of *Assyria. Shamshi-Adad placed his son Ismah-Adad on the throne of Mari, but at Shamshi-Adad's death (*ca.* 1786 B.C.), Iahdun-Lim's son Zimri-Lim regained control. His rule came to an end *ca.* 1765 B.C. when *Hammurabi of Babylon took Mari. In 1748 B.C. it was conquered and destroyed by the *Kassites. It never regained its influential position. Mari served as a garrison town guarding the river crossing for caravan routes during Assyrian times. A village occupied the site when Nebuchadnezzar's Babylon controlled western Asia.

Archaeological interest developed in the Tell Hariri area when bedouin discovered a headless stone statue while quarrying for building material in 1933. Scientific excavation began the same year when Andrè Parrot conducted the first of a series of expeditions on behalf of the Louvre. Six seasons were spent in excavations until work was stopped with the outbreak of World War II. After the war excavations were resumed in a series of campaigns from 1951 to 1956.

A *stratification pit to virgin soil under the temple of Shamash revealed pottery of the same design as the earliest finds at *Nineveh. The earliest buildings dated from ca. 3200 B.C.

During the years prior to World War II, Parrot excavated the ziggurat at Mari with its adjoining shrines. At one site he found superimposed the remains of a succession of four temples to the goddess Ishtar. A temple to Dagan, built during the Isin-Larsa period, was discovered. Its entrance was guarded by two bronze lions with inlaid eyes. Inlay eyes found nearby suggest that there were forty more lions.

The most significant discovery at Mari was the palace complex of Zimri-Lim which covered fifteen acres. Among the three hundred rooms of the palace was the throne room with wall paintings. The royal archives yielded about twenty thousand cuneiform tablets from the time of Iasmah-Adad and Zimri-Lim, including correspondence between Zimri-Lim and Hammurabi. The texts deal largely with administrative matters, but personal and place names provide interesting parallels with the Patriarchal records of Genesis (see Abraham). Most of the Mari texts were in the Akkadian language, but a few were written in *Hurrian, and there were several Sumero-Akkadian bilinguals. The palace included a school for scribes.

The Mari texts mention the *Habiru people and a tribe of Ben-Yamini, a name comparable to the Biblical Benjamin although referring to a different people. *Hazor is the only Palestinian city mentioned, but place names near *Haran have parallels in the Biblical records. Nahur (Nahor), Turahi (Terah) and Sarug (Serug) are places mentioned in the Mari texts which appear to be related to the names of the Patriarchal records (Gen. 11:23-24). Among West-Semitic personal names at Mari we meet an Ariukku (cf. Arioch, Gen. 14:1) and forms like Abraham and Jacob.

Customs reflected in the Mari texts also illustrate life during Patriarchal times. A god had his prophet, sent to make proclamations in the god's name, as Yahweh had Moses as his prophet to Pharaoh and Israel. The census was of religious as well as political and economic significance (cf. II Sam. 24). Tribal land was inalienable, and inheritance was only through members of the family as in Israel. Treaties and covenants were ratified by the killing of an ass, as in the pact between the Shechemites and Jacob (Gen. 33:19; 34:1-3).

BIBLIOGRAPHY. André Parrot, Les fouilles de Mari. Rapports preliminaires des campagnes I a X (1933-55). 10 parts, P. Geuthner, Paris, 1935-55. "Mari et Chagar Bazar," Syria, XIX, 1938, pp. 308-310. Charles Francois Jean, Six campagnes de fouilles à Mari, 1933-39, synthese des resultants, Casterman, Tournai, 1952.

STATUE OF INTUP ILUM, Mari. Courtesy, Aleppo Museum

MARRIAGE.

MARRIAGE. Israelite marriage customs shared much in common with the customs of the other peoples of the Near East. The father, as head of the household, usually selected a bride for his son and made arrangements for the marriage (cf. Gen. 24:4). The girl's role was passive, for she was given as wife to the man her father chose. Romantic love was not necessarily absent, however, and a kindly father would consider the desires of his daughter. We are told, for example, that Michal loved David (I Sam. 18:20).

The concept of *Levirate Marriage may reflect an ancient custom in which a bride is purchased by a father for his son. In the event of the son's death, the bride is given to the next son. The Biblical word *mohar* is used of a gift given to the father (or brothers?) of the bride by the groom, or the groom's father. This might take the form of silver (Deut. 22:29; Exod. 22:16, 17) or services. Jacob served Laban for seven years (Gen. 29:20, 28) for Rachel. As a marriage present for Michal, Saul demanded of David "a hundred foreskins of the Philistines" (I Sam. 18:20-25).

A text from *Ugarit states, "And thou shalt *mhr* her from her father for a thousand [shekels] of silver, and ten thousand of gold." Throughout the Near East it appears that it was customary to give a *mohar* to the bride's father at the time arrangements were made for a wedding. As in the case of Rebekah (Gen. 24) such arrangements must usually have considered the wishes and well-being of the bride. They were not simply commercial transactions, although they had a business aspect.

A second type of gift was the dowry, a gift to the bride (or groom) from her father. This might be a gift of silver and gold, or of servants (Gen. 24:59, 61), or even of land. The Egyptian Pharaoh gave the city of Gezer as a dowry to his daughter who married Solomon (I Kings 9:16).

In addition the bridegroom would provide gifts for the bride (cf. Gen. 24:53) which would be expressive of his wealth and the esteem with which he regarded his beloved. There were doubtless numerous other opportunities for the exchange of gifts among members of the families involved in the wedding proceedings.

Marriage was regarded as a covenant entered into by two families (cf. Prov. 2:17;

Mal. 2:14). The *mohar* gift sealed the covenant between the families, and gave the husband authority (although not absolute control) over his wife.

Prior to the wedding ceremony a contract was drawn up in writing. Many such contracts have been discovered at *Nuzi in which a childless wife agrees to provide an handmaid for her husband in order that he may have children. According to the apocryphal book of Tobit (7:14), the father of the bride drew up a written contract among the Jews. The Mishnah calls this the *ketuba.* Among Aramaic papyri from the fifth century B.C. there are records of contracts between Hebrews and the Egyptians they married.

The wedding itself was a festive occasion. Special attire was worn by the bridal couple, and they were bedecked with ornaments and jewelry. The bride was evidently veiled (cf. Gen. 24:65). Processions accompanied both the bride and the groom from their assembly places and met at a pre-determined location (I Macc. 9:39). To the accompaniment of music they moved on to the house — usually the bridegroom's — where the wedding feast was to be held. The wedding festivities might last seven days or even, as in the book of Tobit (8:20), fourteen.

The ceremony included the spreading of a cloak over the bride, symbolizing that she is taken as a wife of the owner of the cloak. J. L. Burckhardt, a nineteenth century traveler in Arab lands, has noted that one of the bridegroom's relations spreads a cloak over the bride, saying, "None shall cover thee but such a one," naming the bridegroom. In the Biblical story of Ruth, the young woman approached Boaz in the field and asked him to spread his skirt over her (Ruth 3:9) because he was next of kin, and entitled to claim her by the laws of Levirate marriage.

The consummation of the marriage took place in a special tent or room known as the *huppa,* or bridal chamber. A blood stained cloth would then be shown as proof of the bride's virginity (cf. Deut. 22:13-21). After this final ritual, still observed in some places in the Near East, the wedding festivities would continue.

The Mosaic Law made provisions for divorce (Deut. 24:1-4) on the initiative of the husband. Aramaic papyri from *Elephantine indicate that a Jewish bride had the

AIR VIEW OF THE HILL OF MA-
SADA, showing excavated remains.
Courtesy, Israel Office of Information

HEROD'S PALACE AT MASADA. *The pedestals served as bases for columns.*
Courtesy, Israel Information Services

right to obtain a divorce among the Jews in Egypt. When a man divorced his wife he wrote for her a bill, or certificate of divorce, and sent her away. Jesus said that the Mosaic provision for divorce was because of the hardness of men's hearts (Matt. 19:8).

MASADA. South of *En Gedi is a rocky cliff where the Zealots who sought to defy the armies of Rome made their last stand after the destruction of Jerusalem (A.D. 70). The Hasmonean ruler Jonathan had earlier erected a fortress there which he named Masada. King Herod saw the strategic importance of Masada and strengthened its fortifications, making it a secret storehouse for supplies and a refuge for the royal household in the event of revolt.

Masada's hour of fame came during the Jewish revolt (A.D. 66-70) when it was seized by Jewish rebels against Rome and made a base for surprise attacks on Roman troops. In one daring episode, the Zealot Menahem ben Judah of Galilee took the fortress, distributed its weapons among his men, and led them to the gates of Jerusalem.

Deeds of heroism, however, were no match for the Roman legions. The initial victories of the Zealots had the advantage of surprise. When the Roman legions started pouring out of Caesarea with their heavy war machines, the Zealots had to pull back. On

the ninth of Av, A.D. 70, Jerusalem fell to the Romans and in subsequent weeks the city with its temple was completely destroyed.

After the fall of Jerusalem, a heroic Zealot leader, Eleazer Ben Yair, determined to defend Masada. Every other stronghold had fallen to Rome, and when it was obvious that the Zealots could not keep Masada they chose to die by their own hands rather than fall to the enemy. By agreement the women and children were first put to the sword, then the men killed one another. When the Romans eventually broke into the fortress they gazed upon the corpses with amazement. Food supplies had been left as evidence that the people of Masada had died willingly, choosing death to slavery. Archaeological work has brought to light signs of ash in the rubble at Masada, confirming the account of Josephus who mentions that the last of the Zealots completely razed the palace.

The Israel Exploration Society and the Hebrew University have excavated Masada since the 1955-56 season when the Israel Defence Forces and the Department of Antiquity co-operated in its excavation. Yigael Yadin was in charge of the expedition which has uncovered the remains of structures erected on the mountain along with the more prosaic fragments of clothing, utensils, and particles of food. Twelve scrolls have been discovered containing passages from Genesis, Leviticus, and other Biblical and apocryphal books. The 1964 season produced a large piece of a scroll belonging to the long-lost Hebrew original of the Book of Jubilees and a group of sherds inscribed with Hebrew letters. A building which seems to have served as a house of study, with a ritual immersion pool was excavated and fifty-three silver shekels and half-shekels were found.

CORINTHIAN CAPITAL from Herod's Palace, Masada. Courtesy, Israel Information Services

MEDIA, MEDES. Ancient Media occupied the territory west of the Caspian Sea and south of the Zagros Mountains, corresponding to western Iran and southern Azerbaijan today. The Median capital was °Ecbatana.

An Indo-European people, the Medes spoke an Iranian language closely akin to Old Persian. Since they left no written records, our knowledge of the Medes comes largely from Assyrian and Greek sources. They are first mentioned in the annals of the Assyrian ruler Shalmaneser III who raided the Median plain in 886 B.C. and seized the fine horses for which the Medes were famous. Tiglath-pileser III claimed victories over the Medes but Media expanded until, by the time of Sargon (d. 705 B.C.) they ruled all of Persia. From the time of Sargon until the middle of the seventh century B.C. the Medes were subject to the Assyrian kings. Among the places to which Sargon exiled the Israelites were the "cities of the Medes" (II Kings 17:6; 18:11).

Although bound by treaty to Assyria, the Medes joined the Scythians and Cimmerians in besieging Nineveh, which fell in 612 B.C. With freedom restored, the Medes continued as an independent people until Astyages was defeated about the middle of the sixth century by Cyrus, founder of the Persian Empire. Medes were given positions of honor, and their customs and laws were joined with those of the Persians. *See* Persia.

MEDICINE

I. *Mesopotamia.* The library of °Ashurbanipal contained eight hundred tablets providing our main source of information about medicine in the ancient Near East. In the Code of °Hammurabi the word "physician" occurs along with the first laws relating to medical practice. It established both the fees payable to the physicians for satisfactory services and the penalty should their administrations prove harmful. It is noteworthy that the regulations refer mainly to surgery, and that little mention is made of medical practice. Even at that early period there seems to have been a sharp distinction between surgeons and physicians. Medical failure was fraught with danger for the physicians. "If a physician operate on a man (i.e., gentleman) for a severe wound with a bronze lancet and cause the man's death, or open an abscess (in the eye of a man) with a bronze lancet and destroy the man's eye, they shall cut off his fingers."

In Mesopotamia, medicine was a secret, religious craft, based on magic, necromancy, demonology, and divination, and very much under the control of the priestly group. It was taught in special schools within the temples. There were three kinds of medical men, all of them priests. In ancient medicine, physicians were always priests, hence medicine possessed a strong religious flavor. The three kinds of physicians were: (1) herb doctors, who correspond to our modern internists; (2) knife doctors, who correspond to our modern surgeons; and (3) spell doctors, who correspond to our modern psychiatrists. These doctors practiced a highly rudimentary type of medicine and were trained in the temple to diagnose and treat disease. Specialization was rampant. There were men specialized in divination and forecasting, exorcists skilled in incantations to drive away evil spirits, and others skilled in sorcery and the use of drugs.

The market and the temple both played a part in medical practice. Herodotus (I. 80) reports the following: "They bring out their sick to the market place, for they have no physician; then those who pass by the sick person confer with him about the disease, to discover whether they have themselves been afflicted with this same disease as the sick person, or have seen others so afflicted, thus the passers-by confer with him and advise him to have recourse to the same treatment as that by which they escaped a similar disease, or as they have known to cure others. And they are not allowed to pass by a sick person in silence, without inquiring the nature of his distemper." The importance of the temple in Mesopotamian life was powerful. The priest guided everyone, both inside and outside the temple, not only medically and religiously, but also on business matters and other aspects of life. The high priests were also responsible for the "Temple Virgins," or "nurses" who were a combination of priestess, prostitute and medical attendant who tended to the physical and spiritual needs of the temple visitors.

A study of their pharmacopoeia, as reconstructed from the cuneiform tablets of Ashurbanipal's library, revealed 250 vegetable substances and 120 minerals. Wines, fats, oils, honey, wax, and milk were employed in the preparation of various drugs. Many of the agents such as aloes, anise, asafoetida, belladonna, cannabis, cardamon, cassia, castor oil, cinnamon, colocynth, coriander, garlic, henbane, juniper, licorice, mandragora, mint, mustard, myrrh, pomegranate and poppy, are known to us today as having definite therapeutic value. In many instances, the medication prescribed seems, by modern standards, quite rational. Poppy was used for pain and to produce sleep. Belladonna was employed as an anodyne, to check the flow of saliva, to relieve spasms of the bladder, for dysmenorrhea, bronchitis, and asthma. This is consistent with modern materia medica.

But in this curious admixture of the eccentric, bizarre and the valuable, we find other revolting and nauseating remedies to be taken by mouth. Some of these are swine's fat, dog's dung, human excreta and urine. These substances were doubtless given in the hope that they would be revolting to the demons and drive them away.

One curious form of medical diagnosis, widely practiced in Babylon, was hepatoscopy, or inspection of the liver. Mention of both this and the use of divination is made in Ezekiel 21:21: "For the King of Babylon stood at the parting of the waves, at the head of the two waves to use divination: he made his arrows bright, he consulted with images, he looked in the liver." The practice was to take a clay model of a healthy sheep's liver and compare it with the fresh liver of a sacrificed animal. Any alterations on the fresh specimen were carefully marked on the clay model and were later studied at length to determine what type of disease troubled the patient. This, of course, had no practical value for the patient who seemed strangely detached from the comparison, but to the Babylonians, the liver, as a source of blood, was regarded as the seat of the soul.

It has been stated that the people of ancient Mesopotamia differentiated their demons just as we do our germs. There was a demon for wasting diseases, for liver malfunction, for gynecological problems, and every ill man was possessed by a demon. More than six thousand demons were classified in Mesopotamia alone. Disease was not believed to be a pathologic disorder, but either a punishment by the gods for sins committed or possession by demons. The sick man was a sinful man who required expiatory rituals.

The Mesopotamians did, however, give us systematic descriptions of jaundice, ocular diseases and fevers; early notions of contagion, an amazingly modern pharmacopoeia, legal codification of medical practice (as it is contained in the Code of Hammurabi), and early explorations into surgical practices.

F. H. Garrison in the *History of Medicine* (Saunders, 4th Edition, 1929), has complimented them. "The Assyro-Babylonians protected themselves from the fierce sunlight with parasols, from insect pests with fly-flaps, wore semitic plaids wound about the body terrace-wise, went in for boxing and other manly exercises, employed inflated bladders as water wings, knew how to brew beer and to fertilize the date palm, regulated wet-nursing, buried their dead in slipper shaped coffins and fan shaped tombs."

II. *Egypt.* In Egypt a higher brand of medicine was practiced and it is significant that both the Persian Kings, Cyrus and Darius, had Egyptian physicians. Most of our accurate knowledge of Egyptian medicine has been obtained from medical papyri. Some information has been gained from monuments and mummies, the latter revealing arteriosclerosis, gallstones, gout, arthritis and other contemporary, well-known pathologic states. The two most important papyri are the Ebers papyrus and the Edwin-Smith papyrus. The latter is the oldest surgical treatise in the world, and describes forty-eight cases. The Ebers papyrus dealt with internal medical diseases and listed traditional therapies. The Edwin-Smith papyrus found in Luxor by the man whose name it bears, an American Egyptologist, is probably the first scientific document in the history of medicine and contains some amazing surgical commentaries. Here we find the word "brain" recorded for the first time in human language. Here is described "erection" and "seminal emission" following dislocation of the neck (a phenomenon observed today in men executed by hanging). Here, the writer recognized the heart as the center of a system of distributing vessels, stressed the importance of the pulse, and probably counted it. "Its pulsations," writes the author, "is in every vessel of every member." If the author actually counted the pulse which seems probable, it is all the more remarkable since this was twelve centuries before Hippocrates, and it was not until 1628 that William Harvey wrote his *De Motu Cordis,* a publication from which modern cardiology stemmed.

The amazing surgical treatise discussed a great variety of fractures, dislocations, wounds, tumors, ulcers and abscesses. Lint was employed as an absorbent, also plugs and swabs of linen. Adhesive plaster was used for bringing together the lips of a wound. Surgical stitching is mentioned for the first time, according to the Edwin-Smith papyrus, when the author writes, "Thou shouldst draw together for him his gash with stitching." Cauterization is recommended for ulcers and tumors of the breast, and splints were formed of thin wood, padded with linen and molded to the broken limb (probably with plaster or gum). Infected wounds received applications of a decoction of willow which contains salicin; and as astringents there was employed a solution of copper and sodium sulphate. As among the Mesopotamians, some of the Egyptians' applications were not aesthetic or hygienic with dung, grease, and honey frequently applied to wounds.

But there were other medical papyri. The Kahun papyrus was gynecologic in scope. The Hearst papyrus contained a practicing physician's formulary. The London papyrus contained a very large number of magical incantations, in contrast to the loftier medical tone of the other presentations.

Curiously, in the Egyptian papyri, we find probably the earliest description of contraceptive measures. The Kahun papyrus recommends the insertion of a vaginal suppository containing crocodile's dung and honey mixed with sodium carbonate. The papyrus of Ebers prescribes the vaginal insertion of acacia tips. These tips contain gum arabic which dissolves in water forming lactic acid. Many of the contraceptive jellies, widely employed at present, contained lactic acid as a spermaticide.

Macabre concern of the Egyptians with death is the very essence of their increased knowledge of mummification and thus advancement in anatomical knowledge. While the Mesopotamians feared demons and evil spirits, the Egyptians feared death. Mummification in Egypt was developed to a remarkable degree for the Egyptians believed that the Ka or soul returned to the body after death. It was therefore incumbent on the embalmer to prevent putrefaction inside the dead body. This peculiar concept of immortality resulted in the magnificent mausoleums and tombs, decorated and filled with all the necessities, comforts, and appurtenances of life. Every pyramid, every tomb, was really a new home erected to the deceased; a temple to one who thus became like a god.

Their technique of mummification and embalming, in the light of our modern knowledge, is most authentic and accurate. "The brain was first drawn out through the nostrils by an iron hook and the skull cleared of the rest by rinsing with drugs. The abdomen was then incised with a sharp flint knife; eviscerated; cleansed with wine and aromatics; filled with myrrh, cassia, and spices and the wound sewed up. The body was then steeped for seventy days in sodium chloride or bicarbonate (natron), and afterwards washed and completely enveloped in linen bandages smeared together with gum. The relatives put the treated body in a wooden coffin, shaped like a man, which was deposited in the burial chamber along with four Canopic jars containing the viscera. As with our North American Indians, the departed spirit was furnished with food, drink, and other appointments and conveniences, and there was a spiritual ritual or a Book of the Dead which every Egyptian learned by heart as a sort of Baedeker to the other world" (F. H. Garrison, *History of Medicine,* 4th Edition, Saunders, 1929, p. 58).

Because of the medical papyri available, moderns are more familiar with the medicine of ancient Egypt than with that of Mesopotamia. Though still primitive, the Egyptian concept of disease represented an improvement over the Mesopotamian theories. Unlike the Mesopotamian concept, theirs was not based on the role of the liver, but came close to our modern understanding of the vital functions of respiration and circulation. The Egyptians knew that man required two things to survive: air and food. They also knew that the body contained a magic fluid, vital to man; since its loss could be fatal they related this fluid to the pulsations of the heart. Thus, air, food, and blood became the three basic elements of Egyptian physiology. Furthermore, Egyptian medicine was less closely related to the priestly class and religion. True, in Egypt, magico-religious medicine was employed and was the most popular because it was the least expensive. Yet, it coexisted with empirico-rational medicine, employing drugs and diet, but because of the higher cost the latter was unfortunately limited to the wealthy.

Medical practice shared by priests and physicians reached such a high degree of specialization that most physicians became authorities in one disease only. There were eye specialists, dentists, general practitioners, internists, palace- temple- and tomb-physicians, physicians to the miners (industrial physicians), and even assistants to the physicians. This civilization was purgation conscious, bowel conscious, and anal conscious, with even special physicians who were exclusively "guardians of the royal anus" of the Pharaoh.

Popular remedies were enemas and the technique may have been learned by the Egyptians from observing the Ibis, the sacred bird of the Nile. This is a bird which counteracts its constipating diet by using its long bill as a rectal syringe. Treatment was also based on diet, medicinal plants; castor oil, hot sand, and the application of animal fat (particularly ox fat). The Egyptian materia medica was unpredictable and contained seven hundred odd remedies, not necessarily indicating any special advancement in the art of therapeusis. There was intelligent use of certain drugs, well known to us today, and unintelligent use of bizarre remedies. A popular Egyptian pomade for baldness consisted of equal parts of the fats of lion, hippopotamus, crocodile, goose, serpent and ibex. An ointment for the eye consisted of a trituration of antimony in goose fat.

It can be seen, therefore, that Egyptian medicine represented an advancement over Mesopotamian medicine. There was still a strong religious influence and taint. It had improved anatomically, physiologically, and possibly surgically. Specialization was intense, drug therapy a little more thoughtful, and the Egyptian medical legacy profoundly influenced Greek medicine. Egyptian medicine is closely linked to the name of Imhotep, whom Osler described as "the first figure of a physician to stand out clearly from the mist of antiquity." This man who lived a little less than 3,000 years B.C. distinguished himself as a physician, a statesman, an astronomer, and one of the greatest architects of all time. Little is known of his work as a physician except that for many years after his death he was worshipped as the god of medicine. At one time the Greeks identified him with their own Asclepius whose insignia is used by all physicians today.

371

Moses spent many years of his life in Egypt and was exposed to Egyptian medical practices. We can only guess how much he was influenced by the legends, culture, customs and practices of neighboring Mesopotamia and his long residence in Egypt.

III. *Israel.* The principal sources of our knowledge of Israelite medicine are the Bible, the Talmud, and some references from Aprocryphal literature. There are only a few references to physicians in the Old Testament, and it is clear that the priests acted as hygienic police in relation to contagious diseases, but there is not a single reference in the Bible of priests acting as physicians. The latter were a class apart and evaluation of available literature would indicate that the physician had grown through the centuries in esteem as a wise and learned man. It seems clear that the priest and the physician were quite separate professions in Israel. The physician had a special name in Hebrew, *rophe* (from *Rapha;* to heal). God is the Rophe Cholim, the "Healer of the sick." This can be understood from the Biblical expression *Yahweh-rophi,* "The Lord, my Healer."

Physicians are mentioned when Joseph "commanded the servants, the physicians, to embalm his father" (Gen. 50:2). A second reference to physicians is an unfavorable one, noting that King Asa was diseased in his feet (possibly malodorous, painful gangrene) and "sought not to the Lord, but to the physicians" (II Chron. 16:12).

A further reference is more respectful. "Is there no balm in Gilead? Is there no physician there? Why then is not the health of the daughter of my people recovered?" (Jer. 8:22). In the Apocryphal Book of Ecclesiasticus, written by the son of Sirach, we read, "Honor a physician according to thy need of him with honors due unto him. For verily the Lord hath created him." However, this eulogy of the physician was written during the second century B.C., indicating a growing esteem toward physicians. One curious statement occurs in Ecclesiasticus 38:1-15, "He that sinneth before his Maker, let him fall into the hands of the physician." The interpretation of this is difficult and is tempered by a Hebrew version of Ecclesiasticus discovered in 1896 where, in fragments, the verse is given thus: "He that sinneth against God will behave arrogantly before his physician."

Jesus mentions physicians several times. He quoted the popular proverb, "Physician heal thyself" (Luke 4:23) and "They that be whole have no need of a physician but they that are sick . . ." (Matt. 9:12). Another reference in the Gospels tells of the woman with an issue of blood who was healed on the way to Jairus' house. Of her we read that she suffered many things of many physicians, and had spent all that she had and was no better but rather growing worse (Mark 5:26).

Apparently in New Testament times physicians were regarded with a good deal of respect. Afterward, opinion varied. One Rabbi wrote favorably, "A wise man will not live in a town where there is no physician." Yet another Rabbi made the uncomplimentary statement that in his opinion the best of physicians were deserving of hell (*Sanhedrin 17b Kiddushin* 4:14).

Beside the physician and the high priest who acted as public health officer, there were also professional pharmacists (Neh. 3:8) and professional midwives as reported in Genesis 38:27-30 (recording the birth of locked twins, an obviously complicated obstetrical problem). Tamar, the mother, was fortunate to have survived. Midwives are also mentioned in the striking reference to the ancient Oriental usage of the obstetrical chair in labor where Pharaoh commands the midwives to slay all Jewish infants of the male sex: "When ye do the office of a midwife to the Hebrew women, and see them upon the stools" (Exod. 1:16). Undoubtedly the use of a delivery stool or obstetrical chair, was adopted from the Egyptians.

The genius of Jewish medicine rests in the Mosaic code. The broad Mosaic laws consisted of things, both old and new. What was old, the Hebrew undoubtedly received from neighboring peoples and ancient Semitic ancestors, and formally incorporated into their constitution. Much was new, original and scientifically valid. Ancient Hebrew medicine has left us an imperishable code of public health and hygiene in the Mosaic law. Moses recognized that the prevention of disease is usually simpler and invariably far more reaching than the cure of disease. He appointed health officers who taught and supervised hygiene. He introduced census taking, birth certificates, encouraged the fecundity of the race, punished wilful abortion and coitus interruptus. This code of personal and public cleanliness, as recorded in the book of Leviticus, contains wise mandates in regard to touching unclean objects (Fomites); the proper food to be eaten; the purifying of women after childbirth; the hygiene of the menstrual period; the abomination of sexual perversion; and the prevention of contagious diseases. It honored and edified a virtuous woman, and set a standard of sexual morality which has carried down to the present time. The institution of the Sabbath day gave the tired working man a permanent day of rest.

The rite of circumcision, a minor surgical operation, was practiced by many ancient peoples, but in Israel it became religiously significant. As a commandment from God, it was a religious observance at first carried out by the father, later by the *rophe* (physician), and finally by a layman skilled in the operation, the *mohel*. More recently we have learned that there are wise medical reasons for this operative procedure. It prevents phimosis (adherent foreskin); balantis (inflammation); and virtually no cases of cancer of the penis have been reported in individuals circumcised at birth. In ethnic groups where circumcision is not practiced, the incidence of cancer of the penis is significant. Physicians noted the low incidence of cancer of the cervix in Jewish women, especially in the population of hospitals treating almost solely Jewish patients. In racial settings where circumcision is not performed, the incidence of cancer of the cervix is significant. Further investigation has indicated that smegma, a thick secretion found under the foreskin of the uncircumcised male, has cancerogenic activity. It is not present in the circumcised male.

A number of diseases have been recorded in the Bible, and the list of these might well be encyclopedic. The fiery serpents mentioned in Numbers 21:7 may have been the dracunulus (guinea worm), and it is almost universally agreed that the "emerods" in I Samuel 5:6 represented the Bubonic Plague, because the word mice may be translated as rats which die in large numbers at the outbreak of an epidemic of Bubonic Plague. There is a reference to fatal apoplexy from drunkenness (I Sam. 25:36). Modern surgical interpretation would suggest that when Jacob wrestled with the Angel of the Lord (Gen. 32:22-32) the violence of his spiritual turmoil caused a herniated intervertebral disc, producing severe and intractable sciatica from the pressure on the nerve roots. It is known that he had acute pain and lameness in the "hollow of his thigh" and had to limp on the leg afterward. The Hebrews, therefore, will not eat the sciatic nerve of any animal, in respect for their ancestor's memory. Jewish butchers have always pulled out the sciatic nerve as the "gid." In short, medical references in the Bible, well interpreted, would stand as a good, simple, basic textbook of medicine.

The Jewish knowledge of human anatomy was limited. Dissection was forbidden both by law and by the universal feeling of the Hebrews that it was a violation of the dead, a teaching that was rigidly followed for centuries and still persists among many Orthodox Jews. Even now, burial services are carried out promptly and autopsy permission is not easily obtained from survivors in Jewish families. Though Jewish medicine gained from proximity to Egyptian medicine, embalming such as the Egyptians carried out was also prohibited. Hebrew knowledge of internal pathology was greatly enhanced because Mosaic law prohibited eating the flesh of diseased or injured animals, and autopsies made upon slaughtered animals to determine what was *kosher* or *trepha* revealed diseased processes. The ban on pork, an extremely valuable recognition, prevented trichinosis and parasitic infestation due to pork tapeworm (*taenia solium*).

In Deuteronomy, there are strict laws regarding the disposal of human excreta by burying it in the ground. The Jewish individual was enjoined to wash his hands before eating. These two recommendations undoubtedly reduced the incidence of enteric carried diseases.

The contribution of Hebrew medicine lies primarily in the Mosaic Code and the medical profundity of the Mosaic Code lies largely in the field of public health, hygiene and sanitation. Hume summarized it most succinctly, "Moses has been characterized as the greatest sanitary engineer that the world has ever seen. His doctrines, laid down in that fine treatise on hygiene, the book of Leviticus, could be summed up by the objects of sanitation today: pure food, pure water, pure air, pure bodies and pure dwellings" (Edgar Erskine Hume: *The Military Sanitation of Moses in the Light of Modern Knowledge*, Carlisle Barracks, Pennsylvania, Medical Field Service School, 1940).

AIR VIEW OF MEGIDDO   *Courtesy, Oriental Institute*

MEDINET HABU. Medinet Habu is the modern name of the ruins in the southern part of western Thebes at the point where the cultivated land meets the desert. Here a great temple to the sun god was dedicated by Thutmose I and his successors. Many of the Theban kings built their funerary temples around the great temple. Best preserved is Ramesses III's "House of a Million Years." Its walls are adorned with a pictorial record of the Pharaoh's achievements. The earliest known representation of a salt water naval battle is here. Captive Philistines are depicted as they are led by an Egyptian officer into the presence of the Pharaoh. Ramesses III is depicted in heroic size with the falcon sun-god hovering over his head with outstretched wings. In describing the flight of his enemies, Ramesses III wrote, "The stars of the *seshed*- constellation were frightful in

pursuit of them, while the land of Egypt was glad and rejoiced at the sight of his valor: Ramesses III."

BIBLIOGRAPHY. John A. Wilson, *Medinet Habu Studies, 1928/29*, University of Chicago Press, Chicago, 1930.

MEGIDDO. On a hill overlooking the main road through the Plain of Esdraelon, at the head of a mountain pass which leads to the Coastal Plain, is the mound known as Tell el-Mutesellim, the site of the ancient fortress city of Megiddo. Through the centuries a succession of conquerors passed Megiddo — Egyptians, Canaanites, Israelites, Philistines, Assyrians, Persians, Greeks and Romans. As recently as 1918 the strategic importance of Megiddo was evident when the allied forces under Allenby entered northern Palestine through the Megiddo Pass to wrest it from the Turks. The allied commander was sub-

374

sequently given the title Viscount Allenby of Megiddo.

When Edwin Robinson stood on the imposing hill known as Tell el-Mutesellim in 1838, he jotted down in his diary the words, "I wonder where Megiddo could have been." The mound on which he was standing, rising seventy feet above the surrounding plain and occupying an area of ten acres on its summit (with lower levels even larger) soon proved to be the site of Megiddo.

Serious archaeological work began at Tell el-Mutesellim in 1903 when Gottlieb Schumacher began excavating for the German Palestine Society. During nearly three years of work at Megiddo, Schumacher dug a trench across the top of the mound and identified seven occupation levels, the fifth of which was from the Israelite period. Schumacher discovered pottery, a bronze knife and some scarabs set in gold in a stratum which he dated prior to 2000 B.C. Among the Israelite remains he found a seal depicting a lion with the inscription, "Belonging to Shema, the servant of Jeroboam." The seal was found among the remains of an Israelite palace.

Schumacher's work showed the importance of the mound, but the limited knowledge of pottery at the time seriously handicapped scholars in appraising his results. In 1925, however, the Oriental Institute of Chicago, directed by J. H. Breasted, began a series of excavations at Megiddo under the leadership, successively, of C. S. Fisher (1925-27), P. L. O. Guy (1927-35) and G. Loud (1935-39). It was the purpose of the Chicago excavators to clear the entire mound, level by level, to its base. They succeeded in identifying twenty occupational levels, the earliest of which dated to the early part of the fourth millennium B.C. The top four levels were completely removed, but work was stopped by the outbreak of World War II, and the excavation of the pre-Iron Age sites was not completed. In 1958 the Commission for Landscaping and Preservation of Antiquities of the Israel Government re-

sumed work, and Yigael Yadin, an Israeli archaeologist, conducted a brief campaign in 1960.

The first historical reference to Megiddo occurs during the reign of the Egyptian Pharaoh Thutmose III, who defeated a coalition of Canaanite rulers led by the Prince of Kadesh in 1468 B.C. A record of this victory was subsequently inscribed on the walls of a corridor of the temple of Amun at Karnak. Thutmose's son, Amenhotep II, campaigned in the same region thirty years later and boasted that he sat in judgment on "rebellious princes" in the vicinity of Megiddo.

A text discovered at °Taanach, southeast of Megiddo, dating from about 1450 B.C., mentions an Egyptian general who urged the king of Taanach to pay his tribute: "Send me your charioteers and horses, presents for me, and send all your prisoners. Send them tomorrow to Megiddo." Evidently Megiddo was an Egyptian administrative center during the fifteenth century B.C.

Conditions in Megiddo during the fourteenth century B.C. are revealed in the

HORNED ANIMAL INCISED ON A LIMESTONE SLAB. This is a specimen of the art work of the inhabitants of Megiddo before 3000 B.C. Courtesy, Oriental Institute

MODEL RESTORATION OF THE STABLES AT MEGIDDO. Courtesy, Oriental Institute

*Amarna Tablets discovered in Egypt in 1887. Six of the letters were sent to Pharaoh Amenhotep IV (Akhenaton) by Biridiya, king of Megiddo. Biridiya affirmed his unswerving loyalty to Egypt and paid his tribute faithfully. He warned Akhenaton, however, that he needed a contingent of one hundred men to save Megiddo from insurgents in the area. The Amarna age was one in which Egyptian power was waning in Palestine, and Biridiya had difficulty maintaining himself as a vassal to Akhenaton.

During the conquest of Canaan, Joshua effected a temporary victory over the king of Megiddo (cf. Josh. 12:21) and Megiddo was assigned to the tribe of Manasseh (Josh. 18:11). Manasseh was unable to occupy the city (Judg. 1:27) and Canaanite forces continued to control the area.

During the days of Deborah we read that the Canaanites fought "at Taanach by the waters of Megiddo" (Judg. 5:19). No mention is made of the city of Megiddo, and some scholars surmise that the city was unoccupied at the time. Taanach and Megiddo were neighboring cities and there seems to have been an alteration in settlement between the two.

During the heyday of Solomon's reign, however, Megiddo came into its own. Solomon rebuilt and fortified Megiddo during the tenth century B.C. and made it one of his chariot cities (I Kings 9:15). A century later Ahaziah of Judah was struck by an arrow from the bow of Jehu, who brought the Omri dynasty in Israel to an end. Ahaziah reached the fortress of Megiddo and died there (II Kings 9:27). Megiddo was also the site

of the tragic death of Josiah in 610 B.C. Josiah had hastened to Megiddo to prevent Pharaoh Necho of Egypt from coming to the aid of Assyria in resisting the power of the rising Neo-Babylonian or Chaldean empire. The godly Josiah was wounded, "and his servants carried him in a chariot dead from Megiddo, and brought him to Jerusalem, and buried him in his own sepulchre" (II Kings 23:30).

The Hebrew name *Har Megiddon*, "the hill of Megiddo," is the basis for the New Testament Armageddon, the assembly point for the great apocalyptic battle in which God's power is manifested in the destruction of His foes. The scene, described in Revelation 16:16, is comparable with that of Ezekial 39:1-6, where a foe from the north comes "against the mountains of Israel" (verse 4).

Along the path which leads to the northern slope of the mound, a few yards beyond the present Megiddo Museum, is a roadway which served as the main approach to the ancient city. To the left are remains of the double gateway built during the time of Solomon. An enemy which forced its way past the outer gate would find itself in a small paved and walled enclosure, with the great walls and bastions of the real gate into the city still providing an almost insurmountable obstacle. The inner gate, more massive than the outer one, had guard rooms on either side. In plan and style the gate to Megiddo is similar to the gates at Hazor and Gezer, two other of Solomon's chariot cities.

376

The prophet Ezekiel described similar gates as he depicted the eastern wall of the Temple in his prophetic vision: "Then came he unto the gate which looketh toward the East, and went up the stairs thereof, and measured the threshold of the gate. . . . and the little chambers of the gate eastward were three on this side and three on that side . . ." (Ezek. 40:6-10). Ezekiel was probably familiar with the ruins of the Solomonic Temple in Jerusalem, and his vision reflected a similar pattern. The eastern gate of the temple evidently made use of the same architectural pattern that was used in Megiddo and other Solomonic cities.

East of the double gateway at Megiddo are remains of the stone wall of Solomon's city with wide ramparts. Northwest of the Solomonic gateway stood an earlier Canaanite wall, near which were the palaces of the Canaanite kings. In one of these palaces, later removed to expose lower strata, the excavators came upon a collection of 282 carved ivories dating from the thirteenth and twelfth centuries B.C. Included were a pen case, cosmetic dishes, spoons, ivory carved in the form of Egyptian hieroglyphs, and a plaque depicting a royal victory celebration. This plaque gives us a contemporary picture of social life in a Canaanite court. The ruler, seated on a throne with a sphinx-shaped side, is drinking from a bowl. Behind him are two servers, a large jar, and a bird. In front of the king stands an attendant, followed by a woman playing a lyre. Behind her is a procession headed by a soldier armed with shield and spear. Next come two prisoners with hands bound behind them, joined by a rope to a chariot drawn by two horses. Seated in the chariot is a man whose dress and general appearance are similar to the king on his throne. Probably this represents the king returning in victory. Behind the chariot is another soldier with drawn sword. The plaque is both an example of ancient Canaanite art and a document depicting military practices and concepts of luxury among the ancient Canaanites.

At the western edge of the Megiddo

AN IVORY GAME BOARD from Megiddo (ca. 1350-1150 B.C.). Courtesy, Oriental Institute

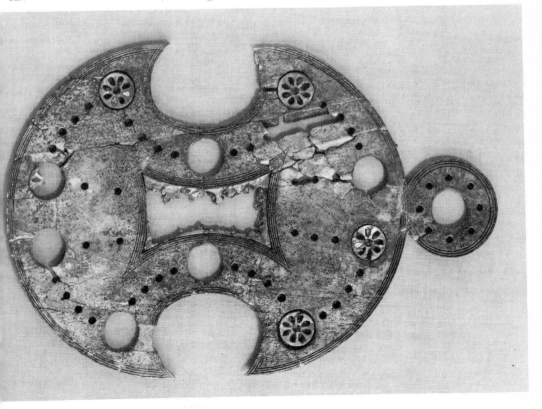

RUINS OF CANAANITE MEGIDDO (foreground) with the Plain of Esdraelon in the background. Courtesy, Israel Office of Information

mound are the well-preserved remains of a water system which dates back to the twelfth century B.C. The ancient engineers sank a shaft to a depth of one hundred twenty feet. From the bottom of the shaft they bored a tunnel through the rock for a distance of three hundred feet to a spring outside the city so that water could be brought into Megiddo even in times of siege. The opening to the spring was hidden by a wall and a covering of earth so that besieging forces would not notice it.

Ruins of stables which once housed Solomon's horses are visible at the southern edge of the mound. They are identical in plan to other stables unearthed near the gate and removed after excavation. In front of the stable compound was an enclosed courtyard, one hundred eighty feet square, with a floor of lime plaster, in the center of which was a huge cistern for watering the horses. The stables themselves can be distinguished from the rows of stone pillars alternating with mangers. The pillars served as supports for the roof as well as tethering posts for the horses. There were five parallel sheds in all, each containing twenty-two stalls in

parallel rows of eleven. East of the stable area, in the southern sector of the mound, are remains of a large building surrounded by a square wall. This building, also dated to the time of Solomon, is believed to have been the residence of the governor of Megiddo.

In the center of the mound are remains of a large eighth century silo, shaped like an inverted cone with steps leading down from two sides. The most ancient buildings, at the east side of the mound, include the ruins of three Canaanite temples from the third milennium B.C. Each consisted of a large chamber with an altar at the southern side, flanked by two large pillar bases. The southeast temple, dated about 2700 B.C., had steps leading to a circular "high place." A second temple, built of mud brick, faces due east, and was probably dedicated to the sun god. Its altar commands a view of the sunrise over Mt. Tabor and the Jordan Valley.

Seldom do all scholars agree on the significance and dating of archaeological discoveries, and Megiddo is no exception. J. W. Crowfoot has urged that the so-called Solo-

378

monic buildings, including the stables, are actually from the time of Omri and Ahab. P. L. O. Guy, however, maintained that they were Solomonic and his interpretation has been generally followed by contemporary archaeologists. Yigael Yadin, following his excavations at Megiddo, attributed the stables to the reign of Ahab who is known to have had a chariot force of two thousand in his battle with Shalmaneser III at °Qarqar. Megiddo is perhaps the most thoroughly studied site of the Bible world, but all of its mysteries have not yet been resolved.

BIBLIOGRAPHY. C. S. Fisher, *The Excavations of Armageddon*, University of Chicago Press, Chicago, 1929. P. L. O. Guy, *New Light from Armageddon*, University of Chicago Press, Chicago, 1935. Robert S. Lamon, *The Megiddo Water System*, University of Chicago Press, Chicago, 1935. Gordon Loud, *The Megiddo Ivories*, University of Chicago Press, Chicago, 1939; *Megiddo II, Seasons 1935-39* (2 vol.), University of Chicago Press, Chicago, 1948. Yigael Yadin, "New Light on Solomon's Megiddo," *BA*, XXIII, 1960, pp. 62-68.

MEIRON. Five miles northwest of Safed is the holy city of Meiron, a town known from Egyptian inscriptions of the second millennium B.C. and conquered by Tiglathpileser III in 732 B.C. It is not mentioned in Scripture, although the Waters of Merom where Joshua defeated the Hazor Confederacy are located nearby. Jewish tradition states that Rabbi Simeon ben Yochai compiled the Zohar ("Book of Splendor") from which Jewish mysticism draws its inspiration, in a cave at nearby Peki'in to which he was forced to flee from Meiron because of outspoken opposition to the Romans. Each year on Lag ba-Omer, twenty-six days after Passover, thousands of orthodox Jews make a pilgrimage from Safed to Meiron where they honor Simeon ben Yochai at his tomb there. Other sages, including Rabbi Hillel and Rabbi Shammai, heads of contending schools of Pharisees during the first century B.C. are allegedly buried on the Meiron hillside. Eliezer, the son of Simeon ben Yochai, buried with his father, shares the honors of the great annual pilgrimage. Meiron contains the ruins of a synagogue from the second century B.C. Its central doorway is made of huge single stones upon which rests the lintel, also a huge monolith, now dangerously cracked. Tradition says that if it falls of its own accord it will presage the coming of the Messiah. We are told that an earth-

quake once moved the lintel slightly and the people began to make merry for they were sure that Messiah would soon come.

MELCARTH STELE. Maurice Dunand, the excavator of Byblos, published a five line Aramaic text under the title "Stèle arameenne dédiée a Melqart," in the *Bulletin de Musée de Beyrouth*, Vol. III, 1941, pp. 65-76. The text, as translated by W. F. Albright reads, "The stele which Bir-Hadad, son of Tab-Ramman son of Hadyan, king of Aram set up for his lord Milqart, (the stele) which he vowed to him when (lit., and) he hearkened to his voice."

Bir-Hadad is the Aramaic equivalent of Ben-Hadad, a contemporary of Asa and Baasha (I Kings 15:16-18). The Biblical text calls Ben-Hadad, "the son of Tabrimmon, the son of Hezion," so that there can be no doubt that both the Bible and the Melcarth Stele refer to the same individual.

The stele depicts the god Melcarth attired in a Syrian loincloth, with a battle-axe and a composite bow, proclaiming the warlike character of the deity. Albright dates the stele *ca.* 850 B.C. and considers it evidence that Ben-Hadad, son of Tabrimmon — the contemporary of Asa and Baasha — is identical with the Ben-Hadad who was a contemporary of Ahab (I Kings 20).

BIBLIOGRAPHY. W. F. Albright, "A Votive Stele Erected by Ben-Hadad I of Damascus to the God Melcarth," *BASOR*, 87, 1942, pp. 23-29.

MEMPHIS. Around 2800 B.C. a ruler named Narmer, or Menes, united the Delta with Upper Egypt and built the city known as White Walls near the spot where Upper Egypt and Lower Egypt meet. Located on the west bank of the Nile, thirteen miles south of modern Cairo, the city came to be known as Memphis. Herodotus wrote:

Menes, who first ruled over Egypt . . . protected Memphis by a mound; for the whole river formerly ran close to the sandy mountain on the side of Libya (i.e. to the west); but Menes, beginning about a hundred furlongs south of Memphis, drained the original channel and diverted it to a new one . . . between the two lines of hills. . . . On the land which had been drained by the diversion of the river, King Menes built the city which is now called Memphis. (Herodotus ii. 99)

The Egyptians called the city Men-nefer, which became Noph or Moph in the Hebrew Bible. Memphis is known to have been the capital of Egypt during the Third Dynasty, when Pharaoh Djoser built the famed step pyramid at Sakkara. At the close of the Fifth Dynasty, however, Memphis declined in power. A period of local dynastic rule, known as the First Intermediate Period, was followed by the powerful Twelfth Dynasty, but the capital was established at *Thebes in Upper Egypt. The Hyksos rulers ruled from Memphis for a time, but they soon moved their capital to Avaris (see Raamses) in the eastern Delta.

Memphis early became a center for the worship of Ptah, and his living emblem, the Apis bull. Even after Memphis lost its political importance, the Ptah sanctuary was regarded as a holy place. In later times the Egyptians looked upon the temples at Thebes, Heliopolis, and Memphis as particularly sacred. According to Memphite theology, Ptah was the oldest of the gods and the creator of mankind.

Memphis, located at the head of the Delta on the main route to Upper Egypt, was frequently exposed to invaders. The city was sacked by the Assyrian rulers Esarhaddon and Ashurbanipal during their attempts to conquer Egypt. Although neither Assyria nor Babylonia succeeded in destroying Egyptian independence, Cambyses, the son of Cyrus, invaded Egypt and incorporated it into the Persian Empire. After gaining a decisive victory at the frontier city of Pelusium, Cambyses marched on Memphis, killed its priests and magistrates and is said to have so wounded the Apis bull that it died. This was regarded as inexcusable sacrilege, and the authenticity of the tradition is often challenged.

Memphis continued to occupy a place of importance until Roman times. Although its great palaces were deserted, it remained prosperous until Emperor Theodosius (A.D. 379-395) in his effort to destroy paganism and establish Christianity, ordered the destruction of the temples of Memphis and the desecration of its statues. The ruin of Memphis was completed when Chalif Omar's general, 'Amr ibn el-'As, captured the city. A new capital was established on the east bank of the Nile and named Cairo. Stones were carried from old Memphis for the buildings of new Cairo.

The destruction of Memphis is without parallel in the ancient world. Nineveh was utterly destroyed, but its ruins remained for the modern archaeologist to excavate. Not so Memphis. Jeremiah's prophecy has been literally fulfilled: "Memphis (A.V. Noph) shall become a waste, a ruin, without inhabitant" (Jer. 46:19). Ezekiel also spoke of the desolations of Memphis: "I will destroy the idols, and put an end to the images, in Memphis" (Ezek. 30:13).

Flinders Petrie excavated at the site of Memphis, as did the Museum of the University of Pennsylvania. Much of Petrie's labors were expended at the site of the Ptah temple, and it did much to corroborate the accuracy of Herodotus. A red granite sphinx dating from *Ramesses II, discovered at the north gate of the temple, is now in the University Museum in Philadelphia.

Two colossal statues of Ramesses II have been excavated at Memphis. The first, discovered by Caviglia and Sonne in 1820, was left in a mud hole for sixty-six years. During the rainy season it was covered with water, but at other times of the year visitors could descend into the hole to examine the statue. Finally, in 1887, Sir Frederick Stephenson collected a sum of money and had the statue raised and placed on a brick pedestal.

The second granite colossus was discovered in 1888, and an alabaster sphinx was excavated nearby in 1912. These two colossi and the sphinx are the only remains of Memphis, at one time the greatest city in the world.

BIBLIOGRAPHY. I. E. S. Edwards, *The Pyramids of Egypt,* Penguin Books, Baltimore, 1961. Alexander Scharff and Anton Moortgat, *'A'gypten und Vorderasien in Altertum,* Verlag F. Bruckmann, Munich, 1950.

MENHIR. The term "menhir" is derived from a French word meaning "a long stone." Menhirs are prehistoric monuments in the form of long stones, standing upright, either in rows, circles, or alone.

MERNEPTAH. Merneptah, son and successor of Ramesses II, ruled Egypt from *ca.* 1224 to *ca.* 1214 B.C. He was called upon to fight to preserve the Egyptian Empire in Libya and to resist the incursion of Mediterranean peoples in the western Delta (see Sea Peoples). His campaign in Palestine, waged during the fifth year of his reign (*ca.* 1220 B.C.) is commemorated on a large black granite stele which was found in Merneptah's mortuary temple in Thebes. At the top is a representation of Merneptah and the god Amun, with Mut, the wife of Amun, and Khonsu, their son in the background. The text itself comprises twenty-eight lines in which the Pharaoh boasts of his triumph over the Libyans and other foreigners, including Israel. Merneptah states:

Israel is laid waste, his seed is not;
Hurru (i.e. Syria) is become a widow
for Egypt.

The stele provides the first mention of Israel on ancient monuments, and provides proof that Israel was in western Palestine by 1220 B.C. In contrast with other enemies, preceded by the determinative for "nation," the word Israel is designated as a "people," suggesting that they were not yet regarded as a settled political unit. Hurru gets its name from the °Hurrians. The statement that Hurru is a widow implies that she is defenceless before the might of Egypt.

MERI-KA-RE, INSTRUCTION FOR.

Meri-ka-Re was a king of the Tenth Dynasty of Egyptian Pharaohs. He reigned at Herakleopolis in the Faiyum ca. 2100 B.C. The text of his "instruction" contains advice in the form of the counsel of a father for his son who is also to be his successor as king. The author is unknown, but it has been suggested that he was Wah-ka-Re Khety II, the father and predecessors of Meri-ka-Re.

Meri-ka-Re lived in the troubled transition time which marked the change from the Old to the Middle Kingdoms in Egyptian history. The once stable world of the Old Kingdom had fallen in ruins. It seemed to be a topsy-turvy world. There was disorder and a scaling down in the social structure. The king was no longer absolutely divine. He could be errantly human and even be rebuked by one of his servants (see Ipuwer, Admonitions of). The scaling down of the kingship was accompanied by a scaling up of the common man and the nobles. The literature from this period shows a strong social consciousness of the rights of the common man. (Unfortunately, this social concern did not survive very long in the Middle Kingdom.) Materialistic foundations were shaken and destroyed. Consequently, there was considerable emphasis on the social, moral, and spiritual values of life. Also, it was an age of free speech and the ability to speak well

was a recognized asset. The right of personal protest was advocated and perhaps accepted to some degree.

Much of the text of the "instruction" can be translated, but it is marred by lucunae and obscure passages. The second part of the treatise is devoted to political affairs and would be of greater interest to historians if better control of the details of translation and reference could be had. The "instruction" includes a variety of subjects but little orderly arrangement. Only the major points will be summarized in the following paragraphs.

First, advice in dealing with *domestic problems* is offered to the new king. He is told to put down rebels without hesitation and to be wary of demagogic agitators. The king himself should be competent in speech

THE MERNEPTAH STELE on which we find the first mention of Israel in Egyptian records. Courtesy, The Cairo Museum

and familiar with the wisdom of the fathers in order to rule well. The tongue of a king is more powerful than his sword — though the king is reminded later that troops are an advantage! Nobles and great men should be advanced to positions of prosperity and security because they are more trustworthy than poor men and less susceptible to bribes. He is admonished to rule with justice, to protect the property rights of dependent classes, and to avoid excessively harsh punishment. Promotion of his servants should be based on ability rather than upon birth and social position. The younger generation should receive special attention and aid from the king. The future depends upon them.

The series of instructions dealing with conditions in the various regions and along the frontiers of the country is difficult to interpret, as noted above. In general, it may be said that the king is advised to follow a vigorous but careful policy of action and defense. He is warned that trouble in the south (a rival dynasty ruled in Thebes) would open the way for invasion from the north. Thus, the frontier to the north should be fortified. The wise king will be aware always of his foes, and he will remember that no king is free from them. Firmness and vigilance will be understood and respected by the enemy.

In a very interesting way, the young king is reminded that he may be personally responsible for damage to his realm by his enemies. This reminder is given in the unprecedented confession of the "father" that the Thinite regions had suffered severely because of his own wrongdoing. The monarch cannot blame his own weakness on the weakness of the god for the misfortune which his reign suffers. He must accept responsibility for his own human errancy.

Second, some *personal instructions* are given to the king. He is cautioned to avoid a violent disposition and to remember that patience is good. He is exhorted to be industrious in religious matters. One passage seems to stress ritualistic piety or even political piety. The king is told to make monuments for the god (though another passage advises him to make for himself a memorial of love in contrast to a memorial of stone) and to be diligent in the cultic acts. But the tone of the passage seems to stress doing these things for purely personal gain.

However, in another passage some basic matters of the divine-human relationship are probed. Here the king is admonished to revere the god (probably to be understood as "the god" of particular circumstances, though this passage is remarkably monotheistic) because none can withstand his creative, yet invisible, hand. Like the irresistible flooding of the Nile, the god performs his will in the world. Men are creatures of the god, and they are made in his image; heaven and earth were made to meet the needs of man, and the divine will controls their operation. The unseen god, who is present with his people, knows every name, he hears the weeping of the distressed, and he punishes for discipline's sake. He made magic for men to use as protection for accidents which might happen in the day or in dreams of the night.

The king should remember that right behavior is important to the gods. When he stands before the judgment council of the gods, his deeds will be placed in heaps beside him. The passage of time will not dim the memory of any of his sins, for a lifetime is but an hour in duration for the gods. Further, he should remember that good character is more acceptable to the gods than the sacrificial ox of an evildoer (*cf.* I Sam. 15:22; Prov. 15:17). The gods are aware of inner motivation and prefer righteous acts rather than propitiatory sacrifices.

These are religious insights which approach the depth and quality of those in the Old Testament. The reader is reminded that Israel did not come to her faith in a spiritual and intellectual vacuum. The great acts of revelation to Israel permitted Israelite prophets, priests, and wise men to learn from many sources. It hardly can be doubted that they learned from the Egyptian wise men.

Historians know little of the reign of Meri-ka-Re. But he received wise counsel. If he failed to heed, the responsibility was his own.

BIBLIOGRAPHY. A. H. Gardiner, *JEA,* I (1914), 20-36. J. A. Wilson, "Egyptian Instructions," *Ancient Near Eastern Texts,* ed. J. B. Pritchard, Princeton University Press, Princeton, 1955, pp. 414-18.

MESHA STELE. *See* Moabite Stone.

METALLURGY. The major sources of metal in the Old Testament world were the mountains of what is today Turkey and Iran. In New Testament times Europe added to the supply of metal used in Palestine. The island of Cyprus actually takes its name from copper which was its major export and which is still mined commercially. The silver mines near Athens were an important economic factor in that city's history and her silver coinage later became par for a good part of the world. Egypt was rich in gold. The metals mentioned in the Bible in the order of the number of references to each are gold, silver, copper, iron, lead and tin. Gold and copper occur as natural nuggets but by Abra-

ham's time most metals had to be extracted from their ores.

The mines of antiquity were open-face cuttings, rooms where pillars of the original rock had been left in place to hold up the roof, horizontal galleries and vertical shafts (Job 28:4). The ability of the Israelites to do tunneling is demonstrated by their work on the *Siloam tunnel in Jerusalem *ca.* 700 B.C. It was 1750 feet long, dug from both ends and maintained the same water grade throughout as it was a water conduit. Here

COPPER MINING IN THE NEGEB. The Promised Land was described as a land "out of whose hills thou mayest dig copper" (Deut. 8:9). Israeli miners still work the copper mines. Courtesy, Consulate General of Israel

GOLD MEDALLION show-
ing a winged lion with horns.
The head is turned back and
lifted into a circle. It is Iranian in origin and dates from
the 6th or 5th century B.C.
Courtesy, Oriental Institute

the problems of surveying and ventilating as well as digging were excellently solved. In mining the rock was split by the action of fires built against it, or wooden wedges were driven into crevices and then soaked with water so they would expand and fracture the rock. Stone tools were used in the early days. Even after the invention of bronze, such tools were so expensive that they only partially replaced stone tools. Iron tools which came into Palestine about the days of David (1000 B.C.) made both earlier tools obsolete.

Mining was largely a government monopoly and the miners were often prisoners of war. David put some of his prisoners of war to work with axes and saws cutting timber for charcoal, others with iron picks worked in the mines and still others labored at the smelting furnaces (*cf.* II Sam. 12:31). The smelting was done on the site when charcoal was available. Charcoal contains twice the heat units of wood and is so light it can be carried long distances economically. The smelting of copper was much easier than that of iron and this is one of the reasons why the use of copper preceded iron although

the iron ore is much more common and widely distributed. Also copper could be worked when cold whereas iron must be heated. Furthermore copper could be cast but the ancients were never able to get enough heat in a furnace to produce cast iron. After copper had been smelted at the mine it was cast into ingots and these were later refined.

The largest ancient refinery that has been discovered is that of Solomon at Ezion-geber. The great winds that sweep down the Jordan valley from lofty Mt. Hermon furnished the forced draft needed for this refinery. By Solomon's day iron had become a strong competitor of copper and Solomon concentrated on the Red Sea lands as a major market for his copper. An interesting description of this refinery and all the copper industry of the Arabah is to be found in Nelson Glueck's *The Other Side of the Jordan*, Chapters III-IV. Smaller refineries and the coppersmiths who worked the metal into final form used the blow torch and the bellows for forced draft. After the discovery of good bronze, closed molds could be used and this made any type of casting possible.

Even for such a small item as an arrow head the Assyrians could use a six piece mold. Slag heaps always identify the ancient smelting sites. Copper slag ran a varied metal content, from that in which most of the metal remained in the slag to the other extreme where virtually all the metal had been extracted. Jeremiah 6:29-30 describes the failure of smelting silver from galena, one of the more common silver ores. For the smelting of iron see IV, below.

A few ores were used commercially in their natural state, i.e., without smelting. Haematite, an iron ore, is a beautiful red stone which was used for weights, jewelry, amulets, etc. Other iron ores such as the ochres, siennas and umbers were used as pigments for paints. A blue pigment came from azurite, a copper ore. Some eye paints were copper carbonate ores ground fine, or galena, a silver ore. A rich iron content in clay gave pottery the finest of reds.

I. *Gold.* This metal, which is mentioned more often in the Bible than any other, is found pure in nature as nuggets and dust, although by Abraham's time most gold was recovered from the ores. It is also found as electrum, a natural alloy of gold and silver. Palestine's major source of gold was the eastern desert of Egypt and Ophir, in the neighborhood of modern Somaliland. Gold is easily worked, is indestructible and does not tarnish. Its most common usage was in jewelry, statuary and tableware. It was also shaped into rings and bars to be used as money. Since gold can be beaten very thin, it was also used as a decorative overlay in furniture and buildings as in the tabernacle and Solomon's temple. Gold can be made into thin threads and interwoven with linen or wool for royal clothing (Ps. 45:13), or for tabernacle hangings (Exod. 39:3). The wedge of gold in Joshua 7:21 was probably an ingot. The literal Hebrew term here is "tongue" and such a lamb-shaped gold tongue was actually found by the German excavators at Jericho. Gold can be cast solid, as was likely the case with the mice of I Sam. 6:4. Aaron's remarks on the golden calf seem to imply that it was cast. In the case of Jeroboam's calves the gold may have been merely an overlay on stone or a baser metal. Gold was also used for heathen idols. The Persians made their gold darics the world's coinage.

II. *Silver.* During most of the Old Testament period silver was a more valuable metal than gold and in the listing of metals in Scripture silver usually precedes gold. Only in Solomon's time is silver depreciated and here the emphasis is on the unbelievable wealth of Solomon (I Kings 10:21, 27). Silver was as common as stones in his capital.

Native silver is rare but the ancients early learned how to smelt the various silver ores both simple and complex (Ezek. 22:18). For the most exacting work the ingots would be further refined (Ps. 12:6, Prov. 25:4). Asia Minor was Palestine's major source of silver. The use of silver was similar to that of gold except that it cannot be beaten into such thin sheets as gold and was therefore less used in decorating furniture and architectural features.

III. *Copper.* The third most common metal mentioned in Scripture is copper. The Hebrew term is confusing as it does not differentiate between copper and the alloys of copper. The term "brass" as it was used when the King James version was translated also meant copper or its alloys. Present day usage of the word "brass" however, is quite different as it is usually reserved for a copper with a zinc alloy. If there is any reference in the Bible to "brass" as we use the term, it is Ezra 8:27 where two unique copper bowls are mentioned which are as precious as gold. Bronze, which is a tin alloy of copper, is the most important of the alloys in Bible times.

Copper was the most useful metal in ancient times and the Sumerians were its best early craftsmen. After David's time a new competitor, iron, challenged copper's monopoly in such items as weapons and tools. (Weapons always seem to precede tools in the history of mankind even in this atomic age.) Although copper occurs as nuggets, virtually all copper was mined long before Abraham's time. The major sources of copper for Palestine were Sinai and the Arabah (Deut. 8:9). One slag dump alone in Sinai is estimated to contain about 100,000 tons of slag. The Sinai ores, however, ran only about 5-15 per cent copper. The Arabah was the area between the south end of the Dead Sea and the north end of the Gulf of Aqabah. The hills on either side of the valley were rich in copper with some ores running 40 per cent copper. The eastern side of the valley belonged to Edom and mining was probably the most profitable income of that state. Edom also had the timber for charcoal to smelt the ores. Anatolia and Cyprus were also rich in copper.

The copper carbonate ores are easily detected because of their unusual colors; malachite is a bright green and azurite a bright blue. Copper is an ideal metal to work with for it can be hammered into shape either hot or cold and it also can be annealed. It can be poured into molds. It is this malleability of copper that made it a rival of flint, the tool that preceded it. Although each has approximately the same cutting quality flint breaks easily and cannot be mended. Copper on the other hand is hard to break and it can be sharpened over and over again by hammering. Furthermore this hammering actually increases the hardness of the cutting edge about 50 per cent. When desired it could be melted down and the whole cycle of use repeated. Bronze is still better than copper as it has the initial hardness of hammered copper and can in turn also take hammering so that a bronze edge can approach the hardness of mild steel.

Copper, which came into use in Palestine *ca.* 4500 B.C. continued to be expensive and it did not replace flint in kitchen usage until about 1700 B.C., which in world history would be the Hyksos period and in Bible history would be about the time of Joseph. After the Hyksos invasion, Palestine's copper technology including its alloys reached its peak, but commercial mass production had to wait until the days of Solomon. The earlier invasion of Transjordan and Sinai, described in Genesis 14, had been primarily for control of the valuable copper mines of those areas.

Chemical analyses of bronzes found in Egypt have usually shown a 2 to 16 per cent tin. For a cutting edge on tools and weapons the tin percentage is 2 to 13 per cent. Such a bronze was the ideal military weapon until the discovery of steel. When copper objects are dug out of the soil they are covered with a corrosion. This makes it impossible even for an expert to tell definitely whether the object is copper or bronze. Even after they are cleaned, only an expert can tell by the color which is which; and only a chemical analysis shows the minor impurities, some of which can modify the quality

of either copper or bronze. As bronze is also stronger than copper it was superior for armor (I Sam. 17:5), shields and battering rams. Wealthy cities covered the great wooden gates of their cities with sheets of bronze so as to make a better defense against the battering ram used to break down the gate (Ps. 107:16). This bronze covering on the gates also made it more difficult for the enemy's fires to destroy the gates.

A tin alloy of more than 13 per cent is best for castings of any kind. The most difficult were statues and such great columns as those in Solomon's temple (I Kings 7:15 ff.). Bronze makes a much better casting than copper and at a much lower temperature. A tin alloy of 24 to 33 per cent produces speculum, a white metal which takes a very high polish and was used in, antiquity for the making of mirrors (II Cor. 3:18; James 1:23). A less used alloy was bell metal which runs 20 to 25 per cent tin. The bells mentioned in Zechariah 14:20 belong in this category. Bell metal was also used for cymbals (I Chron. 15:19; I Cor. 13:1). The humblest use of scrap copper was for shoes for the cattle that treaded out the grain (Micah 4:13). Copper was also the poorman's coin (widow's mite) in inter-Testament and New Testament times (Mark 12:42).

The most famous coppersmiths were the Kenites; indeed that is the literal translation of their name. The Edomites continued this tradition, as the great copper mines were in their land. Hiram of Tyre (I Kings 7:13 ff.) was the most famous worker in copper as demonstrated by his craftsmanship on Solomon's temple. Second only to him would be the craftsmen working on the tabernacle. These Israelite craftsmen doubtless learned their skills in Egypt but they could always have technical consultants in the Kenites who worked the Sinai copper mines. Moses had married a Kenite. The most infamous coppersmith was Alexander (II Tim. 4:14).

The Biblical archaeologist considers copper so significant in ancient history that he has divided the years between 4500 B.C. and 1200 B.C. into the Chalcolithic (copperstone), Early, Middle and Late Bronze Ages.

IV. *Iron.* The earliest iron known in antiquity came from meteors and was sometimes called the "metal of heaven." Such

GOLDEN MASK found by Schliemann at Mycenae. Schliemann thought he had discovered the mask covering the face of Agamemnon, but actually it dates several centuries before the Trojan War. Courtesy, Photo Marburg

iron can be easily identified by its nickel content which averages 7 to 8 per cent but may be as high as 26 per cent. Native ores seldom contain nickel and if so only in very small amounts. The discovery of the smelting of iron seems to have come from Anatolia (modern Turkey) or the mountains to the east of it. Even as late as Jeremiah the best iron came from the north (Jer. 15:12). Although there is some evidence for a very early date for this process, iron did not enter into international commerce until about 1500 B.C. Some 200 years later the Hittites were selling it to the Assyrians and the Syrians. Later the Israelites worked iron ores in the Arabah (Deut. 8:9) and in Gilead near Ajlun. Some of the latter ore is very high grade. This Ajlun district is probably the source of the iron referred to in the book of Joshua, both that captured at Jericho and that used on the chariots in the valley of Esdraelon. Both of these areas are on major trade routes to Gilead. The Philistines were the next to dominate the iron industry in Palestine (I Sam. 13:19-22). It was David's conquest of Syria which made iron cheap in Palestine. The plowshare was now so large that it could be used for deep plowing and thus greatly increased the crops with the resulting population explosion.

Although iron ore is much more widely distributed than copper, iron is much more difficult to work than copper and therefore

also more expensive. It demanded an entirely new set of techniques, some of which were the exact opposite of copper metallurgy. Iron requires a greater heat for a longer time and also the use of a stronger air blast. Many ores also need a flux. The ancients were never able to get a furnace hot enough to pour molten iron as they poured molten copper. Out of their iron furnace came a "bloom" which was a spongy mass of iron, slag and cinders. It had to be hammered to remove the slag, air bubbles, etc. and to consolidate the iron. Then it was forged and reforged into wrought iron (Ecclesiasticus 38:28). Finally came the work of the skilled blacksmiths (I Sam. 13:19-20). They were such valuable prisoners of war that after the capture of Jerusalem they were listed among the prisoners taken to Babylon (II Kings 24:14).

Iron was too soft a metal to compete with bronze as a cutting tool but when a steel edge could be produced then iron became the world's working metal. The Assyrians were the first nation to erect an empire founded on the use of steel in both war and peace. Steel could be produced from a natural ore that contained manganese but such ores were rare. The ancients usually carburized the edges of their iron weapons by placing them in a special charcoal furnace where the iron absorbed enough carbon to make a mild steel. About 900 B.C.

the ancients added quenching to forging to obtain a better cutting edge, but it was not until Roman times that tempering became common. Whetstones were used to sharpen tools (Eccl. 10:10) and razors were honed. Proverbs 27:17 tells of iron sharpening iron. Deuteronomy 27:5 commands that no iron tool be used in building a stone altar. Religion has always been slow in adopting new methods and techniques.

V. *Lead.* Lead and tin ores are easy to smelt and both metals have a low melting point. Lead, however, had the least usage of any of the metals mentioned in Scripture. It was usually a by-product from the smelting of silver ore. It was used for jewelry and the making of small figurines. A cheaper grade of large figurines was made with a lead core covered with gold or silver leaf. Lead was also used for weights (Zech. 5:7-8) and as sinkers for fish nets.

VI. *Tin.* In Palestine tin seems to have been used almost exclusively as an alloy in the making of bronze. It was expensive as can be seen by its listing as an import from Spain (Tarsus) in Ezekial 27:12. These Phoenicians also went even as far as Cornwall in the British Isles to secure tin.

BIBLIOGRAPHY. R. J. Forbes, *Metallurgy in Antiquity,* E. J. Brill, Leiden, 1950. A. Lucas, *Ancient Egyptian Materials and Industries,* Edward Arnold & Co., London, 1962.

MILETUS. Miletus was an important Greek harbor city on the western coast of Asia Minor. Through the years silt from the Maeander River has accumulated and the river itself has shifted with the result that the ruins of Miletus are now five miles from the coast.

Miletus was colonized by Minoans from Crete, after which Mycenaean Greeks made it a fortified outpost. Hittite texts mention a Millawanda on the coasts of western Anatolia. This may be identical with Miletus. The city was destroyed about 1200 B.C., but it subsequently became a center of Ionian culture. By the seventh century B.C. Ionian ships were carrying colonists to the shores of the Black Sea and to Egypt. Miletus was a rival of Lydia, but she chose to make a treaty with the Persians after 546 B.C., thus insuring her territorial integrity.

Thales, Anaximander, and Anaximines were philosophers who came from Miletus. A temple to Apollo was built at Didyma, ten miles south of Miletus, and the cities were joined by a sacred road partially lined with statues. In 499 B.C. Miletus joined other Ionian cities in a revolt against Persia. In 494 the Persians captured the city, killed or deported its people as slaves, and plundered and burned the temple at Didyma.

Following the Persian defeat at Mycala (479 B.C.), Miletus was rebuilt by Hippodamus, a Milesian who laid out the plans of the city according to a regular pattern. Miletus joined the Delian League, was again conquered by Persia and was subject to Caria for a time. In 334 B.C. Alexander the Great captured Miletus and it was thereafter a major Hellenistic port with grandiose architecture and monumental building projects. Miletus continued as a prosperous city under the Romans. Trade continued but the gradual silting up of the harbor proved a threat in later Roman times. When Paul visited Miletus (Acts 20:15-17; II Tim. 4:20) the city had not yet reached the peak of its architectural embellishment. It had, however, two colonnaded market places with an ornate council house between them. The south market was approached by a triple gateway. Overlooking one of the four harbors was a large theater. An inscription shows the place reserved in the theater for Jews and "godfearing" people.

A German expedition sponsored by the Berlin Museum excavated Miletus from 1899 to 1914. Work began again in 1938 and has been conducted intermittently since then. An eighth century (B.C.) house was discovered with a covered stone drain running alongside, indicating a higher culture than was expected for the period. From the same period is an oval platform of rough stones which is nearly seven feet across. It was located under the corner of the later temple of Athena and is thought to have served as an altar — the oldest yet discovered in Greek Asia Minor.

In addition to the ornate council house, excavators discovered remains of a granary over five hundred feet long and the shopping area, six hundred feet long, which was the gift of Antiochus I of Syria.

MINOANS. The civilization of Crete is named for the legendary King Minos of °Cnossus. Until about 1900 ideas about Crete were largely a matter of legend. Since that time scientific excavation has been conducted at Cnossus, Phaistos, Haga Triada and other sites by Sir Arthur Evans and his successors and co-workers Duncan Mackenzie and J. D. S. Pendelbury.

Early Minoan civilization lasted from about 2500 to 2000 B.C. During the earliest years of this period tools and weapons were made of stone and obsidian. By the Middle Minoan period (*ca.* 2000 to 1600 B.C.) the island of Crete has become an important commercial center, and rulers emerged in the fertile central part of the island and built for themselves enormous palaces. They were surrounded by prosperous towns whose citizens lived in comfortable homes surrounded by luxury. Certain palaces and villas were lit by light wells and they had excellent drainage systems. Walls were adorned with colored frescoes depicting landscapes, fish, birds, animals, and scenes from Cretan life. Oil, wine, and grain were stored in huge jars.

The Late Minoan period, beginning around 1600 B.C., was more prosperous yet. Crete carried on trade with °Ugarit in Syria and with Egypt. Some of the most beautiful Minoan vases have been discovered in Egypt. Vases from 1600 to 1400 B.C. are very naturalistic. They often depict sea animals.

About 1400 B.C. Crete was conquered and devastated by Mycenaeans from the Greek mainland. About two centuries later there was another cultural upheaval, associated with the movements of the °Sea Peoples throughout the eastern Mediterranean area. Amos (9:7) stated that the °Philistines came from Caphtor (Crete).

BIBLIOGRAPHY. J. D. S. Pendlebury, *The Archaeology of Crete*, W. W. Norton, New York, 1965.

MIRRORS. The laver of the Tabernacle was made by melting the bronze mirrors of the women who "ministered at the door of the tent of meeting" (Exod. 38:8). Ancient mirrors were made of polished metal, and it was not until late Roman times that glass came into use in making mirrors.

Bronze mirrors have been found in the course of excavations in Palestine. Usually they appear along with jewelry and articles of female apparel. Such mirrors are circular in shape, often with a handle of wood or ivory. The unpolished side of the mirror was usually plain, but a Hellenistic specimen from Gezer has a cluster of grapes in relief on the back.

Mirrors were considered as highly valu-

able objects in antiquity. They are mentioned among lists of presents which kings and princes exchange with one another. A vassal of Pharaoh Akhenaton presented the Egyptian ruler with thirty-two polished bronze mirrors, a fact mentioned in the °Amarna documents. The Hittite king likewise gave him a silver mirror.

Among the luxuries which became widespread during Hellenistic times were mirrors. They ceased to be the exclusive possession of royalty and wealth, becoming a recognized part of every woman's equipment. Paul reminds us of the imperfect reflection in ancient mirrors when he says, "Now we see in a mirror, dimly" (I Cor. 13:12).

MITANNI. About 1500 B.C., when the °Kassites were taking over power in southern Mesopotamia, a people known as °Hurrians, Biblical Horites, became the dominant ethnic element in the north Mesopotamian state of Mitanni. The rulers of Mitanni were Indo-Aryans who worshiped the Vedic gods. They were surrounded by a feudal aristocracy known as *maryannu*, or "chariot warriors," who were the power behind the throne. The Indo-Aryan ruling class intermarried with the dominant Hurrian element in the population.

The Mitannian capital of Wassukkanni has not yet been identified, but it is thought to have been located on the upper Habur River. During Egypt's New Kingdom, or Empire Period, her troops reached the Euphrates and occupied Mitannian territory, which extended from °Alalakh in Syria to °Nuzi and Arrapkha in Assyria. In time, however, relations between Egypt and Mitanni were normalized and the °Amarna Letters tell us that kings of Mitanni gave their daughters as brides to Egyptian Pharaohs. The position of Mitanni was vulnerable, however. She was exposed to the growing Assyrian power to the east and the Hittite Empire seeking to expand beyond its Anatolian stronghold to the northwest. When the Hittite king °Suppiluliumas defeated Tushratta of Mitanni (*ca.* 1350 B.C.) the power of Mitanni was at an end.

BIBLIOGRAPHY. Roger T. O'Callaghan, *Aram Naharaim*, Pontifical Biblical Institute, Rome, 1948.

MIZPAH. Mizpah, meaning "watchtower," was a common Biblical name, for Palestine was constantly being invaded from without

WALLS OF TELL EN-NASBEH. *Reconstruction courtesy of Palestine Institute, Pacific School of Religion*

and struggling internally through dynastic and inter-tribal wars. One such, Mizpah, was located in Benjamin near Gibeon and Ramah (Josh. 18:25-26; I Kings 15:22). Mizpah seems to have been a place of assembly for Israel. In the days of the Judges when a Benjaminite had outraged a Levite's concubine, the men of Israel assembled at Mizpah to plan their punishment (Judg. 20:1, 3; 21:1, 5, 8). In the days of Samuel, Israel gathered at Mizpah for prayer after the ark had been returned by the Philistines (I Sam. 7:5-6). The Philistines attacked the assembled Israelites, but the enemy was repulsed and Samuel was able to erect a stone commemorating divine aid at nearby Ebenezer ("Stone of Help"). Saul, a native of Gibeah, was presented to Israel at Mizpah (I Sam. 10:17) and there acclaimed king.

In his controversies with Baasha of Israel, Asa of Judah fortified Mizpah as an important border town (I Kings 15:22). Following the destruction of Jerusalem. Mizpah had a brief period of importance when it served as the capital ruled by Gedaliah (II Kings 25:23, 25). Jeremiah and other refugees migrated to Mizpah, but a group of Zealots killed Gedaliah and thus brought an end to the last vestige of Israelite independence (Jer. 41).

Mizpah's history continued down into Maccabean times. When Judas the Maccabee realized the strength of his Syrian opposition, he called his partisans together for prayer: "So they assembled and went to Mizpah opposite Jerusalem, because Israel formerly had a place of prayer in Mizpah" (I Macc. 3:46).

The location of Mizpah in Benjamin is still uncertain, although contemporary Biblical scholarship prefers the mound of *Tell en-Nasbeh, about eight miles north of Jerusalem. Traditionally Mizpah has been identified with a mound four and one-half miles northwest of Jerusalem known as Nebi Samwil ("the prophet Samuel"). Nebi Samwil, rising about two thousand fifty feet, was named Mount Joy by the Crusaders because from its summit they caught their first glimpse of the Holy City. It is one of the highest spots in Judaea and is as yet unexcavated. Eusebius identified Nebi Samwil with Mizpah, as did Edward Robinson and George Adam Smith during the nineteenth century.

Since the excavation of Tell en-Nasbeh by W. F. Badé of the Pacific School of Religion, scholars have tended to identify the latter mound with Mizpah. Badé worked on Tell en-Nasbeh for five seasons (1926, 1927, 1929, 1932, and 1935). He died before publication of the results of his work could be begun, but his assistant J. C. Wampler, and C. C. McCown inherited the task of editing the reports.

A number of caves and tombs in the limestone rock of the hill on which Tell en-Nasbeh is located contain pottery, implements, and ornaments of Early Bronze Age settlers. A small town, probably founded by Israelites, existed there during the twelfth century B.C. It was defended by means of a wall about a yard thick built of rubble.

Excavations indicate that much stronger walls, between fifteen and twenty feet thick, were built around 900 B.C., enclosing an area of eight acres. At important salients, towers projected as much as seven feet beyond the wall. They were made of large blocks of stone, fitted together and laid in clay mortar. The outside was covered with lime plaster to a height of fifteen to eighteen feet.

At the northeast side of the city, the ends of the wall overlapped and a large city gate occupied the thirty-foot space between the walls. Inside the gate were guard rooms, and on the outside the court was lined with stone benches. The gate of an oriental city was the place where business and legal transactions were conducted, and the Tell en-Nasbeh gate gives an excellent illustration of that practice (cf. Deut. 22:14; Ruth 4:11; II Sam. 19:8).

Tell en-Nasbeh was occupied down to Hellenistic times, although the population was greatly reduced after the fifth century. Over eighty jar handles from the period shortly before the Exile bear the words "for the king" (Heb. *lemelech*), perhaps an indication that their contents were assigned to the king in payment of taxes. This inscription occurs on other jars from cities of Judah and is evidence that Tell en-Nasbeh belonged to the Southern Kingdom. None

were found at Bethel, but three miles to the north, indicating that the border between North and South lay between the two cities. Pottery of a later, postexilic type, was stamped with the word *Yehud* (Judah), showing that Tell en-Nasbeh belonged to Judah during the Persian period.

Other pottery from the Persian period bears an inscription which may be read *m s h* or *m s p*. Scholars who suggest the reading *m s p* see in the letters the name Mispah, thus identifying the mound. Specimens of the same inscription have been found at Jericho and at Gibeon, so the identification with Mizpah cannot be considered as proved. N. Avigad, an Israeli archaeologist, suggests that the letters refer to the city Mozah (Josh. 18:26), and that products of that town were exported to the places where the inscriptions were found.

BIBLIOGRAPHY. W. F. Albright, "Mizpah and Beeroth," *AASOR*, 1922-23 (vol. IV), pp. 90-111. Chester C. McCown, *Excavations at Tell En-Nasbeh* (2 vol.), American Schools of Oriental Research, New Haven, 1947.

FOUNDATIONS OF CITY GATE AT TELL EN-NASBEH (Mizpah) from the Israelite period. The tower (left) has a slot for the gate bar. In the gatehouse and outside are seats. Model courtesy Palestine Institute, Pacific School of Religion

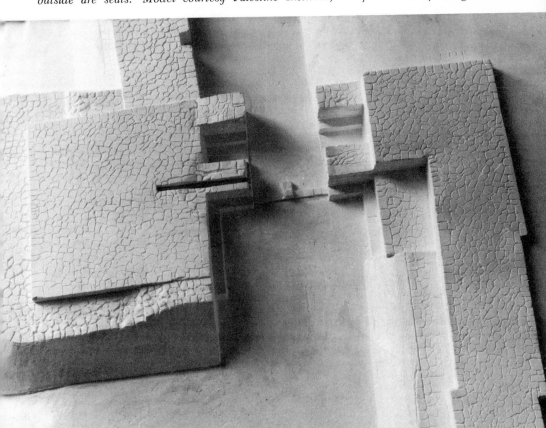

MOAB, MOABITES. Ancient Moab was the country between the Dead Sea and the Syro-Arabian Desert to the east, and the native residents of the Semitic kingdom occupying the region *ca.* 1300-600 B.C. were known as Moabites.

I. *Geography.* On two sides the boundaries of Moab were well-defined and established by geographical barriers; to the west was the Salt Sea (Dead Sea) and the lower reaches of the Jordan; on the south was the great gorge of the Brook Zered dividing Moab from Edom. To the east where the fertile plateau shaded off into the desert wilderness a string of border fortresses roughly outlined the extent of her territory. The deep canyon of the Arnon would seem to have effected similar stability for the northern boundary and, indeed, it did constitute both the traditionally recognized limit of her heartland and a barrier behind which she could retreat in time of trouble. However, it was the fertile plains and plateaus to the north that enticed her to break out from behind her natural barriers and indulge her expansionist ambitions. Consequently, her border on this side fluctuated with the ebb and flow of her political fortunes between the Arnon and the *Wadi Nimrin* opposite Jericho. Even at its greatest extent, however, Moab's territory probably never exceeded 60-65 miles in length and 25-30 miles in width.

Most of the country is a gently rolling plateau, averaging some three thousand feet in elevation and gradually rising and narrowing from north to south. The plateau edge plunges very precipitously toward the Dead Sea on the west, but slopes almost imperceptibly into the desert on the east. Here and there steep-sided valleys cleave the western portion of the tableland in their plunge to the Dead Sea shore. Of these the most spectacular is the gorge of the Arnon which, at its maximum, reaches one-third of a mile in depth and is as much as three miles wide at the rim. The dark reddish-brown soil of the tableland is fertile, especially in the northern part of the country, and the seasonal winter rainfall (averaging sixteen to twenty inches, but diminishing rapidly toward the desert to the east) is usually sufficient for the maturing of wheat and barley. In the dry summers, however, the land is rendered suitable only for the grazing of sheep and goats so that throughout its history sheep have been one of the country's principal products.

Two plains areas adjoining the shore of the °Dead Sea, and quite different in character from the plateau district, are deserving of special note. One is southeast of the peninsula (Lisan) which juts into the Sea about two-thirds the way down its eastern shore; the other, called the "Plains of Moab," extends northward from the Sea to the *Wadi Nimrin* and from the Jordan to the foothills on the east. Each of these plains is only a few feet above the level of the Dead Sea (approximately 1300 feet below sea level) and is therefore extremely hot and practically without rainfall. However, each is traversed by small streams which make an irrigation culture possible. It was in the second of these areas, the Plains of Moab, that Israel was encamped just before crossing the Jordan into Canaan.

The decisive geographical nature and position of Moab predetermined that its major artery of travel should follow a north-south route through the central plateau. The course of this "King's Highway" of the Iron Age was preceded by a Bronze Age route and followed by the Roman Road of Trajan. Today's modern highway is but a successor to these three. The major cities of the country were situated on or nearby this road. Kir Haroseth (modern Kerak), Moab's capital city and major stronghold, dominated the lofty bulwark between the Arnon and the Zered. On the populous plateau north of the Arnon, Dibon, Medeba, and Heshbon were the major Moabite settlements.

II. *Prehistory.* Moab was originally inhabited by a people of gigantic stature called Rephaim in the Bible. The Moabites knew them as Emim (Deut. 2:10f). Such traditions of a race of aboriginal giants were probably inspired in part by the megalithic tombs (dolmens) and huge standing stones (menhirs) from the prehistoric period which are still present in considerable numbers in the Moabite region. Megalithic monuments of this sort are to be found in various parts of the world and wherever traditions about them have been preserved, they inevitably involve giants.

Sedentary occupation appeared in the Moabite plateau during the early centuries of the third millennium B.C. This Early Bronze

Age civilization was characterized by a number of strongly walled sites strategically chosen for their defensive potentialities and accessibility to water, and usually situated to guard the north-south caravan route which traversed the Moabite plateau as well as the whole of the Transjordan highlands. This route provided the path of the invasion of Mesopotamian kings recorded in Genesis 14. These kings are also credited by the Biblical record (Gen. 14:5) with subduing the Rephaim and Emim which they encountered in the progress of their invasion. Exploration and excavation have indicated many sites in Moab to have been occupied during the latter part of the Early Bronze Age (just prior to 2000 B.C.) and two monuments from the region, the stela of Shihan and the stela of Balu'ah, appear to belong to the same period.

Late in the Early Bronze Age, as the third millennium drew to a close, the settled areas of both sides of the Jordan were seriously disrupted by incursions of semi-nomadic elements. Widespread destruction and abandonment of cities and towns reached its peak in the twentieth century and brought the Early Bronze civilization to an end. During the early centuries of the second millennium sedentary occupation was rapidly restored west of the Jordan as the new arrivals settled down, but in the region of Moab, and the rest of southern Transjordan, for some six-hundred years (1900-1300 B.C.) nomadism continued to be the characteristic way of life. Though the identity of the newcomers is veiled in considerable mystery, such of their names as have been preserved in contemporary records suggest that they were a branch of the northwest Semitic Amorites who, at this time, were on the move throughout the Fertile Crescent.

Indeed, it is entirely probable that the name "Amorite" was a rather inclusive designation for the various related peoples from northern Mesopotamia and Syria from whom the Moabites and the Hebrews were later descended. A hint at such a relationship is perhaps contained in the Oracle of Balaam (Num. 24:17) wherein Moab stands parallel to "the Sons of Sheth," who are possibly the roving Semitic tribesmen called *Sutu* in various Mesopotamian and Egyptian texts of the second millennium B.C.

The account of Moabite origins related in the Old Testament (Gen. 19:30-38) is not particularly helpful in clarifying these early relationships and nothing concerning them can be gleaned from the etymology of their name. Moab, the eponymous ancestor of the Moabites, appears in Genesis 19:37 as the son of Lot by the older of his two daughters. The derivation of the name is uncertain. No etymology is given in the Hebrew text, but a popular etymology, derived from the narrative (Gen. 19:30-38), is suggested by the addition of "saying, from my father," following the name "Moab" in the LXX text of verse 37. Only in this reference does the name Moab refer to a person. Elsewhere in the Old Testament and in extra-Biblical literature the name, as such, was used primarily to refer to the people. Customarily, if a writer wished to refer to their country, he used the name in conjunction with some such geographical designation as "land" or "territory." It would appear therefore, that the original usage of the word Moab was to designate a people and that sporadically thereafter the name was used to designate the country, which came to be regarded as their homeland. Whether the Biblical writer preserved this narrative as a reflection of Israelite disdain toward the Moabites or simply because it furnished their traditional origin, in any case, it served to emphasize the relatedness of the two peoples.

In addition to their relationship through Lot, the nephew of Abraham, both language and customs testify that Moabites and Hebrews were of similar Semitic stock. The Hebrew-Phoenician character of the language and script of the *Moabite Stone (ca. 830 B.C.) indicate Moabite to be a dialect of the Northwest Semitic tongue prevailing in Palestine, and practically identical with Hebrew.

III. *History.* Near the close of the Late Bronze Age the various nomadic groups, which during the course of the centuries had become dominant in particular regions of Southern Transjordan, began to adopt a sedentary way of life and establish permanent settlements. It was not until the thirteenth century B.C., therefore, that the organized kingdom of Moab arose (as well as the neighboring kingdoms of Edom, Ammon, and the Amorite Sihon) as indicated by the explorations of Glueck, and supported by the excavations of Dhiban (see Dibon). More-

393

over, the first mention of Moab in contemporary records is found in the thirteenth century Egyptian topographical lists of Ramesses II (*ca.* 1290-1224 B.C.). So, though Moab was relatively young in the Biblical family of nations, it nevertheless antedated Israel, who, as a semi-nomadic group, had to by-pass it in their northward trek through Transjordan on their way to the Promised Land.

By 1300 B.C. Moab's walled cities and strong border fortifications were too formidable for Israel to challenge (Deut. 2:9; Judg. 11:15, 18; II Chron. 20:10). Sometime prior to Israel's arrival on the scene, however, all Moab north of the Arnon was subdued by Sihon, the Amorite ruler of Heshbon, and incorporated into his kingdom (Num. 21:26-30). The Israelites, in turn, dispossessed Sihon of the region (Deut. 2:24-36) and subsequently allotted it to the tribes of Reuben and Gad (Num. 32:2-5; 34-38; Josh. 13:8-10, 15-23) who rebuilt and renamed many former Moabite cities.

Following their conquest of Sihon, Israel encamped in the Plains of Moab east of the Jordan opposite Jericho (Num. 22:1ff). It was while Israel was here that Balak, king of Moab, unsuccessfully sought to bring a curse upon them through the agency of Balaam — resulting in the latter's oracles of blessing upon Israel (Num. 22-24). It was while here, also, that Israel became involved in both adultery and idolatry with Moab and Midian (Num. 25:1-9). From here Moses ascended to Mount Nebo, viewed the Promised Land, died, and was buried in the valley opposite Beth-peor. All of these events are described as taking place in the land of Moab (Num. 22:1, 25:1; Deut. 34:1, 5, 6), suggesting that neither Amorite nor Israelite control of former Moabite territory north of the Arnon seriously curtailed Moabite habitation there.

Moabite dominion over this region was restored during the period of the "judges" and even extended across the Jordan to include Jericho (City of Palms, cf. Judg. 3:12-14) — resulting in an eighteen-year oppression of Israel. From this oppression Israel was delivered in connection with Ehud's assassination of Eglon, king of Moab, and the occupying forces were swiftly dispatched. However, the Moabites apparently remained in control of their East-Jordan holdings and

by the eleventh century had virtually absorbed the tribe of Reuben. That not all was enmity between Moab and Israel during this period, however, is suggested by the friendly portrayal of the Book of Ruth.

Moabite-Israelite relationships during the period of the United Kingdom were generally characterized by the dominance of Israel. Though Saul enjoyed some success against Moab (I Sam. 14:47), David inflicted upon them severe defeat, reducing them to the status of vassal (II Sam. 8:2; I Chron. 18:2, 11). This relationship was apparently maintained under Solomon, who also included Moabite women in his well-stocked harem and built a shrine to their god, Chemosh, within sight of the Temple at Jerusalem (I Kings 11:1, 7).

The dissension and uncertainty following the split of the Israelite monarchy apparently allowed Moab to regain her independence. This was to be rather short-lived, however, for, with the coming of Omri (*ca.* 876) to the throne of the Northern Kingdom, Israel's political fences were mended and Moab was again reduced to a vassal state, having to pay to Israel a heavy annual tribute in sheep and wool (II Kings 3:4).

For the events of the middle of the ninth century B.C. the Old Testament is supplemented by the °Moabite Stone from Dibon, which informs us that Israelites occupied Moabite territory north of the Arnon for forty years beyond the conquest of Omri. Moab successfully rebelled, however, during the reign of Mesha, who threw off the yoke of Israel, rebuilt many captured cities (sometimes using Israelite prisoners), and ruled over them from his capital city of Dibon.

From the Israelite point of view Mesha's revolt reached the brink of disaster in the face of a siege by a coalition of the kings of Israel, Judah, and Edom, and was rescued only by the most drastic of measures — the sacrifice of his son and heir to the throne (II Kings 3:24-27). The end result was the withdrawal of Israel and her allies from Moabite territory. Following this it would appear that marauding bands of Moabites occasionally invaded Israel (II Kings 13:20f).

Moabite fortunes declined with the increased strength of Israel and Judah during the first half of the eighth century B.C., but took a turn for the better in the second half of the century as intrigues and wars weakened her neighbors west of the Jordan. Assyrian domination of the Syro-Palestinian area returned under Tiglath-pileser III (*ca.* 738 B.C.), who proceeded to place Moab (*ca.* 733 B.C.) and her neighbors under tribute. Presumably this tributary relationship continued for more than a century (perhaps not always without benefit) for the Assyrian records of Sennacherib, Esarhaddon, and Ashurbanipal also list Moabite kings among their vassals (*ANET*, pp. 282, 287, 291, 294, 298).

A period of civil strife in Assyria, near the middle of Ashurbanipal's reign (*ca.* 650 B.C.) afforded Arab tribes from the Syrian Desert opportunity to overrun and devastate Moab and much of Transjordan. Though Moab survived the invasion and even sent a captured Arab chief to the Assyrian capital in chains (*ANET*, p. 298), the country was probably sufficiently weakened to seriously accelerate its downfall as an autonomous state. Isaiah 15, 16 and Jeremiah 48 possibly reflect a contemporary dirge describing Moab's fate as related to these events.

Nineveh fell in 612 B.C., and, with the establishment of Babylonian authority over the Syro-Palestinian portion of the collapsed Assyrian Empire in 605 B.C., both Judah and Moab quickly transferred their homage to the new overlord. Three years later Judah rebelled, but bands of Moabites were among the loyal vassals sent to raid Judah in reprisal (II Kings 24:2). A long history of enmity, inhospitality, and collaboration with Judah's enemies brought forth such oracles of judgment against Moab as found in Isaiah 15 and 16, Zephaniah 2:8-11, Jeremiah 48, and Ezekiel 25:8-11.

Soon after 597 B.C. Judah became involved with Moab and others in intrigue against Babylon (Jer. 27:1-11), which eventuated in the rebellion of Judah and the destruction of Jerusalem in 587 B.C. Moab did not suffer a similar devastation at this time, perhaps because she had abandoned the cause she had helped to instigate. Her fate seems not to have been long delayed, however, for Josephus (*Ant.* V. ix.7) preserves an account that Nebuchadnezzar defeated Moab in his 23rd year (582 B.C.), which corresponds to the year in which Nebuzaradan, captain of his guard, deported the third captive group from Judah (Jer. 52:30). Ar-

chaeological exploration and excavation accords with literary evidences that early in the sixth century B.C. Moab as a nation ceased to exist. After more than seven hundred years of organized national life, the land reverted to the domain of the nomad.

IV. *Religion.* Though the sources of information on Moabite religion are few, they contain traces of a close similarity to the religion of the Canaanites. The appearance of such place-names as Bamoth-baal (Num. 22:41), Beth-baal-peor (Josh. 13:20), and Beth-baal-meon (Josh. 13:17; M.I. 30) suggest the worship of the Canaanite Baal or one of his local manifestations. Similarly, sheep and oxen were sacrificed on altars at highplaces and worshippers participated in sacrificial meals (Num. 22:40-23:2; 25:1-3; cf. Rev. 2:14). Sexual orgies accompanying the worship of Baal-peor (Num. 25:3-6; 31: 16; Josh. 22:17) are suggestive of one of the major emphases of Canaanite religion. Moabite fertility figurines representing the mother-goddess Astarte are of the same type as those associated with Canaanite cults and suggest a similar emphasis. Since Ashtar and Astarte seem to represent male and female aspects of the same Canaanite deity, it is perhaps an aspect of this same fertility emphasis which is reflected by the appearance of the compound divine name Ashtar-Chemosh in the Mesha Inscription.

Chemosh, the Moabite national deity, was early regarded as a god of warfare. In the course of time, however, he was understood as having sovereign authority over all aspects of life. In the Mesha Inscription he is referred to (as was Yahweh in the Old Testament) as bringing both good and evil upon his people; he punishes and bestows blessing, and conquers and gives into bondage. His will was mediated to his people by the king (Mesha) who also, like early Canaanite and Israelite kings (II Sam. 6:18; I Kings 8:54f), possessed certain priestly authority. He was satiated by sacrifice (II Kings 3:24-27; M. I. 11) and honored by the practice of *herem* ("ban" or devotion to destruction, M. I., 17). Almost surely he had a temple at Dibon. His name was a common element in Moabite names, even as was Baal in Canaan and Yahweh in Israel. To the Israelites, however, he was merely an abomination whose worship was

THE MOABITE STONE. Courtesy, Oriental Institute

to the Moabites but a weariment (I Kings 11:7; II Kings 23:13).

BIBLIOGRAPHY. W. F. Albright, *The Biblical Period from Abraham to Ezra,* Harper & Row, New York, 1963; *The Archaeology of Palestine,* Pelican Books, Baltimore, Maryland, 1960. Denis Baly, *The Geography of the Bible,* Harper & Brothers, New York, 1957. H. L. Ginsburg, "Judah and the Transjordan States from 734-582 B.C.E.," *Alexander Marx Jubilee Volume,* New York, 1950. Nelson Glueck, *Explorations in Eastern Palestine I-IV, AASOR,* Vol. XIV (1933-34); Vol. XV (1934-35); Vols. XVIII-XIX (1937-39); Vols. XXV-XXVIII (1945-49); *The Other Side of the Jordan,* ASOR, New Haven, Connecticut, 1940. J. B. Pritchard (ed.), *Ancient Near Eastern Texts,* (2nd Ed.), Princeton University Press, Princeton, New Jersey, 1955. A. H. Van Zyl, *The Moabites,* E. J. Brill, Leiden, 1960.

MOABITE STONE. In August, 1868, an Arab sheikh at Dhiban, Biblical Dibon, showed a German missionary, F. Klein, an inscribed slab which was 3 feet 10 inches high, 2 feet wide, and 10½ inches thick. Interest in the discovery was such that both the German and the French consular officials attempted to gain possession of the stele. Sensing that they had an object of value, the Arabs kindled a fire under the black basalt stone and poured water over it to break it into pieces. The fragments then were carried away to bless their grain.

Fortunately the French had been able to obtain a squeeze of the inscription before the stone was destroyed. Efforts were made to recover the fragments that had been scattered, and about two-thirds of the text was recovered — 669 letters out of an estimated 1,100. The stone was then reconstructed and placed in the Louvre. It contains thirty-nine lines of writing in Moabite, a language closely akin to Biblical Hebrew. The alphabet is the old or palaeo-Hebrew script such as was used for the °Siloam Inscription and the °Lachish Letters.

The Moabite king, Mesha, commemorates his revolt against Israel during the latter years of Ahab's reign. Mesha honors Chemosh, the god of Moab, for whom he built an high place. In referring to the relations between Moab and Israel he says:

> Omri, king of Israel, humbled Moab many days because Chemosh was angry at his land. His son followed him, and he also said, "I will humble Moab." In my time he said this, but I have triumphed over him and over his house, while Israel has perished forever. Omri had occupied the land of Medeba and Israel had dwelt there during his time, and half the time of his son [i.e. Ahab], forty years; but Chemosh dwelt there in my time.

The stone goes on to speak of the cities in Moab built by Mesha, and those which he captured from Israel. Mesha is also credited with the building of a palace which was constructed with the aid of Israelite slave labor. The Moabite king also built reservoirs, cisterns and other structures for the defense and prosperity of Moab. He built a highway in the Arnon valley.

The Moabite Stone shows how a people related to Israel looked upon their god Chemosh. Chemosh, like Yahweh, might be angry with his people and deliver them into the hands of their enemies for a time before saving them from their foes. The worship of Chemosh was associated with the "high places" which were denounced by the Israelite prophets.

BIBLIOGRAPHY. E. Ullendorff, "The Moabite Stone," in *Documents from Old Testament Times,* ed. D. Winston Thomas, Nelson, London, 1958.

Bible. It signaled war and peace; it announced the new moons and sabbaths. Its chief function was to make noise. It warned of approaching danger and announced the death of a noble in Israel.

The terms "flute" and "pipe" describe wind instruments of largely secular usage. They were largely associated with sex orgies. A silver flute was discovered at Ur.

An Assyrian relief shows a private band of clarinets and harps at Susa playing homage to King Ashurbanipal. The clarinet, or "double clarinet" served to express both extreme joy and deep mourning. At funerals it accompanied the wailing women. The clarinet was the most popular of woodwind instruments in the Near East. It was regularly used at weddings and banquets.

Similar in usage to the *shophar* was the trumpet, which might be made of metal (bronze, copper, silver, gold), bones, and shell. On the Arch of *Titus we see a trumpet with a mouthpiece added. Signals from trumpets introduced each ceremony and sacrifice in the Temple.

Other instruments used in making noise were gongs (I Cor. 13:1), cymbals, bells (presumably without clapper, Exod. 28:33, 39:25-26), and castanets (II Sam. 6:5, RSV). The castanet, or sistrum, was a rattle type noisemaker used for both joyous and sad occasions. The oldest sistrums were discovered in excavations at *Ur, *Kish, and other Sumerian sites. They came from Mesopotamia, by way of Palestine, to Egypt.

MYCENAE. Mycenae was a Greek city, fourteen miles southwest of Corinth in Argolis. It figured largely in Greek legend and was mentioned in the Iliad as "that well-built city and fortress," the "golden," "wide-wayed" city beloved of Hera. Excavations began at Mycenae by Heinrich Schliemann in 1876-77 who believed that he had discovered the Tomb of Agamemnon among the graves that he cleared with their rich treasure. Work was subsequently done by the Archaeological Society of Athens and the British Archaeological Society. Since World War II the Greek Archaeological Society has continued excavations.

The city comprised an *acropolis occupying the apex of a hill, and the lower town. The acropolis is triangular and surrounded by a massive wall of huge stones known to archaeologists as *cyclopean stones. It is entered by the Gate of Lions, dating to the fourteenth century B.C. The opening of the gate is about ten feet high and wide. Above the huge lintel is a triangular opening with a slab, two feet thick, bearing a relief showing two lions separated by a column. Inside the gate is a double circle of upright stones, eighty feet in diameter, where shaft graves were discovered containing golden ornaments and masks, inlaid sword blades and other objects valued by the ancient Mycenaeans. Schliemann assumed that these were tombs of heroes and heroines of the Trojan War, but modern scholarship suggests that they are much earlier than the time of Agamemnon. While the Trojan War dates to about the twelfth century B.C., the shaft graves of Mycenae were used between the nineteenth and the sixteenth centuries B.C.

Remains of temples and palaces from prehistoric times to later periods have been discovered during excavations of the acropolis. The most important monuments of the lower town are the "beehive tombs" popularly called treasuries. Among these is the so-

THE GOLDEN CUP FROM MYCENAE.
Courtesy, B. Goudis

called "treasury of Atreus," or "the tomb of Agamemnon" being a typical example. The interior is a circle about fifty feet in diameter and slightly less in height. The inner surface of the tomb was probably decorated with metal medallions and painted designs.

Mycenaean art forms, particularly pottery, have turned up in a wide area of the eastern Mediterranean lands. Ornamentation includes geometric decoration, foliage, marine and animal forms, and human figures. The chief objects from Mycenae are at the National Museum in Athens. They include bronze daggers, spears, swords, gold cups, gold ornaments (bands, buttons, and ear clips), beads of semi-precious stones, remains of a leather scabbard, and pottery including painted vases, amphorae, and jars.

N

NABATEANS. The Nabateans were an Arab people who inhabited areas to the east and southeast of the Dead Sea. They are not mentioned specifically in the Old Testament or in the New Testament, although attempts have been made to identify them with Nebaioth, son of Ishmael and brother-in-law of Edom (Gen. 25:13; 28:9). Some writers have linked them with the Nabaiate of the inscriptions of Assurbanipal of Assyria (*ca.* 650 B.C. *Ancient Near Eastern Texts*, ed. J. B. Pritchard, Princeton, 1955, pp. 298, 299). However, since the name Nabaioth is spelled with the Hebrew *t* while the name Nabatean is spelled with the Hebrew *ṭ*, identification of the two groups is uncertain.

I. *History.* There is some evidence that perhaps as early as the sixth century B.C. they began to occupy the territory of the Edomites whom they pushed into the south of Judah. Their original home may have been northwest Arabia. Certainly archaeological remains have been found some 250 miles southeast of Petra at El-Heger, the modern Medain Saleh. Theoretically they fell within the domains of the Persians during the fifth and fourth centuries, although this may have been nominal. They occupied a strategic area astride the trade routes which joined the East to the Mediterranean Sea and were able to attack caravans from their strong posts. Archaeological evidence shows that by the close of the fourth century they had occupied the old areas of Moab and Edom and the area to the south of the Dead Sea. They even infiltrated into part of the Negeb where they built walled strong points at such places as Abde, Kurnub and Sbeita.

By the time of Alexander the Great at the close of the fourth century, they were in-dependent. Already °Petra was occupied to judge from the presence of Greek potsherds there dating to this period. A process of settling down may be postulated. Contact with settled communities to the west during the third and second centuries resulted in the development of many towns and villages. Remarkable systems for water conservation involving dams, cisterns, and conduits were developed and intensive cultivation of the formerly barren areas resulted.

The first recorded date in Nabatean history is 169 B.C. (II Macc. 5:8). Jason, one of the contenders for the position of High Priest in Judaea, sought refuge with Aretas I, king of the Nabateans, in his capital at Petra. This king seems to have organized these erstwhile nomads so as to provide protection for the caravans which plied the deserts between Petra, South Arabia, and the Persian Gulf. From Petra the goods were taken to Gaza and were shipped to a Roman world hungry for spices, silks and luxury goods from the East. Thereafter several Nabatean kings are known from Jewish and Greek sources. A second Aretas is mentioned by Josephus (*Antiq.* XIII. 13.3) *ca.* 96 B.C. During the first century the Nabateans sought to expand southward into the Negeb and northward towards Damascus. Aretas III (*ca.* 70 B.C.) and Aretas IV (*ca.* 9 B.C.–A.D. 40) were strong enough to occupy both these areas and to control East-West trade. It was an officer of Aretas IV who sought to detain Paul in Damascus (II Cor. 11:32). Herod Antipas was married to a daughter of a Nabatean king. When he divorced his wife to marry Herodias, a war ensued (Josephus *Antiq.* XVIII. 5.1), Malicus II (A.D. 40-70) and Rabbel II (A.D.

70-106) made their capital at Bosrah, seventy miles east of Galilee, but on Rabbel's death in A.D. 106 Trajan annexed the Nabatean kingdom as a Roman province.

During the second century A.D. Petra flourished. There was a Christian church here in these days. But the opening up of *Palmyra to the east of Damascus as a trade center, and the redirection of trade routes in the Red Sea area by the Romans, caused the decay of Petra to set in. Finally, the Nabateans became absorbed into the surrounding peoples, although their peculiar script was still used in the fourth century B.C.

II. *Archaeological Evidence of Nabatean Civilization.* Surface surveys, soundings, and a limited amount of excavations have given a good insight into Nabatean culture.

Reference has been made to their remark-able success in conserving water. Complex drainage systems set along hill slopes to direct the water into dams, or among crops, may still be seen. Their dams were well constructed from blocks of stone.

There is evidence that they continued to work the copper and iron mines of old Edom. They had ports on the Gulf of Aqabah and on the Red Sea.

Their pottery vessels are now well known. In particular, their red-painted ware made from fine clay, is some of the most delicate ware that was ever produced in the ancient Near East.

The Nabatean sculptors developed high skill. Their statuary, their clearly cut reliefs with plant designs, their tombs cut out of the solid sandstone in Petra and elsewhere, and the beauty of many of their architectural

NABATEAN INSCRIPTION *from the cornice above the entrance to a tomb at Petra. Courtesy, Matson Photo Service*

features, all bear witness to the outstanding ability of the Nabatean sculptors.

Inscriptions in stone, in a special Nabatean script, but coming from the later period of their kingdom, are written in Aramaic, the *lingua franca* of Palestine in that age. Some inscriptions are written in both Aramaic and Greek. The cursive script such as was used on papyri and parchments is now known from some documents found at Qumran.

Nabatean coins also carry Aramaic inscriptions. They were modeled on Greek and Roman types. Curiously enough, not a single gold coin has yet been found and silver ones are rare.

In architecture the Nabateans were influenced by others. The early Nabatean builders, whose work remains in the many crenellated tombs, were subject to Egyptian and Oriental influences. The classical period of Nabatean architecture, from the first century B.C. to the Roman occupation of 106 B.C., shows Hellenistic decorations. It is represented in a variety of tombs, private houses, shrines and in the large *Ed Deir* temple. Roman and Byzantine influences may be seen in the later buildings.

In religion, the best known and the oldest Nabatean deity is Dushara who was worshipped throughout the Nabatean kingdom. That other gods were later recognized is clear both from excavations carried out at Khirbet et Tannur and Petra, and from the surface surveys of numerous temples, shrines, and high places throughout the Nabatean area. Among these gods were Atargatis (Astarte), the fish goddess, Tyche Allat the Arabian mother goddess, Gad the god of luck, Zeus-Hadad and others. A process of syncretism seems to have gone on through the centuries. However, little is known in detail. That sacrifices were offered is clear from the altars which are found at the high places, notably at the great high place at Petra.

BIBLIOGRAPHY. N. Glueck, *The Other Side of Jordan*, New Haven, 1940, pp. 158-200; *AASOR*, XIV, 1934; XV, 1935; XVIII-XIX, 1939; XXV-XXVIII, 1951. J. Starcky, "The Nabateans: A Historical Sketch," *BA*. XVIII, 1955. pp. 84-106. G. L. Harding, *The Antiquities of Jordan*, London, 1959; *PEQ* LXXXVIII, 1958, pp. 12-15.

NABUNAID, NABONIDUS. Nabunaid, or Nabonidus was the last king of the Neo-Babylonian (°Chaldean) Empire, ruling from 555 to 539 B.C. The so-called Nabonidus Chronicle, first published by T. G. Pinches in 1882, relates events from the accession year of Nabonidus to the fall of °Babylon. It states that the king was at Teima in Arabia during the seventh, ninth, tenth, and eleventh years of his reign, and that his son Belshazzar (Bel-shar-usur) remained behind in control of the government. Nabonidus remained king, but Belshazzar served as regent. In October, 539 B.C., Babylon fell to the Persians when Gobryas (Ugbaru) and the army of Cyrus entered Babylon without battle. Nabonidus was arrested when he returned to Babylon. Daniel 5 relates the account of the fall of Babylon after the impious feast of Belshazzar, who was slain by the Persians as they entered the city.

BIBLIOGRAPHY. J. V. Schiel, "Inscription de Nabonide," *Recueil de Travaux Relatifs á la Philologie et á l'archeologie egyptiennes et assyriennes,* XVIII, 1896, pp. 15-29. Raymond P. Dougherty, *Nabonidus and Belshazzar*, Yale University Press, New Haven, 1929. A. Leo Oppenheim, *ANET,* pp. 305-306. C. J. Gadd, "The Haran Inscription of Nabonidus," *Anatolian Studies*, VIII, 1958, pp. 35-92.

NAG HAMMADI GNOSTIC TEXTS. A collection of Coptic Texts was found in 1945 in Upper Egypt, about sixty miles downstream from Luxor, across the Nile from modern Nag Hammadi. In an ancient cemetery, near the site of St. Pachomius' monastery, peasants unearthed a large jar which, when broken, disclosed thirteen codices (see Codex). Codex I, acquired by a dealer, was finally purchased by a philanthropist and given to the Jung Institute; so it is called "the Jung Codex." The Coptic Museum purchased Codex II in 1946 and acquired the remainder of the texts in 1952. The Jung Codex is in the process of being returned to the Coptic Museum.

The codices are written on papyrus. Eleven of them were enclosed in soft leather bindings resembling modern brief cases. Two of the codices are almost complete; one (Codex I) has considerable lacunae; two others are very fragmentary. The codices vary in size from about 14 x 25 cm. to 15 X 29 cm. The total find contains about one thousand pages of which nearly eight hundred are in good condition. The texts are written in Coptic, the final stage of Egyptian. Ten of the codices are written in the Sahidic dialect, while two more are classified as Sahidic under Achmimic influence. The Jung Codex, however, is written in Sub-Achmimic, or perhaps a new sub-dialect of Sub-Achmimic. The texts thus far studied are translations of Greek originals.

I. *Contents.* These thirteen codices contain from forty-eight to fifty separate works. Discounting duplicates and triplicates, the find discloses at least forty-four different texts. Of these about forty were previously unknown, even by title. The content of the codices is indicated in the following table. The enumeration used by the Coptic Museum is followed with the Codex numbers of Doresse and Puech in parenthesis, sequentially.

CODEX I (XIII, II)
  The Epistle (sometimes called *Apocalypse of Apocryphon*) *of James*
  The Gospel of Truth
  The Discourse of Rheginos
  Treatise concerning the three natures
  Prayers of the Apostle Peter
CODEX II (X, III)
  The Apocryphon of John
  The Gospel of Thomas
  The Gospel of Philip
  The Hypostasis of the Archons
  Untitled revelation devoted to Pistis Sophia
  The Exegesis of the Soul
  The Book of Thomas the Athlete
CODEX III (I, I)
  The Apocryphon of John
  The Gospel of the Egyptians
  The Epistle of Eugnostos
  The Wisdom of Jesus the Christ
  The Dialogue of the Saviour
CODEX IV (II, VIII)
  The Apocryphon of John
  The Gospel of the Egyptians
CODEX V (III, VII)
  The Epistle of Eugnostos
  The Apocalypse of Paul
  The Apocalypse of James
  Another *Apocalypse of James* (the Righteous?)
  The Apocalypse of Adam
CODEX VI (VI, XI) — Mostly Hermetic works
  The Acts of Peter and the Twelve Disciples
  The Gift of the Perfect Mind
  The Authentic Discourse (of Hermes to his Son Tat?)

The Thought of the Great Power
A short, untitled work
An untitled writing (possibly Sethian)
This Is the Prayer Which He Said
Hermetic treatise same as Latin *Asclepius*, par. twenty-one to twenty-nine.
CODEX VII (VII, V)
  Paraphrase of Shem (*Second Treatise of the Great Seth*)
  The Apocalypse of Peter
  The Teachings of Silvanus
  Revelation of Dositheus, or *The Three Pillars of Seth*
CODEX VIII (IV, IX)
  A Revelation without title
  Discourse of Truth by Zoroaster
  Epistle of Peter to Philip
CODEX IX (V, X)
  Revelation Attributed to the Great Seth
  Epistle concerning the Father of the Universe and the Primordial Adam
  Treatise in epistolary form
  Treatise without title against the Scribes and Pharisees concerning John's Baptism
CODEX X (XII, XII)
  Fragments of a treatise on the cosmos
CODEX XI (VIII, VI)
  The Exposition of Gnosis
  The Most High Allogenes
  Revelation of Messos
CODEX XII (XI, XIII)
  Fragments of works dealing with morality and demons
CODEX XIII (IX, IV)
  The Threefold Discourse of the Threefold Protennoia
  A Sethian Revelation in the form of an epistle

II. *Publication.* A photographic reproduction of some missing pages of Codex I and part of Codex II was published by the Coptic Museum (*Coptic Gnostic Papyri in the Coptic Museum at Old Cairo*, Vol. I, ed. by Pahor Labib, Coptic Museum, Cairo, 1956; abbrev. *CGP*, I). Almost simultaneously the Coptic text, with French, German, and English translations of the *Gospel of Truth* appeared (Henri-Charles Peuch; Gilles Quispel; and Michael Malinine, *Evangelium Veritatis*, Rascher, Zurich, 1956). The text edition and translation of *Thomas* appeared simultaneously in French, German, Dutch, and English editions (Antoine Guillaumont, Henri-Charles Puech; Gilles Quispel; Walter

Till, and Yassah 'Abd al Masiḥ, *The Gospel According to Thomas,* Harper, New York, 1959). In 1963 the three variant texts and German translations of the important *Apocryphon of John* appeared (Martin Krause, and Pahor Labib, *Die Drei Versionen des Apocryphon Johannes,* Harrassowitz, Wiesbaden, 1963). Krause and Labib plan to publish *The Exegesis of the Soul* and the *Book of Thomas the Athlete* as Vol. II of the series (*DAIK-Koptische Reihe*) and the *Gospel of the Egyptians* as Vol. III. The Jung Institute has published the *Epistle of Rheginos* (Michael Malinine; Henri-Charles Puech; Gilles Quispel; and Walter Till, *De Resurrectione,* Rascher, Zurich, 1963) and plans to publish the *Epistle of James.* The untitled work of Codex II and some other texts are to be edited and translated by Alexander Bohlig and Pahor Labib. The *Epistle of Eugnostos* and the *Wisdom of Jesus the Christ* are given in the critical apparatus to parallel texts in Codex Berolinensis 8502 (Walter Till, *Die gnostischen Schriften des koptischen Papyrus Berolinensis 8502, TU 60, Akademie Verlag,* Berlin, 1955).

III. *Individual Texts.* Translations or adequate information is available for the following texts.

A. *The Epistle of James* (Codex I. 1: 1—16:30) claims to be a letter written by James to an unnamed recipient. The author says he wrote in Hebrew (*i.e.* Aramaic) characters, but the Greek epistolary style and language indicate that *James* was composed in Greek. It refers to an earlier letter sent to the same addressee, perhaps one of the other two *Epistles of James* in the Nag Hammadi library.

The Church Fathers make no reference to this work, either by title or by quotation. Its contents show that its author did not know the book of Acts, and was not acquainted with Palestinian Christianity. This meager evidence makes it difficult to date the original. Some details indicate a date in the first half of the second century, others point to the second half of the century.

The author is identified as James, the brother of Jesus. However, he is also equated with the leader of Jerusalem Christianity *and* the Apostle James. This blending of the two figures may indicate a late date and/or second hand tradition. However, Clement of Alex-

andria in *Hypotyposes,* the *Gospel of the Hebrews,* and the *Philosophuema* all give James a high place in Christian tradition. The *Gospel of Thomas* (Logion No. 12, Puech enumeration), also places him, along with Thomas, in the Gnostic "inner circle."

The work claims to be a series of revelations given by Jesus to James and Peter 550 days after the resurrection, just before the ascension. Its chief topics are: (1) Redemption through Christ. The Cross is emphasized, but the details are not worked out. However, there is some stress on *gnosis.* (2) Exhortations to steadfastness even unto death in the midst of persecution. (3) The problem of prophecy. What is true prophecy? Who is a true prophet? Jesus answers James' inquiries by saying prophecy came to an end with the death of John the Baptist.

In Christology, the Epistle is not Docetic as many Gnostic works. It lacks eschatology in that there is no reference to the last day, or the return of Christ, or judgment. Entering the kingdom of God is still future, but it is a moral rather than a chronological event. Since many characteristic Gnostic doctrines are missing from the Epistle, it has been called "vague, unreflecting Christianity." If this be true, then it was vague enough to warrant inclusion in the Gnostic library.

B. *The Gospel of Truth* (Latin, *Evangelium Veritatis*) is the chief work found in the Jung Codex. It occupies about thirty-eight pages of text, and was written about A.D. 400. It seems likely that the original composition goes back to about A.D. 140, before Valentinianism sub-divided. Some scholars believe it may have been written by Valentinus himself, just before or after his break with the church.

The *Gospel of Truth* was known to Irenaeus (*ca.* A.D. 180) for in *Adversus Haereses,* iii.11.9 he says:

> But those who are from Valentinus, being, on the other hand, altogether reckless, while they put forth their own compositions, boast that they possess more Gospels than there really are. Indeed, they have arrived at such a pitch of audacity, as to entitle their comparatively recent writing "the Gospel of Truth," although it agrees in nothing with the Gospels of the Apostles, so that they have really no Gospel which is not full of blasphemy. For if what they have published is the Gospel of Truth,

and yet is totally unlike those which have been handed down to us by the Apostles, any who please may learn, as is shown by the Scriptures themselves, that that which has been handed down from the Apostles can no longer be reckoned the Gospel of truth.

The content of this work is a homily or meditation upon the theme, "the Gospel of Truth," which is the means of redemption. This truth, for the Gnostic, is the knowledge that he is "a being from above." The homily says, "Whosoever has knowledge understands from whence he has come and whither he goes." In other words, the *Gospel of Truth* presents the typical gnostic scheme of human redemption through *gnosis*.

The homily summons the reader to introspection so that one may discover himself and return to himself, thus finding *gnosis* and finding God. It posits the thesis that man's difficulty is due to his ignorance, also described as emptiness, illusion, forgetfulness. Salvation consists in "waking up." Christ is the revelation of the truth which brings the transition from nothingness to inclusion in the All. The later Valentinian myth of the Unknown God and the Demiurge with the Aeons between is missing in the *Gospel of Truth*.

The *Gospel of Truth* differs from the canonical Gospels in that it is not an orderly account of the birth, life, deeds, teachings, death, and resurrection of Christ. Like *Philip*, it is sermonic or devotional rather than narrative. It has no Old Testament background, no end-time eschatology, no ethics. Instead of sin, the writer speaks of "ignorance" and "error."

C. *The Apocryphon of John* in three variant texts (Codex II, III, and IV) was found at Nag Hammadi. It was also found in Codex Berolinensis 8502 whose discovery Schmidt announced in 1896. He identified the *Apocryphon* as one of the sources used in Irenaeus' polemic (*Adv. Haer.*) against the Gnostics. Several English translations of *BG* have appeared.

The *Apocryphon* in Codex II (*CGP*, I.47:1–80:10), except for the first eight pages, is remarkably preserved, and is written in beautiful bookhand. It is the most extensive of all texts of the *Apocryphon*, which has led some scholars to date it late, i.e., mid-third century, due to what they consider accretions. However, it is also possible that

it is the earliest, and the others condensed versions. It is closer to the version of Codex IV than it is to that of *BG* or Codex III. The longest passage peculiar to Codex II (*CGP*, I.63:30–67:3) and Codex IV deals with the creation of the various parts of the body by various angels.

The setting of the *Apocryphon* is in Jerusalem. The time is just after the resurrection of Christ. The Apostle John is questioned by a Pharisee, Arimanios, who accuses Christ of misleading His disciples. John turns away in sorrow to a mount (identified through other sources as Olivet) and meditates upon such questions as: "Why was the Saviour appointed? Why was He sent to earth? What is the Aeon like to which we shall go?" In a scene reminiscent of Revelation 1:12-19, Christ appears to John, and announces Himself as the Father, the Mother, and the Son. Christ tells John that He has appeared to teach him, "what now is, and what has been, and what shall be." He instructs John to pass this teaching on to his fellow-spirits, an instruction repeated at the close of the work.

The Savior then delineates the following Gnostic doctrines: (1) The Supreme Being, "the Father of the Universe," is presented, as in the *Gospel of Truth*, in terms of negative attributes. This Supreme Being, by reflection on a sea of light brings forth the Barbēlō (perhaps meaning, "from Arbela"), the Primal female principle. (2) The creation of the Pleroma begins with the creation of four androgynous Aeons: Fore-knowledge, Indestructibility, Eternal Life, and Truth, thus completing the Aeonic Decad. Christ is begotten and given four Lights, each having three attributes, thus constituting twelve Aeons. The *Apocryphon* neglects to inform us concerning the remaining eight Aeons of the Gnostic total of thirty. (3) The Fall of Sophia (Wisdom) results from her desire to produce a work without her consort. Her resultant offspring has the appearance of a dragon and the face of a lion. This defective being is called Yaldabaōth (probably meaning "child of chaos"). The Mother repents and is restored to the Nonad until her defect is remedied. (4) The creation of man occurs when, in response to Yaldabaōth's ignorant boast, "I am God," the Supreme Being revealed his image in the waters. Seeing it, the Archons (Powers)

A PART OF THE GOSPEL ACCORDING TO THOMAS *from the collection known as the Nag Hammadi Gnostic Texts.*

made by Yaldabaōth decided to make a man in that image, citing Genesis 1:26. Each of them created an "essence" of the man. Then follows the passage detailing the parts of the body and the emotions, all created by *daimōns* and angels. Man is lifeless until Yaldabaōth is tricked into breathing into man some of his spirit, obtained from his mother, Sophia. The Archons are jealous and cast him out. God sends Light-Life (Zōē) to assist Adam back to the Plērōma. The Archontic beings make Adam a body of fire, wind, water, and earth. He is imprisoned in this as a tomb, and placed in the paradise of the world. Here he is counselled not to eat of the tree of life since it would give him freedom from the Archons. (5) A typical Gnostic re-interpretation of Genesis 2-9 follows with the Savior teaching Adam to eat of the tree of knowledge, and thus escape the Archons. Eve is created. She begets Cain and Abel by Yaldabaōth, and Seth by Adam. The building of the ark is mentioned. (6) Doctrines of salvation are then elucidated in a series of questions by John and answers by Jesus. All who possess *gnosis* will be saved. Only those "who knew and withdrew" go to the place

of eternal punishment. The Savior departs from John who then goes to share the revelation with his fellow-disciples.

Many of the *Apocryphon's* motifs recur in Manicheism, and survive until the eighth century among the Audians. This work helps modern scholars trace the development of Gnostic mythology, and the inter-relatedness of Gnostic sects. It also provides an excellent example of Gnostic exegesis of the Old Testament.

D. *The Gospel of Thomas* (*CGP*, I.80:10 −99:28) contains, in variant enumerations (here Guillaumont, *et. al.* is followed), 112, 114, or 118 Sayings purporting to be a secret revelation given by Jesus to Didymus Judas Thomas. It contains no record of the deeds of Jesus and is not identical with the previously known *Gospel of Thomas* which describes His childhood. It is a collection of Sayings, or *Logia*, attributed to Jesus, some closely parallelled in the New Testament, others in apocryphal and/or patristic literature. Of the latter, only a few Sayings are strong candidates for acceptance as authentic.

Behind the *Gospel of Thomas* was a Greek (or possibly Syriac) original composed, probably, sometime between A.D. 140-170. Evidence for this is found in the Oxyrhynchus *Papyri (No. 1, 654, and 655) which were found in Egypt in 1897 and 1903. All Oxyrhynchus Sayings are in the *Gospel of Thomas,* albeit in different order, but usually in wording close to the Greek. However, the Greek version, where it varies, is more orthodox; the Coptic is more Gnostic.

Hippolytus (*Refutations* v.7.20) states that *Thomas* was used by the Naasenes. The content has much affinity with their teachings. Thomas evidently came from a Syriac or Aramaic speaking semi-Christian Gnostic community, possibly Edessa. Its variants from the New Testament and/or other sources containing *Logia* are explainable as different translations into Greek of the ambiguous Aramaic originals. *Thomas* followed one translation tradition, the Gospels in Greek followed another.

The Sayings of *Thomas* are somewhat like those of the canonical and apocryphal gospels, including questions, commands, blessings, maledictions, predictions and general statements. It contains twenty-four parables, almost all closely allied to parables in the Synoptics. There are numerous dialogues between Jesus and groups of disciples, or individual disciples. *Thomas* contains a number of doublets: the world as a corpse, 56 and 80; body and soul, 87 and 112; the Kingdom of God is within, 2 and 113; I came to cast fire, 10 and 16; hating one's family, 55 and 101; parable of the robbers, 21b and 103; power to move mountains, 48 and 106.

Some of the Sayings can be interpreted only in an orthodox way; others are open to either orthodox or Gnostic interpretation; still others are clearly Gnostic. The content is anti-Judaistic, anti-Old Testament, anti-ritualistic and almost anti-moralistic. The work is not eschatological: its kingdom of God is not future, but almost exclusively present. As a man "existentially" finds and knows himself, he enters the kingdom.

Close parallels to the *Gospel according to the Hebrews* are found in Sayings 2, 12, and 104; and to the *Gospel of the Egyptians* (not the Nag Hammadi text of the same name) in Sayings 22, 37, and 61. Other parallels are found in the Church Fathers. Attempts to explain the origin of *Thomas* have been unsatisfactory. Some have suggested that it is dependent upon the apoc-

ryphal gospels just mentioned. Others think it preserves an independent oral tradition.

The Sayings can be listed in four broad categories. The first group includes those which are identical, or nearly so, with their New Testament counterparts: e.g. 26 and Matthew 7:3ff.; 34 and Matthew 15:14; 44 and Matthew 12:32. The second group includes Sayings which are paraphrases or independent variants of canonical sayings. Some of these indicate dependence upon oral tradition, but more frequently the canonical gospels are the source. The third category includes Sayings not in the New Testament, but in patristic literature, e.g. Saying 74. Sometimes this literature is citing apocryphal works no longer extant. The last category, about one-half of *Thomas* consists of Sayings previously unknown. All Sayings in this category are very definitely Gnostic in tone, e.g. Sayings 15 and 87.

In his use of the Gospels, Thomas favors Matthew and Luke, dwelling on Matthew 5-7, 13, and Luke 6, 11, and 12. He has no exclusively Markan parallels. His citations and references to John are negligible. Frequently *Thomas* interweaves portions from several Gospels into one Saying, a common practice ridiculed by Irenaeus' statement (*Adv. Haer.* i.8.1) about the Gnostics being like a man who took a mosaic portrait of a king, re-arranged the pieces to make a portrait of a dog or fox and called the result the king's portrait.

E. *The Gospel of Philip* (*CGP*,I.99:29-134:10) consists of approximately 125 Sayings or sermonettes. Many Sayings are joined by word association (e.g. two and three by the word "inheritance"), a phenomenon also found in the *Gospel of Thomas* and the New Testament (cf. Mark 9:33-50). Whether the author gathered Sayings from various sources or originated the Sayings is not yet clear. Wilson (*Gospel of Philip,* p. 10) points out that the chief topic of *Philip,* the "mystery" of the bridal chamber, is not introduced until Saying 60. So evidently the author or compiler maintained a certain reticence about this central "mystery."

The colophon at the end of the work ascribes it to Philip. Perhaps his name is attached to it because he is the only disciple mentioned in the text. However, another Gnostic work, *Pistis Sophia,* 42, charges Philip, Matthew and Thomas with the responsibility of setting down the words and deeds of Jesus, and in Chapter 43 explains this charge by Deuteronomy 19:15. A reputed *Gospel of Philip* quoted by Epiphanius (*Panarion* 26.13.2-) evidently is not the Nag Hammadi treatise.

Philip probably was composed in Greek sometime between A.D. 140 and 200. Present studies would seem to favor a Syrian Christian milieu for its production. The abundant use of allusions, citations, and direct quotations from the New Testament verifies this. Many of its Sayings are paralleled in second century writings of orthodox churchmen. Its attitude toward the Old Testament is not as extreme as the *Apocryphon of John* or Marcion. However, in using Biblical terminology, *Philip* (in Wilson's apt epitome) "transposes it into another key."

At first glance the work seems to be closely related to the Valentinian branch of Gnosticism. A detailed study reveals that is has many affinities with the "great gnostics," especially the Barbelo-gnostics. Since the work contains at least twenty-three parallels to the *Apocryphon of John*, it may answer the perplexing problem, "Which came first, mythological gnosis (Sethians, etc.), or philosophical gnosis (Valentinians)?"

The Sayings, which vary from three to fifty-eight lines of text, deal with many subjects. The chief themes are Adam and Paradise, creation *vs.* begetting, redemption, the five Gnostic sacraments, and the "mystery" of the bridal chamber. The doctrines that *Philip* expounds are, for the most part, those of the early Christian church. However, the exposition is neither Biblical nor concordant with Christian theology of the period. For *Philip,* God is a transcendent being, utterly unknowable to man. Man is created by a lower being and placed in Paradise. He meets death because of his separation (Sayings 71, 78) from the female principle in his creation. Man is redeemed, not by the Cross, but by *gnosis* (Sayings 110, 115), especially the "mysteries" culminating in the bridal chamber where the separation is (symbolically, at least) remedied. Christ came, not to make Atonement, but to restore things to their place (Saying 70), and to "remove the separation" (Saying 78).

Philip enumerates five Gnostic sacraments (Saying 68): Baptism, Chrism, Eucharist,

Redemption, and the Bridal Chamber. Eucharist (communion) is mentioned in Sayings 15, 23, 98, 100, 108 and 53. The Redemption was practiced by the Valentinian Marcosians (Irenaeus, *Adv. Haer.* i.29). It may be mentioned in connection with Baptism in Saying 76. Baptism seemingly was by immersion (Sayings, 59, 101, 109, cf. 120.30). According to Saying 59 the believer receives the Holy Spirit at Baptism (not at confirmation) as attested in ancient Syrian Christianity. The Chrism is superior to Baptism according to Saying 95, and also Saying 76 if one suggested reconstruction is correct. Saying 92 indicates that olive oil was used in this rite. The final sacrament, the Bridal Chamber, seems to be a re-enactment of the archetypal, situation in which the Savior is the bridegroom, the Sophia is the bride, and the Plērōma is the Bridal Chamber. It is difficult to tell when Philip's references to marriage are to be interpreted literally, and when they refer to this sacrament.

F. *The Hypostasis of the Archons* (*CGP,* I. 134:22–145:21) has a bottom corner of each page (three to ten lines) broken away, so readings are frequently uncertain at critical points. Nevertheless, the general ideas of the text are perfectly clear. It probably originated in Ophite or Sethian circles (cf. Irenaeus, *Adv. Haer.* i.30). Many of its motifs are found in the *Apocryphon.* This may indicate a closer relationship between these sects and Barbel-gnosticism than was previously conceded.

Doresse (*Secret Books,* p. 163) says that the *Hypostasis of the Archons* is an abridgement of the *Book of Norea.* In fact, the untitled work which follows it calls it the *Book of Norea.* This untitled work is believed by Doresse (*op. cit.,* p. 195) to be related to the *Epistle of Eugnostos.* Finally, he believes (*loc. cit.*) the *Sophia of Jesus* was fabricated from the *Epistle of Eugnostos.* Final conclusions about dating and relationships must await publication and study of these other texts, but the *Hypostasis of the Archons* may be a later composition than the preceding texts in Codex II.

The work opens by stating its content: "Concerning the Hypostasis of the Powers in the Spirit of the Father of Truth." Then follows a reference to Ephesians 6:12, "The great Apostle said to us, 'We wrestle not against flesh and [blood], but it is against the powers of the wor[ld an]d the spiritual evil.'" The narrative begins with the demiurge, the creator of the lower world, saying in ignorance and pride, "I [am] God. There is none other [except me]." This statement, a quotation of Isaiah 45:5, is also found in the *Apocryphon* (*CGP*, I. 61: 8-9). To it a voice from the Indestructibility answers, "You have erred, Samaēl."

This god then makes the material universe. The powers decide to make man according to an image which had been reflected in the waters below. Adam is created. He names the animals. He is placed in the garden. Eve is created from his side. The Archons (Powers) try to defile her, but she deceives them. Then the serpent beguiles her into eating the forbidden fruit. Adam and Eve hide from God. Finally, they are expelled from the garden.

Cain and Abel are born naturally (*contra, Apocryphon of John*). Then another son, and finally, a daughter, Norea, are born. The demiurge is displeased with men who have multiplied on earth. He instructs Noah to build an ark on mythological Mt. Seir. Norea wants to board the ark, but is not permitted to do so by Noah. She blows upon the ark and burns it, so Noah is forced to rebuild it. Norea cries for help, and the Great Angel, Elelēth, descends to help her. He reassures her, saying, "I was sent so that I should speak with you, and I should rescue you from the hands of these lawless ones [the Archons]. And I shall teach you what is yours."

The story then reverts to "pre-history" with the narrator answering questions about the existence, the essence, and the creation of the Archons. This came about when Sophia (Wisdom) wanted to make a creation on the heavenly prototype without a consort. From the Darkness (Matter) existing below a veil which separated the above from the beneath Sophia formed a "self-willed beast, having a lion aspect, a male-female being." This was the demiurge, Yaldabaōth, also called Samaēl, and Saklas. Yaldabaōth created seven male-female sons to preside over the seven planets as in the *Apocryphon* (*CGP*, I. 58:24–60:26). Sophia's daughter, Zōē, reproved Yaldabaōth for his pride in claiming to be God. She blew on him, and her breath became an angel who cast him into

Tartarus. Yaldabaōth's son, Sabaoth, repented and praised Zoe. He was put in the seventh heaven, just below the veil. He made for himself a four-faced cherubim chariot (in the next treatise these four faces are, as in Ezek. 1:10, lion, ox, man, eagle), and a multitude of angels to praise him. Yaldabaōth was jealous. From his jealousy came death, and from death, sons who were placed over the lower heavens of the chaos.

The interrogator is assured that he belongs to the generation of the Father. He asks, "How long?" (cf. Rev. 5:10). Unfortunately, lacunae in the text obscure the answer, but it seems that some others will be "redeemed" when "the man of Truth [is re]-vealed in the form [of the Spirit of] Truth." The evil powers and demons lament their defeat. The Sons of Light, by contrast, unite in saying, "A righteous One is the Truth of the Father, and the Son over the All, and through every one from eternity to eternity. Holy! Holy! Holy! Amen!"

The following text editions and translations have been announced: *The Gospel of Philip*, edited by the late Walter Till (Walter C., Till, *Das Evangelium nach Phillipos*, De Gruyter, Berlin, 1963); *The Apocalypse of Adam*, the (first) *Apocalypse of James*, the (second) *Apocalypse of James*, and *the Apocalypse of Paul* from Codex V (Alexander Bohlig, and Pahor Labib, *Koptisch-gnostiche Apokalypsen aus Codex V von Nag Hammadi, Wissenschaftliche Zeitschrift d. Martin-Luther-Universitat*, Halle-Wittenberg, 1963); an English translation of the *Apocryphon of John* based on Codex II (Soren Giversen, *The Coptic text of the Apocryphon Johannis in the Nag Hammadi Codex II with translation, introduction and commentary. Act Th. Dan.*, V, 1964.).

IV. *Importance.* The Nag Hammadi texts are important to the Biblical student for at least five reasons:

A. Formation of the Canon. Hitherto the second century has been an obscure period in the history of the canon. These texts reveal one stage in the process, and are themselves one reason for defining the canon. The use of any New Testament book by the Gnostic sectaries demonstrates that the book was authoritative among Christians around A.D. 150 to 200. Turning to the available texts, one finds that these writers knew and used the four Gospels, Acts, most of Paul's epistles, Hebrews, James, I Peter, I John, Revelation, and probably II Peter and Jude. Only the very brief epistles are not quoted or alluded to by these Gnostics, and even they may be cited in the unpublished works. It seems reasonable to infer that the canon of *ca.* A.D. 150 at Rome (*Gospel of Truth*) and in the Oriental Church (*Thomas, Philip,* etc.) was practically identical with that later defined by the church councils.

B. Textual criticism. The Nag Hammadi texts provide many variants from the standard Greek text. This is especially true in *Thomas* and *Philip.* The Gnostics seem to have used a text close to or identical with the so-called "Western" text, or to a "neutral" text. Many passages in *Thomas* parallel variants in Tatian's *Diatesseron.* With the publication of more texts, and the study of those already published, the Nag Hammadi texts may help solve problems of textual transmission.

C. Critical Problems. Solution of some vexing questions in Biblical criticism may come from these texts. The possibility of lost *agrapha* (unrecorded Sayings) of Jesus always exists. Critical scholars are faced with the problem of determining if any of the purported Sayings in the Nag Hammadi texts are genuine. Another problem, the authorship of Revelation, is illuminated by the *Apocryphon* (cf. Andrew Helmbold, "A Note . . ." *NTS,* VIII 1961, pp. 77-79.).

D. Exegesis and New Testament Theology. Here the Nag Hammadi texts make their most important contribution. Careful study of them contradicts the claims of some scholars that the New Testament writers depended upon a pre-existent *gnosis* for such ideas as the First and Last Adam, and shows that Gnosticism appropriated Christian terminology to express its essentially unChristian philosophy. At any rate, the texts reveal how close some forms of Gnosticism were to second century orthodoxy, and how important was the careful delineation of the faith which that situation necessitated.

E. History of Religion. The student can now untangle the web of ancient gnostic movements: Gnosticism in its varied sects, Mandeanism, Manicheism, Hermeticism, etc., and discover the relationships of the various movements. Gnostic ideas which persisted down through the middle ages and into

modern times can be identified and their validity evaluated.

BIBLIOGRAPHY. Jean Doresse, *The Secret Books of the Egyptian Gnostics,* Viking Press, New York, 1960. Robert M. Grant and David Noel Freedman, *The Secret Sayings of Jesus* (with trans. of *Thomas* by Wm. R. Schoedel), Doubleday, Garden City, 1960. Kendrick Grobel, *The Gospel of Truth: A Valentinian Meditation upon the Gospel,* Abingdon, New York, 1960. Edgar Hennecke and Wilhelm Schneemelcher, *New Testament Apocrypha,* Vol. I, Westminster, Philadelphia, 1963. Johannes Leipoldt and Hans-Martin Schenke, *Koptisch-gnostische Schriften aus den Papyrus-Codices von Nag-Hamadi* (transl. of *Thomas, Philip,* and *Hypostasis . . .*), Reich, Hamburg-Bergstadt, 1960. Henri-Charles Puech, Gilles Quispel, and W. C. Van Unnik, *The Jung Codex,* ed. and transl. by F. L. Cross, Mowbrays, London, 1955. W. C. Van Unnik, *Newly Discovered Gnostic Writings,* Allenson, Naperville, 1960; Robert McLachlan Wilson, *The Gospel of Philip,* Harper & Row, New York, 1962.

NAIN. Southeast of Nazareth, at the edge of the Hill of Moreh, is the village of Na'im, probably to be identified with Biblical Nain (Luke 7:11) in which Jesus raised the son of a widow. The Hebrew form of the name, Na'im, means "pleasant," and the village was known to the Arabs at Nain. A Franciscan church marks the traditional site of the miracle.

NARMER, PALETTE OF. *See* Writing.

NATUFIANS. Natufian culture was identified by Professor Dorothy A. E. Garrod in the Wadi en-Natuf near Mount Carmel. The Natufians are thought to have lived around 8000 B.C. They did not make pottery or domesticate animals but they had learned to raise wheat. Straight bone sickles were found with slots into which flint teeth were inserted. The cutting edge of the flints had a gloss which came from the silica of the stems of the grain that was harvested. Flint was also used in making scrapers, borers, and gravers. Natufians carved statuettes, perhaps for magical or religious purposes. In burying their dead the body was placed on its side with legs drawn up. Sometimes ornaments were buried with the dead. *See also* Mugharah.

NAZARETH. About midway between the Sea of Galilee and the Mediterranean, in the hill country north of the Esdraelon Plain, was the boyhood home of Jesus. Nazareth

MARY'S WELL AT NAZARETH. Here
women from the city have gone to draw
water since ancient times. Courtesy, Israel
Office of Information

TRADITIONAL TOMB OF JOSEPH at Nazareth. Courtesy, Phalpot

is situated in a basin shut in by hills except on the south where a narrow rocky gorge leads to the plain. The village itself is on a hillside facing east and southeast. It was a humble village in New Testament times, but its location had many advantages. From the hills surrounding Nazareth, Jesus could have looked northward over rich plains to the snowcapped Mount Hermon. Westward, his eye could take in majestic Mount Carmel, the Bay of Accho, and the Mediterranean. Tabor's wooded heights could be seen on the eastern horizon and, in the distance, the Sea of Galilee. Looking southward, Jesus would have seen the Plain of Esdraelon through which merchants and warriors have passed since time immemorial.

Although in no sense cut off from the world, the Nazareth in which Jesus grew up was a small village with but one spring from which Mary certainly drew water for her household. Today, it is appropriately named Mary's well. The French Bishop Arculf, who visited the Holy Land in the seventh century, described Nazareth as a city of large stone houses and two fine churches. One of these was built over the traditional site of the house of Mary.

Nazareth suffered during the early years of Moslem power. Its religious shrines were desecrated during the tenth century, but the Crusaders took it a century later and made it the political and religious center of Galilee which they ruled until it was recaptured by the Moslems in the thirteenth century. With the expulsion of the Crusaders (or "Franks" as they were called), Nazareth again declined and it is only since the eighteenth

century that it has shown signs of revival. In the days of the British mandate, Nazareth was the center for the administration of Galilee. In July 1948 it was taken by the Israeli army and is now a city of about thirty-two thousand.

About two miles southeast of Nazareth is Jebel Kafsy, the traditional "Mount of Precipitation" from which the people of Nazareth sought to cast Jesus at the time of their rejection of him (Luke 4:29). Like many so-called holy places, the tradition which identifies it cannot be either confirmed or denied.

When Jesus lived at Nazareth, the chief town of the region was situated about four miles northwest at Sepphoris, south of the main Roman road from Ptolemais (Accho) to Tiberias. In 1931, the University of Michigan conducted excavations around the citadel at Sepphoris and discovered important Roman remains. Among these were an amphitheatre and a basilica dating from the second century which were in a poor state of preservation. The small fort standing on top of the mound was built by the Turks in 1745 from ancient stones collected on the spot.

Tradition states that the virgin Mary was a native of Sepphoris, and a church now marks the site of the house of her parents Anna and Joachim. The pilgrim Antoninus Martyr visited Sepphoris in 570 and says, "We adored with reverence the pail and basket of blessed Mary. . . ." The city also became a spiritual center for Palestinian Judaism. Rabbi Judah the Prince compiled and edited the Mishna in Sepphoris during the second century.

NEAPOLIS. Neapolis, "New City," is the modern Kavalla in Greece. In Hellenistic and Roman times it served as the port of °Philippi, ten miles inland. Neapolis is mentioned as a city in Thrace on a fifth century (B.C.) Athenian tribute list. In New Testament times it was important as the city which served as the eastern terminus of the Egnatian Way, the Roman Road across Macedonia. Paul landed at Neapolis on his second missionary journey, but went straight to Philippi without stopping. The absence of a Jewish community at Neapolis probably accounts for Paul's failure to stay at Neapolis, for it was his custom to begin work in a new area

THE HARBOR OF NEAPOLIS. Courtesy, Royal Greek Embassy

among the Jews before going to the gentiles.

A structure from the fourth or fifth centuries B.C. excavated at Neapolis has been identified as the sanctuary of Parthenos, chief deity of the city. Latin inscriptions indicate that in Roman times Neapolis was dependent upon Philippi. Leading persons of Philippi lived at Neapolis. *See also* Macedonia.

NEBI SAMWIL. The traditional site of the tomb of Samuel, Nebi Samwil ("the prophet Samuel") dominates a high ridge above the road which approaches Jerusalem from the west. The Crusaders called the site Mount Joy because they caught their first glimpse of the Holy City from the top of the mount.

NEBI YUNUS. The site of the reputed tomb of the prophet Jonah, Nebi Yunus is one of the two large mounds comprising the remains of ancient °Nineveh.

NEBUCHADNEZZAR. *See* Chaldeans.

NECHO. *See* Egypt.

NEGEB, THE. South of the Judean Shapheleh and Hill Country is an area of arid terrain that appears on modern maps as an inverted triangle. It is bounded on the east by the extension of the Jordan Valley known as the Wadi Arabah, and on the west by the Sinai Peninsula. The apex of the triangle is at the head of the Gulf of Aqaba where the Israeli city of Eilat is located. Nearby, on the Jordan side of the border, is modern Aqaba and Tell el-Kheleifeh, the mound of ancient °Ezion-geber where Solomon maintained refineries for the copper that was mined farther north in the Arabah and in the eastern Negeb. The northern boundary of the Negeb is not clearly defined. It follows an irregular line extending eastward from the Coastal Plain north of °Beersheba to the western shore of the Dead Sea.

Although geologists tell us that heavy rains fell in the Negeb when Europe was experiencing the Ice Age, the area is arid today, and it is necessary to pipe water from a distance to make the land productive. One of the great challenges faced by the State of Israel is to irrigate the Negeb and encourage pioneers to farm this difficult terrain.

The word Negeb (or Negev in Hebrew) means "dry," and it is usually used in the Bible to describe the arid terrain south of Judah where the Biblical patriarchs had sojourned. Abraham settled for a time in the northern Negeb, at Beersheba (Gen. 13:1). As semi-nomads, the patriarchs moved from place to place with their flocks and herds, seeking adequate supplies of water and pasturage.

By the time of the Exodus, the Negeb was inhabited by semi-nomadic Amalekites who were bitter foes of the Israelites. When Israelite spies surveyed the Negeb, they reported that the people there were so mighty that Israel could not hope to enter the Land of Promise through their territory. Although a few, notably Caleb and Joshua, were

413

willing to trust God and move right in to Canaan, the majority prevailed and, after a generation in the wilderness, Joshua's army crossed the Jordan near Jericho and invaded Canaan from the east. The Amalekites who had frightened the spies (Num. 13:29) continued to be inveterate foes of Israel. In the days of Saul the Israelite army defeated the Amalekites and captured Agag their king. Samuel personally slew Agag and rebuked Saul for seeking to spare him (I Sam. 15).

Although assigned to the tribes of Simeon (Josh. 19:1-9) and Judah (Josh. 15:20-31), the Negeb was marginal territory which was not easily controlled. During the time of David's flight from Saul he served as a vassal of the Philistines at Ziklag, northwest of Beersheba (I Sam. 27:6). At that time he "made raids on the Geshurites, the Girzites, and the Amalekites; for these were the inhabitants of the land from of old, as far as Shur, to the land of Egypt" (I Sam. 27:8).

The road from the Judean highlands to Egypt, passing through Beersheba, is known as the Way to Shur. When Hagar, Sarah's Egyptian handmaid, fled from her mistress, she took the road to Shur (Gen. 16:7), doubtless thinking that she should head in the direction of her homeland. After leaving the Negeb, the traveler could continue westward to the borders of Egypt, or turn southwestward into the Sinai Peninsula. Another important road in the Negeb went southeastward toward Ezion-geber and thence into the Arabian Peninsula.

Communities were settled and roads built in those places in the Negeb where there was water. Wells were the most prized of possessions and places such as Beersheba, where water was plentiful, invariably became major settlements. Since 1952 Nelson Glueck has identified hundreds of sites in the Negeb that once were occupied. Some of these date back to Palaeolithic times, and many are from the seventh to fifth millennium B.C., the period known as the Neolithic Age. Most of these are along the Way to Shur.

The Book of Joshua mentions twenty-nine cities in the Negeb (Josh. 15:21-32). Most of these are not known today. Best known is Beersheba which often marked the southern boundary of Israel (cf. Judg. 20:1), and continues today to serve as the metropolis and market town of the northern Negeb.

Archaeological work continues at Arad, east of Beersheba. Southeast of Beersheba is Khirbet Ar'arch, one of three Biblical towns which bore the name Aroer.

The °Nabateans, who founded a kingdom in southern Transjordan with its capital at Petra, settled in the Negeb and by carefully conserving its meager water supply brought it to a high point of productivity. The Nabateans were great traders, and they used the overland route from Aqaba to Gaza, through the Negeb, to reach the Mediterranean. Among the towns which date to Nabatean times are Mampsis (Mamshit), Avdat (Abde), Shivta (Subeita), Nessana (Uja-el-Hafir), Rehovot and Halutza.

The Nabateans were succeeded by the Romans and the Byzantines, but the area continued to prosper. Each city had its reservoirs and wells, some of which were adjacent to private homes. Water from wells, rain, and torrential flooding was collected in carefully planned systems of dams and reservoirs. The Church Father Jerome, who studied in Palestine during the fifth century A.D., speaks of the "vines of Halutza" as particularly fruitful.

Excavations at Mamshit have yielded water cisterns and the remains of the city wall and of churches. Avdat, in the central Negeb was settled by the Nabateans during the third century B.C. At first it was merely a road station, but by the first century B.C. a Nabatean temple occupied a site on the north end of the hill. A potter's house, discovered nearby, yielded evidence of the high standards of Nabatean artisans. A layer of ash serves as evidence that the Romans destroyed the Nabatean city, and Avdat was unoccupied for a century and a half. When the Romans rebuilt the city, they erected temples to Zeus and Aphrodite, waterworks, and a bath house. During the Byzantine period the town reached the peak of its development. Among its buildings were two churches, a monastery, a citadel, and a market. The neighborhood was dotted with farms, and its hundreds of caves were used for processing and storing agricultural produce.

Shivta has left remains of a complete city, with streets, reservoirs, and three beautiful churches. At Nassana archaeologists have studied the remains of a fort, a town wall, and two churches. The site also yielded legal, administrative, and religious documents written on papyri during Greek, Roman, and Arabic times.

During the Arabic period the towns of the Negeb gradually sank into insignificance. There was no policy of destruction, but the Arabs had no need of the difficult roads through the Negeb, and the centers of their culture focused upon Baghdad, Damascus, and Cairo. It has not been until recent times when necessity has forced Israel to seek more farm land and a sea route to Africa and the East, that a fresh attempt has been made to rebuild the Negeb and cause the desert to blossom as the rose.

NEO-BABYLONIAN EMPIRE. *See* Chaldeans.

NEO BABYLONIANS. *See* Chaldeans.

NERO. *See* Rome.

NIMROD, NIMRUD. *See* Calah.

NIMRUD DAGH. Nimrud Dagh is a peak in the Antitaurus Mountains of southeastern Turkey, an area known as Commagene in Classical times and as Kummuh(u) to the Assyrians. Here Antiochus I of Commagene (*ca.* 69-34 B.C.) built an elaborate tomb and sanctuary for himself which the inscriptions refer to as a *hierothesion*. A series of colossal sculptures, representing the deified king, his Greek and Persian ancestors, and his tutelary deities, distinguish the site. Together with its architectural and inscriptional remains, they attest to the intermingling of Iranian, Hellenic, and Anatolian traditions at this time and place, in particular to a religious syncretism which included the Hellenistic cult of divine kingship.

BIBLIOGRAPHY. Theresa Goell, "The Excavation of the 'Hierothesion' of Antiochus I of Commagene on Nemrud Dagh (1953-1956)," *BASOR*, 147, 1957, pp. 4-22. Calvin W. McEwan, *The Oriental Origin of Hellenistic Kingship — Studies in Ancient Oriental Civilizations*, XIII, 1934.

NINEVEH. Nineveh, one of the earliest established cities of mankind is a city whose past remained locked in its mound-ruins until archaeologists dug into its buried secrets and linguists deciphered its fascinating clay tablets. The ruins of Nineveh are located along the Tigris River, opposite Mosul, about 220 miles somewhat to the northwest of Baghdad

IVORY PLAQUE, carved in relief with gold and carnelian inlay. Discovered at Nimrud and dated ca. 710 B.C. *Courtesy, Iraq Museum*

at a point where the Tigris is nearly four hundred feet wide in its meandering course. Between the river and the mountainous region where it has its origin there is an undulating plain deeply cut by water courses made by rivulets from the mountains to the river. One of these rivulets flowed through ancient Nineveh and today divides its ruins into two distinct mounds, *Kuyunjik* to the northwest and *Nebi-Yunus* to the southeast. These mounds are located some little distance from the Tigris. Alteration of the river's course centuries past in all probability accounts for their not being nearer the river's eastern bank.

Ancient Nineveh's mound-ruins are located on a level part of the plain near the river. The rivulet running between them is the Khoser. These are the two largest mounds among a number of smaller mounds located within an 1800-acre area circumscribed by a seven and one-half mile brick-rampart in its ruined state varying from ten to twenty feet in height. Austen Henry Layard among the early excavators surveying this area in 1845 reported that these two mounds lay near the western wall which measured 13,600 feet in length. The north wall measured 7000 feet, the south wall 3000 feet, and the east wall 16,000 feet.

*LION SPRINGING AT ASHURBANIPAL during a lion hunt. From Nineveh.
Courtesy, British Museum*

The appearance and construction of these two mounds is similar to those of other Mesopotamian mounds, for example Khorsabad and Nimrud. Kuyunjik, "the castle of Nineveh," is the larger of the two, perhaps one of the largest among the Assyrian tells. From a distance it has the appearance of a natural eminence as it rises abruptly to a height of ninety feet from the level plain on which it stands. It is about a mile long and 1950 feet wide, very steep on all sides from its base to its top; its base covers nearly one hundred acres. Early explorers often found bricks, pieces of pavement, or other ruins protruding from its sides. R. Campbell Thompson has estimated that there are 14,500,000 tons of debris in Kuyunjik and that it would take one thousand men, each sifting 120,000 tons each year, 124 years to remove the whole mound.

Nebi-Yunus, "the prophet of Jonah," is so named because of the tradition that it is the site of the burial place of Jonah. It is considerably smaller than Kuyunjik, some 100 feet in height but measuring only 430 feet east to west and 355 feet north to south. On its surface are a burial ground, a mosque (formerly a Christian church) reputed to contain Jonah's tomb, and a village clustering around the mosque. Kuyunjik has since the beginning of Mesopotamian archaeology been readily available to the archaeologist's spade; it has been the site of amazing, even fabulous, discoveries. Nebi-Yunus, a sacred site as the presumed burial place of Jonah, has been forbidden territory except in two in-stances: Layard negotiated with one of his native overseers to dig underground summer apartments, with the understanding that he would obtain all ancient objects discovered. In 1954 the Director General of Antiquities of Iraq conducted an excavation on Nebi-Yunus with some very interesting finds.

In Jonah 4:11 there is a statement often interpreted to mean that Nineveh's children up to seven years of age numbered 120,000. This is often taken as an indication of a total population around 600,000. Modern exploration with help from ancient historians has provided both direct and indirect support of the Bible concerning the great size of ancient Nineveh.

Nineveh, "an exceeding great city," can best be understood as Greater Nineveh, that is, Nineveh proper with its outlying suburbs and nearby sister cities. The ancient geographer Diodorus Siculus believed that Nineveh was an area the shape of a quadrangle with a perimeter of 480 stadia of sixty miles. Layard apparently influenced by Siculus thought that Nineveh was a large parallelogram, its corners marked by Nimrod (southwest), Kuyunjik (northwest), Khorsabad (northeast), and Karamles (southeast). The length of the four sides of this parallelogram totalled nearly the sixty miles of the ancient geographer.

Others since Layard have proposed revisions of the area involved but have retained the idea of Greater Nineveh. André Parrot speaks of Greater Nineveh in terms of the Assyrian Triangle (*Nineveh and the Old*

416

Testament, p. 86): Nineveh proper (Kuyunjik and Nebi-Yunus) to Khorsabad, a distance of fourteen miles; Khorsabad to Nimrud (Calah; Gen. 10:11), twenty-six miles; and Nimrud to Nineveh, twenty-three miles. Parrot then estimates that Nineveh's population was around 174,000, Nimrud's around 65,000. He concludes that "the figure of Jonah 4:11 is indirectly confirmed." Karl Friedrich Keil (Keil-Delitzsch Commentary on Jonah 4:11; p. 416) though not discussing the so-called Assyrian Triangle makes it even clearer how 600,000 could well have been the total population of Greater Nineveh.

Nineveh, once a great thriving city, was completely destroyed and passed into oblivion. Although difficult to comprehend, Nahum's prophecy, "Nineveh is laid waste" (Nahum 3:7), and Zephaniah's, "And he . . will make Nineveh a desolation, and dry like the wilderness" (Zeph. 2:13), were fulfilled to the letter. Destruction was so complete that its location was soon forgotten by nearly everyone.

Since 1820 Nineveh has been intermittently the place of exploration and excavation. Claudius James Rich, resident of the East India Company at Baghdad, visited many sites around 1820. It is to him that credit is given for a description and plan of the ruins of Nineveh.

Paul Émile Botta, whose interest was aroused by Rich's report, arrived in Mosul in 1842 as French vice-consul. His appointment was understood in part to be archaeological. Disappointed with meager finds after three months of labor at Kuyunjik, he went to Khorsabad where he discovered the palace of Sargon II. Botta's archaeological career ended in 1848 when he was transfered from Mosul to Jerusalem and then to Tripoli.

Austen Henry Layard, an Englishman of Huguenot descent, was among those whose interest and enthusiasm for Mesopotamian archaeology had been inspired by Botta. He arrived at Mosul in 1845, sponsored by a few friends. He dug at Nimrud, south of Mosul along the Tigris, and discovered a palace similar to the one found by Botta at Khorsabad. As a result he was commissioned by the trustees of the British Museum to work for them. In 1849 he excavated for several months at Kuyunjik, uncovering parts of Sennacherib's palace.

Since 1852, after a period of fierce competition between French and British archaeologists, Nineveh has been excavated for the most part by British and British-authorized archaeologists. Those who have subsequently excavated there have been H. Rassam (1852-54), Boutcher and Loftice (1854-55), George Smith (1872-73, 1876), H. Rassam (1878-82), and E. W. Budge (1888-91). In 1903 L. W. King arrived at Nineveh, to be joined later by R. Campbell Thompson. Together they attempted to establish meaningful order to what had been excavated in a very haphazard and unsystematic way. They endeavored to associate previously-excavated materials with their proper architectural framework and archaeological background.

In 1927 R. Campbell Thompson returned as director of an expedition, assisted by Hutchinson, Hamilton, and Mallowan. Applying recently developed methods they carried on their research from 1927 to 1932. They carefully examined areas that had already been excavated, making stratigraphic soundings, beginning on the surface and going back layer by layer through Assyrian times, into proto-historic times, and to virgin soil. In 1954 the Director of Antiquities of Iraq undertook a small excavation at Nebi-Yunus.

Nineveh and the Bible. The ninety or more feet of debris of Kuyunjik when excavated stratigraphically by R. Campbell Thompson and his staff was found to be the entombment of Nineveh's remains which extended from 612 B.C. back to proto-historic times — between 4000 and 5000 B.C. At many points throughout this long period of time Nineveh's history touches Biblical history either directly or indirectly.

Nineveh is mentioned in the Genesis Table of Nations along with Calah and other cities as one of the towns Nimrod the first empire-builder founded (Gen. 10:10-12). The Bible presents Nineveh in the land of Babylon and Assyria, among the cities built by early man. This has been supported remarkably well through identification and exploration of the mounds which have been the entombment of even the earliest remains of Nineveh and of other ancient Mesopotamian cities.

In assigning dates ancient historians in some instances have suggested that Nimrod (or perhaps Ashur) built Nineveh around 2230 B.C. This however is too late from the standpoint of what is now known about

Nineveh's very early beginnings. The earliest man-made materials of Nineveh were recovered at the bottom of a twenty by fifteen meter pit dug off the northwest corner of the Ishtar temple on the mound of Kuyunjik. These materials have been chiefly fragments of a coarse, poorly-fired, light-gray, unburnished ware with some incised markings — mainly small gouges in parallel or in herringbone patterns. In addition, incised ware with simple painted designs along with some black and some red painted ware has been found.

This pottery has been analyazed as Neolithic, Hassuna phase, represented best by materials found at °Hassuna, a stratified site not far from Mosul, and at Nineveh. It goes back to some time between 4000 and 5000 B.C. and it is the earliest Neolithic pottery to be found, excepting perhaps at Jericho. In giving a general description of the culture represented by Hassuna ware, Ann Perkins (Comparative Archaeology of Early Mesopotamia, p. 15) states that it was a Neolithic village culture, of a time of domestic plants and animals, of clay houses, and of considerable technical development. Burials with objects suggest some concept of afterlife.

Written sources in particular make it clear that Nineveh was dedicated at an early time to the goddess Ishtar (or Inanna), the goddess of love and war and venerated particularly as a warrior. It is this which per-

haps explains Nineveh's blood-thirstiness and lust for conquest.

A °Cappadocian Tablet of the twenty-first century B.C. is one of the earliest sources mentioning Nineveh. It was found at Kultepe and when deciphered was recognized as a part of the correspondence carried on between Semitic merchants colonized there and Assyrians at ancient Ashur. The name Nineveh appears on this tablet as an ideogram, a fish in the middle of a city. This is understood to be an allusion to Ishtar, the goddess of Nineveh, whose emblem was the figure of a fish.

The Code of the °Hammurabi (1728-1683) also mentions Nineveh. In the prologue of the Code, Hammurabi is described as "the king, who made the name of Inanna glorious in Nineveh. . . ."

An inscription of Shamshi-Adad of Ancient °Ashur (1748-1716) shows that Ishtar-worship at Nineveh goes back to the twenty-third century B.C. This inscription refers to the ruinous state of the Temple of Inanna in the land of E-mash-mash (ideogram for Nineveh), and states that this old temple was built by Manishtusu (2295-2281 B.C.), son of Sharrukin (i.e. Sargon), king of Akkad.

Excavated materials supplement these sources. Remains of an Ishtar temple were discovered at Kuyunjik, along with those of a temple dedicated to the god Nabu. Nabu was the god of writing and of the arts and sciences. Devotion to him is strikingly illus

ASHURBANIPAL AND HIS QUEEN *feasting in their garden at Nineveh. Courtesy,* British Museum

trated by the tens of thousands of texts found at Nineveh.

Nineveh always held a place of prominence during the long history of the many Assyrian dynasties who ruled from it and several other cities for more than two thousand years. Along with Nimrud and Ashur it was intermittently the palace-city of Early, Middle, and Late Assyrian kings: Shalmaneser I (1265-1236), Tiglath-pileser I (1116-1078), Adadnirari II (912-892), Tukultininurta II (891-885), and Ashurnazirpal II (884-860). Its splendor equalled that of Ashur and of Nimrud and was not outdone by another royal city until Sargon II (722-706) built by Dur Sharrukin (Sargonsburg or Khorsabad), an entirely new palace-city. However, Sennacherib (705-682) soon restored it to first place among Assyrian cities, making it a city of great splendor and beauty.

Though not permanently the capital city until the time of Sennacherib, Nineveh was nevertheless an important city of Assyrian rulers who threatened, imposed tribute, and finally overthrew Samaria of the Northern Kingdom (Israel). Annals and inscriptions of these rulers for over a century rather strangely refer to Israelite rulers as *Bit Humria* (the House of Omri); further their mention of names and descriptions of events coincide at many points with Scripture passages, especially those of II Kings.

*Sennacherib may rightly be called the mightiest Assyrian ruler. He was apparently a vigorous, ambitious, and forceful person. He strove diligently to promote himself as a builder, warrior, and patron of letters. He succeeded famously along all three lines.

As a builder he made Nineveh, his royal palace, an architectural wonder. Layard found its remains in 1847 and cleared them extensively from 1849-51. His palace was no doubt breathtaking to behold in both its size and its impressive art work. It was built on a platform well above the level of the city. Marble stairs lead up on all four sides to magnificent entrances decorated with colossal stone figures, such as human-headed bulls and winged sphinxes. The palace itself was an enromous building. It had two large halls 40 feet wide and 180 feet long which led into its interior made up of a number of large courts and more than seventy spacious rooms. Its walls were beautifully adorned with sculptured slabs; it has

been estimated that it contained 9,880 feet of decorated walls. Further, the winged bulls of ten to thirty tons each and large lion-sphinxes were a prominent aspect of the decor. In one part of the palace these bulls and sphinxes framed or guarded at least twenty-seven portals. In these and other respects Sennacherib's palace was a veritable art gallery. It approached, if not equalled, the great palace-temple of Karnak in size and splendor.

In further pursuit of his building interest, Sennacherib surrounded his city with an impressive wall. Fifteen strong, bastion gateways led from the main city within to the outlying suburbs and to the other cities of Greater Nineveh. He also built a thirty-mile *aqueduct through hills and over plains in order to bring fresh water into his city. These and other activities provided the basis for Sennacherib's boast of one inscription that he, Sennacherib . . . "king of the universe, king of Assyria" had quarried limestone for mighty protecting bull-colassi, and had gathered many other materials for his magnificent residence.

His many military successes are known from the account of numerous campaigns on clay cylinders or prisms. The Taylor Prism of the British Museum, considered the final edition of his annals, gives an account of eight or more military campaigns. It tells of his moves against Merodach-baladan of Babylonia who rebelled against him, the same Merodach-baladan who sent emissaries to King Hezekiah (see Isa. 39; II Kings 20:12-19) — Berodach-baladan. (The different initial labial is due perhaps to dittography.)

The Taylor Prism related how Sennacherib attacked Lachish, also illustrated by a sculpture which shows him receiving spoils of war from prisoners of the captured city (cf. II Kings 18:13, 17). It gives details of the siege of Jerusalem and of the booty demanded of Hezekiah. A number of these details are the same as those of the Bible (II Kings 18:13-25), with obvious differences. The catastrophe which Sennacherib experienced at Jerusalem, perhaps after a second attack not made clear in the Bible, is understandably not mentioned in his annals. After this crushing defeat he returned to Nineveh and was murdered by two sons older than his favorite, Esarhaddon,

ASHURBANIPAL'S SOLDIERS *lead away prisoners of war. Four women captives
are seated in a cart with spoked-wheels. From the palace of Ashurbanipal at Nineveh. Courtesy, the Louvre*

whom he had designated as his successor
(cf. II Kings 19:36-37).

Sennacherib's temple of Nabu demonstrates
his interest in letters. In the spring of 1851
Layard and Rassam were excavating his
palace. They had occasionally come across
cuneiform tablets or fragments. In the course
of excavating two rooms, one leading into
the other, they found clay tablets on the
floor of these rooms piled to a height of a foot
or more. Many were complete while many
others were broken, apparently being crushed
when the roof and upper part of the building caved in due to fire. These rooms were
part of Sennacherib's temple to Nabu; the
tablets were a portion of his royal library
dedicated to Nabu whom the Assyrians understood was the creator of the arts and
sciences and who knew all the mysteries of
literature and of writing. The thousands of
tablets of this temple became a part of
the valuable materials sent back to the British
Museum.

The noteworthy successors of Sennacherib
at Nineveh were Esarhaddon and Ashurbanipal (the Osnapper of Ezra 4:10). Esarhaddon's palace was discovered during the

brief excavations of Layard at Nebi-Yunus.
As a military leader he could proudly
proclaim that he was "King of the kings
of Egypt." Ashurbanipal conducted many
military campaigns with success but he is
remembered mainly for his cultural interests, particularly for his great library. Rassam and his men cleared the "lion-hunt"
gallery and then proceeded to clear the way
through a doorway into a high-vaulted room.
In both the gallery room and the high-vaulted
room they found the floor piled high with
stacks of clay tablets. They had come upon
the largest part of *Ashurbanipal's library,
some tens of thousands or more copies (perhaps more than 100,000). Among these were
the Babylonian account of creation and of a
great flood.

The fall of Nineveh and shortly thereafter
the complete collapse of Assyria came rather
quickly. Weak rulers followed Ashurbanipal on the throne in Nineveh. At the same
time a descendant of Merodach-baladan,
Nabopolassar, a Chaldean, rose to power in
Babylonia. Nabopolassar ruled from 625 to
605 B.C. According to the Babylonian Chronicle, known as B. M. 21901, Nineveh fell

in Nabopolassar's fourteenth year. Babylonians, Medes, and Scythians joined forces to attack and to besiege the great city of Nineveh; after withstanding siege from May to August it fell. This occurred in 612 B.C. Its spoils were divided among its conquerors. Another king tried to hold on at Haran but he too was defeated by his enemies. Assyria with once mighty monarchs in once fabulous cities ceased to exist.

BIBLIOGRAPHY. Joseph Bonomi, *Nineveh and Its Palaces,* Ingram, Cooke & Co., 1853. C. Gadd, *The Fall of Nineveh,* 1923. Austen H. Layard, *Discoveries in the Ruins of Nineveh and Babylon,* G. P. Putnam and Co., New York, 1853. Daniel David Luckenbill, *The Annals of Sennacherib,* The University of Chicago Press, Chicago, 1924. A. Leo Oppenheim, "Babylonian and Historical Texts," *Ancient Near Eastern Texts,* ed. James B. Pritchard, Princeton University Press, Princeton, 1953. Ann Perkins, *The Comparative Archaeology of Early Mesopotamia,* Studies in Ancient Oriental Civilization, No. 25, The University of Chicago Press, Chicago, 1949. André Parrot, *Nineveh and the Old Testament,* translated by B. E. Hooke, SCM Press, London, 1955.

NIPPUR. Nippur (modern Nuffar) in north central Babylonia, one hundred miles south of Baghdad, was the cultural and religious center of the ancient Sumerians. Enlil of Nippur was the chief god in the Sumerian pantheon, and his temple, the E-kur ("Mountain House") was the leading shrine of Sumer. A Sumerian academy which met at Nippur gave diligent study to the position of Enlil, his wife Ninlil, and their son Ninurta in the religious life of the land. With the decline of Sumerian power, however, Nippur lost its prestige and by the time of Hammurabi, °Babylon became the dominant city in Mesopotamia. The site of Nippur was not abandoned, however, until Parthian times.

Late in the nineteenth century, Americans became interested in Mesopotamian archaeology and their attention was drawn to the site then known as Nuffar. After a preliminary survey (1884-85) an expedition set out in 1888 under the direction of John P. Peters of Philadelphia, an Episcopal clergyman and professor of Hebrew. After two seasons the work was suspended, but it began again in 1893 under the direction of Peters with John H. Hayes as field director. When Peters had to relinquish the work due to new pastoral responsibilities, Herman V. Hilprecht of the University of Pennsylvania took charge. The work under Hilprecht ended in 1900,

but the University Museum of Philadelphia and the Oriental Institute of Chicago resumed excavations at Nippur in 1948 and conducted excavations every other year from 1949 to 1958 under the leadership of Donald E. McCown.

The excavations have produced evidence that Nippur was one of the oldest centers of Mesopotamian civilization, founded by 'Ubaid people around 4000 B.C. Archaeologists have given particular attention to the excavation of the Sumerian temple known as the E-kur, its zigguarat, and the temple complex with the scribal quarters. Another temple, to the goddess Inanna (Semitic Ishtar) has been excavated as well.

Among the 30,000 to 40,000 clay tablets discovered at Nippur are many valuable literary texts. One of these gives the Sumerian account of the flood, a version of the flood story which antedates that contained in the °Gilgamesh Epic written in Semitic Akkadian. There is also a fragment of a Sumerian creation story, and numerous votive inscriptions on vases, bowls, bricks, door sockets, and cuneiform tablets.

A valuable addition to our knowledge of Jewish life in Babylon following the exile is the collection of texts forming the archives of the Murashi Sons, a Jewish mercantile house doing business during the reigns of the Persian kings Artaxerxes I (464-423 B.C.; and Darius II (423-404 B.C.). These texts show how Jews were able to prosper in business during Persian times, and they supplement the picture of Persian Jewry given

in the books of Nehemiah and Esther. In the book of Nehemiah we read of a Jew who served in the Persian court, and Esther is the story of a Jewess who actually became queen. In general the Jews were highly respected by the Persians, and they had many opportunities in government and in private business.

One of the clay tablets from Nippur contains a map of the city, dated to 1500 B.C. The River Chebar, mentioned as the stream on whose banks the exiles built their city of Tell Abib (Ezek. 1:1,3), is probably to be identified with the Grand Canal which left the Euphrates above Babylon, and flowed past Nippur before re-entering the Euphrates. One of the business documents from Nippur mentions a stream bearing the name *nari kabari* which would be translated into Hebrew as the equivalent of our River Chebar.

BIBLIOGRAPHY. Thomas Fish, "The Sumerian City Nippur in the Period of the Third Dynasty of Ur," *Iraq*, V, 1938, pp. 157-179.

NISIBIS. *See* Habor.

NO. *See* Thebes.

NOPH. *See* Memphis.

NUBIA, NUBIANS. Nubia was the land south of the First Cataract of the Nile at *Aswan. At times it extended as far south as Khartoum in the Sudan. Nubia was a land rich in gold (from which it received its name), good quality stone, hard wood, and large cattle. It was the gateway from Egypt to central Africa from which came ivory, ebony, strange animals, and pygmies.

The Nubian people were less civilized than the Egyptians but they were good soldiers. Egyptians colonized and exploited Nubia, but in the process the Nubians were Egyptianized, adopting Egyptian religion, customs, and writing. In a time of Egyptian weakness kings of Nubia conquered the lower Nile Valley and imposed their rule on Egypt for about a century, from about 750 B.C. to 650 B.C. This dynasty is known as Kushite, after the name Kush which the Egyptians gave to the Sudan or, following the Greek tradition, Ethiopian. Taharqa, Biblical Tirhakah, of this Ethiopian dynasty led his Egyptian forces against Sennacherib of Assyria (II Kings 19:9; Isa. 37:9), but was unable effectively to resist him.

NUZI. Excavations at Yorghan Tepe, twelve miles southwest of modern Kirkuk, were conducted by the University Museum (University of Pennsylvania) in cooperation with the American Schools of Oriental Research, the Harvard Semitic Museum and the Iraq Museum from 1925 to 1931 under the direction of Edward Chiera. A number of business documents and a clay map discovered by Chiera date from the Akkadian period (*see* Sargon of Akkad) when the town was known as Gasur. The major discoveries, however, date from the middle of the second millennium B.C. when the site was under *Hurrian domination and bore the name of Nuzi (or Nuzu). More than twenty thousand cuneiform documents from this period give us an insight into four or five generations of Nuzi life during the fifteenth and fourteenth centuries B.C. enabling us to trace the fortunes of its leading citizens.

The Nuzi tablets are written in *Akkadian which was the lingua franca of the Near East during the *Amarna Age. The Hurrian scribes, however, occasionally use Hurrian words with which they were more familiar. As a result the Nuzi tablets are a source of information concerning the Hurrian as well as the Akkadian language.

The Bible student is interested in the Nuzi tablets because they are a primary source for information concerning life in northern Mesopotamia, a district where the Biblical patriarchs lived for a time and to which they sent to find suitable wives for their sons. The customs and values of the Nuzi area, not far from Biblical Paddan-Aram, find reflection in the Biblical stories of the patriarchs.

The modern mind would have difficulty understanding Sarah's action in suggesting that Abraham have sexual relations with Hagar, her slave. The Nuzi tablets present us with striking parallels. Marriage contracts make it clear that no marriage was considered satisfactory if it did not issue in the birth of children. Nuzi texts specify that a barren wife must provide her husband with a slave girl through whom he may have children. Several of the contracts specify that the wife must come from Lulluland, in the mountains to the north, where the best slaves were obtained.

The Bible relates how Sarah presented

BRONZE COAT OF MAIL FROM NUZI
dating from the second millennium B.C.
Courtesy, Iraq Museum

her Egyptian slave, Hagar, to Abraham in the hope that he might have children by her (Gen. 16:1-2). That this is not an isolated event is indicated by the fact that Rachel, concerned about her own lack of fertility, offered her slave Bilhah to Jacob (Gen. 30:1-4). Leah subsequently offered her slave Zilpah because of her desire for additional children (Gen. 30:9). The children in each instance are reckoned to the mistress.

The Nuzi tablets indicate an awareness of the problems that arise when the wife becomes jealous of the slave girl and her children. The law protected the slave and her children under such circumstances by insisting that the child could not be expelled from his father's household. It was only with great reluctance that Abraham agreed to Sarah's demand that Ishmael be sent away (Gen. 21:9-14).

One of the texts contains an interesting parallel to Esau's sale of his birthright to Jacob (Gen. 25:29-34). At Nuzi, a brother sold his birthright for three sheep.

Adoption was a common practice at Nuzi, where a childless couple would adopt a freeborn person or a slave to care for them in old age, to provide a proper burial, and,

eventually to inherit the family property. Abraham seems to have adopted his servant Eliezer of Damascus (Gen. 15:1-4), yet he still hoped for a son of his own.

At times a natural son is born to a couple after they have adopted a child. Nuzi customs anticipated this eventuality by decreeing that an adopted son would be subordinate to a natural son in such instances. The birth of Ishmael removed Eliezer from his position as chief heir, even as subsequently the birth of Isaac to Abraham's wife gave him priority over Ishmael, the child of a slave girl.

A man with daughters but no sons frequently adopted the daughter's husband. When Jacob first appeared in Laban's household there is no hint that Laban had sons. Twenty years later, however, sons of Laban were resentful of Jacob (Gen. 31:1) with the result that Jacob determined to take his family and possessions and return to Canaan. Laban had evidently adopted Jacob, and during the early years of their association, Jacob's services had been indispensable to Laban. After Laban had sons of his own, friction began to be felt.

When Jacob fled from Laban's household,

his wife Rachel stole her father's teraphim, or household gods (Gen. 31:34). At Nuzi the household gods are the rightful possession of the head of the family. They serve as a kind of title deed and evidence of priority. One of the tablets reads:

The adoption tablet of Nashwi son of Arshenni. He adopted Wullu son of Puhishenni. As long as Nashwi lives, Wullu shall be the heir. Should Nashwi beget a son, the latter shall divide equally with Wullu, but only Nashwi's son shall take Nashwi's gods. But if there be no son of Nashwi, then Wullu shall take Nashwi's gods. And Nashwi had given his daughter Nuhuya as a wife to Wullu. And if Wullu takes another wife, he forfeits Nashwi's land and buildings. Whoever breaks the contract shall pay one mina of silver and one mina of gold.

The parallel Biblical account implies that Rachel, Laban's daughter and Jacob's wife, wanted to preserve for her husband the position of head of the household, a position legitimized by the possession of the household gods. Knowing that her brothers would claim headship over Laban's household, Rachel stole the teraphim to secure the chief inheritance for her husband.

At Nuzi, as in many ancient societies, the patriarch of a family might declare his desires concerning the division of his property when on his deathbed. A Nuzi tablet tells of a young man named Tarmiya who sought to maintain his rights against two brothers who tried to prevent his marriage. Tarmiya reports:

My father, Huya, was sick and lying in bed and my father seized my hand and spoke thus to me: "My other older sons have taken wives but thou hast not taken a wife, and I give Zuluishtar to thee as wife."

Cyrus H. Gordon observes that this follows the pattern of Biblical blessings in that it is (a) an oral will, (b) with legal validity, (c) made to a son by a dying father.

The spoken word was accorded the utmost sanctity in the Bible. Even though Jacob had secured his blessing through trickery, Isaac considered himself powerless to effect any change (Gen. 27:35-37). Esau was deprived of the blessing that would normally have been his because Isaac had uttered his word of blessing to Jacob. Later, Jacob specifically designated Judah as his chief heir with the words, "Judah, may thy brothers pay thee homage. . . . may thy

father's sons bow down to thee" (Gen. 49:8).

Adoption customs were often used at Nuzi as a means of circumventing the law. In Nuzi, as in Israel, transfer of property had to take place within the family unit. Israel, too, had a provision whereby sales of property were made conditional on the return of the property to the original owner at the Jubilee year, which recurred on a fifty year cycle (Lev. 25:13-17). A wealthy individual from Nuzi used adoption as a device for securing large amounts of property. For a stated price, the landowner would adopt the person desiring the land, and would thereby become the legal heir of the owner. Property could thus be transferred within the family.

The practice of °levirate marriage was enforced at Nuzi as well as in the Bible (Deut. 25:5-10). In a Nuzi tablet the father specified, in purchasing a wife for his son, that in the event his son died, the girl was to be married to another of his sons.

Infractions of the moral law were met with strict justice at Nuzi, as in the Bible. Hosea (2:4-5) speaks of the treatment meted out to a faithless wife: "Take action against your mother, for she is not my wife and I am not her husband . . . lest I have her stripped naked and set her as on the day she was born." A Nuzi tablet states: "If (my wife) Wishirwi goes to (another) husband and lives (with him), my sons shall strip off the clothes of my wife and drive (her) out of my house." The Biblical expression, "She is not my wife and I am not her husband" is a divorce formula, tantamount to "I disown her."

Several of the Nuzi texts mention a people termed °Habiru. The Habiru at Nuzi were people who entered the service of the king or voluntarily sold themselves into slavery to some other individual. One text reads: "Maridiglat, a Habiru from the land of Assyria, on his own initiative has entered (the house of) Tehiptilla, the son of Puhi-shenni, as a slave."

A Habiru woman is mentioned in another text:

Sin-balti, a Habiru woman, on her own initiative has entered the house of Tehiptilla as a slave. Now if Sin-balti defaults and goes into the house of another, Tehiptilla shall pluck out the eyes of Sin-balti and sell her.

Both the Bible and the Nuzi texts mention two kinds of slavery. A slave may contract to serve his master for a predetermined period of time. This was a means of escaping poverty (cf. Lev. 25:39-46). A slave may, however, elect to serve his master for life (Exod. 21:1-6). In the Nuzi texts, a man who sells himself into temporary servitude must provide a replacement and pay the substitute when the time comes for him to leave his master's employ.

BIBLIOGRAPHY. Richard F. S. Starr, *Nuzi*, Vol. 1., Text. Harvard University Press, Cambridge, 1939. Richard F. S. Starr, *Nuzi,* Vol. 2., Plates and Plans, Harvard University Press, Cambridge, 1937. Francis Rue Steele, *Nuzi Real Estate Transactions,* American Oriental Society, New Haven, 1943. E. A. Speiser, "Notes on Recently Discovered Nuzi Texts," *JAOS,* LV, 1935, pp. 432-443. C. H. Gordon, "Nuzi Tablets Relating to Women," *Miscellanea Orientalia Dedicata Antonio Deimel,* Pontifical Biblical Institute, Rome, 1935; C. H. Gordon, "Nuzi Tablets Relating to Theft," *Orientalia,* V, 1936, pp. 305-330. C. H. Gordon, "Biblical Customs in the Nuzu Tablets," *BA* III (1940).

NYMPHAEUM. A nymphaeum was originally a building dedicated to the nymphs, the daughters of Zeus who animated all of nature. Each spring, mountain, river, and tree had its own nymphs which were venerated in woods and caves, and especially at springs. The simple, rustic nymphaea of early times gave way to ornate, ostentatious structures under the Romans.

O

OCCUPATIONS. Man never ceased being a food gatherer, for hunting and fishing continued as important occupations, but with the development of °agriculture, it became possible to free a large part of the work force for occupations other than food producing, with the result that the great cultures of the Near East developed.

Food producing itself developed a number of specialized occupations.

Fishermen. Fish was one of the cheapest and most abundant articles of food in Bible lands. In fishing we find the use of (1) the casting net, used by a fisherman standing on the shore or wading in water; (2) the drag net, which was worked from two boats to insure a large quantity of fish; (3) the casting hook and line; (4) the spear, used from the shore or from a boat to spear fish.

Millers. The women of the household — mothers, daughters, sisters, and maidservants (Exod. 11:5) — usually served as millers. In most ancient times grain was rubbed in a saddle-shaped rock or quern with a small hand stone. We later find heavy grinding stones, one and a half feet in diameter, used to mill grain. In large communities a professional miller operated large millstones turned by donkey power. Samson was forced to function in place of such an animal at Gaza (Judg. 16:21).

Bakers. Ancient villages often had a public baker who kindled his oven with quick brush fuel and baked the dough (along with other food) brought to him by children on trays balanced on their heads.

Cattle-breeders. In both Egypt and Mesopotamia the herdsman and shepherd occupied an important part in the economy. Theirs was an independent type of life — often wild and indifferent to law — with the result that the more civilized and refined elements of the population looked down on them.

Confectioners. The palace staff of kings in Egypt and Mesopotamia included candy-makers as well as pastry-cooks. Fruit-and-honey cakes were in great demand.

In the construction of temples, palaces, and houses a variety of building trades developed.

Brickmakers and bricklayers. In Mesopotamia, where stone is rare, the common building material was brick which might be fired in a kiln, but more frequently was simply dried in the sun. Brickmakers and stonemasons often travelled from country to country with their measuring-rods, plumb lines, leveling lines, hammers, hoisting ropes, chisels, trowels and baskets for removing earth.

Stonemasons. In Egypt and Palestine, where stone was abundant, quarrying and stone-setting were honored occupations. When the Jerusalem Temple was built, stone was cut at the quarry and brought to the Temple site ready to set up. Mason's tools included the mallet, level, plumb line, square,

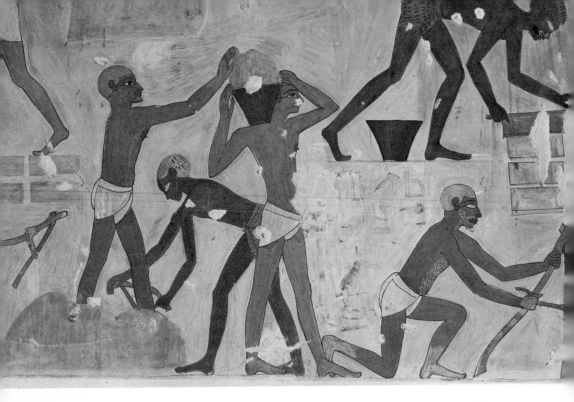

BRICKMAKING in 18th Dynasty Egypt, ca. 1450 B.C. From the tomb of Rehkmire,
Vizier of Upper Egypt. Courtesy, Metropolitan Museum of Art

A MODEL BAKERY from
Middle Kingdom Egypt.
Courtesy, Oriental Institute

AN OLIVE PRESS
FROM CAPERNAUM.
Courtesy, Jerry Vardaman

and chisel. Hammers were used to drive chisels.

Carpenters. Carpenters in antiquity used tools comparable to those of today. Earliest saws consisted of flint teeth with serrated edges mounted in a frame. Other saws were like knives of bronze and iron. The carpenter's hammer was usually of heavy stone, sometimes drilled with a hole for inserting a handle. Palestinian carpenters made doors, window frames, and roof beams for houses of stone or mudbrick. Simple furniture such as stools and low tables, along with yokes and plows were often produced. Egyptian carpenters also trimmed palaces, fashioned mummy cases and constructed boats. *See* Transportation.

Other trades included:

Weavers and dyers. The weaving of tent cloth and garments was frequently the function of the women of the family, but commercial guilds of specialists developed. At °Tell Beit Mirsim excavators have discovered evidence of an elaborate setup for cloth production. Remnants of a dyeing establishment have been found at °Ugarit where Canaanites extracted the dye from murex shellfish.

Potters. See Ceramics.

Miners and smelters. Gold, silver, copper, and iron were mined in the ancient Near East. Mines were operated in the Arabah, south of the Dead Sea, and smelting operations carried on at °Ezion-geber. Egyptians mined copper and turquoise in the Sinai Peninsula. *See* Serabit el-Khadem, Metallurgy.

Traveling smiths. Kenites traveled from

ASSYRIAN FISHING with a line. He stands in a pond with a basket of fish on his back. From Nineveh. *Courtesy, British Museum*

place to place with their asses, bellows, and tools and lived by their craftsmanship. *See* Metallurgy.

Scribes. Since writing was an art known to but few, the scribe was looked upon as the man of education and distinction. He copied legal documents, wrote letters and contracts, and served in general as a public secretary. He could usually be found near the city gate, which served as the city hall. Scribes also wrote religious texts and, in New Testament times the scribe is the authority on Biblical teaching. This ideal was often missed as the New Testament states, when the scribes were more concerned with the minutia of legalism than with the spirit of Scripture.

Priests. In all of the lands of the Near East, priests served as ministrants in the temples. Possessing allegedly supernatural powers they counseled kings on military matters, interpreting the omens such as bird flights and the markings on an animal's liver. Since offerings were brought to the temple in kind, the priests often supervised a temple complex which included storage rooms, manufacturing facilities, and a variety of commercial ventures.

ODEUM. In ancient Greece, and later in Rome, the odeum was a small theater, roofed over, in which poets and musicians submitted their work to the public and contended for prizes. The odeum was smaller than the dramatic theater.

FIRST CENTURY OSSUARY from Azor. Courtesy, Israel Department of Antiquities

OSSUARIES. Ossuaries are small chests used as receptacles for the bones of the dead. Bones were gathered and placed in ossuaries after the flesh had decayed. Hundreds of ossuaries dating from early Roman times have been found in Palestine. Most of them are rectangular limestone chests varying in size from twenty to thirty inches in length, twelve to twenty inches in width, and ten to sixteen inches in depth. The outside was decorated with rosettes and other decorations and often inscribed with a name in Hebrew, Aramaic, or Greek.

Ossuaries have been found in both caves and tombs in the vicinity of Jerusalem. Tombs were often constructed with small niches large enough to hold a single ossuary. A clay ossuary in the Palestine Archaeological Museum in Jerusalem is fashioned in the form of a miniature house. This is thought to date from the Chalcolithic Age (*ca.* 4000-3300 B.C.).

OSTRACON, OSTRACA. Ostraca are pottery fragments which were used as an inexpensive writing material because of their abundance and the high cost of papyrus. Potsherds, inscribed with ink, were used for letters, receipts, and school texts. Important discoveries of ostraca were made at °Lachish and °Samaria.

OXYRHYNCHUS PAPYRI. In the last decade of the nineteenth century and the first decade of the twentieth century numerous papyrus documents have been recovered from the sands of Egypt. One of the most productive sites to be excavated was Oxyrhynchus, the modern Behnesa, located on the edge of the western desert about 120 miles south of Cairo and about 10 miles west of the Nile. The first excavation of this site took place in 1897, principally under the direction of B. P. Grenfell and A. S. Hunt. These men and others have found many thousands of manuscripts and fragments which are still in the process of being published. These have been appearing in a series of volumes under the title *Oxyrhynchus Papyri*, the first volume appearing in 1898, and the latest (Volume 29) in 1963. The total number of items to be published in these twenty-nine volumes is 2506. Most of these are dated in the first nine centuries of our era.

I. *The Contents.* Some of the papyri contain Biblical texts: OP 208 and 1781 = P5 (third century); OP 1228 = P22 (third century); OP 1355 = P27 (third century); OP 1598 = P30 (third century); OP 2 = P1 (third century); OP 1596 = P28 (fourth century); OP 657 = P13 (late third century); OP 209 = P10 (fourth century); OP 1008 = P15 (fourth century); OP 1227 = P21 (fifth century); OP 2383 = P69 (third century); OP 1229 = P23 (fourth century); OP 1171 = P20 (third century); OP 1009 = P16 (fourth century); OP 1079 = P18 (late third century). Most of these are fragments containing only portions of the Biblical text. Four papyri contain collections of sayings of Jesus not found in the canonical gospels: OP 1; OP 654; OP 655; OP 840 (*see below*). A large portion of the papyri are non-literary documents dealing with private and public affairs. The private documents include such things as personal letters, receipts, wills, invitations, memoranda, agreements, accounts and lists. The public documents consist of edicts, orders, petitions, judicial business, codes, and regulations, contracts, nominations and appointments, public announcements, and official acts and declarations. The collection also includes many literary papyri containing portions of Greek poetry and prose from all periods. Fragments of the works of classical authors have added considerable new material for the textual studies of these works. Some of these fragments contain works previously unknown; others provide a text much older than the existing manuscripts. Because of the great variety of material, the Oxyrhynchus Papyri

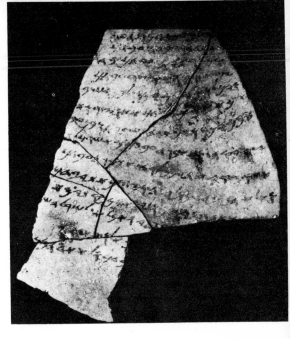

HEBREW LETTER on ostraca, from the time of Christ. Courtesy, Israel Department of Antiquity

are of interest to the classicist, the historian, the theologian, the economist, and the sociologist.

II. *Significance of the Oxyrhynchus Papyri for Biblical Studies.* The discovery of the numerous papyrus documents in Egypt in the last seventy years has brought about a revolution in the field of New Testament studies. The following are some of the areas affected by this remarkable archaeological contribution.

A. Textual Criticism. The Oxyrhynchus Papyri have not contributed material commensurate in size and antiquity with that of the °Chester Beatty Papyri or the °Bodmer Papyri, but numerous fragments from the third and fourth centuries have provided valuable data for specific passages in many of the New Testament books.

B. Sayings of Jesus. Four of the Oxyrhynchus Papyri contain sayings ascribed to Jesus by the simple formula, "Jesus says . . ." These are OP 1, OP 654, OP 655, and OP 840. The first three have been assigned to the third century. OP 1 contains seven sayings of Jesus, six of which are quite legible. Three of these are modifications of canonical sayings, and three are entirely new. OP 654 was more difficult to reconstruct, and it contains sayings only remotely related to the canonical sayings. OP 655 contains expansions of material in Matthew 6 and Luke 11. OP 840 is an unusual document dating from about A.D. 400. It reports a dialogue between Jesus and a chief priest in the temple regarding the matter of purification and defilement. It has no parallel in the New Testament. Jeremias accepts it as authentic, but Schürer, Grant, and Freedman reject it.

The discovery of these collections of sayings confirmed the opinion held for some time before that in the early church there were *logia* of Jesus in circulation in addition to those found in the Gospels. The relationship of these to the *logia* of Papias is still debated, but these collections may well have been the source of the *agrapha* found in Acts 20:35 and I Thessalonians 4:16f.

Renewed interest in the Oxyrhynchus sayings was aroused by the discovery and publication of the Gospel of Thomas in 1959 as part of the large Gnostic library found in 1946 near °Nag Hammadi (ancient Chenoboskion). The Oxyrhynchus Papyri are related to this document which contains 114 sayings attributed to Jesus. OP 1 contains Sayings 27, 28, 30-34, 77 of the Gospel of Thomas; OP 654, the preface and first six sayings; OP 655, Sayings 37-40. The discovery of this Gnostic Gospel has thrown new light on the reconstruction and interpretation of the Oxyrhynchus materials. The Greek version appears to be earlier and not as strongly Gnostic-oriented as the Coptic Gospel of Thomas.

C. New Testament Philological Studies. The German scholar Gustav Adolf Deissmann brought into sharp focus the relevance of the study of papyri for New Testament grammatical and lexical research. He has played such an important role in this respect that some are inclined to divide the history of such studies into pre-Deissmann and post-Deissmann periods. Deissmann began a study of New Testament Greek in terms of the recently-discovered papyri. Two of his major works in this area are available in English translation (*Bible Studies,* Edinburgh: T. & T. Clark, 1903 and *Light from the Ancient East,* London: Hodder & Stoughton, 1910).

The contributions of the papyri to New Testament philological studies can best be understood in the light of the situation in the pre-Deissmann period. The precise identification of New Testament Greek had plagued scholars for years. Its differences from classical Greek were apparent to all. Some scholars went so far as to suggest that New Testament Greek was a special "Holy Ghost language." Others tried to account for its non-classical features in terms of Semitic influence. Still others tried to impose classical Greek categories on the language of the New Testament. More than 500 words in the New Testament could not be paralleled in any other Greek document, making interpretation and analysis of these words extremely difficult. Certain grammatical constructions in the New Testament violated classical usage. All in all, the Greek of the New Testament presented a real puzzle to the Greek grammarian.

The discovery of papyri in the late 1800's and early 1900's provided the answers to many of the problems in New Testament philological studies. In general these documents illustrate the late Greek colloquial language contemporaneous with the New Testament. This language was used by the New Testament writers. Its more literary expression is found in Hebrews; its more colloquial side in Revelation. The new discoveries contained a non-literary form of Koine (the Greek of the first century of our era) in contrast to the literary Koine and the works of the Atticists. The New Testament materials must be classified primarily with the former. The contributions of the new material are found basically in three major areas: vocabulary, lexicography, and grammar.

1. Vocabulary. The list of expressions found only in the New Testament (*hapax legomena*) as given in Thayer's *Greek-English Lexicon* (1889) contains over 500 words. In contrast, Arndt-Gingrich-Bauer's *Greek-English Lexicon* (1957) lists only about seventy such words, with this confident comment: "The fact that the advances in our knowledge have freed one after another of these words from their isolation and demonstrated that they were part of the living language forces upon us the conclusion that the great mass of Biblical words for which we do not yet have secular evidence also belong to that language" (p. xvi). Naturally, there always will remain certain words peculiar to the New Testament because of its unique contents, but the new evidence points conclusively to the fact that the New Testa-

ment authors used the common language of their day more or less colloquially. This was undoubtedly a major factor in the rapid spread of Christianity in the early centuries.

2. Lexicography. The discovery of such a large body of material contemporaneous with the New Testament provided a large number and variety of contexts in which the New Testament vocabulary could be found. Through an examination of these new contexts the connotation and denotation of words has been refined. In this way new possibilities of interpretation have been presented, and in some cases it is possible to recover with confidence the exact concept which the New Testament writer had in mind. For example, it is now obvious that Paul was borrowing terminology from the process of freeing slaves in his description of redemption (Deissmann, *LAE*, pp. 322-34). This adds a significant dimension to the meaning of terms such as "redeem," "slave," "price," "freedom," "ransom," as used by Paul.

The following are a few examples of the illumination that has been cast upon the meaning of New Testament terms and concepts. In Hebrews 11:1 *hypostasis* has been variously translated — "assurance," "substance." In the papyri it occurs in the sense of "title-deed." To use this meaning to describe faith in Hebrews 11:1 is very attractive in the light of the immediate context. To interpret the Greek word *apechō* in Matthew 6:2, 5, 16; Philippians 4:18; Philemon 15; and possibly Mark 16:41 in the sense of "to give a receipt," thereby indicating full payment, certainly makes these passages intelligible. The significance of the use of the Greek *exaleiphō* rather than *chiazō* in Colossians 2:14 is illustrated in the papyri. Both terms are suitable to describe the cancellation of a debt. However the term used here by Paul has the additional connotation of "wiping out," that is, a complete removal leaving no trace of the original writing, rather than a cancellation by lines drawn through (the Greek letter *chi*, from whence *chiazō*, has the shape of an "x"). Thus also in the atoning work of Christ every trace of our debt has been obliterated. Paul describes the Holy Spirit as an *arrabōn* in Ephesians 1:14; II Corinthians 1:22, 5:5, This has been translated "earnest" (AV), "guarantee" (RSV), and "pledge" (NEB). In the papyri this term is used in a context where the meaning is down-payment. In terms of Paul's emphasis upon the present experience of the new life and age, it makes good sense to speak of the Holy Spirit as a "down-payment" or "first installment" of the inheritance (life) to come.

The significance of the papyri in lexicography of the Greek New Testament can be seen in the frequent citations of the papyri in the Arndt-Gingrich-Bauer lexicon. J. H. Moulton and G. Milligan have made these contributions available in a work entitled *The Vocabulary of the Greek Testament, Illustrated from the Papyri and Others Non-literary Sources* (London, 1929; reprinted, Grand Rapids: Eerdmans, 1949).

3. Grammar. Many of the anomalies and non-classical grammatical constructions in the New Testament have been explained by the Greek grammar used in the papyri. Any grammar of New Testament Greek written prior to 1900 is inadequate and out-dated as a result of the papyrus discoveries. James H. Moulton began the new approach with the publication of the first volume of *A Grammar of New Testament Greek* in 1906. The second volume was completed by W. F. Howard, and a third by Turner. In 1914 the first edition of A. T. Robertson's *A Grammar of the Greek New Testament in the Light of Historical Research* appeared (fifth edition was published by Harper and Brothers in 1931). Almost every page of this huge volume testifies to the influence of the papyri. In Germany the chief publication in the twentieth century is the work of Friedrich Blass as continually revised by Albert Debrunner (tenth edition, 1959) under the title *Grammatik des neutestamentlichen Griechisch*. R. W. Funk has prepared an English translation of this with additions under the title *A Greek Grammar of the New Testament* (Chicago: University of Chicago Press, 1961).

The following is a sampling of the fuller understanding of New Testament Greek grammar provided by the papyri. The use of the indicative mood with the Greek conjunction *ean* in the New Testament can now be paralleled in the papyri and is recognized as a legitimate first-century construction. In a similar way the occasional New Testament use of this word *ean* instead of *an* in relative clauses appears to be a normal usage from the papyri. It has been clearly substantiated that the *hina* clauses have a wider range

431

of usage and meaning in the New Testament period than in the classical period. Such clauses, primarily expressing purpose in classical Greek, can function as result clauses (e.g., John 9:2; I John 1:9) or as substantive clauses after verbs of commanding, saying, or exhorting. The New Testament lack of the refined usage of Greek particles as found in classical authors is clearly paralleled in the papyri. The New Testament tendency to express verbs in the active and passive rather than the middle voice can also be seen in the papyri. Unusual inflectional endings of nouns and verbs and unique spellings in the New Testament are also found in the papyri, demonstrating that these are normal first century usages.

This brief survey of the contributions of the papyri to New Testament philological studies indicates that no student of the Bible can afford to ignore this storehouse of data. Some perhaps have been a bit over-enthusiastic on this point, and have over-stressed the non-literary character of New Testament Greek. It has a decided affinity with non-literary Koine, but at times it has definite literary traits. On the other hand, its Semitic background must not be overlooked. The Aramaic influence can be found in varying degrees. In conclusion, in some respects the New Testament will always remain unique because of its new message and way of life which it conveys.

D. New Testament backgrounds. These first century documents also provide information for the reconstruction of the background and environment of the New Testament. Some of the customs and usages reflected in the New Testament can now be clarified from the papyri. The format of a Pauline letter is typical of that found in numerous letters from Oxyrhynchus. Date lines in the papyri clearly show that Luke's reference to the fifteenth year of Tiberias (Luke 3:1) must be dated in the year A.D. 28/29. The fourteen-year census cycle established from the Oxyrhynchus papyri shows that the earliest possible date for the birth of Christ is 9 B.C. The authentication of a letter by the greeting and signature of the author as seen in the papyri explains Paul's practice in I Corinthians 16:21; Colossians 4:18; II Thessalonians 3:17; and Galatians 6:13 ("large letters").

In conclusion it should be observed that the total impact of the papyri has not yet been fully felt in New Testament studies. Certain areas of research must still be investigated. First of all, there is the problem of the assimilation of new material. Over ten volumes of the *Oxyrhynchus Papyri* have appeared since Moulton and Milligan published their *Vocabulary of the Greek Testament*. This material as well as the promised future additional volumes dealing with a large amount of unpublished material must be analyzed. There should be more grammatical and lexical studies dealing with specific aspects. Although these will tend to be technical in nature, their conclusions can be of great value to the exegete. A specific area in need of study is epistolography. A definitive study on the use of amanuenses as displayed in the papyri may contribute considerably to the problems of authorship in the New Testament. A further refinement of Deissmann's distinction between "letter" and "epistle" may provide the interpreter with valuable guide-lines in dealing with the New Testament materials. The discovery of papyri, and especially the large find at Oxyrhynchus, has made and will continue to make phenomenal contributions to New Testament studies.

BIBLIOGRAPHY. B. P. Grenfell, A. S. Hunt, et. al., Oxyrhynchus Papyri Volumes Iff., Egypt Exploration Fund, London, 1898ff. A. Deissmann, Light from the Ancient East, Hodder and Stoughton, London, 1927; Bible Studies, T. and T. Clark, Edinburgh, 1903. Joachim Jeremias, Unknown Sayings of Jesus, S. P. C. K., London, 1958.

P

PALAEONTOLOGY. Palaeontology is the scientific study of extinct forms of life, knowledge of which generally comes through the study of fossils. Palaeontology and °archaeology are distinct sciences in that the first is related to the remains of ancient life, the second to ancient artifacts and the light they throw on culture. The sciences cross when both fossils and artifacts are discovered at the same occupation level.

PALERMO STONE. The Palemro Stone is an Egyptian inscription on black diorite, 17 inches high, 9½ inches wide, and 2½ inches thick, dating from the Fifth Dynasty. It received its name from the Palermo (Italy) Museum where it has been on display since 1899. A smaller fragment of the text is at the Cairo Museum.

The first reference to the Palermo stone was made in 1866 by E. de Rouge in his *Recherches sur les monuments qu' on peut attribuer aux premieres dynasties de Manethon* (p. 145). In 1889 E. Naville visited Palermo, studied the text and published the results in G. Maspero, *Recueil de travaux relatifs a la philologie et a l' archeologie egyptiennes et assyriennes,* XXV (New Series, IX). A more detailed study was made by the German Egyptologists H. Schafer, L. Borchardt, and K. Sethe, whose text formed the basis for J. H. Breasted's translation in *Ancient Records of Egypt, I,* pp. 51-72.

At the top of the Palermo Stone is a row of oblong spaces containing hieroglyphic signs. In the lower section of each space is a figure wearing a red crown and holding a flail. This figure is the well-known sign for a king of Lower Egypt. Nine names of kings of Lower Egypt appear on the top of the Palermo Stone. Others probably were listed on lost portions of the stone, along with a list of kings of Upper Egypt. These kings reigned during predynastic times, before the two Egypts were united into one Empire (*see* Egypt).

While the predynastic kings are mentioned only by name, the records are fuller when First Dynasty rulers are listed. Here the name of the king is given, followed by the principal events of his reign, year by year. In the early years and reigns the events noted are largely religious feasts, but by the Third Dynasty the annals are more detailed. Here there is a reference to the building of ships and the importing of cedar wood, probably from Lebanon. A double palace was built with a name that recalls the union of the two Egypts: "Exalted is the White Crown of Snefru upon the Southern Gate. Exalted is the Red Crown of Snefru upon the Northern Gate." Most of the records of the Fourth Dynasty are missing, but the inscription on

the back of the stone carries us as far as the Fifth Dynasty.

PALMYRA. Palmyra, or Tadmor as it is called in Arabic, was originally an insignificant village, set in a green oasis watered by a copious spring in the midst of the Syrian Desert. The villagers eked a scanty existence from the palm grove which grew around the spring and from the few crops that they managed to raise from its surplus waters. The village lay off the caravan route which skirted the Syrian Desert on the north, and ran along the banks of the Euphrates avoiding the Syrian Desert. Tadmor is mentioned twice in ancient annals: once in the *Cappadocian Tablets which go back to the nineteenth century B.C. and again in the eleventh century when Tiglath-pileser I followed some bedu tribes as far as the village. There is a reference to Tadmor in the Bible where it is stated that Solomon built Tadmor in the wilderness (I Kings 9:18; II Chron. 8:4).

Palmyra is not mentioned again until 41 B.C. when Mark Antony sent a looting expedition against the village, but his legionaires found it deserted. After this incident, Palmyra managed to keep a precarious existence between the warring Parthians and the Romans, and eventually came under Roman protection.

With the coming of the Romans, the inhabitants of Palmyra cleverly diverted the caravan route from the north and made it pass through their city. This brought them untold wealth and suddenly their village grew into a very large city. For almost three centuries, from 30 B.C. to A.D. 273, the inhabitants enjoyed great wealth and prosperity, and built in the heart of the desert, a city which compared in size and magnificence with other cities in the Roman Empire.

Palmyra played a great role in the history of the Near East during the third century A.D. At a time when the Roman Empire was beset by the Goths in Europe, the Parthians under Shapur invaded north Syria and overran Asia Minor as far as the Chalcedon. Roman power in the east seemed at an end and the fate of Syria and Egypt lay in the balance. At this juncture Odenathus, the Prince of Palmyra, came to the rescue and retrieved the fortunes of Rome. He recovered Mesopotamia for the Romans and forced Shapur to withdraw back to Parthia.

Odenathus died in A.D. 266, and was succeeded by his queen Zenobia who viewed matters differently, and instead of supporting what seemed to her a tottering empire, she sought to create an empire of her own. She expelled the Romans from Syria, Asia Minor and Egypt and claimed these countries as her own.

In 270, a new emperor arose, who, after defeating the Goths in Europe, turned his attention to the East to settle scores with Zenobia. Aurelian, the new Emperor, had her forces expelled from Egypt, and he himself swept the Palmyrenes out of Asia Minor and signally defeated them near Homs. He then set out for Palmyra, and after a siege of three months captured the city and took Zenobia captive. On his departure, the Palmyrenes massacred the garrison he left behind. Aurelian returned and destroyed Palmyra, which after a while reverted to an insignificant village.

The present ruins of Palmyra mostly date back to the third century A.D. The city was built on a roughly semicircular plan with the diameter just above a ravine, while the rest of the city sprawled over the area to the north, nestled within a range of low hills, which formed a natural arc around the city. The city walls followed the contours of the surrounding area. On the south the wall formed a roughly straight line from one end of the city to the other, and then swept in a wide arc around the city. The city walls were pierced with one main gate and a number of less important ones. The main gate stood at a slight turn in the wall about three hundred yards from its western extremity. It led into a wide avenue flanked by colonnaded porches on either side and ran dead straight for about 250 yards. At that point it turned sharply to the east. Subsidiary streets branched off at right angles from this main avenue in two directions. At about 650 yards from the beginning of the avenue, there was a monument standing on four piers (tetrapylon), which at one time supported a statue. On the first column on the north beyond the tetrapylon, there is a column bearing a dedicatory inscription to Zenobia inscribed by her generals Zabdas and Zabbaios. To the south of the tetrapylon stands the agora or market place, a

large open court contained within a colonnaded porch. A short distance east of the tetrapylon along the avenue of columns, there is a well preserved theater of the usual Roman type. At the end of the avenue there are the remains of a small temple. Beyond this point, the avenue of columns is brought to an end by a triumphal arch, which is built askew in order to change the direction of the avenue towards the Temple of Bel which stands about three hundred yards to the southeast.

The Temple of Bel was built on a square artificially raised platform (podium) which measured about 215 yards on each side. A flight of stairs on the west side led up to an enclosed porch, which opened on to a vast open court through three doors. The temple area consisted of a relatively small cella set in the midst of the court, which was enclosed on all four sides with a colonnaded porch. The cella itself contained elements of both Graeco-Roman and Oriental architecture. A flight of stairs led up to the entrance which was on the west side. The axis of the cella was very short and the width was considerably greater than the length. The cella was surrounded by a row of columns which had capitals that were cased in metal. The walls of the cella were very thick and at the southwest corner, a stairwell in the body of the wall led up to the roof.

In front of the cella on either side there were two basins for purifying sacrificial animals.

Of less importance than the Temple of Bel is a small temple dedicated to Baalshamin, "Lord of the Skies." It is situated along the subsidiary road that leads from the Tetrapylon towards the north. This temple consists of a cella, with six columns in front (hexa-style).

In addition, the remains of two churches belonging to about the fifth century are still standing off one of the subsidiary streets.

At the extreme end of the city there is a building generally called the Camp of Diocletian. It is approached by a colonnaded street branching from the avenue which starts at the main gate, and consists of a vast enclosure, at the west end of which there is a building fronted by a colonnaded porch and consisting of an audience chamber and other smaller rooms. Its attribution to Di-

PANORAMA OF PALMYRA with the Grand Colonnade and Triumphal Arch in the foreground. Courtesy, Azad, Beyrouth

THE AGORA AT PALMYRA. *Courtesy, Azad, Beirut*

ocletian has been questioned in recent years.

Besides the buildings within the city, Palmyra has another attraction in the monumental tombs outside the city. Some of these are built like towers within which there are long narrow shelves for burial The slabs sealing the tombs generally have a representation of the deceased and a short epitaph in Aramaic. Other tombs lie underground and consist of an outer court, which opens into an underground chamber. Burials are generally grouped around three walls of the chamber, and the cover of each grave is carved with a representation of the funeral feast, showing the deceased reclining and drinking out of a bowl.

PAPYRUS. Papyrus is a rush-like water plant of the sedge variety. It was very common in Egypt and in parts of Palestine. The stems of the papyrus plant were split, beaten, and used as a writing material. Manuscripts made of this material are known collectively as papyri, singular papyrus.

PARTHIA, PARTHIANS. Parthia was the mountainous region southeast of the Caspian Sea conquered by Alexander the Great. It was famous for its horsemen and archers and its people are thought to have been of Scythian stock. About the middle of the third century B.C. a Parthian named Arsaces freed his people from the Seleucids and established an independent Parthian Empire which extended, at its height, from the Euphrates, across Afghanistan to the Indus, and from the Oxus to the Indian Ocean. The chief Parthian cities were *Ecbatana, Ctesiphon, Seleucia, and Hecatompylus. The land was governed by the land-owning aristocracy which controlled trade routes with the Far East.

In 53 B.C. the Parthian cavalry bowmen defeated the Roman consul Crassus and posed a threat to Syria and Asia Minor. The Parthians were often at war with Rome but they retained their independence until A.D. 226 when Ardashir I, founder of the Sassanian Persian Empire administered a decisive defeat. *See also* Persia.

PASARGADAE (PARSAGADA). Pasargadae, or its variant Parsagada, is a name derived from the Pars or Fars tribe which migrated to southwestern Iran from Azarbaijan. Under Cyrus, Pasargadae became capi-

tal of Persia. Its ruins lie fifty-four miles northeast of Persepolis. West of the town is a Muslim cemetery, the central tomb of which bears the colorful name, "The Throne of Solomon's Mother." This tomb is considered to be that of Cyrus, the tomb visited by Alexander the Great. According to Arrian, Alexander read the Persian inscription on the tomb:

O Man, I am Cyrus the son of Cambyses who founded the Persian Empire and was king in Asia. Grudge me not therefore this monument. (Arrian, *Anabasis of Alexander* vi. 29. 8)

Cyrus built his royal residence at Pasargadae on the spot where tradition says he gained a decisive victory over Astyages the Mede. A trilingual inscription (Old Persian, Akkadian, and Elamite) reads, "I am Cyrus, the King, the Achaemenian." Ghirshman suggests that this inscription dates from the time when he was still a vassal under the Medes. A second trilingual inscription gives him the title "Great King," suggesting that by this time Cyrus had conquered Media.

North of the Palace of Cyrus is the so-called Palace Harem where the local guides point out the tomb of Cambyses, the son of Cyrus. A Persian scholar, Djavad Zakataly, has suggested that this is the real tomb of Cyrus because of its proximity to the palace area and the fact that it is aligned in the axis of the palaces (*L'authentique tombeau de Cyrus,* Tehran, 1954.)

Ghirshman has called attention to the composite nature of the art of Pasargadae "with its Assyrian bulls, Hittite orthostats, its Babylonian polychromy and Egyptian symbols." All agree, however, that the fusion is a happy one and that Pasargadae represents the spirit of ancient Persia at its best.

PATINA. Patina is a green rust that covers ancient bronze objects and copper coins and medals. It is formed by oxidation and is usually valued as a sign of antiquity.

PELLA (in Palestine). Egyptian *Execration Texts and *Amarna tablets mention a Palestinian town named Philum, Canaanite *Pahel.* The name does not appear in the Bible, but the records of the Egyptian Pharaohs Thutmose III, Seti I and Ramesses II describe battles in which the people of Pahel took part. Evidently in one of the battles Pahel was destroyed, for the city

THE THEATER OF THE ASCLEPIUM at Pergamum. Courtesy, H. Gökberg

disappeared from historical records until the conquest of the country by Alexander the Great (332 B.C.). Macedonians who colonized the region after Alexander's victory called it Pella, since the old name Pahel reminded them of the Macedonian captial Pella. Palestinian Pella located east of the Jordan, opposite Scythopolis (*Beth-shan) was destroyed by Alexander Jannaeus during the early part of the first century B.C. In 63 B.C. Pompey liberated Pella and other Hellenistic towns, annexed them to the province of Syria and gave them municipal freedom. About A.D. 1 they formed a league for trade and mutual defence known as the *Decapolis.

When the revolt against the Romans broke out in A.D. 66, the Christian community of Jerusalem fled to Pella which became an important Christian center in the years following. The ruins of ancient Pella are known as Khirbet Fahil. There can be seen today the remains of a Roman theater as well as many buildings dating to Hellenistic and Roman times. In the region are caves occupied by anchorites and numerous sepulchres.

PERGAMUM. About sixty-five miles north of Smyrna stood Pergamum on a hill one thousand feet high. Situated eighteen miles from the ocean, it communicated with the Aegean via the Caicus River, which was navigable by small craft. Pergamum dominated not only the Caicus valley but also

a highway into the interior of Asia Minor as well as the western coastal road. Her wealth came from trade, agricultural surplus, stock breeding and the dependent industries of woolen textiles and parchment, and silver mines.

Pergamum was brought to a height of prosperity under the Attalid dynasty during the third and second centuries B.C. Territorial expansion came in large measure through close cooperation with and support of Rome. The last of the Attalids, Attalus III, willed his kingdom to Rome at his death in 133 B.C. In the Empire the kingdom was known as the Province of Asia and encompassed approximately the western third of Asia Minor. Political capital of the province from the beginning, Pergamum gradually lost out to Ephesus which was more easily accessible to Roman governors by sea.

During the second century A.D. a large new section of Pergamum developed at the foot of the hill on which the old city was located, and the hill city became the acropolis. During Byzantine times the city was again confined to the acropolis but now the acropolis is uninhabited and the modern city covers the lower city of Roman imperial times.

Pergamum is one of the most completely excavated of ancient sites. The story began with the efforts of the German architect Carl Humann, who became chief road engineer for the western Ottoman Empire and in 1868 set up his headquarters at Pergamum. In that year he began excavations which German archaeologists have continued almost a century and which now are about 60 per cent complete.

The first major triumph of the German excavators was the location of the great altar of Zeus with its remarkable sculptures. Probably built by King Eumenes (197-159 B.C.) the altar stood on foundations measuring 125 by 115 feet. The altar rested on a great horseshoe shaped plinth thirty feet high, approached by twenty-eight sixty foot steps on the western side. These steps led through an Ionic colonnade into a square court where the altar proper stood. The three outer sides of the monument were sculptured with scenes of struggles between gods and giants and scenes representing the defeat of the Gauls by Eumenes. Another frieze ran around the three inner sides of the altar court on the upper level and depicted events from the life of Telephus, son of Hercules, and mythical ancestor of the Attalid dynasty. The frieze (about four hundred feet long) is only slightly shorter than that of the Parthenon. Humann's export of the altar of Zeus by stealth led the Turkish government to forbid further export of antiquities. The reconstructed altar of Zeus was housed in a Pergamum museum in Berlin, and after being hidden during World War II it has been set up again in East Berlin. Some have thought that the Altar of Zeus is what the Apostle John had in mind when he spoke of "Satan's throne" at Pergamum (Rev. 2:13).

At the foot of the acropolis, Eumenes (apparently) built the lower agora, a paved court 210 by 110 feet surrounded by Doric porticoes giving entrance to shops. Just up the hill from the agora stood a gymnasium complex on three terraces. Above the gymnasium in about the middle of the slope lay the upper agora, above and to the left of which was the Altar of Zeus. As one ascends the western side of the acropolis from the Altar, he comes to the remains of a beautiful temple of Athena surrounded on three sides by the two story library which at one time had been the second in the

RECONSTRUCTION OF ALTAR OF ZEUS at Pergamum. Courtesy, Staatliche Museen zu Berlin

ancient world, boasting some 200,000 volumes (scrolls). But the building was fairly empty in John's day because Antony had given Pergamum's library to Cleopatra and most of the books had been carried off to Alexandria. Against the side of the acropolis adjacent to the temple of Athena lay the theater which was constructed in 170 B.C. and held 15,000 spectators. Four other theaters have been found at Pergamum. At the top of the hill stood the arsenal and just below it one of the five richly decorated palaces of the city.

Just prior to World War II archaeological attention centered on the lower city of Pergamum, now largely overlaid by the modern city of Bergama. And since World War II much work has been done on the Asklepion (on a small plateau above the lower town), the great health center dedicated to *Asclepius, god of healing. This was a famous center in antiquity; even Emperors (Hadrian, Marcus Aurelius and Caracalla) came here. And Galen was one of the greatest physicians to practice here. The center attained its height in the second century A.D. and most of the structures excavated there date to that century. But the Asklepion was founded in Hellenistic times and was impor-

tant in John's day. What it may have looked like then will require further investigation, but it certainly included at the minimum a temple to Asclepius and a dormitory where patients slept.

Although much remains to be done at Pergamum, a student can today range with profit over an excavated acropolis and a partially restored Asklepion. We might have a better idea of a few of the structures if it had not been for vandalism committed during World War II.

PERSEPOLIS. The first Achaemenian king to move his palace from *Pasargadae to Persepolis was Darius the Great, who probably began work on his palace-fortress soon after his accession (522 B.C.). From that time on, Persepolis was the principal capital of Achaemenian Persia.

The Oriental Institute of the University of Chicago conducted archaeological campaigns at Persepolis under the direction of Ernst Herzfeld (1931-34) and Erich F. Schmidt (1935-39). They were able to trace the plan of the ancient city, observing that the palaces and public buildings were erected on a terrace of masonry some distance from the city proper. The entire city was surrounded

THE APADANA AT PERSEPOLIS. Relief from the stairway showing Babylonians and Syrians bringing tribute. Courtesy, Oriental Institute

SILVER DRACHMAE of Alexander the Great from the treasury of Persepolis. Courtesy, Erich F. Schmidt, The Oriental Institute

by a triple fortification system with one row of towers and walls running over the crest of the mountain.

On the masonry terrace stood the palace of Darius with an entrance hall opening across the entire width of the building. The main hall was fifty feet square, adorned with reliefs proclaiming, "I am Darius, great king, king of kings, king of lands, son of Hystaspes the Achaemenian, who constructed this palace."

The building now known as the Tripylon was probably the first reception room in Persepolis. Its stairways depict rows of dignitaries approaching the king. On the eastern gate jambs, Darius I is shown on his throne.

A larger audience hall was the so-called Apadana, begun by Darius I and completed by Xerxes. It was a huge room, 195 feet square, surrounded by vestibules on three sides. The wooden roof was supported by seventy-two stone columns, of which thirteen are still standing. Two monumental sculptured stairways were used to approach the building which was on an elevated platform. The reliefs on the eastern stairway, excavated by Herzfeld, are well preserved. They show envoys of twenty-three subject nations bringing New Year's gifts to the Persian emperor.

A third large reception hall is known as the Hall of One Hundred Columns. It was started by Xerxes and finished by Artaxerxes I. The central unit, a room 229 feet square, was larger than the Apadana. One hundred columns once supported the roof. Huge stone depicting the victory of the king over the bulls flanked the northern portico, and eight stone gateways were ornamented with scenes depicting the victory of the king over the evil powers.

An impressive Gate of Xerxes stood on the terrace above the stairway leading up from the plain. Colossal bulls guarded the entrance. The accompanying inscription reads, "King Xerxes says: By the grace of Ahura Mazda I constructed this gateway called All-Countries."

Erich Schmidt called the complex built largely by Artaxerxes I the treasury, because it contained stone vessels suitable for storing valuables. Alexander the Great seized the valuables from the Persepolis treasury during his victorious march through Persia after the battle of Gaugamala. Diodorus valued the treasure at 120,000 silver talents (*Diodorus* xvii. 71. 1).

Alexander's treatment of Persepolis has puzzled historians, for his usual generosity seems to have left him. The men were slain, the women enslaved, and the property plundered by Alexander's troops. As a climax, the palaces of Persepolis were burned. Some feel that Alexander burned Persepolis in revenge for the burning of Athens by the Persians. Whatever the reason, the evidence of the conflagration is there, and the excavators of Persepolis examined the charred remains of a once beautiful city.

A few miles north of Persepolis, at Naksh-i-Rustam, the Achaemenian kings of Persia, except for Cyrus, are buried. The name Naksh-i-Rustam, meaning picture of Rustam, was mistakenly given to the site because of a monument which was thought to depict the legendary Persian hero Rustam. Actually it depicts Shapur I (A.D. 241-272) standing before the god Ahura-Mazda.

The tomb of Darius bears a trilingual inscription which boasts,

Says Darius the king: By the favor of Ahura Mazda, I am of such a sort that I am a friend to right, I am not a friend to wrong; it is not my desire that the weak man should have wrong done to him by the mighty; nor is that my desire that the mighty man should have wrong done to him by the weak.

To the right and left of the tomb of Darius are similar tombs of Xerxes, Artaxerxes I and Darius II.

See also Persia.

BIBLIOGRAPHY. Roland G. Kent, *JNES* IV, 1945, pp. 39-52

PERSIA. The founder of the Persian army came to the throne of the tiny Elamite prov-

THE GATE OF XERXES IN PERSEPOLIS with guardian man-headed bulls at the eastern doorway. Courtesy, Oriental Institute

ince of Anshan *ca.* 559 B.C. Taking advantage of rebellion in the Median army, Cyrus defeated Astyages, king of the *Medes, and entered his capital city, *Ecbatana. In an amazingly short time, Cyrus extended his borders westward and northward. He threatened the fabulously wealthy kingdom of *Lydia, in Asia Minor, whose king, Croesus sought an alliance with *Nabunaid of Babylon and Amasis II of Egypt. Before help could come, Cyrus struck and added Lydia to his domains. This brought Cyrus into contact with the Greeks of Asia Minor. Later Persia would seek to conquer Greece, itself, but for the moment Cyrus turned eastward toward the Tigris-Euphrates valleys and moved in the direction of *Babylon. After a series of victories north of the capital, Babylon fell to the Persian armies in 538 B.C. There was no fighting, and Cyrus was heralded as a liberator by those who were discontent with the policies of Nabunaid and Belshazzar.

Cyrus made it a point to reverse certain of the basic policies of his predecessors. Captive peoples were permitted to return to their homelands, and idols which had been taken to Babylon were restored to their local shrines. Cyrus granted permission to the Jews to return to Jerusalem and rebuild their temple (Ezra 1:2-3).

Under Cambyses (530-522 B.C.), son and heir of Cyrus, Persian power reached Egypt. Pharaoh Psamtick was defeated at Pelusium (525 B.C.) after which Cambyses sacked the capital at Memphis. The defeat of the Egyptians by Cambyses marked the end of Pharaonic Egypt. Once the ruler of western Asia, she was to become subject to Persians, Greeks, Romans, and their successors. Following his victories in Egypt, Cambyses learned of revolts at home and hastened back to Persia to secure his throne. He died on the way, possibly a suicide.

The period of confusion which marked the last days of Cambyses was ended when Darius Hystaspes (522-486 B.C.) put down all opposition and became one of the strongest of Persian monarchs. Cyrus had tried to rule with a policy of clemency, but Darius found it necessary to exert absolute power. His efficient organization made of Persia a centralized state in which all power was vested in the king. It had been the dream of

442

Persian kings since Cyrus to conquer the Greeks. Darius undertook a European campaign and subdued Thrace and Macedonia north of Greece, with little difficulty. He moved into Greece, but the defeat at Marathon (490 B.C.) proved a major setback and robbed Darius of the prize he sought most. During the reign of Darius the Jews were permitted to continue work on their Temple, and in the sixth year of his reign the Second Temple was dedicated in Jerusalem (Ezra 6:15).

Xerxes I was the son of Darius and Atossa, a daughter of Cyrus. Early in his reign (486-465 B.C.) he put down a rebellion in Egypt, after which he prepared for the invasion of Greece. The campaign got off to a good start. The brave Spartans were defeated at Thermopylae (480 B.C.) and Athens itself was occupied and pillaged. At Salamis, however, the Persians lost their fleet and the tide of battle turned. Xerxes turned over the command of his army to a general, Mardonius, and returned to Asia. Mardonius was unable to recover the initiative in fighting the Greeks, and Xerxes was killed by one of his own guards.

Artaxerxes, a son of Xerxes, succeeded to the throne (465-423 B.C.). During his reign Ezra "the scribe" led a group of exiles back to Jerusalem, and Nehemiah, the king's cupbearer, secured a leave of absence to encourage the Jews to rebuild the walls of Jerusalem. The empire was restive during the reign of Artaxerxes. He was quite successful in putting down rebellion, but the concessions he had to make to the Greeks indicated a weakness which was to grow more pronounced among his successors. The decline in Persian power dates from the reign of Artaxerxes.

The ninety years between the death of Artaxerxes I and the defeat of Darius III at Issus (333 B.C.) saw a series of six Persian rulers, none of whom was able to restore Persia to its former greatness. The most celebrated dynastic quarrel of the period was the rebellion of Cyrus the Younger, a Persian prince who hired an army of Greek mercenaries ("The Ten Thousand") to support his cause in opposition to Artaxerxes II. Cyrus died in the battle of Cunaxa (401 B.C.). Xenophon, one of the "Ten Thousand" who fought their way home, told the story of hardships during this retreat from Persia in the *Anabasis*. Harassed by the Persians, the Greek mercenaries went up the Tigris into Armenia, passing through the mountains and then down to the shores of the Black Sea at Trebizond (Trapezus). Then they were able to make their way home to Greece.

Although there were temporary periods of splendor, the last kings of Persia lived during times of intrigue, rebellion, and bloodshed. In 334 B.C. Alexander of Macedon invaded Asia Minor, and in the following year he defeated a Persian force at Issus in northern Syria. In 331 B.C. the Persian Empire came to an end with Alexander's victory at Gaugemala in Mesopotamia. The last of the Persian kings fled to Bactria where he was assassinated by his own cousin. See also Elam, Behistun Inscription.

BIBLIOGRAPHY. R. Ghirshman, *Iran,* Penguin Books, Baltimore, 1954. A. T. Olmstead, *The History of the Persian Empire,* University of Chicago Press, Chicago, 1948. Richard N. Frye, *The Heritage of Persia,* World Publishing, Cleveland, 1962.

PETRA. The famed capital city of the Nabatean empire was located in a fertile well-watered basin of the Wadi Musa at an elevation of 2700 feet in the Jordanian highlands about fifty miles south of the Dead Sea. The site, approximately one mile long and a half mile wide, is bounded on the east and west by parallel ridges of Nubian sandstone rising one thousand feet above the plateau. To the north and south the area is open and although access to the city is possible over steep and difficult trails from these directions, entry is, and was, generally made through a colorful, narrow, twisting cleft in the eastern ridge known as "the Siq." Rising from the floor of the basin to a height of 950 feet is a huge, rocky acropolis known by the Arabic name Umm el-Biyerah (Mother of Cisterns) which appears to have served as a fortress in Edomitic and Nabatean times. As capital of a trading empire Petra was strategically situated on the trade route linking the port of Ezion-geber with Ammon and Damascus, and was the point where the trade route from Gaza by way of Beersheba and the Ascent of Akkrabim joined the north-south route.

Modern exploration of Petra began in 1812 when, after a six-hundred-year period during which the location of the city was forgotten, the site was rediscovered by a Swiss explorer Johann Ludwig Burckhardt. On the pretext of making a sacrifice at the traditional tomb of Aaron (Jebel Haroun) Burckhardt persuaded a native guide to lead him through the Siq to Petra. The account of his journey including reference to the hundreds of rock-cut tombs with ornate facades, published posthumously in 1822 by John Murray, encouraged other travelers to visit the newly-discovered city and write of their journeys. In 1849, fourteen drawings of Petra were included in a folio of engravings by David Roberts, and in 1904 a detailed description of the elaborate funerary architecture by Rudolf Brünnow and Alfred von Domaszewski appeared.

In 1929 systematic archaeological investigation was begun by George Horsfield under the Petra Exploration Fund Expedition financed by Henry Mond, M.P. Soundings going down to bed rock were made in the Katute and other city dumps. On the basis of Horsfield's findings a pattern for dating was established. In 1934 William F. Albright joined Horsfield under the sponsorship of the Melchett Exploration Fund in excavating the so-called "Conway High Place" named for Agnes Conway (later Mrs. Horsfield) who, with George Horsfield, had published a report on the structure in 1930. The natural outcropping of stone around which a massive circular retaining wall had been built to a diameter of seventy-two feet had been tentatively identified by Miss Conway as an Edomite sanctuary. Albright, in studying the pottery and coinage, concluded that the construction was Nabatean and perhaps represented the earliest of Nabatean shrines. On the basis of more recent study, Peter J. Parr of London has challenged this identification calling attention to the location of the tower at the northwest corner of the city wall, and suggesting that the tower formed part of the defense work of the city and was not a high place but a circular corner bastion.

Important explorations were made during the 1930's by Nelson Glueck, Margaret A. Murray and J. C. Ellis. Horsfield's work was continued under the auspices of the Melchitt Fund and many of the sculptured cliff structures were studied. In 1958 the British School of Archaeology supported excavations directed by Peter J. Parr, and in 1959 this group was joined by an American team led by Philip C. Hammond. Work at the Katute dump was continued, trenches were dug along the Roman street and by the "Triumphal Arch," and a study of the city proper was undertaken. A number of graves were opened and rich finds of complete pottery items, sherds of painted ware and figurine fragments were made. In 1960 Awni Dajani, director of the Department of Antiquities of Jordan, cooperated with the British and Americans in an intensive exploration of Petra. The Roman theater was partially cleared and one piece of statuary, a marble figure of Hercules, was recovered. As a result of archaeological research a partial history of Petra can be given.

Through the discovery by Diana Kirkbride of distinctive hand axes and flints, human habitation at Petra can be traced to the paleolithic period. At nearby Al Barid, flint weapons similar to those known from the earliest levels at Jericho were found, indicating neolithic settlements in the area. During these early periods human habitation seems to have been confined to cave dwellings. In the thirteenth century B.C. the Edomites assumed control of the area and established a fortress on Umm el-Biyerah, where numerous sherds testify to their presence. Since the nineteenth century Umm el-Biyerah has been tentatively identified as the "Rock," "Sela" of the Old Testament (cf. II Kings 14:7-10; II Chron. 25:12; Isa. 16:1; Jer. 49:16-17; Obad. 1:3-4; Pss. 60:9, 108:10; cf. LXX where hă-Selă is rendered tēn Petran, Vulgate Petram). Although the designation is still uncertain, some archaeological support has been given by Nelson Glueck who was able to put Umm el-Biyerah sherds into the context of Edomite pottery. Excavations on the summit disclosed buildings and pottery from Iron II (late eighth to seventh centuries). The narrow trail which led to the top of the rock in Edomite times was broadened by the Nabateans. The Arabic appellation "Mother of Cisterns" has been explained by the discovery of numerous narrow-mouthed, bottle-shaped, plastered cisterns each capable of holding twenty thousand gallons, carved into the rock on the summit.

Some time during the Persian period Petra was deserted by the Edomites. The prophet Obadiah, who wrote probably during the fifth century, seems to refer to the Edomites dwelling in Petra (Obad. 1:3-4). In this same century another prophet referred to the fall of Edom and the usurpation of the Edomite kingdom by the "jackals of the desert" (Mal. 1:3, RSV). If the account by Diodorus Siculus (II:48, XIX:94-100) can be trusted, during the fourth century a nomadic people moved into the Petra area. Known to scholars as Nabatu, these people had been plunderers preying upon Red Sea shipping until their piracy was terminated by the Egyptian navy compelling them to become marauders of caravans and subsequently traders and merchants. By the end of the fourth century they had begun to establish the vast commercial Nabatean empire which at its height extended from Damascus to Medâ'in Saleh, embraced the Negeb and controlled Mediterranean ports. Petra, the central stronghold, was so secure that Antigonus the One-eyed who attacked in 312 B.C. was unable to take the city. Limited excavations have demonstrated that in this early period the Nabatean domiciles were constructed of boulders and *terre pisée*. Natural caves were also used as dwellings and store-chambers. During the first century B.C., under the reign of Aretes III (86-60 B.C.) the Nabateans reached their peak of artistic creativity. Nabatean pottery, renowned for its egg-shell thinness, hardness, and beauty of design, achieved near-perfection. Shallow bowls, with floral leaf patterns imposed on pinkish clay with a red-brown paint, are characteristic. The beautiful monuments carved into the red-rose sandstone to serve as tombs and cult centers for the worship of the dead were decorated externally in a plain style utilizing simple arches and crenelations. Some aspects of Nabatean worship are reflected in the high places such as that known as Zinn 'Atuf which had open altars, cisterns, and carved obelisks, and on a lower level a triclinium which appears to have been associated with the Nabatean funerary cult. Small stone or clay incense burners and portable stone idols which are little more than crudely carved representations of human faces appear to be cultic equipage. An inscription on the Turkamaniya tomb proclaims the dedication of that monument and its halls to Dusares, the Nabatean god.

In the later Nabatean period cruder building forms were abandoned, and the excavation of a house from the first century A.D. has revealed fine ashlar masonry with stuc-

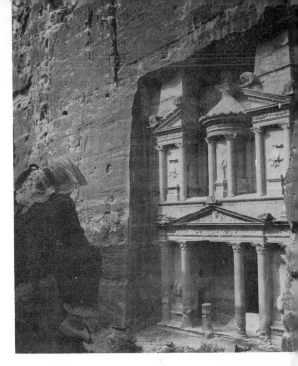

EL KHAZNEH, "The Treasury," is the modern Arabic name for this royal tomb hewn out of the rock at Petra. Courtesy, Jordan Tourist Department

coed walls. The city itself appears to have been laid out with considerable planning. Hellenistic influence seen in imported objects can be traced in changes in pottery styles, particularly in lamps.

Most Nabatean wealth was derived from trade but local industries were developed. Copper ingots found within the city, and the discovery of a smelting site at eş-Şabrah, a suburb of Petra, indicate that copper deposits in the Wadi Arabah were exploited. Terraced hillsides and a complex hydraulic system demonstrate the importance of agriculture. According to Diodorus, bitumen was mined at the Dead Sea for export.

In 106 A.D. the emperor Trajan incorporated Petra into the Roman empire and the city was reduced in size, probably for defense purposes. Ornate features, characteristic of Roman temples and royal buildings, were introduced into the facades of the cliff structures. A theater capable of seating three thousand persons was constructed, a wide, colonnaded street was laid out in Roman style, and Roman statuary was introduced. The one free-standing building remaining in Petra, Qasr el-Bint, is from this period.

Roman power waned in the third century A.D. and Petra began to sink into obscurity. A Byzantine church built during the fifth century, a Greek inscription from A.D. 447 in the so-called Urn Tomb referring to the consecration of a chapel by the Bishop of Petra, and crosses carved on doorways and walls testify to the presence of an active Christian community. It would appear that some Nabatean sacred places were adapted to Christian usage, for at al Deir on the Wadi Deir Christian crosses painted and scored on the walls suggest that this former Nabatean shrine became a Christian place of worship. During the seventh century Petra was engulfed in the expansive movement of Islam. In the twelfth century a crusader fortress was built but when this outpost fell before the Saracen Saladin in 1188-89, Petra disappeared from historical records until its rediscovery in 1812.

There are no references to Petra in the Bible, but it is possible, as noted above, that the passages in the Old Testament which mention Sela as an Edomitic stronghold refer to Umm el-Biyerah. Indirect reference appears in II Corinthians 11:32-33 when Paul mentions Aretas who was King of Petra (9 B.C.-40 A.D.). Recently an old hypothesis linking the activities of Moses to Petra has been revived. It is suggested that Sinai is in the Petra area for the site is known as the "Valley of Moses" (Wadi Musa) and its spring is "The Spring of Moses" ('Ain Musa). Nearby is the mountain where Aaron is said to have been buried (Jebel Haroun), a four-thousand-foot peak so sacred that only Moslems may ascend. The Siq is represented as the cleft in the rock through which the waters gushed when struck by Moses' rod. In the Petra valley pasturage for Hebrew flocks and herds was to be found. Further support for this thesis is derived from the apostle Paul, for in Galatians 4:25 he writes that "Hagar is Mount Sinai in Arabia," and it is argued that the area in which Petra is located was known as Arabia in Paul's time. However, it must be pointed out that there is neither archaeological nor historical support for this hypothesis.

BIBLIOGRAPHY. W. F. Albright, "The Excavation of the Conway High Place at Petra," *BASOR*, No. 57, 1935, pp. 18-26. C. M. Bennett, "The Nabateans in Petra," *Archaeology*, XV, 1962, pp. 233-243. R. E. Brünnow and A. von Domaszewski, *Die Provincia Arabia*, Strassburg, Vol. 1, 1904. R. L. Cleveland, "The Excavation of the Conway High Place (Petra) and Soundings at Khirbet Ader," *AASOR*, XXXIV-XXXV, 1954-5, pp. 57-97. S. I. Curtiss, "High Place and Altar," *PEFQ*, 1900, pp. 350-355. Gustaf Dalman, *Petra und seine Felsheiligtümer*, J. C. Hinrichs, Leipzig, 1908; "The Khazneh at Petra," *PEF*, I, 1911, pp. 95-107. N. Glueck, "Explorations in Eastern Palestine II," *AASOR*, XV, 1934-5; "Explorations in Eastern Palestine III," *AASOR*, XVIII-XIX, 1937-8. P. C. Hammond, "The Nabatean Bitumen Industry at the Dead Sea," *BA*, XXII, 1959, pp. 40-48; "Petra," *BA*, XXIII, 1960, pp. 29-32; "A Classification of Nabatean Fine Ware," *AJA*, LXVI, 1962, pp. 169-180; "Petra, The Excavation of the Main Theater," *The American Scholar*, XXXIII, 1962-3, pp. 93-106. G. Horsfield and A. Conway, "Historical and Topographical Notes on Edom, With an Account of the First Excavation at Petra," *Geographical Journal*, LXXVI, 1930, pp. 369-388. G and A. Horsfield, "Sela-Petra, the Rock of Edom and Nabatene," *QDAP*, VII, 1938, pp. 1-42; VIII, 1938, pp. 87-115; IX, 1941, pp. 105-204. A. Kennedy, *Petra: Its History and Monuments*, Country Life, London, 1925. W. H. Morton, "Umm el-Biyara," *BA*, XIX, 1956, pp. 26-36. M. A. Murray, *Petra, the Rock City of Edom*, Blackie and Son, London, 1939. M. A. Murray and J. C. Ellis, *A Street in Petra*, B. Quaritch, London, 1940. A. Musil, *Arabia Petraea II*. A. Hölder, Vienna, 1907. D. Nielsen, "The Mountain Sanctuaries in Petra and its Environs," *JPOS*, XI, 1931, pp. 222-240; XIII, 1933, pp. 185-208. P. J. Parr, "Recent Discoveries at Petra," *PEQ*, 1957, pp. 5-16; "Rock Engravings from Petra," *PEQ*, 1959, pp. 106-108; "Le 'Haut-Lieu Conway' de Petra," *RB*, LXIX, Jan. 1962, pp. 64-79. S. Perowne, "Petra, the Rock of Ages," *The Geographical Magazine*, XXXV, 1962, pp. 253-266. G. L. Robinson, *The Sarcophagus of an Ancient Civilization*, Macmillan Co., New York, 1930. J. Starcky, "The Nabateans: a Historical Sketch," *BA*, XVIII, 1955, pp. 84-106.

PHARISEES. See Jewish Sects.

PHAROS. See Alexandria.

PHILAE. The island of Philae ("the frontier"), located at the head of the First Cataract, six miles south of Aswan, was once the beauty spot of Upper Egypt. It did not achieve importance before the fourth century B.C., but the Ptolemies and the Romans made of it a holy place second to none. The beautiful temple to Isis was begun by Ptolemy II Philadelphus and his wife Arsinoe.

Osiris worship flourished at Philae until A.D. 453, seventy years after Theodosius issued his edict against the religion of Egypt. Both Egyptians and Ethiopians esteemed Philae as one of the burial places of Osiris.

His left leg was thought to have been buried there, the right leg being at Heracleopolis. The temples of Philae have become a casualty to the need for irrigation in modern Egypt. The Aswan Dam now covers the island, and during much of the year its ancient monuments are under water.

PHILIPPI. Philippi was located on the Egnation Way in eastern Macedonia, ten miles inland from the Aegean. In 356 B.C. Philip II of Macedon enlarged the earlier settlement named Krenides and named it for himself—Philippi, the city of Philip. The wall that Philip built around the city and over the *acropolis can still be traced. The ruins of the Greek *theater built by Philip are at the foot of the hill. In 335 B.C. Alexander passed through Philippi on his trip from Amphipolis to Thrace. The city entered history again in 42 B.C. when Antony and Octavian defeated Brutus and Cassius west of the city. After the Battle of Philippi Antony ordered Roman soldiers settled in Philippi, which became a Roman colony. The city, as a result, had a mixed population: the original Thracians, Greeks, and Romans.

The École Francaise d'Athens excavated Philippi between 1914 and 1938. They discovered the forum in the shape of a rectangle, three hundred feet long and one hundred fifty feet wide along the Egnation Way. At the center of the north side was a podium for speakers. At the northeast and northwest corners of the forum were the ruins of two impressive temples. Elsewhere in the city were a library, colonnades, porticoes, fountains, and monuments. Roman baths were discovered with mosaic pavements which date from the mid-third century A.D.

In Acts 16:13 Paul and his party are described as having gone outside the city of Philippi to a place of prayer where Jewish women were assembled. About a mile west of Philippi are the ruins of a Roman arch, beyond which is the River Gangites. The erection of such an arch often accompanied the founding of a colony. It symbolized the dignity of the city and it could mark the pomerium, a line enclosing an empty space outside the city wall within which building and burial were prohibited, and strange cults were not to be introduced. It may be that Jews were required to meet beyond the arch, because their religion was considered strange to the city fathers of Philippi. The arch may have been there at the time Paul visited Philippi.

Amphipolis was the leading city of the district, but Acts 16:12 states that Philippi was the "leading city of the district of Macedonia, and a colony." Textual variants in Codex Vaticanus and Codex Bezae have been cited to show that the passage was not understood. Perhaps in the original Philippi was described as a "city of the first district of Macedonia, and a colony."

PHILISTINES. The name Palestine is ultimately derived from a people known as Philistines who settled in the southern coastal plain, subsequently known as the Philistine Plain, during the twelfth century before Christ. Their five principal cities, known as the Philistine Pentapolis, were Gaza, Ashkelon, Ashdod, Ekron, and Gath. Mount Carmel formed the northern border of the Philistine country. In times of military strength the Philistines challenged Israelite control of central Palestine, although the proper home of the Philistines was the coastal plain, and that of Israel was the central highland district.

According to the prophet Amos (9:7) the Philistines came to Canaan from Caphtor, generally identified with the island of Crete. During the second millennium B.C. Minoan Crete controlled much of the Aegean area and its high culture spread throughout the Mediterranean world. Beginning about 1400 B.C. a period of decline set in, and archaeological evidence shows that most of the towns in Crete were destroyed. Toward the end of the period of decline (1400-1125 B.C.) Dorian Greeks came to the island and its earlier inhabitants are found in numerous places in the eastern Mediterranean. The "Sea Peoples" ravaged Asia Minor and northern Syria, bringing about the overthrow of the Hittite Empire (ca. 1200 B.C.). The Hittite capital at Hattusas and the Canaanite city-state of Ugarit were both destroyed about this time. The Philistines were among the Sea Peoples who attacked Egypt during the reigns of Merneptah and Ramesses III. Although repulsed by the Egyptians, the Philistines were permitted to settle on the southern coast of Canaan where the warrior overlord class settled with their families.

After their settlement in Canaan, the Philistines seem to have quickly adopted a form of the Canaanite language and Canaanite religious practices. They worshiped Dagon, a deity mentioned in the Ugaritic literature (*see* Ugarit). The fact that the Philistines were uncircumcised (Judg. 14:3; 15:18) marked them off as distinct from the Hebrews. The Israelites entered Canaan from the east and settled in the highlands at about the same time the Philistines settled on the coast lands of southern Palestine. The interests of the two peoples were bound to clash, and it was the Philistine threat that conditioned much of Israelite history during the days of Samuel, Saul, and the early years of David.

Before the time of David the Philistines had a monopoly on iron (I Sam. 13:19-22), giving them technological superiority over the Israelites. Smelting furnaces have been excavated on the fringes of Philistine territory at Tell Qasile, Tell Jemmeh, and 'Ain Shems (Beth Shemesh).

At Medinet Habu in Egypt there are scenes depicting the wagons, chariots, and ships used by the Philistines. A Philistine warrior is pictured wearing an Aegean type kilt. His helmet is a plumed headdress with chin straps, similar to one that appears on the Phaestos Disk from Crete.

In Canaan the Philistines captured Ashkelon, Ashdod, Gath and Gaza from the Canaanites. They may have founded the city of Ekron themselves. The Book of Judges records the prowess of the Judge Shamgar who slew six hundred Philistines and also speaks of Samson who fell in love with a Philistine girl but subsequently became an avowed enemy of the Philistines.

The superior arms of the Philistines enabled them to gain a foothold in the Judean hill country (*ca.* 1050 B.C.). At the battle of Aphek the Israelites were thoroughly humiliated. The sons of Eli were killed and the ark of Yahweh fell into Philistine hands. About this time the Philistines destroyed Shiloh and occupied the strongholds of °Megiddo and °Beth-shan in the Valley of Esdraelon and Gibeah in Benjamin. Following Ebenezer (I Sam. 4), however, the Israelite forces were able to strike back. The Philistine threat in part motivated the Israelite desire for a king, and under Saul, Israel gained victories over their oppressors. The David and Goliath story (I Sam. 12) shows that the Philistines were still able to strike terror in the armies of Israel.

The defeat of Israel's army at Mount Gilboa, at which time Saul and his son Jonathan died, enabled the Philistines to assume control over much of the Israelite territory. David, however, who had lived with the Philistines for a time when Saul was seeking his life, knew their tactics and was able to strike back effectively (II Sam. 5:17-25). He reclaimed the hill country for Israel and restricted the Philistines to the coastal area.

While the Philistines never became a serious menace to Israel again, they continued to cause trouble throughout the history of the divided kingdom. There was periodic fighting on the frontier (cf. I Kings 15:27;

THE ANCIENT PHILISTINE CITY OF ASHKELON was rebuilt by Herod the Great. Courtesy, Phalpot, Israel

16:15). Jehoshaphat received tribute from the Philistines (II Chron. 17:11) but under Jehoram the border town of Libnah was lost to Israel (II Kings 8:22). They were still aggressive in the time of Ahaz (Isa. 9:8-12). The Philistines allied with Egypt against Nebuchadnezzar, but their rulers and populace were deported in much the same way that Judah was taken into exile (cf. Jer. 25:20; 47:2-7; Zeph. 2:4-7; Zech. 9:5-6). The name Philistia, or Palestina, continued to be used for the territory occupied by the Philistines, but by New Testament times the cities were distinctly Hellenistic with mixed population.

Excavations at Philistine centers reveal a distinctively Philistine type of pottery dating to the twelfth and early eleventh centuries. It is an imitation of thirteenth century Mycenaean forms, and has affinities with pottery excavated in Cyprus and Rhodes. Among the chief types are buff colored bowls, spouted beer jugs, cups, and vases covered with a white slip on which geometric designs are painted with reddish purple or black paint. During subsequent years the ceramic styles of the Philistines became indistinguishable from those of other peoples of southern Palestine.

BIBLIOGRAPHY. G. von Rad, "Das Reich Israel und die Philister," *Palästina Jahrbuch,* XXIX, 1933, pp. 30-42. W. A. Heurtley, "The Relation between 'Philistine' and Mycenaean Pottery," *Quarterly, Department of Antiquities of Palestine,* V, 1936, pp. 90-110. J. Bérard, "Philistins et Préhellenes," *Revue Archealogique,* 1951, pp. 129-142. T. Dothan, "Archaeological Reflections on the Philistine Problem," *Antiquity and Survival,* II, 1957, pp. 151-164.

TWO PRISONERS FROM AMONG THE PHILISTINES are brought to be Rameses III who celebrates a victory by carving a relief on the walls of the temple at Medinet Habu. Courtesy, Oriental Institute

PHOENICIAN, PHOENICIANS.

Modern archaeological interest in the Phoenicians begins in the late sixteenth and seventeenth centuries with the collecting and publication of Phoenician inscriptions and coins. At that time the old Canaanite-Phoenician script was still unknown, and so the inscriptions could not be read, even though they were written in a language very closely akin to Hebrew. Then in the middle of the eighteenth century a few bilingual inscriptions written in Greek and Phoenician were found in Kition in Cyprus and taken to Oxford where John Swinton, Keeper of the University Archives, was able to decipher the Phoenician script and recognize the language. Within the next few years the Abbé J.-J. Barthélemy, who had spent some time handling Phoenician coins, and had identified some of the letters on these coins, got hold of the pedestal of a column found in Malta and bearing an inscription in Greek and Phoenician, and with this Barthélemy, working independently of Swinton, completed his decipherment. Actually twin columns and pedestals had been found, bearing the same inscription to Melqart, and this fact is not without interest since it calls to mind the twin columns in Melqart's temple at Tyre mentioned by Herodotus (ii.44) as well as the twin columns of Solomon's Temple erected by Phoenician craftsmen (I Kings 7:13ff.). The personal names in the inscription show Egyptian influence: "To our Lord, to Melqart, Baal of

PHOENICIAN TOMBS amid
the remains of ancient Byblos.
Courtesy, Photo Sport, Beirut

Tyre, that which thy servants, 'Abdosir and his brother Osirshamar, the two sons of Osirshamar, son of 'Abdosir, pledged because he heard their voice. May he bless them!"

Oddly, no one made any great advances over their work until Wilhelm Gesenius painstakingly collected and published the available evidence and wrote a scientific grammar of Phoenician in 1837 (Scriptura linguaeque Phoeniciae monuments quotquot supersunt). During the next few years progress was more rapid. New inscriptions were found in various places in the Mediterranean (e.g. the funerary inscription of Eshmunazar in Sidon and the so-called Sacrificial Tariff of Marseilles). Then in 1860 an outbreak of hostility between Druzes and Christians led the way to French intervention in Lebanon. Along with her troops, France sent a full-scale archaeological expedition under the direction of Ernest Renan. With such support Renan was able to conduct simultaneous excavations at Arvad, Gebal (Byblos), Sidon, and Tyre. Although archaeological methods were then still very imperfect and Renan failed to go deeper than the levels of the Greek period, he returned to Europe with much valuable information, including some additional inscriptions. All this new evidence enabled Paul Schröder to publish a grammar in 1869 (Die phönizische Sprache) which quite surpassed Gesenius' earlier work and remained the standard treatment of the subject for nearly seventy years.

Soon Ernest Renan began what he was later to consider his most important work: the publication of the great Corpus Inscrip-

tionum Semiticarum (beginning in 1881 and still being published today). The Corpus (abbreviated CIS, followed by volume number and inscription number) offers a definitive publication of inscriptions in Phoenician, Aramaic, Hebrew, and Old South Arabian. Work on the Phoenician language and other closely related tongues was now on a very sound footing, and soon the study itself, along with some of its comparative results, was to be made more readily available to students in Mark Lidzbarski's Handbuch der nordsemitischen Epigraphik (1898) and his Ephemeris für semitische Epigraphik (1902-15) and in G. A. Cooke's Text-Book of North-Semitic Inscriptions (1903). Beginning in 1905 the French sped up the circulation of new texts through the Répertoire d'Epigraphie sémitique.

Meanwhile Gesenius was able to use comparative evidence from his study of the Phoenician language in preparing his monumental Hebrew grammar and his great Hebrew lexicon. Both of these works have gone through several editions in German and English, and they remain indispensable in the study of Hebrew today.

In 1936 Zelig S. Harris published his Grammar of the Phoenician Language, following this three years later with his valuable study, The Development of the Canaanite Dialects. Harris' grammar superseded Schröder's work as the standard introduction to Phoenician and held the field exclusively until the publication in 1951 of Johannes Friedrich's Phönizisch-punische Grammatik. Thus analysis of the language of the Phoenician inscriptions has become more and more precise, and the results of this study have been useful not only in terms of understanding the Phoenicians themselves, but also in terms of a better understanding of the Hebrew of the Old Testament.

Side by side with the grammatical study of the Phoenician inscriptions has been their palaeographical study. Since it has long been known that virtually all modern alphabetic writing derives directly from the ancient Phoenician script, the study of the development of the forms of the Phoenician letters is important to every historian of culture. By observing minor changes in the way each letter is formed in different inscriptions, the trained palaeographer can place these inscriptions in chronological order with a surprising degree of success. Great care must be taken in this work, and a dating on palaeographical evidence alone can hardly be considered definitive, especially for periods from which few inscriptions have survived, since there are many factors other than time that can cause minor differences in letter shapes. No two people have identical handwriting, and besides, the traditional shapes of letters differ from one place to another. Thus although the Phoenician and Aramaic alphabets started out practically identical, they gradually diverged so much that they became completely different. About the time of Ezra, the Hebrew scribes, who had been following the Phoenician tradition, changed over to the Aramaic script. Similarly, while they were writing in the same general way, scribes of Tyre may have formed some of their letters a bit differently from scribes of Gebal, or one of the colonies. Considerable progress has been made in the study of Phoenician writing in recent years through the discovery of numerous ancient inscriptions and through the meticulous study of these inscriptions. Outstanding in this field of endeavor in the United States has been the work of William F. Albright and his students.

Much is now known about the history of the Canaanites from early times, but these people are not usually thought of as Phoenicians until the beginning of the Iron Age, about 1200 B.C. Whereas the Canaanites had formerly possessed practically the whole eastern end of the Mediterranean, they were now driven out of their southern holdings by the Israelites and iron-possessing Philistines, and were increasingly being pushed out of the inland areas of the north by Hurrians, Hittites, and Arameans. Soon Canaanites were considered foreigners everywhere except in the narrow strip of coast stretching from the area around Mount Carmel in the South to Arvad in the North.

In this area the cities of Tyre, Sarepta (the Zarephath of I Kings 17:9f.), Sidon, Beirut, Gebal, Simyra, and Arvad were already old and well established. All of these cities were long since known to the Egyptians, who had maintained commercial relations with Gebal since the beginning of the third millennium B.C. Nor had these cities been isolated from the great Mesopotamian culture to the East. The Akkadian language had been studied by scribes at Gebal as early as the Third Dynasty of Ur (beginning of second millennium B.C.). It was natural for these people, confined to an area that had many excellent natural harbors, with plenty of timber on the slopes of the Lebanon for building ships, and few other natural resources, to turn increasingly toward the sea. With their lumber they could also build furniture for trade, and the waters off their coasts abounded both in edible fish and in several species of shellfish (*Murex brandaris, Murex trunculus, Helix ianthina, and Purpura lapillus*) that could be processed to obtain various shades of purple dye. The Phoenicians became highly skilled in the building and sailing of ships and in various aspects of commerce. Their art work became world famous, and their purple textiles were desired throughout the Mediterranean world. It is probable that the Greeks gave them the name "Phoenicians" (Greek *phoinix*, purple) because of these purple fabrics.

The Phoenicians now dealt on more nearly equal terms with the great powers of antiquity. According to the charming Egyptian tale of the Adventures of *Wenamon (ca. 1100 B.C.?), when the expedition of the hero arrived at Gebal to obtain wood for the god Amun, he could not pay for the lumber, and the Phoenician prince made no attempt to veil his disrespect for the Egyptian envoy. The story presents an interesting picture of the ruler of Gebal sitting in his upstairs room looking out at the roaring sea while Wenamon waited for an audience in which to ask for cedar logs on credit.

Roughly contemporary with the journey of Wenamon was a westward march led by Tiglath-pileser I (1115-1077 B.C.), king of the rising state of Assyria. Gebal, Sidon, and Arvad paid tribute, and from Arvad the Assyrian monarch went by sea to Simyra, killing some kind of sea creature (perhaps a dolphin) on the outing. It is unlikely that Assyria exerted any lasting political influence on Phoenicia at this time. It is from this period that our earliest Phoenician inscriptions come. The oldest of these is the funerary inscription of Ahiram of Gebal (first quarter of the tenth century). This inscription was carved in a single line of text around two sides of the lid of Ahiram's sarcophagus. It is in a good state of preservation, with only a few letters needing restoration, but apparently the stone-mason omitted a letter or two. Though not all scholars agree on the meaning of all the words, the following translation certainly captures its general intent: "The coffin that Ittobaal, son of Ahiram, King of Gebal, made for his father as his place in eternity. If any king or any governor or any military commander should attack Gebal and expose this coffin, may his scepter of judgment be broken; may his kingly throne be overturned, and may peace flee from Gebal. As for him, may a wanderer efface his inscription." Scratched on the wall of the tomb shaft was another warning for any would-be plunderer: "Notice! Behold, there is grief for you below here!"

It is clear from this inscription that it was very important to the Phoenicians that their corpses should not be desecrated. Whether the expression "his place in eternity" indicates a belief in an afterlife at this early period is less clear, but in view of Egypt's long influence on Phoenicia, and especially Gebal, it is certainly possible. The desire that one's grave should not be molested was expressed again and again in Phoenician inscriptions, usually with a curse pronounced on any tomb violator, and often with the additional statement that no jewelry or other riches had been buried with the deceased. From the time of Alexander the Great comes an inscription of Tabnit, who was a priest of Ashtart and at the same time "King of the Sidonians." Tabnit, after protesting that nothing of value is buried with him, states that it would be an abomination to Ashtart to disturb him.

Not all extant Phoenician inscriptions are of a funerary nature, and the next oldest royal inscription now known is a building inscription coming from one of Ahiram's immediate successors on the throne of Gebal:

The temple that Yehimilk, King of Gebal, built. He it was who repaired all the ruins of these temples. May Baal-Shamen and Baal-Gebal and the assemblage of the holy gods of Gebal lengthen the days of Yehimilk and his years over Gebal as a rightful king and a true king in the presence of the holy gods of Gebal.

While Ahiram, Ittobaal, and Yehimilk were occupying the throne of Gebal and other rulers were in power in Tyre, Sidon, and the other Phoenician cities, the Israelites were engaged in establishing something that their northern neighbors would never experience for themselves: a unified political state. Solomon (961-922 B.C.), the third ruler of this new monarchy, entered into marriage alliances with many of his neighbors. Among these was probably the king of Sidon (I Kings 11:1), if "Sidonians" in this verse does not refer to Phoenicians in general as it often does in the Old Testament as well as in Homer and other ancient sources. As a result of these foreign marriages Solomon adopted many foreign deities, including Ashtoreth of the Sidonians (I Kings 11:5). The Phoenicians also had a tremendous impact on Israelite art, architecture, and commerce, for Solomon made a particularly sweeping treaty with Hiram, King of Tyre, who had also been an ally of David's (I Kings 5:1ff.). Not only did Solomon join with Hiram in a shipping venture (II Chron. 9:21); he also imported skilled Phoenician architects and craftsmen to carry out the most important building project ever undertaken in ancient Israel. This, of course, was the construction of the Temple in Jerusalem and of the king's palace — the glorious "House of the Forest of Lebanon" (I Kings 7:2ff. RSV). Thus Phoenician influence was felt at the very heart of ancient Israel's worship and government.

A century later, after Solomon's kingdom had split into the northern kingdom of Israel and the southern kingdom of Judah, both Hebrew states were to feel the impact of Phoenician religion even more directly. Ittobaal of Tyre gave his daughter Jezebel in marriage to Ahab, king of Israel (869-850 B.C.). Later Athaliah, daughter of Ahab and Jezebel, married Jehoram, king of Judah. The struggle that ensued between the House of Ahab and the followers of Baal against Elijah the prophet of Yahweh is graphically recorded in I Kings 16:29ff.

Nor was the House of Ittobaal of Tyre completely free from troubles at home. Throughout the period of Phoenician independence, Phoenician traders plied the coasts of the Mediterranean, setting up trading posts and colonies (and leaving inscriptions which attest their presence to modern archaeologists). According to a legend that is thought to have some factual basis, it was the great-granddaughter of Ittobaal, fleeing from a family quarrel in Tyre, who established in 814 the most famous of all Phoenician colonies: Carthage.

The ninth century also saw a revival of Assyrian interest in the West. Ashurnasirpal II (883-859 B.C.) forced the Phoenician cities to pay tribute to Assyria. Aside from several different kinds of wood the tribute included silver, gold, lead, copper, copper vessels, brightly colored woolen garments, linen garments, ivory, and the same kind of sea creature that had provided sport for Tiglath-pileser. Shalmaneser III (858-824 B.C.) continued his father's policy, leading his troops westward on more than one occasion, and though he had to face a coalition of western kings at Qarqar in 853 B.C. (including Ahab of Israel, Hadadezer of Damascus, Matinubaal of Arvad, and others), he collected considerable quantities of tribute from the Phoenician cities. In addition to material booty he took home many Phoenician and Syrian craftsmen. A hoard of fine Phoenician carved ivory dating from this period has recently been recovered from the Assyrian capital of Calah (Nimrud). The fame of the Phoenician craftsmen of this era is also echoed in Homer, who speaks in the Iliad and again in the Odyssey of bowls of Sidonian workmanship.

Many such bowls have been found, including one carved with Egyptian hieroglyphs and motifs dating from the last half of the seventh century discovered at Praeneste, Italy, and bearing the owner's (or maker's) name inscribed in Phoenician: "Eshmunya'ad son of Ashto."

From this general period comes one of the longest Phoenician inscriptions known today. This is the bilingual monument erected by Azitawadd, king of the Danunites, in the Cilician Plain of Adana. It is particularly interesting to note the use of pure

CRUSADER CASTLE AT SIDON. Courtesy, Zion Research Library

Phoenician in an official inscription this far North. Was this little kingdom a Phoenician colony, or had Canaanites been in this area continuously from early times, or was this just a small neo-Hittite kingdom that had somehow come under the influence of the Phoenicians? Whatever the solution of the historical problems raised by this inscription, carved twice in Phoenician and duplicated in hieroglyphic Hittite, it has been helpful in solving some of the problems of the hieroglyphic Hittite writing and it has also illuminated certain aspects of Phoenician grammar.

Assyrian interest in the West fell off for about a century after the death of Shalmaneser III, but it was vigorously resumed by Tiglath-pileser III (745-727 B.C.), who took tribute from Arvad, Gebal, and from Hiram II of Tyre. Since he makes no mention of Sidon, and since a contemporary inscription (CIS.i. 5) erected by the Phoenician governor of Qart-hadasht (New City) in Cyprus speaks of "Hiram, King of the Sidonians," it is generally thought that Tyre and Sidon were united at this time. His successor, Shalmaneser V (727-722 B.C.), received the submission of most of the Phoenician cities (including Sidon), but the island stronghold of Tyre held out. Although the Assyrians besieged the city for five years, and even attacked it by sea with the aid of ships from those cities that had capitulated, Tyre successfully withstood the siege, which ended with a treaty upon Shalmaneser's death. Assyria remained the dominant influence in Phoenician affairs from this time until the overthrow of Nineveh at the hands of the Babylonians. Though even Tyre had submitted for a while to the Assyrians during the reign of Sennacherib (704-681 B.C.), it was again independent when Nebuchadnezzar came to the throne of Babylon (605-562 B.C.). In the year after the fall of Jerusalem (586 B.C.) the Babylonian monarch laid siege to Tyre, and the prophet Ezekiel (chapter 26) confidently stated that he would completely destroy the city. But the siege dragged on for thirteen interminable years and finally ended with Tyre's conditional surrender. A few years later Babylon fell to Persia (539 B.C.), and with it went Phoenicia. But the Phoenician city-states were still unaccustomed to foreign rule, having vacillated in their loyalty throughout the period of Assyro-Babylonian dominance. Several times the Assyrians had put down revolts, and Esarhaddon had destroyed Sidon, although by the Persian period it was again a thriving metropolis. For a long time the Phoenicians were loyal to Persia, and Sidon served as the capital of the Fifth Satrapy. Gradually they became restive, however, and during the reign of Artaxerxes III Ochus a rebellion broke out (345 B.C.), centering at Sidon. Again this ancient city was burned to the ground, and most of its inhabitants perished in its flames.

In the earlier years of their rule, the Persians had made good use of the Phoenician sailors and craftsmen, but when Alexander the Great began his eastward march, Darius III failed to take advantage of the Phoenician maritime strength to attack Alexander in the rear. After defeating Darius at Issus (333 B.C.), Alexander eliminated the possibility of such a rear attack by marching South into Phoenicia. All the cities quickly submitted except Tyre. Although the people of Tyre were willing to accept Alexander as a ruler at a distance and pay tribute to him, they were unwilling to allow him to set foot on their island stronghold. Deciding to set an example against such an independent spirit, Alexander laid siege and constructed a causeway to connect the island to the mainland. After seven months, he completed the causeway, and supported by the navies of the other Phoenician cities, he wantonly destroyed Tyre. In less than a decade Alexander died and his empire was divided by his successors. The Seleucids of Syria and the Ptolemies of Egypt fought for possession of the Phoenician coast, which passed from one to the other without regard to the wishes of the Phoenicians themselves. Sidon was rebuilt and ruled by the dynasty of Tabnit and Eshmunazar, both mentioned above, and according to the funerary inscription of Eshmunazar, the dynasty did much to beautify the city, erecting temples for Ashtart and Eshmun, the chief gods of Sidon. They also extended their control as far south as Dor and Joppa in the fruitful Plain of Sharon south of Carmel.

In the West, Carthage carried on independently, leading the other Phoenician colonies in the struggle with the rising menace of Rome until the Romans were finally victorious in 146 B.C. The Phoenicians con-

---

tinued to maintain enclaves in important commercial cities throughout the Mediterranean and at the Athenian port of Piraeus was found an inscription set up in the first century B.C. by the Sidonian community there in honor of Shama'ba'al son of Magon as a token of gratitude for his public service.

Soon Aramaic was to replace Phoenician as the language of the Canaanite homeland, but the old language, now rather changed and called Neo-Punic, lingered on in North Africa for a long time. St. Augustine said that the people of his day there still called themselves Canaanite.

Today more than five thousand Phoenician inscriptions from all parts of the Mediterranean world are available for study. The majority of these, many of which are exceedingly brief, come from the environs of Carthage. They have been divided by Harris into five linguistic categories: Early Phoenician (before 800 B.C.), Middle Phoenician (800-500 B.C.), Late Phoenician (500 B.C. to the time of Christ in the East), Punic (*ca.* 500-146 B.C. in the West), and Neo-Punic (from the fall of Carthage to the Arabic conquest).

Recent developments have added new aspects and new importance to the study of the Phoenician inscriptions. Among these developments may be mentioned the discovery of hundreds of tablets written in a previously unknown Northwest Semitic language at °Ugarit and the subsequent discussion of the relationships of the language and religion presented in these tablets with the Phoenician language and religion. Much more recent than the discovery of Ugarit has been Cyrus H. Gordon's announcement that he has deciphered the so-called Linear A script from the island of Crete and found the Minoan Linear A tablets to be written in a Northwest Semitic dialect closely related to Phoenician and Hebrew. Subsequent to this he further has maintained that both Eteocretan and Eteocypriote are essentially this same dialect.

BIBLIOGRAPHY. W. F. Albright, "New Light on the Early History of Phoenician Colonization," *BASOR* 83, 1941, pp. 14-22; "The Phoenician Inscriptions of the Tenth Century B.C. from Byblus," *JAOS* 67, 1947, pp. 153-60; "The Role of the Canaanites in the History of Civilization," *The Bible and the Ancient Near East*, ed. G. E. Wright, Doubleday, Garden City, New York, 1961. G. Contenau, *La civilisation phénicienne*, second edition, Payot, Paris, 1949. G. A. Cooke, *A Text-book of North-Semitic Inscriptions*, Oxford, 1903.. Maurice Dunand, *Byblia grammata*, Beyrouth, 1945. Johannes Friedrich, *Phönizisch-punische Grammatik*, Pontificum Institutum Biblicum, Rome, 1951. Cyrus H. Gordon, "Azitawadd's Phoenician Inscription," *JNES* 8, 1949, pp. 108-115; "Newest Frontier in Biblical Studies," *Christianity Today*, vol. 7, number 12, March 15, 1963, pp. 3-8; "Phoenician Inscriptions from Karatepe," *JQR* 39, 1948, pp. 41-50. Donald B. Harden, *The Phoenicians*, Thames and Hudson, London, 1962. Zellig S. Harris, *Development of the Canaanite Dialects*, American Oriental Society, New Haven, 1939; *A Grammar of the Phoenician Language*, American Oriental Society, New Haven, 1936. Philip K. Hitti, *Lebanon in History*, Macmillan, London, 1957. Alexander M. Honeyman, "Phoenician Inscriptions from Karatepe," *Le Muséon*, 61, 1948, pp. 43-57. B. Maisler, "Phoenician Inscriptions from Byblos and the Development of the Phoenician-Hebrew Alphabetic Writing," (in Hebrew) *Leshonenu*, 14, 1946, pp. 166-181. Ralph Marcus and Ignace J. Gelb, "The Phoenician Stele Inscription from Cilicia," *JNES* 8, 1949, pp. 116-120; "A Preliminary Study of the New Phoenician Inscription from Cilicia," *JNES* 7, 1948, pp. 194-198. Th.C. Vriezen and J. H. Hospers, *Palestine Inscriptions (Textus Minores, vol. xvii)*, E. J. Brill, Leiden, 1951.

PHRYGIANS. The Phrygians came from Thrace in the great Aegean migrations *ca.* 1200 B.C. and occupied central Anatolia west of the Halys River. Their capital was at Gordion. The Phrygians worshiped Cybele, the Great Mother who is depicted riding in a chariot drawn by lions. The Cybele cult was introduced into Rome during the third century B.C. A second Phrygian deity was Attis, the god who died as a result of castration, but came back to life. The kingdom of Phrygia lasted from *ca.* 1050 to *ca.* 700 B.C. Their best known king was Mushku, or Midas, who is mentioned in the inscriptions of Sargon II of Assyria and became a figure of classical legend.

PICTOGRAPH. See Writing.

PILATE, PONTIUS. Pontius Pilate, who is mentioned in the New Testament fifty-three times, was the fifth of the Roman procurators. Like his immediate predecessor, Valerius Gratus (A.D. 15-26), Pilate had a rather lengthy rule (A.D. 26-36) as Roman governor of Palestine. His long tenure in office was due to a fixed policy of Tiberius, who believed that it was in the interest of the provinces to leave procurators in office many years both to profit from their experi-

*THEATER INSCRIPTION FROM CAESAREA bearing the name of Pontius Pilate.
Courtesy, Israel Department of Antiquities*

ence and to prevent graft and bribery. He thought that governors acted like "flies upon the body of a wounded animal." If "flies" (or procurators) had once stuffed to the full, they would become less demanding in their exactions. If frequent changes in the office of his governors occurred, Tiberius felt that the people under them would be constantly subjected to fresh greed and unsatisfied rapacity (Josephus, *Antiquites* XVIII. vi. 5). Much information concerning Pilate may be found in Josephus (who describes his career more fully than that of any other procurator), Philo, and Tacitus. Philo records a letter of Agrippa I in which Pilate is spoken of as a person of "inflexible, stubborn, and cruel disposition." According to the same source Pilate's term of service was marked by ". . . venality, violence, thefts, assaults of the people, abusive behavior, frequent executions of untried prisoners, endless and savage ferocity" (Philo, *The Embassy to Gaius*, 38, ed. Smallwood, *infra*, p. 128).

Pilate had been appointed to office by the influence of Sejanus, who was an arch-enemy of the Jews. It was also due to the influence of Sejanus that the expulsion of the Jews from Rome took place in A.D. 19 (Philo, *The Embassy to Gaius*, Sec. 24 [159-161], ed. Smallwood, p. 94). Pilate likewise consistently followed an anti-Semitic policy during his term of office. The coins which were struck during his years of authority display pagan religious symbols (the *lituus* and the *simpulum;* see Reifenberg, *Ancient Jewish Coins*, Nos. 131-133) which must have been offensive to the Jews. Herod the Great had earlier placed an *eagle* on some coins, and the Jews were particularly enraged when he placed an eagle on the temple. The eagle representing the government of Rome, was looked upon as an idolatrous symbol by pious Jews. (Cf. Reifenberg, *op. cit.*; no. 34 and cf. Josephus, *Antiquities* XVII. vi. 2 ff. For the date of Herod's coins, see J. Meyshan, "The Coins of the Herodian Dynasty," *The Dating and Meaning of Ancient Jewish Coins* [Numismatic Studies and Researches, II. Publications of the Israel Numismatic Society, 1958]).

The extra-Biblical information concerning Pontius Pilate is consistent with what we learn of him from the New Testament writers. Josephus informs us (*Antiquites* XVIII. iii. 1) that in disregard for Jewish religious sensitivities, he carried into Jerusalem standards which depicted the portrait of Tiberius. The Jewish people resented this action and marched to Caesarea in great numbers to protest. Pilate let them assemble to the hippodrome, which could accommodate twenty thousand. The theater, which could accommodate smaller crowds, was evidently not large enough. Though his soldiers surrounded the mob and drew swords to intimidate them (to which act the people daringly bared their necks), Pilate was forced to yield to the pressure of this demonstration and withdraw the standards.

Pilate also misappropriated the funds of the Temple offerings by building an aqueduct to Jerusalem from springs somewhat south of Bethlehem, at a spot called Etam, erroneously designated "Solomon's Pools" today. (Cf. Josephus, *Antiquities* XVII, iii. 2; *Wars* II. ix. 4; Eusebius. *Church History*, II 6.; *Jerusalem Yoma* III). When the Jews protested this abuse of the Temple treasury, Pilate had his soldiers club them to death.

Pilate attempted to take votive shields which were inscribed with the name of Tiberius into the palace of Herod at Jerusalem (which also must have been the place where Jesus was tried before Pilate. Cf. Philo, *Embassy to Gaius* 39 [299 ff.]. Smallwood, p. 128). Again, the people protested and certain leading citizens appealed in a petition to Tiberius that this insult might be rectified. Tiberius sternly instructed Pilate to remove these shields from Jerusalem and deposit them in Caesar's temple at Caesarea. The crowning act of Pilate's tyranny led to his removal and to the appointment of Marcellus to take his place. Pilate slaughtered and imprisoned a large number of Samaritans who had gathered at Mount Gerizim, on the report that certain religious objects buried since Moses' time were to be found by a self-appointed false prophet (*Antiquities* XVIII. iv. 1). Pilate's removal came when the Samaritans complained to Vitellius, Roman governor of Syria, who sent Pilate to Rome to answer for his behavior to Tiberius.

The New Testament adds to our knowledge of Pilate's arbitrary temper and tells of his slaying of certain Galileans while they were in the act of offering their sacrifices at the Jerusalem temple (Luke 13:1ff.).

In the Apocryphal Gospels much fanciful material is recorded concerning Pilate. There is no historical basis for his supposed letters to Tiberius, or for the belief that he committed suicide. Some legends state that he was executed under Tiberius (or Nero) and others that he died as a penitent Christian (cf., "The Giving Up of Pontius Pilate," in *Apocryhal Gospels*, Vol. XVI; *Ante-Nicene Christian Library*, 1873, pp. 231-233). In the Ethiopic Church he has even been canonized as a saint! A papyrus text in the Eisenberg Museum of the Southern Baptist Seminary in Louisville mentions a certain early Christian named "Pilate." The popularity of the name among early Christians seems to grow out of such legends.

Of much greater historical worth is a newly discovered inscription from the theatre at Caesarea (found in 1961 as Italian archaeologists were washing and cleaning the area after excavations. See especially the report by Frova, *infra*.).

This text can perhaps be translated ". . . Tiberium [that is a temple dedicated to the worship of Tiberius] (? of the Caesareans?) Pontius Pilate, prefect of the Judea (? has dedicated ?)." This "Tiberium" must have been demolished well before the fourth century A.D. since stones from it were used to rebuild and to repair the theater at Caesarea when it was remodeled to accommodate spectacles on water about that century. The great significance of this new "Pilate inscription," of course, rests in the new information which it affords Biblical students concerning the exact title Pilate bore ["Prefect"] at the time he dedicated a temple in honor of Tiberius. Just where this temple to Tiberius was located at Caesarea is unknown. It was probably near the theater, which was itself close to the temple of Augustus. The small size of the letters on the inscription (6 to 7 cm.) indicate that the "Tiberium" must have been itself quite small. This suggests that it was an annex to the earlier temple to Augustus which Herod had constructed (cf. *Antiquities* XV. ix. 6) and would explain why Tiberius ordered the inscribed shields returned to the "Temple of Caesar" at Caesarea, assuming, as Schürer does, that this event came towards the close of Pilate's career when this temple for emperor worship must certainly have been completed.

Whenever it was that Pilate had the temple to Tiberius' honor built, this new fact about him adds valuable dimensions to the New Testament picture of Jesus' crucifixion. Pilate was anxious to show himself a "friend of Caesar" (cf. John 19:12). This title is a techinical designation for such high officials, as shown by numerous inscriptions and coins. (Cf. the coins of Agrippa I and II with this title. See Reifenberg, *op. cit.*, no. 60, 60a, 62, 63, 74). The enemies of Jesus knew the weak spots in Pilate's defense when they forced him in a corner by the charges they brought against Jesus.

As far as the title "Prefect" is concerned, it should be remembered that this title was widely used in the time of Augustus (cf. Schürer, *infra*. I, Division II, P. 45). By the time of Claudius, the title of "procurator" was the prevailing one. Both Tacitus (*Annals* XV. 44) and Josephus (*Wars* II. ix. 2) call Pilate a "procurator" and there should be little doubt that at some time in his career he must have been so designated (perhaps towards the end of his career). In any case, there is no conflict with the New Testament on this point, since the only designation given there for Pilate is "governor" (a neutral term used for any ruler).

BIBLIOGRAPHY. Emil Schürer, *A History of the Jewish People in the Time of Jesus Christ*, Charles Scribner's Sons, New York, 1891, I, Division II, pp. 81-88 (see Index Volume for other material on Pilate and the older bibliographical sources). E. Mary Smallwood, *Philonis Alexandrini: Legatio ad Gaium*, E. J. Brill, Leiden, 1961. *Bible et Terre Sainte*, 57 (Juin, 1963) — whole issue devoted to various studies on Pontius Pilate (see especially in this issue the article by M. Aristide Calderini, "L'Inscription de Ponce Pilate a Cesarea," pp. 8-10). Antonio Frova, "L'Inscriptione di Ponzio Pilato a Cesarea," *Rendiconti* 95, Instituto Lombardo di Scienze e Lettere, Milano, 1961, pp. 419-434. Jerry Vardaman, "A New Inscription which Mentions Pilate as 'Prefect,'" *JBL*, LXXXI, 1962, pp. 71-73.

PITHOM (PI-TUM). Although the exact location of Pithom is not known, there can be no doubt that it was located in the Wadi Tumilat. In 1883, Edouard Naville began the excavation of Tell el-Maskhuta for the Egypt Exploration Fund. On the basis of inscriptions which he found, Naville was convinced that the place anciently was called Per-Atum, "the house of Atum," a close approximation to Pithom. Years before, Lepsius had identified the site of Tell el-Maskhuta with the other of the two store cities mentioned in Exodus 1:11 — Raamses. Naville found a number of rectangular chambers, without doors, separated from one another by thick walls of crude brick. These he assumed to be the store-rooms which the Hebrews were

SILVER DISHES AND UTENSILS DISCOVERED AT POMPEII. They are on display at the National Museum, Naples. Courtesy, F. Alinari

forced to build during the days of their slavery. Grain, according to the usual Egyptian custom, had been poured into the store rooms through openings in the roof.

The bricks used at Tell el-Maskhuta are of three varieties. Those at the lowest level were mixed with chopped straw; higher up when the straw seems to have been used up, the clay was found to have been mixed with reeds, and at the top level Nile mud was used for the bricks with no binding substance added. It will be remembered that the Egyptian taskmasters withheld straw from their Israelite slaves (Exod. 5:10-21). Nile mud coheres in such a way that bricks can be made without straw, but the Biblical record implies that straw was normally used. Although the bricks of Tell el-Maskhuta cannot be positively identified as Israelite in origin, they illustrate the different kinds of bricks which were used in ancient Egypt.

Alan Gardiner is not satisfied that Tell el-Maskhuta is the site of Biblical Pithom. He prefers a mound eight and one-half miles west known as Tell er-Retaba. To add to the confusion, Flinders Petrie identified Tell er-Retaba with Biblical Raamses. Others identify Tell el-Maskhuta with Succoth, the first stop of the Israelites after they escaped from Pharaoh (Exod. 12:37).

Naville's "store chambers" have been questioned, by later archaeologists who suggest that the walls of the cells which he discovered were really foundations of a strong fortress. T. Eric Peet states, "These late Egyptian fortresses were built up on massive brick platforms containing hollow compartments. No one who examines Naville's plan can remain in doubt as to the real nature of what he found" (*Egypt and the Old Testament*, p. 86, note 2).

Flinders Petrie excavated Tell er-Retaba in 1905-06, finding evidence that the site had been occupied since Old Kingdom times. A temple was discovered, dating to the time of Ramesses II and adorned with red granite and sandstone. A double statue represented Ramesses and the god Atum. Baikie mentions a curious tradition from the fourth century of our era in which a woman pilgrim was told that the statue depicted Moses and Aaron (*Egyptian Antiquities on the Nile Valley*, p. 16).

Petrie noted that human sacrifices had been offered at the dedication of the first wall of the town. This custom was otherwise unknown among the Egyptians but common among the Canaanites. Macalister had discovered evidences of such human sacrifice at Gezer. It appears that Canaanite influence had been exerted at Tell er-Retaba at an early date.

Among the more colorful discoveries of Petrie at Tell er-Retaba was a bowl of blue glaze with nineteen frogs sitting around the bowl and others scrambling up the sides of the interior. In the middle of the inside a large frog sits enthroned upon a pedestal. The bowl dates from the Twenty-second Dynasty.

BIBLIOGRAPHY. *See under* Raamses.

POMPEII. Situated at the foot of Mount Vesuvius, thirteen miles southeast of Naples, Pompeii was a flourishing provincial town before it was hit by an earthquake (A.D. 63) and totally destroyed by an eruption of Mount Vesuvius in A.D. 79. Layers of ash

and pumice covered the city, preserving its ruins practically intact until the present day. Some excavations were made in antiquity in an effort to recover buried treasure, but the city and its ruins were soon forgotten. In 1748 some peasants came upon some works of ancient art in a ruined house at Pompeii, and the rulers of nearby Naples took an interest in the site. Work continued sporadically until the fall of the Bourbon kingdom in 1860. Since that time scientific excavations were conducted by Giuseppe Fiorelli and others. Most of the area within the walls has now been excavated. This comprises about two-fifths of the city which had an area of about 160 acres in A.D. 79.

The Great Theater of Pompeii, dating to the time of Augustus, was semicircular in plan with a diameter of 322 feet. The temple of Isis had adjoining quarters for the priests whose skeletons bear mute evidence that they sought too late to flee. The houses of the city give an insight into the daily lives of the ancient Romans. Many are adorned with murals. The so-called House of the Faun has mosaics instead of the usual wall paintings. The famous *Dancing Faun* and a mosaic of the *Battle of Issus* came from this house.

POTTERY. Pottery was the first artificial stone made by mankind and like all important inventions it has played its part in changing the history of civilization. Ceramics is still expanding its usage in many phases of the modern world and in the space age program. When clay is heated to the proper temperature its chemical composi-

tion is changed and the new substance has a different set of physical properties. Pottery has the permanence of stone and this is one of the basic reasons why the archaeologists of today can interpret the chronology of the Bible. The pottery of Abraham's time is just as good today as when it was made. A second feature of pottery which is of use to the archaeologist is that clay can be fashioned into thousands of forms before it is fired. After that the form is permanent. It is the patient study of these different forms that has enabled the archaeologist to date the years when certain forms come into use and when they go out of circulation. Today most pottery of Bible times can be dated to within fifty years or less if a sufficient variety of dishes is found.

I. *Fashioning clay into pottery.* Most of Palestine had a good grade of red clay which, when properly weathered and washed, could be fashioned into good pottery. Some of these clays had to be modified but the necessary agents for this were well known and available. After the clay was purified, it was mixed with the proper amount of water and treaded well so as to produce a consistent texture and to remove all air bubbles (Isa. 41:25). This clay could then be fashioned by hand into the desired vessel or it could be thrown on the potter's wheel just as we see it done today. Most of the pottery of Bible days was wheel made. The potter's wheel of Old Testament times was either small in diameter, in which case it was usually turned by the potter himself as he shaped the vessel; or this small wheel, on which the potter worked, was set into a larger wheel which could then be turned by an apprentice, thus giving the thrower an opportunity to create better forms. Jer. 18:3 refers to the second or compound wheel. The potter's wheel with its foot-tread such as is used today was invented in inter-Testament times (Ecclesiasticus 38:29-30). After the vessel was hand fashioned or thrown on the wheel, it was set aside to dry before being fired in the kiln. This latter process demanded the highest professional skill, depending upon the clays used, the type of vessels in the kiln, the firing itself and other factors. If he misjudged any of these factors the pottery might be unsalable and would be thrown out as worthless.

Before firing, the pottery could be decorated in various ways. It might be dipped into a clay slip with a heavy iron content which could give it a richer texture and a deeper red color. It might be burnished to give the varying play of light and shadow. Painted patterns could also be applied. The use of the latter was most common just preceding Joshua's conquest, although the Philistines used it and introduced a new set of patterns. It is in striking contrast to the Israelite pottery which was at its worst in the days of the Judges. Occasionally after firing, the vessels were dipped into a vat of liquid colored clay. This thin coating improved the look of poor ware but such decoration quickly wore off, unlike the permanent patterns which had been put on before the ware was fired. The potters of Palestine did not glaze their ware but such vessels could be imported. Glaze is only mentioned once in the Old Testament (Prov. 26:23). The Greeks were the experts in the field of glazed pottery. It is not uncommon

AN ANCIENT EGYPTIAN POTTER. The potter is depicted at his wheel. Three pots are at his side. Courtesy, Oriental Institute

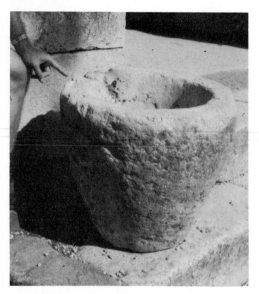

WATER JAR at Capernaum Synagogue.
Courtesy, Jerry Vardaman

to find Greek and Roman glazed pottery when excavating the better homes of New Testament Palestine. The most beautiful of all ceramic forms, however, were made in the Middle Bronze Age, i.e. about the time of Joseph.

II. *Late Israelite pottery as an assembly line product.* About the time of Isaiah the Israelites invented our modern methods of mass production and assembly line techniques in manufacturing their pottery. Thus they, like ourselves were enabled to produce good ware at very cheap prices. They also standardized their vessels in size just as we do today and their ware could be nested just as ours is. Each potter could have his own trade-mark although he used it chiefly on cooking pots, which naturally had the shortest life of all ceramic ware and therefore were the potter's best source of income. The government had its own factory which produced the legal jars for holding taxable liquids. The government never trusted the size of your jar; you used their container. These jars were stamped on the handles with the government seal and the name of the county seat where the taxes were to be paid (I Chron. 4:23). The king also had his own private seal which was used on all royal pottery. Note the distinction between the personal property of the king and the taxable property which was available for the payments of the bureaucrats and the members of the military service.

III. *Pottery kitchen ware.* We think of pottery today primarily as dishes but in Bible times it had a much wider usage. Pottery vats took the place of modern barrels, boxes and bags, all of which were very much more expensive than their pottery counterparts. The hand woven basket was the potter's only economic competitor. Pottery cooking ware was the normal usage in the kitchen for only the rich could afford copper kettles; and it was not until after David's day that an iron skillet could be afforded in wealthy homes. The invention of the pottery cooking pot improved the world's menu for it added boiling and stewing to roasting. Even the latter could be improved by the use of the pottery oven which looked like a small inverted tub without a bottom. Some types of cooking pots were globular in shape with narrow mouths, apparently used primarily for heating water. Most cooking pots, however, were wide and shallow with wide mouths so that the stew or porridge could be watched and stirred. Some cooking vessels resembled a modern casserole. Some were used especially for deep fat frying. There was also a pottery kneading trough for the bread dough.

AN OIL STORAGE JAR from the Jaffa Museum. Courtesy, Gerald Larue

IV. *Pottery dinner ware.* In the days of the prophets water was carried in pitchers similar to those used today. There was also a cylindrical shaped jar with a wide mouth and an antisplash rim used for the same purpose. The latter jar could also serve for the storage of flour. Gideon used one of these jars to carry the charcoal with which to light his torches. Olive oil was stored in a foot tall jar with a built-in funnel so that the dipper could be inverted over the funnel and the expensive oil drained back into the jar. Oil and wine were stored in various sized jars and the contents were removed by pottery dippers. When a large jar was broken the larger pieces could be used as lids for other store jars, as a shovel to carry coals from a neighbor's hearth, or a sherd could serve as stationery on which to write a letter or a legal document. Smaller sherds were often built into the clay walls of an oven to increase the heat. They were also ground very find and used in water-proof plaster for cisterns. Although pottery was very cheap, the poor people were such paupers that they mended their few dishes with copper wire.

At the table bowls of various sizes were employed. These bowls run in size from the great banquet urns to what we would call dessert dishes. Plates were very difficult to make on the wheel, so shallow bowls were used instead of plates until inter-Testament times. Their cups seldom carried a handle; and the cup shape, which we know, was not as widely used then as was a shallow cup more like our cereal bowls. Water was served from a narrow-mouthed decanter similar to the water decanters used on rail-road diners. This aerated the water. Olive oil cruets were of various sizes. If the meal was served after dark it was illuminated by a pottery lamp. In Old Testament times this was about the size of a dessert dish, but it had been pinched in at one point so as to hold a flax wick which rested in the olive oil. The lamp used by the wise and foolish virgins had a Greek ancestry, and was very small, seldom over two inches in diameter.

V. *Pottery in industry.* Pottery was also used in industry. Metallurgy demanded pottery crucibles made from various types of clay depending upon the temperature of the smelting. Large ones were used in smelting the ore at the mine and smaller ones were used by the jeweler in refining the precious metals such as silver and gold. The molten metal from the smelters was poured into pottery ingot molds. When the ingots were refined the metal was poured into pottery molds with a wide variety of patterns depending upon the purpose for which the object was used. In the making of cloth ceramics played its part also. The poor used a pottery spindle whorl when spinning their thread and clay loom weights were used by everyone in the weaving of cloth. If the cloth was dyed pottery vats were often used.

VI. *Pottery in Idolatry.* Pottery idols and other cult objects were common among the Canaanites; only occasionally are they found in Israelite homes. The teraphim of Genesis 31:19 ff. were such idols. Pottery idols were usually those of the fertility goddess Astarte and were used in family shrines. Before Joshua's conquest these idols were in the form of a flat placque about the size of the palm of the hand. These were made on a press mold, i.e. plastic clay was pressed into pottery molds which contained the form of the goddess. In Jezebel's day the body of the idol was fashioned freehand and looked like a snowman about four to six inches high. The head, however, was made in a press mold and when hard was fastened to the body. Pottery statuettes of Baal are rare; they were usually of metal. In front of the idol in the family shrine was a stylized pottery tree holding a lamp in its branches. Pottery incense altars and censers along with fancy flower vases were used in public shrines. Pottery rattles, small pottery doves and bulls and other cultic objects were used in both public and private shrines.

VII. *Writing on pottery.* Most writing was done on large pieces of broken jars for papyrus and leather were very expensive. Government tax receipts, military dispatches and legal documents as well as personal letters were written on pottery. Ink wells were usually pottery. The invention of writing was based upon pictures which were imprinted on clay tablets many of which were something of the size and shape of a shredded wheat biscuit. These pictures were then stylized and became writing, thus giving the world its greatest invention in history. A letter was signed by the owner rolling his decorated stone seal over the wet clay or stamping it with his signet ring. To make any document permanent and to prevent any forgery or change of the contents it was baked and thus became true pottery. These clay tablets are of invaluable help to us in reading the history of the Near East. Maps were also imprinted on clay. Ezekiel 4:1 refers to such a map of Jerusalem.

VIII. *Pottery in the building trades.* Today we use a brick which has been kiln fired but in antiquity Babylonia was the

POTTERY INCENSE STAND from Megiddo. Courtesy, Oriental Institute

chief user of such bricks. These burnt bricks were laid in bitumen thus furnishing the underwater foundations so necessary in irrigated lands. They also used beautiful, glazed, decorative tiles in their great public buildings. Palestine did not use burnt brick, as stone was available near at hand or could be transported cheaper than burnt brick could be made. The bricks that were used in Palestine were only sun-dried bricks which, if exposed to the winter rains, would dissolve into mud. Houses made of sun-dried brick had to be covered with a stucco made of good marly clay which would shed water and thus prevent the house from disintegrating.

IX. *Miscellaneous pottery items.* Among other common usages for pottery were the army canteen (I Sam. 26:11-12) and the pilgrim flask. These were lightly fired so that the water in the canteen was cooled by evaporation through the vessel. Perfume juglets were pottery except for the rich who preferred alabaster jars. By New Testament times the rich had shifted to glass but the poor were still using pottery. Wash basins were also pottery. Children's toys such as dolls, horses, sheep, dishes, lamps, etc. were pottery. In Babylonia they used pottery sling shots and they had learned to make such high grade pottery that they even used it for sickles.

In both the Old and New Testaments spiritual truth is often conveyed by the figurative use of the potter's vocabulary.

BIBLIOGRAPHY. James L. Kelso, *"The Ceramic Vocabulary of the Old Testament,"* BASOR, Supplementary Studies Nos. 5-6, New Haven, Connecticut, 1948.

PRAETORIUM. *See* Jerusalem.

PYRAMIDS. A line of pyramids once stretched all the way from the head of the Delta, near modern Cairo southward to Meroe, between the Fifth and the Sixth Cataract of the Nile, near Khartum. Each of these pyramids was the center of a necropolis. Each had a funerary temple in which offerings were made on behalf of the dead person entombed in the pyramid. Although the Giza pyramids are the best known to the modern traveler, they are but the largest of the many pyramids built by the Pharaohs of ancient *Egypt.

The great epoch of pyramid building was the Egyptian Old Kingdom — Dynasties Three and Four according to Manetho's reckoning, covering the years from about 2660 B.C. to about 2500 B.C. This was at least a half millennium before the time of Abraham, and a millennium before Moses. Although the Pharaohs may have used forced labor batallions in building their pyramids, it is wrong to assume that Israelites worked on them. The great pyramid age ended at least five centuries before Abraham. The Biblical record speaks of Israelite slaves working on "store cities" but there is no hint that Israelites had anything to do with the pyramids.

The Great Pyramid of Khufu (Cheops) was probably built about the middle of the twenty-fifth century before Christ. It covers an area of about thirteen acres and contains more than 2,300,000 blocks of stone, each weighing an average of two and one-half tons. It has been computed that the blocks, if cut to sections one foot square, would reach two-thirds of the way around the earth at the equator.

The physical labor required to construct the Great Pyramid staggers the imagination. The lever, roller, and inclined plain were the only mechanical devices known to the ancient Egyptians. Petrie found evidence that long copper saws, at least nine feet in length, were used to cut the great blocks of stone used in the pyramids. Tubular drills are known to have been used in hollowing out stones such as those used for a royal sarcophagus.

Herodotus reports the tradition that one hundred thousand men worked for twenty years in building the Great Pyramid. They labored, however, only three months a year. This should be reckoned as the period when the Nile floods made work in the fields impossible. Although laborers were certainly forced to work on the royal pyramid of Khufu, the Pharaoh did not entirely disregard the economic needs of his people. While it is true that more productive work could have been accomplished, it is also true that the pyramid construction was limited to the season when agriculture was not possible. The pyramids had religious significance, and the workers doubtless felt that they were contributing to the well being of Egypt as they labored on the Pharaoh's pyramid.

The second pyramid, built for Pharaoh Khafra (Chephren), successor to Khufu (Cheops) ca. 2525 B.C., had a base measurement nearly fifty feet less than that of Cheops, but its perpendicular height was only ten feet less. The second pyramid was first opened in modern times by Belzoni who entered it on March 2, 1818.

Nearby is the famous sphinx, also associated with Khafra. It is in the form of a recumbent lion with a human head adorned with the royal headdress and the uraeus. The sphinx rises 66 feet from the pavement to the crown of its head and is 240 feet long. There are many smaller sphinxes throughout Egypt, but the sculptors of Khafra were able to make use of a natural outcrop of gray and yellowish limestone for their most impressive tribute to the Pharaoh. They shaped the limestone into a portrait of Khafra. The head of the Pharaoh towers above a lion's body with outstretched paws. Through the years it has been weathered and abused by treasure hunters, but it still stands in majestic calm among the pyramids. Under the Mamluke rulers of Egypt the head of the sphinx was actually used for musketry practice!

The desert sands habitually encroach upon the sphinx with the result that its base is periodically covered. An Egyptian record tells us that the sphinx was cleared of desert sand by Pharaoh Thutmose IV (ca. 1440 B.C.). Excavations were again made during Ptolemaic and Roman times. Early in the nineteenth century (1818) an English group paid 450 pounds to have the sphinx cleared, and the work had to be done again by Maspero in 1886. The Egyptian Department of Antiquities undertook a new clearing in 1925-26.

The third pyramid of the Giza group is that of Menkaure, the Mycerinus of Herodotus, who succeeded Pharaoh Khafre. His pyramid, built ca. 2500 B.C. is much smaller than its companions, ranking ninth among existing pyramids.

Of equal interest to the Giza pyramids is the older step pyramid at Saqqara, in the desert west of Memphis. The step pyramid, built by Djoser (ca. 2640 B.C.) is the earliest large stone building known to man. The step pyramid is actually a suc-

GREAT PYRAMID OF KHUFU (Cheops) and Sphinx. Courtesy, E. Anrich

cession of mastabas, or bench-shaped tombs, built one above another. It served as the transition between the mastaba burials of older pharaohs and the pyramids which became characteristic of Djoser's successors.

The ground-plan of the step pyramid measures 413 by 344 feet. It is surmounted by six steps, each set back 6½ feet from the next lower level. The first step is 37½ feet high, but successive steps decrease in size.

The sixth is 29 feet high. The six steps rise 200 feet from the ground.

True pyramids developed when steps were filled in and leveled off, as was done with the Great Pyramid and its successors. The step pyramid forms the architectural transition between the mastaba and the pyramid.

BIBLIOGRAPHY. I. E. S. Edwards, *The Pyramids of Egypt*, Penguin Books, Baltimore, 1961. Ahmed Fakhry, *The Pyramids*, University of Chicago Press, Chicago, 1961.

Q

QALAT SHARQAT. *See* Ashur.

QARQAR. Qarqar was a city on the Orontes River northwest of Hamath in Syria. There, in 853 B.C., Shalmaneser II of °Assyria fought an alliance of Syrian states headed by the Aramean king of °Damascus, and including Ahab of Israel and representatives of Tyre and other Phoenician city-states. The "Monolith Inscription" of Shalmaneser III, now in the British Museum, states that Ben-Hadad of Damascus provided a contingent of 1200 chariots, 1200 horses, and 20,000 infantry. "Ahab, the Israelite" is said to have provided 2000 chariots — more than Bed-Hadad — but only 10,000 infantry. Shalmaneser III boasts of a decisive victory in which he made the blood of his enemies flow down the valleys and scattered their corpses far and wide. In fact he did not send armies into Syria for several years after the battle of Qarqar, and it appears that the victory was both costly and indecisive.

QATNA (EL-MISHRIFEH). El-Mishrifeh, identified with ancient Qatna, is located some thirteen miles northeast of Homs (Emesa), east of the Orontes river in central Syria. Much of the ancient city's importance arose from its position astride a major trade route of the Fertile Crescent. Evidence from °Mari especially indicates that, in addition to the longer route via Aleppo, there was also a shorter, supplementary route directly across the desert from Mari to Qatna via Palmyra.

The site is known to have been visited by various early travelers and explorers, but little was known of it until the French archaeologist, Count du Mesnil du Buisson, excavated it on a large scale in four campaigns between 1924 and 1929. The finds at el-Mishrifeh together with frequent literary mention of Qatna make the identification of the two certain.

I. *History of Occupation.* Combination of information from literary sources with the results of the excavations provides the following picture of the history of Qatna.

Flints found at the nearby Wadi Zorat and pits uncovered under one of Qatna's later temples indicate some occupation of the site in prehistoric (paleolithic and neolithic) periods.

However, there is no sign of major, permanent construction until around the end of the third millennium B.C. Undoubtedly, it is to the Sumerian revival in the Third Dynasty of °Ur and its commercial interests that we must attribute Qatna's initial importance. Cylinder seals from Ur III and various artistic and architectural features establish the predominance of lower Mesopotamian influence in early Qatna.

Especially significant in this connection, however, are the Akkadian cuneiform tablets found in early temple levels. These contained among other records, an inventory of the treasure of the goddess Belit-ekalli ("Lady of the City"). This cult is plainly of °Sumerian origin (although it is interesting to note that Nin-Egal (the Sumerian form of her name) was only a third-rank deity in Ur itself, in contrast to her front rank at Qatna. A second inventory describes the "treasure of the gods of the king," referring to another, private temple for the king.

Egyptian influence is also evident already in this early period, pointing to Qatna's role on the frontier between the Egyptian and Mesopotamian spheres of influence throughout its history. Already the Old Kingdom of °Egypt may have claimed suzerainty over the region, although it is doubtful if control could then be established. However, the excavations at Qatna, as at Byblos and Ugarit, show that later, during the period of the Middle Kingdom or Twelfth Dynasty in phase A of Middle Bronze II (19th and 20th centuries B.C.), Egyptian power and material culture were dominant in Palestine and Phoenicia. This was most graphically demonstrated at Qatna by the finding of two Egyptian sphinxes, one bearing the name of Ita, daughter of Amenemhet II (*ca.* 1929-1895 B.C.).

Mesopotamian influences became dominant again with the °Amorite invasions which swept over most of the ancient Near East in the early centuries of the second millennium B.C. An Amorite dynasty whose kings had Amorite names was installed at Qatna as at most Syrian and Mesopotamian cities. Records from the Amorite kingdoms at Mari and Assyria from the latter half of the eighteenth century bring Qatna into the full light of the history of this period and document its importance. After Shamshi-adad I (1748-1717 B.C.), first Amorite king of Assyria, had temporarily defeated Mari in the course of his westward expansion and installed his son, Yasmaḫ-adad, as his viceroy there, he proceeded to protect his southern flank by negotiating for his son's marriage to the daughter of Ishkhe-Adad, king of Qaṭna, assuring his son that "the house of Mari is famous, and the house of Qaṭna [also] is famous." When Mari regained her independence under Zimri-lim (ca. 1730-1700 B.C.), references in the "Mari letters" make it plain that Qaṭna continued to be an important city.

In the early seventeenth century comes the great southward migration of the °Hurrians (Biblical "Horites") into all parts of the Fertile Crescent, apparently ruled over by an Indo-Aryan aristocracy. Increasingly, at Qaṭna, as at most other places in the region, Hurrian deities and Hurrian personal names began to predominate. Although the exact relationship is not yet clear, this migration must certainly be connected with the "Hyksos" invasion of Egypt and Palestine and rule there during Egypt's "Second Intermediate Period", ca. 1720-1550 B.C. It may be that the initial °Hyksos invaders were really Amorites (Semites) pushed southward by the Hurrians with the latter following themselves in later phases of the Hyksos period.

Qaṭna undoubtedly played a key role in this period of Mesopotamian dominance over Egypt. It is even possible that Qaṭna was one of the Hyksos' major bases for the invasion of Palestine and Egypt. The very appearance of the site of ancient Qaṭna documents this possibility, for el Mishrifeh is not a typical "tell" or mound of the type usually excavated, but instead a classical example of what we now know as typical Hyksos fortifications, such as are found in this period throughout Palestine and Syria, from Tell el-Yahudiyeh and Heliopolis in lower Egypt to the Euphrates and beyond (Hazor probably providing the best example in Palestine proper). El-Mishrifeh takes the form of a vast defended camp, about a thousand yards square, surrounded by steep ramparts of beaten earth some fifty feet high. Openings in these fortifications, generally near the middle of each side, indicate the original entrances. It is fairly universally

accepted that these camps served the purpose of protecting the huge armies of horse-drawn chariots (introduced by the Hyksos to this region) which it was impossible to accommodate within the relatively small walled towns.

The revival of native Egyptian power under the eighteenth dynasty led not only to the expulsion of the Hyksos from Egypt around 1550 B.C., but also, as the Hyksos threat continued in Syria, to Egyptian invasion and domination of the former Hyksos territory, reaching at times as far as the Euphrates. The greatest architect of the Egyptian New Kingdom's empire was Thutmose III (ca. 1490-1435 B.C.) who apparently occupied Qaṭna not long after the famous battle of Megiddo in 1468 B.C. (as he tells us in his inscriptions at Karnak in Upper Egypt). Later pharaohs of the eighteenth dynasty also mention Qaṭna as either conquered or still under their dominion.

However, although Egypt's political control seems not to have been seriously challenged for some time, the dominant cultural influences continue to be Hurrian, now emanating from the great Hurrian state of °Mitanni, northeast of Qaṭna, with which Egypt ultimately became allied during this peaceful interlude of the pax aegyptica. The closeness of the relationship is illustrated by the fact that a high official who exercised Egyptian jurisdiction over Qaṭna in this period bore the name Biriawaza and may have been a Mittanian prince. The Mycenean trade expansion eastward into the Levant during this period of peaceful international commerce is also documented at Qaṭna as elsewhere, by the large numbers of contemporary Greek vases uncovered.

Circumstances changed drastically, however, in the "Amarna Period" in the middle of the fourteenth century because of Pharaoh Akhenaten's neglect of the Egyptian empire and the revival of Hittite power under the able °Suppiluliumas (ca. 1375-1340 B.C.). Several °Amarna Letters sent to Akhenaten's new capital by Akizzi, the loyal king of Qaṭna, graphically illustrate the seriousness of the Hittite threat. (In these letters the name of the city appears in its Amorite form "Qaṭana," shortened to the now familiar Qaṭna instead of the earlier Akkadianized "Qaṭanum," probably witnessing to its diminished political importance.) Akizzi vividly describes the danger to Egypt's entire holdings in Syria, especially in view of a defection from Egypt led by one Aitugama of nearby Kadesh who is attempting to seduce Akizzi as well. The latter pledges his continued loyalty, however (comparing it to that of Damascus), together with other cities even further north.

Nor was Akizzi mistaken, for only a few years later, towards the end of Akhenaten's reign, Suppiluliumas, after eliminating Mitanni, found a pretext to invade central Syria again (his second or third campaign in the (area) and completely looted and razed Qatna. The sequel to Akizzi's letters to Amarna comes in Suppiluliumas' boast that "I also brought Qatna with its possessions and all that they owned to the Hatti land." Du Buisson's excavations graphically illustrate the proportions of this destruction.

Qatna never really recovered from this disaster, in spite of several subsequent (and short-lived) settlements on the ancient site. The excavations indicate some slight reoccupation shortly afterward in the late fourteenth and thirteenth centuries. Both Sethi I and Ramesses II, the first kings of Egypt's nineteenth dynasty, again mention Qatna as captured, although the reference may well be more to the territory than to the city itself. In any event, in spite of some victories (such as the capture of Tunip, Qatna's erstwhile ally), Egypt never succeeded in dislodging the Hittites from the region. That was accomplished only by the invasion of the "Sea Peoples" shortly before 1200, and Qatna's last literary mention appears in a report by Ramesses III (*ca.* 1175-1144 B.C.) of the twentieth dynasty that Qatna and Tunip were among the localities engulfed in the Sea People's invasion.

The site lay vacant for over half a millennium until it experienced a brief revival in the first half of the sixth century, probably because of the commercial interests of the Neo-Babylonian empire — motives virtually identical with those leading to its initial greatness in Sumerian times. However, as soon as those motives ceased to exist in the latter half of the sixth century, the village again vanished. There is no sign of Persian influence, but a treasure of buried Seleucid coins testifies to the brief presence of a village on the site in the second century B.C. for the last time in antiquity. The contemporary village of Mishrifeh was not founded until about A.D. 1850.

II. *Importance for Biblical Studies.* Qatna is never mentioned in the Bible, but its excavation has proved important for Biblical history nonetheless. Above all, the city obviously plays a crucial role in much of the ancient Near East's history in the second millennium B.C. at the dawn of the Biblical period. Many details of this history are still obscure, and increasing information from other sources added to what we already know of Qatna cannot but contribute even further to our understanding of this important period.

Since the age of the patriarchs is almost certainly to be set in the days of Egypt's twelfth dynasty and the Amorite incursions, it is obvious that increasing general knowledge of the period will probably help us better to understand the patriarchs historically. The Israelites' voluntary sojourn in Egypt succeeded by enslavement there is difficult to separate from the Hyksos (Semitic) occupation of Egypt and subsequent expulsion (although the exact relationships are anything but clear). The polyglot composition of at least the later Hyksos helps explain the presence of Hurrians (Horites), Indo-Iranians, and other ethnic groups alongside the older Canaanite and Amorite elements in Palestine at the time of the Israelite invasion.

The temple inventories from Qatna are important written sources for understanding the religion of the ancient Near East. Especially significant for Biblical studies is the prestige which the temple of Belit-ekalli at Qatna enjoyed also in surrounding territories. The Mari letters mention it as a popular goal of religious pilgrimage and the varying origins of the votive offerings found there in the course of the excavations illustrate its great renown. Thus, its role was analogous in many ways to that of Shiloh in later Israel, which had its great central pilgrimage sanctuary like most other ancient Near Eastern countries.

Finally, it may be noted that the characteristic Old Testament idiom, "to cut a covenant," is also found in a text of about the fifteenth century from Qatna, probably indicating the Amorite origins of the phrase.

BIBLIOGRAPHY. Preliminary reports of du Buisson's excavations appeared in Vols. **VII-XI** (1926-1930) of *Syria*. In 1935 appeared the ex-

THE CAVES AT QUMRAN, in the wilderness of Judah. Courtesy, Matson Photo Service

cavator's summary: *Le Site Archéologique De Mishrifé — Qatna,* E. De Bocard, Paris.

QUERN. A quern is a hand mill for grinding grain. It consists of two stone disks, one placed above the other. Querns are among the most common artifacts discovered at Neolithic sites.

QUMRAN. Khirbet Qumran is the ruin, eight miles south of Jericho, near which the *Dead Sea Scrolls were discovered in 1947 and subsequent years. After the announcement of the discovery of the scrolls, excavations were conducted at Qumran under the direction of G. Lankester Harding and Roland deVaux with the co-operation of the Jordan Department of Antiquities and the École Biblique of Jerusalem, Jordan.

Vestiges of occupation in Israelite times (eighth or seventh century B.C.) have been discovered, and it is conjectured that these may mark the site of the City of Salt (Ir-Hammelach) mentioned in Joshua 15:62. The site was abandoned and was not occupied again until the end of the second century B.C. when a Jewish community, usually identified with the Essenes (*see* Jewish Sects) built a large building to serve as a community center. Its central section forms an irregular rectangle, about 120 feet long, and from 80 to 90 feet wide. Around the central building were smaller buildings and cisterns, some of which could have been used as bathing pools. The excavators explain the great cracks in the cisterns as the result of an earthquake which hit the area in 31 B.C. and caused the area to be temporarily abandoned. About the beginning of the Christian era repairs were made to the community center and the Qumran community continued to observe their communal life until A.D 68 when the Tenth Roman Legion occupied the site during the first Jewish-Roman war (*see* Jerusalem, Masada).

The community center had an open inside court and a strong defence tower on the northwest corner. Store rooms were at the front. There was a large hall for meetings and meals and a number of smaller halls, one of which served as the scriptorium in which the Dead Sea Scrolls were copied. A complete potter's workshop was discovered. One room served for laundry purposes.

The Jewish community apparently fled from Qumran at the approach of the Roman soldiers. The center served as a military garrison for several years, during which the Romans modified its interior structure to serve their needs. Jews were there again during the second Jewish-Roman war (The Bar Kochba Revolt, A.D. 132-135), but they were not related to the earlier Essene community. At the end of the war Qumran was again abandoned. Aside from providing shelter for an occasional Arab, it was not again occupied.

BIBLIOGRAPHY. C. F. Pfeiffer, *The Dead Sea Scrolls,* 2nd ed., Baker Book House, Grand Rapids, 1962. Menahem Mansoor, *The Dead Sea Scrolls,* William B. Eerdmans, Grand Rapids, 1964. R. de Vaux, reports on the excavations in *Revue Biblique,* LVI, 1949, pp. 234-237; 586-609; LX, 1953, pp. 83-106; 540-561; LXI, 1954, pp. 206-236; 567-568; LXIII, 1956, pp. 533-577.

DOMESTIC QUARTER AT QUMRAN with mill for grinding grain. Courtesy, Palestine Archaeological Museum

R

RAAMSES (TANIS, ZOAN). Near the northeastern frontier of Egypt on the east bank of the Tanaitic branch of the Nile about thirty miles due west of ancient Pelusium, was the city of Zoan, or Tanis, which had been settled at least as far back as the Sixth Dynasty Pharaoh Pepi I (*ca.* 2300 B.C.). It was rebuilt and enlarged by the Pharaohs of the Twelfth Dynasty (*ca.* 1990-1785 B.C.). Amenemhet and his successors left large statues of themselves in Tanis. Ramesses II (*ca.* 1250 B.C.) practically reconstructed the place, erecting obelisks and statues with pompous inscriptions boasting about his accomplishments — real and fancied.

The Temple at Tanis was one of the largest structures of ancient Egypt. From end to end it measured about a thousand feet. A colossal statue of Ramesses II originally stood ninety-two feet high and weighed about nine hundred tons — the tallest colossus ever erected. Its large toe was the size of a man's body. The stone was all quarried at Aswan and floated hundred of miles down the Nile to Tanis.

The Hyksos invaders of Egypt established their capital at Tanis which bore the name of Avaris during their reign. Its position on the northeast border of Egypt gave them ready access both to their Asiatic holdings and to Egypt.

The store city of Raamses (Exod. 1:11) on which the Israelites were forced to perform slave labor, is identified by most scholars with Tanis (P. Montet, *Le Drame d'Avaris,* Paris, 1940), although others locate it at Qantir, a few miles farther south.

Tanis maintained its importance down to Roman times. Among the bishops who attended the Council of Chalcedon (A.D. 451) we read of Apollonius, Bishop of Tanis. Early Arab writers spoke in glowing terms of the climate of Tanis, but it is now but a heap of ruins in the small village of San — a name reminiscent of ancient Zoan.

San was visited by the French archaeologist Mariette, but extensive excavations did not begin until 1884 when Flinders Petrie reached the mound. In those days such an expedition was virtually cut off from society. Once a week a man was sent on the forty mile journey to Faqus, the nearest town, in order to maintain communications with the outside world and bring needed provisions. This was Petrie's first mission for the Egypt Exploration Fund and he labored under great hardships. He was able to reconstruct much of the town's history, however, and many of his finds are now in the Cairo Museum.

BIBLIOGRAPHY. Pierre Montet, "Avaris, Pi-Ramses, Tanis," *Syria,* XVII, 1936, pp. 200-202. Harold M. Wiener, "Pithom and Raamses," *Ancient Egypt,* VIII, 1923, pp. 75-77. Raymond Weill, "The Problem of the Site of Avaris," *Journal of Egyptian Archaeology,* XXI, 1935, pp. 10-25. Allan H. Gardiner, Pi-Ra'messe: Tanis — A Retraction," *Journal of Egyptian Archaeology,* XIX, 1933, pp. 122-128. Hans Goedicke, "The Route of Sinuhe's Flight," *Journal of Egyptian Archaeology,* XLIII, 1957, pp. 77-85.

RADIO CARBON (Carbon 14) DATING. Of help in dating organic matter discovered in archaeological research is the method developed by W. F. Libby and J. R. Arnold at the Institute of Nuclear Studies, the University of Chicago. This method of dating proceeds from the thesis that all living things absorb from the atmosphere an unstable or radioactive form of carbon with an atomic weight of fourteen. The Carbon 14 thus formed is an isotope of ordinary carbon of atomic weight twelve (C12). Both are contained in the carbon dioxide of the atmosphere in a constant proportion to each other. Once an organism is dead, however, it ceases to take carbon from the atmosphere, and the carbon fourteen content slowly diminishes at a known rate. After 5,600 years (the half-life) only one-half the original amount of Carbon fourteen is left.

By determining experimentally the amount of carbon in living matter, and knowing its half life, it is possible to determine the age of an ancient sample. The surviving proportion of C14 to C12 in a given specimen can be determined in the laboratory, and from it the time elapsed since the death of the organic matter can be calculated. With present techniques, the effective range is about twenty thousand years, with a margin of error of from five to ten percent.

BIBLIOGRAPHY. Willard F. Libby, *Radio Carbon Dating,* University of Chicago Press, Chicago, 1955.

RAMAT RAHEL. Six reasons of excavation under the auspices of the Israel Department of Antiquities, the Israel Exploration Society, the Hebrew University, and the Universita de Roma have produced a rich collection of finds that illuminate the history of this settlement. The tell is about midway between Jerusalem and Bethlehem, both of which can be seen from the summit. The Valley of Rephaim lies to the west, and the Judean wilderness stretches out to the east. In antiquity the road from Jerusalem to Bethlehem passed along its slopes. If the identification with Beth-haccherem, "House of the vineyard," is correct, the name is undoubtedly due to the area's suitability for viticulture, today as in the past. The excavator, Yohanan Aharoni, has now distinguished seven occupational periods at Ramat Rahel which are as follows:

Level V B (eighth-seventh centuries B.C.). No settlement was founded when the Israelites first occupied Canaan. The oldest stratum of human remains dates from the eighth-seventh centuries B.C. The structures and other installations from that period were in a large measure destroyed by the construction of a newer fortress (Level V A). Material from Level V B was found mainly in the fill below floors of the later building and included a significant number of stamped jar handles bearing seal impressions "to the king." Most of these *seals include the "two-winged" symbol, but some have the "four-winged" *scarab.* The total number of examples from these royal seals from Ramat Rahel now exceeds 150, a record second only to that of Lachish.

In the final weeks of the fifth season a new section of ashlar construction was uncovered in the southeastern portion of the tell. Its precise date has not been determined; it not only formed an additional line of the casemate fortification wall but also probably represents the main building of this earliest level. It certainly seems to precede the Judean fortress of Level V A. A dwelling from Level VII also came to light on the northern slope. In it were found two private seal impressions "To Shebna (son of Shahar)," like those examples found at *Lachish and *Tell en-Nasbeh.*

Level V A (ca. 600 B.C.). The most important discovery at Ramat Rahel for Old Testament study is the royal fortress of Level V A. Its main defense was a casemate wall, rectangular in plan (100 x 55 yards). Its general dimensions are similar to those found at other Iron Age sites in both Judah and Israel. Nevertheless, the quality of construction found at Ramat Rahel is exceptionally good. The outside wall is built mostly of headers running through the entire width of the wall. That portion of the interior wall which faced towards the courtyard was made of finely fitted stones laid as headers and stretchers; the technique is identical to that found at Samaria. (*See also* Architecture.)

The foundations of these structures were laid on bedrock, and again like Samaria, the stones laid in courses below floor level, and therefore not visible, were not smoothed completely. The southern section of the casemate wall at Ramat Rahel contains evidence that the inner compartments were used for storage. The floors in some of the chambers were found intact and on their thresholds were holes for the door pivot and for the bolt. A doorway led from the outer courtyard into one of the rooms from which an inner door opened into the next room, and so on. The positions of the respective bolt holes prove that each inner room was locked from the next outer one, and the first was locked from the outside.

There was an underground postern gate leading into the citadel through its northern wall. The outer opening is just wide enough for one person to enter at a time. This is the first example of such a secret entrance that has been found in Palestine; in Judges 1:24-25 an "entrance to the city" was utilized for the conquest of Bethel.

The western side of the citadel was enclosed by a wall about six feet thick built of large stones. From the midway point on this wall a tower projected outward for a distance of over forty feet. It overlooked a "lower citadel" consisting of a sort of "parade ground" of approximately five acres in area. A stone wall ten to twelve feet thick surrounded this lower citadel. Its construction is of unhewn stones, except near the gate where hewn stones were used in a manner similar to the upper citadel. In places this outer wall was built some distance from the natural slope, and the intervening space was taken up by an artificial fill. Thus, the wall itself was given extra strength, and the area

RAMAT RAHEL. A group of archaeologists examine the excavations at Ramat Rahel. Courtesy, Israel Office of Information

of the "parade ground" was widened. The date of this construction is established by the abundance of sherds from very late in the Iron Age. A noteworthy quantity of royal seal impressions of every kind was also found. The lower citadel and the upper citadel of Level VI were established together as part of one royal building project.

Two interesting features of the lower citadel area are a rock quarry located on the northeastern slope and a tunnel on the western side below the citadel walls. The entrance to this latter was discovered in a trial pit just outside of the lower citadel's gate. The tunnel itself is hewn out of the natural rock and seems to lead up into the upper citadel. Until it can be more thoroughly excavated, its purpose and date remain a mystery.

The buildings of the upper citadel were planned around a spacious courtyard adjacent to the southern wall. The court was built upon a fill consisting of earth, stones, and debris (one to three yards deep) laid directly on bedrock; a thick layer of chalk, neatly leveled and tamped, comprised the surface. Buildings surrounded this area on three sides.

The "official building" was apparently on the eastern side of the courtyard. Some of its walls were more than six feet thick, and

the foundations went down to bedrock. As in the courtyard, a thick layer of fill was laid underneath the floor surface. One of the floors consisted of large square stone slabs, the upper parts of which were cracked by the intense heat of the holocaust which marked the citadel's destruction. The outer walls of this structure are built partly of headers in a manner similar to the outer casemate wall and partly of hewn stones with irregular bosses like those found at Samaria. One beautiful section of this wall was preserved underneath the mosaic of the Roman bath house (Level III). Perfectly smoothed and fitted stones laid as headers only comprise the courses visible above floor level. On the stones beneath the floor bosses were left — again demonstrating a knowledge of the "Samaria" building techniques. To the east of it another courtyard was partially uncovered.

The northern building was a storehouse. In one of its rooms, a narrow hall more than thirty feet long, an abundance of beautiful pottery was discovered. Besides many examples of the lovely, late Israelite red-burnished ware and some terra-cotta figurines, two sherds were found from a painted vessel (in black and red). It bears the picture of a royal personage seated on a throne. The scene resembles other examples of seated kings from Assyrian reliefs, but the vessel is of local ware. The man has curled hair and a beard and is attired in an ornamented robe. He holds his hands out before him, the right above the left; and his feet seem to be resting on a footstool. On the second fragment from this vessel is depicted the motif of a Proto-Aeolic capital like the stone capitals found only on royal Israelite installations, e.g., *Samaria, *Megiddo, *Hazor, and as a surface find in Transjordan. Six complete examples of these stone ornaments have also turned up at Ramat Rahel along with fragments of several others. Most of them were strewn about the central courtyard, but the last complete capital to be found was discovered within a Post-exilic burial chamber where it had been commandeered for use as a subterranean altar. More capitals of this type have been found at Ramat Rahel than at any other site. Back in 1930 Mazar (Maisler) and Stekelis found a unique friezestone with designs similar to those on the Proto-Aeolic capitals, but with certain additions such as a column, a lotus, and a volute motif. The architectural designs on this tablet correspond to some of the actual stone decorations discovered in the western building of the citadel complex.

The structure that stood on the west side of the central court (behind the buttress overlooking the "parade ground") was almost completely obliterated by later construction (the Roman villa, see Level III); only some traces of the foundations remain. However, in the northwestern end of the building a pile of debris was found to contain portions from the parapets from beneath the building's windows. These consisted of columnettes decorated with leaves and capitals of the Proto-Aeolic style. Comparison with carved ivories from various other sites depicting the "woman at the window" leaning on a similar parapet leaves no doubt that these new finds are the actual decorations which adorned the building's frontage. Five outstanding features of Jehoiakim's palace are mentioned by Jeremiah: its measurements, its upper rooms, its windows, its cedars, and its colors (Jer. 22:14). The prophet denounced King Jehoiakim for his dishonesty and the oppressive methods he used in building his luxurious house (Jer. 22:13-19). As a consequence he predicted that this king would be buried like an ass, "drawn and cast forth

beyond the gates of Jerusalem" (vs. 19). Aharoni has suggested that this passage contains a satirical reference to Jehoiakim's palace at a spot outside of the Holy City, viz., this magnificent citadel at Ramat Rahel.

A seal impression with the inscription "To Eliakim, steward (?) of Jehoiachin" was discovered in the upper citadel. This new example of that famous seal from *Tell Beit Mirsim and *Beth-shemesh furnishes proof that the fortress at Ramat Rahel was still in use in 597 B.C. If its destruction did not coincide with the captivity of Jehoiachin in that year (II Kings 24:8-17; II Chron. 36:9-10), then it must have been carried out in conjunction with the final devastation of Jerusalem by the Babylonians in 587-6 B.C.

The seal impressions consisting of a simple rosetta design are apparently from this level. Another group of seals with crudely executed animal designs, of which numerous examples were found at *Tell en-Nasbeh, seem to come from the end of the Iron Age and the beginning of the Post-exilic period.

Private seal impressions and other epigraphic inscriptions from the Iron Age have been found during nearly every season's work at Ramat Rahel. For detailed information see the bibliography below.

Level IV B. These excavations have shed considerable light on the period of Persian-Hellenistic rule. Numerous stamped jar handles, more in number than from any other Judean site, have been found here bearing seal impressions from the provincial administration that governed Judea under Persian authority.

The names of two previously unknown Jewish governors have also appeared on some of these official seals: Jehoazar and Ahiyo. Such typical priestly names followed by the title "governor" suggest that the leading priestly families continued to rule the province throughout the Persian period. Three Jewish governors are known from the Bible: Shesbazzar, Zerubbabel, and Nehemiah. A fourth name, Bagohi, is known from the Yeb papyri; he ruled in Judea sometime after Nehemiah, towards the end of the fifth century B.C. That this is a typically Persian name does not preclude his being Jewish (Neh. 7:19; cf. Josephus, Antiquities XI, 7:1). During the fourth century B.C. practically nothing is known about the Judean province from historical sources. However, when records appear again in the third century B.C., the high priest had control. Finally in 1961 the Ramat Rahel expedition succeeded in restoring a complete jar from the fourth century B.C., the handle of which was stamped with an official seal. So it seems most probable that the priestly families maintained their authority during the fourth century as well.

The remains of buildings from Level V are few indeed, having been almost completely annihilated by Byzantine structures (Level II). Most of the pottery and inscriptions were found in pits dispersed over the surface of the tell which had been dug for the disposal of rubbish. A personal seal found in the last season of digging has the inscription: "Azbuk (son of) Zedekiah"; both of these names are known from the Post-exilic period (Neh. 3:16; 10:2).

The Post-exilic settlement came to an end in the third century B.C. at the very latest.

Level IV A (first century B.C.–first century A.D.). A small settlement existed on the site during this period which continued until the destruction of the temple (A.D. 70). Coins found here date down as far as A.D. 69.

On the rocky slope that runs along the northern edge of the upper citadel a row of burial caves was discovered. These were hewn deeply into the natural rock, and a few of them were transformed into water cisterns during the Roman or Byzantine periods. However, one cave was found in its original condition with the stone door still in its place. Glass vessels, decorated lamps, and stone °ossuaries for the collection of bones were extracted from these graves. Some of the ossuaries bear incised decorations and inscriptions. One Hebrew-Aramaic inscription reads "[Shim']on, son of Eleazer." The accompanying Greek inscription mentions: Simonides, Marela, and "the children."

This settlement was evidently wiped out with the destruction of the second temple.

Level III (second-third centuries A.D.). The Roman 10th Legion was camped at Jerusalem from A.D. 70 until the reign of Emperor Diocletian (*ca.* A.D. 300), and Ramat Rahel served as a military installation. The ruins of a handsome Roman villa from this period were discovered.

Numerous examples of tiles with the 10th Legion inscription: LEG(io) X FRE (tensis),

have been found around the Jerusalem area. But the elaborate Roman bath house from Ramat Rahel is the first structure in which such bricks were discovered *in situ*. Some walls of the former Iron Age fortress served as its foundations. The floor of the bath house was paved with interesting mosaic patterns. Six bathing pools of various shapes and three large cisterns were linked together by an inter-connecting system of clay and lead pipes beneath the floor. The inscribed pottery tiles comprised the floor of the hypocaust, the central chamber in which the water was heated.

Level II (fifth-sixth centuries A.D.). A Byzantine church and monastery were erected in about the fifth century A.D. These structures incorporated the Roman bath house described above. The church itself was located on the northeast corner of the Judean fortress from Level VI. The nave and aisles were paved with colored geometric mosaics; gaps in the mosaic floor betray the positions of the two rows of columns that divided the nave and the aisles. A large cruciform stone, probably the altar, was found in the narthex.

Near the church was discovered a long paved corridor which had been roofed over with pottery tiles; it led to a row of rooms that contained stoves and ovens. Two large halls were located west of the church; they had been roofed over by stone arches resting on pilasters along the length of the halls. They seem to have been store rooms since their floor level is lower than the contemporary ground level outside. These store rooms were built directly on top of those from the Judean fortress of Level VI and utilized some of its foundations.

The name of the well on Ramat Rahel's western slope, *Bir Qadismu*, comes from the Greek *Kathisma*, "The Seat," and provided a plausible identification of this church. The "Well of the Seat," where Mary and Joseph are said to have rested on their way to Bethlehem, was located by Theodosios (*ca.* A.D. 530) three miles south of Jerusalem. Antoninus (*ca.* A.D. 570) found a church erected near this well to commemorate the event. The church was built, according to Cyrillus of Scythopolis and Metaphrastes, by a rich woman of Jerusalem *ca.* A.D. 450. St. Theodosius (*ca.* A.D. 460) is said to have lived there.

The church and its monastery were destroyed during the seventh century A.D. Daniel, a Russian monk (A.D. 1115), says that, when he passed this way, he saw the ruins of a big church dedicated to St. Mary.

Level I (seventh-eighth centuries A.D.). On the very top of the mound the remains were from the early Arab period. The Arab settlers apparently re-used some of the monastery rooms, adding an occasional wall or new floor. Evidence from coins found in this level indicate that the settlement lasted only until the eighth century A.D. After that the site remained uninhabited.

A skeleton crew continued to dig at Ramat Rahel throughout the academic year, 1962-63. Thus it has been possible to clarify some of the stratigraphic problems and fill in various details. However, none of the main conclusions reached in November, 1962, has been changed. Study of the artifacts and inscriptions and their preparation for publication are now being carried out.

BIBLIOGRAPHY. Yohanan Aharoni, "Excavations at Ramat Rahel, 1954," *IEJ* 6, 1956, pp. 102-11; "Excavations at Ramat Rahel," *BA* 24, 1961, pp. 98-118; "Ramat Rachel," *Bible et Terre Sainte* No. 37, April, 1961, pp. 4-10; *Excavations at Ramat Rahel, Seasons 1959 and 1960. Roma: Centro di Studi Semitici*, 1962. With contributions by several scholars on special aspects of the discoveries. Similar volumes on each subsequent season, plus a final summary, are now in preparation.

RAMESES (city). See Raamses.

RAMESSES II.

I. *Birth and Background.* The grandfather of Ramesses II was Ramesses I, known before his accession as Pramesse. He had served Haremhab as vizier, and before that in various other capacities. He was an old man when he ascended the throne, and reigned only about two years. Monuments built by him are scanty, but the few reliefs bearing his name near the Second Pylon at Karnak indicate that he was instrumental in changing the style of architecture from Haremhab's open court with a central double line of columns to the great Hypostyle Hall. Ramesses I was succeeded by Seti I, who reigned about a score of years. He built an elaborate temple at Abydos, reputed home of Osiris, and found it necessary to step up the production of gold from the mines near the Red Sea in order to endow the temple which he had built. The warlike scenes depicted upon the exterior north wall of the great Hypostyle Hall at Karnak tell of his successful forays into Canaan and Syria, including victories over the Hittites.

The circumstances surrounding the succession of Ramesses II to the throne of his father are not clear. Ramesses himself claims that he was his father's choice, and that when he was but ten years of age he was given command of an army. He further alleges that when he was fifteen his father presented him with a harem, and allowed him to serve as co-regent. Other accounts hint of a conspiracy. Breasted, in *A History of Egypt*, suggests that an unknown eldest son of Seti I was appointed by his father as crown prince. This prince allegedly had his figure inserted in the Libyan battle scene on the north wall of his father's Karnak Hall,

STELE OF RAMESSES II discovered at Beisan (Beth-shan), in the University Museum, Philadelphia. Courtesy, The University Museum

OSIRIS COLUMNS *in the Great Temple of Ramesses II at Abu Simbel. Courtesy, Foto Marburg*

which was later defaced by Ramesses II upon his accession to the throne. Gardiner, in *Egypt of the Pharaohs,* supports the accuracy of the claim of Ramesses that he was the legitimate crown prince, the proper successor. Seele also has expressed confidence in the accuracy of the claims of Ramesses.

II. *Early Years of the Reign of Ramesses II.* Like his predecessors of the Nineteenth Dynasty, Ramesses II hailed from the Delta. One of the first recorded acts of his reign was a visit to Thebes to take part in Amun's great feast of Ope (Luxor), when the god was carried in state in his ceremonial boat from Karnak to Luxor. From there he went to Abydos, to do reverence to Osiris, and also to give orders to complete the mortuary temple of his father, Seti I. After appointing a new high priest of Amun, he proceeded northward to the Delta, where he established his capital at Pi-Ramesse, Great-of-Victories, the Biblical *Raamses. It was apparently located on the same site as the great Hyksos stronghold of Avaris, later called Tanis by the Greeks and Zoan in the Bible. A monument found here, called the Four Hundred Year Stele, dates the founding of the Hyksos capital at about 1700 B.C. The principal god of the Hyksos was Sutekh, or Seth, and his worship was revived by Ramesses II.

A stele bearing the date "year 3" has been found in Lower Nubia. It records the successful digging of a well to supply water to miners working the rich gold mines of that region. Apparently the heavy endowments of the various mortuary temples begun by his father and himself had drained the treasury of its existing revenues, and had necessitated further exploitation of the Upper Nile region. Also dating from the very early years of his reign is the mention of the capture of the Sherden, pirates from Sardinia, who fought a naval battle near the river-mouths.

III. *Campaigns against the Hittites.* Although Seti I had signed a treaty with the Hittite ruler Mursulis II, it was inevitable that the two great world powers must clash again. Muwatallis had taken advantage of the change of kings in Egypt to push southward into Syria. In the fourth year of the reign of Ramesses the Egyptian army swept up the coast to secure the harbors necessary to insure communication and supply lines for an all-out campaign to be waged later.

The only evidence now extant is a limestone stele near Beirut, on "Dog River," facing the sea. Unfortunately for Ramesses, this alerted the Hittite king, who began to gather a huge army.

The campaign against the *Hittites which was launched in the fifth year of Ramesses is one of the most famous in history. In Karnak and Luxor, in Abydos and Abu-Simbel, Ramesses is lavishly praised for his "victory." The city of Kadesh was reached by about a month's march from Egypt. It had been captured earlier by Seti I, but had since fallen into Hittite hands. Its strategic importance was due to its position near the exit from the high-level valley between the Lebanons, which was the preferred route for a north-bound army rather than the more narrow one which lay along the Phoenician coast. This city was the immediate objective of Ramesses. The Egyptian army was divided into four corps bearing the names of Amun, Re, Ptah, and Sutekh, the chief gods of Egypt. There were approximately twenty thousand soldiers in each of the opposing armies. Apparently Ramesses was deceived by false information given him by captured spies. Supposing that the Hittites had withdrawn from Kadesh toward Aleppo, he threw caution to the winds and marched rapidly to the north of the city, leaving the main force of his army behind. The Hittites then struck from ambush, and quickly cut to pieces two of the Egyptian corps. Ramesses was evidently saved by two events. The Hittite army became undisciplined, looting the wagons and provisions of the Egyptians instead of completing the rout which they had begun. Also, a small but firmly disciplined regiment of Egyptian cadets suddenly appeared, which seemed to be a surprise both to Ramesses and his foes. In spite of the obvious exaggerations in the account, the king probably showed unusual bravery. Ramesses claims to have destroyed 2500 Hittite chariots, each carrying three warriors. On the other side, Muwatallis claims to have pursued the Egyptians as far back as Damascus. The truth probably lies somewhere between these two conflicting claims, but it is obvious that Kadesh was not captured.

After several years of indecisive warfare, in the twenty-first year of the reign of Ramesses II, a nonaggression pact was signed between the two nations. Fortunately, this

RAMESSES II represented as victor. From the Great Temple at Abu Simbel. Courtesy, Foto Marburg

document has been preserved both in the Egyptian hieroglyphic and the Hittite cuneiform version. According to its terms, both states should in the future stand on equal terms, while eternal peace was to prevail between the kings and all their descendants. Confirmation was later given to the treaty by the marriage of Ramesses with a daughter of the Hittite king, Hattusilis, who was a brother of Muwatallis. She was given the title "Great Royal Wife."

IV. *Latter Years of Ramesses II.* Since the treaty with the Hittites was signed about 1280 B.C., the king had nearly a half-century to devote to internal affairs, chiefly building enterprises. Although he was unscrupulous in cutting the names of his predecessors from temple inscriptions and in his tearing down earlier temples to reuse the materials, he was a great builder in his own right. Of the thirty-two obelisks in Egypt, he is said to have erected in whole or in part twenty-one. Of the eight ruined temples in Thebes, he built in whole or in part seven. Beginning in the thirtieth year of his reign, he celebrated festivals of rejuvenation, perhaps a dozen in all. More than a hundred sons are listed, and there were probably more. His

buildings attempted to impress by overpowering size, without concern for artistic quality. At Tanis he built a ninety-foot colossus. In the mortuary temple known as the Ramesseum there was another colossus, made of pink granite and weighing a thousand tons. At Abu-Simbel, between the First and Second Cataracts, he had a facade of a temple hewed out of the natural rock of the cliff. He also had four statues of himself there, each sixty-five feet tall. The mighty Hypostyle Hall at Karnak had 134 gigantic columns, some of 169 feet. Each flares out at the top so that a hundred men can stand on top of one, yet the carving is careless and crude.

While evidence is not decisive, many scholars feel that Ramesses II was the Pharaoh of the Exodus.

After a reign of sixty-seven years, Ramesses II died in 1232 B.C., and was succeeded by his son Merneptah. His corpse is that of a shriveled old man with a long narrow face, massive jaw, and prominent nose, conspicuous also for his well-preserved teeth.

The Aswan High Dam would send the Nile rolling 120 feet above the six-story-high images at Abu-Simbel. To save them, UNESCO has approved a plan of the United Arab Republic, prepared by Swedish engineers, to cut the statues and temples into sections and reassemble them in a natural setting on the plateau above. The United States has provisionally offered to pay a third of the cost.

BIBLIOGRAPHY. James Henry Breasted, *A History of Egypt,* London, Hodder and Stoughton, 1925. Sir Alan Gardiner, *Egypt of the Pharaohs,* Oxford, at the Clarendon Press, Oxford University Press, 1961. Georg Gerster, "Threatened Treasures of the Nile," *National Geographic Magazine,* Vol. 124, No. 4, October, 1963, Melville Bell Grosvenor, Ed., Washington, D. C. Emil Ludwig, *The Nile: The Life-Story of a River,* Trans. by Mary H. Lindsay, The Viking Press, New York, 1937. Margaret A. Murray, *The Splendor That Was Egypt: A General Survey of Egyptian Culture and Civilization,* Sidgwick and Jackson Ltd., London, 1949. George Steindorff and Keith C. Seele, *When Egypt Ruled the East,* Rev. by Keith C. Seele, 2nd Ed., The University of Chicago Press, Chicago, Illinois, 1957. John A. Wilson, *The Burden of Egypt: An Interpretation of Ancient Egyptian Culture,* The University of Chicago Press, Chicago, Illinois, 1951.

RAS SHAMRA. *See* Ugarit.

RELIGION. Temples, cults, objects, and re-

THE GOD HORUS guards the entrance to the Horus Temple at Edfu. Courtesy, E. Anrich

ligious texts form a large part of the material with which *archaeology is concerned. Each of the lands of the ancient Near East had its distinctive religious beliefs but, as the result of trade and the mobility of peoples, religious ideas and the gods themselves came to be accepted over wide areas.

In the earliest days, each Egyptian village looked to its own deity for the blessings of life and protection from hostile powers. The village would boast a shrine to its deity, and the worship of the local god would serve as a unifying influence within the community, and a means of distinguishing one village from another. Ptah was the god of Memphis, Atum of Heliopolis, Hathor the "lady of Dendera," Neith the goddess of Sais. The name of Neith appears in the name Asenath, "she is of Neith," the daughter of Potiphera, priest of On (Heliopolis) who married Joseph (Gen. 41:45).

As small Egyptian communities united to become states (called nomes) local gods gained a wider recognition, and when the empires of Upper and Lower Egypt emerged, two of the local gods — Seth of Ombos and Horus of Behdet — became the gods of the two states. About 3000 B.C. when Egypt became a unified state under Nar-mer (Menes), Upper Egypt emerged as the dominant part of the country and Horus became god of "the two Egypts," as the combined empire of Upper and Lower Egypt was called. The Pharaoh was considered the incarnation and patron of Horus, and was therefore regarded as a god in his own right.

The local gods continued in the affection of the people and, as they moved from place to place they brought their god with them and erected new shrines for his worship. As a result of some supposedly potent cure or display of miraculous intervention the god of a community might gain a reputation for special power. Because of this people from neighboring areas in which his fame was known would make pilgrimages to the god's shrine, or build him new shrines in their own villages. In some such way Neith of Sais acquired a shrine at Esna.

At an early date, local deities were associated with some aspect of their character. The falcon-shaped Montu was worshiped as a war god and Min of Coptos became a god of fertility and harvests and patron of desert travelers. Ptah of Memphis, in whose province the distinctive art of Egypt originated, became patron of artists, smiths, and metal workers. As such he may be compared with the Canaanite Kathar-wa-Khassis, the classical Hephaestus, and the Germanic Vulcan.

Sekhmet of Memphis was a fire goddess who annihilated her enemies, while the more kindly Hathor of Dendera was a goddess of love and joy. The falcon god Horus, identified with the sun, was pictured as a youthful hero in perpetual battle with his evil brother Seth, the storm god. The ibis-headed Thoth of Hermopolis was the moon god who had created the divisions of time and order in the universe. Thoth was "lord of divine words," who had invented hieroglyphic writing and was the god of learning in general. Sobek, the crocodile god, had his home in the water.

In addition to the gods of the state, and the numerous city gods, the Egyptians were concerned about a multitude of lesser gods, demons, or spirits who might help or injure man. There were gods who assisted women in childbirth, gods of the household, and gods of the harvest. In times of illness, spirits provided healing, and other spirits were particularly active in time of war. Ma'at was the goddess of truth and justice.

Many of the Egyptian gods were represented in animal form. Sobek, the crocodile; Thoth, the ibis; Khnum, the ram; Hathor, the cow; and Buto, the serpent are represented in this way. Gods might also be depicted as humans, and it was common for gods which had been depicted as animals to be transformed into human figures with the heads of the animals they represent. Thus Sobek might be depicted as a crocodile, or as a man with the head of a crocodile. Khnum became a man with a ram's head; Horus, a man with the head of a falcon; Thoth, a man with the head of an ibis. The goddess Sekhmet became a woman with the head of a lioness.

Egyptian religion included the worship of a multitude of such gods, often arranged into groups resembling human families. Certain animals, particularly the Apis bull, were venerated and, in addition to the divine Pharaoh, certain outstanding humans had been deified. The phenomena of nature — sun, moon, stars, heaven, earth, the Nile — all had a part in Egyptian religion. The traditional religious ideas were challenged once during the history of the Pharaohs, when *Akhenaton sought to ban all religious activity except that which honored the Aton, a solar deity. Akhenaton's reforms did not long outlive their instigator, and the priests of Amun of Thebes, against whom he had rebelled, were able to re-assert their authority shortly after his death.

The religious ideas of Egypt have parallels in Sumer and in the cultures that derived

DIAGRAM OF A TEMPLE TO THE GOD MEKAL at Beth-shan, excavated by the University of Pennsylvania. Courtesy, the University Museum

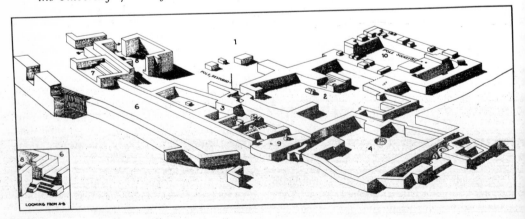

BRONZE MODEL FROM SUSA, 12th century B.C., representing the worship of the dawn. Courtesy, the Louvre

religious ideas from the °Sumerians. There, too, local gods became national and international gods as their cities gained prestige and power. The Sumerians conceived of the universe as subject to a pantheon of gods in charge, respectively, of heaven, earth, air, and water; of the sun, the moon, and the various planets; of wind, storm, and tempest; of the rivers, the mountains, and the plains; of the cities and states; of fields, farms, and irrigation ditches; of the pickax, the brick mold and the plow. There was a hierarchy among the gods, chief of which were the four creating gods: An, the god of heaven; Ki, the god of earth; Enlil, the god of air; and Enki, the god of water. Inanna, goddess of fertility, was a favorite Sumerian deity.

Much of Sumerian religion was absorbed by the Semitic Assyrians and Babylonians whose culture replaced that of Sumer in the Tigris-Euphrates valley. Sumerian gods were often referred to by their Semitic equivalents. Sumerian Utu, the sun god, became Shamash; Nanna or Nannar, the moon god, became Sin. The cult of the moon god was common to °Ur and °Haran. Sumerian Inanna became the mother goddess Ishtar. Marduk, described in the °Enuma Elish as one of the younger gods, was the patron deity of Babylon. With the growth of the Babylonian Empire, Marduk's rank increased. Farther north it was Ashur, the god of the city of Ashur and of its empire, Assyria, who became a creator god.

The Semitic names of the gods of Mesopotamia appear in Palestine and Syria. Town names such as Beth-shemesh ("house of the sun") suggest that a shrine to the sun god once stood there. Our fullest knowledge of Canaanite religion comes from °Ugarit, where El is the father of the gods, and Baal the most popular deity of the second generation. Baal, and his sister Anat are both fertility gods. The ritual prostitution of the Baal cult made it abominable in the eyes of the prophets of Israel.

Hittite religion included some gods indigenous to Asia Minor, others introduced by Indo-Europeans, and still others adopted by the Hittites from their neighbors the °Sumerians. Babylonians, Hurrians, and Canaanites. Early efforts were made to combine deities of similar function and locale into families, and we find a genealogy of the gods which may be compared with the Greek traditions incorporated by Hesiod in his *Theogony*. Most prominent among Hittite deities was the weather god known to the Hurrians as Teshub, controller of both life-giving rain and destructive storm. Shaushka, like the Babylonian Ishtar, was goddess of love, sex, and warfare. The wife of the weather god was the sun goddess who was known as queen of heaven and queen of the Hatti lands. She protected the Hittite king in battle.

Istanu, the sun god, like the Babylonian Shamash was god of right and justice. He was king of the gods and judge of mankind.

See also Ugarit, Egypt, Babylon.

483

RHODES. The island of Rhodes, in the southeastern part of the Aegean, is separated from Asia Minor by a channel about ten miles wide. Rhodes measures forty-two by seventeen miles and is the largest island of the Aegean after Crete. Minoans from Crete founded a colony on the northwestern coast and, later, Mycenaeans built settlements all over the island. In later times Dorian Greeks settled the island.

Rhodes fell to the Persians, but after its liberation it joined the Delian League (477 B.C.). A new city of Rhodes was built in 408 B.C. to serve as capital of the island. The capital was built near the sanctuary of the sun god Helios at the northeast point of the island. In Hellenistic times Rhodes became an important trading center. At the entrance to the harbor stood a bronze statue to Helios, one hundred five feet high, known as the colossus of Rhodes — one of the wonders of the ancient world. The statue was demolished by an earthquake around 227 B.C.

In 43 B.C. Cassius collected all gold and silver from public and private resources and transported it to Rome along with many Rhodian works of art. Although the period of commercial and cultural greatness was past, Rhodes continued as a favorite resort for Roman travelers and political exiles. Travelers including Strabo and Pliny still spoke of its monuments and artistic wealth in the first century A.D.

Because of the extensive rebuilding of the town, little is known of the archaeology of the city of Rhodes. Other cities of the island, Lindos, Kameros and Ialysos are better preserved.

ROADS. Palestine served as a land bridge between Asia Minor and Mesopotamia to the north and east, and Egypt to the south. The most famous road system in the Biblical lands was the Great West Road, or the Road to the Sea. One section of this road went from Capernaum, through the Plain of Esdraelon to Megiddo, then down the coastal plain to Egypt.

A road from Asia Minor ran through Damascus, then south through the plateau east of the Jordan to Arabia. Part of it is known as the King's Highway. Branches led into Palestine at several points.

Hittites, Babylonians, Assyrians, and Persians all built roads for military and commercial purposes. Many roads built by the Romans are still visible, particularly in Jordan. See King's Highway.

ROBINSON'S ARCH. At the western wall of the temple area in °Jerusalem, remnants of the arches of two ancient bridges that connected the Upper City with the Temple area may still be seen. The one near the southwestern corner of the Temple area is known as Robinson's Arch, and the other, farther north, is known as Wilson's Arch. The arches bear the names of pioneer students of Biblical antiquities and travelers in Palestine, Edward Robinson and Charles W. Wilson.

ROME. Hub of the Roman Empire in New Testament times, Rome was ideally located to dominate the peninsula of Italy just as Italy was ideally located to dominate the Mediterranean world. Situated in the center of the peninsula, she could meet her enemies one by one and could prevent them from effectively combining against her.

About sixteen miles from where the Tiber enters the sea it flows through a group of small hills. Between these hills was swampy land until it was drained early in Roman history. Of these hills the Palatine was the best fitted for settlement and was the first of the hills occupied by Latins. Its more or less flat top twenty-five acres in extent and its precipitous and easily defensible sides made it a choice site. Just to the north of the Palatine, where all paths seemed to cross, evolved the Roman Forum.

"The Eternal City" has long enjoyed the detailed attention of archaeologists and historians. Legion are the monuments that have been excavated and/or preserved. Most of them have nothing to do with the Biblical account, and limitations of space prevent consideration of many items of interest here. The principle of selection in this article is threefold: (1) What structures or places is Paul likely to have seen while in Rome? (2) What important structures would have played a part in the lives of Christians during the first century or would have been known to them? (3) How should one evaluate the supposed discovery of Peter's tomb?

When Paul walked through the Porta Capena, the gate by which the Appian Way passed through the old Servian Wall, before him stood the great Circus Maximus. To his right the palaces of the Caesars rose on the Palatine Hill and overlooked the Circus. Farther to his right on the other side of the Palatine lay the Forum, where the Apostle probably stood trial before Caesar. To the east of the Forum Nero later built his Golden House — certainly by the time Paul was martyred. All of these structures require comment in an encyclopedia of Biblical archaeology. Because first century Christians living in Rome would have been impressed with the Colosseum and the tomb of Augustus and would have benefited greatly from the aqueducts and baths, all of those structures are profitably studied here.

I. *The Palaces of the Caesars.*

A. The Palatine Structures. Directly south of the Roman Forum stands the Palatine Hill, the first of the hills of Rome occupied by Latins and subsequently the residence of the emperors. Excavations on the Palatine began about 1725 under the auspices of Francis I of Parma and were continued by the French about a half century later. After sporadic investigations during the first half of the nineteenth century, in 1860 Napoleon III opened a new phase of the work. Under the leadership of Italian archaeologists, numerous campaigns have been conducted there in the twentieth century before World War I, between the wars and since World War II.

Investigations have brought to light the remains of huts of the iron age dating as early as the eighth and seventh centuries B.C. and have demonstrated that during the whole period of the Republic the hill did not have particular importance in the political and economic development of the city. It was simply an exclusive residential area and a place where several temples were erected during the third and second centuries B.C. Among the important residents of the hill during the later Republic were the tribune M. Livius Drusus, Mark Antony and Cicero.

Use of the Palatine changed radically with Augustus (27 B.C.—A.D. 14), who tradition says was born there and lived there as a private citizen. Just where his house was located is a matter of controversy. Tiberius (14-37) built a new palace on the northwest part of the hill, covered almost completely today by the beautiful Farnese Gardens and therefore not excavated. Only

THE OLD APPIAN WAY near Rome. Courtesy, Italian State Tourist Office

AUGUSTUS CAESAR. Courtesy,
National Museum, Naples

a little of the south side of the structure may be seen. Caligula (37-41) extended Tiberius' palace in the direction of the Forum and joined it by a bridge to the Capitoline Hill. Claudius (41-54) may have begun the palace used by Nero (54-68) in the years before the fire (64), located in the central and southern part of the hill.

Domitian (81-96), the emperor who exiled John to the Isle of Patmos, modified the configuration of the hill and demolished and covered many of the older structures with his grandiose new buildings. Principally these included the official palace, the residence and the stadium. The first two follow the usual plan of a Roman house with rooms arranged around an open colonnaded court (peristyle). The residence was more elaborate than the official palace, however, and had two courts. Domitian provided water for his palace (with its fountains) by extending the Claudian Aqueduct from the Caelian Hill to the Palatine. While Trajan and Hadrian did not live on the Palatine, other emperors did. They carried on some construction in their own right but did not greatly modify the plan for which Domitian

and his architect Rabirius were responsible.

Since the visitor to the Palatine today will see primarily the ruins of Domitian's construction (and it is this which is most fully known to archaeologists), a few words of description are in order. On the side facing the Forum (northeast) one enters the official palace through three doors. The one on the left led into a chapel, the one on the right, commonly called the Basilica, seems to have served for the judiciary audiences of the Emperor. It had a row of marble columns along each of the long walls and an apse in the rear wall separated from the rest of the hall by a screen. The great central audience hall (100 by 126 feet) was faced with polychrome marble in which were niches for statues and led directly into the peristyle. Along both sides of the peristyle were rooms of undetermined use and at the rear of it was the dining room.

The private dwelling of the emperor stood adjacent to the official palace on the southeast and consisted of a collection of rooms grouped, as has been noted, around two peristyles — one on the crest of the hill and the other about half way down the hill at a level some forty feet lower. Most of the rooms are not large but there are some larger ones that alternate with smaller ones for passage or rest. Fragments of marble pavements and wall friezes may still be seen in place.

Next to the private palace (on the southeast) lay the stadium of Domitian at a much lower level. About 470 feet long, it is closed on the north by a row of rooms and on the south by a semicircular wall. Probably this was a place for races and games reserved for the private use of the emperor.

The ruins on the Palatine now appear as great masses of brickwork with arched roofs, but during the first century they were magnificently encased in marble.

B. Nero's Golden House. After the great fire of A.D. 64 Nero determined to create for himself a great new palace in the center of the city. The grounds covered the area between the Esquiline, the Palatine and the Caelian hills. Known as the Golden House or Domus Aurea, this Versailles of the ancient world encompassed several palaces, parks, groves, pastures, a pool and a zoo — this vast complex covering 125 acres.

Later emperors did their best to destroy the memory of this monstrosity of Nero. The Flavians filled in the lake on the grounds and built the Colosseum on it; Trajan built his baths on top of the palace on the Oppian Hill. These two emperors and others built temples and other public buildings over the monumental approach to the grounds along the north and east sides of the Forum.

Since 1907, when the German archaeologist F. Weege wormed his way through a hole in the wall of the baths of Trajan and began to explore the Domus Aurea, modern archaeologists have been working on the site. So far eighty-eight rooms of the palace complex have been worked on; much more needs to be done there. The western wing of the palace was a conventional arrangement with rooms grouped around a peristyle with a garden and fountain. The eastern wing is more irregular in plan. The decoration of the rooms is absolutely fantastic and requires an extended on-the-spot examination to appreciate it. A riot of color is employed in the painted ceilings and walls, many of which are still decorated with mythological and erotic scenes. Venus languishing in the arms of Mars, Cupid riding in a chariot drawn by panthers, sphinxes with shrubs growing out of their backs, griffins, satyrs, and centaurs are among the many subjects that make up the riotous decor.

Miss E. B. Van Deman in 1925 was able to restore on paper the 350-foot wide monumental approach to the Domus Aurea from the north side of the Forum. Near the later Arch of Titus stood a colossal statue of Nero 120 feet tall.

II. *The Forum.* In the earliest days the area between the Palatine and Capitoline hills was significant as a crossroads of important highways. Later it became a burial ground for communities on the nearby hills. And as the population on those hills expanded into the valley and the area was rendered habitable by the construction of a great sewer, the valley became the hub of Roman life — religious, political, economic and social. Over the centuries the Forum became increasingly formalized and gradually the more objectionable features of commerce (such as selling of meat, poultry and vegetables) were forced out to other locations. Paving of the area occurred also.

During the Republic the Forum was the scene of political struggles with their impassioned oratory, and exulting crowds at the triumphs of emperors. But all of this changed under the Empire as the life went out of the old Republican forms with increasing imperial autocracy. Various emperors developed building programs to enhance the area and with Julius Caesar began the practice of building other forums nearby to handle expanding business and government at the Capital. Augustus, Domitian, Nerva and Trajan followed the pace set by Julius in building these new centers. But the old Roman Forum never lost its place of primacy in the affections of the people.

As Rome declined the Barbarians wrought considerable destruction in the Forum, but not as much as elsewhere in Rome. Some buildings there were preserved during the early Middle Ages because they were transformed into Christian churches. Severe damage occurred during the ninth to twelfth centuries, however, with papal decline, decline of population and factional strife within the city. During the sixteenth and seventeenth centuries large quantities of stone were removed from the Forum for building

HEAD OF NERO. Courtesy, N. Stoupnapas

elsewhere and much of it disappeared in the lime-kilns.

Archaeological investigation took its first feeble steps in the Forum area in 1788 when the Swedish ambassador in Rome excavated there briefly. Carlo Fea became Commissioner for Roman Antiquities in 1803 and conducted work there for over thirty years. The papal government continued the work during the middle of the century. After the new government of Italy obtained Rome for its capital in 1870, a new phase began in excavation of the Forum. Pietro Rosa directed the work until 1885. Giacomo Boni directed the excavations 1898-1925 and began the practice of excavating down to bedrock. He was followed by Alfonso Bartoli. Work has gone on steadily at the Forum since World War II.

While much is yet to be learned, a general knowledge of the area is now available. Perhaps it would be useful to try to visualize the Forum as the Apostle Paul would have known it. Overhanging it on the west was the Capitoline Hill with its great temple to Jupiter on the summit and the Tabularium or state record office on the eastern slope. At the foot of the Capital adjacent to the Forum was the Mamertine Prison, where Paul was probably incarcerated. It is now under the church of San Giuseppe de' Falegnami. A chamber where noted prisoners (conspirators and others) were kept before execution, it was apparently built in the third century B.C. It was originally a truncated cone twelve feet high but later a vaulted chamber of stone was built above the dungeon and in Tiberius' reign a facade of travertine was built on the Forum front.

As to the Forum itself, it is probably best approached from the east by means of the Sacred Way. The first important building one would pass is the house of the Vestal Virgins with its adjacent temple where was kept the fire that symbolized the perpetuity of the State. In front of the Temple of Vesta stood the Regia or official residence of the head of the state religion. The Sacred Way now turns left past the Temple of Caesar (of the divine Julius) and the Arch of Augustus and leads straight to the steps of the Temple of Castor and Pollux, the sanctuary of horsemen. Now the Sacred Way turns right again and passes the Basilica Julia, where Paul probably stood trial before

Caesar. The structure was 312 feet long by 156 feet wide with a great central hall measuring 234 by 85 feet. Paved with colored marble, this hall was surrounded by a double row of marble faced brick pillars which formed aisles that were vaulted and stuccoed. This hall was the seat of the tribunal of the *centumviri*, who judged civil cases.

As one stood on the Sacred Way alongside the Basilica Julia he could see straight ahead of him in the center of the Forum the Rostra where speakers might address a crowd gathered in the Forum. At one corner of the Rostra was the golden milestone, a marble column covered with gilt bronze, on which the distance from Rome to the principal towns of Italy and the Empire were marked. Next to the golden milestone was the Arch of Tiberius through which a glimpse of the Temple of Saturn could be caught. Directly across the Forum from the Basilica Julia stood the Basilica Aemilia, a great commercial center about 300 by 80 feet, especially used for money changing. Next to that stood the Senate House and the Senate Office Building.

The great fire of A.D. 64 destroyed the shops at the east and northeast edges of the Forum. There Nero built the facade of his Golden House, the memory of which later emperors tried to destroy. Titus built his triumphal arch at the east end of the Forum (after his conquest of Jerusalem in A.D. 70) and Domitian built luxury shops over part of the vestibule of the Golden House.

III. *Recreational Architecture.*

A. Circuses. Greatest of the recreational structures of Rome in Paul's day was the Circus Maximus, and he would have seen this edifice immediately upon entering the city at the Porta Capena. The circus lay between the parallel slopes of the Aventine and Palatine. It had evolved through a process of repeated destruction and rebuilding and was destined to be almost completely rebuilt by Nero after the fire of 64.

The total length of the circus was about 600 yards and the total width not over 200 yards. The arena was about 570 by 85 yards. In the middle of it stood the spina or central barrier around which chariots raced, 345 yards in length. At the west end were twelve carceres or starting places for chariots, and at the east end the circus was curved with

ARCH OF TITUS in Rome. *Courtesy, Italian State Tourist Office*

a gate in the center. This was later re-placed by a monumental gateway in tribute to Titus for his victory in Palestine.

Surrounding the arena was a raised plat-form on which chairs of high officials were placed. From this platform rose three tiers of seats, the lower of stone and the upper and perhaps the middle of wood. Estimates of seating capacity vary greatly, but 200,000 is probably not far from wrong. The ex-terior consisted of a three story arcade with engaged columns, like the Colosseum, and all was covered with marble.

There were at least three other circuses in Rome during the first Christian century. C. Flaminius Nepos in 221 B.C. built one just north of the Capitoline Hill. Its dimen-sions were about 260 by 100 yards. Caligula began a circus which Nero finished on the site where St. Peter's Cathedral now stands. Its size is uncertain. To the northwest of the Pantheon Domitian built a circus which reportedly held 15,000 spectators.

In all of these structures chariot races were commonly held, wild beast hunts or games might occur, and Christians might be martyred.

B. Baths. Under the Empire it was a part of every self-respecting Roman's daily rou-tine to frequent the bath. The story of the evolution of the Roman bath is hardly part of the present study. Suffice it to say that during Augustus' reign occurred the transition from the small simple public baths designed for bathing only to the massive imperial structures which served as great social centers for the whole populace.

These baths were much more than baths. They were places of social gathering — places where one might make appointments to meet his friends. There one could find gymnasia, exercising grounds, sweating rooms, warm and cold baths, rub down rooms, libraries and rooms where poets and philosophers held forth.

With Nero the baths assumed their common form. His was rectangular in form (measuring about 190 by 120 yards) and was entered on the north. In the middle of the north side was the cold bath, in the central hall the warm bath and on the south side the hot bath. On either side of the hot bath were four dressing or lounging rooms. Large colonnaded courts for gymnastic activities were situated to the east and west of the central hall.

JULIUS CAESAR. Courtesy, National Museum, Naples

Another of the great first century baths were those of Titus. Hastily built at the time of the dedication of the Colosseum and opened with magnificent games, they were located just west of the later baths of Trajan on the slope overhanging the Colosseum. The arrangement was similar to that of the baths of Nero, but on a smaller plan (about 105 by 120 yards). Near the end of the century Domitian bestowed a great public bath on the Roman people. Among the great baths of the second century and following are those built by Trajan, Caracalla, Decius, Commodus, Diocletian and Maxentius. Unfortunately, little is known of the details and procedure involved in taking a proper Roman bath, but generally one progressed from the warm to the hot to the cold bath.

C. Amphitheaters. While amphitheaters were built earlier in Rome (the earliest in 46 B.C.), the largest and most famous was the Colosseum. Begun by Vespasian on the site of the lake adjoining Nero's Domus Aurea, it was completed by Titus and dedicated in A.D. 80. It suffered several partial destructions and rebuildings. The last gladiatorial combats occurred there in 404. It was injured by an earthquake in 847 and was thereafter gradually destroyed until the eighteenth century. Since that time it has been protected with increasing care.

The circumference of this elliptical structure is about 1725 feet and the height of its four story walls 158 feet. Its seating capacity was about 45,000 with standing room for 5,000 more. The outer wall of the building rested on eighty piers connected by stone barrel vaults and was faced externally with three-quarter Doric columns, carrying an entablature. These eighty arches afforded access to the amphitheater and all of them were numbered to facilitate the movement of ticket holders. Above the lower arcade were a second and third faced with Ionic and Corinthian columns respectively. Statuary was placed in the second and third arcades. The fourth story consisted of solid walls of masonry faced with pilasters.

At the center of the structure was an arena 287 by 180 feet floored with wood. In the substructure are traces of dens for wild beasts, elevators, and provision for drainage of water. The seating was divided into three vast bands or sections. The first was for the more distinguished citizens, the second for the middle class and the third for the poor and women. The entire structure (including seats) was faced inside and out with marble. Gladiatorial combats and wild beast fights were the entertainments most commonly held there.

IV. *Aqueducts and Mausoleum.*

A. Aqueducts. Without an adequate water supply the great baths and fountains of Rome could not have been maintained. In fact, the city itself with its some 1,500,000 population could not have existed. When the Goths did cut the aqueducts in the sixth century A.D., Rome became an inconsequential town. As the Latin word indicates, an aqueduct was simply a means of "leading water" into a city. The upper portions were simply water channels on the surface of the ground or in underground channels. The first aqueduct built to Rome about 312 B.C. was a ten-mile covered tunnel from springs east of the city. Later, when longer water courses were constructed, when engineering skills and wealth permitted it, and when a desire to supply water for the hills of Rome demanded it, the latter part of the course was carried on high brick and concrete arches across the landscape to the city. The water channel of the famous Claudian aqueduct rested on 110-foot arches. Even then some two-thirds of the water system was carried on or beneath the surface of the ground. It was cheaper and safer that way; an aqueduct below the ground was harder for an enemy to find and cut.

Water was carried to Rome from springs or mountain streams (for as great a distance as sixty-two miles) to large distributing reservoirs in the city and then caused to flow through lead pipe under the streets to public fountains, baths and private houses. In Paul's day eight aqueducts served Rome. By the end of the century there were nine. Ultimately there were eleven early in the third century A.D. At the latter date they provided 250,000,000 gallons of water per day according to Paul MacKendrick (*The Mute Stones Speak*, p. 134), though estimates run as high as 400,000,000 gallons daily. Courses of the major aqueducts of Rome have been plotted by Thomas Ashby of the British School at Rome and Miss Esther B. Van Deman of the American Academy.

B. The Mausoleum of Augustus. In the northwestern section of Rome adjacent to the Tiber, Augustus began in 28 B.C. a huge mausoleum that was designed to resemble an Etruscan burial mound. When the concrete substructure was completed it was to be heaped with earth and planted with cypresses and surmounted with a huge statue of the Emperor.

When Italian excavators stripped the mausoleum of later accretions and excavated it in 1935, they found it to consist of a huge outer wall within which rose to a height of 143 feet a series of concentric vaulted corridors surrounding a hollow cylinder designed to hold the Emperor's ashes. In the passage way around the cylinder were placed marble urns which had once held the ashes of various members of the family, such as Augustus' stepson Drusus and sister Octavia, as well as of Emperors Caligula and Claudius and others. Before the entrance to the tomb stood bronze tablets inscribed with Augustus' autobiography.

V. *The Vatican Excavations.* Most controversial of the excavations in Rome is the work done under the Vatican. According to tradition Constantine built a basilica over the tomb of St. Peter. Through the centuries Constantine's church gradually decayed and was replaced by the present St. Peter's Basilica beginning in 1506. The high altar of the modern church supposedly covered the Apostle's tomb. Finally Pope Pius XII permitted excavations under the Vatican 1940-49, and they were resumed in 1953.

Beneath the church was found an early cemetery with tombs dating mainly from about A.D. 100 to well into the fourth century. But there were burials dating before 100. Under the high altar of the church was found a sort of shrine under which some human bones were found. The official excavation reports published in 1951 set forth the view that this was indeed the tomb of St. Peter.

By way of background it should be noted that Gaius, a churchman of Rome who lived there about A.D. 200, spoke of a memorial shrine to Peter erected there about 160. Under the shrine were traces of an ancient grave which was an object of special veneration.

Actually the finds permit quite different interpretations. Supporters and opponents of the conclusions of the excavators are not

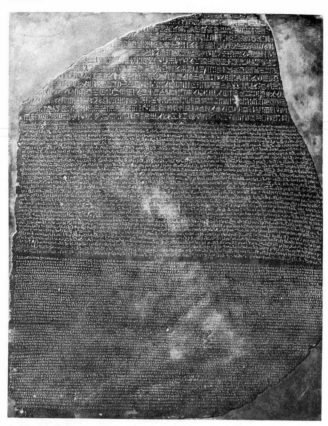

THE ROSETTA STONE, a trilingual inscription which contained the key to the decipherment of hieroglyphics. Courtesy, Oriental Institute

divided strictly along party lines. A number of Roman Catholic scholars, including theologians, reject decisively the conclusions of the official reports and independent archaeologists embrace them.

Oscar Cullmann says, "The grave of Peter cannot be identified" (*Peter*, p. 156). Taking more of a middle ground, Toynbee and Perkins conclude that ". . . although there is nothing to prove that this grave was that of St. Peter, nothing in the archaeological evidence is inconsistent with such an identification" (Jocelyn Toynbee and John Ward Perkins, *The Shrine of St. Peter and the Vatican Excavations*, p. 161). Margherita Guarducci is convinced that the site of Peter's burial was in the Vatican and at the place marked by the shrine under the present high altar. She identifies the shrine under the altar with the memorial shrine of Gaius (*The Tomb of St. Peter*, pp. 180-81). Engelbert Kirschbaum, one of the excavators, feels that the shrine discovered was that spoken

of by Gaius and that St. Peter's grave was located in this portion of the Vatican but that the Apostle's grave was not "discovered" in the same sense (*The Tombs of St. Peter and St. Paul*, p. 118).

In the face of conflicting scholarly opinion, conclusions are difficult. A reading of the evidence does not seem completely convincing that Peter's tomb has been found. On the other hand, it does not seem to close the door conclusively to the possibility that Peter was buried there.

BIBLIOGRAPHY. Axel Boethius, *The Golden House of Nero*, University of Michigan Press, Ann Arbor, 1961. Oscar Cullmann, *Peter*, trans. by Floyd V. Filson, 2nd rev. ed., The Westminster Press, Philadelphia, 1962. Margherita Guarducci, *The Tomb of St. Peter*, trans. by Joseph McLellan, George G. Harrap & Co. Ltd., London, 1960. Engelbert Kirschbaum, *The Tombs of St. Peter and St. Paul*, trans. by John Murray, Secker and Warburg, London, 1959. Paul MacKendrick, *The Mute Stones Speak*, St. Martin's Press, New York, 1960. Samuel B. Platner, *A Topographical Dictionary of Ancient Rome*, Completed and revised by Thomas

Ashby, Oxford University Press, London, 1929. G. T. Rivoira, *Roman Architecture,* trans. by G. McN. Rushforth, at the Clarendon Press, Oxford, 1925. D. M. Robertson, *A Handbook of Greek and Roman Architecture,* Cambridge University Press, Cambridge, 1929. Pietro Romanelli, *The Palatine,* Istituto Poligrafico Dello Stato, Rome, 2d ed., 1956. Pietro Romanelli, *The Roman Forum,* Istituto Poligrafico Dello Stato, Rome, 3d ed., 1959. Jocelyn Toynbee and John Ward Perkins, *The Shrine of St. Peter and the Vatican Excavations,* Longmans, Green & Co., London, 1956.

ROSETTA STONE. The Rosetta Stone is a *stele approximately three feet high and two feet four inches broad, containing inscriptions in Greek and two forms of ancient Egyptian — Demotic, the common script of Egypt, and Hieroglyphic. The stone gets its name from the Egyptian village of Rosetta near which it was discovered in 1798 by an officer of Napoleon's expedition in Egypt.

The Greek text at the bottom of the stone could be read, and scholars attempted to use it as a key to the decipherment of the two Egyptian scripts. Silvester de Sacy of France and J. D. Ackerblad of Sweden identified

Greek personal names in the demotic text — Ptolemy, Berenike, and Arsinoe. An English scholar, Thomas Young, identified the name of Ptolemy in the hieroglyphic section where groups of signs in oval frames, called cartouches, were thought to be king's names. A young French scholar, Jean Francois Champollion (1790-1832), was able to demonstrate the nature of hieroglyphic writing, to formulate an Egyptian grammar and dictionary, and to translate numerous Egyptian texts.

The Rosetta Stone was a decree issued by the priests of Memphis in honor of Ptolemy V, Epiphanes (*ca.* 203-181 B.C.). Its significance is not so much in its contents, however, as in its value in opening the secret of hieroglyphic writing to the world of scholarship. The Rosetta Stone is now in the British Museum, for it came into the possession of the British after the fall of Alexandria and the defeat of the Napoleonic army. For the decipherment of the cuneiform character *see* the Behistun Inscription.

S

SADDUCEES. *See* Jewish Sects.

SAFED. Safed, traditionally identified as the "city that is set on an hill" (Matt. 5:14), is perched high among the mountains of northern Israel. Although not mentioned in Scripture, the Talmud says that it was one of a chain of high places on which beacons were lit to signal the arrival of the New Year. During the sixteenth and seventeenth centuries, Safed gained renown as one of four Holy Cities in Palestine and the center of Cabbalist mysticism. Jews, suffering from persecution in Europe, looked for the rapid appearance of their Messiah, and spiritual leaders found in Safed a center from which to write and teach. In the late sixteenth and early seventeenth centuries there were eighteen Talmudic colleges there. The historian Cecil Roth terms this "the most vital movement in Judaism which had come forth from Palestine since the days of the Second Temple." The first printing press in all Asia was installed in sixteenth century Safed. The

first Hebrew book to be printed in Palestine was published in 1578. Safed is the northernmost city in modern Israel. Its old synagogues still show a concern for the traditions of the past, but its modern artists' colony blends the contemporary with the old.

SAMARIA. About 880 B.C. Omri of Israel moved his capital from Tirzah to a three hundred foot high hill seven miles northwest of Shechem. The hill is located in a wide basin formed by a valley which runs from *Shechem to the coast, and it commands the main trade routes through Esdraelon. The hill was easily defensible, being surrounded by valleys on all sides. From the summit there is a clear view to the Mediterranean.

The work of Omri (I Kings 16:21) was continued by his son Ahab who is known for the ivory palace which he built at Samaria (I Kings 22:39). The reference may be to the rich ivory inlay which was used

REMAINS OF THE CITY GATE of Samaria (cf. II Kings 7:1, 16-20). Courtesy, Matson Photo Service

in the palace furnishings, many of which have been discovered in recent years. Under Ahab, Baalism became a prominent element in the life of Samaria and idolatrous cult objects were erected in the capital (cf. II Kings 3:2).

The city was unsuccessfully besieged by Benhadad of Damascus (I Kings 20; II Kings 6). With the growth in °Assyrian power Menahem thought it wise to pay tribute (II Kings 25:17-20), but Pekah adopted an anti-Assyrian policy, trusting Egypt to offer aid in the event of an emergency. Shalmaneser V besieged Samaria with his Assyrian armies (725-722 B.C.), and the city finally was taken by °Sargon II (II Kings 17:6). Its people were transported to other areas subject to Assyria, and new colonists were settled in Samaria and its environs. It was these settlers (II Kings 17:24), who were augmented from time to time by others (cf. Ezra 4:2, 9, 10) who formed the people later known as Samaritans. The area was also colonized by Greeks following Alexander's conquest (331 B.C.). John Hyrcanus besieged Samaria (111-107 B.C.) and incorporated it into his Hasmonaean Empire. The city was rebuilt by Pompey and Gabinius and later embellished by Herod who named it Sebaste Augusta for his Emperor.

The village still bears the name Sebastiyeh.

Excavations began at Sebastiyeh in 1908 under the auspices of Harvard University. The first director was D. G. Lyon, followed in 1909 and 1910 by G. A. Reisner. Work was resumed in 1931 by J. W. Crowfoot representing Harvard University, the Palestine Exploration Fund, the Hebrew University, and the British School of Archaeology, Jerusalem. Excavations were conducted during the summers of 1931, 1932, and 1933, and part of the 1935 season.

The history of Israelite Samaria began with Omri's purchase of the site, although there is evidence of some occupation during the Early Bronze Age (3000-2000 B.C.). Seven Israelite levels of occupation have been traced, followed by Hellenistic and Roman levels. The two lowest levels (designated I and II) are from the time of Omri and Ahab. They include the city walls — inner walls five feet thick and outer walls nineteen and one-half feet thick. The main gateway had a columned entrance court. The palace also had a wide court and a pool or reservoir, thirty-three and one-half by seventeen feet (cf. I Kings 22:38). The palace has additions from the time of Jeroboam II.

In a storeroom near the palace, about two

hundred plaques and ivory pieces were discovered. Some have Hebrew letters scratched on their back. Many were apparently attached to furniture, but most seem to have been affixed to the wainscoting of the room. They are of Phoenician workmanship with many Egyptian motifs. They may have given rise to the name of the "ivory house" which Ahab is said to have built (I Kings 22:39).

Near the west end of the Israelite citadel, the excavators found about seventy broken pieces of pottery inscribed with official records in the Old Hebrew script. Twenty-two villages in the territory of Manasseh are mentioned, along with several of the revenue officers. They probably date from the reign of Jeroboam II.

The third level marks the period of Jehu, and some of the earlier buildings were adapted for the new dynasty. After an interval, levels four through six cover the period of Jeroboam and the eighth century B.C. The destruction level (VII) marks the fall of the city to the Assyrians.

The Hellenistic remains include a round tower, earlier thought to date from Jeroboam II. Ben Dor of the Hebrew University discovered Hellenistic pottery in the masonry which would date it no earlier than 325 B.C. The same level has yielded remains of a fortress, city wall, stamped jar handles, and Hellenistic pottery. During Hellenistic times the city of Samaria was Greek in culture, while the Semitic Samaritans found their cultural and religious center at Shechem. The jar fragments when pieced together indicate a type of wine jar that was used on the island of Rhodes. Much of the pottery was of an Athenian type. It is obvious that Samaria had commerce with the Hellenistic world and that she had little cultural contact with either the Jew or the Samaritan of the period.

John Hyrcanus destroyed the Hellenistic city and sold its inhabitants into slavery. For nearly half a century, Samaria was unoccupied. Then (63 B.C.) Pompey and his Roman army invaded Judaea and restored Samaria and other non-Jewish districts to their former owners. In 57 B.C. Gabinius, the provincial governor of Syria, rebuilt Samaria on a small scale. In 30 B.C. Octavial, later to become Augustus Caesar, presented Samaria to Herod who settled the city with discharged mercenaries and renamed it Sebaste, the Greek equivalent of Augustus, in honor of his friend and patron. Herod's mercenaries included Gauls, Thracians, and Germans, and the city took upon itself a thoroughly cosmopolitan atmosphere. Over the remains of earlier Israelite palaces, there arose a Roman temple to Augustus. The city boasted a basilica, a forum, a stadium, and an aqueduct — all representative of Roman influence. Roman Samaria boasted a nine hundred yard long colonnaded street with adjacent shops.

BIBLIOGRAPHY. G. A. Reisner, C. S. Fisher, and D. G. Lyon, Harvard Excavations at Samaria, 1908-10, Harvard University Press, Cambridge, 1924. John W. and Grace M. Crowfoot, Early Ivories from Samaria, Palestine Excavation Fund, London, 1938. John W. Crowfoot, Kathleen Kenyon, and E. J. Sukenik, The Buildings at Samaria, Palestine Exploration Fund, London, 1942. J. W. Crowfoot, G. M. Crowfoot, and Kathleen M. Kenyon, The Objects from Samaria, Palestine Exploration Fund, London, 1957. Renè Dussaud, "Samarie au temps d'Achab," Syria, VI, 1925-26, pp. 314-338. J. W. Jack, Samaria in Ahab's Time: Harvard Excavations and their Results, T. and T. Clark, Edinburgh, 1929. André Parrot, Samaria, the Capital of the Kingdom of Israel, S.C.M. Press, London, 1958.

SAMARITAN OSTRACA. During the excavation of Samaria in 1910 G. A. Reisner discovered a uniform group of sixty-five documents written in the ancient Hebrew script on broken pieces of pottery (see Ostraca), These lay on the floor of a room which belonged to the first phase of the second period of palace construction at Samaria. They had been written with a reed pen in black carbon ink in a clear and flowing hand and appeared to be the work of skilled scribes. The words were divided by dots or strokes as in the °Moabite Stone and the °Siloam inscription.

Although these documents contain only scanty information they are of considerable significance for the script, spelling, personal names, topography, religion and administration of the period. A typical ostracon (No. 18) will give a general picture of their contents. It reads, "In the tenth year. From Hazeroth to Gaddiyau; a jar of fine oil."

A number of problems await a final solution. The original excavators attributed the level where they were found to the days of Ahab in the ninth century B.C., but mature consideration of the evidence would give a date in the eighth century. The exact date depends, in large measure, on the interpretation of the symbols used to express the number of the years. In particular the sign has been read as 10, and the sign as 5, so that the combination denotes 15. One combination of signs in ostracon No. 63 has been read for "17 years" where the date formula is then "In the 17th year." On this basis, only those kings during the ninth or eighth century who reigned seventeen years could qualify, namely Jehu (ca. 842-815 B.C.), Jehoahaz (ca. 815-801 B.C.) and Jeroboam (ca. 786-745 B.C.).

More recently Y. Yadin has suggested that the symbols should be read differently and has concluded that the highest regnal year is 9. He argues that the pottery used in the documents may be assigned to periods IV or V at Samaria (K. M. Kenyon, Sebaste, III, p. 470), while the script resembles that of the Siloam inscription more than that of the Mesha Stone. Again, he proposes that the defeat of Menahem by Tiglath-pileser in 738 B.C. (II Kings 15:14-20) and the obligation laid on him to pay heavy tribute would provide a historical explanation of the need to collect taxes in an excessive manner. In that case a date between 745 and 735 B.C. seems possible, a view that has now received the support of W. F. Albright (BASOR, 168, p. 43).

The nature of the documents is not entirely clear. It has been assumed hitherto, that the formula "To X from Y" indicates that the goods were delivered from a certain place to a certain person in charge of the area. Where more than one name is mentioned the reference may be to the fact that wine, oil, etc. from a particular place was designated for several persons. The documents seem to have been written at the receiving end, however, since Nos. 48 and 49 are part of the same vessel although they differ both in their place names and their personal names. Moreover the script suggests that only a small number of scribes wrote the documents. Indeed, one scribe wrote ostraca mentioning various place names. On the other hand Yadin has suggested that the word to on the ostraca means belonging to, so that ostraca 18 would read "In the 10th year. From Hazeroth, belonging to Gaddiyau. A jar of fine oil." The ostraca, on this view, were records written by a court official on receipt of the item in question. Where several names are mentioned the first would indicate the main owner and the others his associates or sub-tenants.

Whatever the final solution, an explanation has to be offered as to why the persons to whose name the preposition to is prefixed are connected with different places and different districts, and why various persons are mentioned in connection with the same place.

The items mentioned are oil and wine. This suggests that we are dealing not so much with annual tribute as with produce from crown properties round Samaria that was sent by tenants of vineyards or gardens to officials for distribution.

The names mentioned in the ostraca are of considerable religious significance. There are, as in the Old Testament, names compounded with 'ab "father," 'ah "brother," 'am "people" and also with the divine names El, Baal, Yah. There were approximately seven Baal names to every eleven names formed with Yah. This would lend support to the Old Testament picture of the great interest in Baal worship in Samaria and the northern parts of Israel. At the same time the presence of numerous Yah names provides evidence of the continuity of Yahweh worship in the north, despite the evil reputation of the kingdom of Israel in the Old Testament.

BIBLIOGRAPHY. G. A. Reisner, C. S. Fisher, and D. G. Lyon, Harvard Excavations at Samaria, 1908-1910, 1924, pp. 227-246. Y. Yadin, "Ancient Judaean Weights and the Date of the Samaria Ostraca," Scripta Hierosolymitana, VIII, Jerusalem, 1961, pp. 9-25. J. W. Jack, Samaria in Ahab's Time, Edinburgh, 1929. Various notes in Israel Exploration Journal, Vol. 9, 1959, pp. 184-187; Vol. 12, 1962, pp. 62-69.

SAMARRA. When Ernst Herzfeld was excavating Samarra, on the Tigris River north of Baghdad, his chief interest was Islamic remains. While studying houses of the Islamic period he was attracted to the five-foot layer of debris between the pavements of the houses and the virgin soil. Digging into the debris he found a number of badly preserved graves containing painted pottery in a variety of forms: plates, dishes on high bases, hemispheric bowls, wide-mouthed pots, and squat jars. The pottery was of medium thickness and much of it was over-fired. It was distinctive in that it was covered with drawings of plants, animals, and

*PHOENICIAN SARCOPH-
AGUS from Byblos. Courtesy
Photo Sport, Beirut*

people in bright red and purple-brown colors. Geometric motifs also appear. Samarra type pottery has been identified at various sites between the Tigris River and northern Syria.

BIBLIOGRAPHY. Ernst Herzfeld, *Geschichte der Stadt Samarra,* Eckardt and Messtorff, Hamburg, 1948.

SARCOPHAGUS. A sarcophagus is a stone coffin. Egyptian sarcophagi, made for mummified bodies, were elaborately sculptured and bore hieroglyphic inscriptions.

SARDIS. Sardis (*Sardeis*), the ancient capital city of Lydia in western Asia Minor, is mentioned in the Bible only in Revelation 1:11; 3:1, 4. It is one of the seven cities of Asia Minor to which specific letters are addressed.

I. *Location.* The city is located thirty-five miles south of Thyatira. It was built at the base of Mt. Tmolus, with the acropolis on Mt. Tmolus about eight hundred feet above the city proper. The acropolis was surrounded by a triple wall, which survives to the present day. The city is located about two and a half miles south of the Hermus River. The Pactolus River, which flows in a general north-south direction through the city, empties into the Hermus. The modern paved road, the Salihli Highway, passes in a northwest-southeast direction through the ruins of the city.

Sardis is perhaps best known as the residence and capital of the wealthy King Croesus. It is here that the earliest evidence of the use of coins has been found. Some have suggested that gold was found in the sands of the Pactolus River, but this is doubtful, since there are no traces of it to be found today. However, there is no reason to doubt the fabled riches of Croesus.

II. *History of Sardis.* W. M. Ramsay (*The Letters to the Seven Churches of Asia,* p. 356) suggests that the earlier name of Sardis was Hyde, the primitive capital of the Hermus Valley as identified by Homer. If this is correct, the beginnings of Sardis would go back to the beginning of the Lydian kingdom, about 1200 B.C. The name Sardis (a plural form in the Greek) is found in Greek literature from the time of Aeschylus and Thucydides on.

The earliest significance of Sardis in world history is as the capital and residence of the Lydian King Croesus. In 546 B.C. its fortress on the acropolis, which Croesus thought impregnable, fell to the mobilized Persian forces under the leadership of Cyrus the Great. Herodotus describes this capture (possibly somewhat embellished) in Book I. For the next two centuries Sardis stood more or less on the dividing line between East and West. Through here the forces of Darius and Xerxes passed in their futile attempts to conquer the Greeks in the early fifth century.

Alexander the Great granted Sardis independent status upon her surrender in 334 B.C.; but this lasted only briefly, ending in 322 B.C. when Antigonus captured the city. Sardis' own evaluation of her role during this period is reflected in the confident inscription on her coins: "Sardis the First Metropolis of Asia, and of Lydia, and of Hellenism."

Seleucid control began in 301 B.C. and continued through the third century. In 190 B.C. Sardis became part of the empire of Pergamos. When the Romans took over this area, Sardis became a part of the province of Asia. Much of her splendor was destroyed by a violent earthquake in A.D. 17. To meet this disaster Emperor Tiberius cancelled the taxes for five years and gave a donation of ten million sesterces.

Sardis regained a position of power after A.D. 295 as the capital of the province of Lydia. In the Byzantine church, Sardis occupied a position of leadership, since her bishop was the Metropolitan and Archbishop of Lydia, the sixth in order of dignity of all the Asiatic and European bishops subject to the Patriarch of Constantinople (Ramsay, *Letters*, p. 368). An influential leader in the second century church was Bishop Melito who resided at Sardis.

Most of the major buildings of the Byzantine period were destroyed by the Sassanian raid about A.D. 615 (Hanfmann, *BASOR* 170, April 1963, p. 48). Final destruction of Sardis occurred in A.D. 1402 when Tamerline, the great Asiatic conquerer, invaded Asia Minor (E. G. Krealing, *Bible Atlas*, Rand McNally and Co., New York, 1956, p. 470).

III. *Excavations of Sardis.* In the early 1900's the now defunct American Society for the Excavation of Sardis was organized under H. C. Butler of Princeton University. Under his direction this society excavated Sardis from 1910 until 1914 when the First World War forced them to discontinue this project. One of the major operations of this expedition was the clearing of the huge temple of Artemis. Only two large columns of this temple were visible, but the work of the expedition revealed a huge building complex covering an area 327 feet by 163 feet. The surviving remains indicate that this was an impressive temple from the Roman period. The native goddess of Sardis was Cybele, who was later identified as Artemis. In the Christian period, a church was constructed at the southeast corner of the temple.

Another major operation of these early excavations was the opening of more than a thousand graves. Although these excavations were never resumed by this society (an attempt in 1922 had to be abandoned because of the war between Turkey and Greece), their publications include some seven comprehensive volumes appearing under the general title *Sardis* (Leyden, 1922 ff.).

In 1958 the Fogg Art Museum of Harvard University and Cornell University, in cooperation with the American Schools of Oriental Research, launched a new project of excavating at Sardis, under the direction of George M. A. Hanfmann of Harvard. Every summer since 1958 extensive excavations have been carried on. Each season's work has been rather extensively reported by Hanfmann in *BASOR* (*see bibliography*).

Areas excavated and under excavation are found on both sides of the Salihli Highway and mainly east of the Pactolus River. Some restoration work was done in 1960 on the Temple of Artemis. This Hellenistic temple had been rebuilt, possibly after the earthquake of A.D. 17. In 1961 the church at the southeast corner of the temple was investigated and partially repaired and restored. This structure appears to have been in use by the middle of the fourth century after Christ continuing until about A.D. 615. The excavators suggest that this small church "is a social, historical, and architectural document of considerable value" (Hanfmann, *BASOR* report the discovery of a number of

Excavations in 1962 just north of the Salihli Highway and east of the Pactolus River uncovered the ruins of a Jewish synagogue. Fragmentary Hebrew inscriptions, inscribed jars, mosaic floors, and Jewish symbols (including a *menorah*) were found in the ruins. Further excavation of the synagogue area in 1963 revealed an extensive and impressive structure. The remains of marble slabs and pillars and massive doorways point to a structure of major importance. It is suggested that this synagogue was constructed in the first half of the third century of our era. "The disrupted mosaic floors, the worn thresholds, and the evidences of remodeling throughout the building testify to a complex history throughout the fourth, fifth, and sixth centuries A.D., with a major remodeling in the fourth century, followed by increasing neglect" (Hanfmann, *BASOR* 170, April 1963, p. 48). The synagogue was flanked by Byzantine shops along the south wall. These were in line with a row of Byzantine shops along the south wall of the gymnasium located west of the synagogue. These later structures were part of a large complex of ornate marble architecture.

Excavations in 1960, 1961, and 1962 on the acropolis gave indication of Byzantine and Lydian remains, as well as a Hellenistic level on the north side of the elevation. Other extensive excavations south of the modern highway have uncovered Lydian, Persian, Hellenistic, Roman, and Byzantine levels of occupation. These were found in various tombs, graves, and building remains. This would indicate practically continuous occupation of Sardis from the ancient period until about the seventh century after Christ. The informative preliminary presentations in BASOR report the discovery of a number of unique objects of relevance in many areas of study.

IV. *Evaluation.* Since these current archaeological excavations at Sardis have not yet been completed, it is impossible to draw any final conclusions regarding Sardis and the archaeological record. However, the evidence of recent excavations makes it necessary to reconsider some of Ramsay's conclusions regarding the city. His epithet "a city of death" for the first century Sardis is hardly appropriate in all respects. From the information in Revelation this phrase would seem to give an accurate description of the spiritual condition of the city. However, her star continued to shine, sometimes dimly, until the seventh century. The fact that she had a role of leadership in the early church (see above) probably indicates that there were those who did "hear what the Spirit says to the churches" (Rev. 3:6). Some apparently did awaken, repent, and strengthen what remained (Rev. 3:2, 3). The threat, "I will come like a thief" (Rev. 3:3) no doubt reminded the people of Sardis of their city's history, for their city had fallen twice when the people had not been alert. The size of the synagogue which has been uncovered would indicate a rather large Jewish population in the early Christian era. This was probably a source of conflict and difficulty for the early church at Sardis.

The Biblical record tells very little about Sardis. But the results of archaeological investigation here have supplied a rather complete background for the Biblical message.

BIBLIOGRAPHY. H. C. Butler, *et al.*, *Sardis*, Volumes Iff., Leyden, 1922ff. W. M. Ramsay, *The Letters to the Seven Churches of Asia*, Hodder and Stoughton, London, 1904. G. M. A. Hanfmann, "Excavations at Sardis, 1958," *BASOR* 154, April 1959, pp. 5-35; "Excavations at Sardis, 1959," *BASOR* 157, February 1960, pp. 8-43; "The Third Campaign at Sardis, 1960," *BASOR* 162, April 1961, pp. 8-49; "The Fourth Campaign at Sardis (1961)," *BASOR* 166, April 1962, pp. 1-57; "The Fifth Campaign at Sardis (1962)," *BASOR* 170, April 1963, pp. 1-65.

SARGON OF AKKAD. Sharru(m)-kin (= Sargon) of Agade, *ca.* 2360-2304 B.C., was the first of several Mesopotamian monarchs to bear this name. The others belong to the much later Assyrian period (cf. Sargon II). Sargon is noted as the first empire-builder in the annals of history. The empire and dynasty which he founded, with Agade, or *Akkad, as its principal city, gave its name to the Semitic language as well as to the Sumero-Semitic culture which Sargon and his successors spread throughout the ancient Near East.

The location of the city of Akkad has not been archaeologically identified, although it must have existed somewhere near the three cities which were located in the "bottle-neck" area between the Euphrates and Tigris rivers: *Babylon, *Kish (*Tell el 'Uhaimir*) and *Sippar (*Abû Habba*). *Hammurabi (*ca.* 1700 B.C.), in the Prologue to his law code, mentions having installed a goddess in her temple built in the square of Akkad.

Until Sargon's rise, lower Mesopotamia was a cluster of Sumerian city-states, although those in the upper part of this area were now in the control of Semites. From time to time the king of one city-state overpowered one or more of the others. Seldom, however, was his rule extended much beyond this area, nor did it unite the area for very long. Lugalzaggisi of Umma (*Tell Jôkha*), who was Sargon's contemporary and predecessor in power over the Sumerian south, conquered *Uruk (*Warka*, Biblical Erech, Gen. 10:10) and *Lagash (Telloh), and destroyed Kish, which was currently in power. He subsequently claimed control of all Sumer and that all Mesopotamia recognized his rule. However, Lugalzaggisi not only did not found an enduring dynasty, but was in his turn overpowered by Sargon, who brought Mesopotamia in its fullest extent under the

CYLINDER SEAL and its impression, from the Akkadian Period, about 2300 B.C. Courtesy, Oriental Institute

direct military and political power of his regime in actuality.

Sargon bequeathed to his successors a unified empire which embraced the whole Mesopotamian area from the head of the Persian Gulf to the mountains of the north and northwest. He brought the Elamite territory east of the Tigris under his control, also, by capturing Susa (the Shushan of Esther and Daniel). These conquests gave the dynasty of Akkad control over the trade routes of the Near East. Trade southwards, mediated through *Dilmun* (the island of Bahrein), was apparently developed with southern Arabia, the Indus river settlements in western India and, perhaps, with the coastal peoples of East Africa. In the northwest, trade was carried on with the peoples of upper Syria, Asia Minor, and probably with the early Minoans via Cyprus and Crete.

I. *Archaeological Attestation.* Attestation of Sargon of Akkad is of two kinds, direct and indirect. "Direct" evidence includes written texts and inscriptions which give details of Sargon's career. The "indirect" attestations come in the form of evidences of commercial and other cultural activities, discovered in sites at levels datable to the Sargonic period, which presuppose the conditions of the Sargonic empire for their existence.

A. Direct Evidence. Direct evidence for Sargon are a number of cuneiform texts and inscriptions, of which the principal ones are: (1) the Sumerian King List; (2) the Sargon Chronicle; (3) inscriptions on statues of Sargon; (4) the so-called "King of Battle Epic"; and (5) the so-called "Legend of Sargon." The statuary inscriptions are believed by their latest translator to date from a time soon after the close of Sargon's dynasty, early in the twenty-second century B.C. Copies of the other texts have been found in sites and strata dating variously from the twenty-second down to the seventh centuries B.C. They have also been found widely distributed geographically: at *Nippur (Niffar), *Babylon, *Nineveh (Kuyunjik), *Ashur (Qalat Sharqat), and other sites in Mesopotamia; at *Amarna in Egypt; and in Hittite sites in eastern Asia Minor.

Secondary attestation of similar kind has come through the inscriptions of Sargon's successors, particularly his illustrious grandson and great-grandson, Naram-Sin and Shargalisharri, which mention him as their predecessor. Further, an inscription of Nabuna'id, or Nabonidus (father of the Biblical Belshazzar, sixth century B.C.), gives an account of his having discovered the foundation platform of a temple which had been erected by Naram-Sin, whom he calls "son" of Sargon.

Although some of these texts are of semilegendary nature, a "hard core" of fairly reliable information persists, whether relating to Sargon's personal background or to his career. The main points seem to be: (1) Sargon was born of a cult priestess, a sort of "wife of the god"; (2) he was brought up humbly, but became cupbearer to Ur-Ilbaba, king of Kish; (3) at an opportune time, perhaps when Lugalzaggisi attacked Kish, Sargon deserted Ur-Ilbaba and founded his own city, Agade or Akkad (cf. Gen. 10:10); (4) he later overthrew Lugalzaggisi, unified Sumer and Akkad under his rule and began a career of empirebuilding that quickly made him master of the entire Mesopotamian area; (5) his rule lasted about fifty-five years; (6) in his time he made numerous military expeditions for the purpose of extending his rule and of pacifying rebels. In the course of these expeditions he crossed the Amanus mountains and reached the coast of the

Mediterranean, and also crossed at least the eastern ranges of the Taurus mountains farther to the north.

B. Indirect Evidence. Excavations at a number of sites, mainly in upper Mesopotamia, have yielded dramatic evidences of the commercial aspects of Sargon's empire. The discoveries at *Yorgan Tepe,* near modern Kirkuk, are illustrative. The earlier excavations discovered the city of *Nuzi, the finds from which were quickly popularized since they witnessed to customs of various kinds which vividly illustrated the patriarchal narratives of the Bible. Later and deeper excavations, however, recovered many of the remains of an earlier city which was known as Gasur. Numerous texts and artifacts revealed that it had been a flourishing mercantile center in Sargonic times. Many of the texts dealt with trading matters, indicating among other things that the merchants of Gasur maintained commercial relations with almost the whole of Mesopotamia.

Similar finds at levels of the Sargonic period in other sites in Mesopotamia help to fill out the picture. They attest to an organized commercial empire with a good system of communications; a busy caravan trade carried on over reasonably well-protected routes; an established banking system with organized credit and regular exchange values (cf. Gen. 23:16); and, finally, the existence of trading enclaves in foreign territories, especially in the northwest, which imply some sort of trade agreement with foreign rulers.

Trade in grain, metals, woods, and manufactured wares was brisk. Along with this went a rise in the standard of living of at least part of the citizens of the empire, and an acceleration of the development and spread of the arts and conveniences of an advancing material culture.

II. *Significance for Biblical Studies.* The archaeologically recovered history of Sargon and his empire is significant for Biblical studies at a number of points, even though his empire rose and fell centuries before Biblical history as such begins.

A. Dominance of the Semites. The people of the Akkad region of lower Mesopotamia, including Sargon, were predominantly Semitic. So were those settled along the middle Euphrates and in much of northern Meso-

potamia at this time. Under Sargon's rule they were made participators in a sort of Semitic super-state. The Amurru (Amorites, or western Semites) eventually gained the dominance, but only to become the heritors and perpetuators of the Akkadian culture. After the downfall of Sargon's dynasty, a little more than a century after his death, the hegemony of Mesopotamia passed to Ur, then to other originally Sumerian city-states of the south. However, a gradual process of semitization both in language and general culture continued in these centers up through the times of Hammurabi, in the eighteenth century B.C. In a very circumstantial way, Japheth had been brought into the tents of Shem (Gen. 9:27). The later empires of the Assyrians and Babylonians were developed on the pattern of the Sargonic conquests and administration.

B. Spread of the Old Babylonian Culture. The style of writing developed by the Sumerians and which the Akkadians adopted was the cuneiform script. Through the pro-

VICTORY STELE of Naram Sin, grandson of Sargon of Akkad. Courtesy, the Louvre

cesses of cultural diffusion set in motion by Sargon's exploits, the Akkadian language and writing were spread throughout the entire Fertile Crescent. They became the medium for international correspondence which continued in general use up to the time of Moses.

Not only was the speech and writing system of Akkad so widely spread, but so was the Sumero-Akkadian system of commerce, political government, legal custom and jurisprudence. Although political and military control changed hands from city to city and monarch to monarch through the centuries, the basic elements of these systems remained intact. These were gradually spread into Syria and Palestine along with features of the material culture which moved over the trade routes. By the time Abraham migrated to Canaan, he had been long preceded by features of culture and social organization with which he was familiar in his homeland. He also could use a common medium of communication, whether with native Canaanites or with Hittite trade-colonists (Gen. 23).

C. Diffusion of Religious Concepts. Probably given wider dispersion by Sargon's conquests were certain religious beliefs indigenous with the Sumerians, as attested by the very early cuneiform religious texts. It has been suggested in late years that these may go back to a pre-Sumerian, Irano-Semitic culture believed to have preceded the Sumerians. However that may be, there were the following ideas corresponding in greater or lesser degree with the truths of Scripture: (1) the belief that the heavens and the earth were formed from an original chaotic state by the will and command of a deity (cf. Gen. 1:1-2); (2) belief in the dynamic effectiveness of the word or command of a deity (cf. Gen. 1:3 ff.); (3) belief that man was a creation of deity, and had the opportunity to become immortal but lost it (cf. Gen. 2 and 3); as well as a tradition that primal man lived in a sort of Paradise from which he was later excluded; (4) that there had been a world-devastating flood from which only one family escaped, due to warning by a deity, to repeople the earth (cf. Gen. 6-9).

It must be remembered that Abraham came from a milieu in which such beliefs and traditions were dominant. It is further noteworthy that, in spite of the sojourn of the Israelites in Egypt, the old Babylonian form of these concepts is closer to the Biblical, than is the Egyptian.

D. The Sargon and Moses Birth-Stories. A strong similarity exists between one or two details of the birth accounts of Sargon and Moses. According to the "Legend of Sargon," his father was an unknown, and his mother a cult-priestess (cf. IA, above) who bore him in secret. His mother made a basket of rushes which she caulked with bitumen, and set him afloat in it on the river. Akki, a gardener, found him and raised him. From such humble beginnings, Sargon rose to fame.

While the story has legendary overtones, it is not necessary to dismiss it as completely fiction. Numerous great men of history have arisen from very obscure beginnings. Grant certain features of culture as regnant in Sargon's day, and his birth-story becomes credible. Since his mother was a cult-priestess, his conception probably resulted from her performance of a cultic act appropriate to her caste. It is significant that at least one text denominates Sargon as "god-begotten." She may have never known the identity of her child's father; or, if she did, would not make it known. Further, since the fiction was maintained that the cult-priestesses were perpetual virgins, a pregnancy would be concealed and a child would have to be disposed of. This Sargon's mother did with as much humanity as was possible in the circumstances. Since numbers of people engaged in agricultural activities along the banks of the rivers and canals which criss-crossed Akkad, putting little Sargon on the river (or canal) was almost to guarantee his discovery.

The parallels of Sargon's birth-story with that of Moses extend chiefly to the detail of the bitumen-caulked basket or "ark." This may be chance resemblance. The ingenuity of Moses' parents may have been stimulated by the persecution of the pharaoh. A further possibility is that, in view of the widespread and persistent popularity of the Sargon story throughout the ancient Near East over a long span of time, acquaintance with it may have actually suggested a means for securing the baby Moses' safety. We shall never know the certainty of these matters; but in the absence of strong con-

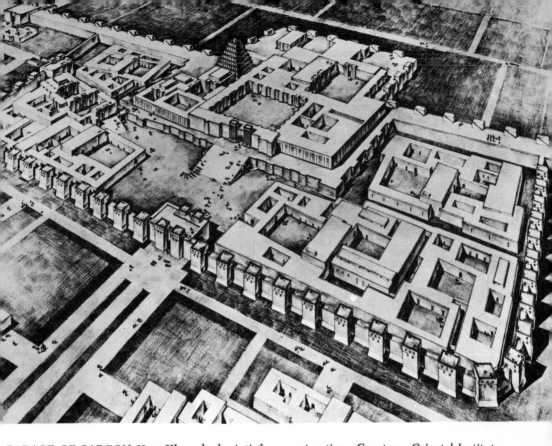

PALACE OF SARGON II at Khorsabad. *Artist's reconstruction.* Courtesy, Oriental Institute

tradictory evidence, there is no necessity to refuse to grant either account a basis in fact.

BIBLIOGRAPHY. H. W. F. Saggs, *The Greatness That Was Babylon*, Sidgwick and Jackson, London, 1962. Sidney Smith, *Early History of Assyria*, Chatto and Windus, London, 1928. W. F. Leemans, *Foreign Trade in the Old Babylonian Period*, E. J. Brill, Leiden, 1960. V. Gordon Childe, *New Light on the Most Ancient East*, 4th ed., Routledge and Kegan Paul, Ltd., London, 1952. A. Leo Oppenheim, "Babylonian and Assyrian Historical Texts," *Ancient Near Eastern Texts*, ed. J. B. Pritchard, Princeton University Press, Princeton, 1950. G. A. Barton, *The Royal Inscriptions of Sumer and Akkad*, Yale University Press, New Haven, 1929. C. J. Gadd, *The Early Dynasties of Sumer and Akkad*, Luzac and Co., London, 1921. Thorkild Jacobsen, *The Sumerian King List*, University of Chicago Press, Chicago, 1939. S. H. Langdon, *Oxford Editions of Cuneiform Inscriptions*, vols. 1 and 2, Oxford University Press, London, 1923. W. F. Albright, *From Stone Age to Christianity*, 2d ed., Doubleday and Co., Inc., New York, 1957. G. A. Barton, *Archaeology and the Bible*, 7th ed., American Sunday-School Union, 1937. Jack Finegan, *Light from the Ancient Past*, 2d ed., Princeton University Press, Princeton, 1959.

SARGON II. Sargon II of Assyria (*ca.* 722/1-705 B.C.) succeeded the short-lived son of Tiglath-pileser III, Shalmaneser V. He is the "Sargon" who is mentioned in Isaiah 20:1; and he is believed by many interpreters to be the "king of Assyria" mentioned in II Kings 17:6. He is thought to have usurped the throne of *Assyria upon the death of Shalmaneser V, although he is inscribed in the official king-list as "son" of Tiglath-pileser III. He himself claims the final destruction of *Samaria and the deportation of its population (cf. II Kings 18:11). His own annals begin with the record of these events. Like the first great king of his name, Sargon of Akkad, Sargon II founded a dynasty which controlled Mesopotamia and the Near East from *ca.* 721-630 B.C. With him and with each of his four major successors the fortunes of the Israelite state of Judah were closely bound up.

I. *Archaeological Attestation.* Prior to 1843, the reference in Isaiah 20:1 was the only place in all classical literature in which the name of Sargon appeared. In the early spring of that year, Paul Emile Botta, the French consular agent stationed at Mosul, began digging at the mound of Khorsabad in the hopes of locating Nineveh. This mound is located about fourteen miles northeast of the actual site of *Nineveh (*Kuyunjik*), in the hilly terrain between the Tigris and the Upper Zab rivers. Botta was exceedingly fortunate, for his initial excavations uncovered remains of a city which Sargon had founded near the close of his reign. It was a city in which he lavished the treasure of his empire, and to which he gave the name of *Dur-Sharrukîn,* "Sargon's Fort." With such fabulous discoveries, the serious study of Assyriology was inaugurated.

Botta and his assistants continued work at Khorsabad for about a year and a half. In that time they worked out the general plan of Sargon's palace. They also recovered (either physically or by drawings and detailed descriptions) a fantastic treasure of artifacts. At the conclusions of his campaign he was able to ship a large number of antiquities to France, including specimens of the huge relief-statues of winged, human-headed bulls of stone which guarded the gates of Dur-Sharrukîn and the king's throne-room.

In 1851 the French government assigned Victor Place to reopen the Khorsabad excavations, and he worked there from then until 1855. Place succeeded in completing the excavation of the palace and in gaining a fair idea of the plan of the town. By the time Place had concluded his operations, scholars were already hard at work translating the inscriptions which Botta had copied and published, thanks to the work of Rawlinson on the cuneiform of the Behistun Rock monument.

Excavations at Khorsabad were again reopened in 1928 by the Oriental Institute of the University of Chicago. This group is credited with having rescued some of the best-preserved reliefs taken from Sargon's palace up to that time. These excavations were continued till 1936. As a result, some corrections in the details of the palace and town plans were made, together with the recovery of a great number of interesting artifacts. Chief among these, and of great historical importance, was a copy of the official list of Assyrian kings from high antiquity down into the seventh century B.C., the famous Khorsabad King List. For many

of the later kings, including Sargon, the years of reign were given in such a way as to make positive dating possible which could be checked with chronological information from the Bible and other sources.

Dur Sharrukîn was the last of Sargon's capital cities, built to his personal specifications. Previously, however, he had used Ashur (*Qalat Sharqat*), Calah (*Nimrud*) and Nineveh (*Kuyunjik*) as his capitals, in that order, and his memorials have been found in each of them, but more lavishly at Dur-Sharrukîn than elsewhere. Bas-reliefs on city walls and inner palace walls depicted with graphic realism various aspects of Assyrian life. Scenes celebrating events in the conquests of the king were numerous. It has been estimated that if the sculptured bas-reliefs found at Dur-Sharrukîn were put end to end they would make a continuous panel a mile in length.

Inscriptions appeared everywhere, commemorating the royal exploits in conquest and battle, together with foundation and dedicatory inscriptions related to buildings. Numerous inscribed clay tablets, dealing with the different affairs of Assyrian common life in the times of Sargon were found here and at other sites.

II. *The Era of Sargon.* During the brief reign of Shalmaneser V, Sargon's immediate predecessor, the Phoenician states and Samaria (or, Israel, the northern kingdom) refused to pay the tribute previously levied on them by Tiglath-pileser. Tyre and Samaria were laid under siege. Tyre won out, but Samaria succumbed after three years. About the time of the downfall of Samaria, Shalmaneser V passed from the scene and Sargon appeared.

From the military point of view, Sargon II was a very energetic and able general. In fifteen of the seventeen years of his reign he led military expeditions into various parts of the empire, primarily to pacify rebellions. A few were to extend the control of the empire still further. Most of these appear to have been successful. Sargon followed the policy of Tiglath-pileser III, deporting the populations of recalcitrant states and repopulating their territories with other conquered peoples from elsewhere. The purpose of this policy was, of course, to reduce the will to rebel by destroying the unity and rootage of the various ethnic groups.

Samaria, with its previous history of intrigue and opposition to Assyria, finally fell victim to this policy when Sargon gained power.

Tiglath-pileser III had pushed the political boundaries of the Mesopotamian state to its greatest extent since the time of Sargon of Akkad. Sargon II extended actual Assyrian political control still farther in the northwest, to beyond the Taurus mountains. He spent his entire life administering this widespread area and maintaining it by military force. Just as for the first Sargon (of Akkad), the prize was complete control, for Assyria, of the natural resources of the Fertile Crescent and of the international routes of trade that crisscrossed the Near East.

Several of Sargon's expeditions were occasioned by the antagonistic activities of Midas of Mushki, in league with the Urartians and Mannaeans (cf. below). One of the main reasons Sargon endeavored to nullify the Mushki-Urartu-Mannaean combine was to insure uninterrupted control of the great trade routes which began at the west coast of Asia Minor, came eastward to junction with the routes which came north from Egypt through Palestine and Syria and those coming up from the Persian Gulf along both the Tigris and Euphrates rivers, and passed thence into the eastern regions. Since all trade with Egypt and south Arabia had to pass through Palestine, Sargon (like his predecessors and successors) found it necessary to interfere in the affairs of the Palestinian states.

The principal beneficiaries of Sargon's military campaigns were the royal treasuries, the temples, and the merchants. Much of the booty which was taken on the military expeditions was returned to the royal coffers and to the temples. Control of the mountainous areas brought their natural resources of various metals, stones for building and for jewelry and fine craft work, and

*FACADE OF THE INNER TEMPLE OF NABU at Khorsabad (ca. 722-705 B.C.)
Courtesy, Oriental Institute*

PROCESSION OF HORSES AND CAPTIVES en route to Sargon's capital at Khorsabad. Courtesy, Oriental Institute

various kinds of woods, into the hands of the merchants. Food and fiber producing areas supplied these necessities under the taxation system. On the other hand much of the wealth taken by conquest was used not only for the personal aggrandizement of the monarch, but also to finance various public works. In large measure, much of this wealth filtered down to the people of Assyria. Those of vassal countries, after having had their land ravaged in many cases, were placed under severe taxes.

Art, in the service particularly of the palace and of the temples, flourished. As noted above, the Assyrian artists were especially adept at producing realistic bas-reliefs. Also, stylized decoration in vivid colors was practiced. Assyrian craftsmen were also expert in working with alabaster, precious and semi-precious stones, the various metals (including iron for implements), and ivory.

Writing (*see* Alphabet) was an art, too, as a glance at cuneiform will attest, and Assyrian inscriptionists had considerable op-

portunity to demonstrate their skill. The royal military retinue included scribes and sculptors, in order that the results of a campaign might be duly given memorial, and stela might be prepared to place in the temple or other public building of a conquered city. Besides the royal annals, religious texts were copied, together with legendary materials. There is some evidence that Sargon began the collection of a library at Dur-Sharrukîn, a project which he did not live to complete. But it apparently was the first of such attempts among the Assyrian monarchs.

III. *Historical Significance.*

A. Importance for General History. When it is remembered that the inscriptions from Dur-Sharrukîn were the first of such records to have been discovered in quantity, their great importance for the historian living in the mid-nineteenth century can be appreciated. For the first time in the Christian era, students of the ancient Near East had at their disposal non-Biblical documents contemporary with the times of the events recorded. These new documents served both as a check upon, and a vast extension of, the information about the ancient Near East as recorded in the Bible and in a few classical sources. Sargon's records disclosed the identity, location and some of the relations sustained between Assyria and the numerous ethnic groups which surrounded it. All of the peoples and many of the places met with frequently in the Old Testament history and the prophetic writings which fall in the period of eighth-sixth centuries B.C. find mention in the Sargonic annals. The countries of Edom, Moab, Egypt, and Elam; the Medes, Philistines, Syrians; the cities of Gaza, Ashdod, Damascus, Tyre, Arpad, Carchemish, and Hamath, all find their places in Sargon's attention, and are seen in their relations one with another and with the great world-power of those times.

Besides this independent attestation to such countries, peoples and places, the character of others whose mention in the Bible was clouded in obscurity came into clearer view. Of these are Ararat (II Kings 19:37 and Isa. 37:38, RSV; Assyr., *Urartu*); Meschech (Ezek. 27:12; 32:26; 38:2, 3; 39:1; Assyr., *Mushki*) and Tubal (Isa. 66:19 and previous refs. in Ezek.; Assyr., *Tabal*); Minni, mentioned with Ararat (Jer. 51:27; the *Mannaeans* of Sargon's records); Kue, or Cilicia (I Kings 10:28; II Chron. 1:16, RSV).

Further, two individuals unexpectedly appeared. The one was Midas, he of the fabled "golden touch" in classical legend. He was known to Sargon as king of the Mushki, or ancient Phrygia in central Asia Minor. Midas (Assyr., *Mita*) continually intrigued with the small states along Assyria's northern frontiers, especially with the Urartians settled in the mountains around Lake Van, and the Mannaeans settled in the Lake Urmia region. Apparently through fear of invading Cimmerians (the *Gomer* of Ezek. 38:6; cf. Gen. 10:2), Midas finally concluded a treaty of amity with Sargon. Urartu remained intractable up to within two or three years of Sargon's death, and was the object of a number of punitive expeditions. However, in 707 B.C., the Cimmerians struck Urartu, forcing an appeal to Sargon for help. Since the invaders were moving westwards, Sargon moved up river in 706 B.C. to engage

the Cimmerians in Tabal, northwest of Carchemish, and to turn them away from the Mesopotamian heartland. In this he was apparently successful, for they moved into interior Asia Minor.

The other individual was Merodach-baladan (Assyr. *Marduk-apal-iddina*) who sought to persuade Hezekiah to rebel against Assyria (II Kings 20:12; Isa. 39:1) in Sennacherib's time. But by this time he had already become a regular "thorn in the flesh" to Assyrian rule in Babylonia, having begun his program of intrigue, rebellion and harassment in the time of Sargon.

B. Relation to Biblical History. As noted above, Sargon II is only once named in the Bible. Isaiah dates one of his oracles by the year in which Sargon sent his commander-in-chief to subdue disaffection at Ashdod, an event which is also duly noted in the annalistic inscriptions. It is clear from the foregoing summary, however, that the reign of Sargon II has a greater importance for the development of Biblical history, and his records have greater importance for Biblical studies, than that single notation indicates.

The total result obtained from the translation of the Khorsabad and other Assyrian documents was the completion of the historical context, a rounding out of Israel's world environment and involvement. Scholars were put in a position to view the history of Israel in the full context of world history for the first time. Further, a controlled chronology of events in the history of Israel and of the Near East became more and more possible through the dovetailing of records from Egypt, Assyria, and the Bible. The interplay of the forces of international diplomacy and intrigue, and Assyrian political interests, which had both direct and indirect effects upon Israel at this period, became much better understood.

As noted above, many of the peoples and places, and some of the personages, of relatively obscure mention in the Bible, were identified and their real importance became evident. Merodach-baladan, for instance, appears as a Chaldean sheikh of considerable influence in southern Babylonia who kept rebellion and intrigue fomented against the Assyrians for practically all of Sargon's rule. In this he had, most of the time, the willing help of Elam and certain other groups east of the Tigris.

Further, during Sargon's reign many of the forces and coalitions of peoples were forming, hard as he tried to prevent them, which ultimately destroyed the Assyrian Empire. With some of these, such as the Chaldeans and, later, the Medes, the sons of Judah were to have direct and harsh dealings. In Palestine itself, the intrigue of the Egyptians, which kept the various petty states disaffected against Assyria and into which Israel and Judah were drawn from time to time, help to explain the numerous interventions of Sargon in Palestinian affairs. It was hearkening to the blandishments of a petty delta prince that led to the downfall of Hoshea of Israel and the sack of Samaria. Prior to this, it was Isaiah who constantly warned the kings of Judah against becoming entangled in any rebellious alliances against Assyria; and after this, he repeatedly warned the princes of Judah of the folly of listening to Egypt.

The Sargonic records relating to these events, including the conspiracies, help clarify the Biblical accounts at many places. They are particularly illuminating for an understanding of the messages of the prophets during this period, especially those of Isaiah. It can safely be said that one who is not well acquainted with Sargon II and his times is hardly in a position to appreciate fully either the political and religious history of the Divided Monarchy, or the early ministry and messages of the great prophet Isaiah.

BIBLIOGRAPHY. D. D. Luckenbill, *Ancient Records of Assyria and Babylonia*, Vol. II, University of Chicago Press, 1926. James B. Pritchard, *Ancient Near Eastern Texts Relating to the Old Testament*, Princeton University Press, Princeton, 1950; *The Ancient Near East in Pictures*, Princeton University Press, 1954. H. V. Hilprecht, *Explorations in Bible Lands During the 19th Century*, A. J. Holman and Co., Philadelphia, 1903. A. T. Olmstead, *History of Assyria*, University of Chicago Press, Chicago, 1951. H. W. F. Saggs, *The Greatness That Was Babylon*, Sidgwick and Jackson, London, 1962. Gordon Loud, *Khorsabad, Part I: Excavations in the Palace and at a City Gate*, University of Chicago Press, Chicago, 1936. G. Loud and Chas. B. Altman, *Khorsabad, Part II: The Citadel and the Town*, University of Chicago Press, Chicago, 1938. C. J. Gadd, *The Stones of Assyria*, Chatto and Windus, London, 1936. Arno Poebel, "The Assyrian King List from Khorsabad," *JNES* II 1943, pp. 56-90; Edwin R. Thiele, "The Chronology of the Kings of Judah and Israel," *JNES* III 1944, pp. 137-186.

SCARABS

I. *Origin, Use, Shape and Purpose.* The scarab is of Egyptian origin, and served as amulet and seal. In the early dynasties of Egyptian history the cylinder seal taken over from Mesopotamia was the exclusive instrument of sealing documents or objects. Very soon a stamp seal in the form of a button seal came into use and served not only as a seal but also as a charm, being worn like a bead on a chain or necklace. In the Sixth Dynasty the first scarabs made their appearance, but they were uninscribed, which is an indication that they were merely used as amulets. By the time of the Egyptian Middle Kingdom, Dynasties Eleven and Twelve, the scarabs bore inscriptions and from then on served as seals as well as amulets. In this double function scarabs were produced for more than fifteen centuries in Egypt, also imitated in Palestine and Phoenicia, from which countries specimens were spread to many other lands of the ancient world.

Scarabs were stone images of the black dung-beetle (*Ateuchus sacer*) which the ancient Egyptians called *ḫprr* (perhaps pronounced *kheprer*). The scarab was believed to be a manifestation of the creator-god who was "brought into existence by himself." It was also considered to be a representative of the sun-god, since the dung-beetle rolled a large ball of dung over the ground just as the sun-god moved the sun disk across the firmament. In the hieroglyphic script the picture of the scarab was used as a word sign (*ḫpr*) with the meaning "to be," "to become," and "to come into existence." This meaning of the beetle as a hieroglyph explains why the scarab-shaped seal became a popular amulet or talisman for many centuries.

Scarabs were made of stone, such as steatite, limestone, or hematite, or of faïence, and in size ranged from one to ten centimeters, although the smaller sized scarabs are more common than the large ones. The true scarabs are quite natural images of the beetle, showing clearly marked wing-cases and a head on the upper side, with its legs beneath resting on a base into which a design or an inscription (or both) was engraved.

Aside from the scarab, the most common Egyptian stamp seal, several other types of stamp seals existed which must briefly be described. First there was the button-seal which has already been mentioned. Then came the scarab, and afterwards the scaraboid, a modified scarab. It retained the oval shape of the scarab and its engraved base, but its top was either left smooth, showing no trace of wings, head and legs of the beetle, or it bears the image of another animal or even a human head. Another seal is the cowroid, having a lentoid or ellipsoidal shape. Originally this seal was made in imitation of the form of a cowry-shell, but later it lost all traces of its original form. Finally, mention should be made of flat, plaque-shaped seals of a square or oblong shape inscribed in the same manner as seal-scarabs.

All these seals were perforated lengthwise. Hence they could be worn on a cord or chain of a necklace, especially if used as an amulet. Some were mounted on a signet-ring as a bezel, or a metal wire was passed through the hole and secured to a ring.

Because of the wide use and popularity of scarabs, their workmanship varied greatly. Many are beautiful pieces of art work, while others are so poorly made that one can be sure of their genuineness only if they have been found in controlled excavations. Speaking of genuineness, it may be useful to point out that it is extremely difficult to be sure of the ancient origin of any scarab that was not found by archaeologists, because the demand of tourists for these small fine objects has been so great that the falsification of ancient scarabs has for many years been a lucrative business in modern Egypt, where a number of scarab factories produce imitation scarabs that are put on the market as genuine specimens. There probably does not exist a single sizable collection of scarabs in this world that can claim to be entirely free of fakes.

II. *Scarabs with Names.* Scarabs used as private seals were inscribed with the name and title of the owner, who was in many cases an official. However, many scarabs are inscribed with royal names because of the protective qualities of such names. Since the royal names were usually sentences that had a significant meaning, scarabs with such names were in great demand for long periods of time — in many cases for centuries after the death of the king whose

(inscription)

(side view)

A COMMEMORATIVE SCARAB issued in 1422 B.C. on the occasion of the construction of a pleasure lake for Queen Tiy by Pharaoh Amenhotep III. Discovered at Thebes. Courtesy, Metropolitan Museum of Art

name appears on the scarab. The prenomen of Thutmose III (fifteenth century B.C.) may serve as an example. That name, *Mn-ḫpr-Rˁ* meaning "May (the sun-god) Re continue to bring into existence," expressed the meaning of the beetle so well that scarabs with that name were copied thousands of times for centuries. During his excavations at Giza, G. A. Reisner found scarabs of this king on mummies of the second century

A.D. on which they had been used as protective amulets sixteen centuries after the death of Thutmose III. This is the reason that scarabs are poor criteria for chronological purposes. At best they may serve to indicate the earliest date that can be given to the archaeological context in which they were found. Many archaeological reports suffer from the misconception that dated scarabs can help to settle historical questions of archaeological remains.

Another class of scarabs were commemorative issues. The most famous of these are the large scarabs (up to 10 cm. in length) of Amenhotep III of the Eighteenth Dynasty. Some were issued at the occasion of the king's marriage with Tiy, others after a wild cattle hunt, then some after having hunted lions for ten years. Later scarabs were issued when he married Giluhepa of Mitanni, and finally after his construction of a pleasure lake at Thebes. The commemorative scarabs were sent as gifts to many foreign kings and have consequently been found during excavations in several countries, among them Palestine (Lachish, Beth-shemesh and Gezer). Small scarabs referring with a few words to great events during their reign were occasionally issued by other kings; for example, Thutmose III refers to the erection of obelisks and the capture of Kadesh, on small commemorative scarabs.

III. *Scarabs without Names.* Aside from scarabs which carry either private or royal names, there are many scarabs without names of individuals. In the first place the large heart-scarabs must be mentioned. They are usually made of a hard stone or of faïence, and flanked with falcons' wings. They were placed in the mummy wrappings and were often inscribed with the 30th chapter of the "Book of the Dead" to make sure that the heart would be a favorable witness before the judges of the nether world. Secondly, there are many scarabs inscribed with wishes or devout phrases clearly indicating their talismanic character. On them we find inscriptions such as these: "Establish the city beloved by Amen," "May Re behold him," or "May I find in my heart that which I ought to do." Thirdly, there is a large group of design scarabs. They carry either no inscription or unreadable hieroglyphs, but show a great variety of decorative designs, such as geometric patterns, scrolls, twisted ropes, plants, animals or birds. These scarabs became very popular during the Hyksos period and remained in use until late dynastic times.

IV. *Scarabs Found in Palestine.* Practically everything that has been said with regard to the Egyptian scarabs is true of those found in Palestine. The only category not yet found there is the heart-scarabs. All other scarabs became so popular in Palestine, especially in cities which had strong connections with Egypt, that some sites in southern Palestine have brought to light a far greater number of scarabs than has any one site in Egypt. Flinders Petrie, for example, found in *Tell el-'Ajjûl* more than a thousand scarabs (mostly of the Hyksos type), of which about five hundred show good workmanship. In fact, many of the Hyksos scarabs found in Palestine are better specimens than those found in Egypt, which leads to the conclusion that they were native Canaanite products and were not imported from Egypt. The largest number of scarabs have been found in the coastal cities of southern Palestine, such as the southern *Tell el-Fâr'ah* (probably ancient Sharuhen), *Tell Jemmeh, Tell el-'Ajjûl,* also at Lachish, an important city in the foothills of the mountains of Judah, and furthermore at Megiddo and Bethshan in the Plain of Jezreel. All these cities had strong ties with Egypt during the Middle Kingdom period, under the Hyksos kings, and especially under the kings of the Eighteenth, Nineteenth and Twentieth Dynasties. On the other hand, excavations of inland cities have produced a much smaller number of scarabs. For example at Shechem, an extremely important city of central Palestine during the second and first millennia B.C., only about fifty scarabs and scaraboids have been found in more than ten seasons of excavations.

The earliest scarabs found in Palestine come from the Twelfth Dynasty, but since most of them are local products, the royal names are usually found on them in an abbreviated or corrupt form. However, the majority of all Palestinian scarabs come from the Hyksos period, although New Kingdom scarabs also turn up in fairly large numbers. Comparatively few scarabs date from the Twenty-first and Twenty-second Dynasties, and hardly any from the later dynasties. This shows quite clearly that the ties between Egypt and Palestine were of a very loose nature during the first millennium B.C.

Most Palestinian scarabs probably served as charms and amulets. That some, however, were used as stamp seals, is clearly revealed by the occurrence of jar handles found at various sites, into which scarabs had been impressed before the jar was baked. The use of scarabs as seals in Palestine is also proved by the fact that scarabs mounted on finger rings have come to light in several Palestinian excavations.

See also Seals.

BIBLIOGRAPHY. P. E. Newberry, *An Introduction to the Study of Egyptian Seals and Signet Rings*, London, 1908. H. R. Hall, *Catalogue of Egyptian Scarabs, etc. in the British Museum*, London, 1913. W. M. Flinders Petrie, *Scarabs and Cylinders with Names*, London, 1917. Flinders Petrie, *Buttons and Design Scarabs*, London, 1925. Alan Rowe, *A Catalogue of Egyptian Scarabs, Scaraboids, Seals and Amulets in the Palestine Archaeological Museum*, Cairo, 1936. See also the excavation reports on Lachish, Megiddo, and other Palestinian sites mentioned above.

SCYTHOPOLIS. *See* Beth-shan.

SEALS.
I. *Words Used in the Bible.* The most common word for "seal" in Hebrew is *ḥōtām,* a loan word from the Egyptian *ḥtm* (T. O. Lambdin, *JAOS*, 73, 1953, p. 151). *Ḥôtām* designates the cylinder seal as well as the stamp seal, just as the verb *ḥōtām,* "to seal," does not indicate the kind of seal used in the sealing process. The seal of Judah (Gen. 38:18, 25) must have been a cylinder seal, the most common type of seal in Mesopotamia and Palestine during the patriarchal age. On the other hand the *ḥôtām* of Jeremiah 22:24 definitely designates a "signet ring," since it is said to be worn on the "right hand."

Another Hebrew designation for seal is *ṭabbaʿat,* also a loan word, from the Egyptian *db't* (Lambdin, *ibid.*), which is used exclusively as a designation of the "signet ring" (Gen. 41:42). The Hebrew *ṭabbaʿat* was eventually used to designate any ring, even rings attached to pieces of temple furniture to hold staves by means of which they could be carried (Exod. 25:12 ff.). Once the Aramaic *ʿizqāʾ,* "seal," occurs in the Bible (Dan. 6:18). In the New Testament the common words are *sphragis,* "seal," and *sphragizō,* "to seal."

II. *Use of the seal in the Bible.*

IMPRESSION OF A CYLINDER SEAL from the Old Babylonian Period —the 19th or 18th century B.C. The text reads, "Manum, the Diviner and Servant of the god Enki (= Ea). Courtesy, British Museum

A. Conveyance of authority. Royal directives, especially when written by a deputy of a king, were sealed with the royal seal. Examples for this custom are the "letters" written by Queen Jezebel in Ahab's name through which she gave orders to the officials of Jezreel to prosecute Naboth (I Kings 21:8), also the decrees issued by Haman and Mordecai in the name of King Ahasuerus (Esth. 3:10, 12; 8:2, 8, 10). Such documents containing royal seal impressions have repeatedly been found in the excavations of ancient Near Eastern cities. As examples one may mention the many sealed royal documents from Ugarit discussed and depicted by Claude F.-A. Schaeffer in *Ugaritica III*, Paris, 1956, pp. 1 ff.

B. Legalization of Documents. Legal documents such as agreements or contracts were not only signed by the principal partners of such agreements but also sealed for validation. Jeremiah describes this process with regard to a deed of purchase that was signed and sealed at the time of purchase of a piece of property (Jer. 32:10-11, 14, 44). Also a covenant between the people of Judah and God made in the time of Nehemiah was sealed by the governor as well as by representatives of the people (Neh. 9:38; 10:1). Sealed ancient treaties contracted between kings have been found in Ugarit (Schaeffer, *ibid.*) and elsewhere. A study of the seals attached to the treaties between King Esarhaddon of Assyria and some princes of Media, found at Nimrud, has been made by D. J. Wiseman in *Iraq*, 20, 1958, 14-23.

C. Sealing of Structures. Sometimes doors or entrances to certain structures were sealed to make sure that no unauthorized individual would gain access. Biblical examples for this practice are the sealing of the entrance to the cage of lions into which Daniel had been thrown (Dan. 6:17 [Hebr. v. 18]), and the sealing of the stone of Joseph's tomb into which Jesus was laid (Matt. 27:66). This practice in ancient times can be demonstrated from the tomb of Tutankhamun. When this tomb was discovered in November 1922, its entrance was found to be walled up with masonry covered with plaster into which official seals had been impressed. In the same way the doorway between the antechamber and the sepulchral chamber as well as the doorway leading to the annex were walled up and sealed; also the doors of the inner shrines of the king's sarcophagus in which his golden coffin lay were protected by seals (Howard Carter and A. C. Mace, *The Tomb of Tut-ankh-Amen*, vol. I, New York, 1923, pp. 134, 148, 152, 247, 250, and Plates XIV, XLI-XLV).

D. Figurative Use. Numerous texts, especially in the New Testament, speak of sealing activities in a figurative sense. Some of the imagery is borrowed from real life occurrences, while others are unreal. In Isaiah 29:11 an obscure vision is compared with "the words of a book that is sealed." Reference is here undoubtedly made to a papyrus scroll such as those found at Elephantine, which were rolled up and then folded in on the center from each end, after which a string was wound around it. Moist clay was then put on the knot and a seal was impressed into the wet clay (E. G. Kraeling, *The Brooklyn Museum Aramaic Papyri*, New Haven, 1953, Pl. XXI). For the explanation of some texts that speak of a sealing work no parallels from real life can be found. To this category of texts belongs, for example, Revelation 7:3, which speaks of a seal worn by the servants of God on their forehead. The author evidently had slave marks in mind. These were put on a slave by either branding or tattooing, or a slave received an identifying tag which he had to carry around his neck or wrist by means of a chain (I. Mendelsohn, *Slavery in the Ancient Near East*, New York, 1949, pp. 42-50).

III. *Seals Used.*

A. Cylinder Seals. The original home of the cylinder seal seems to have been Sumeria in the lower Mesopotamian valley, where the earliest and most archaic cylinder seals have been found. That the cylinder seal originated among the Sumerians is also due to the fact that they invented writing on clay tablets, for the cylinder seal is best suited to make an impression on clay. Egypt, which in the earliest stages of its history took over many cultural accomplishments from the Sumerians, got the cylinder seal from them and used it for several centuries before developing its own typical Egyptian stamp seal. Other ancient nations of the Near East also adopted the cylinder seal together with writing on clay tablets.

The materials most frequently used for

making cylinder seals were steatite and he-matite, but also limestone, lapis lazuli, serpentine, basalt, marble, and other stones were used, and occasionally even wood or ivory. The majority of cylinder seals have a length of 20-30 mm and a diameter of 10-15 mm, but some are as small as 15 mm in length or as large as 65 mm, and the diameter can vary from 7 to 50 mm. Most of the cylinders are perforated lengthwise so that they could be worn on a cord or chain as Judah did (Gen. 38:18 RSV). Some, however, were provided with a metal loop by means of which the seal could be held and suspended. The outer face was engraved with a design in reverse. When the cylinder was rolled over moist clay it produced a continuous impression of the cylinder's engraved design. Virtually every seal is different, and there are hardly two seals alike among the many thousands that have so far come to light. These differences in design were necessary to make identification with the seal's owner possible and to prevent fraud. It was for this reason that in later times the law of Greece forbade seal cutters to make a duplicate of a seal or to keep an impression of a manufactured seal in their possession.

Hence we find a great variety of motifs represented on cylinder seals. Some show geometric designs, others simple patterns of flowers or plants, also animals and humans in simple formations. A popular motif was a scene arranged around a sacred tree, or a scene borrowed from a mythological story or from the realm of religion. Therefore we find humans depicted in the presence of gods, heroes fighting against dragons, or people in the posture of adoration. The majority of cylinder seals found in Palestine show Mesopotamian motifs, although some contain Egyptian hieroglyphs and imitations of Egyptian designs. A few seals reveal a hybrid art in which Mesopotamian and Egyptian designs or inscriptions are found on the same seal.

Only a few cylinder seals contain a design as well as a personal name. One of the oldest such seals found in Palestine comes from Taanach. Its cuneiform inscription gives the name of its owner as "Atanah-ili, son of Habsim, servant of Nergal." This seal assigned to the early second millennium B.C. bears also some Egyptian hieroglyphs

and an adoration scene (J. Nougayrol, *Cylindressceaux et empreintes de cylindres trouvés en Palestine*, Paris, 1939, pp. 37-39, Pl. XII). A most interesting cylinder seal of faïence was found at Bethel in an ancient dump. Dated to the Nineteenth Egyptian dynasty, it is inscribed with the name ʿstrt, "ʿAstart," in Egyptian hieroglyphs. This goddess is depicted as standing on one side of the inscription while Baʿal with a scimitar in his right hand faces her on the other side of the inscription (W. F. Albright, *BASOR*, No. 56, Dec. 1934, pp. 7-8, Fig. 1). Another interesting seal of the thirteenth century was found at Bethshan. This unusually large cylinder (69 x 52 mm) of beautiful serpentine bears the cartouche of Ramesses II, who is shown in battle helmet shooting arrows at Canaanite foes tied up below a standard, which is a target on a pole with three arrows piercing it. On the other side of the standard is the god Resheph holding a scimitar in his left hand and the hieroglyph for "life" in his right hand (Nougayrol, *op. cit.*, pp. 63-65, Pl. VII).

Cylinder seals with names engraved in Phoenician script from the Assyrian, Babylonian and Persian periods have come to light in Mesopotamia, Syria and Palestine. However, not one of the twenty-five such seals studied by K. Galling (*ZDPV*, 64, 1941, pp. 161-165, 194-198, Plates 9-11) was found in controlled excavations, and the provenience of many is unknown. Practically all of them seem to have belonged to Arameans who lived in Syria or northern Mesopotamia.

B. Cone Seals. Conical stamp seals have usually a rounded perforated top, and at the lower end a slightly convex circular or oval base with the design engraved into it. The origin of the cone seal is sought in Syria-Palestine or Egypt (G. E. Wright, *BASOR*, No. 167, Oct. 1962, pp. 11-13). In Palestine cone seals begin to show up not earlier than in the tenth century B.C. and seem to have been in use only up to the end of the Babylonian empire period. In Assyria and Babylonia such seals were used from the eighth century B.C. on. The Palestinian cone seals are usually smaller than the Mesopotamian seals and are most frequently made of black stones. The stamping surface is usually flat, since they were used on writing materials other than clay. The most common designs found on cone seals

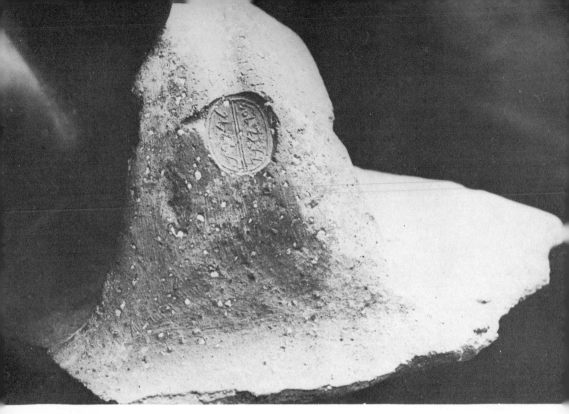

SEAL IMPRESSION ON A JAR HANDLE from Tell Beit Mirsim. The seal identifies the steward of King Jehoiachin (ca. 597 B.C.). Courtesy, Matson Photo Service

are quadrupeds, scorpions, and other creatures. Inscriptions are seldom found on such seals.

C. Scarabs. *See* Scarabs.

D. Scaraboid Seals. This name is usually given to oval stamp seals, which have a flat underside bearing a design or inscription, and a curved upper side that generally does not show any engravings. Since these seals have nothing in common with the Egyptian scaraboids (*see* Scarabs), the name "scaraboid" is somewhat confusing. Therefore the substitute terms "hemioroid seals" (A. Procopé-Walter, *AFO*, 6, 1930-31, p. 66) or "oval seals" (K. Galling, *ZDPV*, 64, 1941, p. 126) have been proposed, although without much success. The scaraboid seals are perforated lengthwise, and were either worn on a chain or cord around the neck or wrist, or mounted on a ring. The material used for these seals is usually harder than that used for scarabs. In many cases they were made of semi-precious stones such as chalcedony, agate, jasper, carnelian, amethyst, and onyx. The size of the scaraboid seals varies greatly, and they also show no standard ratio between length and width. The length of the seals varies from 11 to 40 mm and the width from 8 to 30 mm. According to the engravings on the lower side, the scaraboid seals can be divided into three classes: (1) seals which bear only a pictorial design; (2) seals which bear only an inscription; and (3) seals which bear both a pictorial design and an inscription.

The pictorial motifs of the scaraboid seals represent sphinxes and various animals among which the lion was most popular. On some seals appears the Egyptian uraeus serpent, or the winged sun; furthermore there are found deities, and humans standing in front of gods as adorants.

The inscriptions deal exclusively with the names and offices of the owners. Of the many such seals known, only a few will be mentioned here. Inscribed seals of commoners who were not royal officers usually carry the name and father's name of the owner, as for example one inscribed *Ishm'yhw bn 'zryhm*, "Belonging to Shemayahu, the son of Azaryahu" (D. Diringer, *Le iscrizioni antico-ebraiche palestinesi*, Florence, 1934, pp. 199-200, No. 40). Seals of royal officers generally mention their title, such as the beautiful lion seal from Megiddo, inscribed *lshmʿ ʿbd yrbʿm*, "Belonging to Shema, the minister of Jeroboam" (Diringer, *op. cit.*, pp. 224-228, No. 68). For a long time it was thought that the Jeroboam mentioned on this seal was King Jeroboam II, but recently weighty arguments have been advanced by S. Yeivin in favor of attributing this seal to the reign of Jeroboam I (*JNES*, 19, 1960, pp. 205-212). From *ca.* 600 B.C. comes a seal found at *Tell en-Nasbeh that shows a fighting cock and the inscription, *lyʾznyhw ʿbd hmlk*, "Belonging to Yaazanyahu, the minister of the king" (Diringer, *op. cit.*, p. 229, No. 69). This Yaazanyahu may be the individual mentioned in II Kings 25:23 and Jeremiah 40:8. During the excavations of Lachish the impression of a seal came to light inscribed *lgdlyhw ʿshr ʿl hbyt*, "Gedalyahu who is over the house." Gedalyahu was probably the individual whom the Chaldeans after the destruction of Jerusalem appointed as governor over Judah (Jer. 41:1 ff.), but the seal impression found at Lachish comes from a time when he was still a high palace official of King Zedekiah, as his title "who is over the house (= palace)" indicates. Identical seal impressions found at Tell Beit Mirsim (probably Debir), Bethshemesh, and Ramat Raḥel bear the inscription *lʿlyqm nʿr ywkn*, "Belonging to Elyakim, steward of Jaukin (= King Jehoiachin)" (Diringer, *op. cit.*, p. 126, No. 9). During the excavations of Ezion-geber (Elath) a seal was found enclosed in a copper casing which depicts a ram and carries the inscription *lytm*, "Belonging to Jotham." Since the inscription lacks title as well as patronymic, it has been suggested that the seal belonged to King Jotham of Judah, perhaps during the time when he acted for his father as governor of Elath (N. Glueck, *BASOR*, 79, Oct. 1940, pp. 13-15).

E. Royal Seal Impressions. Hundreds of jar handles have been found in excavations of Judean sites that contain impressions of royal seals, but an actual seal with which the impressions were made has so far not turned up. The impressions are of two types: the earlier ones show a four-winged scarabaeus with an inscription, while the later ones show a two-winged symbol, variously interpreted to represent a bird, a winged sun-disk, or a flying scroll. All these seals contain the inscription *lmlk*, "Belonging to the king," and the name of one of the following four cities, Hebron, Siph, Socoh or *Mmsht*. The first three cities are known and their sites have been identified, but *Mmsht* remains enigmatic, for no city of that name is known. Some scholars have suggested that *mmsht* is an abbreviation of *memshelet*, "government," and designates Jerusalem as an administrative center of a district. Also the function of the seal impressions on the hundreds of jars is not certain. Some think that the four cities mentioned on the seals are places where royal potteries were located, and that the seal impressions indicated that the size of the jars in question or their volume was approved or guaranteed by the government. Others consider the four cities to have been centers of administrative districts into which the kingdom of Judah was divided during the last two centuries of its existence. The seals are usually dated to the eighth and seventh centuries B.C. (Y. Aharoni, *Excavations at Ramat Raḥel*, Rome, 1962, pp. 51-56).

F. Post-exilic Government Seal Impressions. From post-exilic sites located in Judah, jar handles have been recovered bearing impressions on seals which usually are inscribed with the word "Judah," sometimes in an abbreviated form. From Ramat Raḥel come some seal impressions that have even revealed two new names of Jewish governors of the province of Judah during the Persian period. One inscription reads *yhwd yhwʿzr phwʾ*, "Judah, Yehoezer the governor," while another reads *lʾhyw phwʾ*, "Belonging to Ahiyo the governor." All these seals have variously been dated from the fifth to the second century B.C. The most recent evidence seems to favor a third/second century B.C. date (Aharoni, *op. cit.*, pp. 56-59; G. Garbini, *ibid.*, pp. 61-68).

SEA PEOPLES. In the fifth year of *Merneptah, tribes of Aegean origin known collectively as Sea Peoples moved in force upon Egypt. Merneptah was able to protect Egypt from their incursions, but they posed a threat to the entire eastern Mediterranean. Among the Sea Peoples, Merneptah lists (1) the Shardina, who were to give their name at a later time to Sardinia; (2) the 'Aqiwasha, known historically as the Achaeans; (3)

the Turusha, later known as the Tyrsenians and the Etruscans; (4) the Ruka (or Luka), the historical Lycians; and (5) the Shakarusha.

These invasions took place around 1220 B.C. and reflect the political situation prior to or during the Trojan War, a phase of the happenings reflected in the Iliad and the Odyssey. A casualty of the activities of the Sea Peoples was the Hittite Empire which came to an end about 1200 B.C. The Hittite texts mention the people of Ahhiyawa, which some scholars identify with the Achaeans of Homer, the Mycenaean Greeks.

Waves of Sea Peoples continued to attack Egypt. Ramesses III lists them as (1) Perasata (Pelasata), the Philistines from whom Palestine was ultimately named; (2) Danauna, the Danaeans; (3) Washasha; (4) Shakarusha; and (5) Tjikar (Tsikal), the Sikel, possibly the Sicilians of the Odyssey. Ramesses boasted victory over these Sea Peoples but he was not able to keep them out of his provinces in Asia. They swarmed down the Mediterranean coast from °Ugarit to Ashkelon and Ramesses had to accept them as nominal vassals. The °Philistines and the Tsikal remained in southern Palestine.

SELA. The ancient stronghold of Sela is to be identified with *Umm el-Bayyara,* the rocky eminence which dominated the city of °Petra. It was, indeed, the fortress *par excellence* of both the Edomites and the °Nabateans. In the Old Testament it was the fortified city which the Psalmist longed to conquer (Ps. 108:10), the rocky home and the lofty nest of the arrogant Edomites for whom both Obadiah and Jeremiah prophesied judgment (Obad. 3, 4; Jer. 49:16, 17). Amaziah, king of Judah, once stormed and took this stronghold and changed its name to Joktheel (II Kings 14:7; cf. II Chron. 25:12), and Isaiah, referring to the coming judgment on Moab, spoke of fugitive Moabites sending tribute to Judah from distant Sela (Isa. 16:1).

Archaeological investigation of the site began in 1929 with a surface survey by the Melchett Expedition (*QDAP* VII, p. 4, n.1). But Nelson Glueck conducted soundings there in 1933 and was subsequently able to check the pottery evidence against the pottery found on his survey of Edom in

March-July 1934 (*AASOR* XIV). Then in 1955 W. H. Morton returned to the site and conducted further soundings. He was able to supplement earlier investigations by the evidence of pottery, cisterns, rock carvings, and the outline of building foundations. The pottery showed that the site was occupied during the Iron I and II periods (1200-600 B.C.), that is, during the days of the Edomites, during the Nabatean period, and perhaps, spasmodically, during the later Byzantine and Arab periods. The building remains appear to be all Nabatean. The cisterns which had an estimated capacity of twenty thousand gallons suggest that the site was equipped to stand a siege, but neither these nor the rock carvings can be dated with certainty. It is possible to postulate a period of occupation from perhaps 1200 B.C. until the early Christian centuries with, no doubt, periods of interruption. Thereafter, for many centuries, Sela was forgotten.

BIBLIOGRAPHY. N. Glueck, *AASOR* XIV, 1933-4, pp. 77 f. W. H. Morton, *"Umm el Biyara", BA,* XIX, 1956, pp. 26 f. F. M. Abel, *Géographie de la Palestine,* II, Paris, 1933, p. 407.

SENJIRLI. See Zinjerli.

SENNACHERIB. Sennacherib, son of Sargon II, was king of °Assyria from 705 to 681 B.C. He faced a serious challenge in 703 B.C. when Merodach-baladan attempted to unite the warring °Chaldean and °Aramean tribes against Sennacherib and Assyria. With Elamite help Merodach-baladan took over Babylonia, and he sought to strengthen his position by sending messengers to the Assyrian vassals in the west in order to incite them to rebel (cf. Isa. 39). Sennacherib defeated the Elamites and Chaldeans near °Kish and took control of Babylonia. The kings of Sidon and Tyre, however, took advantage of Sennacherib's troubles in the East and refused to pay tribute. Farther south, Hezekiah of Judah, who had received a message from Merodach-baladan (II Kings 20:12, 13), seized the pro-Assyrian ruler of Ekron.

Sennacherib appeared with his army and resistance in °Phoenicia quickly collapsed. The Philistine cities of Ekron, Ashdod, and Ashkelon fought, however, and Egypt sent an army against Sennacherib. At Eltekeh Sennacherib defeated the Egyptians, and from his camp at Lachish, Sennacherib insisted that Hezekiah surrender and pay tribute.

The events of Sennacherib's siege are recorded in II Kings 18 and in Sennacherib's own annals. The final edition of Sennacherib's annals has been preserved on the Oriental Institute Prism, and on the so-called Taylor Prism in the British Museum. Sennacherib's scribes tell of forty-six of Hezekiah's cities which fell to the Assyrians "by the assaults of battering-rams and the blows of engines, the attack of foot-soldiers, sappers, breaches, axes." Of Hezekiah he writes, "Himself, like a bird in a cage in the midst of Jerusalem, his royal city, I shut up." Although Sennacherib received tribute from Hezekiah, it is clear that he was not able to take Jerusalem.

Of the forty-six cities taken, *Lachish seems to have offered the most resistance. In one of the rooms of the palace discovered by A. H. Layard at Nineveh in 1849 there were thirteen stone slabs in bas relief depicting an attack on a well fortified city. In front of the king who was enthroned on a hill before the besieged city, was a short cuneiform inscription stating that Sennacherib sat on the throne as he reviewed the booty taken from Lachish.

BIBLIOGRAPHY. D. D. Luckenbill, *The Annals of Sennacherib,* University of Chicago Press, Chicago, 1924. A. Leo Oppenheim, *ANET,* pp. 287-288.

SERABIT EL-KHADEM. A number of inscriptions dating from *ca.* 1500 B.C. have been discovered on monuments and rocks at Serabit el-Khadem about fifty miles from the traditional site of *Sinai in the Sinai Peninsula. In 1904 and 1905 W. M. Flinders Petrie discovered the first of the Proto-Sinaitic inscriptions. Others were discovered in the years 1927, 1929, 1930, and 1935. As a member of the University of California African Expedition, W. F. Albright studied them again in 1948.

In the region of Serabit el-Khadem there were turquoise mines which had been worked by Egyptians since the third millennium B.C. The inscriptions are thought to have been written by Semitic people whose home was in Egypt and who worked in the mines. There are about fifty inscriptions in all. They contain appeals to the gods and ask the overseers to provide offerings on behalf of deceased persons.

Albright considers the Proto-Sinaitic script to be normal alphabetic Canaanite from the early fifteenth century B.C. The inscriptions are termed Proto-Semitic to distinguish them from *Nabatean inscriptions from the same area which date from the first few centuries of the Christian era.

BIBLIOGRAPHY. W. F. Albright, "The Early Alphabetic Inscriptions from Sinai and their Decipherment," *BASOR,* 110, 1948, pp. 6-22.

SERAPEUM. *See* Alexandria.

SHAGAR BAZAR. *See* Habor.

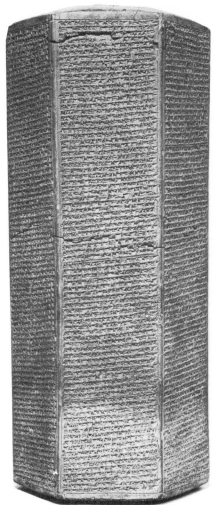

CLAY PRISM containing the annals of Sennacherib, the Assyrian king who besieged Jerusalem in the days of Hezekiah. Courtesy, British Museum

SHALMANESER, BLACK OBELISK OF.
See Black Obelisk of Shalmaneser III.

SHALMANESER III. See Ashur, Assyria.

SHECHEM (TELL BALATA)

I. *Geographical Location.* Shechem's geographical position virtually assures it a prominent role in the history of Palestine. It is situated in the "navel" of the land (Judg. 9:37) at the eastern end of the pass between Mt. Ebal and Mt. Gerizim, some forty miles north of Jerusalem. The mound (Tell Balâta) beside the modern village of Balâta overlooks a large plain to the east. Because of the mountainous terrain, this location controls all roads through the central hill country of Palestine. However, its own unguarded position facing the plain on the lower southeastern slopes of Mt. Ebal (thus the probable meaning of Shechem: "shoulder(s)") made exceptionally strong defenses imperative, as seen in the excavations.

II. *Role in Bible.* The prominent role which Shechem plays in many Biblical narratives inevitably makes it a focal point of archaeological interest in Palestine. It figures prominently especially in those early periods when the problems of historical interpretation are the greatest, and where, as a result, the services of the archaeologist are most needed.

The site is first mentioned in Genesis 12:6 as a "place" (probably in the technical sense of "shrine") where Abram first stopped in Canaan and built an altar. But it is especially the patriarch Jacob whose activities center in this region. Jacob is reported (Gen. 33:18-20) to have purchased peacefully a parcel of land from "the sons of Hamor, Shechem's father" after his return from Haran. However, Genesis 48:22 seems to preserve a tradition of military conquest of the region also. Perhaps this latter tradition is related to the account of the rape of Dinah and the ensuing vengeance upon Shechem by her brothers in Genesis 34.

Joseph is reported on the site in Genesis 37:12-14 somewhat after his brothers had herded their flocks nearby. Joshua 24:32 also records Joseph's burial at Shechem (the traditional spot is a Moslem shrine today).

Joshua's "farewell speech" (Josh. 24) at the conclusion of his battles of conquest and the renewal of the covenant by the tribes (often interpreted in modern scholarship as the inauguration of the twelve-tribe "amphictyony" at its first center in Shechem) takes place here. This ceremony of covenant-making at Shechem reminds one of the ceremony of antiphonal blessing and cursing on Mt. Gerizim and Mt. Ebal respectively, commanded to the Israelites upon arrival in Deuteronomy 11:26 ff. and Deuteronomy 27, and the execution of the command reported in Joshua 8:30-35.

Judges 9 reports how the "judge" Abimelech became "king of Israel" at Shechem (his mother's home) apparently at first with the support of the rulers of Shechem in spite of an abortive plot engineered by Gaal. A later revolt resulted in the destruction and razing of the city (vv. 42 ff.).

Rehoboam was crowned and subsequently established his first capital at Shechem temporarily (I Kings 12), but after this the city receives no further significant mention in the Bible. It was designated as one of the six "cities of refuge" (Josh. 20:7) and one of the forty-eight Levitical cities (Josh. 21:21). Other Biblical allusions contribute little certain information.

However, we know that in the post-exilic period the Samaritans built their temple atop Mt. Gerizim, which became the focal point of Samaritan opposition to the returning exiles' attempts to rebuild the walls of Jerusalem (Neh. 4) and to the later Jewish state. Jesus was at or near the site at least once (John 4) in his conversation with the woman of Samaria at Jacob's well in "Sychar" (possibly a textual corruption of "Shechem").

III. *Literary References Outside the Bible.* Shechem apparently appears in an Egyptian "execration text" of the Twelfth Dynasty (Middle Bronze II A period in the nineteenth century B.C. — probably also the beginning of the "patriarchal age") as a defeated enemy of the pharaoh. Similarly, the Khu-Sebek inscription from about the same period seems to describe the city's capture by Pharaoh *Senusert* III (*ca.* 1880-40 B.C.). These references, if correctly interpreted, may indicate Shechem's importance already in the early Middle Bronze age as a center of opposition to Egypt. The city figures prominently also in the Late Bronze (1500-1200 B.C.) *Amarna letters as the center of the notorious Lab'ayu in confederation with the invading Habiru and his intrigues against the decaying empire of the Pharaohs and against other Canaanite city-states.

IV. *History of Excavation.* Considering the site's obvious importance and its potential usefulness to Biblical scholarship, its checkered early history of excavation is unfortunate (although due, in part, to the infancy of the science of archaeology at the time).

A. Early German Excavations. The site of Tell Balâta was first identified as that of ancient Shechem by the German scholar, Hermann Thiersch, in 1903. Most subsequent, early excavations were directed by Ernst Sellin with various assistants, but rarely adequately staffed. Very few good records were kept of the first campaigns in 1913 and 1914, in spite of the occasional presence of the Greek archaeologist, G. Welter. After the war Sellin returned again in 1926, 1927 and (briefly) in 1928. When Welter began making serious charges against Sellin's work, Sellin was discharged, but when Welter's work, apparently in 1928 and 1932 or 1933, proved to be even less satisfactory, Sellin was reinstated as director. He returned in 1934 with H. Steckeweh. Two further campaigns were planned, but never materialized.

Sellin concentrated his investigations on the city fortifications which Thiersch had already noted protruding from the tell on the west. On the northwest side of the mound he uncovered a large city gate (the "Northwest Gate") with three successive entryways, each constructed of two parallel blocks a short space apart. On its south the gate was bonded into the great "cyclopean" wall (i.e., made of huge, unhewn stones leaning inward against a thick earth fill). In contrast, the East Gate had only two entryways, made by two parallel and projecting orthostats and was connected with a different type of wall with alternate projecting and recessing sections.

On the western side of the mound just inside the cyclopean wall Sellin unearthed a huge building which he identified (doubtless correctly) as a temple. It was built upon deep fill (as the most prominent feature of the city) like that behind the cyclopean wall and approached by a ramp from below. Sellin also discovered that some broken, flat stones lying in front of the temple fit into the depressions cut into large stone blocks on each side of the door. Concluding

that these were the *masseboth* (sacred standing stones) often associated with Canaanite temples (also confirmed by later investigators), Sellin pieced these together again. (Later, Welter derided this interpretation and toppled the stones; they were not re-erected until 1962.)

B. Recent (American) Excavations. The Drew-McCormick expedition under the direction of G. Ernest Wright was organized largely to salvage as much as possible from the earlier excavations and to establish scientifically the stratigraphy and chronology of the site. The first brief and preliminary campaign in 1956 concentrated on the problems of the East Gate. Slowly its complicated history began to emerge. Apparently, it had been built during the Hyksos period (*ca.* 1750-1550 B.C.) to strengthen earlier fortifications and violently destroyed when the Egyptians destroyed Shechem and expelled the Hyksos about 1550 B.C. Rebuilt again in the succeeding Late Bronze period it was destroyed again in the eighth century, probably in connection with the Assyrian destruction of Samaria. It was rebuilt a third time about 325 B.C. by the Samaritans and destroyed again towards the end of the second century B.C., after which the ancient mound was never again occupied. Thus the broad outlines of the history of ancient Shechem began to become clear.

Subsequent campaigns were made in the summers of 1957, 1960, 1962 and 1964 under the direction of G. Ernest Wright of Harvard. The major efforts concentrated in four areas: the fortifications (gate and walls), the temple, the "palace" area (below the temple to the northeast), and an attempt to obtain a complete stratigraphical history of the site's occupation by beginning at the top of the mound in an area undisturbed by earlier excavations.

During the second campaign it became clear that both the temple and the cyclopean wall had been built in the latter half of the Hyksos period (in the century after 1650 B.C.). The entire city changed appearance in this period; the sharp break in architectural traditions may be associated with the probable Hurrian (Horite) and/or Indo-European infusion into the earlier Hyksos stock about this time (cf. Gen. 34:2, where "Horite" should probably replace "Hivite"). In general, this was the period of greatest prosperity for Shechem.

Continued probes at the East Gate showed how the city's defenses at this vulnerable point were repeatedly strengthened throughout this period. Here the outer defense system (called the "A system" by the excavators) consisted of *two* parallel walls joined by transverse walls forming a series of rooms where any invader might easily be trapped. The outer wall of this "A system" appears to be the massive cyclopean wall also traceable on the other side of the mount with its Northwest Gate. Soon after its completion another wall ("B") was constructed inside and above it, and into the latter the East Gate was built. The Gate consisted of two huge rectangular towers, each with a narrow guard room inside. The approach to this inner gate was on a ramp between the inner and outer walls, turning at a right angle into the city at the gate itself.

In spite of its strength, the East Gate was destroyed three times in its brief existence of only fifty years. The subsequent Late Bronze age occupants apparently built their wall behind the ruins of the earlier ones and the continuity of Late Bronze and Iron I (Israelite) strata, without an intervening destruction layer, indicated plainly that the incoming Israelites used essentially the same wall and gate. At the beginning of the Hellenistic period the Samaritans more ambitiously cleared away debris down to the Hyksos levels and, in fact, used the old "B" wall as the foundation for their own fortifications.

The temple proved to have been built in the later Hyksos period also, but had been destroyed at some later date (presumably in Abimelech's time, as recorded in Judg. 9) and abandoned for a considerable time. Sometime in the Israelite period, probably about 800 B.C., another structure, oriented in a slightly different direction, had been built above the temple. Its heavy plaster floor was found directly over the tops of the column bases on the earlier temple. Apparently, this later structure was a granary, indicating Shechem's importance as an administrative center in the northern kingdom.

The campaigns in 1960 and 1962 devoted much time and effort to further investigation of the problems of the temple area (the largest extant pre-Roman temple remains in Palestine). The interpretation of these finds could not be separated from the intensive work in the nearby "palace" area.

First of all, it soon became clear that the Israelite granary was not built directly upon Middle Bronze (Hyksos) temple walls, but on the walls of a slighter structure built by the Late Bronze occupants about a century after the Egyptian destruction of the first temple about 1550 B.C. It was this second temple (followed later by the granary) which had been first reoriented in a different direction (perhaps in connection with some solar cult practiced there). The orientation of the huge *massebah* and stone altar showed that they had also been planned and constructed by the builders of this later (Late Bronze) temple (replacing two smaller pillars and an earthen altar in front of the earlier temple). Absence of all signs of destruction at the end of the Late Bronze period (as at the East Gate) indicated that it was probably this later temple which was used by the early Israelites at Shechem (until Abimelech).

Several strange pits, either cylindrical or flask-shaped and usually unlined, were found to have been dug through the temple floors in early Israelite times. Their function remains uncertain, although they were probably used for storage of some sort.

Excavations under the walls of the early temple demonstrated that no temple stood on this site at all before about 1650 B.C. Far below the fill (over twenty feet deep) on which the temple was built, five Chalcolithic (fourth millennium B.C.) occupation levels were discovered, and below these, just above bedrock, a claylined Chalcolithic living pit. Under the later temple was also discovered a double wall, probably part of an early defense system. Apparently, when the Cyclopean wall ("A") was built, the city limits were enlarged and a tremendous amount of earth was moved, both for the wall and to form an elevation for a new temple.

Previously, an entirely different temple type had existed here. The evidence for this came from the "palace" area nearby, which had been levelled by the Hyksos in connection with their fill operations. Sellin had already exposed a heavy wall running north and south to the east of the temple, which apparently served to separate the sacred area from the rest of the city. A short distance west of this wall three phases of an early building were disclosed.

The uppermost "palace" structure had been largely removed by the German excavations, but under one floor a jar burial with the skeletons of children was found. Six column bases were also found, apparently supporting a courtyard roof originally. The next lower building, differing in various features from the later structure, yielded two jar burials. The lowest structure, a much simpler building than those which followed it, was built about 1750 B.C. in the Amorite period. Slightly earlier in the same MB IIA period, when real building activity first began at Shechem, there came to light a large earthen platform of unascertained function, retained by a wall parallel to the later wall enclosing the inner city.

However, now it became possible to relate this series of building with the temple itself. Instead of "palaces" as interpreted earlier, it became necessary to understand them as early *temple* predecessors to, but of a different "courtyard" type from the massive fortress-temples of later times. Their rooms were all to the north of a "great court," the center and axis of which was a small "central court." The latter was precisely below the later temple's altar and sacred pillar, which were surely intended as its successors. Throughout the earlier periods a small shelter, probably housing an open-air shrine, had stood here.

Thus, in aggregate, there seems to have been a total of at least *eight* temples (or at least remodelings) in this area, four of the courtyard type between *ca.* 1750 and 1650 B.C., and four of the fortress-temple type between *ca.* 1650 and 1100 B.C. (with about a century intervening, *ca.* 1500-1450 B.C., between the two late Middle Bronze structures and the two Late Bronze buildings).

This evidence of earlier temple traditions can hardly be separated from the persistent traditions of patriarchal theophanies and covenants at the "place" (shrine) at Shechem, sometimes in connection with an altar and a sacred tree. Present evidence also indicates that the earliest shrine was outside the city, as indicated in the patriarchal narratives. In fact, the archaeological evidence suggests that a sacred pillar was associated also with this early shrine; while the Bible mentions none explicitly at Shechem (but cf. the "great stone" of Josh. 24:26 and the "oak of the *pillar*" in Judg. 9:6), they frequently appear elsewhere in the patriarchal accounts, understood probably as "witnesses" to the covenant, perhaps also as celebrated and renewed in later liturgies.

The other major effort of the last campaigns was in a residential area between the temple and the East Gate. By starting at the top of the mound at the end of the city's history where there had been no previous excavations, and digging down to meet or overlap with the earlier strata exposed underneath the German excavations, it was hoped to obtain a complete stratigraphical history of Shechem. By the end of the 1962 season, however, this goal had not yet been reached: a tenth stratum had been probed, possibly reaching back to the period of the United Monarchy in the tenth century, but, if so, still some two centuries from the days of Abimelech. Above it were structures of the following strata (some with more than one phase): (1) IX of the early ninth century, possibly destroyed by the Arameans; (2) VIII, poorly preserved, but perhaps destroyed in the reign of King Menahem of Israel (748-738 B.C.); (3) VII, closely related to the preceding, and violently destroyed, doubtless by the Assyrians about 723 B.C.; (4) VI, representing a reoccupation during the eighth and seventh centuries, betraying the Assyrian presence by much "Assyrian palace ware," but again violently destroyed, perhaps in later revolts against the Assyrians; (5) V, later dating from the sixth century, but badly eroded by the long abandonment of the tell during most of the Persian period (from *ca.* 500-330 B.C.); (6) IV, representing the first Samaritan occupation of the site *ca.* 330-250 B.C. (probably because Alexander had paganized the city of Samaria and deprived them of authority there after they had revolted against him) and also for the first time datable by coins found in the debris; (7) III, *ca.* 250-190 B.C., the best preserved of the Samaritan levels and contributing a large number of Ptolemaic coins; (8) II, *ca.* 190-150 B.C., representing the Seleucid occupation of Palestine in the Maccabean period, but rather fragmentarily preserved because of erosion and surface cultivation; and (9) I, *ca.* 150-107 B.C. repre-

521

sented by little more than surface debris. Coins found make it certain that the city was not destroyed when John Hyrcanus first captured Shechem in 128 B.C. and destroyed the Samaritan temple on Mt. Gerizim (as earlier supposed), but probably during Hyrcanus' later campaign against Samaria in 107 B.C. However, especially from the western walls, it is clear that a vast amount of earth was moved again, as in Hyksos days, but this time because of Hyrcanus' determination that these defenses should never be used again.

Hyrcanus' actions had their intended effect, for with this destruction a century before Christ, occupation of the ancient mound apparently ceased forever. However, small villages have probably always clustered around the excellent spring just southeast of the *tell*, today the center of the village of Balâtah; perhaps this was the case in Christ's time. During the reign of Vespasian in A.D. 72 the Romans replaced the ancient town with Neapolis ("new city" of which the modern "Nablus" is a corruption) on a new site to the west.

V. *Results and Comparison with the Biblical Accounts.* It will not escape notice that the first major structures discovered at Shechem date from the same "Amorite" period (*ca.* 1900ff. B.C.) in which Shechem is first mentioned in Egyptian records and in which the patriarchs are now usually dated (*cf.* Gen. 48:22). Some of the cultic installations discovered in early Shechem also seem to find reliable echo in the early Biblical traditions, as noted above. Shechem's tremendous fortifications answer to the known turmoil of the Hyksos period in which the Jacob traditions are probably to be set.

The absence in the Bible of any tradition of an Israelite conquest of Shechem plus the prominent role which Shechem plays in the earliest days of the Israelite occupation of Canaan is strikingly paralleled by the absence of any signs of destruction or other discontinuity (such as Philistine occupation) between the Late Bronze ("Habiru" occupation) and Iron I (early Israelite) levels. Many problems remain in the interpretation of the accounts of Abimelech's brief rule over Shechem in Judges 9. Nevertheless, it seems certain that the gate referred to in verses 35ff. is the archaeologists' "East

Gate" and that the temple reported destroyed in that episode represents the last Late Bronze phase of the fortress-temple. The deity of the temple is named "Baal-berith" (vs. 4) or "El-berith" (vs. 46), that is, the "god (or lord) of the covenant"; the name is reminiscent of the Biblical accent on covenants (often made or renewed in early times at Shechem) and is very similar to other names given to God in patriarchal times.

Jeroboam's "building" (rebuilding or fortification) of Shechem as his first capital (I Kings 12:25) also seems to find confirmation in the archaeological evidence.

Further information and clarification will certainly be forthcoming from the subsequent excavations.

BIBLIOGRAPHY. Preliminary reports of the first four campaigns in 1956, 1957, 1960 and 1962 may be found, respectively, in the following numbers of *BASOR*: 144, 1956, pp. 9-20; 148, 1957, pp. 11-28; 161, 1961, pp. 11-54; and 169, 1963, pp. 1-60 (the first two written by G. Ernest Wright alone; the last two together with Lawrence E. Toombs, Associate Director of these campaigns). The following issues of *BA*, reporting the same campaigns more popularly, are devoted largely to Shechem: XX, 1, 1957; XX 4, 1957; XXIII, 4, 1960; and XXVI, 1, 1963; these are edited by Edward F. Campbell, Assistant director of the American campaigns. Also G. E. Wright, "The Samaritans at Shechem," *The Harvard Theological Review*, LV, 1962, pp. 357-366. Siegfried H. Horn, "Scarabs from Shechem," *JNES*, XXI, 1962, pp. 1-14. O. R. Sellers, "Coins of the 1960 Excavations at Shechem," *BA* XXV, 3, 1962 pp. 87-96. James F. Ross and Lawrence C. Toombs, "Three Campaigns at Biblical Shechem," *Archaeology*, XIV, 1961, pp. 171-179.

SHESHON. See Shisak.

SHILOH. On a hilltop three miles east of the main road, about twelve miles south of °Shechem, is the Arab village of Seilun, occupying the site of ancient Shiloh (cf. Judg. 21:19). In this isolated spot the Israelites assembled after the division of Canaan among the tribes and set up the Tabernacle which was to serve as their national shrine (Josh. 18:1). The Tabernacle, or "tent of meeting," had been a portable sanctuary during the years of wandering, but at Shiloh it became the more permanent structure (Judg. 18:31) to which pilgrims came for their annual feasts (I Sam. 1:3). Although the nature of this "house of God" at Shiloh is not known, we read of "the doorpost of the temple of the Lord" (I Sam. 1:9) beside which Eli the priest sat.

Scripture does not mention the destruction of Shiloh, but it is clearly implied. The sacred ark was taken by Israel into battle at Aphek and fell into the hands of the Philistines (I Sam. 4). When they determined to return it to Israel, it was not returned to Shiloh, but instead was placed in the house of a man named Abinadab at Kirjath-jearim, west of Jerusalem. It is probable that Shiloh was destroyed during the Philistine wars, a fact which seems to have been well known in the time of Jeremiah, for the prophet addressed the Jerusalemites of his generation with the warning concerning the Temple, ". . . then I will make this house like Shiloh . . ." (Jer. 26:6; cf. 7:12; 26:9).

In September 1922, H. Kjaer and Aage Schmidt sank a number of trial pits through the debris at Seilun and found pottery from the Arabic, Graeco-Roman, and Early Israelite (1200-1050 B.C.) periods. Schmidt periodically renewed the excavation of Shiloh until his death in 1952. Although no major discoveries were reported, the evidence from pottery tallies perfectly with what we might expect from the Biblical record. There is no evidence that there was ever a Canaanite settlement at Shiloh. It seems to have been purposely selected as a centrally located place for the ark, and the town then grew up around the sanctuary which was built to house the ark. After the ark was taken by the Philistines, the priesthood seems to have settled at Nob (I Sam. 22:11), in the environs of Jerusalem. The pottery indicates no settlement at Shiloh from about 1050 B.C. to about 300 B.C., although the possibility of an unimportant town at the site cannot be ruled out. The prophet who told Jeroboam that he would become king of the ten tribes is named "Ahijah the Shilonite" (I Kings 10:29), a name which suggests that there was some community at Shiloh as late as the time of Solomon. Subsequently, however, the town existed only in the memory of Israel's prophets and Psalmists (cf. Ps. 78:60).

BIBLIOGRAPHY. A. T. Richardson, "The Site of Shiloh," *PEQ*, LIX, 1927, pp. 85-88. H. Kjaer, "The Danish Excavation of Shiloh, Preliminary Report," *PEQ*, LIX, 1927, pp. 202-213. "The Excavation of Shiloh, 1929," *JPOS*, X, 1930, pp. 87-174. "Shiloh. A Summary Report of the Second Danish Expedition, 1929," *PEQ*, LXIII, 1931, pp. 71-88. W. F. Albright, "The Danish Excavations at Seilun — A Correction," *PEQ*, LIX, 1927, pp. 157-158.

SHINAR. Biblical Shinar was the land in which the great cities of Erech, Akkad, and Babylon were located (Gen. 10:10). The name Shinar was used for the place to which the Jews were exiled (Isa. 11:11; Dan. 1:2). The Septuagint equates Shinar with Babylonia. Although the country around Baghdad is known as *Sen'ar* in Syriac, no earlier Semitic name for Babylonia corresponding to Shinar is known. The identification of its cities, however, leaves no question that Biblical Shinar is the land that later comprised Babylonia.

SHIPWRECKED SAILOR, THE. By the end of the third millennium B.C. the Egyptians had developed the art of storytelling into a literary genre. One of the most charming pieces is the story of the Shipwrecked Sailor. It is actually a tale within a tale, since it is a yarn put into the mouth of one of the principal characters in the main narrative. Unfortunately, the latter is not complete, inasmuch as the sole source for our knowledge, a manuscript in the Hermitage Museum at Leningrad, though otherwise perfectly preserved, lacks the beginning.

I. *The Story.* From the extant material we can surmise that the lost portion probably described the outcome of an expedition into Nubia via the Nile River and gave the reasons for the leader's misgivings about the report which he must make in person to the King of Egypt. It happens that what has been preserved takes up precisely where a "trustworthy retainer" attempts to cheer up the leader: "May it please you, Prince, we have reached home! The mallet has been taken, the mooring post pounded in, and the front-hawser placed on land. Praise and thanksgiving have been offered. They are all embracing one another. Our crew has arrived safely; our party has suffered no loss." Prince to address the King with composure and to answer without stammering. "A man's mouth saves him; his speech obtains indulgence for him. But do as you like. Talking to you is making you weary."

We may detect at this juncture a trace of the humor which permeates the story. For, having indicated that he feels there is no point in saying more, the retainer at once launches out on a fantastic tale which, he assures his listener, is "a similar experience which happened to me when I went to Sinai for the sovereign." Expeditions to the mines of Sinai are not uncommon in Egyptian annals, but the story which unfolds certainly lay beyond the limits of reality (though one must not conclude that it seemed so to the Egyptians).

It was while sailing across the Red Sea toward Sinai that disaster struck, so the retainer's story goes. He had set out in a good sized ship (about 206 feet x 70 feet) manned by 120 of Egypt's best sailors. His men "could foresee a storm before it came, a tempest before it arose," yet they were caught on the high sea by a hurricane. All these brave men perished, but miraculously the storyteller was washed ashore on an island. His haven turned out to be as fertile as any garden along the Nile, so that his survival was in effect guaranteed. In thanksgiving he fashioned a firedrill and kindled a flame with which to offer sacrifices to the gods.

Scarcely had the shipwrecked sailor attended to his religious duty when he was startled by a thunderous noise reminding him of the catastrophe which had so recently been his lot. The earth was shaking and trees were snapped in two. Our hero cowered in fear with his face covered. When he ventured to look about, he found an immense serpent approaching. His body was plated with gold and his eyebrows were of the valued blue stone known as lapis lazuli. He wore a long beard and appeared to be highly intelligent. To the Egyptian he could be nothing other than a god.

The marooned sailor prostrated himself before the snake, who proceeded to belabor the refugee: "What brought you? What brought you, little one? What brought you? If you delay in telling me what brought you to this island, I will bring you to your senses, though you will be but ashes. You will have become one who cannot be seen." But the wretched man did not hear the threat. In his excitement he had lost consciousness.

The serpent carries him in his mouth to his lair where he obtains the story of the shipwreck. Then the man is assured that he has nothing to fear. At the end of four

months a ship will arrive from Egypt and take him home.

The serpent helps the sailor to forget his distress by telling his own tale of woe. "I was here with my kinsmen, and there were children among them. We totaled 75 snakes, my offspring and my kinsmen, without my mentioning to you a little daughter whom I had obtained by prayer. Then a star fell and they perished in its flame. It just happened that I was not involved in this conflagration, since I was not in their midst. But I went into shock when I found them a single corpse."

The serpent goes on to reassure his shaken guest that a different fate lay in store for him. "If you have the strength, pull yourself together: you will hug your children to your bosom and you will kiss your wife."

The sailor tries to show his gratitude by promising the serpent that he will acquaint the Pharaoh with his greatness and will send gifts of perfumes, spices, and incense, as well as the commodities for which Egypt was noted, "as should be done for a god who loves people when they are in a land distant from their own, even though the people don't know him." It is apparent here again that the storyteller envisages a deity in the form of the serpent.

In response to the sailor's outburst the serpent laughs as though the offer seemed ridiculous to him. He points out that he has no need for such gifts since he possesses them in more abundance than do the Egyptians. "It shall come about, moreover, that when you take your departure from this place nevermore will you see this island; it will have become waves."

Four months later a boat appeared. From a tall tree the sailor recognized acquaintances from Egypt. He hurried to report this to the serpent but found that the latter already knew it. The snake wished him a safe journey and provided him with a cargo of valuable goods: myrrh and spices, perfumes and eyepaint, giraffes' tails, incense, ivory, hounds and monkeys and apes, to mention only a few. In return he asked of the sailor, "Let my repute be good in your town, that is my due from you."

The sailor brings his tale to a close by telling that upon his return to Egypt he was promoted by the king to the rank of "retainer." Then he admonishes the Prince to whom he had narrated his story, "Hearken to my utterance, for it is good to listen to people."

But the Prince finds no encouragement in the retainer's good fortune and retorts, "Don't set yourself up as an example, friend. Does one give water to a bird at dawn when it is going to be killed later in the morning?" And with this allusion to the Prince's predicament the author concludes one of the most delightful stories from ancient Egypt.

II. *The Historical Setting.* We have no grounds for attempting to establish historicity for any part of the story, but there are internal clues which enable us to fit it into the framework of Egyptian history. The shipwreck episode, for one thing, reflects a period when the Pharaoh was sending expeditions to the Red Sea. Especially significant in this regard is the serpent's claim to the lordship of Punt, a region on the east coast of Africa reached via the Red Sea. Punt was noted as a source for commodities which were scarce or unavailable in Egypt. When the sailor offered to send gifts upon his return to the homeland, the serpent replies, "You don't have much myrrh. And have you become the owner of incense? I am the ruler of Punt and myrrh belongs to me." It is most likely that such a declaration would have been incorporated into a story at a time when connections between Egypt and Punt were strong. There is no evidence of traffic with Punt for two centuries following the decay of the Sixth Dynasty around 2200 B.C. It is thus improbable that the story was created earlier than 2000 B.C. The surviving manuscript must be dated no later than the Thirteenth Dynasty, and it may have been produced as early as the Twelfth Dynasty (1990-1780 B.C.). The first two centuries of the second millennium would accordingly appear to be the period during which the story was created.

The serpent in the story is a deity and as such he is patterned after the king of Egypt. His external features (i.e., gold-covered body, lapis lazuli eyebrows, and beard) reflect the official characterization of the Pharaoh. The sailor obviously intends to depict him to the Prince as the counterpart of their king. Indeed, the purpose of his tale is to nerve the Prince for an audience awaiting him at the court.

The serpent's personality agrees with the public image of the Egyptian ruler during the Twelfth Dynasty. Merely to be in his presence is enough to strike fear into the bravest heart. He has all power to destroy the one who does not speak up when addressed, but at the same time he is basically kind-hearted and benevolent. He is in other words the good god. He can experience misfortunes familiar to all men and consequently is able to sympathize with his subjects. This description would be particularly apt for the era suggested above for the story's creation.

Since the story is incomplete in the Leningrad manuscript, we cannot be certain with respect to its ultimate objective. That it is entertaining cannot be doubted, but to say that amusement was the author's primary aim is to go beyond the evidence. In fact, it is known that several other compositions from the Middle Kingdom were written as propaganda for the king. We need to refer only to the tale of *Sinuhe which the Egyptians themselves must have regarded as diverting literature but which in reality was intended for aggrandizement of Sesostris I, son of the founder of the Twelfth Dynasty.

It is possible that the story of the Shipwrecked Sailor is also entertainment with a moral — a moral which would have been much more readily apparent to its ancient audience than to its modern readers. We can suggest that it was the author's intention to develop rapport between royalty and officials. Achievement of this goal was desirable, even necessary, at the beginning of the Twelfth Dynasty. We know that the founder of the dynasty did indeed effect a balance between royal power and princely ambition, a trick not easily accomplished. One of the devices which he employed to bolster his position, was propaganda. If the Shipwrecked Sailor fulfilled this function, it would help to explain why the story, unlike the Sinuhe romance, has no personal names. Both officials in the tale are referred to by their titles. "Retainer," literally "follower," is here and in Sinuhe a rank bestowed after the recipient has survived unusual and harrowing experiences. "Prince" does not denote the son of the king but rather a local ruler or monarch. The rulers of the nomes benefited greatly when Egypt

was reorganized under Ammenemes I shortly after the Eleventh Dynasty had come to an end. The import of the Shipwrecked Sailor may well have been intended primarily for these officials. If so, anonymity of the retainer and the Prince would certainly have aided in exerting maximum influence upon them.

III. *Literary Affinities*. It would be a mistake to treat the Shipwrecked Sailor, or for that matter any Egyptian literary work, in isolation from other East Mediterranean literature. The story is noteworthy for anticipating by many centuries motifs in Homer's *Odyssey*. True, both are tales of the sea, but the parallels are striking because of agreement in detail.

The Egyptian tale presents a hero who like Odysseus finds himself stranded upon a strange island after narrowly escaping a watery grave. Shipwrecks are not uncommon in marine saga, but in these two instances it is easy to demonstrate an unusually close tie.

When the Egyptian was cast upon the beach, he sought shelter beneath a bower of branches. Odysseus likewise took refuge in an arbor upon his arrival at the Phaeacian coast: "He made his way to the woods . . . and he crept beneath two bushes which grew from the same spot. . . . Through these the force of the wet winds could not blow, nor the rays of the bright sun beat, nor the rain penetrate, so closely did they grow, intertwining one with the other" (*Odyssey* V. 475 ff.).

It is predicted that the island of the Phaeacians will vanish after Odysseus' departure. Even so does the serpent foretell his island's disappearance beneath the billowy waves. Needless to say, the notion of an island which will never be seen again is a clever device against checking the storyteller's veracity.

It is also noteworthy that both the Egyptian sailor and Odysseus leave the enchanted isle after being lavished with gifts of friendship (*cf. Odyssey* XIII. 10-15).

Even in the account of the shipwreck there appears to be a detail which anticipates

a Homeric episode. The Egyptian text is much more concise, but following the description of a huge wave which capsized the boat, there is a difficult phrase in which there occurs a common word variously rendered as "wood," "tree," "pole," or "mast." The context is strikingly like that in the *Odyssey* XII. 415-25. Odysseus' ship was torn to pieces by the waves, and he alone escaped by riding out the storm on a makeshift raft made from mast and keel. Most interpreters have seen in the obscure Egyptian text a reference to the means whereby the hero was able to survive. It is not at all impossible that he kept himself from drowning by clinging to the mast.

BIBLIOGRAPHY. Adolf Erman, *The Literature of the Ancient Egyptians*, London, 1927. W. Golénischeff, *Le conte du naufragé*, Imprimerie de l'institut francais d'archéologie orientale, Cairo, 1912. Battiscombe Gunn, "The Island of the Serpent," *Land of Enchanters*, ed. Bernard Lewis, Harvill Press, London, 1948. William C. Hayes, "The Middle Kingdom in Egypt. Internal history from the rise of the Heracleopolitans to the death of Ammenemes III," *The Cambridge Ancient History*, revised edition, Cambridge University Press, Cambridge, 1961. Gustave Lefebvre, *Romans et contes égyptiens de l'époque pharaonique*, Librairie d'Amerique et d'Orient, Paris, 1949. G. A. Wainwright, "Zeberged: the Shipwrecked Sailor's Island," *Journal of Egyptian Archaeology* 32 (1946), p. 31.

SHISHAK. Pharaoh Shishak (940-915 B.C.), known in Egyptian as Sheshonk, was a member of a powerful family in the Faiyum who founded the Twenty-second Dynasty and sought to restore Egypt's lost prestige. During the fifth year of Rehoboam, Shishak invaded Palestine and took temple treasures from Jerusalem as tribute (cf. I Kings 14:25-26).

At the temple of Amun, in Thebes, he left a triumphal relief scene in which he lists towns both in Judah and Israel which he plundered.

In March 1939 M. Pierre Montet discovered a mummy in a golden mummy case, with an outer case of silver, at Tanis in the eastern Delta. Jewelry was strewn around the floor and the walls of the chamber were covered with paintings. This was first thought to be the tomb of Shishak, but archaeologists now think it may be the tomb of a later king of the same dynasty.

ECORD OF SHISHAK'S CAMPAIGN IN ALESTINE carved on the temple walls at rnak, Egypt. Courtesy, Matson Photo rvice

SHURUPPAK. Shuruppak (Tell Fara) was

a Sumerian town north of Uruk. According to the *Sumerian King List, Ubar-Tutu of Shuruppak was the last ruler before the flood. In the Sumerian version of the flood story (see Gilgamesh Epic) Ziusudra, son of Ubar-Tutu, was warned of an impending flood and urged to build a huge boat to save himself and his family. Although the Sumerian version of the story is fragmentary, Ziusudra appears in greater detail in the Akkadian version where he bears the name Utnapishtim.

Excavations were conducted by the University of Pennsylvania at Shuruppak under the direction of H. V. Hilprecht, and the Deutsche Orient-Gesellschaft worked there under Robert Koldewey in the 1902-03 season. Pottery of the *Jemdet Nasr type was discovered, along with early buildings, seals, and tablets. A flood deposit, two feet thick, has been dated to the end of the Jemdet Nasr period.

SIDON. Sidon, an ancient Phoenician city twenty-five miles north of °Tyre, was built on a small hill projecting out into the Mediterranean. The land side was protected by a wall, and the northern harbor of Sidon was particularly good. The Bible indicates that Sidon was the first of the Phoenician cities to be founded (cf. Gen. 10:19) and the term Sidonian is often used of all the inhabitants of Phoenicia (cf. I Kings 5:6; 16:31).

The *Amarna Letters suggest that Zimri-Adda of Sidon defected from Egypt (ca. 1390 B.C.). Later kings evidently tried to expand Sidonian power southward as far as Dor, but the Philistines retaliated and destroyed Sidon (ca. 1150 B.C.). Under Tiglath-pileser I of Assyria (ca. 1100 B.C.) Sidon and other coastal cities had to pay tribute to the Assyrians. With the rise of Tyre, Sidon lost its importance as a Phoenician port, and it had to struggle against a succession of Assyrian, Babylonian, and Persian conquerors during the first millennium B.C. Shalmaneser III received tribute from Sidon, Nebuchadnezzar captured it, and the Persians used its fleet in their campaigns against the Greeks. The Sidonians rose up against Artaxerxes III (Ochus) but the city was betrayed. Forty thousand perished in the battle that followed, and the survivors burned the city and the fleet. The forti-

fications were never rebuilt. Sidon surrendered to Alexander without a fight and actually aided in his siege of Tyre.

In New Testament times the inhabitants of Sidon were mainly Greek and the city became famous as a center of philosophical learning. Many coins bear the names of Sidonian rulers. Archaeological discoveries in the area include a number of buildings from the port area dating back to New Testament times. The *sarcophagus of Eshmunazar (ca. 300 B.C.) is of interest because of its inscription.

BIBLIOGRAPHY. A. Poidebard and J. Lauffray, *Sidon,* 1951.

SILOAM INSCRIPTION. In ancient times, the proposed location of a new city was based primarily on two important factors: ease of fortification, and a nearby abundant water supply. The site of *Jerusalem enjoyed such magnificent natural impregnability that its earliest inhabitants were willing to put up with the enforced inconvenience of bringing in water by various methods from the only important natural spring in the immediate vicinity of the city. The spring itself is located in the Kidron valley against the eastern side of the Ophel hill and, although it discharges its waters intermittently because of a peculiar siphoning arrangement of underground caverns, it provided an ample supply for the first settlers, even in its undeveloped state. Referred to as "Gihon" in the Old Testament (cf., e.g., I Kings 1:33), the spring is today generally called "the Virgin's Fountain" by Christians and "the Spring of the Stairway" by Moslems.

Although the waters of the Gihon are now said to be highly unpalatable, having become more and more brackish through the centuries, they undoubtedly were originally pure and sweet. Prior to the Israelite occupation of the land of Palestine, the Canaanites had dug a tunnel from within the city to a point from which it was possible to lower containers to a pool formed by the Gihon, thus making more efficient use of the available water supply. It is not known whether Joab and his cohorts penetrated Jebusite Jerusalem via this conduit (cf. II Sam. 5:8; I Chron. 11:6), for the crucial word translated "gutter" in II Samuel (RSV: "water shaft") has been recently interpreted as meaning "scaling-hook." At any rate, at

528

THE POOL OF SILOAM in the Kidron Valley, connected with En Rogel by the Siloam Tunnel. Courtesy, Matson Photo Service.

some time after the capture of Jerusalem by the Israelites a trench was dug in the Ophel hillside leading from the Gihon pool (which, in the course of time, became known as the "upper pool") to a reservoir (later called the "lower pool") at the southern end of the city. Since this open-air channel ran outside the city walls for most of its course. it could easily be damned up in time of siege. It is therefore not surprising that a second conduit was discovered in 1886 by Conrad Schick, a German architect then residing in Jerusalem. This latter conduit had been built to carry the Gihon waters down the western side of the Kidron valley to the lower pool. But it was only partly cut through the Ophel rock, the other part being scarcely more than a ditch covered with flat stones. Since it was still outside the walls, this aqueduct, like the former, could be obstructed with relatively little difficulty. It was at the end of this "conduit of the upper pool in the highway of the fuller's field" (Isa. 7:3) that Isaiah interviewed Ahaz, and it is probably also to these "waters of Shiloah that go softly" (8:6) that Isaiah refers as he compares them metaphorically to the destructive "waters of the [Euphrates] river" (8:7) which would soon virtually inundate the tiny kingdom of Judah in the persons of the Assyrian king, Sennacherib, and his armies.

The significance of the Assyrian conquest of Damascus (732 B.C.) and Samaria, the capital of the northern Kingdom of Israel (722/1 B.C.), was not lost on Hezekiah, who succeeded Ahaz as sole ruler of the southern Kingdom of Judah ca. 715 B.C. For a time Hezekiah remained a faithful vassal of Assyria but, as Judah began to grow stronger and more prosperous under his benevolent leadership, "he rebelled against the king of Assyria, and served him not" (II Kings 18:7). Anticipating Assyrian reprisal in the form of invasion, Hezekiah then set about to strengthen the fortifications of Jerusalem (II Chron. 32:5). At the same time he "took counsel with his princes and his mighty men to stop the waters of the fountains which were without the city" (32:3). A large group of workmen "stopped all the fountains, and the brook that ran through the midst of the land, saying, Why should the kings of Assyria come, and find much water?" (32:4). Having "closed the upper outlet of the waters of Gihon," Hezekiah then "directed them down to the west side of the city of David" (32:30 RSV) through the now-famous tunnel that conducts water from the Virgin's Fountain to the Pool of Siloam. In one master stroke, the king of Judah thus assured a plentiful supply of water for Jerusalem while denying it to the enemy.

The construction of "the pool and the conduit" by means of which Hezekiah "brought water into the city" (II Kings 20:20 RSV) is justly recognized as one of the great engineering feats of antiquity. He first built the Siloam reservoir itself, enclosing it within fortifications located in the southwest quarter of Jerusalem (cf. Isa. 22:9, 11 RSV) and intending then to divert the Gihon waters from the "old" or "lower" pool (the site of the modern Birket el Ḥamrā or "Red Pool") into it through the Siloam tunnel. It has been surmised that the actual hewing of the rock was being done at the very time that the emissaries of Sennacherib were standing "by the [already blocked?] conduit of the [already concealed?] upper pool, which is in the highway of the fuller's field" (II Kings 17:17; cf. Isa. 36:2). If so, the people standing on the city wall who were listening to the taunts and threats of the Rab-shakeh and his companions must have laughed inwardly when they were warned that they would die "by thirst" (II Chron. 32:11) if they refused to surrender. While there can be no doubt that it was the power of the Lord that preserved Jerusalem from destruction (701 B.C.) and slew the Assyrian troops (32:21; II Kings 19:35; Isa. 37:36), we cannot but admire Hezekiah for his foresight in guaranteeing an adequate water supply for the beleaguered city.

Hezekiah's tunnel has continued to bring water into Jerusalem from the time of its construction to the present day. The writer of the Apocryphal Book of Ecclesiasticus mentions it (48:17), apparently indicating that its existence and purpose were still known in the second century B.C. By the first century A.D., however, it would seem that the tunnel itself had been all but forgotten for Josephus, in a detailed description of Jerusalem and its environs, refers only to the "fountain" of Siloam (modern 'Ain Silwân) which he locates correctly at the mouth of the Tyropoeon valley, "the

530

valley of the Cheese-mongers" (*De Bello Judaico* V.iv.1). Josephus thus evidently considered the "fountain" to be a spring rather than the lower end of a tunnel, which by his time had doubtless begun to fill with calcareous deposits. The tunnel was apparently first rediscovered in the thirteenth century but was by no means generally known until the nineteenth. Its first modern explorer was the American scholar, Edward Robinson, who, together with his friend, Eli Smith, a missionary in Syria, traversed its entire length in April of 1838. They discovered the fact that the tunnel, through portions of which it was necessary to crawl, had not been cut in a straight line but wound a serpentine course through the rock. The reason for the zig-zag route is still unknown; it has been supposed that the diggers tried to avoid royal tombs that were in the vicinity, or that they attempted to follow natural fissures or soft veins of limestone in the rock. Perhaps their surveying methods were inadequate. At any rate, Robinson noted that two gangs of workmen had done the actual labor of excavation, proceeding toward each other through Ophel hill, one starting from inside the city by the Siloam pool, the other from outside by the Gihon spring. He measured the results of their work as an aqueduct 1750 feet long, an estimate which strikes an average between more recent longer and shorter measurements, the differences being due to choice of starting point and finishing point.

In December of 1867 Captain Charles Warren explored the entire tunnel with great care, spending four hours in its waters. At times he found himself crawling through sections in which there were just four inches of air space. It was not until the year 1909 that the expedition of Captain Montague Parker began to completely excavate, explore, survey, and measure the Siloam tunnel, doing a far more accurate piece of work than had ever been attempted. Together with his staff of British engineers and with financial backing of about 25,000 pounds, Parker cleaned out the tunnel and restored it to its original width and height. He confirmed the measurement of length already determined by Robinson, and observed that the average height was just under six feet, while the total fall in elevation from spring to reservoir was seven feet two inches. The

width varies from twenty-three to twenty-six inches. It was further determined that when the two original gangs of tunnelers had been about ninety-eight feet apart they had first heard each others' pickax blows and begun to cut toward each other. At the point of breakthrough (944 feet from the Siloam end, according to an earlier surveyor, C. R. Conder) the floor of the southern half was about a foot higher than that of the northern half. French Dominican Père L. H. Vincent has estimated that approximately 850 cubic yards of rock had been removed and that the total length of time necessary to complete the task had been between six and seven months. The southern crew had been supplied with air for breathing through a single shaft cut about 460 feet from the Siloam pool, while the northern crew simply breathed the air that seeped in through the Gihon aperture. It is quite likely that several crews labored around the clock to complete the task, since there was room for only one man at a time to work at the head of the excavation.

The Pool of Siloam (modern *Birket Silwân*) to which the third-of-a-mile-long tunnel leads emerging today under an arch, was excavated by Frederick J. Bliss. The original pool had been seventy-one feet north to south by seventy-five feet east to west and had been mostly dug in the solid rock. Bliss uncovered a flight of steps along the western edge of the pool, which was surrounded by an arcade twelve feet wide and over twenty-two feet high and bisected by a central arcade which perhaps separated a section for men from one for women. Since these constructions were probably from the time of Herod or earlier, they represent the appearance of the area when Jesus, having anointed the eyes of a blind man with clay, said to him, "Go, wash in the pool of Siloam" (John 9:6, 7).

Interesting though Hezekiah's tunnel and pool are in themselves, however, they are most important because of a remarkable discovery that was made about twenty feet inside the Siloam end of the aqueduct. In June of 1880 a pupil of the aforementioned Conrad Schick was playing in the tunnel with some friends. His foot slipped and he fell into the water. Upon rising to his feet, he noticed an inscription incised on a smoothed portion of the tunnel wall about

531

three feet above the floor on the east side. The inscription itself proved to be about two and one-half feet long, the text being about the size of a modern newspaper page. It was written in fine classical Hebrew and, until the discovery of the °Gezer calendar in 1908, it was the oldest known Hebrew inscription of any length.

The Siloam inscription was written in flowing characters that are independently datable to the time of Hezekiah, so that 700 B.C. cannot be too far from the actual year of its engraving, probably by a member of one of the crews that dug the tunnel. Its first decipherer was A. H. Sayce who read it by candlelight, sitting in the water for a long period of time to do so. The inscription, the first part of which seems to be missing, reads as follows:

[. . .] the breakthrough. Now this is the manner of the breakthrough. While still [. . .] the axe, each toward his fellow, and while three cubits still remained to be tunne[led], the

voice of a man [was hea]rd calling to his fellow, for there was a fissure(?) in the rock on the right [. . .]. Now when the tunnel was cut through, each of the excavators hewed through to meet his fellow, axe against axe, and the waters began flowing from the source toward the reservoir for 1200 cubits, 100 cubits being the height of the rock above the heads of the excavators.

The 1200-cubit figure given as the length of the tunnel is an excellent round-number statement of the true measurements, for a cubit of just under eighteen inches is well known from other sources. Likewise, Ophel hill rises to a height of 150 feet and more above the roof of the aqueduct, confirming the "100 cubits" of the inscription. More important than these data, however, is the significance of the Siloam inscription for the study of the development of Hebrew orthography. Like the °Mesha stone, this inscription is characterized by dots which separate words from each other. The script itself

INSIDE THE SILOAM TUNNEL. Courtesy, Matson Photo Service

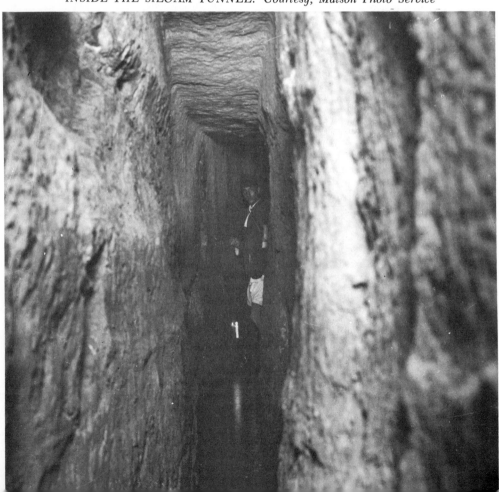

is a beautifully executed form of the cursive Phoenician consonantal alphabet, no vowel sounds being represented in ancient Hebrew. Although certain consonants were used as vowel indicators in later times, such use is virtually non-existent in the Siloam inscription except at word-end. The translation of the word provisionally rendered "fissure" above is still a matter of debate, but every other word is found in one form or other in the Hebrew Bible.

The discovery of the inscription was an immediate cause of excitement in the scholarly world. In 1881 Hermann Guthe obtained a gypsum cast of it and published a photograph, with an accompanying description, in 1882. Guthe also removed the lime incrustations from the letters of the inscription with dilute hydrochloric acid, soon after which several additional excellent "squeezes" and transcriptions of it were made. The importance of these copying efforts soon became evident, for in 1890 vandals removed the Siloam inscription from its place in the tunnel, apparently breaking it into six or seven pieces in the process. Some months after their removal they were found in the possession of a Greek citizen of Jerusalem, who claimed that he had purchased them from an unknown Arab for thirty-five napoleons. The Turkish government subsequently acquired the pieces and transferred them to the Museum of the Ancient Orient in Istanbul where, again pieced together, the Siloam inscription may be seen to the present day.

BIBLIOGRAPHY. J. B. Pritchard, *Archaeology and the Old Testament,* Princeton University Press, Princeton, 1958, pp. 36-42. G. E. Wright, *Biblical Archaeology,* The Westminster Press, Philadelphia, 1957, pp. 169-171. See also the excellent motion picture, *Hezekiah's Water Tunnel* (Griffon Graphics, Inc., 1963, 27½ minutes).

SINAI. The Sinai Peninsula comprises a barren wilderness south of the land bridge which connects Egypt with the lands of the Fertile Crescent. The Brook of Egypt, or Wadi el-'Arish, flowing northward from the Wilderness of Paran, marks the geographical boundary between Canaan and Egypt. Contact between the two lands was continuous, for the distance between major cities was relatively short. Kantara, in the eastern Delta, is but 117 miles from Raphia in southern Canaan. The Roman general Titus took but

five days to march from Sile in Egypt to Gaza.

Three ancient roads traverse the land bridge between Egypt and her Asiatic neighbors. Skirting the Mediterranean is the *Via Maris,* "the way of the sea," which was used by the armies of Egypt when they campaigned in Asia. Scripture calls it, "The Way of the Land of the Philistines" (Exod. 13:17-18), asserting that the Israelites avoided this road at the direction of God. The former slaves to Pharaoh were in no condition to wage full scale warfare, which would have been unavoidable had the route of the Exodus followed the coastal route.

South of the *Via Maris* was the "Way to Shur" (Gen. 16:7), the road which Hagar took as she fled from her mistress Sarah. Hagar, an Egyptian, was evidently on the way to her homeland when an angel stopped her and told her to return to the home of Abraham. The Egyptians maintained a wall at the frontier to control traffic from the East. As the word "Shur" means "wall," the road seems to have terminated at the check point garrisoned by Egyptian troops. The Egyptian terminus was in the region of modern Ismailia, on the Suez Canal. In southern Canaan it connected with roads leading northward to Beer-sheba, Hebron, and Jerusalem.

A third route, known in modern times as the *Darb el-Haj,* "the Pilgrim's Way," runs across the Sinai Peninsula from the head of the Gulf of Suez, to Ezion-geber (Elath) at the head of the Gulf of Aqaba. These two gulfs, extending like rabbit ears in a northwesterly and a northeasterly direction from the Red Sea, bound the Sinai Peninsula.

The Exodus did not take Israel along any of the well traveled roads, and it is difficult for modern geographers to trace the route of the Exodus with any certainty. The starting point was Raamses in the Eastern Delta (Num. 33:5), identified with Egyptian *Per-Ramses,* the capital city which Ramesses II built at or near the site of ancient Tanis. It was in this region that the patriarch Jacob had settled some centuries before (Gen. 47:11) when it was described as the "choicest part of the land."

Stops were made at Succoth (Exod. 12:37), Egyptian *tkw,* in the eastern part of the Wadi Tumilat, and at Etham "in the edge of the wilderness" (Exod. 13:20), a site

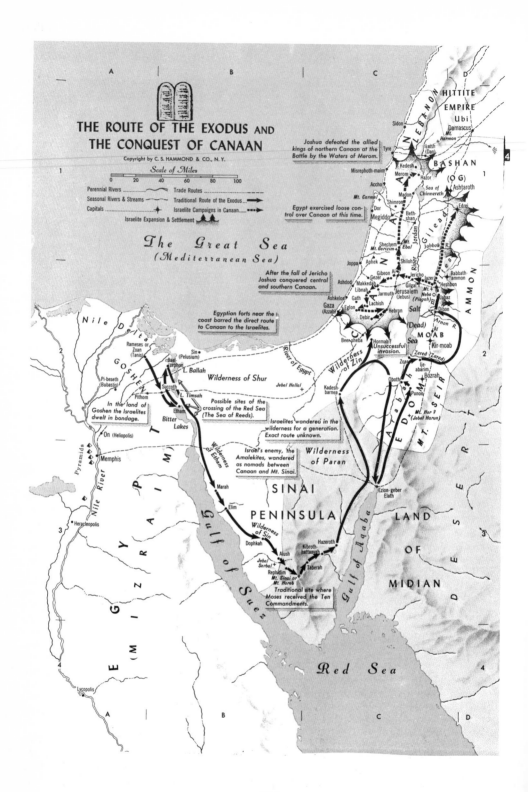

THE ROUTE OF THE EXODUS AND THE CONQUEST OF CANAAN

Copyright by C. S. HAMMOND & CO., N.Y.

Scale of Miles

0   20   40   60   80   100

Perennial Rivers

Seasonal Rivers & Streams

Capitals

Israelite Expansion & Settlement

Trade Routes

Traditional Route of the Exodus

Israelite Campaigns in Canaan

The Great Sea
(Mediterranean Sea)

Joshua defeated the allied kings of northern Canaan at the Battle by the Waters of Merom.

Egypt exercised loose control over Canaan at this time.

After the fall of Jericho Joshua conquered central and southern Canaan.

Egyptian forts near the coast barred the direct route to Canaan to the Israelites.

In the land of Goshen the Israelites dwelt in bondage.

Possible sites of the crossing of the Red Sea (The Sea of Reeds).

Israelites wandered in the wilderness for a generation. Exact route unknown.

Israel's enemy, the Amalekites, wandered as nomads between Canaan and Mt. Sinai.

Unsuccessful invasion.

Wilderness of Shur

Wilderness of Etham

Wilderness of Paran

Wilderness of Sin

Wilderness of Zin

SINAI PENINSULA

Traditional site where Moses received the Ten Commandments.

Nile Delta

GOSHEN

Pyramids

Nile River

E G Y P T (M I Z R A I M)

Gulf of Suez

Gulf of Aqaba

LAND OF MIDIAN

Red Sea

LEBANON

HITTITE EMPIRE
Ubi
Damascus

BASHAN (OG)

Gilead

AMMON

MOAB

EDOM

MT. SEIR

Arabah

DESERT

Salt (Dead) Sea

Rameses or Zoan (Tanis)
Pi-beseth (Bubastis)
Pithom
On (Heliopolis)
Memphis
Heracleopolis
Lycopolis

Sin (Pelusium)
Baal-zephon
L. Ballah
Succoth
L. Timsah
Etham
Bitter Lakes
Marah
Elim
Dophkah
Alush
Jebel Serbal
Rephidim
Mt. Sinai or Mt. Horeb
Taberah
Kibroth-hattaavah
Hazeroth
Ezion-geber Elath

River of Egypt
Jebel Helal
Kadesh-barnea
Hormah?
Beer-sheba
Gaza (Azzah)
Ashkelon
Ashdod
Joppa
Aphek
Gezer
Makkedah
Libnah
Gath
Eglon
Lachish
Debir
Hebron
Jarmuth
Jerusalem (Jebus)
Gibeon Ai
Jericho
Gilgal
Shiloh
Shechem
Mt. Gerizim
Mt. Ebal
Jordan River
Jabbok R.
Jazer
Rabbath-ammon
Heshbon
Nebo (Pisgah)
Jahaz
Dibon
Arnon R.
Zered (Zared)
Kir-moab
Ije-abarim
Oboth
Zoar
Bozrah
Punon
Mt. Hor? (Jebel Harun)

Sidon
Tyre
Accho
Dor
Megiddo
Beth-shan
Misrephoth-maim
Merom
Hazor
Madon
Shimron
Mt. Carmel
Sea of Chinnereth
Ashtaroth
Edrei
Kedesh
Laish (Dan)
Mt. Hermon

534

which has not been identified. From Etham they turned back to Pi-Hahiroth, which may have been the name of a canal linking the Bitter Lakes to the Nile. The Israelite encampment was "by the sea beside Pi-Hahiroth, in front of Baal-zephon" (Exod. 14:9). Baal-zephon is a Semitic name meaning, "Baal of the North." In Hellenistic times a temple to Zeus Casius was located there. Nearby was another place bearing a Semitic name, Migdol, meaning tower. Migdol was a common place name, for the ancient world had many watch towers. We read of a Tower of Seti and a Tower of Merneptah, identified with modern Tell el-Heir, five miles north of Sile between Qantara and Pelusium. It was in the northern sector of the ancient Wall of Egypt.

Israel left Egypt "by the way of the Red Sea" (Exod. 13:18), but the exact location of the crossing is not known. Although traditionally known as the Red Sea, the Hebrew text of Exodus is clear that it was the "Sea of Reeds" which Israel crossed to escape from Egypt and Pharaoh's armies. The term aptly describes the lake region north of the Gulf of Suez comprising the Bitter Lakes and Lake Timsah. The crossing must have taken place north of the Sinai Peninsula, for the Israelites found themselves in the Wilderness of Shur after crossing the Sea (Exod. 15:22). The Wilderness of Shur covers the area south of the Mediterranean coast, extending from the Wadi el-Arish (The "Brook of Egypt") to the line of the modern Suez Canal. All of the direct routes from Egypt to Canaan passed through the Wilderness of Shur.

Instead of taking one of the direct routes eastward, however, the Israelites turned southward into the Sinai Peninsula, taking a route parallel to the Gulf of Suez. Brief stops were made at Mareh, where the bitter waters were made sweet (Exod. 15:23-26) and the oasis of Elim (Exod. 15:27) with its twelve springs and seventy palm trees.

In the heart of the Sinai Peninsula, south of the Wilderness of Shur, is the region known as the Wilderness of Sin in which Dophkah was located (Num. 33:12). Dophkah is thought to have been located near the famed copper and turquoise mines which were operated by Pharaoh from early dynastic times. In the center of the mining region was the famed temple to the goddess Hathor at Serabit el-Khadem. Hundreds of inscriptions have been identified at the temple and at the entrances to the mines. Although most of them are in hieroglyphic Egyptian characters, about forty are in the so-called Proto-Sinaitic alphabetic script from the fifteenth century B.C. They represent one of the earliest attempts at developing a purely alphabetic means of writing.

The last stop before Mount Sinai was at Rephidim (Exod. 17:1), possibly modern Wadi Refayid in the southwestern part of the Peninsula. Here Moses smote the rock (Exod. 17:1-7) in order to bring forth water to supply the demands of his people. Shortly afterward the Israelites met their first enemies, the Amalekites, and gained a victory after a difficult battle (Exod. 17:8-16).

Tradition has located Mount Sinai in the southern part of the Sinai Peninsula since the fourth century A.D. A legend states that Catherine of Alexandria, after her martyrdom, was carried by angels to the top of the mountain which now bears her name. A monastery has been located there continuously since the fourth century, although the Christians have undergone periods of severe persecution. The Moslem conquest brought with it anti-Christian feeling, and massacres are recorded in the time of the monk Ammonius (A.D. 373) and some years later in the days of St. Nilus (A.D. 390). The present Monastery of St. Catherine, on the northwest slope of Jebel Musa — a 7,500 foot high mountain — was founded about A.D. 527 under the Emperor Justinian who established it on the site where Helena, the mother of Constantine, had erected a small church two centuries earlier.

Approaching Jebel Musa from Serabit el-Khadem, the traveler enters a wide valley called er-Raha, two miles long and one-third to two-thirds of a mile wide. This would be the natural place for Israel to have encamped (Exod. 19:1-2; Num. 33:15). Towering above the plain are three summits, Ras es-Safsaf to the northwest, Jebel Musa to the southeast, and, still higher, Jebel Katarin rising 8,500 feet to the southwest. While Gebel Musa, which means "the mount of Moses," is the favored location, we cannot be positive concerning the original Sinai. The church historian Eusebius preferred still

535

another site, Jebel Serbal, west of the Wadi Feiran, and some scholars abandon the Sinai peninsula entirely, preferring a site in northwestern Arabia or in the vicinity of Kadesh-barnea. The southern part of the Sinai Peninsula is still favored, however, and Gebel Musa may well be the real Mount Sinai, or Horeb, where the Law was received by Moses.

After the encampment at Sinai, the Israelites moved northeastward and entered the Wilderness of Paran, which is bordered on the east by the extension of the Jordan-Dead Sea valley known as the Arabah, and its southern extension, the Gulf of Aqabah. To this Wilderness of Paran, Hagar and Ishmael fled after they were expelled from the household of Abraham (Gen. 21:21), and from the same region Moses sent men to spy out the land of Canaan (Num. 10:12; 12:16). On the northern border of the Wilderness of Paran, where it touches the Wilderness of Zin, was Kadesh-barnea (Num. 20:1, 22). Kadesh-barnea was evidently an ancient holy place, known by the alternate name En Mishpat ("Spring of Judgment") at the time of Abraham (Gen. 14:7). In 1842 Rowlands discovered a spring with the name Ain Qudeis about fifty miles southwest of Beersheba, and scholars have tended to equate this with Biblical Kadesh-barnea. The paucity of water at the site argues against the identification, however. A more suitable location would be Ain Qudeirat, five miles northwest of Ain Qudeis, which has an abundance of water and vegetation. It must have been somewhere in this general area that Israel encamped several times during the period of wilderness wandering (Num. 13:26; 20:1; Deut. 1:19, 46). Here Miriam died and was buried (Num. 20:1), and Aaron was buried in nearby Mt. Hor (Num. 20:22-29).

Kadesh-barnea might well have served as a base for the invasion of Canaan, had not the Israelites accepted the report of the majority of the spies who expressed fear that they could not overcome the enemy (Num. 13:25-14:3). An attempt was made to penetrate southern Canaan (Num. 14:45) but Israel suffered defeat at the hand of the Amalekites and the Canaanites. The generation which had left Egypt did not enter the land of Promise. Most of the years of wandering seem to have been spent in the vicinity of Kadesh. When the time came for making a fresh attempt to enter Canaan, the direct route from the south was rejected and the tribes crossed the Arabah and circled around Edom (Num. 21:4) as they prepared to enter Canaan from the east.

SINUHE. The Egyptian romance in which the hero bears the name Sinuhe evolved from political developments in Egypt during the twentieth century B.C. Sinuhe was serving, so the story goes, with a military expedition led by the king's son and coregent Senusert I. The troops had quelled certain Libyan tribes on the frontier of the western delta and had begun the march back to the Nile valley with their booty when late one evening news arrived from the palace that King Amenemhet I, founder of the Twelfth Dynasty, had been assassinated, the victim of harem intrigue.

Senusert departed at once for the royal residence (situated near the modern village of El-Lisht) without notifying his men, but Sinuhe learned of the sudden turn of events by chancing to overhear a treasonous conversation between a messenger and another of the king's sons whom the conspirators intended to place on the throne. The import of their words left Sinuhe panic-stricken and he immediately resorted to flight lest he become a casualty in the civil strife which could ensue.

Sinuhe crossed the Nile just south of the delta and struck out on foot for the northeastern frontier, where he managed to slip past the border outposts. Thirst overtook him in the desert, but in the nick of time a band of nomads came by and saved him from his plight. He wandered from place to place in Canaan, eventually reaching Byblos and thence heading inland and settling down in a fertile region called Qedem where his services were engaged by a Syrian ruler. The prince's question, "Why is it that you have come here?" (natural enough in East Mediterranean epic), brings the story to a virtual standstill, for the narrator uses Sinuhe's reply to bring in a lengthy eulogy lauding the new Pharaoh, Senusert.

The prince gave his eldest daughter as a bride to Sinuhe, a development strikingly similar to that which occurred when Moses fled from Egypt to seek asylum in the land of Midian (Exod. 2:15-21). Sinuhe was also

JEBEL MUSA (Arabic for Mount Moses) in the southern part of the Sinai Peninsula is the traditional Mount Sinai or Horeb where Moses received the law. Courtesy, Matson Photo Service

entrusted with a frontier territory noted for its fertility: "It is a good land called Ya'a. It produces figs and grapes. It has more wine than water. Honey is plentiful and olive oil abounds. All kinds of fruit are on its trees. Barley and emmer are there, as well as countless cattle of every species." The description follows the same pattern as the Biblical characterization of the promised land (Deut. 8:7-9). The custom of bestowing a frontier buffer region upon an able refugee is embedded in Homeric epic as well; cf. the experience of Phoenix (*Iliad* IX:478-84).

In time Sinuhe was promoted to a more prominent position, and later when his own sons grew to manhood, they too were numbered among the ruling aristocracy. When nomads encroached upon the territory of the city states, Sinuhe was the leading tactician in overcoming them. He himself led troops on many combat missions and gained distinction with success after success.

The esteem and favor which had come to Sinuhe could not help but incite the jealousy of some ambitious warrior and soon a challenge to single combat rang out at the door of Sinuhe's domicile. Sinuhe made clear his distate for fighting a man with whom he had no quarrel, but he agreed to a duel on the following morning. At daybreak virtually the whole land had gathered to witness the clash. Sinuhe, though considered the underdog, made short work of his opponent: "He charged at me and I shot him, my arrow sticking in his neck. He screamed and fell on his nose. I dispatched him with his own battle-axe, and on his back I let out my war-cry. . . . What he had planned to do to me, I did to him."

There are many features in this episode which remind us of details in cognate epic materials. No doubt some of the closest parallels are in the account of David's triumph over Goliath (I Sam. 17), originating, to be sure, some nine centuries later but before the heroic age had run its course in

Israel. The Biblical narrative relates that Goliath, mortally wounded, fell flat on his face and was then decapitated with his own sword. Even the vindictive mood ascribed to Sinuhe crops up again in East Mediterranean saga, for the Philistine warriors declare that they had come to bind Samson "to do to him as he has done to us," while Samson in turn explains his actions by saying, "As they had done to me, thus I have done to them" (Judg. 15:10-11). It is noteworthy that the famous New Testament injunction, "Do unto others as you would have them do unto you," takes exception to the standards of heroic behavior in the ancient epics.

With the defeat of his challenger Sinuhe increased in fame and fortune. And yet, when it occurred to him that his repute would reach the Egyptian court, he was beset by nostalgia. He had grown old in exile and yearned for repatriation. A prayer voicing his desire brings out the underlying theme of the story: a hero abroad who wants more than anything else to return to his homeland. The subject was popular in ancient Egyptian literature. Other tales employing it are °*Shipwrecked Sailor, Doomed Prince*, and °*Two Brothers*. Within the realm of reality the theme finds in the report of °*Wenamon* a setting in East Mediterranean seaports. The tradition has its most elaborate expression in the Homeric *Odyssey*.

Sinuhe's prayers were answered. Senusert did hear about the hero's circumstances and gifts were forwarded to the exile in Syria to assure him of Pharaoh's good will. And then one day Sinuhe received a royal letter urging him at great length to return to Egypt where he could live out his life at the capital and be accorded a decent burial. He was deeply moved by the message and promptly sent off a reply extolling the king and excusing himself for having left Egypt in the first place. He indicated his willingness to relinquish his position in Ya'a and requested that he be allowed to bring with him three princes of renown: Meki from South Qedem, Ya'ush of Keshu, and Menus from the lands of the Phoenicians. The latter may be an allusion to Minos, the legendary ruler of Crete, who according to Greek tradition was the son of a Phoenician princess. This equation, however, is not devoid of problems.

Within a day Sinuhe had turned over his estate to his children and appointed his eldest son as fratriarch. Then he undertook the journey southward to the Egyptian garrison. There the officer in charge of border patrols sent word to Pharaoh that Sinuhe had arrived and Senusert dispatched ships laden with gifts for the Syrians who had escorted him to Egypt. Sinuhe himself was taken aboard a well-staffed vessel and transported to the capital.

Early the next day Sinuhe was conducted to the palace and ushered in before the king, who greeted him kindly. The excitement was too much for the former expatriate. He fainted away and had to be helped to his feet. Only after His Majesty reprimanded him for his lack of decorum did Sinuhe find his tongue and even then he could only admit his discomposure. Then the queen and her offspring entered but were taken aback by the sight which met their eyes. They had to be assured that the bearded old man in Asiatic garb was really Sinuhe. The latter was soon directed to luxurious quarters and re-initiated into the pleasurable life at the Egyptian court: "Years were made to pass away from my body. I was shaved, and my hair was combed. A load (of dirt) was given back to the desert, my clothes to the bedouin. I was clothed in fine linen and anointed with fine oil. I slept in a bed. I relinquished the sand to those who dwell thereon, and wood-oil to him who anoints himself therewith." Sinuhe was provided with a country estate, newly renovated, and meals were brought to him from the palace. He was to spend the remainder of his days with every available comfort.

The narrative draws to a close with a description of the construction of the hero's final resting place. The sepulchre was endowed with priests and choice fields and was embellished with a gold-covered statue of Sinuhe. A prince would not have expected more: "It was His Majesty who brought this to pass. There is no poor man for whom the like has been done."

I. *The Literary Aspect.* The tale of Sinuhe is obviously the effort of an exceptional writer rather than the product of oral improvisation. It was put into writing at the start; there is no evidence of an extended developmental period. This is not to deny that the composition marks the culmination of a rich literary tradition nor that long and hard thought is implied. To the contrary, the author's heritage and talent must have been remarkable indeed. Were his name known, he would be listed among those who have bequeathed to posterity the classics of world literature. His work is a milestone in the history of civilization.

The language employed is not the vernacular of the time but rather the fruit borne by a stream of tradition whose fountainheads are shrouded in the mists of an uncharted past. The story unfolds in elegant prose interspersed with poetical passages. Every sentence is carefully phrased for vividness and variety. In a work only some 2700 words in length there are more than seven hundred lexical items. The rich vocabulary affords piquancy, freshness and color. Synonyms and alternative morphemes abound. Repetitive formulae are lacking. At no point does the tale drift into monotony.

We have no way of knowing to what extent professional storytellers circulated the account of Sinuhe's adventures. Suffice it to say that most likely it was told and retold as entertainment for the upper classes of Egyptian society, at least as long as the Twelfth Dynasty lasted (i.e., until 1786 B.C.). We do know that it was a favorite with scribes during the second millennium B.C., inasmuch as more than a score of documents, none of which preserves the tale in its entirety, have already come to light. The most important and earliest copy dates from about 1800 B.C., a century and a half after the historical events described in the narrative, and lacks only the beginning, which is supplied by another papyrus originating not much later in date. The other attestations, mostly quite fragmentary but all earlier than 1100 B.C., testify to a persisting popularity among men of letters.

II. *The Historical Nucleus.* Although the story is copiously supplied with embellishments, we cannot assert that it is sheer fabrication and devoid of historical content. The author does in fact display a thorough acquaintance with details pertaining to the early Twelfth Dynasty. For him to utilize the names of rulers proves nothing in itself, but he knows even the names of their pyramids and the name of a queen as well. He gives the correct length (thirty years) for the reign of Amenemhet I. The stationing of garrisons at the northeastern border out-

posts is a verifiable practise for the period, and friendly relations between Egypt and peoples to the northeast are attested elsewhere specifically for the reign of Sesostris I. In actuality, there is nothing in the story which conflicts with external evidence bearing on the history of the time in which it is set.

III. *The Purpose.* From beginning to end the romance extols Senusert I and likely was composed during this Pharaoh's incumbency (about 1962-1928 B.C.). He is first portrayed as the ideal monarch when Sinuhe assured his Syrian host that Egypt was in good hands after Amenemhet's death. This panegyric is in the form of a hymn to the new god-king and must have been the work of a contemporary writer. Elsewhere in the tale the author repeatedly brings up the deification of Senusert with epithets such as "the falcon," "the good god," "great god," and "peer" of Ra [the sun god]." Alongside this, another aspect of the king is quite evident in the last half of the story. There the author takes pains to portray Senusert as an amicable and kind human being, interested only in the welfare of his subjects. No longer is he the distant god, but rather a beneficent and understanding friend. He sent gifts to Sinuhe in Syria and urged him to spend his last days in Egypt, pointing out that our hero was guilty of no wrong. All was forgiven. A royal welcome awaited Sinuhe at It-towy, where Pharaoh resided. The story comes to a close with Sinuhe giving full credit to Senusert for the unexpected change in his circumstances. Here indeed is a sovereign for whom his subjects can only have praise.

That the two-fold depiction of Senusert in the tale of Sinuhe is an instance of propagandism can be taken as fairly certain. Senusert's predecessor, having founded a new dynasty by a *coup d'état,* had strengthened his claim to the throne by a "prophecy" foretelling his rise to power. Sesostris appears to have been no less wily a politician than Amenemhet, for he too had employed literary propaganda to bolster his position at the beginning of his reign: words put in the mouth of his deceased father tell of the latter's assassination and urge Sesostris to exercise caution as king of the land. It is in keeping with this tradition, then, for the tale of Sinuhe to have been composed on behalf of Pharaoh to augment the esteem which he desired from his courtiers and provincial rulers. Sinuhe eulogizes: "He is such a master of charm and so great in kindness that he has taken over by love. His city loves him more than itself; it is prouder of him than of its god. Men and women enthusiastically acclaim him now that he is king." Though these sentiments were first propagated at the beginning of his reign Senusert had much to gain by having them reiterated in his old age. Nearing the end of his reign he followed the practice of his father in sharing the throne with a son in order to secure the succession. It may be that he was taking no chances in view of the fate which had befallen his father. At any rate, whoever devised the tale about Sinuhe had in mind primarily the exaltation of Senusert I, and it could have been brought into being at the behest of the king himself.

IV. *The Hero.* It is altogether probable that the story was based upon an autobiographical inscription in the tomb of the hero. It begins, as is typical of the funerary texts, with a recitation of the titles which Sinuhe bore at the time of his death. It closes with him referring to his own demise, "I was the recipient of the king's favors until the day of mooring came," again in harmony with the tomb inscriptions.

Sinuhe's resting place has not been found and until it is there must remain the possibility that he is only a fictitious character. But if we assume that the hero had actually been associated with Senusert I, as seems more likely, the course of his life can be sketched from the information provided by the story.

The narrative opens with Sinuhe in a military capacity with the Libyan expeditionary force. To judge from his experiences in Syria, he was already a seasoned warrior of no mean ability, whether in single combat or at the head of troops. He was also adept in mapping out strategy. The art of warfare had apparently been a vital part of his early training at the court, where he served Amenemhet's daughter, Nefrou, who had been married to Senusert. At the time of the Libyan campaign he must have been a young man. He was born in all probability within a few years after Amen-

emhet founded the Twelfth Dynasty around 1991 B.C.

Sinuhe remained in exile long enough to establish a family and see his children grow to maturity. More than a score of years must have elapsed before he returned to his native land. He was by then an old man who abhorred, as could be expected of an Egyptian, the thought of burial outside the land of the Nile. We can surmise that he had passed the half-century mark when he again saw his sovereign's face. The story intimates that he died a few years thereafter, perhaps around 1930 B.C. He was interred in the burial place which had been prepared for him near El-Lisht.

The romance of Sinuhe would have been composed simultaneously with the hero's autobiographical tomb inscription. But even if the latter were to come to light, it would undoubtedly lack many elements found in the literary treatment which we presently have.

V. *The Land of Exile.* Apart from its worth as a literary masterpiece and a cleverly contrived bit of propaganda, the saga must be treasured for enabling us to realize how the Egyptians of the twentieth century B.C. viewed their neighbors to the north. The information provided therein concerning Syro-Palestine, though not abundant, can safely be regarded as trustworthy. The scantiness of details may be accounted for partly by the author's apparent lack of first-hand acquaintance with the places he described. The autobiography in Sinuhe's tomb could not have made up this deficiency, since it would have been devoted almost wholly to the courtier's relations with Senusert. Another factor which should not be overlooked in this regard is that whoever adapted the funerary inscription was writing for a generation which was not obsessed with curiosity about foreign lands. Four centuries later when Egypt expanded its empire into Asia under the kings of the Tuthmoside succession, the situation was quite different; then the Egyptians could not hear enough about the newly conquered states.

The author, being associated with the royal court, was in a good position to acquire accurate information about Syro-Palestine through the visits of envoys, merchants and others. That his knowledge is authoritative can be demonstrated. He depicts Syria, for instance, as a region divided politically into city states which have to contend with encroachments of non-sedentary peoples. This picture accords precisely with what archaeology has taught us concerning the history of the region during that era. The author's reliability carries even into the realm of onomastica: the prince with whom Sinuhe found asylum in Syria bears a Semitic name (Ammi-enshi) of a type now attested in Egyptian magical curses inscribed on pottery and clay figurines and dating from a century or two later than Sinuhe. (*See* Execration texts.) These same texts mention the land Keshu, the home of one of the three princes whom Sinuhe wished to bring with him on his return trip to Egypt.

It is not beyond the realm of possibility that sophisticated Egyptians at the pharaonic court had at this time a familiarity with epics of the peoples to the north. Sinuhe's three companions from Asia may have been known to the author of the romance as heroic figures of saga. It is difficult to account for their inclusion in the story on other grounds.

Embedded in the tale is the manner in which Senusert regarded his neighbors in Asia. From his point of view they are kindly disposed towards him and indeed towards Egyptians in general. This is brought out by a number of incidents. When Sinuhe was on the brink of death in the desert, his life was saved by a passing Bedouin tribe: "An attack of thirst had overtaken me. I was parched and my throat felt like dust. I thought that this was the taste of death. Then I took courage and pulled myself together, for I heard the bleating of flocks. Then I caught sight of some nomads. The sheik among them, who had been in Egypt, recognized me. He gave me water and heated milk for me. I went with him to his people and they treated me well." Perhaps it was the friendliness of Asiatics towards Egyptians in this period which had prompted Sinuhe to seek a haven among them in the first place.

Ammi-enshi, overlord of a region which Egyptians called Upper Retenu, assured Sinuhe, "You will prosper with me, and you will be hearing the language of Egypt," and again, "You shall stay with me and I will treat you well." We have every reason to believe that conditions among the peoples

of Syro-Palestine were so favorable that Egyptian colonists had settled in their midst. We are told that Ammi-enshi was anxious for Sinuhe to join him because "he knew my character and had heard of my capabilities; Egyptians who were there with him had vouched for me."

To be sure, Sinuhe encountered opposition in Syria, but even when he fought a Retenu warrior singlehandedly, most of the spectators were on his side. When he won, they hurrahed and Ammi-enshi embraced him.

That diplomatic exchanges were part of the picture is clear from Sinuhe's reception and entertainment of envoys going to and from the capital of Egypt. It is by this means, in fact, that the exile kept informed about conditions in his native land and that Senusert learned of Sinuhe's situation. Pharaoh was obviously maintaining close contact with the countries to the north.

BIBLIOGRAPHY. John W. B. Barns, *The Ashmolean Ostracon of Sinuhe*, Griffith Institute, Oxford, 1952. Alan H. Gardiner, *Notes on the Story of Sinuhe*, Librairie Honoré Champion, Paris, 1916. Cyrus H. Gordon, *Before the Bible*, Harper & Row, New York, 1962. Hermann Grapow, *Untersuchungen zur ägyptischen Stilistik. I. Der stilistische Bau der Geschichte des Sinuhe*, Akademie-Verlag, Berlin, 1952. Battiscombe Gunn, "The Adventures of Sinuhe," *Land of Enchanters*, ed. Bernard Lewis, Harvill Press, London, 1948. G. Posener, *Littérature et politique dans l'Égypte de la XIIᵉ Dynastie*, Librairie Ancienne Honoré Champion, Paris, 1956. John Wilson, "The Story of Sinuhe," *The Ancient Near East*, ed. James B. Pritchard, Princeton University Press, 1958.

SIPPAR. Sippar (Abu Habba) was a town on the Euphrates River in central Mesopotamia. It is one of five cities mentioned on the °Sumerian King List as having a dynasty of rulers before the flood. Hormuzd Rassam, best known for his excavation of Ashurbanipal's palace and library at Nineveh, began the search for Sippar in December 1880. Convinced that Abu Habba was the site, he began excavations in 1881, and on the very first day workmen brought out fragments of a barrel cylinder and of inscribed bricks. During the following eighteen months Rassam excavated a temple to the god Shamash, the sun god, which contained about 60,000 inscribed clay tablets. Unfortunately they were not baked, and thousands of them crumbled to pieces before they could be removed. They are largely business records,

*JEBEL USDUM is believed by many to mark the locale of ancient
Sodom. Courtesy, Charles F. Pfeiffer*

referring to the administration of the temple and its property. We read of the daily sacrifices to Shamash and other gods, the weaving of garments and the manufacture of jewelry and vessels, the building and repair of houses, and the execution of orders given in connection with the worship of the gods and the maintenance of the priesthood.

Since tithes were frequently paid in kind, depots were established along the principal canals where scribes stored and registered everything that came in. Among goods thus received were vegetables, meat, and other perishable objects which had to be sold or exchanged before they decayed or decreased in value. An ancient temple shared many functions with a mercantile establishment.

Literary tablets were found among the documents from Sippar. Astronomical and mathematical texts, hymns, mythological fragments, and a bilingual version of the creation story (*see* Enuma Elish), sign lists and grammatical exercises have come to light.

The °Nabonidus Chronicle tells how the army of Cyrus reached Sippar seventeen days before °Babylon fell. Sippar had continued from Sumerian to Chaldean times as a center of the worship of Shamash and a cultural center. The work begun by Rassam on behalf of the British Museum in excavating Sippar was continued by V. Scheil for the Ottoman Museum in 1894. In 1927 a German campaign was conducted by W. Andrae.

BIBLIOGRAPHY. Hormuzd Rassam, *Asshur and the Land of Nimrod,* Eaton and Mains, New York, 1897. Jean Vincent Scheil, *Une saisen de fouilles à Sippar,* L'Institut francois d' archeologie orientale, Cairo.

SIRQU. *See* Terqa.

SMYRNA. There are two Smyrnas. The first city, which lay at the northeast edge of the Gulf of Smyrna, was destroyed by the Lydians in the sixth century B.C. The inhabitants fled to nearby villages and their town lay in ruins until the fourth century, when, in the days of Alexander the Great, Smyrna was refounded — but this time at the southeast edge of the Gulf. This city, to which John addressed a message in the Revelation, lay about forty-two miles north of Ephesus by Roman road on a very excellent double harbor. The outer harbor was a portion of the gulf which served as a mooring ground; the inner harbor, now silted in and occupied by bazaars, had a narrow entrance that could be blocked by a chain.

The city itself curved around the edge of the bay at the foot of 525-foot Mount Pagus, its splendid acropolis. Its streets were excellently paved and drawn at right angles.

The city had several squares and porticoes, a public library, numerous temples and other buildings. Its aqueduct insured an ample water supply. This commercial center had a population which may have reached nearly 200,000 by the time John sent a message to its church.

The recovery of New Testament Smyrna by means of archaeological research is virtually impossible. The modern city covers the ancient one; and to make matters worse, the city was virtually destroyed by an earthquake in A.D. 178. The Emperor Marcus Aurelius rebuilt large areas of the metropolis.

In spite of the difficulty of excavation in Smyrna, the Turkish Historical Association has conducted numerous seasons of excavation there between World Wars I and II and since World War II. Their efforts have largely centered on the agora area, where much is yet to be done. Finds there date to the reconstruction of Marcus Aurelius and therefore have no bearing on New Testament times. A few remains of walls on the acropolis date back to the first century, as do ruins of the aqueduct and theater.

SODOM and GOMORRAH.

No traces of Sodom and Gomorrah have been found, but the site is thought to be in the area now submerged under the waters of the Dead Sea south of the peninsula el-Lisan ("the tongue"). That area was doubtless known as the Valley of Siddim, originally a fertile plain watered by the five streams which now flow from the east and southeast to this part of the Dead Sea. This is implied in the explanation, "the Valley of Siddim, that is, the Salt Sea" (Gen. 14:3).

Along the southern end of the west side of the Dead Sea is the 700 foot high mountain known as Jebel Usdum ("Mount Sodom"), largely a mass of crystalline salt about five miles long. Its name reflects the tradition that Sodom was located in this area.

The destruction of Sodom, Gomorrah, and the other cities of the valley may have been the result of lightning igniting the petroleum seepages and the gas which was plentiful in the region. About five miles from the shore of the Dead Sea at an elevation of five hundred feet, southeast of the Lisan Peninsula is °Bab ed-Dra', which served as a religious shrine for inhabitants of the area. Pottery indicates that the site was frequented from ca. 2300 to ca. 1900 B.C. This seems to indicate that Sodom and Gomorrah were destroyed ca. 1900 B.C., during the lifetime of Abraham. From near Hebron, Abraham looked in the direction of Sodom and Gomorrah and he saw that "the smoke of the land went up like the smoke of a furnace."

BIBLIOGRAPHY. J. Penrose Harland, "Sodom and Gomorrah: The Location and Destruction of the Cities of the Plain," *BA,* V, 1942, pp. 17-32; *BA,* VI, 1943, pp. 41-54.

SPHINX.

In Egyptian mythology a sphinx is a wingless monster with the body of a lion and the head of a man, a ram, or a hawk. The Sphinx at Gizeh is a monument two hundred feet long carved out of a natural outcropping of rock. At Sakkara there is an alley of one hundred forty sphinxes. In Greek mythology, a sphinx is a winged monster with a woman's head and breasts and a lion's body.

STELE, STELA.

The word stele is derived from the Greek *stele,* meaning "a standing block" or "a slab." As an archaeological term it refers to an upright stone slab bearing an inscription or a sculptured design. The Code of °Hammurabi was inscribed on a diorite stele which was set up in the temple of Marduk (the Esagila) in Babylon where it could be read by the people. Eannatum, an ancient king of Lagash (*ca.* 2500 B.C.)

STELE OF ESARHADDON showing the seed plow and other implements. Courtesy, British Museum

STELE OF SETI I, erected at Beth-shan by the Egyptian conqueror, and discovered during the campaign of the University Museum at Beisan (ancient Beth-shan). Courtesy, the University Museum

commemorated his victory over nearby Umma by erecting a limestone monument popularly known as the "Stele of the Vultures" which depicts the soldiers of Lagash marching to victory in a solid phalanx protected by shields, while vultures carry the corpses of the enemy from the field of slaughter. A basalt stele commemorating the victories of Mesha, King of Moab, over his Israelite foes (ca. 835 B.C.) was discovered at Dibon in 1868 (see Moabite Stone). Although stelae were commonly used by Israel's ancient neighbors, no Israelite stele has been excavated. A fragment containing but one Hebrew word was discovered at the site of ancient °Samaria.

STELE OF THE VULTURES. See Lagash.

STRATIGRAPHY. Stratigraphy is a term which archaeology has borrowed from geology. The study of stratigraphy in geology is based on the assumption that in the normal sequence of rock formation, the lower layers (or strata) are older. In archaeological work, likewise, it is assumed that pottery, implements, or other artifacts found in the upper strata are more recent than those found in lower strata. In the excavation of a mound, or °tell, careful archaeologists study the materials from each level separately, seeking to understand each artifact in the light of its proper sequence.

SULTAN TEPE. See Haran.

SUMER. At the dawn of history a people known as Sumerians had established themselves at the head of the Persian Gulf in southern Mesopotamia. Scholars suggest that they migrated into the lower Tigris-Euphrates Valley from the Caucasus Mountain region. In the Sumerian language the words for "country" and "mountain" are identical, and it was probably the Sumerians who built the first artificial mountains known as °ziggurats. They speak of themselves as "the black-headed people," in contrast to neighboring peoples of light-colored hair. It was the Sumerian invention of writing (see Alphabet) that marks the transition from prehistory to history, although a high culture had developed in prehistoric times.

The millennium from 3500 to 2500 B.C. saw the establishment of the first true cities along the banks of the Tigris and the Euphrates. The great cities of °Ur, °Nippur, °Lagash, °Uruk (Biblical Erech), °Kish, and Khafajah were built with massive walls and fortifications. Each was devoted to the worship of one of the Sumerian deities. Nippur was the city of Enlil and Ninlil; Uruk of Anu and Inanna; Ur of the moon god Nanna and his wife Ningal. A monumental temple dominated each city, and the local *ensi*, or ruler, was regarded as the viceroy of the city god. Unlike Egypt, where the Pharaoh was a god in his own right, the Sumerian *ensi* was a servant of the city god, charged with responsibility for looking after his interests.

The temple was the most important building of a Sumerian city. Farmers either brought a fixed portion of their produce to the temple, or served as temple employees. The temple maintained workshops where craftsmen were busy with carpentry, weaving, brewing, metal work, stone cutting, or jewel setting. They received their wages in barley and other commodities from the temple storehouses. The surplus products of Sumer — barley, wool, sesame oil, dates — were taken northward by caravan to be ex-

changed for stone and wood, neither of which were native to southern Mesopotamia.

From time to time the Sumerian states fought with one another, or with foreign powers. The first battles were probably fought over land and water rights. Warfare served as an impetus for developing metallurgy in ancient Sumer, as it has for developing nuclear power in modern times. A victorious conqueror considered the foreigners, or the fellow-Sumerians defeated in battle as part of the spoils of war. As a result, a slave class developed in the Sumerian city-states.

The Sumerians were not the only ethnic group in the territory north of the Persian Gulf. Iranians from the mountain districts east of the Tigris, and Semites from the west shared the valley with them. Properly speaking, Sumer was the territory from modern Baghdad south to the Persian Gulf and, after the dynasty of °Akkad the territory north of Sumer was called Akkad. In time, as Sumerians, Akkadians, and other peoples lived side by side, the culture of the lower Tigris-Euphrates valley became unified.

The Sumerian states arose as a result of the need for maintaining a system of dams

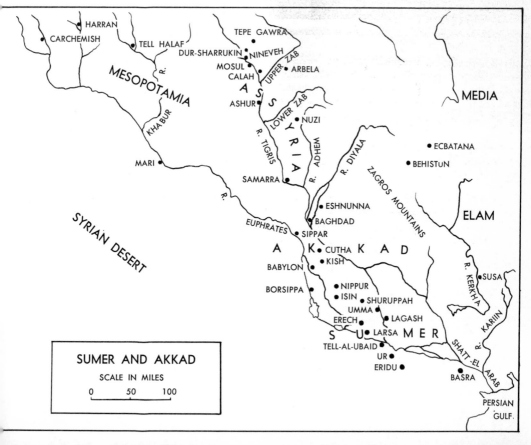

SUMER AND AKKAD
SCALE IN MILES
0   50   100

STANDING MALE FIGURE in the act of worship. From Tell Asmar. Courtesy, Oriental Institute

and canals to make use of the waters of the Tigris and the Euphrates. The terrain of southern Mesopotamia was such that materials for such farm equipment as hoes, sickles, spades, and hammers had to be imported from a distance. Each farmer was dependent upon trade for necessities as well as luxuries, with the result that he willingly submitted to the measure of government control that made trade possible. The temple, which was the center of business and government as well as religion, adopted a system of standard measurements which regulated all business transactions. When Abraham purchased a burial plot for his wife he "weighed out for Ephron the silver which he had named in the hearing of the Hittites, four hundred shekels of silver, according to the weights current among the merchants" (Gen. 23:17).

The first Sumerian ruler whose deeds are recorded was a legendary king of Kish named Etana. He is celebrated as "the man who stabilized all the lands," suggesting that he ruled over a wide area. Some years later we read of a king named Meskiaggasher who founded a dynasty at Erech. His son Enmerkar campaigned at "Aratta," a state which is thought to have been located west of the Caspian Sea in an area known for its rich deposits of metal and stone.

One of Enmerkar's warriors, Lugalbanda, succeeded him to the throne of Uruk. The exploits of Enmerkar and Lugalbanda form the basis for a series of Sumerian epic tales. By the end of Lugalbanda's reign, Uruk was threatened by the city-state of Kish which was rising to dominance in the south. Enmebaraggesi of Kish is known for his conquest of Elam, to the east of Sumer, and for the great temple which he built to the Sumerian god of the air, Enlil, in Nippur. Enmebaraggesi's dynasty was shortlived, however. His son Agge was checked by Mes-Anne-Pada of the rising state of Ur.

The Classical Sumerian Period (2700-2250 B.C.) is the time when the cities of Ur, Kish, Umma, and Lagash flourished. According to the °Sumerian King List, the first king of Ur, Mes-Anne-Pada, reigned for eighty years. He was a powerful ruler who saw to it that the state of Ur was furnished with an adequate supply of raw materials. A temple inscription states, "A-anne-pada, son of Mes-Anne-Pada, has built a temple for Ninhursag." Since A-anne-pada is not mentioned in the King List, it appears probable that the eighty year reign of the father included that of the son. Thus Mes-Anne-Pada's eighty years are to be taken as the period of his dynasty.

The remarkable "Royal Cemetery" excavated by C. Leonard Woolley during his 1927-30 campaign at Ur, probably dates from the time of Mes-Anne-Pada. Under a layer of graves containing seals and inscriptions from the Akkad dynasty (2360-2180 B.C.) were tombs which are thought to date from around 2500 B.C. Many graves of

SUMER

commoners were found with bodies wrapped in matting or placed in coffins of wood, wickerwork, or clay. The graves contained the personal belongings of the deceased — bracelets, necklaces, vanity cases, tools, and weapons, — besides food and drink. Most of the bodies were placed on their sides in a sleeping position. Their hands held a cup to the mouth.

As Woolley continued his excavating he came upon the so-called "Royal tombs" in rooms made of brick or of stone. One tomb contained a cylinder seal with the name Abargi. Against the tomb wall stood a silver model of a boat similar to those which can still be seen plying the marshes of southern Mesopotamia.

Above the vault of Abargi was the tomb of a lady who was identified by a lapis lazuli cylinder as Shubad. Her body had been placed on a wooden bier, and she had a golden cup in her hand. She wore an elaborate headdress made with nine yards of gold band. The comb in her hair had five points which ended in golden flowers with centers of lapis lazuli. Crescent-shaped earrings added a further touch of ornamentation.

Connected with the tombs of both Abargi and Shubad were death pits which reveal the least attractive side of Sumerian culture. These, along with other pits nearby, contained the remains of chariots which had been driven into them. Treasures were there, in honor of the deceased. The remains of large numbers of people who died at the time of the funeral were also in the pits. Some suggest that these bodies were of priests and priestesses sacrificed in fertility rites (cf. E. A. Speiser in *Antiquity*, VIII, 1934, p. 45). Others suggest that servants of a king (or priest) would willingly accompany him in death with the hope that they might continue to be of service in the next life. Evidence indicates that the victims went into the death pit willingly.

We gain some knowledge of music in ancient Sumer from the harps or lyres found in the tombs. The animal heads used for ornamentation include a bearded bull, a cow, and a stag. Each of two statuettes from Ur represented a goat standing in front of a bush from which it appears to be eating leaves. Woolley likened these to the Biblical "ram caught in a thicket" (Gen.

22:13) although the Sumerian figures are at least half a millennium earlier than Abraham.

A beautiful golden dagger came from the tomb of a warrior identified as "Meskalamdug, hero of the Good Land." The hero's body was in the usual burial position, and between his hands there was a beautiful cup of heavy gold. The dagger was hanging from a broad silver belt at his side. Over the skull was a helmet in the form of a wig, with locks of hair hammered in relief, and individual hairs engraved in delicate lines.

In one of the large stone tombs, Woolley discovered the "Standard of Ur," a wooden panel, 22 inches long by 9 inches high, which was probably carried by the Sumerians on a pole during ceremonial or military processions. It was inlaid with mosaic work on both sides, one of which depicted scenes of war, and the other scenes of peace. The wooden background had rotted away, but

A SUMERIAN PRIEST from Tell Asmar. Courtesy, Oriental Institute

547

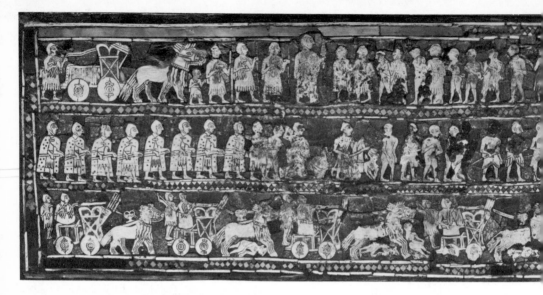

THE STANDARD OF UR (showing scenes of war). Courtesy, British Museum

the pieces of inlay kept their relative positions, and skillful work on the part of the archaeologists made it possible to restore the mosaics with perfect fidelity. Each side comprised three rows made of shell figures set in a lapis lazuli background.

The "war" side shows the king, distinguished by his height, dismounted from his chariot. Soldiers are bringing him a group of naked captives with arms tied behind their backs. In the second row, the phalanx of the royal army is advancing. The men, armed with axes, wear long cloaks and copper helmets. Ahead of them light infantrymen, without cloaks but armed with axes or short javelins, are fighting. On the third row we see chariots of javelin throwers who break into an excited gallop as they encounter corpses strewn on the ground.

The reverse side, showing a peaceful motif, depicts the king and his family enjoying a feast. Musicians are playing, and servants bring food for the banquet. The spoils of war are in evidence. The people are dressed in characteristic Sumerian sheepskin kilts, with the upper parts of their bodies bare.

Other Sumerian states came to the fore in the decades following the reign of Mes-Anne-Pada. Uruk had the great Gilgamesh as its ruler, and in later Sumerian history and legend he would be remembered as Sumer's supreme hero. Lugalannemunda of Adab is said to have ruled from the Iranian mountains to the Mediterranean, from the Taurus Range to the Persian Gulf. Mesilim of Kish

is remembered for the temples he built at Adab and Lagash. As overlord of Sumer he was called upon to settle a border dispute between Lagash and Umma. He measured off a just boundary and had a stele erected to mark the spot for the benefit of future generations. Lagash and Umma were traditional rivals. Eannatum of Lagash gained hegemony over all Sumer, and his successor Urukagina is known for his social reforms. As an ideal king he is said to have espoused the cause of the poor, to have helped the widow and the orphan, and to have sought to limit the bureaucracy of his day. Urukagina was overthrown by Lugalzaggesi of Umma who destroyed Lagash and claims to have gained the loyalty of fifty princes throughout the land. Lugalzaggesi, however, proved no match for the energetic Semite, Sargon of Akkad whose conquests brought the Classical Sumerian period to an end.

The last great period of Sumerian power and civilization is known as the third dynasty of Ur (Ur III), founded by Ur-Nammu and lasting from about 2110 to 2015 B.C. Ur-Nammu was able to wrest power from the Gutians, a little-known mountain people who had overrun lower Mesopotamia following the breakup of the Akkadian dynasty. He rebuilt the walls of Ur and restored the city's ziggurat, palace, and numerous public buildings.

A contemporary record of the building of the °ziggurat is given on the Stele of Ur-Nammu, a slab of white limestone nearly five feet across and ten feet high. The top panel depicts the king in an attitude of prayer. Above him are flying angels carrying vases from which water is flowing. This, so far as is known, is our first artistic representation of angels. The king appears to be thanking his god for the gift of water, so needful in southern Mesopotamia. A series of panels is then devoted to the building of the ziggurat. In the first of these, Ur-Nammu stands before the goddess Ningal and the god Nanna receiving orders for the building. The next panel shows him with compasses, mortar basket, pick and trowel, going forth to the work. The final panel is poorly preserved, but on it a workman can be seen leaning against the side of the rising structure.

As other buildings were erected around the ziggurat, an extensive sacred area developed. One of these buildings, the Gigparku temple, dedicated to Ningal, had a well equipped kitchen. Included in its furnishings were a well for water, fireplaces for boiling the water, a bitumen-covered brick table for cutting up the carcase of an animal, a flat-topped cooking range, and a domed oven. The kitchen was an important part of ancient temples, since animals were offered in sacrifice and the cooked flesh was shared among the god, his priests, and the worshipers.

Our knowledge of business life in the Ur III period comes largely from about two thousand cuneiform tablets which record the offerings and taxes given to Nannar, the moon god. Records were carefully kept by the temple scribes, and weekly, monthly, and annual reports were assembled. The excavators came upon the records of a weaving factory which produced twelve varieties of woolen cloth. The tablets give the names of the women who did the weaving, the rations allotted to them, the quantity of wool issued to each, and the amount of cloth manufactured.

Fragments of the law code of Ur-Nammu have been identified among the Sumerian texts at the Museum of the Ancient Orient, Istanbul. The texts state that Ur-Nammu was chosen by the god Nannar to rule over Ur and Sumer. Ur-Nammu had removed dishonesty and corruption, and had established honest weights and measures. The few laws which are legible mention fines to be imposed upon men who have caused specified injuries to others.

The Sumerian law court met in the temple area. The Dublal-mah, the "Great House of Tablets," was the building in which the records of legal decisions were preserved on clay tablets. From the door of the Dublal-mah, judges announced their decisions to the waiting crowds.

Following the death of Ur-Nammu, the city of Ur began to lose its prestige. His son Shulgi proclaimed himself "the divine Shulgi, god of his land," but his greatest

THE STANDARD OF UR (showing scenes of peace). Courtesy, British Museum

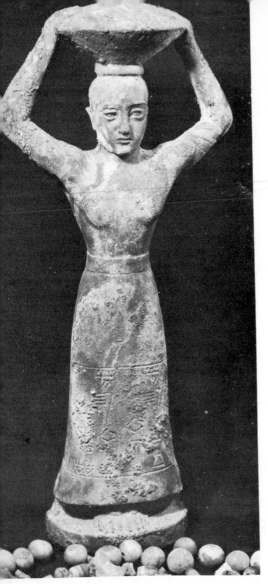

Ibi-Sin was taken captive. About 1720 B.C., Hammurabi, an Amorite ruler of Babylon, defeated Rim-Sin of Larsa in extending Babylonian power throughout southern Mesopotamia.

During the two and one-half centuries during which Isin and Larsa vied for dominance, there were several attempts at rebuilding Ur. Ishme-Dagon of Isin dedicated his daughter as high priestess to Nannar, and rebuilt the Nannar temple in Ur. Warad-Sin of Larsa undertook to rebuild the ziggurat at Ur. When Ur rebelled against Hammurabi's son Samsuiluna, he destroyed the city and we hear no more of it for centuries. Sumer was part of the Babylonian empire and Sumerian history, as such, was at an end.

The end of Sumerian political history did not mean the end of Sumerian culture, for Sumerian culture had a relationship to the lands of western Asia analogous to the relationship between Graeco-Roman culture and the life of Europe. The Sumerians developed a system of °cuneiform writing which was subsequently adopted by Babylonians, Assyrians, and Hittites, and adapted for use in the Canaanite alphabet of °Ugarit. Cuneiform writing, beginning among the Sumerians before 3000 B.C. continued in use until the first century B.C. when it was finally displaced by the less cumbersome alphabetic writing (see Alphabet).

In the field of mathematics, the Sumerians have given us our sexagesimal system, which finds modern expression in the sixty-second minute, the sixty-minute hour and the 360 degree circle. In the area of law, the Code of °Hammurabi written in Semitic Akkadian rests on earlier Sumerian precedent, as exemplified in the Ur-Nammu and Lipit Ishtar Sumerian codes.

Later Akkadian literature owes a continuing debt to the earlier Sumerian texts. The °Enuma Elish and the °Gilgamesh Epic can be traced to Sumerian antecedents. The gods of the Sumerians re-appear in Semitic guise. Sumerian Nannar becomes Semitic Sin; Sumerian Innana becomes Semitic Ishtar; in the same way in which Greek Zeus corresponds to Roman Jupiter. Sumerian loan words entered the Semitic languages of the Near East, and some appear in our Hebrew Bible. The Sumerians called a temple or a palace an É GAL, literally "big

BRONZE STATUETTE OF KING UR-NAMMU, depicting the king as a humble basket carrier during the building of a temple. About 2100 B.C. Courtesy, Oriental Institute

monument was his mortuary temple and sepulchre, which Woolley excavated. Shulgi was followed successively by Bur-Sin, Gimil-Sin, and Ibi-Sin.

Drastic changes were taking place in southern Mesopotamia during the days of Ibi-Sin. Ishbi-Irra, an Amorite from °Mari overran Akkad and occupied Isin. Elamites crossed the Tigris, took Sumer and placed their vassal, an Amorite named Naplanum on the throne of Larsa. Ur was sacked, and

house." Ultimately this became Hebrew *hekal*, also meaning palace or temple.

BIBLIOGRAPHY, Samuel N. Kramer, *History Begins at Sumer*, Thames and Hudson, London, 1961. *Sumerian Mythology*, Harper and Brothers, New York, 1961; *The Sumerians: Their History Culture, and Character*, University of Chicago Press, Chicago, 1963. George A. Barton, *The Royal Inscriptions of Sumer and Akkad*, Yale University Press, New Haven, 1929. Edward Chiera, *Sumerian Epics and Myths*, University of Chicago Press, Chicago, 1934. *Sumerian Religious Texts*, Crozier Theological Seminary, Upland, Pa., 1924. Edmund I. Gordon, *Sumerian Proverbs*, University Museum, Philadelphia, 1959. *See also* under Ur.

SUMERIAN KING LIST.

The first fragments of the Sumerian King list were published in 1906. Since 1923 the standard text has been the Weld-Blundell prism which became the basis for the publication of the List by S. Langdon in the *Oxford Edition of Cuneiform Texts*, Vol. II, Oxford, 1923, plates I-IV, pp. 13ff. A detailed study of the Weld-Blundell prism and its variants from other sources appears in *The Sumerian King List* by Thorkild Jacobsen, Assyriological Studies No. 11, Chicago, 1939.

The King List was compiled sometime between 2250 and 2000 B.C., probably during the reign of Utu-hegal of Uruk. Utu-hegal liberated Sumer from the Gutians, and may have wished to show that his country had always been ruled by one king even though different capital cities were the centers of successive dynasties. The compiler of the list made use of records available to him which named the kings, along with the places and the lengths of their reigns. He also had a body of epic texts and local traditions concerning the heroes of Sumerian antiquity. The result is a list which becomes more reliable the closer it comes to the time of Utu-hegal, but which has value even in its earlier records to the extent that they throw light on Sumerian traditions concerning a long past heroic age.

The King List begins with the statement: "When kingship was lowered from heaven kingship was (first) in Eridu." There follows the list of eight kings who reigned a total of 241,200 years before the flood. They appear in the following order:

CITY	KING	YEARS OF RULE
Eridu	Alulim	28,800
	Alalgar	36,000
Bad-tibira	En-men-lu-Anna	43,200
	En-men-gal-Anna	28,800
	Dumu-zi	36,000
Larak	En-sipa-zi-Anna	28,800
Sippar	En-men-dur-Anna	21,000
Shuruppak	Ubar-Tutu	18,600

The King List then inserts a summary: "These are five cities, eight kings ruled them for 241,000 years. (Then) the Flood swept over (the earth)."

After the flood "when kingship was lowered (again) from heaven, kingship was (first) in Kish." Seventy-eight kings are named as rulers of various dynasties in Kish, Uruk, Ur, Awan, Hamazi, Adab, Mari and Akshak. The kings include names familiar from Sumerian mythology such as Etana, Gilgamesh, Emmerkar, and Lugalbanda. A

THE SUMERIAN KING LIST gives the earliest tradition of rulers who reigned before the flood, and of later rulers whose reigns reached to historical times. Courtesy, Ashmolean Museum

Sumerian poem entitled "Gilgamesh and Agga" treats the two as contemporary, although the King List names Gilgamesh as fifth ruler of the First Dynasty of Uruk whereas Agga is listed as last king of the First Dynasty of Kish. This suggests that the dynasties of the King List overlap.

*Berossos, a priest of Marduk at Babylon during the reign of Antiochus I (281-261 B.C.), compiled a list of ten antediluvian kings which has many points of comparison with the list of eight in the Sumerian text. Berossos includes Xisouthros, the hero of the flood who is not in the Sumerian list, and two corruptions of the name En-men-lu-Anna. Except for the inflation in numbers (a total of 432,000 years in Berossos as compared with 241,209 in the Sumerian List), the two are otherwise substantially the same.

The Bible lists ten patriarchs prior to the flood (Adam, Seth, Enosh, Kenan, Mahalalel, Jared, Enoch, Methuselah, Lamech, and Noah) but it is difficult to find direct relationships between the Biblical names and those in the Sumerian King List or Berossos. That longevity was believed to have been greater before the flood is attested among the Sumerians as well as in the Biblical records. Methuselah, who lived 969 years according to Genesis 5:27, had a life span much shorter than that of any of the rulers of the Sumerian List, only one of whom (Ubar-Tutu) reigned less than 20,000 years. In general the longevity of the Sumerian rulers is reduced as the historical period is reached. Within the Bible, too, there is a general reduction in longevity in the period after the flood. Abraham's life span was 175 years (Gen. 25:7); that of Moses, 120 (Deut. 34:7); and subsequently seventy (Psalm 90:10) was regarded as the norm.

BIBLIOGRAPHY. Thorkild Jacobsen, *The Sumerian King List,* University of Chicago Press, Chicago, 1939. Arno Poebel, *The Second Dynasty of Isin according to a New King List Tablet,* University of Chicago Press, Chicago, 1955.

SUPPILULIUMAS.

Suppiluliumas, a Hittite king who reigned from 1375-1335 B.C., has been called the Charlemagne of the Near East. The archives of *Boghazköy indicate that the city was at one time merely the headquarters of one tribe or section of the Hittite confederacy, but when its king became the Great King of all the Hittites, his city became the capital of an empire and the repository of the official correspondence between the Hittites and surrounding nations. His father Hattusilis is called simply "King of the city of Kussar," a name otherwise unknown. Suppiluliumas succeeded in uniting the Hittite tribes into a powerful state and founded a dynasty. He was apparently a military genius, but also possessed an unusual sense of religious tolerance and political justice.

The excavations at Amarna have brought to light a letter from Suppiluliumas to Akhenaton, congratulating him on his succession to the throne of Egypt. This king, also known as Amenhotep IV, ruled Egypt *ca.* 1370-1350 B.C., and is noted for his attempts to reform the worship of Egypt from its polytheism to the worship of the sun's disc, Aton. Sayce attributed the source of this inspiration to the mother of Amenhotep IV, who was from Mitanni. The Hittite monuments bear witness to the prevalence of this worship in Northern Syria, and at Boghazköy the winged solar disc has been carved by Hittite sculptors upon the rock. Suppiluliumas was fond of referring to himself in treaties as "My Sunship." Other titles were "Labarnas, the Great King, the Favorite of the Weather-god." Whatever may have been the origin of the worship of the sun's disc in Egypt, this religious reform by Akhenaton so weakened the country that the Hittites were not hindered by Egypt in their empire-building during this period.

Early in the reign of Suppiluliumas, about 1370 B.C., he led his army in an invasion through the Taurus passes into Syria which was repulsed with heavy losses. Tushratta, King of Mitanni, was able to forward a part of the loot to his ally, the King of Egypt. The next attack was more carefully planned. The Hittites crossed the Euphrates at Malatya in order to take the Mitannian kingdom from the rear. In order to secure peace on his left flank, Suppiluliumas married his sister to the ruler of Hayasa. The lost province of Isuwa was soon recovered, and the Mitannian capital, Wassaukkanni, was entered and sacked. The Syrian princes then made peace with the Hittites, except for the ruler of Kadesh, who was overwhelmed by the Hittite chariotry. Suppiluliumas then penetrated as far south as Abina, the Hobah of Genesis 14:15. As a result of this brilliant expedition, Halap (Aleppo) and Alalakh (Atchana) became Hittite. However, Carchemish, which controlled the main Euphrates crossing, remained hostile. At this point Suppiluliumas was recalled to his capital by pressing affairs at home.

Documents show that when he married his sister to the king of the land of Hayasa, he sent along with the bride her half-sisters. Since her husband was Hurrian, he observed some customs which were barbaric by Hittite standards. He therefore found it necessary to warn the groom that sibling marriage and freedom of sexual relations among kinsfolk could not be tolerated. "In Hattusas anyone who commits such an act does not keep his life; he is killed."

When Suppiluliumas returned about 1340 B.C. to complete his task, a siege of only eight days was required to reduce the fortress of Carchemish, and Syria from the Euphrates to the sea became a Hittite protectorate. While he was encamped before Carchemish he received an unusual request from the queen of Egypt, widow of Tutankhamun: "My husband has died and I have no son, but of you it is said that you have many sons. If you would send me one of your sons, he could become my husband." After thorough investigation, Suppiluliumas decided the request was sincere, and sent one of his sons. The Hittite prince was murdered upon his arrival in Egypt, apparently by the priestly party there.

Suppiluliumas appointed his son Telepinus "priest" of Kizzuwatna, which may have meant an outright annexation of some part of this territory or an attempt to gain religious influence there by occupation of this decisive position. This city was probably on Syria's border, outside of Anatolia proper, because the treaty which Suppiluliumas made with Sunassuras, the ruler of the city, existed both in an Akkadian and a Hittite version. The former language was reserved for countries outside Anatolia. The country of Kizzuwatna is required by the treaty to aid Suppiluliumas if attacked by Hurri or Arzawa, adjoining countries. Its territory probably was that later known as Cilicia, with the possibility that Tarsus is to be identified with the city of Kizzuwatna.

The treaty which Suppiluliumas made with Mattiwaza, a king of Mitanni, affords a parallel to the blessings and curses of Deuteronomy 28. A portion of this treaty is quoted below:

(These gods) by the words of this treaty shall be present, and shall be witnesses: If you, Mattiwaza, the son of the king, and the Kharri-people with your land, your wives, and all your possessions, the lords of the oath shall destroy. . . . And you, Mattiwaza, together with the other wife whom you shall take, and the Kharri-people with their wives, their children and their lands, shall have no posterity. And these gods, the lords of the oath, shall bring poverty and misery upon you.

If you, Mattiwaza, the son of the king, and the Kharri-people keep this treaty, then shall you, Mattiwaza, with thy wife (daughter of the Hittite king), thy sons and thy grandchildren, you, the Kharri-people with their wives, their children, these gods will guard, and the land of Mitanni shall as formerly . . . lie peaceful in its place.

Suppiluliumas and his eldest son Arnuwandas III died during a pestilence in 1435 B.C., four years after the death of Tutankhamun. Mursilis II became the next Hittite king. (See Hittites.)

BIBLIOGRAPHY. C. W. Ceram (Pseudonym), Kurt W. Marek, *Narrow Pass, Black Mountain: The Discovery of the Hittite Empire,* Trans. by Richard and Clara Winston, Victor Gollanz Ltd., in assoc. with Sidgwick and Jackson Ltd., London, 1956. A. E. Cowley, *The Hittites, The Schweich Lectures for 1918,* Pub. for the British Academy by Humphrey Milford, Oxford University Press, London, 1926. John Garstang, *The Hittite Empire,* Constable and Co., London, 1929; *The Land of the Hittites,* Constable and Co. Ltd., 1910. Albrecht Goetze, *Kizzuwatna and the Problem of Hittite Geography, Yale Oriental Series,* Researches, Vol. XXII, Yale University Press, New Haven, 1940. O. R. Gurney, *The Hittites,* A Pelican Book, Penguin Books, Ltd., Harmondsworth, Middlesex, 1952. David George Hogarth, *Kings of the Hittites, The Schweich Lectures for 1924,* Published for the British Academy by Humphrey Milford, Oxford University Press, London, 1926. Ira Maurice Price, Ovid R. Sellers, and E. Leslie Carlson, *The Monuments and the Old Testament,* The Judson Press, Philadelphia, 1958.

SUSA. Susa, the capital of ancient Susiana, had a geographical and historical orientation which differed from the other cities of ancient Persia. It was located about 150 miles north of the Persian Gulf in the steppe country east of the Tigris which is really a continuation of the southern Mesopotamian plain. The mountains of Luristan begin north of Susa, but the city itself is situated on a low spur of gravel and clay which is naturally

THE MOUND OF SUSA from the air. Courtesy, Oriental Institute

raised above normal floods but conveniently situated for exploiting the alluvial plain of the Karum River (the Biblical Ulai, Dan. 8:2).

Excavations began at Susa over a century ago when William K. Loftus dug there in connection with his Warka (*see* Uruk) excavation. Although the work was primitive by modern standards, Loftus proved that he had located Biblical Shushan (Susa). His conclusions were published in his book *Travels and Researches in Chaldea and Susiana* (London and New York, 1857). In 1884 Marcel Dieulafoy excavated the Susa acropolis and sent back to the Louvre the Archer Frieze and bull capital.

The great name in the archaeology of Susa is the French scholar Jacques de Morgan, who made an archaeological survey of Persia in 1889 and resigned his post as director of antiquities in Egypt (1897) to head the *Delegation en Perse* which was working at Susa. The most spectacular discovery of the early years of de Morgan's labors was the diorite stele of the Code of °Hammurabi which was found in three pieces in December 1901 and January 1902. Early in 1902 the stele was transported to Paris, and in

September of the same year Pere Victor Scheil, a Dominican Assyriologist, published the text with a transliteration and a translation.

Roland de Mocquenem became architect for the Susa expedition in 1903, and he took over its direction from 1912 to 1939. In 1946, Roman Ghirshman became his successor.

The excavations have provided evidence that Susa was occupied from about 4000 B.C. to A.D. 1200. The remains of the earliest settlements are about twenty-seven yards beneath the top of the citadel mound. There are two archaic levels, separated by about twelve yards each with a distinctive type of painted pottery. During the latter part of the fourth millennium B.C a sizable village was located at Susa. About two thousand graves have been identified in the cemetery. Copper utensils were in use at this time, and potters had learned to use the wheel in producing their ceramic ware.

Before 3000 B.C. an undeciphered proto-Elamite type of writing was used at Susa. The script was semi-pictographic and, although it seems to have originated under Mesopotamian influence, it was distinct in its development. From Susa it penetrated to the heart of the Iranian plateau and continued in use for many centuries.

By the first quarter of the third millennium B.C., people known as *Elamites occupied the plains of Susiana. The Semitic conqueror *Sargon of Akkad seems to have conquered Susa (*ca.* 2360 B.C.) for his stele was excavated there. Shortly afterward, however, Elamites built installations at the center of the acropolis hill.

De Morgan discovered the victory stele of Sargon's grandson Naram-Sin at Susa. Naram-Sin was called upon to put down revolts throughout his empire, and Susa was governed by one of his appointees. Akkadian began to supplant Elamite as the state language and Semitic names became common. Assimilation was far from complete, however. A local governor, Puzur-Inshushinak, who had been appointed by Naram-Sin, developed a nationalist movement, and soon Elam embarked on its own policy of conquest. At the death of Naram-Sin, Puzur-Inshushinak proclaimed his independence and invaded Babylonia.

The hill peoples north of Susa took advantage of the weakness of the last kings of the Akkadian dynasty, and *ca.* 2180 B.C. the *Gutians overran Lower Mesopotamia. A little more than a century later (*ca.* 2070) the Sumerians experienced a period of cultural and political revival in what is known as the Third Dynasty of Ur. After about a century, Ur itself was attacked by Elamites, and Elamite power continued unchecked until the reign of Hammurabi of Babylon (1728-1686 B.C.).

Elamites and Babylonians alike were dominated by the Kassites from the mountains of Luristan from about 1650 to 1175 B.C. During the twelfth century B.C., however, Elam entered her golden age. Under Shilhak-Inshushinak (1165-1151 B.C.) and his successors, the sanctuaries of Susa were embellished by trophies of war. It was at this time that the stele bearing the Code of Hammurabi reached Susa, along with the Naram Sin stele and a statue of the Babylonian god Marduk.

With the reign of Nebuchadnezzar I of Babylon, Elam again met serious opposition. Nebuchadnezzar I ruled at the end of the second millennium B.C. (*n.b.* He should not be confused with Nebuchadnezzar II,

the Neo-Babylonian or Chaldean ruler who conquered Jerusalem, 587 B.C.). He attacked Elam, seized Susa, and restored the statue of Marduk to his temple at Babylon.

About 900 B.C. the Medes began a series of attacks upon Elam. In quick succession the Assyrians and the Babylonians considered Susa legitimate prey. Sargon II and Sennacherib both attacked the city and Ashurbanipal boasted that he had destroyed it. In the winter of 596 B.C. the Chaldean ruler Nebuchadnezzar II attacked Susa (cf. Jer. 59:34-38).

When Cyrus of Anshan began the series of conquests which were to produce the mighty Persian Empire, the position of Susa was radically altered. Under the successors of Cyrus, Susa shared with Persepolis, Ecbatana, and Ctesiphon the honors of being a royal city. Nehemiah was at Susa as a palace servant to Artaxerxes I when he received the disturbing report concerning affairs in Jerusalem (Neh. 2:1). It was to Susa that Esther was brought in the days of Ahasuerus (Xerxes I), and in the palace there that she prevailed upon the king to issue an edict which would permit the Jews to defend themselves from the attack of their enemies.

A tradition dating back to Benjamin of Tudela (A.D. 1170) places the tomb of Daniel in a mosque north of Susa. There is actually no evidence that Daniel ever visited Susa, but we are told that he was there "in a vision" (Dan. 8:2). Louis Ginzberg in his *Legends of the Jews* (IV, 350) tells of dissension that is said to have broken out among the Jews of Susa because the grave of Daniel was on the side of the city in which the wealthy Jews lived. The poor citizens who lived on the other side of the river wanted to share the good fortune that Daniel's grave would bring. It was determined that the bier of Daniel would be moved back and forth on alternate years, until the Persian king had the bier suspended from chains precisely in the middle of the bridge spanning the river!

SYCHAR. John 4 records the encounter of Jesus with a Samaritan woman from the town of Sychar who came to draw water from the well named for the patriarch Jacob. The name Sychar does not appear elsewhere in Scripture, and it has been traditionally identified with Shechem. Excavations at Shechem indicate that the town was not occupied in New Testament times, and current scholarship tends to identify Sychar with the village El-Askar, on the eastern slope of Mount Ebal about half a mile north of Jacob's well.

SYNAGOGUE. Philo, Josephus, and the New Testament regularly use the word synagogue to designate Jewish places of worship distinct from the Temple in Jerusalem. Jews of the exile and the dispersion, deprived of access to the Temple, gathered for prayer and the study of the Scriptures. Such gatherings, doubtless informal in the beginning, developed into the institution of the synagogue which continued as a focal point of Jewish life in Palestine as well as abroad.

In the first century A.D. most cities and villages had synagogues (cf. Matt. 4:23; 9:25). On the sabbath day Jesus regularly attended the synagogue at Nazareth (Luke 4:16), and, later, at Capernaum (Luke 4:31). A synagogue excavated at *Capernaum, dating from the second or third centuries, A.D., is probably built on the site of the synagogue in which Jesus ministered.

Archaeological excavations have brought to light the remains of fifty synagogues in Palestine. Most of them are in Galilee and dated from the time that the bulk of the Jewish population moved to Galilee — from the end of the second century onward. See Capernaum, Dura Europus.

SYRACUSE. Syracuse, a city on the east coast of Sicily, was colonized by Greeks in the eighth century B.C. The Romans took the city in 212 B.C., after which Syracuse became the residence of the governor of

SEVEN BRANCHED CANDLESTICK with the shophar (right) and lulab (left). From a synagogue of New Testament times at Kefr Birim. Courtesy, the Louvre.

Sicily. In 21 B.C. Augustus gave the city the rank of a colony. Cicero described Syracuse as the largest of Greek cities and the largest of all cities. On the island were temples to Diana and Minerva and the palace of the governors. On the mainland were the forum, town hall, senate house, and temple to Olympian Zeus (Roman Jupiter).

The ruins of Syracuse include the temple of Athena, built in the fifth century B.C. and transformed into a Christian cathedral in the seventh century A.D. There is a large fifth century B.C. theater and an amphitheater built by Augustus. Christian catacombs of the third and fourth century have also been preserved.

T

TAANACH. The ancient Canaanite and later Israelite city of Taanach occupied the mound now known as Tell Ta'annek. This mound rises sharply 150 feet above the southern edge of the rich Esdraelon plain and has a summit measuring eleven acres. It lies five miles southeast of *Megiddo and six miles northwest of modern Jenin. It

commanded several ancient roads, one leading from Shechem and Samaria to the plain of Acre, the other from the plain of Sharon to the plain of Esdraelon.

Tell Ta'annek was first excavated in 1902-04 by Ernst Sellin, then professor at Vienna. Though his methods of digging, recording, and pottery analysis were primitive by

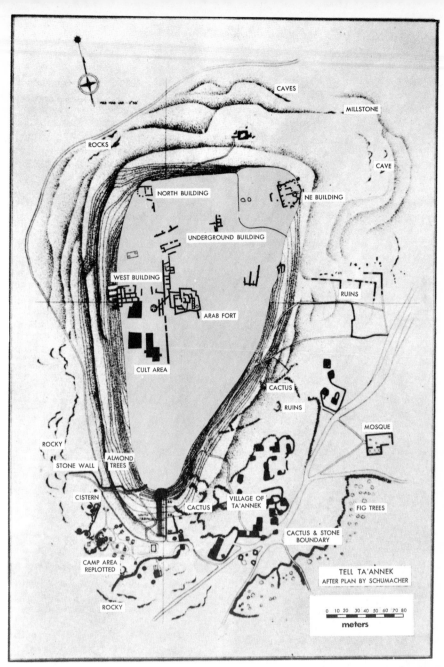

CAVES

MILLSTONE

ROCKS

CAVE

NORTH BUILDING

NE BUILDING

UNDERGROUND BUILDING

WEST BUILDING

RUINS

ARAB FORT

CULT AREA

CACTUS

RUINS

MOSQUE

ROCKY

ALMOND
TREES

STONE WALL

CISTERN

CACTUS

VILLAGE OF
TA'ANNEK

FIG TREES

CAMP AREA
REPLOTTED

CACTUS & STONE
BOUNDARY

TELL TA'ANNEK
AFTER PLAN BY SCHUMACHER

ROCKY

0 10 20 30 40 50 60 70 80

meters

present-day standards, his report does not suffer from comparison with contemporary reports in the then infant science of Palestinian archaeology. Sellin cut a patchwork of trenches in an attempt to find the fortifications and the main plan of the city. He was never able to discover a city wall and so incorrectly assumed that Taanach had no defense other than that afforded by various larger buildings on the mound which he termed "fortresses."

The site was again dug in 1963 in the first of a projected series of seasons by a Concordia-American School of Oriental Research team under the direction of Paul Lapp, director of the American School in Jerusalem. The American expedition restricted its work to the southwestern quadrant of the mound, excavating four areas. They checked the German excavations at three points: the West Building, the environs of the cultic incense stand, and the south trench.

I. *Taanach in Ancient Literature.* Taanach is first mentioned in the fifteenth century B.C. when Pharaoh Thutmose III reports that he chose not to go through the pass at Taanach before his famous battle at Megiddo (*ANET* pp. 235f.). He also listed Taanach among the many cities of Palestine which he conquered (*ANET* p. 243). A broken passage in an Amarna letter (248:14) probably mentions the men of Taanach.

In the Bible the king of Taanach is listed among those defeated by the Israelites (Josh. 12:31) although Manasseh, to which Taanach was allotted, was unable to drive out the Canaanite inhabitants to take the city (Josh. 17:11-12; I Chron. 7:29). Israel's great victory over the Canaanites, celebrated in Deborah's Song, occurred at "Taanach by the waters of Megiddo" (Judg. 5:19). Under Solomon Taanach was one of five major cities in the administrative district under

BUILDING FROM TAANACH, ca. 1450 B.C. Possibly a pottery. Courtesy, Paul Lapp

Baana (I Kings 4:12). It was also a Levitical city assigned to the Kohathites (Judg. 21:25).

Pharaoh Shishak I lists Taanach among his conquests in his Palestinian campaign of 918 B.C. (*ANET* p. 243). Taanach is not mentioned again in ancient literature until post-biblical times in Eusebius' *Onomastica* (157:11).

II. *The Early Bronze Age at Taanach* (2700-2500 B.C.). Taanach first became a settled city during the Early Bronze Age, the period in which the first walled cities and city-states were founded in Palestine. Khirbet-Kerak ware and other characteristic pottery indicate an occupation during the twenty-seventh to twenty-sixth centuries. A series of three massive fortification systems on the south and two on the west as well as occupational debris five feet thick in the center of the mound show that Taanach flourished during this brief period. Remains of a wall and a tower from the first defensive system on the south were discovered in 1963. The wall of the second system was twelve feet thick and remains to a height of eight feet. On the west the earliest defense consisted of two parallel walls with an intervening passageway, a construction with striking parallels at Tell Farah (N), Ai, and Byblos from the same age. Later this outer wall was abandoned and the inner wall widened.

In the north Sellin discovered a curious installation with walls of huge stones set on bedrock and an underground, rock-hewn stairway, covered with large stone slabs, leading down into several chambers beneath. A channel for liquid ran down the side of the steps. Sellin suggested that this was a fifteenth century cultic installation for a chthonic or earth deity. Albright interprets it as an Early Bronze tomb of the style of the third-dynasty Egyptian king Djoser which was then later reused as a cistern for storing water.

Taanach was apparently destroyed about 2500 B.C. and was not extensively occupied again for over 800 years. This was a period of incursions by semi-nomadic groups during which every walled city in Palestine was destroyed and lay unoccupied for some time.

III. *The Second Period* (1650-1468 B.C.). Late in the Middle Bronze period (Middle Bronze IIC, 1650-1550 B.C.), when the Hyksos controlled Egypt and Palestine, Taanach

DEBRIS FROM STOREROOM of "cultic structure" from 10th Century B.C. A pile of doughnut-shaped "loom weights" is at left center. Courtesy, Paul Lapp

was rebuilt on a grand scale. A series of earthen glacis foundations, such as are typical in Palestine in Hyksos times, were found on the north, south, and west of Tell Ta' annek. In such a glacis, earth was packed extremely hard on the sharply sloping (twenty-five to fifty degree angle) side of the mound. This presented a very steep surface which was difficult for attackers to negotiate. Some of the glacis which ring the entire mound of Taanach are up to five feet thick at points and extend as much as sixty feet down the side of the mound. Their construction involved moving staggering amounts of earth fill and offers eloquent witness to the strength of the political organization needed to direct such work.

The largest building found at Taanach from pre-Islamic times is the West Building. It was set into the third phase of the west glacis and its western wall was firmly founded on earlier Early Bronze walls beneath. Made of hard limestone blocks, some as much as five feet long, it measures seventy by sixty

feet with walls four feet thick. Characteristically, a large court with a deep cistern forms the northeastern corner of the building. Nine almost square rooms, a corridor, and the foundation for a stairway to the upper story complete the ground plan of the building. Its huge size and strength indicate it was the home of a ruling nobleman and may have served some public administrative function also.

A large number of burials within the city, especially of children, may be attributed to this or a slightly later period. The mortality rate in ancient times was excessive. Infants were often placed in large storage jars, sometimes with a bowl covering the jar's mouth, which were then buried near or even inside the home beneath the dirt floor. Usually one or more small juglets were interred in or with the large jar. A whole "cemetery" of sixteen infants under the age of two was found in the northeast of the mound, perhaps mute witness to a plague. Another group of various ages was found near the West Building, and individual burials were scattered over the mound.

When the Egyptians drove the Hyksos overlords out of Egypt in the mid-sixteenth century, they also destroyed many of the Hyksos cities in Palestine. There is no clear evidence yet that they destroyed Taanach at this time, however. Taanach's prosperity may simply have continued uninterrupted into the first part of the Late Bronze Age. Painted pottery reported to have been found in the West Building suggests it was used in the fifteenth century. At about 1500 B.C. a rather complex structure was erected south of the West Building. It adjoined a street which was resurfaced at least four times. This structure has yielded seven rooms so far, six of which once had fine plaster floors, and the other a cistern. They appear to have been store or work rooms about a court and may have formed an industrial installation, though the lack of objects precludes certainty.

A group of six skeletons, apparently of a woman and her five children who were killed when their home was suddenly destroyed, may belong to this stratum. Since the house was destroyed while still in use, it contained many objects used in daily life. Of chief interest, however, is the unusual find of jewelry, including eight simple gold rings, plus two each of bronze and silver, beads, several objects of precious stone, and a silver pin. Such finds of precious metal and stone are not uncommon in Egypt and Mesopotamia but are quite rare in Palestine and then, significantly, almost always come from the richer Canaanite period, not from Israelite times.

This prosperous period of Taanach's history came to an end with the destruction of the city during one of Thutmose III's campaigns, most likely in connection with the battle of nearby Megiddo in 1468 B.C.

IV. *Cuneiform Tablets.* In 1903 Sellin found a building very near the underground stairway mentioned above but of uncertain relationship to it. This building yielded four clay tablets bearing Akkadian cuneiform writing. He returned in 1904 for the sole purpose of searching for more tablets. He found two by sifting the debris taken from the building the year before, and six more by clearing out the building more completely. These twelve tablets, some of them frag-

mentary, are written in the universal diplomatic language of the day, Babylonian. They date from sometime in the fifteenth century when Egypt was in control of Palestine. Most of them are letters addressed from cities near Taanach to a certain Re-Washsha, apparently the king of Taanach. The fact that he bears an Egyptian name, Re-Washsha (meaning "the god Re is mighty"), may indicate that he was a vassal of the Egyptians.

The details of daily administration of government are reflected in two letters from a higher Egyptian official, Amenophis, who is sometimes in nearby Megiddo, sometimes in Gaza, the main Egyptian headquarters in the south. He gives directives to Re-Washsha regarding supplies of troops, arms, and equipment, as well as in regard to the disposition of captives taken in battle.

ASTARTE FIGURINE MOLD with modern cast. Courtesy, Paul Lapp

The tablets also afford a glimpse of Canaanite religious belief and practice. The male and female deities, Baal and Asherah, so well known in the Old Testament, are mentioned, as well as the practice of divination prohibited in Deuteronomy 18:10-14. Letters 5 and 6 open with the greeting, "May Baal protect thy life." The author of letter 1 suggests "If there is a wizard of Ashera, let him tell our fortunes and let me hear quickly; and the (oracular) sign and interpretation send to me."

Several administrative lists of names were also found, perhaps for military conscription or taxes. The ethnic characteristics of the names indicate a mixture of Hurrian, Egyptian, Babylonian, and Hittite influences in the Canaanite city of Taanach.

Taanach is mentioned again as a settled place in a broken early fourteenth century letter found in Egypt among the famous *Amarna letters. Jadashta, the brother of the king of Megiddo, to whom he has fled for asylum, writes the king of Egypt for help. He complains that the men of Taanach have robbed the gifts and cattle which the king of Egypt had given him.

V. *The Thirteenth and Twelfth Centuries.* The next datable structures discovered belong to the thirteenth-twelfth century stratum. Here the patterns of Late Bronze culture continue into the Iron Age in the twelfth century. This reflects the Biblical statement that the Canaanite cities of the northern plain, such as Megiddo, Taanach, and Beth-Shean, withstood the invading Israelites longer than did many cities in the southern hill country (Judg. 1:27). There cities such as Bethel and Debir were destroyed and experienced a cultural shift already at the end of the thirteenth century.

A large room from this stratum was found at the southern tip of the mound. Its most striking and peculiar feature is a vertical clay "drainpipe" seven inches in diameter which remains to a height of six feet. There are pairs of handles at its base and at its midpoint. It may have served to drain water from the roof to a cistern below.

Another building of this age was partly uncovered in 1963 immediately south of the West Building. Its outlines were sizable enough to suggest that it was not just a private home but some larger structure. In its burnt debris appeared a perfectly preserved cylindrical cuneiform clay tablet, about half the size of a cigar. Significantly, it is not written in the usual syllabic writing, but in an alphabetic script closely related to that used in the tablets from Ugarit, but only rarely found in Palestine. The tablet has not yet been fully deciphered. The size of the building and the presence of such

a tablet suggest that it served some public administrative function.

Both of these structures were violently destroyed in the latter part of the twelfth century. It is possible that the Israelites carried out this destruction after their victory over the coalition of Canaanite kings "at Taanach, by the waters of Megiddo" (Judg. 5:19). The Canaanites should have had tactical superiority in a battle in the level plain because they possessed chariots. Providential rains, however, swelled the brook Kishon, made the plain a sea of mud, and so rendered the chariots ineffective (Judg. 4:12-16; 5:21). In this light it is interesting to note Sellin's report that spring rains made travel for his supply wagons difficult in the muddy plain. In fact, three of his horses drowned in that same swollen Kishon in 1903.

Albright believes that the Biblical phrase, "at Taanach, by the waters of Megiddo," implies that the battle occurred at a time when Megiddo was not a settled city. The battle could thus be dated to a time when Megiddo was not occupied, but Taanach was. This would place the Israelite victory not very far from 1125 B.C.

VI. *The Period of the United Monarchy (Tenth Century).* Taanach is named as one of the cities in Solomon's administrative district for the Esdraelon plain headed by the governor Baana (I Kings 4:12). It is just barely possible that Taanach was the residence of the governor, for it heads the list of cities and is centrally located. *Megiddo is usually regarded as the governor's residence, however, since it served as the provincial capital in other periods and was the site of much Solomonic construction, perhaps including a governor's palace.

Several structures of Solomonic Taanach have been unearthed. Just south of the West Building remains of three occupational phases of this period were found. The last of these included a cistern reaching forty feet below the surface, around which there was an open plastered court and two basins made of plastered flagstones. Several walls of the "cuneiform tablet" building of the preceding period were reused at this time.

In his south-central trench Sellin found a small clay stand or altar for burning incense. It bears ornamental relief of animal figures, a "tree of life," and a snake, all of which are common in Canaanite religious art.

*INCENSE ALTAR FROM TAANACH,
about 36 inches high, discovered in 1902.
Courtesy, Carl Graesser, Jr.*

In the hope of finding more of the building in which this incense altar was discovered, the Concordia-ASOR team opened the area adjacent to Sellin's trench. This exposed the northwest corner of a tenth century building which Sellin had partially uncovered, though there is no longer any way of showing stratigraphically that it was the same one in which the incense stand was found.

This building was destroyed while still in use. Its debris yielded a small museum of objects: eighty small and large clay vessels of many types, including storage jars containing burned wheat and a number of bowls of unusually fine quality, over fifty complete loom weights, several knives and other iron objects, weights, many grinding stones, several bone spatulas, 108 pig ankle bones in three caches, a brazier, an Astarte figurine, and a complete Astarte figurine mold. Some of this suggests storage on a large scale or a shop. The pig bones, the figurine mold and the incense stand almost necessitate

some religious or cultic interpretation. A goodsized, well-dressed megalith which was found nearby would serve well as a standing pillar (*maṣṣēbāh*) in a cultic context. Lapp has suggested that these are the remains of a sanctuary storehouse or that they may even reflect combined cultic and commercial activities by a group of enterprising priests.

This tenth century stratum came to a violent end, presumably at the hands of Pharaoh Shishak I, who claims conquest of Taanach about 918 B.C. Strangely enough, no city walls or fortifications of this period (or any period after the first two Early and Middle Bronze periods) have yet been discovered.

VII. *Later Periods.* Sellin's North Outwork and Northeast Building contain fine dressed masonry and surely date to the time of Solomon or later. More accurate dating and interpretation await further excavation, however. Abundant pottery indicates a sizable occupation in the seventh-sixth centuries, though only one coherent structure has been found in the south, a building reusing a portion of the tenth century "cult" building. Evidences of a scattered occupation in the Persian period (fifth-fourth centuries B.C.) and a few Hellenistic sherds comprise the whole of material found on the mound dating to the period between the sixth century B.C. and the ninth century A.D. In Roman (New Testament) times the village had moved down to the plain. Since Roman military strength insured peace, there was no longer any need of a heavily fortified walled city up on the mound.

The Islamic occupation, dating to the ninth-tenth centuries A.D., includes two strata and is limited to the central portion of the mound. Its center is a palace or villa, measuring ninety by ninety-five feet, with over twenty-five rooms, constructed of soft dressed limestone, some of it reused from Hellenistic times. A large vaulted hypocaust supplied heated water to several baths in this palace and probably to another fine plastered bath uncovered in 1963 near the West Building.

BIBLIOGRAPHY. E. Sellin, "Tell Ta'annek," *Denkschriften der Kaiserlichen Akademie der Wissenschaften* 50, 4, Wien, 1904; "Eine Nachlese auf den Tell Ta'annek in Palästina," *Denkschriften* 52, 3, Wien, 1906. P. Lapp, "The 1963 Excavation at Ta'annek," *BASOR,* 173, 1964, pp. 4-44. W. F. Albright, "A Prince of Taanach in the Fifteenth

Century B. C.," *BASOR*, 94, 1944, pp. 12-27. J. A. Knudtzon, *Die El-Amarna Tafeln*, Vol. I, Hinrichs, Leipzig, 1915, No. 248:14. J. B. Pritchard, ed., *ANET*, pp. 235-36, 243, 490. G. van Beek, *The Interpreter's Dictionary of the Bible*, Vol. III, ed. G. A. Buttrick, New York, Abingdon, 1962, p. 497.

TADMOR. *See* Palmyra.

TAHPANHES. In the eastern Delta, twelve miles north of Tell el-Mashkutah is the mound known as Tell Defenneh, located on the Pelusiac branch of the Nile. Tell Defenneh is thought to mark the site of ancient Tahpanhes, the Egyptian city to which the Jews of Jeremiah's day fled in order to escape the wrath of Nebuchadnezzar (Jer. 40-41). Jeremiah subsequently prophesied to the Jewish community in Tahpanhes. An oracle of the Lord came to the prophet, saying:

Take in your hands large stones, and hide them in the mortar in the pavement which is at the entrance to Pharaoh's palace at Tahpanhes, in the sight of the men of Judah, and say to them, "Thus says the Lord of hosts, the God of Israel: Behold I will send and take Nebuchadnezzar the king of Babylon, my servant, and he will set his throne above these stones which I have hid, and he will spread his royal canopy over them. He shall come and smite the land of Egypt, giving to the pestilence those who are doomed to the pestilence, to captivity those who are doomed to captivity, and to the sword those who are doomed to the sword . . ." (Jer. 43:8-11).

Flinders Petrie arrived at Tell Defenneh in the spring of 1886 and learned that the largest mound in the area bore the name Qasr Bint el-Yahudi, "The Palace of the Jew's Daughter." Remembering the Biblical reference to the Jewish settlement at Tahpanhes, Petrie's interest in the site quickened.

The pavement of which Jeremiah spoke seems to have been part of the complex of fortifications discovered during Petrie's excavation. Petrie came upon a large platform of brickwork which seems to have been used for loading and unloading baggage and other work connected with the garrison. This platform, much like the familiar bench-shaped mastaba early used for Egyptian burials, would have been an ideal place for the hiding of Jeremiah's stones.

Tell Defenneh may also have been the location of Baal-zephon, one of the places at which Israel stopped at the time of the Exodus (Exod. 14:2). A Phoenician papyrus found in Egypt speaks of "Baal-zephon and all the gods of Talphanhes."

Herodotus is our witness to the fact that Egyptian garrisons were stationed at Daphnae to repel Arabians and Syrians (*Histories* ii. 30). Petrie's excavation of the mound Kasr Bint el-Yahudi gave evidence that a strong fortress had once been located there to guard the eastern frontier of Egypt. The foundation deposit of the excavated fort bore the name of Pharaoh Psammetechus, but there were also traces of bricks dating back to the Ramesside period.

Herodotus states that Psammetechus established garrisons of Ionians and Carians "near the sea, a little below the city of Bubastis, on that which is called the Pelusiac mouth of the Nile . . . these were the first people of a different language who settled in Egypt."

Greek occupation of Daphnae found abundant attestation in Petrie's excavations. Pottery indicated a curious combination of Greek and Egyptian motifs. The Greek influences at Daphnae ended, however, in 564 B.C. when Ahmase decreed that Naucratis, in the western Delta, should be the sole Greek Treaty Port.

TANIS. *See* Raamses.

TELEILAT GHASSUL. *See* Ghassulian Culture.

TELL. Tell, an Arabic word meaning "high," is used in the technical sense to designate a mound which was occupied by a succession of cities or towns. The mounds, or tells (*tulul* is the Arabic plural of *tell*, but the word has been Anglicized), were built up over many centuries as a result of the accumulation of the debris of successive cities. After destruction by war or fire, a new city would be built on the ruins of the old and the mound grew successively higher. The word *tell* appears in the Hebrew of Joshua 11:13, speaking of "the cities that stood on their mounds." The word *tepe* is used instead of *tell* in areas where Turkish is spoken.

TELL AHMAR. *See* Til-Barsib.

TELL AL 'UBAID. The ruins of Tell al 'Ubaid, on the lower Euphrates River north

STEP TRENCH AT TELL JEDEIDAH, SYRIA. The excavator of a tell is apt to find a series of civilizations superimposed on one another. At Tell Jedeidah fourteen distinct levels of occupation have been identified from 5500 B.C. to A.D. 600. Typical objects are shown from each level. Courtesy, Oriental Institute

I. A.D. 600-300. The level of an early Christian church. On a near-by site are even later Byzantine ruins and bronze crosses of the priests.

II. A.D. 300-64 B.C. A village partly contemporary with Paul and early Christian missionary activity in Antioch. Coins of the Caesars and Roman lamps.

III. ca. 64-500 B.C. An occupation of the period of the Persian Empire and of the Greek empires which followed the conquests of Alexander the Great.

IV. ca. 500-1000 B.C. Layers of the Syrian Hittite kingdom, contemporary with the later Assyrian Empire and the Babylonian Nebuchadnezzar. Hittite Hieroglyphs.

V. ca. 1000-1200 B.C. Ceramic traces of the "Peoples of the Sea," some of whom are known as the Philistines, others as the Achaeans who sacked Troy.

VI. ca. 1200-1600 B.C. A period rich in imported pottery of Cypriote and Aegean type, contemporary with the culture at Ugarit.

VII. ca. 1600-1900 B.C. The beginning of marked technological advances in the second millennium B.C. Grotesque "mother-goddess" figurines are characteristic of this period.

VIII. ca. 1900-2000 B.C. A period of transition (probably of a relatively short time) during which certain distinct types of pottery were manufactured.

IX. ca. 2000-2300 B.C. A time of brilliant work in metal and pottery, climaxing the technological achievements of the third millennium B.C.

X. ca. 2300-2600 B.C. The beginnings of a range of goblets and small drinking vessels; a period rich in connections with the south and east.

XI. ca. 2600-3000 B.C. A range marked by a fine red-and-black pottery series, by excellent metalwork, and by cylinder seals of Mesopotamian type.

XII. ca. 3000-3500 B.C. A period of technological advancement, at the end of which appear the earliest known castings of human figures in metal. Links to both Egypt and Mesopotamia.

XIII. ca. 3500-3900 B.C. Levels yielding rather drab pottery but the earliest types of tectonically conceived metal tools. The technological traditions have links to the east.

GAP

XIV. ca. 5000-5500 B.C.(?) Traces of materials in the range of the earliest known villages of Syro-Cilicia. Hand-made, polished pottery; simple tools in bone and flint.

VIRGIN SOIL   Six feet under the present water level.

of Ur were discovered by H. R. Hall in 1919. C. Leonard Woolley conducted systematic excavations at the site for the Joint Expedition of the British Museum and the University of Pennsylvania from 1923 to 1924 and in 1937.

Characteristic 'Ubaid pottery is pale green in color, painted with free geometric designs in black or dark brown. Some of it was formed by hand, and the remainder was fashioned on a slow, hand-turned wheel. Human and animal figurines were also moulded in clay. The 'Ubaid period follows that of *Tell Halaf and dates from about 4100 to 3500 B.C.

'Ubaid type pottery has been found at Ur, Erech, Eridu, Lagash, Susa, Persepolis and numerous other places. The discovery of a peculiar variety in the fourteenth to eighteenth levels at *Eridu has caused some scholars to suggest that there is a proto- or pre-'Ubaid period which was contemporary with Tell Halaf. 'Ubaid pottery, although for the most part later than that of Tell Halaf, is aesthetically less attractive. The use of the wheel and the ability to maintain uniform heat in a closed oven were, however, important technological advances in the ceramic art.

Houses at 'Ubaid were made of reeds plastered with mud. Larger buildings were made of the sun-dried bricks characteristic of southern Mesopotamia. Mud-plastered walls were decorated with mosaics of small, slender, pencil-like cones of baked clay. The ends, some of which were painted, provided valuable waterproofing for the houses and served as decoration for otherwise drab walls.

BIBLIOGRAPHY. C. L. Woolley, *Al-'Ubaid*, 1927.

TELL AMUDA. *See* Habor.

TELL ARPACHIYA. The prehistoric mound of Tell Arpachiya, four miles north of Nineveh, was first noted by R. Campbell Thompson who examined potsherds on its surface in 1932 and determined that it had been occupied since chalcolithic times. The British School of Archaeology in Iraq conducted an expedition there in 1933-34 under the direction of M. E. L. Mallowan. Pottery remains from the upper levels of the mound were similar to those found at al-'Ubaid

and remains from the lower levels resembled those of Tell Halaf (*Gozan).

A craftsman's shop from the sixth level was evidently burned and its pottery broken and strewn around in the ashes. One large bowl was reconstructed from the seventy-six pieces into which it had been broken. In the rubble was a piece of red ochre clay, flat palettes for mixing paint, and bone tools for shaping clay. Jugs and bowls were decorated with geometric designs, flowers, trees, and dancing girls.

The 'Ubaid culture of the upper levels may indicate the invasion of new peoples who seized and occupied the mound. The name Arpachiya may be related to the Biblical Arphaxad, a descendant of Shem (Gen. 10:22-24).

TELL ARAQ EL MENSHIYEH. *See* Tell Sheikh el Areini.

TELL 'ASHARA. *See* Terqa.

TELL ASMAR. *See* Eshnunna.

TELL BARI. *See* Habor.

TELL BEIT MIRSIM. *See* Debir.

TELL ED-DUWEIR. *See* Lachish.

TELL EL-AMARNA. *See* Amarna.

TELL EL-FAR'AH. *See* Tirzah.

TELL EL FUL. *See* Gibeah.

TELL EL-HESY. In the history of Palestinian archaeology, the excavation of Tell el-Hesy is one of the most significant chapters. This mound lies about seven miles southwest of Tell ed-Duweir (*Lachish) at the edge of a group of foothills which jut out into the coastal plain due west of Hebron. It was strategically located at the opening of a valley which led up into the hill country. The span of occupation extends from about 2600 B.C. until about 400 B.C.

I. *Identification of the Site.* Tell el-Hesy was believed for many years to be the site of ancient Lachish. This was the identification given to it by C. R. Conder, and that which was accepted by its excavators, Flinders Petrie and Frederick J. Bliss. However, the excavation of Tell ed-Duweir from 1932-38 by the Wellcome-Marston expedition, under the direction of J. L. Starkey, revealed that this was the real location of Lachish.

Since that time, Tell el-Hesy has generally been identified with the Canaanite royal city of Eglon, although Tell en-Nagila, which lies three miles to the southeast, has also been suggested.

II. *Excavation.* The excavation of Tell el-Hesy was first undertaken by Flinders Petrie who received permission to excavate in southern Palestine in 1890. He worked for six weeks at the site and was able, during this time, to reveal the stratification of seven levels of the tell. After Petrie, the work was continued by Frederick Jones Bliss in 1891-93.

III. *Archaeological Significance.* Scientific archaeology was greatly advanced in 1890 when Petrie dug at Tell el-Hesy. This was the first time the stratigraphic method of excavation was applied in Palestine. He brought with him the knowledge gained through his forty-five years of study in Egypt. While Petrie was in error in identifying the site as Lachish and his surveying methods and system of dating has been much criticized, his insight into the nature of a Palestinian tell established this excavation as one of the foremost achievements in archaeological research.

At Tell el-Hesy, Petrie demonstrated the importance of the stratigraphic study of ancient mounds. He was aware that most important sites in southwestern Asia consist of superimposed layers of debris which had collected during the successive periods of occupation, destruction and re-occupation. By the study of the artifacts contained in these layers, they may be dated and a history of the site reconstructed. In this way, Petrie was able to show that the relation of objects to one another within the layer of deposit in which they occur can be the basis of archaeological chronology.

Petrie observed that the styles and fashions of pottery differed at various levels in the mound. He therefore states positively that each period had its own typical pottery which could be distinguished from that of earlier or later periods.

In order to establish the dates of the finds at Tell el-Hesy, Petrie related the wares found there with those from datable Egyptian burials. From this study a chronology of the site was constructed by Petrie and Bliss which was dependent on the correspondence with Egyptian archaeology. This chronology, which they worked out in 1894, was correct almost to the century as far back as *ca.* 1500 B.C., but prior to that there was considerable inaccuracy because Petrie's dates for the earlier Egyptian dynasties were too high.

Petrie was succeeded at Tell el-Hesy by Bliss, who was able to establish the dependability of Petrie's proposals on dating through the study of the strata in which the various artifacts were located. The significance of this contribution is seen in G. Ernest Wright's comment that all scientific modern archaeology is based on the application of the two basic principles of stratigraphy, the study of the physical relation of artifacts in the levels in which they

A PALESTINIAN TELL, Tell el-Mutesellim, the mound of Megiddo. Courtesy, Oriental Institute

REVETMENT built to strengthen the wall at Tell en-Nasbeh (Mizpah). Courtesy, Palestine Institute, Pacific School of Religion

occur, and typology, the study of the relation of forms of objects (*The Westminster Historical Atlas to the Bible*, Rev. ed., The Westminster Press, Philadelphia, 1956, p. 10a).

When judged by modern criteria, Petrie's excavation of Tell el-Hesy is open to serious criticism. He attacked his projects vigorously and often dispensed with equipment which most modern excavators require. C. C. McCown describes his method in this way: "He has had different methods of working and of reporting results — a shorthand method, on the one hand, evolved through years of tedious labor, and a popular method on the other, due to the necessity of raising funds by private subscription. His reports often, not always, enable the critic to reach his own conclusions" (*The Ladder of Progress in Palestine*, Harper and Brothers, New York, 1943).

On the other hand, Palestinian archaeology was still in its infancy when Petrie began his work at Tell el-Hesy. Whatever the shortcomings of his work may be, the value of it must be judged in terms of the advancement which was made through the application of stratigraphic method of excavation in Palestine.

III. *Occupation and Discoveries.* The tell revealed the remains of eight successive settlements. In the lowest level, an axehead of crescentic form was found in a group of copper weapons. This axehead is almost the same as one found in a late Early Bronze III tomb at Jericho. This serves to establish the earliest occupation of Tell el-Hesy at about 2600 B.C.

During the Middle Bronze period the city was well fortified. The fortifications were distinguished by the wall having a strong, sloping stone foundation plastered with hard packed clay or lime plaster. This same type of fortification is also found at °Taanach, °Schechem and °Tell Beit Mirsim.

From the work of Petrie and Bliss it is

568

known that the city was destroyed about 1200 B.C., about the same time as Lachish, Bethel and Debir. This evidence of destruction suggests a planned campaign such as that depicted in Joshua 10, where there are references to the destruction of Makkedah, Libnah, Lachish, Eglon, Hebron and Debir. Eglon was made a part of the tribe of Judah (Josh. 15:39), and the city was rebuilt and became a stronghold in that area. The development of the culture at Eglon is demonstrated in Stratum V (ca. tenth century B.C.) where there is a structure similar to the stable at Megiddo employing quoin construction.

An important area in which information was provided by Tell el-Hesy is that of writing and the alphabet. Bliss found a cuneiform tablet from the fourteenth century B.C. This tablet links the place with Tell el-Amarna and is an illustration of the crosscurrents of culture in Palestine at the time. Perhaps even more important was the discovery in 1892, of an inscribed potsherd with three early West Semitic characters similar to the proto-Sinaitic characters in the inscription at Serabit el-Khadem. This sherd belongs to the twelfth or thirteenth century B.C., but the history of this writing system begins about the eighteenth or nineteenth century B.C. This discovery at Tell el-Hesy, along with those at Gezer, Shechem, Lachish, Megiddo and Beth-shemesh, demonstrates that the Canaanite inhabitants of Palestine had their own alphabet(s) beside those of Egypt and Babylon.

IV. *Relevance to Biblical Study.* Eglon was one of the cities in the Amorite coalition, led by Adonizedek of Jerusalem, which attacked Gibeon after Joshua had made a covenant of peace with the Gibeonites (Josh. 10). This offensive was repulsed by Joshua; and the leaders, including Debir, king of Eglon, were executed. The inhabitants of the city were slain (Josh. 10:34-35), and possession of the city taken by the Israelites (Josh. 12:7, 12). It was made a part of the tribe of Judah (Josh. 15:39) and continued to be occupied until ca. 400 B.C. The city was not large, the Israelite settlement occupying only about two and one-half acres, but its location was sufficient to insure it a degree of importance.

Perhaps the most important feature, Biblically, is the correspondence of the archae-ological evidence for destruction and the reference to Joshua's campaign in this area (Josh. 10).

BIBLIOGRAPHY. W. Flinders Petrie, *Tell el Hesy (Lachish),* A. P. Watt, London, 1891.

TELL EL-HUSN. See Beth-shan.

TELL EL-MUTESSELLIM. See Megiddo.

TELL EL-YAHUDIYA. See Leontopolis.

TELL EN-NASBEH. This tell occupies the summit of a large, rounded limestone hill about eight miles north of Jerusalem beside the highway that runs to Nablus, just south of the modern village of Ramallah. It has a commanding view of the area; and, from the site, one can see to er-Ram (Ramah), Tell el-Fûl (Gibeah), el-Jib (Gibeon), and Nebi Samwîl.

I. *Excavation.* The excavation of Tell en-Nasbeh was undertaken in 1926 under the direction of W. F. Badè of the Pacific School of Religion who founded a "Palestinian Institute" to carry on the project. The work continued through five seasons, the last being conducted in 1935. During the last season, Badè was so overtaxed physically that he fell ill on the return trip and subsequently died in March, 1936. The work of co-ordinating the results of the expedition was passed on to J. C. Wampler, who had been Badè's assistant through the last three seasons, and C. C. McCown, Badè's successor as director of the Palestine Institute of the Pacific School of Religion. The final results of the expedition were published in 1947 as a joint publication of the Pacific School of Religion and the American School of Oriental Research.

A. Levels of occupation. When the excavation of Tell en-Nasbeh was undertaken, Badè was convinced that the walls which were visible were from the Middle Bronze period (ca. 2000-1500 B.C.). Upon further investigation, however, it was found that there were only two architectural levels: Middle Iron (ca. eleventh-eighth centuries B.C.) and Late Iron (ca. seventh-fourth centuries B.C.). From deposits in tombs on top of the mound it was found that there had been a brief occupation of the site during the Early Bronze period (ca. 3000 B.C.). Only one tomb yielded pottery from the Middle Bronze period. The settlement of the hill, in a permanent manner, did not occur until about 1100 B.C. The site was then occupied until about 300 B.C. The Roman and Byzantine tombs at Tell en-Nasbeh do not belong to a settlement there, but probably go with nearby Khirbet esh-Shuweikeh, where the mosaic floor of a church has been found.

The location of the town and its fortifications indicate the importance of the place. The major road from Jerusalem to Samaria passes Tell en-Nasbeh. In the past it has sometimes been on the east and sometimes on the west, but at all times very near. The town, therefore, occupied a strategic location as the guardian of the trade route. Also, the discovery of inscribed jar handles with the letters l-m-l-k (lᵉmelek, "belonging to the king") indicates that, during the period of the Divided Kingdom, this was a northern outpost of Judah.

B. Fortifications. The most important single discovery was the fortifications. The walls of the city, which were about fifteen to twenty feet thick, enclosed an area of a little less than eight acres. At intervals towers were erected, projecting about seven feet beyond the line of the wall. The base of the wall and towers were constructed of massive stones, and the outside was covered with lime plaster to a height of fifteen to eighteen feet to discourage scaling of the wall. The walls, which perhaps rose to a height of thirty-five to forty feet originally, were preserved to a height of twenty-five feet when Badè began his work.

The gate was disclosed in the fourth season. It was a double gate which was oriented toward the north rather than the south, toward Jerusalem, as might be expected of a town belonging to the Southern Kingdom. The walls of the gate were preserved to a height of six to nine feet; and the sill, pivots for the leaves of the gate, and the stops against which they closed were in situ. The gate was formed by the wall running up from the south overlapping the wall running down from the north with a space of about thirty feet between the two walls. The area formed by the overlapping of the walls made an external court about thirty feet square. On either side of the gate a massive tower protected the gate enclosure. The walls of the external court and the interior guard rooms were lined

with stone benches and offer a classic example of how the varied business could be conducted, according to many Old Testament passages, "in the gate."

II. Identification. The identification of Tell en-Nasbeh is a particularly difficult problem. Abbé Raboisson identified the site as that of Mizpah of Benjamin (Les Maspeh, 1897). Badè thought this identification was correct, and James Muilenberg also identifies it as °Mizpah. W. F. Albright, however, rejects this view, preferring to locate Mizpah at nearby Nebi Samwil, as suggested by Edward Robinson in 1838. (For a complete discussion see: James Muilenberg, "Survey of the Literature on Tell En-Nasbeh," Tell en-Nasbeh, I, pp. 13-22.)

The most serious difficulty in identifying Tell en-Nasbeh with Mizpah arises from topographical problems in tracing the route of Ishmael in Jeremiah 41. The strongest evidence is gained from I Kings 15:16-22. King Baasha of Israel fortifies Ramah (er-Ram), which lies to the southeast of Tell en-Nasbeh, "that he might not suffer any to go out or come in to Asa king of Judah." Asa, however, appealed to Ben-hadad of Damascus who attacked Israel and forced Baasha to retire from Ramah. Asa then imposed a conscription on Judah, carried away Baasha's building material from Ramah and fortified Geba of Benjamin and Mizpah. This information coincides very well with the fact that the thin rubble wall at Tell en-Nasbeh was strengthened to the impressive proportions described about 900 B.C.

A significant factor in the identification of the site arises from the discovery of twenty-eight jar handles which bear the letters m-s-p or m-s-h. There is uncertainty about the reading of the last letter for it is unclear. Badè thought the last letter was pe and used the inscription as an indication of the place name. Others have chosen to read the last letter as he although the meaning in this case is unclear. (The only other specimen of this kind of handle was found at Jericho.)

III. Relevance to Biblical Studies. If Tell en-Nasbeh may be regarded as the site of Mizpah the connection with Biblical history is very evident. Until the time of the monarchy, Mizpah served as a national sanctuary or meeting place for Israel in times of danger (Judg. 20:1, 3; 21:1; 5, 8; I Sam. 7:5ff.;

0:17). The first significant occupation be-
an about the eleventh century B.C. At
rst it was only a weakly fortified country
illage; but, in the tenth century, Asa made
a fortress to guard the northern border
f his kingdom (I Kings 15:16-22). When
erusalem fell to the Babylonians, Mizpah
ecame the residence of Gedaliah, who was
ppointed governor of Judah by Nebuchad-
ezzar (Jer. 40-41). Nehemiah 3:7, 15, 19
uggest that Mizpah was the capital of a
istrict in Judah after the Babylonian Exile.
t served as the rallying point for the faithful
ews after the desecration of the Temple
y Antiochus Epiphanes (I Macc. 3:46).

The information about Tell en-Nasbeh
vhich has been gained through archaeology
ccords very well with the Biblical narratives
vhich mention Mizpah. However, in view
f the difficulties which arise (see: G. Ernest
Vright, "Tell en-Nasbeh," BA, X, pp. 73-77),
ny identification must be held as tentative
ntil Nebi Samwil can be thoroughly in-
estigated.

BIBLIOGRAPHY. William Frederic Badè, A
1anual of Excavation in the Near East, University
f California Press, Berkeley, 1934. C. C. McCown
nd J. C. Wampler, Tell En-Nasbeh, 2 vols., The
'alestine Institute of the Pacific School of Religion
nd the American School of Oriental Research,
erkeley and New Haven, 1947. G. Ernest Wright,
Tell en-Nasbeh," The Biblical Archaeologist, X,
947, pp. 69-77.

'ELL ER-RETABA. See Pithom.

'ELL ES-SULTAN. See Jericho (Old Testa-
1ent).

'ELL EZ-ZAKARIYEH. See Azekah.

'ELL FAKHARIYA. See Gozan.

'ELL HALAF. See Gozan.

'ELL HAMUDI. See Habor.

'ELL HARIRI. See Mari.

'ELL HASSUNA. Tell Hassuna, a prehis-
oric site near ancient Ashur, on the Tigris
liver twenty-five miles south of Mosul was
xcavated by the Iraq Museum in 1943-44.
n the lowest level the excavators came upon
int tools and coarse earthenware jugs.
tone axes discovered at this level were
robably used for breaking the ground in a
rimitive type of agriculture. Hassuna il-

STELE FROM TELL HALAF, showing a
wheeled chariot. Courtesy, Aleppo Museum

lustrates the existence of a village culture
based on small farming in the period before
metal came into use. A coarse type of pottery
was discovered at Hassuna. It is similar
in form to pottery discovered in Cilicia,
Syria and Palestine. Weapons and tools at
Hassuna were made of flint and obsidian.

Remains from seven other layers of culture
were discovered above the earliest Hassuna
settlement. In these later settlements we find
people living in houses with several rooms
and an open courtyard. Pottery is improved in design and texture. Some of it
has incised or painted decorations. Flint-
toothed sickles were used for reaping and
grain was stored in spherical clay bins. The
women ground their flour between flat rub-
bing stones and baked their bread in clay
ovens. Infants were buried in pottery jars,
and other jars — perhaps for food and water
— were placed nearby. Beads, amulets, and
figurines used in the fertility cult help us to
reconstruct the manner of life in prehistoric
Hassuna. The upper levels of the mound
yielded pottery of a type first identified at
*Samarra.

TELL KHELEIFEH. See Ezion-geber.

TELL NAGILA. Because the so-called Tell
Gath has been proven not to be the site
of the famous Philistine city (cf. Tell Sheikh
el-Areini), Binyamin Mazar suggested that
Gath might be located at Tell Nagila. Surface studies had produced an abundance
of Iron Age pottery, and this led S. Buelow and R. A. Mitchell to make a further
investigation of the site. They found that
the outlines of a large building were visible

on the surface of the tell which they took to be an Iron Age fort. Excavations carried out by Ruth Amiran in the summers of 1962 and 1963 have shown that this cannot be Gath of the Philistines.

The large building noted by Buelow and Mitchell was an Arab caravanserei dating from somewhere between the twelfth to the fourteenth centuries A.D.

The next earliest period of occupation was apparently in the early part of Iron Age II as indicated by the pottery finds. The main evidence for this period still consists of pits full of sherds and ashes which have appeared in various places on the mound. In the second season a few ovens and one wall were found which point to some kind of settlement at that time. On a nearby hill were found ruins of a typical seventh century B.C. Israelite house with another large building nearby. This work was done by R. Gofna who had suggested after the first season at Nagila that the tell had been used for a small farming community like several others in the region around *Tell el-Hesy.

No Philistine occupation was found in any part of the excavation, and no Philistine pottery has ever been found there during surface explorations. Neither have buildings of the Late Bronze Age turned up thus far. However, occasional pieces of pottery from that period suggest that some occupation may have existed there.

The most important finds have been from the Middle Bronze Age II. The tell was fortified by a so-called "Hyksos rampart," in this case consisting of a ramp of brown dirt with a brick wall on its innermost side.

This latter wall served as a retaining wall for subsequent layers of various local soils. On top of the slope and over the retaining wall was built a high wall of which only a few courses remain. In another area the excavators have uncovered part of the town's living quarters. Two narrow streets have been excavated with small dwellings opening onto them along both sides. The dwelling units consist of one small room and a court. Four thin strata of occupation were discerned which together were included in a depth of one to one and a half yards. The houses continued in use throughout the entire Middle Bronze II period with only minor repairs being made. They were usually made of undressed stones but occasionally of unfired brick. Remains of a large building from the same period have appeared towards the middle of the tell which enjoyed at least three phases of occupation. The excavation here, though most cursory, brought to light a large zoomorphic vessel in the form of an ox and covered with a red burnished slip decorated in black and white.

A large Middle Bronze II grave consisting of three rooms and containing about forty burials was also found. It has produced an abundance of sherds, alabaster and faience, and also bronze daggers, pins and many scarabs. One Tell el-Yehudeiyeh juglet and a Cypriot jug of the red-on-black type were also found here.

Beneath the Middle Bronze dwellings were preserved two strata of Early Bronze II and III. There is a possibility that another stratum is represented in a few "pockets" right on bedrock. This requires further investigation.

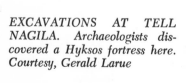

EXCAVATIONS AT TELL NAGILA. Archaeologists discovered a Hyksos fortress here. Courtesy, Gerald Larue

BIBLIOGRAPHY. Y. Aharoni and R. Amiran, "The Tells of the Western Negev," *Bulletin of the Israel Exploration Society* 17, 1952, pp. 53-54 (Hebrew). R. Amiran, "A Preliminary Note of the First Season of Excavations at Tell Nagila, 1962," *Christian News from Israel* 13, 1962, pp. 24-26; "Tell Nagila," *Hadashot Arkhiologiot* 4, Oct., 1962, pp. 8-10 (Hebrew); "The Second Season of Excavations at Tell Nagila," *Hadashot Arkhiologiot* 8, Oct., 1963, pp. 9-12; "Tell Nagila," in Notes and News, *Israel Exploration Journal* 13, 1963, pp. 143-145. S. Buelow and R. A. Mitchell, "An Iron Age II Fortress on Tel Nagila," *Israel Exploration Journal* 11, 1961, pp. 101-110. R. Gofna, "Haserim" Settlement in the Northern Negev," *Yediot* 27, 1963, pp. 173-180. B. Mazar, "Gath and Gittaim," *Israel Exploration Journal* 4, 1954, pp. 227-235.

TELLOH. See Lagash.

TELL QASILE. On the north bank of the Yarkon, near Tel Aviv, on the border of the Plain of Sharon, is the mound of Tell Qasile which the Israel Exploration Society excavated from 1948 to 1950 with the help of the Municipality of Tel Aviv. Benjamin Mazar directed the excavation which uncovered remains of the Philistine, Israelite (Iron Age), Persian, Hellenistic, and Roman periods.

From Philistine times smelting furnaces have been discovered which were used for copper and iron. The Philistines possessed a monopoly of iron, and it was necessary for the Israelites to go to the Philistines to have their agricultural implements sharpened (I Sam. 13:19, 20). A Philistine building from Tell Qasile has rooms bisected by a row of pillars built of bricks on stone foundations. The pillars supported the ceiling. Samson, in Philistine Gaza, leaned on such pillars and destroyed the house and all who were in it (Judg. 16:25-29).

Tell Qasile was destroyed by fire at the beginning of the tenth century, probably at the time the coastal region north of the Yarkon was conquered by David. An Israelite settlement was built on the ruins of the earlier city and continued until the second half of the eighth century B.C. when the armies of Tiglath-pileser III overran the northern and western provinces of Judah.

After the destruction of the Israelite settlement, Tell Qasile was unoccupied until the postexilic period when a large building was erected on the ruins. The building is thought to have served as an administrative and economic center for the area. Pottery is typical of the Persian period, but it includes Attic sherds from Greece as well. Tell Qasile was occupied continuously from Persian to Arab times. We do not, however, know the ancient name of the city that was located there.

BIBLIOGRAPHY. B. Maisler, "Excavation at Tell Qasile," *BA*, XIV, 1951, pp. 43-49.

TELL SHAGAR BAZAR. See Habor.

TELL SHEIKH EL-AREINI. This tell stands in the coastal plain, about fifteen miles inland from Ashkelon almost on a line between it and Hebron. It is one of a chain of tells which form a wide curving line running north and south to the west of the Judean shephela. In the literature it is sometimes called Tell Araq el-Menshiyeh after the Arab village which formerly stood nearby. Albright had proposed to locate the Biblical Gath of the Philistines at this site, and it has subsequently been designated "Tell Gath." However, recent investigations have shown that this identification can hardly be correct.

Excavations have been carried out on Tell Sheikh el-Areini in six seasons (from 1956 to 1961) under the direction of S. Yeivin. The site consists of: a lower terrace surrounding the tell and merging into the surrounding plain; a higher terrace about 62½ acres in area on the west, south, and southeast; and an "acropolis." Because of the discontinuity between the strata on the higher terrace and the acropolis, the levels of each were numbered separately. On the higher terrace they begin with I at the top (towards the end of Early Bronze II, *ca.* 2600 B.C.) and go down to XII which dates to the Middle Chalcolithic period (*ca.* 3500 B.C.). Stratum V has provided a special group of intrusive foreign pottery and a sherd, or perhaps two, bearing the name of Narmer, a king of the First Egyptian Dynasty.

The last ancient level on the acropolis was Hellenistic, but it was greatly disturbed by an Arab cemetery (seventh to fifteenth cent. A.D.). Over fifteen strata were subsequently uncovered. Levels XIV-IV all date to the Israelite period and represent several stages of rebuilding and refortifying. Level XV contains traces of a tenth century fortification, and below it there is pre-Israelite material. A trail trench which was

TEPE GAWRA. The archaeologists have reached stratum 18. Parts of stratum 17 are in the center foreground. Courtesy, University Museum, Philadelphia

dug in the last season to clarify the stratification of these earlier fortifications found traces of a stratum from the eleventh-twelfth centuries B.C. There is evidence of settlement during the Late Bronze Age, but so far none from Middle Bronze. Philistine sherds have been found, but usually in pits or cisterns. It would seem, then, that the site was abandoned *ca.* 2600 B.C. because the surrounding swamps had dried up. Re-occupation was only possible in Late Bronze, when the technique of gathering water in cisterns had been developed. The excavations have not yet reached the top level of the high terrace, but there remains very little room for a Middle Bronze Age stratum.

At least it is clear that the settlement on this tell during the late Canaanite and Philistine periods was very small, being confined to the citadel only. It is therefore most improbable that this could have been the mighty Philistine center indicated by the Bible.

The presence of jar handles stamped with seal impressions "to the king" (*see* Seals)

in the Iron Age II citadel show that this was a Judean town during the seventh and sixth centuries B.C. Sargon II mentions Gath as an independent city during his campaign of 713-712 B.C., which he conquered and reconstituted as an Assyrian colony. It is most unlikely that Judah could have annexed it afterwards since she, too, had become a dependency of the Assyrians.

BIBLIOGRAPHY. W. F. Albright, "The Sites of Ekron, Gath, and Libna," *AASOR* 2-3, 1921-1922, p. 11. A. Ciasca, "Tell Gat," *Oriens Antiquus* 2, 1962, pp. 23-39 (Italian). Israel Department of Antiquities, [Short reports on the Excavations at Tell Gat] *IEJ* 9, 1959, pp. 269-271; *IEJ* 10, 1960, pp. 122-123; *IEJ* 11, 1961, p. 191. S. Yeivin, "Early Contacts between Canaan and Egypt," *IEJ* 10, 1960, pp. 193-203; *First Preliminary Report on the Excavations at Tel "Gat" (Tell Sheikh 'Ahmed el-'Areyny) Seasons 1956-1958.* Jerusalem: Dept of Antiquities, Ministry of Education and Culture 1961; "Further Evidence of Narmer at 'Gat,'" *Oriens Antiquus* 2, 1963, pp. 205-213; [Short report of the 1959-60 Seasons at Tell Gat] *Revue Biblique* 67, 1960, pp. 391-4 (French).

TELL TA'ANNEK. See Taanach.

TELL TA'YINAT. A medium-sized mound just north of the Orontes River and the Syrian frontier in the Turkish Hatay, Tell Ta'yīnāt is one of several sites excavated by the Oriental Institute of Chicago between 1932 and 1938 in the marshy plain of Antioch called Unqi by the Assyrians and 'Amuq today. It is close to Tell 'Atshānah, the ancient *Alalakh, as to preclude the possibility that both flourished at the same time. In fact, Tell Ta'yīnāt's principal remains date from the "Syro-Hittite" period in the early first millennium when the area, still independent, was known to the Assyrians as Hattina. The discovery of a royal palace suggests the identification of Ta'yīnāt with Taia, one of the capitals of Hattina whose capture Shalmaneser III claimed in his first regnal year (858 B.C.). Among the fragmentary Hieroglyphic Hittite monuments found at the site is a colossal inscribed statue depicting, or at least mentioning, Halparuntas, identical with the Kal/rparu(n)da of Hattina (or his namesake at Gurgum) whose tribute Shalmaneser claims to have received in 853 B.C., just before he fought the great Battle of Qarqar against the more intransigent western states, and again in 848 B.C.; his "portrait" appears on Shalmaneser's famous "black obelisk" together with that of Jehu of Israel and other tributaries, though not in the same attitude of abject prostration (*see* Black Obelisk of Shalmaneser). A column base of twin crouching lions from Ta'yīnāt is perhaps the most highly developed example of Syro-Hittite sculpture in the round yet found.

Adjacent to the royal palace, the excavators came upon a small chapel of the eighth century (B.C.) kings of the city. This is the only temple contemporary with the kings of Israel ever discovered in Syria or Palestine. Like Solomon's temple it was a rectangle. A portico with two columns stood at the front. Next was a main hall, behind which was a cella, or shrine, with a raised platform. The Tell Ta'yānīt shrine was two-thirds as long as Solomon's temple and it was probably lined with cedar.

BIBLIOGRAPHY. Calvin W. McEwan, "The Syrian Expedition of The Oriental Institute of the University of Chicago," *AJA*, XLI, 1937, pp. 8-16. Robert J. and Linda S. Braidwood, *Excavations in the Plain of Antioch I* = Oriental Institute Publications, LXI, 1960.

TEMENOS. A temenos is a sacred enclosure, the area marked off and assigned to the use of a god. It is used of the altar and the land surrounding the altar which was regarded as holy. In a broader sense it can be used of all lands belonging to the cult of a god.

TEMPLE. *See* Architecture.

TEPE GAWRA. The site of Tepe Gawra, fifteen miles northeast of Musul, was discovered by Ephraim Speiser and excavated in 1927 and from 1931 to 1938 by the American Schools of Oriental Research, the University of Pennsylvania Museum, and Dropsie College. Our oldest known brass ax came to light during these excavations. Metal was introduced from some unknown mountain area and was first used for weapons, while stone continued to be used for household utensils. The ax came from the 'Ubaid (*see* Tell al 'Ubaid) level, while the oldest pottery is of the Halaf type (*see* Gozan).

In all twenty-four levels and sublevels were excavated, showing occupation from the fifth to the second millennium B.C. The more recent upper levels were not distinctive, but in the lower levels archaeologists can trace the chronological sequence from the Tell Halaf period (*ca.* 5000 B.C.) through the 'Ubaid (4100-3500 B.C.) and *Jemdet Nasr (3500-3000 B.C.) periods. Three remains of temples on an acropolis of the thirteenth level represent the finest architecture on the site. A circular construction of the eleventh level was probably a citadel.

BIBLIOGRAPHY. Charles Bache, "Tepe Gawra, 1934-35," *AJA*, 1935, XXXIX 185-188; "Fouilles de Tepe Gawra," *Syria*, 1937, XVIII, p. 317. E. A. Speiser, *Excavations at Tepe Gawra* I and II, University of Pennsylvania Press, Philadelphia, 1935, 1950; "Closing the Gap at Tepe Gawra," Annual Report, 1939, Smithsonian Institute, Washington, 1940; "Historical Significance of Tepe Gawra," Annual Report, 1933, Smithsonian Institute, Washington, 1935; "The Joint Excavation at Tepe Gawra," *AJA*, 1932, XXXVI, pp. 564-568; "New Discoveries at Tepe Gawra and Khafaje," *AJA*, 1937, XLI, pp. 190-193; "The Bearing of the Excavations at Tell Billis and at Tepe Gawra upon the ethnic problems of Ancient Mesopotamia," *AJA*, 1932, XXXVI, pp. 29-35; "Traces of the Oldest Cultures of Babylonia and Assyria," *Archiv für Orientforschung*, 1928-29, V, pp. 62-164; "Preliminary Excavations at Tepe Gawra," *AASOR*, 1927-28, IX, pp. 17-94. A. J. Tobler, *Excavations at Tepe Gawra*, Vol. II, 1950.

TEPE SIYALK. About midway on the road from Tehran to Isfahan in modern Iran is the oasis of Kashan, the site of Tepe Siyalk which was excavated by Roman Ghirshman between 1933 and 1937. Siyalk contained the earliest traces of human settlement in the Iranian plateau. The earliest inhabitants left traces discovered above the virgin soil at the bottom of the mound. They lived in huts made from the branches of trees. Soon, however, we find evidences of more permanent structures, and agriculture is added to hunting as a way of life. Bones of domesticated oxen and sheep give evidence that stock breeding was practiced by the prehistoric residents of Siyalk.

At Siyalk, Ghirshman was able to trace the development of Iranian pottery from very crude beginnings. During the earliest period, known to archaeologists as Siyalk I, pottery was black, smoked, and made by hand without the use of a wheel. Later a red ware appeared with black patches caused by accidents of firing in a primitive oven. Next appears painted pottery, with geometric designs which suggest an imitation of basket work. The early inhabitants of Siyalk had evidently learned to weave baskets before they developed the ceramic arts and the early pots imitated the earlier basket designs. Spindle whorls made of baked clay and stone provide evidence that a textile industry was in operation at a very early date. There were also numerous stone tools, flint knife blades, sickle blades, polished axes and scrapers. By the end of the period small hammered objects began to appear. The properties of metal were evidently understood, but the art of casting had not been discovered. The Siyalk civilization dates to the end of the neolithic age.

Both men and women took delight in adorning themselves with rings, bracelets, and necklaces during the Siyalk I period. Along with jewelry, Ghirshman found small pestles and miniature mortars used for the grinding of body paints. The neolithic artists made use of bone for carving, and tool handles were often decorated with the head of a gazelle or a hare. One of the oldest of Near Eastern figurines is a Siyalk knife handle representing a man wearing a cap and a loin cloth fastened by a belt.

The inhabitants of Siyalk I believed in a life after death, and they buried their dead under the floors of their houses so that the spirits of the deceased could share in the family life. Trade with neighboring villages had been developed as early as the Siyalk I community, as evidenced by the fact that shells were imported from the Persian Gulf, six hundred miles away. Itinerant peddlers probably traveled from village to village selling luxury wares such as shells used for jewelry.

The Siyalk II period (fourth millennium B.C.) presents an advance on the earliest settlements. Tools are more refined and the houses are decorated and improved. Sun-dried bricks served as building material and the interiors were decorated with red paint made from a mixture of iron oxide and fruit juice. Pottery was also much improved, some of it decorated with pictures of birds and animals. Metal became more plentiful. Commerce continued to increase, and Iranian traders introduced barley and wheat, both indigenous to Iran, into both Egypt and Europe.

Siyalk III comprises a large number of superimposed levels comprising much of the history of the site during the fourth millennium B.C. Among technological advances are rectangular, molded bricks and the potter's wheel. Writing had not yet begun on the Iranian plateau, but the pictorial representations which came to characterize Iranian ceramic ware may well have contributed to the development of the pictographic Sumerian syllabary which developed in southern Mesopotamia before 3000 B.C.

During the Siyalk III period, copper was smelted and cast, and metals began slowly to supplant stone in the making of tools and weapons. Jewelry became more varied as carnelian, turquoise, lapis lazuli and jade were used along with the shell of earlier times. Plain discs with slightly raised borders served as mirrors. Stamp seals made first with geometric, and later with pictorial designs, were used to provide evidence of ownership. During the middle of the fourth millennium B.C., the civilization of northern Mesopotamia (later to be known as Assyria) adopted the ceramic tradition of Iran with its chalice shape and painted decoration. Siyalk provides some of the best examples of these.

Excavations indicate a gap of nearly two

THE ACROPOLIS AT TEPE GAWRA. *Courtesy, University Museum, Philadelphia*

thousand years in the occupation of Siyalk. With the beginnings of the first millennium B.C. Indo-European peoples whom we know as Iranians began to penetrate the Iranian plateau, and Siyalk was again occupied. The Iranians were a pastoral and agricultural people who took pride in the breeding and training of horses. Chariotry and cavalry made possible their phenomenal success on the battlefield. At this time Siyalk was occupied by an invading prince who built an imposing residence on top of the mound. Then he surrounded the town, including the houses at the foot of the mound, with a wall flanked with towers. The new settlers buried their dead in a vast cemetery several hundred yards from the town.

Pottery from Iranian Siyalk depicts fighting men. A cylinder seal shows a fighting man on horseback fighting a monster, and another depicts a man riding in a horse-drawn chariot, shooting an arrow at an animal. Siyalk by this time was a fortified town with local princes who prepared to fight the Assyrians and other western peoples. Urban life had come to Siyalk.

BIBLIOGRAPHY. Roman Ghirshman, "At Sialk: Prehistoric Iran," *Asia*, 1938, XXXIII, pp. 645-650; "Les Fouilles de Sialk et des civilisations prehistoriques de l'Iran," *Bulletin des Musees de France*, 1935, 7 anee, pp. 123-24; *Fouilles de Sialk pres de Kashan*, P. Geutner, Paris, 1933-37.

TERQA (Tell 'Ashara). A major station on the middle Euphrates, Terqa was the principal seat of the worship of the god Dagan (Biblical Dagon) in Mesopotamia. It rose to prominence under Shamshi-Adad I of Assyria and Zimri-Lim or Mari, and probably became the capital of the independent state of Hana after Hammurabi.

I. *Name and Location.* According to the cuneiform geographical lists, there were at least three ancient Mesopotamian towns known as Terqa, and variant spellings such as Sirqa, Sirku and Tirga suggest an etymology based on Semitic words for irrigation. The principal Terqa (or Tirqa), today named Tell 'Ashara after a local tribe, suits this etymology, since it is located on the Euphrates between a network of ancient canals paralleling that river, and about fifteen miles below the confluence of the *Habor River. It lies in modern Syria, about forty-five miles above the Iraqi border. Like the ancient cities of Mari, (H)anat and Tuttul farther downstream, it lay on the right bank of the Euphrates; together with these cities, it constituted a buffer zone between Syria and Babylonia.

II. *Exploration.* Tell 'Ashara was first visited by Herzfeld in 1910, and identified by him with Terqa on the basis of an inscription found at the site. It was briefly excavated by Thureau-Dangin and Dhorme in 1923, but since then the excavations at nearby *Mari have taken precedence over it, though at the same time throwing much light on Terqa too. In 1948, a stele of Tukulti-Ninurta II was discovered at the site, whose proximity to the Euphrates constantly threatens to wash away its remains.

III. *History of the Site.*

A. Terqa in the Third Millennium. The Middle Euphrates entered the orbit of Sumerian culture at an early date, as revealed both by the excavations at Mari, which have turned up architecture, sculpture and artifacts in the best Early Dynastic style, and by the native Sumerian traditions, which include an early ruler of Mari in their King Lists and record the destruction of the city by Eannatum of Lagash (*ca.* 2450 B.C.). In return, the region bequeathed to Sumer (as it did later to Philistia and the West) its worship of the grain-god Dagan. Thus *Sargon of Akkad (*ca.* 2333-2283 B.C.) worshipped Dagan at Tuttul to assure himself of access to the "Upper Country" and similarly his grandson Naram-Sin (*ca.* 2252-2216 B.C.) credits his conquests in North Syria to Dagan. By the neo-Sumerian period (ca. 2111-2004 B.C.), personal names composed with Dagan become common in Mesopotamia, and his worship became part of the official cult, at least at Şillush-Dagan, the great livestock-center of the religious capital at Nippur. A text from this site mentioning people from "Tirga" is the earliest documentary evidence for the city.

B. Terqa in the Mari Age. The earliest rulers of Terqa may be preserved for us in an unexpected source: the Assyrian King List. This includes a list of the ancestors of Shamshi-Adad I of Assyria (*ca.* 1815-1782 B.C.), beginning with Apiashal and ending with Ila-kabkabi, and including such typically Amorite names as Yazlu-ili and a theophoric name Ilu-Mer which is at home in the Middle Euphrates region. According to the same source, Shamshi-Adad established himself in Babylonia while Naram-Sin of Eshnunna was ruling Ashur; when Erishu II succeeded Naram-Sin at Ashur, Shamshi-Adad drove him from the throne and established himself as ruler of Ashur. At the same time he remained mindful of his "Hanaean" origins, sacrificing to his ancestral spirits in Terqa and (re)building the great temple of Dagan there. Mari shared Ashur's fate, for here the native dynast Yahdun-Lim, an old antagonist of Ila-kabkabi and of Shamshi-Adad, was killed in a palace revolt, his son Zimri-Lim fleeing to Aleppo and Shamshi-Adad installed his own younger son Yashmah-Adad as viceroy. Since the region of Ashur was similarly assigned to the Crown-prince Ishme-Dagan at Ekallatum, while Shamshi-Adad himself seems to have ruled the Habor Region from Shubat-Enlil, it appears that the entire area between the Middle Euphrates and the Middle Tigris was united under these Hanaeans from Terqa about 1800 B.C.

The special privileges which Terqa apparently enjoyed under Shamshi-Adad came to an end at his death (*ca.* 1782 B.C.), for Zimri-Lim soon regained Mari for himself, and Terqa became a province of the restored kingdom. Its governor, Kibri-Dagan, maintained a lively correspondence with his sovereign and colleagues at Mari, and almost a hundred of his letters are preserved in the archives of Mari. They provide a vivid picture of provincial administration in the Mari Age. Other letters, too, deal with Terqa at this time; one of the most interesting details the dream of an official in the temple of Dagan at Terqa in which this deity interrogated and instructed him concerning the chiefs of the "Benjaminite" nomads with whom Zimri-Lim was constantly concerned. The defeat of Mari by Hammurabi of Babylon (*ca.* 1792-1750) in *ca.* 1760 B.C., and its destruction two years later, once more changed Terqa's fortunes. It briefly became part of the empire of Hammurabi and his successor Samsu-iluna (*ca.* 1749-1712) but, with Mari reduced, the stage was set for Terqa's independence.

C. The Kingdom of Hana. As presumed capital of the independent kingdom of Hana which inherited the Middle Euphrates when the empire of Hammurabi collapsed under his successor, Terqa boasts one of the few documented dynasties in a period (*ca.* 1740-1570 B.C.) when most of the surrounding area was being gradually plunged into a prolonged eclipse. Even so, we know little more than the names of the rulers, and not even their order is certain. Those attested by date formulas, seal impressions or both are: Ishar-Lim, Is(h)ih-Dagan, Hammurabi, Shumuh-rammu and his son Ammi-madar, and Kashtili-ashu. The first five names and, as far as preserved, their patronymics — which may or may not identify reigning kings — are of the Amorite type already familiar from the Mari period; the last is clearly Kassite — indeed it is a name borne by four separate kings of the Kassite dynasty, a dynasty which the traditional native sources date *ca.* 1740-1160 B.C. If these sources are taken at their word, then the Kassite Kashtiliashu I and II ruled *ca.* 1704-1675 B.C., i.e., they were contemporary with Abi-eshuh (*ca.* 1711-1684 B.C.) and Ammi-ditana (*ca.* 1683-1647 B.C.), the successors of Shamshu-iluna at Babylon, and it becomes reasonable to identify one of them with the ruler of Hana. Thus the conclusion that the first Kassite kings ruled at Terqa (for which there are also some other, if ambiguous, indications) would solve one of the knottiest problems of Mesopotamian chronology, for it enables us to say that they extended their rule to Babylon itself only after that city had been sacked by the Hittites about 1595 B.C. The Kassite sources themselves seem to imply as much when they state that their king Agum II (*ca.* 1592-1565 B.C.) brought Marduk, the god of Babylon, back from the land of the Hanaeans (i.e., Terqa) after he had been in Hittite captivity for twenty-four years.

D. Terqa in the Assyrian period. For Terqa, the Dark Ages began only with the removal of the Kassite capital to Babylon, for the Terqa which, in the treaty between Hittites and Mitannians, was assigned to Piya-shilli of *Carchemish is surely the one to the east of that city. Two isolated kings of Hana are known for the late second millennium, Tukulti-Mer and Ilu-iqîsha, but it was under the name of Laqe that the area around the confluence of the Habor and Euphrates Rivers first appears in the Assyrian records, where Terqa is referred to as Sirqu. Since the traditional route of early Assyrian campaigns went down the Tigris or the Wadi Tartar and back up along the Middle Euphrates and Habor, it is understandable that the land of "Hana and Mari" had a foretaste of the Assyrian armies as early as the second millennium. But these expedi-

tions were little more than raids to collect booty, and it was not until the ninth century that Assyrian expansion resumed in earnest, beginning precisely in this area (*see also* Til-Barsip III B). In his annals, Tukulti-Ninurta II (890-884 B.C.) was the first to record the submission of Terqa, then ruled by a certain Mudad (or Iddin-Dada) who had already figured in the annals of his predecessor, Adad-nirari II (911-891 B.C.). A stele found in Terqa itself in 1948 also celebrates the Assyrian conquest of the city in 886 B.C.; it is a most remarkable monument, inscribed by Tukulti-Ninurta in Assyrian cuneiform and decorated with reliefs in the purest "Syro-Hittite" style. One could regard it as a most precisely dated example of this style (so Albright) if reliefs and inscriptions were demonstrably executed at the same time. Ashur-nasir-pal II (883-859 B.C.) mentions the city again and it was probably under Shalmaneser III (858-824 B.C.) that it was definitively incorporated into the Assyrian provincial system, for Nergal-eresh, governor of Raṣappa from at least 803-775 B.C. (according to the eponym lists) records Terqa as one of the parts of his extensive province in an inscription in honor of his king, Adad-nirari III (810-783 B.C.). This is to date the last reference to the city in the cuneiform documents.

BIBLIOGRAPHY. François Thureau-Dangin and Édouard Dhorme, "*Cinq jours de fouilles a 'Asharah*," *Syria*, V, 1924, pp. 265-293 and pls. lvii-lx. Jean Nougayrol, "*Une nouvelle tablette de Hana*," *ibid.*, XXXVII, 1960, pp. 205-209; "*Un nouveau roi de Hana*," *Revue d'Assyriologie*, XLI, 1947, pp. 42-46. Ernst Herzfeld, "*Hana et Mari*," *ibid.*, XI, 1914, pp. 131-139. Ferris J. Stephens, "A cuneiform tablet from Dura-Europas," *ibid.*, XXXIV, 1937, pp. 183-190. Georges Dossin, "*Une révélation du dieu Dagan a Terqa*," *ibid.*, XLII, 1948, pp. 125-134. Jean-Robert Kupper, "*Un gouvernement provincial dans le royaume de Mari.*" *ibid.*, XLI, 1947, pp. 150-183; *Correspondance de Kibri-Dagan* = *Archives Royales de Mari*, III, 1950; "*Le canal Ishim-Iahdunlim*," *Bibliotheca Orientalis*, IX, 1952, pp. 168f.; *Les Nomades en Mésopotamie au temps de Rois de Mari* = *Bibliothèque de la Faculté de Philosophie et Lettres de l'Université de Liège*, CXLII, 1957. Édouard Dhorme, "*Les atavars du dieu Dagon*," *Revue de l'Histoire des Religions*, CXXXVIII, 1950, pp. 129-144 and *Recueil Édouard Dhorme*, 1951, pp. 745-754. R. J. Tournay and Soubhi Saouaf, "*Stèle de Tukulti-Ninurta II*," *Les Annales Archéologiques de Syrie*, II, 1952, pp. 169-190 and pls. i-iii.

THEATER. The theater is first known in the fifth century B.C. in Greece where it was used

ROMAN AMPHITHEATER at Caesarea. Courtesy, Israel Office of Information

to present dramatic performances which developed from the religious songs and dances in honor of the god Dionysus. It also served as an assembly place for the citizens of a Hellenistic community (Acts 19:29-41). The theater was built on a natural ground slope. The auditorium was semicircular in form, with a circular orchestra or chorus space in the center and a raised wooden stage for the actors. Spectators sat on tiers of seats cut from rock, stone, wood, or marble slabs, separated into two or more sections by gangways.

The best preserved Greek theater is at Epidaurus in the Peloponnesus. It was built in the fourth century B.C. and may have accommodated up to fourteen thousand spectators. It is used today in the presentation of Greek drama.

The theater built by Herod the Great at *Caesarea has recently been excavated by Israeli archaeologists. Other theaters which he built are still visible in Damascus, Gadara, Kanatha, Scythopolis (Beth-shan) and Philadelphia (Amman). According to Josephus, Herod built a theater and an *amphitheater

in Jerusalem. Remains of Greek and Roman theaters survive in Philippi, Athens, Corinth, Miletus, Ephesus, and Rome. The theater at Ephesus is said to have accommodated 24,500 persons.

THEBES. During the four centuries between the expulsion of the Hyksos (*ca.* 1575 B.C.) and the death of Ramesses III (*ca.* 1151 B.C.), Thebes was Egypt's capital and, during much of that time, the political center of an empire which extended to the Euphrates. Unlike the cities of Babylon and Nineveh, whose remains were hidden until modern times in mounds of rubbish, the glory of Thebes was always visible in the ruins of its great temples which are still standing on the east bank of the Nile, 450 miles south of Cairo.

The modern city of Luxor occupies a small portion of the area occupied by ancient Thebes. The name Luxor is derived from the Arabic *El-Uqsur,* "the castles," a reference to the ruins of the great temples which still dominate the site. In ancient times the city and district of Thebes bore the

THE TEMPLE OF AMUN AT KARNAK. *Courtesy, Matson Photo Service*

name Weset, or Newt ("The city"). From the latter name the Bible designates the city as No (Ezek. 30:14-16) and No-Amon (i.e. the city of the god of Amun, Nahum 3:8).

Another ancient name for Thebes was "the two apts," a reference to the two districts of the city corresponding to the ruins of Karnak and Luxor. Some Egyptologists suggest that the Greeks called the city Thebes (after Grecian Thebes) because of the native *ta ape*, Tape ("the apts"). Egyptian Thebes was familiar to the Greeks as early as Homer. The Iliad speaks of "hundred gated Thebes from which valiant men issue forth on missions of conquest."

The Greeks identified the great Egyptian god Amun with their Zeus and referred to Thebes as Diospolis Magna, "the great city of the god." Across the river from Thebes was Weset Amentet ("Western Thebes") or Per Hathor ("House of Hathor") the city of the dead in which the tombs of the pharaohs were located.

Although the origins of Thebes go back to predynastic times, it was not until the Eleventh Dynasty that a Theban prince took to himself the title "King of Upper and Lower Egypt." Thebes maintained its importance during the period of Hyksos rule in Egypt, although its local ruler was forced to admit the suzerainty of the hated foreigners. It was a Theban prince, Kamose, who ultimately freed Middle Egypt of Hyksos power. Ahmose I, founder of the Eighteenth Dynasty, succeeded in driving the Hyksos from their Delta stronghold at Avaris. Egypt once again was ruled by her own dynasty. Ahmose restored Luxor, and the Pharaohs Amenhotep I and Thutmose I built monuments at Karnak which still stand. Queen Hatshepsut is favored by an obelisk at Karnak. Her successor Thutmose III extended Egyptian power in Asia and returned with trophies of victory that made Thebes the grandest capital in the ancient world.

At this time Amun, the god of Thebes, attained the position of chief deity of Egypt. Prior to the Twelfth Dynasty, Amun was a lesser god of Thebes. It may have been Amenemhet I, founder of the Twelfth Dynasty, who first raised the Amun cult to a place of importance. Temples to Amun began to arise at Karnak during his reign. The conquests of Thutmose III brought

added glory to the Amun temple at Karnak. Under Amenhotep II, Thutmose IV, and Amenhotep III the city of Thebes continued to expand and the glory of Amun was enhanced.

Amenhotep III connected the temples of Luxor and Karnak by a wide avenue beautified by flower gardens and bordered with sphinxes. Across the river he built a mortuary temple of which the so-called colossi of Memmon are the remaining monuments. A palace for himself, another for his favorite wife, Tiy, and a pleasure lake on which he and his wife could sail, were among the other building operations of Amenhotep III.

Under Amenhotep IV (Akhenaton), Thebes was abandoned as a royal city. The son of Amenhotep III renounced the Amun priests, left Thebes, and built his new capital Akhetaton at Tell El-Amarna. For about a dozen years Thebes was purposely neglected and Aton of Akhetaton replaced Amun of Thebes as the royal deity.

At the death of Akhenaton the Amarna revolt was ended. His successor Haremhab moved the capital back to Thebes and made additions to the temples at Luxor and Karnak. Ramesses I, Seti I, and Ramesses II added to the huge Hypostle Hall which became the most noteworthy feature of the Karnak temple. West of the Nile funerary temples continued to be built by successive Pharaohs. The Ramesseum of Ramesses II was adorned with the largest granite colossus of ancient Egypt.

After Ramesses II, however, the power of Egypt quickly declined, and with it the glory of Thebes. Ramesses III built the gigantic Medinet Habu temple, but he could not arrest the decay in Egyptian prestige. The priests of Amun gained power and the high priest Herihor was able to dethrone the last of the Ramesside rulers. The wealth of Egypt was largely controlled by the Amun priesthood and, as a result, both Thebes and Egypt suffered.

With the rise in power of the Amun priests of Thebes, a rival dynasty was established at Tanis in the Delta. The god Amun continued to be reverenced, and Thebes was recognized as a religious center, but government was administered from the Delta. Under the Ethiopian Pharaohs of the Twenty-fifth Dynasty the seat of government was returned to Thebes but the results were disastrous. Interference in the affairs of Syria and Palestine brought about the wrath of Assyria. Ashurbanipal sacked Thebes in 661 B.C.

The prophet Nahum taunted proud Nineveh by reminding the Assyrian capital of the fate of Thebes:

Are you better than Thebes that sat by the Nile,
with water around her, her rampart a sea,
and water her wall? Ethiopia was her strength
Egypt too, and that without limit;
Put and the Libyans were her helpers.

(Nahum 3:8-9)

After the sack of Thebes efforts were made to restore the city but it never regained its strategic importance. Cambyses, the son of Cyrus the Persian, sacked Thebes 136 years after Ashurbanipal's expedition.

The Ptolemies sought to enhance Thebes, but the city lived in the afterglow of former glories. When Diodorus visited the town in 57 B.C., he was shown its splendid ruins. "The Thebans boast," he observes, "that they were the most ancient philosophers and astrologers of any people in the world, and the first that found out exact rules for the improvement both of philosophy and astrology" (I, 45, 46).

In 24 B.C. Strabo visited the city. He observed: "Vestiges of its magnitude still exist, which extend 80 stadia [about 9 miles] in length. There are a great number of temples, many of which Cambyses mutilated. The spot is at present occupied by villages" (XVII. i. 46).

From Roman times to the present Thebes has served as a tourist attraction. Its temples have been desecrated by Moslem and Christian alike, and nature has also taken its toll of the monuments of Egypt's past. Still the city remains one of the living witnesses to the fact that human glory is short-lived, that earthly fame lasts at most but a few generations.

BIBLIOGRAPHY. Elizabeth Riegstahl, *Thebes in the time of Amunhotep III*, University of Oklahoma Press, Norman 1964. Alexander Scharff and Anton Moortgat, '*Agypten und Vorderasien im Altertum*, Verlag F. Bruckmann, Munich, 1950.

THERAPEUTAE. *See* Jewish Sects.

BAS RELIEF FROM THE AMUN TEMPLE at Karnak. Courtesy, Foto Marburg

TIBERIAS. Tiberias, the chief town along the western shore of the Sea of Galilee, was built by Herod Antipas around A.D. 25 to serve as capital of the tetrarchy of Galilee and Perea, and named for Tiberius Caesar. The city had not been built when Jesus was a boy, and in his manhood he seems never to have visited it.

South of Tiberias are sulphur springs which were used by the Romans and evidently had been known as early as Joshua who mentions a town of Hammath (Josh. 19:35) in the region. The Romans called the place Therma. During the building of Tiberias, the workmen came upon an ancient cemetery, presumably from Therma, and the Jews considered the city unclean for that reason. Before the destruction of Jerusalem, A.D. 70, Tiberias was a strictly gentile city, but subsequently it became a center of Talmudic Judaism. The Palestinian Talmud was compiled there and, significantly, the great medieval Jewish scholar Maimonides was buried at Tiberias in the twelfth century.

Tiberias gave its name to the Sea of Galilee which became known as the Lake of Tiberias. The city is mentioned only once in the New Testament when the followers of Jesus took Tiberian boats to journey from the east site of the Sea of Capernaum (John 6:23).

Its geographical position, surrounded by mountains and the waters of the Sea, made Tiberias easy to defend, a fact which probably caused Herod Antipas to choose the site for his capital. The region around Tiberias has few other advantages, for it is almost seven hundred feet below sea level and the summer heat is almost unbearable.

TIL-BARSIB (Tell Ahmar). The modern village of Tell Ahmar ("red mound") occupies part of the site of ancient Til-Barsib which guarded an important crossing of the Euphrates River and served as capital (?) of the independent state of Bit-Adini, the Biblical Beth-eden (Amos 1:5), until conquered by Assyria in the ninth century B.C., when it was renamed Kar-Shulmanu-asharid ("Quay of Shalmaneser").

I. *Location.* Til-Barsib is located on the left, or Assyrian, bank of the Euphrates, a dozen miles inside the modern Syrian border. It is the natural terminus of the Assyrian trade and military route leading westward through

*Gozan, *Haran and Hadatu, for it lies midway between *Carchemish to the north, for long an effective buffer against Assyrian ambitions, and the inhospitable desert of Osrhoene to the south. By the same token, it served as the Assyrian gateway to Syria and the Mediterranean when it did not mark the westernmost extension of Assyrian hegemony.

II. *History of Discovery.* The first modern archaeologist to visit Tell Ahmar was D. G. Hogarth, who already in 1908 proposed to identify the site with cuneiform Til-Barsib. The identification was confirmed three years later by Thompson, who visited the site together with T. E. Lawrence, on the basis of two identical Assyrian inscriptions carved on a pair of winged lions flanking the northeastern gate which gave one the direct route to Assyria. The inscriptions, commemorating the lions "in the great gate of Kar-Shulmanu-asharid," were published by Thompson in 1912 (see Bibliography). In 1927 and 1928, Thureau-Dangin made some initial soundings at the site which he published in 1929, and from 1929-31 he conducted systematic excavations there which led to an improved edition of the lion inscriptions in 1930 and to the definitive publication of the site, with Dunan and others, in 1936 (see Bibliography).

III. *History of the Site.*

A. Before the First Millennium. The site of Til-Barsib was occupied during the fourth and third millennia B.C. on the testimony of vestigial remains, chiefly of pottery, which can be approximately dated by comparison with artifacts from other Mesopotamian sites. The first alleged mention of the site in cuneiform text occurs in the inscriptions of Gudea of Lagash (*ca.* 2136-1121 B.C.), who mentions the mountain of Bar-sib (or Bar-me) as the source of the otherwise unknown na-lu-a stone; but it is equally possible that he is here referring to the Babylonian city of Borsippa or, more likely, to Barmeum east of the Tigris. Throughout the second millennium, more or less datable graves and grave deposits attest to the continued occupation of the site.

B. Period of Independence. Sometime around 1000 B.C., Til-Barsib emerged as the, or a, capital of the Arameo-Hittite state of Bit-Adini, which had taken advantage of a period of Assyrian weakness to gain control of both sides of the Euphrates below Carchemish and may have extended eastward at least as far as *Haran on the Balikh River.

TIBERIAS on the Sea of Galilee. Courtesy, Consulate General of Israel

Two native inscriptions in Hieroglyphic Hittite, edited by Meriggi in 1935 and Hrozný in 1937 (see Bibliography) throw some light on this period. Although their final interpretation remains uncertain, they seem to show a succession of late Hittite royal names ruling the Aramean state of Bit-Adini and its neighbors approximately as follows: Hapadalas-Ahunas-Maluiwadas-Hamatas. Of these names, the second is familiar from Assyrian sources as Ahuni, last independent ruler of Bit-Adini (see below), while his grandson (?) ruled Bit-Haluppi on the Habor River as governor of Suru under his Assyrianized name of Hamatai until murdered in 884 B.C. at the instigation of Ahuni. He may also have been identical with the Hamatai of Laqe (*see* Terqa) who paid tribute to Tukulti-Ninurta II of Assyria in the same year.

C. The Struggle with °Assyria. The resurgence of Assyria (*ca.* 930-830 B.C.) brought Bit-Adini inexorably into conflict with its more powerful neighbor. At first the Assyrian armies, busy with conquests nearer home,

contented themselves with punitive raids and the collection of tribute, but their ambitions eyed the rich lands west of the Euphrates, and Bit-Adini blocked their path. Ahuni confronted Ashurnasirpal as early as 878 and 877 B.C., and his successor Shalmaneser III in 858 B.C. Allied with his more distant neighbors of Sam'al, Hattina and Carchemish, he at first managed to check the new conqueror at the battle of Lutibu, but in the next three years he had to endure the Assyrian onslaught alone. In successive campaigns, he was chased from his capital, deprived of his kingdom and finally captured. The cities of Bit-Adini were given Assyrian names, with Til-Barsib itself renamed after its conqueror (above) who built there a royal residence for his own temporary sojourns. His triumph ushered in three decades of almost continuous campaigns against the west and its impact was not lost on Israel and Judah, where it was still recalled a century later (Amos 1:5) and more (II Kings 19:12–Isa. 37:12).

D. Interregnum. Shamshi-Adad V (823-

585

811 B.C.) was not able to maintain the pace of his father's conquests, and Til-Barsib now became the westernmost outpost of Assyrian influence. It remained in Assyrian hands, but at a price: the Assyrian governor of Til-Barsib at Haran who, as *turtanu* (Hebrew *tartan*: II Kings 18:17; Isa. 20:1), was second only to the king himself, assumed a stance of virtual autonomy. He is prominently featured in some of the Assyrian wall-paintings, among the finest yet recovered, which probably date from this period. One of them, Shamshi-ilu by name (*ca.* 780-752), inscribed the gate lions of Til-Barsib in quasi-royal style without even deigning to mention his nominal Assyrian sovereign. He boasted of taming numerous enemies, among them Urartu (Armenia); but if so, his success was short-lived, for between 781 and 774 B.C. Shalmaneser IV of Assyria (783-774 B.C.) fought no less than six campaigns against Urartu and its aggressive king Argishti I. These were clearly defensive in nature, and ended in the loss of Til-Barsib and all of northern Syria to Urartu; the last dated evidence of Assyrian occupation of Til-Barsib is a tablet from Calah dated 778 B.C.

E. Pax Assyriaca. Urartu was not to be dislodged until a new Assyrian conqueror arose. In 743 B.C., Tiglath-pileser III (744-727 B.C.) dealt it a crushing blow at the battle of Kummuh and reconquered the entire area. At the same time he made sure of the loyalty of his governors by separating Til-Barsib from Haran and making it the seat of a small new prefecture, while restoring the royal residence of Shalmaneser III. The city itself, however, was not restored to its former grandeur until Esarhaddon (680-669 B.C.) rebuilt it. His inscription at Til-Barsib was found on a stele done in the Aramaeo-Hittite style of the period and probably commemorated his victory over Sidon in 676 B.C.; it is perhaps the largest Assyrian stele yet known. Henceforth little is known of the city, though it probably remained loyal to Assyria to the very end (610 B.C.). The site continued to be occupied even after this, for it has yielded graves of the Achaemenid period and a small Hellenistic sanctuary. The geographer Ptolemy recorded it as Bersiba in his Mesopotamian itineraries.

BIBLIOGRAPHY. R. Campbell Thompson, "Til-Barsib and its Cuneiform Inscriptions," *Proceedings of the Society of Biblical Archaeology*, XXXIV, 1912, pp. 66-74 and pls. iv-vi. Francois Thureau-Dangin, "Tell Ahmar," *Syria*, X, 1929, pp. 185-205 and pls. xxviii-xxxv; "Un Specimen des Peintures Assyriennes de Til-Barsib," *ibid.*, XI, 1930, pp. 113-132 and pls. xxiif.; "L'Inscription des Lions de Til-Barsib," *Revue d'Assyriologie*, XXVII, 1930, pp. 11-21; "A propos des peintures de Til-Barsib: une question de date,' *ibid.*, XXXI, 1934, pp. 193f.; *Til-Barsib*, Librairie Orientaliste Paul Geuthner, Paris, 1936 (with Maurice Dunand). Pietro Meriggi, "Sur deux inscriptions en hiéroglyphs de Tell Ahmar," *Revue Hittite et Asianique*, III, 1935, pp. 45-57 and pls. 2-4. Bedrich Hrozny, "Les deux stèles 'Hittites' hiéroglyphiques de Tell Ahmar," *Monografie Archivu Orientálního*, I, 1937, pp. 465-490. Abraham Malamat, "*Amos* 1:5 in the light of the Til-Barsip Inscriptions," *BASOR*, 129, 1953, pp. 25f.

TIRZAH. The town of Tirzah was originally a Canaanite town noted for its beauty (S. of Sol. 6:4). It was captured by Joshua (Josh. 12:24) and later became the capital of Israel in the days of Jeroboam I (I Kings 14:17), Baasha (I Kings 15:21, 33; 16:6), Elah and Zimri (I Kings 16:8, 9, 15). Zimri burned the palace over his own head when besieged there by Omri (I Kings 16:17, 18). After six years Omri moved the capital to Samaria. A later resident of Tirzah, Menahem, overthrew Shallum and usurped the throne (II Kings 15:14, 16).

I. *Identification.* The exact location of Tirzah is difficult to decide from Old Testament evidence. One might suspect a location in the general region of Samaria and a number of large mounds in the area have been suggested, among them being *Tulluza* to the north of Mt. Ebal, *Teyasir* farther north and *Jemma'in* seven miles south of Shechem. Two of these have names resembling Tirzah. The strongest claimant is, however, °*Tell el-Far'ah* (Mound of the Elevated Ridge), some 600 meters long and 300 meters wide, situated on the road from Shechem to Bethshan and Damascus at the head of the *Wadi el Far'ah* where the road from Transjordan reaches the central highlands. Already in 1931 W. F. Albright had suggested this identification (*Journal of the Palestine Oriental Society*, XI, pp. 241 ff.). A surface survey suggested a period of occupation which would agree with the literary evidence.

II. *Excavation.* Since 1946, a series of campaigns have been undertaken by the Dominican École Biblique under the direction of Père R. de Vaux, assisted by Père A. M. Steve. A clear picture has now become available. *Tell el-Far'ah* was first occupied during the Middle Chalcolithic period (middle of the fourth millennium B.C.) down to about 600 B.C. Five periods of occupation are distinguished for the Early Bronze Age Level (*ca.* 3200-2100 B.C.). The remains of the Middle and Late Bronze ages are rather sparse because the town was severely destroyed in these days. A small sanctuary from the Middle Bronze age (*ca.* 2100-1550 B.C.) has been discovered. Iron Age I (*ca.* 1200-900 B.C.) and II (*ca.* 900-600 B.C.) are represented by four periods of occupation, which the excavators describe as: level I, the end of Iron Age II (*ca.* 723-600 B.C.); level II, the first part of Iron II age (eighth century to 723 B.C.); intermediate level (ninth century); level III, the Iron I age (end of the eleventh to the beginning of the ninth century B.C.). The Israelite occupation during the days of the Northern Kingdom of Israel is represented by levels I to III. The destruction of level III may well represent the time of Omri's attack (I Kings 16:17) in 885 B.C. After the abandonment of Tirzah in favor of Samaria some deterioration of the town would be expected and this is reflected in the poor settlement of the intermediate level dating to the ninth century B.C. During the eighth century Tirzah entered upon a new phase. Level II (eighth century down to 723 B.C.) revealed a number of fine houses, a great administrative building, a massive gate into the walled city, and alongside all this many smaller and poorer houses. This confirms the picture drawn by the eighth century prophets (Amos 5:11, Isa. 9:8-10). This phase of the city's life ended with the Assyrian invasion of 723-721 B.C. The last period of the city, Level I, represents the final days of its life during the years of Assyrian domination and culminating in the destruction of the city at the end of the seventh century, possibly at the hands of Nebuchadnezzar. It was a poor city in comparison with that represented by Level II.

Comparison of the archaeological facts from Tirzah with those from Samaria provides an interesting correlation of the occupation sequence in the two sites which accords closely with the Old Testament evidence.

BIBLIOGRAPHY. W. F. Albright, "The site of Tirzah and the Topography of Western Manasseh," *Journal of the Palestine Exploration Society*, XI, 1930, pp. 241-251. G. E. Wright, "The Excavation at Tell El-Far'ah," *Biblical Archaeologist*, XII, 3,

1949, pp. 66-68. Articles in *Revue Biblique* by R. de Vaux and A. M. Steve, from 1947 (Vol. LIV) onwards, especially Vol. LXII, 1955, pp. 587-589.

TITUS, ARCH OF. Shortly before Passover, A.D. 70, the Roman armies began the siege which brought about the fall and destruction of Jerusalem. Late in the summer, with food supplies exhausted, the city capitulated. Titus, the Roman general, ordered the city razed, the temple burned, and the people slaughtered indiscriminately. In Rome, the following year, Titus celebrated his triumph, accompanied by seven hundred Jewish prisoners and the spoils of war which, according to Josephus, included the golden table of showbread, the golden lampstand, and a copy of the Jewish law from the temple.

The Arch of Titus was completed and dedicated in Rome after the death of the emperor (A.D. 81). It depicts Titus' triumph in relief, showing Roman soldiers without weapons crowned with laurel, and carrying the sacred furniture including the seven-armed lampstand and the table of showbread. The arch is still standing near the colosseum in Rome.

TRANSPORTATION. The Nile, the Tigris-Euphrates river system, and the eastern Mediterranean were waterways that the ancients early learned to use for trade, commerce, and other purposes. Boats were usually made of wood, which normally does not survive except in a dry, desert climate. Models of boats are frequently discovered in Egyptian tombs, however, and ancient artists depicted boats on the tomb walls of Egypt and the bas reliefs of Mesopotamian palaces.

A relief from Nineveh depicts a coracle, a round boat made of skins stretched tight on a wooden framework. The coracle is manned by four oarsmen who were transporting a heavy cargo. The modern *guffa*, still used on the Tigris and Euphrates, is similar to the ancient coracle. Dugout canoes and bark canoes were also used in ancient times.

For long voyages, particularly on the Nile and the Mediterranean, sail boats were used. Before 3000 B.C. Egypt had learned to use the sail. A journey from the Nile Delta to °Byblos could be made in four days if winds were favorable. The return journey had to be made with the use of oars, and it took about ten days. The earliest ships to

COVERED WAGON excavated at Tepe Gawra. Courtesy, University Museum, Philadelphia

use the Mediterranean were from seventy to one hundred feet long. By the Egyptian Middle Kingdom they were as much as two hundred feet long and sixty-eight feet wide. One hundred men might be carried on such a vessel.

*Phoenicians, *Minoans, and *Myceneans were sea-going peoples. The Mediterranean did not serve to divide peoples, but rather to provide easy access for men and supplies.

The Sumerians used four-wheeled carts as early as the third millennium B.C. Examples from the tomb of Lady Shubad at *Ur had solid-disc wheels, with leather tires. At *Tepe Gawra, level VIII, we have the oldest artistic representation of a wheeled conveyance in the form of a covered wagon.

In rugged mountain terrain wheeled vehicles were impractical. Kings and nobles would ride instead in elaborate palanquins. The gold casing of the palanquin of Queen Hetep-heres, mother of Khufu, builder of the Great *Pyramid, was found near the pyramid and is now restored and on display in the Cairo Museum.

Two-wheeled chariots were used as an important part of the equipment of military campaigns. Egyptian and early Assyrian chariots were manned by two men, the driver and the warrior. The Hittites also used a shieldbearer, and this pattern was adopted by the later Assyrians, Syrians, and, probably, the Hebrews. Chariots were normally drawn by two horses. A third, not yoked to the chariot, often was taken along as a spare.

The body of the chariot itself was probably made of a light wood. It had a high dashboard, to which was attached a box for spears. The horse-drawn chariot played an important part in building the Egyptian, Hittite, and later Assyrian empires. In ordinary life they served to enhance the pomp and pleasure of kings and their officers.

TURRET. A turret is a small tower rising above a larger structure such as a wall or a palace. In ancient times turrets served as lookout posts and signaling stations.

TUT-ANKH-AMUN. See Egypt.

TWO BROTHERS, STORY OF THE. The Egyptian Story of the Two Brothers has been preserved on a hieratic manuscript in the British Museum (#10183) known as the Papyrus d'Orbiney. It was written for Seti II of the Nineteenth Dynasty and dates from the thirteenth century B.C. The story itself is probably much older. Its chief characters Anubis (or Anpu) and Bata bear the names of Egyptian gods, and the story may be classified as mythology.

Early in the story, Bata the young unmarried brother lived with his older brother Anubis. The younger brother tended the cattle and made himself generally useful on his older brother's farm. One day when Anubis sent Bata to the house on an errand, the wife of Anubis attempted to seduce Bata. The young man, like the Biblical Joseph in a similar circumstance, was horrified at the suggestion and repulsed the temptress. When Anubis returned home, however, his wife pretended to have been attacked by Bata and insisted that her husband kill his younger brother.

Believing the false evidence presented by his wife, Anubis stood behind the door, spear in hand, ready to strike Bata when he would return in the evening. As the cows entered the cowhouse they warned Bata of the intent of his brother. Bata looked under the door and saw his brother standing, spear in hand. Thereupon Bata fled and Anubis ran after him.

While in flight Bata prayed that the sun

BOATS TRANSPORTING LOGS, some carried on board and some towed behind. The logs are from the famed cedars of Lebanon. Relief from the palace of Sargon at Khorsabad. Courtesy, the Louvre

god might vindicate him, and the prayer was answered as Re-Harachti created a river full of crocodiles between the brothers. Bata then called to his brother on the other side of the river and told Anubis the truth concerning his wife. Bata castrated himself and declared that he was going to the Valley of the Cedars (in Lebanon).

When he would arrive in the Valley of Cedars, Bata said, he would take out his heart and place it in a tree. If the cedar should be cut down, Bata would die. His brother Anubis would be warned of what had happened by a sign: If a mug of beer given to Anubis would foam up, he would know that the tree had fallen and his brother had died. Then it would be the responsibility of Anubis to come to rescue him, finding his heart and placing it in a jar of cold water.

Anubis realized his error, killed his wife for her treachery, and mourned for his younger brother. In the meantime Bata, in the Valley of the Cedars, received a wife from the gods. She was the fairest woman on earth, and in her dwelt the essence of all the gods.

Bata's story was not to end happily, however. The sea brought a lock of his wife's hair to Egypt; the Pharaoh smelled the fragrance and sent messengers to find the girl and bring her back to Egypt. Bata killed the first messengers, but Pharaoh sent others, including a woman who enticed Bata's wife with beautiful ornaments and lured her to Egypt. In Egypt the faithless wife prevailed upon Pharaoh to order the cedar tree which bore Bata's heart cut down. The heart fell and Bata died.

When a mug of beer was set before Anubis, it foamed up and he knew that his brother had died. Anubis then journeyed to the Valley of the Cedars, found his brother's heart (in the form of a berry), and placed it in a jar of cold water. Bata revived, but he quickly transformed himself into a bull so that he might return to Egypt to punish his wife. Anubis rode the beautiful bull into Egypt, and both he and the bull were highly honored. In the royal dining room the bull introduced himself to his wife as Bata, after which she asked the Pharaoh to allow her to eat some of the bull's liver. A great feast was proclaimed, during which the bull was sacrificed. The bull, however, shook its neck and two drops of blood fell beside the two door jambs of Pharaoh's palace. These grew into two large persea trees. One day as his wife was sitting under one of the trees, Bata again identified himself. His wife again made a request to Pharaoh: "Have the two persea trees cut down and made into beautiful furniture." She stood by as the trees were being cut, and a splinter accidentally was thrown into her mouth. She became pregnant and bore a son who quickly won the hearts of all the people. He was made Viceroy of Nubia, and on the death of Pharaoh, succeeded to the throne of all Egypt. Thereupon the new Pharaoh — who was actually but a reincarnation of Bata — gathered the royal officials and accused his wife of the crimes she had committed. The officials agreed with Bata and (presumably) his faithless wife was condemned to death. The Pharaoh reigned thirty years.

The opening of the story has many points of comparison with the Biblical story of Joseph (Gen. 39). Joseph, like the younger brother, was trusted. Potiphar's wife, like Bata's sister-in-law, suggested an illicit relationship. Joseph, like Bata, resisted the temptation and maintained his moral integrity. Potiphar's wife, like Bata's sister-in-law, charged her intended victim with the crime he was unwilling to commit.

The latter part of the story contains mythological elements which are wholly removed from the Biblical manner of expression. It may be noted, however, that the Pharaoh was ever ready to add a fair woman to his harem, sending to the Valley of the Cedars to find one who was known to him only by the scent of a lock of her hair. When famine drove Abraham into Egypt (Gen. 12:10-16), the patriarch feared that Pharaoh might want to add Sarah to his harem so, to protect himself, he declared that she was his sister. The reputation of the Pharaohs was evidently wide-spread in this regard.

BIBLIOGRAPHY. John A. Wilson, "Egyptian Myths, Tales, and Mortuary Texts," ANET, pp. 23-25.

TYRE. Tyre, the principal Phoenician seaport, is located on the Mediterranean, twenty-five miles south of Sidon and thirty-five miles north of Mount Carmel. In ancient times a distinction was made between the mainland port city, Old Tyre or *Ushu* (in Assyrian texts), and the island city of Tyre (Assyrian Ṣurru). Alexander the Great laid siege to the island city for seven months (332 B.C.), and captured it only after he built a mole to connect the island with the mainland. This change in the topography of Phoenicia was permanent, and Tyre is no longer an island.

The early history of Tyre is not known. During the *Amarna Age its king, Abimilki, remained loyal to Egypt while charging that the king of Sidon had joined the Amorite Aziru in fomenting rebellion. When the Philistines plundered Sidon (*ca.* 1200 B.C.) many of its people fled to Tyre which became the principal Phoenician port in subsequent centuries.

In the days of the Israelite United Kingdom, Hiram of Tyre had friendly commercial relations with both David and Solomon (II Sam. 5:11; I Kings 5:1; I Chron. 14:1). Hiram provided building materials for the Jerusalem Temple (II Chron. 2:3-16) and Tyrians assisted in the building of the Temple. A man named Hiram (not the king) was responsible for the bronze work (I Kings 7:13-14).

Hiram of Tyre built the first causeway linking the mainland to the island, and during his reign the Tyrians built a great temple to their god Melkart, the Tyrian Baal whose name means "king of the city," and the goddess Astarte. Hiram also assisted Solomon in the development of the port of Ezion-geber for trade with the eastern shore of Africa and the Indian Ocean territories (I Kings 9:27-28). The age of Hiram was the golden age of Tyre, when her ships plied the Mediterranean carrying her Tyrian purple dyes, made from the murex shellfish, and her manufactured glass to the islands and coastlands of the eastern Mediterranean. During the ninth century B.C. Tyrians founded Carthage ("new town") in North Africa. Its legendary founder was Dido, whose story Virgil gives in the Aeneid. The ninth century also saw Jezebel, a daughter of Ethbaal (Itobal) the Tyrian kingpriest, married to Ahab of Israel. The purpose of the marriage was assuredly political, serving to cement relations between Tyre and Israel, but Jezebel's Baalism precipitated a major religious crisis in Israel.

With the rise of Assyrian power in western Asia, Tyre was continually threatened. Usually she maintained a degree of autonomy by paying tribute. In 722 B.C., however, Tyre along with Samaria fell to Sargon II.

With the decline of Assyrian power, Tyre regained her autonomy and her sea trade prospered. Nebuchadnezzar besieged Tyre, and finally she fell to the Babylonians. Tyre continued to be a major port city in the centuries that followed. Alexander, by building a mole, was able to subdue Tyre, but the city soon recovered. In Roman times Herod I rebuilt the main temple of Tyre.

The principal ruins of Tyre date to Crusader times. Many coins minted at Tyre from the fifth century B.C. onward bear testimony to the greatness of Tyre in the lands of the eastern Mediterranean. Excavations since 1921 have traced some of the early foundations of the city.

BIBLIOGRAPHY. A. Poidebard and L. Cayeux, *Un grand Port disparu, Tyr,* 1939.

U

UGARIT; RAS SHAMRA. The ancient city of Ugarit occupied the mound now known as Ras Shamra ("Fennel Head") situated in northern Syria fifty nautical miles east of the point of the island of Cyprus. It was located on a bay known to the Greeks as *Leucos Limen* ("White Harbor"), modern *Minet el-Beida.* Ugarit was the important Bronze Age port through which copper ore passed en route from Cyprus to Mesopotamia. It had important contacts with the Hittites and the Egyptians and served as the crossroads between Mediterranean culture and the Sumero-Akkadian world. With the coming of the Iron Age to the Near East, copper lost its importance and Ugaritic influence vanished.

The modern discovery of Ras Shamra dates from 1928 when a Syrian peasant accidentally plowed up a flagstone which

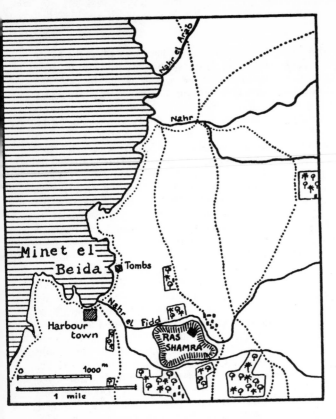

MAP OF UGARIT (Ras Shamra)
and its immediate environs

covered a subterranean passageway. Charles Virolleaud, Director of Archaeological Works in Syria and Lebanon, was sent to excavate the site which proved to be a burial chamber. Pieces of Cypro-Mycenean pottery were found in the tomb, but the initial dig was not otherwise productive.

In the spring of 1929 a French archaeological expedition directed by Claude F. A. Schaeffer of the Strasbourg Museum and his associate, George Chenet, began the systematic excavation of Ras Shamra. Work was carried on for several months each year until the outbreak of World War II. It was resumed in 1950. Only a small part of the mound has been excavated to date, yet it has already proved to be one of the major archaeological discoveries of the twentieth century.

Excavations have brought to light the royal tombs of Ugarit, two large temples, and numerous artifacts which reflect contacts between Ugarit and Egypt, Mesopotamia, the Hittites, and the Cretan-Mycenaean areas. The most significant discovery was that of a library containing inscriptions in a wide variety of Near Eastern languages

including a previously unknown Semitic language which used an alphabetic cuneiform script. Through the labors of Charles Virolleaud, Édouard Dhorme of the École Biblique, and Hans Bauer of Halle the cuneiform alphabet was deciphered, and the work of translating the texts was begun. An American scholar, Cyrus H. Gordon, now of Brandeis University, has published a grammar of Ugaritic along with a glossary and a transliteration of the extant Ugaritic texts.

A. *Levels of Occupation.* Excavations at Ras Shamra indicate that the site has had a history extending back to the Neolithic Age — perhaps the fifth or sixth millennium B.C. Schaeffer has noted five levels of occupation which are numbered from the top down. Level five contains the flint and bone implements of the first occupants of the site, a pre-pottery Neolithic people. The fourth, or Chalcolithic level, has yielded several fine examples of painted Halafian ceramics. During the course of the occupation of Level three (the latter half of the third millennium B.C.) the city was destroyed by fire. The people who subsequently occupied the site used the so-called Khirbet Kerak ware.

Most of Schaeffer's work has been on the two topmost strata, numbered two (2100-1600 B.C.) and one (1600-1200 B.C.). During both of these periods Ras Shamra bore the name Ugarit. The great literary and cultural achievements of Ugarit occurred during the period represented by Level one.

B. *The Major Epics.* Of several hundred Ugaritic texts which have been studied, none is of greater interest than the three major epics discovered in the library of Ugarit and dated during the reign of King Niqmad II who is known to have paid tribute to the Hittite king Shuppiluliumas (1375-1340 B.C.). The epics may have had a prior oral form, but our copies date from the fourteenth century B.C.

1. Aqhat. The hero of the Aqhat Epic was the son of the pious King Danel (a variant of the Biblical Daniel). Aqhat accidentally acquired a bow which had been made for the goddess Anat. The goddess was so anxious to get the bow from the lad that she offered him riches or immortality in exchange for it. Aqhat, however, refused to part with his bow under any circumstances. Undaunted, Anat determined to use force to get back her bow, and secured the services of a ruffian to insure success. The ruffian secured the bow from Aqhat, but the bow was dropped into the sea and lost, and Aqhat was killed. The corpse of Aqhat was consumed by a vulture. Danel, Aqhat's father, and Pughat, his sister mourned for a period of seven years. All this time Pughat determined to avenge the death of her brother. Here the story breaks off. If we had the ending it would probably tell of Pughat's success in bringing about the death of the ruffian who had killed her brother.

2. Keret. In the Keret Epic we read of a prosperous and godly king who was distressed because he had no heir. He had lost a succession of wives and wept at the thought that his line would soon be extinct. The kindly god El appeared to him in a dream suggesting that he mobilize his forces and march to the land of Udm and demand the hand of Huriya, the beautiful daughter of King Pabil. Keret, after making appropriate vows to Athirat, marched against Udm and besieged the capital city of King Pabil. Although tribute was offered, Keret insisted that he would lift the siege only on condition that he be given the fair Huriya. Reluctantly Pabil gave his daughter to Keret, and in due time Keret was blessed with sons and daughters of his own.

Keret, however, forgot the vow he had made to Athirat, and the goddess caused him to fall sick. The youngest son and daughter, Elhu and Thitmanet, were genuinely grieved at their father's condition, but the firstborn Yassib only thought of his own prospects. Kindly El intervened to restore Keret's health. Here the epic breaks off but its conclusion is fairly obvious. Faithless Yassib would certainly have been deprived of his rights as firstborn. On the other hand the faithful Elhu and Thitmanet would be rewarded. Doubtless Elhu succeeded his father to the throne.

3. ʿBaal. The Baal Epic tells how the fertility god Baal (or Hadad) received an house for himself and recognition as supreme lord of the earth. In the early part of the epic Yam (the sea god) had an house and Baal did not. The two were rivals and they engaged in furious combat. It looked as though the battle might end in a draw until Kathir-and-Khasis (god of arts and crafts) gave Baal two magic maces with which to attack his rival. The result was

UGARITIC TEXT WITH THE LEGEND OF AQHAT. Courtesy, the Louvre

the domain of Mot, and finally she was successful. The sun goddess who goes to the netherworld each night brought him back on one of her appointed rounds. Accompanied by bountiful showers Baal returned to his domains above.

C. *Relevance to Biblical Studies.*

1. Historical Backgrounds. From the time of Israel's entrance into Canaan under Joshua to the fall of Jerusalem (587 B.C.), the worship of Baal and other Canaanite religious rites proved a temptation to Israel. The Biblical prophets spared no invective in denouncing the licentious Baal cult. With the discovery of the Ugaritic epics we now can read the literature of the ancient Canaanites and get a clearer view of the culture and attitudes of the people who were in Canaan at the time of the conquest.

2. Vocabulary. Because Ugaritic is a Semitic language, closely related to Biblical Hebrew, the use of words in Ugaritic texts often throws light on their Biblical usage. The word *bamôth* often appears in the Old Testament in the sense of "high places." The word is used in Ugaritic to signify the back of an animal or person (Cyrus H. Gordon, *Ugaritic Textbook*, Glossary, word 480). This usage makes good sense in Deut. 33:29 which would read, "Thy enemies shall be discomfited before thee; Thou shalt tread upon their backs (*bamôth*)." Artistic portrayals from the ancient Near East frequently depict a conqueror with his foot on the back of his victim. The rendering "backs" is more meaningful than "high places" in Deut. 33:29.

When King Uzziah was stricken with leprosy he was placed in a "several house" according to the traditional rendering of II Kings 15:5 and II Chronicles 26:21. The American Standard and the Revised Standard Versions read "a separate house." The word appears in the Ugaritic texts to describe the place to which Aleyan Baal descended before proceeding to the netherworld. This suggests that Uzziah may have been confined in a cave or cellar, or even in the palace basement.

3. Textual Studies. David's lament over Saul and Jonathan following their death on Mount Gilboa contains the lines:

Ye mountains of Gilboa, let there be no dew nor rain upon you, neither fields of offerings (II Sam. 1:21 A.V.).

A GOD FROM UGARIT, wearing a high crown similar to the white crown of Upper Egypt. The figure is made of bronze, covered with gold and silver and dates from the 15th or 14th century B.C. Courtesy, the Louvre

unchallenged victory for Baal. His friends celebrated while his sister Anat fell upon his foes to exterminate them.

After some hesitation, El ordered that materials be gathered to provide an house for Baal. Cedars were brought from Lebanon and other materials gathered from remote places. It took Kathir-and-Khasis just seven days to build the house for Baal. After the house was completed he journeyed from city to city claiming each as part of his realm. He even sent messengers to the netherworld to inform Mot ("death") of his right to the throne. Mot, however, challenged Baal to meet him in the netherworld and Baal reluctantly did so. During Baal's absence the earth languished and the gods mourned. The ever faithful Anat was busy seeking means of bringing Baal up from

Biblical scholars have been puzzled over the expression "fields of offering," but H. L. Ginsberg has proposed a reading which is widely accepted. In the Aqhat Epic we read a curse which is similar to that which David uttered:

Seven years may Baal fail
Even eight, the rider of the clouds;
Nor dew, nor rain, nor upsurging of the deep,
Nor sweetness of the voice of Baal.

The Hebrew word for "fields" is similar to the Ugaritic word for "upsurging" and Hebrew "offering" is similar to Ugaritic "deep." Ginsberg suggests, on the basis of this parallel, that David prayed:

Ye mountains of Gilboa, let there be no dew nor rain upon you, neither upsurging of the deep.

The Revised Standard Version has accepted this interpretation. The "upsurgings of the deep" were the mountain springs, as we know from Ugaritic texts. Dew, rain, and mountain springs were the three sources of moisture in Syria and Palestine. David prayed that Mount Gilboa might be barren as a sign of mourning for Saul and Jonathan.

The people of Ugarit used a white glaze which is termed *spsg*. The word appears in Proverbs 26:23 although ancient scribes did not recognize it and made two words of it. In the light of Ugaritic usage the passage can be read: "Burning lips and a wicked heart are like white glaze covered over a pot."

4. Legal Terminology. Many of the sacrifices mentioned in the Ugaritic texts have names which are identical with those described in Leviticus. In Ugarit we read of the Burnt Offering, Whole Burnt Offering, Trespass Offering, Wave Offering, Peace Offering, Offering for Expiation, Tribute Offering, First Fruits Offering and New Moon Offering. Ugaritic sacrifices, like those of the Bible, had to be "without blemish."

The similarities are largely on the surface, however. The sacrifices of Ugarit were offered to Baal and to a host of other gods, while those of the Hebrews were offered to Yahweh alone. Biblical sacrifices did not begin with the Levitical laws, but are traced back to the earliest times. Cain, Abel (Gen. 4:3-4), Noah (Gen. 8:20) and the line of Abraham (Gen. 15:9-10) all offered pre-Levitical sacrifices.

There is reason to believe that some ele-

STELE FROM UGARIT depicting two officials with offerings for the god El. Courtesy, Aleppo Museum, Syrian Arab Republic

ments in the Mosaic law were offered as a polemic against Canaanite practices. The Ugaritic epic entitled "The Birth of the Beautiful and Gracious Gods" describes the rite of seething a kid in its mother's milk in order to procure rain for the parched soil of Canaan. The rite was specifically forbidden in Israelite law (Exod. 23:1; 34:26). The prophetic leaders of Israel were concerned that the people resist the temptation to adopt Canaanite practices.

5. Literary Allusions. The poetic language of the Bible and Ugarit makes use of similar figurative expressions, drawing on a common stock of metaphors. Baal, like Yahweh, rides the clouds (cf. Psalm 68:4, 33). Thunder is his voice (cf. Psalm 29:3). When the writer of the Biblical flood story wanted to describe the torrents of rain which fell on

the earth he used the poetic expression (Gen. 7:11). In Ugarit we read how the god Baal opened a window of his celestial house, uttered his voice and thus brought a thunderstorm to the world (Baal II. vi. 25-35).

The mythological figure Lotan (Biblical Leviathan) appears in the Ugaritic texts as an enemy of Baal. The Baal Epic says, "When thou smotest Lotan, the slippery (serpent) (and) madest an end of the wriggling serpent, the tyrant (with seven heads) . . ." (Baal I. i. 28-30). The words are reminiscent of Isaiah 27:1: "In that day the Lord [i.e. Yahweh] with his great and strong sword will punish Leviathan, the twisting serpent, and he will slay the dragon that is in the sea." Biblical Leviathan, like Ugaritic Lotan, had a multiplicity of heads: "Thou didst crush the heads of Leviathan" (Psalm 74:14). It should be noted, however, that Biblical Leviathan, unlike his Ugaritic counterpart, was not a god. Leviathan was a rebellious creature of Yahweh. He represents the forces of evil which come under divine judgment. The high ethical monotheism of the Israelites is not paralleled in Ugarit even though both peoples have a common linguistic and cultural heritage.

6. Historical Matters. When King Hezekiah was sick with a boil, the prophet Isaiah directed that a cake, or lump of figs be placed on the boil (II Kings 20:7; Isa. 38:21). We learn from one of the veterinary treatises at Ugarit that lumps of figs were used as poultices for horses. The medicinal use of figs was evidently known in a wide area of the Middle East.

The prophet Ezekiel mentioned three godly men who were the epitome of righteousness: Noah, Daniel, and Job (Ezek. 14:14-20). Both Noah and Job were men of the ancient past at the time of Ezekiel's prophecy, but the Daniel of our canonical book of Daniel was a young contemporary of Ezekiel. It has long seemed unusual to link Daniel with the worthies of the distant past, but the Ugaritic texts now give us reason to think that Ezekiel was referring to an earlier Daniel — the Danel of Ugarit who

. . . judged (the cause of the widow (and) he) tried (the case of the orphan) (Aqhat I, i, 23-25).

King David purchased the threshing floor of a man designated as "Araunah the Jebu-

site" (II Sam. 24:18). The Ugaritic texts contain a word *iwr*, meaning "lord." It forms a part of several personal names including *iwrn*, which became Hebrew Araunah. Thus the name Araunah appears to have been a title rather than a personal name.

BIBLIOGRAPHY. G. R. Driver, *Canaanite Myths and Legends*, Edinburgh: T. & T. Clark, 1956. H. L. Ginsberg, "Ugaritic Myths and Legends." *Ancient Near East Texts*, ed. J. B. Pritchard, Princeton: Princeton University Press, 1953. Cyrus H. Gordon, *Ugaritic Literature*, Rome: Pontifical Biblical Institute, 1949; *Ugaritic Textbook*, Rome: Pontifical Biblical Institute, 1965. John Gray, *The Legacy of Canaan*, Leiden: E. J. Brill, 1965. Edmond Jacob, *Ras Shamra et L'Ancien Testament*, Neuchatel: Editions Delachaux et Niestle, 1960. Marvin H. Pope, *El in the Ugaritic Texts*, Leiden: E. J. Brill, 1955. Claude F. A. Schaeffer, *The Cuneiform Texts of Ras Shamra-Ugarit*. The Schweich Lectures, 1936, London: The British Academy (Oxford), 1939.

UMMA. Umma (Tell Jokha) was located fifteen and one-half miles northwest of °Lagash, a city with which it waged constant civil war. Lugalzaggisi of Umma, who ruled in the twenty-fourth century B.C., plundered Lagash and ultimately became king of Uruk and Ur as well. In his triumphal inscription discovered at °Nippur, Lugalzaggisi boasts that his conquests reached the Mediterranean.

UR. Although there are several cities which have used the root form, Ur, the most outstanding site is located in Southern Mesopotamia. The main mound, called Tell el-Muqaiyar ("Mound of Pitch") in the Arabic, is located 160 miles from the present head of the Persian Gulf and 220 miles south southeast of Baghdad. It stands ten miles west of the present course of the Euphrates River although originally occupying a prominent position on the east bank before the river changed its course.

The site is composed of a number of sand covered mounds, occupying an oval space 1000 by 800 yards. The long axis of the oval points generally north-south. The entire landscape is dominated by the °ziggurat or temple tower with its sacred enclosure area around it. This artificial hill, composed of bricks and bitumen, originally covered an area of 200 by 150 yards and was 70 yards high. It is the best preserved example of an ancient ziggurat in Mesopotamia.

I. *Archaeological Work.* The site was first carefully examined in modern times by J. E.

THE RUINS OF UR *showing the ziggurat in the left background. Courtesy, The University Museum, Philadelphia*

Taylor who was British consul at Basra. He was commissioned by the British Museum to investigate the ruined cities in Southern Mesopotamia in 1854. At once he was attracted to the site by the imposing appearance of the artificial mound — the ziggurat. After driving a shaft to the heart of the brick mass to make certain that the hill was solid brick, Taylor decided to dig into the corners of the structure. This move was most fortunate because he quickly discovered cylinders of baked clay with cuneiform inscriptions (*see* Seal). These cylinders had been fashioned by the workmen of Nabonidus, the last king of Babylon (556-539 B.C.). Upon them, Nabonidus commemorated his rebuilding of the ziggurat while attributing the original structure to much earlier kings, Ur-Nammu and his son. The identification of the site was clearly established by Nabonidus as he called the structure "The Ziggurat of E-gish-shir-gal in Ur."

Although J. E. Taylor published his findings in the *Journal of the Royal Asiatic Society* (XV, 1855, p. 260 ff.), the city of Ur remained abandoned for more than sixty years. In 1918, R. Campbell Thompson, a captain in the British Intelligence, made preliminary soundings at Ur for one week before moving on to the site of ancient Eridu. The next year, H. R. Hall moved in for more serious effort: (1) He excavated part of a large burnt-brick building which he labeled "B" (later to be called HT or Hall's Temple).

(2) He further cleared part of the southeast face of the ziggurat down to the floor level of Nabonidus. (3) He uncovered a section of the wall which surrounded the sacred area. (4) He exposed many tombs and house walls. (5) He discovered and began clearing the site of Al-'Ubaid, four miles to the west.

As a consequence of the work of H. R. Hall, a joint expedition was planned by the British Museum and the Museum of the University of Pennsylvania under the direction of Charles Leonard Woolley. Twelve full seasons of work were devoted to the site between 1922 and 1934. Although much of the old city still remains untouched, systematic excavation was carried out in the most strategic areas. The bulk of the work concerned the sacred area, harbors, city walls, palaces, cemeteries, and scattered residential areas. Deep soundings were made in the royal cemetery and other areas to examine the stratigraphy. The work on the ziggurat was spread over many years since the expedition was financed by museums which desired more than architectural information. Part of the time in nine out of twelve seasons was devoted to work on the great ziggurat. The thoroughness of Woolley's work is clearly indicated in the voluminous official reports of both the excavations and the texts. See Bibliography at end of this article.

II. *History of the Site.* The earliest settlement of the area which became the prosperous city of Ur goes back into the Protoliterate, Warka, and Ubaid Periods. Handmade pottery of the type found at Al 'Ubaid from 4000 B.C. showed up in the Ur-Ubaid level, a layer of clean earth eight feet thick. Woolley sank five pits seeking similar material but was able to find such deposits in only two pits. A later phase of Ubaid culture covered this layer of earth. Woolley's interpretation of this as illustrative of the great flood mentioned in Genesis led many to seek similar evidence. However, the layers of clean earth found at several other Mesopotamian sites do not coincide in date with each other.

Much evidence was uncovered which relates to the Early Dynastic Period at Ur. The Royal Tombs, dating about 2500 B.C., give extensive background for the powerful dynasty at Ur which represented the last and culminating phase of the Early Dynastic Period in Mesopotamia. These tombs were remarkable for their architecture, contents, and the light which they shed on customs even though there was no reference to the known kings of this dynasty (Mes-Anne-pada, A-Anne-pada, Meskiag-Nanna, Elulu, and Balulu).

Little is known about the Second Dynasty at Ur either from the excavations at Ur or other sources. However, following the strong Semitic Dynasty of Agade (2350-2150 B.C.) and the cultural eclipse when the land was controlled by the Gutians (2150-2070 B.C.), the Third Dynasty at Ur (2070-1960 B.C.) led in a Sumerian renaissance. Strong kings of this dynasty (Ur-Nammu, Shulgi, Amar-Sin, Shu-Sin, Ibbi-Sin) extended Ur's influence over all of Mesopotamia, even reaching out to the Lebanons in the territory later to be known as Syria. The population of Ur has been estimated at more than one-half million during this period. The mightiest building work was the erection of the ziggurat by Ur-Nammu and his son, Shulgi.

The powerful Third Dynasty at Ur came to an end when the Amorites of Mari overran much of Central and Northern Mesopotamia and the Elamites took over Southern Mesopotamia where Ur was located. The city was later controlled by *Hammurabi (1728-1686 B.C.) and was destroyed by his son, Samsuiluna, when it rebelled against the Amorite power. The whole land was further wasted by the barbarian Kassites, causing Ur to enter an eclipse which lasted several centuries.

While there was some rebuilding of the city by Kurigalzu of Babylon and later by Marduk-Nadin-akhe, Ur was restored to splendor by Nebuchadnezzar II and Naboni-

THE ZIGGURAT OF UR-NAMMU at Ur. A restoration. Courtesy, The University Museum, Philadelphia

GAME BOARD from Ur. Courtesy, British Museum

dus. The redesigned ziggurat was the crown of Nabonidus' labors. Further improvements were made by the Persians under Cyrus.

The latest tablets from Ur found *in situ* come from the middle of the fifth century B.C. in the remains of a few Persian houses. Cyrus was the only Persian king whose name appears stamped on any of the bricks. Seemingly, the city reached a point when it was economically and politically of little importance. Many writers have linked this with the changed course of the Euphrates River. While no date can be established for the shifting of the river bed, such a change would produce economic disaster for a city which had enjoyed trade from the up-river regions as well as from the Persian Gulf. Likewise the changed course of the river would destroy the carefully dug canal systems used for irrigation of the farm land. Coupled with this should be recognized the changing religious situation as the Persian kings adopted the Zoroastrian monotheism, rejecting images and idolatrous temples. Whatever happened, the end came swiftly and completely.

III. *Design of the City.* The city walls of Ur were oval in shape, enclosing several mounds which averaged about thirty feet in height. The highest point in the city was the top of the ziggurat rising from the plain along the Euphrates to a height of seventy feet. Included within the outer walls were two harbors, one due north of the center of the city and one almost due west. Openings in the wall brought small boats into the city complex itself.

The sacred area occupied a central position within the city walls, covering the middle third of the northern half of the site. It was continually expanded, redesigned, and rebuilt with the rising and falling fortunes of Ur. A separate temenos wall enclosed the several religious shrines and cemeteries. The major orientation was toward the northeast where the main entrance was located. Inside a large towered gateway was a rectangular forecourt surrounded by rooms. Across the forecourt, stairs led up into an inner court, also rectangular in shape with rooms on all four sides. It was within this inner court where the ziggurat stood. The great Temple of Ningal was located immediately to the southeast of the ziggurat while the Temple of E-nun-makh was hidden away in a complex of stairs and chambers. The latter was rebuilt in a wide open fashion by Nebuchadnezzar with a courtyard in front. At the east corner of the ziggurat platform the Dublal-makh, a two roomed sanctuary, was situated.

The location of the ziggurat was kept constant during the many building phases of the city. However, the design was changed in regard to the appearance and size of the upper stages. Below the outstanding structure of Ur-Nammu was a First Dynasty ziggurat as well as the remains of an older structure of similar character. No attempt was made by Woolley to investigate systematically these older structures although their general plan was recovered. They stood in a walled terrace enclosure with chambers and small buildings around the edges.

The plan used by Ur-Nammu demands more description. The artificial hill was composed of solid brick — an inner core of mud bricks with an outer surface of burnt bricks eight feet thick. The bricks were fourteen to sixteen inches square by seven inches thick and weighed an average of eighteen pounds each. No attempt was made to bond the outer bricks to the mud brick core. Ur-Nammu's ziggurat was built in three stages or steps with connecting stairways on the northeast side. Three staircases of one hundred steps each led up to the first level. One staircase led up from a monumental gateway to the shrine on the third level.

Nabonidus found only the lowest stage of the Ur-Nammu ziggurat standing and built upon it. Raising the first level by one meter, he had to raise the threefold stairway in like manner. According to Herodotus, Nabonidus placed six stages on the base, making a total of seven levels rather than the three levels of Ur-Nammu. Special red bricks and others covered with blue glaze seem to distinguish further the work by Nabonidus. Woolley saw some astrological significance in the colors used, suggesting that the shrine was bright blue glaze, the upper stage red, the lower stages black (dark gray clay painted black) and the facade of the courtyard whitewashed.

House and street planning also showed up clearly in the excavations. A large group of houses was found northwest of the sacred area from the twentieth and nineteenth centuries B.C. Another large residential area northeast of the West Harbor dated from the same period with some houses extending into the Old Babylonian Period (nineteenth to sixteenth centuries, B.C.). Two other areas of housing to the southwest of the sacred area illustrated later housing down

GOLD DAGGER AND SHEATH
from Ur. Courtesy, The University Museum, Philadelphia

to the Neo-Babylonian Period under Nebuchadnezzar and Nabonidus.

The streets at Ur were unpaved, undrained, narrow, and winding with blank house walls facing on the street. The houses were made of brick — burnt brick at the bottom with crude mud bricks above. They were then plastered over and whitewashed. Many of the houses had two stories originally although one story houses for the poor were evident. The typical plan consisted of an entrance hall leading into a paved courtyard surrounded by rooms. A staircase in one corner of the courtyard led up to a balcony which was supported by wooden pillars. The houses had flat roofs and no windows on the lower floor. In many cases there was a family mausoleum beneath the house.

IV. *Outstanding Discoveries.* The outstanding artifacts came from the royal tombs of the Early Dynastic Period at Ur (*ca.*

2500 B.C.) although some showed up in the palaces, temples, and public buildings. The following are illustrative of the many objects found:

(1) Personal jewels of fine gold filigree
(2) A head attire made from nine yards of gold band
(3) A golden tumbler and libation cup
(4) Both the original and a replica of a golden helmet of Mes-Kalam-dug, made like a wig with locks of hair hammered up in relief and individual hairs delicately engraved
(5) Gold and silver mounted harps and lyres, carefully decorated with the heads of animals
(6) Statuettes of gold, silver, shell, and lapis lazuli which once supported an offering table
(7) A two-sided mosaic illustrating war and peace which vividly illustrates civilian and military dress (On one side is pictured the king with his army, chariots, and captives while the other side portrays the king and royal family at a feast with his musicians and servants.)
(8) Numerous cylinder seals from various periods
(9) Clay tablets bearing mathematical cube roots
(10) Word lists in Sumerian cuneiform on clay tablets
(11) Temple receipts for tithes and taxes
(12) Business records demonstrating the extensive nature of Ur's commerce
(13) A limestone stele of Ur-Nammu (*ca.* 2050 B.C.) depicting his exploits in war, his sacrifice to the gods, and his preparations for building the great ziggurat

Many other discoveries related directly to the burial practices of the early Sumerians. There was much evidence of servants and attendants being buried alive with the rulers. In one tomb at least sixty-eight court women and six other servants joined their ruler in death. The quiet repose of the attendants suggests that they were either drugged before being placed in the tomb or voluntarily

GOLD HELMET OF MES-KALAM-DUG. Courtesy, The University Museum, Philadelphia

UR

took sleeping potions. Soldiers with spears, musicians with costly harps, and servants with the royal ox cart paid the supreme price.

Actually, most of the graves were of common people buried in rectangular pits. However, these graves have received little attention since few objects of value were found. Suffice it to say that these bodies were put in clay coffins or were wrapped in reed matting. The body was always on its side in an attitude of one asleep with a bowl often held up to the mouth.

V. *Relation to the Patriarchs.* The location of Ur has always been important to the Biblical student because of several passages which point to Ur as the home of Abram (*cf.* Gen. 11:26, 31; 15:7; Neh. 9:7). However, other passages also reflect a North

GOAT EATING LEAVES. A figure from Ur, ca. 2500 B.C. The figure has been likened to the "ram caught in the thicket" (Gen. 22:13) but it is at least five hundred years earlier than the time of Abraham. Courtesy, University Museum, Philadelphia

Mesopotamian origin for Abraham's family. It should be noted that every patriarchal contact after Abram's arrival in Canaan is with the northern area.

The terminology used in the Hebrew of the above passages, '*Ur Kasdîm,* is usually translated "Ur of the Chaldees" (KJ) or "Ur of the Chaldeans" (RSV). This must be an anachronism if a South Mesopotamian site is accepted, since the Chaldeans did not arrive in this area until the last of the second millennium B.C. or later. However, such anachronisms were common among the ancients. A greater problem arises in the LXX translation of this phrase. The LXX makes no mention of the city of Ur but merely suggests that Abram came "from the country of the Chaldeans."

The location of Abram's original home has long been debated. Eusebius quotes Eupolemus (150 B.C.) as saying that Abraham came from a city "Kamarina of Babylon, called by some the city Urie." Stephen followed the LXX in referring to the land of the Chaldeans (Acts 7:4). However, the Moslems have traditionally believed that Abram's Ur was Urfa, a city twenty miles northwest of Haran called Edessa by the Greeks. This equation of Ur with Urfa was based on similarity of name, classical and Arab tradition, and the interpretation of "beyond the river" in Joshua 24:2 as referring to Syria. The southern identification of Ur of the Chaldees began during the latter part of the nineteenth century when many references to Ur were being found in recently deciphered inscriptions. Further emphasis was given to the theory by the extensive work of Woolley at Ur. However the argument has been opened again by C. H. Gordon and others. Rather than Urfa, Gordon points to Ura, a town north or east of Haran under the control of the Hittites. It was described as the home town of merchants who traded with Ugarit in Akkadian documents from Ugarit. Gordon treats Abraham as a merchant-prince or *Tamkarum* from the realm of the Hittites. His three main arguments are: (1) There is strong tradition connecting Ur of the Chaldees with Northern Mesopotamia. (2) The picture of the patriarchs as city-merchants fits known facts. (3) The term "Chaldees" can be adequately applied to Northern Mesopotamia (*cf.* C. H. Gordon, *JNES*, XVII, pp.

28-31 with the answer of H. W. F. Saggs, "Ur of the Chaldees, A Problem of Identification," *Iraq*, XXII, pp. 200-209, Spring-Autumn 1960).

VI. *Religious Background.* Any connection of the Sumerian Ur with Abram makes the religious background of the city of great import. That Ur was a religious city is obvious from any examination of the complex of buildings in the sacred area. These significant shrines made Ur a place of pilgrimage and a desired place for burial. Throughout the history of Babylonia until the sixth century B.C., the sacred area linked to the great ziggurat was the most important temple area in Mesopotamia.

The chief god at Ur was the Moon-god Nanna (known as "Sin" among the Semites). He was the city's lord and king, ruling in war and peace. When Ur dominated the land of Mesopotamia, Nanna was recognized as king of the gods. The human ruler was his protégé or steward. When Ur held the ascendency, the consent of Enlil was considered necessary before the human king could represent the god-king. Even though there were temples and shrines dedicated to other gods scattered throughout Ur, the city was truly dedicated to Nanna, its patron god. The only member of the pantheon to share his splendor was Ningal, his wife. Her temple was one of the outstanding structures in the city, standing in the shadow of the ziggurat.

In addition to the temples, there were other places of worship. Four public chapels of the Larsa period were uncovered during the 1930-31 season. These wayside shrines were used as places of prayer and meditation. Special household chapels were found in many of the houses with small altars and hearths. Closely associated with the chapel was the family god, probably quite distinct from those worshipped at the great shrines. The burial custom of placing relatives beneath the floor of the house may emphasize the close ties within the family circle of worship. Strangely enough, no statue of a family god was found in any of the rooms designated as household chapels by the excavators. Likewise, the royal tombs produced no images although some terra cotta figurines depicting broad-shouldered females with slit-eyes were found in earlier levels.

BIBLIOGRAPHY.
1. Official Reports of the Joint Expedition. C. L. Woolley and H. R. Hall, *Ur Excavations I: Al 'Ubaid*, 1927. C. L. Woolley, *Ur Excavations II: The Royal Cemeteries*, 1934. L. Legrain, *Ur Excavations III: Archaic Seal-impressions*, 1936. C. L. Woolley, *Ur Excavations IV: The Early Periods*, 1955; *Ur Excavations V: The Ziggurat and Its Surroundings*, 1939; *Ur Excavations VI: The Ur III Period: Ur Excavations VII: The Larsa Period; Ur Excavations VIII: The Kassite Period; Ur Excavations IX: The Neo-Babylonian and Persian Period*, 1960. L. Legrain, *Ur Excavations X: Seal Cylinders*, 1951. C. J. Gadd and L. Legrain, *Ur Excavations Texts: Royal Inscriptions*, 1928. Eric Burrows, *Ur Excavations Texts: Archaic Texts*, 1935. L. Legrain, *Ur Excavations Texts: Business Documents of the Third Dynasty*, 1937. *Ur Excavations Texts: Business Documents of the Neo-Babylonian Period*, 1949. H. Figulla, *Ur Excavations Texts: Letters and Documents of the Old Babylonian Period*, 1953. C. J. Gadd and S. N. Kramer, *Ur Excavations Texts: Sumerian Literary Texts*.
2. Books and Articles. C. J. Gadd, *History and Monuments of Ur*, Chatto & Windus, London, 1929. H. R. Hall, *A Season's Work at Ur*, Methuen & Co., London, 1930. T. Jacobsen, "Ur," *The Interpreter's Dictionary of the Bible*, Abingdon, New York, 1962. Guillame Janneau, *Une Dynastie Chaldeenne; les Rois D'Ur*, P. Geuthner, Paris, 1911. M. E. L. Mallowan and D. J. Wiseman, "Ur in Retrospect" *Iraq*, XXII, 1-236, Spring-Autumn 1960 (28 important articles). E. Porada, "Ur Excavations," *AJA*, LVIII, 339-342, Oct. 1954. C. L. Woolley, *Abraham*, Scribners, New York, 1936; *Antiquaries Journal*, vol. III through XIV, Oct. 1923 - Oct. 1934 (preliminary reports of each season); *Antiquities at Ur*, University Press, London, 1929; *The Excavation at Ur and the Hebrew Records*, Allen and Unwin, London, 1929; *Excavations at Ur, A Record of Twelve Years' Work*, L. E. Benn, London, 1954; *Ur of the Chaldees*, Ernest Benn, London, 1929.

URA. Two towns by the name of Ura occur in the Hittite texts, one a fortress of the land Azzi in the extreme northeast of Anatolia, the other a Cilician seaport, possibly at the mouth of the Gyuk Su (Calycadmus River) southwest of Tarsus. The latter Ura was in frequent contact with *Ugarit in the period of the Hittite Empire (*ca.* 1400 B.C.), and several tablets from Ugarit mention the merchants of Ura. One in particular regulates their status at Ugarit, where they apparently enjoyed "extra-territorial" rights under Hittite protection. Gordon has attempted to identify one of these Ura's with the Biblical "Ur of the Chaldees" (Gen. 11:28, 31; 15:7; Neh. 9:7). See Ur.

BIBLIOGRAPHY. Cyrus H. Gordon, "Abraham and the Merchants of Ura," *JNES*, XVII, 1958, pp.

THE UR-NAMMU STELE DEPICTS THE KING *receiving directions for building a ziggurat. In successive registers he completes the task assigned by his god. Courtesy, The University Museum, Philadelphia*

28-31. William F. Albright, "Abraham and the Caravan Trade," *BASOR*, 163, 1961, pp. 44-54.

URARTU. Assyrian historical records mention the land of Urartu, the region which has its geographical center in Lake Van. Shalmaneser III of °Assyria captured Urartian mountain fortresses, but following his death the Urartians were able to expand their own power. They built citadels of a combination of masonry and rock cuttings. The Urartians devised a system of irrigation, constructing aqueducts to carry water.

Assyrians regained control of the region under Tiglath-pileser III (745-727 B.C.). Sargon (722-705 B.C.) increased Assyrian

power over Urartu, and in subsequent centuries Urartu was invaded by Cimmerians, Scythians, and Medes. By the end of the sixth century B.C., Urartu ceased to exist as an independent ethnic and political unit.

In modern times explorers from Turkey, Russia, and Iran have studied the Urartu region. The architectural style of Urartu has affinities to that of Asia Minor. Hittite and Phrygian elements may be traced in Urartu.

Urartu is of interest to the Biblical scholar because it is the locale of Mount Ararat (Gen. 8:4). The mountains in the north of Urartu give us our Biblical name, Ararat.

BIBLIOGRAPHY. R. D. Barnett, "The Excavations of the British Museum at Toprak Kale Near Van," *Iraq*, XII, 1950, pp. 1-43. C. A. Burney, "Urartian Fortresses and Towns in the Van Region," *Anatolian Studies* VII, 1957, pp. 37-53.

URFA. *See* Edessa.

URKISH. *See* Habor.

UR-NAMMU. Ur-Nammu was the founder of the Third Dynasty of °Ur and reigned from *ca.* 2044 to 2007 B.C. The cities of southern Mesopotamia had fallen into ruin under the °Gutians, but Ur-Nammu began the task of reconstruction. C. Leonard Woolley cleared the ziggurat of Ur during his campaign of 1922-23. While part of the ziggurat antedated Ur-Nammu, and later sections were built by °Nabonidus, the bulk of the construction was the work of Ur-Nammu himself as is evident from his name and title stamped on the bricks. The ziggurat was a mass of brickwork, 200 feet long, 150 feet wide, and 70 feet high. Originally the shrine of Nanna (or Nannar) the moon god, stood on the topmost stage of the ziggurat.

The stele of Ur-Nammu presents a contemporary record of the building of the ziggurat. The stele is a slab of white limestone, nearly five feet across and ten feet high. At the top the king stands in an attitude of prayer. Above him are figures of angels with vases from which flow the streams of life. This is our earliest known artistic representation of angels.

Three panels of the stele are devoted to the building of the ziggurat. In the first Ur-Nammu stands before the goddess Ningal and before the god Nanna, receiving the command to build the ziggurat. In the next panel the king is setting out with compasses, mortar basket, pick and trowel, and in the third little has been preserved except a portion of one of the ladders used by the workmen as the structure was rising.

Among the Sumerian texts at the Museum of the Ancient Orient at Istanbul is a law code promulgated by Ur-Nammu. This code, three centuries older than Hammurabi, is the oldest code known at present. It is recorded on cuneiform tablets, eight by five inches in size, with five legible paragraphs.

The text states that the god Nanna chose Ur-Nammu to rule over Ur and Sumer as his earthly representative. The king was to remove those who seized the citizens' livestock, and establish honest weights and measures. He was to defend orphans and widows against those who would prey upon them in their need. The code spells out penalties for bodily injury. A man who had cut off another's nose could make amends by paying two-thirds of a mina of silver.

URSUM. *See* Carchemish.

URUK (ERECH). In southern Mesopotamia, forty miles northwest of Ur and four miles east of the present course of the Euphrates, is a group of mounds known to the Arabs as Warka, known as Uruk to the ancient Akkadians and as Erech to the Israelites (*cf.* Gen. 10:10). As early as 1850, William Kenneth Loftus investigated the Warka mounds, and in 1857 he wrote of his discoveries in his *Travels and Researches in Chaldaea and Susiana.* Henry C. Rawlinson, the British Consul-General at Baghdad, also visited Warka periodically between 1851 and 1855.

Scientific excavations began at Warka in 1912 when the German Orient Society sent Julius Jordan to the field. A temple of the goddess Ishtar was uncovered, along with portions of the city wall, when the work was interrupted by World War I. Work began again in 1928 and continued until 1939 when World War II again interrupted the excavations. In 1954, however, the Germans were ready to resume their work, and they have sent out a series of expeditions since that time. Two ziggurats have been cleared, along with several temples from the late fourth and early third millennium B.C. At one point a shaft was dug to virgin soil

seventy feet below the surface, revealing eighteen levels of occupation. The original village, Kullab, was founded by 'Ubeid people around 4000 B.C. Sumerian Uruk dates from the time of Meskiaggasher early in the third millennium. His successors included such heroes as Enmerkar, Lugalbanda, and Gilgamesh.

The pottery of prehistoric Uruk was made on a spinning potter's wheel and baked in a kiln, smothered down to make the smoke penetrate and color the clay. The pottery was highly polished but unpainted.

Limestone blocking from Uruk forms the small pavement which is our oldest stone structure in Mesopotamia. The Uruk ziggurat is the oldest staged temple tower.

Uruk's most notable contribution to cultural history, however, comes from its introduction of the cylinder seal and cunei-

STELE SHOWING A LION-HUNTING SCENE *from Uruk. Courtesy, Iraq Museum*

ASSYRIAN ARCHERS and siege engines fighting for Tiglath-pileser III. Courtesy, British Museum

form script. Stone stamp seals were impressed in clay to indicate ownership as early as the *Tell Halaf period. The earliest flat seals were replaced by a domelike shape during the 'Ubaid era. (*See* Tell al 'Ubaid.) At Uruk, however, we find the first seals made by cutting a design into a small stone cylinder so that it would leave an impression when rolled across a soft surface. The seals introduced a new art form, for each seal had to have a distinctive design to identify its owner and his property. The religion and mythology of the day provided motifs which artists carved into their cylinder seals.

In one of the temples excavated at Uruk, the archaeologists discovered a number of flat clay tablets inscribed in a crude pictographic script, representing the earliest stage of the cuneiform syllabary which was used throughout the Fertile Crescent until Persian times. The language of these earliest tablets was Sumerian, but the cuneiform syllabary was later adopted by Babylonians, Assyrians, Hittites and other peoples.

BIBLIOGRAPHY. Walter Andrae, "The Story of Uruk," *Antiquity*, 1936, X, pp. 133-145. Julius Jordon, "The Excavations at Warka, Mesopotamia," *Antiquity*, IV, pp. 109-111. J. Jordan, *Uruk-Warka*, 1928.

URUKAGINA. *See* Lagash.

W

WADI MURABBA'AT. *See* Dead Sea Scrolls.

WARFARE. *See* Arms and Weapons.

WARKA. *See* Uruk.

WEAPONS. *See* Arms and Weapons.

WENAMON. The story of the voyage of Wenamon to Phoenicia was found on two pages of papyrus presently in the Moscow Museum. The first page is only partly preserved with three pieces presently remaining. The remainder of page one and all of page three, which originally contained the conclusion of the story, are lost. The text itself dates from the early twenty-first dynasty of Egypt (*ca.* 1075 B.C.) only shortly after the events described.

As is usual in Egyptian papyri, the text is written in the hieratic script. It is of great significance to the student of ancient Egyptian language in that it is written in a natural colloquial style almost free of the literary stylisms which are generally found in Late-Egyptian texts.

Perhaps the outstanding literary characteristic of the story is the writer's sense of irony and humor. Wenamon's great speeches are described as "a great testimony of words" (II, 60). The humor of Wenamon's position is evident despite the fact that this humor is usually at Egypt's expense. Yet Wenamon never becomes a mere buffoon.

At the time of Wenamon's journey (*ca.* 1100 B.C.) Egyptian unity had collapsed. In Upper Egypt Heri-Hor ruled as an independent king although he was nominally subject to Ramesses XI, the last king of the Twentieth Dynasty, for a time. In the Delta, Smendes (Ne-su-Ba-neb-Ded) ruled with equal independence.

Mention of two other events will help to place Wenamon in a historical setting meaningful for Biblical students. About one hundred years earlier (*ca.* 1192) Ramesses III had repulsed a great wave of migrating Sea Peoples from Egypt. Two of these, the Philistines and the Teucrians (*Tjeker*) subsequently were given permission to settle on the Southern Palestinian coast, an event of significance for Biblical history as well as for Wenamon.

Little more than one hundred years later, Sheshonk I of Egypt (A. V., Shishak) invaded Palestine on a plundering raid and returned with booty from the temple in Jerusalem (I Kings 14:25-26).

Wenamon's voyage took place within a few decades of the rule of Saul over ancient Israel. Thus, the story pictures the state of affairs in Palestine during the time of the late Judges and the early Hebrew monarchy. Due to Egypt's decline and disunity her hold on Palestine had long ceased, although much of her traditional prestige remained.

Since the other major powers had been either destroyed or weakened in the migrations of the late thirteenth century, there was no external political force capable of interfering with the independent evolution of Palestine.

The story tells of Wenamon, an official of the temple of Amon-Re in Upper Egypt, who was sent to Byblos to buy wood for the sacred boat of Amon. He was given only five *deben* of gold and thirty-one *deben* of silver for a task which previously had cost one thousand *deben* of silver augmented by other goods if Zakar-Baal's records are to be trusted (II,29). Wenamon's money has been estimated at 1.2 pounds troy of gold and 7.5 pounds troy of silver. After securing a pledge of assistance from Smendes he travelled by ship to Dor, in the territory of the Teucrians, where he was robbed by a member of the crew. At first the prestige of the envoy from Egypt was shown by the manner in which Beder, the ruler of Dor, sent provisions to Wenamon. A lack of respect for Egypt was displayed by Beder's refusal to reimburse Wenamon for the money stolen from him while he was under the jurisdiction of Dor's ruler. Beder's pretext for failing to make restitution was that the thief was a member of the boat's crew and therefore not one of Beder's own subjects: the reason was that Egypt was no longer strong enough to demand the ordinary privileges for foreign mercantile representatives.

After some argument with Beder over this matter, Wenamon made his way to Byblos where he apparently succeeded in stealing thirty *deben* of silver from a Teucrian ship at Byblos in retaliation for the theft of his own money at Dor. This much seems clear despite the broken condition of the text at this point. The Teucrians apparently left Wenamon alone for a time following this incident.

About this point Amon-of-the road is first mentioned. This was a portable idol of Amon which could be carried and used for performance of cult practices while travelling. For twenty-nine days Zakar-Baal, ruler of Byblos, refused to see Wenamon. He sent daily instructing Wenamon to leave his harbor. However, at this point in the story, one of Zakar-Baal's attendants suffered a prophetic frenzy in which he instructed Zakar-Baal to grant a hearing to Amon-of-the-road and to Wenamon.

Zakar-Baal then summoned Wenamon for a hearing, but treated him in a rude manner despite the divine instructions. Thus when Wenamon greeted Zakar-Baal with a polite greeting, instead of courteously returning the greeting, Zakar-Baal immediately began discussing business. Such behavior is still bad manners in the Near East!

After pointing out several weaknesses in Wenamon's position, his lack of proper documents, his lack of sufficient money, and the questionable behavior on the part of Smendes, Zakar-Baal sent several selected pieces of wood to Egypt. The return voyage brought a payment, perhaps only partial, in silver, gold, linen, cowhides, papyrus, ropes, lentiles, and fish. After receiving this payment, Zakar-Baal set out in earnest to provide Wenamon with the wood.

Eventually the lumber was cut, seasoned, and stacked on the shore for shipment. By this time Heri-Hor seems to have provided Wenamon with adequate transport. However Wenamon's difficulties were not finished. At that moment eleven Teucrian ships appeared and demanded that Wenamon be surrendered to them. Zakar-Baal was unwilling to violate the custom of guest protection so he both maintained his honor and satisfied the demands of the Teucrians by expelling Wenamon from his harbor free, but at the mercy of the Teucrians.

Wenamon somehow escaped to Alashiya (Cyprus) where he sought refuge with its ruler. The text ends here, but Wenamon apparently made his way safely back to Egypt since the story is told in the first person.

The decline of Egyptian power and the disintegration of Egypt itself is clearly shown during the course of the story. A strong Egypt would never have tolerated the rise of the Hebrew monarchy. As it happened, the substantial opposition to the Hebrew monarchy was offered by the Philistines and the Aramean kingdoms of Syria. Egyptian weakness was responsible for the disrespectful treatment given Wenamon by both the Teucrians and Zakar-Baal.

The story reflects the distribution of power among the coastal city states. More political power, as well as control of more trade, lay in the hands of the Philistines and their Teucrian allies. Thus when the Teucrians demanded that Wenamon be given to them, Zakar-Baal had to yield to them though by means of a face-saving subterfuge. This balance of power was upset by the rise of Israel under David. The resulting Philistine weakness also coincided with the rise of Tyre and Sidon to mercantile leadership. Fear of a common enemy, the Philistines, perhaps contributed to Hebrew-Tyrian friendship.

The story of Wenamon demonstrates the political fragmentation of coastal Palestine into independent mercantile city states. Local leagues such as the Philistine league might be formed, but the independent city state was the rule. Each was ruled by its own king, thus accounting for the large number of kings conquered in the book of Judges. These kings were frequently assisted in their responsibilities by an assembly of elders. Each city state took great pride in its independence so that each ruler could share Zakar-Baal's protest of independence from Egypt.

Egypt's influence upon Palestine and Phoenicia is evident throughout the story. "Craftsmanship" and "learning" came from Egypt. An Egyptian singer came to cheer Wenamon. Zakar-Baal's butler had an Egyptian name, Pen-Amon. The supremacy of Amun is freely acknowledged although this statement should be interpreted in the light of the internationalization of deities.

The use of the Semitic word ḥbr for trade relationships shows that the influence could flow from Palestine to Egypt as well.

The character of commercial life is shown. Trade could be either for cash or by bartering goods. Wenamon originally took with him precious metals, but the payment from Egypt which verified the transaction consisted of goods as well as precious metals. Merchants were entitled to protection for themselves and for their goods. Thus Wenamon asked restitution from the ruler of Dor, and Zakar-Baal hesitated to hand Wenamon directly to the Teucrians.

Trade was frequently regarded as a ruler-to-ruler relationship, a condition reflected in Solomon's commercial ties with Hiram of Tyre (I Kings 5; cf. also I Kings 10:1-13). When trade relationships with Lower Egypt are discussed, they are spoken of as relationships with Smendes himself. Reference is made to commercial ties with Werket-El, king of Sidon.

In this context it should be noted that ancient documents were not precise in their use of terms such as "tribute," "gifts," and "trade." In Egyptian records all commercial imports are recorded as tribute, for Pharaoh's glory, regardless of origin. Similarly the "gifts" between Solomon and the Queen of Sheba should be regarded as mercantile barter of goods.

The "prophetic frenzy" of Zakar-Baal's attendant is the same phenomenon which happened to Saul (I Sam. 10:11-12).

A last point of interest to Biblical students

WRITING EQUIPMENT OF AN EGYPTIAN SCRIBE. A palette, with two circular sections hollowed out, is attached to a writing reed and a water jar. The palette is original; the other objects are reconstructed. This combination of writing equipment served as the hieroglyph for the word "scribe." Courtesy, Oriental Institute

is the manner in which the internationalization of formerly national gods is shown. Amun and Seth were national gods of Egypt; the corresponding national gods of the Phoenicians were El and Baal. These gods had been internationalized by becoming identified with their counterparts from other lands. In the story, the gods were referred to as "Amun" and "Seth" even while Zakar-Baal was speaking. Whether Zakar-Baal actually used these names or the Phoenician ones is beside the point. The deities were identified so that conversation was meaningful and understood regardless of the names used. This same phenomenon is probably involved in Necho's usage of the term *elohim* (II Chron. 35:21).

BIBLIOGRAPHY. Alan Gardiner, *Late-Egyptian Stories*, Brussels: Édition de la Fondation Égyptologique Reine Elisabeth, 1932, pp. xi-xii. John Wilson, *The Culture of Ancient Egypt*, Chicago: University of Chicago Press, 1951, pp. 289-292; "The Journey of Wen-Amon to Phoenicia," ANET, pp. 25-29.

WILSON'S ARCH. See Robinson's Arch.

WRITING. By 3000 B.C. both the Sumerians of the lower Tigris-Euphrates Valley and the Egyptians of the Nile Valley had developed systems of writing which began as a type of picture writing and developed into conventionalized symbols. The cuneiform, or wedge-shaped characters which the Sumerians and their successors incised into clay or stone was pictorial in its earliest stage. In time, however, the concrete came to represent the abstract. The solar disc would represent not only the sun, but also the concepts of day and time. This usage is called the ideograph, or, more correctly, the word sign. In a further development cuneiform characters came to represent the phonetic value of words, without regard to their meaning as a picture, as though a picture of a pine and an apple were joined to give us the word "pineapple." This last stage is the phonogram which provides the material from which a syllabary can be developed.

As finally developed the cuneiform system had certain characters which we designate as polyphones, i.e. those with more than one phonetic value. Others are homophones, characters representing differing objects yet pronounced with the same phonetic value. In addition, cuneiform writ-

THE PALETTE of NARMER. The obverse (right) contains a circular recess for grinding cosmetics. The reverse (left) depicts Narmer with mace in hand ready to smite an enemy. Courtesy, Cairo Museum

ing used determinatives, signs which appear in front of or after certain words without being read themselves. Such word classes as deities, countries, mountains, birds, and plurals are regularly indicated by determinatives. Most of them are placed in front of the word they designate but some, particularly those of Sumerian origin, are placed after the word. A further device for safeguarding the reading of ambiguous signs is the phonetic complement. Since, for example, the same sign may be read either as "god" or "heaven" a phonetic complement giving the final syllable of the word intended may be appended.

One of the oldest specimens of Egyptian writing is the slate palette of Narmer (Menes), the Pharaoh who united Egypt and founded the First Dynasty, according to Manetho. At the top of the palette the name of the king is written between two heads of Hathor. Narmer's name is written by the use of two pictures — the *n'ar* —

fish, and the *mer* — chisel. The palette commemorates a victory of the king over people in the Egyptian delta.

The early history of hieroglyphic writing parallels that of the cuneiform, yet Egypt was more conservative in its approach to language. The earliest known hieroglyphic inscriptions present essentially the same method of writing as do inscriptions which are dated three thousand years later. Along with this oldest form known as hieroglyphic, or sacred writing, the Egyptians developed two cursive scripts known as hieratic and demotic. Hieroglyphs continued to be used for the monuments. The priests used the hieratic script in copying literary compositions such as the °Book of the Dead. Demotic was the popular script during the time of the Ptolemies. Unlike the cuneiform syllabaries which were in use throughout the Fertile Crescent, the Egyptian script was essentially national. *See* Alphabet.

Z

ZAKIR STELE. The Zakir Stele, discovered by Pognon in 1903 near Aleppo, describes the inner conflicts among Aramean states in Syria during the eighth century B.C. Zakir was evidently seeking to build an empire for himself, for he began as king of *Hamath, and subsequently took the title and functions of "king of Hamath and Lu'ash." The capital of Lu'ash was Hazrek (Biblical Hadrach, II Chron. 9:1). Benhadad II of Damascus and his allies besieged Hazrek, but Zakir boasts in his stele that he prayed to Baal-Shamain ("Baal of Heaven") and received the reply, "Fear not! It is I who caused you to reign and it is I who will be with you. It is I who will deliver you from all these kings which have set up siege against you. . . ."

Zakir was delivered, but the inner conflicts among the Aramean states permitted Israel a period of relative rest. Joash of Israel (*ca.* 801 - 786 B. C.) was able to re-establish Israel's prestige, and his successor, Jeroboam II, enjoyed a period of remarkable prosperity.

ZALMAQUM. *See* Haran.

ZEALOTS. *See* Jewish Sects.

ZENO PAPYRI. The Zeno papyri comprise the business files of Zeno, secretary to Apollonius the finance minister of Ptolemy II (Philadelphus), including their records of tax collections and commercial transactions between Egypt and her officials in Syria and Palestine.

Among the letters are two which can be precisely dated to May 12, 259 B.C. One of these is addressed to Apollonius and the other to Ptolemy himself. The letter begins, "To King Ptolemy, greeting: Tubias," and it goes on to enumerate a number of animals which Tubias is sending to the Egyptian king: two horses, six dogs, one half-wild ass bred from an ass, two white Arabian asses ("beasts of burden"), two foals bred from a half-wild ass, one foal bred from a wild ass.

Tobias sent a eunuch and four "well-bred slave boys" to Apollonius whose description follows. Two were circumcised, and two not.

The Tubias of the Zeno Papyri is probably to be identified with the Tobias who was buried at *Araq el-Emir, a descendant of the Ammonite Tobiah who gave trouble Nehemiah.

ZIGGURAT. The Akkadian word *ziqqur* from a root meaning "to be high," gives us word ziggurat which designates the arti mountains or staged towers which were acteristic of ancient Mesopotamian The artificial mountain served as a place for the god whose temple was l on its summit. More than two doz gurats have been identified, the ear which was built in the city of *Uruk, Erech.

ZINJERLI. Zinjerli (or Singerli) Samal, is located near Antioch in S site was excavated from 1888 to 1 German expedition under Von Discoveries indicate that Zinje *Hittite state in northern Syria Arameans entered the area around The sculptures are of Hittite inscriptions are in Aramaic.

Tirhakah, Egyptian Taharqo, war against Sennacherib duri

THE ZIGGURAT AT UR towered eighty feet above the Sumerian plain. Courtesy, A. Marguerite Smith Collection, Zion Research Library

paign in Judah (II Kings 19:9), suffered defeat at the hands of Esarhaddon of *Assyria. A victory stele, set up at Zinjerli, was discovered in 1888 by the German excavators. It depicts the king with a mace his left hand and in his right hand a cup n which he has poured a libation. From eft hand extend ropes which pass through ps of the two figures at his feet. The ng figure, with both hands and feet d, is doubtless Taharqo. The inscriptes, "I fought daily, without intervery bloody battles against Tirhakah, Egypt and Ethiopia, the one acall the great gods. Five times I the point of my arrows inflicting

s
e
to

tu,
our
icial
char-
ities.
high
cated
n zig-
iest of
Biblical

ancient
ria. The
891 by a
Luschan.
li was a
and that
1300 B.C.
design, but

who waged
ng his cam-

wounds from which he should not recover, and then I laid siege to Memphis, his royal residence, and conquered it in half a day by means of mines, breaches, and assault ladders. I destroyed it, tore down its walls and burnt it down."

ZIUSUDRA. Ziusudra, a label name meaning "Life-day prolonged," is described in Sumerian texts as the Son of Ubar-Tutu of *Shuruppak. As Utnapishtim he is the hero of the *Gilgamesh Epic who gained immortality by surviving the flood.

ZOAN. *See* Raamses.

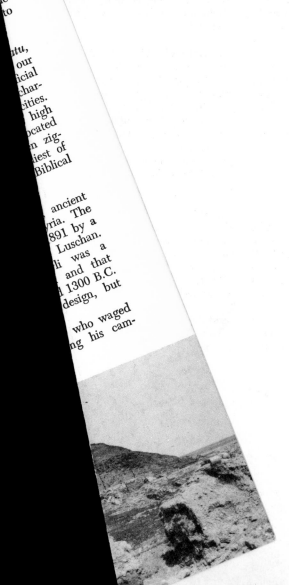

DISCARD